21 Years 2025-2005

ISC

CHAPTERWISE - TOPICWISE QUESTION BANK

Mathematics

Class 12

Mathematics

21 Years 2025-2005

ISC

CHAPTERWISE - TOPICWISE QUESTION BANK

Mathematics

Class 12

Author
Laxman Prasad

arihant
SUCCESS AND NOTHING LESS

arihant
SUCCESS AND NOTHING LESS

ARIHANT PRAKASHAN
(School Division Series)

卐 ADMINISTRATIVE & PRODUCTION OFFICES

Regd. Office
'Ramchhaya' 4577/15, Agarwal Road, Darya Ganj, New Delhi -110002
Tele: 011- 47630600, 43518550

Head Office
Kalindi, TP Nagar, Meerut (UP) - 250002, Tel: 0121-7156203, 7156204

卐 SALES & SUPPORT OFFICES

Agra, Ahmedabad, Bengaluru, Bareilly, Chennai, Delhi, Guwahati, Hyderabad, Jaipur, Jhansi, Kolkata, Lucknow, Nagpur & Pune.

卐 **PO No :** TXT-XX-XXXXXXX-X-XX

Published By Arihant Publications (India) Ltd.

For further information about the books published by Arihant, log on to www.arihantbooks.com or e-mail at info@arihantbooks.com

卐 **PRICE** ₹395.00

Follow us on

Achieving 99+
Marks in Board Exams

Achieving 99+ marks in board exams is definitely an ambitious goal, but with the right approach and these 7 tips from toppers, you can definitely increase your chances of success!

Here are the 7 Topper Tips to ace your board exams:

1. Master the art of consistency

Consistency builds understanding and confidence, both crucial for excelling in exams.

2. Build a winning study strategy

Create a personalised timetable that prioritises subjects based on your strengths and weaknesses.

3. Befriend the syllabus

Focus on high-weightage topics and prioritise mastering core concepts before moving on to advanced ones.

4. Embrace active learning

Explain concepts to yourself or in study groups to solidify understanding.

5. Conquer the past

Solve Past years' papers and Sample Papers under timed conditions to practice time management and understand paper pattern.

6. Seek help, when needed!

Don't hesitate to clarify doubts with teachers, tutors, or study groups. Asking questions strengthens your understanding and prevents confusion.

7. Prioritise well-being

Eat nutritious meals, get enough sleep, regular exercise practice stress management techniques like meditation to stay calm and focused during exams.

These tips are just a starting point, and you can personalise them to fit your learning style and preferences.

Description of

Newly Added Features

01

Relations and Functions

TREND ANALYSIS 3 YEARS

TOPIC 01 Relations and Functions

Average No. of Questions Across all Sets

Types of Questions	2024	2023	2020
1 Mark	3	4	–
2 Marks	2	3	–
3/4 Marks	–	–	–
5/6 Marks	–	–	–
1 Mark	–	4	–

Trend Analysis

At the start of each chapter, Trend Analysis is given to indicate the types of Questions asked from different topics of the chapter. This feature helps students to know the importance of different topics of the given chapter from exam point of view and helps them to prepare accordingly.

21. If $A = \{1, 2, 3, \ldots, 9\}$ and R is the relation in $A \times A$ defined by $(a, b)\ R\ (c, d)$, if $a + d = b + c$ for $(a, b), (c, d)$ in $A \times A$. Prove that R is an equivalence relation. Also, obtain the equivalence class $[(2, 5)]$.

22. Show that the function f in $A = R - \left\{\frac{2}{3}\right\}$ defined as $f(x) = \dfrac{4x+3}{6x-4}$ is one-one and onto. Hence, find f^{-1}.

23. Consider $f : R^+ \to [4, \infty)$ given by $f(x) = x^2 + 4$. Show that f is invertible with the inverse f^{-1} of f given by $f^{-1}(y) = \sqrt{y-4}$, where R^+ is the set of all non-negative real numbers.

KEY CONCEPT
To show $f(x)$ is an invertible function, we will show that f is both one-one and onto function.

Key Concept

'Key Concept' is given with selected questions with the purpose to help students to get the approach 'to answer the question'. This feature help students to develop the systematic approach to answer difficult/ complex questions.

12. (i) (a) $\because$ Ramu Paid ₹ 16 for 5 pens, 3 bags an 1 instrument box and x, y and z represent th of a pen, a bag and an instrument box, respectively

$\therefore \quad 5x + 3y + z = 16$

(ii) (a) Given, $A = \begin{bmatrix} 5 & 3 & 1 \\ 2 & 1 & 3 \\ 1 & 2 & 4 \end{bmatrix}$

Common Mistake For finding the adjoint of a matrix, find cofactors by taking proper sign.

Common Mistakes

It focuses on some of the general but critical mistakes that students commit while answering the questions. This feature helps students to develop the habit of avoiding mistakes while answering questions.

21. Given a relation R in $A \times A$, where $A = \{1, 2, 3, \ldots, 9\}$, defined as $(a, b)\ R\ (c, d)$, if $a + d = b + c$.

Reflexive Let (a, b) be any arbitrary element of $A \times A$.

i.e. $\quad (a, b) \in A \times A$, where $a, b \in A$.

Now, as $\quad a + b = b + a \quad$ [$\because$ addition is commutative]

$\therefore \quad (a, b) R (a, b)$

So, R is reflexive.

Symmetric Let $(a, b), (c, d) \in A \times A$, such that $(a, b) R (c, d)$.

Then, $\quad a + d = b + c$

$\Rightarrow \quad b + c = a + d$

$\Rightarrow \quad c + b = d + a$

$\Rightarrow \quad (c, d) R (a, b)$

So, R is symmetric.

Concept Enhancer A relation R is said to be an equivalence relation, if it is simultaneously reflexive, symmetric and transitive on A.

Concept Enhancer

Concept Enhancer gives the brief description of the concept, which has been used to answer the question. This feature provides revision of important concept along with practice of question solving.

Most Important Topics
from each Chapter

On the basis of analysis of last 4 Years' Board Examination Papers, we have identified Important Topics from each chapter.

Chapter Name	Important Topics	Weightage in Last 3 Years' Boards			
		2025	2024	2023	2020
Relations and Functions	Relations And Functions	1M(2Q)	1M(3Q), 2M(2Q)	1M(4Q), 2M(3Q)	
Inverse Trigonometric Functions	Principal Value of Inverse Trigonometric Functions		1M		2M
	Formulae Related to Inverse Trigonometric Functions	2M, 6M	3M(2Q)	2M, 3M	3M
Matrices	Matrices	1M(2Q), 2M	1M(2Q)	1M	2M
Determinants	Determinants and Its Properties	1M, 4M	2M	1M, 2M, 4M	2M, 4M
	Adjoint and Inverse of a Matrix		6M	6M	6M
Continuity and Differentiability	Continuity and Differentiability	1M	1M, 2M	1M	
	Differentiation	2M(2Q), 4M	1M	3M	2M
	Differentiationof Some Special Functions		3M	3M	4M
Application of Derivatives	Rate Measure, Increasing and Decreasing Functions	1M(2Q)	1M(2Q)	1M	2M
	Tangents and Normals	2M, 4M	2M	1M	4M
	Maxima and Minima	2M	6M	6M	6M
Integrals	Indefinite Integrals	1M, 4M(2Q), 6M	1M, 3M(2Q)	1M(2Q), 2M(2Q) 6M(2Q)	3M(2Q), 6M(2Q)
	Definite Integrals	1M, 6M	1M(2Q), 2M	1M(2Q)	2M
Differential Equations	Order and Degree of Differential Equations		1M		
	Solutions of Differential equations	2M, 6M(2Q)		1M	3M
	Homogeneous and linear Differential Equations	1M	6M(2Q)	3M(2Q)	3M
Probability	Probability	1M, 4M	1M, 2M	1M, 2M, 3M	2M(2Q), 3M
	Conditional Probability with Baye's Theorem	1M, 6M	3M	3M	
	Random Variables and probability Distributions	1M	6M	3M	
Vectors	Algebra of Vectors	4M	1M(3Q)	2M	2M
	Scalar and Vector Product of Two Vectors	1M	2M(2Q)	1M(3Q), 2M	3M
Three Dimensional Geometry	Line	1M, 2M	1M(2Q), 3M	3M	2M, 3M
	Plane	1M, 2M(2Q)	3M	1M(2Q), 3M	2M
Application of Integrals	Applications of Integrals	4M(2Q)	3M(2Q)	3M	6M
Application of Calculus	Application of Calculus	1M, 4M(2Q)	1M(3Q), 2M(2Q)	1M(3Q), 2M(2Q)	2M(3Q), 3M
Linear Regression	Linear Regression	1M(2Q), 2M(2Q)	1M(2Q), 3M(2Q)	1M(2Q), 3M(2Q)	1M(2Q), 3M(2Q)
Linear Programming	Linear Programming	4M	3M	3M	6M

Dream, Believe, Achieve Insights from ISC Toppers

Follow all the 5P's

• Persistence • Passion • Perseverance • Purpose • Practice

MANYA GUPTA
ISC Topper (99.75%)

"Aim for high marks, that's what I was doing. I convinced myself that if I aim for 100 I will at least get a 95. That was my logic, but I ended up getting a 100. "I studied with the help of my school and tuition classes. I didn't study daily much, but before the exams, I used to pull all-nighters and study".

ARYAAN
ISC Topper (99.75%)

"Studying for 3-4 hours every day along with six hours of school helped me secure 399 out of 400 marks, scoring 99.75%,"
I'm very active on all social media platforms but it has never hindered my studies. I strike a balance between hard work and fun,".

POOJA KEJRIWAL
ISC Topper (97.5%)

the degree of toughness of any subject is merely a subjective outlook. I made sure that I incentivised myself at times when I didn't feel like sitting at my study table, especially for theoretical subjects

I simply believe in revising the concepts which were taught at school or tuitions that very day and minimise backlogs as much as I could.

DEVANG KUMAR
ISC Topper

I believe there is no substitute to hard work. There was no fixed hours of preparation, I read a topic till the time I completely understood it. I had to be satisfied with the topic covered,"

See it is important to take breaks and everyone has their own way of entertainment. I do chat with friends on social media. I think it is fine until it becomes as addiction.

There is no secret formula as such, but one should not panic and have faith in his/her preparation.

DIMPLE KOTHARI
ISC Topper (97.5%)

- Don't run behind marks, crave for knowledge, experience because ultimately that's gonna help you.
- Don't let peer pressure dominate you.
- If you want to obtain good marks, leave all social media-This is a myth. I was active on Instagram & WhatsApp before my examinations, and even during my examinations. It's just that you need to remember that everyone has the same 24 hours, it's how you utilize it as well as enjoy it better than others.
- Both early morning and late night studies are best ~ you need to choose what's better for you.
- Don't hesitate to ask questions. If you have any doubts, please clarify. Everyone has different learning styles and speed, so it's nothing to be ashamed of.
- Never give up.

Please Note that all the information is collected from different websites.

Contents

ISC Chapterwise Topicwise Question Bank 2025-2005

Latest Syllabus

Class XII (2024-25)

There will be two papers in the subject :

Paper I : Theory (3 hours) 80 Marks

Paper II : Project work 20 Marks

Paper I : Theory **80 Marks**

The syllabus is divided into three sections A, B and C.

Section A is compulsory for all candidates. Candidates will have a choice of attempting questions from **EITHER** Section B **OR** Section C.

DISTRIBUTION OF MARKS FOR THE THEORY PAPER.

S.No.	Unit Name	Total Weightage
	Section A : 65 Marks	
1.	Relations and Functions	10 Marks
2	Algebra	10 Marks
3.	Calculus	32 Marks
4.	Probability	13 Marks
	Section B : 15 Marks	
5.	Vectors	5 Marks
6.	Three-Dimensional Geometry	6 Marks
7.	Applications of Integrals	4 Marks
	OR Section C : 15 Marks	
8.	Applications of Calculus	5 Marks
9.	Linear Regression	6 Marks
10.	Linear Programming	4 Marks
	Total	**80 Marks**

SECTION A

1. Relations and Functions

(i) Types of relations: reflexive, symmetric, transitive and equivalence relations. One to one and onto functions, inverse of a function.

- **Relations as**
  - – Relation on a set A
  - – Identity relation, empty relation, universal relation.
  - – Types of Relations: reflexive, symmetric, transitive and equivalence relation.
- **Functions**
  - – As special relations, concept of writing "y is a function of x" as $y = f(x)$.
  - – Types: one to one, many to one, into, onto.
  - – Real Valued function.
  - – Domain and range of a function.
  - – Conditions of invertibility.
  - – Invertible functions (algebraic functions only).

(ii) Inverse Trigonometric Functions

Definition, domain, range, principal value branch. Elementary properties of inverse trigonometric functions.

- Principal values.
- $\sin^{-1} x, \cos^{-1} x, \tan^{-1} x$, etc.
- $\sin^{-1} x = \cos^{-1}\sqrt{1-x^2} = \tan^{-1}\dfrac{x}{\sqrt{1-x^2}}$
- $\sin^{-1} x = \operatorname{cosec}^{-1}\dfrac{1}{x}$; $\sin^{-1} x + \cos^{-1} x = \dfrac{\pi}{2}$ and similar relations for $\cot^{-1} x, \tan^{-1} x$, etc.

$$\sin^{-1} x \pm \sin^{-1} y = \sin^{-1}(x\sqrt{1-y^2} \pm y\sqrt{1-x^2})$$
$$\cos^{-1} x \pm \cos^{-1} y = \cos^{-1}(xy \mp \sqrt{1-y^2}\sqrt{1-x^2})$$

Similarly,

$$\tan^{-1} x + \tan^{-1} y = \tan^{-1}\frac{x+y}{1-xy}, xy<1,$$
$$\tan^{-1} x - \tan^{-1} y = \tan^{-1}\frac{x-y}{1+xy}, xy>-1$$

Formulae for $2\sin^{-1}x$, $2\cos^{-1}x$, $2\tan^{-1}x$, $3\tan^{-1}x$ etc. and application of these formulae.

2. Algebra

Matrices and Determinants

(i) Matrices

Concept, notation, order, equality, types of matrices, zero and identity matrix, transpose of a matrix, symmetric and skew-symmetric matrices. Operation on matrices: Addition and multiplication and multiplication with a scalar. Simple properties of addition, multiplication and scalar multiplication. Non-commutativity of multiplication of matrices and existence of non-zero matrices whose product is the zero matrix (restrict to square matrices of order upto 3). Invertible matrices and proof of the uniqueness of inverse, if it exists (here all matrices will have real entries).

(ii) Determinants

Determinant of a square matrix (up to 3 x 3 matrices), properties of determinants, minors, co-factors and applications of determinants in finding the area of a triangle. Adjoint and inverse of a square matrix. Consistency, inconsistency and number of solutions of system of linear equation by examples. Solving system of linear equations in two or three variables (having unique solution) using inverse of a matrix.

- – Types of matrices ($m \times n$; $m, n \leq 3$), order; Identity matrix, Diagonal matrix.
- – Symmetric, Skew-symmetric.
- – Operation – addition, subtraction, multiplication of a matrix with scalar, multiplication of two matrices (the compatibility).

e.g. $\begin{bmatrix}1 & 1\\0 & 2\\1 & 1\end{bmatrix}\begin{bmatrix}1 & 2\\2 & 2\end{bmatrix} = AB$ (say) but BA is not possible.

- Singular and non-singular matrices.
- Existence of two non-zero matrices whose product is a zero matrix.

Inverse $(2 \times 2, 3 \times 3)\ A^{-1} = \dfrac{\text{adj } A}{|A|}$

- *Martin's Rule (i.e. using matrices)*

$a_1x + b_1y + c_1z = d_1$
$a_2x + b_2y + c_2z = d_2$
$a_3x + b_3y + c_3z = d_3$

$$A = \begin{bmatrix} a_1 & b_1 & c_1 \\ a_2 & b_2 & c_2 \\ a_3 & b_3 & c_3 \end{bmatrix}, B = \begin{bmatrix} d_1 \\ d_2 \\ d_3 \end{bmatrix}, X = \begin{bmatrix} x \\ y \\ z \end{bmatrix}$$

$$AX = B \Rightarrow X = A^{-1}B$$

Problems based on above.

***Note :** The conditions for consistency of equations in two and three variables using matrices are to be covered.*

- *Determinants*
  - *Order.*
  - *Minors.*
  - *Cofactors.*
  - *Expansion.*
  - *Application of determinants is finding the area or triangle and collinearity.*
  - *Properties of determinants. Problems based on properties of determinants.*

3. Calculus

(viii) Continuity, Differentiability and Differentiation. Continuity and differentiability, derivative of composite functions, chain rule, derivatives of inverse trigonometric functions, derivative of implicit functions. Concept of exponential and logarithmic functions.

Derivatives of logarithmic and exponential functions. Logarithmic differentiation, derivative of functions expressed in parametric forms. Second order derivatives.

- *Continuity*
  - *Continuity of a function at a point $x = a$.*
  - *Continuity of a function in an interval.*
  - *Algebra of continuous function.*
  - *Removable discontinuity.*
- *Differentiation*
  - *Concept of continuity and differentiability of $|x|$, $[x]$, etc.*
  - *Derivatives of trigonometric functions.*
  - *Derivatives of exponential functions.*
  - *Derivatives of logarithmic functions.*
  - *Derivatives of inverse trigonometric functions - differentiation by means of substitution.*
  - *Derivatives of implicit functions and chain rule for composite functions.*
  - *Derivatives of Parametric functions.*
  - *Differentiation of a function with respect to another function e.g. differentiation of $\sin x^3$ with respect to x^3.*
  - *Logarithmic Differentiation - Finding dy/dx when $y = x^{x^x}$*
  - *Successive differentiation upto 2nd order.*

***Note :** Derivatives of composite functions using chain rule.*

(ii) Applications of Derivatives

Applications of derivatives: rate of change of bodies, increasing/decreasing functions, tangents and normals, maxima and minima (first derivative test motivated geometrically and second derivative test given as a provable tool). Simple problems (that illustrate basic principles and understanding of the subject as well as real-life situations).

- *Equation of Tangent and Normal.*
- *Rate measure.*
- *Increasing and decreasing functions.*
- *Maxima and minima*
  - *Stationary/turning points.*
  - *Absolute maxima/minima.*
  - *Local maxima/minima.*
  - *First derivatives test and second derivatives test.*
  - *Application problems based on maxima and minima.*

(iii) Integrals

Integration as inverse process of differentiation. Integration of a variety of functions by substitution, by partial fractions and by parts, Evaluation of simple integrals of the following types and problems based on them.

Fundamental Theorem of Calculus (without proof). Basic properties of definite integrals and evaluation of definite integrals.

- *Indefinite integral*
  - *Integration as the inverse of differentiation.*
  - *Anti-derivatives of polynomials and functions $(ax+b)^n$, $\sin x$, $\cos x$, $\sec^2 x$, $\operatorname{cosec}^2 x$ etc .*
  - *Integrals of the type $\sin^2 x$, $\sin^3 x$, $\sin^4 x$, $\cos^2 x$, $\cos^3 x$, $\cos^4 x$.*
  - *Integration of $1/x$, e^x.*
  - *Integration by substitution.*
  - *Integrals of the type $f'(x)[f(x)]^n$, $\dfrac{f'(x)}{f(x)}$*
  - *Integration of $\tan x$, $\cot x$, $\sec x$, $\operatorname{cosec} x$.*
  - *Integration by parts.*
  - *Integration using partial fractions.*

Expressions of the form $\dfrac{f(x)}{g(x)}$, when, degree of $f(x)$ < degree of $g(x)$.

e.g. $\dfrac{x+2}{(x-3)(x+1)} = \dfrac{A}{x-3} + \dfrac{B}{x+1}$,

$$\frac{x+2}{(x-2)(x-1)^2} = \frac{A}{x-1} + \frac{B}{(x-1)^2} + \frac{C}{x-2}$$

$$\frac{x+1}{(x^2+3)(x-1)} = \frac{Ax+B}{x^2+3} + \frac{C}{x-1}$$

When degree of $f(x) \geq$ degree of $g(x)$,

e.g. $\dfrac{x^2+1}{x^2+3x+2} = 1 - \left(\dfrac{3x+1}{x^2+3x+2}\right)$

Integrals of the type :

$$\int \frac{dx}{x^2 \pm a^2}, \int \frac{dx}{\sqrt{x^2 \pm a^2}}, \int \frac{px+q}{ax^2+bx+c}dx,$$

$$\int \frac{px+q}{\sqrt{ax^2+bx+c}}dx \text{ and } \int \sqrt{a^2 \pm x^2}\,dx, \int \sqrt{x^2 - a^2}\,dx,$$

$$\int (px+q)\sqrt{ax^2+bx+c}\,dx \int \sqrt{ax^2+bx+c}\,dx,$$

integrations reducible to the above forms.

- Integrals of the form

$$\int \frac{dx}{a\cos x + b\sin x}, \int \frac{dx}{a + b\cos x}, \int \frac{dx}{a + b\sin x},$$

$$\int \frac{dx}{a\cos x + b\sin x + c}, \int \frac{(a\cos x + b\sin x)}{c\cos x + d\sin x}dx,$$

$$\int \frac{dx}{a\cos^2 x + b\sin^2 x + c}, \int \frac{1 \pm x^2}{1 + x^4}dx, \int \frac{dx}{1 + x^4},$$

$$\int \sqrt{\tan x}\,dx, \int \sqrt{\cot x}\,dx \text{ etc.}$$

- Definite integral
  - Fundamental theorem of calculus (without proof).
  - Properties of definite integrals.

Problems based on the following properties of definite integrals are to be covered.

$$\int_a^b f(x)\,dx = \int_a^b f(t)\,dt$$

$$\int_a^b f(x)\,dx = -\int_b^a f(x)\,dx$$

$$\int_a^b f(x)\,dx = \int_a^c f(x)\,dx + \int_c^b f(x)\,dx, \text{ where } a < c < b$$

$$\int_a^b f(x)\,dx = \int_a^b f(a + b - x)\,dx$$

$$\int_0^a f(x)\,dx = \int_0^a f(a - x)\,dx$$

$$\int_0^{2a} f(x)\,dx = \begin{cases} 2\int_0^a f(x)\,dx, & \text{if } f(2a - x) = f(x) \\ 0, & \text{if } f(2a - x) = -f(x) \end{cases}$$

$$\int_{-a}^a f(x)\,dx = \begin{cases} 2\int_0^a f(x)\,dx, & \text{if } f \text{ is an even function} \\ 0, & \text{if } f \text{ is an odd function} \end{cases}$$

(iv) Differential Equations

Definition, order and degree, general and particular solutions of a differential equation. Solution of differential equations by method of separation of variables solutions of homogeneous differential equations of first order and first degree.

Solutions of linear differential equation of the type: $\frac{dy}{dx} + py = q$, where p and q are functions of x or constants. $\frac{dx}{dy} + px = q$, where p and q are functions of y or constants.

- Differential equations, order and degree.
- Formation of differential equation by eleminating arbitrary constant (s).
- Solution of differential equations.
- Variable separable.
- Homogeneous equations.
- Linear form $\frac{dy}{dx} + Py = Q$, where P and Q are functions.

of x only. Similarly for dx/dy.

Note 1 : Equations reducible to variable separable type are included.

Note 2 : The second order differential equations are excluded.

4. Probability

Conditional probability, multiplication theorem on probability, independent events, total probability, Bayes' theorem, Random variable and its probability distribution, mean and variance of random variable.

- Independent and dependent events, conditional events.
- Laws of probability, addition theorem, multiplication theorem, conditional probability.
- Theorem of Total Probability.
- Baye's theorem.
- Theoretical probability distribution, probability distribution function; mean of random variable.

SECTION B

5. Vectors

Vectors and scalars, magnitude and direction of a vector. Direction cosines and direction ratios of a vector. Types of vectors (equal, unit, zero, parallel and collinear vectors), position vector of a point, negative of a vector, components of a vector, addition of vectors, multiplication of a vector by a scalar, position vector of a point dividing a line segment in a given ratio. Definition, Geometrical Interpretation, properties and application of scalar (dot) product of vectors, vector (cross) product of vectors.

- *As directed line segments.*
- *Magnitude and direction of a vector.*
- *Types: equal vectors, unit vectors, zero vector.*
- *Position vector.*
- *Components of a vector.*
- *Vectors in two and three dimensions.*
- *i, j, k as unit vectors along the X, Y and Z-axes; expressing a vector in terms of the unit vectors.*
- *Operations: Sum and Difference of vectors; scalar multiplication of a vector.*
- *Section formulae.*
- *Scalar (dot) product of vectors and its geometrical significance.*
- *Cross product - its properties - area of a triangle, area of parallelogram, collinear vectors.*

Note *Proofs of geometrical theorems by using Vector algebra are excluded.*

6. Three Dimensional Geometry

Direction cosines and direction ratios of a line joining two points. Cartesian equation and vector equation of a line, coplanar and skew lines, shortest distance between two lines. Cartesian and vector equation of a plane. Angle between (i) two lines, (ii) two planes, (iii) a line and a plane. Distance of a point from a plane.

- *Equation of X-axis, Y-axis, Z-axis and lines parallel to them.*
- *Equation of XY-plane, YZ-plane, ZX-plane.*
- *Direction cosines, direction ratios.*
- *Angle between two lines in terms of direction cosines /direction ratios.*
- *Condition for lines to be perpendicular/ parallel.*

- ***Lines***
  - *Cartesian and vector equations of a line through one and two points.*
  - *Coplanar and skew lines.*
  - *Conditions for intersection of two lines.*
  - *Distance of a point from a line.*
  - *Shortest distance between two lines.*

- ***Planes***
  - *Cartesian and vector equation of a plane.*
  - *Direction ratios of the normal to the plane.*
  - *One point form.*
  - *Normal form.*
  - *Intercept form.*
  - *Distance of a point from a plane.*
  - *Intersection of the line and plane.*
  - *Angle between two planes, a line and a plane.*

7. Application of Integrals

Application in finding the area bounded by simple curves and coordinate axes. Area enclosed between two curves.

– *Application of definite integrals - area bounded by curves, lines and coordinate axes is required to be covered.*
Simple curves: lines, circles/ parabolas/ ellipses, simple polynomial functions, modulus function.

SECTION C

8. Application of Calculus

Application of Calculus in Commerce and Economics in the following:

– *Cost function,*
– *average cost,*
– *marginal cost and its interpretation*
– *demand function,*
– *revenue function,*
– *marginal revenue function and its interpretation,*
– *Profit function and breakeven point.*
– *Rough sketching of the following curves: AR, MR, R, C, AC, MC and their mathematical interpretation using the concept of maxima & minima and increasing- decreasing functions.*
– *Self-explanatory*

Note : *Application involving differentiation, increasing and decreasing function and maxima and minima to be covered.*

9. Linear Regression

– *Lines of regression of x on y and y on x.*
– *Scatter diagrams*
– *The method of least squares.*
– *Lines of best fit.*
– *Regression coefficient of x on y and y on x.*
– $b_{xy} \times b_{yx} = r^2,\ 0 \le b_{xy} \times b_{yx} \le 1$
– *Identification of regression equations*
– *Properties of regression lines.*
– *Estimation of the value of one variable using the value of other variable from appropriate line of regression.*
– *Self-explanatory*

10. Linear Programming

Introduction, related terminology such as constraints, objective function, optimization, different types of Linear Programming (LP) problems, mathematical formulation of LP problems, graphical method of solution for problems in two variables, feasible and infeasible regions (bounded and unbounded), feasible and infeasible solutions, optimal feasible solutions (up to three non-trivial constraints).

Introduction, definition of related terminology such as constraints, objective function, optimization, advantages of linear programming; limitations of linear programming; application areas of linear programming; different types of Linear Programming (LP) problems, mathematical formulation of LP problems, graphical method of solution for problems in two variables, feasible and infeasible regions, feasible and infeasible solutions, optimum feasible solution.

01

Relations and Functions

TREND ANALYSIS 3 YEARS

TOPIC 01 Relations and Functions

Average No. of Questions Across all Sets

Types of Questions	2024	2023	2020
1 Mark	3	4	—
2 Marks	2	3	—
3/4 Marks	—	—	—
5/6 Marks	—	—	—

TOPIC 1

Relations and Functions

Relation

A relation R from a set X to a set Y is defined as a subset of the cartesian product $X \times Y$

i.e. $R \subseteq X \times Y$

Relation on a Set A

A relation R from A to itself i.e. a subset of $A \times A$ is called a relation on set A.

Domain and Range of a Relation

The set of first elements of all ordered pairs in R, i.e. $\{x : (x, y) \in R\}$ is called the domain of relation R and the set of second elements of all ordered pairs in R, i.e. $\{y : (x, y) \in R\}$ is called the range of relation R.

NOTE If $n(A) = p$ and $n(B) = q$, then $n(A \times B) = pq$ and number of relations from set A to set $B = 2^{pq}$.

Types of Relation

(i) **Empty (or Void) Relation** A relation R in a set X is called an empty relation, if no element of X is related to any element of X

i.e. $R = \phi \subset X \times X$.

(ii) **Identity Relation** Relation R in a set A is called an identity relation, if each element of A is related to itself only and it is denoted by I_A

i.e. $I_A = \{(a, a) : a \in A\}$.

(iii) **Universal Relation** A relation R in a set X is called universal relation, if each element of X is related to every element of X

i.e. $R = X \times X$.

(iv) **Reflexive Relation** A relation R defined on a set A is said to be reflexive, if $(x, x) \in R, \forall x \in A$

or $xRx, \forall x \in A$

(v) **Symmetric Relation** A relation R defined on a set A is said to be symmetric,

if $(x, y) \in R$

$\Rightarrow (y, x) \in R, \forall x, y \in A$

or $xRy \Rightarrow yRx, \forall x, y \in A$.

(vi) **Transitive Relation** A relation R defined on a set A is said to be transitive, if $(x, y) \in R$ and $(y, z) \in R$ $\Rightarrow (x, z) \in R, \forall x, y, z \in A$

or xRy and yRz

$\Rightarrow xRz, \forall x, y, z \in A$.

(vii) **Equivalence Relation** A relation R defined on a set A is said to be an equivalence relation, if R is reflexive, symmetric and transitive.

Function

Let X and Y be two non-empty sets. A function or mapping f from X into Y written as $f: X \to Y$ is a rule by which each element $x \in X$ is associated to a unique element $y \in Y$. It should be noted that if f associates $x \in A$ to $y \in B$, then y is known as the image of x under the mapping f and denoted by $f(x)$, i.e. $y = f(x)$.

Domain, Codomain and Range of Function

The elements of X are called the **domain** of f and the elements of Y are called the **codomain** of f. The images of the elements of X is called the range of f which is a subset of Y.

NOTE Every function is a relation but every relation is not a function.

Types of Function

(i) **One-one** (or Injective) **and Many-one Function** A function $f: X \to Y$ is said to be a one-one function, if the images of distinct elements of X under f are distinct. Thus, f is one-one iff $f(x_1) = f(x_2)$
$\Rightarrow x_1 = x_2$ for all $x_1, x_2 \in X$ or f is one-one iff $x_1 \neq x_2$
$\Rightarrow f(x_1) \neq f(x_2)$ for all $x_1, x_2 \in X$.
A function which is not one-one, is known as many-one function.

(ii) **Onto** (or Surjective) **and Into Function** A function $f: X \to Y$ is said to be an onto function, if every element of Y is image of some element of set X under f, i.e. for every $y \in Y$, there exists an element x in X such that $f(x) = y$.
In other words, a function is called an onto function, if its range is equal to codomain. A function $f: X \to Y$ is said to be into function, if there exists atleast one element in Y, which do not have any pre-image in X.

(iii) **Bijective Function** A function $f: X \to Y$ is said to be a bijective function, if it is both one-one and onto.

(iv) **Real Valued function** It is a function that assigns a real number to each member of its domain.

Invertible Function

A function $f: X \to Y$ is said to be invertible, if there exists a function $g: Y \to X$ such that $gof = I_x$ and $fog = I_y$. The function g is called inverse of function f and is denoted by f^{-1}.

Condition of Invertibility

A function is said to be invertible iff it is both one-one and onto i.e. bijective.

NOTE (i) The inverse of a bijective function is also a bijective function.
(ii) If f is an invertible function, then $(f^{-1})^{-1} = f$.
(iii) If $f: X \to Y$ and $g: Y \to Z$ are two invertible functions, then gof is also invertible with $(gof)^{-1} = f^{-1}og^{-1}$.

Domain and Range of Some Useful Functions

S.No.	Function	Domain	Range
1.	Polynomial function	R	R (if degree is odd) and subset of R (if degree is even)
2.	Rational function	All real values except for which denominator = 0.	Depends on particular rational function.
3.	Exponential function, $a^x, a > 0$	R	$(0, \infty)$
4.	Logarithmic function, $\log_a x$, $a > 0$ and $a \neq 1$	$(0, \infty)$	R
5.	Identity function, $y = x$	R	R
6.	Modulus function, $\|x\|$	R	$[0, \infty)$
7.	Signum function, $\begin{cases} \frac{\|x\|}{x}, & x \neq 0 \\ 0, & x = 0 \end{cases}$	R	$\{-1, 0, 1\}$
8.	Greatest integer function, $[x]$	R	Set of integers (I)

PYQs Previous Years Questions

1 Mark Questions

1. Let L be a set of all straight lines in a plane. The relation R on L defined as 'perpendicular to' is **ISC 2024**

(a) Symmetric and Transitive
(b) Transitive
(c) Symmetric
(d) Equivalence

2. Let A be a non-empty set.

Statement I Identity relation on A is reflexive.

Statement II Every reflexive relation on A is an identity relation. **ISC 2024**

(a) Both the statements are true.
(b) Both the statements are false.
(c) Statement I is true and Statement II is false.
(d) Statement I is false and Statement II is true.

3. Which one of the following graphs is a function of x? **ISC 2024**

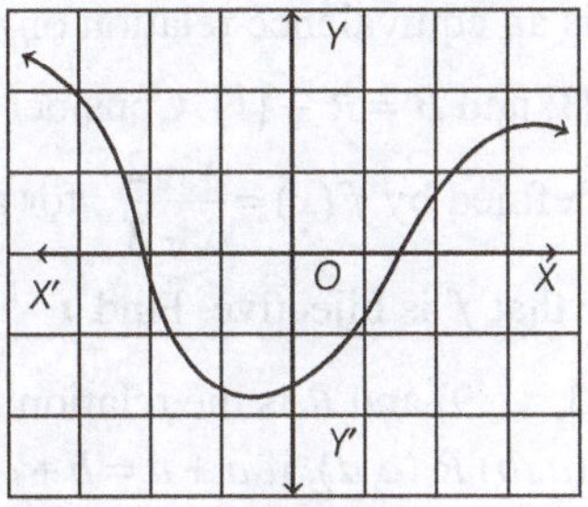

Graph A

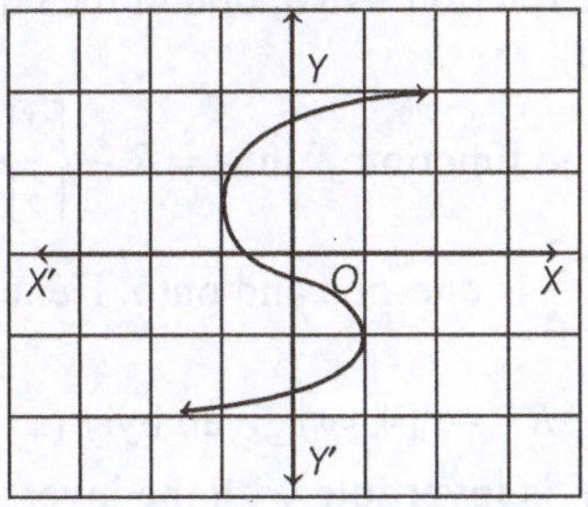

Graph B

4. **Statement 1** The function $f : N \to N$ given by $f(x) = 5x$ is one to one and onto.

Statement 2 The function $f : R \to R$ given by $f(x) = 5x$ is one to one and onto.

Which one of the following options is correct? **ISC Specimen 2024**

(a) Both the statements are true.
(b) Both the statements are false.
(c) Statement 1 is true and Statement 2 is false.
(d) Statement 1 is false and Statement 2 is true.

5. The function $f : X \to Y$ is not invertible. State the reason. **ISC Specimen 2024**

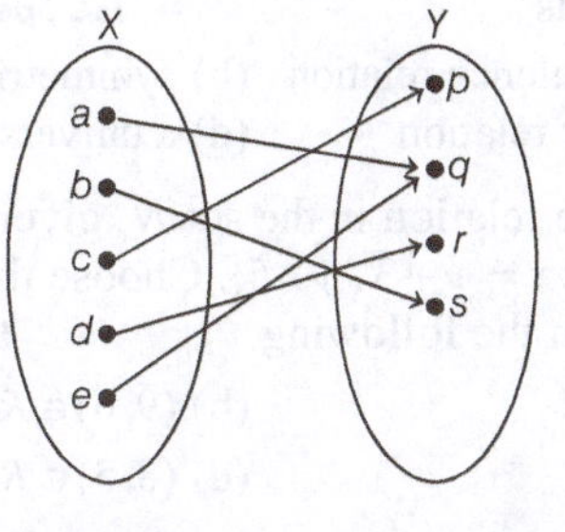

6. If a relation R on the set $A = \{1,2,3\}$ be defined by $R = \{(1,2),(2,1)\}$, then classify the function R. **ISC Specimen 2024**

7. A relation R on $\{1, 2, 3\}$ is given by $R = \{(1, 1), (2, 2), (1, 2), (3, 3), (2, 3)\}$. Then, the relation R is **ISC 2023**

(a) reflexive
(b) symmetric
(c) transitive
(d) symmetric and transitive

8. Let $f(x) = x^3$ be a function with domain $\{0, 1, 2, 3\}$. Then, domain of f^{-1} is **ISC 2023**

(a) $\{3, 2, 1, 0\}$
(b) $\{0, -1, -2, -3\}$
(c) $\{0, 1, 8, 27\}$
(d) $\{0, -1, -8, -27\}$

9. Which of the following is not an equivalence relation of Z? **ISC Specimen 2023**

(a) $aRb \Leftrightarrow a + b$ is an even integer
(b) $aRb \Leftrightarrow a - b$ is an even integer
(c) $aRb \Leftrightarrow a < b$
(d) $aRb \Leftrightarrow a = b$

10. Let A be the set of all 50 cards numbered from 1 to 50. Let $f : A \to N$ be a function defined by $f(x)$ = card number of the card x. Then, the function 'f' is **ISC Specimen 2023**

(a) one to one but not onto.
(b) onto but not one to one.
(c) neither one to one nor onto.
(d) one to one and onto.

11. The function $f : R \to R$ defined by $f(x) = \sin(3x + 2)$, $\forall\, x \in R$ is **ISC Specimen Sem-I 2022**

(a) One-One
(b) Onto
(c) Neither one-one nor onto
(d) One-One but not onto

12. If set A contains 5 elements and set B contains 6 elements, then the number of one-one onto mapping from A to B is **ISC Specimen Sem-I 2022**
(a) 720 (b) 120
(c) 0 (d) None of these

13. Let A be the set of all students of a boy's school. Then, the relation R in A defined by $R = \{(a, b) : a$ is sister of $b\}$ is **ISC Specimen Sem-I 2022**
(a) an equivalence relation (b) symmetric relation
(c) an empty relation (d) a universal relation

14. Let R be the relation in the set N, given by $R = \{(x, y) : x = y + 3, y > 5\}$. Choose the correct answer from the following **ISC Specimen 2021**
(a) $(7, 4) \in R$ (b) $(9, 6) \in R$
(c) $(4, 1) \in R$ (d) $(8, 5) \in R$

15. If $A = \{1, 2, 3\}$, $B = \{x, y\}$, then the number of functions from A to B is **ISC Specimen 2021**
(a) 3 (b) 6 (c) 8 (d) 12

16. Write total number of functions from set A to set B, where $A = \{1, 2, 3\}$, $B = \{p, q, r, s\}$. **ISC Specimen 2021**

2 Marks Questions

17. Let $f : R - \left\{\frac{-1}{3}\right\} \to R - \{0\}$ be defined as $f(x) = \frac{5}{3x+1}$ is invertible. Find $f^{-1}(x)$. **ISC 2024**

18. If $f : R \to R$ is defined by $f(x) = \frac{2x-7}{4}$, show that $f(x)$ is one-one and onto. **ISC 2024**

19. If $f(x) = [4 - (x-7)^3]^{\frac{1}{5}}$ is a real invertible function, then find $f^{-1}(x)$. **ISC 2023**

20. Let $A = R - \{2\}$ and $B = R - \{1\}$. If $f : A \to B$ is a function defined by $f(x) = \frac{x-1}{x-2}$, then show that f is a one-one and an onto function. **ISC 2023**

21. Let $f : R \to R$ defined as $f(x) = 2x - 3$. Find
(i) $f^{-1}(x)$
(ii) domain and range of $f^{-1}(x)$ **ISC Specimen 2023**

22. Show that the function $f : N \to N$, defined by $f(x) = 5x - 3$, $\forall x \in N$, is one-one function but not onto function. **ISC Specimen 2021**

3/4 Marks Questions

23. Let R^+ be the set of all positive real numbers and $f : R^+ \to [4, \infty) : f(x) = x^2 + 4$. Show that inverse of f exists and find f^{-1}. **ISC Specimen 2021**

24. If $f : A \to A$ and $A = R - \left\{\frac{8}{5}\right\}$, show that the function $f(x) = \frac{8x+3}{5x-8}$ is one-one onto. Hence, find f^{-1}. **ISC 2019**

25. If the function $f(x) = \sqrt{2x-3}$ is invertible, then find its inverse. **ISC 2018**

26. If $f : W \to W$ is defined as $f(x) = x - 1$, if x is odd and $f(x) = x + 1$, if x is even. Show that f is invertible. Find the inverse of f, where W is the set of all whole numbers.

27. If R is a relation defined on the set of natural numbers N as follows
$R = \{(x, y) : x \in N, y \in N$ and $2x + y = 24\}$, then find the domain and range of the relation R. Also, find whether R is an equivalence relation or not.

28. If $A = R - \{3\}$ and $B = R - \{1\}$. Consider the function $f : A \to B$ defined by $f(x) = \frac{x-2}{x-3}$, for all $x \in A$.
Then, show that f is bijective. Find $f^{-1}(x)$.

29. If $A = \{1, 2, 3, \ldots, 9\}$ and R is the relation in $A \times A$ defined by $(a, b)\, R\, (c, d)$, if $a + d = b + c$ for $(a, b), (c, d)$ in $A \times A$. Prove that R is an equivalence relation. Also, obtain the equivalence class $[(2, 5)]$.

30. Show that the function f in $A = R - \left\{\frac{2}{3}\right\}$ defined as $f(x) = \frac{4x+3}{6x-4}$ is one-one and onto. Hence, find f^{-1}.

31. Consider $f : R^+ \to [4, \infty)$ given by $f(x) = x^2 + 4$. Show that f is invertible with the inverse f^{-1} of f given by $f^{-1}(y) = \sqrt{y-4}$, where R^+ is the set of all non-negative real numbers.

> **KEY CONCEPT**
> To show $f(x)$ is an invertible function, we will show that f is both one-one and onto function.

32. Show that $f : N \to N$, given by

$$f(x)=\begin{cases} x+1, & \text{if } x \text{ is odd} \\ x-1, & \text{if } x \text{ is even}\end{cases}$$

is bijective (both one-one and onto).

33. If $f : N \to N$ is defined by

$$f(n)=\begin{cases} \frac{n+1}{2}, & \text{if } n \text{ is odd} \\ \frac{n}{2}, & \text{if } n \text{ is even}\end{cases} \quad \text{for all } n \in N.$$

Find whether the function f is bijective.

5/6 Marks Questions

34. Consider the mapping $f : A \to B$ is defined by $f(x)=\frac{x-1}{x-2}$ such that $f(x)$ is one-one onto.

Based on the above information, answer the following questions by choosing the correct option.

ISC Specimen Sem-I 2022

(i) Domain of $f(x)$ is.

(a) $R-\{2\}$ (b) R

(c) $R-\{1, 2\}$ (d) $R-\{0\}$

(ii) Range of $f(x)$ is

(a) $R-\{2\}$ (b) R

(c) $R-\{1\}$ (d) $R-\{0\}$

(iii) If $g(x)=2f(x)-1$, then $g(x)$ in terms of x is

(a) $\frac{x+2}{x}$ (b) $\frac{x+1}{x-2}$

(c) $\frac{x-2}{x}$ (d) $\frac{x}{x-2}$

(iv) A function $f(x)$ is said to be one-one, if

(a) $f(x_1)=f(x_2) \Rightarrow x_1=x_2$

(b) $f(-x_1)=f(-x_2) \Rightarrow -x_1=x_2$

(c) $f(x_1)=f(x_2) \Rightarrow -x_1=x_2$

(d) $-f(x_1)=f(x_2) \Rightarrow x_1=x_2$

35. Consider $f : R_+ \to [-5, \infty)$ given by $f(x)=9x^2+6x-5$. Show that f is invertible with

$$f^{-1}(y)=\left(\frac{\sqrt{y+6}-1}{3}\right).$$

Hence, find

(i) $f^{-1}(10)$

(ii) y, if $f^{-1}(y)=\frac{4}{3}$

where R_+ is the set of all non-negative real numbers.

36. Consider $f : R-\left\{-\frac{4}{3}\right\} \to R-\left\{\frac{4}{3}\right\}$ given by $f(x)=\frac{4x+3}{3x+4}$. Show that f is bijective. Find the inverse of f and hence find $f^{-1}(0)$ and x such that $f^{-1}(x)=2$.

37. Let $f : N \to N$ be a function defined as $f(x)=9x^2+6x-5$. Show that $f : N \to S$, where S is the range of f is invertible. Find the inverse of f and hence find $f^{-1}(43)$ and $f^{-1}(163)$.

38. If N denotes the set of all natural numbers and R be the relation on $N \times N$ defined by $(a, b) R (c, d)$, if $ad(b+c)=bc(a+d)$. Show that R is an equivalence relation.

Explanations

1. (c) Given, the relation R is defined as

$R=\{(L_1, L_2) : L_1 \perp L_2\}$

Now, R is not reflexive as every line is not perpendicular to itself.

Since, $L_1 \perp L_2$, therefore L_2 is also perpendicular to L_1.

Thus, relation is symmetric.

Also, $L_1 \perp L_2$ and $L_2 \perp L_3$.

Then, L_1 may or may not be perpendicular to L_3.

So, R is not transitive.

2. (c) Let A be a non-empty set.

Statement I Identity relation on A is reflexive.

Consider an example.

Let $A=\{1, 2, 3\}$

Now, a relation R defined as

$R=\{(1,1), (2,2), (3,3)\}$ is an identity relation which is reflexive.

But $R'=\{(1, 1), (1, 3), (3, 3), (2, 2), (2, 3)\}$ is a reflexive relation but not identity relation.

So, Statement II is not necessarily true.

3. By the definition of function

If A and B are any two sets, then a function $f : A \to B$ is a rule that assigns to each element of A exactly one element of B.

So, Graph A represents a function of x but Graph B is not a function because at $x = 0$, we get three values of y.

4. (d) **Statement I** $f : N \to N$

$$f(x) = 5x$$

Let $y = 5x \Rightarrow x = \frac{y}{5}$

Here, if $y = 12$, then $x = 2.4 \notin N$

Hence, f is not onto.

Statement II $f : R \to R$

$$f(x) = 5x$$

Now, $f(x_1) = f(x_2)$

$\Rightarrow \quad 5x_1 = 5x_2 \Rightarrow x_1 = x_2$

$\therefore$ f is one to one.

Let $y = 5x \Rightarrow x = \frac{y}{5} \in R$ for each $y \in R$.

$\therefore$ f is onto.

5. Here, element a and e have same image

$\therefore$ f is not one-one.

and hence f is not invertible.

6. We have, $A = \{1, 2, 3\}$

and $R = \{(1, 2), (2, 1)\}$

$(1, 1) \notin R$

$\therefore$ R is not reflexive.

$(1, 2) \in R$ and $(2, 1) \in R$

$\therefore$ R is symmetric.

$(1, 2) \in R$ and $(2, 1) \in R$ but $(1, 1) \notin R$

$\therefore$ R is not transitive.

7. (a) Given, $R = \{(1, 1), (2, 2), (1, 2), (3, 3), (2, 3)\}$.

Since, $(1, 1), (2, 2)$ and $(3, 3) \in R$.

Hence, R is reflexive.

$(1, 2) \in R$ but $(2, 1) \notin R$.

Hence, R is not symmetric.

$(1, 2) \in R, (2, 3) \in R$ but $(1, 3) \notin R$.

Hence, R is not transitive.

8. (c) $f(x) = x^3$

$$f(0) = 0,\ f(1) = 1,\ f(2) = 8,\ f(3) = 27$$

$$f^{-1}(0) = 0,\ f^{-1}(1) = 1,\ f^{-1}(8) = 2,\ f^{-1}(27) = 3$$

$\therefore$ Domain of $f^{-1} = \{0, 1, 8, 27\}$

9. (c) According to option (c), $aRb \Leftrightarrow a < b$

As, $a < b$ does not imply $b < a$, which make the relation a symmetric and thus, it is not an equivalence relation.

10. (a) A is the set of all 50 cards number from 1 to 50.

Number on each card will be unique.

Now, $51 \in N$ but $51 \notin A$

So, there is no pre-image of 51 in A.

Therefore, f must be one-one.

11. (c) Let $h(x) = \sin x$ and $g(x) = 3x + 2$

$\therefore \quad f(x) = hog(x)$

$g(x) = 3x + 2$ is one-one and onto function but $h(x)$ is oscillatory.

So, $h(x)$ is neither one-one nor onto function.

Hence, $f(x) = hog(x)$ is also neither one-one nor onto function.

12. (c) $n(A) = 5$ and $n(B) = 6$

We know that, the number of one-one and onto from A into B can only be possible when provided $n(A) \geq n(B)$.

But in this case, $n(A) < n(B)$.

Hence, the number of one-one onto mappings from A to $B = 0$.

13. (c) Since, it is a boys school, there are no girls student.

So, there cannot be sister of any student.

Hence, R is an empty relation.

14. (b) Given, $R = \{x, y : x = y + 3, y > 5\}$

Here, $\quad y > 5$

So, $\quad y = 6$

when $y = 6$, then $\quad x = 6 + 3 = 9$

Hence, $(9, 6) \in R$

15. (c) Given, $A = \{1, 2, 3\}, B = \{x, y\}$

Here, $m = 3, n = 2$

So, number of function from A to $B = n^m = 2^3 = 8$

16. Given, $A = \{1, 2, 3\}, B = \{p, q, r, s\}$

So, $n(A) = 3$ and $n(B) = 4$

Number of function from set A to set $B = (n(B))^{n(A)}$

$$= 4^3 = 64$$

17. Let $f : R - \left\{\frac{-1}{3}\right\} \longrightarrow R - \{0\}$ be defined as

$$f(x) = \frac{5}{3x + 1}$$

Assume that $y=\dfrac{5}{3x+1}$

$\Rightarrow \quad 3xy+y=5$

$\Rightarrow \quad 3xy=5-y$

$\Rightarrow \quad x=\dfrac{5-y}{3y}=f(y)$

Thus, $f^{-1}(x)=\left(\dfrac{5-x}{3x}\right)$

which is the required solution.

18. A mapping $f:R\longrightarrow R$ is defined by

$$f(x)=\frac{2x-7}{4}$$

Let $x_1, x_2 \in R$, then for one-one

$$f(x_1)=f(x_2)$$

$\Rightarrow \quad \dfrac{2x_1-7}{4}=\dfrac{2x_2-7}{4}$

$\Rightarrow \quad 2x_1-7=2x_2-7 \Rightarrow x_1=x_2$

Thus, f is one-one.

Now, let $\quad y=\dfrac{2x-7}{4}$

Then, $\quad 4y=2x-7$

$\Rightarrow \quad 2x=4y+7$

$$x=\frac{4y+7}{2}=f(y)$$

Clearly, for each $y\in R$, there exists

$$x=\frac{4y+7}{2}\in R \text{ such that}$$

$$f(x)=f\left(\frac{4y+7}{2}\right)=\frac{1}{4}\left[2\left(\frac{4y+7}{2}\right)-7\right]$$

$$=\frac{1}{4}[4y+7-7]=y$$

$\Rightarrow f$ is onto.

Hence, f is one-one and onto i.e. f is bijective.

19. We have, $f(x)=[4-(x-7)^3]^{1/5}$

We know that $f(f^{-1}(x))=x$

$\therefore \quad f(f^{-1}(x))=[4-(f^{-1}(x)-7)^3]^{1/5}$

$\Rightarrow \quad x=[4-(f^{-1}(x)-7)^3]^{1/5}$

$\Rightarrow \quad x^5=4-(f^{-1}(x)-7)^3$

$\Rightarrow \quad (f^{-1}(x)-7)^3=4-x^5$

$\Rightarrow \quad f^{-1}(x)-7=(4-x^5)^{1/3}$

$\Rightarrow \quad f^{-1}(x)=7+(4-x^5)^{1/3}$

20. Given, $f(x)=\dfrac{x-1}{x-2}$

For one-one function

Let $x_1, x_2 \in R, \forall x \in A$

Now, $\quad f(x_1)=\dfrac{x_1-1}{x_1-2}$ and $f(x_2)=\dfrac{x_2-1}{x_2-2}$

$$f(x_1)=f(x_2)$$

$\Rightarrow \quad \dfrac{x_1-1}{x_1-2}=\dfrac{x_2-1}{x_2-2}$

$\Rightarrow x_1x_2-2x_1-x_2+2=x_1x_2-x_1-2x_2+2$

$\Rightarrow \quad x_1=x_2$

Now, $\quad f(x_1)=f(x_2)$

$\Rightarrow \quad x_1=x_2$

Here, f is one-one function.

For onto function Let $f(x)=y$

$\therefore \quad y=\dfrac{x-1}{x-2} \Rightarrow xy-2y=x-1$

$\Rightarrow \quad xy-x=2y-1 \Rightarrow x=\dfrac{2y-1}{y-1}, y\neq 1$

$\therefore$ For onto function,

Range = Codomain

$$f(x)=\frac{x-1}{x-2}$$

$\Rightarrow \quad f(x)=\dfrac{\dfrac{2y-1}{y-1}-1}{\dfrac{2y-1}{y-1}-2}=\dfrac{2y-1-y+1}{2y-1-2y+2}=y$

$$f(x)=y$$

$\therefore f$ is onto function.

21. (i) Given, function $f(x)=2x-3$ and $f:R\rightarrow R$

Let $a, b\in R$

$$f(a)=f(b)$$

$\Rightarrow \quad 2a-3=2b-3$

$\Rightarrow \quad 2a=2b$

$\Rightarrow \quad a=b\ \forall\ a, b\in R$

$\therefore f$ is one-one function.

Let $y\in R$ (codomain)

$$f(x)=y \Rightarrow 2x-3=y$$

$\Rightarrow \quad x=\dfrac{3+y}{2}\in R\ \forall y\in R$

So, pre-image for each value of y exists in domain R.

Thus, f is onto function.

Therefore, f is one-one onto function.

Hence, $f^{-1}\ R:R\to R$ exists.

Let $x\in R$ (domain of f)

and $y\in R$ (codomain of f)

Let $f(x)=y$, then $f^{-1}(y)=x$

$\Rightarrow\quad f(x)=y$

$\Rightarrow\quad 2x-3=y$

$\Rightarrow\quad x=\dfrac{y+3}{2}\in R$

$\Rightarrow\quad f^{-1}(y)=\dfrac{y+3}{2}$

$\Rightarrow\quad f^{-1}(x)=\dfrac{x+3}{2},\ \forall\, x\in R$

(ii) Domain of $f^{-1}(x)=$ Range of $f(x)$

Here, $y=2x-3\Rightarrow \dfrac{y+3}{2}=x$

Range of $f(x)=R$

and range of $f^{-1}(x)=$ domain of $f(x)$

$y=2x-3$

Domain of $f(x)=R$.

22. Given a function $f:N\to N$ defined by $f(x)=5x-3$

For one-one

Let $x_1, x_2\in N$ such that

$f(x_1)=f(x_2)$

$\Rightarrow\quad 5x_1-3=5x_2-3$

$\Rightarrow\quad 5x_1=5x_2\Rightarrow x_1=x_2$

So, f is one-one.

For onto

Let $y\in N$ (codomain) be any arbitrary constant.

Then, $\quad y=f(x)$

$\Rightarrow\quad y=5x-3\Rightarrow y+3=5x$

$\Rightarrow\quad x=\dfrac{y+3}{5}$

Now, for $y=1, x=\dfrac{4}{5}\notin N$

Thus, $y=1\in N$ (codomain) does not have a pre-image in domain (N).

So, f is not onto.

23. Given, $f:R^+\to[4,\infty)$ is defined as $f(x)=x^2+4$

For one-one Let $f(x_1)=f(x_2)$, for some

$x_1, x_2\in R^+\Rightarrow x_1^2+4=x_2^2+4$

$\Rightarrow\quad x_1^2-x_2^2=0\Rightarrow(x_1+x_2)(x_1-x_2)=0$

$\Rightarrow\quad x_1=x_2, x_1\neq -x_2; x_1, x_2\in(R^+)$

Thus, $\quad f(x_1)=f(x_2)$

$\Rightarrow\quad x_1=x_2; x_1, x_2\in R^+$

So, $f(x)$ is one-one function.

For onto Let $y=x^2+4\Rightarrow x=\sqrt{y-4}$ ...(i)

Since, $x\in R^+, \forall\ y\in[4,\infty)$

So, range of $f(x)=[4,\infty)$

$\therefore$ Range $=$ Codomain

So, $f(x)$ is onto function.

Hence, $f(x)$ is bijective inverse of $f(x)$ exists.

From Eq. (i), $f^{-1}(y)=\sqrt{y-4}$

$[\because y=f(x)\Rightarrow f^{-1}(y)=x]$

or $\quad f^{-1}(x)=\sqrt{x-4}$

24. We have, $f:A\to A, A=R-\left\{\dfrac{8}{5}\right\}$

and $\quad f(x)=\dfrac{8x+3}{5x-8}$

For one-one Let $x_1, x_2\in A$ such that

$f(x_1)=f(x_2)$

$\Rightarrow\quad \dfrac{8x_1+3}{5x_1-8}=\dfrac{8x_2+3}{5x_2-8}$

$\Rightarrow\ (8x_1+3)(5x_2-8)=(5x_1-8)(8x_2+3)$

$\Rightarrow\ 40x_1x_2-64x_1+15x_2-24$

$=40x_1x_2+15x_1-64x_2-24$

$\Rightarrow\quad 15x_1+64x_1=15x_2+64x_2$

$\Rightarrow\quad 79x_1=79x_2$

$\Rightarrow\quad x_1=x_2$

$\therefore$ $f(x)$ is one-one function.

For onto Let y be an arbitrary element of A (codomain).

Then, $f(x)=y$

$\Rightarrow\quad \dfrac{8x+3}{5x-8}=y$

$\Rightarrow\quad 5xy-8y=8x+3$

$\Rightarrow\quad x(5y-8)=3+8y$

$\Rightarrow\quad x=\dfrac{8y+3}{5y-8},\ y\neq\dfrac{8}{5}$ ...(i)

Clearly, $x=\dfrac{8y+3}{5y-8}$ is a real number for all $y\neq\dfrac{8}{5}$.

Thus, for every $y\in A$ (codomain) there exists,

$x=\dfrac{8y+3}{5y-8}\in A$ (domain) such that

$$f(x)=f\left[\frac{8y+3}{5y-8}\right]=\frac{8\left(\frac{8y+3}{5y-8}\right)+3}{5\left(\frac{8y+3}{5y-8}\right)-8}$$

$$=\frac{64y+24+15y-24}{40y+15-40y+64}=\frac{79y}{79}=y$$

$\Rightarrow f(x)$ is onto function.

Since, $f(x)$ is a bijective function, so its inverse exists.

From Eq. (i), we get

$$x=\frac{8y+3}{5y-8}$$

$$\Rightarrow \quad f^{-1}(y)=\frac{8y+3}{5y-8} \quad [\because y=f(x) \Rightarrow x=f^{-1}(y)]$$

$$\therefore \quad f^{-1}(x)=\frac{8x+3}{5x-8}, x\neq\frac{8}{5}$$

25. Given, $f(x)=\sqrt{2x-3}$ is invertible function.

Let $f(x)=y$

$\Rightarrow f^{-1}(y)=x$

$\therefore \quad y=\sqrt{2x-3}$

$\Rightarrow y^2=2x-3$

$\Rightarrow \quad x=\frac{y^2+3}{2}$

$\Rightarrow f^{-1}(y)=\frac{y^2+3}{2}$

$\Rightarrow f^{-1}(x)=\frac{x^2+3}{2}$

$\therefore$ Inverse of $f(x)$ is $\frac{x^2+3}{2}$.

26. Given, $f: W\rightarrow W$ is defined as

$$f(x)=\begin{cases}x-1, \text{ if } x \text{ is odd}\\ x+1, \text{ if } x \text{ is even}\end{cases}$$

One-one function Let $x_1, x_2 \in W$ be any two numbers such that $f(x_1)=f(x_2)$.

***Case* I** When x_1 and x_2 are odd.

Then, $\quad f(x_1)=f(x_2)$

$\Rightarrow \quad x_1-1=x_2-1$

$\Rightarrow \quad x_1=x_2$

***Case* II** When x_1 and x_2 are even.

Then, $\quad f(x_1)=f(x_2)$

$\Rightarrow \quad x_1+1=x_2+1$

$\Rightarrow \quad x_1=x_2$

Thus, in both cases, $f(x_1)=f(x_2) \Rightarrow x_1=x_2$

***Case* III** When x_1 is odd and x_2 is even.

Then, $x_1\neq x_2$

Also, $f(x_1)$ is even and $f(x_2)$ is odd.

So, $f(x_1)\neq f(x_2)$

Thus, $\quad x_1\neq x_2 \Rightarrow f(x_1)\neq f(x_2)$

Hence, from cases I, II and III, we can observe that, $f(x)$ is a one-one function.

Onto function Clearly, any odd number $2y+1$ in the codomain W, is the image of $2y$ in the domain W.

Also, any even number $2y$ in the codomain W, is the image of $2y+1$ in the domain W.

Thus, every element in W (codomain) has a pre-image in W (domain). So, f is onto.

Therefore, f is bijective and so it is invertible.

Let $\quad f(x)=y$

$\Rightarrow \quad x-1=y$, if x is odd

and $\quad x+1=y$, if x is even

$$\therefore \quad f^{-1}(y)=x=\begin{cases}y+1, \text{ if } y \text{ is even}\\ y-1, \text{ if } y \text{ is odd}\end{cases}$$

or $$f^{-1}(x)=\begin{cases}x+1, \text{ if } x \text{ is even}\\ x-1, \text{ if } x \text{ is odd}\end{cases}$$

27. Given, $R=\{(x, y): x\in N, y\in N \text{ and } 2x+y=24\}$

Now, $x=1 \Rightarrow y=22$;

$x=2 \Rightarrow y=20$; $\quad [\because y=24-2x]$

$x=3 \Rightarrow y=18$; $x=4 \Rightarrow y=16$;

$x=5 \Rightarrow y=14$; $x=6 \Rightarrow y=12$;

$x=7 \Rightarrow y=10$; $x=8 \Rightarrow y=8$

$x=9 \Rightarrow y=6$; $x=10 \Rightarrow y=4$

and $x=11 \Rightarrow y=2$

So, domain of $R=\{1,2,3,\ldots,11\}$

and range of $R=\{2,4,6,8,10,12,14,16,18,20,22\}$

and $R=\{(1,22),(2,20),(3,18),(4,16),(5,14),$
$(6,12),(7,10),(8,8),(9,6),(10,4),(11,2)\}$

Reflexive Since, for $1\in$ domain of R, $(1,1)\notin R$. So, R is not reflexive.

Symmetric We observe that $(1, 22)\in R$ but $(22, 1)\notin R$. So, R is not symmetric.

Transitive We observe that $(7, 10)\in R$ and $(10, 4)\in R$ but $(7, 4)\notin R$.

So, R is not transitive.

Thus, R is neither reflexive nor symmetric nor transitive.

Hence, R is not an equivalence relation.

28. Given, a function $f : A \to B$, where $A = R - \{3\}$ and $B = R - \{1\}$, defined by $f(x) = \dfrac{x-2}{x-3}$.

One-one function

Let $x_1, x_2 \in A$ such that $f(x_1) = f(x_2)$

Then, $\dfrac{x_1 - 2}{x_1 - 3} = \dfrac{x_2 - 2}{x_2 - 3}$

$\Rightarrow \quad (x_1 - 2)(x_2 - 3) = (x_2 - 2)(x_1 - 3)$

$\Rightarrow \quad x_1x_2 - 3x_1 - 2x_2 + 6 = x_1x_2 - 3x_2 - 2x_1 + 6$

$\Rightarrow \quad -3x_1 - 2x_2 = -3x_2 - 2x_1$

$\Rightarrow \quad -3(x_1 - x_2) + 2(x_1 - x_2) = 0$

$\Rightarrow \quad -(x_1 - x_2) = 0$

$\Rightarrow \quad x_1 - x_2 = 0$

$\Rightarrow \quad x_1 = x_2$

Thus, $\quad f(x_1) = f(x_2)$

$\Rightarrow \quad x_1 = x_2, \forall x_1, x_2 \in A$

So, $f(x)$ is an one-one function.

Onto function Let $y \in B = R - \{1\}$ be any arbitrary element.

Then, $\quad f(x) = y$

$\Rightarrow \quad \dfrac{x-2}{x-3} = y$

$\Rightarrow \quad x - 2 = xy - 3y$

$\Rightarrow \quad x - xy = 2 - 3y$

$\Rightarrow \quad x(1 - y) = 2 - 3y$

$\Rightarrow \quad x = \dfrac{2-3y}{1-y}$

or $\quad x = \dfrac{3y-2}{y-1}$ ...(i)

Clearly, $x = \dfrac{3y-2}{y-1}$ is a real number for all $y \neq 1$.

Also, $\dfrac{3y-2}{y-1} \neq 3$ $\quad \left[\because \dfrac{3y-2}{y-1} = 3 \Rightarrow 3y - 2 = 3y - 3 \Rightarrow 2 = 3 \text{ which is absurd.}\right]$

Thus, for each $y \in B$, there exists $x = \dfrac{3y-2}{y-1} \in A$

such that $f(x) = f\left(\dfrac{3y-2}{y-1}\right)$

$$= \frac{\left(\frac{3y-2}{y-1}\right) - 2}{\frac{3y-2}{y-1} - 3} = \frac{3y-2-2y+2}{3y-2-3y+3} = y$$

Hence, $f(x)$ is an onto function.

Therefore, $f(x)$ is a bijective function.

From Eq. (i), we get

$$f^{-1}(y) = \frac{3y-2}{y-1}$$

or $\quad f^{-1}(x) = \dfrac{3x-2}{x-1}$

which is the inverse function of $f(x)$.

Concept Enhancer A function is said to be bijective or bijection, if a function $f : A \to B$ satisfies both the injective (one-one function) and surjective function (onto function) properties.

29. Given a relation R in $A \times A$, where $A = \{1, 2, 3, \ldots, 9\}$, defined as $(a, b)\, R\, (c, d)$, if $a + d = b + c$.

Reflexive Let (a, b) be any arbitrary element of $A \times A$.

i.e. $\quad (a, b) \in A \times A$, where $a, b \in A$.

Now, as $a + b = b + a$ $\quad$ [$\because$ addition is commutative]

$\therefore \quad (a, b) R (a, b)$

So, R is reflexive.

Symmetric Let $(a, b), (c, d) \in A \times A$, such that $(a, b)R(c, d)$.

Then, $\quad a + d = b + c$

$\Rightarrow \quad b + c = a + d$

$\Rightarrow \quad c + b = d + a$

$\Rightarrow \quad (c, d) R (a, b)$

So, R is symmetric.

Transitive Let $(a, b), (c, d), (e, f) \in A \times A$ such that $(a, b) R (c, d)$ and $(c, d) R (e, f)$.

Then, $a + d = b + c$ and $c + f = d + e$

On adding the above equations, we get

$$a + d + c + f = b + c + d + e$$

$\Rightarrow \quad a + f = b + e$

$\Rightarrow \quad (a, b) R (e, f)$

So, R is transitive.

Thus, R is reflexive, symmetric and transitive. Hence, R is an equivalence relation.

Now, for $[(2, 5)]$, we will find $(c, d) \in A \times A$ such that $2 + d = 5 + c$ or $d - c = 3$

Clearly, $(2, 5) R (1, 4)$ as $4 - 1 = 3$

$(2, 5) R (2, 5)$ as $5 - 2 = 3$

$(2, 5) R (3, 6)$ as $6 - 3 = 3$

$(2, 5) R (4, 7)$ as $7 - 4 = 3$

$$(2,5)R(5,8) \text{ as } 8-5=3$$
and $$(2,5)R(6,9) \text{ as } 9-6=3$$
Hence, equivalence class $[(2,5)]$
$$= \{(1,4), (2,5), (3,6), (4,7), (5,8), (6,9)\}.$$

Concept Enhancer A relation R is said to be an equivalence relation, if it is simultaneously reflexive, symmetric and transitive on A.

30. Given, $f(x) = \dfrac{4x+3}{6x-4}$,

where $x \in A = R - \left\{\dfrac{2}{3}\right\}$

One-one function Let $x_1, x_2 \in A = R - \left\{\dfrac{2}{3}\right\}$ such that

$f(x_1) = f(x_2)$.

Then, $$\frac{4x_1+3}{6x_1-4} = \frac{4x_2+3}{6x_2-4}$$
$$\Rightarrow (4x_1+3)(6x_2-4) = (4x_2+3)(6x_1-4)$$
$$\Rightarrow 24x_1x_2 - 16x_1 + 18x_2 - 12 = 24x_1x_2 - 16x_2 + 18x_1 - 12$$
$$\Rightarrow -34x_1 = -34x_2$$
$$\Rightarrow x_1 = x_2$$
So, f is one-one function.

Onto function Let y be an arbitrary element of A (codomain).

Then, $$f(x) = y$$
$$\Rightarrow \frac{4x+3}{6x-4} = y$$
$$\Rightarrow 4x+3 = 6xy - 4y$$
$$\Rightarrow 4x - 6xy = -4y - 3$$
$$\Rightarrow x(4-6y) = -(4y+3)$$
$$\Rightarrow x = \frac{-(4y+3)}{4-6y}$$
$$\Rightarrow x = \frac{4y+3}{6y-4}$$

Clearly, $x = \dfrac{4y+3}{6y-4}$ is a real number for all $y \neq \dfrac{4}{6} = \dfrac{2}{3}$.

Also, $\dfrac{4y+3}{6y-4} \neq \dfrac{2}{3}$ $\left[\because \dfrac{4y+3}{6y-4} = \dfrac{2}{3} \Rightarrow 12y+9 = 12y-8 \Rightarrow 9 = -8, \text{ which is absurd}\right]$

Thus, for each $y \in A$ (codomain), there exists $x = \dfrac{4y+3}{6y-4} \in A$ (domain) such that

$$f(x) = f\left(\frac{4y+3}{6y-4}\right) = \frac{4\left(\frac{4y+3}{6y-4}\right)+3}{6\left(\frac{4y+3}{6y-4}\right)-4}$$
$$= \frac{16y+12+18y-12}{24y+18-24y+16}$$
$$= \frac{34y}{34} = y$$

Hence, f is onto function.

Since, f is bijective function, so its inverse exists.

$$\therefore \quad x = f^{-1}(y) = \frac{3+4y}{6y-4}$$

or $f^{-1}(x) = \dfrac{3+4x}{6x-4}, x \neq \dfrac{2}{3}$

31. Here, function $f : R^+ \to [4, \infty)$ is given by $f(x) = x^2 + 4$.

One-one function Let $x, y \in R^+$, such that $f(x) = f(y)$.
$$\Rightarrow x^2 + 4 = y^2 + 4$$
$$\Rightarrow x^2 = y^2$$
$$\Rightarrow x = y$$
[$\because$ we take only positive sign as $x, y \in R^+$]

Therefore, f is a one-one function.

Onto function For $y \in [4, \infty)$, let $y = x^2 + 4$
$$\Rightarrow x^2 = y - 4 \geq 0 \quad [\because y \geq 4]$$
$$\Rightarrow x = \sqrt{y-4} \geq 0$$
[we take only positive sign, as $x \in R^+$]

Therefore, for any $y \in R^+$, (codomain), there exists $x = \sqrt{y-4} \in R^+$ (domain) such that
$$f(x) = f(\sqrt{y-4}) = (\sqrt{y-4})^2 + 4 = y - 4 + 4 = y$$

Therefore, f is onto function.

Since, f is one-one and onto and therefore f^{-1} exists.
$$\therefore \quad x = f^{-1}(y) = \sqrt{y-4}$$
or $$f^{-1}(x) = \sqrt{x-4}, x \in [4, \infty)$$

Alternate Method

Let us define $g : [4, \infty) \to R^+$, by $g(y) = \sqrt{y-4}$.

Now, $gof(x) = g(f(x)) = g(x^2+4)$

$$= \sqrt{(x^2+4)-4} = \sqrt{x^2} = x$$

and $fog(y) = f[g(y)] = f(\sqrt{y-4})$

$$= (\sqrt{y-4})^2 + 4 = (y-4)+4 = y$$

Thus, $gof = I_{R^+}$ and $fog = I_{[4,\infty)}$.

$\Rightarrow f$ is invertible and its inverse function is g.

$\therefore \quad f^{-1}(y) = g(y) = \sqrt{y-4}$ or $f^{-1}(x) = \sqrt{x-4}$

32. Given function is $f: N \to N$ such that

$$f(x) = \begin{cases} x+1, & \text{if } x \text{ is odd} \\ x-1, & \text{if } x \text{ is even} \end{cases}$$

One-one function

From the given function, we observe that

***Case* I** when x is odd.

Let $f(x_1) = f(x_2) \Rightarrow x_1+1 = x_2+1 \Rightarrow x_1 = x_2$

$\because \quad f(x_1) = f(x_2) \Rightarrow x_1 = x_2, \forall x_1, x_2 \in N$

So, $f(x)$ is one-one.

***Case* II** when x is even.

Let $f(x_1) = f(x_2) \Rightarrow x_1 - 1 = x_2 - 1 \Rightarrow x_1 = x_2$

$\because \quad f(x_1) = f(x_2)$

$\Rightarrow \quad x_1 = x_2, \forall x_1, x_2 \in N$

So, $f(x)$ is one-one.

Hence, from case I and case II, we observe that,

$f(x_1) = f(x_2) \Rightarrow x_1 = x_2, \forall x_1, x_2 \in N$

Therefore, $f(x)$ is one-one.

Onto function Let $y \in N$ (codomain) be any arbitrary number.

If y is odd, then there exists an even number $y+1 \in N$ (domain) such that

$$f(y+1) = (y+1) - 1 = y$$

If y is even, then there exists an odd number $y-1 \in N$ (domain) such that

$$f(y-1) = (y-1)+1 = y$$

Thus, every element in N (codomain) has a pre-image in N (domain).

Therefore, $f(x)$ is an onto function.

Hence, the function $f(x)$ is bijective.

33. The given function is $f: N \to N$ such that

$$f(n) = \begin{cases} \dfrac{n+1}{2}, & \text{if } n \text{ is odd} \\ \dfrac{n}{2}, & \text{if } n \text{ is even} \end{cases}$$

One-one function Here, $f(1) = \dfrac{1+1}{2} = \dfrac{2}{2} = 1$ $\left[\text{put } n = 1 \text{ in } f(n) = \dfrac{n+1}{2}\right]$

and $f(2) = \dfrac{2}{2} = 1$ $\left[\text{put } n = 2 \text{ in } f(n) = \dfrac{n}{2}\right]$

$\therefore f(n)$ is not a one-one function because at two distinct values of domain (N), $f(n)$ has same image.

Onto function If n is an odd natural number, then $2n-1$ is also an odd natural number.

Now, $f(2n-1) = \dfrac{2n-1+1}{2} = n$ ...(i)

Again, if n is an even natural number, then $2n$ is also an even natural number. Then,

$$f(2n) = \frac{2n}{2} = n \quad \text{...(ii)}$$

From Eqs. (i) and (ii), we observe that for each n (whether even or odd) there exists its pre-image in N.

i.e. Range = Codomain

Therefore, f is onto.

Hence, $f(x)$ is not one-one but it is onto.

So, it is not a bijective function.

34. (i) (a) The denominator of the function $f(x) = \dfrac{x-1}{x-2}$ should not be zero.

So, x cannot be equal to 2. $[\because 2-2=0]$

Therefore, domain of $f(x) = R - \{2\}$.

(ii) (c) Let $f(x) = y$

$$\therefore \quad y = \frac{x-1}{x-2}$$

$$\Rightarrow \quad xy - 2y = x - 1$$

$$\Rightarrow \quad xy - x = 2y + 1$$

$$\Rightarrow \quad x(y-1) = 2y+1$$

$$\Rightarrow \quad x = \frac{2y-1}{y-1}$$

Now, $y - 1 \neq 0$

$y \neq 1$

Hence, range of $f(x) = R - \{1\}$.

(iii) (d) $g(x) = 2\left(\dfrac{x-1}{x-2}\right) - 1 = \dfrac{2x-2}{x-2} - 1$

$$= \frac{2x-2-x+2}{x-2} = \frac{x}{x-2}$$

(iv) (a) A function is said to be one-one if each element of set A has a unique element on set B.

So, the function $f(x)$ will be one-one, if

$$f(x_1) = f(x_2)$$

$$\Rightarrow \quad x_1 = x_2$$

35. Here, function $f: R_+ \to [-5, \infty)$ is given as

$$f(x) = 9x^2 + 6x - 5$$

Let y be any arbitrary element of $[-5, \infty)$.

Let $\quad y = 9x^2 + 6x - 5$

$$\Rightarrow \quad y = (3x+1)^2 - 1 - 5 = (3x+1)^2 - 6$$

$$= (3x+1)^2 = y + 6$$

$$\Rightarrow \quad 3x + 1 = \sqrt{y+6}, \text{ as } y \ge -5 \Rightarrow y + 6 \ge 0$$

$$\Rightarrow \quad x = \frac{\sqrt{y+6} - 1}{3}$$

Therefore, f is onto, thereby range $f = [-5, \infty)$

Let us define $g: [-5, \infty) \to R_+$

as $\quad g(y) = \dfrac{\sqrt{y+6} - 1}{3}$

Now, $(gof)(x) = g[f(x)] = g(9x^2 + 6x - 5)$

$$= \frac{\sqrt{(3x+1)^2 - 6 + 6} - 1}{3} = \frac{3x + 1 - 1}{3} = x$$

and $(fog)(y) = f[g(y)] = f\left(\dfrac{\sqrt{y+6} - 1}{3}\right)$

$$= \left[3\left(\frac{\sqrt{y+6} - 1}{3}\right) + 1\right]^2 - 6$$

$$= (\sqrt{y+6})^2 - 6 = y + 6 - 6 = y$$

Therefore, $gof = I_{R+}$ and $fog = I[-5, \infty)$

Hence, f is invertible and the inverse of f is given by

$$f^{-1}(y) = g(y) = \frac{\sqrt{y+6} - 1}{3}$$

(i) $\therefore \; f^{-1}(10) = \dfrac{\sqrt{10+6} - 1}{3} = \dfrac{\sqrt{16} - 1}{3} = \dfrac{4 - 1}{3} = 1$

(ii) If $f^{-1}(y) = \dfrac{4}{3}$

$$\Rightarrow \quad y = f(4/3) = 9(4/3)^2 + 6(4/3) - 5$$

$$= 16 + 8 - 5 = 19$$

36. Given, $f: R - \left\{-\dfrac{4}{3}\right\} \to R - \left\{\dfrac{4}{3}\right\}$

defined by $f(x) = \dfrac{4x+3}{3x+4}$

Let $x_1, x_2 \in R - \left\{-\dfrac{4}{3}\right\}$ such that $f(x_1) = f(x_2)$

$$\Rightarrow \quad \frac{4x_1 + 3}{3x_1 + 4} = \frac{4x_2 + 3}{3x_2 + 4}$$

$$\Rightarrow \quad (4x_1 + 3)(3x_2 + 4) = (3x_1 + 4)(4x_2 + 3)$$

$$\Rightarrow \quad 12x_1x_2 + 16x_1 + 9x_2 + 12 = 12x_1x_2 + 9x_1 + 16x_2 + 12$$

$$\Rightarrow \quad 7x_1 = 7x_2$$

$$\Rightarrow \quad x_1 = x_2$$

$\Rightarrow$ f is one-one.

Let $y \in R - \left\{\dfrac{4}{3}\right\}$, then $y \ne \dfrac{4}{3}$

The function f is onto if there exist

$x \in R - \left\{\dfrac{-4}{3}\right\}$, such that $f(x) = y$

Now, $f(x) = y \Rightarrow \dfrac{4x+3}{3x+4} = y$

$$\Rightarrow \quad 4x + 3 = y(3x + 4)$$

$$\Rightarrow \quad 4x + 3 = 3xy + 4y \Rightarrow 4x - 3xy = 4y - 3$$

$$\Rightarrow \quad x(4 - 3y) = 4y - 3$$

$$\Rightarrow \quad x = \frac{4y - 3}{4 - 3y} \in R - \left\{\frac{-4}{3}\right\} \left(y \ne \frac{4}{3}\right)$$

Thus, for any $y \in R - \left\{\dfrac{4}{3}\right\}$, there exist

$\dfrac{4y-3}{4-3y} \in R - \left\{\dfrac{-4}{3}\right\} \Rightarrow f$ is onto.

$$f^{-1}(y) = \frac{4y - 3}{4 - 3y} \in R - \left\{-\frac{4}{3}\right\}$$

$$f^{-1}(x) = \frac{4x - 3}{4 - 3x}$$

$$\Rightarrow \quad f^{-1}(0) = \frac{0 - 3}{4 - 0} = \frac{-3}{4}$$

and also $\quad f^{-1}(x) = 2 \Rightarrow \dfrac{4x - 3}{4 - 3x} = 2$

$$\Rightarrow \quad 4x - 3 = 2(4 - 3x)$$

$$\Rightarrow \quad 4x - 3 = 8 - 6x$$

$$\Rightarrow \quad 10x = 8 + 3 = 11 \Rightarrow x = \frac{11}{10}$$

Concept Enhancer If a function $f: A \to B$ is a bijective function i.e. it is one-one and onto function. Then, we define $g: B \to A$, such that $f(x) = y \Rightarrow g(y) = x$, g is called inverse of f and *vice-versa*.

Thus, $f(x) = y \Rightarrow f^{-1}(y) = x$

37. We have a mapping $f: N \to N$ given by

$$f(x) = 9x^2 + 6x - 5$$

One-one function Let $x_1, x_2 \in N$, such that

$$f(x_1) = f(x_2)$$

Then, $9x_1^2 + 6x_1 - 5 = 9x_2^2 + 6x_2 - 5$

$$\Rightarrow \quad 9x_1^2 + 6x_1 = 9x_2^2 + 6x_2$$

$$\Rightarrow \quad 9(x_1^2 - x_2^2) + 6(x_1 - x_2) = 0$$

$$\Rightarrow 3(x_1 - x_2)(x_1 + x_2) + 2(x_1 - x_2) = 0 \quad \text{[divide by 3]}$$

$$\Rightarrow \quad (x_1 - x_2)(3x_1 + 3x_2 + 2) = 0$$

$$\Rightarrow \quad x_1 - x_2 = 0 \text{ or } 3x_1 + 3x_2 + 2 = 0$$

But $3x_1 + 3x_2 + 2 \neq 0$ $[\because x_1, x_2 \in N]$

$$\therefore \quad x_1 - x_2 = 0$$

$$\Rightarrow \quad x_1 = x_2$$

So, f is one-one function.

Onto function Obviously, $f: N \to S$ is an onto function, because S is the range of f.

Thus, $f: N \to S$ is one-one and onto function.

$\Rightarrow f$ is invertible function, so its inverse exists.

Let $f(x) = y$, then

$$y = 9x^2 + 6x - 5$$

$$\Rightarrow \quad y = (3x)^2 + 2 \cdot 3x \cdot 1 + 1 - 6$$

$$\Rightarrow \quad y = (3x + 1)^2 - 6$$

$$\Rightarrow \quad (3x + 1)^2 = y + 6$$

$$\Rightarrow \quad 3x + 1 = \sqrt{y + 6}$$

[taking positive square root as $x \in N$]

$$\Rightarrow \quad x = \frac{\sqrt{y+6} - 1}{3}$$

$$\therefore \quad f^{-1}(y) = \frac{\sqrt{y+6} - 1}{3}$$

or $f^{-1}(x) = \dfrac{\sqrt{x+6} - 1}{3}$, where $x \in S$

Now, $f^{-1}(43) = \dfrac{\sqrt{43+6} - 1}{3}$

$$= \frac{\sqrt{49} - 1}{3} = \frac{7 - 1}{3} = 2$$

and $f^{-1}(163) = \dfrac{\sqrt{163+6} - 1}{3} = \dfrac{\sqrt{169} - 1}{3}$

$$= \frac{13 - 1}{3}$$

$$= \frac{12}{3} = 4$$

38. We have, a relation R on $N \times N$ defined by $(a, b) R (c, d)$, if $ad(b + c) = bc(a + d)$.

Reflexive Let $(a, b) \in N \times N$ be any arbitrary element.

We have to show $(a, b) R (a, b)$, i.e. to show $ab(b + a) = ba(a + b)$ which is trivally true as natural numbers are commutative under usual multiplication and addition.

Since, $(a, b) \in N \times N$ was arbitrary, therefore R is reflexive.

Symmetric Let $(a, b), (c, d) \in N \times N$ such that $(a, b) R (c, d)$, i.e. $ad(b + c) = bc(a + d)$ ...(i)

To show, $(c, d) R (a, b)$,

i.e. to show $cb(d + a) = da(c + b)$

From Eq.(i), we have

$$ad(b + c) = bc(a + d) \Rightarrow da(c + b) = cb(d + a)$$

[$\because$ natural numbers are commutative under usual addition and multiplication]

$$\Rightarrow cb(d + a) = da(c + b) \Rightarrow (c, d) R (a, b)$$

Thus, R is symmetric.

Transitive Let $(a, b), (c, d)$ and $(e, f) \in N \times N$ such that $(a, b) R (c, d)$ and $(c, d) R (e, f)$.

Now, $(a, b) R (c, d) \Rightarrow ad(b + c) = bc(a + d)$

$$\Rightarrow \quad \frac{b + c}{bc} = \frac{a + d}{ad}$$

$$\Rightarrow \quad \frac{1}{b} + \frac{1}{c} = \frac{1}{a} + \frac{1}{d} \quad \text{...(ii)}$$

and $(c, d) R (e, f) \Rightarrow cf(d + e) = de(c + f)$

$$\Rightarrow \quad \frac{d + e}{de} = \frac{c + f}{cf}$$

$$\Rightarrow \quad \frac{1}{d} + \frac{1}{e} = \frac{1}{c} + \frac{1}{f} \quad \text{...(iii)}$$

On adding Eqs. (ii) and (iii), we get

$$\left(\frac{1}{b} + \frac{1}{c}\right) + \left(\frac{1}{d} + \frac{1}{e}\right) = \left(\frac{1}{a} + \frac{1}{d}\right) + \left(\frac{1}{c} + \frac{1}{f}\right)$$

$$\Rightarrow \quad \frac{1}{b} + \frac{1}{e} = \frac{1}{a} + \frac{1}{f}$$

$$\Rightarrow \quad \frac{e + b}{be} = \frac{f + a}{af}$$

$$\Rightarrow \quad af(e + b) = be(f + a)$$

$$\Rightarrow \quad af(b + e) = be(a + f)$$

$$\Rightarrow \quad (a, b) R (e, f)$$

$\Rightarrow R$ is transitive.

Thus, R is reflexive, symmetric and transitive, hence R is an equivalence relation.

CHAPTER TEST

1 Mark Questions

1. The number of all one-one functions from set $A = \{1, 2, 3\}$ to itself is

(a) 2 (b) 6

(c) 3 (d) 1

2. The inverse of the function $f: R \to [a \in R : a < 1]$, defined by $f(a) = \dfrac{e^a - e^{-a}}{e^a + e^{-a}}$, is

(a) $\dfrac{1}{2}\log\dfrac{1+a}{1-a}$ (b) $\dfrac{1}{2}\log\dfrac{2+a}{2-a}$

(c) $\dfrac{1}{2}\log\dfrac{1-a}{1+a}$ (d) None of these

3. Let R be a relation from R to R the set of real numbers defined by $R = \{(x, y): x, y \in R$ and $x - y + \sqrt{3}$ is an irrational number$\}$. Then, R is

(a) reflexive

(b) transitive

(c) symmetric

(d) an equivalence relation

2 Marks Questions

4. State whether the function $f: R \to R$, defined by $f(x) = 3 - 4x$ is onto or not.

5. Show that the function $f: N \to N$, given by $f(x) = 2x$ is one-one but not onto.

6. Consider $f: \{1, 2, 3\} \to \{a, b, c\}$ given by $f(1) = a$, $f(2) = b$, $f(3) = c$. Find f^{-1}. Show that $(f^{-1})^{-1} = f$.

3/4 Marks Questions

7. Let N be the set of all natural numbers and let R be a relation in N, defined by

$$R = \{(a, b): a \text{ is a multiple of } b\}.$$

Show that R is reflexive and transitive but not symmetric.

8. Show that relation R in the set of real numbers, defined as $R = \{(a, b): a \le b^2\}$ is neither reflexive nor symmetric nor transitive.

5/6 Marks Questions

9. Consider $f: R^+ \to [-9, \infty)$ given by $f(x) = 5x^2 + 6x - 9$. Prove that f is invertible with

$$f^{-1}(y) = \left(\frac{\sqrt{54 + 5y} - 3}{5}\right)$$

[where, R^+ is the set of all non-negative real numbers].

Answers

1. (b) 2. (a) 3. (a)

4. f is onto

02

Inverse Trigonometric Functions

TREND ANALYSIS 3 YEARS

		Average No. of Questions Across all Sets		
	Types of Questions	2024	2023	2020
TOPIC 01 Principal Values of Inverse Trigonometric Functions	1 Mark	1	—	—
	2 Marks	—	—	1
	3/4 Marks	—	—	—
	5/6 Marks	—	—	—
TOPIC 02 Formulae Related to Inverse Trigonometric Functions	1 Marks	—	—	—
	2 Marks	—	1	—
	3/4 Marks	2	1	1
	5/6 Marks	—	—	—

TOPIC 1

Principal Values of Inverse Trigonometric Functions

If a function f is one-to-one and onto i.e. bijective from A to B, then function g which associates each element $y \in B$ to one and only one element $x \in A$, such that $y = f(x)$, then g is called the **inverse function** of f and it is denoted by $x = g(y)$.

Usually, we denote $g = f^{-1}$ [read as f inverse]

or $x = f^{-1}(y)$

Thus, a function f is invertible iff f is one-one and onto.

Inverse Trigonometric Functions

As we know that, trigonometric functions are periodic functions, so these functions are many-one over their domains. These functions are not one-one and onto over their natural domain and range, so their inverse does not exist but if we restrict their domain and range, then their inverse exists. All inverse trigonometric functions are $\sin^{-1} x, \cos^{-1} x, \tan^{-1} x$, $\text{cosec}^{-1} x, \sec^{-1} x$ and $\cot^{-1} x$.

Domain and Range

The range of trigonometric functions becomes the domain of inverse trigonometric functions and restricted domain of trigonometric functions becomes range or principal value branch of inverse trigonometric functions.

Principal Value

The value of an inverse trigonometric functions, which lies in its range or principal value branch is called the principal value of the inverse trigonometric function.

(i) $\sin^{-1} y \neq (\sin y)^{-1}, \sin^{-1} y \neq \sin^{-1}\left(\frac{1}{y}\right), \sin^{-1} y \neq \frac{1}{\sin y}$.

The same holds for other inverse trigonometric functions.

(ii) Whenever no branch of an inverse trigonometric function is mentioned, we consider the principle value branch of that function.

Tabular Representation of Domain and Principal value branch of Inverse Trigonometric Functions

Functions	Domain	Principal value branch (Range)
$y=\sin^{-1}x$	$-1\le x\le 1$ or $[-1,1]$	$-\frac{\pi}{2}\le y\le\frac{\pi}{2}$ or $\left[\frac{-\pi}{2},\frac{\pi}{2}\right]$
$y=\cos^{-1}x$	$-1\le x\le 1$ or $[-1,1]$	$0\le y\le\pi$ or $[0,\pi]$
$y=\tan^{-1}x$	All real numbers $(-\infty<x<\infty)$	$-\frac{\pi}{2}<y<\frac{\pi}{2}$ or $\left(\frac{-\pi}{2},\frac{\pi}{2}\right)$
$y=\cot^{-1}x$	All real numbers $(-\infty<x<\infty)$	$0<y<\pi$ or $(0,\pi)$
$y=\sec^{-1}x$	$x\ge 1$ or $x\le -1$ or $R-(-1,1)$	$0\le y\le\pi,\ y\ne\frac{\pi}{2}$ or $[0,\pi]-\left\{\frac{\pi}{2}\right\}$
$y=\text{cosec}^{-1}x$	$x\ge 1$ or $x\le -1$ or $R-(-1,1)$	$-\frac{\pi}{2}\le y\le\frac{\pi}{2},\ y\ne 0$ or $\left[\frac{-\pi}{2},\frac{\pi}{2}\right]-\{0\}$

Elementary Properties of Inverse Trigonometric Functions

(i) $\sin^{-1}(\sin\theta)=\theta,\ \forall\ \theta\in\left[-\frac{\pi}{2},\frac{\pi}{2}\right]$

(ii) $\cos^{-1}(\cos\theta)=\theta,\ \forall\ \theta\in[0,\pi]$

(iii) $\tan^{-1}(\tan\theta)=\theta,\ \forall\ \theta\in\left(-\frac{\pi}{2},\frac{\pi}{2}\right)$

(iv) $\text{cosec}^{-1}(\text{cosec}\,\theta)=\theta,\ \forall\ \theta\in\left[-\frac{\pi}{2},\frac{\pi}{2}\right]-\{0\}$

(v) $\sec^{-1}(\sec\theta)=\theta,\ \forall\ \theta\in[0,\pi],-\left\{\frac{\pi}{2}\right\}$

(vi) $\cot^{-1}(\cot\theta)=\theta,\ \forall\ \theta\in(0,\pi)$

(vii) $\sin(\sin^{-1}x)=x,\ \forall x\in[-1,1]$

(viii) $\cos(\cos^{-1}x)=x,\ \forall x\in[-1,1]$

(ix) $\tan(\tan^{-1}x)=x,\ \forall x\in R$

(x) $\text{cosec}(\text{cosec}^{-1}x)=x,\ \forall x\in R-(-1,1)$

(xi) $\sec(\sec^{-1}x)=x,\ \forall x\in R-(-1,1)$

(xii) $\cot(\cot^{-1}x)=x,\ \forall x\in R$

PYQs Previous Years Questions

1 Mark Questions

1. The value of $\text{cosec}\left(\sin^{-1}\left(\frac{-1}{2}\right)\right)-\sec\left(\cos^{-1}\left(\frac{-1}{2}\right)\right)$ is equal to *ISC 2024*

(a) -4 (b) 0 (c) -1 (d) 4

2. What is the value of $\cot\left(\frac{\pi}{2}+\tan^{-1}\frac{1}{\sqrt{2}}\right)$? *ISC Specimen 2024*

(a) $\frac{1}{\sqrt{2}}$ (b) $\frac{\pi}{2}$ (c) -1 (d) $-\frac{1}{\sqrt{2}}$

3. The value of $\tan^{-1}\sqrt{3}-\sec^{-1}(-2)$ is equal to *ISC Specimen 2023*

(a) $\frac{\pi}{3}$ (b) $\frac{2\pi}{3}$ (c) $\frac{-\pi}{3}$ (d) $\frac{\pi}{4}$

4. What will be the principal value of $\text{cosec}^{-1}(-\sqrt{2})$? *ISC Specimen Sem-I 2022*

(a) $\frac{3\pi}{4}$ (b) $-\frac{\pi}{6}$ (c) $\frac{\pi}{4}$ (d) $-\frac{\pi}{4}$

5. Simplified value of $\sin\left[\frac{\pi}{2}-\sin^{-1}\left(-\frac{\sqrt{3}}{2}\right)\right]$ is *ISC Specimen 2021*

(a) $\frac{1}{2}$ (b) $\frac{1}{\sqrt{2}}$ (c) $\frac{\sqrt{3}}{2}$ (d) $-\frac{\sqrt{3}}{2}$

2 Marks Questions

6. Find the domain of the function $\cos^{-1}x+\sin x$. *ISC Specimen 2024*

7. Prove that $\tan^2(\sec^{-1}2)+\cot^2(\text{cosec}^{-1}3)=11$. *ISC 2020*

> **KEY CONCEPT**
> Use trigonometric identities
> $\tan^2\theta=\sec^2\theta-1$ and $\cot^2\theta=\text{cosec}^2\theta-1$.

8. Solve for x

$$\sin(2\tan^{-1}x)=1$$ *ISC 2019, 11*

9. Solve $\sin^{-1}\cos(\sin^{-1}x)=\frac{\pi}{3}$. *ISC Specimen 2018*

3/4 Marks Questions

10. Prove that $\cos[\tan^{-1}\{\cot(\sin^{-1}x\}]=x$. *ISC Specimen 2024*

11. If $\sec^{-1} x = \text{cosec}^{-1} y$, then show that $\frac{1}{x^2} + \frac{1}{y^2} = 1$. **ISC 2019**

12. Prove that $\sec^2(\tan^{-1} 2) + \text{cosec}^2(\cot^{-1} 3) = 15$. **ISC 2012**

5/6 Marks Questions

13. Prove that $\cot\left(\frac{\pi}{4} - 2\cot^{-1} 3\right) = 7$. **ISC 2005**

KEY CONCEPT
Let $\cos^{-1} 3 = \theta$ and use identity
$\tan(A-B) = \frac{\tan A - \tan B}{1 + \tan A \tan B}$ and $\tan 2A = \frac{2\tan A}{1-\tan^2 A}$.

14. Show that $\tan^{-1}\left(\frac{\cos x}{1+\sin x}\right) = \frac{\pi}{4} - \frac{x}{2}, \frac{-\pi}{2} < x < \frac{\pi}{2}$.

Explanations

1. (b) We have,

$$\text{cosec}\left[\sin^{-1}\left(\frac{-1}{2}\right)\right] - \sec\left[\cos^{-1}\left(\frac{-1}{2}\right)\right]$$

$$= \text{cosec}\left[\sin^{-1}\left\{\sin\left(\frac{-\pi}{6}\right)\right\}\right] - \sec\left[\cos^{-1}\left\{\cos\left(\frac{2\pi}{3}\right)\right\}\right]$$

$$\left[\because -\sin\frac{\pi}{6} = \sin\left(\frac{-\pi}{6}\right) = \frac{-1}{2} \text{ and } \cos\left(\frac{2\pi}{3}\right) = \frac{-1}{2}\right]$$

$$= \text{cosec}\left[\frac{-\pi}{6}\right] - \sec\left[\frac{2\pi}{3}\right]$$

$$= -2 - (-2) = 0$$

2. (d) $\cot\left(\frac{\pi}{2} + \tan^{-1}\frac{1}{\sqrt{2}}\right)$

$$= -\tan\left(\tan^{-1}\frac{1}{\sqrt{2}}\right)$$

$$\left[\because \cot\left(\frac{\pi}{2} + \theta\right) = -\tan\theta\right]$$

$$= -\frac{1}{\sqrt{2}}$$

3. (c) Let $\tan^{-1}\sqrt{3} = x \Rightarrow \tan x = \sqrt{3} = \tan\frac{\pi}{3}$

Since, the principal value branch of $\tan^{-1}$ is $\left(-\frac{\pi}{2}, \frac{\pi}{2}\right)$

and $x = \frac{\pi}{3} \in \left(-\frac{\pi}{2}, \frac{\pi}{2}\right)$

So, the principal value of $\tan^{-1}\sqrt{3}$ is $\frac{\pi}{3}$.

Again, let $\sec^{-1}(-2) = y$

$$\Rightarrow \quad \sec y = -2 = -\sec\frac{\pi}{3}$$

$$\Rightarrow \quad \sec y = \sec\left(\pi - \frac{\pi}{3}\right) = \sec\frac{2\pi}{3}$$

Since, the principal value branch of $\sec^{-1}(-2)$ is $[0, \pi] - \left\{\frac{\pi}{2}\right\}$ and $x = \frac{2\pi}{3} \in [0, \pi] - \left\{\frac{\pi}{2}\right\}$.

So, the principal value of $\sec^{-1}(-2)$ is $\frac{2\pi}{3}$.

Hence, $\tan^{-1}\sqrt{3} - \sec^{-1}(-2) = \frac{\pi}{3} - \frac{2\pi}{3} = \frac{-\pi}{3}$

4. (d) Let $\quad y = \text{cosec}^{-1}(-\sqrt{2})$

$$\Rightarrow \quad \text{cosec } y = -\sqrt{2}$$

$$\Rightarrow \quad \text{cosec } y = \text{cosec}\left(-\frac{\pi}{4}\right)$$

We know that the range of the principal value branch of $\text{cosec}^{-1} x$ is $\left[-\frac{\pi}{2}, \frac{\pi}{2}\right] - \{0\}$.

$$\therefore \quad y = -\frac{\pi}{4}$$

Therefore, the principal value of $\text{cosec}^{-1}(-\sqrt{2})$ is $-\frac{\pi}{4}$.

5. (a) $\sin\left[\frac{\pi}{2} - \sin^{-1}\left(-\frac{\sqrt{3}}{2}\right)\right]$

$$= \sin\left[\frac{\pi}{2} - \left(-\sin^{-1}\left(\frac{\sqrt{3}}{2}\right)\right)\right]$$

$$= \sin\left[\frac{\pi}{2} + \sin^{-1}\frac{\sqrt{3}}{2}\right]$$

$$= \sin\left[\frac{\pi}{2} + \frac{\pi}{3}\right]$$

$$= \cos\frac{\pi}{3} = \frac{1}{2}$$

6. Let $f(x)=\cos^{-1}x+\sin x$

We have, domain of $\cos^{-1}x$ as $[-1,1]$

and domain of $\sin x$ as R.

$\therefore$ Domain of $f(x)$ will be common value of domain of $\cos^{-1}x$ and $\sin x$.

$\therefore$ Domain of $f(x)$ is $[-1,1]$.

7. We have,

$$\text{LHS}=\tan^2(\sec^{-1}2)+\cot^2(\text{cosec}^{-1}3)$$
$$=\{\sec(\sec^{-1}2)\}^2-1+\{\text{cosec}(\text{cosec}^{-1}3)\}^2-1$$
$$[\because \tan^2\theta=\sec^2\theta-1 \text{ and } \cot^2\theta=\text{cosec}^2\theta-1]$$
$$=(2)^2-1+(3)^2-1 \quad [\because \sec(\sec^{-1}\theta)=\theta \text{ and } \text{cosec}(\text{cosec}^{-1}\theta)=\theta]$$
$$=4-1+9-1=11=\text{RHS}$$ **Hence proved.**

8. Given, $\sin(2\tan^{-1}x)=1$

$$\Rightarrow \sin(2\tan^{-1}x)=\sin\frac{\pi}{2}$$
$$\Rightarrow 2\tan^{-1}x=\frac{\pi}{2}\Rightarrow \tan^{-1}x=\frac{\pi}{4}$$
$$\therefore x=\tan\frac{\pi}{4}=1$$

9. We have, $\sin^{-1}\cos(\sin^{-1}x)=\dfrac{\pi}{3}$

$$\Rightarrow \cos(\sin^{-1}x)=\sin\frac{\pi}{3}$$
$$\Rightarrow \cos(\sin^{-1}x)=\frac{\sqrt{3}}{2}$$
$$\Rightarrow \sin^{-1}x=\cos^{-1}\left(\frac{\sqrt{3}}{2}\right)$$
$$\Rightarrow \sin^{-1}x=\frac{\pi}{6}$$
$$\Rightarrow x=\sin\frac{\pi}{6}\Rightarrow x=\frac{1}{2}$$

10. We have, $\cos[\tan^{-1}\{\cot(\sin^{-1}x)\}]$

Let $\sin^{-1}x=\theta\Rightarrow\sin\theta=x=\cos[\tan^{-1}(\cot\theta)]$

$$=\cos\left[\tan^{-1}\left(\tan\left(\frac{\pi}{2}-\theta\right)\right)\right]$$
$$=\cos\left(\frac{\pi}{2}-\theta\right)$$
$$=\sin\theta$$
$$=x$$ **Hence proved.**

11. We have, $\sec^{-1}x=\text{cosec}^{-1}y$ ...(i)

To show $\dfrac{1}{x^2}+\dfrac{1}{y^2}=1$

Let $\text{cosec}^{-1}y=\theta\Rightarrow\text{cosec}\,\theta=y$

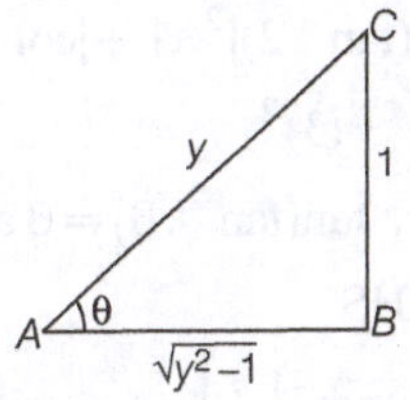

In right angled ΔABC, using Pythagoras theorem,

$$AB=\sqrt{y^2-1}$$
$$\therefore \sec\theta=\frac{y}{\sqrt{y^2-1}}$$
$$\Rightarrow \theta=\sec^{-1}\frac{y}{\sqrt{y^2-1}}$$
$$\Rightarrow \text{cosec}^{-1}y=\sec^{-1}\frac{y}{\sqrt{y^2-1}} \quad [\because y=\text{cosec}\,\theta]$$

$\therefore$ From Eq. (i), $\sec^{-1}x=\sec^{-1}\dfrac{y}{\sqrt{y^2-1}}$

$$\Rightarrow x=\frac{y}{\sqrt{y^2-1}}\Rightarrow x(\sqrt{y^2-1})=y$$

On squaring both sides, we get

$$x^2(y^2-1)=y^2$$
$$\Rightarrow x^2y^2-x^2=y^2$$
$$\Rightarrow x^2+y^2=x^2y^2$$
$$\Rightarrow \frac{1}{y^2}+\frac{1}{x^2}=1$$
$$\text{or} \quad \frac{1}{x^2}+\frac{1}{y^2}=1$$ **Hence proved.**

12. $\text{LHS}=\sec^2(\tan^{-1}2)+\text{cosec}^2(\cot^{-1}3)$

Let $\tan^{-1}2=\theta$ and $\cot^{-1}3=\phi$

$\Rightarrow \tan\theta=2$ and $\cot\phi=3$

Then, $\text{LHS}=\sec^2\theta+\text{cosec}^2\phi$

$$=(1+\tan^2\theta)+(1+\cot^2\phi)$$
$$[\because \sec^2A=1+\tan^2A \text{ and } \text{cosec}^2A=1+\cot^2A]$$
$$=(1+4)+(1+9)=5+10$$
$$=15=\text{RHS}$$ **Hence proved.**

Alternate Method

$$\text{LHS} = \sec^2(\tan^{-1} 2) + \text{cosec}^2 (\cot^{-1} 3)$$

$$= [1+\tan^2 (\tan^{-1} 2)] + [1+\cot^2 (\cot^{-1} 3)]$$

$$[\because \sec^2\theta = 1 + \tan^2\theta \text{ and } \text{cosec}^2\theta = 1+\cot^2\theta]$$

$$= 1+[\tan (\tan^{-1} 2)]^2 + 1 + [\cot (\cot^{-1} 3)]^2$$

$$= 2+(2)^2 + (3)^2$$

$$[\because \tan(\tan^{-1}\theta) = \theta \text{ and } \cot(\cot^{-1}\theta) = \theta]$$

$$= 15 = \text{RHS}$$

Hence proved.

13. $\text{LHS} = \cot\left(\frac{\pi}{4} - 2\cot^{-1} 3\right)$

Let $\cot^{-1} 3 = \theta$

$\Rightarrow \quad \cot\theta = 3$

Then, $\tan\theta = \frac{1}{3}$

$$\therefore \cot\left(\frac{\pi}{4} - 2\cot^{-1} 3\right) = \cot\left(\frac{\pi}{4} - 2\theta\right)$$

$$= \frac{1}{\tan\left(\frac{\pi}{4} - 2\theta\right)}$$

$$= \frac{1+\tan\frac{\pi}{4}\cdot\tan 2\theta}{\tan\frac{\pi}{4} - \tan 2\theta}$$

$$\left[\because \tan(A-B) = \frac{\tan A - \tan B}{1+\tan A \cdot \tan B}\right]$$

$$= \frac{1+\tan 2\theta}{1-\tan 2\theta}$$

$$= \frac{1+\frac{2\tan\theta}{1-\tan^2\theta}}{1-\frac{2\tan\theta}{1-\tan^2\theta}}$$

$$\left[\because \tan\frac{\pi}{4} = 1 \text{ and } \tan 2A = \frac{2\tan A}{1-\tan^2 A}\right]$$

$$= \frac{1+\frac{2\cdot(1/3)}{1-(1/9)}}{1-\frac{2\cdot(1/3)}{1-(1/9)}}$$

$$= \frac{1+\left(\frac{2}{3}\right)\cdot\left(\frac{9}{8}\right)}{1-\left(\frac{2}{3}\right)\cdot\left(\frac{9}{8}\right)} = \frac{1+\frac{3}{4}}{1-\frac{3}{4}} = \frac{7}{1}$$

$$= 7 = \text{RHS}$$

Hence proved.

14. $\text{LHS} = -\tan^{-1}\left(\frac{\cos x}{1+\sin x}\right)$

$$= \tan^{-1}\left(\frac{\cos^2\frac{x}{2} - \sin^2\frac{x}{2}}{\cos^2\frac{x}{2} + \sin^2\frac{x}{2} + 2\sin\frac{x}{2}.\cos\frac{x}{2}}\right)$$

$$\left[\begin{array}{l}\because \cos 2A = \cos^2 A - \sin^2 A, \\ \cos^2 A + \sin^2 A = 1 \\ \text{and } \sin 2A = 2\sin A\cos A\end{array}\right]$$

$$= \tan^{-1}\left[\frac{\left(\cos\frac{x}{2} - \sin\frac{x}{2}\right)\left(\cos\frac{x}{2} + \sin\frac{x}{2}\right)}{\left(\cos\frac{x}{2} + \sin\frac{x}{2}\right)^2}\right]$$

$$[\because a^2 - b^2 = (a+b)(a-b)$$
$$\text{and } (a^2 + b^2 + 2ab) = (a+b)^2]$$

$$= \tan^{-1}\left(\frac{\cos\frac{x}{2} - \sin\frac{x}{2}}{\cos\frac{x}{2} + \sin\frac{x}{2}}\right)$$

$$= \tan^{-1}\left(\frac{1-\tan\frac{x}{2}}{1+\tan\frac{x}{2}}\right)$$

$$\left[\text{dividing numerator and denominator by } \cos\frac{x}{2}\right]$$

$$= \tan^{-1}\left\{\tan\left(\frac{\pi}{4} - \frac{x}{2}\right)\right\}$$

$$\left[\because \tan\left(\frac{\pi}{4} - \theta\right) = \left(\frac{1-\tan\theta}{1+\tan\theta}\right)\right]$$

$$= \frac{\pi}{4} - \frac{x}{2} \qquad [\because \tan^{-1}(\tan\theta) = \theta]$$

Hence proved.

TOPIC 2

Formulae Related to Inverse Trigonometric Functions

Addition Formulae

(i) $\sin^{-1} x + \sin^{-1} y = \sin^{-1}[x\sqrt{1-y^2} + y\sqrt{1-x^2}]$,

if $-1 \le x,\ y \le 1$ and $x^2 + y^2 \le 1$

(ii) $\cos^{-1} x + \cos^{-1} y = \cos^{-1}[xy - \sqrt{1-x^2}\sqrt{1-y^2}]$,

if $-1 \le x,\ y \le 1$ and $x + y \ge 0$

(iii) $\tan^{-1} x + \tan^{-1} y = \tan^{-1} \frac{x+y}{1-xy}$, if $xy < 1$

Subtraction Formulae

(i) $\sin^{-1} x - \sin^{-1} y = \sin^{-1}[x\sqrt{1-y^2} - y\sqrt{1-x^2}]$,

if $-1 \le x,\ y \le 1$ and $x^2 + y^2 \le 1$

(ii) $\cos^{-1} x - \cos^{-1} y = \cos^{-1}[xy + \sqrt{1-x^2}\sqrt{1-y^2}]$,

if $-1 \le x,\ y \le 1$ and $x \le y$

(iii) $\tan^{-1} x - \tan^{-1} y = \tan^{-1} \frac{x-y}{1+xy}$, if $xy > -1$

Other Important Formulae

(i) $\sin^{-1}(-x) = -\sin^{-1} x,\ x \in [-1,1]$

(ii) $\cos^{-1}(-x) = \pi - \cos^{-1} x,\ x \in [-1,1]$

(iii) $\tan^{-1}(-x) = -\tan^{-1} x,\ x \in R$

(iv) $\cot^{-1}(-x) = \pi - \cot^{-1} x,\ x \in R$

(v) $\text{cosec}^{-1}(-x) = -\text{cosec}^{-1} x,\ x \in R - (-1,1)$

(vi) $\sec^{-1}(-x) = \pi - \sec^{-1} x,\ x \in R - (-1,1)$

(vii) $\sin^{-1} x + \cos^{-1} x = \frac{\pi}{2},\ x \in [-1, 1]$

(viii) $\sec^{-1} x + \text{cosec}^{-1} x = \frac{\pi}{2},\ x \in R - (-1,1)$

(ix) $\tan^{-1} x + \cot^{-1} x = \frac{\pi}{2},\ x \in R$

(x) $2\sin^{-1} x = \sin^{-1}[2x\sqrt{1-x^2}],\ \frac{-1}{\sqrt{2}} \le x \le \frac{1}{\sqrt{2}}$

(xi) $2\cos^{-1} x = \cos^{-1}[2x^2 - 1],\ 0 \le x \le 1$

$= 2\pi - \cos^{-1}(2x^2 - 1),\ -1 \le x \le 0$

(xii) $2\tan^{-1} x = \begin{cases} \sin^{-1} \frac{2x}{1+x^2}, & x \in [-1,1] \\ \cos^{-1} \frac{1-x^2}{1+x^2}, & x \ge 0 \\ \tan^{-1} \frac{2x}{1-x^2}, & -1 < x < 1 \end{cases}$

(xiii) $3\sin^{-1} x = \sin^{-1}[3x - 4x^3],\ \frac{-1}{2} \le x \le \frac{1}{2}$

(xiv) $3\cos^{-1} x = \cos^{-1}[4x^3 - 3x],\ \frac{1}{2} \le x \le 1$

(xv) $3\tan^{-1} x = \tan^{-1}\left(\frac{3x - x^3}{1 - 3x^2}\right)$, if $-\frac{1}{\sqrt{3}} < x < \frac{1}{\sqrt{3}}$

Relation between Inverse Trigonometric Functions

(i) $\sin^{-1} x = \text{cosec}^{-1} \frac{1}{x},\ x \in [-1, 1]$

(ii) $\cos^{-1} x = \sec^{-1} \frac{1}{x},\ x \in [-1, 1]$

(iii) $\tan^{-1} x = \cot^{-1} \frac{1}{x},\ x > 0$

(iv) $\sin^{-1} x = \cos^{-1}\sqrt{1-x^2} = \tan^{-1} \frac{x}{\sqrt{1-x^2}}$

$= \cot^{-1} \frac{\sqrt{1-x^2}}{x} = \sec^{-1} \frac{1}{\sqrt{1-x^2}} = \text{cosec}^{-1} \frac{1}{x}$

(v) $\cos^{-1} x = \sin^{-1}\sqrt{1-x^2} = \tan^{-1} \frac{\sqrt{1-x^2}}{x}$

$= \cot^{-1} \frac{x}{\sqrt{1-x^2}} = \sec^{-1} \frac{1}{x}$

$= \text{cosec}^{-1} \frac{1}{\sqrt{1-x^2}}$

(vi) $\tan^{-1} x = \sin^{-1} \frac{x}{\sqrt{1+x^2}} = \cos^{-1} \frac{1}{\sqrt{1+x^2}} = \cot^{-1} \frac{1}{x}$

$= \text{cosec}^{-1} \frac{\sqrt{1+x^2}}{x} = \sec^{-1}\sqrt{1+x^2}$

PYQs Previous Years Questions

1 Mark Questions

1. If $\alpha \le 2\sin^{-1}x + \cos^{-1}x \le \beta$, then (α, β) is **ISC Specimen Sem-I 2022**

(a) $(0, \pi)$ (b) $\left(-\frac{\pi}{2}, \frac{\pi}{2}\right)$

(c) $\left(-\frac{3\pi}{2}, \frac{\pi}{2}\right)$ (d) None of these

2. For all $x \in R$, $\cot^{-1}(-x)$ is equal to **ISC Specimen Sem-I 2022**

(a) $\pi - \cot^{-1}x$ (b) $-\tan^{-1}x$

(c) $-\cot^{-1}x$ (d) $\pi + \cot^{-1}x$

2 Marks Questions

3. Solve for x $5\tan^{-1}x + 3\cot^{-1}x = 2\pi$. **ISC 2023**

4. Solve $3\tan^{-1}x + \cot^{-1}x = \pi$. **ISC 2018**

3/4 Marks Questions

5. Solve for x: $\sin^{-1}\left(\frac{x}{2}\right) + \cos^{-1}x = \frac{\pi}{6}$ **ISC 2024**

6. If $\sin^{-1}x + \sin^{-1}y + \sin^{-1}z = \pi$, show that $x^2 - y^2 - z^2 + 2yz\sqrt{1-x^2} = 0$. **ISC 2024**

7. If $\tan^{-1}\left(\frac{x-1}{x+1}\right) + \tan^{-1}\left(\frac{2x-1}{2x+1}\right) = \tan^{-1}\left(\frac{23}{36}\right)$, then prove that $24x^2 - 23x - 12 = 0$. **ISC 2023**

8. If $\cos^{-1}\frac{x}{a} + \cos^{-1}\frac{y}{b} = \alpha$, prove that

$$\frac{x^2}{a^2} - \frac{2xy}{ab}\cos\alpha + \frac{y^2}{b^2} = \sin^2\alpha.$$

ISC Specimen 2023

9. Evaluate $\cos(2\cos^{-1}x + \sin^{-1}x)$ at $x = \frac{1}{5}$. **ISC 2020**

10. If $\tan^{-1}a + \tan^{-1}b + \tan^{-1}c = \pi$, prove that $a + b + c = abc$. **ISC 2018**

11. Prove that $\frac{1}{2}\cos^{-1}\left(\frac{1-x}{1+x}\right) = \tan^{-1}\sqrt{x}$ **ISC 2017**

> **KEY CONCEPT**
>
> (i) Firstly arrange in formats $\cos^{-1}\frac{1-A^2}{1+A^2}$.
>
> (ii) Further, use the identity $2\tan^{-1}A = \cos^{-1}\frac{1-A^2}{1+A^2}$, $x \ge 0$.

12. Solve for x, if $\tan(\cos^{-1}x) = \frac{2}{\sqrt{5}}$ **ISC 2016**

13. Solve for x $\cos^{-1}(\sin(\cos^{-1}x)) = \frac{\pi}{6}$ **ISC 2015**

14. Evaluate $\tan\left[2\tan^{-1}\frac{1}{2} - \cot^{-1}3\right]$. **ISC 2014**

15. Prove that $\tan^{-1}\frac{1}{4} + \tan^{-1}\frac{2}{9} = \frac{1}{2}\sin^{-1}\frac{4}{5}$. **ISC 2013**

16. Prove that $2\left(\tan^{-1}1 + \tan^{-1}\frac{1}{2} + \tan^{-1}\frac{1}{3}\right) = \pi$. **ISC 2004**

17. Show that $\sin^{-1}\frac{4}{5} + \cos^{-1}\frac{2}{\sqrt{5}} = \cot^{-1}\frac{2}{11}$. **ISC 2003**

> **KEY CONCEPT**
>
> (i) First, convert the $\sin^{-1}x$ and $\cos^{-1}x$ in terms of $\tan^{-1}x$.
>
> (ii) Further, use the identity
>
> $\tan^{-1}x + \tan^{-1}y = \tan^{-1}\left(\frac{x+y}{1-xy}\right)$
>
> and $\tan^{-1}x = \cot^{-1}\frac{1}{x}$.

18. Solve $\tan^{-1}(2+x) + \tan^{-1}(2-x) = \tan^{-1}\frac{2}{3}$. **ISC 2001**

19. Prove that $\sin^{-1}\frac{x}{\sqrt{1+x^2}} + \cos^{-1}\frac{x+1}{\sqrt{x^2+2x+2}} = \tan^{-1}(x^2+x+1)$. **ISC 2000**

> **KEY CONCEPT**
>
> First, convert the inverse trigonometric functions $\sin^{-1}x$ and $\cos^{-1}x$ in terms of $\tan^{-1}x$ and then use identity $\tan^{-1}x + \tan^{-1}y = \tan^{-1}\left(\frac{x+y}{1-xy}\right)$, simplify to get the required expression.

20. If $\cos^{-1}\frac{x}{2} + \cos^{-1}\frac{y}{3} = \theta$, then prove that $9x^2 - 12xy\cos\theta + 4y^2 = 36\sin^2\theta$.

21. Solve for x $\tan^{-1}\left(\frac{x-1}{x-2}\right) + \tan^{-1}\left(\frac{x+1}{x+2}\right) = \frac{\pi}{4}$.

5/6 Marks Questions

22. Solve for x, $\sin^{-1}x + \sin^{-1}(1-x) = \cos^{-1}x$. **ISC 2017, 13**

23. If $\sin^{-1}x+\tan^{-1}x=\frac{\pi}{2}$, then prove that $2x^2+1=\sqrt{5}$ **ISC 2016**

24. Solve the equation for x $\sin^{-1}\frac{5}{x}+\sin^{-1}\frac{12}{x}=\frac{\pi}{2}, x\neq 0$ **ISC 2015**

25. If $\cos^{-1}x+\cos^{-1}y+\cos^{-1}z=\pi$, then prove that $x^2+y^2+z^2+2xyz=1.$ **ISC 2014**

> **KEY CONCEPT**
> (i) First, shift any one $\cos^{-1}$ function to the right hand side.
> (ii) Use the identity
> $$\cos^{-1}x+\cos^{-1}y=\cos^{-1}\left[xy-\sqrt{1-x^2}\sqrt{1-y^2}\right]$$
> and simplify it to prove the result.

26. Prove that

$$\cos^{-1}\frac{63}{65}+2\tan^{-1}\frac{1}{5}=\sin^{-1}\frac{3}{5}.$$ **ISC 2012**

27. Prove that

$$2\tan^{-1}\frac{1}{5}+\cos^{-1}\frac{7}{5\sqrt{2}}+2\tan^{-1}\frac{1}{8}=\frac{\pi}{4}.$$ **ISC 2011**

28. Prove that

$$\sin\left[2\tan^{-1}\frac{3}{5}-\sin^{-1}\frac{7}{25}\right]=\frac{304}{425}.$$ **ISC 2010**

29. If $\sin^{-1}x+\sin^{-1}y+\sin^{-1}z=\pi$, then prove that $x^2-y^2-z^2+2yz\sqrt{1-x^2}=0.$ **ISC 2009**

Explanations

1. (a) We know that $-\frac{\pi}{2}\leq\sin^{-1}x\leq\frac{\pi}{2}$

On adding $\frac{\pi}{2}$ in each term of the inequality

$-\frac{\pi}{2}\leq\sin^{-1}x\leq\frac{\pi}{2}$, we have

$$\frac{\pi}{2}-\frac{\pi}{2}\leq\sin^{-1}x+\frac{\pi}{2}\leq\frac{\pi}{2}+\frac{\pi}{2}$$

$$\Rightarrow\quad 0\leq\sin^{-1}x+\frac{\pi}{2}\leq\pi$$

$$\Rightarrow\quad 0\leq\sin^{-1}x+(\sin^{-1}x+\cos^{-1}x)\leq\pi$$

$$\left[\because \sin^{-1}\theta+\cos^{-1}\theta=\frac{\pi}{2}\right]$$

$$\therefore\quad 0\leq 2\sin^{-1}x+\cos^{-1}x\leq\pi$$

Therefore, $\alpha=0, \beta=\pi$ or $(\alpha,\beta)=(0,\pi)$.

2. (a) Let $\cot^{-1}(-x)=\theta$

$$\Rightarrow\quad \cot\theta=-x$$

$$\Rightarrow\quad \cot(\pi-\theta)=x$$

$$\Rightarrow\quad \pi-\theta=\cot^{-1}x$$

$$\Rightarrow\quad \theta=\pi-\cot^{-1}x$$

$$\therefore\quad \cot^{-1}(-x)=\pi-\cot^{-1}x\ \forall x\in R$$

3. Given, $5\tan^{-1}x+3\cot^{-1}x=2\pi$

$$\Rightarrow 2\tan^{-1}x+3(\tan^{-1}x+\cot^{-1}x)=2\pi$$

$$\Rightarrow\quad 2\tan^{-1}x+3\left(\frac{\pi}{2}\right)=2\pi$$

$$\left[\because \tan^{-1}\theta+\cot^{-1}\theta=\frac{\pi}{2}\right]$$

$$\Rightarrow\quad 2\tan^{-1}x=2\pi-\frac{3\pi}{2}$$

$$\Rightarrow\quad 2\tan^{-1}x=\frac{\pi}{2}$$

$$\Rightarrow\quad \tan^{-1}x=\frac{\pi}{4}$$

$$\Rightarrow\quad x=\tan\frac{\pi}{4}=1$$

4. We have, $3\tan^{-1}x+\cot^{-1}x=\pi$

$$\Rightarrow\quad 3\tan^{-1}x+\frac{\pi}{2}-\tan^{-1}x=\pi$$

$$\left[\because \tan^{-1}\theta+\cot^{-1}\theta=\frac{\pi}{2}\right]$$

$$\Rightarrow\quad 2\tan^{-1}x=\frac{\pi}{2}$$

$$\Rightarrow\quad \tan^{-1}x=\frac{\pi}{4}$$

$$\Rightarrow\quad x=\tan\frac{\pi}{4}\Rightarrow x=1$$

Hence, the value of x is 1.

5. We have, $\sin^{-1}\dfrac{x}{2}+\cos^{-1}x=\dfrac{\pi}{6}$

$$\Rightarrow \cos^{-1}x=\frac{\pi}{6}-\sin^{-1}\frac{x}{2}$$

$$\Rightarrow x=\cos\left(\frac{\pi}{6}-\sin^{-1}\frac{x}{2}\right)$$

$$\Rightarrow x=\cos\frac{\pi}{6}\cos\left(\sin^{-1}\frac{x}{2}\right)+\sin\frac{\pi}{6}\sin\left(\sin^{-1}\frac{x}{2}\right)$$

$$\Rightarrow x=\frac{\sqrt{3}}{2}\cos\left(\sin^{-1}\frac{x}{2}\right)+\frac{1}{2}\cdot\frac{x}{2}$$

Let $\sin^{-1}\dfrac{x}{2}=\theta \Rightarrow \dfrac{x}{2}=\sin\theta$

$$\Rightarrow \cos\theta=\sqrt{1-\frac{x^2}{4}}$$

$$\Rightarrow \theta=\cos^{-1}\sqrt{1-\frac{x^2}{4}}$$

$$\therefore x=\frac{\sqrt{3}}{2}\cos\left(\cos^{-1}\sqrt{1-\frac{x^2}{4}}\right)+\frac{x}{4}$$

$$=\frac{\sqrt{3}}{2}\sqrt{1-\frac{x^2}{4}}+\frac{x}{4}$$

$$\Rightarrow x-\frac{x}{4}=\frac{\sqrt{3}}{2}\sqrt{1-\frac{x^2}{4}}$$

$$\Rightarrow \frac{3x}{4}=\frac{\sqrt{3}}{2}\sqrt{1-\frac{x^2}{4}}$$

$$\Rightarrow \frac{9x^2}{16}=\frac{3}{4}\left(1-\frac{x^2}{4}\right)$$

$$\Rightarrow \frac{9x^2}{16}+\frac{3x^2}{16}=\frac{3}{4}\Rightarrow\frac{3}{4}x^2=\frac{3}{4}$$

$$\Rightarrow x^2=1\Rightarrow x=\pm1$$

But $x=-1$, does not satisfy the given equation.

Hence, $x=1$ is the required solution.

6. We have, $\sin^{-1}x+\sin^{-1}y+\sin^{-1}z=\pi$

$$\Rightarrow \sin^{-1}x+\sin^{-1}y=\pi-\sin^{-1}z$$

$$\Rightarrow \sin^{-1}(x\sqrt{1-y^2}+y\sqrt{1-x^2})=\pi-\sin^{-1}z$$

$$\Rightarrow x\sqrt{1-y^2}+y\sqrt{1-x^2}=\sin(\pi-\sin^{-1}z)$$

$$\Rightarrow x\sqrt{1-y^2}+y\sqrt{1-x^2}=\sin\pi\cos(\sin^{-1}z)-\cos\pi\sin(\sin^{-1}z)$$

$$\Rightarrow x\sqrt{1-y^2}+y\sqrt{1-x^2}=0+z$$

$$\Rightarrow x\sqrt{1-y^2}=z-y\sqrt{1-x^2}$$

On squaring both sides, we get

$$x^2(1-y^2)=z^2+y^2(1-x^2)-2yz\sqrt{1-x^2}$$

$$\Rightarrow x^2-x^2y^2=z^2+y^2-x^2y^2-2yz\sqrt{1-x^2}$$

$$\Rightarrow x^2-y^2-z^2+2yz\sqrt{1-x^2}=0$$ **Hence proved.**

7. We have, $\tan^{-1}\left(\dfrac{x-1}{x+1}\right)+\tan^{-1}\left(\dfrac{2x-1}{2x+1}\right)=\tan^{-1}\left(\dfrac{23}{36}\right)$

$$\Rightarrow \tan^{-1}\left[\frac{\frac{x-1}{x+1}+\frac{2x-1}{2x+1}}{1-\frac{(x-1)(2x-1)}{(x+1)(2x+1)}}\right]=\tan^{-1}\left[\frac{23}{36}\right]$$

$$\left[\because \tan^{-1}x+\tan^{-1}y=\tan^{-1}\left(\frac{x+y}{1-xy}\right)\right]$$

$$\Rightarrow \frac{(x-1)(2x+1)+(2x-1)(x+1)}{(x+1)(2x+1)-(x-1)(2x-1)}=\frac{23}{36}$$

$$\Rightarrow \frac{2x^2-x-1+2x^2+x-1}{2x^2+3x+1-2x^2+3x-1}=\frac{23}{36}$$

$$\Rightarrow \frac{4x^2-2}{6x}=\frac{23}{36}$$

$$\Rightarrow \frac{2(2x^2-1)}{6x}=\frac{23}{36}$$

$$\Rightarrow 24x^2-23x-12=0$$

8. Given, $\cos^{-1}\dfrac{x}{a}+\cos^{-1}\dfrac{y}{b}=\alpha$

We know that

$$\cos^{-1}x+\cos^{-1}y=\cos^{-1}(xy-\sqrt{(1-x^2)(1-y^2)})$$

$$\Rightarrow \cos^{-1}\left(\frac{x}{a}\cdot\frac{y}{b}-\sqrt{\left(1-\frac{x^2}{a^2}\right)\left(1-\frac{y^2}{b^2}\right)}\right)=\alpha$$

$$\Rightarrow \cos\alpha=\frac{xy}{ab}-\sqrt{\left(1-\frac{x^2}{a^2}\right)\left(1-\frac{y^2}{b^2}\right)}$$

$$\Rightarrow \sqrt{\left(1-\frac{x^2}{a^2}\right)\left(1-\frac{y^2}{b^2}\right)}=\left(\frac{xy}{ab}-\cos\alpha\right)$$

On squaring both sides, we get

$$\Rightarrow \left(1-\frac{x^2}{a^2}\right)\left(1-\frac{y^2}{b^2}\right)=\left(\frac{xy}{ab}\right)^2-\frac{2xy}{ab}\cos\alpha+\cos^2\alpha$$

$$\Rightarrow 1-\frac{y^2}{b^2}-\frac{x^2}{a^2}+\left(\frac{xy}{ab}\right)^2=\left(\frac{xy}{ab}\right)^2-\frac{2xy}{ab}\cos\alpha+\cos^2\alpha$$

$\Rightarrow \quad 1-\cos^2\alpha = \dfrac{x^2}{a^2} - \dfrac{2xy}{ab}\cos\alpha + \dfrac{y^2}{b^2}$

$\Rightarrow \quad \sin^2\alpha = \dfrac{x^2}{a^2} - \dfrac{2xy}{ab}\cos\alpha + \dfrac{y^2}{b^2}$

Hence proved.

9. We have, $\cos(2\cos^{-1}x + \sin^{-1}x)$

$= \cos(\cos^{-1}x + \cos^{-1}x + \sin^{-1}x)$

$= \cos\left(\cos^{-1}x + \dfrac{\pi}{2}\right)$ $\left[\because \cos^{-1}\theta + \sin^{-1}\theta = \dfrac{\pi}{2}\right]$

$= \cos\left(\dfrac{\pi}{2} + \cos^{-1}x\right)$

$= -\sin(\cos^{-1}x)$ $\left[\because \cos\left(\dfrac{\pi}{2}+\theta\right) = -\sin\theta\right]$

$= -\sin(\sin^{-1}\sqrt{1-x^2})$

$[\because \cos^{-1}\theta = \sin^{-1}\sqrt{1-\theta^2}]$

$= -\sqrt{1-x^2}$

$= -\sqrt{1-\left(\dfrac{1}{5}\right)^2}$ $\left[\because x = \dfrac{1}{5}\right]$

$= -\sqrt{1-\dfrac{1}{25}}$

$= -\sqrt{\dfrac{24}{25}}$

$= -\dfrac{2\sqrt{6}}{5}$

10. Given, $\tan^{-1}a + \tan^{-1}b + \tan^{-1}c = \pi$

Let $\tan^{-1}a = x \Rightarrow a = \tan x$,

$\tan^{-1}b = y \Rightarrow b = \tan y$,

and $\tan^{-1}c = z \Rightarrow c = \tan z$

$\therefore \; x+y+z = \pi \Rightarrow x+y = \pi - z$

$\Rightarrow \quad \tan(x+y) = \tan(\pi - z)$ [taking tan both sides]

$\Rightarrow \quad \dfrac{\tan x + \tan y}{1-\tan x \tan y} = -\tan z$ $[\because \tan(\pi-\theta) = -\tan\theta]$

$\Rightarrow \quad \dfrac{a+b}{1-ab} = -c$

$\Rightarrow \quad a+b = -c + abc$

$\Rightarrow \quad a+b+c = abc$ **Hence proved.**

Concept Enhancer

For any triangle, sum of all three angles is 180°.

$\therefore x+y+z = 180° = \pi$

$\Rightarrow \quad x+y = \pi - z \Rightarrow \tan(x+y) = \tan(\pi - z)$

$= \dfrac{\tan x + \tan y}{1-\tan x \cdot \tan y} = -\tan z$

$[\because \tan(\pi-\theta) = -\tan\theta]$

11. LHS $= \dfrac{1}{2}\cos^{-1}\left(\dfrac{1-x}{1+x}\right) = \dfrac{1}{2}\cos^{-1}\left(\dfrac{1-(\sqrt{x})^2}{1+(\sqrt{x})^2}\right)$

$= \dfrac{1}{2}\times 2\tan^{-1}(\sqrt{x})$

$\left[\because 2\tan^{-1}A = \cos^{-1}\dfrac{1-A^2}{1+A^2}, x \geq 0\right]$

$= (\tan^{-1}\sqrt{x}) = $ RHS **Hence proved.**

12. Given, $\tan(\cos^{-1}x) = \dfrac{2}{\sqrt{5}}$

$\Rightarrow \tan\left(\tan^{-1}\dfrac{\sqrt{1-x^2}}{x}\right) = \dfrac{2}{\sqrt{5}}$

$\left[\because \cos^{-1}A = \tan^{-1}\dfrac{\sqrt{1-A^2}}{A}\right]$

$\Rightarrow \quad \dfrac{\sqrt{1-x^2}}{x} = \dfrac{2}{\sqrt{5}}$ $[\because \tan(\tan^{-1}\theta) = \theta]$

$\Rightarrow \quad \sqrt{5}\sqrt{1-x^2} = 2x$

$\Rightarrow \quad 5(1-x^2) = 4x^2$ [squaring both sides]

$\Rightarrow \quad 5-5x^2 = 4x^2$

$\Rightarrow \quad 9x^2 - 5 = 0$

$\Rightarrow \quad x^2 = \dfrac{5}{9} \Rightarrow x = \pm\dfrac{\sqrt{5}}{3}$

[taking square roots both sides]

13. Given, $\cos^{-1}(\sin(\cos^{-1}x)) = \dfrac{\pi}{6}$

$\Rightarrow \quad \sin(\cos^{-1}x) = \cos\dfrac{\pi}{6}$

$\Rightarrow \quad \sin(\sin^{-1}\sqrt{1-x^2}) = \dfrac{\sqrt{3}}{2}$

$[\because \cos^{-1}A = \sin^{-1}(\sqrt{1-A^2})]$

$\Rightarrow \quad \sqrt{1-x^2} = \dfrac{\sqrt{3}}{2}$ $[\because \sin(\sin^{-1}\theta) = \theta]$

On squaring both sides, we get

$$1-x^2=\frac{3}{4} \Rightarrow x^2=1-\frac{3}{4} \Rightarrow x^2=\frac{1}{4} \Rightarrow x=\pm\frac{1}{2}$$

14. We have, $\tan\left[2\tan^{-1}\frac{1}{2}-\cot^{-1}3\right]$

$$=\tan\left[\tan^{-1}\frac{2\left(\frac{1}{2}\right)}{1-\left(\frac{1}{2}\right)^2}-\tan^{-1}\frac{1}{3}\right]$$

$$\left[\because 2\tan^{-1}x=\tan^{-1}\frac{2x}{1-x^2} \text{ and } \cot^{-1}x=\tan^{-1}\frac{1}{x}\right]$$

$$=\tan\left[\tan^{-1}\frac{1}{\frac{3}{4}}-\tan^{-1}\frac{1}{3}\right]$$

$$=\tan\left[\tan^{-1}\frac{4}{3}-\tan^{-1}\frac{1}{3}\right]$$

$$=\tan\left[\tan^{-1}\frac{\frac{4}{3}-\frac{1}{3}}{1+\frac{4}{3}\cdot\frac{1}{3}}\right]$$

$$\left[\because \tan^{-1}x-\tan^{-1}y=\tan^{-1}\left(\frac{x-y}{1+xy}\right)\right]$$

$$=\tan\left[\tan^{-1}\left(\frac{\frac{4-1}{3}}{\frac{9+4}{9}}\right)\right]$$

$$=\frac{3}{3}\cdot\frac{9}{13}=\frac{9}{13} \qquad [\because \tan(\tan^{-1}x)=x]$$

15. LHS $=\tan^{-1}\frac{1}{4}+\tan^{-1}\frac{2}{9}$

$$=\tan^{-1}\left(\frac{\frac{1}{4}+\frac{2}{9}}{1-\frac{1}{4}\cdot\frac{2}{9}}\right)=\left(\frac{\frac{9+8}{36}}{\frac{36-2}{36}}\right)$$

$$\left[\because \tan^{-1}x+\tan^{-1}y=\tan^{-1}\left(\frac{x+y}{1-xy}\right)\right]$$

$$=\tan^{-1}\left(\frac{\frac{17}{36}}{\frac{34}{36}}\right)=\tan^{-1}\frac{17}{34}=\tan^{-1}\frac{1}{2} \qquad \ldots(i)$$

$$=\tan^{-1}\frac{1}{2}=\frac{1}{2}\sin^{-1}\left[\frac{2\times\frac{1}{2}}{1+\left(\frac{1}{2}\right)^2}\right]$$

$$\left[\because 2\tan^{-1}x=\sin^{-1}\left(\frac{2x}{1+x^2}\right)\right]$$

$$=\frac{1}{2}\sin^{-1}\left(\frac{1}{\frac{1+4}{4}}\right)=\frac{1}{2}\sin^{-1}\left(\frac{4}{5}\right)=\text{RHS}$$

Hence proved.

16. LHS $=2\left[\tan^{-1}1+\tan^{-1}\frac{1}{2}+\tan^{-1}\frac{1}{3}\right]$

$$=2\left[\tan^{-1}\left(\frac{1+\frac{1}{2}}{1-\frac{1}{2}}\right)+\tan^{-1}\frac{1}{3}\right]$$

$$\left[\because \tan^{-1}x+\tan^{-1}y=\tan^{-1}\left(\frac{x+y}{1-xy}\right)\right]$$

$$=2\left[\tan^{-1}3+\tan^{-1}\frac{1}{3}\right]=2\left[\tan^{-1}\left(\frac{3+\frac{1}{3}}{1-3\cdot\frac{1}{3}}\right)\right]$$

$$=2\tan^{-1}\frac{10}{0}=2\tan^{-1}\infty$$

$$=2\cdot\frac{\pi}{2}=\pi=\text{RHS}\left[\because \tan\frac{\pi}{2}=\infty\right]$$ **Hence proved.**

17. LHS $=\sin^{-1}\frac{4}{5}+\cos^{-1}\frac{2}{\sqrt{5}}$

$$=\tan^{-1}\left(\frac{4/5}{\sqrt{1-16/25}}\right)+\tan^{-1}\left(\frac{\sqrt{1-4/5}}{2/\sqrt{5}}\right)$$

$$\left[\begin{array}{l}\because \sin^{-1}x=\tan^{-1}\frac{x}{\sqrt{1-x^2}}\\ \text{and } \cos^{-1}x=\tan^{-1}\frac{\sqrt{1-x^2}}{x}\end{array}\right]$$

$$=\tan^{-1}\frac{4}{\sqrt{9}}+\tan^{-1}\frac{1}{2}=\tan^{-1}\frac{4}{3}+\tan^{-1}\frac{1}{2}$$

$$=\tan^{-1}\left(\frac{\frac{4}{3}+\frac{1}{2}}{1-\frac{4}{3}\cdot\frac{1}{2}}\right) \qquad \left[\begin{array}{l}\because \tan^{-1}x+\tan^{-1}y\\ =\tan^{-1}\left(\frac{x+y}{1-xy}\right)\end{array}\right]$$

$$=\tan^{-1}\left(\frac{8+3}{6-4}\right)$$

$$=\tan^{-1}\left(\frac{11}{2}\right)$$

$$=\cot^{-1}\frac{2}{11}=\text{RHS} \qquad \left[\because \tan^{-1}x=\cot^{-1}\frac{1}{x}\right]$$

Hence proved.

18. Given, $\tan^{-1}(2+x)+\tan^{-1}(2-x)=\tan^{-1}\left(\frac{2}{3}\right)$

$$\Rightarrow \tan^{-1}\left[\frac{2+x+2-x}{1-(2+x)(2-x)}\right]=\tan^{-1}\left(\frac{2}{3}\right)$$

$$\left[\because \tan^{-1}A+\tan^{-1}B=\tan^{-1}\left(\frac{A+B}{1-AB}\right)\right]$$

$$\Rightarrow \tan^{-1}\left[\frac{4}{1-(4-x^2)}\right]=\tan^{-1}\left(\frac{2}{3}\right)$$

$$\Rightarrow \tan^{-1}\frac{4}{x^2-3}=\tan^{-1}\left(\frac{2}{3}\right)$$

$$\Rightarrow \tan^{-1}\frac{4}{x^2-3}=\tan^{-1}\frac{2}{3} \Rightarrow \frac{4}{x^2-3}=\frac{2}{3}$$

$$\Rightarrow 6=x^2-3 \Rightarrow x^2=9$$

$$\therefore x=\pm 3$$

19. $\text{LHS}=\sin^{-1}\frac{x}{\sqrt{1+x^2}}+\cos^{-1}\frac{x+1}{\sqrt{x^2+2x+2}}$

$$=\tan^{-1}\left(\frac{\frac{x}{\sqrt{1+x^2}}}{\sqrt{1-\frac{x^2}{1+x^2}}}\right)+\tan^{-1}\left(\frac{\sqrt{1-\frac{x^2+2x+1}{x^2+2x+2}}}{\frac{x+1}{\sqrt{x^2+2x+2}}}\right)$$

$$\left[\because \sin^{-1}y=\tan^{-1}\frac{y}{\sqrt{1-y^2}} \text{ and } \cos^{-1}y=\tan^{-1}\frac{\sqrt{1-y^2}}{y}\right]$$

$$=\tan^{-1}\left(\frac{x}{\sqrt{1+x^2}}\times\frac{\sqrt{1+x^2}}{\sqrt{1}}\right)$$

$$+\tan^{-1}\left(\frac{\sqrt{1}}{\sqrt{x^2+2x+2}}\times\frac{\sqrt{x^2+2x+2}}{x+1}\right)$$

$$\left[\because \tan^{-1}A+\tan^{-1}B=\tan^{-1}\left(\frac{A+B}{1-AB}\right)\right]$$

$$=\tan^{-1}\frac{x}{1}+\tan^{-1}\frac{1}{x+1}=\tan^{-1}\left(\frac{x+\frac{1}{x+1}}{1-\frac{x}{x+1}}\right)$$

$$=\tan^{-1}\left(\frac{x^2+x+1}{x+1}\times\frac{x+1}{1}\right)=\tan^{-1}\left(\frac{x^2+x+1}{1}\right)$$

$$=\tan^{-1}(x^2+x+1)$$

= RHS **Hence proved.**

20. We have, $\cos^{-1}\frac{x}{2}+\cos^{-1}\frac{y}{3}=\theta$

$$\Rightarrow \cos^{-1}\left[\left(\frac{x}{2}\times\frac{y}{3}\right)-\sqrt{1-\frac{x^2}{4}}\sqrt{1-\frac{y^2}{9}}\right]=\theta$$

$$[\because \cos^{-1}x+\cos^{-1}y=\cos^{-1}(xy-\sqrt{1-x^2}\sqrt{1-y^2})]$$

$$\Rightarrow \frac{xy}{6}-\sqrt{\left(1-\frac{x^2}{4}\right)\left(1-\frac{y^2}{9}\right)}=\cos\theta$$

$$\Rightarrow \frac{xy}{6}-\cos\theta=\sqrt{\left(1-\frac{x^2}{4}\right)\left(1-\frac{y^2}{9}\right)}$$

On squaring both sides, we get

$$\frac{x^2y^2}{36}-\frac{xy\cos\theta}{3}+\cos^2\theta=\left(1-\frac{x^2}{4}\right)\left(1-\frac{y^2}{9}\right)$$

$$\Rightarrow \frac{x^2y^2}{36}-\frac{xy\cos\theta}{3}+\cos^2\theta=1-\frac{x^2}{4}-\frac{y^2}{9}+\frac{x^2y^2}{36}$$

$$\Rightarrow \frac{x^2}{4}+\frac{y^2}{9}-\frac{xy\cos\theta}{3}=1-\cos^2\theta$$

$$\Rightarrow 9x^2+4y^2-12xy\cos\theta=36\sin^2\theta$$

Hence proved.

21. We have, $\tan^{-1}\left(\frac{x-1}{x-2}\right)+\tan^{-1}\left(\frac{x+1}{x+2}\right)=\frac{\pi}{4}$

$$\Rightarrow \tan^{-1}\left[\frac{\frac{x-1}{x-2}+\frac{x+1}{x+2}}{1-\left(\frac{x-1}{x-2}\right)\left(\frac{x+1}{x+2}\right)}\right]=\frac{\pi}{4}, \left(\frac{x-1}{x-2}\right)\left(\frac{x+1}{x+2}\right)<1$$

$$\left[\because \tan^{-1}x+\tan^{-1}y=\tan^{-1}\left(\frac{x+y}{1-xy}\right), \text{ if } xy<1\right]$$

$$\Rightarrow \tan^{-1}\left[\frac{(x-1)(x+2)+(x+1)(x-2)}{(x-2)(x+2)-(x-1)(x+1)}\right]$$

$$=\frac{\pi}{4}, \frac{x^2-1}{x^2-4}-1<0$$

$$\Rightarrow \frac{(x^2+x-2)+(x^2-x-2)}{x^2-4-(x^2-1)}=\tan\frac{\pi}{4}, \frac{3}{x^2-4}<0$$

$$\Rightarrow \frac{2x^2-4}{-3}=1, \frac{3}{x^2-4}<0$$

$$\Rightarrow 2x^2-4=-3, x^2-4<0$$

$$\Rightarrow 2x^2=1, x^2<4$$

$$\Rightarrow x=\pm\frac{1}{\sqrt{2}}, -2<x<2$$

Hence, both values of x satisfy the given equation.

22. Given, $\sin^{-1} x + \sin^{-1}(1-x) = \cos^{-1} x$

$\therefore \sin^{-1}[x\sqrt{1-(1-x)^2} + (1-x)\sqrt{1-x^2}] = \cos^{-1} x$

$\left[\because \sin^{-1} A + \sin^{-1} B = \sin^{-1}(A\sqrt{1-B^2} + B\sqrt{1-A^2})\right]$

$\Rightarrow \sin^{-1}[x\sqrt{1-(1+x^2-2x)} + (1-x)\sqrt{1-x^2}] = \sin^{-1}\sqrt{1-x^2}$

$[\because \cos^{-1} A = \sin^{-1}\sqrt{1-A^2}]$

$\Rightarrow x\sqrt{2x-x^2} + (1-x)\sqrt{1-x^2} = \sqrt{1-x^2}$

$\Rightarrow x\sqrt{2x-x^2} = (1-1+x)\sqrt{1-x^2}$

$\Rightarrow x\sqrt{2x-x^2} = x\sqrt{1-x^2}$

$\Rightarrow x\sqrt{2x-x^2} - x\sqrt{1-x^2} = 0$

$\Rightarrow x[\sqrt{2x-x^2} - \sqrt{1-x^2}] = 0$

$\Rightarrow x = 0$ or $\sqrt{2x-x^2} - \sqrt{1-x^2} = 0$

Now, $\sqrt{2x-x^2} - \sqrt{1-x^2} = 0$

$\Rightarrow \sqrt{2x-x^2} = \sqrt{1-x^2}$

On squaring both sides, we get

$2x - x^2 = 1 - x^2 \Rightarrow 2x = 1$

$\therefore x = \frac{1}{2}$

Hence, $x = 0, \frac{1}{2}$

23. Given, $\sin^{-1} x + \tan^{-1} x = \frac{\pi}{2}$

$\Rightarrow \tan^{-1} x = \left(\frac{\pi}{2} - \sin^{-1} x\right)$

$\Rightarrow \tan^{-1} x = \cos^{-1} x$

$\left[\because \cos^{-1}\theta + \sin^{-1}\theta = \frac{\pi}{2}\right]$

$\Rightarrow \tan^{-1} x = \tan^{-1}\frac{\sqrt{1-x^2}}{x}$

$\left[\because \cos^{-1}\theta = \tan^{-1}\frac{\sqrt{1-\theta^2}}{\theta}\right]$

$\Rightarrow x = \tan\left(\tan^{-1}\frac{\sqrt{1-x^2}}{x}\right)$

$\Rightarrow x = \frac{\sqrt{1-x^2}}{x}$ $[\because \tan(\tan^{-1}\theta) = \theta]$

$\Rightarrow x^2 = \sqrt{1-x^2}$

$\Rightarrow (x^2)^2 = 1 - x^2$ [squaring both sides]

$\Rightarrow x^4 = 1 - x^2$

$\Rightarrow x^4 + x^2 - 1 = 0$

$\therefore x^2 = \frac{-1 \pm \sqrt{5}}{2}$ $\left[\because x = \frac{-b \pm \sqrt{b^2-4ac}}{2a}\right]$

$\Rightarrow 2x^2 + 1 = \pm\sqrt{5}$

$\Rightarrow 2x^2 + 1 = \sqrt{5}$

$[\because 2x^2 + 1 > 0 \Rightarrow 2x^2 + 1 = -\sqrt{5}$ is not possible$]$

Hence proved.

> **Concept Enhancer** Given, $\sin^{-1} x + \tan^{-1} x = \frac{\pi}{2}$ ...(i)
>
> On using formulae $\cos^{-1} x + \sin^{-1} x = \frac{\pi}{2}$ and $\cos^{-1} x = \tan^{-1}\frac{\sqrt{1-x^2}}{x}$, we get from Eq. (i) a quadratic equation $x^4 + x^2 - 1 = 0$.
>
> For solving this, use Shridharacharya method
>
> i.e. If $ax^2 + bx + c = 0$, $x = \frac{-b \pm \sqrt{b^2-4ac}}{2a}$

24. Given, $\sin^{-1}\frac{5}{x} + \sin^{-1}\frac{12}{x} = \frac{\pi}{2}$

Now, $\sin^{-1}\frac{5}{x} + \cos^{-1}\sqrt{1-\left(\frac{12}{x}\right)^2} = \frac{\pi}{2}$ ...(i)

$[\because \sin^{-1}\theta = \cos^{-1}\sqrt{1-\theta^2}]$

We know that $\sin^{-1}\theta + \cos^{-1}\theta = \frac{\pi}{2}$

$\therefore \frac{5}{x} = \sqrt{1-\frac{144}{x^2}}$

On squaring both sides, we get

$\frac{25}{x^2} = 1 - \frac{144}{x^2}$

$\Rightarrow \frac{25+144}{x^2} = 1$

$\Rightarrow \frac{169}{x^2} = 1$

$\Rightarrow x^2 = 169 \Rightarrow x = \pm 13$

But $x = -13$ does not satisfy the given equation.
Hence, required value of x is 13.

25. Given, $\cos^{-1}x+\cos^{-1}y+\cos^{-1}z=\pi$

$\Rightarrow \quad \cos^{-1}x+\cos^{-1}y=\pi-\cos^{-1}z$

$\Rightarrow \quad \cos^{-1}[xy-\sqrt{1-x^2}\sqrt{1-y^2}]=\pi-\cos^{-1}z$

$[\because \cos^{-1}A+\cos^{-1}B=\cos^{-1}(AB-\sqrt{1-A^2}\sqrt{1-B^2})]$

$\Rightarrow \quad xy-\sqrt{1-x^2}\sqrt{1-y^2}=\cos(\pi-\cos^{-1}z)$

$\Rightarrow \quad xy-\sqrt{1-x^2}\sqrt{1-y^2}=-\cos(\cos^{-1}z)$

$[\because \cos(\pi-\theta)=-\cos\theta]$

$\Rightarrow \quad xy-\sqrt{1-x^2}\sqrt{1-y^2}=-z$

$[\because \cos(\cos^{-1}\theta)=\theta]$

$\Rightarrow \quad \sqrt{1-x^2}\sqrt{1-y^2}=xy+z$

On squaring both sides, we get

$$(1-x^2)(1-y^2)=(xy+z)^2$$

$\Rightarrow \quad 1-x^2-y^2+x^2y^2=x^2y^2+z^2+2xyz$

$\therefore \quad x^2+y^2+z^2+2xyz=1$ **Hence proved.**

26. LHS $=\cos^{-1}\left(\frac{63}{65}\right)+2\tan^{-1}\left(\frac{1}{5}\right)$

$$=\sin^{-1}\sqrt{1-\left(\frac{63}{65}\right)^2}+\sin^{-1}\left[\frac{2\times\frac{1}{5}}{1+\left(\frac{1}{5}\right)^2}\right]$$

$\left[\because \cos^{-1}x=\sin^{-1}\sqrt{1-x^2} \text{ and } 2\tan^{-1}x=\sin^{-1}\frac{2x}{1+x^2}\right]$

$$=\sin^{-1}\sqrt{\frac{(65)^2-(63)^2}{(65)^2}}+\sin^{-1}\left(\frac{\frac{2}{5}}{\frac{25+1}{25}}\right)$$

$$=\sin^{-1}\sqrt{\frac{(65-63)(65+63)}{(65)^2}}+\sin^{-1}\left(\frac{2}{5}\times\frac{25}{26}\right)$$

$[\because a^2-b^2=(a-b)(a+b)]$

$$=\sin^{-1}\sqrt{\frac{2\times128}{(65)^2}}+\sin^{-1}\left(\frac{5}{13}\right)$$

$$=\sin^{-1}\sqrt{\frac{256}{(65)^2}}+\sin^{-1}\left(\frac{5}{13}\right)$$

$$=\sin^{-1}\left(\frac{16}{65}\right)+\sin^{-1}\left(\frac{5}{13}\right)$$

$$=\sin^{-1}\left[\frac{16}{65}\sqrt{1-\left(\frac{5}{13}\right)^2}+\frac{5}{13}\sqrt{1-\left(\frac{16}{65}\right)^2}\right]$$

$[\because \sin^{-1}A+\sin^{-1}B=\sin^{-1}(A\sqrt{1-B^2})+B\sqrt{1-A^2})]$

$$=\sin^{-1}\left[\frac{16}{65}\sqrt{\frac{13^2-5^2}{13^2}}+\frac{5}{13}\sqrt{\frac{65^2-16^2}{65^2}}\right]$$

$$=\sin^{-1}\left[\frac{16}{65}\sqrt{\frac{(13-5)(13+5)}{(13)^2}}+\frac{5}{13}\sqrt{\frac{(65-16)(65+16)}{(65)^2}}\right]$$

$$=\sin^{-1}\left[\frac{16}{65}\sqrt{\frac{8\times18}{(13)^2}}+\frac{5}{13}\sqrt{\frac{49\times81}{(65)^2}}\right]$$

$$=\sin^{-1}\left[\frac{16\times4\times3}{13\times65}+\frac{5}{13}\times\frac{7\times9}{65}\right]$$

$$=\sin^{-1}\left[\frac{192+315}{65\times13}\right]=\sin^{-1}\left(\frac{507}{65\times13}\right)=\sin^{-1}\left(\frac{3}{5}\right)$$

= RHS **Hence proved.**

27. LHS $=2\tan^{-1}\frac{1}{5}+\cos^{-1}\frac{7}{5\sqrt{2}}+2\tan^{-1}\frac{1}{8}$

$$=\tan^{-1}\left(\frac{2\left(\frac{1}{5}\right)}{1-\frac{1}{25}}\right)+\tan^{-1}\left(\frac{\sqrt{1-\frac{49}{50}}}{\frac{7}{5\sqrt{2}}}\right)+\tan^{-1}\left(\frac{2\left(\frac{1}{8}\right)}{1-\frac{1}{64}}\right)$$

$\left[\because 2\tan^{-1}x=\tan^{-1}\left(\frac{2x}{1-x^2}\right) \text{ and } \cos^{-1}x=\tan^{-1}\left(\frac{\sqrt{1-x^2}}{x}\right)\right]$

$$=\tan^{-1}\left(\frac{2}{5}\times\frac{25}{24}\right)+\tan^{-1}\left(\frac{1}{5\sqrt{2}}\times\frac{5\sqrt{2}}{7}\right)+\tan^{-1}\left(\frac{1}{4}\times\frac{64}{63}\right)$$

$$=\tan^{-1}\left(\frac{5}{12}\right)+\tan^{-1}\left(\frac{1}{7}\right)+\tan^{-1}\left(\frac{16}{63}\right)$$

$$=\tan^{-1}\left(\frac{5}{12}\right)+\tan^{-1}\left(\frac{\frac{1}{7}+\frac{16}{63}}{1-\frac{1}{7}\times\frac{16}{63}}\right)$$

$\left[\because \tan^{-1}x+\tan^{-1}y=\tan^{-1}\left(\frac{x+y}{1-xy}\right)\right]$

$$=\tan^{-1}\left(\frac{5}{12}\right)+\tan^{-1}\left(\frac{63+112}{441-16}\right)$$

$$=\tan^{-1}\frac{5}{12}+\tan^{-1}\frac{175}{425}$$

$$= \tan^{-1}\frac{5}{12} + \tan^{-1}\frac{7}{17} = \tan^{-1}\left(\frac{\frac{5}{12}+\frac{7}{17}}{1-\frac{5}{12}\cdot\frac{7}{17}}\right)$$

$$\left[\because \tan^{-1}x + \tan^{-1}y = \tan^{-1}\left(\frac{x+y}{1-xy}\right)\right]$$

$$= \tan^{-1}\left(\frac{85+84}{204-35}\right) = \tan^{-1}\left(\frac{169}{169}\right)$$

$$= \tan^{-1}(1) \qquad \left[\because \tan\frac{\pi}{4} = 1\right]$$

$$= \frac{\pi}{4} = \text{RHS}$$ **Hence proved.**

28. To prove, $\sin\left[2\tan^{-1}\frac{3}{5} - \sin^{-1}\frac{7}{25}\right] = \frac{304}{425}$

i.e. $2\tan^{-1}\frac{3}{5} - \sin^{-1}\frac{7}{25} = \sin^{-1}\frac{304}{425}$

$$\text{LHS} = 2\tan^{-1}\frac{3}{5} - \sin^{-1}\frac{7}{25}$$

$$= \tan^{-1}\frac{3}{5} + \tan^{-1}\frac{3}{5} - \sin^{-1}\frac{7}{25}$$

$$= \sin^{-1}\left(\frac{\frac{3}{5}}{\sqrt{1+\frac{9}{25}}}\right) + \sin^{-1}\left(\frac{\frac{3}{5}}{\sqrt{1+\frac{9}{25}}}\right) - \sin^{-1}\frac{7}{25}$$

$$\left[\because \tan^{-1}x = \sin^{-1}\frac{x}{\sqrt{1+x^2}}\right]$$

$$= \sin^{-1}\frac{3}{\sqrt{34}} + \sin^{-1}\frac{3}{\sqrt{34}} - \sin^{-1}\frac{7}{25}$$

$$= \sin^{-1}\left[\frac{3}{\sqrt{34}}\sqrt{1-\frac{9}{34}} + \frac{3}{\sqrt{34}}\sqrt{1-\frac{9}{34}}\right] - \sin^{-1}\frac{7}{25}$$

$$\left[\because \sin^{-1}x + \sin^{-1}y = \sin^{-1}(x\sqrt{1-y^2} + y\sqrt{1-x^2})\right]$$

$$= \sin^{-1}\left[\frac{6}{\sqrt{34}}\cdot\frac{5}{\sqrt{34}}\right] - \sin^{-1}\frac{7}{25}$$

$$= \sin^{-1}\frac{30}{34} - \sin^{-1}\frac{7}{25}$$

$$= \sin^{-1}\left[\frac{30}{34}\sqrt{1-\frac{49}{625}} - \frac{7}{25}\sqrt{1-\frac{900}{1156}}\right]$$

$$[\because \sin^{-1}x - \sin^{-1}y = \sin^{-1}(x\sqrt{1-y^2} - y\sqrt{1-x^2})]$$

$$= \sin^{-1}\left[\frac{30}{34}\sqrt{\frac{625-49}{625}} - \frac{7}{25}\sqrt{\frac{1156-900}{1156}}\right]$$

$$= \sin^{-1}\left[\frac{30}{34}\sqrt{\frac{576}{625}} - \frac{7}{25}\sqrt{\frac{256}{1156}}\right]$$

$$= \sin^{-1}\left[\frac{30}{34}\cdot\frac{24}{25} - \frac{7}{25}\cdot\frac{16}{34}\right] = \sin^{-1}\left[\frac{720-112}{850}\right]$$

$$= \sin^{-1}\frac{608}{850} = \sin^{-1}\frac{304}{425} = \text{RHS}$$ **Hence proved.**

Alternate Method

We have to prove, $\sin\left[2\tan^{-1}\frac{3}{5} - \sin^{-1}\frac{7}{25}\right] = \frac{304}{425}$

i.e. $2\tan^{-1}\frac{3}{5} - \sin^{-1}\frac{7}{25} = \sin^{-1}\frac{304}{425}$

Let $\text{LHS} = 2\tan^{-1}\frac{3}{5} - \sin^{-1}\frac{7}{25}$

$$= \sin^{-1}\left(\frac{2\cdot\frac{3}{5}}{1+\frac{9}{25}}\right) - \sin^{-1}\frac{7}{25}$$

$$\left[\because 2\tan^{-1}x = \sin^{-1}\frac{2x}{1+x^2}\right]$$

$$= \sin^{-1}\left(\frac{6/5}{34/25}\right) - \sin^{-1}\frac{7}{25}$$

$$= \sin^{-1}\frac{30}{34} - \sin^{-1}\frac{7}{25}$$

$$= \sin^{-1}\left[\frac{30}{34}\sqrt{1-\frac{49}{625}} - \frac{7}{25}\sqrt{1-\frac{900}{1156}}\right]$$

$$[\because \sin^{-1}x - \sin^{-1}y = \sin^{-1}(x\sqrt{1-y^2} - y\sqrt{1-x^2})]$$

$$= \sin^{-1}\left[\frac{30}{34}\cdot\frac{24}{25} - \frac{7}{25}\cdot\frac{16}{34}\right]$$

$$= \sin^{-1}\left[\frac{720-112}{850}\right] = \sin^{-1}\frac{608}{850}$$

$$= \sin^{-1}\frac{304}{425} = \text{RHS}$$ **Hence proved.**

29. Given, $\sin^{-1}x + \sin^{-1}y + \sin^{-1}z = \pi$

$$\Rightarrow \sin^{-1}x + \sin^{-1}y = \pi - \sin^{-1}z$$

$$\Rightarrow \sin^{-1}[x\sqrt{1-y^2} + y\sqrt{1-x^2}] = \pi - \sin^{-1}z$$

$$\Rightarrow x\sqrt{1-y^2} + y\sqrt{1-x^2} = \sin(\pi - \sin^{-1}z)$$

$$\Rightarrow x\sqrt{1-y^2} + y\sqrt{1-x^2} = \sin(\sin^{-1}z)$$

$$[\because \sin(\pi - \theta) = \sin\theta]$$

$$\Rightarrow x\sqrt{1-y^2} + y\sqrt{1-x^2} = z$$

$$\Rightarrow x\sqrt{1-y^2} = z - y\sqrt{1-x^2}$$

On squaring both sides, we get

$$x^2(1-y^2) = z^2 + y^2(1-x^2) - 2zy\sqrt{1-x^2}$$

$$\Rightarrow x^2 - x^2y^2 = z^2 + y^2 - x^2y^2 - 2zy\sqrt{1-x^2}$$

$$\therefore \quad x^2 - y^2 - z^2 + 2zy\sqrt{1-x^2} = 0$$

CHAPTER TEST

1 Mark Questions

1. The domain in which sine function will be one-one, is

(a) $\left[-\frac{\pi}{2}, \frac{\pi}{2}\right]$ (b) $\left[\frac{\pi}{2}, \frac{3\pi}{2}\right]$

(c) $[0, \pi]$ (d) Both (a) and (b)

2. If $\sin^{-1} x + \sin^{-1} y + \sin^{-1} z = \frac{3\pi}{2}$, then the value of $x^{100} + y^{100} + z^{100} - \frac{9}{x^{101} + y^{101} + z^{101}}$ is

(a) 0 (b) 1 (c) 2 (d) 3

3. The value of $\sin^{-1}\left\{\cot\left(\sin^{-1}\frac{\sqrt{2-\sqrt{3}}}{2} + \cos^{-1}\frac{\sqrt{12}}{4} + \sec^{-1}\sqrt{2}\right)\right\}$ is

(a) 0 (b) $\frac{\pi}{2}$ (c) $\frac{\pi}{3}$ (d) $\frac{\pi}{4}$

4. If $0 \le x < 1$, then $\sin\left\{\tan^{-1}\left(\frac{1-x^2}{2x}\right) + \cos^{-1}\left(\frac{1-x^2}{1+x^2}\right)\right\}$ is equal to

(a) 1 (b) -1 (c) 0 (d) 2

5. The value of $\cos[\tan^{-1}\{\sin(\cot^{-1} x)\}]$ is

(a) $\frac{1}{\sqrt{x^2+2}}$ (b) $\sqrt{\frac{x^2+2}{x^2+1}}$

(c) $\sqrt{\frac{x^2+1}{x^2+2}}$ (d) $\frac{1}{\sqrt{x^2+1}}$

2 Marks Questions

6. Find the domain of the function $\cos^{-1}(2x-1)$.

7. Write the value of the following.

(i) $\sin^{-1}(\sin 1550°)$ (ii) $\tan^{-1}\left[\tan\left(\frac{15\pi}{4}\right)\right]$

8. If $\tan^{-1} x + \tan^{-1} y = \frac{4\pi}{5}$, then find $\cot^{-1} x + \cot^{-1} y$.

9. If $\tan^{-1}(\sqrt{3}) + \cot^{-1} x = \frac{\pi}{2}$, then find x.

10. Show that $\sin^{-1} 2x\sqrt{1-x^2} = 2\sin^{-1} x, -\frac{1}{\sqrt{2}} \le x \le \frac{1}{\sqrt{2}}$.

3/4 Marks Questions

11. Find the value of $\sin[\cot^{-1}\{\tan(\cos^{-1} x)\}]$.

12. Solve for x, $\sin^{-1}\left(\frac{2a}{1+a^2}\right) + \sin^{-1}\left(\frac{2\beta}{1+\beta^2} = 2\tan^{-1} x\right)$.

13. Prove that $\tan^{-1}\left(\frac{1-x}{1+x}\right) - \tan^{-1}\left(\frac{1-y}{1+y}\right) = \sin^{-1}\left(\frac{y-x}{\sqrt{1+x^2}\sqrt{1+y^2}}\right)$.

5/6 Marks Questions

14. Prove that $\tan^{-1}\left[\frac{\sqrt{1+x^2}+\sqrt{1-x^2}}{\sqrt{1+x^2}-\sqrt{1-x^2}}\right] = \frac{\pi}{4} + \frac{1}{2}\cos^{-1} x^2$.

15. If $\tan^{-1} x + \tan^{-1} y + \tan^{-1} z = \pi$, then prove that $x + y + z = xyz$.

16. Prove that

$$\tan^{-1}\sqrt{x} = \frac{1}{2}\cos^{-1}\left(\frac{1-x}{1+x}\right), x \in [0, 1].$$

17. Prove that

$$\frac{9\pi}{8} - \frac{9}{4}\sin^{-1}\left(\frac{1}{3}\right) = \frac{9}{4}\sin^{-1}\left(\frac{2\sqrt{2}}{3}\right).$$

Answers

1. (d) **2.** (a) **3.** (a)

4. (a) **5.** (c)

6. $x \in [0, 1]$

7. (i) 70° (ii) $-\frac{\pi}{4}$

8. $\frac{\pi}{5}$

9. $\sqrt{3}$

11. x

12. $\frac{\alpha+\beta}{1-\alpha\beta}$

03

Matrices

TREND ANALYSIS 3 YEARS

TOPIC 01 Matrices

Average No. of Questions Across all Sets

Types of Questions	2024	2023	2020
1 Mark	2	1	—
2 Marks	—	—	1
3/4 Marks	—	—	—
5/6 Marks	—	—	—

TOPIC 1

Matrices

A matrix is an ordered **rectangular array** of numbers or functions, enclosed by [ ] or ( ). The numbers (real or complex) or functions are called the **elements** or the **entries** of a matrix.

A matrix is represented by a single **capital letter** like A, B, X, Y, etc., and elements of a matrix are represented by the small letters $a, b, c, \ldots$, etc. In a matrix, horizontal lines are called **rows** and vertical lines are called **columns**.

Order of Matrix

If a matrix have m rows and n columns, then its order is written as $m \times n$ and read as m by n matrix.

In general, $m \times n$ matrix has the following rectangular array:

$$A = \begin{bmatrix} a_{11} & a_{12} & \ldots & a_{1n} \\ a_{21} & a_{22} & \ldots & a_{2n} \\ \vdots & \vdots & \ldots & \vdots \\ a_{m1} & a_{m2} & \ldots & a_{mn} \end{bmatrix}_{m \times n}$$

Notation of Matrix

It can be rewritten as $A = [a_{ij}]_{m \times n}$, where $1 \le i \le m, 1 \le j \le n$ and $i, j \in N$. In general, a_{ij} or (i, j) th is an element lying in the ith row and jth column.

Types of Matrices

(i) **Column matrix** A matrix which has only one column and many rows, is called a column matrix.

e.g. $\begin{bmatrix} 1 \\ 0 \\ -5 \end{bmatrix}$.

In general,

$A = [a_{ij}]_{m \times 1}$ is a column matrix of order $m \times 1$.

(ii) **Row matrix** A matrix which has only one row and many columns , is called a row matrix.
e.g. $[1 \ \ 5 \ \ 9]$.

In general,

$A = [a_{ij}]_{1 \times n}$ is a row matrix of order $1 \times n$.

(iii) **Square matrix** A matrix which has equal number of rows and columns, is called a square matrix.

e.g. $\begin{bmatrix} 3 & -1 \\ 5 & 2 \end{bmatrix}$.

In general, $A = [a_{ij}]_{m \times m}$ is a square matrix of order m.

NOTE The diagonal elements of above matrix are 3 and 2.

(iv) **Diagonal matrix** A square matrix whose all the elements except the diagonal elements are zeros, is called a diagonal matrix.

e.g. $\begin{bmatrix} 3 & 0 & 0 \\ 0 & -3 & 0 \\ 0 & 0 & -8 \end{bmatrix}$.

In general, $A = [a_{ij}]_{m \times m}$ is a diagonal matrix, if $a_{ij} = 0$, when $i \neq j$.

(v) **Scalar matrix** A diagonal matrix whose all the diagonal elements are same (non-zero), is called a scalar matrix.

e.g. $\begin{bmatrix} 2 & 0 & 0 \\ 0 & 2 & 0 \\ 0 & 0 & 2 \end{bmatrix}$.

In general, $A = [a_{ij}]_{n \times n}$ is a scalar matrix, if $a_{ij} = 0$, when $i \neq j$ and $a_{ij} = k$ (constant), when $i = j$.

NOTE A scalar matrix is a diagonal matrix but a diagonal matrix may or may not be a scalar matrix.

(vi) **Unit or Identity matrix** A diagonal matrix in which all the diagonal elements are '1' and its non-diagonal elements are zeros, is called an identity matrix. It is denoted by I.

e.g. $I = \begin{bmatrix} 1 & 0 & 0 \\ 0 & 1 & 0 \\ 0 & 0 & 1 \end{bmatrix}$

In general, $A = [a_{ij}]_{n \times n}$ is an identity matrix, if $a_{ij} = 1$, when $i = j$ and $a_{ij} = 0$, when $i \neq j$.

(vii) **Zero matrix or Null matrix** A matrix is said to be a zero matrix, if its all elements are zeros. It is denoted by O.

e.g. $O = \begin{bmatrix} 0 & 0 \\ 0 & 0 \end{bmatrix}$ or $\begin{bmatrix} 0 & 0 & 0 \\ 0 & 0 & 0 \\ 0 & 0 & 0 \end{bmatrix}$

In general, $A = [a_{ij}]_{n \times n}$ is a zero or null matrix, if $a_{ij} = 0, \forall\, i$ and j.

(viii) **In a square matrix** If $a_{ij} = 0, \forall\, [i > j]$, then it is called an **upper triangular matrix** and if $a_{ij} = 0, \forall i < j$, then it is called a **lower triangular matrix.**

e.g. $\begin{bmatrix} 0 & 1 & 2 \\ 0 & 0 & -1 \\ 0 & 0 & 0 \end{bmatrix}$ Upper triangular matrix $\qquad \begin{bmatrix} 1 & 0 & 0 \\ 2 & 1 & 0 \\ 1 & 1 & 1 \end{bmatrix}$ Lower triangular matrix

A matrix, in upper or lower triangular, is called a **triangular matrix.** A triangular matrix $A = [a_{ij}]_{m \times m}$ is called **strictly** triangular, if $a_{ii} = 0, \forall 1 \leq i \leq m$.

Operation on Matrices

Between two or more than two matrices, following operations are worked out :

1. Addition of Matrices

Let $A = [a_{ij}]_{m \times n}$ and $B = [b_{ij}]_{m \times n}$ be two matrices of same order, then

$$A + B = [a_{ij} + b_{ij}],\ \forall\, i = 1, 2, 3, \ldots, m \text{ and } j = 1, 2, 3, \ldots, n.$$

Let A, B and C be three matrices of same order, then the properties of addition of matrices are

(i) **Commutative law** $A + B = B + A$

(ii) **Associative law** $(A + B) + C = A + (B + C)$

(iii) **Additive identity** $A + O = A = O + A$

(iv) **Additive inverse** $A + (-A) = O = (-A) + A$

(v) **Cancellation laws**

(a) $A + B = A + C \Rightarrow B = C$ [left cancellation law]

(b) $B + A = C + A \Rightarrow B = C$ [right cancellation law]

2. Subtraction of Matrices

Let A and B be two matrices of same order $m \times n$, then

$$A - B = [a_{ij} - b_{ij}]_{m \times n}$$

Let A, B and C be three matrices of same order, then properties of subtraction of matrices are

(i) Non-commutative $A - B \neq B - A$

(ii) Non-associative $A - (B - C) \neq (A - B) - C$

3. Multiplication of a Matrix by a Scalar

Let $A = [a_{ij}]$ be an $m \times n$ matrix and k be any scalar. Then, the matrix obtained by multiplying each element of A by k is called the scalar multiple of A by k.

Let A and B be two matrices of same order, then the properties of multiplication of a matrix by scalar are

(i) $k\,(A + B) = kA + kB$ (ii) $(k_1 + k_2)A = k_1 A + k_2 A$

(iii) $(kl)A = k(lA) = l(kA)$ (iv) $(-I)A = -A$

(v) $I\,(A) = A$

4. Multiplication of Matrices

Let $A = [a_{ij}]_{m \times n}$ and $B = [b_{ij}]_{n \times p}$ be two matrices such that number of columns of A is equal to the number of rows of B, then the product matrix is $C = [c_{ij}]$ of order $m \times p$.

where, $c_{ij} = \sum_{k=1}^{n} a_{ik} b_{kj}$

To get the (i, k) th element c_{ik} of the matrix C, take the ith row of A and k th column of B, multiply them elementwise and take the sum of all these products.

e.g.

(i) Let $A=\begin{bmatrix} a & b \\ c & d \end{bmatrix}$ and $B=\begin{bmatrix} e & f \\ g & h \end{bmatrix}$

Then, $AB=\begin{bmatrix} ae+bg & af+bh \\ ce+dg & cf+dh \end{bmatrix}$

(ii) Let $A=\begin{bmatrix} a & b & c \\ d & e & f \\ g & h & i \end{bmatrix}$ and $B=\begin{bmatrix} l & m & n \\ p & q & r \\ x & y & z \end{bmatrix}$

Then, $AB=\begin{bmatrix} al+bp+cx & am+bq+cy & an+br+cz \\ dl+ep+fx & dm+eq+fy & dn+er+fz \\ gl+hp+ix & gm+hq+iy & gn+hr+iz \end{bmatrix}$

Let A, B and C be three matrices of order $m \times n$, $n \times p$ and $p \times k$, then the properties of multiplication of matrices are

(i) **Non-commutative** $AB \neq BA$
(ii) **Associative** $(AB)C = A(BC)$
(iii) **Multiplicative Identity** $IA = A = AI$
(iv) **Multiplicative Distributive** $A(B+C) = AB + AC$ and $(A+B)C = AC + BC$
(v) If A and B be suitable matrices and λ is a scalar, then $\lambda(AB) = (\lambda A)B = A(\lambda B)$.
(vi) Existence of non-zero matrices whose product is the zero matrix (restrict to square matrices of order upto 3) i.e. $AB = O$, where A, B are non-zero matrices and O is a zero matrix.

NOTE (i) If the product AB is defined for any two matrices A and B, then it is not necessary that BA is also defined.

e.g. Take $A=\begin{bmatrix} 1 & 1 \\ 0 & 2 \\ 1 & 1 \end{bmatrix}$ and $B=\begin{bmatrix} 1 & 2 \\ 2 & 2 \end{bmatrix}$.

Then, AB is defined but BA is not defined.

(ii) If the product of two matrices is a zero matrix, then it is not necessary that one of the matrices is a zero matrix.

e.g. Take $A=\begin{bmatrix} 0 & -1 \\ 0 & 2 \end{bmatrix}$ and $B=\begin{bmatrix} 3 & 5 \\ 0 & 0 \end{bmatrix}$

Then, $AB=\begin{bmatrix} 0 & 0 \\ 0 & 0 \end{bmatrix}$.

5. Equality of Matrices

Two matrices $A=[a_{ij}]$ and $B=[b_{ij}]$ are said to be equal, if they are of same order and all the corresponding elements are equal i.e. $[a_{ij}]=[b_{ij}]\ \forall\ i, j$.

Remark If $f(x) = a_0x^m + a_1x^{m-1} + \ldots + a_{m-1}x + a_m$ is a polynomial in x and A is a square matrix of order n, then we called $f(A) = a_0A^m + a_1A^{m-1} + \ldots + a_{n-1}A + a_mI_n$ is a matrix polynomial.

6. Equivalent Matrices

Two matrices A and B are said to be equivalent, if one is obtained from the other by one or more elementary operations and we write $A \sim B$.

Transpose of a Matrix

Let $A=[a_{ij}]$ be an $m \times n$ matrix, then transpose of A, denoted by A' or A^T, is the matrix obtained from A by interchanging its rows and columns.

Clearly, A' is an $n \times m$ matrix whose

(j, i)th element $= (i, j)$th element of A.

i.e. $A' = [b_{ji}]$,

where $b_{ji} = a_{ij}, 1 \leq i \leq m, 1 \leq j \leq n$.

e.g. Let $A=\begin{bmatrix} 1 & -1 \\ 2 & 3 \\ 3 & 5 \end{bmatrix}$, then the transpose of $A=\begin{bmatrix} 1 & 2 & 3 \\ -1 & 3 & 5 \end{bmatrix}$.

Important Results

- If A and B are two matrices of order $m \times n$, then $(A \pm B)' = A' \pm B'$.
- If k is a scalar, then $(kA)' = kA'$.
- $(A')' = A$
- $(AB)' = B'A'$
- $(A^n)' = (A')^n$

Symmetric Matrix

A square matrix A is called a symmetric matrix, if it satisfies the relation $A' = A$.

e.g. $A=\begin{bmatrix} 2 & 1 \\ 1 & 2 \end{bmatrix}$ is a symmetric matrix as $A'=\begin{bmatrix} 2 & 1 \\ 1 & 2 \end{bmatrix} = A$.

Skew-Symmetric Matrix

A square matrix A is called skew-symmetric matrix, if it satisfies the relation $A' = -A$.

e.g. $A=\begin{bmatrix} 0 & -1 \\ 1 & 0 \end{bmatrix}$ is a skew-symmetric matrix as

$$A'=\begin{bmatrix} 0 & 1 \\ -1 & 0 \end{bmatrix} = -\begin{bmatrix} 0 & -1 \\ 1 & 0 \end{bmatrix} = -A$$

NOTE
- For a square matrix A, $A + A'$ is symmetric matrix and $A - A'$ is skew-symmetric matrix.
- Every square matrix can be uniquely expressed as the sum of symmetric and skew-symmetric matrix.

i.e. $A = \frac{1}{2}(A + A') + \frac{1}{2}(A - A')$

Important Results

Symmetric Matrix

- If A and B are two symmetric matrices of the same order, then
  (i) AB is symmetric if and only if $AB = BA$.
  (ii) $A \pm B$, $AB + BA$ are also symmetric matrices.
- If A is symmetric matrix, then A^{-1} will also be a symmetric matrix.

Skew-Symmetric Matrix

- If A and B are two skew-symmetric matrices, then
  (i) $A \pm B$, $AB - BA$ are also skew-symmetric matrices.
  (ii) $AB + BA$ is a symmetric matrix.
- Determinant of skew-symmetric matrix of odd order is zero.

Invertible Matrices

A square matrix A of order m is said to be invertible, if there exists another square matrix B of same order m, such that $AB = BA = I$, where I is a unit matrix of same order m.

The matrix B, is called the inverse of matrix A and is denoted by A^{-1}.

Important Theorem

Theorem 1st (uniqueness of inverse) Inverse of a square matrix, if it exists, is unique.

Theorem 2nd If A and B are invertible matrices of the same order, then $(AB)^{-1} = B^{-1}A^{-1}$, where A and B are matrices of the same order.

NOTE (i) A rectangular matrix does not possess inverse matrix.
(ii) If B is the inverse of A, then A is also the inverse of B.

PYQs Previous Years Questions

1 Mark Questions

1. **Assertion** (A) Let the matrices $A = \begin{pmatrix} -3 & 2 \\ -5 & 4 \end{pmatrix}$ and $B = \begin{pmatrix} 4 & -2 \\ 5 & -3 \end{pmatrix}$ be such that $A^{100}B = BA^{100}$ *ISC 2024*

   Reason (R) $AB = BA$ implies $A^nB = BA^n$ for all positive integers n.
   (a) Both Assertion and Reason are true and Reason is the correct explanation for Assertion.
   (b) Both Assertion and Reason are true but Reason is not the correct explanation for Assertion.
   (c) Assertion is true but Reason is false.
   (d) Assertion is false but Reason is true.

2. If A and B are symmetric matrices of the same order, then $AB - BA$ is *ISC 2024*
   (a) Skew-symmetric matrix
   (b) Symmetric matrix
   (c) Diagonal matrix
   (d) Identity matrix

3. P and Q are two matrices such that $[P + Q]^T = \begin{bmatrix} 7 & -8 \\ 3 & 0 \end{bmatrix}$. If $P = \begin{bmatrix} -1 & 1 \\ 3 & 2 \end{bmatrix}$, which one of the following is Q? *ISC Specimen 2024*
   (a) $\begin{bmatrix} 8 & -9 \\ 0 & 2 \end{bmatrix}$ (b) $\begin{bmatrix} -8 & -2 \\ 11 & 2 \end{bmatrix}$
   (c) $\begin{bmatrix} 8 & 2 \\ -11 & -2 \end{bmatrix}$ (d) $\begin{bmatrix} 8 & -11 \\ 2 & -2 \end{bmatrix}$

4. Matrix P is a skew-symmetric matrix of odd order.
   Assertion The inverse of matrix P does not exist.
   Reason The determinant of matrix P is zero. *ISC Specimen 2024*
   (a) Both Assertion and Reason are true and Reason is the correct explanation for Assertion.
   (b) Both Assertion and Reason are true but Reason is not the correct explanation for Assertion.
   (c) Assertion is true but Reason is false.
   (d) Assertion is false but Reason is true.

5. If $A=\begin{pmatrix}5 & x\\ y & 0\end{pmatrix}$ and A is symmetric, then write the relation between x and y. **ISC Specimen 2024**

6. For what value of k, the matrix $\begin{bmatrix}0 & k\\ -6 & 0\end{bmatrix}$ is a skew-symmetric matrix? **ISC 2023**

7. If $\begin{pmatrix}3 & 5\\ 7 & 9\end{pmatrix}=X+Y$, where X is skew-symmetric matrix and Y is symmetric matrix. Find $|X|$. **ISC Specimen 2023**

8. If $A=\begin{pmatrix}1 & b\\ 0 & 1\end{pmatrix}$, then A^n $(n\in N)$ is equal to **ISC Specimen 2023**

(a) $\begin{pmatrix}1 & nb\\ 0 & 1\end{pmatrix}$ (b) $\begin{pmatrix}1 & b^n\\ 0 & 1\end{pmatrix}$

(c) $\begin{pmatrix}1 & n^b\\ 0 & 1\end{pmatrix}$ (d) $\begin{pmatrix}1 & nb\\ 0 & 0\end{pmatrix}$

9. What is the transpose of a column matrix? **ISC Specimen Sem-I 2022**

(a) Zero matrix (b) Diagonal matrix
(c) Column matrix (d) Row matrix

10. If A and B are two non-singular matrices and AB exists, then $(AB)^{-1}$ is **ISC Specimen Sem-I 2022**

(a) $A^{-1}B^{-1}$ (b) $B^{-1}A^{-1}$
(c) AB (d) None of these

11. From the matrix equation $AB=AC$, it can be concluded that $B=C$ provided **ISC Specimen Sem-I 2022**

(a) A is singular matrix
(b) A is non-singular matrix
(c) A is a symmetric matrix
(d) A is a skew-symmetric matrix

12. If $A=\begin{bmatrix}0 & 1\\ 1 & 0\end{bmatrix}$, then A^2 is equal to **ISC Specimen 2021**

(a) $\begin{bmatrix}0 & 1\\ 1 & 0\end{bmatrix}$ (b) $\begin{bmatrix}1 & 0\\ 0 & 1\end{bmatrix}$ (c) $\begin{bmatrix}1 & 0\\ 1 & 0\end{bmatrix}$ (d) $\begin{bmatrix}0 & 0\\ 1 & 1\end{bmatrix}$

2 Marks Questions

13. If $\begin{pmatrix}2 & 3\\ 5 & 7\end{pmatrix}\begin{pmatrix}1 & -3\\ -2 & 4\end{pmatrix}=\begin{pmatrix}-4 & 6\\ -9 & x\end{pmatrix}$, then find x. **ISC 2020**

14. Show that $(A+A')$ is symmetric matrix, if $A=\begin{bmatrix}2 & 4\\ 3 & 5\end{bmatrix}$. **ISC 2019**

15. If $A=\begin{bmatrix}5 & a\\ b & 0\end{bmatrix}$ and A is symmetric matrix, then show that $a=b$. **ISC 2018**

3/4 Marks Questions

16. Find the value of k, if $M=\begin{bmatrix}1 & 2\\ 2 & 3\end{bmatrix}$ and $M^2-kM-I_2=O$. **ISC Specimen 2018, ISC 2015**

17. If the matrix $\begin{bmatrix}6 & -x^2\\ 2x-15 & 10\end{bmatrix}$ is symmetric, then find the value of x. **ISC 2017**

18. If $A=\begin{bmatrix}3 & 1\\ 7 & 5\end{bmatrix}$, then find the values of x and y, such that $A^2+xI_2=yA$. **ISC 2014**

> **KEY CONCEPT**
> First, find A^2 by using multiplicative property

19. If $(A-2I)(A-3I)=O$, where $A=\begin{bmatrix}4 & 2\\ -1 & x\end{bmatrix}$ and $I=\begin{bmatrix}1 & 0\\ 0 & 1\end{bmatrix}$, then find the value of x. **ISC 2013**

5/6 Marks Questions

20. Solve the matrix equation $A\begin{bmatrix}3 & 4\\ -1 & 2\\ 2 & 1\end{bmatrix}=\begin{bmatrix}0 & 15\\ 1 & -2\end{bmatrix}$ **ISC Specimen 2021**

21. Evaluate :

$$\begin{bmatrix}3 & -2 & 3\\ 2 & 1 & -1\\ 4 & -3 & 2\end{bmatrix}\begin{bmatrix}-1 & -5 & -1\\ -8 & -6 & 9\\ -10 & 1 & 7\end{bmatrix}$$

Hence, solve the system of equations, $3x-2y+3z=8$, $2x+y-z=1$ and $4x-3y+2z=4$. **ISC Specimen 2018**

Explanations

1. (a) We have,

$$A = \begin{bmatrix} -3 & 2 \\ -5 & 4 \end{bmatrix} \text{ and } B = \begin{bmatrix} 4 & -2 \\ 5 & -3 \end{bmatrix}$$

Here, $AB = \begin{bmatrix} -3 & 2 \\ -5 & 4 \end{bmatrix}\begin{bmatrix} 4 & -2 \\ 5 & -3 \end{bmatrix} = \begin{bmatrix} -2 & 0 \\ 0 & -2 \end{bmatrix}$

and $BA = \begin{bmatrix} 4 & -2 \\ 5 & -3 \end{bmatrix}\begin{bmatrix} -3 & 2 \\ -5 & 4 \end{bmatrix} = \begin{bmatrix} -2 & 0 \\ 0 & -2 \end{bmatrix}$

We know that if $AB = BA$, then by mathematical induction $A^n B = BA^n$, n is positive integers.

For $n = 100$, we get

$$A^{100} B = BA^{100}$$

Hence, both Assertion (A) and Reason (R) are true and Reason (R) is the correct explanation of Assertion (A).

2. (a) Given, A and B are two symmetric matrices.

Then, $A' = A$ and $B' = B$

Now, $(AB - BA)' = (AB)' - (BA)'$

$= (B'A' - A'B')$

$= (BA - AB)$

$= -(AB - BA)$

Hence, $(AB - BA)$ is skew-symmetric matrix.

3. (c) Given, $(P+Q)^T = \begin{bmatrix} 7 & -8 \\ 3 & 0 \end{bmatrix}$ and $P = \begin{bmatrix} -1 & 1 \\ 3 & 2 \end{bmatrix}$

$\therefore \quad P^T + Q^T = \begin{bmatrix} 7 & -8 \\ 3 & 0 \end{bmatrix}$

$\Rightarrow \quad \begin{bmatrix} -1 & 1 \\ 3 & 2 \end{bmatrix}^T + Q^T = \begin{bmatrix} 7 & -8 \\ 3 & 0 \end{bmatrix}$

$\Rightarrow \quad Q^T = \begin{bmatrix} 7 & -8 \\ 3 & 0 \end{bmatrix} - \begin{bmatrix} -1 & 3 \\ 1 & 2 \end{bmatrix}$

$\Rightarrow \quad Q^T = \begin{bmatrix} 8 & -11 \\ 2 & -2 \end{bmatrix}$

$\therefore \quad Q = \begin{bmatrix} 8 & 2 \\ -11 & -2 \end{bmatrix}$

4. (a) Let P be any skew-symmetric matrix of odd order given by

$$P = \begin{bmatrix} 0 & a & b \\ -a & 0 & c \\ -b & -c & 0 \end{bmatrix}$$

$\therefore \quad |P| = 0(0+c^2) - a(0+bc) + b(ac-0)$

$= -abc + abc = 0$

$\because \quad |P| = 0$

$\therefore \quad P^{-1}$ does not exist.

5. We have, $A = \begin{bmatrix} 5 & x \\ y & 0 \end{bmatrix}$

$\because$ A is symmetric.

$\therefore \quad A^T = A \Rightarrow \begin{bmatrix} 5 & y \\ x & 0 \end{bmatrix} = \begin{bmatrix} 5 & x \\ y & 0 \end{bmatrix} \Rightarrow x = y$

6. Given, $\begin{bmatrix} 0 & k \\ -6 & 0 \end{bmatrix}$ is skew-symmetric matrix.

Let $A = \begin{bmatrix} 0 & k \\ -6 & 0 \end{bmatrix}$

Since, A is skew-symmetric matrix.

$\therefore \quad A = -A'$

$\Rightarrow \quad \begin{bmatrix} 0 & k \\ -6 & 0 \end{bmatrix} = \begin{bmatrix} 0 & 6 \\ -k & 0 \end{bmatrix} \Rightarrow -k = -6 \Rightarrow k = 6$

7. Let $A = \begin{pmatrix} 3 & 5 \\ 7 & 9 \end{pmatrix} = X + Y$

where, X is skew-symmetric matrix.

i.e. $\quad X = \frac{1}{2}(A - A^T)$

and Y is symmetric matrix

i.e. $\quad Y = \frac{1}{2}(A + A^T)$

$\therefore \quad A = \begin{pmatrix} 3 & 5 \\ 7 & 9 \end{pmatrix}$ and $A^T = \begin{pmatrix} 3 & 7 \\ 5 & 9 \end{pmatrix}$

$\Rightarrow \quad X = \frac{1}{2}(A - A^T) = \frac{1}{2}\left[\begin{pmatrix} 3 & 5 \\ 7 & 9 \end{pmatrix} - \begin{pmatrix} 3 & 7 \\ 5 & 9 \end{pmatrix}\right]$

$\Rightarrow \quad X = \frac{1}{2}\begin{bmatrix} 3-3 & 5-7 \\ 7-5 & 9-9 \end{bmatrix} = \frac{1}{2}\begin{bmatrix} 0 & -2 \\ 2 & 0 \end{bmatrix}$

$\Rightarrow \quad X = \begin{bmatrix} 0 & -1 \\ 1 & 0 \end{bmatrix}$

$\therefore \quad |X| = 0 - (-1) = 1$

8. (a) Here, $A = \begin{pmatrix} 1 & b \\ 0 & 1 \end{pmatrix}$

$$A^2 = A \cdot A = \begin{pmatrix} 1 & b \\ 0 & 1 \end{pmatrix}\begin{pmatrix} 1 & b \\ 0 & 1 \end{pmatrix}$$

$$= \begin{pmatrix} 1+0 & b+b \\ 0+0 & 0+1 \end{pmatrix} = \begin{pmatrix} 1 & 2b \\ 0 & 1 \end{pmatrix}$$

$$A^3 = A^2 \cdot A = \begin{pmatrix} 1 & 2b \\ 0 & 1 \end{pmatrix}\begin{pmatrix} 1 & b \\ 0 & 1 \end{pmatrix}$$

$$= \begin{pmatrix} 1+0 & b+2b \\ 0+0 & 0+1 \end{pmatrix} = \begin{pmatrix} 1 & 3b \\ 0 & 1 \end{pmatrix}$$

Similarly, $A^n = \begin{pmatrix} 1 & nb \\ 0 & 1 \end{pmatrix}$

9. (d) The transpose of a column matrix is a row matrix.

10. (b) We know that if A^{-1}, B^{-1} and $(AB)^{-1}$ exists, then $(AB)^{-1} = B^{-1}A^{-1}$.

11. (b) Given, $AB = AC$

$$\Rightarrow \quad B = C$$

On pre-multiplying by A^{-1} on both sides of the equation $AB = AC$, we get

$$A^{-1}AB = A^{-1}AC$$

$$\Rightarrow \quad IB = IC \Rightarrow B = C$$

So, A is non singular matrix.

12. (b) Given, $A = \begin{bmatrix} 0 & 1 \\ 1 & 0 \end{bmatrix}$

Now, $A^2 = A \cdot A$

$$= \begin{bmatrix} 0 & 1 \\ 1 & 0 \end{bmatrix}\begin{bmatrix} 0 & 1 \\ 1 & 0 \end{bmatrix}$$

$$= \begin{bmatrix} 0+1 & 0+0 \\ 0+0 & 1+0 \end{bmatrix} = \begin{bmatrix} 1 & 0 \\ 0 & 1 \end{bmatrix}$$

13. Given, $\begin{bmatrix} 2 & 3 \\ 5 & 7 \end{bmatrix}\begin{bmatrix} 1 & -3 \\ -2 & 4 \end{bmatrix} = \begin{bmatrix} -4 & 6 \\ -9 & x \end{bmatrix}$

$$\Rightarrow \begin{bmatrix} 2-6 & -6+12 \\ 5-14 & -15+28 \end{bmatrix} = \begin{bmatrix} -4 & 6 \\ -9 & x \end{bmatrix}$$

$$\Rightarrow \begin{bmatrix} -4 & 6 \\ -9 & 13 \end{bmatrix} = \begin{bmatrix} -4 & 6 \\ -9 & x \end{bmatrix}$$

On comparing the corresponding element, we get

$$x = 13$$

14. We have, $A = \begin{bmatrix} 2 & 4 \\ 3 & 5 \end{bmatrix}$

Now, $A + A' = \begin{bmatrix} 2 & 4 \\ 3 & 5 \end{bmatrix} + \begin{bmatrix} 2 & 3 \\ 4 & 5 \end{bmatrix} = \begin{bmatrix} 4 & 7 \\ 7 & 10 \end{bmatrix}$

$$\therefore \quad (A + A')' = \begin{bmatrix} 4 & 7 \\ 7 & 10 \end{bmatrix}' = \begin{bmatrix} 4 & 7 \\ 7 & 10 \end{bmatrix} = A + A'$$

Hence, $(A + A')$ is symmetric matrix.

15. Given, $A = \begin{bmatrix} 5 & a \\ b & 0 \end{bmatrix}$, $A' = \begin{bmatrix} 5 & b \\ a & 0 \end{bmatrix}$

A is symmetric matrix. [given]

$$\therefore \quad A = A'$$

$$\Rightarrow \quad \begin{bmatrix} 5 & a \\ b & 0 \end{bmatrix} = \begin{bmatrix} 5 & b \\ a & 0 \end{bmatrix}$$

On comparing the corresponding element, we get

$$a = b$$

Hence proved.

16. Given, $M = \begin{bmatrix} 1 & 2 \\ 2 & 3 \end{bmatrix}$

$$M^2 = \begin{bmatrix} 1 & 2 \\ 2 & 3 \end{bmatrix}\begin{bmatrix} 1 & 2 \\ 2 & 3 \end{bmatrix} = \begin{bmatrix} 5 & 8 \\ 8 & 13 \end{bmatrix}$$

Also, $I_2 = \begin{bmatrix} 1 & 0 \\ 0 & 1 \end{bmatrix}$

$$\because \quad M^2 - kM - I_2 = O$$

$$\begin{bmatrix} 5 & 8 \\ 8 & 13 \end{bmatrix} - \begin{bmatrix} k & 2k \\ 2k & 3k \end{bmatrix} - \begin{bmatrix} 1 & 0 \\ 0 & 1 \end{bmatrix} = O$$

$$\Rightarrow \begin{bmatrix} 5-k-1 & 8-2k-0 \\ 8-2k-0 & 13-3k-1 \end{bmatrix} = O$$

$$\Rightarrow \begin{bmatrix} 4-k & 8-2k \\ 8-2k & 12-3k \end{bmatrix} = \begin{bmatrix} 0 & 0 \\ 0 & 0 \end{bmatrix}$$

On comparing the elements, we get

$$4 - k = 0$$

$$\Rightarrow \quad k = 4$$

17. Let $A = \begin{bmatrix} 6 & -x^2 \\ 2x-15 & 10 \end{bmatrix}$

Given, matrix A is symmetric.

$$\therefore \quad A = A' \quad \ldots\text{(i)}$$

[here, A' is transpose of matrix A]

Clearly, $A' = \begin{bmatrix} 6 & 2x-15 \\ -x^2 & 10 \end{bmatrix}$

From Eq. (i),

$$\begin{bmatrix} 6 & -x^2 \\ 2x-15 & 10 \end{bmatrix} = \begin{bmatrix} 6 & 2x-15 \\ -x^2 & 10 \end{bmatrix}$$

$\because$ Both matrices are equal.

$\therefore \quad -x^2 = 2x - 15$

$\Rightarrow \quad x^2 + 2x - 15 = 0$

$\Rightarrow \quad x^2 + 5x - 3x - 15 = 0$

$\Rightarrow \quad x(x+5) - 3(x+5) = 0$

$\Rightarrow \quad (x+5)(x-3) = 0$

$\therefore \quad x = -5$ or $x = 3$

Concept Enhancer When matrix A is symmetric, then $A = A'$

18. Given, $A = \begin{bmatrix} 3 & 1 \\ 7 & 5 \end{bmatrix}$

Now, $A^2 = A \cdot A = \begin{bmatrix} 3 & 1 \\ 7 & 5 \end{bmatrix}\begin{bmatrix} 3 & 1 \\ 7 & 5 \end{bmatrix}$

$$= \begin{bmatrix} 9+7 & 3+5 \\ 21+35 & 7+25 \end{bmatrix} = \begin{bmatrix} 16 & 8 \\ 56 & 32 \end{bmatrix}$$

Also given, $A^2 + xI_2 = yA$

$$\therefore \quad \begin{bmatrix} 16 & 8 \\ 56 & 32 \end{bmatrix} + x\begin{bmatrix} 1 & 0 \\ 0 & 1 \end{bmatrix} = y\begin{bmatrix} 3 & 1 \\ 7 & 5 \end{bmatrix}$$

$$\Rightarrow \quad \begin{bmatrix} 16 & 8 \\ 56 & 32 \end{bmatrix} + \begin{bmatrix} x & 0 \\ 0 & x \end{bmatrix} = \begin{bmatrix} 3y & y \\ 7y & 5y \end{bmatrix}$$

$$\Rightarrow \quad \begin{bmatrix} 16+x & 8 \\ 56 & 32+x \end{bmatrix} = \begin{bmatrix} 3y & y \\ 7y & 5y \end{bmatrix}$$

[by addition property]

On equating the corresponding elements, we get

$y = 8$ and $32 + x = 5y$

$\Rightarrow \quad 32 + x = 5 \times 8$

$\Rightarrow \quad 32 + x = 40$

$\Rightarrow \quad x = 40 - 32$

$\therefore \quad x = 8$

Hence, $x = 8$ and $y = 8$.

19. Given, $A = \begin{bmatrix} 4 & 2 \\ -1 & x \end{bmatrix}$ and $I = \begin{bmatrix} 1 & 0 \\ 0 & 1 \end{bmatrix}$,

Also given, $(A - 2I)(A - 3I) = O$

$$\left\{\begin{bmatrix} 4 & 2 \\ -1 & x \end{bmatrix} - \begin{bmatrix} 2 & 0 \\ 0 & 2 \end{bmatrix}\right\}\left\{\begin{bmatrix} 4 & 2 \\ -1 & x \end{bmatrix} - \begin{bmatrix} 3 & 0 \\ 0 & 3 \end{bmatrix}\right\} = \begin{bmatrix} 0 & 0 \\ 0 & 0 \end{bmatrix}$$

$$\Rightarrow \quad \begin{bmatrix} 4-2 & 2-0 \\ -1-0 & x-2 \end{bmatrix}\begin{bmatrix} 4-3 & 2-0 \\ -1-0 & x-3 \end{bmatrix} = \begin{bmatrix} 0 & 0 \\ 0 & 0 \end{bmatrix}$$

[by subtraction property]

$$\Rightarrow \quad \begin{bmatrix} 2 & 2 \\ -1 & x-2 \end{bmatrix}\begin{bmatrix} 1 & 2 \\ -1 & x-3 \end{bmatrix} = \begin{bmatrix} 0 & 0 \\ 0 & 0 \end{bmatrix}$$

$$\Rightarrow \quad \begin{bmatrix} 2-2 & 4+2x-6 \\ -1-x+2 & -2+x^2-5x+6 \end{bmatrix} = \begin{bmatrix} 0 & 0 \\ 0 & 0 \end{bmatrix}$$

[by multipliction property]

$$\Rightarrow \quad \begin{bmatrix} 0 & 2x-2 \\ -x+1 & x^2-5x+4 \end{bmatrix} = \begin{bmatrix} 0 & 0 \\ 0 & 0 \end{bmatrix}$$

On equating the corresponding elements, we get

$2x - 2 = 0$

$\Rightarrow \quad x - 1 = 0 \Rightarrow x = 1$

Hence, the value of x is 1.

NOTE Suppose if we take $x^2 - 5x + 4 = 0$, then

$(x-4)(x-1) = 0 \Rightarrow x = 1, 4$

But $x = 4$ does not satisfy the $2x - 2 = 0$. So, please be careful while taking the equation.

20. Given, $A\begin{bmatrix} 3 & 4 \\ -1 & 2 \\ 2 & 1 \end{bmatrix} = \begin{bmatrix} 0 & 15 \\ 1 & -2 \end{bmatrix}$ ...(i)

The right side of given matrix equation is of order 2×2, so left side of the given matrix equation should be of 2×2. It is clear that product of A with 3×2 matrix is 2×2 matrix.

Therefore, A is of order 2×3.

Let $A = \begin{bmatrix} u & w & y \\ v & x & z \end{bmatrix}$

$\therefore$ From Eq. (i), we have

$$\begin{bmatrix} u & w & y \\ v & x & z \end{bmatrix}\begin{bmatrix} 3 & 4 \\ -1 & 2 \\ 2 & 1 \end{bmatrix} = \begin{bmatrix} 0 & 15 \\ 1 & -2 \end{bmatrix}$$

$$\Rightarrow \quad \begin{bmatrix} 3u - w + 2y & 4u + 2w + y \\ 3v - x + 2z & 4v + 2x + z \end{bmatrix} = \begin{bmatrix} 0 & 15 \\ 1 & -2 \end{bmatrix}$$

On comparing the elements from both the side, we get

$3u - w + 2y = 0$, $4u + 2w + y = 15$;

$3v - x + 2z = 1$ and $4v + 2x + z = -2$

On solving, we get

$u = 1$, $w = 5$, $y = 1$, $v = 1$, $x = -2$, $z = -2$

So, $A = \begin{bmatrix} 1 & 5 & 1 \\ 1 & -2 & -2 \end{bmatrix}$

21. Let $A=\begin{bmatrix}3 & -2 & 3\\ 2 & 1 & -1\\ 4 & -3 & 2\end{bmatrix}$;

$$B=\begin{bmatrix}-1 & -5 & -1\\ -8 & -6 & 9\\ -10 & 1 & 7\end{bmatrix}$$

$$AB=\begin{bmatrix}3 & -2 & 3\\ 2 & 1 & -1\\ 4 & -3 & 2\end{bmatrix}\begin{bmatrix}-1 & -5 & -1\\ -8 & -6 & 9\\ -10 & 1 & 7\end{bmatrix}$$

$$=\begin{bmatrix}-3+16-30 & -15+12+3 & -3-18+21\\ -2-8+10 & -10-6-1 & -2+9-7\\ -4+24-20 & -20+18+2 & -4-27+14\end{bmatrix}$$

$$=\begin{bmatrix}-17 & 0 & 0\\ 0 & -17 & 0\\ 0 & 0 & -17\end{bmatrix}$$

$$AB=-17I$$

On pre-multiplying by A^{-1} on both sides, we get

$$(A^{-1}A)\,B=-\,A^{-1}(17I)$$

$$\Rightarrow \quad A^{-1}=\frac{-1}{17}B=\frac{-1}{17}\begin{bmatrix}-1 & -5 & -1\\ -8 & -6 & 9\\ -10 & 1 & 7\end{bmatrix}$$

Given, system of equation can be written as

$$AX=C \Rightarrow X=A^{-1}C,$$

where $A=\begin{bmatrix}3 & -2 & 3\\ 2 & 1 & -1\\ 4 & -3 & 2\end{bmatrix}, C\begin{bmatrix}8\\ 1\\ 4\end{bmatrix}, X=\begin{bmatrix}x\\ y\\ z\end{bmatrix}$

$$X=\frac{-1}{17}\begin{bmatrix}-1 & -5 & -1\\ -8 & -6 & 9\\ -10 & 1 & 7\end{bmatrix}\begin{bmatrix}8\\ 1\\ 4\end{bmatrix}$$

$$\Rightarrow \quad X=-\frac{1}{17}\begin{bmatrix}-8-5-4\\ -64-6+36\\ -80+1+28\end{bmatrix}$$

$$\Rightarrow \quad \begin{bmatrix}x\\ y\\ z\end{bmatrix}=\frac{-1}{17}\begin{bmatrix}-17\\ -34\\ -51\end{bmatrix}=\begin{bmatrix}1\\ 2\\ 3\end{bmatrix}$$

$\therefore \quad x=1,\ y=2,\ z=3$

CHAPTER TEST

1 Mark Questions

1. For any two matrices A and B, we have
(a) $AB = BA$ (b) $AB \neq BA$
(c) $AB = O$ (d) None of these

2. If matrix $A = [a_{ij}]_{2\times 2}$, where $a_{ij} = \begin{cases} 1, \text{ if } i \neq j \\ 0, \text{ if } i = j \end{cases}$. Then, A^2 is equal to
(a) I (b) A
(c) O (d) None of these

3. If $A = \begin{bmatrix} \alpha & \beta \\ \gamma & -\alpha \end{bmatrix}$ is such that $A^2 = I$, then
(a) $1+\alpha^2+\beta\gamma = 0$ (b) $1-\alpha^2+\beta\gamma = 0$
(c) $1-\alpha^2-\beta\gamma = 0$ (d) $1+\alpha^2-\beta\gamma = 0$

2 Marks Questions

4. If $A = \begin{bmatrix} \cos\alpha & -\sin\alpha \\ \sin\alpha & \cos\alpha \end{bmatrix}$, then for what value of α, A is an identity matrix?

5. Show that all the diagonal elements of a skew-symmetric matrix are zero.

6. Show that $A'A$ and AA' are both symmetric matrices for any matrix A.

3/4 Marks Questions

7. From the following matrix equation, find the value of x and y.

$$\begin{bmatrix} x+y & 4 \\ -5 & 3y \end{bmatrix} = \begin{bmatrix} 3 & 4 \\ -5 & 6 \end{bmatrix}$$

8. Find the product and hence find the order of product matrices $\begin{bmatrix} 1 \\ 2 \\ 3 \end{bmatrix}[2 \ \ 3 \ \ 4]$.

9. If $\begin{bmatrix} 1 & 2 \\ 3 & 4 \end{bmatrix}\begin{bmatrix} 3 & 1 \\ 2 & 5 \end{bmatrix} = \begin{bmatrix} 7 & 11 \\ k & 23 \end{bmatrix}$, then find the value of k.

5/6 Marks Questions

10. For the following matrices A and B, verify that $(AB)' = B'A'$;

$$A = \begin{bmatrix} 1 \\ -4 \\ 3 \end{bmatrix}, \quad B = [-1 \ \ 2 \ \ 1]$$

11. Express the following matrix as a sum of a symmetric and a skew-symmetric matrix and verify your result.

$$\begin{bmatrix} 3 & -2 & -4 \\ 3 & -2 & -5 \\ -1 & 1 & 2 \end{bmatrix}$$

Answers

1. (d) **2.** (a) **3.** (c)

4. $\alpha = 0°$ **7.** $x = 1$, $y = 2$

8. The product of matrix is $\begin{bmatrix} 2 & 3 & 4 \\ 4 & 6 & 8 \\ 6 & 9 & 12 \end{bmatrix}$ and its order is 3×3. **9.** $k = 17$

11. Symmetric matrix $= \frac{1}{2}\begin{bmatrix} 6 & 1 & -5 \\ 1 & -4 & -4 \\ -5 & -4 & 4 \end{bmatrix}$

and skew-symmetric matrix $= \frac{1}{2}\begin{bmatrix} 0 & -5 & -3 \\ 5 & 0 & -6 \\ 3 & 6 & 0 \end{bmatrix}$

04

Determinants

TREND ANALYSIS 3 YEARS

		Average No. of Questions Across all Sets			
		Types of Questions	2024	2023	2020
TOPIC 01	Determinant and Its Properties	1 Mark	—	1	—
		2 Marks	1	1	1
		3/4 Marks	—	1	1
		5/6 Marks	—	—	—
TOPIC 02	Adjoint and Inverse of Matrix	1 Mark	—	—	—
		2 Marks	—	—	—
		3/4 Marks	—	—	—
		5/6 Marks	1	1	1

TOPIC 1

Determinant and Its Properties

Square Matrix

A rectangular array of mn numbers in the form of m horizontal lines (i.e. rows) and n vertical lines (i.e. columns) is called a matrix of order $m \times n$. If $m = n$, then matrix is called **square matrix**.

Any square matrix A is denoted by

$$A = \begin{bmatrix} a_{11} & a_{12} & \cdots & a_{1n} \\ a_{21} & a_{22} & \cdots & a_{2n} \\ \vdots & \vdots & \vdots & \vdots \\ a_{n1} & a_{n2} & \cdots & a_{nn} \end{bmatrix} = [a_{ij}]_{n \times n}$$

where, $i = 1, 2, 3, \ldots, n$ and $j = 1, 2, 3, \ldots, n$.

Determinant of a Square Matrix

To every square matrix of order n, a number (real or complex) can be associated, which is called **determinant** of the square matrix.

If A is a n rowed square matrix, then $|A|$ [or det (A)] is called the determinant of matrix A, only square matrix has determinant. Its value may be positive, negative or zero.

Expansion of a Determinant of Order 2

A determinant of order 2 is expanded in the following manner

$$|A| = \begin{vmatrix} a_{11} & a_{12} \\ a_{21} & a_{22} \end{vmatrix} = a_{11} \cdot a_{22} - a_{21} \cdot a_{12}$$

Expansion of a Determinant of Order 3

A determinant of order 3 is expanded in the following manner

$$|A| = \begin{vmatrix} a_{11} & a_{12} & a_{13} \\ a_{21} & a_{22} & a_{23} \\ a_{31} & a_{32} & a_{33} \end{vmatrix}$$

$$= a_{11}(a_{22}a_{33} - a_{32}a_{23}) - a_{12}(a_{21}a_{33} - a_{31}a_{23}) + a_{13}(a_{21}a_{32} - a_{31}a_{22})$$

or $$= a_{11}(a_{22}a_{33} - a_{32}a_{23}) + a_{12}(a_{31}a_{23} - a_{21}a_{33}) + a_{13}(a_{21}a_{32} - a_{31}a_{22})$$

NOTE While expanding the determinant, we use the following (+,−) signs

i.e. $\begin{vmatrix} + & - & + \\ - & + & - \\ + & - & + \end{vmatrix}$

Minors and Cofactors

Let $A=[a_{ij}]$ be a square matrix of order n. Then, minor of an element a_{ij} is the determinant obtained by deleting the row and column in which that element lies and it is denoted by M_{ij}.

If $A=\begin{bmatrix} a_{11} & a_{12} & a_{13} \\ a_{21} & a_{22} & a_{23} \\ a_{31} & a_{32} & a_{33} \end{bmatrix}$, then minor of $a_{11}=M_{11}=\begin{vmatrix} a_{22} & a_{23} \\ a_{32} & a_{33} \end{vmatrix}$

and minor of $a_{12}=M_{12}=\begin{vmatrix} a_{21} & a_{23} \\ a_{31} & a_{33} \end{vmatrix}$ and so on.

If the minor M_{ij} is multiplied by $(-1)^{i+j}$, then we obtain the cofactor of a_{ij}. It is denoted by A_{ij} or C_{ij}

i.e. $A_{ij}=(-1)^{i+j}M_{ij}$, where $1\le i\le 3$ and $1\le j\le 3$.

Then, cofactor of $a_{11}=A_{11}=(-1)^{1+1}M_{11}=\begin{vmatrix} a_{22} & a_{23} \\ a_{32} & a_{33} \end{vmatrix}$

and cofactor of $a_{12}=A_{12}=(-1)^{1+2}M_{12}=-\begin{vmatrix} a_{21} & a_{23} \\ a_{31} & a_{33} \end{vmatrix}$

and so on.

Properties of Determinants

(i) If each element of a row (or column) is zero, then determinant becomes zero.

(ii) If any two rows and columns of a determinant are interchanged, then sign of determinant is changed but its numerical value remains the same.

(iii) If two rows (or columns) of a determinant are identical, then the value of the determinant is zero.

(iv) If each element in a row (or column) of a determinant is multiplied by the same constant, then the determinant gets multiplied by the same constant.

i.e. $\begin{vmatrix} ka & kb & kc \\ p & q & r \\ u & v & w \end{vmatrix}=k\begin{vmatrix} a & b & c \\ p & q & r \\ u & v & w \end{vmatrix}$, where $k\in R-\{0\}$.

(v) The value of a determinant remains unchanged, if any multiple of any row or any column is added to another row or column, respectively

i.e. $\begin{vmatrix} a & b & c \\ p & q & r \\ u & v & w \end{vmatrix}=\begin{vmatrix} a & b & c \\ p+ka & q+kb & r+kc \\ u & v & w \end{vmatrix}$,

where k is a positive constant.

(vi) If each element of a row (or column) of determinant is the sum of the two more terms, then the determinant can be expressed as the sum of the two on more determinants

i.e. $\begin{vmatrix} a_1+a_2 & b & c \\ p_1+p_2 & q & r \\ u_1+u_2 & v & w \end{vmatrix}=\begin{vmatrix} a_1 & b & c \\ p_1 & q & r \\ u_1 & v & w \end{vmatrix}+\begin{vmatrix} a_2 & b & c \\ p_2 & q & r \\ u_2 & v & w \end{vmatrix}$

(vii) $\det(AB)=\det(A)\times\det(B)$

(viii) $\det(kA)=k^n\det(A)$, where A is of order $n\times n$, for any scalar (or constant) k.

(ix) $\det(A^n)=(\det A)^n$, when $n\in I^+$

Applications of Determinant in Geometry

Area of a Triangle

Let the vertices of a ΔABC are $A(x_1, y_1)$, $B(x_2, y_2)$ and $C(x_3, y_3)$.

Then, in the form of determinant,

$$\text{Area of } \Delta ABC=\frac{1}{2}\begin{vmatrix} x_1 & y_1 & 1 \\ x_2 & y_2 & 1 \\ x_3 & y_3 & 1 \end{vmatrix}$$

$$=\frac{1}{2}[x_1(y_2-y_3)+x_2(y_3-y_1)+x_3(y_1-y_2)]$$

NOTE a. Area is a positive quantity, so we take the absolute value of determinant.

b. If area is given, then take both negative and positive values of determinant for calculation.

Condition of Collinearity of Three Points

Three points $A(x_1, y_1)$, $B(x_2, y_2)$ and $C(x_3, y_3)$ are collinear, if and only if the area of triangle formed by these three points is zero.

i.e. $\frac{1}{2}\begin{vmatrix} x_1 & y_1 & 1 \\ x_2 & y_2 & 1 \\ x_3 & y_3 & 1 \end{vmatrix}=0 \Rightarrow \begin{vmatrix} x_1 & y_1 & 1 \\ x_2 & y_2 & 1 \\ x_3 & y_3 & 1 \end{vmatrix}=0$

Equation of a Line Through Two Points

Let $A(x_1, y_1)$ and $B(x_2, y_2)$ be two given points, then the line joining A and B is given by considering any point P (x, y) on the line, so that the points P, A and B are collinear.

Thus, we have $\frac{1}{2}\begin{vmatrix} x & y & 1 \\ x_1 & y_1 & 1 \\ x_2 & y_2 & 1 \end{vmatrix}=0 \Rightarrow \begin{vmatrix} x & y & 1 \\ x_1 & y_1 & 1 \\ x_2 & y_2 & 1 \end{vmatrix}=0$

which gives the required equation of line.

PYQs Previous Years Questions

1 Mark Questions

1. $2\begin{vmatrix} x & y & z \\ p & q & r \\ a & b & c \end{vmatrix} + \begin{vmatrix} x & y & z \\ s & t & u \\ 2a & 2b & 2c \end{vmatrix}$, which one of the following is equal to the above sum? **ISC Specimen 2024**

(a) $\begin{vmatrix} 3x & 3y & 3z \\ 2p+s & 2q+t & 2r+u \\ 4a & 4b & 4c \end{vmatrix}$ (b) $\begin{vmatrix} x & y & z \\ p+s & q+t & r+u \\ 2a & 2b & 2c \end{vmatrix}$

(c) $\begin{vmatrix} 2x & 2y & 2z \\ 2p+s & 2q+t & 2r+u \\ 2a & 2b & 2c \end{vmatrix}$ (d) $\begin{vmatrix} 2x & 2y & 2z \\ p+s & q+t & r+u \\ 4a & 4b & 4c \end{vmatrix}$

2. If A is a square matrix of order 3, then $|2A|$ is equal to **ISC 2023**

(a) $2|A|$ (b) $4|A|$
(c) $8|A|$ (d) $6|A|$

3. If $\begin{bmatrix} 3 & 5 \\ 7 & 9 \end{bmatrix} = X + Y$, where X is skew- symmetric matrix and Y is symmetric matrix. Find $|X|$. **ISC Specimen 2023**

4. The value of $\begin{vmatrix} 1 & \log_a b \\ \log_b a & 1 \end{vmatrix}$ is **ISC Specimen Sem-I 2022**

(a) $1 - \log ab$
(b) $1 - \dfrac{\log b}{\log a}$
(c) 0
(d) $\log ab - 1$

5. If $\Delta = \begin{vmatrix} a & b & c \\ x & y & z \\ p & q & r \end{vmatrix}$, then $\begin{vmatrix} ka & kb & kc \\ kx & ky & kz \\ kp & kq & kr \end{vmatrix}$ is **ISC Specimen Sem-I 2022**

(a) Δ (b) $k\Delta$
(c) $3k\Delta$ (d) $k^3\Delta$

6. What will be the value of x for the determinant equation $\begin{vmatrix} 3-x & 6 & 3 \\ -6 & 3-x & 3 \\ 3 & 3 & 3-x \end{vmatrix} = 0$? **ISC Specimen Sem-I 2022**

(a) 6 (b) 3
(c) 0 (d) – 6

7. Which of the following statement is correct? **ISC Specimen 2021**

(a) Determinant is number associated to a matrix.
(b) Determinant is a square matrix.
(c) Determinant is a number associated to a square matrix.
(d) None of the above

8. If A is square matrix of order 3, with $|A| = 4$, then write the value of $|-2A|$. **ISC Specimen 2021**

2 Marks Questions

9. Using determinants, find the values of k, if the area of triangle with vertices (–2, 0), (0, 4) and (0, k) is 4 sq units. **ISC 2019**

3/4 Marks Questions

10. Using properties of determinants, prove that

$$\begin{vmatrix} x & x^2 & 1+px^3 \\ y & y^2 & 1+py^3 \\ z & z^2 & 1+pz^3 \end{vmatrix} = (1+pxyz)(x-y)(y-z)(z-x),$$

where p is any scalar. **ISC Specimen 2018**

11. Using properties of determinants, find the value of the determinant $\begin{vmatrix} x^3 & x^2 & x \\ y^3 & y^2 & y \\ z^3 & z^2 & z \end{vmatrix}$. **ISC 2003**

12. Find the area of the triangle, whose vertices are (3, 8), (– 4, 2) and (5, 1).

13. If area of the triangle with vertices (–3, 0), (3, 0) and (0, k) is 9 sq units, then find the value of k.

> **KEY CONCEPT**
>
> Determine the area of triangle formed by given points and equate to given area along with (±) sign to get required value of k.

14. If the points (2, – 3), (λ, – 1) and (0, 4) are collinear, then find the value of λ.

15. Find the equation of line joining (2, 3) and (–1, 2) using determinants.

Explanations

1. (b) We have,

$$2\begin{vmatrix} x & y & z \\ p & q & r \\ a & b & c \end{vmatrix} + \begin{vmatrix} x & y & z \\ s & t & u \\ 2a & 2b & 2c \end{vmatrix}$$

$$= \begin{vmatrix} x & y & z \\ p & q & r \\ 2a & 2b & 2c \end{vmatrix} + \begin{vmatrix} x & y & z \\ s & t & u \\ 2a & 2b & 2c \end{vmatrix}$$

$$= \begin{vmatrix} x & y & z \\ p+s & q+t & r+u \\ 2a & 2b & 2c \end{vmatrix}$$

2. (c) We know that $|kA| = k^n |A|$, where n is order of A.

$\therefore \quad |2A| = 2^3 |A| \quad$ [$\because$ order of A is 3]

$= 8|A|$

3. Let $A = \begin{bmatrix} 3 & 5 \\ 7 & 9 \end{bmatrix} = X + Y$

where, X is skew-symmetric matrix i.e. $X = \frac{1}{2}(A - A^T)$

and Y is symmetric matrix i.e.

$$Y = \frac{1}{2}(A + A^T)$$

$\therefore \quad A = \begin{bmatrix} 3 & 5 \\ 7 & 9 \end{bmatrix}$ and $A^T = \begin{bmatrix} 3 & 7 \\ 5 & 9 \end{bmatrix}$

$$\Rightarrow \quad X = \frac{1}{2}(A - A^T) = \frac{1}{2}\left[\begin{pmatrix} 3 & 5 \\ 7 & 9 \end{pmatrix} - \begin{pmatrix} 3 & 7 \\ 5 & 9 \end{pmatrix}\right]$$

$$\Rightarrow \quad X = \frac{1}{2}\begin{bmatrix} 3-3 & 5-7 \\ 7-5 & 9-9 \end{bmatrix} = \frac{1}{2}\begin{bmatrix} 0 & -2 \\ 2 & 0 \end{bmatrix}$$

$$\Rightarrow \quad X = \begin{bmatrix} 0 & -1 \\ 1 & 0 \end{bmatrix}$$

$\therefore \quad |X| = 0 - (-1) = 1$

4. (c) Given, $\begin{vmatrix} 1 & \log_a b \\ \log_b a & 1 \end{vmatrix}$

$= 1 \times 1 - (\log_b a) \cdot (\log_a b)$

$= 1 - \dfrac{\log a}{\log b} \times \dfrac{\log b}{\log a}$ [change of base formula]

$= 1 - 1 = 0$

5. (d) We know that if each element of a column is multiplied by the same constant, then the determinant gets multiplied by the same constant.

So, $\begin{vmatrix} ka & kb & kc \\ kx & ky & kz \\ kp & kq & kr \end{vmatrix} = (k \cdot k \cdot k)\begin{vmatrix} a & b & c \\ x & y & z \\ p & q & r \end{vmatrix} = k^3 \Delta$

6. (b) Let $x = 3$

Now, $\Delta = \begin{vmatrix} 3-x & 6 & 3 \\ -6 & 3-x & 3 \\ 3 & 3 & 3-x \end{vmatrix} = \begin{vmatrix} 0 & 6 & 3 \\ -6 & 0 & 3 \\ 3 & 3 & 0 \end{vmatrix}$

On expanding along R_1, we get

$\Delta = 0(0-9) - 6(0-9) + 3(-18-0)$

$\Delta = 0 + 54 - 54 = 0$

$\therefore \quad x = 3$

7. (c) Determinant is a number associated to a square matrix.

8. Given, A is a square matrix of order 3 and also, $|A| = 4$

Now, $|-2A| = (-2)^3 |A| = -8|A| = -8 \times 4 = -32$

9. Given, area of a triangle with vertices $(-2, 0)$, $(0, 4)$ and $(0, k)$ is 4 sq units.

$\therefore \quad \frac{1}{2}\begin{vmatrix} -2 & 0 & 1 \\ 0 & 4 & 1 \\ 0 & k & 1 \end{vmatrix} = \pm 4 \Rightarrow \begin{vmatrix} -2 & 0 & 1 \\ 0 & 4 & 1 \\ 0 & k & 1 \end{vmatrix} = \pm 8$

Expanding along C_1, we get

$-2(4-k) = \pm 8 \Rightarrow -8 + 2k = \pm 8$

Taking '+' sign,

$-8 + 2k = 8 \Rightarrow 2k = 16 \Rightarrow k = 8$

Taking '–' sign,

$-8 + 2k = -8 \Rightarrow 2k = 0 \Rightarrow k = 0$

Hence, the values of k are 0 and 8.

Concept Enhancer Area of $\Delta ABC = \frac{1}{2}\begin{vmatrix} x_1 & y_1 & 1 \\ x_2 & y_2 & 1 \\ x_3 & y_3 & 1 \end{vmatrix}$

10. Let LHS $= \begin{vmatrix} x & x^2 & 1+px^3 \\ y & y^2 & 1+py^3 \\ z & z^2 & 1+pz^3 \end{vmatrix}$

$$= \begin{vmatrix} x & x^2 & 1 \\ y & y^2 & 1 \\ z & z^2 & 1 \end{vmatrix} + \begin{vmatrix} x & x^2 & px^3 \\ y & y^2 & py^3 \\ z & z^2 & pz^3 \end{vmatrix}$$

On taking common p from C_3, x from R_1, y from R_2 and z from R_3 of second determinant, we get

$$= \begin{vmatrix} x & x^2 & 1 \\ y & y^2 & 1 \\ z & z^2 & 1 \end{vmatrix} + pxyz \begin{vmatrix} 1 & x & x^2 \\ 1 & y & y^2 \\ 1 & z & z^2 \end{vmatrix}$$

$$= (1 + pxyz) \begin{vmatrix} 1 & x & x^2 \\ 1 & y & y^2 \\ 1 & z & z^2 \end{vmatrix}$$

On expanding along R_1, we get

$$= (1 + pxyz)\,[1(yz^2 - zy^2) - x(z^2 - y^2) + x^2(z - y)]$$
$$= (1 + pxyz)\,[yz(z - y) - x(z - y)(z + y) + x^2(z - y)]$$
$$= (1 + pxyz)(z - y)[yz - xz - xy + x^2]$$
$$= (1 + pxyz)(z - y)[z(y - x) - x(y - x)]$$
$$= (1 + pxyz)(z - y)(y - x)(z - x)$$
$$= (1 + pxyz)(x - y)(y - z)(z - x)$$
$$= \text{RHS}$$

11. Given, $\Delta = \begin{vmatrix} x^3 & x^2 & x \\ y^3 & y^2 & y \\ z^3 & z^2 & z \end{vmatrix}$

On taking x, y and z common from R_1, R_2 and R_3 respectively $= xyz \begin{vmatrix} x^2 & x & 1 \\ y^2 & y & 1 \\ z^2 & z & 1 \end{vmatrix}$

On expanding along R_1, we get

$$\Delta = (xyz)\,[x^2(y - z) - x(y^2 - z^2) + 1(y^2 z - z^2 y)]$$
$$= (xyz)\,[x^2(y - z) - x(y + z)(y - z) + yz(y - z)]$$
$$= (xyz)(y - z)[x^2 - xy - xz + yz]$$
$$= (xyz)(y - z)[x(x - y) - z(x - y)]$$
$$= (xyz)(y - z)(x - y)(x - z)$$
$$= (xyz)(x - y)(z - x)(z - y)$$

12. Given vertices of a triangle are (3, 8), (– 4, 2) and (5, 1).

Let $(x_1, y_1) = (3, 8)$, $(x_2, y_2) = (-4, 2)$ and $(x_3, y_3) = (5, 1)$

Then, area of triangle

$$= \frac{1}{2}\begin{vmatrix} x_1 & y_1 & 1 \\ x_2 & y_2 & 1 \\ x_3 & y_3 & 1 \end{vmatrix} = \frac{1}{2}\begin{vmatrix} 3 & 8 & 1 \\ -4 & 2 & 1 \\ 5 & 1 & 1 \end{vmatrix}$$

$$= \frac{1}{2}\left[3\begin{vmatrix} 2 & 1 \\ 1 & 1 \end{vmatrix} - 8\begin{vmatrix} -4 & 1 \\ 5 & 1 \end{vmatrix} + 1\begin{vmatrix} -4 & 2 \\ 5 & 1 \end{vmatrix}\right]$$

$$= \frac{1}{2}[3(2 - 1) - 8(-4 - 5) + 1(-4 - 10)]$$

$$= \frac{1}{2}[3 + 72 - 14] = \frac{61}{2} \text{ sq units}$$

13. Given, area of a triangle with vertices (–3, 0), (3, 0) and (0, k) is 9 sq units.

$\therefore$ We have, $\dfrac{1}{2}\begin{vmatrix} -3 & 0 & 1 \\ 3 & 0 & 1 \\ 0 & k & 1 \end{vmatrix} = \pm 9 \Rightarrow \begin{vmatrix} -3 & 0 & 1 \\ 3 & 0 & 1 \\ 0 & k & 1 \end{vmatrix} = \pm 18$

$$\Rightarrow -3(0 - k) - 0 + 1(3k - 0) = \pm 18$$
$$\Rightarrow 3k + 3k = \pm 18$$
$$\Rightarrow 6k = \pm 18 \Rightarrow k = \pm 3$$

Common Mistake Do consider both the positive and negative sign of given area.

14. Given points (2, – 3), (λ, – 1) and (0, 4) are collinear. So, area of triangle formed by these three points will be zero.

$$\therefore \frac{1}{2}\begin{vmatrix} 2 & -3 & 1 \\ \lambda & -1 & 1 \\ 0 & 4 & 1 \end{vmatrix} = 0$$

$$\Rightarrow \begin{vmatrix} 2 & -3 & 1 \\ \lambda & -1 & 1 \\ 0 & 4 & 1 \end{vmatrix} = 0$$

Now, expanding along R_1, we get

$$2(-1 - 4) + 3(\lambda - 0) + 1(4\lambda - 0) = 0$$
$$-10 + 3\lambda + 4\lambda = 0$$
$$7\lambda = 10$$
$$\Rightarrow \lambda = \frac{10}{7}$$

Hence, the required value of λ is $\dfrac{10}{7}$.

Concept Enhancer When three points are collinear, then area of ΔABC is zero.

15. Equation of line is given by $\begin{vmatrix} x & y & 1 \\ x_1 & y_1 & 1 \\ x_2 & y_2 & 1 \end{vmatrix} = 0$

Consider, $(x_1, y_1) = (2, 3)$ and $(x_2, y_2) = (-1, 2)$

$$\therefore \begin{vmatrix} x & y & 1 \\ 2 & 3 & 1 \\ -1 & 2 & 1 \end{vmatrix} = 0$$

$$\Rightarrow x(3 - 2) - y(2 + 1) + 1(4 + 3) = 0$$

[expanding along R_1]

$$\Rightarrow x - 3y + 7 = 0$$

which is the required equation.

TOPIC 2

Adjoint and Inverse of Matrix

Singular and Non-Singular Matrix

If A is a square matrix and $|A| = 0$, then A is known as singular matrix.

If A is a square matrix and $|A| \neq 0$, then A is known as non-singular matrix.

Adjoint of a Matrix

Let $A = [a_{ij}]_{n \times n}$ be a square matrix of order n and C_{ij} (or A_{ij}) be the cofactor of a_{ij} in the determinant $|A|$.

Then, the adjoint of A is defined as the transpose of the cofactor matrix and it is denoted by adj(A).

e.g. If $A = \begin{bmatrix} a_{11} & a_{12} & a_{13} \\ a_{21} & a_{22} & a_{23} \\ a_{31} & a_{32} & a_{33} \end{bmatrix}$, then adj $A = \begin{bmatrix} A_{11} & A_{21} & A_{31} \\ A_{12} & A_{22} & A_{32} \\ A_{13} & A_{23} & A_{33} \end{bmatrix}$,

where A_{ij}'s are cofactors of A.

Properties of Adjoint of a Matrix

If A is a square matrix of order $n \times n$, then

(i) $A(\text{adj } A) = (\text{adj } A)A = |A| I_n$

(ii) $|\text{adj } A| = |A|^{n-1}$, provided $|A| \neq 0$

(iii) adj $(A^T) = (\text{adj } A)^T$

Inverse of a Square Matrix

Let A be a non-singular (i.e. $|A| \neq 0$) square matrix. Then, a square matrix B, such that $AB = BA = I$ is called inverse of A and it is denoted by A^{-1}

i.e. $$A^{-1} = \frac{1}{|A|} \text{adj}(A).$$

Properties of Inverse Matrix

Let A and B be square matrices of same order, then

(i) A square matrix is invertible if and only if it is non-singular.

(ii) $(A^{-1})^{-1} = A$

(iii) $(A')^{-1} = (A^{-1})'$

(iv) $(AB)^{-1} = B^{-1}A^{-1}$

(v) $|A^{-1}| = |A|^{-1}$

(vi) $AA^{-1} = A^{-1}A = I$

(vii) $(kA)^{-1} = \frac{1}{k} A^{-1}$, if $k \neq 0$

Solutions of System of Linear Equations (Martin's Rule)

Let system of linear equations in three variables be

$$a_1x + b_1y + c_1z = d_1,$$
$$a_2x + b_2y + c_2z = d_2$$

and $$a_3x + b_3y + c_3z = d_3$$

It can be written in the matrix form as

$$\begin{bmatrix} a_1 & b_1 & c_1 \\ a_2 & b_2 & c_2 \\ a_3 & b_3 & c_3 \end{bmatrix} \begin{bmatrix} x \\ y \\ z \end{bmatrix} = \begin{bmatrix} d_1 \\ d_2 \\ d_3 \end{bmatrix} \quad \text{or} \quad AX = B$$

where, $A = \begin{bmatrix} a_1 & b_1 & c_1 \\ a_2 & b_2 & c_2 \\ a_3 & b_3 & c_3 \end{bmatrix}$, $X = \begin{bmatrix} x \\ y \\ z \end{bmatrix}$ and $B = \begin{bmatrix} d_1 \\ d_2 \\ d_3 \end{bmatrix}$

If $|A| \neq 0$, then solution of system of linear equations is given by $X = A^{-1}B$.

This method of solving a system of linear equations is also known as **matrix method.**

Test of Consistency of above System of Equations

Non-homogeneous System of Equations (i.e. where $B \neq O$)

- If $|A| \neq 0$, then the system of equations is **consistent** and has a unique solution.
- If $|A| = 0$ and (adj A) $B \neq O$, then the system of equations is inconsistent and has no solution.
- If $|A| = 0$ and (adj A) $B = O$, then the system of equations is consistent and has infinite number of solutions.

Homogeneous System of Equations (i.e. where $B = O$)

- If $|A| \neq 0$, then the system of equations have only trivial solution i.e. $x = y = z = 0$.
- If $|A| = 0$, then the system of equations has infinite number of solutions.

NOTE A homogeneous system of equations is never inconsistent.

PYQs Previous Years Questions

1 Mark Questions

1. If A is a 3×3 matrix such that $A(\text{adj } A) = \begin{bmatrix} 3 & 0 & 0 \\ 0 & 3 & 0 \\ 0 & 0 & 3 \end{bmatrix}$, then the value of $|A^T|$ will be **ISC Specimen 2023**

(a) 27 (b) 9 (c) 3 (d) –3

2. What is the multiplicative inverse of matrix A? **ISC Specimen Sem-I 2022**

(a) A (b) A^2 (c) $|A|$ (d) $\dfrac{\text{adj } A}{|A|}$

3. For what value of k inverse does not exist for the matrix $\begin{bmatrix} 1 & 2 \\ k & 6 \end{bmatrix}$? **ISC Specimen 2021**

(a) 2 (b) 3 (c) 6 (d) 5

3/4 Marks Questions

4. Find the matrix X for which

$$\begin{bmatrix} 5 & 4 \\ 1 & 1 \end{bmatrix} X = \begin{bmatrix} 1 & -2 \\ 1 & 3 \end{bmatrix}$$

ISC 2016

5. If $A = \begin{bmatrix} 3 & -2 \\ 4 & -2 \end{bmatrix}$, then find x such that $A^2 = xA - 2I$.

Hence, find A^{-1}. **ISC 2011**

> **KEY CONCEPT**
>
> (i) First, find A^2 by multiplication property.
>
> (ii) Simplify, the given matrix and equating the corresponding elements to get the value of x.
>
> (iii) Further, put the value of x in the given equation and multiplying both sides of A^{-1} and then simplify it, to get the required result.

6. If the matrix $A = \begin{bmatrix} 6 & x & 2 \\ 2 & -1 & 2 \\ -10 & 5 & 2 \end{bmatrix}$ is a singular matrix, then find the value of x. **ISC 2010**

7. If $A = \begin{bmatrix} \cos x & \sin x \\ -\sin x & \cos x \end{bmatrix}$ and

$A \cdot (\text{adj}A) = k \begin{bmatrix} 1 & 0 \\ 0 & 1 \end{bmatrix}$, then find the value of k. **ISC 2005**

> **KEY CONCEPT**
>
> (i) First, find cofactors of $|A|$ and then determine adj (A) by using formula $\text{adj} A = \begin{bmatrix} A_{11} & A_{21} \\ A_{12} & A_{22} \end{bmatrix}$.
>
> (ii) Simplify, the given matrix equation and equating the corresponding element to get the required value.

8. If the matrix $A = \begin{bmatrix} 2 & 3 \\ 5 & -2 \end{bmatrix}$, then show that $A^{-1} = \dfrac{1}{19} A$. **ISC 2004**

9. Find the inverse of the matrix $A = \begin{bmatrix} 3 & 1 \\ 4 & 2 \end{bmatrix}$. **ISC 2002**

5/6 Marks Questions

10. A furniture factory uses three types of wood namely, teakwood, rosewood and satinwood for manufacturing three types of furniture, that are table, chair and cot.

The wood requirements (in tonnes) for each type of furniture are given below

	Table	Chair	Cot
Teakwood	2	3	4
Rosewood	1	1	2
Satinwood	3	2	1

It is found that 29 tonnes of teakwood, 13 tonnes of rosewood and 16 tonnes of satinwood are available to make all three types of furniture.

Using the above information, answer the following questions:

(i) Express the data given in the table above in the form of a set of simultaneous equations.

(ii) Solve the set of simultaneous equations formed in subpart (i) by matrix method.

(iii) Hence, find the number of table(s), chair(s) and cot(s) produced. **ISC 2024**

11. Garima owns a cafe that serves burgers, samosas and juice bottles. On a particular day, 100 items in total were sold. The number of burgers sold was thrice the number of samosas sold. Also, the number of samosas sold was 10 more than the number of juice bottles sold. **ISC Specimen 2024**

(i) Form a set of simultaneous equations for the above information.

(ii) Solve the set of equations formed in (i) by matrix method.

(iii) Hence, find the number of items sold in each category.

12. Use matrix method to solve the following system of equations.

$$\frac{2}{x}+\frac{3}{y}+\frac{10}{z}=4,\quad \frac{4}{x}-\frac{6}{y}+\frac{5}{z}=1,\quad \frac{6}{x}+\frac{9}{y}-\frac{20}{z}=2$$

ISC 2023, 11

13. Find A^{-1}, if $A=\begin{bmatrix}1 & 2 & 0\\ -2 & -1 & -2\\ 0 & -1 & 1\end{bmatrix}$. Using A^{-1}, solve the system of linear equations

$x-2y=10, 2x-y-z=8, -2y+z=7$

ISC Specimen 2023

14. Ramu purchased 5 pens, 3 bags and 1 instrument box and paid ₹ 16. From the same shop Venkat purchased 2 pens, 1 bag and 3 instrument boxes and paid ₹ 19 while Gopi purchased 1 pen, 2 bags and 4 instrument boxes and paid ₹ 25. Using the concept of matrices and determinants to answer the following questions by choosing the correct option:

(i) If x, y and z respectively denotes the cost of pen, bag and instrument box, then which of the following is true?

(a) $5x+3y+z=16$ (b) $2x+y+3z=19$

(c) $x+2y+4z=25$ (d) All of these

(ii) If $A=\begin{bmatrix}5 & 3 & 1\\ 2 & 1 & 3\\ 1 & 2 & 4\end{bmatrix}$, $|A|$ is

(a) – 22 (b) 22 (c) 0 (d) 20

(iii) If $A=\begin{bmatrix}5 & 3 & 1\\ 2 & 1 & 3\\ 1 & 2 & 4\end{bmatrix}$ and adj $A=\begin{bmatrix}-2 & x & 8\\ -5 & 19 & -13\\ 3 & -7 & y\end{bmatrix}$, then missing value of x and y are

(a) $x=-10$ and $y=-1$ (b) $x=10$ and $y=-1$

(c) $x=-10$ and $y=1$ (d) $x=10$ and $y=1$

(iv) The cost of one pen is **ISC Specimen Sem-I 2022**

(a) ₹ 2 (b) ₹ 5 (c) ₹ 1 (d) ₹ 3

15. Using matrices, solve the following system of equations

$2x-3y+5z=11,$

$3x+2y-4z=-5$

and $x+y-2z=-3.$ **ISC Specimen 2021, ISC 2018**

16. Solve the following system of linear equations using matrices.

$$x-2y=10,\quad 2x-y-z=8,$$
$$-2y+z=7$$

ISC 2020

17. Solve the following system of linear equations using matrix method

$$\frac{1}{x}+\frac{1}{y}+\frac{1}{z}=9,\ \frac{2}{x}+\frac{5}{y}+\frac{7}{z}=52,\ \frac{2}{x}+\frac{1}{y}-\frac{1}{z}=0.$$

ISC 2019

18. Given that $A=\begin{bmatrix}1 & -1 & 0\\ 2 & 3 & 4\\ 0 & 1 & 2\end{bmatrix}$ and $B=\begin{bmatrix}2 & 2 & -4\\ -4 & 2 & -4\\ 2 & -1 & 5\end{bmatrix}$, find AB. Using this result, solve the following system of equation $x-y=3, 2x+3y+4z=17$ and $y+2z=7$.

ISC 2017

19. Solve the following system of linear equations by using matrix method.

$3x+y+z=1, 2x+2z=0, 5x+y+2z=2$ **ISC 2016**

20. Given two matrices A and B,

$$A=\begin{bmatrix}1 & -2 & 3\\ 1 & 4 & 1\\ 1 & -3 & 2\end{bmatrix} \text{ and } B=\begin{bmatrix}11 & -5 & -14\\ -1 & -1 & 2\\ -7 & 1 & 6\end{bmatrix};$$

AB and use this result to solve the following system of equations

$x-2y+3z=6, x+4y+z=12, x-3y+2z=1.$

ISC 2015

21. Using the matrix method, solve the following system of equations

$x-2y=10, 2x+y+3z=8$ and $-2y+z=7.$ **ISC 2014**

22. Find A^{-1}, where $A=\begin{bmatrix}4 & 2 & 3\\ 1 & 1 & 1\\ 3 & 1 & -2\end{bmatrix}$.

Then, solve the following system of linear equations $4x+2y+3z=2, x+y+z=1$ and $3x+y-2z=5.$

ISC 2013

KEY CONCEPT

(i) First, solve the given matrix by property of inverse of matrix. i.e. $A^{-1}=\frac{1}{|A|}\text{adj}(A)$

(ii) Then, convert the system of equations in matrix form and put the value of inverse of matrix (A^{-1}).

(iii) Further, we will get the required result of the equations.

Explanations

1. (c) Given, A is 3×3 matrix and $A(\text{adj } A)=\begin{bmatrix}3&0&0\\0&3&0\\0&0&3\end{bmatrix}$

We know that $A(\text{adj } A)=|A|I_3$

$\because \begin{bmatrix}3&0&0\\0&3&0\\0&0&3\end{bmatrix}=|A|I_3$

$\Rightarrow 3\begin{bmatrix}1&0&0\\0&1&0\\0&0&1\end{bmatrix}=|A|I_3$

$\Rightarrow 3I_3=|A|I_3 \Rightarrow |A|=3$

$\therefore |A^T|=3$ $[\because |A^T|=|A|]$

2. (d) The multiplicative inverse of matrix A is $\dfrac{\text{adj } A}{|A|}$.

3. (b) For $A=\begin{bmatrix}1&2\\k&6\end{bmatrix}$

If $|A|=0$, then inverse does not exist

$\therefore \begin{vmatrix}1&2\\k&6\end{vmatrix}=0$

$\Rightarrow 6-2k=0 \Rightarrow 2k=6$

$\Rightarrow 2k=6 \Rightarrow k=3$

4. Given, $\begin{bmatrix}5&4\\1&1\end{bmatrix}X=\begin{bmatrix}1&-2\\1&3\end{bmatrix}$

Let $A=\begin{bmatrix}5&4\\1&1\end{bmatrix}$ and $B=\begin{bmatrix}1&-2\\1&3\end{bmatrix}$

Then, $|A|=\begin{vmatrix}5&4\\1&1\end{vmatrix}=(5\times1)-(1\times4)=5-4=1\neq0$

So, A^{-1} exists.

Now, cofactors of elements of matrix A are given below:

$A_{11}=1, A_{12}=-1, A_{21}=-4$ and $A_{22}=5$

Now, $\text{adj}(A)=\begin{bmatrix}1&-1\\-4&5\end{bmatrix}^T=\begin{bmatrix}1&-4\\-1&5\end{bmatrix}$

$\therefore A^{-1}=\dfrac{1}{|A|}\text{adj }(A)=\dfrac{1}{1}\begin{bmatrix}1&-4\\-1&5\end{bmatrix}$

$\Rightarrow A^{-1}=\begin{bmatrix}1&-4\\-1&5\end{bmatrix}$

So, the given matrix equation is

$AX=B \Rightarrow A^{-1}(AX)=A^{-1}B$

$\Rightarrow (A^{-1}A)X=A^{-1}B$

$\Rightarrow IX=A^{-1}B$

$\Rightarrow X=A^{-1}B$

$\Rightarrow X=\begin{bmatrix}1&-4\\-1&5\end{bmatrix}\begin{bmatrix}1&-2\\1&3\end{bmatrix}$

$\Rightarrow X=\begin{bmatrix}1\times1+(-4)\times1 & 1\times(-2)+(-4)\times3\\ -1\times1+5\times1 & (-1)\times(-2)+5\times3\end{bmatrix}$

$\Rightarrow X=\begin{bmatrix}1-4&-2-12\\-1+5&2+15\end{bmatrix}$

$\Rightarrow X=\begin{bmatrix}-3&-14\\4&17\end{bmatrix}$

5. Given, $A=\begin{bmatrix}3&-2\\4&-2\end{bmatrix}$

Now, $A^2=A\cdot A=\begin{bmatrix}3&-2\\4&-2\end{bmatrix}\begin{bmatrix}3&-2\\4&-2\end{bmatrix}$

$=\begin{bmatrix}9-8&-6+4\\12-8&-8+4\end{bmatrix}$

[by multiplication property]

$=\begin{bmatrix}1&-2\\4&-4\end{bmatrix}$ ...(i)

Now, $xA=x\begin{bmatrix}3&-2\\4&-2\end{bmatrix}=\begin{bmatrix}3x&-2x\\4x&-2x\end{bmatrix}$ ...(ii)

$-2I=-2\begin{bmatrix}1&0\\0&1\end{bmatrix}=\begin{bmatrix}-2&0\\0&-2\end{bmatrix}$ ...(iii)

Also given,

$A^2=xA-2I$

or $A^2=xA+(-2I)$

$\Rightarrow \begin{bmatrix}1&-2\\4&-4\end{bmatrix}=\begin{bmatrix}3x&-2x\\4x&-2x\end{bmatrix}+\begin{bmatrix}-2&0\\0&-2\end{bmatrix}$

[using Eqs. (i), (ii) and (iii)]

$\Rightarrow \begin{bmatrix}1&-2\\4&-4\end{bmatrix}=\begin{bmatrix}3x-2&-2x\\4x&-2x-2\end{bmatrix}$

On equating the corresponding elements, we get

$3x-2=1 \Rightarrow 3x=3 \Rightarrow x=1$

$\because A^2=xA-2I$ [given]

$\therefore A^2=A-2I$ $[\because x=1]$

$\Rightarrow A^2-A+2I=O$ ...(iv)

On pre-multiplying both sides by A^{-1} in Eq. (iv), we get

$$A^{-1}\cdot A^2 - A^{-1}\cdot A + 2A^{-1}\cdot I = A^{-1}\cdot O$$

$$\Rightarrow \quad (A^{-1}\cdot A)A - I + 2A^{-1} = O$$

$$[\because A^{-1}A = I \text{ and } A^{-1}I = A^{-1}]$$

$$\Rightarrow \quad I\cdot A - I + 2A^{-1} = O$$

$$\Rightarrow \quad 2A^{-1} = I - A$$

$$\Rightarrow \quad 2A^{-1} = \begin{bmatrix}1 & 0\\ 0 & 1\end{bmatrix} - \begin{bmatrix}3 & -2\\ 4 & -2\end{bmatrix}$$

$$\Rightarrow \quad 2A^{-1} = \begin{bmatrix}1-3 & 0+2\\ 0-4 & 1+2\end{bmatrix} = \begin{bmatrix}-2 & 2\\ -4 & 3\end{bmatrix}$$

[by subtraction property]

Hence, $A^{-1} = \frac{1}{2}\begin{bmatrix}-2 & 2\\ -4 & 3\end{bmatrix} = \begin{bmatrix}-1 & 1\\ -2 & 3/2\end{bmatrix}$

6. Given, $A = \begin{bmatrix}6 & x & 2\\ 2 & -1 & 2\\ -10 & 5 & 2\end{bmatrix}$

Since, A is a singular matrix.

Therefore, it means $|A| = 0$

i.e. $\begin{vmatrix}6 & x & 2\\ 2 & -1 & 2\\ -10 & 5 & 2\end{vmatrix} = 0$ [given]

Expanding LHS along R_1, we get

$$6[-2-10] - x[4+20] + 2[10-10] = 0$$

$$\Rightarrow \quad -72 - 24x + 0 = 0 \Rightarrow 24x = -72$$

$$\Rightarrow \quad x = \frac{-72}{24} = -3$$

Hence, the value of x is -3.

Concept Enhancer When matrix A is a singular matrix, then $|A| = 0$.

7. Given, $A = \begin{bmatrix}\cos x & \sin x\\ -\sin x & \cos x\end{bmatrix}$

Now, cofactors of $|A|$ are

$$A_{11} = (-1)^{1+1}\cos x = \cos x,$$

$$A_{12} = (-1)^{1+2}(-\sin x) = \sin x,$$

$$A_{21} = (-1)^{2+1}\sin x = -\sin x$$

and $$A_{22} = (-1)^{2+2}\cos x = \cos x$$

$$\therefore \quad \text{adj}(A) = \begin{bmatrix}A_{11} & A_{21}\\ A_{12} & A_{22}\end{bmatrix} = \begin{bmatrix}\cos x & -\sin x\\ \sin x & \cos x\end{bmatrix}$$

Now, $A\cdot(\text{adj}\,A) = \begin{bmatrix}\cos x & \sin x\\ -\sin x & \cos x\end{bmatrix}\begin{bmatrix}\cos x & -\sin x\\ \sin x & \cos x\end{bmatrix}$

$$= \begin{bmatrix}\cos x^2 + \sin^2 x & -\sin x\cos x + \cos x\sin x\\ -\sin x\cos x + \cos x\sin x & \sin^2 x + \cos^2 x\end{bmatrix}$$

[by product rule]

$$= \begin{bmatrix}1 & 0\\ 0 & 1\end{bmatrix} \quad [\because \sin^2 x + \cos^2 x = 1] \ldots\text{(i)}$$

Also given, $A\cdot(\text{adj}\,A) = k\begin{bmatrix}1 & 0\\ 0 & 1\end{bmatrix}$ [given]

$$\Rightarrow \quad \begin{bmatrix}1 & 0\\ 0 & 1\end{bmatrix} = k\begin{bmatrix}1 & 0\\ 0 & 1\end{bmatrix}$$

$$\Rightarrow \quad \begin{bmatrix}1 & 0\\ 0 & 1\end{bmatrix} = \begin{bmatrix}k & 0\\ 0 & k\end{bmatrix} \quad \text{[from Eq. (i)]}$$

$$\therefore \quad k = 1$$

8. Given, $A = \begin{bmatrix}2 & 3\\ 5 & -2\end{bmatrix}$

Now, $|A| = \begin{vmatrix}2 & 3\\ 5 & -2\end{vmatrix} = -4 - 15 = -19 \neq 0$

Since, A is a non-singular matrix, so A^{-1} exists.

Now, cofactors of $|A|$ are

$$A_{11} = (-1)^{1+1}(-2) = -2,$$

$$A_{12} = (-1)^{1+2}(5) = -5,$$

$$A_{21} = (-1)^{2+1}(3) = -3$$

and $$A_{22} = (-1)^{2+2}(2) = 2$$

Now, $\text{adj}(A) = \begin{bmatrix}A_{11} & A_{21}\\ A_{12} & A_{22}\end{bmatrix} = \begin{bmatrix}-2 & -3\\ -5 & 2\end{bmatrix}$

$$\therefore \quad A^{-1} = \frac{1}{|A|}\text{adj}(A) = \frac{1}{-19}\begin{bmatrix}-2 & -3\\ -5 & 2\end{bmatrix}$$

$$= \frac{1}{19}\begin{bmatrix}2 & 3\\ 5 & -2\end{bmatrix} = \frac{1}{19}A$$

9. Given, $A = \begin{bmatrix}3 & 1\\ 4 & 2\end{bmatrix}$

Now, $|A| = 3\cdot 2 - 1\cdot 4 = 6 - 4 = 2 \neq 0$

Since, A is a non-singular matrix, so A^{-1} exists.

Now, cofactors of $|A|$ are

$$A_{11} = (-1)^{1+1}(2) = 2,$$

$$A_{12} = (-1)^{1+2}(4) = -4,$$

$$A_{21} = (-1)^{2+1}(1) = -1$$

and $$A_{22} = (-1)^{2+2}(3) = 3$$

Now, $\text{adj}(A) = \begin{bmatrix} A_{11} & A_{21} \\ A_{12} & A_{22} \end{bmatrix} = \begin{bmatrix} 2 & -1 \\ -4 & 3 \end{bmatrix}$

$$A^{-1} = \frac{1}{|A|}\text{adj}(A)$$

$$= \frac{1}{2}\begin{bmatrix} 2 & -1 \\ -4 & 3 \end{bmatrix} = \begin{bmatrix} 1 & -1/2 \\ -2 & 3/2 \end{bmatrix}$$

10. (i) Let x, y and z be the number of tables, chairs and cots, respectively produced by factory. The wood requirements (in tonnes) for each type of furniture are given below.

	Table	Chair	Cot	Availability
Teakwood	2	3	4	29
Rosewood	1	1	2	13
Satinwood	3	2	1	16
	x	y	z	

Mathematical formulation of the above data is

$$2x + 3y + 4z = 29$$
$$x + y + 2z = 13$$
$$3x + 2y + z = 16$$

which is the required set of simultaneous equations.

(ii) The obtained set of equations

$$2x + 3y + 4z = 29$$
$$x + y + 2z = 13$$
$$3x + 2y + z = 16$$

Re-write the system into matrix form $AX = B$

$$\begin{bmatrix} 2 & 3 & 4 \\ 1 & 1 & 2 \\ 3 & 2 & 1 \end{bmatrix}\begin{bmatrix} x \\ y \\ z \end{bmatrix} = \begin{bmatrix} 29 \\ 13 \\ 16 \end{bmatrix}$$

where, $A = \begin{bmatrix} 2 & 3 & 4 \\ 1 & 1 & 2 \\ 3 & 2 & 1 \end{bmatrix}, X = \begin{bmatrix} x \\ y \\ z \end{bmatrix}, B = \begin{bmatrix} 29 \\ 13 \\ 16 \end{bmatrix}$

Now, $|A| = \begin{vmatrix} 2 & 3 & 4 \\ 1 & 1 & 2 \\ 3 & 2 & 1 \end{vmatrix}$

$$= 2(1-4) - 3(1-6) + 4(2-3)$$
$$= -6 + 15 - 4 = 5 \neq 0$$

Now, we find the adjoint of matrix A.

$$C_{11} = -3, C_{12} = 5, C_{13} = -1$$
$$C_{21} = 5, C_{22} = -10, C_{23} = 5$$
$$C_{31} = 2, C_{32} = 0, C_{33} = -1$$

$$\therefore \text{adj}(A) = \begin{bmatrix} -3 & 5 & -1 \\ 5 & -10 & 5 \\ 2 & 0 & -1 \end{bmatrix}^T = \begin{bmatrix} -3 & 5 & 2 \\ 5 & -10 & 0 \\ -1 & 5 & -1 \end{bmatrix}$$

So, $A^{-1} = \frac{1}{|A|}\text{adj}(A) = \frac{1}{5}\begin{bmatrix} -3 & 5 & 2 \\ 5 & -10 & 0 \\ -1 & 5 & -1 \end{bmatrix}$

Thus, $X = A^{-1}B$

$$= \frac{1}{5}\begin{bmatrix} -3 & 5 & 2 \\ 5 & -10 & 0 \\ -1 & 5 & -1 \end{bmatrix}\begin{bmatrix} 29 \\ 13 \\ 16 \end{bmatrix} = \frac{1}{5}\begin{bmatrix} -87+65+32 \\ 145-130+0 \\ -29+65-16 \end{bmatrix}$$

$$\begin{bmatrix} x \\ y \\ z \end{bmatrix} = \frac{1}{5}\begin{bmatrix} 10 \\ 15 \\ 20 \end{bmatrix} = \begin{bmatrix} 2 \\ 3 \\ 4 \end{bmatrix}$$

Hence, $x = 2$, $y = 3$ and $z = 4$.

(iii) The number of tables is 2, number of chairs is 3 and the number of cots is 4.

11. Let x, y and z be the number of burgers, samosas and juice bottles sold, respectively.

(i) $x + y + z = 100, x = 3y \Rightarrow x - 3y = 0$

and $\quad y = z + 10 \Rightarrow y - z = 10$

(ii) Let $A = \begin{bmatrix} 1 & 1 & 1 \\ 1 & -3 & 0 \\ 0 & 1 & -1 \end{bmatrix}, B = \begin{bmatrix} 100 \\ 0 \\ 10 \end{bmatrix}$ and $X = \begin{bmatrix} x \\ y \\ z \end{bmatrix}$

$$|A| = 1(3-0) - 1(-1-0) + 1(1-0)$$
$$= 3 + 1 + 1 = 5 \neq 0$$

$\therefore$ A^{-1} exist.

$$A_{11} = (3-0) = 3, A_{12} = -(-1-0) = 1,$$
$$A_{13} = (1-0) = 1$$
$$A_{21} = -(-1-1) = 2, A_{22} = (-1-0) = -1,$$
$$A_{23} = -(1-0) = -1$$
$$A_{31} = (0+3) = 3, A_{32} = -(0-1) = 1,$$
$$A_{33} = (-3-1) = -4$$

$$\text{adj } A = \begin{bmatrix} 3 & 2 & 3 \\ 1 & -1 & 1 \\ 1 & -1 & -4 \end{bmatrix}$$

Now, $A^{-1} = \frac{1}{|A|}(\text{adj } A) = \frac{1}{5}\begin{bmatrix} 3 & 2 & 3 \\ 1 & -1 & 1 \\ 1 & -1 & -4 \end{bmatrix}$

$$\therefore X = A^{-1}B = \frac{1}{5}\begin{bmatrix} 3 & 2 & 3 \\ 1 & -1 & 1 \\ 1 & -1 & -4 \end{bmatrix}\begin{bmatrix} 100 \\ 0 \\ 10 \end{bmatrix} = \frac{1}{5}\begin{bmatrix} 330 \\ 110 \\ 60 \end{bmatrix}$$

$$\therefore \begin{bmatrix} x \\ y \\ z \end{bmatrix} = \begin{bmatrix} 66 \\ 22 \\ 12 \end{bmatrix}$$

$\therefore \quad x = 66, y = 22$ and $z = 12$

(iii) Number of burgers, samosas and juice bottles sold respectively are 66, 22 and 12.

12. Given equation,

$$\frac{2}{x}+\frac{3}{y}+\frac{10}{z}=4,$$
$$\frac{4}{x}-\frac{6}{y}+\frac{5}{z}=1$$

and $$\frac{6}{x}+\frac{9}{y}-\frac{20}{z}=2$$

Equation written in matrix form

$$\begin{bmatrix}2 & 3 & 10\\ 4 & -6 & 5\\ 6 & 9 & -20\end{bmatrix}\begin{bmatrix}\frac{1}{x}\\ \frac{1}{y}\\ \frac{1}{z}\end{bmatrix}=\begin{bmatrix}4\\1\\2\end{bmatrix},$$

where, $A=\begin{bmatrix}2 & 3 & 10\\ 4 & -6 & 5\\ 6 & 9 & -20\end{bmatrix}, X=\begin{bmatrix}\frac{1}{x}\\ \frac{1}{y}\\ \frac{1}{z}\end{bmatrix}$ and $B=\begin{bmatrix}4\\1\\2\end{bmatrix}$

$\therefore \quad AX=B \Rightarrow X=A^{-1}B$

Now, $A=\begin{bmatrix}2 & 3 & 10\\ 4 & -6 & 5\\ 6 & 9 & -20\end{bmatrix}$

$\Rightarrow \quad |A|=2(120-45)-3(-80-30)+10(36+36)$
$=150+330+720=1200$

$\Rightarrow \quad |A|\neq 0$

So, A^{-1} exists.

Now, $A_{11}=75,\ A_{12}=110,\ A_{13}=72$
$A_{21}=150,\ A_{22}=-100,\ A_{23}=0,$
$A_{31}=75,\ A_{32}=30,\ A_{33}=-24$

$$\therefore\ \text{adj}|A|=\begin{bmatrix}75 & 110 & 72\\ 150 & -100 & 0\\ 75 & 30 & -24\end{bmatrix}^T=\begin{bmatrix}75 & 150 & 75\\ 110 & -100 & 30\\ 72 & 0 & -24\end{bmatrix}$$

$$\therefore\ A^{-1}=\frac{1}{|A|}\text{adj}|A|=\frac{1}{1200}\begin{bmatrix}75 & 150 & 75\\ 110 & -100 & 30\\ 72 & 0 & -24\end{bmatrix}$$

Now, $X=A^{-1}B$

$$X=\frac{1}{1200}\begin{bmatrix}75 & 150 & 75\\ 110 & -100 & 30\\ 72 & 0 & -24\end{bmatrix}\begin{bmatrix}4\\1\\2\end{bmatrix}$$

$$\Rightarrow \begin{bmatrix}\frac{1}{x}\\ \frac{1}{y}\\ \frac{1}{z}\end{bmatrix}=\frac{1}{1200}\begin{bmatrix}300+150+150\\ 440-100+60\\ 288+0-48\end{bmatrix}=\frac{1}{1200}\begin{bmatrix}600\\400\\240\end{bmatrix}=\begin{bmatrix}\frac{1}{2}\\ \frac{1}{3}\\ \frac{1}{5}\end{bmatrix}$$

On comparing, we get

$x=2,\ y=3$ and $z=5$

13. Here, $A=\begin{bmatrix}1 & 2 & 0\\ -2 & -1 & -2\\ 0 & -1 & 1\end{bmatrix}$

$|A|=1(-1-2)-2(-2+0)+0=-3+4=1$

Let C_{ij} be the cofactors of the elements a_{ij} in $A=[a_{ij}]$.

Then, $C_{11}=(-1)^{1+1}\begin{vmatrix}-1 & -2\\ -1 & 1\end{vmatrix}=-3,$

$C_{12}=(-1)^{1+2}\begin{vmatrix}-2 & -2\\ 0 & 1\end{vmatrix}=2,$

$C_{13}=(-1)^{1+3}\begin{vmatrix}-2 & -1\\ 0 & -1\end{vmatrix}=2,$

$C_{21}=(-1)^{2+1}\begin{vmatrix}2 & 0\\ -1 & 1\end{vmatrix}=-2,$

$C_{22}=(-1)^{2+2}\begin{vmatrix}1 & 0\\ 0 & 1\end{vmatrix}=1,$

$C_{23}=(-1)^{2+3}\begin{vmatrix}1 & 2\\ 0 & -1\end{vmatrix}=1,$

$C_{31}=(-1)^{3+1}\begin{vmatrix}2 & 0\\ -1 & -2\end{vmatrix}=-4,$

$C_{32}=(-1)^{3+2}\begin{vmatrix}1 & 0\\ -2 & -2\end{vmatrix}=2$

and $C_{33}=(-1)^{3+3}\begin{vmatrix}1 & 2\\ -2 & -1\end{vmatrix}=3$

$$\therefore\ \text{adj}\,A=\begin{bmatrix}-3 & 2 & 2\\ -2 & 1 & 1\\ -4 & 2 & 3\end{bmatrix}^T=\begin{bmatrix}-3 & -2 & -4\\ 2 & 1 & 2\\ 2 & 1 & 3\end{bmatrix}$$

$$A^{-1}=\frac{1}{|A|}\text{adj}\,A=\frac{1}{1}\begin{bmatrix}-3 & -2 & -4\\ 2 & 1 & 2\\ 2 & 1 & 3\end{bmatrix}$$

We know that $(A^T)^{-1}=(A^{-1})^T$

Here, $C=A^T$

$$C=\begin{bmatrix}1 & -2 & 0\\ 2 & -1 & -1\\ 0 & -2 & 1\end{bmatrix}$$

$$\therefore \quad C^{-1}=\begin{bmatrix}-3 & 2 & 2\\ -2 & 1 & 1\\ -4 & 2 & 3\end{bmatrix} \text{ or } CX=B$$

where, $C=\begin{bmatrix}1 & -2 & 0\\ 2 & -1 & -1\\ 0 & -2 & 1\end{bmatrix}, X=\begin{bmatrix}x\\ y\\ z\end{bmatrix}$ and $B=\begin{bmatrix}10\\ 8\\ 7\end{bmatrix}$

Now, $X=C^{-1}B$

$$\Rightarrow \quad X=\begin{bmatrix}-3 & 2 & 2\\ -2 & 1 & 1\\ -4 & 2 & 3\end{bmatrix}\begin{bmatrix}10\\ 8\\ 7\end{bmatrix}$$

$$X=\begin{bmatrix}-30+16+14\\ -20+8+7\\ -40+16+21\end{bmatrix}$$

$$\Rightarrow \quad \begin{bmatrix}x\\ y\\ z\end{bmatrix}=\begin{bmatrix}0\\ -5\\ -3\end{bmatrix}$$

$\therefore \quad x=0, y=-5$ and $z=-3$

Common Mistake For finding the adjoint of a matrix, find cofactors by taking proper sign.

14. (i) (a) $\because$ Ramu Paid ₹ 16 for 5 pens, 3 bags and 1 instrument box and x, y and z represent the cost of a pen, a bag and an instrument box, respectively.

$\therefore \quad 5x+3y+z=16$

(ii) (a) Given, $A=\begin{bmatrix}5 & 3 & 1\\ 2 & 1 & 3\\ 1 & 2 & 4\end{bmatrix}$

So, $|A|=5(4-6)-3(8-3)+1(4-1)$
$=5(-2)-3(5)+1(3)$
$=-10-15+3=-22$

(iii) (a) Given, $A=\begin{bmatrix}5 & 3 & 1\\ 2 & 1 & 3\\ 1 & 2 & 4\end{bmatrix}$

and $\quad \text{adj } A=\begin{bmatrix}-2 & x & 8\\ -5 & 19 & -13\\ 3 & -7 & y\end{bmatrix}$

We know that

$$A_{12}=C_{21} \text{ and } A_{33}=C_{33}$$

$$\Rightarrow \quad x=(-1)^{2+1}\begin{vmatrix}3 & 1\\ 2 & 4\end{vmatrix} \text{ and } y=(-1)^{3+3}\begin{vmatrix}5 & 3\\ 2 & 1\end{vmatrix}$$

$\Rightarrow \quad x=-1(12-2)$ and $y=1(5-6)$

$\Rightarrow \quad x=-10$ and $y=-1$

(iv) (c) Let $A=\begin{bmatrix}5 & 3 & 1\\ 2 & 1 & 3\\ 1 & 2 & 4\end{bmatrix}, X=\begin{bmatrix}x\\ y\\ z\end{bmatrix}$ and $B=\begin{bmatrix}16\\ 19\\ 25\end{bmatrix}$.

Now, $AX=B \Rightarrow X=A^{-1}B=\dfrac{1}{|A|}(\text{adj } A)B$

$$\begin{bmatrix}x\\ y\\ z\end{bmatrix}=\frac{1}{-22}\begin{bmatrix}-2 & -10 & 8\\ -5 & 19 & -13\\ 3 & -7 & -1\end{bmatrix}\begin{bmatrix}16\\ 19\\ 25\end{bmatrix}$$

$$=\frac{1}{-22}\begin{bmatrix}-22\\ -44\\ -110\end{bmatrix}=\begin{bmatrix}1\\ 2\\ 5\end{bmatrix}$$

$\Rightarrow \quad x=1$

$\therefore$ The cost of one pen is ₹ 1.

15. The given system of equation is

$$2x-3y+5z=11,$$
$$3x+2y-4z=-5$$
and $$x+y-2z=-3$$

In matrix form, $AX=B$ $\quad \ldots$(i)

where, $A=\begin{bmatrix}2 & -3 & 5\\ 3 & 2 & -4\\ 1 & 1 & -2\end{bmatrix}, X=\begin{bmatrix}x\\ y\\ z\end{bmatrix}$ and $B=\begin{bmatrix}11\\ -5\\ -3\end{bmatrix}$

Now, $|A|=\begin{vmatrix}2 & -3 & 5\\ 3 & 2 & -4\\ 1 & 1 & -2\end{vmatrix}$

$=2(-4+4)+3(-6+4)+5(3-2)$
$=2(0)+3(-2)+5(1)$
$=0-6+5$
$=-1$
$\neq 0$

Thus, A is a non-singular matrix.

So, A^{-1} exists cofactors of elements of $|A|$ are

$$C_{11}=(-1)^{1+1}\begin{vmatrix}2 & -4\\ 1 & -2\end{vmatrix}=(-4+4)=0$$

$$C_{12}=(-1)^{1+2}\begin{vmatrix}3 & -4\\ 1 & -2\end{vmatrix}=-(-6+4)=2$$

$$C_{13}=(-1)^{1+3}\begin{vmatrix}3 & 2\\ 1 & 1\end{vmatrix}=3-2=1$$

$$C_{21}=(-1)^{2+1}\begin{vmatrix}-3 & 5\\ 1 & -2\end{vmatrix}=-(6-5)=-1$$

$$C_{22}=(-1)^{2+2}\begin{vmatrix}2 & 5\\ 1 & -2\end{vmatrix}=(-4-5)=-9$$

$$C_{23}=(-1)^{2+3}\begin{vmatrix}2 & -3\\ 1 & 1\end{vmatrix}=-(2+3)=-5$$

$$C_{31}=(-1)^{3+1}\begin{vmatrix}-3 & 5\\ 2 & -4\end{vmatrix}=(12-10)=2$$

$$C_{32}=(-1)^{3+2}\begin{vmatrix}2 & 5\\ 3 & -4\end{vmatrix}=-(-8-15)=23$$

$$C_{33}=(-1)^{3+3}\begin{vmatrix}2 & -3\\ 3 & 2\end{vmatrix}=4+9=13$$

Then, $\text{adj } A=\begin{bmatrix}C_{11} & C_{12} & C_{13}\\ C_{21} & C_{22} & C_{23}\\ C_{31} & C_{32} & C_{33}\end{bmatrix}^T$

$$=\begin{bmatrix}0 & 2 & 1\\ -1 & -9 & -5\\ 2 & 23 & 13\end{bmatrix}^T=\begin{bmatrix}0 & -1 & 2\\ 2 & -9 & 23\\ 1 & -5 & 13\end{bmatrix}$$

Now, $A^{-1}=\frac{1}{|A|}\text{adj}(A)$

$$=\frac{1}{-1}\begin{bmatrix}0 & -1 & 2\\ 2 & -9 & 23\\ 1 & -5 & 13\end{bmatrix}=\begin{bmatrix}0 & 1 & -2\\ -2 & 9 & -23\\ -1 & 5 & -13\end{bmatrix}$$

and the solution of Eq. (i) is given by $X=A^{-1}B$

$$\therefore \quad \begin{bmatrix}x\\ y\\ z\end{bmatrix}=\begin{bmatrix}0 & 1 & -2\\ -2 & 9 & -23\\ -1 & 5 & -13\end{bmatrix}\begin{bmatrix}11\\ -5\\ -3\end{bmatrix}$$

$$=\begin{bmatrix}0-5+6\\ -22-45+69\\ -11-25+39\end{bmatrix}=\begin{bmatrix}1\\ 2\\ 3\end{bmatrix}$$

On comparing elements, we get

$x=1$, $y=2$ and $z=3$

16. Given system of equations

$$x-2y=10,\ 2x-y-z=8,\ -2y+z=7$$

The given system of equations can also be written in matrix form as

$$\begin{bmatrix}1 & -2 & 0\\ 2 & -1 & -1\\ 0 & -2 & 1\end{bmatrix}\begin{bmatrix}x\\ y\\ z\end{bmatrix}=\begin{bmatrix}10\\ 8\\ 7\end{bmatrix}$$

i.e. $AX=B \Rightarrow X=A^{-1}B$

where, $A=\begin{bmatrix}1 & -2 & 0\\ 2 & -1 & -1\\ 0 & -2 & 1\end{bmatrix}, X=\begin{bmatrix}x\\ y\\ z\end{bmatrix}, B=\begin{bmatrix}10\\ 8\\ 7\end{bmatrix}$

Now, $|A|=\begin{vmatrix}1 & -2 & 0\\ 2 & -1 & -1\\ 0 & -2 & 1\end{vmatrix}$

$$=1(-1-2)-(-2)(2-0)+0=1$$
$$\neq 0$$

Since, A is non-singular matrix, so the system of equation has unique solution.

Now, cofactors of A are

$$A_{11}=-3,\ A_{12}=-2,\ A_{13}=-4,$$
$$A_{21}=2,\ A_{22}=1,\ A_{23}=2,$$
$$A_{31}=2,\ A_{32}=1,\ A_{33}=3$$

Now, $\text{adj}(A)=\begin{bmatrix}A_{11} & A_{21} & A_{31}\\ A_{12} & A_{22} & A_{32}\\ A_{13} & A_{23} & A_{33}\end{bmatrix}=\begin{bmatrix}-3 & 2 & 2\\ -2 & 1 & 1\\ -4 & 2 & 3\end{bmatrix}$

$$A^{-1}=\frac{1}{|A|}\text{adj}(A)=\begin{bmatrix}-3 & 2 & 2\\ -2 & 1 & 1\\ -4 & 2 & 3\end{bmatrix}$$

$$X=A^{-1}B=\begin{bmatrix}-3 & 2 & 2\\ -2 & 1 & 1\\ -4 & 2 & 3\end{bmatrix}\begin{bmatrix}10\\ 8\\ 7\end{bmatrix}$$

$$=\begin{bmatrix}-30+16+14\\ -20+8+7\\ -40+16+21\end{bmatrix}=\begin{bmatrix}0\\ -5\\ -3\end{bmatrix}$$

On comparing elements, we get

$\therefore \quad x=0,\ y=-5,\ z=-3$

17. Given system of equations is

$$\frac{1}{x}+\frac{1}{y}+\frac{1}{z}=9,\ \frac{2}{x}+\frac{5}{y}+\frac{7}{z}=52$$

and $\frac{2}{x}+\frac{1}{y}-\frac{1}{z}=0$

Let $\frac{1}{x}=u$, $\frac{1}{y}=v$ and $\frac{1}{z}=w$.

Then, the given system of equations become

$$u+v+w=9,$$
$$2u+5v+7w=52$$

and $2u+v-w=0$

This system of equations can be written in matrix form as

$$AX=B \Rightarrow X=A^{-1}B \quad \text{...(i)}$$

where, $A=\begin{bmatrix}1&1&1\\2&5&7\\2&1&-1\end{bmatrix}$,

$$X=\begin{bmatrix}u\\v\\w\end{bmatrix} \text{ and } B=\begin{bmatrix}9\\52\\0\end{bmatrix}$$

Now, $|A|=\begin{vmatrix}1&1&1\\2&5&7\\2&1&-1\end{vmatrix}$

$$=1(-5-7)-1(-2-14)+1(2-10)$$
$$=-12+16-8=-20+16=-4$$

Since, $|A|\neq 0$, so unique solution exists.

Now, cofactors of $|A|$ are

$$C_{11}=(-1)^2\begin{vmatrix}5&7\\1&-1\end{vmatrix}=(-5-7)=-12$$

$$C_{12}=(-1)^3\begin{vmatrix}2&7\\2&-1\end{vmatrix}=-(-2-14)=16$$

$$C_{13}=(-1)^4\begin{vmatrix}2&5\\2&1\end{vmatrix}=(2-10)=-8$$

$$C_{21}=(-1)^3\begin{vmatrix}1&1\\1&-1\end{vmatrix}=-(-1-1)=2$$

$$C_{22}=(-1)^4\begin{vmatrix}1&1\\2&-1\end{vmatrix}=(-1-2)=-3$$

$$C_{23}=(-1)^5\begin{vmatrix}1&1\\2&1\end{vmatrix}=-(1-2)=1$$

$$C_{31}=(-1)^4\begin{vmatrix}1&1\\5&7\end{vmatrix}=(7-5)=2$$

$$C_{32}=(-1)^5\begin{vmatrix}1&1\\2&7\end{vmatrix}=-(7-2)=-5$$

and $C_{33}=(-1)^6\begin{vmatrix}1&1\\2&5\end{vmatrix}=(5-2)=3$

$$\therefore \quad \text{adj}(A)=\begin{bmatrix}C_{11}&C_{21}&C_{31}\\C_{12}&C_{22}&C_{32}\\C_{13}&C_{23}&C_{33}\end{bmatrix}=\begin{bmatrix}-12&2&2\\16&-3&-5\\-8&1&3\end{bmatrix}$$

$$\therefore \quad A^{-1}=\frac{\text{adj }(A)}{|A|}=\frac{1}{-4}\begin{bmatrix}-12&2&2\\16&-3&-5\\-8&1&3\end{bmatrix}$$

On putting the values of A^{-1} and B in Eq. (i), we get

$$X=-\frac{1}{4}\begin{bmatrix}-12&2&2\\16&-3&-5\\-8&1&3\end{bmatrix}\begin{bmatrix}9\\52\\0\end{bmatrix}$$

$$=-\frac{1}{4}\begin{bmatrix}-108+104+0\\144-156+0\\-72+52+0\end{bmatrix}$$

$$\begin{bmatrix}u\\v\\w\end{bmatrix}=-\frac{1}{4}\begin{bmatrix}-4\\-12\\-20\end{bmatrix}=\begin{bmatrix}1\\3\\5\end{bmatrix}$$

On equating the corresponding elements, we get

$$u=1, v=3, w=5$$

$$\Rightarrow \quad \frac{1}{x}=1, \frac{1}{y}=3, \frac{1}{z}=5 \Rightarrow x=1, y=\frac{1}{3}, z=\frac{1}{5}$$

18. Given, $A=\begin{bmatrix}1&-1&0\\2&3&4\\0&1&2\end{bmatrix}$ and $B=\begin{bmatrix}2&2&-4\\-4&2&-4\\2&-1&5\end{bmatrix}$

$$\therefore \quad AB=\begin{bmatrix}1&-1&0\\2&3&4\\0&1&2\end{bmatrix}\begin{bmatrix}2&2&-4\\-4&2&-4\\2&-1&5\end{bmatrix}$$

$$=\begin{bmatrix}2+4+0&2-2-0&-4+4+0\\4-12+8&4+6-4&-8-12+20\\0-4+4&0+2-2&0-4+10\end{bmatrix}$$

[by multiplication property]

$$\Rightarrow \quad AB=\begin{bmatrix}6&0&0\\0&6&0\\0&0&6\end{bmatrix}=6I_3 \quad \text{...(i)}$$

Now, the given system of equations can be written in matrix form as

$$\begin{bmatrix}1&-1&0\\2&3&4\\0&1&2\end{bmatrix}\begin{bmatrix}x\\y\\z\end{bmatrix}=\begin{bmatrix}3\\17\\7\end{bmatrix}$$

i.e. $AX=C \Rightarrow X=A^{-1}C$ ...(ii)

where, $A=\begin{bmatrix}1&-1&0\\2&3&4\\0&1&2\end{bmatrix}$,

$$X=\begin{bmatrix}x\\y\\z\end{bmatrix} \text{ and } C=\begin{bmatrix}3\\17\\7\end{bmatrix}$$

From Eq. (i), we have

$$AB = 6I_3$$

$$\Rightarrow A\left(\frac{B}{6}\right) = I_3 \Rightarrow A^{-1} = \frac{1}{6}B$$

$$\Rightarrow \quad A^{-1} = \frac{1}{6}\begin{bmatrix} 2 & 2 & -4 \\ -4 & 2 & -4 \\ 2 & -1 & 5 \end{bmatrix}$$

On putting value of A^{-1} in Eq. (ii), we get

$$X = \frac{1}{6}\begin{bmatrix} 2 & 2 & -4 \\ -4 & 2 & -4 \\ 2 & -1 & 5 \end{bmatrix}\begin{bmatrix} 3 \\ 17 \\ 7 \end{bmatrix}$$

$$= \frac{1}{6}\begin{bmatrix} 6+34-28 \\ -12+34-28 \\ 6-17+35 \end{bmatrix}$$

$$= \frac{1}{6}\begin{bmatrix} 12 \\ -6 \\ 24 \end{bmatrix} = \begin{bmatrix} 2 \\ -1 \\ 4 \end{bmatrix}$$

$$\Rightarrow \quad \begin{bmatrix} x \\ y \\ z \end{bmatrix} = \begin{bmatrix} 2 \\ -1 \\ 4 \end{bmatrix}$$

$\therefore \quad x = 2, \; y = -1$ and $z = 4$

19. Given system of linear equations is

$$3x + y + z = 1$$

$$2x + 2z = 0$$

and $\quad 5x + y + 2z = 2$

So, we can rewrite it as

$$\begin{bmatrix} 3 & 1 & 1 \\ 2 & 0 & 2 \\ 5 & 1 & 2 \end{bmatrix}\begin{bmatrix} x \\ y \\ z \end{bmatrix} = \begin{bmatrix} 1 \\ 0 \\ 2 \end{bmatrix}$$

where, $A = \begin{bmatrix} 3 & 1 & 1 \\ 2 & 0 & 2 \\ 5 & 1 & 2 \end{bmatrix}, X = \begin{bmatrix} x \\ y \\ z \end{bmatrix}$ and $B = \begin{bmatrix} 1 \\ 0 \\ 2 \end{bmatrix}$

Now, $|A| = \begin{vmatrix} 3 & 1 & 1 \\ 2 & 0 & 2 \\ 5 & 1 & 2 \end{vmatrix}$

$$= 3(0 \times 2 - 1 \times 2) - 1\,(2 \times 2 - 5 \times 2) + 1(2 \times 1 - 5 \times 0)$$

$$= 3(0-2) - 1(4-10) + 1(2-0)$$

$$= 3 \times (-2) - 1 \times (-6) + 1 \times 2$$

$$= -6 + 6 + 2$$

$$= 2 \neq 0$$

So, A^{-1} exists and the given system has a unique solution.

$$\therefore \quad X = A^{-1}B$$

To find A^{-1}, we have cofactors of the elements of matrix A are

$$A_{11} = \begin{vmatrix} 0 & 2 \\ 1 & 2 \end{vmatrix} = 0 - 2$$

$$= -2$$

$$A_{12} = -\begin{vmatrix} 2 & 2 \\ 5 & 2 \end{vmatrix} = -(4-10) = 6$$

$$A_{13} = \begin{vmatrix} 2 & 0 \\ 5 & 1 \end{vmatrix} = 2 - 0 = 2$$

$$A_{21} = -\begin{vmatrix} 1 & 1 \\ 1 & 2 \end{vmatrix} = -(2-1) = -1$$

$$A_{22} = \begin{vmatrix} 3 & 1 \\ 5 & 2 \end{vmatrix} = 6 - 5 = 1$$

$$A_{23} = -\begin{vmatrix} 3 & 1 \\ 5 & 1 \end{vmatrix} = -(3-5) = 2$$

$$A_{31} = \begin{vmatrix} 1 & 1 \\ 0 & 2 \end{vmatrix} = 2 - 0 = 2$$

$$A_{32} = -\begin{vmatrix} 3 & 1 \\ 2 & 2 \end{vmatrix} = -(6-2) = -4$$

$$A_{33} = \begin{vmatrix} 3 & 1 \\ 2 & 0 \end{vmatrix} = 0 - 2 = -2$$

Now, $\operatorname{adj}(A) = \begin{bmatrix} -2 & 6 & 2 \\ -1 & 1 & 2 \\ 2 & -4 & -2 \end{bmatrix}^T$

$$= \begin{bmatrix} -2 & -1 & 2 \\ 6 & 1 & -4 \\ 2 & 2 & -2 \end{bmatrix}$$

$$\therefore \quad A^{-1} = \frac{1}{|A|}\operatorname{adj}(A) = \frac{1}{2}\begin{bmatrix} -2 & -1 & 2 \\ 6 & 1 & -4 \\ 2 & 2 & -2 \end{bmatrix}$$

$$= \begin{bmatrix} -2/2 & -1/2 & 2/2 \\ 6/2 & 1/2 & -4/2 \\ 2/2 & 2/2 & -2/2 \end{bmatrix}$$

$$= \begin{bmatrix} -1 & -1/2 & 1 \\ 3 & 1/2 & -2 \\ 1 & 1 & -1 \end{bmatrix}$$

$$\therefore \quad X = A^{-1}B = \begin{bmatrix} -1 & -1/2 & 1 \\ 3 & 1/2 & -2 \\ 1 & 1 & -1 \end{bmatrix} \begin{bmatrix} 1 \\ 0 \\ 2 \end{bmatrix}$$

$$= \begin{bmatrix} -1\times1+\left(-\frac{1}{2}\right)\times0+1\times2 \\ 3\times1+\left(\frac{1}{2}\right)\times0+(-2)\times2 \\ 1\times1+1\times0+(-1)\times2 \end{bmatrix}$$

$$= \begin{bmatrix} -1-0+2 \\ 3+0-4 \\ 1+0-2 \end{bmatrix}$$

$$\Rightarrow \quad X = \begin{bmatrix} 1 \\ -1 \\ -1 \end{bmatrix} \Rightarrow \begin{bmatrix} x \\ y \\ z \end{bmatrix} = \begin{bmatrix} 1 \\ -1 \\ -1 \end{bmatrix}$$

$\therefore \quad x = 1, y = -1$ and $z = -1$

20. Do same as Q 18. **Ans.** $x = 1$, $y = 2$ and $z = 3$.

21. Do same as Q 15. **Ans.** $x = 4$, $y = -3$ and $z = 1$.

22. Given, system of equations $4x + 2y + 3z = 2$,
$x + y + z = 1$ and $3x + y - 2z = 5$

The given system of equations can also be written in matrix form as

$$\begin{bmatrix} 4 & 2 & 3 \\ 1 & 1 & 1 \\ 3 & 1 & -2 \end{bmatrix} \begin{bmatrix} x \\ y \\ z \end{bmatrix} = \begin{bmatrix} 2 \\ 1 \\ 5 \end{bmatrix}$$

i.e. $\quad AX = B \Rightarrow X = A^{-1}B$

where, $A = \begin{bmatrix} 4 & 2 & 3 \\ 1 & 1 & 1 \\ 3 & 1 & -2 \end{bmatrix}, X = \begin{bmatrix} x \\ y \\ z \end{bmatrix}$ and $B = \begin{bmatrix} 2 \\ 1 \\ 5 \end{bmatrix}$

Now, $|A| = \begin{vmatrix} 4 & 2 & 3 \\ 1 & 1 & 1 \\ 3 & 1 & -2 \end{vmatrix}$

$$= 4[-2-1] - 2[-2-3] + 3[1-3]$$
$$= 4[-3] + 2[5] + 3[-2]$$
$$= -12 + 10 - 6$$
$$= -8 \neq 0$$

Since, A is a non-singular matrix, so system of equations has unique solution.

Now, cofactors of $|A|$ are

$$A_{11} = (-1)^{1+1} \begin{vmatrix} 1 & 1 \\ 1 & -2 \end{vmatrix} = [-2-1] = -3$$

$$A_{12} = (-1)^{1+2} \begin{vmatrix} 1 & 1 \\ 3 & -2 \end{vmatrix} = -[-2-3] = 5$$

$$A_{13} = (-1)^{1+3} \begin{vmatrix} 1 & 1 \\ 3 & 1 \end{vmatrix} = [1-3] = -2$$

$$A_{21} = (-1)^{2+1} \begin{vmatrix} 2 & 3 \\ 1 & -2 \end{vmatrix} = -[-4-3] = 7$$

$$A_{22} = (-1)^{2+2} \begin{vmatrix} 4 & 3 \\ 3 & -2 \end{vmatrix} = [-8-9] = -17$$

$$A_{23} = (-1)^{2+3} \begin{vmatrix} 4 & 2 \\ 3 & 1 \end{vmatrix} = -[4-6] = 2$$

$$A_{31} = (-1)^{3+1} \begin{vmatrix} 2 & 3 \\ 1 & 1 \end{vmatrix} = [2-3] = -1$$

$$A_{32} = (-1)^{3+2} \begin{vmatrix} 4 & 3 \\ 1 & 1 \end{vmatrix} = -[4-3] = -1$$

$$A_{33} = (-1)^{3+3} \begin{vmatrix} 4 & 2 \\ 1 & 1 \end{vmatrix} = [4-2] = 2$$

Now, $\text{adj}(A) = \begin{bmatrix} A_{11} & A_{21} & A_{31} \\ A_{12} & A_{22} & A_{32} \\ A_{13} & A_{23} & A_{33} \end{bmatrix} = \begin{bmatrix} -3 & 7 & -1 \\ 5 & -17 & -1 \\ -2 & 2 & 2 \end{bmatrix}$

$$\therefore \quad A^{-1} = \frac{1}{|A|}\text{adj}(A) = \frac{1}{-8} \begin{bmatrix} -3 & 7 & -1 \\ 5 & -17 & -1 \\ -2 & 2 & 2 \end{bmatrix}$$

[from Eq. (i)]

$$X = A^{-1}B$$

$$\Rightarrow \quad \begin{bmatrix} x \\ y \\ z \end{bmatrix} = \frac{1}{-8} \begin{bmatrix} -3 & 7 & -1 \\ 5 & -17 & -1 \\ -2 & 2 & 2 \end{bmatrix} \begin{bmatrix} 2 \\ 1 \\ 5 \end{bmatrix}$$

$$= \frac{1}{-8} \begin{bmatrix} -6+7-5 \\ 10-17-5 \\ -4+2+10 \end{bmatrix} = \frac{1}{-8} \begin{bmatrix} -4 \\ -12 \\ 8 \end{bmatrix}$$

[by multiplication property]

$$\Rightarrow \quad \begin{bmatrix} x \\ y \\ z \end{bmatrix} = \begin{bmatrix} 1/2 \\ 3/2 \\ -1 \end{bmatrix}$$

Hence, $x = \frac{1}{2}$, $y = \frac{3}{2}$ and $z = -1$.

CHAPTER TEST

1 Mark Questions

1. Let A be the non-singular square matrix of order 3×3, then $|\text{adj } A|$ is equal to **NCERT**

(a) $|A|$ (b) $|A|^2$ (c) $|A|^3$ (d) $3|A|$

2. If A is an invertible matrix of order 2, then $\det(A^{-1})$ is equal to **NCERT**

(a) $\det(A)$ (b) $\frac{1}{\det(A)}$ (c) 1 (d) zero

3. A square matrix A is said to be non-singular, if

(a) $|A| = 0$ (b) $|A| \neq 0$ (c) $|A| = -1$ (d) $|A| = 1$

4. If A and B are square matrices of same order, then

(a) $|AB| = |A| \cdot |B|$ (b) $|AB| \neq |A| \cdot |B|$

(c) $|AB| = \frac{|A|}{|B|}, |B| \neq 0$ (d) $|AB| = \frac{|B|}{|A|}, |A| \neq 0$

5. The adjoint of the matrix $A = \begin{bmatrix} 1 & 2 \\ 3 & 4 \end{bmatrix}$ is

(a) $\begin{bmatrix} 4 & 2 \\ 3 & 1 \end{bmatrix}$ (b) $\begin{bmatrix} -4 & 2 \\ 3 & -1 \end{bmatrix}$ (c) $\begin{bmatrix} 4 & -2 \\ -3 & 1 \end{bmatrix}$ (d) $\begin{bmatrix} 1 & -2 \\ -3 & 4 \end{bmatrix}$

2 Marks Questions

6. Let A be a square matrix of order 3×3. Write the value of $|2A|$, where $|A| = 4$.

7. Evaluate $\begin{vmatrix} \cos 15° & \sin 15° \\ \sin 75° & \cos 75° \end{vmatrix}$.

8. Evaluate $\begin{vmatrix} a+ib & c+id \\ -c+id & a-ib \end{vmatrix}$.

9. Find the area of triangle whose vertices are $(-2, -3)$, $(3, 2)$ and $(-1, -8)$.

10. Find the equation of the line joining $(1, 2)$ and $(3, 6)$ using determinants.

3/4 Marks Questions

11. If area of a triangle is 35 sq units with vertices $(2, -6)$, $(5, 4)$ and $(k, 4)$, then find the values of k.

12. Using determinants, find the area of the triangle whose vertices are $(1, 4)$, $(2, 3)$ and $(-5, -3)$. Are the given points collinear?

5/6 Marks Questions

13. For positive numbers x, y and z, show that

$$\begin{vmatrix} 1 & \log_x y & \log_x z \\ \log_y x & 1 & \log_y z \\ \log_z x & \log_z y & 1 \end{vmatrix} = 0$$

14. Using the matrix method, solve the following system of equations

$$x - y + 2z = 7,\ 3x + 4y - 5z = -5 \text{ and } 2x - y + 3z = 12.$$

15. Using the matrix method, solve the following system of equations

$$4x + 3y + 2z = 60,\ x + 2y + 3z = 45 \text{ and } 6x + 2y + 3z = 70.$$

16. Use product $\begin{bmatrix} 1 & -1 & 2 \\ 0 & 2 & -3 \\ 3 & -2 & 4 \end{bmatrix}, \begin{bmatrix} -2 & 0 & 1 \\ 9 & 2 & -3 \\ 6 & 1 & -2 \end{bmatrix}$ to solve the system of equations

$$x - y + 2z = 1,\ 2y - 3z = 1 \text{ and } 3x - 2y + 4z = 2.$$

17. If $A = \begin{bmatrix} 3 & -4 & 2 \\ 2 & 3 & 5 \\ 1 & 0 & 1 \end{bmatrix}$, then find A^{-1} and hence solve the system of equations

$$3x - 4y + 2z = -1,\ 2x + 3y + 5z = 7 \text{ and } x + z = 2.$$

Answers

1. (b) **2.** (b) **3.** (b)

4. (a) **5.** (c) **6.** 32

7. 0 **8.** $(a^2 + b^2 + c^2 + d^2)$

9. 15 sq units

10. $y = 2x$ **11.** $k = 12, -2$ **12.** $\frac{13}{2}$, No

14. $x = 2$, $y = 1$ and $z = 3$

15. $x = 5$, $y = 8$ and $z = 8$

16. $x = 0$, $y = 5$ and $z = 3$

17. $A^{-1} = -\frac{1}{9}\begin{bmatrix} 3 & 4 & -26 \\ 3 & 1 & -11 \\ -3 & -4 & 17 \end{bmatrix}$; $x = 3$, $y = 2$ and $z = -1$

05

Continuity and Differentiation

TREND ANALYSIS 3 YEARS

		Average No. of Questions Across all Sets			
		Types of Questions	2024	2023	2020
TOPIC 01	Continuity and Differentiability	1 Mark	1	1	—
		2 Marks	1	—	—
		3/4 Marks	—	—	—
		5/6 Marks	—	—	—
TOPIC 02	Differentiation	1 Mark	1	1	—
		2 Marks	—	—	1
		3/4 Marks	—	—	—
		5/6 Marks	—	—	—
TOPIC 03	Differentiation of Some Special Functions	1 Mark	—	—	—
		2 Marks	—	—	—
		3/4 Marks	1	1	1
		5/6 Marks	—	—	—

TOPIC 1

Continuity and Differentiability

Continuity of a Function

A function $f(x)$ is said to be continuous at a point $x = a$, if

$$(\text{LHL})_{x=a} = (\text{RHL})_{x=a} = f(a) \text{ or } \lim_{x \to a} f(x) = f(a)$$

where, $$(\text{LHL})_{x=a} = \lim_{x \to a^-} f(x) \text{ and } (\text{RHL})_{x=a} = \lim_{x \to a^+} f(x)$$

NOTE To evaluate LHL and RHL of a function $f(x)$ at $x = a$, put $x = a - h$ and $x = a + h$ respectively, where $h \to 0$.

Continuity of a Function in an Interval

A function $y = f(x)$ is said to be continuous in an interval (a, b) iff $f(x)$ is continuous at every point in that interval and f is said to be continuous in the interval $[a, b]$ iff f is continuous in the interval (a, b) and also at the point a from the right and at the point b from the left.

NOTE A function is said to be continuous, if it is continuous on the whole of its domain.

Useful Results for Continuity

(i) Every identity function is continuous.
(ii) Every constant function is continuous.
(iii) Every polynomial function is continuous.
(iv) Every rational function is continuous in their domain.
(v) All trigonometric functions are continuous in their domain.
(vi) Modulus function is continuous.

Standard Results on Limits

(i) $\lim\limits_{x \to a} \dfrac{x^n - a^n}{x - a} = na^{n-1}$

(ii) $\lim\limits_{x \to 0} \dfrac{\sin x}{x} = 1$

(iii) $\lim\limits_{x \to 0} \dfrac{\tan x}{x} = 1$

(iv) $\lim\limits_{x \to 0} \dfrac{e^x - 1}{x} = 1$

(v) $\lim\limits_{x \to \infty} \dfrac{1}{x^p} = 0, p \in (0, \infty)$

(vi) $\lim\limits_{x \to 0} \dfrac{\log (1 + x)}{x} = 1$

(vii) $\lim\limits_{x \to 0} \dfrac{a^x - 1}{x} = \log_e a$

(viii) $\lim\limits_{x \to 0} (1 + x)^{1/x} = e$

(ix) $\lim\limits_{x \to \infty} \left(1 + \dfrac{1}{x}\right)^x = e$

(x) $\lim\limits_{x \to \infty} \sin x$ and $\lim\limits_{x \to \infty} \cos x$ oscillate between -1 to 1.

Algebra of Continuous Functions

Suppose f and g are two real functions, continuous at real number c. Then,

(i) $f + g$ is continuous at $x = c$.
(ii) $f - g$ is continuous at $x = c$.
(iii) $f \cdot g$ is continuous at $x = c$.
(iv) kf is continuous at $x = c$, where k is any constant.
(v) $\left(\dfrac{f}{g}\right)$ is continuous at $x = c$ [provided $g(c) \neq 0$].

Composition of Two Continuous Functions

Suppose f and g are two real valued functions such that (fog) is defined at c. If g is continuous at c and f is continuous at $g(c)$, then (fog) is continuous at c.

Discontinuity of a Function at a Point

A function $f(x)$ is said to be discontinuous at $x = a$, if it is not continuous at $x = a$ i.e. when any of the following cases arise:

(i) $\lim\limits_{x \to a^+} f(x)$ or $\lim\limits_{x \to a^-} f(x)$ or $\lim\limits_{x \to a} f(x)$ does not exist.

(ii) $\lim\limits_{x \to a^-} f(x) \neq \lim\limits_{x \to a^+} f(x)$

(iii) $\lim\limits_{x \to a^-} f(x) \neq \lim\limits_{x \to a^+} f(x) \neq f(a)$ or $\lim\limits_{x \to a} f(x) \neq f(a)$

Differentiability

A function $f(x)$ is said to be differentiable at a point $x = a$, if Left hand derivative at $(x = a)$ equals to Right hand derivative at $(x = a)$ i.e. **LHD at $(x = a)$ = RHD (at $x = a$),** where Right hand derivative,

$$Rf'(a) = \lim_{h \to 0} \frac{f(a + h) - f(a)}{h}$$

Left hand derivative, $Lf'(a) = \lim\limits_{h \to 0} \dfrac{f(a - h) - f(a)}{-h}$

NOTE (i) The common value of $Rf'(a)$ and $Lf'(a)$ is denoted by $f'(a)$ and it is known as the derivative of $f(x)$ at $x = a$.
(ii) Every differentiable functions are continuous but every continuous function need not to be differentiable.

Useful Results for Differentiability

(i) Every polynomial, exponential and constant functions are differentiable.
(ii) Logarithmic functions are differentiable in their domain.
(iii) Trigonometric and inverse trigonometric functions are differentiable in their domain.
(iv) Modulus functions are differentiable everywhere except at the corner points.

PYQs Previous Years Questions

1 Mark Questions

1. The graph of the function f is shown below

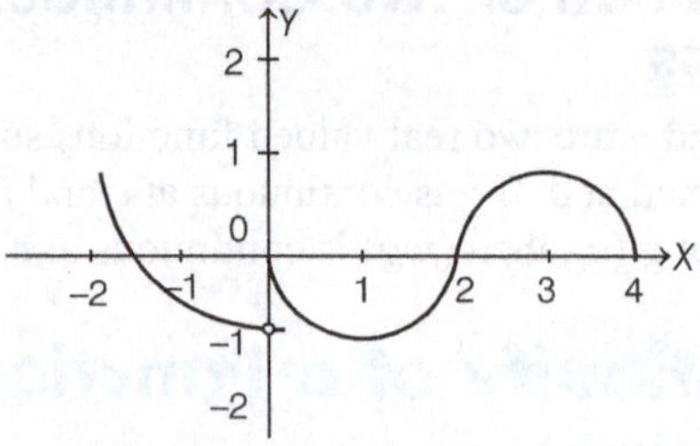

Of the following options, at what values of x is the function f not differentiable? **ISC 2024**

(a) At $x = 0$ and $x = 2$ (b) At $x = 1$ and $x = 3$

(c) At $x = -1$ and $x = 1$ (d) At $x = -1.5$ and $x = 1.5$

2. Given, below are the graphs of $f(x)$ along with the statements. Which one of the following statements is NOT correct about the graphs? **ISC Specimen 2024**

(a) $\lim_{x \to x_0^+} f(x) \neq \lim_{x \to x_0^-} f(x)$

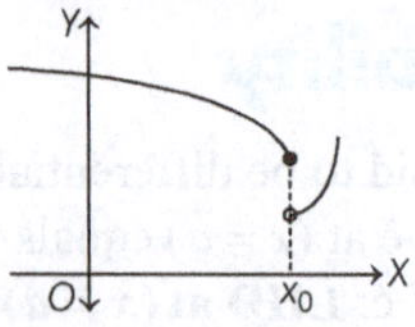

(b) $f(x)$ is not defined at $x = x_0$

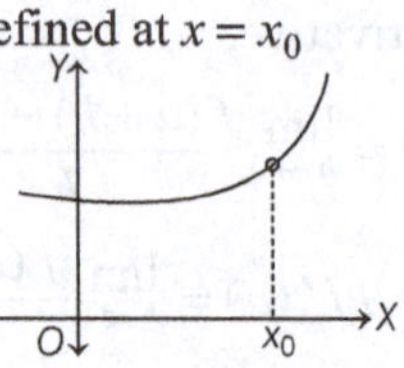

(c) $f(x)$ is not continuous at $x = x_0$

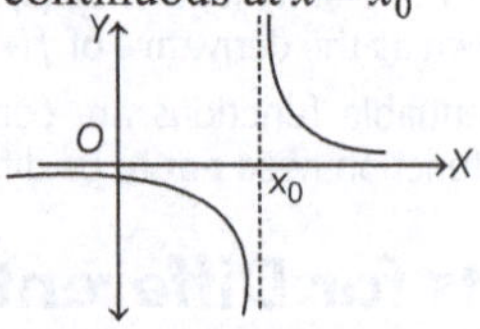

(d) $f(x)$ is continuous at $x = x_0$

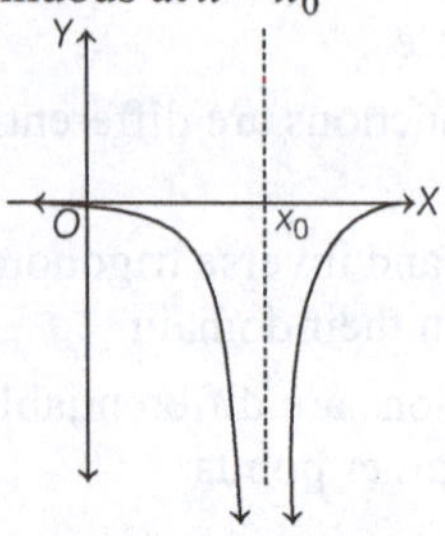

3. Shown below is the graph of a function, $g(x)$.

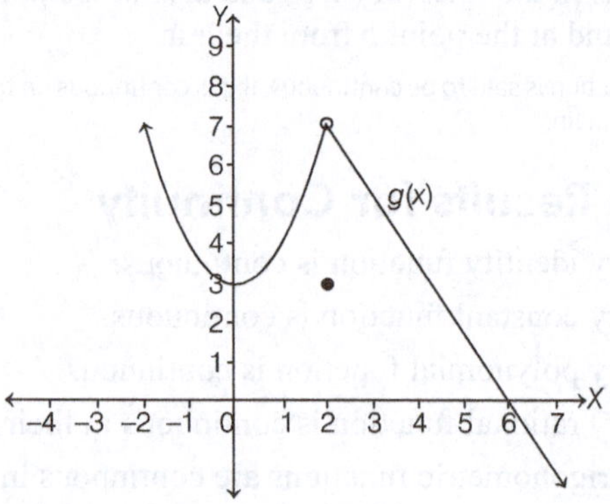

Which of the following is true? **ISC Specimen 2024**

(a) $g(x)$ is continuous and differentiable at $x = 2$

(b) $g(x)$ is continuous but not differentiable at $x = 2$

(c) $g(x)$ is not continuous but differentiable at $x = 2$

(d) $g(x)$ is neither continuous nor differentiable at $x = 2$

4. If the following function is continuous at $x = 2$, then the value of k will be

$$f(x) = \begin{cases} 2x+1, & \text{if } x < 2 \\ k, & \text{if } x = 2 \\ 3x-1, & \text{if } x > 2 \end{cases}$$

ISC 2023

(a) 2 (b) 3 (c) 5 (d) -1

5. If $f(x) = \dfrac{4-x^2}{4x-x^3}$, then the function is **ISC Specimen 2023**

(a) discontinuous at only one point.

(b) discontinuous at exactly two points.

(c) discontinuous at exactly three points.

(d) discontinuous at exactly four points.

6. The set of points, where the function $f(x) = x|x|$ is differentiable in **ISC Specimen Sem-I 2022**

(a) $(-\infty, \infty)$ (b) $(-\infty, 0) \cup (0, \infty)$

(c) $(0, \infty)$ (d) $[0, \infty)$

2 Marks Questions

7. Determine the value of k for which the following function is continuous at $x = 3$. **ISC 2024**

$$f(x) = \begin{cases} \dfrac{(x+3)^2 - 36}{x-3}; & x \neq 3 \\ k; & x = 3 \end{cases}$$

8. $f(x)=\dfrac{x^2-9}{x-3}$ is not defined at $x=3$. What value should be assigned to $f(3)$ for continuity of $f(x)$ at $x=3$? **ISC 2019**

9. Find the value of constant 'k' so that the function $f(x)$ defined as

$$f(x)=\begin{cases}\dfrac{x^2-2x-3}{x+1}, & x\neq -1\\ k, & x=-1\end{cases}$$ is continuous at $x=-1$. **ISC 2018**

3/4 Marks Questions

10. Show below is a function which is differentiable at $x=3$

$$f(x)=\begin{cases}-\log(4-x), & \text{if } x<3\\ p-qx, & \text{if } x\geq 3\end{cases}$$

Find the values of p and q, where they are real numbers. Show your steps and give a valid reason. **ISC Specimen 2024**

11. Show that the function $f(x)=|x-4|,\ x\in R$ is continuous but not differentiable at $x=4$. **ISC 2019**

12. Show that the function $f(x)=\begin{cases}x^2, & x\leq 1\\ \dfrac{1}{x}, & x>1\end{cases}$ is continuous at $x=1$ but not differentiable. **ISC 2018**

13. Prove that the function $f(x)=|x-1|,\ x\in R$, is continuous at $x=1$ but not differentiable. **ISC Specimen 2018**

5/6 Marks Questions

14. Find the values of p and q for which

$$f(x)=\begin{cases}\dfrac{1-\sin^3 x}{3\cos^2 x}, & \text{if } x<\dfrac{\pi}{2}\\ p, & \text{if } x=\dfrac{\pi}{2}\\ \dfrac{q(1-\sin x)}{(\pi-2x)^2}, & \text{if } x>\dfrac{\pi}{2}\end{cases}$$

is continuous at $x=\dfrac{\pi}{2}$.

15. If $f(x)=\begin{cases}\dfrac{\sin(a+1)x+2\sin x}{x}, & x<0\\ 2, & x=0\\ \dfrac{\sqrt{1+bx}-1}{x}, & x>0\end{cases}$

is continuous at $x=0$, then find the values of a and b.

16. Find the value of k, so that the function

$$f(x)=\begin{cases}\left(\dfrac{1-\cos 4x}{8x^2}\right), & \text{if } x\neq 0\\ k, & \text{if } x=0\end{cases}$$

is continuous at $x=0$.

> **KEY CONCEPT**
>
> A function $f(x)$ is said to be continuous at point $x=a$, if LHL at $(x=a)=$ RHL at $(x=a)=f(a)$. So, to find the value of k, we equate anyone of LHL or RHL to $f(a)$ and solve it.

17. If $f(x)=\begin{cases}\dfrac{1-\cos 4x}{x^2}, & \text{when } x<0\\ a, & \text{when } x=0\\ \dfrac{\sqrt{x}}{\sqrt{16+\sqrt{x}}-4}, & \text{when } x>0\end{cases}$

and f is continuous at $x=0$, then find the value of a.

18. Find the value of k, for which

$$f(x)=\begin{cases}\dfrac{\sqrt{1+kx}-\sqrt{1-kx}}{x}, & \text{if } -1\leq x<0\\ \dfrac{2x+1}{x-1}, & \text{if } 0\leq x<1\end{cases}$$

is continuous at $x=0$.

19. Find the value of k, so that the following function is continuous at $x=2$.

$$f(x)=\begin{cases}\dfrac{x^3+x^2-16x+20}{(x-2)^2}, & x\neq 2\\ k, & x=2\end{cases}$$

20. Find the value of k, so that the function f defined by

$$f(x)=\begin{cases}\dfrac{k\cos x}{\pi-2x}, & \text{if } x\neq\dfrac{\pi}{2}\\ 3, & \text{if } x=\dfrac{\pi}{2}\end{cases}$$

is continuous at $x=\dfrac{\pi}{2}$.

21. Find the value of a for which the function f is defined as

$$f(x)=\begin{cases}a\sin\dfrac{\pi}{2}(x+1), & x\leq 0\\ \dfrac{\tan x-\sin x}{x^3}, & x>0\end{cases}$$

is continuous at $x=0$.

22. If the function $f(x)$ given by

$$f(x)=\begin{cases} 3ax+b, & \text{if } x>1 \\ 11, & \text{if } x=1 \\ 5ax-2b, & \text{if } x<1 \end{cases}$$

is continuous at $x=1$, then find the values of a and b.

23. Find the values of a and b such that the following function $f(x)$ is a continuous function.

$$f(x)=\begin{cases} 5, & x\le 2 \\ ax+b, & 2<x<10 \\ 21, & x\ge 10 \end{cases}$$

Explanations

1. (a) Given, graph of the function f is

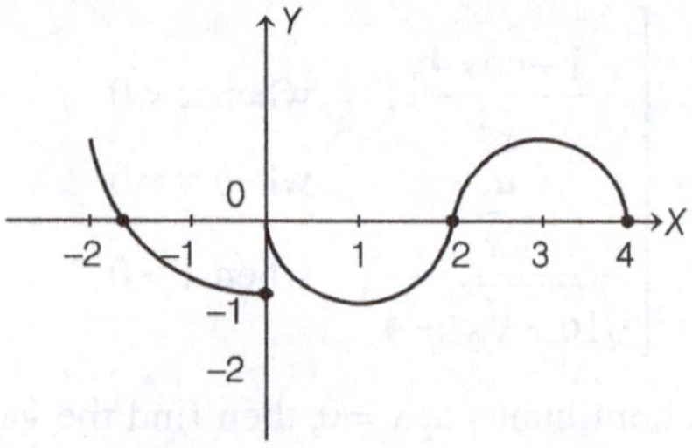

At $x=0$, we cannot draw a tangent, therefore the function is not differentiable at $x=0$.

Similarly, at $x=2$, we cannot draw a tangent. Therefore, function is not differentiable at $x=2$.

2. (d)

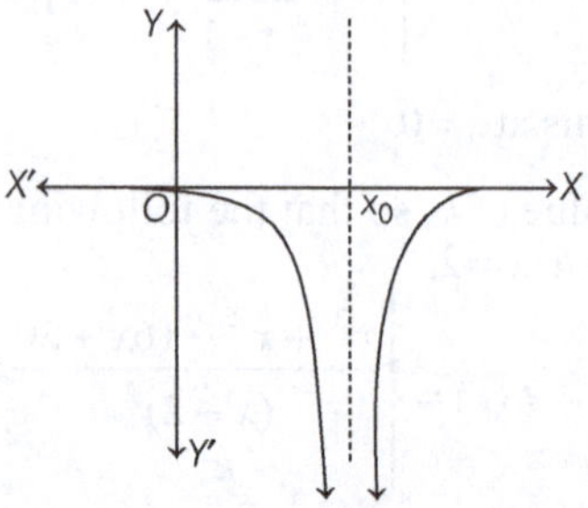

In above graph, we have asymptote, at $x=x_0$

$\therefore$ $f(x)$ is not continuous at $x=x_0$

3. (d) From the graph it can be clearly seen that $g(x)$ is neither continuous nor differentiable at $x=2$

4. (c) $f(x)$ is continuous at $x=2$

$\because \quad \lim_{x\to 2^-}(2x+1)=k$

$\Rightarrow \quad 2(2)+1=k \Rightarrow k=5$

5. (c) Here, $f(x)=\dfrac{4-x^2}{4x-x^3}$

This is a rational function, so it wil be discontinuous at points, where denominator becomes zero.

$$4x-x^3=0$$

$$\Rightarrow \quad x(4-x^2)=0$$

$$\Rightarrow \quad x(2^2-x^2)=0$$

$$\Rightarrow \quad x(2+x)(2-x)=0$$

$$\therefore \quad x=0,\ x=-2 \text{ and } x=2$$

Hence, the function $f(x)=\dfrac{4-x^2}{4x-x^3}$ will be discontinuous at exactly three points $0, -2$ and 2.

6. (a) Given, function can be written as

$$f(x)=\begin{cases} x^2, & \text{if } x>0 \\ -x^2, & \text{if } x<0 \\ 0, & \text{if } x=0 \end{cases}$$

Now, it is clear that the function $f(x)$ is differentiable at all non-zero values of x.

Also, $Lf'(0)=Rf'(0)=f(0)=0$

$\Rightarrow f(x)$ is differentiable at $x=0$

$\therefore\ f(x)=x|x|$ is differentiable in $(-\infty,\infty)$.

7. Given, $f(x)=\begin{cases} \dfrac{(x+3)^2-36}{x-3}; & x\ne 3 \\ k; & x=3 \end{cases}$

$$\text{LHL}=\lim_{x\to 3^-} f(x)=\lim_{h\to 0} f(3-h)$$

$$=\lim_{h\to 0}\frac{(3-h+3)^2-36}{3-h-3}$$

$$=\lim_{h\to 0}\frac{(6-h)^2-36}{-h}$$

$$=\lim_{h\to 0}\frac{36+h^2-12h-36}{-h}$$

$$=\lim_{h\to 0}\frac{h^2-12h}{-h}=\lim_{h\to 0}(12-h)=12$$

$$\text{RHL}=\lim_{x\to 3^+} f(x)=\lim_{h\to 0} f(3+h)$$

$$=\lim_{h\to 0}\frac{(3+h+3)^2-36}{3+h-3}$$

$$= \lim_{h \to 0} \frac{36 + h^2 + 12h - 36}{h}$$

$$= \lim_{h \to 0} (h + 12) = 12$$

and $f(3) = k$

Since, f is continuous at $x = 3$.

Therefore, LHL = RHL = $f(3)$

$\Rightarrow \quad 12 = 12 = k$

Hence, $\quad k = 12$

8. We have, $f(x) = \dfrac{x^2 - 9}{x - 3}$

Now, $\text{RHL} = \lim_{x \to 3^+} f(x) = \lim_{x \to 3^+} \dfrac{x^2 - 9}{x - 3}$

On putting $x = 3 + h$ as $x \to 3^+$ when $h \to 0$

$$= \lim_{h \to 0} \frac{(3+h)^2 - 9}{3 + h - 3} = \lim_{h \to 0} \frac{9 + h^2 + 6h - 9}{h}$$

$$= \lim_{h \to 0} (6 + h) = 6$$

and $\text{LHL} = \lim_{x \to 3^-} f(x) = \lim_{x \to 3^-} \dfrac{x^2 - 9}{x - 3}$

On putting $x = 3 - h$ as $x \to 3^-$ when $h \to 0$

$$= \lim_{h \to 0} \frac{(3-h)^2 - 9}{3 - h - 3}$$

$$= \lim_{h \to 0} \frac{(9 + h^2 - 6h) - 9}{-h}$$

$$= \lim_{h \to 0} (6 - h) = 6$$

Thus, to make $f(x)$ continuous, $f(3)$ should be equal to 6.

9. Given, $f(x) = \begin{cases} \dfrac{x^2 - 2x - 3}{x + 1}, & x \neq -1 \\ k, & x = -1 \end{cases}$

is continuous at $x = -1$.

Since, $f(x)$ is continuous at $x = -1$.

$\therefore \quad \lim_{x \to -1} f(x) = f(-1)$

$\Rightarrow \quad \lim_{x \to -1} \dfrac{x^2 - 2x - 3}{x + 1} = k \quad [\because f(-1) = k]$

$\Rightarrow \quad \lim_{x \to -1} \dfrac{(x+1)(x-3)}{(x+1)} = k$

$\Rightarrow \quad \lim_{x \to -1} x - 3 = k$

$\Rightarrow \quad -1 - 3 = k$

$\Rightarrow \quad k = -4$

Hence, the value of k is -4.

10. We have, $f(x) = \begin{cases} -\ln(4 - x), & x < 3 \\ p - qx, & x \geq 3 \end{cases}$

$\because f(x)$ is continuous at $x = 3$

$\therefore \quad \text{LHL} = \text{RHL} \quad \ldots(\text{i})$

$$\text{LHL} = \lim_{x \to 3^-} [-\ln(4 - x)] = \lim_{h \to 0} [-\ln(4 - (3 - h))]$$

$$= \lim_{h \to 0} [-\ln(1 + h)] = 0$$

$$\text{RHL} = \lim_{x \to 3^+} (p - qx) = \lim_{h \to 0} [p - q(3 + h)]$$

$$= \lim_{h \to 0} (p - 3q - qh)$$

$$= p - 3q$$

$\therefore$ From Eq. (i), we get

$p - 3q = 0 \quad \ldots(\text{ii})$

$f(x)$ is differentiable at $x = 3$

$\therefore \quad \text{LHD} = \text{RHD} \quad \ldots(\text{iii})$

$$\text{LHD} = \lim_{h \to 0} \frac{f(3 - h) - f(3)}{-h}$$

$$= \lim_{h \to 0} \frac{-\ln(4 - (3 - h)) - (p - 3q)}{-h}$$

$$= \lim_{h \to 0} \frac{-\ln(1 + h)}{-h} = 1 \quad [\because p - 3q = 0]$$

$$\text{RHD} = \lim_{h \to 0} \frac{f(3 + h) - f(3)}{h}$$

$$= \lim_{h \to 0} \frac{p - q(3 + h) - (p - 3q)}{h}$$

$$= \lim_{h \to 0} \frac{p - 3q - qh - p + 3q}{h}$$

$$= \lim_{h \to 0} \left(\frac{-qh}{h} \right)$$

$$= \lim_{h \to 0} -q = -q$$

From Eq. (iii), we get

$-q = 1 \Rightarrow q = -1$

$\therefore \quad p - 3(-1) = 0 \Rightarrow p = -3$

$\therefore \quad p = -3$ and $q = -1$

11. We have, $f(x) = |x - 4| = \begin{cases} x - 4, & x \geq 4 \\ 4 - x, & x < 4 \end{cases}$

Check continuity at $x = 4$

$$\text{LHL} = \lim_{x \to 4^-} f(x) = \lim_{h \to 0} f(4 - h)$$

$$= \lim_{h \to 0} [4 - (4 - h)] = \lim_{h \to 0} h = 0$$

$$\text{RHL} = \lim_{x \to 4^+} f(x) = \lim_{h \to 0} f(4 + h)$$

$$= \lim_{h \to 0} \{(4 + h) - 4\} = \lim_{h \to 0} h = 0$$

and $f(4) = 4 - 4 = 0$

Here, LHL = RHL = $f(4) = 0$

Hence, $f(x)$ is continuous at $x = 4$

Check differentiability at $x = 4$

$$\text{LHD} = \lim_{h\to 0}\frac{f(4-h)-f(4)}{-h}$$

$$= \lim_{h\to 0}\frac{4-(4-h)-(4-4)}{-h} = \lim_{h\to 0}\left(-\frac{h}{h}\right) = -1$$

$$\text{RHD} = \lim_{h\to 0}\frac{f(4+h)-f(4)}{h}$$

$$= \lim_{h\to 0}\frac{(4+h)-4-(4-4)}{h} = \lim_{h\to 0}\frac{h}{h} = 1$$

Here, LHD $\neq$ RHD

Hence, $f(x)$ is not differentiable at $x = 4$.

12. Given, $f(x) = \begin{cases} x^2, & x \le 1 \\ \dfrac{1}{x}, & x > 1 \end{cases}$

Continuity at $x = 1$

$$\text{LHL} = \lim_{x\to 1^-} f(x) = \lim_{h\to 0} f(1-h)$$

$$= \lim_{h\to 0}(1-h)^2 = 1$$

$$\text{RHL} = \lim_{x\to 1^+} f(x) = \lim_{h\to 0} f(1+h)$$

$$= \lim_{h\to 0}\frac{1}{1+h} = 1$$

and $f(1) = 1$

$\therefore \lim_{x\to 1^-} f(x) = \lim_{x\to 1^+} f(x) = f(1)$

Hence, $f(x)$ is continuous at $x = 1$.

Differentiability at $x = 1$

$$\text{LHD} = \lim_{h\to 0}\frac{f(1-h)-f(1)}{-h} = \lim_{h\to 0}\frac{(1-h)^2-1}{-h}$$

$$= \lim_{h\to 0}\frac{1-2h+h^2-1}{-h} = \lim_{h\to 0}\frac{-h(2-h)}{-h} = 2$$

$$\text{RHD} = \lim_{h\to 0}\frac{f(1+h)-f(1)}{h} = \lim_{h\to 0}\frac{\frac{1}{1+h}-1}{h}$$

$$= \lim_{h\to 0}\frac{1-1-h}{h(1+h)} = \lim_{h\to 0}\left(-\frac{1}{1+h}\right) = -1$$

Since, LHD $\neq$ RHD.

Hence, f is not differentiable at $x = 1$.

13. We have, $f(x) = |x-1| \Rightarrow f(x) = \begin{cases} x-1, & x \ge 1 \\ 1-x, & x < 1 \end{cases}$

Test for continuity at $x = 1$

$$f(1) = 1 - 1 = 0$$

$$\text{LHL} = \lim_{x\to 1^-} f(x) = \lim_{x\to 1^-}(1-x) = 0$$

$$\text{RHL} = \lim_{x\to 1^+} f(x) = \lim_{x\to 1^+}(x-1) = 0$$

Thus, LHL = RHL = $f(1) = 0$

Hence, $f(x)$ is continuous at $x = 1$.

Test for differentiability at $x = 1$

$$Lf'(1) = \lim_{h\to 0}\frac{f(1-h)-f(1)}{-h}$$

$$= \lim_{h\to 0}\frac{1-(1-h)-0}{-h} = \lim_{h\to 0}\frac{h}{-h} = -1$$

and $$Rf'(1) = \lim_{h\to 0}\frac{f(1+h)-f(1)}{h}$$

$$= \lim_{h\to 0}\frac{1+h-1-0}{h} = \lim_{h\to 0}\frac{h}{h} = 1$$

$\because \quad Lf'(1) \neq Rf'(1)$

Hence, f is not differentiable at $x = 1$.

14. Given, $f(x) = \begin{cases} \dfrac{1-\sin^3 x}{3\cos^2 x}, & \text{if } x < \dfrac{\pi}{2} \\ p, & \text{if } x = \dfrac{\pi}{2} \\ \dfrac{q(1-\sin x)}{(\pi-2x)^2}, & \text{if } x > \dfrac{\pi}{2} \end{cases}$

is continuous at $x = \dfrac{\pi}{2}$.

$$\therefore (\text{LHL})_{x=\frac{\pi}{2}} = (\text{RHL})_{x=\frac{\pi}{2}} = f\left(\frac{\pi}{2}\right) \quad \text{...(i)}$$

Now, $$\text{LHL} = \lim_{x\to \frac{\pi}{2}^-} f(x) = \lim_{h\to 0} f\left(\frac{\pi}{2}-h\right)$$

$\left[\text{put } x = \dfrac{\pi}{2} - h; \text{ when } x \to \dfrac{\pi}{2}^-, \text{ then } h \to 0\right]$

$$= \lim_{h\to 0}\frac{1-\sin^3\left(\frac{\pi}{2}-h\right)}{3\cos^2\left(\frac{\pi}{2}-h\right)} = \lim_{h\to 0}\frac{1-\cos^3 h}{3\sin^2 h}$$

$\left[\because \cos\left(\dfrac{\pi}{2}-\theta\right) = \sin\theta, \sin\left(\dfrac{\pi}{2}-\theta\right) = \cos\theta\right]$

$$= \lim_{h\to 0}\frac{(1-\cos h)(1^2+\cos^2 h + 1\times\cos h)}{3(1-\cos^2 h)}$$

$$= \lim_{h\to 0}\frac{(1-\cos h)(1+\cos^2 h+\cos h)}{3(1-\cos h)(1+\cos h)}$$

$$= \lim_{h\to 0} \frac{(1+\cos^2 h+\cos h)}{3(1+\cos h)}$$

$$= \frac{1+\cos^2 0+\cos 0}{3(1+\cos 0)}$$

$$= \frac{1+(1)^2+1}{3(1+1)} = \frac{3}{3\times 2} = \frac{1}{2}$$

and $\quad \text{RHL} = \lim_{x\to \frac{\pi}{2}^+} f(x) = \lim_{h\to 0} f\left(\frac{\pi}{2}+h\right)$

$$\left[\text{put } x = \frac{\pi}{2}+h;\text{ when } x\to\frac{\pi^+}{2}, \text{ then } h\to 0\right]$$

$$= \lim_{h\to 0} \frac{q\left[1-\sin\left(\frac{\pi}{2}+h\right)\right]}{\left[\pi-2\left(\frac{\pi}{2}+h\right)\right]^2}$$

$$= \lim_{h\to 0} \frac{q(1-\cos h)}{(\pi-\pi-2h)^2} = \lim_{h\to 0}\frac{q(1-\cos h)}{4h^2}$$

$$= \lim_{h\to 0} \frac{q\left(2\sin^2\frac{h}{2}\right)}{4h^2} \quad \left[\because \cos x = 1-2\sin^2\frac{x}{2}\right]$$

$$= \frac{q}{8}\lim_{h\to 0}\left[\frac{\sin\left(\frac{h}{2}\right)}{\frac{h}{2}}\right]^2$$

$$= \frac{q}{8}\times(1)^2 = \frac{q}{8} \quad \left[\because \lim_{h\to 0}\frac{\sin h}{h}=1\right]$$

From Eq.(i), $\frac{1}{2} = \frac{q}{8} = p \quad [\because f(\pi/2) = p]$

$\Rightarrow \quad \frac{1}{2} = \frac{q}{8}$ and $\frac{1}{2} = p$

$\therefore \quad q = 4$ and $p = \frac{1}{2}$

Concept Enhancer A function $f(x)$ is said to be continuous at point $x = \frac{\pi}{2}$.

If LHL at $\left(x=\frac{\pi}{2}\right)$ = RHL at $\left(x=\frac{\pi}{2}\right) = f\left(\frac{\pi}{2}\right)$

15. Given, $f(x) = \begin{cases} \dfrac{\sin(a+1)x+2\sin x}{x}, & x<0 \\ 2, & x=0 \\ \dfrac{\sqrt{1+bx}-1}{x}, & x>0 \end{cases}$

is continuous at $x=0$.

$\therefore \quad (\text{LHL})_{x=0} = (\text{RHL})_{x=0} = f(0) \quad \ldots(i)$

Now, $\quad \text{LHL} = \lim_{x\to 0^-} f(x) = \lim_{h\to 0} f(0-h)$

$$[\text{put } x = 0-h;\text{ when } x\to 0^-, \text{ then } h\to 0]$$

$$= \lim_{h\to 0}\frac{\sin(a+1)(0-h)+2\sin(0-h)}{(0-h)}$$

$$= \lim_{h\to 0}\frac{-\sin(a+1)h-2\sin h}{-h}$$

$$[\because \sin(-\theta) = -\sin\theta]$$

$$= \lim_{h\to 0}\frac{\sin(a+1)h+2\sin h}{h}$$

$$= \lim_{h\to 0}\frac{\sin(a+1)h}{h} + \lim_{h\to 0} 2\frac{\sin h}{h}$$

$$= \lim_{h\to 0}\frac{\sin(a+1)h}{(a+1)h}\times(a+1) + 2\lim_{h\to 0}\frac{\sin h}{h}$$

$$= 1\times(a+1)+2\times 1 \quad \left[\because \lim_{x\to 0}\frac{\sin x}{x}=1\right]$$

$$= a+1+2 = a+3$$

and $\quad \text{RHL} = \lim_{x\to 0^+} f(x) = \lim_{h\to 0} f(0+h)$

$$[\text{put } x = 0+h;\text{ when } x\to 0^+, \text{ then } h\to 0]$$

$$= \lim_{h\to 0}\frac{\sqrt{1+b(0+h)}-1}{0+h} = \lim_{h\to 0}\frac{\sqrt{1+bh}-1}{h}$$

$$= \lim_{h\to 0}\frac{\sqrt{1+bh}-1}{h}\times\frac{\sqrt{1+bh}+1}{\sqrt{1+bh}+1}$$

[multiplying numerator and denominator by $\sqrt{1+bh}+1$]

$$= \lim_{h\to 0}\frac{(1+bh)-1}{h(\sqrt{1+bh}+1)}$$

$$= \lim_{h\to 0}\frac{bh}{h(\sqrt{1+bh}+1)}$$

$$= \lim_{h\to 0}\frac{b}{(\sqrt{1+bh}+1)} = \frac{b}{\sqrt{1+0}+1} = \frac{b}{2}$$

From Eq. (i), we get

$$a+3 = \frac{b}{2} = 2 \quad [\because f(0) = 2]$$

$\Rightarrow \quad a+3 = 2$ and $\frac{b}{2} = 2$

$\therefore \quad a = -1$ and $b = 4$

16. Given, $f(x)=\begin{cases}\left(\dfrac{1-\cos 4x}{8x^2}\right), & \text{if } x\neq 0\\ k, & \text{if } x=0\end{cases}$

is continuous at $x=0$.

$\therefore \quad (\text{LHL})_{x=0}=(\text{RHL})_{x=0}=f(0) \qquad \ldots\text{(i)}$

Here, $\text{LHL}=\lim_{x\to 0^-} f(x)=\lim_{x\to 0^-}\dfrac{1-\cos 4x}{8x^2}$

$$=\lim_{h\to 0}\frac{1-\cos 4(0-h)}{8(0-h)^2}$$

[put $x=0-h$; when $x\to 0^-$, then $h\to 0$]

$$=\lim_{h\to 0}\frac{1-\cos 4h}{8h^2} \qquad [\because \cos(-\theta)=\cos\theta]$$

$$=\lim_{h\to 0}\frac{2\sin^2 2h}{8h^2} \qquad [\because 1-\cos 2\theta=2\sin^2\theta]$$

$$=\lim_{h\to 0}\frac{\sin^2 2h}{4h^2}=\lim_{h\to 0}\left(\frac{\sin 2h}{2h}\right)^2=1^2=1$$

$$\left[\because \lim_{x\to 0}\frac{\sin x}{x}=1\right]$$

At $x=0, f(0)=k$

Now, from Eq. (i), we have

$$\text{LHL}=f(0) \Rightarrow 1=k$$

Hence, for $k=1$, the given function $f(x)$ is continuous at $x=0$.

Alternate Method

Let $f(x)=\begin{cases}\left(\dfrac{1-\cos 4x}{8x^2}\right), & \text{if } x\neq 0\\ k, & \text{if } x=0\end{cases}$ is continuous at $x=0$.

Here, $f(0)=k$

and $\lim_{x\to 0} f(x)=\lim_{x\to 0}\dfrac{1-\cos 4x}{8x^2}=\lim_{x\to 0}\dfrac{2\sin^2 2x}{8x^2}$

$$=\lim_{x\to 0}\left(\frac{\sin 2x}{2x}\right)^2=(1)^2=1$$

$\because f(x)$ is continuous at $x=0$.

$\Rightarrow \quad \lim_{x\to 0} f(x)=f(0)$

$\therefore \quad 1=k\Rightarrow k=1$

17. Given, $f(x)=\begin{cases}\dfrac{1-\cos 4x}{x^2}, & \text{when } x<0\\ a, & \text{when } x=0\\ \dfrac{\sqrt{x}}{\sqrt{16+\sqrt{x}}-4}, & \text{when } x>0\end{cases}$

Since, $f(x)$ is continuous at $x=0$.

$\therefore \quad \lim_{x\to 0^-} f(x)=\lim_{x\to 0^+} f(x)=f(0) \qquad \ldots\text{(i)}$

Here, $\lim_{x\to 0^-} f(x)=\lim_{x\to 0^-}\dfrac{1-\cos 4x}{x^2}$

$$=\lim_{h\to 0}\frac{1-\cos 4(0-h)}{(0-h)^2}$$

[put $x=0-h$; when $x\to 0^-$, then $h\to 0$]

$$=\lim_{h\to 0}\frac{1-\cos 4h}{h^2} \qquad [\because \cos(-\theta)=\cos\theta]$$

$$=\lim_{h\to 0}\frac{2\sin^2 2h}{h^2} \qquad [\because 1-\cos 2\theta=2\sin^2\theta]$$

$$=2\lim_{h\to 0}\left(\frac{\sin 2h}{2h}\right)^2\times 4$$

$$=2\times(1)^2\times 4 \qquad \left[\because \lim_{h\to 0}\frac{\sin h}{h}=1\right]$$

$$=8$$

Now, from Eq. (i), we have $\lim_{x\to 0^-} f(x)=f(0)$

$\Rightarrow \quad 8=a$

$\therefore \quad a=8$

18. Let $f(x)=\begin{cases}\dfrac{\sqrt{1+kx}-\sqrt{1-kx}}{x}, & \text{if } -1\le x<0\\ \dfrac{2x+1}{x-1}, & \text{if } 0\le x<1\end{cases}$

is continuous at $x=0$.

Here, $f(0)=\dfrac{2\cdot 0+1}{0-1}=\dfrac{1}{-1}=-1$

and $\quad \text{LHL}=\lim_{h\to 0} f(0-h)$

$$=\lim_{h\to 0}\frac{\sqrt{1-kh}-\sqrt{1+kh}}{-h}$$

$$=\lim_{h\to 0}\frac{\sqrt{1-kh}-\sqrt{1+kh}}{-h}\times\frac{(\sqrt{1-kh}+\sqrt{1+kh})}{(\sqrt{1-kh}+\sqrt{1+kh})}$$

$$=\lim_{h\to 0}\frac{(1-kh)-(1+kh)}{-h(\sqrt{1-kh}+\sqrt{1+kh})}$$

$$[\because (a+b)(a-b)=a^2-b^2]$$

$$=\lim_{h\to 0}\frac{-2kh}{-h(\sqrt{1-kh}+\sqrt{1+kh})}$$

$$=\lim_{h\to 0}\frac{2k}{\sqrt{1-kh}+\sqrt{1+kh}}=\frac{2k}{1+1}=\frac{2k}{2}=k$$

$\because$ $f(x)$ is continuous at $x=0$.

$\Rightarrow \quad f(0) = \text{LHL} \Rightarrow -1 = k$

$\therefore \quad k = -1$

19. Let $f(x) = \begin{cases} \dfrac{x^3 + x^2 - 16x + 20}{(x-2)^2}, & x \neq 2 \\ k, & x = 2 \end{cases}$

is continuous at $x = 2$. Here, we have $f(2) = k$

and $\lim\limits_{x \to 2} f(x) = \lim\limits_{x \to 2} \dfrac{x^3 + x^2 - 16x + 20}{(x-2)^2}$

$= \lim\limits_{x \to 2} \dfrac{(x-2)(x^2 + 3x - 10)}{(x-2)^2}$

$= \lim\limits_{x \to 2} \dfrac{(x-2)(x+5)(x-2)}{(x-2)^2}$

$= \lim\limits_{x \to 2} (x+5) = 2 + 5 = 7$

$\because$ $f(x)$ is continuous at $x = 2$.

$\therefore$ $\lim\limits_{x \to 2} f(x) = f(2) \Rightarrow 7 = k$

$\therefore \quad k = 7$

20. Let $f(x) = \begin{cases} \dfrac{k \cos x}{\pi - 2x}, & \text{if } x \neq \dfrac{\pi}{2} \\ 3, & \text{if } x = \dfrac{\pi}{2} \end{cases}$

is continuous at $x = \pi/2$.

Then, at $x = \dfrac{\pi}{2}$, $\text{LHL} = \text{RHL} = f\left(\dfrac{\pi}{2}\right)$ ...(i)

Here, $\text{LHL} = \lim\limits_{x \to \frac{\pi}{2}^-} f(x) = \lim\limits_{x \to \frac{\pi}{2}^-} \dfrac{k \cos x}{\pi - 2x}$

$\Rightarrow \quad \text{LHL} = \lim\limits_{h \to 0} \dfrac{k \cos\left(\dfrac{\pi}{2} - h\right)}{\pi - 2\left(\dfrac{\pi}{2} - h\right)}$

$\left[\text{put } x = \dfrac{\pi}{2} - h; \text{ when } x \to \dfrac{\pi^-}{2}, \text{ then } h \to 0\right]$

$= \lim\limits_{h \to 0} \dfrac{k \sin h}{\pi - \pi + 2h} \quad \left[\because \cos\left(\dfrac{\pi}{2} - \theta\right) = \sin\theta\right]$

$= \lim\limits_{h \to 0} \dfrac{k \sin h}{2h}$

$= \dfrac{k}{2} \lim\limits_{h \to 0} \dfrac{\sin h}{h}$

$\Rightarrow \quad \text{LHL} = \dfrac{k}{2} \times 1 = \dfrac{k}{2} \quad \left[\because \lim\limits_{h \to 0} \dfrac{\sin h}{h} = 1\right]$

Also, from the given function, we get

$$f\left(\dfrac{\pi}{2}\right) = 3$$

From Eq. (i), we have

$$\text{LHL} = f\left(\dfrac{\pi}{2}\right) \Rightarrow \dfrac{k}{2} = 3$$

$\therefore \quad k = 6$

21. Let $f(x) = \begin{cases} a \sin \dfrac{\pi}{2}(x+1), & x \leq 0 \\ \dfrac{\tan x - \sin x}{x^3}, & x > 0 \end{cases}$

is continuous at $x = 0$.

$\therefore \quad \text{LHL} = \text{RHL} = f(0)$ ...(i)

Here, $\quad \text{LHL} = \lim\limits_{x \to 0^-} a \sin \dfrac{\pi}{2}(x+1)$

$\Rightarrow \quad \text{LHL} = \lim\limits_{h \to 0} a \sin \dfrac{\pi}{2}(0 - h + 1)$

[put $x = 0 - h$; when $x \to 0^-$, then $h \to 0$]

$= a \sin \dfrac{\pi}{2} = a \quad \left[\because \sin \dfrac{\pi}{2} = 1\right]$

$f(0) = a \sin \dfrac{\pi}{2} = a$

Now, we need to evaluate RHL at $x = a$.

[$\because$ LHL $= f(0) = a$ and from this, we can not find the value of a]

Here, $\quad \text{RHL} = \lim\limits_{x \to 0^+} \dfrac{\tan x - \sin x}{x^3}$

$\Rightarrow \quad \text{RHL} = \lim\limits_{h \to 0} \dfrac{\tan h - \sin h}{h^3}$

[put $x = 0 + h = h$; when $x \to 0^+$, then $h \to 0$]

$= \lim\limits_{h \to 0} \dfrac{\dfrac{\sin h}{\cos h} - \sin h}{h^3}$

$= \lim\limits_{h \to 0} \dfrac{\sin h - \sin h \cos h}{h^3 \cos h}$

$= \lim\limits_{h \to 0} \dfrac{\sin h (1 - \cos h)}{h^3 \cos h}$

$= \lim\limits_{h \to 0} \dfrac{\sin h}{h} \cdot \lim\limits_{h \to 0} \dfrac{1 - \cos h}{h^2} \cdot \lim\limits_{h \to 0} \dfrac{1}{\cos h}$

$= 1 \times \lim\limits_{h \to 0} \dfrac{1 - \cos h}{h^2} \times 1$

$\left[\because \lim\limits_{h \to 0} \dfrac{\sin h}{h} = 1 \text{ and } \lim\limits_{h \to 0} \dfrac{1}{\cos h} = \dfrac{1}{\cos 0} = \dfrac{1}{1} = 1\right]$

$$= \lim_{h\to 0} \frac{1-\cos h}{h^2}$$

$$= \lim_{h\to 0} \frac{2\sin^2 \frac{h}{2}}{h^2} \quad \left[\because 1-\cos x = 2\sin^2 \frac{x}{2}\right]$$

$$= \lim_{h\to 0} \frac{2\times \sin^2 \frac{h}{2}}{\left(\frac{h^2}{4}\times 4\right)} = \lim_{h\to 0} \frac{2}{4} \times \lim_{h\to 0} \frac{\sin^2 \frac{h}{2}}{\frac{h^2}{4}}$$

$$= \frac{1}{2}\times \lim_{h\to 0}\left(\frac{\sin \frac{h}{2}}{\frac{h}{2}}\right)^2 = \frac{1}{2}\times (1)^2 \quad \left[\because \lim_{x\to 0}\frac{\sin x}{x} = 1\right]$$

$\therefore \quad \text{RHL} = \frac{1}{2}$

From Eq. (i), we have LHL = RHL

$\therefore \quad a = \frac{1}{2}$

22. Given, $f(x) = \begin{cases} 3ax+b, & \text{if } x>1 \\ 11, & \text{if } x=1 \\ 5ax-2b, & \text{if } x<1 \end{cases}$

is continuous at $x=1$.

$\therefore \quad \text{LHL} = \text{RHL} = f(1) \quad \ldots\text{(i)}$

Here, $\text{LHL} = \lim_{x\to 1^-} f(x) = \lim_{x\to 1^-} (5ax-2b)$

$= \lim_{h\to 0} [5a(1-h)-2b]$

[put $x=1-h$; when $x\to 1^-$, then $h\to 0$]

$= \lim_{h\to 0} (5a-5ah-2b)$

$= 5a-2b$

and $\text{RHL} = \lim_{x\to 1^+} (3ax+b)$

$= \lim_{h\to 0} [3a(1+h)+b]$

[put $x=1+h$; when $x\to 1^+$, then $h\to 0$]

$= \lim_{h\to 0} (3a+3ah+b)$

$= 3a+b$

Also, given that $f(1)=11$

Now, from Eq. (i), we have

$\text{RHL} = f(1) \Rightarrow 3a+b=11 \quad \ldots\text{(ii)}$

and $\text{LHL} = f(1) \Rightarrow 5a-2b=11 \quad \ldots\text{(iii)}$

On multiplying Eq. (ii) by 5 and Eq. (iii) by 3 and then subtracting, we get

$$\begin{array}{r} 15a+5b=55 \\ 15a-6b=33 \\ - \quad + \quad - \\ \hline 11b=22 \end{array}$$

$\Rightarrow \quad b=2$

On putting the value of b in Eq. (ii), we get

$3a+2=11 \Rightarrow 3a=9 \Rightarrow a=3$

Hence, $a=3$ and $b=2$.

23. Given, $f(x) = \begin{cases} 5, & x\le 2 \\ ax+b, & 2<x<10 \\ 21, & x\ge 10 \end{cases}$

is a continuous function.

So, it is continuous at $x=2$ and at $x=10$.

$\therefore$ By definition,

$(\text{LHL})_{x=2} = (\text{RHL})_{x=2} = f(2) \quad \ldots\text{(i)}$

and $(\text{LHL})_{x=10} = (\text{RHL})_{x=10} = f(10) \quad \ldots\text{(ii)}$

Now, let us calculate LHL and RHL at $x=2$.

$\text{LHL} = \lim_{x\to 2^-} f(x) = \lim_{x\to 2^-} 5$

$\Rightarrow \quad \text{LHL} = 5$

and $\text{RHL} = \lim_{x\to 2^+} f(x) = \lim_{x\to 2^+} (ax+b)$

$= \lim_{h\to 0} \{a(2+h)+b\} = \lim_{h\to 0} (2a+ah+b)$

[put $x=2+h$; when $x\to 2^+$, then $h\to 0$]

$= 2a+b$

From Eq. (i), we have

LHL = RHL

$\Rightarrow \quad 2a+b=5 \quad \ldots\text{(iii)}$

Now, we have to find LHL and RHL at $x=10$.

$\text{LHL} = \lim_{x\to 10^-} f(x) = \lim_{x\to 10^-} (ax+b)$

$= \lim_{h\to 0} [a(10-h)+b]$

[put $x=10-h$; when $x\to 10^-$, then $h\to 0$]

$= \lim_{h\to 0} (10a-ah+b)$

$\Rightarrow \quad \text{LHL} = 10a+b$

and $\text{RHL} = \lim_{x\to 10^+} f(x) = \lim_{x\to 10^+} 21 = 21$

Now, from Eq. (ii), we have

$\text{LHL} = \text{RHL} \Rightarrow 10a+b=21 \quad \ldots\text{(iv)}$

On subtracting Eq. (iv) from Eq. (iii), we get

$-8a = -16 \Rightarrow a=2$

On putting $a=2$ in Eq. (iv), we get

$20+b=21 \Rightarrow b=1$

Hence, $a=2$ and $b=1$.

TOPIC 2

Differentiation

The process of finding derivative of a function is called differentiation.

Fundamental Rules for Derivative

(i) The derivative of a constant function is zero

i.e. $\frac{d}{dx}(c) = 0,$

where c is a constant.

(ii) The derivative of constant times a function is constant times the derivative of the function

i.e. $\frac{d}{dx}\{c \cdot f(x)\} = c\frac{d}{dx}\{f(x)\},$

where c is a constant.

(iii) The derivative of the sum or difference of two functions is the sum or difference of their derivatives

i.e. $\frac{d}{dx}\{f(x) \pm g(x)\} = \frac{d}{dx}\{f(x)\} \pm \frac{d}{dx}\{g(x)\}$

(iv) **Product Rule for Derivative** The derivative of the product of two functions is defined as

$$\frac{d}{dx}\{f(x) \cdot g(x)\} = f(x) \cdot \frac{d}{dx}\{g(x)\} + g(x) \cdot \frac{d}{dx}\{f(x)\}$$

= (First function) × (Derivative of second function) + (Second function) × (Derivative of first function)

(v) **Quotient Rule for Derivative** The derivative of the quotient of two functions is defined as

$$\frac{d}{dx}\left\{\frac{f(x)}{g(x)}\right\} = \frac{g(x) \cdot \frac{d}{dx}\{f(x)\} - f(x) \cdot \frac{d}{dx}\{g(x)\}}{\{g(x)\}^2}$$

$$= \frac{(\text{Denominator} \times \text{Derivative of numerator}) - (\text{Numerator} \times \text{Derivative of denominator})}{(\text{Denominator})^2}$$

NOTE If f, g and h are three differentiable functions at x, then

$$\frac{d}{dx}[f(x) \cdot g(x) \cdot h(x)] = f(x)\, g(x) \frac{d}{dx} h(x) + f(x)\, h(x) \frac{d}{dx} g(x) + g(x)\, h(x) \frac{d}{dx}[f(x)]$$

Derivatives of Some Standard Functions

There are some derivatives of standard functions given below

Algebraic Functions

(i) $\frac{d}{dx}(x^n) = nx^{n-1}$ (ii) $\frac{d}{dx}\left(\frac{1}{x^n}\right) = -nx^{-n-1}$

(iii) $\frac{d}{dx}(\sqrt{x}) = \frac{1}{2\sqrt{x}}$

Trigonometric Functions

(i) $\frac{d}{dx}(\sin x) = \cos x$ (ii) $\frac{d}{dx}(\cos x) = -\sin x$

(iii) $\frac{d}{dx}(\tan x) = \sec^2 x$ (iv) $\frac{d}{dx}(\cot x) = -\text{cosec}^2 x$

(v) $\frac{d}{dx}(\sec x) = \sec x \tan x$

(vi) $\frac{d}{dx}(\text{cosec}\, x) = -\text{cosec}\, x \cot x$

Exponential Functions

(i) $\frac{d}{dx}(e^x) = e^x$

(ii) $\frac{d}{dx}(a^x) = a^x \log_e a, a > 0.$

Logarithmic Functions

(i) $\frac{d}{dx}(\log_e x) = \frac{1}{x}, x > 0.$

(ii) $\frac{d}{dx}(\log_a x) = \frac{1}{x \log_e a}; x > 0, a > 0$ and $a \neq 1$

Inverse Trigonometric Functions

(i) $\frac{d}{dx}(\sin^{-1} x) = \frac{1}{\sqrt{1-x^2}}; |x| < 1$

(ii) $\frac{d}{dx}(\cos^{-1} x) = \frac{-1}{\sqrt{1-x^2}}; |x| < 1$

(iii) $\frac{d}{dx}(\tan^{-1} x) = \frac{1}{1+x^2}; x \in R$

(iv) $\frac{d}{dx}(\cot^{-1} x) = \frac{-1}{1+x^2}; x \in R$

(v) $\frac{d}{dx}(\sec^{-1} x) = \frac{1}{x\sqrt{x^2-1}}; |x|>1$

(vi) $\frac{d}{dx}(\text{cosec}^{-1} x) = \frac{-1}{x\sqrt{x^2-1}}; |x|>1$

The following formulae will be helpful to solve the problems involving inverse trigonometric functions.

(i) $\sin 2x = 2\sin x \cos x = \frac{2\tan x}{1+\tan^2 x}$

(ii) $\cos 2x = 2\cos^2 x - 1 = 1 - 2\sin^2 x$

$= \cos^2 x - \sin^2 x = \frac{1-\tan^2 x}{1+\tan^2 x}$

(iii) $\tan 2x = \frac{2\tan x}{1-\tan^2 x}$

(iv) $\frac{1 \pm \tan x}{1 \mp \tan x} = \tan\left(\frac{\pi}{4} \pm x\right)$

Differentiation by Substitution

Substitution is useful to reduce the function into simple form. For problems involving inverse trigonometric functions, first try for a suitable substitution to simplify it and then differentiate it. If no substitution is found, then differentiate directly.

Some standard substitutions are given below

Expressions	Substitutions
$\sqrt{a^2+x^2}$	$x = a\tan\theta$ or $x = a\cot\theta$
$\sqrt{a^2-x^2}$	$x = a\sin\theta$ or $x = a\cos\theta$
$\sqrt{x^2-a^2}$	$x = a\sec\theta$ or $x = a\,\text{cosec}\,\theta$
$\frac{a+x}{a-x}$ or $\frac{a-x}{a+x}$	$x = a\tan\theta$
$\sqrt{\frac{a+x}{a-x}}$ or $\sqrt{\frac{a-x}{a+x}}$	$x = a\cos 2\theta$
$\frac{2x}{1+x^2}$ or $\frac{2x}{1-x^2}$	$x = \tan\theta$
$a\sin x + b\cos x$	$a = r\cos\alpha, b = r\sin\alpha$
$\sqrt{x-\alpha}$	$x = \alpha\sin^2\theta$
$\sqrt{\beta-x}$	$x = \beta\cos^2\theta$
$\sqrt{2ax-x^2}$	$x = a(1-\cos\theta)$

Differentiation of Implicit Function

If the relation between the variables x and y is given by an equation containing both of the form $\phi(x, y) = 0$ and this equation is not immediately solvable for y i.e. it is not possible to express y as a function of x in the form $y = \phi(x)$, then y is called an **implicit function** of x.

In such a case to find dy/dx, differentiate both sides of the given relation with respect to x keeping in mind that the derivative of $f(y)$ w.r.t. x is $\frac{d[f(y)]}{dy} \cdot \frac{dy}{dx}$.

e.g. (i) $\frac{d}{dx}(\tan y) = \sec^2 y \cdot \frac{dy}{dx}$

(ii) $\frac{d}{dx}(y^4) = 4y^3 \cdot \frac{dy}{dx}$

Differentiation of Parametric Functions

Sometimes x and y are separately given as functions of a single variable t (called a parameter)

i.e. $y = f(t)$ and $x = g(t)$.

In this case,

Derivative, $\frac{dy}{dx} = \frac{dy/dt}{dx/dt} = \frac{f'(t)}{g'(t)}$

Differentiation of Composite Functions

Derivative of a composite function can be find out by chain rule.

Chain Rule

Chain rule is applied, when the given function is the function of function i.e. a function is in the form of $[fog(x)]$ of $f[g(x)]$.

Let y be a real valued function which is a composite of two functions say $y = f(u)$ and $u = g(x)$.

Then, $\frac{dy}{dx} = \frac{dy}{du} \cdot \frac{du}{dx} = f'(u) \cdot g'(x)$

i.e. $\frac{d}{dx}[f\{g(x\}] = f'\{g(x)\} \cdot g'(x)$

Extension of Chain Rule Extension of chain rule is applied, when the given function say y is a composite of there functions.

e.g. $f[g(h(x))]$

If $y = f(u), u = g(v)$ and $v = h(x)$, then

$\frac{dy}{dx} = \frac{dy}{du} \cdot \frac{du}{dv} \cdot \frac{dv}{dx} = f'(u) \cdot g'(v) \cdot h'(x)$

Differentiation of a Function with Respect to Another Function

If $y = f(x)$ and $z = g(x)$ are two functions of x. Then, to find the derivative of $f(x)$ with respect to $g(x)$

i.e. $\frac{dy}{dz}$ use the following formula, $\frac{dy}{dz} = \frac{dy/dx}{dz/dx} = \frac{f'(x)}{g'(x)}$

PYQs Previous Years Questions

1 Mark Questions

1. Find the derivative of $y = \log x + \frac{1}{x}$ with respect to x. **ISC 2024**

2. The derivative of $\log x$ with respect to $\frac{1}{x}$ is **ISC 2023**

(a) $\frac{1}{x}$ (b) $\frac{-1}{x^3}$ (c) $\frac{-1}{x}$ (d) $-x$

3. If $\sin^{-1} x + \sin^{-1} y = \frac{\pi}{2}$, then $\frac{dy}{dx}$ is equal to **ISC Specimen 2023 ; ISC Specimen Sem-I 2022**

(a) $\frac{x}{y}$ (b) $-\frac{x}{y}$ (c) $\frac{y}{x}$ (d) $-\frac{y}{x}$

4. If $y = t^2$ and $t = x + 3$, then $\frac{dy}{dx}$ is equal to **ISC Specimen Sem-I 2022**

(a) $(x+3)^2$ (b) $2(x+3)$
(c) $2t$ (d) $2(x+3)^2$

5. What will be the derivative of $\sin^{-1}\left(\frac{2x}{1+x^2}\right)$ with respect to $\cos^{-1}\left(\frac{1-x^2}{1+x^2}\right)$? **ISC Specimen Sem-I 2022**

(a) -1 (b) 1 (c) 2 (d) 4

2 Marks Questions

6. If $y = \sqrt{\sin x + y}$, then find $\frac{dy}{dx}$. **ISC Specimen 2023**

7. Differentiate the function with reference to x:

$f(x) = \cos^{-1}\left(\sqrt{\frac{1-\cos x}{2}}\right)$. **ISC Specimen 2021**

8. Find $\frac{dy}{dx}$, if $x = at^2$ at $y = 2at$. **ISC Specimen 2021, 2018**

9. Find $\frac{dy}{dx}$, if $x^3 + y^3 = 3axy$. **ISC 2020**

3/4 Marks Questions

10. Find the derivative of $\sin x^2$ with respect to x^3. **ISC 2009**

11. If $y = \sqrt{\frac{1-\cos x}{1+\cos x}}$, then find $\frac{dy}{dx}$. **ISC 2008**

> **KEY CONCEPT**
> (i) Firstly, multiply numerator and denominator by $\sqrt{1-\cos x}$ and simplify it.
> (ii) Further, differentiate and get the required result.

12. If $y = e^{\sin x^2}$, then find $\frac{dy}{dx}$. **ISC 2006**

> **KEY CONCEPT**
> (i) Firstly, assuming $y = e^z$, where $z = \sin t$ and $t = x^2$, so that it comes in differentiable form.
> (ii) Further, differentiate it by using chain rule of derivative use.

13. If $\sin xy + \cos xy = 1$ and $\tan xy \neq 1$, then show that $\frac{dy}{dx} = \frac{-y}{x}$. **ISC 2005**

14. If $x = a\sin^3 t$ and $y = a\cos^3 t$, then find dy/dx. **ISC 2004**

15. If $y = \tan^{-1}\left(\frac{2x}{1-x^2}\right)$, then prove that $\frac{dy}{dx} = \frac{2}{1+x^2}$. **ISC 2003**

> **KEY CONCEPT**
> (i)Firstly , substitute $x = \tan\theta$, so that becomes an identity $\tan^{-1}(\tan\theta) = \theta$.
> (ii)Further, substitute the value of θ and differentiate w.r.t. x, to get prove the result.

16. If $y=e^x \log \tan 2x$, then find dy/dx. **ISC 2002**

17. If $y=\log\sqrt{\dfrac{1-\cos x}{1+\cos x}}$, then find dy/dx. **ISC 2000**

5/6 Marks Questions

18. If $y=\dfrac{x\sin^{-1}x}{\sqrt{1-x^2}}$, then prove that

$$(1-x^2)\frac{dy}{dx}=x+\frac{y}{x}.$$

ISC 2014

19. Using a suitable substitution, find the derivative of $\tan^{-1}\sqrt{\dfrac{a-x}{a+x}}$ with respect to x. **ISC 2010**

Explanations

1. We have, $y=\log x+\dfrac{1}{x}$

On differentiating w.r.t. x, we get

$$\frac{dy}{dx}=\frac{d}{dx}(\log x)+\frac{d}{dx}\left(\frac{1}{x}\right)=\frac{1}{x}-\frac{1}{x^2}$$

2. (d) Let $u=\log x$ and $v=\dfrac{1}{x}$

$$\therefore \quad \frac{du}{dx}=\frac{1}{x} \text{ and } \frac{dv}{dx}=\frac{-1}{x^2} \Rightarrow \frac{du}{dv}=\frac{1/x}{-1/x^2}=-x$$

3. (b) Given, $\sin^{-1}x+\sin^{-1}y=\dfrac{\pi}{2}$

$$\Rightarrow \quad \sin^{-1}x=\frac{\pi}{2}-\sin^{-1}y$$

$$\Rightarrow \quad \sin^{-1}x=\cos^{-1}y \quad \left[\because \cos^{-1}\theta=\frac{\pi}{2}-\sin^{-1}\theta\right]$$

$$\Rightarrow \quad y=\sqrt{1-x^2} \quad \ldots\text{(i)}$$

On differentiating both sides w.r.t x, we get

$$\frac{dy}{dx}=\frac{1(-2x)}{2\sqrt{1-x^2}}=\frac{-x}{\sqrt{1-x^2}}$$

$$\Rightarrow \quad \frac{dy}{dx}=\frac{-x}{y} \quad \left[\text{from Eq. (i) } y=\sqrt{1-x^2}\right]$$

4. (b) We have, $y=t^2 \Rightarrow \dfrac{dy}{dt}=2t$

and $t=x+3 \Rightarrow x=t-3$

$$\Rightarrow \quad \frac{dx}{dt}=1$$

$$\therefore \quad \frac{dy}{dx}=\frac{dy/dt}{dx/dt}=\frac{2t}{1}=2t=2(x+3)$$

NOTE $\dfrac{dy}{dx}$ cannot be a function of t.

5. (b) Let $u=\sin^{-1}\left(\dfrac{2x}{1+x^2}\right)$

and $v=\cos^{-1}\left(\dfrac{1-x^2}{1+x^2}\right)$

Now, let $x=\tan\theta$

On evaluating $\dfrac{du}{d\theta}$ and $\dfrac{dv}{d\theta}$, we get

$$\frac{du}{d\theta}=\frac{d}{d\theta}\sin^{-1}\left(\frac{2\tan\theta}{1+\tan^2\theta}\right)$$

$$=\frac{d}{d\theta}\sin^{-1}(\sin 2\theta)$$

$$=\frac{d}{d\theta}(2\theta)=2$$

$$\frac{dv}{d\theta}=\frac{d}{d\theta}\cos^{-1}\left(\frac{1-\tan^2\theta}{1+\tan^2\theta}\right)$$

$$=\frac{d}{d\theta}\cos^{-1}(\cos 2\theta)=\frac{d}{d\theta}(2\theta)=2$$

$$\therefore \quad \frac{du}{dv}=\frac{du/d\theta}{dv/d\theta}=\frac{2}{2}=1$$

6. We have, $y=(\sin x+y)^{1/2}$

On differentiating both sides w.r.t. x, we get

$$\frac{dy}{dx}=\frac{1}{2}\cdot\frac{1}{(\sin x+y)^{1/2}}\cdot\left(\cos x+\frac{dy}{dx}\right)$$

$$\Rightarrow \quad \frac{dy}{dx}=\frac{1}{2y}\left(\cos x+\frac{dy}{dx}\right) \quad [\because \text{put } (\sin x+y)^{1/2}=y]$$

$$\Rightarrow \quad \frac{dy}{dx}\left(1-\frac{1}{2y}\right)=\frac{\cos x}{2y}$$

$$\therefore \quad \frac{dy}{dx}=\frac{\cos x}{2y}\cdot\frac{2y}{2y-1}=\frac{\cos x}{2y-1}$$

7. Let $y=\cos^{-1}\sqrt{\dfrac{1-\cos x}{2}}$

$$=\cos^{-1}\sqrt{\frac{2\sin^2\frac{x}{2}}{2}}$$

$$=\cos^{-1}\sqrt{\sin^2\frac{x}{2}}$$

$$=\cos^{-1}\left(\sin\frac{x}{2}\right)$$

$$=\cos^{-1}\left[\cos\left(\frac{\pi}{2}-\frac{x}{2}\right)\right]$$

$$y=\frac{\pi}{2}-\frac{x}{2}$$

On differentiating both sides w.r.t. x, we obtain

$$\frac{dy}{dx}=\frac{-1}{2}$$

8. Given that, $x=at^2$, $y=2at$

On differentiating both functions w.r.t. t, we get

$$\frac{dx}{dt}=2at \text{ and } \frac{dy}{dt}=2a$$

Now, $$\frac{dy}{dx}=\frac{\frac{dy}{dt}}{\frac{dx}{dt}}=\frac{2a}{2at}=\frac{1}{t}$$

9. We have, $x^3+y^3=3axy$

On differentiating w.r.t. x both sides, we get

$$3x^2+3y^2\frac{dy}{dx}=3a\left(x\frac{dy}{dx}+y\right)$$

$$\Rightarrow \quad 3x^2+3y^2\frac{dy}{dx}=3ax\frac{dy}{dx}+3ay$$

$$\Rightarrow \quad 3y^2\frac{dy}{dx}-3ax\frac{dy}{dx}=3ay-3x^2$$

$$\Rightarrow \quad \frac{dy}{dx}(3y^2-3ax)=3ay-3x^2$$

$$\Rightarrow \quad \frac{dy}{dx}=\frac{3(ay-x^2)}{3(y^2-ax)}$$

$$\Rightarrow \quad \frac{dy}{dx}=\frac{ay-x^2}{y^2-ax}$$

10. Let $u=\sin x^2$ and $v=x^3$

To find $\dfrac{du}{dv}$.

Now, $\quad u=\sin x^2$

On differentiating both sides w.r.t. x, we get

$$\frac{du}{dx}=\frac{d}{dx}(\sin x^2)$$

$$=\frac{d(\sin x^2)}{d(x^2)}\times\frac{d(x^2)}{dx}=2x\cos x^2 \quad \ldots\text{(i)}$$

and $\quad v=x^3$

On differentiating both sides w.r.t. x, we get

$$\frac{dv}{dx}=\frac{d(x^3)}{dx}=3x^2 \quad \ldots\text{(ii)}$$

Now, $$\frac{du}{dv}=\frac{du}{dx}\times\frac{dx}{dv}=2x\cos x^2\times\frac{1}{3x^2}$$

[from Eqs. (i) and (ii)]

$$=\frac{2\cos x^2}{3x}$$

Alternate Method

Now, $u=\sin x^2$ and $v=x^3$

$$\Rightarrow \quad \frac{du}{dx}=\frac{d}{dx}(\sin x^2) \text{ and } \frac{dv}{dx}=\frac{d}{dx}(x^3)$$

$$\Rightarrow \quad \frac{du}{dx}=\cos x^2\frac{d}{dx}(x^2)$$

and $$\frac{dv}{dx}=3x^2 \Rightarrow \frac{du}{dx}=2x\cos x^2$$

and $$\frac{dv}{dx}=3x^2$$

$$\therefore \quad \frac{du}{dv}=\frac{du/dx}{dv/dx}=\frac{2x\cos x^2}{3x^2}=\frac{2\cos x^2}{3x}$$

11. Given, $y=\sqrt{\dfrac{1-\cos x}{1+\cos x}}$

On multiplying and dividing by $\sqrt{1-\cos x}$ on RHS, we get

$$y=\sqrt{\frac{(1-\cos x)(1-\cos x)}{(1+\cos x)(1-\cos x)}}$$

$$\Rightarrow \quad y=\sqrt{\frac{(1-\cos x)^2}{1-\cos^2 x}}=\sqrt{\frac{(1-\cos x)^2}{\sin^2 x}}$$

$[\because 1-\cos^2 x=\sin^2 x]$

$$\Rightarrow \quad y=\frac{(1-\cos x)}{\sin x}$$

$$\Rightarrow \quad y=\frac{1}{\sin x}-\frac{\cos x}{\sin x} \Rightarrow y=\operatorname{cosec} x-\cot x$$

On differentiating both sides w.r.t. x, we get

$$\frac{dy}{dx}=-\operatorname{cosec} x\cot x+\operatorname{cosec}^2 x$$

12. Given, $y = e^{\sin x^2}$

Let $y = e^z$, where $z = \sin t$ and $t = x^2$

On differentiating both sides of t w.r.t. x, we get

$$\frac{dt}{dx} = 2x \quad \text{...(i)}$$

On differentiating both sides of z w.r.t. t, we get

$$\frac{dz}{dt} = \cos t \quad \text{...(ii)}$$

On differentiating both sides of y w.r.t. z, we get

$$\frac{dy}{dz} = e^z \quad \text{...(iii)}$$

Using chain rule of derivative,

$$\frac{dy}{dx} = \frac{dy}{dz} \times \frac{dz}{dt} \times \frac{dt}{dx} = e^z \times \cos t \times 2x$$

[from Eqs. (i), (ii)and (iii)]

$$= 2x\, e^{\sin t} \cos t = 2x\, e^{\sin x^2} \cos x^2$$

13. Given, $\sin xy + \cos xy = 1$

On differentiating both sides w.r.t. x, we get

$$\frac{d}{dx}[\sin xy + \cos xy] = \frac{d(1)}{dx}$$

$$\Rightarrow \frac{d}{dxy}(\sin xy)\frac{d}{dx}(xy) + \frac{d}{dxy}(\cos xy)\frac{d}{dx}(xy) = 0$$

$$\Rightarrow \frac{d}{d(xy)}[\sin xy + \cos xy] \times \frac{d(xy)}{dx} = 0$$

$$\Rightarrow \left[\frac{d\sin(xy)}{d(xy)} + \frac{d\cos(xy)}{d(xy)}\right] \times \left(x\frac{dy}{dx} + y\frac{dx}{dx}\right) = 0$$

$$\left[\frac{d}{dx}\{f(x)\cdot g(x)\} = f(x)\cdot\frac{d}{dx}\{g(x)\} + g(x)\cdot\frac{d}{dx}\{f(x)\}\right]$$

$$\Rightarrow (\cos xy - \sin xy)\left(x\frac{dy}{dx} + y\right) = 0$$

$$\Rightarrow \left(1 - \frac{\sin xy}{\cos xy}\right)\left(x\frac{dy}{dx} + y\right) = 0$$

[divide by $\cos xy$]

$$\Rightarrow (1 - \tan xy)\left(x\frac{dy}{dx} + y\right) = 0$$

$$\Rightarrow x\frac{dy}{dx} + y = 0$$

[$\because \tan xy \neq 1$, given]

$$\therefore x\frac{dy}{dx} = -y \Rightarrow \frac{dy}{dx} = \frac{-y}{x}$$

Hence proved.

14. Given, $x = a\sin^3 t$ and $y = a\cos^3 t$

Now, differentiating both sides of x w.r.t. t, we get

$$\frac{dx}{dt} = a\frac{d}{dt}(\sin^3 t) = a\frac{d(\sin^3 t)}{d(\sin t)} \times \frac{d(\sin t)}{dt}$$

$$= a \times 3\sin^2 t \times \cos t = 3a\sin^2 t\cos t \quad \text{...(i)}$$

Now, differentiating both sides of y w.r.t. t, we get

$$\frac{dy}{dt} = a\frac{d(\cos^3 t)}{dt} = a\frac{d(\cos^3 t)}{d(\cos t)} \times \frac{d(\cos t)}{dt}$$

$$= a \times 3\cos^2 t \times (-\sin t)$$

$$= -3a\sin t\cos^2 t \quad \text{...(ii)}$$

Now, $\frac{dy}{dx} = \frac{dy}{dt} \times \frac{dt}{dx} = \frac{-3a\sin t\cos^2 t}{3a\sin^2 t\cos t}$

[using Eqs. (i) and (ii)]

$$= \frac{-\cos t}{\sin t} = -\cot t$$

15. Let $y = \tan^{-1}\left(\frac{2x}{1-x^2}\right)$

On putting $x = \tan\theta$, then $y = \tan^{-1}\left(\frac{2\tan\theta}{1-\tan^2\theta}\right)$

$$= \tan^{-1}(\tan 2\theta)$$

$$\left[\because \tan 2a = \frac{2\tan a}{1-\tan^2 a}\right]$$

$$= 2\theta \quad [\because \tan^{-1}(\tan a) = a]$$

$$\Rightarrow y = 2\tan^{-1} x$$

$[\because x = \tan\theta \Rightarrow \theta = \tan^{-1} x]$

On differentiating both sides w.r.t. x, we get

$$\therefore \frac{dy}{dx} = 2\frac{d}{dx}(\tan^{-1} x) = \frac{2}{1+x^2}$$

Hence proved.

16. Given, $y = e^x \log\tan 2x$

On differentiating both sides w.r.t. x, we get

$$\frac{dy}{dx} = e^x\frac{d}{dx}(\log\tan 2x) + (\log\tan 2x)\frac{d(e^x)}{dx}$$

[product rule of derivative]

$$= e^x\frac{d(\log\tan 2x)}{d(\tan 2x)} \times \frac{d(\tan 2x)}{d(2x)} \times \frac{d(2x)}{dx} + e^x\log\tan 2x$$

[by chain rule of derivative]

$$= \frac{2e^x\sec^2 2x}{\tan 2x} + e^x\log\tan 2x$$

$$= \frac{2e^x}{\sin 2x \cos 2x} + e^x \log \tan 2x$$

$$= \frac{2 \times 2e^x}{2 \sin 2x \cos 2x} + e^x \log \tan 2x$$

$$= \frac{4e^x}{\sin 4x} + e^x \log \tan 2x \quad [\because \sin 2x = 2 \sin x \cos x]$$

$$= 4e^x \operatorname{cosec} 4x + e^x \log \tan 2x$$

$$= e^x [4 \operatorname{cosec} 4x + \log (\tan 2x)]$$

17. Given, $y = \log \sqrt{\frac{1-\cos x}{1+\cos x}}$

$$\Rightarrow \quad y = \frac{1}{2} \log \left(\frac{1-\cos x}{1+\cos x}\right) \quad [\because \log m^n = n \log m]$$

$$\Rightarrow \quad y = \frac{1}{2} [\log (1-\cos x) - \log (1+\cos x)]$$

$$\left[\because \log \frac{m}{n} = \log m - \log n\right]$$

On differentiating both sides w.r.t. x, we get

$$\frac{dy}{dx} = \frac{1}{2}\left[\frac{1}{1-\cos x} \times \frac{d}{dx}(1-\cos x) - \frac{1}{1+\cos x} \times \frac{d}{dx}(1+\cos x)\right]$$

$$\Rightarrow \quad \frac{dy}{dx} = \frac{1}{2}\left[\frac{0-(-\sin x)}{1-\cos x} - \frac{0+(-\sin x)}{1+\cos x}\right]$$

$$= \frac{1}{2}\left[\frac{\sin x (1+\cos x + 1 - \cos x)}{1-\cos^2 x}\right]$$

$$= \frac{1}{2}\left(\frac{2 \sin x}{\sin^2 x}\right) \quad [\because \sin^2 x + \cos^2 x = 1]$$

$$= \frac{1}{\sin x} = \operatorname{cosec} x$$

18. Given, $y = \frac{x \sin^{-1} x}{\sqrt{1-x^2}}$

On differentiating both sides w.r.t. x, we get

$$\frac{dy}{dx} = \frac{\sqrt{1-x^2}\frac{d}{dx}(x \sin^{-1} x) - (x \sin^{-1} x)\frac{d}{dx}(\sqrt{1-x^2})}{(\sqrt{1-x^2})^2}$$

$$\left[\text{using quotient rule of deriative i.e. } \frac{d}{dx}\left(\frac{f(x)}{g(x)}\right) = \frac{g(x)\frac{d}{dx}f(x) - f(x)\frac{d}{dx}g(x)}{[g(x)]^2}\right]$$

$$= \frac{\sqrt{1-x^2}\left[\sin^{-1} x \frac{d}{dx}(x) + x \frac{d}{dx}(\sin^{-1} x)\right] - (x \sin^{-1} x)\left[\frac{\frac{d}{dx}(1-x^2)}{2\sqrt{1-x^2}}\right]}{(\sqrt{1-x^2})^2}$$

$$\frac{dy}{dx} = \frac{\sqrt{1-x^2}\left\{\sin^{-1} x + \frac{x}{\sqrt{1-x^2}}\right\} - \frac{(x \sin^{-1} x)(-2x)}{2\sqrt{1-x^2}}}{(1-x^2)}$$

$$\Rightarrow \quad (1-x^2)\frac{dy}{dx} = \sqrt{1-x^2} \sin^{-1} x + x + \frac{x^2 \sin^{-1} x}{\sqrt{1-x^2}}$$

$$= x + \left[\frac{(1-x^2) \sin^{-1} x + x^2 \sin^{-1} x}{\sqrt{1-x^2}}\right]$$

$$= x + \frac{\sin^{-1} x}{\sqrt{1-x^2}}$$

$$= x + \frac{y}{x} \quad \left[\because \text{given, } y = \frac{x \sin^{-1} x}{\sqrt{1-x^2}}\right]$$

19. Let $\quad y = \tan^{-1} \sqrt{\frac{a-x}{a+x}}$

On putting $x = a \cos 2\theta$, we get

$$y = \tan^{-1} \sqrt{\frac{a - a \cos 2\theta}{a + a \cos 2\theta}} = \tan^{-1} \sqrt{\frac{a (1-\cos 2\theta)}{a (1+\cos 2\theta)}}$$

$$= \tan^{-1} \sqrt{\frac{2 \sin^2 \theta}{2 \cos^2 \theta}} = \tan^{-1} \sqrt{\tan^2 \theta}$$

$$\left[\begin{array}{l}\because \cos 2x = 2\cos^2 x - 1 \\ \text{and } \cos 2x = 1 - 2\sin^2 x\end{array}\right]$$

$$= \tan^{-1}(\tan \theta) = \theta \quad [\because \tan^{-1}(\tan x) = x]$$

$$= \frac{1}{2} \cos^{-1} \frac{x}{a}$$

$$\left[\because x = a \cos 2\theta \Rightarrow \theta = \frac{1}{2} \cos^{-1} \frac{x}{a}\right]$$

On differentiating both sides w.r.t. x, we get

$$\frac{dy}{dx} = \frac{1}{2} \times \frac{-1}{\sqrt{1-\frac{x^2}{a^2}}} \times \frac{1}{a} = \frac{-1}{2\sqrt{a^2 - x^2}}$$

TOPIC 3

Differentiation of Some Special Functions

Logarithmic Differentiation

The functions, which can be evaluated by using logarithmic differentiation, are of type

$$y=[f(x)]^{g(x)}$$

or $$y=f_1(x)\,f_2(x)\,f_3(x)\cdots$$

or $$y=\frac{f_1(x)f_2(x)\,f_3(x)\cdots}{g_1(x)\,g_2(x)\,g_3(x)\cdots}$$

For this type of function firstly we take the logarithm in the following way given below and then differentiate both sides

(i) If the function is given as the product of a number of functions like $y=u(x)\,v(x)\,w(x)$, then taking log on both sides, we get
$\log y=\log u(x)+\log v(x)+\log w(x)$

(ii) If the function is given as the division of two functions like $y=\dfrac{u(x)}{v(x)}$, then taking log on both sides, we get $\log\ y=\log u(x)-\log v(x)$

(iii) If the function is given as one function is a power of other function like $y=[f(x)]^{g(x)}$, then taking log on both sides, we get $\log y=g(x)\log[f(x)]$

Thus, the derivative of such function can be easily obtained by taking the logarithm of the function. This process is called logarithmic differentiation.

Here, $\dfrac{d}{dx}(\log y)=\dfrac{1}{y}\cdot\dfrac{dy}{dx}$

Successive Differentiation

If the function $y=f(x)$ is differentiated with respect to x, then the result $\dfrac{dy}{dx}$ or $f'(x)$, so obtained is a function of x (or may be a constant).

Hence, $\dfrac{dy}{dx}$ can again be differentiated with respect to x.

The differential coefficient of $\dfrac{dy}{dx}$ with respect to x is written as $\dfrac{d}{dx}\left(\dfrac{dy}{dx}\right)=\dfrac{d^2y}{dx^2}$ or $f''(x)$.

Again, the differential coefficient of $\dfrac{d^2y}{dx^2}$ with respect to x is written as

$$\frac{d}{dx}\left(\frac{d^2y}{dx^2}\right)=\frac{d^3y}{dx^3}\text{ or } f'''(x).$$

Here, $\dfrac{dy}{dx},\dfrac{d^2y}{dx^2},\dfrac{d^3y}{dx^3},\ldots$ are respectively known as first, second, third, ... order differential coefficients of y with respect to x.

These are alternatively denoted by $f'(x), f''(x), f'''(x),\ldots$ or $y_1, y_2, y_3,\ldots$, respectively.

The process of differentiating a function more than once is called **successive differentiation.**

NOTE $\dfrac{dy}{dx}=\dfrac{dy/d\theta}{dx/d\theta}$ but $\dfrac{d^2y}{dx^2}\neq\dfrac{d^2y/d\theta^2}{d^2x/d\theta^2}$

PYQs Previous Years Questions

1 Mark Question

1. The second derivative of $y=x^3-5x^2+x$ is

ISC Specimen Sem-I 2022

(a) $10x-5$
(b) $6x-10$
(c) $3x^2-10x$
(d) $3x^2-10x+1$

3/4 Marks Questions

2. If $y=3\cos(\log x)+4\sin(\log x)$, show that

$$x^2\frac{d^2y}{dx^2}+x\frac{dy}{dx}+y=0$$

ISC 2024

3. If $x=a\left(\frac{1-t^2}{1+t^2}\right)$ and $y=\frac{2at}{1+t^2}$, prove that $\frac{dy}{dx}=-\frac{x}{y}$.

Hence, prove that $\frac{d^2y}{dx^2}=-\left(\frac{x^2+y^2}{y^3}\right)$. **ISC Specimen 2024**

4. If $y=e^{ax}\cos bx$, then prove that

$$\frac{d^2y}{dx^2}-2a\frac{dy}{dx}+(a^2+b^2)y=0.$$

ISC 2023

5. If $y=(x+\sqrt{1+x^2})^n$, then prove that

$$(1+x^2)\frac{d^2y}{dx^2}+x\frac{dy}{dx}=n^2y.$$

ISC Specimen 2023

6. If $x=\tan\left(\frac{1}{a}\log y\right)$, prove that

$$(1+x^2)\frac{d^2y}{dx^2}+(2x-a)\frac{dy}{dx}=0.$$

ISC Specimen 2021, ISC 2018

7. If $y=e^{m\sin^{-1}x}$, prove that $(1-x^2)\frac{d^2y}{dx^2}-x\frac{dy}{dx}=m^2y$.

ISC 2020

8. If $y=e^{\sin^{-1}x}$ and $z=e^{-\cos^{-1}x}$, prove that $\frac{dy}{dz}=e^{\pi/2}$.

ISC 2019

9. If $y=e^{a\cos^{-1}x}$, where $-1\le x\le 1$, then show that $(1-x^2)y_2-xy_1-a^2y=0$. **ISC Specimen 2018**

10. If $e^{x+y}=xy$, then show that $\frac{dy}{dx}=\frac{y(1-x)}{x(y-1)}$.

ISC 2007

> **KEY CONCEPT**
> Firstly, taking log on both sides, then further differentiate it.

11. If $x^y y^x=5$, then show that $\frac{dy}{dx}=-\left(\frac{\log y+\frac{y}{x}}{\log x+\frac{x}{y}}\right)$.

ISC 2004

12. If $y=(\cos x)^{\cos x}$, then find $\frac{dy}{dx}$.

ISC 2001

> **KEY CONCEPT**
> (i) Firstly, take log on both sides of equation.
> (ii) Use product rule of derivative to get required result.

5 Marks Questions

13. If $y=\cos(\sin x)$, show that

$$\frac{d^2y}{dx^2}+\tan x\frac{dy}{dx}+y\cos^2 x=0.$$

ISC 2017

14. If $\log y=\tan^{-1}x$, then prove that

$$(1+x^2)\frac{d^2y}{dx^2}+(2x-1)\frac{dy}{dx}=0.$$

ISC 2016

15. If $y=e^{m\cos^{-1}x}$, then prove that

$$(1-x^2)\frac{d^2y}{dx^2}-x\frac{dy}{dx}=m^2y.$$

ISC 2015, 13

> **KEY CONCEPT**
> (i) Firstly, taking log on both sides.
> (ii) Use inverse trigonometric differentiation and quotient rule to get required result.

16. If $y=(\cot^{-1}x)^2$, then show that

$$(1+x^2)^2\frac{d^2y}{dx^2}+2x(1+x^2)\frac{dy}{dx}=2.$$

ISC 2013

Explanations

1. (b) Given, $y = x^3 - 5x^2 + x$

On differentiating w.r.t. x, we get

$$\frac{dy}{dx} = \frac{d}{dx}(x^3 - 5x^2 + x)$$

$$= 3x^2 - 5(2x) + 1 = 3x^2 - 10x + 1$$

$$\therefore \quad \frac{dy}{dx} = 3x^2 - 10x + 1$$

Again, on differentiating w.r.t. x, we get

$$\frac{d^2y}{dx^2} = \frac{d}{dx}\left(\frac{dy}{dx}\right)$$

$$= \frac{d}{dx}(3x^2 - 10x + 1)$$

$$= 3(2x) - 10(1) + 0 = 6x - 10$$

2. We have, $y = 3\cos(\log x) + 4\sin(\log x)$ ...(i)

On differentiating w.r.t 'x', we get

$$\frac{dy}{dx} = \frac{-3}{x}\sin(\log x) + \frac{4}{x}\cos(\log x) \quad \text{...(ii)}$$

On multiplying by 'x' both sides, we get

$$x\frac{dy}{dx} = -3\sin(\log x) + 4\cos(\log x) \quad \text{...(iii)}$$

Again, on differentating Eq. (ii) w.r.t x, we get

$$\frac{d^2y}{dx^2} = \frac{3}{x^2}\sin(\log x) - \frac{3}{x^2}\cos(\log x) - \frac{4}{x^2}\cos(\log x) - \frac{4}{x^2}\sin(\log x)$$

On multiplying x^2 both sides, we get

$$x^2\frac{d^2y}{dx^2} = 3\sin(\log x) - 3\cos(\log x) - 4\cos(\log x) - 4\sin(\log x)$$

$$= -[-3\sin(\log x) + 4\cos(\log x)] - [3\cos(\log x) + 4\sin(\log x)]$$

$$\Rightarrow x^2\frac{d^2y}{dx^2} = -x\frac{dy}{dx} - y \quad \text{[using Eqs. (i) and (iii)]}$$

$$\Rightarrow x^2\frac{d^2y}{dx^2} + x\frac{dy}{dx} + y = 0$$

Hence proved.

3. Given, $x = a\left(\frac{1-t^2}{1+t^2}\right)$ and $y = \frac{2at}{1+t^2}$

Let $t = \tan\theta$

$$\therefore \quad x = a\left(\frac{1-\tan^2\theta}{1+\tan^2\theta}\right) = a\cos 2\theta$$

and $y = \frac{2a\tan\theta}{1+\tan^2\theta} = a\sin 2\theta$

Now, $\frac{dy}{dx} = \frac{(dy/d\theta)}{(dx/d\theta)} = \frac{2a\cos 2\theta}{-2a\sin 2\theta} = -\frac{\cos 2\theta}{\sin 2\theta} = -\frac{x}{y}$

Now, $\frac{d^2y}{dx^2} = -\left[\frac{y \times 1 - x\left(\frac{dy}{dx}\right)}{y^2}\right] = -\left[\frac{y - x\left(\frac{-x}{y}\right)}{y^2}\right]$

$$= -\left[\frac{y^2 + x^2}{y^3}\right]$$

$$\frac{d^2y}{dx^2} = -\left(\frac{x^2 + y^2}{y^3}\right)$$

Hence proved.

4. We have, $y = e^{ax}\cos bx$ ...(i)

On differentiating w.r.t. x, we get

$$\frac{dy}{dx} = be^{ax}(-\sin bx) + ae^{ax}\cos bx$$

$$\Rightarrow \frac{dy}{dx} = -be^{ax}\sin bx + ay \quad \text{[from Eq. (i)] ...(ii)}$$

Again, on differentiating w.r.t. x, we get

$$\frac{d^2y}{dx^2} = -b^2e^{ax}\cos bx - abe^{ax}\sin bx + \frac{a\,dy}{dx}$$

$$\Rightarrow \frac{d^2y}{dx^2} = -b^2y + a\left(\frac{dy}{dx} - ay\right) + a\frac{dy}{dx}$$

[from Eqs. (i) and (ii)]

$$\Rightarrow \frac{d^2y}{dx^2} = -b^2y + a\frac{dy}{dx} - a^2y + a\frac{dy}{dx}$$

$$\Rightarrow \frac{d^2y}{dx^2} - 2a\frac{dy}{dx} + (a^2 + b^2)\,y = 0$$

5. Given, $y = (x + \sqrt{1+x^2})^n$

On differentiating both sides w.r.t x, we get

$$\frac{dy}{dx} = n(x + \sqrt{1+x^2})^{n-1}\frac{d}{dx}(x + \sqrt{1+x^2})$$

$$\Rightarrow \frac{dy}{dx} = n(x + \sqrt{1+x^2})^{n-1} \cdot \left(1 + \frac{1 \times 2x}{2\sqrt{1+x^2}}\right)$$

$$\Rightarrow \quad \frac{dy}{dx} = \frac{n(x+\sqrt{1+x^2})^{n-1}(x+\sqrt{1+x^2})}{\sqrt{1+x^2}}$$

$$\Rightarrow \quad \frac{dy}{dx} = \frac{n(x+\sqrt{1+x^2})^n}{\sqrt{1+x^2}} = \frac{ny}{\sqrt{1+x^2}}$$

$$\Rightarrow \quad \sqrt{1+x^2}\frac{dy}{dx} = ny \qquad \ldots\text{(i)}$$

Again, on differentiating both sides w.r.t. x, we get

$$\sqrt{1+x^2}\frac{d^2y}{dx^2} + \frac{1}{2\sqrt{1+x^2}}(2x)\frac{dy}{dx} = n\frac{dy}{dx}$$

$$\Rightarrow \quad \sqrt{1+x^2}\frac{d^2y}{dx^2} + \frac{x}{\sqrt{1+x^2}}\frac{dy}{dx} = \frac{n^2y}{\sqrt{1+x^2}}$$

[on putting $\frac{dy}{dx} = \frac{ny}{\sqrt{1+x^2}}$ from Eq. (i)]

On multiplying both sides with $\sqrt{1+x^2}$, we get

$$(1+x^2)\frac{d^2y}{dx^2} + x\frac{dy}{dx} = n^2y$$ **Hence proved.**

6. Given that $x = \tan\left(\frac{1}{a}\log y\right)$

So, $\tan^{-1}x = \frac{1}{a}\log y$

$$a\tan^{-1}x = \log y$$

On differentiating both sides w.r.t. x, we obtain

$$\frac{a}{1+x^2} = \frac{1}{y}\cdot\frac{dy}{dx}$$

$$\frac{dy}{dx} = \frac{ay}{1+x^2}$$

$$(1+x^2)\frac{dy}{dx} = ay$$

Again, on differentiating both sides w.r.t. x, we obtain

$$(1+x^2)\frac{d^2y}{dx^2} + 2x\frac{dy}{dx} = a\cdot\frac{dy}{dx}$$

$$(1+x^2)\frac{d^2y}{dx^2} + (2x-a)\frac{dy}{dx} = 0$$

7. We have, $y = e^{m\sin^{-1}x}$

Taking log on both sides, we get

$$\log y = \log e^{m\sin^{-1}x}$$

$$\Rightarrow \quad \log y = m\sin^{-1}x\log e$$

$$\Rightarrow \quad \log y = m\sin^{-1}x \qquad [\because \log e = 1]$$

On differentiating w.r.t. x both sides, we get

$$\frac{1}{y}\frac{dy}{dx} = \frac{m}{\sqrt{1-x^2}}$$

$$\Rightarrow \quad \sqrt{1-x^2}\frac{dy}{dx} = my$$

On squaring both sides, we get

$$(1-x^2)\left(\frac{dy}{dx}\right)^2 = m^2y^2$$

On differentiating w.r.t. x both sides, we get

$$(1-x^2)\left(2\frac{dy}{dx}\right)\left(\frac{d^2y}{dx^2}\right) - 2x\left(\frac{dy}{dx}\right)^2 = m^2\left(2y\frac{dy}{dx}\right)$$

On dividing both sides by $\left(2\frac{dy}{dx}\right)$, we get

$$(1-x^2)\frac{d^2y}{dx^2} - x\frac{dy}{dx} = m^2y$$

Hence proved.

8. We have, $y = e^{\sin^{-1}x}$ and $z = e^{-\cos^{-1}x}$

On differentiating both sides w.r.t. x, we get

$$\frac{dy}{dx} = e^{\sin^{-1}x}\frac{d}{dx}(\sin^{-1}x)$$

and $$\frac{dz}{dx} = e^{-\cos^{-1}x}\frac{d}{dx}(-\cos^{-1}x)$$

[using chain rule of derivative]

$$\therefore \quad \frac{dy}{dx} = e^{\sin^{-1}x}\times\frac{1}{\sqrt{1-x^2}}$$

and $$\frac{dz}{dx} = e^{-\cos^{-1}x}\times\left(-\frac{-1}{\sqrt{1-x^2}}\right)$$

$$= e^{-\cos^{-1}x}\times\frac{1}{\sqrt{1-x^2}}$$

$$\therefore \quad \frac{dy}{dz} = \frac{\frac{dy}{dx}}{\frac{dz}{dx}} = \frac{e^{\sin^{-1}x}\times\frac{1}{\sqrt{1-x^2}}}{e^{-\cos^{-1}x}\times\frac{1}{\sqrt{1-x^2}}}$$

$$\Rightarrow \quad \frac{dy}{dz} = e^{\sin^{-1}x+\cos^{-1}x} = e^{\frac{\pi}{2}}$$

$$\left[\because \sin^{-1}x + \cos^{-1}x = \frac{\pi}{2}\right]$$

9. We have, $y = e^{a\cos^{-1}x}$

Taking log on both sides, we get

$$\log y = a\cos^{-1}x\log e \Rightarrow \log y = a\cos^{-1}x$$

On differentiating w.r.t. x, we get

$$\frac{1}{y}\frac{dy}{dx}=-\frac{a}{\sqrt{1-x^2}}$$

$$\Rightarrow \quad \sqrt{1-x^2}\,dy=-ay$$

$$\Rightarrow \quad (1-x^2)\left(\frac{dy}{dx}\right)^2=a^2y^2$$

Again, differentiating w.r.t. x, we get

$$(1-x^2)\,2\left(\frac{dy}{dx}\right)\frac{d^2y}{dx^2}-2x\left(\frac{dy}{dx}\right)^2=a^2\left(2y\frac{dy}{dx}\right)$$

On dividing by $\frac{2dy}{dx}$, we get

$$(1-x^2)\frac{d^2y}{dx^2}-x\frac{dy}{dx}=a^2y$$

$$\Rightarrow (1-x^2)y_2-xy_1-a^2y=0$$ **Hence proved.**

10. Given, $e^{x+y}=xy$

Taking log on both sides, we get

$$x+y=\log_e(xy)=\log_e x+\log_e y$$

$$\left[\because \log_e x^y = y\log_e x,\ \log_e xy=\log_e x+\log_e y\right]$$

On differentiating both sides w.r.t. x, we get

$$1+\frac{dy}{dx}=\frac{d}{dx}(\log_e x)+\frac{d}{dx}(\log_e y)$$

$$\Rightarrow \quad 1+\frac{dy}{dx}=\frac{1}{x}+\frac{d(\log_e y)}{d(y)}\frac{dy}{dx}$$

$$\Rightarrow \quad 1+\frac{dy}{dx}=\frac{1}{x}+\frac{1}{y}\frac{dy}{dx}$$

$$\Rightarrow \quad \left(1-\frac{1}{y}\right)\frac{dy}{dx}=\frac{1}{x}-1\Rightarrow \frac{(y-1)}{y}\frac{dy}{dx}=\frac{1-x}{x}$$

$$\therefore \quad \frac{dy}{dx}=\frac{y\,(1-x)}{x\,(y-1)}$$ **Hence proved.**

11. Given, $x^y y^x=5$

Taking log on both sides, we get

$$\log x^y y^x=\log 5$$

$$\Rightarrow \quad \log x^y+\log y^x=\log 5$$

$$[\because \log(mn)=\log m+\log n]$$

$$\Rightarrow \quad y\log x+x\log y=\log 5$$

On differentiating both sides w.r.t. x, we get

$$y\cdot\frac{1}{x}+\log x\frac{dy}{dx}+\log y+\frac{x}{y}\frac{dy}{dx}=0$$

[using product rule of derivative]

$$\Rightarrow \quad \frac{dy}{dx}\left(\log x+\frac{x}{y}\right)=-\log y-\frac{y}{x}$$

$$\Rightarrow \quad \frac{dy}{dx}=-\frac{\left(\frac{y}{x}+\log y\right)}{\left(\frac{x}{y}+\log x\right)}$$ **Hence proved.**

12. Given, $y=(\cos x)^{\cos x}$

Taking log on both sides, we get

$$\log y=\cos x\log(\cos x)$$

On differentiating both sides w.r.t. x, we get

$$\frac{1}{y}\frac{dy}{dx}=\cos x\frac{d}{dx}\log(\cos x)+\log(\cos x)\frac{d}{dx}(\cos x)$$

[using product rule of derivative]

$$\Rightarrow \quad \frac{1}{y}\frac{dy}{dx}=\cos x\frac{d[\log(\cos x)]}{d(\cos x)}\times\frac{d(\cos x)}{dx}-\sin x\log(\cos x)$$

$$\Rightarrow \quad \frac{1}{y}\frac{dy}{dx}=\frac{\cos x}{\cos x}\times(-\sin x)-\sin x\log(\cos x)$$

$$\left[\because \frac{d}{dx}(\log y)=\frac{1}{y}\cdot\frac{dy}{dx}\right]$$

$$\Rightarrow \quad \frac{1}{y}\frac{dy}{dx}=-\sin x-\sin x\log(\cos x)$$

$$\Rightarrow \quad \frac{dy}{dx}=y[-\sin x-\sin x\log(\cos x)]$$

$$\therefore \quad \frac{dy}{dx}=(\cos x)^{\cos x}[-\sin x\{1+\log(\cos x)\}]$$

$$[\text{put } y=(\cos x)^{\cos x}]$$

13. Given, $y=\cos(\sin x)$ ...(i)

On differentiating both sides w.r.t. x, we get

$$\frac{dy}{dx}=\frac{d}{dx}\cos(\sin x)=\frac{d\{\cos(\sin x)\}}{d(\sin x)}\times\frac{d(\sin x)}{dx}$$

$$=-\sin(\sin x)\times\cos x \quad \text{...(ii)}$$

On differentiating again w.r.t. x, we get

$$\frac{d^2y}{dx^2}=\frac{d}{dx}\{-\sin(\sin x)\cos x\}$$

$$=\cos x\frac{d\{-\sin(\sin x)\}}{d(\sin x)}\times\frac{d(\sin x)}{dx}+\{-\sin(\sin x)\}\frac{d(\cos x)}{dx}$$

$$=\cos x\{-\cos(\sin x)\times\cos x\}-\sin(\sin x)(-\sin x)$$

$$=-\cos^2 x\cos(\sin x)+\sin x\cdot\sin(\sin x)$$

...(iii)

Now, LHS $= \dfrac{d^2y}{dx^2} + \tan x \dfrac{dy}{dx} + y\cos^2 x$

$$= -\cos^2 x \cdot \cos(\sin x) + \sin x \cdot \sin(\sin x) + \tan x\{-\sin(\sin x)\cdot \cos x\} + \cos(\sin x)\cdot \cos^2 x$$

[from Eqs. (i), (ii) and (iii)]

$$= \sin x \cdot \sin(\sin x) - \frac{\sin x}{\cos x}\cdot \{\sin(\sin x)\cdot \cos x\}$$

$\left[\because \tan\theta = \dfrac{\sin\theta}{\cos\theta}\right]$

$$= \sin x \cdot \sin(\sin x) - \sin x \cdot \sin(\sin x)$$

$= 0 =$ RHS **Hence proved.**

14. Given, $\log y = \tan^{-1} x$

On differentiating both sides w.r.t. x, we get

$$\frac{1}{y}\cdot\frac{dy}{dx} = \frac{1}{1+x^2}$$

$$\Rightarrow \quad \frac{dy}{dx} = \frac{y}{1+x^2} \Rightarrow (1+x^2)\frac{dy}{dx} = y$$

Again, on differentiating w.r.t. x, we get

$$(1+x^2)\frac{d^2y}{dx^2} + \frac{dy}{dx}(2x) = \frac{dy}{dx}$$

$$\Rightarrow \quad (1+x^2)\frac{d^2y}{dx^2} + (2x-1)\frac{dy}{dx} = 0$$

Hence proved.

15. Given, $y = e^{m\cos^{-1}x}$ ...(i)

Taking log on both sides, we get

$\log y = m\cos^{-1}x$ $[\because \log_e e = 1]$

On differentiating both sides w.r.t. x, we get

$$\frac{1}{y}\frac{dy}{dx} = m \times \left(\frac{-1}{\sqrt{1-x^2}}\right) \Rightarrow \frac{dy}{dx} = \frac{-me^{m\cos^{-1}x}}{\sqrt{1-x^2}} \quad \text{...(ii)}$$

$[\text{put } y = e^{m\cos^{-1}x}]$

On differentiating both sides w.r.t. x, we get

$$\frac{d^2y}{dx^2} = -m\left[\frac{\sqrt{1-x^2}\dfrac{d}{dx}(e^{m\cos^{-1}x}) - e^{m\cos^{-1}x}\dfrac{d}{dx}(\sqrt{1-x^2})}{(\sqrt{1-x^2})^2}\right]$$

$$\left[\because \frac{d}{dx}\left\{\frac{f(x)}{g(x)}\right\} = \frac{g(x)f'(x) - f(x)g'(x)}{\{g(x)\}^2}\right]$$

$$\Rightarrow \frac{d^2y}{dx^2} = -m\left[\frac{\sqrt{1-x^2}\,(e^{m\cos^{-1}x})\dfrac{d}{dx}(m\cos^{-1}x) - e^{m\cos^{-1}x} \times \dfrac{\frac{d}{dx}(1-x^2)}{2\sqrt{1-x^2}}}{(\sqrt{1-x^2})^2}\right]$$

$$\Rightarrow \frac{d^2y}{dx^2} = -m\left[\frac{-\dfrac{\sqrt{1-x^2}\times me^{m\cos^{-1}x}}{\sqrt{1-x^2}} + e^{m\cos^{-1}x} \times \dfrac{2x}{2\sqrt{1-x^2}}}{1-x^2}\right]$$

$$\Rightarrow (1-x^2)\frac{d^2y}{dx^2} = -\frac{mx\,e^{m\cos^{-1}x}}{\sqrt{1-x^2}} + m^2e^{m\cos^{-1}x}$$

$$\Rightarrow (1-x^2)\frac{d^2y}{dx^2} = x\frac{dy}{dx} + m^2 y \quad \text{[using Eqs. (i) and (ii)]}$$

$$\therefore \quad (1-x^2)\frac{d^2y}{dx^2} - x\frac{dy}{dx} = m^2 y$$

Hence proved.

16. Given, $y = (\cot^{-1} x)^2$

On differentiating both sides w.r.t. x, we get

$$\frac{dy}{dx} = 2(\cot^{-1}x)^{2-1}\frac{d}{dx}(\cot^{-1}x)$$

[using chain rule of derivative]

$$\Rightarrow \quad \frac{dy}{dx} = 2\cot^{-1}x \times \left(\frac{-1}{1+x^2}\right)$$

$$\Rightarrow \quad (1+x^2)\frac{dy}{dx} = -2\cot^{-1}x$$

Again, on differentiating w.r.t. x, we get

$$(1+x^2)\frac{d^2y}{dx^2} + 2x\frac{dy}{dx} = -2\times\left(\frac{-1}{1+x^2}\right)$$

$$\Rightarrow \quad (1+x^2)^2\frac{d^2y}{dx^2} + 2x(1+x^2)\frac{dy}{dx} = 2$$

Hence proved.

CHAPTER TEST

1 Mark Questions

1. If $y = \log x^x$, then the value of $\frac{dy}{dx}$ is

(a) $x^x (1 + \log x)$ (b) $\log ex$

(c) $\log \frac{e}{x}$ (d) $\log \left(\frac{x}{e}\right)$

2. If $f(x) = \begin{cases} mx + 1, \text{ if } x \le \frac{\pi}{2} \\ \sin x + n, \text{ if } x > \frac{\pi}{2} \end{cases}$ is continuous at $x = \frac{\pi}{2}$, then

(a) $m = 1, n = 0$ (b) $m = \frac{n\pi}{2} + 1$

(c) $n = \frac{m\pi}{2}$ (d) $m = n = \frac{\pi}{2}$

3. If $y = \log_7 (\log x)$, then $\frac{dy}{dx}$ is equal to

(a) $\frac{1}{x \log x \log 7}$ (b) $\frac{-1}{x \log x \log 7}$

(c) $\frac{1}{x \log x}$ (d) None of these

4. If $f(x) = |\cos x|$, then

(a) f is everywhere differentiable

(b) f is everywhere continuous but not differentiable at $x = n\pi, n \in Z$

(c) f is everywhere continuous but not differentiable at $x = (2n+1)\frac{\pi}{2}, n \in Z$

(d) None of the above

2 Marks Questions

5. Find the derivative of $xe^x \sin x$ w.r.t. x.

6. Differentiate $\frac{a^x}{1 + a^x}$ w.r.t. a^x.

7. Find the second derivative of function $y = \log \log x$.

3/4 Marks Questions

8. Determine the value of k for which the following function is continuous at $x = 3$

$$f(x) = \begin{cases} \frac{(x+3)^2 - 36}{x - 3}, & x \ne 3 \\ k, & x = 3 \end{cases}$$

9. Find the values of a and b such that the function defined as follows is continuous.

$$f(x) = \begin{cases} x + 2, & x \le 2 \\ ax + b, & 2 < x < 5 \\ 3x - 2, & x \ge 5 \end{cases}$$

10. If $y = 3\cos(\log x) + 4\sin(\log x)$, then show that $x^2 y_2 + xy_1 + y = 0$.

5/6 Marks Questions

11. Differentiate the following function w.r.t. x,

$$\tan^{-1}\left(\frac{\sqrt{1+x} - \sqrt{1-x}}{\sqrt{1+x} + \sqrt{1-x}}\right).$$

12. If $y = (\tan^{-1} x)^2$, then show that

$$(x^2 + 1)^2 \frac{d^2 y}{dx^2} + 2x(x^2 + 1)\frac{dy}{dx} = 2.$$

13. If $\sin y = x \sin(a + y)$, then prove that $\frac{dy}{dx} = \frac{\sin^2(a + y)}{\sin a}$.

Answers

1. (b) **2.** (c) **3.** (a) **4.** (c)

5. $xe^x \cos x + (x+1)e^x \sin x$ **6.** $\frac{1}{(1 + a^x)^2}$

7. $\frac{-(1 + \log x)}{(x \log x)^2}$ **8.** $k = 12$

9. $a = 3, b = -2$ **11.** $\frac{1}{2\sqrt{1 - x^2}}$

06

Application of Derivatives

TREND ANALYSIS 3 YEARS

Topic	Average No. of Questions Across all Sets			
	Types of Questions	2024	2023	2020
TOPIC 01 Rate Measure and Increasing-Decreasing Functions	1 Mark	2	1	—
	2 Marks	—	—	1
	3/4 Marks	—	—	—
	5/6 Marks	—	—	—
TOPIC 02 Tangents and Normals	1 Mark	—	1	—
	2 Marks	1	—	—
	3/4 Marks	—	—	1
	5/6 Marks	—	—	—
TOPIC 03 Maxima and Minima	1 Mark	—	—	—
	2 Marks	—	—	—
	3/4 Marks	—	—	—
	5/6 Marks	2	2	1

TOPIC 1

Rate Measure and Increasing-Decreasing Functions

Rate of Change of Quantities

Let $y = f(x)$ be a function of x. Then, $\frac{dy}{dx}$ represents the rate of change of y with respect to x.

Also, $\left(\frac{dy}{dx}\right)_{\text{at } x=x_0}$ represents the rate of change of y with respect to x at $x = x_0$.

Rate of Change of Two Variables

If two variables x and y are varying with respect to another variable t i.e. $x = f(t)$ and $y = g(t)$, then

$$\frac{dy}{dx} = \frac{dy}{dt} \Big/ \frac{dx}{dt}$$

where, $\frac{dx}{dt} \neq 0$.

In other words, the rate of change of y with respect to x can be calculated using the rate of change of y and that of x both with respect to t.

NOTE $\frac{dy}{dx}$ is positive, if y increases as x increases and it is negative, if y decreases as x decreases.

Increasing and Decreasing Functions

1. Let I be an open interval contained in the domain of a real valued function f. Then, f is said to be
   (i) **increasing on I,** if $x_1 < x_2$ in I
   $\Rightarrow f(x_1) \le f(x_2), \forall x_1, x_2 \in I.$
   (ii) **strictly increasing on I,** if $x_1 < x_2$ in I
   $\Rightarrow f(x_1) < f(x_2), \forall x_1, x_2 \in I.$
   (iii) **decreasing on I,** if $x_1 < x_2$ in I
   $\Rightarrow f(x_1) \ge f(x_2), \forall x_1, x_2 \in I.$
   (iv) **strictly decreasing on I,** if $x_1 < x_2$ in I
   $\Rightarrow f(x_1) > f(x_2), \forall x_1, x_2 \in I.$

NOTE For a given interval $I \subseteq R$, function f increase for some values in I and decrease for other values in I, then we say function is neither increasing nor decreasing.

2. Let f be continuous on $[a, b]$ and differentiable on the open interval (a, b).
   Then,
   (i) f is increasing in $[a, b]$, if $f'(x) > 0$ for each $x \in (a, b)$.
   (ii) f is decreasing in $[a, b]$, if $f'(x) < 0$ for each $x \in (a, b)$.
   (iii) f is a constant function in $[a, b]$, if $f'(x) = 0$ for each $x \in (a, b)$.

NOTE (i) f is strictly increasing in (a,b), if $f'(x) > 0$ for each $x \in (a,b)$.
(ii) f is strictly decreasing in (a,b), if $f'(x) < 0$ for each $x \in (a,b)$.

Monotonic Function

A function which is either increasing or decreasing in a given interval I, is called monotonic function.

PYQs Previous Years Questions

1 Mark Questions

1. In which one of the following intervals is the function $f(x) = x^3 - 12x$ increasing? **ISC 2024**

(a) $(-2, 2)$
(b) $(-\infty, -2) \cup (2, \infty)$
(c) $(-2, \infty)$
(d) $(-\infty, 2)$

2. Given that $\frac{1}{y} + \frac{1}{x} = \frac{1}{12}$ and y decreases at a rate of $1\ \text{cms}^{-1}$, find the rate of change of x when $x = 5$ cm and $y = 1$ cm. **ISC 2024**

3. The interval in which the function $f(x) = 5 + 36x - 3x^2$ increases will be **ISC 2023**

(a) $(-\infty, 6)$ (b) $(6, \infty)$
(c) $(-6, 6)$ (d) $(0, -6)$

4. The function $f(x) = x^3 - 3x$ is strictly decreasing on **ISC Specimen 2021**

(a) $-1 < x < 1$ (b) $-1 \le x \le 1$
(c) $1 \le x < \infty$ (d) $-\infty < x < -1$

2 Marks Questions

5. If $f(x) = x^3 - 48x$, find the interval where $f: R \to R$ is decreasing. **ISC Specimen 2024**

6. The edge of a variable cube is increasing at the rate of 10 cm/s. How fast is the volume of the cube increasing when the edge is 5 cm long? **ISC 2020**

7. Prove that the function $f(x) = x^3 - 6x^2 + 12x + 5$ is increasing on R. **ISC 2019**

8. Find the intervals in which the function $f(x)$ is strictly increasing where, $f(x) = 10 - 6x - 2x^2$. **ISC Specimen 2018**

3/4 Marks Questions

9. A 13 m long ladder is leaning against a wall, touching the wall at a certain height from the ground level. The bottom of the ladder is pulled away from the wall, along the ground, at the rate of 2 m/s. How fast is the height on the wall decreasing when the foot of the ladder is 5 m away from the wall? **ISC 2019**

10. Water is dripping out from a conical funnel of semi-verticle angle $\frac{\pi}{4}$ at the uniform rate of 2 cm^2/s in the surface, through a tiny hole at the vertex of the bottom. When the slant height of the water level is 4 cm, find the rate of decrease of the slant height of the water. *ISC 2018*

11. A circular disc of radius 3 cm is heated. Due to expansion its radius increases at the rate of 0.05 cm/s. Find the rate at which its area increases when the radius is 3.2 cm. *ISC Specimen 2018*

12. The side of an equilateral triangle is increasing at the rate of 2 cm/s. At what rate is its area increasing, when the side of the triangle is 20 cm?

13. Find the intervals in which the function $f(x)=3x^4-4x^3-12x^2+5$ is
(i) strictly increasing.
(ii) strictly decreasing.

14. Find the value(s) of x for which $y=[x(x-2)]^2$ is an increasing function.

15. A ladder 5 m long is leaning against a wall. Bottom of ladder is pulled along the ground away from wall at the rate of 2 m/s. How fast is the height on the wall decreasing, when the foot of ladder is 4 m away from the wall?

> **KEY CONCEPT**
> Firstly, draw a rough figure of a right angled triangle, then use Pythagoras theorem. Further differentiate the relation between sides with respect to t and simplify it.

16. Show that $y=\log(1+x)-\frac{2x}{2+x}, x>-1$ is an increasing function of x, throughout its domain.

17. Find the intervals in which the function given by $f(x)=\sin x+\cos x, 0\le x\le 2\pi$ is
(i) increasing.
(ii) decreasing.

18. Sand is pouring from the pipe at the rate of 12 cm^3/s. The falling sand forms a cone on a ground in such a way that the height of cone is always one-sixth of radius of the base. How fast is the height of sand cone increasing when the height is 4 cm?

19. Find the intervals in which the function $f(x)=(x-1)^3(x-2)^2$ is
(i) increasing.
(ii) decreasing.

20. Find the intervals in which the function $f(x)=2x^3+9x^2+12x+20$ is
(i) increasing.
(ii) decreasing.

21. The length x of a rectangle is decreasing at the rate of 5 cm/min and the width y is increasing at the rate of 4 cm/min. When $x=8$ cm and $y=6$ cm, find the rate of change of
(i) the perimeter.
(ii) area of rectangle.

> **KEY CONCEPT**
> Using the relation perimeter of rectangle, $P=2(x+y)$ and area of rectangle, $A=xy$, differentiate both sides with respect to t and put them in rate of change value and get the result.

5/6 Marks Questions

22. Prove that $y=\frac{4\sin\theta}{2+\cos\theta}-\theta$ is an strictly increasing function in $\left(0,\frac{\pi}{2}\right)$.

> **KEY CONCEPT**
> To prove that given function is increasing, prove that $\frac{dy}{d\theta}>0$, for all values of x.

23. Find the intervals in which the function $f(x)=\sin 3x-\cos 3x, 0<x<\pi$, is strictly increasing or strictly decreasing.

24. Prove that the function f defined by $f(x)=x^2-x+1$ is neither increasing nor decreasing in (–1, 1). Hence, find the intervals in which $f(x)$ is
(i) strictly increasing.
(ii) strictly decreasing.

Explanations

1. (b) We have, $f(x) = x^3 - 12x$

$$f'(x) = 3x^2 - 12$$

For increasing,

$$f'(x) > 0$$
$$3x^2 - 12 > 0$$
$$3(x^2 - 4) > 0$$
$$3(x-2)(x+2) > 0$$

Now, sign of $f'(x)$

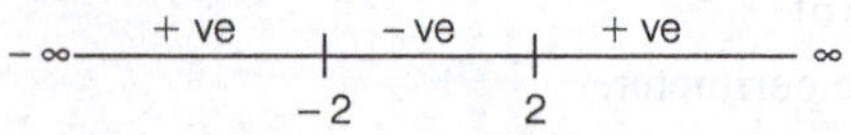

Function is increasing on $(-\infty, -2)$ and $(2, \infty)$.

Hence, the function is increasing in the interval $(-\infty, -2) \cup (2, \infty)$.

2. We have, $\frac{1}{y} + \frac{1}{x} = \frac{1}{12}$ ...(i)

and $\frac{dy}{dt} = -1$ cm/s

On differentiating Eq. (i) w.r.t. 't', we get

$$-\frac{1}{y^2}\frac{dy}{dt} - \frac{1}{x^2}\frac{dx}{dt} = 0$$

$$\Rightarrow \frac{1}{y^2} - \frac{1}{x^2}\frac{dx}{dt} = 0 \quad \left[\because \frac{dy}{dt} = -1\right]$$

$$\Rightarrow \frac{dx}{dt} = \frac{x^2}{y^2}$$

When $x = 5$ cm and $y = 1$ cm, then

$$\frac{dx}{dt} = \frac{5^2}{1^2} = 25 \text{ cm/s}$$

Hence, the rate of change of x i.e. $\frac{dx}{dt}$ is 25 cm/s.

3. (a) Given, $f(x) = 5 + 36x - 3x^2$

$$f'(x) = 36 - 6x$$

$f(x)$ increases.

$\therefore \quad f'(x) > 0 \Rightarrow 36 - 6x > 0$

$\Rightarrow \quad x < 6$

$\therefore \quad x \in (-\infty, 6)$

4. (a) Let $f(x) = x^3 - 3x$

So, $f'(x) = 3x^2 - 3$

For decreasing, $f(x) < 0$

Hence, $3x^2 - 3 < 0$ i.e. $x^2 - 1 < 0 \Rightarrow (x-1)(x+1) < 0$

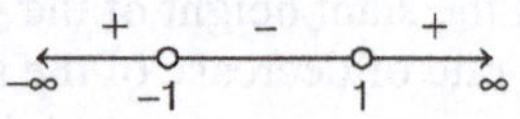

which is valid if $-1 < x < 1$.

5. We have, $f(x) = x^3 - 48x$

$\therefore \quad f'(x) = 3x^2 - 48 = 3(x^2 - 16)$

Now, for $f(x)$ to be decreasing,

$$f'(x) \le 0$$

$\therefore \quad 3(x^2 - 16) \le 0$

$\Rightarrow \quad x^2 - 16 \le 0$

$\Rightarrow \quad (x-4)(x+4) \le 0$

$\Rightarrow \quad x \in [-4, 4]$

6. Let x be the edge of cube and V be it's volume.

Given, $\frac{dx}{dt} = 10$ cm/s

Now, $V = x^3$

$$\Rightarrow \frac{dV}{dt} = 3x^2 \frac{dx}{dt}$$

To find $\frac{dV}{dt}$, when $x = 5$ is given by

$$\left(\frac{dV}{dt}\right)_{x=5} = 3(5)^2(10) \quad \left[\because \frac{dx}{dt} = 10 \text{ cm/s}\right]$$

$$\Rightarrow \frac{dV}{dt} = 750 \text{ cm}^3\text{/s}$$

Thus, the volume of cube is increasing at the rate of 750 cm^3/s.

7. We have, $f(x) = x^3 - 6x^2 + 12x + 5$

On differentiating both sides w.r.t. x, we get

$$f'(x) = 3x^2 - 12x + 12$$
$$= 3(x^2 - 4x + 4)$$
$$= 3(x-2)^2 \ge 0$$

$\therefore \; f'(x) \ge 0, \forall x \in R$

Hence, $f(x)$ is an increasing function.

8. We have, $f(x) = 10 - 6x - 2x^2$

On differentiating w.r.t. x, we get

$$f'(x) = -6 - 4x$$

$f(x)$ is strictly increasing, if

$$f'(x) > 0$$

$\because \quad -6-4x>0$

$\Rightarrow \quad 4x+6<0$

$\Rightarrow \quad x<\dfrac{-3}{2}$

Hence, $f(x)$ is strictly increasing when $x \in \left(-\infty, \dfrac{-3}{2}\right)$.

9. Let $AC=13$ m be the length of ladder and AB be the distance of the ladder from the wall at any time t, such that $AB=x$ and $BC=y$.

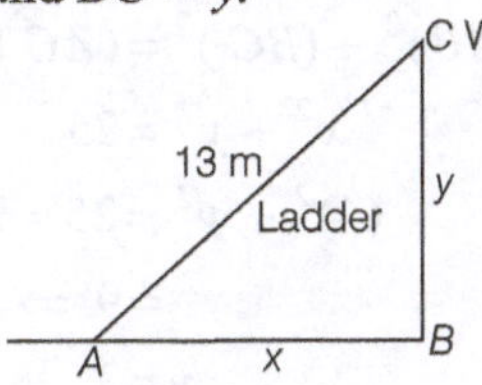

Given, $x=5$ m and $\dfrac{dx}{dt}=2$ m/s

In right angled ΔABC, we get

$$AB^2+BC^2=AC^2 \quad \text{[by Pythagoras theorem]}$$

$$\therefore \quad x^2+y^2=(13)^2 \Rightarrow x^2+y^2=169 \quad \text{...(i)}$$

When $x=5$, then

$$5^2+y^2=169$$

$$\Rightarrow \quad y^2=169-25=144 \Rightarrow y=12$$

On differentiating Eq. (i) w.r.t. t, we get

$$2x\frac{dx}{dt}+2y\frac{dy}{dt}=0 \Rightarrow x\frac{dx}{dt}+y\frac{dy}{dt}=0$$

$$\Rightarrow \quad 5\times 2+12\times\frac{dy}{dt}=0 \Rightarrow \frac{dy}{dt}=\frac{-10}{12}=-\frac{5}{6}\text{ m/s}$$

Hence, the height of ladder on the wall is decreasing at the rate of $\dfrac{5}{6}$ m/s, when ladder is 5 m away from the wall.

10. Let r be the radius, l be the slant height, α be the semi-vertical angle of the cone and S be the curved surface area of the cone.

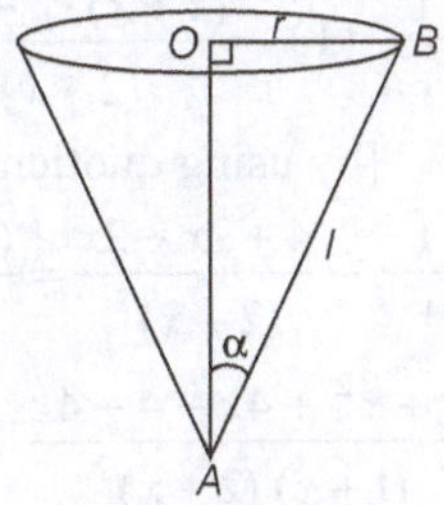

Given, $\dfrac{dS}{dt}=-2\text{ cm}^2/\text{s}$, $l=4$ cm and $\alpha=\dfrac{\pi}{4}$

In ΔOAB,

$$\sin\alpha=\frac{r}{l} \Rightarrow \sin\frac{\pi}{4}=\frac{r}{l} \Rightarrow r=\frac{l}{\sqrt{2}}$$

$\therefore$ Curved surface area of cone $=\pi rl$

i.e. $$S=\pi rl=\frac{\pi l^2}{\sqrt{2}} \quad \left[\because r=\frac{l}{\sqrt{2}}\right]$$

On differentiating w.r.t. t, we get

$$\frac{dS}{dt}=\frac{2}{\sqrt{2}}\pi l\frac{dl}{dt}$$

$$\Rightarrow \quad -2=\frac{2}{\sqrt{2}}\pi(4)\frac{dl}{dt} \Rightarrow \frac{dl}{dt}=\frac{-\sqrt{2}}{4\pi}\text{ cm/s}$$

Hence, the rate at which the water level decreasing is $\dfrac{\sqrt{2}}{4\pi}$ cm/s.

11. Let r be the radius of circular disc and A be the area of circular disc.

Also, rate of change of radius with respect to time is 0.05 cm/s.

$$\because \quad \frac{dr}{dt}=0.05$$

Now, $A=\pi r^2$

On differentiating w.r.t. t both side, we get

$$\frac{dA}{dt}=\pi(2r)\frac{dr}{dt} \Rightarrow \frac{dA}{dt}=2\pi r(0.05)=0.1\pi r$$

When radius $r=3.2$ cm

$$\frac{dA}{dt}=0.1\pi(3.2)=0.32\pi\text{ cm}^2/\text{s}$$

Hence, the required rate of increase of the area is 0.32π cm^2/s.

12. Let a be the side of an equilateral triangle and A be the area of an equilateral triangle.

Then, $\dfrac{da}{dt}=2$ cm/s

We know that area of an equilateral triangle,

$$A=\frac{\sqrt{3}}{4}a^2$$

On differentiating both sides w.r.t. t, we get

$$\frac{dA}{dt}=\frac{\sqrt{3}}{4}\times 2a\times\frac{da}{dt}$$

$$\Rightarrow \quad \frac{dA}{dt}=\frac{\sqrt{3}}{4}\times 2\times 20\times 2 \quad \text{[given, } a=20\text{]}$$

$$\therefore \quad \frac{dA}{dt}=20\sqrt{3}\text{ cm}^2/\text{s}$$

Thus, the rate of area increasing is $20\sqrt{3}$ cm^2/s.

13. Given, function is

$$f(x)=3x^4-4x^3-12x^2+5$$

On differentiating both sides w.r.t. x, we get

$$f'(x)=12x^3-12x^2-24x$$

For strictly increasing or strictly decreasing, putting $f'(x)=0$, we get

$$12x^3-12x^2-24x=0$$
$$\Rightarrow \quad 12x(x^2-x-2)=0$$
$$\Rightarrow \quad 12x[x^2-2x+x-2]=0$$
$$12x(x+1)(x-2)=0$$
$$\therefore \quad x=0,-1 \text{ or } 2$$

Now, we find intervals in which $f(x)$ is strictly increasing or strictly decreasing.

Interval	$f'(x)=12x(x+1)(x-2)$	Sign of $f'(x)$
$x<-1$	(–)(–)(–)	– ve
$-1<x<0$	(–)(+)(–)	+ ve
$0<x<2$	(+)(+)(–)	– ve
$x>2$	(+)(+)(+)	+ ve

We know that a function $f(x)$ is said to be strictly increasing, if $f'(x)>0$ and it is said to be strictly decreasing, if $f'(x)<0$. So, the given function $f(x)$ is

(i) strictly increasing on the intervals $(-1, 0)$ and $(2, \infty)$.

(ii) strictly decreasing on the intervals $(-\infty, -1)$ and $(0, 2)$.

14. Given, function is $y=[x(x-2)]^2=[x^2-2x]^2$

On differentiating both sides w.r.t. x, we get

$$\frac{dy}{dx}=2(x^2-2x)\frac{d}{dx}(x^2-2x)$$
$$=2(x^2-2x)(2x-2)=4x(x-2)(x-1)$$

On putting $\frac{dy}{dx}=0$, we get

$$4x(x-2)(x-1)=0 \Rightarrow x=0,1 \text{ and } 2$$

Now, we find interval in which $f(x)$ is strictly increasing or strictly decreasing.

Interval	$\frac{dy}{dx}=4x(x-2)(x-1)$	Sign of $f'(x)$
$(-\infty, 0)$	(–)(–)(–)	– ve
$(0, 1)$	(+)(–)(–)	+ ve
$(1, 2)$	(+)(–)(+)	– ve
$(2, \infty)$	(+)(+)(+)	+ ve

Hence, y is strictly increasing in $(0, 1)$ and $(2, \infty)$.
Also, y is a polynomial function, so it continuous at $x=0$, 1 and 2.
Hence, y is increasing in $[0,1]\cup[2,\infty)$.

15. Let AC be the ladder, BC be x. and height of the wall, AB be y.

As the ladder is pulled along the ground away from the wall at the rate of 2 m/s.

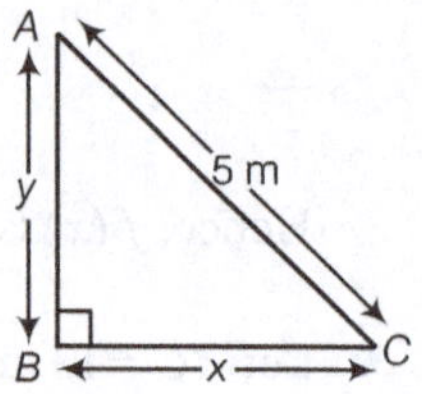

So, $\frac{dx}{dt}=2$ m/s

To find $\frac{dy}{dt}$, when $x=4$.

In right angled ΔABC, by Pythagoras theorem, we get

$$(AB)^2+(BC)^2=(AC)^2$$
$$\Rightarrow \quad x^2+y^2=25 \quad \text{...(i)}$$
$$\Rightarrow \quad (4)^2+y^2=25 \Rightarrow 16+y^2=25$$
$$\Rightarrow \quad y^2=9 \Rightarrow y=\sqrt{9}$$
$$\therefore \quad y=3$$

On differentiating both sides of Eq. (i) w.r.t. t, we get

$$2x\frac{dx}{dt}+2y\frac{dy}{dt}=0$$
$$\Rightarrow \quad x\frac{dx}{dt}+y\frac{dy}{dt}=0 \quad \text{...(ii)}$$

[dividing both sides by 2]

On substituting the values of x, y and $\frac{dx}{dt}$ in Eq. (ii), we get

$$(4\times 2)+3\times\frac{dy}{dt}=0 \Rightarrow 8+3\times\frac{dy}{dt}=0$$
$$\therefore \quad \frac{dy}{dt}=\frac{-8}{3} \text{ m/s}$$

Hence, the height of the wall is decreasing at the rate of $\frac{8}{3}$ m/s.

NOTE In a rate of change of a quantity, +ve sign shows that it is increasing and – ve sign shows that it is decreasing.

16. Given, function is $y=\log(1+x)-\frac{2x}{2+x}$.

On differentiating both sides w.r.t. x, we get

$$\frac{dy}{dx}=\frac{1}{1+x}(1)-\frac{(2+x)\cdot 2-2x\cdot 1}{(2+x)^2}$$

[by using quotient rule of derivative]

$$=\frac{1}{1+x}-\frac{4+2x-2x}{(2+x)^2}=\frac{(2+x)^2-4(1+x)}{(1+x)(2+x)^2}$$
$$=\frac{4+x^2+4x-4-4x}{(1+x)(2+x)^2}$$
$$\Rightarrow \quad \frac{dy}{dx}=\frac{x^2}{(1+x)(2+x)^2} \quad \text{...(i)}$$

Now, x^2, $(2+x)^2$ are always positive, also $1+x>0$ for $x>-1$.

From Eq. (i), $\frac{dy}{dx}>0$ for $x>-1$.

Hence, the function increases for $x>-1$.

Common Mistake Square of any positive or negative number gives always positive, so never take negative for any square result.

In expression $\frac{x^2}{(1+x)(2+x)^2}$, x^2 and $(2+x)^2$ are always positive, also $1+x>0$ for $x>-1$.

17. Given, function is $f(x)=\sin x+\cos x$.

On differentiating both sides w.r.t. x, we get

$$f'(x)=\cos x-\sin x$$

Now, put $f'(x)=0 \Rightarrow \cos x-\sin x=0$

$$\Rightarrow \tan x=1 \Rightarrow x=\frac{\pi}{4}, \frac{5\pi}{4}, \text{ as } 0\le x\le 2\pi$$

Now, we find the intervals in which $f(x)$ is strictly increasing or strictly decreasing.

Interval	Test value	$f'(x) = \cos x - \sin x$	Sign of $f'(x)$
$0<x<\frac{\pi}{4}$	At $x=\frac{\pi}{6}$	$\cos\frac{\pi}{6}-\sin\frac{\pi}{6} = \frac{\sqrt{3}}{2}-\frac{1}{2}=\frac{\sqrt{3}-1}{2}$	+ve
$\frac{\pi}{4}<x<\frac{5\pi}{4}$	At $x=\frac{\pi}{2}$	$\cos\frac{\pi}{2}-\sin\frac{\pi}{2} =0-1=-1$	−ve
$\frac{5\pi}{4}<x<2\pi$	At $x=\frac{3\pi}{2}$	$\cos\frac{3\pi}{2}-\sin\frac{3\pi}{2} =0-(-1)=1$	+ve

Here, we see that $f'(x)>0$ in $\left(0,\frac{\pi}{4}\right)$, $f'(x)<0$ in $\left(\frac{\pi}{4},\frac{5\pi}{4}\right)$ and $f'(x)>0$ in $\left(\frac{5\pi}{4},2\pi\right)$.

Since, $f(x)$ is a trigonometric function, so it is continuous at $x=0, \frac{\pi}{4}, \frac{5\pi}{4}$ and 2π.

Hence, the function is

(i) increasing in $\left[0,\frac{\pi}{4}\right]$ and $\left[\frac{5\pi}{4},2\pi\right]$.

(ii) decreasing in $\left[\frac{\pi}{4},\frac{5\pi}{4}\right]$.

18. Let V be the volume of cone, h be the height and r be the radius of base of the cone.

Given, $\frac{dV}{dt}=12\text{ cm}^3/\text{s}$ ...(i)

Also, height of cone = 1/6 (radius of base of cone)

$$\therefore \quad h=\frac{1}{6}r \quad\text{or}\quad r=6h \qquad \text{...(ii)}$$

We know that volume of cone is given by

$$V=\frac{1}{3}\pi r^2 h \qquad \text{...(iii)}$$

On putting $r=6h$ from Eq. (ii) in Eq. (iii), we get

$$V=\frac{1}{3}\pi(6h)^2\cdot h \Rightarrow V=\frac{\pi}{3}\cdot 36h^3$$

$$\Rightarrow \quad V=12\pi h^3$$

On differentiating both sides w.r.t. t, we get

$$\frac{dV}{dt}=12\pi\times 3h^2\cdot\frac{dh}{dt}$$

$$\Rightarrow \quad \frac{dV}{dt}=36\pi h^2\cdot\frac{dh}{dt}$$

On putting $\frac{dV}{dt}=12\text{ cm}^3/\text{s}$ and $h=4$ cm, we get

$$12=36\pi\times 16\times\frac{dh}{dt} \Rightarrow \frac{dh}{dt}=\frac{12}{36\pi\times 16}$$

$$\therefore \quad \frac{dh}{dt}=\frac{1}{48\pi}\text{ cm/s}$$

Hence, the height of sand cone is increasing at the rate of $1/48\pi$ cm/s.

19. Given, $f(x)=(x-1)^3(x-2)^2$

On differentiating both sides w.r.t. x, we get

$$f'(x)=(x-1)^3\cdot\frac{d}{dx}(x-2)^2+(x-2)^2\cdot\frac{d}{dx}(x-1)^3$$

$$\left[\because \frac{d}{dx}(uv)=u\frac{dv}{dx}+v\frac{du}{dx}\right]$$

$$\Rightarrow f'(x)=(x-1)^3\cdot 2(x-2)+(x-2)^2\cdot 3(x-1)^2$$

$$=(x-1)^2(x-2)[2(x-1)+3(x-2)]$$

$$=(x-1)^2(x-2)(2x-2+3x-6)$$

$$\Rightarrow f'(x)=(x-1)^2(x-2)(5x-8)$$

Now, put $f'(x)=0 \Rightarrow (x-1)^2(x-2)(5x-8)=0$

Either $(x-1)^2=0$ or $x-2=0$ or $5x-8=0$

$$\therefore \quad x=1, \frac{8}{5}, 2$$

Now, we find intervals and check in which interval $f(x)$ is strictly increasing and strictly decreasing.

Interval	$f'(x)=(x-1)^2(x-2)(5x-8)$	Sign of $f'(x)$
$x<1$	(+)(−)(−)	+ve
$1<x<\frac{8}{5}$	(+)(−)(−)	+ve
$\frac{8}{5}<x<2$	(+)(−)(+)	−ve
$x>2$	(+)(+)(+)	+ve

We know that a function $f(x)$ is said to be an strictly increasing function, if $f'(x)>0$ and strictly decreasing, if $f'(x)<0$. So, the given function $f(x)$ is increasing on the intervals $(-\infty, 1)\left(1, \frac{8}{5}\right)$ and $(2, \infty)$ and decreasing on $\left(\frac{8}{5}, 2\right)$.

Since, $f(x)$ is a polynomial function, so it is continuous at $x=1, \frac{8}{5}, 2$.

Hence, $f(x)$ is

(i) increasing on intervals $\left(-\infty, \frac{8}{5}\right]$ and $[2, \infty)$.

(ii) decreasing on interval $\left[\frac{8}{5}, 2\right]$.

20. Given, function is

$$f(x)=2x^3+9x^2+12x+20$$

On differentiating both sides w.r.t. x, we get

$$f'(x)=6x^2+18x+12$$

On putting $f'(x)=0$, we get

$$6x^2+18x+12=0$$

$$\Rightarrow \quad 6(x^2+3x+2)=0$$

$$\Rightarrow \quad 6(x+1)(x+2)=0$$

$$\Rightarrow \quad (x+1)(x+2)=0$$

$$\Rightarrow \quad x+1=0 \text{ or } x+2=0$$

$$\therefore \quad x=-2, -1$$

Now, we find intervals and check in which interval $f(x)$ is strictly increasing and strictly decreasing.

Interval	f'(x) = 6 (x + 1)(x + 2)	Sign of f'(x)
$x<-2$	(+)(−)(−)	+ve
$-2<x<-1$	(+)(−)(+)	−ve
$x>-1$	(+)(+)(+)	+ve

We know that a function $f(x)$ is said to be an increasing function, if $f'(x)>0$ and decreasing, if $f'(x)<0$. So, given function is increasing on intervals $(-\infty, -2]$ and $[-1, \infty)$ and decreasing on interval $(-2, -1)$.

Since, $f(x)$ is a polynomial function, so it is continuous at $x=-1, -2$.

Hence, the given function is

(i) increasing on intervals $(-\infty, -2]$ and $[-1, \infty)$.

(ii) decreasing on interval $[-2, -1]$.

21. Given that length x of a rectangle is decreasing at the rate of 5 cm/min.

$$\therefore \quad \frac{dx}{dt}=-5 \text{ cm/min} \quad \ldots\text{(i)}$$

Also, the breadth y of rectangle is increasing at the rate of 4 cm/min.

$$\therefore \quad \frac{dy}{dt}=4 \text{ cm/min} \quad \ldots\text{(ii)}$$

(i) Here, we have to find rate of change of perimeter i.e. dP/dt

and we know that perimeter $P=2(x+y)$

On differentiating both sides w.r.t. t, we get

$$\frac{dP}{dt}=2\left(\frac{dx}{dt}+\frac{dy}{dt}\right)$$

$$\Rightarrow \quad \frac{dP}{dt}=2(-5+4)=2(-1)=-2 \text{ cm/min}$$

[from Eqs. (i) and (ii)]

Hence, the perimeter of rectangle is decreasing at the rate 2 cm/min.

(ii) Here, we have to find rate of change of area $\frac{dA}{dt}$.

We know that area of rectangle $A=xy$

On differentiating both sides w.r.t. t, we get

$$\frac{dA}{dt}=x\cdot\frac{dy}{dt}+y\cdot\frac{dx}{dt}$$

[by using product rule of derivative]

Now, we have $x=8$ cm and $y=6$ cm

$$\frac{dx}{dt}=-5 \text{ cm/min and } \frac{dy}{dt}=4 \text{ cm/min}$$

$$\therefore \quad \frac{dA}{dt}=(8\times 4)+[6\times(-5)]=32-30$$

$$\Rightarrow \quad \frac{dA}{dt}=2 \text{ cm/min}$$

Hence, the area of rectangle is increasing at the rate 2 cm/min.

Concept Enhancer

(i) If x and y are the length and breadth of a rectangle respectively, then $\frac{dx}{dt}$ and $\frac{dy}{dt}$ are equal to rate of decreasing or increasing respectively. If P is perimeter, then increasing or decreasing rate of perimeter

$$\frac{dP}{dt}=2\left(\frac{dx}{dt}+\frac{dy}{dt}\right) \quad [\because P=2(x+y)]$$

(ii) Area of rectangle, $A=x\times y$

Then, rate of change of area, $\frac{dA}{dt}=x\frac{dy}{dt}+y\frac{dx}{dt}$

22. Given function is $y = \dfrac{4\sin\theta}{2+\cos\theta} - \theta$ ...(i)

We know that a function $y = f(x)$ is said to be an increasing function, if $\dfrac{dy}{dx} > 0$, for all values of x.

On differentiating both sides of Eq. (i) w.r.t. θ, we get

$$\frac{dy}{d\theta} = \frac{\left[(2+\cos\theta)\times\frac{d}{d\theta}(4\sin\theta) - 4\sin\theta\times\frac{d}{d\theta}(2+\cos\theta)\right]}{(2+\cos\theta)^2} - 1$$

[by using quotient rule of derivative]

$$= \frac{(2+\cos\theta)(4\cos\theta) - 4\sin\theta(0-\sin\theta)}{(2+\cos\theta)^2} - 1$$

$$= \frac{\left[8\cos\theta + 4\cos^2\theta + 4\sin^2\theta - (2+\cos\theta)^2\right]}{(2+\cos\theta)^2}$$

$$= \frac{\left[8\cos\theta + 4(\cos^2\theta + \sin^2\theta) - (4+\cos^2\theta + 4\cos\theta)\right]}{(2+\cos\theta)^2}$$

$[\because (a+b)^2 = a^2 + b^2 + 2ab]$

$$= \frac{8\cos\theta + 4 - 4 - \cos^2\theta - 4\cos\theta}{(2+\cos\theta)^2}$$

$[\because \sin^2\theta + \cos^2\theta = 1]$

$$= \frac{4\cos\theta - \cos^2\theta}{(2+\cos\theta)^2}$$

$$\Rightarrow \frac{dy}{d\theta} = \frac{\cos\theta(4-\cos\theta)}{(2+\cos\theta)^2}$$

Now, as $\cos\theta > 0, \forall\, \theta \in \left(0, \dfrac{\pi}{2}\right)$ and $(2+\cos\theta)^2$ being a perfect square is always positive for all $\theta \in \left(0, \dfrac{\pi}{2}\right)$.

Also, for $\theta \in \left(0, \dfrac{\pi}{2}\right)$, we know that

$$0 < \cos\theta < 1$$

$\therefore 4 - \cos\theta > 0$ for all $\theta \in \left(0, \dfrac{\pi}{2}\right)$

Thus, we conclude that

$$\frac{\cos\theta(4-\cos\theta)}{(2+\cos\theta)^2} > 0, \forall\, \theta \in \left(0, \frac{\pi}{2}\right)$$

$$\Rightarrow \frac{dy}{d\theta} > 0, \forall\, \theta \in \left(0, \frac{\pi}{2}\right)$$

Now, as y is continuous at $\theta = 0$ and $\dfrac{\pi}{2}$.

$\therefore$ y is an increasing function in $\left(0, \dfrac{\pi}{2}\right)$.

23. Given, $f(x) = \sin 3x - \cos 3x, 0 < x < \pi$

On differentiating both sides w.r.t. x, we get

$f'(x) = 3\cos 3x + 3\sin 3x$

On putting $f'(x) = 0$, we get

$$\sin 3x = -\cos 3x \Rightarrow \tan 3x = -1$$

$$\Rightarrow 3x = \frac{3\pi}{4}, \frac{7\pi}{4}, \frac{11\pi}{4}$$

[∵ tan θ is negative in IInd and IVth quadrants]

$$\Rightarrow x = \frac{\pi}{4}, \frac{7\pi}{12}, \frac{11\pi}{12}$$

Now, we find intervals and check in which intervals $f(x)$ is strictly increasing or strictly decreasing.

Interval	Test value	$f'(x) = 3(\cos 3x + \sin 3x)$	Sign of $f'(x)$
$0 < x < \frac{\pi}{4}$	At $x = \frac{\pi}{6}$	$3\left(\cos\frac{\pi}{2} + \sin\frac{\pi}{2}\right) = 3(0+1) = 3$	+ ve
$\frac{\pi}{4} < x < \frac{7\pi}{12}$	At $x = \frac{\pi}{3}$	$3(\cos\pi + \sin\pi) = 3(-1+0) = -3$	− ve
$\frac{7\pi}{12} < x < \frac{11\pi}{12}$	At $x = \frac{3\pi}{4}$	$3\left(\cos\frac{9\pi}{4} + \sin\frac{9\pi}{4}\right) = 3\left(\frac{1}{\sqrt{2}} + \frac{1}{\sqrt{2}}\right) = 3\sqrt{2}$	+ ve
$\frac{11\pi}{12} < x < \pi$	At $x = \frac{23\pi}{24}$	$3\left(\cos\frac{23\pi}{8} + \sin\frac{23}{8}\pi\right) = 3\left[\cos\left(3\pi - \frac{\pi}{8}\right) + \sin\left(3\pi - \frac{\pi}{8}\right)\right] = 3\left(-\cos\frac{\pi}{8} + \sin\frac{\pi}{8}\right) = 3\left(\sin\frac{\pi}{8} - \cos\frac{\pi}{8}\right) < 0$	− ve

Here, we see that $f'(x) > 0$, for $0 < x < \dfrac{\pi}{4}$ and $\dfrac{7\pi}{12} < x < \dfrac{11\pi}{12}$, so $f(x)$ is strictly increasing in the intervals $\left(0, \dfrac{\pi}{4}\right)$ and $\left(\dfrac{7\pi}{12}, \dfrac{11\pi}{12}\right)$

While $f'(x) < 0$ in $\dfrac{\pi}{4} < x < \dfrac{7\pi}{12}$ and $\dfrac{11\pi}{12} < x < \pi$

So, $f(x)$ is strictly decreasing in the intervals $\left(\dfrac{\pi}{4}, \dfrac{7\pi}{12}\right)$ and $\left(\dfrac{11\pi}{12}, \pi\right)$.

24. Given, function is $f(x)=x^2-x+1$

On differentiating both sides w.r.t. x, we get

$f'(x)=2x-1$

On putting $f'(x)=0$

$\Rightarrow \quad 2x-1=0$

Now, we find intervals in which $f(x)$ is strictly increasing or strictly decreasing.

Interval	$f'(x)=(2x-1)$	Sign of $f'(x)$
$x<\frac{1}{2}$	(−)	− ve
$x>\frac{1}{2}$	(+)	+ ve

Here, $f(x)$ is strictly increasing on $\left(\frac{1}{2}, \infty\right)$ and $f(x)$ is strictly decreasing on $\left(-\infty, \frac{1}{2}\right)$.

Hence, $f(x)$ is neither increasing nor decreasing in $(-1, 1)$.

Concept Enhancer $f(x)$ is strictly increasing in (a, b), if $f'(x)>0, \forall x \in (a, b)$ and $f(x)$ is strictly decreasing in (a, b), if $f'(x)<0, \forall x \in (a, b)$.

Here, interval $(-1, 1) \notin \left(\frac{1}{2}, \infty\right)$ or $\left(-\infty, \frac{1}{2}\right)$.

So, $f(x)$ is neither increasing nor decreasing in $(-1, 1)$.

TOPIC 2

Tangents and Normals

A line which touches the curve at a single point is called **tangent** at a point and if a line is perpendicular to the tangent at the point of contact, then it is called **normal**.

Slope of Tangent and Normal

(i) The slope of a tangent at the point of contact to the curve $y=f(x)$ at the point (x_1, y_1) is given by

$$\left(\frac{dy}{dx}\right)_{(x_1, y_1)} \quad \text{or} \quad f'(x_1)$$

(ii) The slope of a normal to the curve $y=f(x)$ at the point (x_1, y_1) is given by $\dfrac{-1}{\left(\frac{dy}{dx}\right)_{(x_1, y_1)}}$.

NOTE If a tangent line to the curve $y=f(x)$ makes an angle θ with X-axis in the positive direction, then $\frac{dy}{dx}$ = Slope of the tangent = $\tan\theta$.

Equations of Tangent and Normal

(i) The equation of tangent to the curve $y=f(x)$ at the point $P(x_1, y_1)$ is given by $y-y_1=m(x-x_1)$, where $m=\frac{dy}{dx}$ at point (x_1, y_1).

(ii) The equation of normal to the curve $y=f(x)$ at the point $Q(x_1, y_1)$ is given by $y-y_1=\frac{-1}{m}(x-x_1)$, where $m=\frac{dy}{dx}$ at point (x_1, y_1).

Some Important Points

(i) If slope of the tangent line is zero, then $\tan\theta=0$, so $\theta=0$, which means that tangent line is parallel to the X-axis and then equation of tangent at the point (x_1, y_1) is $\boldsymbol{y=y_1}$.

(ii) If $\theta \to \frac{\pi}{2}$, then $\tan\theta \to \infty$, which means that tangent line is perpendicular to the X-axis i.e. parallel to the Y-axis and then equation of the tangent at the point (x_1, y_1) is $\boldsymbol{x=x_1}$.

(iii) Suppose m_1 and m_2 are slopes of tangent to the curves. The condition for two curves to be perpendicular (orthogonal), is $\boldsymbol{m_1 m_2=-1}$.

(iv) The angle of intersection between two curves is the angle between the tangents to the curves at the point of intersection.

PYQs Previous Years Questions

1 Mark Questions

1. For the curve $y^2 = 2x^3 - 7$, the slope of the normal at (2, 3) is **ISC 2023**

(a) 4 (b) $\frac{1}{4}$

(c) – 4 (d) $\frac{-1}{4}$

2. Any tangent to the curve $y = 3x^7 + 5x + 3$ **ISC Specimen Sem-I 2022**

(a) is parallel to X-axis

(b) is parallel to Y-axis

(c) makes an acute angle with X-axis

(d) makes an obtuse angle with Y-axis

3. Identify from the given options the slope of the normal to the curve $x^2 + 3y + y^2 = 5$ at (1, 1) **ISC Specimen 2021**

(a) $-\frac{2}{5}$ (b) $\frac{5}{2}$

(c) $\frac{2}{5}$ (d) $-\frac{5}{2}$

2 Marks Questions

4. Find a point on the curve $y = (x-2)^2$ at which the tangent is parallel to the line joining the chord through the points (2,0) and (4,4). **ISC 2024**

5. Find the point on the curve $y = x^2 + 2x - 1$, where the tangent is parallel to X-axis. **ISC Specimen 2024**

6. Find the point on the curve $y^2 = 4x + 8$ for which the abscissa and ordinate changes at the same rate. **ISC Specimen 2023**

7. The function f is defined for all $x \in R$. The line with equation $y = 6x - 1$ is the tangent to the graph of f at $x = 4$.

(i) Write down the value of $f'(4)$.

(ii) Find $f(4)$. **ISC Specimen 2023**

3/4 Marks Questions

8. The equation of tangent at (2, 3) on the curve $y^2 = px^3 + q$ is $y = 4x - 7$. Find the values of p and q. **ISC 2020**

> **KEY CONCEPT**
> Given curve passes through (2, 3). So, put $x = 2$, $y = 3$ in given curve and find relation between p and q. Now, find $\frac{dy}{dx}$ at point (2, 3). Also, find $\frac{dy}{dx}$ from equation of tangent of curve.

9. Find the points on the curve $y = 4x^3 - 3x + 5$ at which the equation of the tangent is parallel to the X-axis. **ISC 2018**

10. Find the equations of the normals to the curve $y = x^3 + 2x + 6$, which are parallel to the line $x + 14y + 4 = 0$. **ISC Specimen 2018**

11. Find the point on the curve $9y^2 = x^3$, where the normal to the curve makes equal intercepts on the axes.

12. Find the equations of the tangent and normal to the curves $x = a\sin^3\theta$ and $y = a\cos^3\theta$ at $\theta = \frac{\pi}{4}$.

13. Find the points on the curve $x^2 + y^2 - 2x - 3 = 0$ at which tangent is parallel to X-axis.

> **KEY CONCEPT**
> As tangent is parallel to X-axis, put $\frac{dy}{dx} = 0$ and find value of x from it. Then, put this value of x in the equation of the given curve and find value of y.

14. Find the points on the curve $y = x^3$ at which the slope of the tangent is equal to y-coordinate of the point.

> **KEY CONCEPT**
> Firstly, determine the derivative and put $\frac{dy}{dx} = y$ and then find the value of x from it. Further, put this value of x in the equation of the given curve and find the value of y.

15. Find the equations of tangents to the curve $y = (x^2 - 1)(x - 2)$ at the points, where the curve cuts the X-axis.

> **KEY CONCEPT**
> The curve cuts the X-axis, so put $y = 0$ and get the corresponding values of x.
> Further, differentiate and determine the slopes at different points. And then use the equation of tangent $y - y_1 = m(x - x_1)$.

16. Find the equation of tangent to the curve $y=\frac{x-7}{x^2-5x+6}$ at the point, where it cuts the X-axis.

17. Find the equations of the normal to the curve $y=x^3+2x+6$, which are parallel to line $x+14y+4=0$.

5/6 Marks Questions

18. Find the angle of intersection of the curves $y^2=4ax$ and $x^2=4by$.

19. Find the equation of tangents to the curve $y=\cos(x+y)$, $-2\pi\le x\le 2\pi$ that are parallel to the line $x+2y=0$.

20. Find the value of p for which the curves $x^2=9p(9-y)$ and $x^2=p(y+1)$ cut each other at right angles.

21. Find the equations of the tangent to the curve $y=x^2-2x+7$ which is

(i) parallel to the line $2x-y+9=0$.

(ii) perpendicular to the line $5y-15x=13$.

Explanations

1. (d) We have, $y^2=2x^3-7$

$$2y\frac{dy}{dx}=6x^2$$

$$\Rightarrow \frac{dy}{dx}=\frac{3x^2}{y}$$

Slope of tangent at (2, 3) is $\left(\frac{dy}{dx}\right)_{(2,3)}=\frac{12}{3}=4$

$\therefore$ Slope of normal at (2, 3) $=-\frac{1}{dy/dx}=\frac{-1}{4}$

2. (c) We have, $y=3x^7+5x+3$

On differentiating w.r.t. x, we get

$$\frac{dy}{dx}=21x^6+5$$

It is clear that x^6 is always positive for any real value.

So, $x^6>0\Rightarrow\frac{dy}{dx}>0$

Consequently, $\tan\theta>0$

So, θ lies in first quadrant.

Hence, the tangent to curve makes an acute angle.

3. (b) We have, $x^2+3y+y^2=5$

On differentiating w.r.t. x, we obtain

$$\frac{d}{dx}(x^2+3y+y^2)=\frac{d}{dx}(5)$$

$$\Rightarrow 2x+3\frac{dy}{dx}+2y\frac{dy}{dx}=0$$

$$\Rightarrow 2x+\frac{dy}{dx}(3+2y)=0$$

$$\Rightarrow \frac{dy}{dx}=\frac{-2x}{(3+2y)}$$

$$\Rightarrow \left.\frac{dy}{dx}\right|_{(1,1)}=\frac{-2}{3+2}=\frac{-2}{5}$$

Now, slope of normal $=-\frac{1}{\frac{dy}{dx}}$

$$=\frac{-1}{\left(-\frac{2}{5}\right)}=\frac{5}{2}$$

4. Given, equation of curve is $y=(x-2)^2$ ...(i)

Let (h, k) be the point at which the tangent is parallel to the line joining the chord through the points (2, 0) and (4, 4).

Then, $y'=2(x-2)$

At point (h, k)

$$\left.\frac{dy}{dx}\right|_{(h,k)}=2(h-2)$$

Also, slope of the chord joining the points (2, 0) and (4, 4)

$$=\frac{4-0}{4-2}=\frac{4}{2}=2$$

Since, tangent line is parallel to chord, therefore,

$$2(h-2)=2$$

$$\Rightarrow h=3$$

Also, the point (h, k) will lie on the curve (i), then

$$k=(h-2)^2$$

$$=(3-2)^2 \quad [\because h=3]$$

$$k=1$$

Hence, the required point is (3, 1).

5. Given, $y=x^2+2x-1$

$\therefore \quad \dfrac{dy}{dx}=2x+2=2(x+1)$

Let at (x_1, y_1) tangent is parallel to X-axis.

$\therefore \quad \left(\dfrac{dy}{dx}\right)_{(x_1, y_1)}=0$

$\Rightarrow \quad 2(x_1+1)=0 \Rightarrow x_1=-1$

$\therefore \quad y_1=(-1)^2+2(-1)-1$

$=1-2-1=1-3=-2$

$\therefore (x_1, y_1)=(-1,-2)$

6. Let the required point (x, y).

Given, $\dfrac{dy}{dt}=\dfrac{dx}{dt}$ ...(i)

and $y^2=4x+8$ ...(ii)

On differentiating both sides of equation w.r.t. t, we get

$$2y\frac{dy}{dt}=4\frac{dx}{dt}$$

$\Rightarrow \quad 2y=4 \quad \left[\text{from Eq. (i), } \dfrac{dy}{dt}=\dfrac{dx}{dt}\right]$

$\Rightarrow \quad y=2$

On putting $y=2$ in Eq. (ii), we get

$(2)^2=4x+8 \Rightarrow x=-1$

Hence, the required point is $(-1, 2)$.

7. Given, $y=6x-1$ is the tangent line at $x=4$

(i) $y=6x-1$

On differentiating w.r.t. x, we get

$$\frac{dy}{dx}=6$$

Therefore, $f'(4)=6$

(ii) The tangent line touches the function at $x=4$

$f(x)=6x-1$

$\Rightarrow \quad f(4)=6\times 4-1=23$

8. Given, curve is $y^2=px^3+q$.

Since, its passes through (2, 3).

$\therefore \quad (3)^2=p(2)^3+q$

$\Rightarrow \quad 8p+q=9$ ... (i)

Now, $y^2=px^3+q$

$\Rightarrow \quad 2y\dfrac{dy}{dx}=3px^2$

$\Rightarrow \quad \dfrac{dy}{dx}=\dfrac{3px^2}{2y}$

$\Rightarrow \quad \left(\dfrac{dy}{dx}\right)_{(2, 3)}=\dfrac{3p(2)^2}{2(3)}=2p$

Equation of tangent of curve $y^2=px^3+q$ is

$y=4x-7$

$\therefore \quad \dfrac{dy}{dx}=4=2p$

$\Rightarrow \quad p=2$

Now, putting the value of p in Eq. (i), we get

$8(2)+q=9$

$\Rightarrow \quad q=9-16=-7$

$\therefore \quad p=2$ and $q=-7$

9. Given, equation of curve is $y=4x^3-3x+5$.

On differentiating both side w.r.t. x, we get

$$\frac{dy}{dx}=12x^2-3$$

It is given that equation of tangent is parallel to X-axis

$\therefore \quad \dfrac{dy}{dx}=0$

$\Rightarrow \quad 12x^2-3=0 \Rightarrow x^2=\dfrac{3}{12} \Rightarrow x=\pm\dfrac{1}{2}$

When $x=\dfrac{1}{2}$, then $y=4$ and $x=-\dfrac{1}{2}$, then $y=6$

$\therefore$ The point on the curve are $\left(\dfrac{1}{2},4\right)$ and $\left(-\dfrac{1}{2},6\right)$.

10. Given equation of curve is

$y=x^3+2x+6$ ...(i)

and equation of line is

$x+14y+4=0$ ...(ii)

On differentiating both side of Eq. (i) w.r.t. x, we get

$$\frac{dy}{dx}=3x^2+2$$

$\therefore$ Slope of normal $=\dfrac{-1}{\left(\dfrac{dy}{dx}\right)}=\dfrac{-1}{3x^2+2}$

Also, slope of the line $x+14y+4=0$ is $-\dfrac{1}{14}$

$\left[\because \text{slope of the line } Ax+By+C=0 \text{ is } \left(-\dfrac{A}{B}\right)\right]$

Since, the normal to the curve is parallel to the line.

$\therefore$ Slope of line = Slope of normal

$\Rightarrow \quad \dfrac{-1}{14}=\dfrac{-1}{3x^2+2} \Rightarrow 3x^2+2=14$

$\Rightarrow \quad 3x^2=12 \Rightarrow x^2=4 \Rightarrow x=\pm 2$

From Eq. (i), at $x = 2$, we get

$$y = (2)^3 + 2(2) + 6 = 8 + 4 + 6 = 18$$

and at $x = -2$, we get

$$y = (-2)^3 + 2(-2) + 6$$
$$= -8 - 4 + 6 = -6$$

$\therefore$ Normal passes through the points (2, 18) and (−2, −6).

Also, slope of normal $= \frac{-1}{14}$.

Hence, the equation of normal at point (2, 18) is

$y - y_1 =$ Slope of normal $\times (x - x_1)$

$$\Rightarrow \quad y - 18 = \frac{-1}{14}(x - 2)$$

$$\Rightarrow \quad 14y - 252 = -x + 2$$

$$\Rightarrow \quad x + 14y = 254$$

and equation of normal at point (−2, −6) is

$$y + 6 = -\frac{1}{14}(x + 2)$$

$$\Rightarrow \quad 14y + 84 = -x - 2$$

$$\Rightarrow \quad x + 14y = -86$$

Hence, the two equations of normal are $x + 14y = 254$ and $x + 14y = -86$.

11. Given, curve is $9y^2 = x^3$ ...(i)

On differentiating both sides w.r.t. x, we get

$$9 \times 2y \frac{dy}{dx} = 3x^2$$

$$\Rightarrow \quad \frac{dy}{dx} = \frac{3x^2}{18y} = \frac{x^2}{6y}$$

Let (x_1, y_1) be the required point on the curve (i).

Then, slope of normal to the curve (i) at point (x_1, y_1)

$$= -\frac{1}{(dy/dx)_{(x_1, y_1)}} = \frac{-6y_1}{x_1^2} \quad \text{...(ii)}$$

Since, the normal makes equal intercept on the axes.

$\therefore$ Slope of normal $= \tan \frac{\pi}{4}, \tan \frac{3\pi}{4} = \pm 1$

Hence, $\frac{-6y_1}{x_1^2} = \pm 1$ [from Eq. (ii)]

$$\Rightarrow \quad y_1 = \pm \frac{x_1^2}{6} \quad \text{...(iii)}$$

Again, point (x_1, y_1) lies on curve (i).

$$\therefore \quad 9y_1^2 = x_1^3$$

$$\Rightarrow \quad 9\left(\pm \frac{x_1^2}{6}\right)^2 = x_1^3 \quad \text{[using Eq. (iii)]}$$

$$\Rightarrow \quad \frac{9x_1^4}{36} = x_1^3$$

$$\Rightarrow \quad \frac{x_1}{4} = 1 \Rightarrow x_1 = 4$$

$$\therefore \quad y_1 = \pm \frac{x_1^2}{6} = \pm \frac{16}{6} = \pm \frac{8}{3}$$

Hence, the required points are $\left(4, \frac{8}{3}\right)$ and $\left(4, \frac{-8}{3}\right)$.

Note that $x_1 \neq 0$, as $x_1 = 0$, then $y_1 = 0$.

So, the normal will pass through (0, 0), which is not possible.

12. Given, $x = a \sin^3 \theta$ ...(i)

On differentiating both sides w.r.t. θ, we get

$$\frac{dx}{d\theta} = a(3 \sin^2 \theta \cos \theta)$$

$$\Rightarrow \quad \frac{dx}{d\theta} = 3a \sin^2 \theta \cos \theta$$

and $y = a \cos^3 \theta$ ...(ii)

On differentiating both sides w.r.t. θ, we get

$$\frac{dy}{d\theta} = -3a \cos^2 \theta \sin \theta$$

Then, $$\frac{dy}{dx} = \frac{\frac{dy}{d\theta}}{\frac{dx}{d\theta}} = \frac{-3a \cos^2 \theta \sin \theta}{3a \sin^2 \theta \cos \theta}$$

$$\Rightarrow \quad \frac{dy}{dx} = -\cot \theta$$

$$\therefore \quad \left(\frac{dy}{dx}\right)_{\theta = \frac{\pi}{4}} = -\cot \frac{\pi}{4} = -1$$

Also, at $\theta = \frac{\pi}{4}$, from Eqs. (i) and (ii), we get

$$x = a\left(\sin \frac{\pi}{4}\right)^3, y = a\left(\cos \frac{\pi}{4}\right)^3$$

$$\Rightarrow \quad x = a\left(\frac{1}{2}\right)^{3/2}, y = a\left(\frac{1}{2}\right)^{3/2}$$

$$\left[\because \sin \frac{\pi}{4} = \frac{1}{\sqrt{2}} \text{ and } \cos \frac{\pi}{4} = \frac{1}{\sqrt{2}}\right]$$

Now, equation of tangent at the point $\left(\frac{a}{(2)^{3/2}}, \frac{a}{(2)^{3/2}}\right)$ is $y - y_1 = \frac{dy}{dx}(x - x_1)$

$$\Rightarrow \quad y - \frac{a}{(2)^{3/2}} = (-1)\left(x - \frac{a}{2^{3/2}}\right)$$

$$\Rightarrow \quad y+x=\frac{2a}{(2)^{3/2}}$$

$$\Rightarrow \quad y+x=\frac{a}{\sqrt{2}} \Rightarrow x+y-\frac{a}{\sqrt{2}}=0$$

Clearly, slope of normal $=\dfrac{-1}{\text{Slope of tangent}}$

$\Rightarrow$ Slope of normal $=\dfrac{-1}{-1}=1$

Now, equation of normal at the point $\left(\dfrac{a}{(2)^{3/2}}, \dfrac{a}{(2)^{3/2}}\right)$ is

$$y-\frac{a}{(2)^{3/2}}=(1)\left(x-\frac{a}{2^{3/2}}\right)$$

$$\therefore \quad x-y=0$$

13. Given, equation of curve is

$$x^2+y^2-2x-3=0 \quad \ldots(i)$$

On differentiating both sides of Eq. (i) w.r.t. x, we get

$$2x+2y\frac{dy}{dx}-2=0$$

$$\Rightarrow \quad 2y\frac{dy}{dx}=2-2x$$

$$\Rightarrow \quad \frac{dy}{dx}=\frac{2-2x}{2y} \Rightarrow \frac{dy}{dx}=\frac{1-x}{y}$$

We know that when a tangent to the curve is parallel to X-axis, then $\dfrac{dy}{dx}=0.$

On putting $\dfrac{dy}{dx}=0$, we get

$$1-x=0 \Rightarrow x=1$$

Now, on putting $x=1$ in Eq. (i), we get

$$1+y^2-2-3=0$$

$$\Rightarrow \quad y^2-4=0$$

$$\Rightarrow \quad y^2=4 \Rightarrow y=\pm 2$$

Hence, the required points are (1, 2) and (1, –2).

14. Given, equation of curve is $y=x^3 \quad \ldots(i)$

On differentiating both sides w.r.t. x, we get

$$\frac{dy}{dx}=3x^2$$

$\therefore$ Slope of tangent at any point (x, y) is

$$\frac{dy}{dx}=3x^2$$

Now, given that

Slope of tangent = y-coordinate of the point

$$\Rightarrow \quad \frac{dy}{dx}=y$$

$$\Rightarrow \quad 3x^2=y \quad \left[\because \frac{dy}{dx}=3x^2\right]$$

$$\Rightarrow \quad 3x^2=x^3 \quad [\because y=x^3]$$

$$\Rightarrow \quad 3x^2-x^3=0 \Rightarrow x^2(3-x)=0$$

$\Rightarrow$ Either $x^2=0$ or $3-x=0$

$$\therefore \quad x=0, 3$$

Now, on putting $x=0$ and $x=3$ in Eq. (i), we get

$$y=(0)^3=0 \quad [\text{at } x=0]$$

and $$y=(3)^3=27 \quad [\text{at } x=3]$$

Hence, the required points are (0, 0) and (3, 27).

15. Given, equation of the curve is

$$y=(x^2-1)(x-2) \quad \ldots(i)$$

Since, the curve cuts the X-axis, so at that point y-coordinate will be zero.

So, on putting $y=0$, we get

$$(x^2-1)(x-2)=0$$

$$\Rightarrow \quad x^2=1 \text{ or } x=2$$

$$\therefore \quad x=\pm 1 \text{ or } 2 \Rightarrow x=-1, 1, 2$$

Thus, the given curve cuts the X-axis at points (–1, 0), (1, 0) and (2, 0).

On differentiating both sides of Eq. (i) w.r.t. x, we get

$$\frac{dy}{dx}=(x^2-1)\cdot 1+(x-2)\cdot 2x$$

[by using product rule of derivative]

$$\Rightarrow \quad \frac{dy}{dx}=x^2-1+2x^2-4x$$

$$\Rightarrow \quad \frac{dy}{dx}=3x^2-4x-1$$

Now, slope of tangent at (–1,0) is

$$m_1=\left(\frac{dy}{dx}\right)_{(-1,\,0)}=3(-1)^2-4(-1)-1$$

$$=3+4-1=6$$

Slope of tangent at (1,0) is

$$m_2=\left(\frac{dy}{dx}\right)_{(1,\,0)}=3(1)^2-4(1)-1$$

$$=3-4-1=-2$$

Slope of tangent at (2,0) is

$$m_3=\left(\frac{dy}{dx}\right)_{(2,\,0)}=3(2)^2-4(2)-1$$

$$=12-8-1=3$$

We know that equation of tangent at the point (x_1, y_1) is given by $y-y_1=m(x-x_1)$.

Here, we get three equations of tangents.

Equation of tangent at point (–1, 0) having slope, $m_1 = 6$, is

$$y - 0 = 6(x + 1)$$

$$\Rightarrow \quad y = 6x + 6 \Rightarrow 6x - y = -6$$

Equation of tangent at point (1, 0) having slope, $m_2 = -2$, is

$$y - 0 = -2(x - 1)$$

$$\Rightarrow \quad y = -2x + 2 \Rightarrow 2x + y = 2$$

and equation of tangent at point (2, 0) having slope, $m_3 = 3$, is

$$y - 0 = 3(x - 2)$$

$$\Rightarrow \quad y = 3x - 6$$

$$\therefore \quad 3x - y = 6$$

16. Given, equation of curve is

$$y = \frac{x-7}{x^2 - 5x + 6} \quad \text{...(i)}$$

On differentiating both sides w.r.t. x, we get

$$\frac{dy}{dx} = \frac{(x^2 - 5x + 6)\cdot 1 - (x - 7)(2x - 5)}{(x^2 - 5x + 6)^2}$$

$$\left[\because \frac{d}{dx}\left(\frac{u}{v}\right) = \frac{v\frac{du}{dx} - u\frac{dv}{dx}}{v^2}\right]$$

$$\Rightarrow \quad \frac{dy}{dx} = \frac{\left[(x^2 - 5x + 6) - y(x^2 - 5x + 6)(2x - 5)\right]}{(x^2 - 5x + 6)^2}$$

$$\left[\begin{array}{l} \because \quad y = \dfrac{x-7}{x^2 - 5x + 6} \\ \therefore \quad (x - 7) = y(x^2 - 5x + 6) \end{array}\right]$$

$$\Rightarrow \quad \frac{dy}{dx} = \frac{1 - (2x - 5)\,y}{x^2 - 5x + 6} \quad \text{...(ii)}$$

[dividing numerator and denominator by $x^2 - 5x + 6$]

Also, given that curve cuts X-axis, so its y-coordinate is zero.

Put $y = 0$ in Eq. (i), we get

$$\frac{x-7}{x^2 - 5x + 6} = 0$$

$$\Rightarrow \quad x = 7$$

So, curve passes through the point (7, 0).

Now, slope of tangent at (7,0) is

$$m = \left(\frac{dy}{dx}\right)_{(7,\,0)} = \frac{1 - 0}{49 - 35 + 6} = \frac{1}{20}$$

Hence, the required equation of tangent passing through the point (7, 0) having slope 1/20 is

$$y - 0 = \frac{1}{20}(x - 7)$$

$$\Rightarrow \quad 20y = x - 7$$

$$\therefore \quad x - 20y = 7$$

17. Given, equation of curve is

$$y = x^3 + 2x + 6 \quad \text{...(i)}$$

and the given equation of line is

$$x + 14y + 4 = 0$$

On differentiating both sides of Eq. (i) w.r.t. x, we get

$$\frac{dy}{dx} = 3x^2 + 2$$

$$\therefore \text{ Slope of normal} = \frac{-1}{\left(\frac{dy}{dx}\right)} = \frac{-1}{3x^2 + 2}$$

Also, slope of the line $x + 14y + 4 = 0$ is $-\frac{1}{14}$.

$$\left[\because \text{slope of the line } Ax + By + C = 0 \text{ is } -\frac{A}{B}\right]$$

We know that if two lines are parallel, then their slopes are equal.

$$\therefore \quad -\frac{1}{3x^2 + 2} = -\frac{1}{14} \Rightarrow 3x^2 + 2 = 14$$

$$\Rightarrow \quad 3x^2 = 12$$

$$\Rightarrow \quad x^2 = 4 \Rightarrow x = \pm 2$$

When $x = 2$, then from Eq. (i),

$$y = (2)^3 + 2(2) + 6 = 8 + 4 + 6 = 18$$

and when $x = -2$, then from Eq. (i),

$$y = (-2)^3 + 2(-2) + 6$$

$$= -8 - 4 + 6 = -6$$

$\therefore$ Normal passes through (2, 18) and (–2, –6).

Also, slope of normal $= \frac{-1}{14}$

Hence, the equation of normal at point (2, 18) is

$$y - 18 = \frac{-1}{14}(x - 2)$$

$$\Rightarrow \quad 14y - 252 = -x + 2 \Rightarrow x + 14y = 254$$

and equation of normal at point (–2, –6) is

$$y + 6 = -\frac{1}{14}(x + 2)$$

$$\Rightarrow \quad 14y + 84 = -x - 2 \Rightarrow x + 14y = -86$$

Hence, the two equations of normal are

$$x + 14y = 254 \text{ and } x + 14y = -86.$$

18. Given, equations of curves are

$$y^2 = 4ax \quad \ldots(i)$$

and $$x^2 = 4by \quad \ldots(ii)$$

Clearly, the angle of intersection of curves (i) and (ii) is the angle between the tangents to the curves at the point of intersection.

So, let us first find the intersection point of given curves.

On substituting the value of y from Eq. (ii) in Eq. (i), we get

$$\left(\frac{x^2}{4b}\right)^2 = 4ax \Rightarrow \frac{x^4}{16b^2} = 4ax \Rightarrow x^4 = 64ab^2x$$

$$\Rightarrow x^4 - 64ab^2x = 0 \Rightarrow x(x^3 - 64ab^2) = 0$$

$$\Rightarrow \quad x = 0 \text{ or } x = 4a^{1/3}b^{2/3}$$

Clearly, when $x = 0$, then from Eq. (i), $y = 0$

and when $x = 4a^{1/3}b^{2/3}$, then from Eq. (i),

$$y^2 = 16a^{4/3}b^{2/3} \Rightarrow y = 4a^{2/3}b^{1/3}$$

Thus, the points of intersection are (0, 0) and $(4a^{1/3}b^{2/3}, 4a^{2/3}b^{1/3})$.

Now, let us find the angle of intersection at (0, 0) and $(4a^{1/3}b^{2/3}, 4a^{2/3}b^{1/3})$.

Let m_1 be the slope of tangent to the curve (i) and m_2 be the slope of tangent to the curve (ii).

Angle of intersection at (0, 0)

Now, $$m_1 = \left(\frac{dy}{dx}\right)_{\text{at }(0,0)} = \left(\frac{2a}{y}\right)_{\text{at }(0,0)} = \infty$$

and $$m_2 = \left(\frac{dy}{dx}\right)_{\text{at }(0,0)} = \left(\frac{x}{2b}\right)_{\text{at }(0,0)} = 0$$

⇒ Tangent to the curve (i) is parallel to Y-axis and tangent to the curve (ii) is parallel to X-axis.

∴ Angle between these curves two is $\frac{\pi}{2}$.

⇒ The angle of intersection of the curves is $\frac{\pi}{2}$.

Angle of intersection at

$$(4a^{1/3}b^{2/3}, 4a^{2/3}b^{1/3})$$

Here, $$m_1 = \frac{2a}{4a^{2/3}b^{1/3}} = \frac{1}{2}\cdot\frac{a^{1/3}}{b^{1/3}} = \frac{1}{2}\left(\frac{a}{b}\right)^{1/3}$$

and $$m_2 = \frac{4a^{1/3}b^{2/3}}{2b} = 2\left(\frac{a}{b}\right)^{1/3}$$

Let θ be the angle between the tangents.

Then, $$\tan\theta = \left|\frac{m_2 - m_1}{1 + m_1m_2}\right| = \left|\frac{2\left(\frac{a}{b}\right)^{1/3} - \frac{1}{2}\left(\frac{a}{b}\right)^{1/3}}{1 + 2\left(\frac{a}{b}\right)^{1/3}\frac{1}{2}\left(\frac{a}{b}\right)^{1/3}}\right|$$

$$= \left|\frac{\frac{3}{2}\left(\frac{a}{b}\right)^{1/3}}{1 + \left(\frac{a}{b}\right)^{2/3}}\right| = \left|\frac{\frac{3}{2}\left(\frac{a}{b}\right)^{1/3}\cdot b^{2/3}}{b^{2/3} + a^{2/3}}\right|$$

$$= \left|\frac{3\,(ab)^{1/3}}{2\,(a^{2/3} + b^{2/3})}\right|$$

$$\Rightarrow \quad \theta = \tan^{-1}\left\{\frac{3\,(ab)^{1/3}}{2\,(a^{2/3} + b^{2/3})}\right\}$$

Hence, the angles of intersection of the curves are $\frac{\pi}{2}$ and $\tan^{-1}\left\{\frac{3\,(ab)^{1/3}}{2\,(a^{2/3} + b^{2/3})}\right\}$.

Concept Enhancer We know that the angle of intersection of two curves is the angle between the tangents to the curves at the point of intersection. If m_1 and m_2 are the slopes of tangents to the curves and let θ be the angle between the tangents, then $\tan\theta = \left|\frac{m_2 - m_1}{1 + m_1 \cdot m_2}\right|$.

19. Given, equation of curve is

$$y = \cos(x + y), \; -2\pi \le x \le 2\pi \quad \ldots(i)$$

and equation of line is

$$x + 2y = 0 \quad \ldots(ii)$$

Clearly, slope of tangents to the curve is $\frac{-1}{2}$.

Let (x_1, y_1) be the point of contact, then we have

$$y_1 = \cos(x_1 + y_1) \quad \text{[from Eq. (i)]} \ldots(iii)$$

and slope of tangent $$= \left(\frac{dy}{dx}\right)_{(x_1, y_1)} = \frac{-\sin(x_1 + y_1)}{1 + \sin(x_1 + y_1)}$$

$$\left[\begin{aligned} &\because \frac{dy}{dx} = -\sin(x + y)\left(1 + \frac{dy}{dx}\right) \\ &\Rightarrow \frac{dy}{dx} + \sin(x + y)\frac{dy}{dx} = -\sin(x + y) \\ &\Rightarrow \frac{dy}{dx} = \frac{-\sin(x + y)}{1 + \sin(x + y)} \end{aligned}\right]$$

$$\Rightarrow \quad \frac{dy}{dx} = \frac{-\sin(x_1 + y_1)}{1 + \sin(x_1 + y_1)}$$

$$\therefore \quad \frac{-1}{2}=\frac{-\sin(x_1+y_1)}{1+\sin(x_1+y_1)}$$

[$\because$ lines are parallel, so slope will be equal]

$$\Rightarrow \quad 1+\sin(x_1+y_1)=2\sin(x_1+y_1)$$

$$\Rightarrow \quad \sin(x_1+y_1)=1 \quad \ldots(\text{iv})$$

On squaring and adding Eqs. (iii) and (iv), we get

$$\cos^2(x_1+y_1)+\sin^2(x_1+y_1)=1+y_1^2$$

$$\Rightarrow \quad 1+y_1^2=1 \Rightarrow y_1^2=0 \Rightarrow y_1=0$$

On putting $y_1=0$ in Eq. (iii), we get $\cos x_1=0$

$$\Rightarrow \quad x_1=\frac{\pi}{2},\frac{3\pi}{2},\frac{-\pi}{2},\frac{-3\pi}{2} \quad [\because -2\pi \le x \le 2\pi]$$

But only $x_1=\frac{\pi}{2}$ and $\frac{-3\pi}{2}$ satisfy Eq. (iv).

Hence, the points of contact are $\left(\frac{\pi}{2},0\right)$ and $\left(\frac{-3\pi}{2},0\right)$

$\therefore$ Equations of tangents are

$$y-0=\frac{-1}{2}\left(x-\frac{\pi}{2}\right) \text{ and } y-0=-\frac{1}{2}\left(x+\frac{3\pi}{2}\right)$$

$\therefore$ $2x+4y=\pi$ and $2x+4y=-3\pi$

20. Given, equations of curves are

$$x^2=9p(9-y) \quad \ldots(\text{i})$$

and $$x^2=p(y+1) \quad \ldots(\text{ii})$$

As, these curves cut each other at right angle, therefore their tangent at point of intersection are perpendicular to each other.

So, let us first find the point of intersection and slope of tangents to the curves.

From Eqs. (i) and (ii), we get

$$9p(9-y)=p(y+1)$$

$$\therefore \quad 9(9-y)=y+1$$

[$\because p\neq 0$, as if $p=0$, then curves becomes straight, which will be parallel]

$$\Rightarrow \quad 81-9y=y+1 \Rightarrow 80=10y \Rightarrow y=8$$

On substituting the value of y in Eq. (i),we get

$$x^2=9p \Rightarrow x=\pm 3\sqrt{p}$$

Thus, the point of intersection are $(3\sqrt{p},8)$ and $(-3\sqrt{p},8)$.

Now, consider Eq.(i),we get

$$\frac{x^2}{9p}=9-y \Rightarrow \quad y=9-\frac{x^2}{9p}$$

On differentiating both sides w.r.t. x, we get

$$\frac{dy}{dx}=\frac{-2x}{9p} \quad \ldots(\text{iii})$$

From Eq. (ii), we get

$$\frac{x^2}{p}=y+1 \Rightarrow y=\frac{x^2}{p}-1$$

On differentiating both sides w.r.t. x, we get

$$\frac{dy}{dx}=\frac{2x}{p} \quad \ldots(\text{iv})$$

Now, for intersection point $(3\sqrt{p},8)$, we have slope of tangent to the first curve

$$=\frac{-2(3\sqrt{p})}{9p}=\frac{-6\sqrt{p}}{9p} \quad [\text{using Eq. (iii)}]$$

and slope of tangent to the second curve

$$=\frac{2(3\sqrt{p})}{p}=\frac{6\sqrt{p}}{p} \quad [\text{using Eq. (iv)}]$$

$\because$ Tangents are perpendicular to each other.

Then, slope of first curve × Slope of second curve = −1

$$\therefore \quad \frac{-6\sqrt{p}}{9p}\times\frac{6\sqrt{p}}{p}=-1$$

$$\Rightarrow \quad \frac{4}{p}=1 \Rightarrow p=4$$

And for intersection point $(-3\sqrt{p},8)$, we have slope of tangent to the first curve

$$=\frac{-2(-3\sqrt{p})}{9p}=\frac{6\sqrt{p}}{9p} \quad [\text{using Eq. (iii)}]$$

and slope of tangent to the second curve

$$=\frac{2(-3\sqrt{p})}{p}=\frac{-6\sqrt{p}}{p} \quad [\text{using Eq. (iv)}]$$

$\because$ Tangents are perpendicular to each other. Then,

$$\frac{6\sqrt{p}}{9p}\times\frac{-6\sqrt{p}}{p}=-1 \quad [\because m_1 m_2=-1]$$

$$\Rightarrow \quad \frac{4}{p}=1 \Rightarrow p=4$$

Hence, the value of p is 4.

Common Mistake When curves cut each other at right angle, then not forgot to assume that their tangents at point of intersection are perpendicular to each other or multiplication of slopes of tangents equal to −1.

21. Given, equation of curve is

$$y=x^2-2x+7 \quad \ldots(\text{i})$$

On differentiating both sides w.r.t. x, we get

$$\frac{dy}{dx}=2x-2$$

(i) Given, equation of the line is

$$2x - y + 9 = 0 \Rightarrow y = 2x + 9$$

which is of the form $y = mx + c$.

$\therefore$ Slope of the line is $m = 2$.

If a tangent is parallel to the line, then slope of tangent is equal to the slope of the line.

Therefore, $\frac{dy}{dx} = m$

$\Rightarrow \quad 2x - 2 = 2 \Rightarrow x = 2$

When $x = 2$, then from Eq. (i), we get

$$y = 2^2 - 2 \times 2 + 7$$

$\Rightarrow \quad y = 7$

The point on the given curve at which tangent is parallel to given line is (2, 7) and the equation of the tangent is

$$y - 7 = 2(x - 2) \quad [\because y - y_1 = m(x - x_1)]$$

$\Rightarrow 2x - y + 3 = 0$

Hence, the equation of the tangent line to the given curve which is parallel to line $2x - y + 9 = 0$ is $y - 2x - 3 = 0$.

(ii) The equation of the given line is

$$5y - 15x = 13 \Rightarrow y = \frac{15x + 13}{5} = 3x + \frac{13}{5}$$

which is of the form $y = mx + c$.

$\therefore$ Slope of the given line is 3.

If a tangent is perpendicular to the line $5y - 15x = 13$.

Then, the slope of the tangent $= -\frac{1}{3}$

$$\therefore \; 2x - 2 = \frac{-1}{3} \Rightarrow 2x = \frac{5}{3} \Rightarrow x = \frac{5}{6}$$

When $x = \frac{5}{6}$, then from Eq. (i), we get

$$y = \left(\frac{5}{6}\right)^2 - 2\left(\frac{5}{6}\right) + 7$$

$$= \frac{25}{36} - \frac{10}{6} + 7 = \frac{25 - 60 + 252}{36} \Rightarrow y = \frac{217}{36}$$

$\therefore$ The point on the given curve at which tangent is perpendicular to given line is $\left(\frac{5}{6}, \frac{217}{36}\right)$ and the equation of the tangent is

$$y - \frac{217}{36} = \frac{-1}{3}\left(x - \frac{5}{6}\right)$$

$$[\because y - y_1 = m(x - x_1)]$$

$$\Rightarrow \quad \frac{36y - 217}{36} = \frac{-x}{3} + \frac{5}{18}$$

$$\Rightarrow \quad \frac{36y - 217}{36} = \frac{-12x + 10}{36}$$

$\therefore \; 12x + 36y - 227 = 0$

Hence, the equation of the tangent line to the given curve which is perpendicular to the line $5y - 15x = 13$, is

$$36y + 12x - 227 = 0$$

TOPIC 3
Maxima and Minima

Maximum and Minimum Value of a Function

Let f be a function define on an interval I. Then,

(i) f is said to have a **maximum value** in I, if there exists a point c in I such that $f(c) \geq f(x), \forall x \in I$. The number $f(c)$ is called the maximum value of f in I and the point c is called a **point of maximum value** of f in I.

(ii) f is said to have a **minimum value** in I, if there exists a point c in I such that $f(c) \leq f(x), \forall x \in I$. The number $f(c)$ is called the minimum value of f in I and the point c is called a **point of minimum value** of f in I.

(iii) f is said to have an extreme value in I, if there exists a point c in I such that $f(c)$ is either a maximum value or a minimum value of f in I. The number $f(c)$ is called an **extreme value** of f in I and the point c is called an **extreme point**.

Local Maxima and Local Minima

(i) A point C in the interior of the domain of f, is called local maxima, if there exists a $\delta > 0$ such that $f(x) \leq f(a), \forall x \in (a - \delta, a + \delta)$. Here, $f(a)$ is called the local maximum value of $f(x)$ at the point $x = a$.

(ii) A point C in the interior of the domain of f, is called local minima, if there exists $\delta > 0$ such that $f(x) \geq f(a), \forall x \in (a - \delta, a + \delta)$. Here, $f(a)$ is called the local minimum value of $f(x)$ at the point $x = a$.

Some Important Points

(i) The points at which a function changes its nature from decreasing to increasing or *vice-versa* are called **turning points.**

NOTE (i) Through the graphs, we can even find maximum/minimum value of a function at a point at which it is not even differentiable.

(ii) Every monotonic function assumes its maximum/minimum value at the end points of the domain of definition of the function.

(ii) Every continuous function on a closed interval has a maximum and a minimum value.

(iii) Let f be a function defined on an open interval I. Suppose $c \in I$ is any point. If f has a local maxima or a local minima at $x = c$, then either $f'(c) = 0$ or f is not differentiable at c.

(iv) **Critical Point** A point c in the domain of a function f at which either $f'(c) = 0$ or f is not differentiable, is called a critical point of f.

Method to Find Maxima and Minima by First Derivative Test

Let f be a function defined on an open interval I and f be continuous at a critical point c in I. Then,

(i) If $f'(x)$ changes sign from positive to negative as x increases through c, then c is a point of **local maxima.**

(ii) If $f'(x)$ changes sign from negative to positive as x increases through c, then c is a point of **local minima.**

Method to Find Maxima and Minima by Second Derivative Test

Let $f(x)$ be a function defined on an interval I and $c \in I$. Let f be twice differentiable at c. Then,

(i) $x = c$ is a point of local maxima, if $f'(c) = 0$ and $f''(c) < 0$.

(ii) $x = c$ is a point of local minima, if $f'(c) = 0$ and $f''(c) > 0$.

(iii) the test fails, if $f'(c) = 0$ and $f''(c) = 0$.

NOTE (i) If the test fails, then we go back to the first derivative test and find whether c is a point of local maxima, local minima or a point of inflection.

(ii) If we say that f is twice differentiable at a, then it means second order derivative exist at a.

Maximum and Minimum Value of Function in a Closed Interval

If a function $f(x)$ is continuous on a closed interval $[a, b]$, then it attains the maximum value (minimum value) which is called the absolute maximum value or global maximum (absolute minimum value or global minimum), at critical points or at the end points of the interval $[a, b]$.

Let f be a continuous function on a closed interval $I = [a, b]$. Then, f has the absolute maximum value and f attains it atleast once in I. Also, f has the absolute minimum value and attains it atleast once in I.

Working Rule for Finding Absolute Maxima and Absolute Minima

***Step* I** Find all the critical points of f in the given interval.

***Step* II** At all these points and at the end points of the interval, calculate the values of f.

***Step* III** Identify the maximum and minimum values of f out of the values calculated in Step II. The maximum value will be the absolute maximum value of f and the minimum value will be the absolute minimum value of f.

PYQs Previous Years Questions

1 Mark Question

1. The function $f(x) = \sin x + \cos x, x \in \left(0, \frac{\pi}{2}\right)$;
Maximum value of the $f(x)$ is **ISC Specimen 2021**
(a) 1 (b) 2 (c) $\frac{1}{\sqrt{2}}$ (d) $\sqrt{2}$

3/4 Marks Questions

2. Show that the surface area of a closed cuboid with square base and given volume is minimum when it is a cube. **ISC 2017**

3. A rectangle is inscribed in a semi-circle of radius r with one of its sides on the diameter of the semi-circle. Find the dimensions of the rectangle to get maximum area. Also, find the maximum area. **ISC 2016**

4. Show that the rectangle of maximum perimeter which can be inscribed in a circle of radius 10 cm is a square of side $10\sqrt{2}$ cm. **ISC 2015**

5. A wire of length 50 m is cut into two pieces. One piece of the wire is bent in the shape of a square and the other in the shape of a circle. What should be the length of each piece so that the combined area of the two is minimum? **ISC 2014**

5/6 Marks Questions

6. Mrs. Roy designs a window in her son's study room, so that the room gets maximum sunlight. She designs the window in the shape of a rectangle surmounted by an equilateral triangle. If the perimeter of the window is 12 m, find the dimensions of the window that will admit maximum sunlight into the room. **ISC 2024**

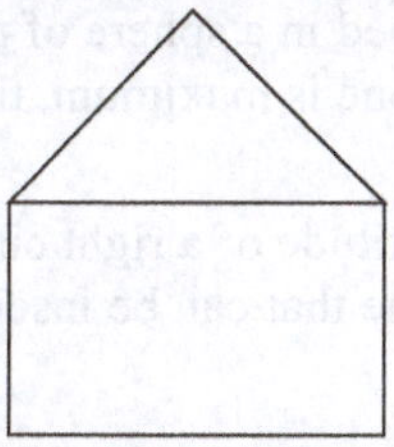

7. Sumit has bought a closed cylindrical dustbin. The radius of the dustbin is r cm and height is h cm. It has a volume of 20π cm^3. **ISC 2024**

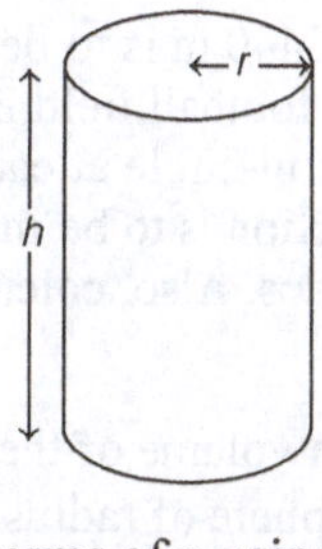

(a) Express h in terms of r, using the given volume.
(b) Prove that the total surface area of the dustbin is $2\pi r^2 + \frac{40\pi}{r}$.
(c) Sumit wants to paint the dustbin. The cost of painting the base and top of the dustbin is ₹ 2 per cm^2 and the cost of painting the curved side is ₹ 25 per cm^2. Find the total cost in terms of r, for painting the outer surface of the dustbin including the base and top.
(d) Calculate the minimum cost for painting the dustbin.

8. A village chief wants to build a cuboidal water tank with a square base and an open top to store 50,000 L of water. The cost of the stainless-steel sheet required for construction is ₹ 60,000 per square meter.

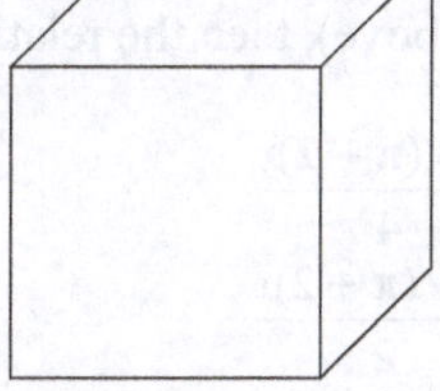

Find the dimensions of the tank that will minimise the cost of the stainless-steel sheet and determine the minimum cost. **ISC Specimen 2024**

9. A paper weight manufacturer is designing a paper weight in the form of a cylinder inscribed in a sphere. He wants to keep the volume of the cylinder to be maximum. The radius of the sphere is $3\sqrt{3}$ cm. Find the maximum volume of the cylinder. **ISC Specimen 2024**

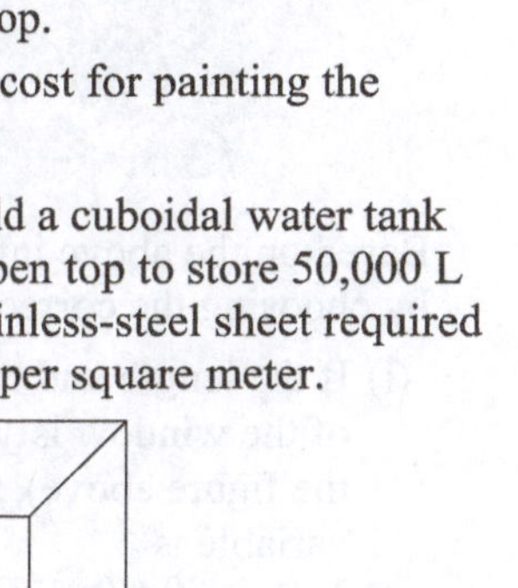

10. Prove that the semi-vertical angle of the right circular cone of given volume and least curved area is $\cot^{-1}\sqrt{2}$. **ISC 2023**

11. A running track of 440 m is to be laid out enclosing a football field. The football field is in the shape of a rectangle with a semi-circle at each end. If the area of the rectangular portion is to be maximum, then find the length of its sides. Also, calculate the area of the football field. **ISC 2023**

12. Find the maximum volume of the cylinder which can be inscribed in a sphere of radius $3\sqrt{3}$ cm. (find the answer in terms of π) **ISC Specimen 2023**

13. A Norman window is constructed by adjoining a semicircle to the top of an ordinary rectangular window as shown in the figure given below. The total perimeter of the window is 10 m.

Based on the above information answer the following by choosing the correct option. **ISC Specimen Sem-I 2022**

(i) If the length and breadth of the rectangle portion of the window is y and x respectively (as shown in the figure above), then the relation between the variable is

(a) $y = \dfrac{20 + (\pi - 2)x}{4}$

(b) $y = \dfrac{20 - (\pi + 2)x}{2}$

(c) $y = \dfrac{20 - (\pi + 4)x}{4}$

(d) $y = \dfrac{20 - (\pi + 2)x}{4}$

(ii) Let A be the area of the Norman window which admits the sunlight. Then, A expressed in terms of x as

(a) $A = 5x + \dfrac{\pi}{4}x^2 - 2x^2$

(b) $A = 5x + \dfrac{\pi}{8}x^2 - \dfrac{1}{2}x^2$

(c) $A = 5x - \dfrac{\pi}{8}x^2 - \dfrac{1}{2}x^2$

(d) $A = 5x - \dfrac{\pi}{2}x^2 - \dfrac{1}{4}x^2$

(iii) For the maximum value of A what will be the radius of the semicircle?

(a) $\dfrac{10}{2+\pi}$ (b) $\dfrac{10}{\pi - 2}$

(c) $\dfrac{10}{4+\pi}$ (d) $\dfrac{20}{4-\pi}$

(iv) For maximum value of A, the length of the rectangle represented by y will be equal to

(a) $\dfrac{10}{4+\pi}$ (b) $\dfrac{10}{\pi - 2}$

(c) $\dfrac{20}{4+\pi}$ (d) $\dfrac{20}{4-\pi}$

14. A cone is inscribed in a sphere of radius 12 cm. If the volume of the cone is maximum, then find its height. **ISC Specimen 2021**

15. Show that the radius of a closed right circular cylinder of given surface area and maximum volume is equal to half of its height. **ISC 2020**

> **KEY CONCEPT**
>
> Total surface area of cylinder, $S = 2\pi r^2 + 2\pi rh$
>
> and volume, $V = \pi r^2 h$
>
> Find $\dfrac{dV}{dr}$ and put it equal to zero and find value of r.
>
> Again, differentiate it and find $\dfrac{d^2V}{dr^2} < 0$, also find relation in r and h by using above formula.

16. Find the point on the straight line $2x + 3y = 6$, which is closest to the origin. **ISC 2019**

17. The volume of a closed rectangular metal box with a square base is 4096 cm^3. The cost of polishing the outer surface of the box is ₹ 4 per cm^2. Find the dimensions of the box for the minimum cost of polishing it. **ISC 2019**

18. A cone is inscribed in a sphere of radius 12 cm. If the volume of the cone is maximum, then find its height. **ISC 2018**

19. Show that the altitude of a right circular cone of maximum volume that can be inscribed in a sphere of radius r is $\dfrac{4r}{3}$. **ISC Specimen 2018**

20. An open topped box is to be made by removing equal squares from each corner of a 3 m by 8 m rectangle sheet of aluminium and by folding up the sides. Find the volume of the largest such box. **ISC Specimen 2018**

Explanations

1. (d) Given, $f(x) = \sin x + \cos x$

$$f'(x) = \cos x - \sin x$$

For maximum value, $f'(x) = 0$

$$\Rightarrow \quad \cos x - \sin x = 0$$

$$\Rightarrow \quad \cos x = \sin x$$

$$\Rightarrow \quad \tan x = 1$$

$$\Rightarrow \quad \tan x = \tan \frac{\pi}{4}$$

$$\Rightarrow \quad x = \frac{\pi}{4}$$

Now, $f''(x) = -\sin x - \cos x$

$$= -(\sin x + \cos x)$$

$$f''\left(\frac{\pi}{4}\right) = -\left(\sin\frac{\pi}{4} + \cos\frac{\pi}{4}\right)$$

$$= -\left(\frac{1}{\sqrt{2}} + \frac{1}{\sqrt{2}}\right)$$

$$= -\frac{2}{\sqrt{2}}$$

$$= -\sqrt{2} < 0$$

Thus, $f(x)$ is maximum cot $x = \frac{\pi}{4}$.

Hence, the maximum value $= f\left(\frac{\pi}{4}\right) = \sin\frac{\pi}{4} + \cos\frac{\pi}{4}$

$$= \frac{1}{\sqrt{2}} + \frac{1}{\sqrt{2}} = \sqrt{2}$$

2. Let V be the volume of a closed cuboid having length a, breadth a and height h.

Also, let A be the surface area of the closed cuboid.

Then, $V = (a \times a \times h)$ or $h = \frac{V}{a^2}$ ...(i)

Now, $A = 2(a^2 + ah + ah) = 2(a^2 + 2ah)$

$$= 2\left(a^2 + \frac{2V}{a}\right) \quad \text{[using Eq. (i)]}$$

$$\therefore \quad \frac{dA}{da} = 2\left(2a - \frac{2V}{a^2}\right) \text{ and } \frac{d^2A}{da^2} = \left(4 + \frac{8V}{a^3}\right)$$

For maxima and minima, put

$$\frac{dA}{da} = 0 \Rightarrow V = a^3$$

$$\Rightarrow \quad a \times a \times h = a^3 \Rightarrow h = a$$

Now, when $V = a^3$ or $a = V^{1/3}$

$$\left[\frac{d^2A}{da^2}\right] = 4 + \frac{8V}{V} = 12 > 0$$

$\therefore$ A is minimum when length $= a$, breadth $= a$ and height $= a$ i.e. when it is cube. **Hence proved.**

3. Let $ABCD$ be a rectangle inscribed in a semi-circle of radius r.

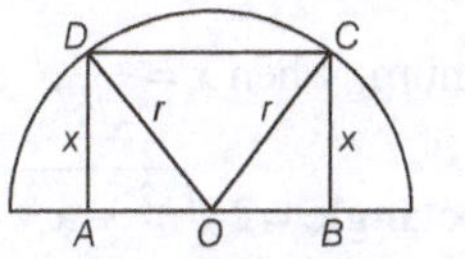

Let $AD = BC = x$

$$\therefore \quad OA = OB = \sqrt{r^2 - x^2}$$

Now, $AB = OA + OB = 2\,OB = 2\sqrt{r^2 - x^2}$

$\therefore$ Area of rectangle, $A = AB \times BC$

$$\Rightarrow \quad A = (2\sqrt{r^2 - x^2}) \times x$$

On differentiating w.r.t. x, we get

$$\frac{dA}{dx} = 2x \times \frac{1}{2\sqrt{r^2 - x^2}}(-2x) + \sqrt{r^2 - x^2} \cdot 2$$

$$\Rightarrow \quad \frac{dA}{dx} = \frac{-2x^2}{\sqrt{r^2 - x^2}} + 2\sqrt{r^2 - x^2}$$

$$\Rightarrow \quad \frac{dA}{dx} = \frac{-2x^2 + 2(r^2 - x^2)}{\sqrt{r^2 - x^2}} = \frac{-4x^2 + 2r^2}{\sqrt{r^2 - x^2}}$$

For maximum or minimum, put

$$\frac{dA}{dx} = 0$$

$$\Rightarrow \quad \frac{-4x^2 + 2r^2}{\sqrt{r^2 - x^2}} = 0 \Rightarrow -4x^2 + 2r^2 = 0$$

$$\Rightarrow \quad x^2 = \frac{r^2}{2} \Rightarrow x = \frac{r}{\sqrt{2}}$$

Now,

$$\frac{d^2A}{dx^2} = \frac{\sqrt{r^2 - x^2}\,(-8x) - (2r^2 - 4x^2) \cdot \dfrac{-2x}{2\sqrt{r^2 - x^2}}}{r^2 - x^2}$$

$$\Rightarrow \quad \frac{d^2A}{dx^2} = \frac{-8x\sqrt{r^2 - x^2} + \dfrac{(2r^2 - 4x^2)x}{\sqrt{r^2 - x^2}}}{(r^2 - x^2)}$$

$$\Rightarrow \quad \frac{d^2A}{dx^2} = \frac{-8x\,(r^2-x^2)+(2r^2-4x^2)\,x}{(r^2-x^2)^{3/2}}$$

$$\therefore \quad \left(\frac{d^2A}{dx^2}\right)_{x=\frac{r}{\sqrt{2}}} = \frac{-8\frac{r}{\sqrt{2}}\left(\frac{r^2}{2}\right)+0}{\left(\frac{r^2}{2}\right)^{3/2}} = -\frac{\frac{4r^3}{\sqrt{2}}}{\frac{r^3}{2\sqrt{2}}}$$

$$= -4\frac{r^3}{\sqrt{2}} \times \frac{2\sqrt{2}}{r^3} = -8 < 0$$

So, A is maximum, when $x = \frac{r}{\sqrt{2}}$.

$\therefore$ Length of rectangle $= 2\sqrt{r^2-x^2} = \sqrt{2}r$

and breadth of rectangle $= \frac{r}{\sqrt{2}}$

$\therefore$ Maximum area $= r^2$

4. Let $ABCD$ be the rectangle which is inscribed in the fixed circle whose centre at O and radius 10 cm.

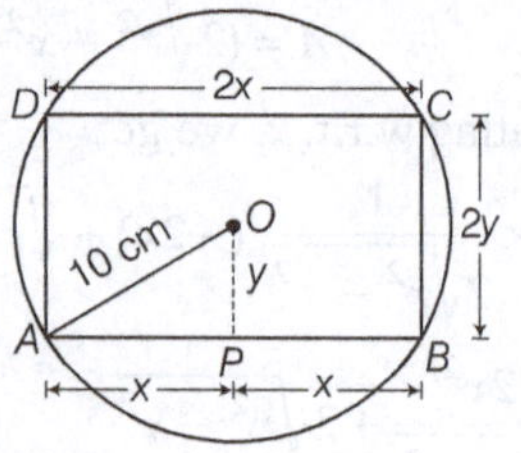

Let $AB = 2x$ and $BC = 2y$

In right angled ΔOPA,

$$x^2 + y^2 = 10^2$$

$$\Rightarrow \quad y^2 = 100 - x^2$$

$$\Rightarrow \quad y = \sqrt{100-x^2} \quad \text{...(i)}$$

Let A be the area of rectangle.

$$\therefore \quad A = 2x \times 2y = 4xy$$

$$\Rightarrow \quad A = 4xy$$

$$\Rightarrow \quad A = 4x\sqrt{100-x^2}$$

On differentiating both sides w.r.t. x, we get

$$\frac{dA}{dx} = 4x\frac{d}{dx}(\sqrt{100-x^2}) + \sqrt{100-x^2}\frac{d}{dx}(4x)$$

$$= 4x \times \frac{-2x}{2\sqrt{100-x^2}} + \sqrt{100-x^2} \times 4$$

$$= 4\left[\frac{100-x^2-x^2}{\sqrt{100-x^2}}\right] = 4\left[\frac{100-2x^2}{\sqrt{100-x^2}}\right]$$

For maxima or minima, put $\frac{dA}{dx} = 0$

$$\therefore \quad 4\left[\frac{100-2x^2}{\sqrt{100-x^2}}\right] = 0$$

$$\Rightarrow \quad 100 - 2x^2 = 0$$

$$\Rightarrow \quad x^2 = \frac{100}{2}$$

$$\Rightarrow \quad x^2 = 50 \Rightarrow x = \pm 5\sqrt{2}$$

Now, $$\frac{d^2A}{dx^2} = \frac{d}{dx}\left[4(100-2x^2)(100-x^2)^{-\frac{1}{2}}\right]$$

$$= 4\left[(100-2x^2)\frac{d}{dx}(100-x^2)^{-\frac{1}{2}} + (100-x^2)^{-\frac{1}{2}}\frac{d}{dx}(100-2x^2)\right]$$

$$= 4\left[(100-2x^2)\left(-\frac{1}{2}\right)(100-x^2)^{-\frac{3}{2}}(-2x) + (100-x^2)^{-\frac{1}{2}}(-4x)\right]$$

$$= 4\left[\frac{x(100-2x^2)}{(100-x^2)^{\frac{3}{2}}} - \frac{4x}{(100-x^2)^{\frac{1}{2}}}\right]$$

Put $x = 5\sqrt{2}$, we get

$$\frac{d^2A}{dx^2} = 4\left[5\sqrt{2}\frac{[100-2\times 50]}{(100-50)^{\frac{3}{2}}} - \frac{4\times 5\sqrt{2}}{(100-50)^{\frac{1}{2}}}\right]$$

$$= 4\left[0 - \frac{20\sqrt{2}}{(50)^{\frac{1}{2}}}\right] = 4\left[\frac{-20\sqrt{2}}{5\sqrt{2}}\right] = -16 < 0$$

$\because \frac{d^2A}{dx^2} < 0$, so A is maximum at $x = 5\sqrt{2}$.

Now, put $x = 5\sqrt{2}$ in Eq. (i), we get

$$y = \sqrt{100-(5\sqrt{2})^2} = \sqrt{100-50} = \sqrt{50} = 5\sqrt{2}$$

$$\therefore \quad x = y = 5\sqrt{2} \text{ cm} \Rightarrow 2x = 2y = 10\sqrt{2} \text{ cm}$$

Hence, area of rectangle is maximum, when $2x = 2y$ i.e. when rectangle is a square of side $10\sqrt{2}$ cm.

5. Let x be the radius of circle and y be the side of square.

Circumference of circle $= 2\pi x$

Perimeter of square $= 4y$

Also, given,

$$2\pi x + 4y = 50 \quad \ldots\text{(i)}$$

Let A be the sum of the area of circle and square.

Then, $A = \pi x^2 + y^2$

$$= \pi x^2 + \left(\frac{50 - 2\pi x}{4}\right)^2 \quad \text{[from Eq. (i)]}$$

On differentiating both sides w.r.t. x, we get

$$\frac{dA}{dx} = 2\pi x + 2\frac{(50 - 2\pi x)}{4}\frac{d}{dx}\left(\frac{50 - 2\pi x}{4}\right)$$

$$= 2\pi x + \frac{2(50 - 2\pi x)}{4} \times \left(\frac{-2\pi}{4}\right)$$

$$= 2\pi x - \frac{(50 - 2\pi x)\pi}{4}$$

$$= 2\pi x - \frac{50\pi}{4} + \frac{\pi^2 x}{2}$$

For maxima or minima, put $\frac{dA}{dx} = 0$

$\Rightarrow \quad 2\pi x - \frac{50\pi}{4} + \frac{\pi^2 x}{2} = 0$

$\Rightarrow \quad 8\pi x - 50\pi + 2\pi^2 x = 0$

$\Rightarrow \quad 8x - 50 + 2\pi x = 0$

$\Rightarrow \quad \pi x + 4x = 25$

$\therefore \quad x = \frac{25}{4 + \pi}$

Now, $\frac{d^2A}{dx^2} = 2\pi + \frac{\pi^2}{2}$ which is always positive.

So, A is minimum when $x = \frac{25}{4 + \pi}$.

Then, $4y = 50 - \frac{2\pi \times 25}{4 + \pi}$ [from Eq. (i)]

$\Rightarrow \quad 4y = \frac{200 + 50\pi - 50\pi}{4 + \pi}$

$\therefore \quad y = \frac{50}{4 + \pi}$

Hence, A is minimum when

$$y = 2x$$

i.e. Side of square = Diameter of circle.

Therefore, the length of the wire bent in the shape of square should be of $\frac{200}{(4 + \pi)}$ m and the length of the wire in the shape of circle should be $\frac{50\pi}{4 + \pi}$ m.

6. Let x be the length and y be the width of the rectangular portion of the window as shown in the figure.

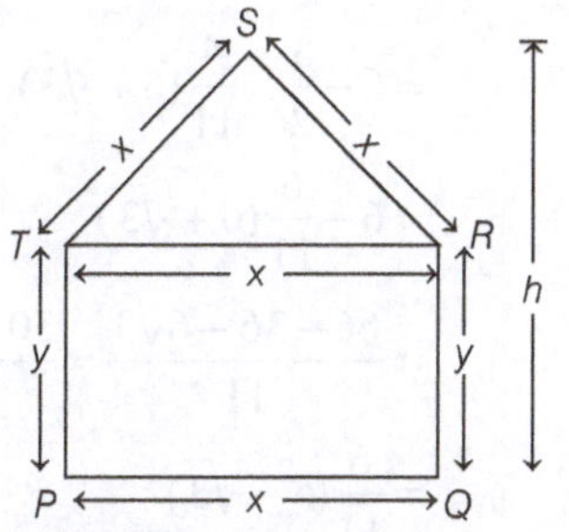

An equilateral triangle with side x placed on the rectangular shape.

$\because$ Perimeter of window $= PQ + QR + RS + ST + TP$

$$12 = x + y + x + x + y$$

$$12 = 3x + 2y \quad \ldots\text{(i)}$$

Now, the area of the window

A = Area of rectangle + Area of equilateral triangle

$$= xy + \frac{\sqrt{3}}{4}x^2$$

$$= x\left[\frac{12 - 3x}{2}\right] + \frac{\sqrt{3}}{4}x^2 \quad [\because \text{using Eq. (i)}]$$

$$= 6x - \frac{3}{2}x^2 + \frac{\sqrt{3}}{4}x^2$$

$$= x^2\left(\frac{\sqrt{3}}{4} - \frac{3}{2}\right) + 6x$$

For maximum sunlight, area of window should be maximum.

Now, $\frac{dA}{dx} = 2x\left(\frac{\sqrt{3}}{4} - \frac{3}{2}\right) + 6 = x\left(\frac{\sqrt{3}}{2} - 3\right) + 6$

For maximum, $\frac{dA}{dx} = 0$

$\Rightarrow x\left(\frac{\sqrt{3}}{2} - 3\right) + 6 = 0$

$\Rightarrow \quad x = \frac{6}{\left(3 - \frac{\sqrt{3}}{2}\right)} = \left(\frac{12}{6 - \sqrt{3}}\right) \times \frac{6 + \sqrt{3}}{6 + \sqrt{3}}$

$$= \frac{4}{11}(6 + \sqrt{3}) \text{ m}$$

Also, $\frac{d^2A}{dx^2} = \left(\frac{\sqrt{3}}{2} - 3\right) < 0$

Hence, the area is maximum at $x = \frac{4}{11}(6 + \sqrt{3})$.

So, from Eq. (i),

$$y=\frac{12-3x}{2}$$
$$=6-\frac{3}{2}\times\frac{4}{11}(6+\sqrt{3})$$
$$=6-\frac{6}{11}(6+\sqrt{3})$$
$$=\frac{66-36-6\sqrt{3}}{11}=\frac{30-6\sqrt{3}}{11}$$
$$=\frac{6}{11}(5-\sqrt{3})$$

Hence, the length of window (rectangular portion) is $\frac{4}{11}(6+\sqrt{3})$ m and the width of (rectangular portion) is $\frac{6}{11}(5-\sqrt{3})$ m and the height of the window

$$h=y+\text{Height of triangle}$$
$$=\frac{6}{11}(5-\sqrt{3})+\frac{\sqrt{3}}{2}\times\frac{4}{11}(6+\sqrt{3})$$
$$=\frac{30}{11}-\frac{6\sqrt{3}}{11}+\frac{12\sqrt{3}}{11}+\frac{6}{11}$$
$$=\frac{36}{11}+\frac{6\sqrt{3}}{11}$$
$$=\frac{6}{11}(6+\sqrt{3})\text{ m}$$

7. Given, volume of closed cylindrical dustbin $=20\pi$ cm^3

Also, given r and h are the radius and height of the dustbin, respectively.

(a) We have,

$$V=20\pi \text{ cm}^3$$
$$\Rightarrow \quad \pi r^2 h=20\pi$$
$$\Rightarrow \quad r^2 h=20$$
$$\Rightarrow \quad h=\frac{20}{r^2}$$

(b) Total surface area of closed dustbin

$$S=\text{Area of top and bottom} + \text{Curved surface area}$$
$$=2\pi r^2+2\pi rh$$
$$=2\pi r^2+2\pi r\times\frac{20}{r^2} \quad \left[\because h=\frac{20}{r^2}\right]$$
$$=2\pi r^2+\frac{40\pi}{r}$$
$$S=2\pi r^2+\frac{40\pi}{r}$$ **Hence proved.**

(c) Given, the cost of painting the base and top of the dustbin = ₹ 2/cm^2

and the cost of painting the curved surface area of dustbin = ₹ 25/cm^2

$$\therefore \text{Total cost of painting}=2\times 2\pi r^2+25\times\frac{40\pi}{r}$$
$$=₹4\pi r^2+₹\frac{1000\pi}{r}$$
$$=₹\left(4\pi r^2+\frac{1000\pi}{r}\right)$$

(d) Let the total cost of painting

$$C(r)=4\pi r^2+\frac{1000\pi}{r}$$
$$\Rightarrow \quad C'(r)=8\pi r-\frac{1000\pi}{r^2}$$

For minimum and maximum cost, we take

$$C'(r)=0$$
$$\Rightarrow 8\pi r-\frac{1000\pi}{r^2}=0$$
$$\Rightarrow \quad 8r^3-1000=0$$
$$\Rightarrow \quad (2r)^3=(10)^3$$
$$\Rightarrow \quad 2r=10 \Rightarrow r=5$$

Again, $C''(r)=8\pi+\frac{2000\pi}{r^3}$

At $r=5$, $C''(5)=\left(8\pi+\frac{2000\pi}{125}\right)>0$

Hence, the cost is minimum at $r=5$ cm.

$$\therefore \; C(5)=4\pi(5)^2+\frac{1000\pi}{5}$$
$$=100\pi+200\pi=300\pi=300\times\frac{22}{7}$$
$$=₹\,942.85 \text{ (approx)}$$

Thus, the minimum cost of painting is ₹ 942.85 (approx).

8. Let the length, width and height of the open tank be x, x and y units respectively.

$\therefore$ Volume $(V)=x^2y=50$ ...(i)

Total surface area $S=x^2+4xy$ ...(ii)

From Eqs. (i) and (ii), we get

$$S=x^2+4x\left(\frac{50}{x^2}\right)=x^2+\frac{200}{x}$$
$$\therefore \quad \frac{dS}{dx}=2x-\frac{200}{x^2}$$

Now, $\frac{dS}{dx}=0 \Rightarrow 2x-\frac{200}{x^2}=0$

$\Rightarrow \quad x=(100)^{1/3}$

$\Rightarrow \quad \frac{d^2S}{dx^2}=2+\frac{400}{x^3}$

$\therefore \quad \left.\frac{d^2S}{dx^2}\right|_{x=(100)^{1/3}}$ is positive.

$\therefore$ Surface area will be minimum at $x=(100)^{1/3}$

$\therefore \quad y=\frac{50}{(100)^{2/3}}$

$\therefore$ Minimum surface area,

$$S=(100)^{2/3}+4(100)^{1/3}\cdot\frac{50}{(100)^{2/3}}$$

$$S=(100)^{2/3}+\frac{200}{(100)^{1/3}}$$

$\therefore$ Total minimum cost

$$=₹\left((100)^{2/3}+\frac{200}{(100)^{1/3}}\right)\times 60000$$

$$=₹\ 3877982.4$$

9. Let 'V' be the volume of the cylinder

$\therefore \quad V=\pi r^2 h \quad \ldots$(i)

From figure,

$$\left(\frac{h}{2}\right)^2+r^2=(3\sqrt{3})^2 \Rightarrow \frac{h^2}{4}+r^2=27$$

$\Rightarrow \quad r^2=\left(27-\frac{h^2}{4}\right) \quad \ldots$(ii)

From Eqs. (i) and (ii), we get

$$V=\pi\left(27-\frac{h^2}{4}\right)h$$

$$V=\pi\left(27h-\frac{h^3}{4}\right)$$

$$\frac{dV}{dh}=\pi\left(27-\frac{3h^2}{4}\right)$$

Now, $\frac{dV}{dh}=0 \Rightarrow 27=\frac{3h^2}{4}$

$\Rightarrow \quad h^2=36 \Rightarrow h=6$ cm

$$\frac{d^2V}{dh^2}=\pi\left(-\frac{6h}{4}\right)$$

$\therefore \quad \left.\frac{d^2V}{dh^2}\right|_{h=6}$ is negative.

$\therefore$ Volume V is maximum, when $h=6$ cm.

From Eq. (ii), we get

$$r^2=27-\frac{36}{4}=27-9=18$$

$\Rightarrow \quad r=3\sqrt{2}$ cm

$\therefore$ Maximum volume, $V=\pi(3\sqrt{2})^2(6)$

$$V=108\pi \text{ cm}^3$$

10. Let r be the radius and h be the height of given cone.

Then, volume $(V)=\frac{1}{3}\pi r^2 h$

$\Rightarrow \quad h=\frac{3V}{\pi r^2}$

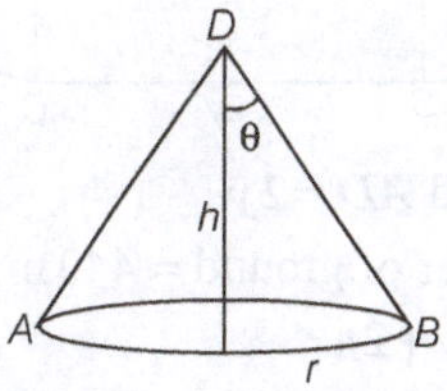

Let C be the curved surface area of the cone.

Then, $\quad C=\pi r l$

$\Rightarrow \quad C^2=\pi^2 r^2 l^2=\pi^2 r^2(r^2+h^2)$ $[\because l^2=r^2+h^2]$

Let $\quad C^2=S$

$\therefore \quad S=\pi^2(r^4+r^2h^2)$

$\Rightarrow \quad S=\pi^2\left[r^4+r^2\left(\frac{9V^2}{\pi^2 r^4}\right)\right]$ $\left[\because h=\frac{3V}{\pi r^2}\right]$

$\Rightarrow \quad S=\pi^2\left(r^4+\frac{9V^2}{\pi^2 r^2}\right)$

C is maximum or minimum according to S is maximum or minimum.

$\therefore \quad \frac{dS}{dr}=\pi^2\left(4r^3-\frac{18V^2}{\pi^2 r^3}\right)$

For maximum or minimum, we must have

$$\frac{dS}{dr}=0 \Rightarrow \pi^2\left(4r^3-\frac{18V^2}{\pi^2 r^3}\right)=0 \Rightarrow V^2=\frac{2}{9}\pi^2 r^6$$

Again, on differentiating w.r.t. r, we get

$$\frac{d^2S}{dr^2}=\pi^2\left(12r^2+\frac{54V^2}{\pi^2 r^4}\right)>0$$

[by second derivative test]

So, S is minimum when $V^2 = \frac{2}{9}\pi^2 r^6$

$$\Rightarrow \quad \frac{2}{9}\pi^2 r^6 = \frac{1}{9}\pi^2 r^4 h^2 \quad \left[\because V = \frac{1}{3}\pi r^2 h\right]$$

$$\Rightarrow \quad 2r^2 = h^2 \Rightarrow h = \sqrt{2}r$$

$$\Rightarrow \quad \frac{h}{r} = \sqrt{2} \Rightarrow \cot\theta = \sqrt{2}$$

$$\Rightarrow \quad \theta = \cot^{-1}\sqrt{2}$$

Hence, the curved surface area is minimum when $\theta = \cot^{-1}\sqrt{2}$.

11. Let $ABCD$ be a rectangle and let the semi-circle be described on side AB and CD as diameter respectively.

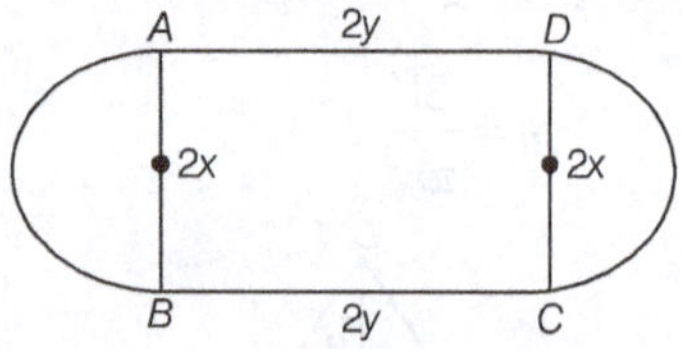

Let $AB = 2x$ and $AD = 2y$

Given, perimeter of ground = 440 m

Then, $440 = 4y + 2\pi x$ ...(i)

A = Area of rectangular field

$$\therefore \quad A = 2x \cdot 2y = 4xy$$

$$\Rightarrow \quad A = x4y = x(440 - 2\pi x) \quad \text{[from Eq. (i)]}$$

$$\Rightarrow \quad A = 440x - 2\pi x^2$$

$$\Rightarrow \quad \frac{dA}{dx} = 440 - 4\pi x \Rightarrow \frac{d^2A}{dx^2} = -4\pi < 0$$

$\therefore$ Area of rectangular field is maximum.

$\therefore$ For maxima or minimum, put $\frac{dA}{dx} = 0$

$$\Rightarrow \quad 440 - 4\pi x = 0 \Rightarrow x = \frac{440}{4\pi} = \frac{110}{\pi}$$

$$\Rightarrow \quad x = \frac{110 \times 7}{22} = 35$$

On substitute $x = 5$ in Eq. (i), we get

$$440 = 4y + 2 \times \pi \times 35$$

or $$4y = 440 - 2 \times \frac{22}{7} \times 35 \quad \text{[from Eq. (i)]}$$

$$\Rightarrow \quad 4y = 440 - 220 = 220 \Rightarrow y = \frac{220}{4} = 55$$

Length of sides = 55 m and 35 m

Area of football field $= 4xy + \pi x^2$

$$= 4 \times 35 \times 55 + \frac{22}{7} \times 35 \times 35$$

$$= 7700 + 3850 = 11550 \text{ m}^2$$

12. Let h units be the height of the cylinder and R units be the radius of the cylinder

Given, $3\sqrt{3}$ cm is the radius of the sphere

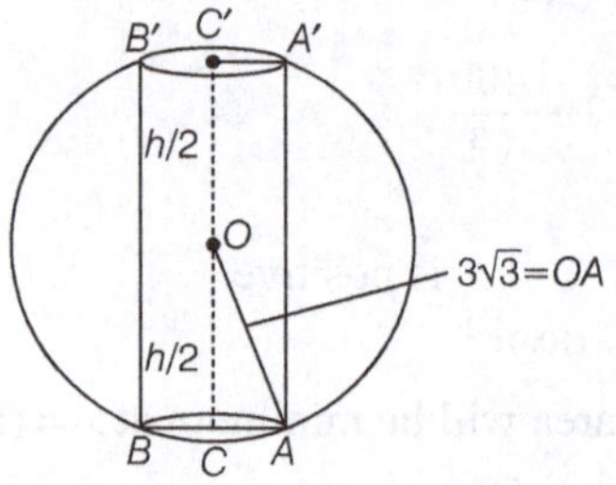

If V is the volume of the cylinder, then

$$V = \pi R^2 h \quad \text{...(i)}$$

Let O be the centre of the sphere and $C'OC \perp B'A'$ as well as BA.

From right angled ΔOCA,

$$(3\sqrt{3})^2 = \left(\frac{h}{2}\right)^2 + R^2 \Rightarrow R^2 = 27 - \frac{h^2}{4} \quad \text{...(ii)}$$

On putting the value of R^2 in Eq. (i), we get

$$V = \pi\left(27 - \frac{h^2}{4}\right) \times h = 27\pi h - \pi\frac{h^3}{4}$$

$$\therefore \quad \frac{dV}{dh} = 27\pi - \frac{3\pi h^2}{4} \text{ and } \frac{d^2V}{dh^2} = \frac{-6\pi h}{4}$$

For maxima/minima, $\frac{dV}{dh} = 0$

$$\therefore \; 27\pi = \frac{3\pi h^2}{4} \Rightarrow h^2 = \frac{4 \times 27}{3} \Rightarrow h^2 = 36 \Rightarrow h = 6, -6$$

and $$\left(\frac{d^2V}{dh^2}\right)_{h=6} = \frac{-6\pi \times 6}{4} < 0$$

$\therefore$ V is maximum, when $h = 6$, on putting $h = 6$ in Eq. (ii), we get

$$R^2 = 27 - \frac{36}{4} \Rightarrow R^2 = 18$$

From Eq. (i), $V = \pi R^2 h = \pi \times 18 \times 6$

$$\therefore \quad V = 108\pi \text{ cm}^3$$

Concept Enhancer For the maximum volume of the cylinder which inscribed in a sphere, the centre of sphere will divide the height of cylinder in equal two parts. If V is the volume of the cylinder, then $V = \pi R^2 h$, (where h is height and R is radius of cylinder).

For maxima and minima, $\frac{dV}{dh} = 0$ ...(i)

If $\frac{d^2V}{dh^2} = -\text{ve} < 0$, then V is maximum at the value of h.

13. Given, diameter of semi-circle $= x$

So, radius of semi-circle $= \frac{x}{2}$

and perimeter of window $= 10$ m

(i) (d) $x + 2y + \pi\left(\frac{x}{2}\right) = 10$

$$2x + 4y + \pi x = 20 \quad \text{[multiplying by 2]}$$

$$\Rightarrow \quad 4y = 20 - \pi x - 2x$$

$$\Rightarrow \quad y = \frac{20 - (\pi + 2)x}{4} \quad \ldots(\text{i})$$

(ii) (c) Area of window

= Area of rectangle + Area of semi-circle

$$A = xy + \frac{1}{2}\pi\left(\frac{x}{2}\right)^2$$

$$= x\left[\frac{20 - (\pi+2)x}{4}\right] + \frac{1}{2} \times \frac{\pi x^2}{4} \quad \text{[from Eq. (i)]}$$

$$= 5x - \frac{\pi x^2}{4} - \frac{1}{2}x^2 + \frac{\pi x^2}{8}$$

$$A = 5x - \frac{\pi x^2}{8} - \frac{1}{2}x^2$$

(iii) (c) $\frac{dA}{dx} = 5 - \frac{\pi x}{4} - x$

Putting $\frac{dA}{dx} = 0$

$$0 = 5 - \frac{\pi x}{5} - x \Rightarrow x + \frac{\pi x}{4} = 5$$

$$\Rightarrow \quad x = \frac{5}{\left(1 + \frac{\pi}{4}\right)} = \frac{20}{\pi + 4}$$

Now, $\frac{d^2A}{dx^2} = -1 - \frac{\pi}{4} < 0$

So, $\frac{d^2A}{dx^2} < 0$ at $x = \frac{20}{\pi + 4}$

Hence, A is maximum when $x = \frac{20}{\pi + 4}$

Therefore, radius of semi-circle $= \frac{x}{2} = \frac{10}{\pi + 4}$

(iv) (a) Substituting the value of x into Eq. (i) to find the value of y.

$$y = \frac{20 - (\pi + 2)\left(\frac{20}{\pi + 4}\right)}{4}$$

$$= 5 - \frac{20}{\pi + 4}\left(\frac{2 + \pi}{4}\right) = 5 - 5\frac{(2 + \pi)}{\pi + 4}$$

$$= 5\left(1 - \frac{2 + \pi}{\pi + 4}\right) = 5\left(\frac{\pi + 4 - 2 - \pi}{\pi + 4}\right)$$

$$= 5\left(\frac{2}{\pi + 4}\right)$$

$$y = \frac{10}{\pi + 4}$$

14. Let the radius of cone be x cm and its height be h cm.

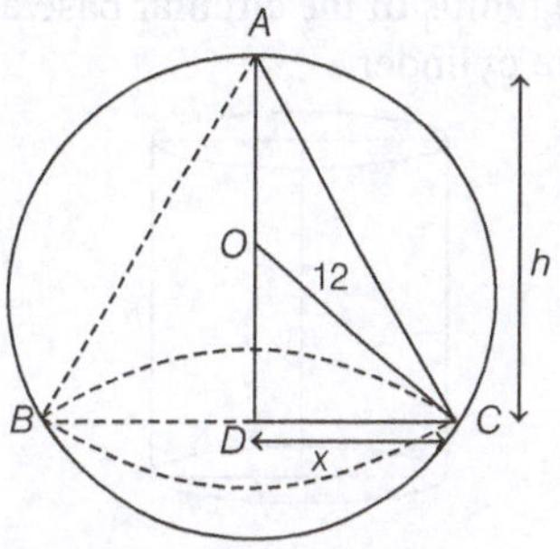

Here, $AD = h$ cm, $OA = OC = 12$ cm

$DC = x$ cm, $OD = h - 12$ cm

Now, in ΔODC,

$$OD^2 + DC^2 = OC^2$$

$$\Rightarrow \quad (h - 12)^2 + x^2 = (12)^2$$

$$\Rightarrow \quad x^2 = (12)^2 - (h - 12)^2$$

$$\Rightarrow \quad x^2 = 24h - h^2 \quad \ldots(\text{i})$$

Volume of cone, $V = \frac{1}{3}\pi x^2 h$

$$= \frac{1}{3}\pi(24h - h^2)h \quad \text{[by Eq. (i)]}$$

$$= \frac{1}{3}\pi(24h^2 - h^3)$$

On differentiating w.r.t. h, we obtain

$$\frac{dV}{dh} = \frac{1}{3}\pi[24(2h) - 3h^2]$$

$$= \frac{\pi}{3}[48h - 3h^2] = \pi[16h - h^2]$$

On $\frac{dV}{dh} = 0 \Rightarrow \pi[16h - h^2] = 0$

$$\Rightarrow \quad h^2 - 16h = 0 \Rightarrow h(h - 16) = 0$$

$$\Rightarrow \quad h = 0, 16$$

So, $h = 16$ $[\because h \neq 0]$

$$\frac{dV}{dh} = \pi(16h - h^2)$$

Again, on differentiating w.r.t. h, we obtain

$$\frac{d^2v}{dh^2} = \pi[16-2h]$$

$$\Rightarrow \left.\frac{d^2v}{dh^2}\right|_{h=16} = \pi[16-32]$$

$$\Rightarrow \left.\frac{d^2v}{dh^2}\right|_{h=16} < 0\,(-\text{ve})$$

Hence, the value will be maximum at height $h = 16$ cm.

15. Let r be the radius of the circular base and h be the height of the cylinder.

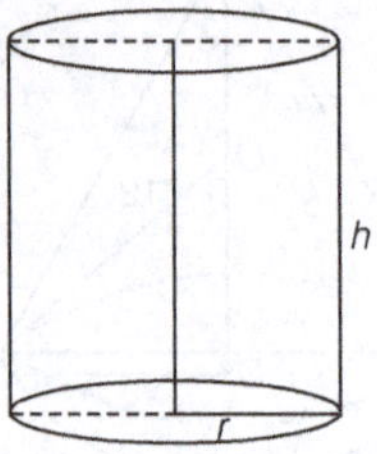

Let S (given) and V denotes its surface area and volume of cylinder. Then,

$$S = 2\pi r^2 + 2\pi rh \Rightarrow h = \frac{S-2\pi r^2}{2\pi r} \quad \ldots\text{(i)}$$

$$\therefore \quad V = \pi r^2 h = \pi r^2\left(\frac{S-2\pi r^2}{2\pi r}\right)$$

$$\Rightarrow \quad V = \frac{1}{2}(Sr - 2\pi r^3)$$

On differentiating it w.r.t. r, we get

$$\frac{dV}{dr} = \frac{1}{2}(S-6\pi r^2) \text{ and } \frac{d^2V}{dr^2} = -6\pi r$$

For maxima or minima,

$$\frac{dV}{dr} = 0 \Rightarrow S - 6\pi r^2 = 0 \Rightarrow r^2 = \frac{S}{6\pi} \Rightarrow r = \sqrt{\frac{S}{6\pi}}$$

At $r = \sqrt{\frac{S}{6\pi}}$, $\frac{d^2V}{dr^2} = -6\pi\sqrt{\frac{S}{6\pi}} < 0$

$\Rightarrow V$ is maximum at $r = \sqrt{\frac{S}{6\pi}}$

Now, putting the value of $S = 6\pi r^2$ in Eq. (i), we get

$$h = \frac{6\pi r^2 - 2\pi r^2}{2\pi r} = \frac{4\pi r^2}{2\pi r} = 2r \Rightarrow r = \frac{h}{2}$$

Hence, the volume is maximum when $r = \frac{h}{2}$.

Hence proved.

16. Let $P(h, k)$ be the point on the straight line $2x + 3y = 6$, so it is satisfied.

$$\therefore \quad 2h + 3k = 6 \quad \ldots\text{(i)}$$

Now, distance between origin and P is

$$d = \sqrt{(h-0)^2 + (k-0)^2}$$

$$\Rightarrow \quad d^2 = h^2 + k^2 = h^2 + \left(\frac{6-2h}{3}\right)^2 \quad \text{[from Eq. (i)]}$$

$$= h^2 + \left(\frac{36+4h^2-24h}{9}\right)$$

$$\text{Let } D = d^2 = \frac{13h^2 - 24h + 36}{9} \quad \ldots\text{(ii)}$$

On differentiating both sides of Eq. (ii) w.r.t. h, we get

$$\frac{dD}{dh} = \frac{26h-24}{9} \text{ and } \frac{d^2D}{dh^2} = \frac{26}{9}$$

For closest (minimum) distance, put $\frac{dD}{dh} = 0$

$$\Rightarrow \quad 26h - 24 = 0$$

$$\Rightarrow \quad h = \frac{24}{26} = \frac{12}{13}$$

$$\therefore \quad \frac{d^2D}{dh^2} = \frac{26}{9} > 0,$$

so it is minimum.

On putting $h = \frac{12}{13}$ in Eq. (i), we get

$$2 \times \frac{12}{13} + 3k = 6$$

$$\Rightarrow \quad 3k = 6 - \frac{24}{13}$$

$$\Rightarrow \quad 3k = \frac{78-24}{13} = \frac{54}{13}$$

$$\Rightarrow \quad k = \frac{18}{13}$$

Hence, the closest point is $\left(\frac{12}{13}, \frac{18}{13}\right)$.

17. Let the length of side of the square base of closed rectangular metal box be x cm with and its height be y cm.

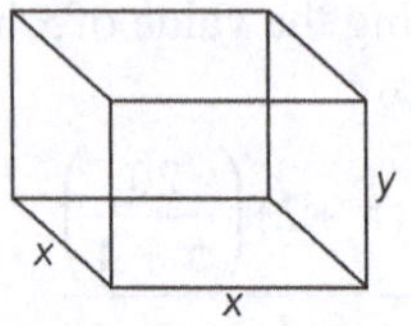

Then, volume of rectangular box $= x \times x \times y$

$$= x^2 y$$

$$\Rightarrow \quad 4096 = x^2 y$$

$$\Rightarrow \quad y = \frac{4096}{x^2}$$

Let C denotes the cost of the box in outer surface area

$$C = 4 \times 2x^2 + 4 \times 4xy$$

$$= 8x^2 + 16x \cdot \frac{4096}{x^2}$$

$$= 8x^2 + \frac{65536}{x} \quad \text{...(i)}$$

On differentiating both sides w.r.t. x, we get

$$\frac{dC}{dx} = 16x - \frac{65536}{x^2} \quad \text{...(ii)}$$

Now, $\frac{dC}{dx} = 0$

$$\Rightarrow \quad 16x - \frac{65536}{x^2} = 0$$

$$\Rightarrow \quad 16x^3 = 65536$$

$$\Rightarrow \quad x^3 = 4096 = 16^3$$

$$\Rightarrow \quad x = 16$$

Again, on differentiating Eq. (ii) w.r.t. x, we get

$$\frac{d^2C}{dx^2} = 16 - 65536(-2) \cdot \frac{1}{x^3} = 16 + \frac{131072}{x^3} > 0$$

So, for $x = 16$, cost is minimum.

$$\therefore \quad y = \frac{4096}{x^2} = \frac{4096}{16^2} = 16$$

Hence, dimensions of the box for the minimum cost of polishing is 16 cm, 16 cm and 16 cm.

18. Let r be the radius and h be the height of cone, which inscribed in a sphere of radius 12 cm.

$$\therefore \quad OD = h - 12 \qquad [\because AD = h]$$

$$\Rightarrow \quad x = h - 12$$

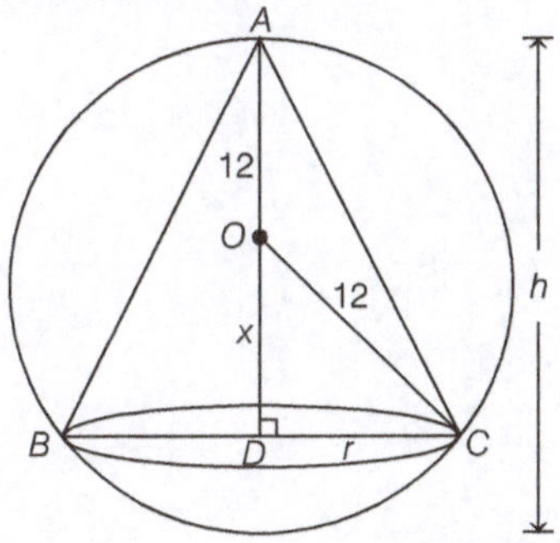

In ΔOCD, $12^2 = x^2 + r^2$

$$\Rightarrow \quad 144 = (h-12)^2 + r^2$$

$$\Rightarrow \quad r^2 = 144 - h^2 + 24h - 144$$

$$\Rightarrow \quad r^2 = 24h - h^2$$

Now, volume of cone,

$$V = \frac{1}{3}\pi r^2 h$$

$$V = \frac{\pi}{3}(24h - h^2)h$$

$$= \frac{\pi}{3}(24h^2 - h^3)$$

On differentiating both sides w.r.t. h, we get

$$\frac{dV}{dh} = \frac{\pi}{3}(48h - 3h^2)$$

For maxima or minima, putting $\frac{dV}{dh} = 0$

$$\Rightarrow \quad 48h - 3h^2 = 0$$

$$\Rightarrow \quad h = 16$$

Again, differentiating w.r.t. h, we get

$$\frac{d^2V}{dh^2} = \pi(16 - 2h)$$

$$\Rightarrow \quad \left(\frac{d^2V}{dh^2}\right)_{h=16} = \pi(16 - 32) < 0$$

Volume is maximum when $h = 16$ cm

19. Let R be the radius and h be the height of cone, which is inscribed in a sphere of radius r.

$$\therefore \quad OA = h - r$$

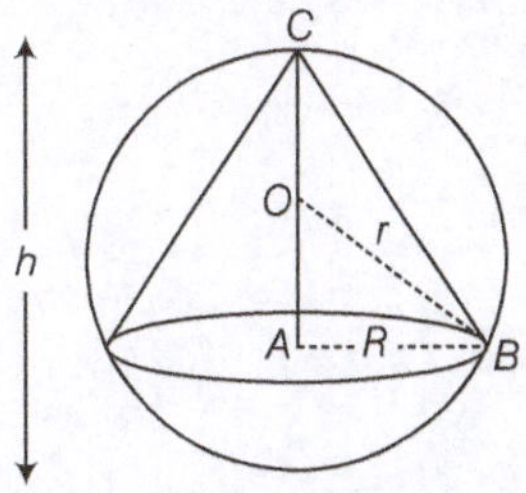

In ΔOAB, by Pythagoras theorem, we get

$$r^2 = R^2 + (h - r)^2$$

$$\Rightarrow \quad r^2 = R^2 + h^2 + r^2 - 2rh$$

$$\Rightarrow \quad R^2 = 2rh - h^2 \quad \text{...(i)}$$

The volume of sphere $= \frac{4}{3}\pi r^3$

and the volume of the cone, $V = \frac{1}{3}\pi R^2 h$

$\Rightarrow \quad V = \frac{1}{3}\pi h(2rh - h^2)$ [from Eq. (i)]

$\Rightarrow \quad V = \frac{1}{3}\pi(2rh^2 - h^3)$ ...(ii)

On differentiating both sides of Eq. (ii) w.r.t. h, we get

$$\frac{dV}{dh} = \frac{1}{3}\pi(4rh - 3h^2) \quad \text{...(iii)}$$

For maximum or minimum value, putting

$$\frac{dV}{dh} = 0 \Rightarrow 4rh = 3h^2 \Rightarrow 4r = 3h$$

$\Rightarrow \quad h = \frac{4r}{3}$ $[\because h \neq 0]$

Again, differentiating both side of Eq. (iii) w.r.t. h, we get

$$\frac{d^2V}{dh^2} = \frac{1}{3}\pi(4r - 6h)$$

At $h = \frac{4r}{3}$, $\left[\frac{d^2V}{dh^2}\right]_{h=\frac{4r}{3}} = \frac{1}{3}\pi\left(4r - 6 \times \frac{4r}{3}\right)$

$$= \frac{\pi}{3}(4r - 8r) = -\frac{4r\pi}{3} < 0$$

$\Rightarrow V$ is maximum at $h = \frac{4r}{3}$. **Hence proved.**

20. Let the side of square piece to be cut x m.

$\therefore$ Length of box $= (8 - 2x)$ m

Breadth of box $= (3 - 2x)$ m

Height of box, $h = x$

Volume of box, $V = lbh$

$\therefore \quad V = (8 - 2x)(3 - 2x)x$

$\Rightarrow \quad V = (24 - 22x + 4x^2)x$

$\Rightarrow \quad V = 24x - 22x^2 + 4x^3$

On differentiating V w.r.t. x, we get

$$\frac{dV}{dx} = 24 - 44x + 12x^2$$

For maxima or minima, putting $\frac{dV}{dx} = 0$

$\Rightarrow \quad 24 - 44x + 12x^2 = 0$

$\Rightarrow \quad 3x^2 - 11x + 6 = 0$ [divide by 4]

$\Rightarrow \quad (x - 3)(3x - 2) = 0$

$\Rightarrow \quad x = 3$ and $x = \frac{2}{3}$

But $x = 3$ is not possible.

Again, on differentiating w.r.t. x, we get

$$\frac{d^2V}{dx^2} = -44 + 24x$$

At $x = \frac{2}{3}$, $\left(\frac{d^2V}{dx^2}\right)_{x=\frac{2}{3}} = -44 + 16 = -28 < 0$

So, volume is maximum at $x = \frac{2}{3}$ m.

$\therefore$ Maximum volume $= \left(8 - \frac{4}{3}\right)\left(3 - \frac{4}{3}\right)\left(\frac{2}{3}\right)$

$$= \frac{20}{3} \times \frac{5}{3} \times \frac{2}{3}$$

$$= \frac{200}{27}\text{ m}^3$$

CHAPTER TEST

1 Mark Questions

1. The distance covered by a particle in time t is given by $x = 3 + 8t - 4t^2$. After 1s, its velocity will be
(a) 0 unit/s (b) 3 units/s
(c) 4 units/s (d) 7 units/s

2. If $f: R \to R$ be defined by $f(x) = 2x + \cos x$, then f
(a) has a minimum at $x = \pi$
(b) has a maximum at $x = 0$
(c) is a decreasing function
(d) is an increasing function

3. Let $g(x) = 2f\left(\frac{x}{2}\right) + f(2-x)$ and $f''(x) < 0$ for all $x \in (0, 2)$. Then, $g(x)$ is
(a) increasing on $(4/3, 2)$ and increasing on $(0, 4/3)$
(b) decreasing on $(0,4/3)$ and increasing on $(4/3, 2)$
(c) increasing on $(0, 4/3)$ and decreasing on $(4/3, 2)$
(d) None of the above

2 Marks Questions

4. The volume of a sphere is increasing at the rate of $3 \text{ cm}^3/\text{s}$. Find the rate of increase of its surface area when the radius is 2 cm.

5. The sides of an equilateral triangle are increasing at the rate of 2 cm/s. Find the rate at which the area increases, when the side is 10 cm.

6. Show that the function $f(x) = 4x^3 - 18x^2 + 28x - 7$ is always increasing on R.

7. Find the intervals in which the function $f(x) = 2x^3 - 15x^2 + 36x + 17$ is increasing or decreasing.

8. Find the intervals in which the function $f(x) = (x-1)(x-1)^2$ is increasing or decreasing.

3/4 Marks Questions

9. Find the equation of tangent and normal to the curves $\frac{x^2}{a^2} - \frac{y^2}{b^2} = 1$ at the point $(\sqrt{2}a, b)$.

10. Find the equation of tangent to the curve $y = \sqrt{3x-2}$, which is parallel to the line $4x - 2y + 5 = 0$.

11. Find the equation of tangent and normal to the curve $x = 1 - \cos\theta,\ y = \theta - \sin\theta$ at $\theta = \frac{\pi}{4}$.

12. Show that a cylinder of a given volume which is open at the top has minimum total surface area, when its height is equal to the radius of its base.

5/6 Marks Questions

13. Find the area of the greatest rectangle that can be inscribed in an ellipse $\frac{x^2}{a^2} + \frac{y^2}{b^2} = 1$.

14. Show that the height of a closed right circular cylinder of given surface and maximum volume is equal to diameter of base.

15. Prove that radius of right circular cylinder of greatest curved surface area which can be inscribed in a given cone is half of that of the cone.

Answers

1. (a) 2. (d) 3. (c)
4. $3 \text{ cm}^2/\text{s}$ 5. $10\sqrt{3} \text{ cm}^2/\text{s}$
7. The function increasing in $(-\infty, 2] \cup [3, \infty)$ and decreasing $(2, 3)$.
8. Increasing on $(-\infty, 4/3]$ and $[2, \infty)$, decreasing on $[4/3, 2]$.
9. Equation of tangent $\sqrt{2}bx - ay - ab = 0$,
Normal $= ax + \sqrt{2}by = \sqrt{2}(a^2 + b^2)$
10. $48x - 24y = 23$
11. Equation of tangent
$= (8 - 4\sqrt{2})x - 4\sqrt{2}y = 16 - \sqrt{2}\pi - 8\sqrt{2}$,
Equation of normal $= 4\sqrt{2}x + (8 - 4\sqrt{2})y = \pi(2 - \sqrt{2})$
13. $2ab$

07 Integrals

TREND ANALYSIS 3 YEARS

Average No. of Questions Across all Sets

Topic	Types of Questions	2024	2023	2020
TOPIC 01 Indefinite Integrals	1 Mark	1	2	—
	2 Marks	—	2	—
	3/4 Marks	2	—	2
	5/6 Marks	—	2	2
TOPIC 02 Definite Integrals	1 Mark	2	2	—
	2 Marks	1	—	1
	3/4 Marks	—	—	—
	5/6 Marks	—	—	—

TOPIC 1

Indefinite Integrals

Integration as the Inverse Process of Differentiation

In the differential calculus, we are given a function and we have to find the derivative or differential of this function, but in the integral calculus, we have to find a function whose differential is given. Thus, integration is the inverse process of differentiation.

Suppose $\frac{d}{dx}[F(x)] = f(x)$, then

$$\int f(x)\,dx = F(x) + C.$$

These integrals are called indefinite integrals or general integrals and C is an arbitrary constant by varying which one gets different anti-derivatives of the given function.

NOTE Derivative of a function is unique but a function can have infinite anti-derivatives or integrals.

Properties of Indefinite Integral

(i) $\int [f(x) \pm g(x)]\,dx = \int f(x)\,dx \pm \int g(x)\,dx$.

(ii) For any real number k, $\int k\,f(x)\,dx = k\int f(x)\,dx$.

(iii) In general, if $f_1, f_2, \ldots, f_n$ are functions and $k_1, k_2, \ldots, k_n$ are real numbers, then

$$\int [k_1 f_1(x) + k_2 f_2(x) + \ldots + k_n f_n(x)]\,dx$$
$$= k_1\int f_1(x)\,dx + k_2\int f_2(x)\,dx + \ldots + k_n\int f_n(x)\,dx.$$

Basic Formulae of Integrals

1. $\int x^n\,dx = \frac{x^{n+1}}{n+1} + C, n \neq -1$
2. $\int e^x\,dx = e^x + C$
3. $\int e^{ax}\,dx = \frac{e^{ax}}{a} + C$
4. $\int a^x\,dx = \frac{a^x}{\log a} + C$

5. $\int \frac{1}{x} dx = \log|x| + C$

6. $\int \sin x \, dx = -\cos x + C$

7. $\int \cos x \, dx = \sin x + C$

8. $\int \tan x \, dx = -\log|\cos x| + C = \log|\sec x| + C$

9. $\int \cot x \, dx = \log|\sin x| + C = -\log|\operatorname{cosec} x| + C$

10. $\int \sec x \, dx = \log|\sec x + \tan x| + C$

$= \log\left|\tan\left(\frac{\pi}{4} + \frac{x}{2}\right)\right| + C$

11. $\int \operatorname{cosec} x \, dx = \log|\operatorname{cosec} x - \cot x| + C$

$= \log\left|\tan\frac{x}{2}\right| + C$

12. $\int \sec x \tan x \, dx = \sec x + C$

13. $\int \operatorname{cosec} x \cot x \, dx = -\operatorname{cosec} x + C$

14. $\int \sec^2 x \, dx = \tan x + C$

15. $\int \operatorname{cosec}^2 x \, dx = -\cot x + C$

16. $\int \frac{1}{\sqrt{1-x^2}} dx = \sin^{-1} x + C$

17. $\int \frac{-1}{\sqrt{1-x^2}} dx = \cos^{-1} x + C$

18. $\int \frac{1}{1+x^2} dx = \tan^{-1} x + C$

19. $\int \frac{-1}{1+x^2} dx = \cot^{-1} x + C$

20. $\int \frac{1}{x\sqrt{x^2-1}} dx = \sec^{-1} x + C$

21. $\int \frac{-1}{x\sqrt{x^2-1}} dx = \operatorname{cosec}^{-1} x + C$

22. $\int \frac{dx}{\sqrt{a^2-x^2}} = \sin^{-1}\frac{x}{a} + C$

23. $\int \frac{dx}{\sqrt{x^2-a^2}} = \log|x + \sqrt{x^2-a^2}| + C$

24. $\int \frac{dx}{\sqrt{x^2+a^2}} = \log|x + \sqrt{x^2+a^2}| + C$

25. $\int \frac{1}{a^2+x^2} dx = \frac{1}{a}\tan^{-1}\left(\frac{x}{a}\right) + C$

26. $\int \frac{1}{a^2-x^2} dx = \frac{1}{2a}\log\left|\frac{a+x}{a-x}\right| + C$

27. $\int \frac{dx}{x^2-a^2} = \frac{1}{2a}\log\left|\frac{x-a}{x+a}\right| + C$

28. $\int \sqrt{x^2-a^2} \, dx = \frac{x}{2}\sqrt{x^2-a^2} - \frac{a^2}{2}$

$\log|x + \sqrt{x^2-a^2}| + C$

29. $\int \sqrt{x^2+a^2} \, dx = \frac{x}{2}\sqrt{x^2+a^2}$

$+ \frac{a^2}{2}\log\left|x + \sqrt{x^2+a^2}\right| + C$

30. $\int \sqrt{a^2-x^2} \, dx = \frac{x}{2}\sqrt{a^2-x^2} + \frac{a^2}{2}\sin^{-1}\frac{x}{a} + C$

31. $\int (ax+b)^n \, dx = \frac{1}{a}\frac{(ax+b)^{n+1}}{n+1} + C, n \neq -1$

Integration by Substitution

The method of reducing a given integral into one or other standard integral by changing the independent variable is called method of substitution.

Thus, $\int f(x)\,dx = \int [f\{g(t)\} \cdot g'(t)]\,dt$, if we substitute $x = g(t)$, such that

$$dx = g'(t)\,dt$$

(i) $\int [\{f(x)\}^n \cdot f'(x)]\,dx = \frac{\{f(x)\}^{n+1}}{n+1} + C, n \neq -1$

(ii) $\int \frac{f'(x)}{f(x)} dx = \log|f(x)| + C, f(x) \neq 0$

Substitutions to evaluate integrals of the form $\int \frac{\phi(x)}{P\sqrt{Q}} dx$

(i) If P and Q both are linear functions of x, put $Q = t^2$

(ii) If P is quadratic and Q is a linear function of x, put $Q = t^2$

(iii) If P is linear and Q is quadratic function of x, put $P = \frac{1}{t}$

(iv) If P and Q both are pure quadratic of the form $P = ax^2 + b$ and $Q = cx^2 + d$, then substitute $x = \frac{1}{t}$ and then $c + dt^2 = u^2$.

Integration Using Trigonometric Identities

Sometimes when the integrand involves some trigonometric functions, we use the following identities to find the integral

(i) $2\sin A \cdot \cos B = \sin(A+B) + \sin(A-B)$

(ii) $2\cos A \cdot \sin B = \sin(A+B) - \sin(A-B)$

(iii) $2\cos A \cdot \cos B = \cos(A+B) + \cos(A-B)$

(iv) $2\sin A \cdot \sin B = \cos(A-B) - \cos(A+B)$

(v) $2\sin A \cdot \cos A = \sin 2A = \dfrac{2\tan A}{1+\tan^2 A}$

(vi) $\cos 2A = \cos^2 A - \sin^2 A$
$= 2\cos^2 A - 1$
$= 1 - 2\sin^2 A$
$= \dfrac{1-\tan^2 A}{1+\tan^2 A}$

(vii) $\sin^2 A = \dfrac{1-\cos 2A}{2}$

(viii) $\cos^2 A = \dfrac{1+\cos 2A}{2}$

(ix) $\sin^3 A = \dfrac{3\sin A - \sin 3A}{4}$

(x) $\cos^3 A = \dfrac{3\cos A + \cos 3A}{4}$

(xi) $\sin^4 x = \dfrac{\cos 4x - 4\cos 2x + 3}{8}$

(xii) $\cos^4 x = \dfrac{\cos 4x + 4\cos 2x + 3}{8}$

Some Special Substitutions

$a^2 + x^2$	$x = a\tan\theta$ or $a\cot\theta$
$a^2 - x^2$	$x = a\sin\theta$ or $a\cos\theta$
$x^2 - a^2$	$x = a\sec\theta$ or $a\operatorname{cosec}\theta$
$\sqrt{\dfrac{a-x}{a+x}}$ or $\sqrt{\dfrac{a+x}{a-x}}$	$x = a\cos 2\theta$
$\sqrt{\dfrac{x-a}{b-x}}$ or $\sqrt{(x-a)(x-b)}$	$x = a\cos^2\theta + b\sin^2\theta$
$\sqrt{\dfrac{x}{a-x}}$ or $\sqrt{\dfrac{a-x}{x}}$	$x = a\sin^2\theta$ or $x = a\cos^2\theta$
$\sqrt{\dfrac{x}{a+x}}$ or $\sqrt{\dfrac{a+x}{x}}$	$x = a\tan^2\theta$ or $x = a\cot^2\theta$

Integration by Partial Fractions

A rational function is a ratio of two polynomials of the form $\dfrac{p(x)}{q(x)}$, where $p(x)$ and $q(x)$ are polynomials in x and $q(x) \neq 0$. If degree of $p(x) >$ degree of $q(x)$, then we may divide $p(x)$ by $q(x)$, so that $\dfrac{p(x)}{q(x)} = t(x) + \dfrac{p_1(x)}{q(x)}$, where $t(x)$ is a polynomial in x which can be integrated easily and degree of $p_1(x)$ is less than the degree of $q(x)$.

Now, $\dfrac{p_1(x)}{q(x)}$ can be integrated by expressing $\dfrac{p_1(x)}{q(x)}$ as the sum of partial fractions of the following types:

(i) $\dfrac{px+q}{(x-a)(x-b)} = \dfrac{A}{x-a} + \dfrac{B}{x-b}, a \neq b$

(ii) $\dfrac{px+q}{(x-a)^2} = \dfrac{A}{x-a} + \dfrac{B}{(x-a)^2}$

(iii) $\dfrac{px^2+qx+r}{(x-a)(x-b)(x-c)} = \dfrac{A}{x-a} + \dfrac{B}{x-b} + \dfrac{C}{x-c}, a \neq b \neq c$

(iv) $\dfrac{px^2+qx+r}{(x-a)^2(x-b)} = \dfrac{A}{x-a} + \dfrac{B}{(x-a)^2} + \dfrac{C}{(x-b)}, a \neq b$

(v) $\dfrac{px^2+qx+r}{(x-a)(x^2+bx+c)} = \dfrac{A}{x-a} + \dfrac{Bx+C}{x^2+bx+c}$, where x^2+bx+c cannot be factorised further.

Integration by Parts

For given functions $f(x)$ and $g(x)$, we have

$$\int [\underset{\text{I}}{f(x)} \cdot \underset{\text{II}}{g(x)}]\,dx = f(x) \cdot \int g(x)\,dx - \int \{f'(x) \cdot \int g(x)\,dx\}\,dx$$

Here, we can choose first function according to its position in **ILATE**, where

I = Inverse trigonometric function
L = Logarithmic function
A = Algebraic function
T = Trigonometric function
E = Exponential function

[The function which comes first in ILATE should taken as first function and other as second function.]

NOTE (i) Keep in mind, ILATE is not a rule, as all questions of integration by parts cannot be solve by above method.

(ii) It is worth mentioning that integration by parts is not applicable to product of functions in all cases. For instance, the method does not work for $\int \sqrt{x}\sin x\,dx$. The reason is that there does not exist any function whose derivative is $\sqrt{x}\sin x$.

Some Special Types of Integrals

Type I Important Forms Transformed into Standard Forms

(i) **Form I** Integrals of the types $\int \frac{dx}{ax^2+bx+c}$ or $\int \frac{dx}{\sqrt{ax^2+bx+c}}$ can be transformed into standard form by expressing

$$ax^2+bx+c = a\left[x^2+\frac{b}{a}x+\frac{c}{a}\right]$$

$$= a\left[\left(x+\frac{b}{2a}\right)^2+\left(\frac{c}{a}-\frac{b^2}{4a^2}\right)\right].$$

(ii) **Form II** Integrals of the types $\int (px+q)\sqrt{ax^2+bx+c}\,dx$ or $\int \frac{px+q}{ax^2+bx+c}dx$ or $\int \frac{px+q}{\sqrt{ax^2+bx+c}}dx$ can be transformed into standard form by expressing

$$px+q = A\frac{d}{dx}(ax^2+bx+c)+B = A(2ax+b)+B,$$

where A and B are determined by comparing coefficients and constants on both sides.

(iii) **Form III** Integral of the type $\int e^x[f(x)+f'(x)]dx$, if the given integrand is of the form $e^x[f(x)+f'(x)]$, then we can directly write the integral as

$$\int e^x[f(x)+f'(x)]dx = e^x f(x)+C.$$

(iv) **Form IV** $\int e^{ax}\sin(bx+c)dx = \frac{e^{ax}}{a^2+b^2}[a\sin(bx+c) - b\cos(bx+c)]+C$

(v) **Form V** $\int e^{ax}\cos(bx+c)dx$

$$= \frac{e^{ax}}{a^2+b^2}[a\cos(bx+c)+b\sin(bx+c)]+C$$

where, C is a constant of integration.

Type II Important Forms to be Converted into Special Integrals

(i) **Form I** $\int \frac{1}{ax^2+bx+c}dx$ or $\int \frac{1}{\sqrt{ax^2+bx+c}}dx$

Express ax^2+bx+c as sum or difference of two squares.

i.e. $ax^2+bx+c = a\left[\left(x+\frac{b}{2a}\right)^2+\frac{4ac-b^2}{4a^2}\right]$

(ii) **Form II** $\int \frac{px+q}{ax^2+bx+c}dx$ or $\int \frac{px+q}{\sqrt{ax^2+bx+c}}dx$

or $\int (px+q)\sqrt{ax^2+bx+c}\,dx$

Put $px+q = \lambda\cdot\frac{d}{dx}(ax^2+bx+c)+\mu$

Now, find values of λ and μ and integrate it.

(iii) **Form III** $\int \frac{P(x)}{ax^2+bx+c}dx$ when $P(x)$ is a polynomial of degree 2 or more than 2, then firstly divide $P(x)$ by ax^2+bx+c and write $bx+c$ in the form $\frac{P(x)}{ax^2+bx+c} = Q(x)+\frac{R(x)}{ax^2+bx+c}$, where $R(x)$ is a linear expression or constant, and $Q(x)$ is quotient, then integral reduces to the forms discussed earlier.

Type III

(i) **Form I** $\int \frac{dx}{a+b\sin^2 x}, \int \frac{dx}{a+b\cos^2 x},$

$\int \frac{dx}{a\sin^2 x+b\cos^2 x}, \int \frac{dx}{a\sin^2 x+b\cos^2 x+c},$

$\int \frac{dx}{(a\sin x+b\cos x)^2}$

To evaluate the above type of integrals, we proceed as follows:

(a) Divide numerator and denominator by $\cos^2 x$.

(b) Replace $\sec^2 x$ if any in denominator by $1+\tan^2 x$.

(c) Put $\tan x = t \Rightarrow \sec^2 x\,dx = dt$, then the given integral becomes standard form of integrals in t variables.

(d) After integration, convert t variables in terms of x variables.

(ii) **Form II** $\int \frac{dx}{a+b\sin x}, \int \frac{dx}{a+b\cos x},$

$\int \frac{dx}{a\sin x+b\cos x}, \int \frac{dx}{a\sin x+b\cos x+c}$

To evaluate the above type of integrals, we proceed as follows

(a) Put $\sin x = \frac{2\tan\frac{x}{2}}{1+\tan^2\frac{x}{2}}$ and $\cos x = \frac{1-\tan^2\frac{x}{2}}{1+\tan^2\frac{x}{2}}$

(b) Replace $1+\tan^2\frac{x}{2}$ by $\sec^2\frac{x}{2}$.

(c) Put $\tan\frac{x}{2}=t \Rightarrow \frac{1}{2}\sec^2\frac{x}{2}\,dx=dt$

i.e. $\sec^2\frac{x}{2}\,dx=2\,dt$,

then the given integral becomes standard form of integrals in t variables.

(d) After integration, convert t variables in terms of x variables.

(iii) **Form III** $\int \frac{a\sin x+b\cos x}{c\sin x+d\cos x}dx$,

Write numerator $=\lambda$ (differentiation of denominator) $+\mu$ (denominator)

i.e. $a\sin x+b\cos x=\lambda\,(c\cos x-d\sin x)+\mu\,(c\sin x+d\cos x)$

$$\int \frac{a\sin x+b\cos x}{c\sin x+d\cos x}dx=\lambda\int\frac{c\cos x-d\sin x}{c\sin x+d\cos x}dx+\mu\int\frac{c\sin x+d\cos x}{c\sin x+d\cos x}dx$$

$$=\lambda\log|c\sin x+d\cos x|+\mu x+C$$

(iv) **Form IV** $\int \frac{a\sin x+b\cos x+c}{p\sin x+q\cos x+r}dx$

Write numerator $=\lambda$ (differentiation of denominator) $+\mu$ (denominator) $+\gamma$

i.e. $a\sin x+b\cos x+c=\lambda\,(p\cos x-q\sin x)+\mu\,(p\sin x+q\cos x+r)+\gamma$

$$\int\frac{a\sin x+b\cos x+c}{p\sin x+q\cos x+r}dx=\lambda\int\frac{p\cos x-q\sin x}{p\sin x+q\cos x+r}dx+\mu\int\frac{p\sin x+q\cos x+r}{p\sin x+q\cos x+r}dx+\gamma\int\frac{1}{p\sin x+q\cos x+r}dx$$

$$=\lambda\log|p\sin x+q\cos x+r|+\mu x+\gamma\int\frac{1}{p\sin x+q\cos x+r}dx$$

Type IV

(i) **Form I** $\int\frac{x^2+1}{x^4+\lambda x^2+1}dx$,

$\int\frac{x^2-1}{x^4+\lambda x^2+1}dx$, $\int\frac{1}{x^4+\lambda x^2+1}dx$,

$\int\frac{1\pm x^2}{1+x^4}dx$, $\int\frac{dx}{1+x^4}$

To evaluate this type of integrals, we proceed as follows

(a) Divide numerator and denominator by x^2.

(b) Express the denominator of integrands either of the form of $\left(x+\frac{1}{x}\right)^2\pm k^2$ or $\left(x-\frac{1}{x}\right)^2\pm k^2$.

(c) Introduce $d\left(x+\frac{1}{x}\right)$ or $d\left(x-\frac{1}{x}\right)$ or both in numerator.

(d) Put $x+\frac{1}{x}=t$ or $x-\frac{1}{x}=t$ as the case may be required.

(e) Integral reduced to the form of $\int\frac{1}{x^2+a^2}dx$ or $\int\frac{1}{x^2-a^2}dx$.

(f) For the integrals

$\int\frac{x^2+a^2}{x^4+kx^2+a^4}dx$ or $\int\frac{x^2-a^2}{x^4+kx^2+a^4}dx$

After dividing both numerator and denominator by x^2.

Put $x-\frac{a^2}{x}=t$ or $x+\frac{a^2}{x}=t$, then the given integral becomes standard form of integrals in t variables.

(g) After integration, convert t variables in terms of x variables.

(ii) **Form II** $\int\sqrt{\tan x}\,dx$, $\int\sqrt{\cot x}\,dx$, $\int\frac{dx}{\sin^4 x+\cos^4 x}$,

$\int\frac{dx}{\sin^6 x+\cos^6 x}$, $\int\frac{\pm\sin x\pm\cos x}{a+b\sin x\cdot\cos x}dx$

Put $\tan x=t^2 \Rightarrow d(\tan x)=d(t^2)\Rightarrow \sec^2 x\,dx=2t\,dt$,

then the given integral becomes standard form of integrals in t variables.

PYQs Previous Years Questions

1 Mark Questions

1. If $\int (\cot x - \text{cosec}^2 x)e^x dx = e^x f(x) + C$, then $f(x)$ will be **ISC 2024**

(a) $\cot x + \text{cosec}\, x$ (b) $\cot^2 x$
(c) $\cot x$ (d) $\text{cosec}\, x$

2. If $\int \sin^{-1}(\cos x)\, dx = g(x) - \frac{x^2}{2} + C$, then g($x$) will be **ISC Specimen 2024**

(a) $\frac{\pi}{2}x$ (b) $\frac{-\pi}{2}x$ (c) 0 (d) $\frac{x}{2}$

3. Evaluate $\int \frac{x}{x^2+1}\, dx.$ **ISC 2023**

(a) $2\log(x^2+1)+C$ (b) $\frac{1}{2}\log(x^2+1)+C$
(c) $e^{x^2+1}+C$ (d) $\log x + \frac{x^2}{2} + C$

4. Evaluate $\int \frac{1+\cos x}{\sin^2 x}\, dx.$ **ISC 2023**

5. If $\int \log 2x dx = x \log 2x - k + C$, where k is a function of x, then find k. **ISC Specimen 2023**

6. $\int a^{3x+2} dx$ is equal to **ISC Specimen Sem-II 2022**

(a) $\left(\frac{e^{3x}}{3\log_e a}\right)+C$ (b) $a^2 x + \left(\frac{a^{3x}}{3\log_e a}\right)+C$
(c) $a^2\left(\frac{a^{3x}}{3\log_e a}\right)+C$ (d) $a^2\left(\frac{a^{3x}}{\log_e a}\right)+C$

7. $\int e^{\sin x} \cos x\, dx$ is equal to **ISC Specimen Sem-II 2022**

(a) $e^{\cos x}+C$ (b) $e^{\sin x}+C$
(c) $\frac{\sin^2 x}{2}+C$ (d) $e^{\sin^2 x}+C$

8. $\int \frac{\sin 2x}{\cos x}\, dx$ is equal to **ISC Specimen Sem-II 2022**

(a) $-2\cos x + C$ (b) $2\cos x + C$
(c) $\frac{-\cos x}{2}+C$ (d) $\frac{\cos x}{2}+C$

9. Evaluate $\int \left(\sqrt{x}+\frac{1}{\sqrt{x}}\right)^2 dx.$ **ISC Specimen Sem-II 2022**

10. Evaluate $\int \frac{1}{\sin^2 x \cos^2 x}\, dx.$ **ISC Specimen Sem-II 2022**

11. If $\int \frac{(\log x)^2}{x}\, dx = \frac{(\log x)^k}{k} + C$, then the value of k is **ISC Specimen Sem-II 2022**

(a) 3 (b) 2
(c) 1 (d) None of these

12. Given $\int e^x \left(\frac{x-1}{x^2}\right) dx = e^x f(x) + C$. Then, $f(x)$ satisfying the equation is **ISC Specimen Sem-II 2022**

(a) x (b) x^2
(c) $\frac{1}{x}$ (d) None of these

2 Marks Questions

13. Evaluate $\int \frac{5-3x^2}{6-x^3+5x}\, dx.$ **ISC Specimen 2024**

14. Evaluate $\int xe^x\, dx.$ **ISC Specimen 2024**

15. Evaluate $\int \cos^{-1}(\sin x)\, dx.$ **ISC 2023**

16. If $\int x^5 \cos(x^6) dx = k \sin(x^6) + C$, then find the value of k. **ISC 2023**

17. Evaluate $\int [\sin(\log x) + \cos(\log x)] dx.$ **ISC Specimen 2023**

18. Evaluate $\int \frac{x^3 - x^2 + x - 1}{x-1}\, dx.$ **ISC Specimen Sem-II 2022**

19. Evaluate $\int \log_{10} x\, dx.$ **ISC Specimen Sem-II 2022**

20. Evaluate $\int \frac{\sec^2 x}{\text{cosec}\, x}\, dx.$ **ISC Specimen 2021, 19**

21. Evaluate $\int \frac{x^3+5x^2+4x+1}{x^2}\, dx.$ **ISC 2018**

3/4 Marks Questions

22. Evaluate $\int x^2 \cos x\, dx$ **ISC 2024**

23. Evaluate $\int \frac{x+7}{x^2+4x+7}\, dx$ **ISC 2024**

24. Evaluate $\int \frac{9x^3+63x^2}{x^4+14x^3-9x^2}\,dx.$ **ISC Specimen 2024**

25. Evaluate $\int \sqrt{\operatorname{cosec} x-1}\,dx.$ **ISC Specimen 2023**

26. Evaluate $\int x\tan^{-1} x\,dx.$ **ISC Specimen Sem-II 2022**

27. Evaluate $\int \frac{dx}{x[(\log x)^2+5\log x+6]}.$ **ISC Specimen Sem-II 2022**

28. Evaluate $\int \frac{1+\sin x}{1-\sin x}\,dx.$ **ISC Specimen Sem-II 2022**

29. Evaluate $\int \sin^3 x\cos^4 x\,dx.$ **ISC 2020**

30. Evaluate $\int \frac{dx}{\sqrt{5x-4x^2}}.$ **ISC 2020**

31. Evaluate $\int \frac{x(1+x^2)}{1+x^4}\,dx.$ **ISC 2019**

32. Evaluate $\int \tan^{-1}\sqrt{x}\,dx.$ **ISC 2018**

33. Evaluate $\int \frac{6x+7}{\sqrt{(x-5)(x-4)}}\,dx.$ **ISC Specimen 2018**

34. Evaluate $\int \frac{\sin 2x}{(1+\sin x)(2+\sin x)}\,dx.$ **ISC 2017**

35. Evaluate $\int \frac{1}{x^2}\sin^2\left(\frac{1}{x}\right)dx.$ **ISC 2017**

36. Evaluate $\int \frac{2y^2}{y^2+4}\,dy.$ **ISC 2017**

> **KEY CONCEPT**
>
> Firstly, adding and subtracting 8 in numerator of integrand and simplify the integral, so it becomes in standard form of integral. Further integrate it and get the result.

37. Evaluate $\int \tan^3 x\,dx.$ **ISC 2016**

38. Evaluate $\int \frac{\sin x+\cos x}{\sqrt{9+16\sin 2x}}\,dx.$ **ISC 2016**

39. Evaluate $\int \frac{\sec x}{1+\operatorname{cosec} x}\,dx.$ **ISC 2015**

40. Evaluate $\int \frac{x+\sin x}{1+\cos x}\,dx.$ **ISC 2014**

> **KEY CONCEPT**
>
> Firstly, convert the given integral in $I=I_1+I_2$ form, then integrate one by one using integration by part method to get required result.

41. Evaluate $\int e^x\frac{(2+\sin 2x)}{\cos^2 x}\,dx.$ **ISC 2014**

42. Evaluate $\int \frac{1}{x+\sqrt{x}}\,dx.$ **ISC 2013**

> **KEY CONCEPT**
>
> To solve this problem, we use the concept of method of substitution. Here, first of all put $x=t^2$, then apply the formula i.e. $\int \frac{1}{x}\,dx=\log|x|+C.$

43. Evaluate $\int \frac{\cos^{-1} x}{x^2}\,dx.$ **ISC 2013**

44. Evaluate $\int \frac{dx}{x\{6(\log x)^2+7\log x+2\}}.$ **ISC 2012**

45. Evaluate $\int e^x(\tan x+\log\sec x)\,dx.$ **ISC 2012**

46. Evaluate $\int \frac{\operatorname{cosec} x}{\log\tan\left(\frac{x}{2}\right)}\,dx.$ **ISC 2011**

> **KEY CONCEPT**
>
> (i) Firstly, put $\log\left(\tan\frac{x}{2}\right)=t$, then whole differentiation is cosec x.
>
> (ii) Further integrate it and substitute the value of t.

5 Marks Questions

47. Evaluate $\int \frac{x^2}{x^4+1}\,dx.$ **ISC Specimen 2024**

48. Evaluate $\int \frac{3e^{2x}-2e^x}{e^{2x}+2e^x-8}\,dx.$ **ISC 2023**

49. Evaluate $\int \frac{2}{(1-x)(1+x^2)}\,dx.$ **ISC 2023**

50. Evaluate $\int \frac{1}{\sin^4 x+\cos^4 x}\,dx.$ **ISC Specimen 2023**

51. Evaluate $\int \frac{dx}{\sin x+\sin 2x}.$ **ISC Specimen Sem-II 2022**

52. Evaluate $\int \tan^{-1}\sqrt{x}\,dx.$ **ISC Specimen 2021**

53. Evaluate $\int \tan^{-1}\sqrt{\frac{1-x}{1+x}}\,dx.$ **ISC 2020**

54. Evaluate $\int \frac{2x+7}{x^2-x+2}\,dx.$ **ISC 2020**

55. Evaluate $\int \frac{x-1}{\sqrt{x^2-x}}\,dx.$ **ISC 2018**

56. Evaluate $\int \frac{3x+5}{x^3-x^2-x+1}\,dx.$ **ISC Specimen 2018**

Explanations

1. (c) We have,

$$\int(\cot x-\operatorname{cosec}^2 x)e^x\,dx=e^x f(x)+C$$

Taking LHS

$$\int(\cot x-\operatorname{cosec}^2 x)e^x\,dx$$
$$=\int e^x\cot x\,dx-\int e^x\operatorname{cosec}^2 x\,dx$$

Integrating by parts, we get

$$=e^x\cot x+\int \operatorname{cosec}^2 x\cdot e^x dx-\int e^x\operatorname{cosec}^2 x\,dx$$
$$=e^x\cot x+C$$

On comparing with RHS, we get

$$f(x)=\cot x$$

2. (a) Given, $\int \sin^{-1}(\cos x)\,dx=g(x)-\frac{x^2}{2}+C$ ... (i)

$\because$ $\sin^{-1}x+\cos^{-1}x=\frac{\pi}{2}$

$\therefore$ $\sin^{-1}(\cos x)+\cos^{-1}(\cos x)=\frac{\pi}{2}$

$\Rightarrow \sin^{-1}(\cos x)=\frac{\pi}{2}-\cos^{-1}(\cos x)=\frac{\pi}{2}-x$

$\therefore$ $\int\sin^{-1}(\cos x)\,dx=\int\left(\frac{\pi}{2}-x\right)dx=\frac{\pi x}{2}-\frac{x^2}{2}+C$ ...(ii)

$\therefore$ From Eqs. (i) and (ii), we get

$$g(x)=\frac{\pi x}{2}$$

3. (b) Let $I=\int\frac{x}{x^2+1}\,dx$

Put $x^2+1=t\Rightarrow 2x\,dx=dt$

$\therefore$ $I=\frac{1}{2}\int\frac{dt}{t}=\frac{1}{2}\log|t|+C=\frac{1}{2}\log|x^2+1|+C$

4. Let $I=\int\frac{1+\cos x}{\sin^2 x}\,dx$

$\Rightarrow I=\int(\operatorname{cosec}^2 x+\operatorname{cosec}x\cot x)\,dx$

$\Rightarrow I=-\cot x-\operatorname{cosec}x+C$

5. Let $I=\int\log 2x\,dx$

$\therefore$ On putting $2x=k\Rightarrow 2dx=dk\Rightarrow dx=\frac{dk}{2}$

So, $\int\log 2x\,dx=\int\log k\frac{dk}{2}=\frac{1}{2}\int\log k\cdot 1\,dk$

$$=\frac{1}{2}[k\log k-k]+C$$
$$=\frac{1}{2}[2x\log(2x)-2x]+C$$

$\Rightarrow$ $\int\log 2x\,dx=x\log 2x-x+C$

On comparing with $\int\log 2x\,dx=x\log 2x-k+C$, we get

$$k=x$$

6. (c) Let $I=\int a^{3x+2}dx=\int a^{3x}a^2\,dx=a^2\int a^{3x}dx$

$$=a^2\cdot\frac{a^{3x}}{3\log_e a}+C$$

7. (b) Let $I=\int e^{\sin x}\cos x\,dx$

Put $\sin x=t$, then $\cos x\,dx=dt$

$$=\int e^t\,dt=e^t+C=e^{\sin x}+C$$

8. (a) Let $I=\int\frac{\sin 2x}{\cos x}\,dx=\int\frac{2\sin x\cdot\cos x}{\cos x}\,dx$

$$=\int 2\sin x\,dx$$
$$=2\int\sin dx$$
$$=-2\cos x+C$$

9. Let $I=\int\left(\sqrt{x}+\frac{1}{\sqrt{x}}\right)^2dx=\int\left(x+\frac{1}{x}+2\right)dx$

$$=\int x\,dx+\int\frac{1}{x}\,dx+2\int 1\,dx$$
$$=\frac{x^2}{2}+\log|x|+2x+C$$

10. Let $I=\int \frac{1}{\sin^2 x\cos^2 x}\,dx=\int \frac{\sin^2 x+\cos^2 x}{\sin^2 x\cos^2 x}\,dx$

$[\because \sin^2\theta+\cos^2\theta=1]$

$$=\int\left(\frac{1}{\cos^2 x}+\frac{1}{\sin^2 x}\right)dx$$

$$=\int(\sec^2 x+\operatorname{cosec}^2 x)\,dx=\tan x-\cot x+C$$

11. (a) Let $I=\int \frac{(\log x)^2}{x}\,dx$

On putting $\log x=t\Rightarrow \frac{1}{x}\,dx=dt$

$\therefore\quad I=\int t^2 dt=\frac{t^3}{3}+C$

$\Rightarrow\quad I=\frac{(\log x)^3}{3}+C$

$\therefore\quad \int \frac{(\log x)^2}{x}\,dx=\frac{(\log x)^3}{3}+C\Rightarrow k=3$

12. (c) Given, $\int e^x\left(\frac{x-1}{x^2}\right)dx=e^x f(x)+C$ ...(i)

Let $\quad I=\int e^x\left(\frac{x-1}{x^2}\right)dx$

$$=\int e^x\left\{\frac{1}{x}-\frac{1}{x^2}\right\}dx$$

$$=\int e^x\left\{\frac{1}{x}+\left(\frac{-1}{x^2}\right)\right\}dx=e^x\left(\frac{1}{x}\right)+C$$

$[\because \int e^x[f(x)+f'(x)]dx=e^x f(x)+C]$

$\therefore\ \int e^x\left(\frac{x-1}{x^2}\right)dx=e^x\left(\frac{1}{x}\right)+C$ ...(ii)

On comparing Eqs. (i) and (ii), we get

$$f(x)=\frac{1}{x}$$

13. Let $I=\int \frac{5-3x^2}{(6-x^3+5x)}\,dx$

Let $6-x^3+5x=t\Rightarrow(-3x^2+5)dx=dt$

$\therefore\quad I=\int \frac{dt}{t}=\log|t|+C$

$\therefore\quad I=\log|6-x^3+5x|+C$

14. Let $I=\int xe^x dx=x\int e^x dx-\int\left(\frac{d}{dx}(x)\int e^x dx\right)dx$

$$=xe^x-\int(1.e^x)dx=xe^x-e^x+C$$

15. Let $I=\int \cos^{-1}(\sin x)\,dx$

$$=\int \cos^{-1}\left(\cos\left(\frac{\pi}{2}-x\right)\right)dx=\int\left(\frac{\pi}{2}-x\right)dx$$

$\left[\because \cos\left(\frac{\pi}{2}-\theta\right)=\sin\theta \text{ and } \cos^{-1}(\cos\theta)=\theta,\ \theta\in[0,\pi]\right]$

$\Rightarrow\ I=\frac{\pi}{2}x-\frac{x^2}{2}+C$

16. Given, $\int x^5\cos(x^6)dx=k\sin(x^6)+C$ ...(i)

Let $I=\int x^5\cos(x^6)\,dx$

On putting $x^6=t\Rightarrow 6x^5dx=dt$

$\therefore\quad I=\frac{1}{6}\int\cos t\,dt=\frac{1}{6}\sin t+C=\frac{1}{6}\sin x^6+C$

$\Rightarrow\ \int x^5\cos(x^6)\,dx=\frac{1}{6}\sin^6 x+C$ ...(ii)

On comparing Eqs. (i) and (ii), we get

$$k=\frac{1}{6}$$

17. Let $I=\int[\sin(\log x)+\cos(\log x)]dx$

$$=[\sin(\log x)]\cdot\int 1\,dx-\int\left[\left(\frac{d}{dx}(\sin(\log x))\right)\cdot\int 1\,dx\right]dx+\int\cos(\log x)\,dx+C$$

[integrating by parts]

$$=[\sin(\log x)]\cdot x-\int\left[\cos(\log x)\cdot\frac{1}{x}\cdot x\right]dx+\int\cos(\log x)\,dx+C$$

$$=x\sin(\log x)-\int\cos(\log x)dx+\int\cos(\log x)dx$$

$$=x\sin(\log x)+C$$

18. Let $I=\int\frac{x^3-x^2+x-1}{x-1}\,dx$

$$=\int\frac{x^2(x-1)+1(x-1)}{x-1}\,dx$$

$$=\int\frac{(x-1)(x^2+1)}{x-1}\,dx$$

$$=\int(x^2+1)\,dx$$

$$=\int x^2dx+\int 1\,dx$$

$\therefore\quad I=\frac{x^3}{3}+x+C$

19. Let $I = \int \log_{10} x\, dx = \int \frac{\log_e x}{\log_e 10} dx$

$$= \frac{1}{\log_e 10} \int \underset{\text{II}}{1} \cdot \underset{\text{I}}{\log_e x}\, dx$$

$$= \frac{1}{\log_e 10} \left[\log_e x \int 1\, dx - \int \left\{ \frac{d}{dx} (\log_e x) \cdot \int 1\, dx \right\} dx \right] + C$$

[integrating by parts]

$$= \frac{1}{\log_e 10} \left[(\log_e x)(x) - \int \frac{1}{x} \times x\, dx \right] + C$$

$$= \frac{x \log_e x - x}{\log_e 10} + C$$

20. Let $I = \int \frac{\sec^2 x}{\operatorname{cosec}^2 x} dx = \int \frac{1}{\cos^2 x} \times \frac{\sin^2 x}{1} dx$

$$= \int \tan^2 x\, dx$$

$$= \int (\sec^2 x - 1)\, dx$$

$$= \int \sec^2 x\, dx - \int 1\, dx = \tan x - x + C$$

21. Let $I = \int \frac{x^3 + 5x^2 + 4x + 1}{x^2} dx$

$$\Rightarrow I = \int \left(x + 5 + \frac{4}{x} + \frac{1}{x^2} \right) dx$$

$$\Rightarrow I = \frac{x^2}{2} + 5x + 4 \log |x| - \frac{1}{x} + C$$

22. Let $I = \int x^2 \cos x\, dx$

Integrating by parts, we get

$$= x^2 \sin x - \int 2x \sin x\, dx$$

$$= x^2 \sin x - 2[-x \cos x + \int \cos x\, dx]$$

$$= x^2 \sin x + 2x \cos x - 2 \sin x + C$$

Hence, $\int x^2 \cos x\, dx$

$$= x^2 \sin x + 2x \cos x - 2 \sin x + C$$

where, C is an integrating constant.

23. Let $I = \int \frac{x+7}{x^2 + 4x + 7} dx$

Let us assume that

$$x + 7 = A \frac{d}{dx}(x^2 + 4x + 7) + B$$

$$= A(2x + 4) + B$$

On comparing the coefficients of x and constant terms both sides, we get

$$2A = 1$$

$$\Rightarrow A = \frac{1}{2}$$

and $4A + B = 7$

$$\Rightarrow B = 5$$

So, $x + 7 = \frac{1}{2}(2x + 4) + 5$

$$\therefore I = \int \frac{\frac{1}{2}(2x+4) + 5}{x^2 + 4x + 7} dx$$

$$= \frac{1}{2} \int \frac{2x + 4}{x^2 + 4x + 7} dx + 5 \int \frac{1}{x^2 + 4x + 7} dx$$

$$= \frac{1}{2} \ln |x^2 + 4x + 7| + 5 \int \frac{1}{(x+2)^2 + 3} dx$$

$$= \frac{1}{2} \ln |x^2 + 4x + 7| + \frac{5}{\sqrt{3}} \tan^{-1} \left(\frac{x+2}{\sqrt{3}} \right) + C$$

Hence, $\int \frac{x+7}{x^2 + 4x + 7} dx$

$$= \frac{1}{2} \ln |x^2 + 4x + 7| + \frac{5}{\sqrt{3}} \tan^{-1} \left(\frac{x+2}{\sqrt{3}} \right) + C$$

where, C is an integrating constant.

24. Let $I = \int \frac{9x^3 + 63x^2}{x^4 + 14x^3 - 9x^2} dx$

$$I = \int \frac{9x^2 (x + 7)}{x^2 (x^2 + 14x - 9)} dx$$

$$I = \int \frac{9(x+7)}{(x^2 + 14x - 9)} dx$$

Let $x^2 + 14x - 9 = t$

$$\Rightarrow (2x + 14) dx = dt$$

$$\Rightarrow (x + 7) dx = \frac{dt}{2}$$

$$\therefore I = \frac{9}{2} \int \frac{dt}{t} = \frac{9}{2} \log |t| + C$$

$$= \frac{9}{2} \log |x^2 + 14x - 9| + C$$

25. Let $I = \int \sqrt{(\operatorname{cosec} x - 1)}\, dx$

$$= \int \sqrt{\frac{1}{\sin x} - 1}\, dx$$

$$= \int \frac{\sqrt{1 - \sin x}}{\sqrt{\sin x}} dx$$

$$= \int \frac{\sqrt{\cos^2\frac{x}{2} + \sin^2\frac{x}{2} - 2\sin\frac{x}{2}.\cos\frac{x}{2}}}{\sqrt{\sin x}}\,dx$$

$$= \int \frac{\sqrt{\left(\cos\frac{x}{2} - \sin\frac{x}{2}\right)^2}}{\sqrt{\sin x}}\,dx$$

$$= \int \frac{\left(\cos\frac{x}{2} - \sin\frac{x}{2}\right)}{\sqrt{\sin x}}\,dx$$

$$= \sqrt{2}\int \frac{\frac{1}{\sqrt{2}}\cos\frac{x}{2} - \frac{1}{\sqrt{2}}\sin\frac{x}{2}}{\sqrt{\sin x}}\,dx$$

$$= \sqrt{2}\int \frac{\sin\frac{\pi}{4}\cos\frac{x}{2} - \cos\frac{\pi}{4}\sin\frac{x}{2}}{\sqrt{\cos\left(\frac{\pi}{2} - x\right)}}\,dx$$

$$\Rightarrow \quad I = \int \frac{\sqrt{2}\sin\left(\frac{\pi}{4} - \frac{x}{2}\right)}{\sqrt{2\cos^2\left(\frac{\pi}{4} - \frac{x}{2}\right) - 1}}\,dx \quad \ldots\text{(i)}$$

Let $\sqrt{2}\cos\left(\frac{\pi}{4} - \frac{x}{2}\right) = t$

$$\Rightarrow -\sqrt{2}\sin\left(\frac{\pi}{4} - \frac{x}{2}\right)\left(\frac{-1}{2}\right)dx = dt$$

$$\Rightarrow \quad \sin\left(\frac{\pi}{4} - \frac{x}{2}\right)dx = \sqrt{2}\,dt$$

On substituting these values in Eq. (i), we get

$$I = \int \frac{2}{\sqrt{t^2 - 1}}\,dt \qquad \left[\because t = \sqrt{2}\cos\left(\frac{\pi}{4} - \frac{\pi}{2}\right)\right]$$

$$= 2\log|t + \sqrt{t^2 - 1}| + C$$

$$= 2\log\left|\sqrt{2}\cos\left(\frac{\pi}{4} - \frac{x}{2}\right) + \sqrt{2\cos^2\left(\frac{\pi}{4} - \frac{x}{2}\right) - 1}\right| + C$$

$$= 2\log\left|\begin{array}{l}\sqrt{2}\left(\cos\frac{\pi}{4}\cos\frac{x}{2} + \sin\frac{\pi}{4}\sin\frac{x}{2}\right) \\ + \sqrt{\cos\left(2\left(\frac{\pi}{4} - \frac{x}{2}\right)\right)}\end{array}\right| + C$$

$$\Rightarrow \quad I = 2\log\left|\cos\frac{x}{2} + \sin\frac{x}{2} + \sqrt{\sin x}\right| + C$$

26. Let $I = \int \underset{\text{II}}{x} \cdot \underset{\text{I}}{\tan^{-1} x}\,dx$

$$= (\tan^{-1} x)\left(\frac{x^2}{2}\right) - \int \frac{1}{1+x^2}\cdot\frac{x^2}{2}\,dx + C$$

[integration by parts]

$$= \frac{x^2}{2}\tan^{-1} x - \frac{1}{2}\int \frac{x^2}{x^2+1}\,dx + C$$

$$= \frac{x^2}{2}\tan^{-1} x - \frac{1}{2}\int \frac{x^2+1-1}{1+x^2}\,dx + C$$

$$= \frac{x^2}{2}\tan^{-1} x - \frac{1}{2}\int \frac{1+x^2}{1+x^2}\,dx + \frac{1}{2}\int \frac{1}{1+x^2}\,dx + C$$

$$\Rightarrow \quad I = \frac{x^2}{2}\tan^{-1} x - \frac{1}{2}x + \frac{1}{2}\tan^{-1} x + C$$

27. Let $I = \int \frac{dx}{x[(\log x)^2 + 5\log x + 6]}$

On putting $\log x = t \Rightarrow \frac{1}{x}dx = dt$

$$\therefore \int \frac{dx}{x\{(\log x)^2 + 5\log x + 6\}} = \int \frac{dt}{(t^2 + 5t + 6)}$$

$$= \int \frac{dt}{(t^2 + 2t + 3t + 6)}$$

$$= \int \frac{dt}{t(t+2) + 3(t+2)}$$

$$= \int \frac{dt}{(t+2)(t+3)}$$

Let $\frac{1}{(t+2)(t+3)} = \frac{A}{(t+2)} + \frac{B}{(t+3)}$

[using partial fraction]

$$\Rightarrow \quad 1 = A(t+3) + B(t+2)$$

On putting $t = -3$, we get

$$B = -1$$

On putting $t = -2$, we get

$$A = 1$$

$$\int \frac{dt}{(t+2)(t+3)} = \int \frac{1}{t+2}\,dt + \int \frac{-1}{t+3}\,dt$$

$$= \log|t+2| - \log|t+3| + C$$

$$= \log\left|\frac{t+2}{t+3}\right| + C$$

$$= \log\left|\frac{\log x + 2}{\log x + 3}\right| + C \qquad [\because t = \log x]$$

28. Let $I=\int \frac{1+\sin x}{1-\sin x}dx$

$$=\int \frac{1}{1-\sin x}dx+\int \frac{\sin x}{1-\sin x}dx$$

$$=\int \frac{(1+\sin x)}{1-\sin^2 x}dx+\int \frac{(1+\sin x)\sin x}{1-\sin^2 x}dx$$

$$=\int \frac{(1+\sin x)}{\cos^2 x}dx+\int \frac{(\sin x+\sin^2 x)}{\cos^2 x}dx$$

$$=\int \sec^2 x\,dx+\int \sec x\tan x\,dx+\int \sec x\tan x\,dx+\int \tan^2 x\,dx$$

$$=\int \sec^2 x\,dx+2\int \sec x\tan x\,dx+\int (\sec^2 x-1)\,dx$$

$$=\int \sec^2 x\,dx+2\int \sec x\tan x\,dx+\int \sec^2 x\,dx-\int 1\,dx$$

$$=2\int \sec^2 x\,dx+2\int \sec x\tan x\,dx-\int 1\,dx$$

$$\Rightarrow I=2\tan x+2\sec x-x+C$$

29. Let $I=\int \sin^3 x\cos^4 x\,dx$

$$=\int \sin^2 x\cos^4 x\sin x\,dx$$

$$=\int (1-\cos^2 x)\cos^4 x\sin x\,dx$$

On putting $\cos x=t\Rightarrow -\sin x\,dx=dt$

$$\therefore\quad I=-\int (1-t^2)t^4\,dt$$

$$=\int (t^6-t^4)\,dt$$

$$=\frac{t^7}{7}-\frac{t^5}{5}+C$$

$$\Rightarrow\quad I=\frac{\cos^7 x}{7}-\frac{\cos^5 x}{5}+C \quad [\because t=\cos x]$$

30. Let $I=\int \frac{dx}{\sqrt{5x-4x^2}}$

$$=\frac{1}{2}\int \frac{dx}{\sqrt{\frac{5}{4}x-x^2}}$$

$$=\frac{1}{2}\int \frac{dx}{\sqrt{\frac{25}{64}-\frac{25}{64}+\frac{5x}{4}-x^2}}$$

$$=\frac{1}{2}\int \frac{dx}{\sqrt{\frac{25}{64}-\left(x^2-\frac{5}{4}x+\frac{25}{64}\right)}}$$

$$=\frac{1}{2}\int \frac{dx}{\sqrt{\left(\frac{5}{8}\right)^2-\left(x-\frac{5}{8}\right)^2}}=\frac{1}{2}\sin^{-1}\left[\frac{x-\frac{5}{8}}{5/8}\right]+C$$

$$\left[\because \int \frac{dx}{\sqrt{a^2-x^2}}=\sin^{-1}\frac{x}{a}+C\right]$$

$$=\frac{1}{2}\sin^{-1}\left(\frac{8x-5}{5}\right)+C$$

Concept Enhancer Integral of the types $\int \frac{ax}{\sqrt{ax^2+bx+c}}$ can be transformed into standard form by expressing $ax^2+bx+c=a\left[x^2+\frac{b}{a}x+\frac{c}{a}\right]$

$$=a\left[\left(x+\frac{b}{2a}\right)^2+\left(\frac{c}{a}-\frac{b^2}{4a^2}\right)\right]$$

31. Let $I=\int \frac{x(1+x^2)}{1+x^4}dx=\int \frac{x}{1+x^4}dx+\int \frac{x^3}{1+x^4}dx$

On putting $x^2=t$ in first integral

$$\Rightarrow 2x\,dx=dt\Rightarrow x\,dx=\frac{dt}{2}$$

and $1+x^4=u$ in second integral

$$\Rightarrow\quad 4x^3\,dx=du$$

$$\therefore\quad I=\int \frac{1}{2(1+t^2)}dt+\frac{1}{4}\int \frac{du}{u}$$

$$=\frac{1}{2}\times\tan^{-1}t+\frac{1}{4}\log|u|+C$$

$$=\frac{1}{2}\tan^{-1}x^2+\frac{1}{4}\log|1+x^4|+C$$

32. Let $I=\int \tan^{-1}\sqrt{x}\,dx$

On putting $x=t^2\Rightarrow dx=2t\,dt$

$$\therefore\quad I=\int 2t\tan^{-1}t\,dt$$

Using integration by part, we get

$$I=2\left[\tan^{-1}t\int t\,dt-\int\left(\frac{d}{dt}(\tan^{-1}t)\int t\,dt\right)dt\right]+C$$

$$=2\left[(\tan^{-1}t)\cdot\frac{t^2}{2}-\int \frac{1}{1+t^2}\times\frac{t^2}{2}\,dt\right]+C$$

$$=t^2\tan^{-1}t-\int \frac{t^2+1}{t^2+1}dt+\int \frac{1}{1+t^2}dt+C$$

$$= t^2 \tan^{-1} t - \int 1\,dt + \int \frac{1}{1+t^2}\,dt + C$$
$$= t^2 \tan^{-1} t - t + \tan^{-1} t + C$$
$$= (t^2+1)\tan^{-1} t - t + C$$
$$\Rightarrow \quad I = (x+1)\tan^{-1}\sqrt{x} - \sqrt{x} + C$$

Common Mistake In solving the integral problems by using by parts method, choose first function and second function very carefully.

33. We have, $I = \int \frac{6x+7}{\sqrt{(x-5)(x-4)}}dx$

$$\Rightarrow \quad I = \int \frac{6x+7}{\sqrt{x^2-9x+20}}\,dx$$

Let $6x+7 = A\frac{d}{dx}(x^2-9x+20)+B$

$\Rightarrow \quad 6x+7 = A(2x-9)+B$

$\Rightarrow \quad 6x+7 = 2Ax - 9A + B$

Equating the coefficients of x and constant terms, we get

$$A = 3 \text{ and } B = 34$$

$$\therefore \quad I = \int \frac{3(2x-9)}{\sqrt{x^2-9x+20}}\,dx + \int \frac{34}{\sqrt{x^2-9x+20}}dx$$
$$= \int \frac{3(2x-9)}{\sqrt{x^2-9x+20}}\,dx + \int \frac{34}{\sqrt{\left(x-\frac{9}{2}\right)^2 - \frac{1}{4}}}\,dx$$

On putting $x^2-9x+20 = t \Rightarrow (2x-9)\,dx = dt$, we get

$$I = \int \frac{3dt}{\sqrt{t}} + 34\left[\log\left|\left(x-\frac{9}{2}\right)+\sqrt{\left(x-\frac{9}{2}\right)^2-\frac{1}{4}}\right|\right] + C$$
$$= 6\sqrt{t} + 34\log\left[\left(x-\frac{9}{2}\right)+\sqrt{x^2-9x+20}\right] + C$$
$$\Rightarrow \quad I = 6\sqrt{x^2-9x+20}$$
$$+ 34\log\left|\left(x-\frac{9}{2}\right)+\sqrt{x^2-9x+20}\right| + C$$

34. Let $I = \int \frac{\sin 2x}{(1+\sin x)(2+\sin x)}\,dx$

$$= \int \frac{2\sin x \cdot \cos x}{(1+\sin x)(2+\sin x)}\,dx$$

On putting $\sin x = t \Rightarrow \cos x\,dx = dt$

$$\therefore \quad I = 2\int \frac{t\,dt}{(1+t)(2+t)} \quad \ldots\text{(i)}$$

Let $\frac{t}{(1+t)(2+t)} = \frac{A}{(1+t)} + \frac{B}{(2+t)}$

$\Rightarrow \quad t = A(2+t) + B(1+t)$

On putting $t = -1$, we get

$$A = -1$$

and on putting $t = -2$, we get

$$B = 2$$

$$\therefore \quad \frac{t}{(1+t)(2+t)} = \frac{-1}{(1+t)} + \frac{2}{(2+t)}$$

$\therefore$ From Eq. (i),

$$I = 2\int\left(\frac{-1}{1+t} + \frac{2}{2+t}\right)dt$$
$$= 2\int \frac{-1}{1+t}\,dt + 4\int \frac{1}{2+t}\,dt$$
$$= -2\log|1+t| + 4\log|2+t| + C$$
$$\Rightarrow \quad I = -2\log|1+\sin x| + 4\log|2+\sin x| + C$$
$[\because t = \sin x]$

35. Let $I = \int \frac{1}{x^2}\sin^2\left(\frac{1}{x}\right)dx$

On putting $\frac{1}{x} = t$ and on differentiating both sides w.r.t. x, we get

$$\frac{-1}{x^2}\,dx = dt \Rightarrow \frac{1}{x^2}\,dx = -\,dt$$

$$\therefore \quad I = \int (\sin^2 t)(-dt) = -\int \sin^2 t\,dt$$
$$= -\int \frac{1-\cos 2t}{2}\,dt$$
$$= -\left[\int \frac{1}{2}\,dt - \frac{1}{2}\int \cos 2t\,dt\right]$$
$$= -\left[\frac{1}{2}t - \frac{1}{2}\frac{\sin 2t}{2}\right] + C$$
$$= \frac{1}{4}\sin 2t - \frac{1}{2}t + C$$

Now, by putting value of t, we get

$$I = \frac{1}{4}\sin\left(\frac{2}{x}\right) - \left(\frac{1}{2x}\right) + C$$

36. Let $I = \int \frac{2y^2}{y^2+4}\,dy = \int \frac{2y^2+8-8}{y^2+4}\,dy$

[adding and subtracting 8 in numerator of integrand]

$$= \int \frac{2(y^2+4)-8}{y^2+4}\,dy = \int 2dy - 8\int \frac{1}{y^2+4}\,dy$$
$$= 2y - 8\cdot\frac{1}{2}\tan^{-1}\left(\frac{y}{2}\right) + C = 2y - 4\tan^{-1}\left(\frac{y}{2}\right) + C$$

37. Let $I = \int \tan^3 x\, dx = \int \tan^2 x \tan x\, dx$

$= \int (\sec^2 x - 1) \tan x\, dx$

$= \int (\tan x \sec^2 x - \tan x)\, dx$

$= \int \tan x \sec^2 x\, dx - \int \tan x\, dx$

On putting $\tan x = t$ and $\sec^2 x\, dx = dt$ in first integral, we get

$$I = \int t\, dt - \int \tan x\, dx$$

$$\Rightarrow \quad I = \frac{t^2}{2} + \log|\cos x| + C$$

$$\therefore \int \tan^3 x\, dx = \frac{1}{2}\tan^2 x + \log|\cos x| + C$$

38. Let $I = \int \frac{\sin x + \cos x}{\sqrt{9 + 16 \sin 2x}}\, dx$

On putting $\sin x - \cos x = t \Rightarrow (\cos x + \sin x)\, dx = dt$

Again, $(\sin x - \cos x)^2 = t^2$

$\Rightarrow \sin^2 x + \cos^2 x - 2 \sin x \cos x = t^2$

$\Rightarrow 1 - 2 \sin x \cos x = t^2$

$\Rightarrow 1 - \sin 2x = t^2$

$\Rightarrow \sin 2x = 1 - t^2$

$$\therefore \quad I = \int \frac{dt}{\sqrt{9 + 16(1 - t^2)}} = \int \frac{dt}{\sqrt{9 + 16 - 16t^2}}$$

$$= \int \frac{dt}{\sqrt{25 - 16t^2}}$$

$$= \int \frac{dt}{4\sqrt{\left(\frac{5}{4}\right)^2 - (t)^2}}$$

$$= \frac{1}{4}\int \frac{dt}{\sqrt{(5/4)^2 - t^2}}$$

$$= \frac{1}{4}\sin^{-1}\frac{4t}{5} + C \quad \left[\because \int \frac{dx}{\sqrt{a^2 - x^2}} = \sin^{-1}\frac{x}{a} + C\right]$$

$$\Rightarrow I = \frac{1}{4}\sin^{-1}\left[\frac{4}{5}(\sin x - \cos x)\right] + C$$

$[\because t = \sin x - \cos x]$

39. Let $I = \int \frac{\sec x}{1 + \operatorname{cosec} x}\, dx = \int \frac{\sin x}{\cos x(1 + \sin x)}\, dx$

$$= \int \frac{\sin x}{\cos x(1 + \sin x)} \times \frac{\cos x}{\cos x}\, dx$$

$$= \int \frac{\sin x \cos x}{\cos^2 x(1 + \sin x)} dx$$

$$= \int \frac{\sin x \cos x}{(1 - \sin^2 x)(1 + \sin x)} dx$$

$$= \int \frac{\sin x \cos x}{(1 + \sin x)^2 (1 - \sin x)} dx$$

On putting $\sin x = t \Rightarrow \cos x\, dx = dt$

$$\therefore \quad I = \int \frac{t}{(1 + t)^2 (1 - t)} dt$$

By using partial fraction, consider

$$\frac{t}{(1 + t)^2 (1 - t)} = \frac{A}{(1 + t)} + \frac{B}{(1 + t)^2} + \frac{C}{(1 - t)}$$

$$\Rightarrow \quad t = A(1 + t)(1 - t) + B(1 - t) + C(1 + t)^2$$

$$\Rightarrow \quad t = A(1 - t^2) + B(1 - t) + C(1 + t^2 + 2t)$$

On equating the coefficient of t^2, t and constant, we get

$$0 = -A + C, 1 = -B + 2C \text{ and } 0 = A + B + C$$

On solving, we get

$$A = \frac{1}{4}, B = -\frac{1}{2} \text{ and } C = \frac{1}{4}$$

$$\therefore \quad \frac{t}{(1 + t)^2 (1 - t)} = \frac{1}{4(1 + t)} - \frac{1}{2(1 + t)^2} + \frac{1}{4(1 - t)}$$

$$\therefore I = \int \left[\frac{1}{4(1 + t)} - \frac{1}{2(1 + t)^2} + \frac{1}{4(1 - t)}\right] dt$$

$$= \frac{1}{4}\log|1 + t| - \frac{1}{2}\frac{(1 + t)^{-2+1}}{-2 + 1} - \frac{1}{4}\log|1 - t| + C$$

$$= \frac{1}{4}\log|1 + t| + \frac{1}{2(1 + t)} - \frac{1}{4}\log|1 - t| + C$$

$$= \frac{1}{4}\log\left|\frac{1 + t}{1 - t}\right| + \frac{1}{2(1 + t)} + C$$

$$\left[\because \log m - \log n = \log\left(\frac{m}{n}\right)\right]$$

$$\Rightarrow I = \frac{1}{4}\log\left|\frac{1 + \sin x}{1 - \sin x}\right| + \frac{1}{2(1 + \sin x)} + C \quad [\because t = \sin x]$$

Concept Enhancer If the integral problem is of the form $\int \frac{px^2 + qx + r}{(x - a)^2 (x - 6)}$, then by using partial fraction, we consider

$$\frac{px^2 + qx + r}{(x - a)^2 (x - b)} = \frac{A}{x - a} + \frac{B}{(x - a)^2} + \frac{C}{x - b}$$

40. Let $I=\int \frac{x+\sin x}{1+\cos x}\,dx$

Then, $I=\int \frac{x}{1+\cos x}\,dx+\int \frac{\sin x}{1+\cos x}\,dx$

$\Rightarrow \quad I=I_1+I_2$ [say] ...(i)

Now, $I_1=\int \frac{x}{1+\cos x}\,dx$

$$=\int \frac{x}{2\cos^2 x/2}\,dx \quad \left[\because \cos\theta=2\cos^2\frac{\theta}{2}-1\right]$$

$$=\frac{1}{2}\int \underset{\text{I}}{x}\,\underset{\text{II}}{\sec^2}\frac{x}{2}\,dx$$

Using integration by parts, we get

$$I_1=\frac{1}{2}\left[x\cdot\tan\frac{x}{2}\cdot 2-\int 1\cdot\tan\frac{x}{2}\cdot 2\,dx\right]$$

$$\left[\because \int \underset{\text{I}}{f(x)}.\underset{\text{II}}{g(x)}\,dx=f(x)\int g(x)-\int\left(\frac{d}{dx}f(x)\int g(x)dx\right)dx\right]$$

$$=\frac{1}{2}\left[2x\tan\frac{x}{2}-2\int\tan\frac{x}{2}\,dx\right]$$

$$\Rightarrow \quad I_1=x\tan\frac{x}{2}-\int\tan\frac{x}{2}\,dx$$

and $I_2=\int \frac{\sin x}{1+\cos x}\,dx$

$$=\int \frac{2\sin x/2\cdot\cos x/2}{2\cos^2 x/2}\,dx$$

$$\left[\because \sin\theta=2\sin\frac{\theta}{2}\cos\frac{\theta}{2}\text{ and }\cos\theta=2\cos^2\frac{\theta}{2}-1\right]$$

$$\Rightarrow \quad I_2=\int \tan x/2\,dx$$

From Eq. (i),

$$I=I_1+I_2$$

$$\Rightarrow \quad I=x\tan\frac{x}{2}-\int\tan\frac{x}{2}\,dx+\int\tan\frac{x}{2}\,dx$$

$$\Rightarrow \quad I=x\tan\frac{x}{2}+C$$

41. Let $I=\int e^x\frac{(2+\sin 2x)}{\cos^2 x}\,dx=\int e^x\frac{(2+2\sin x\cos x)}{\cos^2 x}\,dx$

$[\because \sin 2\theta=2\sin\theta\cos\theta]$

$$=2\int e^x\left[\frac{1}{\cos^2 x}+\frac{\sin x\cos x}{\cos^2 x}\right]dx$$

$$=2\int e^x(\sec^2 x+\tan x)\,dx$$

$$=2\int e^x(\tan x+\sec^2 x)dx$$

$$\Rightarrow \quad I=2e^x\tan x+C$$

$$\left[\because \int e^x[f(x)+f'(x)]\,dx=e^x f(x)+C\right]$$

42. Let $I=\int \frac{1}{x+\sqrt{x}}\,dx$

On putting $x=t^2 \Rightarrow dx=2t\,dt$

$$I=\int\frac{2t\,dt}{t^2+t}$$

$$=2\int\frac{1}{1+t}\,dt$$

$$=2\log|1+t|+C \quad \left[\because \int\frac{1}{x}\,dx=\log|x|+C\right]$$

$$=2\log|1+\sqrt{x}|+C$$

43. Let $I=\int\frac{\cos^{-1}x}{x^2}\,dx$

On putting $x=\cos\theta \Rightarrow dx=-\sin\theta\,d\theta$ and $\theta=\cos^{-1}x$

$$\therefore \quad I=\int\left[-\left(\theta\cdot\frac{\sin\theta}{\cos\theta}\cdot\frac{1}{\cos\theta}\right)\right]d\theta$$

$$\Rightarrow \quad I=-\int \underset{\text{I}}{\theta}\cdot(\tan\underset{\text{II}}{\theta}\cdot\sec\theta)\,d\theta$$

Using integration by parts, we get

$$I=-[\theta\cdot\sec\theta-\int 1\cdot\sec\theta\,d\theta]$$

$$\left[\because \int \underset{\text{I}}{f(x)}.\underset{\text{II}}{g(x)}\,dx=f(x)\int g(x)-\int\left(\frac{d}{dx}f(x)\int g(x)dx\right)dx\right]$$

$$=-\theta\sec\theta+\int\sec\theta\,d\theta$$

$$=-\theta\sec\theta+\log|\sec\theta+\tan\theta|+C$$

$$=-\cos^{-1}x\cdot\frac{1}{x}+\log\left|\left(\frac{1}{x}+\sqrt{\sec^2\theta-1}\right)\right|+C$$

$$\left[\text{on putting }\cos\theta=x\Rightarrow\sec\theta=\frac{1}{x}\right]$$

$$=\frac{-\cos^{-1}x}{x}+\log\left|\frac{1}{x}+\sqrt{\frac{1}{x^2}-1}\right|+C$$

$$\Rightarrow \quad I=\frac{-\cos^{-1}x}{x}+\log\left|\frac{1}{x}+\frac{\sqrt{1-x^2}}{x}\right|+C$$

44. Let $I=\int \dfrac{dx}{x\{6(\log x)^2+7\log x+2\}}$

On putting $\log x=t \Rightarrow \dfrac{1}{x}dx=dt$

$$\therefore \quad I=\int \frac{dt}{6t^2+7t+2}=\int \frac{dt}{6t^2+4t+3t+2}$$

$$=\int \frac{dt}{2t(3t+2)+1(3t+2)}$$

$$\Rightarrow \quad I=\int \frac{dt}{(3t+2)(2t+1)} \quad \ldots\text{(i)}$$

Let $\dfrac{1}{(3t+2)(2t+1)}=\dfrac{A}{(3t+2)}+\dfrac{B}{(2t+1)}$

[using partial fraction method]

$$\Rightarrow \quad 1=A(2t+1)+B(3t+2) \quad \ldots\text{(ii)}$$

On putting $t=-1/2$ in Eq. (ii), we get

$$1=0+B\left[3\times\left(-\frac{1}{2}\right)+2\right]$$

$$\Rightarrow \quad 1=B\left(\frac{-3+4}{2}\right) \Rightarrow 1=\frac{B}{2} \Rightarrow B=2$$

Put $t=-2/3$ in Eq. (ii), we get

$$1=A\left[2\times\left(-\frac{2}{3}\right)+1\right]$$

$$\Rightarrow \quad 1=A\left(\frac{-4+3}{3}\right) \Rightarrow 1=-\frac{A}{3} \Rightarrow A=-3$$

Now, from Eq. (i),

$$I=\int \frac{dt}{(3t+2)(2t+1)}$$

$$=\int\left(\frac{-3}{(3t+2)}+\frac{2}{(2t+1)}\right)dt$$

$$=-3\log|3t+2|\left(\frac{1}{3}\right)+2\log|2t+1|\left(\frac{1}{2}\right)+C$$

$$=-\log|3t+2|+\log|2t+1|+C$$

$$=\log\left|\frac{2t+1}{3t+2}\right|+C$$

$$\Rightarrow \quad I=\log\left|\frac{2\log x+1}{3\log x+2}\right|+C \quad [\because t=\log x]$$

45. Let $I=\int e^x(\tan x+\log\sec x)\,dx$

$$=\int e^x\left[\log\sec x+\frac{d}{dx}(\log\sec x)\right]dx$$

$$\left[\because \frac{d}{dx}\log\sec x=\frac{1}{\sec x}\cdot\sec x\tan x=\tan x\right]$$

Using $\int e^x[f(x)+f'(x)]\,dx=e^x f(x)+C$

$$I=e^x\log\sec x+C$$

46. Let $I=\int \dfrac{\operatorname{cosec} x}{\log\tan\left(\dfrac{x}{2}\right)}dx$

On putting $\log\tan\left(\dfrac{x}{2}\right)=t$,

$$\Rightarrow \quad \frac{1}{\tan x/2}\left(\left(\sec^2\frac{x}{2}\right)\frac{1}{2}\right)dx=dt$$

$$\Rightarrow \quad \frac{1\cdot\cos x/2\,dx}{2\sin x/2\cdot\cos^2 x/2}=dt$$

$$\Rightarrow \quad \frac{1\,dx}{2\sin x/2\cdot\cos x/2}=dt$$

$$\Rightarrow \quad \frac{1}{\sin x}dx=dt$$

$[\because \sin 2\theta=2\sin\theta\cdot\cos\theta]$

$$\Rightarrow \quad \operatorname{cosec} x\,dx=dt$$

$$\therefore \quad I=\int\frac{\operatorname{cosec} x\,dx}{\log\tan\left(\frac{x}{2}\right)}=\int\frac{dt}{t}$$

$$=\log|t|+C$$

$$=\log\left|\log\tan\left(\frac{x}{2}\right)\right|+C \quad \left[\because t=\log\tan\left(\frac{x}{2}\right)\right]$$

47. Let $I=\int\dfrac{x^2}{1+x^4}dx$

$$I=\int\frac{1}{x^2+\frac{1}{x^2}}dx$$

$$=\frac{1}{2}\int\frac{\left(1+\frac{1}{x^2}\right)+\left(1-\frac{1}{x^2}\right)}{x^2+\frac{1}{x^2}}dx$$

$$I=\frac{1}{2}\int\frac{\left(1+\frac{1}{x^2}\right)}{x^2+\frac{1}{x^2}}dx+\frac{1}{2}\int\frac{\left(1-\frac{1}{x^2}\right)}{x^2+\frac{1}{x^2}}dx$$

$$I=I_1+I_2$$

$$I_1=\frac{1}{2}\int\frac{\left(1+\frac{1}{x^2}\right)}{\left(x^2+\frac{1}{x^2}\right)}dx$$

$$=\frac{1}{2}\int\frac{\left(1+\frac{1}{x^2}\right)dx}{\left(x-\frac{1}{x}\right)^2+2}$$

Let $x-\frac{1}{x}=t\Rightarrow\left(1+\frac{1}{x^2}\right)dx=dt$

$$I_1=\frac{1}{2}\int\frac{dt}{t^2+2}=\frac{1}{2}\left[\frac{1}{\sqrt{2}}\tan^{-1}\left(\frac{t}{\sqrt{2}}\right)\right]+C_1$$

$$=\frac{1}{2\sqrt{2}}\tan^{-1}\left(\frac{x^2-1}{\sqrt{2}x}\right)+C_1$$

$$I_2=\frac{1}{2}\int\frac{\left(1-\frac{1}{x^2}\right)dx}{\left(x^2+\frac{1}{x^2}\right)}$$

$$=\frac{1}{2}\int\frac{\left(1-\frac{1}{x^2}\right)dx}{\left(x+\frac{1}{x}\right)^2-2}$$

Let $x+\frac{1}{x}=t\Rightarrow\left(1-\frac{1}{x^2}\right)dx=dt$

$$I_2=\frac{1}{2}\int\frac{dt}{t^2-2}=\frac{1}{2}\int\frac{dt}{t^2-(\sqrt{2})^2}$$

$$I_2=\frac{1}{2}\left[\frac{1}{2\sqrt{2}}\log\left|\frac{t-\sqrt{2}}{t+\sqrt{2}}\right|\right]+C_2$$

$$I_2=\frac{1}{4\sqrt{2}}\log\left|\frac{x+\frac{1}{x}-\sqrt{2}}{x+\frac{1}{x}+\sqrt{2}}\right|+C_2$$

$$I_2=\frac{1}{4\sqrt{2}}\log\left|\frac{x^2-\sqrt{2}x+1}{x^2+\sqrt{2}x+1}\right|+C_2$$

$\therefore\quad I=I_1+I_2$

$$\Rightarrow\quad I=\frac{1}{2\sqrt{2}}\tan^{-1}\left(\frac{x^2-1}{\sqrt{2}x}\right)+\frac{1}{4\sqrt{2}}\log\left|\frac{x^2-\sqrt{2}x+1}{x^2+\sqrt{2}x+1}\right|+C$$

48. Let $I=\int\frac{3e^{2x}-2e^x}{e^{2x}+2e^x-8}dx=\int\frac{e^x(3e^x-2)}{e^{2x}+2e^x-8}dx$

On putting $e^x=t\Rightarrow e^x dx=dt$

$$\therefore\quad I=\int\frac{3t-2}{t^2+2t-8}dt$$

Let $3t-2=\lambda\frac{d}{dt}(t^2+2t-8)+\mu$

$\Rightarrow\ 3t-2=\lambda(2t+2)+\mu$

$\Rightarrow\ 3t-2=2\lambda t+2\lambda+\mu$

Equating the coefficient of t and constant term, we get

$$3=2\lambda \text{ and } 2\lambda+\mu=-2$$

$$\lambda=\frac{3}{2}\text{ and }\mu=-5$$

$$\therefore\quad I=\int\frac{\frac{3}{2}(2t+2)\,dt}{t^2+2t-8}+\int\frac{-5}{t^2+2t-8}dt$$

$$\Rightarrow\quad I=\frac{3}{2}\log(t^2+2t-8)-5\int\frac{dt}{(t+1)^2-(3)^2}$$

$$\Rightarrow\quad I=\frac{3}{2}\log(t^2+2t-8)-5\times\frac{1}{6}\log\left|\frac{t+1-3}{t+1+3}\right|+C$$

$$\left[\because\int\frac{dx}{x^2-a^2}=\frac{1}{2a}\log\left|\frac{x-a}{x+a}\right|+C\right]$$

$$\Rightarrow\quad I=\frac{3}{2}\log|t^2+2t-8|-\frac{5}{6}\log\left|\frac{t-2}{t+4}\right|+C$$

$$\Rightarrow\quad I=\frac{3}{2}\log|e^{2x}+2e^x-8|-\frac{5}{6}\log\left|\frac{e^x-2}{e^x+4}\right|+C$$

$[\because t=e^x]$

49. Let $I=\int\frac{2}{(1-x)(1+x^2)}dx$

Again, let $\frac{2}{(1-x)(1+x^2)}=\frac{A}{1-x}+\frac{Bx+C}{1+x^2}$

[using partial decomposition]

$\Rightarrow\ 2=A(1+x^2)+(Bx+C)(1-x)$

$\Rightarrow\ 2=Ax^2-Bx^2+(B-C)x+A+C$

Equating the coefficient of x^2, x and constant terms, we obtain

$A-B=0$ ...(i)

$B-C=0$ ...(ii)

$A+C=2$ ...(iii)

On solving Eqs. (i), (ii) and (iii), we get

$$A=1,\ B=1\text{ and }C=1$$

$$\therefore\ \int\frac{2}{(1-x)(1+x^2)}dx=\int\frac{dx}{1-x}+\int\frac{x+1}{x^2+1}dx$$

$$=\int\frac{1}{1-x}dx+\int\frac{x}{x^2+1}dx+\int\frac{dx}{x^2+1}$$

$$=-\log|1-x|+\frac{1}{2}\log|x^2+1|+\tan^{-1}x+C$$

50. Let $I=\int \frac{1}{\sin^4 x+\cos^4 x}dx=\int \frac{\sec^4 x}{1+\tan^4 x}dx$

On putting $\tan x = t \Rightarrow \sec^2 x\, dx = dt$

$$\therefore\ I=\int \frac{1+t^2}{1+t^4}dt=\int \frac{t^2\left(1+\frac{1}{t^2}\right)}{t^2\left(t^2+\frac{1}{t^2}\right)}dt$$

$$=\int \frac{1+\frac{1}{t^2}}{t^2+\frac{1}{t^2}-2+2}dt=\int \frac{1+\frac{1}{t^2}}{\left(t-\frac{1}{t}\right)^2+(\sqrt{2})^2}dt$$

Again, let $t-\frac{1}{t}=v \Rightarrow \left(1+\frac{1}{t^2}\right)dt=dv$

$$I=\int \frac{dv}{(\sqrt{2})^2+(v)^2}=\frac{1}{\sqrt{2}}\tan^{-1}\left(\frac{v}{\sqrt{2}}\right)+C$$

$$=\frac{1}{\sqrt{2}}\tan^{-1}\left[\frac{\tan^2 x-1}{\sqrt{2}\tan x}\right]+C$$

$$\left[\because v=t-\frac{1}{t} \text{ and } t=\tan x\right]$$

51. Let $I=\int \frac{dx}{\sin x+\sin 2x}=\int \frac{dx}{\sin x+2\sin x\cos x}$

$$=\int \frac{dx}{\sin x\,(1+2\cos x)}=\int \frac{\sin x\, dx}{(1-\cos^2 x)(1+2\cos x)}$$

On putting $\cos x = t \Rightarrow \sin x\, dx = -dt$

$$\therefore\ I=\int \frac{-dt}{(1-t^2)(1+2t)}$$

$$=\int \frac{-dt}{(1-t)\,(1+t)\,(1+2t)}$$

Let $\frac{-1}{(1+t)\,(1-t)\,(1+2t)}=\frac{A}{1+t}+\frac{B}{1-t}+\frac{C}{1+2t}$

$\Rightarrow -1 = A(1-t)\,(1+2t)+B\,(1+t)\,(1+2t)$
$+C(1+t)\,(1-t)$ ... (i)

On putting $t=1$ in Eq. (i), we get

$$-1=6B$$

$$\Rightarrow \quad B=-\frac{1}{6}$$

On putting $t=-1$ in Eq. (i), we get

$$-1=-2A$$

$$\Rightarrow \quad A=\frac{1}{2}$$

On putting $t=-\frac{1}{2}$ in Eq. (i), we get

$$-1=\frac{3}{4}C$$

$$\Rightarrow \quad C=-\frac{4}{3}$$

On substituting the values of A, B and C in Eq. (i), we get

$$\frac{-1}{(1+t)\,(1-t)\,(1+2t)}=\frac{1}{2(1+t)}-\frac{1}{6\,(1-t)}-\frac{4}{3\,(1+2t)}$$

On integrating both sides, we get

$$I=\frac{1}{2}\int \frac{1}{1+t}dt-\frac{1}{6}\int \frac{1}{1-t}dt-\frac{4}{3}\int \frac{1}{1+2t}dt$$

$$\Rightarrow \quad I=\frac{1}{2}\log|1+t|+\frac{1}{6}\log|1-t|-\frac{2}{3}\log|1+2t|+C$$

$$\Rightarrow \quad I=\frac{1}{2}\log|1+\cos x|+\frac{1}{6}\log|1-\cos x|$$
$$-\frac{2}{3}\log|1+2\cos x|+C$$

52. Let $I=\int \tan^{-1}\sqrt{x}\,dx$

On putting $x=\tan^2\theta$, then $dx = 2\tan\theta\sec^2\theta\, d\theta$

$$\therefore\quad I=2\int \underset{\text{I}}{\theta}\,\underbrace{\tan\theta\sec^2\theta}_{\text{II}}\,d\theta$$

$$=2\left[\theta\cdot\frac{\tan^2\theta}{2}-\int \frac{\tan^2\theta\cdot 1}{2}d\theta\right]$$

$$=[\theta\tan^2\theta-\int(\sec^2\theta-1)\,d\theta]$$

$$=[\theta\tan^2\theta-\tan\theta+\theta]+C$$

$$=[x\tan^{-1}\sqrt{x}-\sqrt{x}+\tan^{-1}\sqrt{x}]+C$$

$$\Rightarrow \quad I=[(x+1)\tan^{-1}\sqrt{x}-\sqrt{x}]+C$$

53. Let $I=\int \tan^{-1}\sqrt{\frac{1-x}{1+x}}\,dx$

On putting $x=\cos 2\theta$

$$\Rightarrow \quad dx=-2\sin 2\theta\, d\theta$$

$$\therefore\quad I=\int \tan^{-1}\sqrt{\frac{1-\cos 2\theta}{1+\cos 2\theta}}\,(-2\sin 2\theta)\,d\theta$$

$$=\int \tan^{-1}\sqrt{\frac{2\sin^2\theta}{2\cos^2\theta}}\,(-2\sin 2\theta)\,d\theta$$

$$=-2\int \tan^{-1}(\tan\theta)\sin 2\theta\, d\theta$$

$$=-2\int \theta\sin 2\theta\, d\theta$$

$$= -2\left[\theta\int \sin 2\theta\, d\theta - \int\left[\frac{d}{d\theta}\theta \int \sin 2\theta\, d\theta\right]\cdot d\theta\right] + C$$

$$= -2\left[-\frac{\theta\cos 2\theta}{2} + \int \frac{\cos 2\theta}{2}\, d\theta\right] + C$$

$$= \theta\cos 2\theta - \frac{1}{2}\sin 2\theta + C$$

$$\Rightarrow \quad I = \frac{x}{2}\cos^{-1} x - \frac{\sqrt{1-x^2}}{2} + C \qquad \left[\because \theta = \frac{1}{2}\cos^{-1} x\right]$$

54. Let $I = \int \frac{2x+7}{x^2-x+2}\, dx$

$$= \int \frac{2x-1}{x^2-x+2}\, dx + \int \frac{8}{x^2-x+2}\, dx$$

$$= \int \frac{d(x^2-x+2)}{x^2-x+2} + \int \frac{8}{x^2-x+\frac{1}{4}+2-\frac{1}{4}}\, dx$$

$$= \log(x^2-x+2) + 8\int \frac{dx}{\left(x-\frac{1}{2}\right)^2 + \left(\frac{\sqrt{7}}{2}\right)^2}$$

$$= \log(x^2-x+2) + 8 \times \frac{1}{\frac{\sqrt{7}}{2}} \tan^{-1}\left(\frac{x-\frac{1}{2}}{\frac{\sqrt{7}}{2}}\right) + C$$

$$\Rightarrow \quad I = \log(x^2-x+2) + \frac{16}{\sqrt{7}}\tan^{-1}\left(\frac{2x-1}{\sqrt{7}}\right) + C$$

55. We have,

$$I = \int \frac{x-1}{\sqrt{x^2-x}}\, dx$$

$$= \frac{1}{2}\int \frac{2x-2}{\sqrt{x^2-x}}\, dx$$

$$= \frac{1}{2}\left[\int \frac{2x-1}{\sqrt{x^2-x}}\, dx - \int \frac{1}{\sqrt{x^2-x}}\, dx\right]$$

$$= \frac{1}{2}\left[\int \frac{2x-1}{\sqrt{x^2-x}}\, dx - \int \frac{dx}{\sqrt{x^2-x+\frac{1}{4}-\frac{1}{4}}}\right]$$

$$= \frac{1}{2}\left[\int \frac{1}{\sqrt{t}}\, dt - \int \frac{dx}{\sqrt{\left(x-\frac{1}{2}\right)^2 - \left(\frac{1}{2}\right)^2}}\right]$$

$[\because$ putting $x^2 - x = t \Rightarrow (2x-1)dx = dt]$

$$= \frac{1}{2}\left[2\sqrt{t} - \log\left|\left(x-\frac{1}{2}\right) + \sqrt{x^2-x}\right|\right] + C$$

$$\Rightarrow \quad I = \sqrt{x^2-x} - \frac{1}{2}\log\left|\left(x-\frac{1}{2}\right) + \sqrt{x^2-x}\right| + C$$

56. Let $\quad I = \int \frac{3x+5}{x^3-x^2-x+1}\, dx$

$$\Rightarrow \quad I = \int \frac{3x+5}{(x+1)(x-1)^2}\, dx$$

Here, integrand is a proper rational function, so using partial fraction. We write as

$$\frac{3x+5}{(x+1)(x-1)^2} = \frac{A}{x+1} + \frac{B}{x-1} + \frac{C}{(x-1)^2}$$

$$\Rightarrow \quad 3x+5 = A(x-1)^2 + B(x+1)(x-1) + C(x+1) \quad \ldots(i)$$

On putting $x = 1$ in Eq. (i), we get

$$8 = 2C \Rightarrow C = 4$$

On putting $x = -1$ in Eq. (i), we get

$$2 = A(-2)^2 \Rightarrow A = \frac{1}{2}$$

On putting $x = 0$ in Eq. (i), we get

$$5 = A - B + C$$

$$\Rightarrow \quad 5 = \frac{1}{2} - B + 4 \Rightarrow B = -\frac{1}{2}$$

$$\therefore \quad I = \frac{1}{2}\int \frac{dx}{x+1} - \frac{1}{2}\int \frac{dx}{x-1} + 4\int \frac{dx}{(x-1)^2}$$

$$= \frac{1}{2}\log|x+1| - \frac{1}{2}\log|x-1| - \frac{4}{x-1} + C$$

$$\Rightarrow \quad I = \frac{1}{2}\log\left|\frac{x+1}{x-1}\right| - \frac{4}{x-1} + C$$

TOPIC 2

Definite Integral

An integral of the form of $\int_a^b f(x)\,dx$ is known as **definite integral** and is given by $\int_a^b f(x)\,dx = g(b) - g(a)$, where $f(x)$ is derivative of $g(x)$, a and b are respectively the lower and upper limits of a definite integral.

First Fundamental Theorem of Integral Calculus

Theorem 1 Let f be a continuous function defined on the closed interval $[a, b]$ and $A(x)$ be the area of function i.e. $A(x) = \int_a^x f(x)dx$.

Then, $A'(x) = f(x)$, for all $x \in [a, b]$.

Second Fundamental Theorem of Integral Calculus

Theorem 2 Let f be a continuous function defined on the closed interval $[a, b]$ and F be an anti-derivative of f.

Then, $\int_a^b f(x)\,dx = [F(x)]_a^b = F(b) - F(a)$

In other words,

$\int_a^b f(x)\,dx$

= Value of the anti-derivative F of f at the upper limit b – Value of the same anti-derivative at the lower limit a.

Steps for Calculating Definite Integral

Step I Firstly, find the indefinite integral $\int f(x)\,dx$. Let this be $F(x)$. There is no need to keep integration constant C because if we consider $F(x) + C$ instead of $F(x)$, we get

$$\int_a^b f(x)dx = [F(x) + C]_a^b$$
$$= [F(b) + C] - [F(a) + C]$$
$$= F(b) - F(a)$$

Thus, the arbitrary constant disappears in evaluating the value of definite integral.

Step II Evaluate $\int_a^b f(x)dx = [F(x)]_a^b$

$$= F(b) - F(a).$$

Step III Calculate $F(b) - F(a)$.

Properties of Definite Integral

(i) $\int_a^b f(x)\,dx = \int_a^b f(t)\,dt$

(ii) $\int_a^b f(x)\,dx = -\int_b^a f(x)\,dx$

(iii) $\int_a^b f(x)\,dx = \int_a^c f(x)\,dx + \int_c^b f(x)\,dx$, where $a < c < b$

(iv) $\int_a^a f(x)\,dx = 0$

(v) $\int_0^a f(x)\,dx = \int_0^a f(a-x)\,dx$

(vi) $\int_a^b f(x)\,dx = \int_a^b f(a+b-x)\,dx$

(vii) $\int_0^{2a} f(x)\,dx = \int_0^a f(x)\,dx + \int_0^a f(2a-x)\,dx$

(viii) $\int_0^{2a} f(x)\,dx = \begin{cases} 2\int_0^a f(x)\,dx, & \text{if } f(2a-x) = f(x) \\ 0, & \text{if } f(2a-x) = -f(x) \end{cases}$

or $\int_a^b f(x)\,dx$

$$= \begin{cases} 0, & \text{if } f(a+x) = -f(b-x) \\ 2\int_a^{\frac{a+b}{2}} f(x)\,dx, & \text{if } f(a+x) = f(b-x) \end{cases}$$

(ix) $\int_{-a}^a f(x)\,dx = \int_0^a [f(x) + f(-x)]dx$

$$= \begin{cases} 2\int_0^a f(x)\,dx, & \text{if } f(x) \text{ is even i.e. } f(-x) = f(x) \\ 0, & \text{if } f(x) \text{ is odd i.e. } f(-x) = -f(x) \end{cases}$$

Evaluation of Definite Integrals by Substitution

Consider a definite integral of the following form

$\int_a^b \{f[g(x)] \cdot g'(x)\}\,dx$

Step I Substitute $g(x) = t$

$\Rightarrow \quad g'(x)\,dx = dt$

Step II Find the limits of integration in new system of variable i.e. the lower limit $g(a)$ and the upper limit $g(b)$ and the given integral becomes $\int_{g(a)}^{g(b)} f(t)\,dt$.

Step III Evaluate the integral, so obtained by usual method.

Some Useful Results

(i) $1+2+\ldots+(n-1)=\dfrac{n(n-1)}{2}$

(ii) $1^2+2^2+\ldots+(n-1)^2=\dfrac{n(n-1)(2n-1)}{6}$

(iii) $1^3+2^3+\ldots+(n-1)^3=\dfrac{[(n-1)n]^2}{4}$

(iv) $a+ar+ar^2+\ldots+ar^{n-1}=\dfrac{a(r^n-1)}{r-1}, r\neq 1$ [for GP series]

(v) $a+(a+d)+(a+2d)+\ldots+\{a+(n-1)d\}$

$=\dfrac{n}{2}[2a+(n-1)d]$ [for AP series]

(vi) $\sin(a)+\sin(a+h)+\ldots+\sin(a+(n-1)h)$

$$=\frac{\sin\left\{a+\left(\frac{n-1}{2}\right)h\right\}\sin\left(\frac{nh}{2}\right)}{\sin\left(\frac{h}{2}\right)}$$

(vii) $\cos(a)+\cos(a+h)+\ldots+\cos[a+(n-1)h]$

$$=\frac{\cos\left\{a+\left(\frac{n-1}{2}\right)h\right\}\sin\left(\frac{nh}{2}\right)}{\sin\left(\frac{h}{2}\right)}$$

PYQs Previous Years Questions

1 Mark Questions

1. The value $\int_1^{\sqrt{3}}\dfrac{dx}{1+x^2}$ is **ISC 2024**

(a) $\dfrac{\pi}{2}$ (b) $\dfrac{2\pi}{3}$

(c) $\dfrac{\pi}{6}$ (d) $\dfrac{\pi}{12}$

2. Evaluate $\int_0^6|x+3|\,dx$ **ISC 2024**

3. Evaluate $\int_{-1}^1 x^{17}\cos^4 x\,dx.$ **ISC 2023**

(a) ∞ (b) 1 (c) -1 (d) 0

4. Evaluate $\int_0^1|2x+1|\,dx.$ **ISC 2023**

5. $\int_0^{2a} f(x)dx=\int_0^a f(x)dx+\int_0^a f(k-x)dx$, then the value of k is **ISC Specimen Sem-II 2022**

(a) a (b) $2a$

(c) independent of a (d) None of these

2 Marks Questions

6. Evaluate $\int_0^{2\pi}\dfrac{1}{1+e^{\sin x}}\,dx$ **ISC 2024**

7. Evaluate $\int_{-\pi/2}^{\pi/2}|\sin x|\,dx.$ **ISC Specimen 2024**

8. Evaluate $\int_0^{\frac{\pi}{2}}\dfrac{a\sin x+b\cos x}{\sin x+\cos x}\,dx.$ **ISC Specimen 2023**

9. Evaluate $\int_2^8\dfrac{\sqrt{10-x}}{\sqrt{x}+\sqrt{10-x}}dx.$ **ISC Specimen Sem-II 2022**

10. Evaluate $\int_0^{\pi/2}\dfrac{\sin^{\frac{3}{2}}x}{\sin^{\frac{3}{2}}x+\cos^{\frac{3}{2}}x}\,dx.$ **ISC Specimen 2021**

11. Evaluate $\int_4^5|x-5|\,dx.$ **ISC 2020**

12. Evaluate $\int_0^{\frac{\pi}{4}}\log(1+\tan\theta)\,d\theta.$ **ISC 2017, 07**

13. Using properties of definite integrals, evaluate $\int_0^{\pi/2}\dfrac{\sin x-\cos x}{1+\sin x\cos x}\,dx.$ **ISC 2016**

14. Evaluate $\int_0^3 f(x)dx$, where $f(x)=\begin{cases}\cos 2x, & 0\le x\le\dfrac{\pi}{2}\\ 3, & \dfrac{\pi}{2}<x\le 3\end{cases}$ **ISC 2015**

3/4 Marks Questions

15. Evaluate $\int_{-1}^{2}|x^3 - x|\,dx.$ **ISC Specimen 2023**

16. Evaluate $\int_{1}^{4}|x-2|\,dx.$ **ISC Specimen Sem-II 2022**

17. Evaluate $\int_{-6}^{3}|x+3|\,dx.$ **ISC Specimen 2021**

18. Evaluate $\int_{0}^{\pi}\frac{x\tan x}{\sec x+\tan x}\,dx.$ **ISC Specimen 2021**

19. Evaluate $\int_{-6}^{1}|x+3|\,dx.$ **ISC 2019**

20. Using properties of definite integrals, evaluate

$$\int_{0}^{\pi/2}\frac{\sqrt{\sin x}}{\sqrt{\sin x}+\sqrt{\cos x}}\,dx.$$

ISC 2014

21. Evaluate $\int_{0}^{1}\log\left(\frac{1}{x}-1\right)dx.$ **ISC 2013**

> **KEY CONCEPT**
>
> (i) First apply the property of definite integral
> i.e. $\int_0^a f(x)\,dx = \int_0^a f(a-x)\,dx$
> Further adding the equations and use the property of logarithm i.e. $\log m+\log n=\log mn$.
>
> (ii) Finally integrate and simplify it to get the required result.

22. Evaluate $\int_{1}^{2}\frac{\sqrt{x}}{\sqrt{3-x}+\sqrt{x}}\,dx.$ **ISC 2012**

23. Evaluate $\int_{0}^{1}\frac{xe^x}{(1+x)^2}\,dx.$ **ISC 2011**

> **KEY CONCEPT**
>
> (i) Firstly, adding and subtracting 1 and convert the integrand in two parts such that it become of the form $[e^x[f(x)+f'(x)]$.
>
> (ii)Further use the property
> $\int e^x[f(x)+f'(x)]dx = e^x f(x)+C$ and simplify it.

5 Marks Questions

24. Evaluate $\int_{0}^{\pi/4}\log(1+\tan x)dx.$ **ISC Specimen Sem-II 2022**

25. Evaluate $\int_{-\pi/2}^{\pi/2}\frac{\cos x}{1+e^x}\,dx.$ **ISC Specimen 2021**

26. Evaluate $\int_{0}^{\pi}\frac{x\tan x}{\sec x+\tan x}\,dx.$ **ISC 2019**

27. Evaluate $\int_{0}^{\pi/2}\frac{\cos^2 x}{1+\sin x\cos x}\,dx.$ **ISC 2018**

28. Evaluate $\int_{0}^{9}f(x)\,dx$, where $f(x)$ is defined by

$$f(x)=\begin{cases}\sin x, & \text{if } 0\le x\le \pi/2\\ 1, & \text{if } \frac{\pi}{2}<x\le 5\\ e^{x-5}, & \text{if } 5<x\le 9\end{cases}$$

ISC 2008

> **KEY CONCEPT**
>
> Firstly, expand the given integrand by using expansion property, then integrate it to get required result.

Explanations

1. (d) Let $I=\int_1^{\sqrt{3}}\frac{dx}{1+x^2}$

$=[\tan^{-1}x]_1^{\sqrt{3}}\quad\left[\because \int\frac{1}{x^2+a^2}dx=\frac{1}{a}\tan^{-1}\left(\frac{x}{a}\right)\right]$

$=\tan^{-1}(\sqrt{3})-\tan^{-1}(1)$

$=\frac{\pi}{3}-\frac{\pi}{4}$

$=\frac{\pi}{12}$

2. We have, $\int_0^6|x+3|\,dx$

Here, $f(x)=\begin{cases}x+3, & x\ge -3\\ -(x+3) & x<-3\end{cases}$

By the property of definite integral, we get

$\int_a^b f(x)\,dx=\int_a^c f(x)\,dx+\int_c^b f(x)\,dx$

where, $a<c<b$

Now, $\int_0^6|x+3|\,dx=\int_0^{-3}-(x+3)\,dx+\int_{-3}^6(x+3)\,dx$

$=-\left[\frac{x^2}{2}+3x\right]_0^{-3}+\left[\frac{x^2}{2}+3x\right]_{-3}^{6}$

$=-\left[\frac{9}{2}-9\right]+\left[18+18-\frac{9}{2}+9\right]$

$=\frac{9}{2}+45-\frac{9}{2}=45$

3. (d) Let $I=\int_{-1}^{1}x^{17}\cos^4 x\,dx$

$f(x)=x^{17}\cos^4 x$

$\therefore f(-x)=(-x)^{17}\cos^4(-x)=-x^{17}\cos^4 x=-f(x)$

Hence, $f(x)$ is an odd function.

$\therefore\ I=0\quad[\int_{-a}^{a}f(x)\,dx=0;\because f(x)$ is an odd function$]$

4. Let $I=\int_0^1|2x+1|\,dx$

$=\int_0^1(2x+1)\,dx\qquad[\because 2x+1>0;\ x\in(0,1)]$

$=[x^2+x]_0^1$

$=(1+1)-0=2$

5. (b) Given,

$$\int_0^{2a}f(x)\,dx=\int_0^a f(x)\,dx+\int_0^a f(k-x)\,dx\quad\ldots\text{(i)}$$

We know that,

$$\int_0^{2a}f(x)\,dx=\int_0^a f(x)\,dx+\int_0^a f(2a-x)\,dx\quad\ldots\text{(ii)}$$

On comparing Eqs. (i) and (ii), we get

$k=2a$

6. Let

$$I=\int_0^{2\pi}\frac{1}{1+e^{\sin x}}dx\quad\ldots\text{(i)}$$

We know that

$\int_0^a f(x)\,dx=\int_0^a f(a-x)\,dx$

$\therefore\quad I=\int_0^{2\pi}\frac{1}{1+e^{\sin(2\pi-x)}}dx$

$=\int_0^{2\pi}\frac{1}{1+e^{-\sin x}}dx$

$$\Rightarrow\quad I=\int_0^{2\pi}\frac{e^{\sin x}}{1+e^{\sin x}}dx\quad\ldots\text{(ii)}$$

On adding Eqs. (i) and (ii), we get

$2I=\int_0^{2\pi}\frac{1+e^{\sin x}}{1+e^{\sin x}}dx$

$=\int_0^{2\pi}1\cdot dx$

$=[x]_0^{2\pi}=2\pi$

$\Rightarrow\quad I=\pi$

Hence, $\int_0^{2\pi}\frac{1}{1+e^{\sin x}}dx=\pi$

7. Let $I=\int_{-\pi/2}^{\pi/2}|\sin x|\,dx$

$\because |\sin x|$ is an even function.

$\therefore\quad I=2\int_0^{\pi/2}|\sin x|\,dx$

$=2\int_0^{\pi/2}\sin x\,dx$

$=2[-\cos x]_0^{\pi/2}$

$=2\left[-\cos\frac{\pi}{2}+\cos 0\right]$

$=2[0+1]=2$

8. Let $I = \int_0^{\frac{\pi}{2}} \frac{a\sin x + b\cos x}{\sin x + \cos x} dx$ ...(i)

$$= \int_0^{\frac{\pi}{2}} \frac{a\sin\left(\frac{\pi}{2} - x\right) + b\cos\left(\frac{\pi}{2} - x\right)}{\sin\left(\frac{\pi}{2} - x\right) + \cos\left(\frac{\pi}{2} - x\right)} dx$$

$$\left[\because \int_0^a f(x)\,dx = \int_0^a f(a-x)\,dx\right]$$

$\Rightarrow I = \int_0^{\frac{\pi}{2}} \frac{a\cos x + b\sin x}{\cos x + \sin x} dx$ ...(ii)

On adding Eqs. (i) and (ii), we get

$$2I = \int_0^{\frac{\pi}{2}} \frac{a\sin x + b\cos x}{\cos x + \sin x} dx + \int_0^{\frac{\pi}{2}} \frac{a\cos x + b\sin x}{\cos x + \sin x} dx$$

$$= \int_0^{\frac{\pi}{2}} \frac{(a+b)(\sin x + \cos x)}{(\cos x + \sin x)} dx$$

$$\Rightarrow 2I = (a+b)[x]_0^{\frac{\pi}{2}} \Rightarrow I = \frac{\pi}{4}(a+b)$$

9. Let $I = \int_2^8 \frac{\sqrt{10-x}}{\sqrt{x} + \sqrt{10-x}} dx$ ...(i)

$\therefore \quad I = \int_2^8 \frac{\sqrt{10-(2+8-x)}}{\sqrt{2+8-x} + \sqrt{10-(2+8-x)}} dx$

$$\left[\because \int_a^b f(x)\,dx = \int_a^b f(a+b-x)\,dx\right]$$

$\therefore \quad I = \int_2^8 \frac{\sqrt{x}}{\sqrt{10-x} + \sqrt{x}} dx$ ...(ii)

On adding Eqs. (i) and (ii), we get

$$2I = \int_2^8 \frac{\sqrt{10-x} + \sqrt{x}}{\sqrt{10-x} + \sqrt{x}} dx = \int_2^8 1\,dx = [x]_2^8$$

$$\Rightarrow \quad 2I = 8 - 2 = 6 \Rightarrow I = 3$$

10. Let $I = \int_0^{\pi/2} \frac{\sin^{3/2} x}{\sin^{3/2} x + \cos^{3/2} x} dx$ ...(i)

$$= \int_0^{\pi/2} \frac{\sin^{3/2}\left(\frac{\pi}{2} - x\right)}{\sin^{3/2}\left(\frac{\pi}{2} - x\right) + \cos^{3/2}\left(\frac{\pi}{2} - x\right)} dx$$

$$\left[\because \int_0^a f(x)\,dx = \int_0^a f(a-x)\,dx\right]$$

$= \int_0^{\pi/2} \frac{\cos^{3/2} x}{\cos^{3/2} x + \sin^{3/2} x} dx$ ...(ii)

On adding Eqs. (i) and (ii), we get

$$2I = \int_0^{\pi/2} \frac{\sin^{3/2} x + \cos^{3/2} x}{\sin^{3/2} x + \cos^{3/2} x} dx$$

$$= \int_0^{\pi/2} dx = [x]_0^{\pi/2} = \frac{\pi}{2} - 0$$

$$\Rightarrow \quad 2I = \frac{\pi}{2} \Rightarrow I = \frac{\pi}{4}$$

11. Let $I = \int_4^5 |x-5|\,dx$

$$= -\int_4^5 (x-5)\,dx \qquad [\because x - 5 < 0 \text{ when } x \in (4, 5)]$$

$$= -\left[\frac{x^2}{2} - 5x\right]_4^5$$

$$= -\left[\left(\frac{25}{2} - 25\right) - \left(\frac{16}{2} - 20\right)\right]$$

$$\Rightarrow I = -\left[-\frac{25}{2} + 12\right] = \frac{1}{2}$$

12. Let $I = \int_0^{\frac{\pi}{4}} \log(1 + \tan\theta)\,d\theta$ ...(i)

By using the property,

$\int_0^a f(x)\,dx = \int_0^a f(a-x)\,dx$, we get

$$I = \int_0^{\frac{\pi}{4}} \log\left[1 + \tan\left(\frac{\pi}{4} - \theta\right)\right]$$

$$= \int_0^{\frac{\pi}{4}} \log\left[1 + \frac{1 - \tan\theta}{1 + \tan\theta}\right] d\theta$$

$$= \int_0^{\frac{\pi}{4}} \log\left(\frac{2}{1 + \tan\theta}\right) d\theta$$

$$= \int_0^{\frac{\pi}{4}} [\log 2 - \log(1 + \tan\theta)]\,d\theta$$

$= \log 2 \int_0^{\frac{\pi}{4}} d\theta - \int_0^{\frac{\pi}{4}} \log(1 + \tan\theta)\,d\theta$ ...(ii)

Now, on adding Eqs. (i) and (ii), we get

$$2I = (\log 2)\int_0^{\frac{\pi}{4}} d\theta$$

$$= (\log 2)[\theta]_0^{\frac{\pi}{4}} = \frac{\pi}{4}(\log 2)$$

$$\therefore \quad I = \frac{\pi}{8}(\log 2)$$

13. Let $I = \int_0^{\pi/2} \frac{\sin x - \cos x}{1 + \sin x \cos x} dx$

$\Rightarrow I = \int_0^{\pi/2} \frac{\sin(\pi/2 - x) - \cos(\pi/2 - x)}{1 + \sin(\pi/2 - x)\cos(\pi/2 - x)} dx$

$[\because \int_0^a f(x)\,dx = \int_0^a f(a-x)\,dx]$

$\Rightarrow I = \int_0^{\pi/2} \frac{\cos x - \sin x}{1 + \cos x \sin x} dx$

$\Rightarrow I = -\int_0^{\pi/2} \frac{\sin x - \cos x}{1 + \sin x \cos x} dx = -I$

$\Rightarrow 2I = 0 \Rightarrow I = 0$

14. Given, $f(x) = \begin{cases} \cos 2x, & 0 \le x \le \frac{\pi}{2} \\ 3, & \frac{\pi}{2} < x \le 3 \end{cases}$

Let $I = \int_0^3 f(x)dx$

$= \int_0^{\pi/2} f(x)dx + \int_{\pi/2}^3 f(x)\,dx$

$= \int_0^{\pi/2} \cos 2x dx + \int_{\pi/2}^3 3\,dx$

$= \left[\frac{\sin 2x}{2}\right]_0^{\frac{\pi}{2}} + [3x]_{\frac{\pi}{2}}^3$

$= \frac{1}{2}\left[\sin\left(2 \times \frac{\pi}{2}\right) - \sin 0\right] + 3\left[3 - \frac{\pi}{2}\right]$

$= \frac{1}{2}[\sin \pi - 0] + \frac{3}{2}(6 - \pi)$

$= \frac{1}{2}[0] + \frac{3}{2}(6 - \pi)$

$\Rightarrow I = \frac{3}{2}(6 - \pi)$

Concept Enhancer We know that

$\int_a^b f(x)dx = \int_a^c f(x)dx + \int_c^b f(x)dx,$

where $a < c < b$.

15. Let $I = \int_{-1}^{2} |x^3 - x|\,dx$

$|x^3 - x| = |x(x^2 - 1)| = |x||(x-1)(x+1)|$

$= |x||x-1||x+1|$

Thus, $x = 0, x = 1$ and $x = -1$

$\therefore |x^3 - x| = \begin{cases} (-x)(-(x-1))(-(x+1)), & \text{if } x < -1 \\ (-x)(-(x-1))(x+1), & \text{if } -1 \le x < 0 \\ (x)(-(x-1))(x+1), & \text{if } 0 \le x < 1 \\ (x)(x-1)(x+1), & \text{if } x \ge 1 \end{cases}$

Using the property, $\int_a^c f(x)dx = \int_a^b f(x)dx + \int_b^c f(x)dx$

$\int_{-1}^{2} |x^3 - x|\,dx = \int_{-1}^{0} (x^3 - x)dx - \int_0^1 (x^3 - x)dx + \int_1^2 (x^3 - x)dx$

$= \left[\frac{x^4}{4} - \frac{x^2}{2}\right]_{-1}^{0} - \left[\frac{x^4}{4} - \frac{x^2}{2}\right]_0^1 + \left[\frac{x^4}{4} - \frac{x^2}{2}\right]_1^2$

$= 0 - \left[\frac{1}{4} - \frac{1}{2}\right] - \left[\frac{1}{4} - \frac{1}{2}\right] + 0 + \left[\frac{16}{4} - \frac{4}{2} - \frac{1}{4} + \frac{1}{2}\right]$

$= -2\left[\frac{1-2}{4}\right] + \left[\frac{16 - 8 - 1 + 2}{4}\right] = \frac{11}{4}$

16. We know,

$|x - 2| = \begin{cases} -(x-2) & 1 \le x < 2 \\ (x-2) & 2 \le x \le 4 \end{cases}$

Let $I = \int_1^4 |x - 2|\,dx$

$= \int_1^2 [-(x-2)]\,dx + \int_2^4 (x-2)\,dx$

$\Rightarrow I = \left[-\frac{x^2}{2} + 2x\right]_1^2 + \left[\frac{x^2}{2} - 2x\right]_2^4$

$\Rightarrow I = [-2 + 4] - \left[-\frac{1}{2} + 2\right] + [8 - 8] - [2 - 4]$

$= \left[2 - \frac{3}{2}\right] + 2$

$\Rightarrow I = \frac{1}{2} + 2 \Rightarrow I = \frac{5}{2}$

17. $\int_{-6}^{3} |x + 3|\,dx = \int_{-6}^{-3} |x + 3|\,dx + \int_{-3}^{3} |x + 3|\,dx$

$= -\int_{-6}^{-3} (x + 3)\,dx + \int_{-3}^{3} (x + 3)\,dx$

$= -\left[\frac{x^2}{2} + 3x\right]_{-6}^{-3} + \left[\frac{x^2}{2} + 3x\right]_{-3}^{3}$

$= -\left[\left(\frac{9}{2} - 9\right) - \left(\frac{36}{2} - 18\right)\right] + \left[\left(\frac{9}{2} + 9\right) - \left(\frac{9}{2} - 9\right)\right]$

$= -\left[\frac{9}{2} - 9 - 18 + 18\right] + \left[\frac{9}{2} + 9 - \frac{9}{2} + 9\right]$

$= -\frac{9}{2} + 9 + 18 = 27 - \frac{9}{2} = \frac{54 - 9}{2} = \frac{45}{2}$

18. Let $I=\int_0^{\pi}\frac{x\tan x}{\sec x+\tan x}dx$ ...(i)

$\therefore\quad I=\int_0^{\pi}\frac{(\pi-x)\tan(\pi-x)}{\sec(\pi-x)+\tan(\pi-x)}dx$

$\left[\because\int_0^a f(x)\,dx=\int_0^a f(a-x)\,dx\right]$

$=\int_0^{\pi}\frac{-(\pi-x)\tan x}{-\sec x-\tan x}dx$

$\Rightarrow\quad I=\int_0^{\pi}\frac{(\pi-x)\tan x}{\sec x+\tan x}dx$ ...(ii)

On adding Eqs. (i) and (ii), we get

$2I=\pi\int_0^{\pi}\frac{\tan x}{\sec x+\tan x}dx$

$=\pi\int_0^{\pi}\frac{\tan x(\sec x-\tan x)}{(\sec x+\tan x)(\sec x-\tan x)}dx$

$=\pi\int_0^{\pi}\frac{\tan x\cdot\sec x-\tan^2 x}{\sec^2 x-\tan^2 x}dx$

$=\pi\left[\int_0^{\pi}\sec x\cdot\tan x\,dx-\int_0^{\pi}\tan^2 x\,dx\right]$

$[\because\sec^2 x-\tan^2 x=1]$

$=\pi\{[\sec x]_0^{\pi}-\int_0^{\pi}(\sec^2 x-1)\,dx\}$

$=\pi\{[\sec\pi-\sec 0]-[\tan x-x]_0^{\pi}\}$

$=\pi\{[-1-1]-[(\tan\pi-\pi)-(\tan 0-0)]\}$

$=\pi\{-2-[(0-\pi)-0]\}=\pi(\pi-2)$

$\Rightarrow\quad I=\frac{\pi}{2}(\pi-2)$

19. Let $I=\int_{-6}^{1}|x+3|\,dx$

$=\int_{-6}^{-3}[-(3+x)]dx+\int_{-3}^{1}(x+3)\,dx$

$=-\left[3x+\frac{x^2}{2}\right]_{-6}^{-3}+\left[\frac{x^2}{2}+3x\right]_{-3}^{1}$

$=-\left[-9+\frac{9}{2}\right]+\left[3\times(-6)+\frac{36}{2}\right]+\left[\frac{1}{2}+3-\left(\frac{9}{2}-9\right)\right]$

$=\frac{9}{2}+0+\left[\frac{1}{2}-\frac{9}{2}+12\right]$

$=\frac{9}{2}+[-4+12]$

$=\frac{9}{2}+8=\frac{25}{2}$

20. Let $I=\int_0^{\pi/2}\frac{\sqrt{\sin x}}{\sqrt{\sin x}+\sqrt{\cos x}}dx$ ...(i)

$\therefore\quad I=\int_0^{\pi/2}\frac{\sqrt{\sin(\pi/2-x)}\,dx}{\sqrt{\sin(\pi/2-x)}+\sqrt{\cos(\pi/2-x)}}$

$[\because\int_0^a f(x)\,dx=\int_0^a f(a-x)\,dx]$

$\Rightarrow\quad I=\int_0^{\pi/2}\frac{\sqrt{\cos x}}{\sqrt{\cos x}+\sqrt{\sin x}}dx$ ...(ii)

On adding Eqs. (i) and (ii),we get

$2I=\int_0^{\pi/2}\frac{\sqrt{\sin x}+\sqrt{\cos x}}{\sqrt{\sin x}+\sqrt{\cos x}}dx$

$=\int_0^{\pi/2}1dx=[x]_0^{\pi/2}$

$=(\pi/2-0)$

$\Rightarrow\quad 2I=\pi/2$

$\Rightarrow\quad I=\pi/4$

21. Let $I=\int_0^1\log\left(\frac{1}{x}-1\right)dx$

$\Rightarrow\quad I=\int_0^1\log\left(\frac{1-x}{x}\right)dx$ ...(i)

Using $\int_0^a f(x)\,dx=\int_0^a f(a-x)\,dx$, we get

$I=\int_0^1\log\left(\frac{1-(1-x)}{(1-x)}\right)dx$

$\Rightarrow\quad I=\int_0^1\log\left(\frac{x}{1-x}\right)dx$ ...(ii)

On adding Eqs. (i) and (ii), we get

$2I=\int_0^1\log\left(\frac{1-x}{x}\right)dx+\int_0^1\log\left(\frac{x}{1-x}\right)dx$

$=\int_0^1\log\left[\left(\frac{1-x}{x}\right)\left(\frac{x}{1-x}\right)\right]dx$

[using product rule of logarithm i.e. $\log m+\log n=\log mn$]

$=\int_0^1\log 1\,dx=0$ $[\because\log 1=0]$

$\Rightarrow\quad 2I=0$

$\Rightarrow\quad I=0$

22. Let $I=\int_1^2\frac{\sqrt{x}}{\sqrt{3-x}+\sqrt{x}}dx$ ...(i)

Using $\int_a^b f(x)\,dx=\int_a^b f(a+b-x)\,dx$, we get

$$I=\int_1^2 \frac{\sqrt{3-x}}{\sqrt{3-3+x}+\sqrt{3-x}}\,dx$$

$$\Rightarrow \quad I=\int_1^2 \frac{\sqrt{3-x}}{\sqrt{x}+\sqrt{3-x}}\,dx \qquad \ldots\text{(ii)}$$

On adding Eqs. (i) and (ii),we get

$$2I=\int_1^2 \frac{\sqrt{x}+\sqrt{3-x}}{\sqrt{x}+\sqrt{3-x}}\,dx=\int_1^2 1\,dx$$

$$\Rightarrow \quad 2I=[x]_1^2=(2-1) \Rightarrow 2I=1 \Rightarrow I=\frac{1}{2}$$

23. Let $I=\int_0^1 \frac{xe^x}{(1+x)^2}\,dx$

$$=\int_0^1 \frac{[(1+x)-1]\,e^x}{(1+x)^2}\,dx$$

[adding and subtracting 1 in numerator]

$$=\int_0^1 \left(\frac{e^x}{(1+x)}-\frac{e^x}{(1+x)^2}\right)dx$$

$$=\int_0^1 e^x\left(\frac{1}{(1+x)}-\frac{1}{(1+x)^2}\right)dx$$

$$=\left[e^x\,\frac{1}{(1+x)}\right]_0^1$$

[using $\int e^x\{f(x)+f'(x)\}\,dx=e^x f(x)+C$]

$$=\left(\frac{e^1}{2}-\frac{e^0}{1+0}\right)$$

$$\Rightarrow \quad I=\left(\frac{e}{2}-1\right)$$

24. Let $I=\int_0^{\pi/4} \log(1+\tan x)\,dx \qquad \ldots\text{(i)}$

$$=\int_0^{\pi/4} \log\left[1+\tan\left(\frac{\pi}{4}-x\right)\right]dx$$

$$\left[\because \int_0^a f(x)\,dx=\int_0^a f(a-x)\,dx\right]$$

$$=\int_0^{\pi/4} \log\left[1+\frac{\tan\frac{\pi}{4}-\tan x}{1+\tan\frac{\pi}{4}\tan x}\right]dx$$

$$=\int_0^{\pi/4} \log\left[1+\frac{1-\tan x}{1+\tan x}\right]dx$$

$$=\int_0^{\pi/4} \log\left[\frac{2}{1+\tan x}\right]dx \qquad \ldots\text{(ii)}$$

On adding Eqs. (i) and (ii), we get

$$2I=\int_0^{\pi/4}\left[\log(1+\tan x)+\log\left(\frac{2}{1+\tan x}\right)\right]dx$$

$$\Rightarrow 2I=\int_0^{\pi/4} \log\left[(1+\tan x)\left(\frac{2}{1+\tan x}\right)\right]dx$$

$$=\int_0^{\pi/4} \log 2\,dx$$

$$\Rightarrow \quad I=\frac{1}{2}\log 2[x]_0^{\pi/4}=\frac{\log 2}{2}\left[\frac{\pi}{4}-0\right]=\frac{\pi}{8}\log 2$$

25. Let $I=\int_{-\pi/2}^{\pi/2} \frac{\cos x}{1+e^x}\,dx$

$$=\int_{-\pi/2}^{0} \frac{\cos x}{1+e^x}\,dx+\int_0^{\pi/2} \frac{\cos x}{1+e^x}\,dx$$

Again, let $I_1=\int_{-\pi/2}^{0} \frac{\cos x}{1+e^x}\,dx$

Put $\quad x=-t$

So, $\quad dx=-\,dt$

When $x=0$, then $t=0$ and when $x=-\frac{\pi}{2}$, then $t=\frac{\pi}{2}$

Now, $I_1=\int_{\pi/2}^{0} \frac{\cos(-t)}{1+e^{-t}}\,(-dt)$

$$=\int_0^{\pi/2} \frac{\cos t}{1+e^{-t}}\,dt$$

$$=\int_0^{\pi/2} \frac{\cos t}{\frac{e^t+1}{e^t}}\,dt$$

$$=\int_0^{\pi/2} \frac{e^t\cos t}{1+e^t}\,dt$$

$$=\int_0^{\pi/2} \frac{e^x\cos x}{1+e^x}\,dx \quad \left[\because \int_0^a f(x)\,dx=\int_0^a f(t)\,dt\right]$$

So, $\quad I=\int_0^{\pi/2} \frac{e^x\cos x}{1+e^x}+\int_0^{\pi/2} \frac{\cos x}{1+e^x}\,dx$

$$=\int_0^{\pi/2} \frac{e^x\cos x+\cos x}{1+e^x}\,dx$$

$$=\int_0^{\pi/2} \frac{\cos x\,(e^x+1)}{(e^x+1)}\,dx$$

$$=\int_0^{\pi/2} \cos x\,dx$$

$$=[\sin x]_0^{\pi/2}$$

$$=\sin\frac{\pi}{2}-\sin(0)=1$$

26. Let $I=\int_0^{\pi}\frac{x\tan x}{\sec x+\tan x}dx$ ...(i)

$\therefore\quad I=\int_0^{\pi}\frac{(\pi-x)\tan(\pi-x)}{\sec(\pi-x)+\tan(\pi-x)}dx$

$$\left[\because \int_0^a f(x)\,dx=\int_0^a f(a-x)\,dx\right]$$

$\Rightarrow\quad I=\int_0^{\pi}\frac{(\pi-x)\tan x}{\sec x+\tan x}dx$ ...(ii)

On adding Eqs. (i) and (ii), we get

$$2I=\pi\int_0^{\pi}\frac{\tan x}{\sec x+\tan x}dx$$

$$=\pi\int_0^{\pi}\frac{\tan x(\sec x-\tan x)}{(\sec x+\tan x)(\sec x-\tan x)}dx$$

$$=\pi\int_0^{\pi}\frac{\tan x\cdot\sec x-\tan^2 x}{\sec^2 x-\tan^2 x}dx$$

$$=\pi\left[\int_0^{\pi}\sec x\cdot\tan x\,dx-\int_0^{\pi}\tan^2 x\,dx\right]$$

Since, tan x is not defined at $x=\frac{\pi}{2}$, so given integral should be break at $x=\frac{\pi}{2}$.

$$2I=\pi\left[\int_0^{\pi/2}\sec x\tan x\,dx+\int_{\pi/2}^{\pi}\sec x\tan x\,dx\right.$$
$$\left.-\left\{\int_0^{\pi/2}(\sec^2 x-1)\,dx+\int_{\pi/2}^{\pi}(\sec^2 x-1)\,dx\right\}\right]$$

$$=\pi\left[(\sec x)_0^{\pi/2}+(\sec x)_{\pi/2}^{\pi}\right.$$
$$\left.-\left\{(\tan x-x)_0^{\pi/2}+(\tan x-x)_{\pi/2}^{\pi}\right\}\right]$$

$$\Rightarrow 2I=\pi\left[-(1)+(-1)-\left\{\lim_{x\to\pi/2}\tan x-\frac{\pi}{2}\right.\right.$$
$$\left.\left.+\tan\pi-\pi-\left(\lim_{x\to\pi/2}\tan x-\frac{\pi}{2}\right)\right\}\right]$$

$\Rightarrow\quad I=\frac{\pi}{2}[-2+\pi]$

27. Let $I=\int_0^{\pi/2}\frac{\cos^2 x}{1+\sin x\cos x}dx$ ...(i)

$\Rightarrow\quad I=\int_0^{\pi/2}\frac{\cos^2\left(\frac{\pi}{2}-x\right)}{1+\sin\left(\frac{\pi}{2}-x\right)\cos\left(\frac{\pi}{2}-x\right)}dx$

$$\left[\because \int_0^a f(x)\,dx=\int_0^a f(a-x)\,dx\right]$$

$\Rightarrow\quad I=\int_0^{\pi/2}\frac{\sin^2 x}{1+\cos x\sin x}dx$ ...(ii)

On adding Eqs. (i) and (ii), we get

$2I=\int_0^{\pi/2}\frac{dx}{1+\sin x\cos x}$ $\quad[\because \sin^2\theta+\cos^2\theta=1]$

$\Rightarrow\quad 2I=\int_0^{\pi/2}\frac{dx}{1+\sin x\cos x}$

$\Rightarrow\quad 2I=\int_0^{\pi/2}\frac{\sec^2 x}{\sec^2 x+\tan x}dx$ $\quad$[divide by $\cos^2 x$]

$$=\int_0^{\pi/2}\frac{\sec^2 x}{\tan^2 x+\tan x+1}dx$$

On putting $\tan x=t\Rightarrow\sec^2 x\,dx=dt$,

when $x=0,\ t=0$

and when $x=\frac{\pi}{2},\ t=\infty$

$\therefore\quad 2I=\int_0^{\infty}\frac{dt}{t^2+t+1}$

$$=\int_0^{\infty}\frac{dt}{t^2+t+\frac{1}{4}+1-\frac{1}{4}}$$

$\Rightarrow\quad 2I=\int_0^{\infty}\frac{dt}{\left(t+\frac{1}{2}\right)^2+\left(\frac{\sqrt{3}}{2}\right)^2}$

$$=\frac{2}{\sqrt{3}}\left[\tan^{-1}\frac{2t+1}{\sqrt{3}}\right]_0^{\infty}$$

$\Rightarrow\quad 2I=\frac{2}{\sqrt{3}}\left(\tan^{-1}\infty-\tan^{-1}\frac{1}{\sqrt{3}}\right)$

$$=\frac{2}{\sqrt{3}}\left(\frac{\pi}{2}-\frac{\pi}{6}\right)=\frac{2\pi}{3\sqrt{3}}$$

$\Rightarrow\quad I=\frac{\pi}{3\sqrt{3}}$

28. Given, integrand is

$$f(x)=\begin{cases}\sin x, & \text{if } 0\le x\le\pi/2\\ 1, & \text{if } \pi/2<x\le 5\\ e^{x-5}, & \text{if } 5<x\le 9\end{cases}$$

Now, $\int_0^9 f(x)=\int_0^{\pi/2}\sin x\,dx+\int_{\pi/2}^5 1\,dx+\int_5^9 e^{x-5}\,dx$

$$=-[\cos x]_0^{\pi/2}+[x]_{\pi/2}^5+[e^{x-5}]_5^9$$

$$=-(\cos\pi/2-\cos 0)+(5-\pi/2)+(e^4-e^0)$$

$$=0+1+5-\pi/2+e^4-1$$

$$=5-\pi/2+e^4$$

CHAPTER TEST

1 Mark Questions

1. $\int_0^{\pi/2} \sqrt{1-\sin 2x}\, dx$ is equal to

(a) $2\sqrt{2}$ (b) $2(\sqrt{2}+1)$
(c) 2 (d) $2(\sqrt{2}-1)$

2. $\int \frac{1}{x^2+2x+2}\, dx$ is equal to

(a) $x\tan^{-1}(x+1)+C$ (b) $\tan^{-1}(x+1)+C$
(c) $(x+1)\tan^{-1}x+C$ (d) $\tan^{-1}x+C$

3. $\int \frac{1}{\sqrt{9x-4x^2}}\, dx$ is equal to

(a) $\frac{1}{9}\sin^{-1}\left(\frac{9x-8}{8}\right)+C$ (b) $\frac{1}{2}\sin^{-1}\left(\frac{8x-9}{9}\right)+C$
(c) $\frac{1}{3}\sin^{-1}\left(\frac{9x-8}{8}\right)+C$ (d) $\frac{1}{2}\sin^{-1}\left(\frac{9x-8}{9}\right)+C$

4. $\int \frac{e^x(1+x)}{\cos^2(e^x x)}\, dx$ is equal to

(a) $-\cot(ex^x)+C$ (b) $\tan(xe^x)+C$
(c) $\tan(e^x)+C$ (d) $\cot(e^x)+C$

5. If $\int_0^1 \frac{e^t}{1+t}\, dt = a$, then $\int_0^1 \frac{e^t}{(1+t)^2}\, dt$ is equal to

(a) $a-1+\frac{e}{2}$ (b) $a+1-\frac{e}{2}$
(c) $a-1-\frac{e}{2}$ (d) $a+1+\frac{e}{2}$

2 Marks Questions

6. Evaluate $\int \sqrt{\tan x}\,(1+\tan^2 x)dx$.

7. Evaluate $\int \frac{\sin^4 x+\cos^4 x}{\sin^3 x+\cos^3 x}\, dx$.

8. Evaluate $\int_2^8 |x-5|\, dx$.

9. Evaluate $\int_0^{\pi} \left(\sin^2\frac{x}{2}-\cos^2\frac{x}{2}\right) dx$.

10. Evaluate $\int_0^2 x\sqrt{x+2}\, dx$.

3/4 Marks Questions

11. Evaluate $\int \tan^{-1}(\sec x+\tan x)\, dx, 0 \le x \le \frac{\pi}{2}$.

12. Evaluate $\int \frac{\sec^2(2\tan^{-1}x)\, dx}{1+x^2}$.

13. Evaluate $\int \sin^{-1}\left(\frac{2x}{1+x^2}\right) dx$.

14. Evaluate $\int \sin^{-1}\left(\sqrt{\frac{x}{a+x}}\right) dx$.

15. Evaluate $\int \frac{3x-2}{(x+1)^2(x+3)}\, dx$.

16. Evaluate $\int_0^{\pi/4} \sec x\sqrt{\frac{1-\sin x}{1+\sin x}}\, dx$.

5/6 Marks Questions

17. Evaluate $\int_0^{\pi} \frac{x\sin x}{1+\cos^2 x}\, dx$.

18. Evaluate $\int_{\pi/6}^{\pi/3} \frac{dx}{1+\sqrt{\tan x}}$.

19. Evaluate $\int_0^a \frac{\sqrt{x}}{\sqrt{x}+\sqrt{a-x}}\, dx$.

20. Evaluate $\int_{-1}^{2} |x^3-x|\, dx$.

Answers

1. (d) **2.** (b) **3.** (b) **4.** (b) **5.** (b)

6. $\frac{2}{3}(\tan x)^{3/2}+C$

7. $\log|\sec x+\tan x|+\log|\operatorname{cosec} x-\cot x|+C$

8. 9 **9.** 0 **10.** $\frac{16\sqrt{2}}{15}(\sqrt{2}+1)$ **11.** $\frac{x}{4}(\pi+x)+C$

12. $\frac{1}{2}\tan(2\tan^{-1}x)+C$ **13.** $2x\tan^{-1}x-\log(1+x^2)+C$

14. $(a+x)\tan^{-1}\left(\sqrt{\frac{x}{a}}\right)-\sqrt{ax}+C$

15. $\frac{11}{4}\log\left|\frac{x+1}{x+3}\right|+\frac{5}{2(x+1)}+C$

16. $2-\sqrt{2}$ **17.** $\frac{\pi^2}{4}$ **18.** $\frac{\pi}{12}$ **19.** $\frac{a}{2}$ **20.** $\frac{11}{4}$

08

Differential Equations

TREND ANALYSIS 3 YEARS

Average No. of Questions Across all Sets

Topic	Types of Questions	2024	2023	2020
TOPIC 01 Order and Degree of Differential Equations	1 Mark	1	—	—
	2 Marks	—	—	—
	3/4 Marks	—	—	—
	5/6 Marks	—	—	—
TOPIC 02 Solution of Differential Equations	1 Mark	—	1	—
	2 Marks	—	—	—
	3/4 Marks	—	—	—
	5/6 Marks	—	—	—
TOPIC 03 Homogeneous and Linear Differential Equations	1 Mark	—	—	—
	2 Marks	—	—	—
	3/4 Marks	—	2	1
	5/6 Marks	2	—	—

TOPIC 1

Order and Degree of Differential Equations

An equation involving independent variable, dependent variable, derivatives of dependent variable with respect to one (or more) independent variable and constant is called a **differential equation**.

e.g. $$x\frac{dy}{dx}+xy\frac{d^2y}{dx^2}+4=0.$$

Ordinary Differential Equation

An equation involving derivatives of the dependent variable with respect to only one independent variable is called an ordinary differential equation.

e.g. $$\frac{dy}{dx}+\frac{d^2y}{dx^2}-2=0.$$

From any given relation between the dependent and independent variables, a differential equation can be formed by differentiating it with respect to the independent variable and eliminating arbitrary constants involved.

Order of a Differential Equation

Order of a differential equation is defined as the order of the highest order derivative of the dependent variable with respect to the independent variable involved in the given differential equation.

NOTE Order of the differential equation cannot be more than the number of arbitrary constants in the equation.

Degree of a Differential Equation

The highest exponent of the highest order derivative is called degree of a differential equation provided exponent of each derivative appearing in the differential equation is a non-negative integer.

NOTE (i) Order and degree (if defined) of a differential equation are always positive integers.

(ii) The differential equation is a polynomial equation in derivatives.

(iii) If the given differential equation is not polynomial equation in its derivatives, then its degree is not defined.

e.g. $\frac{d^2y}{dx^2}+\sin\frac{dy}{dx}=0$,

here, we cannot defined the degree because this differential equation is not a polynomial equation in its derivatives.

(iv) If the differential equation have radical (like $\sqrt{\ }, \sqrt[3]{\ }$ etc) and fractions $\left(\text{like } \frac{1}{\frac{dy}{dx}}, \frac{1}{\sqrt{1+\frac{d^2y}{dx^2}}} \text{ etc}\right)$, then to find degree, first made it free from radicals and fractions by simplifying it.

PYQs Previous Years Questions

1 Mark Questions

1. The order and the degree of differential equation $1+\left(\frac{dy}{dx}\right)^2=\frac{d^2y}{dx^2}$ are

ISC 2024

(a) 2 and $\frac{3}{2}$ (b) 2 and 3

(c) 3 and 4 (d) 2 and 1

2. The degree of the differential equation $\frac{d^2y}{dx^2}+3\left(\frac{dy}{dx}\right)^2=x^2\log\left(\frac{d^2y}{dx^2}\right)$ is

ISC Specimen 2023

(a) 2 (b) 1 (c) 3 (d) Not defined

3. The order and degree of the differential equation $\frac{d^3y}{dx^3}+\frac{d^2y}{dx^2}+\left(\frac{dy}{dx}\right)^2=3$ is

ISC Specimen Sem-II 2022

(a) order 3 and degree 1

(b) order 1 and degree 3

(c) order 2 and degree 1

(d) order 2 and degree 2

4. The degree of the differential equation $\frac{d^2y}{dx^2}+3\left(\frac{dy}{dx}\right)^2=x^2\left(\frac{d^2y}{dx^2}\right)^2$ is

ISC Specimen Sem-II 2022

(a) 1 (b) 2 (c) 3 (d) 4

5. Find the sum of order and degree of the differential equation:

$$\left(\frac{dy}{dx}\right)^5+3xy\left(\frac{d^3y}{dx^3}\right)^2+y^2\left(\frac{d^2y}{dx^2}\right)^3=0$$

ISC Specimen 2021

6. Write the sum of the order and degree of the differential equation $\frac{d}{dx}\left\{\left(\frac{dy}{dx}\right)^3\right\}=0$.

KEY CONCEPT

The degree of the differential equation is the degree of the highest order derivative, when differential coefficients are made free from radicals and fractions sign.

Explanations

1. (d) Given, $1+\left(\frac{dy}{dx}\right)^2=\frac{d^2y}{dx^2}$

Here, the highest order derivative is $\frac{d^2y}{dx^2}$.

So, the order of given differential equation $=2$

and the degree of given differential equation $=1$

2. (d) Given, $\frac{d^2y}{dx^2}+3\left(\frac{dy}{dx}\right)^2=x^2\log\left(\frac{d^2y}{dx^2}\right)$

Here, degree is not defined because this differential equation is not a polynomial equation in its derivatives.

3. (a) $\frac{d^3y}{dx^3}+\frac{d^2y}{dx^2}+\left(\frac{dy}{dx}\right)^2=3$

The order of highest derivative is 3 and its power is 1. Hence, the required order of differential equation is 3 and degree is 1.

4. (b) Given, $\frac{d^2y}{dx^2}+3\left(\frac{dy}{dx}\right)^2=x^2\left(\frac{d^2y}{dx^2}\right)^2$ ...(i)

$\because$ Given, differential equation has highest order derivative of 2 and its power is 2.

$\therefore$ Degree of given differential equation is 2.

5. Given, differential equation is

$$\left(\frac{dy}{dx}\right)^5+3xy\left(\frac{d^3y}{dx^3}\right)^2+y\left(\frac{d^2y}{dx^2}\right)^3=0$$

Clearly, highest order derivative occuring in the differential equation is $\frac{d^3y}{dx^3}$.

So, its order is 3 and degree is 2.

Now, required sum $=3+2=5$

6. Given, differential equation is $\frac{d}{dx}\left\{\left(\frac{dy}{dx}\right)^3\right\}=0$.

$$\Rightarrow \quad 3\left(\frac{dy}{dx}\right)^{3-1}\frac{d}{dx}\left(\frac{dy}{dx}\right)=0$$

$$\Rightarrow \quad 3\left(\frac{dy}{dx}\right)^2\frac{d^2y}{dx^2}=0$$

Here, order $=2$ and degree $=1$

$\therefore$ Sum of the order and degree $=2+1=3$

TOPIC 2

Solution of Differential Equations

The solution of a differential equation is a relation between dependent and the independent variables which satisfies the given differential equation

i.e. when this relation is substituted in given differential equation, make left hand and right hand side identically equal.

General Solution

It is the solution which contains the number of arbitrary constants equal to the order of the differential equation. It is also called **complete primitive**.

Particular Solution

A particular solution of a differential equation is a solution obtained from the general solution by giving particular values to the arbitrary constant.

Solution of Differential Equation with Variable Separable Method

If the given differential equation can be expressed in the form $\quad g(y)\,dy=f(x)\,dx$,

we say that the variables are separable and such differential equations can be solved by integrating both sides.

The general solution is given by $\int g(y)\,dy=\int f(x)\,dx+C$

where, C is an arbitrary constant.

Solution of Differential Equations Reducible to Variable Separable Method

Differential equation of the form $\frac{dy}{dx}=f(ax+by+c)$ can be reduced to variable separable form by substitution $ax+by+c=v$ and it will reducible to variable separable and then separate the variables v and x.

PYQs Previous Years Questions

1 Mark Questions

1. Solve the differential equation $\frac{dy}{dx} = \text{cosec } y$. **ISC 2023**

2. Solve $\frac{dy}{dx} = \sin x - x$ **ISC Specimen Sem-II 2022**

3. Solve $\frac{dy}{dx} + 2x = e^{3x}$. **ISC Specimen Sem-II 2022**

2 Marks Questions

4. Solve the differential equation $(1+y^2)(1+\log x)dx + xdy = 0$. **ISC Specimen 2023**

> **KEY CONCEPT**
> (i) Firstly, separting the variables, x, y along dx and dy.
> (ii) Further, integrate both sides by using the method of substitution and then simplify it.

5. Solve the differential equation $\text{cosec}^3 x\, dy - \text{cosec } y\, dx = 0$. **ISC Specimen Sem-II 2022**

6. Solve the differential equation $\frac{dy}{dx} = 2^{-y}$. **ISC Specimen Sem-II 2022**

7. Solve $\frac{dy}{dx} = 1 - xy + y - x$. **ISC Specimen 2021, ISC 17**

3/4 Marks Questions

8. Solve the differential equation $\frac{dy}{dx} = \frac{x+y+2}{2(x+y)-1}$. **ISC 2019**

9. Solve the differential equation $\sin^{-1}\left(\frac{dy}{dx}\right) = x + y$. **ISC 2015**

10. Solve the differential equation $(x+1)dy - 2xydx = 0$. **ISC 2014**

11. Solve the differential equation $\log(dy/dx) = 2x - 3y$. **ISC 2013**

12. Solve the differential equation $(xy^2 + x)\, dx + (x^2 y + y)dy = 0$. **ISC 2012**

13. Solve the differential equation $\frac{dy}{dx} = e^{x+y} + x^2 e^y$. **ISC 2011**

14. Solve the differential equation $(x \cos y)dy = e^x (x \log x + 1)dx$. **ISC 2009**

> **KEY CONCEPT**
> (i) Firstly, separating the variables x and y along dx and dy respectively.
> (ii) Further, integrate both sides and get the required result.

15. Solve the differential equation $\tan y\, dx + \sec^2 y \tan x\, dy = 0$. **ISC 2007**

16. Solve the differential equation $x(x^2 - x^2y^2)dy + y(y^2 + x^2y^2)\, dx = 0$. **ISC 2006**

17. Solve the differential equation $dy/dx - e^{y+x} = e^{x-y}$. **ISC 2005**

18. Solve $\frac{dy}{dx} = \frac{(1+\cos^2 x)\sin^2 y}{(1+\sin^2 y)\cos^2 x}$. **ISC 2003**

19. Solve $e^y\,(1+x^2)\, dy - \frac{x}{y}\, dx = 0$. **ISC 2002**

20. Solve $(x - y - 2)dx - (2x - 2y - 3)\, dy = 0$. **ISC 2001**

21. Solve $dy/dx = e^{x-y} + x^2 e^{-y}$.

5 Marks Questions

22. Solve: $(x^2 - yx^2)dy + (y^2 + xy^2)dx = 0$. **ISC 2017, 01**

Explanations

1. Given, $\frac{dy}{dx} = \text{cosec } y \Rightarrow \sin y\, dy = dx$

On integrating both sides, we get

$$\int \sin y\, dy = \int dx$$

$\Rightarrow$ $-\cos y = x + C$

$\Rightarrow$ $x + \cos y + C = 0$

2. $\frac{dy}{dx} = \sin x - x$

$dy = (\sin x - x)\, dx$

On integrating both sides, we get

$$\int dy = \int (\sin x - x) dx$$

$\Rightarrow$ $y = -\cos x - \frac{x^2}{2} + C$

3. We have, $\frac{dy}{dx} + 2x = e^{3x}$

$\Rightarrow$ $\frac{dy}{dx} = e^{3x} - 2x$

$\Rightarrow$ $dy = (e^{3x} - 2x)\, dx$

On integrating both sides, we get

$$\int dy = \int (e^{3x} - 2x)\, dx$$

$\Rightarrow$ $y = \frac{e^{3x}}{3} - \frac{2x^2}{2} + C$

$\Rightarrow$ $y = \frac{e^{3x}}{3} - x^2 + C$

4. Given, $(1 + y^2)(1 + \log x)dx + xdy = 0$

$\Rightarrow$ $\frac{(1 + \log x)dx}{x} = \frac{-dy}{1 + y^2}$

On integrating both sides, we get

$$\int \frac{1 + \log x}{x}\, dx = \int \frac{-dy}{1 + y^2}$$

Let $\log x = t$, so $\frac{dx}{x} = dt$

$\Rightarrow$ $\int (1 + t)dt = \int \frac{-dy}{1 + y^2}$

$\Rightarrow$ $t + \frac{t^2}{2} = -\tan^{-1} y + C$

$\Rightarrow$ $\log x + \frac{(\log x)^2}{2} = -\tan^{-1} y + C$

$\Rightarrow$ $\log x + \frac{(\log x)^2}{2} + \tan^{-1} y = C$

5. Given, $\text{cosec}^3 x\, dy - \text{cosec } y\, dx = 0$

$\Rightarrow$ $\text{cosec}^3 x\, dy = \text{cosec } y\, dx$

$\Rightarrow$ $\frac{dy}{\sin^3 x} = \frac{dx}{\sin y} \Rightarrow \sin y\, dy = \sin^3 x\, dx$

$\Rightarrow$ $\sin y\, dy = \left(\frac{3\sin x - \sin 3x}{4}\right) dx$

On integrating both sides, we get

$$\int \sin y\, dy = \int \left(\frac{3\sin x - \sin 3x}{4}\right) dx$$

$$= \frac{3}{4}\int \sin x\, dx - \frac{1}{4}\int \sin 3x\, dx$$

$\Rightarrow$ $-\cos y = -\frac{3}{4}\cos x + \frac{\cos 3x}{12} + C$

$\Rightarrow$ $-12\cos y = -9\cos x + \cos 3x + 12C$

$\Rightarrow$ $12\cos y + \cos 3x - 9\cos x + C' = 0$ $\quad [\because C' = 12C]$

6. Given, $\frac{dy}{dx} = 2^{-y} \Rightarrow 2^y dy = dx$

On integrating both sides, we get

$$\int 2^y dy = \int 1\, dx \Rightarrow \frac{2^y}{\log 2} = x + C$$

$\Rightarrow$ $2^y = x \log 2 + C \log 2$

$\Rightarrow$ $2^y = x \log 2 + C'$ $\quad [\because C' = C \log 2]$

7. Given, $\frac{dy}{dx} = 1 - xy + y - x$

$\frac{dy}{dx} = 1 - x + y - xy$

$\frac{dy}{dx} = (1 - x) + y(1 - x) = (1 - x)(1 + y)$

$\frac{dy}{dx} = (1 - x)(1 + y)$

$\frac{dy}{(1 + y)} = (1 - x)\, dx$

On integrating both sides, we get

$$\int \frac{dy}{(1 + y)} = \int (1 - x) dx$$

$\Rightarrow$ $\log(1 + y) = x - \frac{x^2}{2} + C$

which is the required solution.

8. We have, $\frac{dy}{dx}=\frac{x+y+2}{2(x+y)-1}$ ...(i)

On putting $x+y=u$

$$\Rightarrow \quad 1+\frac{dy}{dx}=\frac{du}{dx}$$

$$\Rightarrow \quad \frac{dy}{dx}=\frac{du}{dx}-1$$

$\therefore$ From Eq. (i), we get

$$\frac{du}{dx}-1=\frac{u+2}{2(u)-1}$$

$$\Rightarrow \quad \frac{du}{dx}=\frac{u+2}{2u-1}+1$$

$$\Rightarrow \quad \frac{du}{dx}=\frac{3u+1}{2u-1}$$

$$\Rightarrow \left(\frac{2u-1}{3u+1}\right)du=dx \Rightarrow \left(\frac{2}{3}-\frac{5/3}{3u+1}\right)du=dx$$

$$\Rightarrow \frac{2}{3}\left(1-\frac{5/2}{3u+1}\right)du=dx$$

On integrating both sides, we get

$$\frac{2}{3}\int\left[1-\frac{5}{2(3u+1)}\right]du=dx$$

$$\Rightarrow \quad \frac{2}{3}\left[u-\frac{5}{2}\frac{\log|3u+1|}{3}\right]=x+C$$

$$\Rightarrow \frac{2}{3}\left[x+y-\frac{5}{6}\log|3x+3y+1|\right]=x+C \quad [\because u=x+y]$$

$$\Rightarrow \quad x-\frac{2}{3}x-\frac{2}{3}y+\frac{5}{9}\log|3x+3y+1|+C=0$$

$$\Rightarrow \quad \frac{x}{3}-\frac{2}{3}y+\frac{5}{9}\log|3x+3y+1|+C=0$$

9. Given, differential equation can be rewritten as

$$\frac{dy}{dx}=\sin(x+y) \quad ...(i)$$

On putting $x+y=v \Rightarrow 1+\frac{dy}{dx}=\frac{dv}{dx}$

$$\Rightarrow \quad \frac{dy}{dx}=\frac{dv}{dx}-1$$

$\therefore$ Eq. (i) becomes,

$$\frac{dv}{dx}-1=\sin v \Rightarrow \frac{dv}{dx}=1+\sin v$$

$$\Rightarrow \quad \frac{dv}{1+\sin v}=dx$$

On integrating both sides, we get

$$\int\left[\frac{1}{1+\sin v}\times\frac{1-\sin v}{1-\sin v}\right]dv=\int dx$$

$$\Rightarrow \quad \int\frac{1-\sin v}{1-\sin^2 v}dv=\int dx$$

$$\Rightarrow \quad \int\frac{1-\sin v}{\cos^2 v}dv=\int dx$$

$$\Rightarrow \quad \int(\sec^2 v-\tan v\sec v)dv=\int dx$$

$$\Rightarrow \quad [\tan v-\sec v]=x+c$$

$$\Rightarrow \quad \tan(x+y)-\sec(x+y)=x+c$$

[putting $v=x+y$]

10. Given, $(x+1)dy-2xy\,dx=0$

$$\Rightarrow \quad (x+1)dy=2xy\,dx$$

$$\Rightarrow \quad \frac{dy}{dx}=\frac{2xy}{x+1} \Rightarrow \frac{dy}{y}=\frac{2x\,dx}{x+1}$$

On integrating both sides, we get

$$\int\frac{dy}{y}=2\int\frac{(x+1-1)\,dx}{x+1}$$

$$\Rightarrow \quad \log y=2\left[\int dx-\int\frac{dx}{x+1}\right]$$

$$\therefore \quad \log y=2[x-\log|x+1|]+C,$$

where, C is constant of integration.

11. Given, $\log\left(\frac{dy}{dx}\right)=2x-3y$

$$\Rightarrow \quad \frac{dy}{dx}=e^{2x-3y} \quad [\because \log_a b=c \Rightarrow a^c=b]$$

$$\Rightarrow \quad \frac{dy}{dx}=e^{2x}\cdot e^{-3y} \Rightarrow e^{3y}dy=e^{2x}dx$$

On integrating both sides, we get

$$\int e^{3y}dy=\int e^{2x}dx$$

$$\therefore \quad \frac{e^{3y}}{3}=\frac{e^{2x}}{2}+C$$

where, C is constant of integration.

12. Given, $(xy^2+x)\,dx+(x^2y+y)\,dy=0$

$$\Rightarrow \quad x(y^2+1)\,dx+y(x^2+1)\,dy=0$$

$$\Rightarrow \quad \frac{x}{x^2+1}dx+\frac{y}{y^2+1}dy=0$$

On integrating both sides, we get

$$\frac{1}{2}\int\frac{2x}{x^2+1}dx+\frac{1}{2}\int\frac{2y}{y^2+1}dy=0$$

[multiplying numerator and denominator by 2]

$$\Rightarrow \quad \frac{1}{2}\log|x^2+1|+\frac{1}{2}\log|y^2+1|=C$$

$$\left[\because \int \frac{2x}{x^2+1}dx=\log|x^2+1|\right]$$

$$\Rightarrow \quad \log\sqrt{x^2+1}+\log\sqrt{y^2+1}=C$$

$$\Rightarrow \quad \log(\sqrt{x^2+1}\sqrt{y^2+1})=C$$

$$\Rightarrow \quad \sqrt{x^2+1}\sqrt{y^2+1}=e^C$$

$$[\because \log_a b=c \Rightarrow b=a^c]$$

On squaring both sides, we get

$$(x^2+1)(y^2+1)=e^{2C}$$

$$\Rightarrow \quad (x^2+1)(y^2+1)=C' \text{ where, } e^{2C}=C'$$

13. Given, $\frac{dy}{dx}=e^{x+y}+x^2e^y \Rightarrow \frac{dy}{dx}=e^x\cdot e^y+x^2e^y$

$$\Rightarrow \quad e^{-y}dy=(e^x+x^2)dx$$

[multiplying both sides by e^{-y}]

On integrating both sides, we get

$$\int e^{-y}dy=\int(e^x+x^2)dx$$

$$\Rightarrow \quad -e^{-y}=e^x+\frac{x^3}{3}+C_1$$

$$\Rightarrow \quad e^{-y}=-e^x-\frac{x^3}{3}-C_1$$

or $\quad e^{-y}=-e^x-\frac{x^3}{3}+C_1,$

where, $C=-C_1$

14. Given, $(x\cos y)\,dy=e^x(x\log x+1)\,dx$

$$\Rightarrow \quad \cos y\,dy=e^x\left(\frac{x\log x+1}{x}\right)dx$$

$$\Rightarrow \quad \cos y\,dy=e^x\left(\log x+\frac{1}{x}\right)dx$$

On integrating both sides, we get

$$\int\cos y\,dy=\int \underset{\text{II}}{e^x}\ \underset{\text{I}}{\log x}\,dx+\int\frac{e^x}{x}dx$$

$$\Rightarrow \quad \int\cos y\,dy=(\log x)\int e^x dx-\int\left\{\frac{d(\log x)}{dx}\int e^x dx\right\}dx+\int\frac{e^x}{x}dx$$

[using integration by parts method]

$$\Rightarrow \quad \sin y=e^x\log x-\int\frac{e^x dx}{x}+\int\frac{e^x}{x}dx+C$$

$$\Rightarrow \quad \sin y=e^x\log x+C$$

15. Given, $\tan y\,dx+\sec^2 y\tan x\,dy=0$

$$\Rightarrow \quad \tan y\,dx=-\sec^2 y\tan x\,dy$$

$$\Rightarrow \quad \frac{1}{\tan x}dx=\frac{-\sec^2 y}{\tan y}dy$$

[dividing both sides by $\tan x\tan y$]

On integrating both sides, we get

$$-\int\cot x\,dx=\int\frac{\sec^2 y}{\tan y}dy$$

$$\Rightarrow \quad -\log|\sin x|=\log|\tan y|+\log|C_1|$$

$$\Rightarrow \quad \log|\sin x|+\log|\tan y|+\log C_1=0$$

$$\Rightarrow \quad \log|\sin x\cdot\tan y\cdot C_1|=0$$

$$\Rightarrow \quad \sin x\cdot\tan y\cdot C_1=e^0$$

$$\Rightarrow \quad \sin x\cdot\tan y=\frac{1}{C_1} \quad [\because \log_a b=c\Rightarrow b=a^c]$$

$$\Rightarrow \quad \sin x\cdot\tan y=C, \text{ where } \frac{1}{C_1}=C$$

16. Given, $x(x^2-x^2y^2)\,dy+y(y^2+x^2y^2)\,dx=0$

$$\Rightarrow \quad x^3(1-y^2)\,dy+y^3(1+x^2)\,dx=0$$

$$\Rightarrow \quad \frac{(1-y^2)}{y^3}dy+\frac{(1+x^2)}{x^3}dx=0$$

$$\Rightarrow \quad \left(\frac{1}{y^3}-\frac{1}{y}\right)dy+\left(\frac{1}{x^3}+\frac{1}{x}\right)dx=0$$

On integrating both sides, we get

$$\int\left(\frac{1}{y^3}-\frac{1}{y}\right)dy+\int\left(\frac{1}{x^3}+\frac{1}{x}\right)dx=0$$

$$\Rightarrow \quad \frac{-1}{2y^2}-\log|y|-\frac{1}{2x^2}+\log|x|=C$$

$$\Rightarrow \quad \log|y|-\log|x|+C=-\left(\frac{1}{2x^2}+\frac{1}{2y^2}\right)$$

$$\Rightarrow \quad \log\left|\frac{y}{x}\right|+C=-\left(\frac{1}{2x^2}+\frac{1}{2y^2}\right)$$

$$\left[\because \log m-\log n=\log\frac{m}{n}\right]$$

17. Given, $\frac{dy}{dx}-e^{x+y}=e^{x-y}$

$$\Rightarrow \quad \frac{dy}{dx}-e^x\cdot e^y=e^x\cdot e^{-y}$$

$$\Rightarrow \quad \frac{dy}{dx}=e^x\cdot e^y+e^x\cdot e^{-y}$$

$$\Rightarrow \quad \frac{dy}{dx}=e^x(e^y+e^{-y})$$

$$\Rightarrow \quad \frac{dy}{e^y+e^{-y}}=e^x dx$$

$$\Rightarrow \quad \frac{e^y\,dy}{1+e^{2y}} = e^x\,dx$$

On integrating both sides, we get

$$\int \frac{e^y}{1+e^{2y}}\,dy = \int e^x\,dx$$

$$\Rightarrow \quad \int \frac{dt}{1+t^2} = e^x + C$$

[putting $e^y = t \Rightarrow e^y\,dy = dt$]

$$\Rightarrow \quad \tan^{-1} t = e^x + C$$

$$\Rightarrow \quad \tan^{-1}(e^y) = e^x + C \qquad [\text{putting } t = e^y]$$

$$\therefore \quad e^y = \tan(e^x + C)$$

18. Given, $\dfrac{dy}{dx} = \dfrac{(1+\cos^2 x)\sin^2 y}{(1+\sin^2 y)\cos^2 x}$

$$\Rightarrow \quad \frac{(1+\sin^2 y)\,dy}{\sin^2 y} = \frac{(1+\cos^2 x)\,dx}{\cos^2 x}$$

On integrating both sides, we get

$$\int \frac{(1+\sin^2 y)}{\sin^2 y}\,dy = \int \frac{(1+\cos^2 x)}{\cos^2 x}\,dx$$

$$\Rightarrow \quad \int (\operatorname{cosec}^2 y + 1)\,dy = \int (\sec^2 x + 1)\,dx$$

$$\Rightarrow \quad -\cot y + y = \tan x + x + C$$

$$\Rightarrow \quad y - x = \tan x + \cot y + C$$

19. Given, $e^y(1+x^2)\,dy - \dfrac{x}{y}\,dx = 0$

$$\Rightarrow \quad y \cdot e^y\,dy - \frac{x}{1+x^2}\,dx = 0$$

$$\Rightarrow \quad y \cdot e^y\,dy = \frac{x}{1+x^2}\,dx$$

On integrating both sides, we get

$$\int (\underset{\text{I}}{y} \cdot \underset{\text{II}}{e^y})\,dy = \frac{1}{2}\int \frac{2x}{1+x^2}\,dx$$

$$\Rightarrow \quad y\int e^y\,dy - \int \left[\frac{d(y)}{dy}\left\{\int e^y\,dy\right\}\right]dy = \frac{1}{2}\log|1+x^2| + C$$

[using integration by parts in left integral]

$$\Rightarrow \quad ye^y - \int (1 \cdot e^y)\,dy = \log\sqrt{1+x^2} + C$$

$$\Rightarrow \quad ye^y - e^y = \log\sqrt{1+x^2} + C$$

$$\Rightarrow \quad e^y(y-1) - \log\sqrt{1+x^2} = C$$

20. Given, $(x-y-2)dx - (2x-2y-3)\,dy = 0$

$$\Rightarrow \quad (x-y-2) - [2(x-y-2)+1]\frac{dy}{dx} = 0$$

On putting $x - y - 2 = t$

$$\Rightarrow \quad 1 - \frac{dy}{dx} = \frac{dt}{dx}$$

$$\Rightarrow \quad \frac{dy}{dx} = 1 - \frac{dt}{dx}$$

Therefore, given differential equation becomes

$$t - (2t+1)\left(1 - \frac{dt}{dx}\right) = 0$$

$$\Rightarrow \quad t - 2t - 1 + (2t+1)\frac{dt}{dx} = 0$$

$$\Rightarrow \quad -t - 1 + (2t+1)\frac{dt}{dx} = 0$$

$$\Rightarrow \quad (2t+1)\frac{dt}{dx} = t+1$$

$$\Rightarrow \quad dx = \frac{(2t+1)}{t+1}\,dt$$

$$\Rightarrow \quad dx = \frac{(2t+2-1)}{t+1}\,dt$$

$$\Rightarrow \quad dx = \frac{2(t+1)}{t+1}\,dt - \frac{dt}{t+1}$$

On integrating both sides, we get

$$\int dx = 2\int dt - \int \frac{dt}{t+1}$$

$$\Rightarrow \quad x = 2t - \log|t+1| + C$$

$$\Rightarrow \quad x = 2(x-y-2) - \log|x-y-2+1| + C$$

[putting $t = x - y - 2$]

$$\Rightarrow \quad x = 2(x-y-2) - \log|x-y-1| + C$$

$$\Rightarrow \quad (2y - x + 4) + \log|x-y-1| = C$$

21. Given, $\dfrac{dy}{dx} = e^{x-y} + x^2 e^{-y}$

$$\Rightarrow \quad \frac{dy}{dx} = e^x \cdot e^{-y} + x^2 e^{-y}$$

$$\Rightarrow \quad \frac{dy}{dx} = (e^x + x^2)\,e^{-y}$$

$$\Rightarrow \quad e^y\,dy = (e^x + x^2)\,dx$$

On integrating both sides, we get

$$\int e^y\,dy = \int (e^x + x^2)\,dx$$

$$\Rightarrow \quad e^y = e^x + \frac{x^3}{3} + C$$

22. Given, $(x^2 - yx^2)\,dy + (y^2 + xy^2)\,dx = 0$

$\Rightarrow \quad x^2(1-y)\,dy + y^2(1+x)\,dx = 0$

$$\Rightarrow \quad \frac{(1-y)}{y^2}\,dy + \frac{(1+x)}{x^2}\,dx = 0$$

On integrating both sides, we get

$$\int\left(\frac{1-y}{y^2}\right)dy + \int\left(\frac{1+x}{x^2}\right)dx = 0$$

$$\Rightarrow \quad \int \frac{1}{y^2}\,dy - \int \frac{1}{y}\,dy + \int \frac{dx}{x^2} + \int \frac{dx}{x} = 0$$

$$\Rightarrow \quad \frac{-1}{y} - \log|y| - \frac{1}{x} + \log|x| = C_1$$

$$\Rightarrow \quad -\left(\frac{1}{x} + \frac{1}{y}\right) = \log|y| - \log|x| + C_1$$

$$\Rightarrow \quad \left(\frac{x+y}{xy}\right) = \log\left|\frac{x}{y}\right| + C \quad [\text{where } C = -C_1]$$

TOPIC 3

Homogeneous and Linear Differential Equation

Homogeneous Function

A function $f(x, y)$ is called homogeneous function of degree n (a non-negative integer), if

$$f(\lambda x, \lambda y) = \lambda^n f(x, y)$$

where, λ is some non-zero real number.

e.g.

(i) $f(x, y) = x^2 - 4xy + 3y^2$ is homogeneous function of degree 2, because

$$f(\lambda x, \lambda y) = (\lambda x)^2 - 4\lambda x(\lambda y) + 3(\lambda y)^2$$
$$= \lambda^2 x^2 - 4\lambda^2 xy + 3\lambda^2 y^2$$
$$= \lambda^2 (x^2 - 4xy + 3y^2)$$
$$= \lambda^2 f(x, y)$$

(ii) $f(x, y) = 3x^2 + \sin 2x$ is not homogeneous,because

$f(\lambda x, \lambda y) = 3(\lambda x)^2 + \sin 2(\lambda x) \neq \lambda^n f(x, y)$ for any n.

Homogeneous Differential Equations

A differential equation of the form

$$\frac{dy}{dx} = \frac{f(x, y)}{g(x, y)}$$

where, $f(x, y)$ and $g(x, y)$ are homogeneous functions of the same degree is said to be homogeneous differential equation.

Method to Solve $\frac{dy}{dx} = \frac{f(x,y)}{g(x,y)}$

(i) Put $y = vx$.

(ii) Differentiate it w.r.t. x, we get

$$\frac{dy}{dx} = v + x\frac{dv}{dx}.$$

(iii) Substitute the value of $\frac{dy}{dx}$ and y in the given differential equation which reduces the equation to the variable separable form.

(iv) Integrate and simplify it. Further substitute $v = \frac{y}{x}$ to get the required solution.

Linear Differential Equations

A differential equation either of the form $\frac{dy}{dx} + Py = Q$, where P and Q are either constants or functions of x (and not of y) or of the form $\frac{dx}{dy} + Px = Q$, where P and Q are either constants or functions of y (and not of x) is said to be linear differential equation of the first order.

Method to Solve Linear Differential Equation

***Step* I** Write the given differential equation either in the form $\frac{dy}{dx} + Py = Q$, where P and Q are either constants or functions of x only or of the form $\frac{dx}{dy} + Px = Q$, where P and Q are constants or functions of y (and not of x).

***Step* II** Find the integrating factor $\text{IF} = e^{\int P dx}$

or $\text{IF} = e^{\int P dy}$.

***Step* III** Write the solution of the given differential equation as

$$y \times (\text{IF}) = \int (Q \times \text{IF})\,dx + C$$

or $$x \times (\text{IF}) = \int Q \times (\text{IF})\,dy + C$$

PYQs Previous Years Questions

1 Mark Question

1. For what value of n is the given a homogenous differential equation? **ISC Specimen 2024**

$$\frac{dy}{dx}=\frac{x^3-y^3}{x^n y+xy^n}$$

(a) 1 (b) 3 (c) 0 (d) 2

3/4 Marks Questions

2. Solve the differential equation.
$$(1+y^2)dx=(\tan^{-1}y-x)\,dy$$ **ISC 2023**

3. Solve the differential equation.
$$(x^2-y^2)dx+2xydy=0$$ **ISC 2023**

4. Solve the differential equation
$$(1+x^2)\frac{dy}{dx}=4x^2-2xy.$$ **ISC 2020**

5. Solve $\sin x\frac{dy}{dx}-y=\sin x\tan\frac{x}{2}$. **ISC 2018**

6. Solve the following differential equation
$$x\frac{dy}{dx}+2y=x^2\log x.$$ **ISC Specimen 2018**

7. Solve the differential equation
$$x\frac{dy}{dx}+y=3x^2-2.$$

8. Solve the differential equation
$$(x+1)\frac{dy}{dx}-y=e^{3x}(x+1)^2.$$ **ISC 2008**

9. Solve the differential equation
$(1-x^2)\frac{dy}{dx}-xy=x$, gives $y=2$, when $x=0$. **ISC 2004**

10. Solve $(1+y+x^2y)\,dx+(x+x^3)\,dy=0$. **ISC 2003**

11. Solve $\cos^2 x\frac{dy}{dx}+y=\tan x$. **ISC 2002**

12. Solve $\frac{dy}{dx}+\frac{2x}{1+x^2}y=\frac{1}{(1+x^2)^2}$. **ISC 2001**

13. Solve $x(x-y)\,dy+y^2dx=0$. **ISC 2000**

5/6 Marks Questions

14. Solve the following differential equation
$$2ye^{\frac{x}{y}}dx+\left(y-2xe^{\frac{x}{y}}\right)dy=0,\text{ given } x=0 \text{ and } y=1.$$ **ISC 2024**

15. Solve the following differential equation
$$x(x^2-1)\frac{dy}{dx}=1,\ y=0,\text{ given } x=2.$$ **ISC 2024**

16. Solve $x^3dy+(xy-1)\,dx=0$. **ISC Specimen 2024**

Given $y=3-e$ when $x=\frac{1}{2}$, then find y when $x=1$

17. Find the particular solution of the differential equation given below
$(1+x^2)dy=(\tan^{-1}x-y)dx$, given that $y=1$, when $x=0$ **ISC Specimen 2023**

18. Write a particular solution of the differential equation,
$\frac{dy}{dx}=\frac{y^2}{xy-x^2}$, when $x=1$, $y=1$ **ISC Specimen Sem-II 2022**

19. Write a particular solution of the differential equation.
$(1+x^2)\frac{dy}{dx}+2xy=\frac{1}{1+x^2}$, when $y=0$, $x=0$. **ISC Specimen Sem-II 2022**

> **KEY CONCEPT**
> Divide the given differential equation by (x^2+1) to convert it into the form of linear differential equation and then solve it.

20. Solve the differential equation
$x^2\,dy+(xy+y^2)\,dx=0$, when $x=1$ and $y=1$. **ISC 2016**

21. Solve the differential equation
$$e^{\frac{x}{y}}\left(1-\frac{x}{y}\right)+\left(1+e^{\frac{x}{y}}\right)\frac{dx}{dy}=0,\text{ when } x=0,\ y=1.$$ **ISC 2015**

22. Solve the following differential equation
$(3xy+y^2)\,dx+(x^2+xy)\,dy=0$. **ISC 2014**

23. Solve the following differential equation
$ye^y dx=(y^3+2xe^y)\,dy$ given that $x=0$, $y=1$. **ISC 2013**

Explanations

1. (d) Given, $\dfrac{dy}{dx}=\dfrac{x^3-y^3}{x^n y+xy^n}$

Let $f(x, y)=\dfrac{x^3-y^3}{x^n y+xy^n}$

If $n=2$, then $f(x, y)=\dfrac{x^3-y^3}{x^2 y+xy^2}$

Now, on putting $x=\lambda x$ and $y=\lambda y$, we get

$$f(\lambda x, \lambda y)=\frac{\lambda^3(x^3-y^3)}{\lambda^3(x^2 y+xy^2)}=\lambda^0 f(x, y)$$

Hence, for $n=2$, $f(x, y)$ is a homogeneous differential equation.

2. We have, $(1+y^2)\,dx=(\tan^{-1} y-x)\,dy$

$$\Rightarrow \quad \frac{dx}{dy}=\frac{\tan^{-1} y}{1+y^2}-\frac{x}{1+y^2}$$

$$\Rightarrow \quad \frac{dx}{dy}+\frac{x}{1+y^2}=\frac{\tan^{-1} y}{1+y^2}$$

This is a linear differential equation in form

$$\frac{dx}{dy}+Px=Q,$$

where $P=\dfrac{1}{1+y^2}$ and $Q=\dfrac{\tan^{-1} y}{1+y^2}$

$$\text{IF}=e^{\int P dy}=e^{\int \frac{1}{1+y^2}dy}=e^{\tan^{-1} y}$$

Solution of the given differential equation is

$$x\cdot \text{IF}=\int Q\cdot \text{IF}\,dy$$

$$\Rightarrow xe^{\tan^{-1} y}=\int \frac{\tan^{-1} y}{1+y^2}e^{\tan^{-1} y}\,dy$$

On putting $\tan^{-1} y=t \Rightarrow \dfrac{1}{1+y^2}dy=dt$

$$\therefore \quad xe^{\tan^{-1} y}=\int te^t\,dt$$

Integrating by parts in RHS, we have

$$xe^{\tan^{-1} y}=t\int e^t\,dt-\int\left[\frac{d}{dt}(t)\cdot\int e^t\cdot dt\right]dt$$

$$\Rightarrow \quad xe^{\tan^{-1} y}=te^t-\int e^t\,dt+C$$

$$\Rightarrow \quad xe^{\tan^{-1} y}=te^t-e^t+C$$

$$\Rightarrow \quad xe^{\tan^{-1} y}=e^{\tan^{-1} y}[(\tan^{-1} y)-1]+C$$

$[\because\ t=\tan^{-1} y]$

$$\Rightarrow \quad x=\tan^{-1} y-1+Ce^{-\tan^{-1} y}$$

Concept Enhancer Solution of the differential equation of the type $\dfrac{dx}{dy}+Px=Q$ is given by $x(\text{IF})=\int Q(\text{IF})dy+C$, where $\text{IF}=e^{\int P\cdot dy}$

3. Given, $(x^2-y^2)\,dx+2xy\,dy=0$

$$\Rightarrow \quad 2xy\,dy=(y^2-x^2)\,dx$$

$$\Rightarrow \quad \frac{dy}{dx}=\frac{y^2-x^2}{2xy}$$

which is a homogeneous differential equation.

On putting $y=vx \Rightarrow \dfrac{dy}{dx}=v+x\dfrac{dv}{dx}$

$$\therefore \quad v+\frac{xdv}{dx}=\frac{v^2x^2-x^2}{2x(vx)}=\frac{x^2(v^2-1)}{2x^2v}=\frac{v^2-1}{2v}$$

$$\Rightarrow \quad x\frac{dv}{dx}=\frac{v^2-1}{2v}-v$$

$$\Rightarrow \quad x\frac{dv}{dx}=\frac{v^2-1-2v^2}{2v}=\frac{-(1+v^2)}{2v}$$

$$\Rightarrow \quad \frac{2v}{v^2+1}dv=-\frac{dx}{x}$$

On integrating both sides,

$$\int\frac{2v}{v^2+1}dv=-\int\frac{dx}{x}$$

$$\Rightarrow \quad \log|v^2+1|=-\log x+\log C$$

$$\Rightarrow \log|v^2+1|+\log x=\log C$$

$$\Rightarrow \quad \log[(v^2+1)x]=\log C$$

$$\Rightarrow \quad (v^2+1)x=C$$

$$\Rightarrow \quad \left(\frac{y^2}{x^2}+1\right)x=C \qquad \left[\because v=\frac{y}{x}\right]$$

$$\Rightarrow \quad (y^2+x^2)=Cx \Rightarrow x^2+y^2-Cx=0,$$

where C is an arbitrary constant.

4. We have, $\quad (1+x^2)\dfrac{dy}{dx}=4x^2-2xy$

$$\Rightarrow \quad \frac{dy}{dx}+\frac{2xy}{1+x^2}=\frac{4x^2}{1+x^2}$$

This is linear differential equation of the form.

$$\frac{dy}{dx}+Py=Q,$$

where $P=\dfrac{2x}{1+x^2}$ and $Q=\dfrac{4x^2}{1+x^2}$

$\therefore \quad \text{IF} = e^{\int P dx} = e^{\int \frac{2x}{1+x^2} dx}$

$= e^{\log(1+x^2)} = 1 + x^2$

Solution of the given differential equation is

$\Rightarrow \quad y(1+x^2) = \int \frac{4x^2}{1+x^2} \times (1+x^2)\, dx + C$

$\Rightarrow \quad y(1+x^2) = \int 4x^2 dx + C$

$\Rightarrow \quad y(1+x^2) = \frac{4x^3}{3} + C$

5. We have, $\sin x \frac{dy}{dx} - y = \sin x \tan \frac{x}{2}$

$\Rightarrow \quad \frac{dy}{dx} - y \operatorname{cosec} x = \tan \frac{x}{2}$

This is the form of $\frac{dy}{dx} + Py = Q$,

where $P = -\operatorname{cosec} x$ and $Q = \tan \frac{x}{2}$

Now, $\text{IF} = e^{\int P\, dx} = e^{\int -\operatorname{cosec} x\, dx} = e^{-\log \tan \frac{x}{2}}$

$= \frac{1}{\tan x/2}$

and the solution of the given differential equation is

$y \cdot \text{IF} = \int Q \cdot \text{IF}\, dx + C$

$\frac{y}{\tan \frac{x}{2}} = \int \tan \frac{x}{2} \cdot \frac{1}{\tan \frac{x}{2}}\, dx + C$

$\Rightarrow \quad \frac{y}{\tan \frac{x}{2}} = \int dx + C = x + C$

$\Rightarrow \quad y = x \tan \frac{x}{2} + C \tan \frac{x}{2}$

6. We have,

$x \frac{dy}{dx} + 2y = x^2 \log x$

$\Rightarrow \quad \frac{dy}{dx} + \frac{2y}{x} = x \log x$

This is the form of $\frac{dy}{dx} + Py = Q$,

where $P = \frac{2}{x}$ and $Q = x \log x$

$\therefore \text{IF} = e^{\int P dx} = e^{\int \frac{2}{x} dx} = e^{2 \log x} = e^{\log x^2} = x^2$

Solution of the given differential equation is

$y \cdot x^2 = \int \underset{\text{II}}{x^3} \underset{\text{I}}{\log x}\, dx + C$

$x^2 y = \log x \int x^3 dx - \int \left\{ \frac{d}{dx} (\log x) \int x^3 dx \right\} dx + C$

[by using integration by parts]

$\Rightarrow \quad x^2 y = \log x \left(\frac{x^4}{4} \right) - \int \frac{1}{x} \cdot \frac{x^4}{4}\, dx + C$

$\Rightarrow \quad x^2 y = \frac{x^4}{4} \log x - \int \frac{x^3}{4}\, dx + C$

$\Rightarrow \quad x^2 y = \frac{x^4}{4} \log x - \frac{x^4}{16} + C$

$\Rightarrow \quad y = \frac{x^2}{4} \log x - \frac{x^2}{16} + \frac{C}{x^2}$

7. Given, differential equation is

$x \frac{dy}{dx} + y = 3x^2 - 2$

$\Rightarrow \quad \frac{dy}{dx} + \frac{1}{x} \cdot y = 3x - \frac{2}{x} \quad \ldots(\text{i})$

On comparing it with the standard form $\frac{dy}{dx} + Py = Q$,

we get

$P = \frac{1}{x}$ and $Q = 3x - \frac{2}{x}$

So, Eq. (i) is linear in y.

$\therefore \quad \text{IF} = e^{\int P dx} = e^{\int \frac{1}{x} dx} = e^{\log x} = x$

Therefore, solution of Eq. (i) is

$y \cdot x = \int \left(3x - \frac{2}{x} \right) x\, dx + C$

$\Rightarrow \quad y \cdot x = \int (3x^2 - 2)\, dx + C$

$\Rightarrow \quad yx = 3 \cdot \frac{x^3}{3} - 2x + C$

$\Rightarrow \quad yx = x^3 - 2x + C$

$\Rightarrow \quad y = x^2 - 2 + Cx^{-1}$,

where C is arbitrary constant.

8. Given, $(x+1) \frac{dy}{dx} - y = e^{3x} (x+1)^2$

$\Rightarrow \quad \frac{dy}{dx} - \frac{y}{x+1} = e^{3x} (x+1) \quad \ldots(\text{i})$

On comparing, above equation with the linear differential equation $\frac{dy}{dx}+Py=Q$, we get

$$P=\frac{-1}{x+1} \text{ and } Q=e^{3x}\ (x+1)$$

$$\therefore \quad \text{IF}=e^{\int P dx}=e^{-\int \frac{1}{x+1}dx}=e^{-\log|x+1|}$$

$$=e^{\log\left(\frac{1}{x+1}\right)}=\frac{1}{x+1} \qquad [\because e^{\log x}=x]$$

$\therefore$ The solution is $y\times \text{IF}=\int Q\times \text{IF}\, dx+C$

$$\Rightarrow \quad y\times\frac{1}{x+1}=\int\frac{e^{3x}(x+1)\,dx}{x+1}+C$$

$$\Rightarrow \quad \frac{y}{x+1}=\frac{e^{3x}}{3}+C$$

$$\Rightarrow \quad y=\frac{e^{3x}}{3}(1+x)+C\ (1+x)$$

Alternate Solution

Given, differential equation can be rewritten as

$$\left(\frac{dy}{dx}-\frac{y}{x+1}\right)\frac{1}{x+1}=e^{3x} \Rightarrow \frac{d}{dx}\left(\frac{y}{x+1}\right)=e^{3x}$$

On integrating both sides, we get

$$\int\frac{d}{dx}\left(\frac{y}{x+1}\right)dx=\int e^{3x}dx$$

$$\Rightarrow \quad \frac{y}{x+1}=\frac{e^{3x}}{3}+C$$

$$\Rightarrow \quad y=\frac{e^{3x}}{3}(x+1)+C\ (x+1)$$

9. Given, $(1-x^2)\frac{dy}{dx}-xy=x$

$$\Rightarrow \quad \frac{dy}{dx}-\frac{x}{1-x^2}y=\frac{x}{1-x^2}$$

On comparing above equation with the linear differential equation $\frac{dy}{dx}+Py=Q$, we get

$$P=\frac{-x}{1-x^2} \text{ and } Q=\frac{x}{1-x^2}$$

$$\therefore \text{IF}=e^{\int P\,dx}=e^{\int\frac{-x}{1-x^2}dx}=e^{\frac{1}{2}\int\frac{-2x}{1-x^2}dx}$$

$$=e^{\frac{1}{2}\log|1-x^2|}=e^{\log\sqrt{1-x^2}}=\sqrt{1-x^2} \quad [\because a^{\log_a x}=x]$$

$\therefore$ Solution is $y\times \text{IF}=\int(Q\times \text{IF})dx+C$

$$\Rightarrow \quad y\sqrt{1-x^2}=\int\frac{x}{1-x^2}\times\sqrt{1-x^2}\,dx+C$$

$$\Rightarrow \quad y\sqrt{1-x^2}=\int\frac{x\,dx}{\sqrt{1-x^2}}+C$$

On putting $t=\sqrt{1-x^2} \Rightarrow t^2=1-x^2$

$$\Rightarrow \quad 2t\,dt=-2x\,dx \Rightarrow t\,dt=-x\,dx$$

$$\therefore \quad y\sqrt{1-x^2}=\int\frac{-t\,dt}{t}+C$$

$$\Rightarrow \quad y\sqrt{1-x^2}=-t+C$$

$$\Rightarrow \quad y\sqrt{1-x^2}=-\sqrt{1-x^2}+C \qquad \ldots\text{(i)}$$

$$\therefore \quad 2=-1+C$$

$$[\because y=2 \text{ when } x=0]$$

$$\Rightarrow \quad C=3$$

On putting $C=3$ in Eq. (i), we get

$$y\sqrt{1-x^2}=-\sqrt{1-x^2}+3$$

$$\Rightarrow \quad y\sqrt{1-x^2}+\sqrt{1-x^2}=3$$

10. Given, $(1+y+x^2y)\,dx+(x+x^3)\,dy=0$

$$\Rightarrow \quad 1+y+x^2y+(x+x^3)\frac{dy}{dx}=0$$

$$\Rightarrow \quad 1+y(1+x^2)+x(1+x^2)\frac{dy}{dx}=0$$

$$\Rightarrow \quad \frac{dy}{dx}+\frac{y(1+x^2)}{x(1+x^2)}+\frac{1}{x(1+x^2)}=0$$

$$\Rightarrow \quad \frac{dy}{dx}+\frac{y}{x}=\frac{-1}{x(1+x^2)}$$

On comparing above equation with the linear differential equation $\frac{dy}{dx}+Py=Q$, we get

$$P=\frac{1}{x} \text{ and } Q=\frac{-1}{x(1+x^2)}$$

$$\text{IF}=e^{\int P\,dx}=e^{\int\frac{1}{x}dx}=e^{\log|x|}=x \qquad [\because a^{\log_a x}=x]$$

$\therefore$ The solution is

$$y\times \text{IF}=\int(Q\times \text{IF})\,dx+C$$

$$\Rightarrow \quad yx=\int\frac{-1}{x(1+x^2)}\times x\,dx+C$$

$$\Rightarrow \quad yx=-\int\frac{dx}{1+x^2}+C$$

$$\Rightarrow \quad yx=-\tan^{-1}x+C$$

11. Given, $\cos^2 x \dfrac{dy}{dx} + y = \tan x$

$$\Rightarrow \frac{dy}{dx} + \frac{y}{\cos^2 x} = \frac{\tan x}{\cos^2 x}$$

[dividing both sides by $\cos^2 x$]

$$\Rightarrow \frac{dy}{dx} + \sec^2 x\, y = \tan x \cdot \sec^2 x$$

On comparing above equation with linear differential equation $\dfrac{dy}{dx} + P\,y = Q$, we get

$$P = \sec^2 x \text{ and } Q = \tan x \cdot \sec^2 x$$

$$\text{IF} = e^{\int P\,dx} = e^{\int \sec^2 x\,dx} = e^{\tan x}$$

$\therefore$ The solution is

$$y \times \text{IF} = \int (Q \times \text{IF})\,dx + C$$

$$\Rightarrow ye^{\tan x} = \int [\tan x \cdot \sec^2 x\, e^{\tan x}]dx + C$$

On putting $\tan x = t \Rightarrow \sec^2 x\,dx = dt$

$$\therefore \quad ye^{\tan x} = \int \underset{\text{I}}{t} \cdot \underset{\text{II}}{e^t}\, dt + C$$

$$= t\int e^t\,dt - \int\left[\frac{d(t)}{dt}\int e^t\,dt\right]dt + C$$

[using integration by parts]

$$= te^t - \int (1 \cdot e^t)\,dt + C$$

$$= te^t - e^t + C = e^t(t-1) + C$$

$$\therefore \quad ye^{\tan x} = e^{\tan x}(\tan x - 1) + C \quad [\text{putting } t = \tan x]$$

12. Given, $\dfrac{dy}{dx} + \dfrac{2x}{1+x^2}\,y = \dfrac{1}{(1+x^2)^2}$

On comparing above equation with linear differential equation $\dfrac{dy}{dx} + P\,y = Q$, we get

$$P = \frac{2x}{1+x^2} \text{ and } Q = \frac{1}{(1+x^2)^2}$$

$$\therefore \quad \text{IF} = e^{\int P\,dx} = e^{\int \frac{2x}{1+x^2}dx} = e^{\log|1+x^2|} \qquad [\because a^{\log_a x} = x]$$

$$= 1 + x^2$$

$\therefore$ The solution is

$$y \times \text{IF} = \int (Q \times \text{IF})\,dx + C$$

$$\Rightarrow y(1+x^2) = \int \frac{1}{(1+x^2)^2} \times (1+x^2)\,dx + C$$

$$\Rightarrow y(1+x^2) = \int \frac{1}{1+x^2}\,dx + C$$

$$\Rightarrow y(1+x^2) = \tan^{-1} x + C$$

13. Given, $x(x-y)\,dy + y^2\,dx = 0$

$$\Rightarrow x(x-y)\frac{dy}{dx} + y^2 = 0$$

$$\Rightarrow x(x-y)\frac{dy}{dx} = -y^2$$

$$\Rightarrow \frac{dy}{dx} = \frac{-y^2}{x^2 - xy}$$

[homogeneous form]

Since, degree of numerator and denominator is same, thus it is a homogeneous differential equation.

On putting $y = vx$

Then, $\dfrac{dy}{dx} = v + x\dfrac{dv}{dx}$

Now, $v + x\dfrac{dv}{dx} = \dfrac{-(vx)^2}{x^2 - x \cdot vx}$

$$\Rightarrow v + x\frac{dv}{dx} = \frac{-v^2x^2}{x^2(1-v)}$$

$$\Rightarrow v + x\frac{dv}{dx} = \frac{-v^2}{1-v}$$

$$\Rightarrow x\frac{dv}{dx} = \frac{-v^2}{1-v} - v$$

$$\Rightarrow x\frac{dv}{dx} = \frac{-v^2 - v + v^2}{1-v}$$

$$\Rightarrow x\frac{dv}{dx} = \frac{-v}{1-v}$$

$$\Rightarrow \frac{(1-v)\,dv}{v} = \frac{-dx}{x}$$

On integrating both sides, we get

$$\int\left(\frac{1}{v} - 1\right)dv = -\int \frac{dx}{x}$$

$$\Rightarrow \log|v| - v = -\log|x| + C$$

$$\Rightarrow \log\frac{y}{x} - \frac{y}{x} + \log x = C \quad \left[\text{putting } v = \frac{y}{x}\right]$$

$$\Rightarrow \log y - \log x - \frac{y}{x} + \log x = C$$

[using quotient rule of logarithm]

$$\Rightarrow \log y - \frac{y}{x} = C$$

14. The given differential equation is

$2ye^{x/y}dx + (y - 2xe^{x/y})\,dy = 0$, with $y(0) = 1$

$$\Rightarrow \frac{dx}{dy} = \frac{2xe^{x/y} - y}{2ye^{x/y}}$$

On putting $x = vy$ and $\frac{dx}{dy} = v + y\frac{dv}{dy}$, we get

$$v + y\frac{dv}{dy} = \frac{2vye^v - y}{2ye^v} = \frac{2ve^v - 1}{2e^v}$$

$$\Rightarrow \quad y\frac{dv}{dy} = \frac{2ve^v - 1}{2e^v} - v = \frac{-1}{2e^v} \Rightarrow \frac{dy}{y} = -2e^v dv$$

On integrating both sides, we get

$$\int \frac{dy}{y} = \int -2e^v dv$$

$$\Rightarrow \quad \log y = -2e^v + C$$

$$\Rightarrow \quad \log y + 2e^v = C \Rightarrow \log y + 2e^{x/y} = C$$

On applying the given condition, $y(0) = 1$, we get

$$0 + 2e^0 = C \Rightarrow C = 2$$

$$\therefore \log y + 2e^{x/y} - 2 = 0$$

which is the required solution.

15. The given differential equation is

$$x(x^2 - 1)\frac{dy}{dx} = 1 \text{ with } y(2) = 0$$

$$\Rightarrow \quad \frac{dx}{x(x^2-1)} = dy \Rightarrow \frac{dx}{x(x-1)(x+1)} = dy$$

By partial fraction, we get

$$\left[\frac{-1}{x} + \frac{1}{2(x-1)} + \frac{1}{2(x+1)}\right] dx = dy$$

On integrating, we get

$$\int \left(\frac{-1}{x}\right) dx + \frac{1}{2}\int \frac{1}{x-1} dx + \frac{1}{2}\int \frac{1}{x+1} dx = \int dy + K$$

$$\Rightarrow \quad -\ln|x| + \frac{1}{2}\ln|x-1| + \frac{1}{2}\ln|x+1| = y + K \quad \ldots\text{(i)}$$

On applying the initial condition $y(2) = 0$, we get

$$-\ln|2| + \frac{1}{2}\ln|1| + \frac{1}{2}\ln|3| = K$$

$$\Rightarrow \quad K = \ln(\sqrt{3}) - \ln|2|$$

$$K = \ln\left|\frac{\sqrt{3}}{2}\right|$$

On substituting the value of K in Eq. (i), we get

$$-\ln|x| + \frac{1}{2}\ln|x-1| + \frac{1}{2}\ln|x+1| = y + \ln\left|\frac{\sqrt{3}}{2}\right|$$

$$\Rightarrow \quad y = -\ln|x| + \ln\left|\sqrt{x^2-1}\right| - \ln\left|\frac{\sqrt{3}}{2}\right|$$

$$= \ln\left|\frac{\sqrt{(x^2-1)}}{x}\right| - \ln\left|\frac{\sqrt{3}}{2}\right|$$

$$\therefore \quad y = \ln\left|\frac{2}{x}\sqrt{\left(\frac{x^2-1}{3}\right)}\right|$$

which is the required solution.

16. We have, $x^3 dy + (xy - 1)\, dx = 0$

$$x^3\frac{dy}{dx} + xy - 1 = 0$$

$$\Rightarrow \quad x^3\frac{dy}{dx} + xy = 1$$

$$\Rightarrow \quad \frac{dy}{dx} + \frac{y}{x^2} = \frac{1}{x^3},$$

which is linear differential equation of the form

$$\frac{dy}{dx} + P \cdot y = Q.$$

$$\therefore \text{ IF} = e^{\int P\,dx} = e^{\int \frac{1}{x^2}dx} = e^{-\frac{1}{x}}$$

$\therefore$ Solution is given by

$$y \cdot (\text{IF}) = \int Q(\text{IF})\, dx + C$$

$$ye^{-1/x} = \int \frac{1}{x^3} e^{-1/x}\, dx + C \quad \ldots\text{(i)}$$

Let $\quad I = \int \frac{1}{x^3} e^{-1/x} dx$

Let $\frac{-1}{x} = t \Rightarrow \frac{1}{x^2}dx = dt$

$$\therefore \quad I = -\int te^t\, dt$$

$$I = -\left[t\int e^t dt - \int\left(\frac{d}{dt}(t)\int e^t dt\right) dt\right]$$

$$I = -[te^t - e^t] = e^t - te^t$$

$$I = e^{-1/x} + \frac{1}{x}e^{-1/x}$$

$\therefore$ From Eq. (i), we get

$$ye^{-1/x} = e^{-1/x} + \frac{1}{x}e^{-1/x} + C$$

Given, $y = 3 - e$ when $x = \frac{1}{2}$

$$\therefore \quad (3 - e)\, e^{-2} = e^{-2} + 2e^{-2} + C$$

$$\Rightarrow \quad 3e^{-2} - e^{-1} = 3e^{-2} + C$$

$$\Rightarrow \quad -e^{-1} = C$$

$$\therefore \quad ye^{-1/x} = e^{-1/x} + \frac{1}{x}e^{-1/x} - e^{-1}$$

Now, on putting $x = 1$, we get

$$ye^{-1} = e^{-1} + e^{-1} - e^{-1} \Rightarrow y = 1$$

17. Given, $(1+x^2)\dfrac{dy}{dx}=(\tan^{-1}x-y)$

$$\Rightarrow \quad \frac{dy}{dx}=\frac{\tan^{-1}x}{1+x^2}-\frac{y}{1+x^2}$$

$$\Rightarrow \quad \frac{dy}{dx}+\frac{y}{1+x^2}=\frac{\tan^{-1}x}{1+x^2}$$

On comparing it with general linear differential equation $\dfrac{dy}{dx}+yP(x)=Q(x)$

$$\therefore \quad P(x)=\frac{1}{1+x^2} \text{ and } Q(x)=\frac{\tan^{-1}x}{1+x^2}$$

Integrating factor, IF $=e^{\int P(x)dx}$

$$=\int\frac{1}{1+x^2}\,dx=\tan^{-1}x$$

$$\therefore \quad \text{IF}=e^{\tan^{-1}x}$$

We know that solution of the differential equation

$$y\cdot\text{IF}=\int Q(x)\cdot\text{IF}\,dx$$

$$y\cdot e^{\tan^{-1}x}=\int\frac{\tan^{-1}x}{1+x^2}e^{\tan^{-1}x}\,dx$$

On putting $\tan^{-1}x=t$

$$\Rightarrow \quad \frac{1}{1+x^2}dx=dt$$

$$=\int \underset{\text{I}}{t}\,\underset{\text{II}}{e^t}\,dt=t\,e^t-e^t+C$$

$$=(t-1)e^t+C$$

$$y\cdot e^{\tan^{-1}x}=[\tan^{-1}x-1]e^{\tan^{-1}x}+C \quad \text{...(i)}$$

Where, $x=0$, $y=1$

Then, $1\cdot e^{\tan^{-1}0}=[\tan^{-1}0-1]e^{\tan^{-1}0}+C$

$$1=-1+C$$

$$\Rightarrow \quad C=2$$

On substituting $C=2$ in Eq. (i), we get

$$y\cdot e^{\tan^{-1}x}=(\tan^{-1}x-1)e^{\tan^{-1}x}+2$$

or $$y=\tan^{-1}x-1+2e^{-\tan^{-1}x}$$

18. Given, $\dfrac{dy}{dx}=\dfrac{y^2}{xy-x^2}$

On putting $y=xv \Rightarrow \dfrac{dy}{dx}=v+x\dfrac{dv}{dx}$

$$\therefore \quad v+x\frac{dv}{dx}=\frac{v^2x^2}{x\cdot xv-x^2}$$

$$\Rightarrow \quad v+x\frac{dv}{dx}=\frac{v^2}{v-1}$$

$$\Rightarrow \quad x\frac{dv}{dx}=\frac{v^2}{v-1}-v \Rightarrow x\frac{dv}{dx}=\frac{v}{v-1}$$

$$\Rightarrow \quad \int\frac{dx}{x}=\int\left(\frac{v-1}{v}\right)dv$$

$$\Rightarrow \quad \int\frac{dx}{x}=\int\left(1-\frac{1}{v}\right)dv$$

$$\Rightarrow \quad \log x=v-\log v+C$$

$$\Rightarrow \quad \log x=\frac{y}{x}-\log\left(\frac{y}{x}\right)+C \quad \left[\because v=\frac{y}{x}\right]$$

$$\Rightarrow \quad \log x=\frac{y}{x}-\log y+\log x+C$$

$$\Rightarrow \quad \log y=\frac{y}{x}+C$$

$$\Rightarrow \quad x\log y-y=Cx$$

$$\Rightarrow \quad x\log y=y+Cx$$

At $x=y=1$, $C=-1$ $\quad [\because \log 1=0]$

$\therefore$ Eq. (i) becomes

$$x\log y=y-x$$

19. Given, differential equation is

$$(x^2+1)\frac{dy}{dx}+2xy=\frac{1}{x^2+1}$$

On dividing both sides by (x^2+1), we get

$$\frac{dy}{dx}+\frac{2x}{x^2+1}y=\frac{1}{(x^2+1)^2}$$

which is a linear differential equation of the form $\dfrac{dy}{dx}+Py=Q$,

here $P=\dfrac{2x}{x^2+1}$ and $Q=\dfrac{1}{(x^2+1)^2}$

Now, IF $=e^{\int Pdx}+e^{\int\frac{2x}{x^2+1}dx}=e^{\log|x^2+1|}=x^2+1$

$$\left[\begin{array}{l}\text{putting } x^2+1=t\Rightarrow 2x\,dx=dt\text{, then}\\ \displaystyle\int\frac{2x}{x^2+1}dx=\int\frac{1}{t}dt=\log|t|=\log|x^2+1|\end{array}\right]$$

So, the required general solution is

$$y\times\text{IF}=\int(Q\times\text{IF})\,dx+C$$

$$\Rightarrow \quad y(x^2+1)=\int\left[\frac{1}{(x^2+1)^2}\times(x^2+1)\right]dx+C$$

$$\Rightarrow \quad y(x^2+1)=\int\frac{1}{x^2+1}dx+C$$

$$\Rightarrow \quad y(x^2+1)=\tan^{-1}x+C \quad \text{...(i)}$$

When $x=0$, then

$$y=0$$

$$\therefore \quad 0=\tan^{-1}0+C$$

$$\Rightarrow \quad C=0$$

Now, $y(x^2+1)=\tan^{-1}x$ [from Eq. (i)]

which is the required differential equation.

20. Given, differential equation is

$$x^2dy+(xy+y^2)\,dx=0$$

$$\Rightarrow \quad \frac{dy}{dx}=\frac{-(xy+y^2)}{x^2} \quad \text{...(i)}$$

The given differential equation is homogeneous.

On putting $y=vx \Rightarrow \frac{dy}{dx}=v+x\frac{dv}{dx}$

On substituting the values of y and $\frac{dy}{dx}$ in Eq. (i), we get

$$v+x\frac{dv}{dx}=-\frac{(xvx+v^2x^2)}{x^2}$$

$$\Rightarrow \quad x\frac{dv}{dx}=-v-(v+v^2)=-2v-v^2$$

$$\Rightarrow \quad \frac{dv}{2v+v^2}=-\frac{dx}{x}$$

$$\Rightarrow \quad \frac{dv}{(v+1)^2-1}+\frac{dx}{x}=0$$

On integrating, we get

$$\frac{1}{2}\log\left|\frac{(v+1)-1}{(v+1)+1}\right|+\log|x|=C$$

$$\Rightarrow \quad \log\left|\frac{v}{v+2}\right|+2\log|x|=2C$$

$$\Rightarrow \quad \left|\frac{vx^2}{v+2}\right|=e^{2C} \Rightarrow \frac{vx^2}{v+2}=\pm e^{2C}=A \quad \text{[say]}$$

$$\Rightarrow \quad \frac{\frac{y}{x}\cdot x^2}{\frac{y}{x}+2}=A$$

$$\Rightarrow \quad x^2y=A(y+2x) \quad \text{...(ii)}$$

Given that $y=1$, when $x=1$

$$\Rightarrow \quad 3A=1$$

$$\Rightarrow \quad A=\frac{1}{3}$$

On substituting this value of A in Eq. (ii), we get

$$y+2x=3x^2y$$

which is the required solution.

21. Given, differential equation is

$$(1+e^{\frac{x}{y}})\frac{dx}{dy}+e^{\frac{x}{y}}\left(1-\frac{x}{y}\right)=0$$

$$\Rightarrow \quad \frac{dx}{dy}=\frac{-e^{\frac{x}{y}}\left(1-\frac{x}{y}\right)}{(1+e^{\frac{x}{y}})} \quad \text{...(i)}$$

On putting $\frac{x}{y}=v \Rightarrow x=vy$, then $\frac{dx}{dy}=v+y\frac{dv}{dy}$ ...(ii)

From Eqs. (i) and (ii), we get

$$v+y\frac{dv}{dy}=-e^v\frac{(1-v)}{(1+e^v)}$$

$$\Rightarrow \quad y\frac{dv}{dy}=\frac{-e^v(1-v)}{(1+e^v)}-v$$

$$\Rightarrow \quad y\frac{dv}{dy}=\frac{-e^v(1-v)-v(1+e^v)}{(1+e^v)}$$

$$\Rightarrow \quad y\frac{dv}{dy}=\frac{-e^v+ve^v-v-ve^v}{1+e^v}$$

$$\Rightarrow \quad y\frac{dv}{dy}=-\frac{(v+e^v)}{(1+e^v)}$$

On separating the variables, we get

$$\frac{(1+e^v)}{(v+e^v)}dv=-\frac{1}{y}dy$$

On integrating both sides, we get

$$\int\frac{(1+e^v)}{(v+e^v)}dv=-\int\frac{dy}{y}$$

$$\Rightarrow \quad \log|v+e^v|=-\log|y|+\log|C|$$

$$\left[\begin{array}{l}\because \text{ putting } v+e^v=t \Rightarrow (1+e^v)dv=dt \\ \therefore \int\frac{1+e^v}{v+e^v}dv=\int\frac{1}{t}dt=\log|t|=\log|v+e^v|\end{array}\right]$$

$$\Rightarrow \quad \log\left|\frac{x}{y}+e^{\frac{x}{y}}\right|+\log|y|=\log|C| \quad \left[\text{putting } v=\frac{x}{y}\right]$$

$$\Rightarrow \quad \log\left|y\left(\frac{x}{y}+e^{\frac{x}{y}}\right)\right|=\log|C| \Rightarrow x+ye^{\frac{x}{y}}=C \quad \text{...(iii)}$$

Also, given, $x=0$, $y=1$

Then, from Eq. (iii), we get

$$0+1e^0=C \Rightarrow C=1$$

$\therefore$ Required equation is $x+ye^{\frac{x}{y}}=1$.

22. Given, $(3xy+y^2)\,dx+(x^2+xy)\,dy=0$

$$\Rightarrow \quad (x^2+xy)\,dy=-(3xy+y^2)\,dx$$

$$\Rightarrow \quad \frac{dy}{dx}=-\frac{3xy+y^2}{x^2+xy}$$

It is a homogeneous differential equation, because numerator and demominator both have same degree.

On putting $y=vx$

Then, $\dfrac{dy}{dx}=v+x\dfrac{dv}{dx}$

$$\therefore \quad v+x\frac{dv}{dx}=-\frac{[3x\cdot vx+(vx)^2]}{[x^2+x\cdot vx]}$$

$$\Rightarrow \quad v+x\frac{dv}{dx}=-\frac{[3vx^2+v^2x^2]}{[x^2+vx^2]}$$

$$\Rightarrow \quad v+x\frac{dv}{dx}=-\frac{[3v+v^2]x^2}{[1+v]x^2}$$

$$\Rightarrow \quad x\frac{dv}{dx}=-\frac{[3v+v^2]}{1+v}-v$$

$$\Rightarrow \quad x\frac{dv}{dx}=\frac{-3v-v^2-v-v^2}{1+v}$$

$$\Rightarrow \quad x\frac{dv}{dx}=\frac{-2v^2-4v}{1+v}$$

$$\Rightarrow \quad \frac{(1+v)\,dv}{2\,(v^2+2v)}=-\frac{dx}{x} \qquad \ldots\text{(i)}$$

$$\Rightarrow \quad \frac{(v+1)\,dv}{v\,(v+2)}=-2\frac{dx}{x}$$

Let $\dfrac{v+1}{v\,(v+2)}=\dfrac{A}{v}+\dfrac{B}{v+2}$

[using partial fraction]

$$\Rightarrow \quad v+1=A\,(v+2)+Bv$$

$\Rightarrow \quad A+B=1$

[comparing coefficient of v both sides]

and $\quad 2A=1$

[comparing constant term both sides]

i.e. $\quad A=\dfrac{1}{2}$ and $B=\dfrac{1}{2}$

Eq. (i) becomes,

$$\frac{dv}{2v}+\frac{dv}{2\,(v+2)}=-\frac{2dx}{x}$$

On integrating both sides, we get

$$\frac{1}{2}\int\frac{dv}{v}+\frac{1}{2}\int\frac{dv}{v+2}=-2\int\frac{dx}{x}$$

$$\Rightarrow \frac{1}{2}\log|v|+\frac{1}{2}\log|v+2|=-2\log|x|+\log|C|$$

$$\Rightarrow \quad \log|v|+\log|v+2|=-4\log|x|+2\log|C|$$

$$\Rightarrow \quad \log|v(v+2)|=\log\left|\frac{C^2}{x^4}\right|$$

$$\Rightarrow \quad v\,(v+2)=\frac{C^2}{x^4}, \text{ where } C^2=C'$$

$$\Rightarrow \quad \frac{y}{x}\left(\frac{y}{x}+2\right)=\frac{C'}{x^4} \qquad \left[\text{putting } v=\frac{y}{x}\right]$$

$$\Rightarrow \quad y\,(y+2x)=\frac{C'}{x^2}$$

23. $\because \quad ye^y\,dx=(y^3+2xe^y)\,dy$

$$\Rightarrow \quad \frac{dx}{dy}=\frac{y^3+2xe^y}{ye^y}$$

$$\Rightarrow \quad \frac{dx}{dy}=y^2e^{-y}+\frac{2x}{y}$$

$$\Rightarrow \quad \frac{dx}{dy}-\frac{2x}{y}=y^2e^{-y} \qquad \ldots\text{(i)}$$

It is a linear differential equation of the form $\dfrac{dx}{dy}+Px=Q$, we get

$$\therefore \quad P=\frac{-2}{y} \text{ and } Q=y^2e^{-y}$$

$$\therefore \quad \text{IF}=e^{\int P dy}=e^{\int \frac{-2}{y}dy}=e^{-2\log y}$$

$$=e^{\log y^{-2}}=\frac{1}{y^2},\ y\neq 0 \qquad [\because a^{\log_a x}=x]$$

$\therefore$ The solution is $x\times \text{IF}=\int(\text{IF}\times Q)\,dy+C$

$$\Rightarrow \quad \frac{x}{y^2}=\int\frac{y^2e^{-y}}{y^2}dy+C \Rightarrow \frac{x}{y^2}=\int e^{-y}dy+C$$

$$\Rightarrow \quad \frac{x}{y^2}=-e^{-y}+C \qquad \ldots\text{(ii)}$$

Also, given $x=0$ and $y=1$

$$\therefore \quad \frac{0}{1^2}=-e^{-1}+C$$

$$\Rightarrow \quad C=e^{-1}$$

$$\Rightarrow \quad C=\frac{1}{e}$$

On putting $C=\dfrac{1}{e}$ in Eq. (ii), we get

$$\frac{x}{y^2}=-e^{-y}+\frac{1}{e}$$

$$\Rightarrow \quad x=y^2\,(e^{-1}-e^{-y}),$$

which is the required solution.

CHAPTER TEST

1 Mark Questions

1. If m and n are the order and degree of the differential equation $\left(\frac{d^2y}{dx^2}\right)^5 + 4\frac{\left(\frac{d^2y}{dx^2}\right)^3}{\frac{d^3y}{dx^3}} + \frac{d^3y}{dx^3} = x^2 - 1$, then

(a) $m = 3, n = 3$ (b) $m = 3, n = 2$
(c) $m = 3, n = 5$ (d) $m = 3, n = 1$

2. The order of the differential equation satisfying $\sqrt{1-x^2} + \sqrt{1-y^2} = a(x-y)$ is

(a) 1 (b) 2
(c) 3 (d) None of these

3. The solution of $\frac{dy}{dx} - y = 1$, $y(0) = 1$ is given by

(a) $xy = -e^x$ (b) $xy = -e^{-x}$
(c) $xy = -1$ (d) $y = 2e^x - 1$

4. The differential equation $y\frac{dy}{dx} + x = C$ represents

(a) family of hyperbolas (b) family of parabolas
(c) family of ellipses (d) family of circles

5. The integrating factor of differential equation $\frac{dy}{dx} + y\tan x - \sec x = 0$ is

(a) $\cos x$ (b) $\sec x$ (c) $e^{\cos x}$ (d) $e^{\sec x}$

2 Marks Questions

6. State whether $y = e^{-x}(x+a)$ is a solution of differential equation $\frac{dy}{dx} + y = e^{-x}$.

7. Show that the function $y = (A + Bx)\,e^{3x}$ is a solution of the equation $\frac{d^2y}{dx^2} - 6\frac{dy}{dx} + 9y = 0$.

3/4 Marks Questions

8. Solve the differential equation $\frac{dy}{dx} = e^{x-y} + x^2e^{-y}$.

9. Solve the differential equation $y + x\frac{dy}{dx} = x - y\frac{dy}{dx}$.

10. Solve the differential equation $(y + 3x^2)\frac{dx}{dy} = x$.

5/6 Marks Questions

11. Solve the equation $x\,dy - y\,dx = \sqrt{x^2 + y^2}\,dx$.

12. Find the particular solution of the differential equation $x(x^2-1)\frac{dy}{dx} = 1$, $y = 0$ when $x = 2$.

13. Solve the differential equation $x\frac{dy}{dx} = y - x\tan\left(\frac{y}{x}\right)$.

14. Solve the differential equation $(1 + x^2)\frac{dy}{dx} + y = \tan^{-1} x$.

15. Solve $\frac{dy}{dx} = \cos(x+y) + \sin(x+y)$.

16. Solve the differential equation $\frac{dy}{dx} - 3y\cot x = \sin 2x$, given $y = 2$, when $x = \frac{\pi}{2}$.

17. Solve the differential equation $\left[y - x\cos\left(\frac{y}{x}\right)\right]dy + \left[y\cos\left(\frac{y}{x}\right) - 2x\sin\left(\frac{y}{x}\right)\right]dx = 0$.

Answers

1. (b) **2.** (a) **3.** (d)
4. (d) **5.** (b) **6.** Yes

8. $e^y = e^x + \frac{x^3}{3} + c$ **9.** $y^2 + 2xy - x^2 = C$

10. $y = 3x^2 + Cx$ **11.** $y + \sqrt{x^2 + y^2} = Cx^2$

12. $y = \frac{1}{2}\log\left|\frac{x^2-1}{x^2}\right| + \log\frac{2}{\sqrt{3}}$

13. $x\sin\frac{y}{x} = C$

14. $y = \tan^{-1} x - 1 + Ce^{-\tan^{-1} x}$

15. $\log\left|1 + \tan\left(\frac{x+y}{2}\right)\right| = x + c$

16. $y = -2\sin^2 x + 4\sin^3 x$

17. $y^2 - 2x^2\sin\left(\frac{y}{x}\right) = C$

09

Probability

TREND ANALYSIS 3 YEARS

Average No. of Questions Across all Sets

Topic		Types of Questions	2024	2023	2020
TOPIC 01	Probability	1 Mark	1	1	—
		2 Marks	1	1	2
		3/4 Marks	—	1	1
		5/6 Marks	—	—	—
TOPIC 02	Conditional Probability with Baye's Theorem	1 Mark	—	—	—
		2 Marks	—	—	—
		3/4 Marks	1	1	—
		5/6 Marks	—	—	—
TOPIC 03	Random Variable and Probability Distribution	1 Mark	—	—	—
		2 Marks	—	—	—
		3/4 Marks	—	1	—
		5/6 Marks	1	—	—

TOPIC 1

Probability

Before understanding probability, we should understand some basic terms, which are discussed below

- **Experiment** When we conduct a trial to obtain some statistical information, it is called an experiment.
- **Deterministic Experiment** Sometime result is unique. For example, if any quadrilateral is given then without knowing the four angles, we can definitely say that the sum of their measure is 360°. Such experiments are called deterministic experiments.
- **Random Experiment** Sometimes the outcomes may not be unique is called random experiment such as tossing a coin.
- **Sample space** The collection of all possible outcomes of a random experiment is called sample space. it is denoted by S.

e.g. when we toss a coin once, it may come up in either of two ways -head and tail. So, there are two possible outcomes of the random experiment. If we denoted by H and T, then sample space $(S) = \{H,T\}$

- **Events** The possible outcomes of a trial/experiment are called events. Events are generally denoted by capital letters A, B, C, etc.
- **Occurrence of an Event** An event associated to a random experiment is said to occur, if anyone of the elementary events associated to it happens.

- **Simple Event** A single possible outcome of an experiment is called simple event.
- **Compound Event** A combined occurrence of two or more simple events is called compound event.
- **Sure Event** The whole sample space S is also a subset of S and hence it represents a sure event.
  e.g. when we throw a die, then sample space $(S) = \{1, 2, 3, 4, 5, 6\}$, and then getting a number less than 7 is a sure event.
- **Impossible Event** The empty set ϕ is also a subset of the sample space (S) and it represents an impossible event.
  e.g. when we throw a die, getting a number higher than 6 is an impossible event.
- **Equally Likely Events** The events are said to be equally likely, if the chance of happening of each event is equal or same.
- **Mutually Exclusive Events** Two events are said to be mutually exclusive when they cannot happen simultaneously in a single trial.
- **Exhaustive Events** A set of events is said to be exhaustive, if the performance of the experiment always results in occurrence of atleast one of them.
- **Complementary Events** Let there be two events A and B, then A is called the complementary event of B and B is called the complementary event of A, if A and B are mutually exclusive and exhaustive events. It is denoted by A' or $\overline{A}$.
- **Independent Events** Two events are said to be independent if the occurrence of one event does not affect the occurrence of the other event.
- **Dependent Events** Two events are said to be dependent when the occurrence of one affects the occurrence of the other events.
- **Conditional Events** Dependent event that occurs only if another event on which it depends has occured.

Algebra of Events

(i) **The Event 'A or B'** In set theory, union of two sets A and B denoted by $A \cup B$ contains all those elements which are either in A or in B or in both.

(ii) **The Event 'A and B'** In set theory, intersection of two sets A and B denoted by $A \cap B$ contains all those elements which are common to both A and B.

(iii) **The Event 'A but not B'** In set theory, $A - B$ is the set of all those elements which are in A but not in B.

$$\therefore \quad A - B = A \cap B'$$

Mathematical Definition of Probability

According to the Laplace, "Probability is the ratio of the favourable cases to the total number of equally likely cases."

$$P(A) = p = \frac{\text{Number of favourable cases}}{\text{Total number of equally likely cases}} = \frac{m}{n}$$

where, $P(A)$ = Probability of occurrence of an event A

m = Number of favourable cases

n = Total number of equally likely cases

If $\overline{A}$ is the complement event of A, then

$$P(A) + P(\overline{A}) = 1$$

Similarly, $P(\overline{A}) = 1 - P(A) = 1 - \frac{m}{n}$

where $P(\overline{A}) = q$ = Probability of non-occurrence of an event A.

From the above definition, it is clear that the sum of the probability of happening of an event called **success** (p) and the probability of non-happening of an event called **failure** (q) is always one, i.e. $p + q = 1$.

The values of p and q lie from 0 to 1. i.e. $0 \le p \le 1$ and $0 \le q \le 1$. If an event can happen in m ways and fail to happen in n ways, then probability of **success** is $\frac{m}{m+n}$ and that of its **failure** to happen is $\frac{n}{m+n}$.

The probability of an event always lies from 0 to 1, i.e. $0 \le p \le 1$. If the event cannot take place, i.e. impossible event, then its probability will be zero, i.e. $P(E) = 0$ and if the event is sure to occur, then its probability will be one i.e. $P(E) = 1$.

Odds in Favour/Against

Probabilities are often expressed in terms of 'odds'. Suppose an outcome A occurs m times out of n equally likely outcomes in an experiment.

$$\text{Odds in favour of } A = \frac{\text{Number of times } A \text{ occurs}}{\text{Number of times } A \text{ does not occur}} = \frac{m}{n-m}$$

$$\text{and odds in against } A = \frac{\text{Number of times } A \text{ does not occur}}{\text{Number of times } A \text{ occurs}} = \frac{n-m}{m}$$

Addition Law of Probability

Addition law of probability is given below:

Addition Law for not Mutually Exclusive Events

If A and B are not mutually exclusive events, then the probability of the occurrence of either A or B or both is equal to the probability that event A occurs, plus the probability that event B occurs minus the probability that events common to both A and B occur.

$$P(A \text{ or } B \text{ or both}) = P(A) + P(B) - P(AB)$$

Generalisation The law can be extended to three or more not mutually exclusive events. If A, B and C are not mutually exclusive events, then

$$P(\text{Either } A \text{ or } B \text{ or } C) = P(A) + P(B) + P(C) - P(AB) - P(AC) - P(BC) + P(ABC)$$

Addition Law for Mutually Exclusive Events

If A and B are two mutually exclusive events, then the probability of occurrence of either A or B is the sum of the individual probabilities of A and B.

Symbolically,

$$P(A \text{ or } B) = P(A \cup B) = P(A) + P(B)$$

Generalisation The law can be extended to three or more mutually exclusive events. If A, B and C are three mutually exclusive events, then

$$P(A \text{ or } B \text{ or} C) = P(A \cup B \cup C) = P(A) + P(B) + P(C)$$

NOTE $P(AB) = P(A \cap B) = P(A \text{ and } B)$,

$P(ABC) = P(A \cap B \cap C) = P(A \text{ and } B \text{ and } C)$

Important Results

(i) If A and B are two events associated to a random experiment, then

$P(A \cap B) \le P(A) \le P(A \cup B) \le P(A) + P(B)$

(ii) If A and B are two events associated with a random experiment, then

(a) $P(\bar{A} \cap B) = P(B) - P(A \cap B)$

(b) $P(A \cap \bar{B}) = P(A) - P(A \cap B)$

(c) $P[(A \cap \bar{B}) \cup (\bar{A} \cap B)]$

$= P(A) + P(B) - 2P(A \cap B)$

(d) $P(\bar{A} \cap \bar{B}) = 1 - P(A \cup B)$

(e) $P(\bar{A} \cup \bar{B}) = 1 - P(A \cap B)$

(f) $P(A) = P(A \cap B) + P(A \cap \bar{B})$

(g) $P(B) = P(A \cap B) + P(B \cap \bar{A})$

(iii) (a) P (exactly one of A, B occurs)

$= P(A) + P(B) - 2P(A \cap B)$

$= P(A \cup B) - P(A \cap B)$

(b) P (neither A nor B) $= P(\bar{A} \cap \bar{B}) = 1 - P(A \cup B)$

(iv) P (exactly one of A, B, C occurs)

$= P(A) + P(B) + P(C) - 2P(A \cap B) + 3P(A \cap B \cap C) - 2P(B \cap C) - 2P(A \cap C)$

(v) (a) $P(A \cup \bar{A}) = P(S)$

(b) $P(\phi) = 0$

Multiplication Law of Probability

Multiplication law of probability is given below.

Multiplication Law for Independent Events

Multiplication law states that if A and B are two independent events, then the probability of the simultaneous occurrence of A and B is equal to the product of their individual probabilities.

Symbolically,

$$P(A \cap B) = P(AB) = P(A) \times P(B)$$

Generalisation

The law can be extended to three or more independent events. If A, B and C are three independent events, then

$$P(A \cap B \cap C) = P(ABC) = P(A) \times P(B) \times P(C)$$

NOTE If A and B are independent events, then

(i) A' and B' are also independent events.

(ii) A' and B are also independent events.

(iii) A and B' are also independent events.

Probability of Happening of Atleast One Event in Case of *n* Independent Events

If we are given n independent events $A_1, A_2, A_3, \ldots, A_n$ with respective probabilities of happening as $p_1, p_2, p_3, \ldots, p_n$, then the probability of happening of atleast one of independent events $A_1, A_2, A_3, \cdots, A_n$ is given by

P (happening of atleast one of the events)

$= 1 - P$ (happening of none of the events)

$= 1 - [(1 - p_1) \cdot (1 - p_2) \cdot (1 - p_3) \ldots (1 - p_n)]$

PYQs Previous Years Questions

1 Mark Questions

1. Teena is practising for an upcoming Rifle Shooting tournament. The probability of her shooting the target in the 1st, 2nd, 3rd and 4th shots are 0.4, 0.3, 0.2 and 0.1, respectively. Find the probability of atleast one shot of Teena hitting the target. **ISC 2024**

2. Bhuvan is preparing chapati and curry for a dinner party at his home.
Let event $A =$ Bhuvan prepares chapati well.
Let event $B =$ Bhuvan cooks curry well.
Given, $P(A) = 0.40$, $P(B) = 0.30$ and P (A and B) $= 0.20$
Which one of the following is true about the events A and B? **ISC Specimen 2024**
(a) They are mutually exclusive but not independent.
(b) They are independent but not mutually exclusive.
(c) They are both mutually exclusive and independent.
(d) They are neither mutually exclusive nor independent.

3. A company has estimated that the probabilities of success for three products introduced in the market are 1/3, 2/5 and 2/3, respectively. Assuming independence, find the probability that at least one product is successful. **ISC Specimen 2024**

4. Dobleron, a chocolate is known for its distinctive shape and its taste. The quality assurance team of the brand undertakes quality test in two steps
   - **Step I** 30 out of every 990 chocolate bars are randomly picked for physical examination, where the shape of the bar is examined.
   - **Step II** For every 30 chocolate bars whose shape is examined, 1 chocolate bar is randomly picked for chemical examination, where the composition and taste of the chocolate is examined.

   If one chocolate bar is randomly picked out of 990 bars, what is the probability that it was not chemically examined, provided it was physically examined? **ISC Specimen 2024**

5. A bag contains 19 tickets, numbered from 1 to 19. Two tickets are drawn randomly in succession with replacement. Find the probability that both tickets drawn are even numbers. **ISC 2023**

6. A speaks truth in 60% of cases and B speaks truth in 90% of the cases. In what percentage of cases are they likely to contradict each other in stating the same fact? **ISC Specimen 2023**

7. A bag contains 9 red, 7 white and 4 black balls. If two balls are drawn at random without replacement, the probability that both balls are red will be **ISC Specimen Sem-II 2022**
(a) $\frac{11}{95}$ (b) $\frac{15}{95}$ (c) $\frac{18}{95}$ (d) $\frac{18}{23}$

8. Two cards are drawn out randomly from a pack of 52 cards one after the other, without replacement. The probability of first card being a king and second card not being a king is **ISC Specimen Sem-II 2022**
(a) $\frac{48}{663}$ (b) $\frac{24}{663}$ (c) $\frac{12}{663}$ (d) $\frac{4}{663}$

9. If two balls are drawn from a bag containing 3 white, 4 black and 5 red balls. Then, the probability that the drawn balls are of different colours is **ISC Specimen Sem-II 2022**
(a) $\frac{1}{66}$ (b) $\frac{3}{66}$ (c) $\frac{19}{66}$ (d) $\frac{47}{66}$

10. A and B appeared for an interview for two vacancies. The probability of A's selection is $\frac{4}{5}$ and B's selection is $\frac{1}{3}$. Find the probability that none of them will be selected. **ISC Specimen 2021**

11. If A and B are independent events such that $P(A) = \frac{1}{4}$ and $P(B) = \frac{2}{3}$. Find $P(A \cap B)$. **ISC Specimen 2021**

2 Marks Questions

12. Evaluate $P(A \cup B)$, if $2P(A) = P(B) = \frac{5}{13}$ and $P\left(\frac{A}{B}\right) = \frac{2}{3}$. **ISC 2024**

13. The probability of the event A occurring is $\frac{1}{3}$ and of the event B occurring is $\frac{1}{2}$. If A and B are independent events, then find the probability of neither A nor B occurring. **ISC 2023**

14. A bag contains 5 white, 7 red and 4 black balls. If four balls are drawn one by one with replacement, what is the probability that none is white? **ISC 2020**

15. Let A and B be two events such that

$P(A)=\frac{1}{2}, P(B)=p$ and $P(A \cup B)=\frac{3}{5}$

Find p, if A and B are independent events. **ISC 2020**

16. If events A and B are independent, such that $P(A)=\frac{3}{5}$ and $P(B)=\frac{2}{3}$, then find $P(A \cup B)$. **ISC 2019**

17. In a race, the probabilities of A and B winning the race are $\frac{1}{3}$ and $\frac{1}{6}$, respectively. Find the probability of neither of them winning the race. **ISC 2018**

18. Given that the events A and B are such that $P(A)=\frac{1}{2}$, $P(A \cup B)=\frac{3}{5}$ and $P(B)=k$. Find k, if

(a) A and B are mutually exclusive.

(b) A and B are independent. **ISC Specimen 2018**

3/4 Marks Questions

19. A problem in Mathematics is given to three students A, B and C. Their chances of solving the problem are $\frac{1}{2}, \frac{1}{3}$ and $\frac{1}{4}$, respectively. Find the probability that

(a) exactly two students will solve the problem.

(b) atleast two of them will solve the problem. **ISC 2023**

20. A candidate takes three tests in succession and the probability of passing the first test is $\frac{1}{2}$. The probability of passing each succeeding test is $\frac{1}{2}$ or $\frac{1}{4}$ depending on whether he passes or fails in the preceding one. The candidate is selected, if he passes at least two tests. Find the probability that the candidate is selected. **ISC Specimen 2023**

21. Two horses are considered for race. The probability of selection of first horse is $\frac{1}{5}$ and that of second is $\frac{2}{3}$.

Find the probability that **ISC Specimen Sem-II 2022**

(i) both will be selected

(ii) only one of them will be selected

(iii) none of them will be selected

(iv) at least one of them will be selected

22. A bag contains 3 red and 4 white balls and another bag contains 2 red and 3 white balls. If one ball is drawn from the first bag and 2 balls are drawn from the second bag, then find the probability that all three balls are of the same colour. **ISC Specimen Sem-II 2022**

23. Bag A contains 4 white balls and 3 black balls, while Bag B contains 3 white balls and 5 black balls. Two balls are drawn from Bag A and placed in Bag B. Then, what is the probability of drawing a white ball from Bag B. **ISC Specimen 2021**

24. Three persons A, B and C shoot to hit a target. Their probabilities of hitting the target $\frac{5}{6}, \frac{4}{5}$ and $\frac{3}{4}$, respectively. Find the probability that **ISC 2020**

(i) exactly two persons hit the target.

(ii) atleast one person hits the target.

25. A speaks truth in 60% of the cases, while B in 40% of the cases. In what percent of cases are they likely to contradict each other in stating the same fact? **ISC 2018**

26. A problem is given to three students whose chances of solving it are $\frac{1}{4}, \frac{1}{5}$ and $\frac{1}{3}$, respectively. Find the probability that the problem is solved. **ISC 2017, 03**

27. A pair of dice is thrown. What is the probability of getting an even number on the first die or a total of 8? **ISC 2016**

28. A pair of dice is thrown. If the two numbers appearing on them are different, find the probability that the sum of the numbers appearing is 6. **ISC 2016**

29. A card is drawn from a well shuffled pack of playing cards. What is the probability that it is either a spade or an ace or both? **ISC 2015**

30. A bag contains 20 balls numbered 1 to 20. One ball is drawn at random from the bag. What is the probability that the ball drawn is marked with a number which is multiple of 3 or 4? **ISC 2014**

31. If two balls are drawn from a bag containing three red balls and four blue balls, find the probability that

(i) they are of the same colour.

(ii) they are of different colours. **ISC 2013**

32. Three persons A, B and C shoot to hit a target. If in trials A hits the target 4 times in 5 shots, B hits 3 times in 4 shots and C hits 2 times in 3 trials. Find the probability that

(i) exactly two persons hit the target.

(ii) atleast two persons hit the target. **ISC 2012**

33. A word consists of 9 different alphabets, in which there are 4 consonants and 5 vowels. Three alphabets are chosen at random. What is the probability that more than one vowel will be selected? **ISC 2011**

34. A fair die is thrown once. What is the probability that either an even number or a number greater than three will turn up? **ISC 2010**

35. Two horses are considered for a race. The probability of selection of the first horse is 1 / 4 and that of the second is 1/3. What is the probability that

(i) both of them will be selected?
(ii) only one of them will be selected?
(iii) none of them will be selected? **ISC 2009**

> **KEY CONCEPT**
>
> (a) Use the concept of independent events.
> i.e. $P(A \cap B) = P(A)P(B)$ etc.
>
> (b) Futher use the formula
> (i) $P(AB) = P(A)P(B)$
> (ii) $P(A\bar{B}) + P(\bar{A}B) = P(A)P(\bar{B}) + P(\bar{A})P(B)$
> (iii) $P(\overline{AB}) = P(\bar{A})P(\bar{B})$, where A and B are the selection of Ist and IInd horse respectively.

36. In a single throw of two dice, find the probability of getting a total of atmost 9. **ISC 2008**

37. Kamal and Monica appear for an interview for two vacancies. The probability of Kamal's selection is 1/3 and that of Monica's selection is 1/5. Find the probability that only one of them will be selected. **ISC 2007**

38. The probability of A, B and C solving a problem are $\frac{1}{3}, \frac{2}{7}$ and $\frac{3}{8}$, respectively. If all try and solve the problem simultaneously, find the probability that only one of them will solve it. **ISC 2006**

39. Tickets numbered from 1 to 20 are mixed up together and then a ticket is drawn at random. What is the probability that the ticket has a number which is a multiple of 3 or 7? **ISC 2005**

40. What is the probability that a leap year has 53 Sunday? **ISC 2004**

41. A bag has 4 red and 5 black, a second bag has 3 red and 7 black balls. One ball is drawn from first bag and two balls are drawn from second bag. Find the probability that two balls are black and one is red. **ISC 2004**

42. One number is chosen at random from the numbers 1 to 21. Find the probability that it may be a prime number. **ISC 2003**

43. The probability that a contractor will get a plumbing contract is $\frac{2}{3}$ and electric contract is $\frac{4}{9}$.
If the probability of getting atleast one contract is $\frac{4}{5}$, find the probability that he will get both the contracts. **ISC 2003**

44. There are 10 persons who are to be seated together around a circular table. Find the probability that two particular person will always sit together. **ISC 2002**

> **KEY CONCEPT**
>
> Use the concept of circular arrangement i.e. if n peoples are to be seated in a circular arrangement, then there are $(n-1)!$ ways to arrange them. Further find the required probability.

45. A bag contains 20 balls marked 1 to 20. One ball is drawn at random from the bag. What is the probability that the ball drawn is marked with a number which is a multiple of 5 or 7? **ISC 2001**

5/6 Marks Questions

46. A, B and C throw a die one after the other in the same order till one of them gets a '6' and wins the game. Find their respective probability of winning, if A starts the game. **ISC Specimen 2018**

47. In a class of 60 students, 30 opted for Mathematics, 32 opted for Biology and 24 opted for both Mathematics and Biology. If one of these students is selected at random, find the probability that **ISC 2017**

(i) the student opted for Mathematics or Biology.
(ii) the student has opted neither Mathematics nor Biology.
(iii) the student has opted Mathematics but not Biology.

48. An urn contains 10 white and 3 black balls while another urn contains 3 white and 5 black balls. Two balls are drawn from the first urn and put into the second urn and then a ball is drawn from the second urn. Find the probability that the ball drawn from the second urn is a white ball. **ISC 2016**

49. A committee of 4 persons has to be chosen from 8 boys and 6 girls, consisting of atleast one girl. Find the probability that the committee consists of more girls than boys. **ISC 2016**

50. Three persons A, B and C shoot to hit a target. If A hits the target four times in five trials. B hits it three times in four trials and C hits it two times in three trials, find the probability that

(i) exactly two persons hit the target.
(ii) atleast two persons hit the target.
(iii) none hit the target. **ISC 2015**

51. A bag contains 5 white and 4 black balls and another bag contains 7 white and 9 black balls. A ball is drawn from the first bag and two balls drawn from the second bag. What is the probability of drawing one white and two black balls? **ISC 2014**

52. Bag A contains three red and four white balls; bag B contains two red and three white balls. If one ball is drawn from bag A and two balls from bag B, find the probability that

(i) one ball is red and two balls are white.

(ii) all the three balls are of the same colour. **ISC 2013**

53. Three persons, Aman, Bipin and Mohan attempt a Mathematics problem independently. The odds in favour of Aman and Mohan solving the problem are 3 : 2 and 4 : 1, respectively and the odds against Bipin solving the problem are 2 : 1. Find **ISC 2013**

(i) the probability that all the three persons will solve the problem.

(ii) the probability that problem will be solved.

> **KEY CONCEPT**
>
> Use the concept of odds in favour
>
> $= \dfrac{\text{Number of times event occurs}}{\text{Number of times event does not occurs}}$

54. A box contains 30 bolts and 40 nuts. Half of the bolts and half of the nuts are rusted. If two items are drawn at random from the box, then what is the probability that either both are rusted or both are bolts? **ISC 2012**

55. A bag contains 8 red and 5 white balls. Two successive draws of 3 balls are made at random from the bag without replacements. Find the probability that the first draw yields 3 white balls and the second draw 3 red balls. **ISC 2012**

56. Aman and Bhuwan throw a pair of dice alternatively. In order to win, they have to get a sum of 8. Find their respective probabilities of winning, if Aman starts the game. **ISC 2011**

57. A purse contains 4 silver and 5 copper coins. A second purse contains 3 silver and 7 copper coins. If a coin is taken out at random from one of the purses, then what is the probability that it is a copper coin? **ISC 2011**

> **KEY CONCEPT**
>
> Firstly find the probability of bags and then find the probability of coins.

58. Akhil and Vijay appear for an interview for two vacancies. The probability of Akhil's selection is $\frac{1}{4}$ and Vijay's selection is $\frac{2}{3}$. Find the probability that only one of them will be selected. **ISC 2010**

Explanations

1. Given probability of her shooting the target in

$P(\text{1st shot}) = 0.4$

$P(\text{2nd shot}) = 0.3$

$P(\text{3rd shot}) = 0.2$

and $P(\text{4th shot}) = 0.1$

$\therefore$ The probability of atleast one shot of Teena hit the target

$= 1 -$ Probability of none of the shot hitting the target

$= 1 - [(1-0.4)(1-0.3)(1-0.2)(1-0.1)]$

$= 1 - (0.6 \times 0.7 \times 0.8 \times 0.9)$

$= 1 - 0.3024$

$= 0.6976$

2. (d) Here, $P(A) \cdot P(B) = 0.4 \times 0.3 = 0.12 \neq P(A \cap B)$

$\therefore$ A and B are not independent and $P(A \cap B) \neq 0$

$\therefore$ A and B are not mutually exclusive .

3. Let $P(A) = \frac{1}{3}, P(B) = \frac{2}{5}$ and $P(C) = \frac{2}{3}$

$\therefore$ P (atleast one product is successful)

$= 1 - P$ (none product is successful)

$= 1 - \left(\frac{2}{3} \times \frac{2}{5} \times \frac{1}{3}\right) = 1 - \frac{4}{45} = \frac{41}{45}$

4. To find the probability that a chocolate bar was not chemically examined given that it was physically examined, we need to calculate the conditional probability.

Let A : Event that a chocolate bar is physically examined.

B : Event that a chocolate bar is chemically examined.

We need to find $P\left(\frac{B'}{A}\right)$, which represents the probability of B' (not B) given A.

According to the problem statement, 30 out of every 990 chocolate bars and randomly picked for physical examination.

Then, the probability of a chocolate bar being physically examined is

$$P(A)=\frac{30}{990}=\frac{1}{33}$$

In Step II For every 30 chocolate bars whose shape is examined (A), the composition and taste of the chocolate is examined (B). This indicates that all the chocolate bars that pass Step I (physically examined) also go through Step II (chemically examined).

Therefore, $P\left(\frac{B}{A}\right)=\frac{1}{30}$

Now, we calculate the probability that a chocolate bar was not chemically examined given that it was physically examined.

$$P\left(\frac{B'}{A}\right)=1-P\left(\frac{B}{A}\right)=1-\frac{1}{30}=\frac{29}{30}$$

5. There are 9 even number from 1 to 19.

Probability of both tickets drawn are even numbers

$$=\frac{9}{19}\times\frac{9}{19}=\frac{81}{361}$$

6. Let $E=$ The event of A speaking truth

and $F=$ The event of B speaking truth.

$\therefore\ P(E)=\frac{60}{100}=\frac{6}{10}$ and $P(F)=\frac{90}{100}=\frac{9}{10}$

Probability of A and B contradicting each other $P(E\overline{F}$ or $\overline{F}E)$

$$P(E\overline{F})+P(\overline{E}F)=P(E)P(\overline{F})+P(\overline{E})P(F)$$

$$=P(E)(1-P(F))+(1-P(E))P(F)$$

$$=\frac{6}{10}\left(1-\frac{9}{10}\right)+\left(1-\frac{6}{10}\right)\frac{9}{10}$$

$$=\frac{6}{10}\times\frac{1}{10}+\frac{4}{10}\times\frac{9}{10}=\frac{6+36}{100}=\frac{42}{100}$$

$\therefore$ A and B are likely to contradicts each other in 42% cases.

7. (c) There are 20 balls in the bag

Total possible outcomes of getting two balls

$$={}^{20}C_2=190$$

Favourable number of outcomes of getting both red balls $={}^{9}C_2=36$

So, required probability $=\frac{36}{190}=\frac{18}{95}$

8. (a) Required probability

$=P$ (first cards being a king and second card not being a king)

$$=\frac{^{4}C_1}{^{52}C_1}\times\frac{^{48}C_1}{^{51}C_1}$$

$$=\frac{4}{52}\times\frac{48}{51}=\frac{48}{663}$$

9. (d) There are 3 white, 4 black and 5 red balls in a bag.

$\therefore$ Total number of balls $=3+4+5=12$

$\therefore$ Required Probability

$=P$ (two drawn balls are of different colours)

$$=\frac{(^{3}C_1\times{}^{4}C_1\times{}^{5}C_0)}{^{12}C_2}+\frac{(^{3}C_1\times{}^{5}C_1\times{}^{4}C_0)}{^{12}C_2}+\frac{(^{4}C_1\times{}^{5}C_1\times{}^{3}C_0)}{^{12}C_2}$$

$$=\frac{3\times4\times1}{66}+\frac{3\times5\times1}{66}+\frac{4\times5\times1}{66}$$

$$=\frac{12}{66}+\frac{15}{66}+\frac{20}{66}=\frac{47}{66}$$

10. Given that, $P(A)=\frac{4}{5}$ and $P(B)=\frac{1}{3}$

So, $P(\overline{A})=\frac{1}{5}$ and $P(\overline{B})=\frac{2}{3}$

Now, probability that none is selected

$$=P(\overline{A}\cap\overline{B})=P(\overline{A})\times P(\overline{B})=\left(\frac{1}{5}\right)\times\left(\frac{2}{3}\right)=\frac{2}{15}$$

11. Given, $P(A)=\frac{1}{4}$ and $P(B)=\frac{2}{3}$

Since, A and B are independent events.

So, $P(A\cap B)=P(A)\cdot P(B)=\left(\frac{1}{4}\right)\cdot\left(\frac{2}{3}\right)=\frac{1}{6}$

12. Given, $2P(A)=P(B)=\frac{5}{13}$

and $P\left(\frac{A}{B}\right)=\frac{2}{5}$

We know that

$$P\left(\frac{A}{B}\right)=\frac{P(A\cap B)}{P(B)}$$

$$\Rightarrow\quad \frac{2}{5}=\frac{P(A\cap B)}{5/13}$$

$$\Rightarrow\quad P(A\cap B)=\frac{2}{13}$$

$$\therefore \quad P(A \cup B) = P(A) + P(B) - P(A \cap B)$$
$$= P(A) + 2P(A) - P(A \cap B)$$
$$= 3P(A) - P(A \cap B)$$
$$= \frac{15}{26} - \frac{2}{13} = \frac{11}{26}$$

Hence, $P(A \cup B) = \frac{11}{26}$

13. Given, $P(A) = \frac{1}{3}$ and $P(B) = \frac{1}{2}$,

where A and B are independent events.

$$\therefore P(A \cap B) = P(A) \cdot P(B) = \frac{1}{3} \times \frac{1}{2} = \frac{1}{6}$$

$$\therefore P(A \cup B)' = 1 - P(A \cup B)$$
$$= 1 - (P(A) + P(B) - P(A \cap B))$$
$$= 1 - \frac{1}{3} - \frac{1}{2} + \frac{1}{6} = \frac{6-2-3+1}{6} = \frac{2}{6} = \frac{1}{3}$$

14. There are 5 white, 7 red and 4 black balls in a bag.

$\therefore$ Total number of balls $= 5 + 7 + 4 = 16$

The probability of four balls are drawn with replacement that none is white $= \frac{11}{16} \times \frac{11}{16} \times \frac{11}{16} \times \frac{11}{16}$

$$= \left(\frac{11}{16}\right)^4$$

15. Given, $P(A) = \frac{1}{2}$, $P(B) = p$ and $P(A \cup B) = \frac{3}{5}$,

where A and B are independent events.

$$\therefore P(A \cap B) = P(A) \times P(B) = \frac{1}{2} \times p = \frac{p}{2}$$

We know that

$$P(A \cup B) = P(A) + P(B) - P(A \cap B)$$
$$\Rightarrow \quad \frac{3}{5} = \frac{1}{2} + p - \frac{p}{2} \Rightarrow \frac{p}{2} = \frac{3}{5} - \frac{1}{2}$$
$$\Rightarrow \quad \frac{p}{2} = \frac{1}{10} \Rightarrow p = \frac{1}{5}$$

16. Given, $P(A) = \frac{3}{5}$ and $P(B) = \frac{2}{3}$

Since, events A and B are independent.

Therefore, $P(A \cap B) = P(A)P(B)$

Now, $\quad P(A \cup B) = P(A) + P(B) - P(A \cap B)$

$$= \frac{3}{5} + \frac{2}{3} - \frac{3}{5} \times \frac{2}{3} = \frac{9+10-6}{15} = \frac{13}{15}$$

Concept Enhancer If two events A and B are independent, then $P(A \cap B) = P(A) \times P(B)$

17. Given, $P(A) = \frac{1}{3}$ and $P(B) = \frac{1}{6}$

So, $\quad P(A') = 1 - \frac{1}{3} = \frac{2}{3}$ and $P(B') = 1 - \frac{1}{6} = \frac{5}{6}$

$\therefore$ Required probability $= P(A') \times P(B') = \frac{2}{3} \times \frac{5}{6} = \frac{5}{9}$

18. Given, $P(A) = \frac{1}{2}$, $P(A \cup B) = \frac{3}{5}$ and $P(B) = k$

(a) Since, A and B are mutually exclusive events.

$\therefore P(A \cap B) = 0$

Now, $P(A \cup B) = P(A) + P(B) - P(A \cap B)$

$$\Rightarrow \quad \frac{3}{5} = \frac{1}{2} + k \Rightarrow k = \frac{3}{5} - \frac{1}{2} = \frac{1}{10}$$

(b) Since, A and B are independent events.

$\therefore \quad P(A \cap B) = P(A) \times P(B)$

Now, $\quad P(A \cup B) = P(A) + P(B) - P(A \cap B)$

$$\Rightarrow \quad \frac{3}{5} = \frac{1}{2} + k - \frac{1}{2}k$$
$$\Rightarrow \quad \frac{1}{2}k = \frac{3}{5} - \frac{1}{2} = \frac{1}{10} \Rightarrow k = \frac{1}{5}$$

19. Consider the events

$A =$ Problem solved by A

$B =$ Problem solved by B

$C =$ Problem solved by C

Given, $P(A) = \frac{1}{2}$, $P(B) = \frac{1}{3}$, $P(C) = \frac{1}{4}$

So, $\quad P(\bar{A}) = \frac{1}{2}$, $P(\bar{B}) = \frac{2}{3}$, $P(\bar{C}) = \frac{3}{4}$

(a) P(exactly two students will solve the problem)

$$= P(AB\bar{C}) + P(A\bar{B}C) + P(\bar{A}BC)$$
$$= P(A) \times P(B) \times P(\bar{C}) + P(A) \times P(\bar{B}) \times P(C) + P(\bar{A}) \times P(B) \times P(C)$$
$$= \frac{1}{2} \times \frac{1}{3} \times \frac{3}{4} + \frac{1}{2} \times \frac{2}{3} \times \frac{1}{4} + \frac{1}{2} \times \frac{1}{3} \times \frac{1}{4}$$
$$= \frac{3+2+1}{24} = \frac{6}{24} = \frac{1}{4}$$

(b) P (atleast two of them will solve the problem)

$$= P(AB\bar{C}) + P(A\bar{B}C) + P(\bar{A}BC) + P(ABC)$$
$$= P(A) \times P(B) \times P(\bar{C}) + P(A) \times P(\bar{B}) \times P(C) + P(\bar{A}) \times P(B) \times P(C) + P(A) \times P(B) \times P(C)$$
$$= \frac{1}{2} \times \frac{1}{3} \times \frac{3}{4} + \frac{1}{2} \times \frac{2}{3} \times \frac{1}{4} + \frac{1}{2} \times \frac{1}{3} \times \frac{1}{4} + \frac{1}{2} \times \frac{1}{3} \times \frac{1}{4}$$
$$= \frac{3+2+1+1}{24} = \frac{7}{24}$$

20. Candidate will be selected in following cases

I. PPP [P means passed]

II. PPF [F means failed]

III. PFP

IV. FPP

$$\therefore \quad P(\text{I})=\frac{1}{2}\cdot\frac{1}{2}\cdot\frac{1}{2}=\left(\frac{1}{2}\right)^3=\frac{1}{8},$$

$$P(\text{II})=\frac{1}{2}\times\frac{1}{2}\times\left(1-\frac{1}{2}\right)=\frac{1}{8},$$

$$P(\text{III})=\frac{1}{2}\times\left(1-\frac{1}{2}\right)\times\frac{1}{4}=\frac{1}{16},$$

$$\text{and } P(\text{IV})=\left(1-\frac{1}{2}\right)\times\frac{1}{4}\times\frac{1}{2}=\frac{1}{16}$$

$$\therefore \text{ Probability of success}=\frac{1}{8}+\frac{1}{8}+\frac{1}{16}+\frac{1}{16}$$

$$=\frac{2+2+1+1}{16}=\frac{6}{16}=\frac{3}{8}$$

21. Let A and B be the events of selecting first and second horse, respectively.

$$\therefore\ P(A)=\frac{1}{5} \text{ and } P(B)=\frac{2}{3}$$

(i) P (both will be selected)

$$=P(AB)=P(A)\,P(B)$$

[since, A and B are independent events]

$$=\frac{1}{5}\times\frac{2}{3}=\frac{2}{15}$$

(ii) P (only one of them will be selected)

$$=P(A\overline{B})+P(\overline{A}B)$$

$$=P(A)\,P(\overline{B})+P(\overline{A})\,P(B)$$

$$=\left(\frac{1}{5}\right)\left(1-\frac{2}{3}\right)+\left(1-\frac{1}{5}\right)\left(\frac{2}{3}\right)$$

$$=\left(\frac{1}{5}\right)\left(\frac{1}{3}\right)+\left(\frac{4}{5}\right)\left(\frac{2}{3}\right)$$

$$=\frac{1}{15}+\frac{8}{15}=\frac{9}{15}=\frac{3}{5}$$

(iii) P (none of them selected)

$$=P(\overline{A}\,\overline{B})=P(\overline{A})P(\overline{B})$$

$$=\left(1-\frac{1}{5}\right)\left(1-\frac{2}{3}\right)=\frac{4}{5}\times\frac{1}{3}=\frac{4}{15}$$

(iv) P (at least one selected)

$$=1-P\text{ (none selected)}$$

$$=1-\frac{4}{15}=\frac{15-4}{15}=\frac{11}{15}$$

22.

3 Red, 4 White	2 Red, 3 White
Bag I	Bag II

$\therefore$ Required Probability,

P (all three balls are of the same colour)

$=P$ (1 red ball from bag I and 2 red balls from bag II) $+\,P$ (1 white ball from bag I and 2 white balls from bag II)

$$=\left(\frac{{}^3C_1}{{}^7C_1}\times\frac{{}^2C_2}{{}^5C_2}\right)+\left(\frac{{}^4C_1}{{}^7C_1}\times\frac{{}^3C_2}{{}^5C_2}\right)$$

$$=\left(\frac{3}{7}\times\frac{2\times1}{5\times4}\right)+\left(\frac{4}{7}\times\frac{3\times2}{5\times4}\right)$$

$$=\frac{6}{140}(1+4)=\frac{6\times5}{140}=\frac{3}{14}$$

23. Here, we have three cases

Case I Two balls drawn from Bag A are white.

Case II Two balls drawn from Bag A are black.

Case III Two balls drawn from Bag A are one white and other black.

So, required probability

$$=\frac{{}^4C_2}{{}^7C_2}\times\frac{5}{10}+\frac{{}^3C_2}{{}^7C_2}\times\frac{3}{10}+\frac{{}^4C_1\times{}^3C_1}{{}^7C_2}\times\frac{4}{10}$$

$$=\frac{2}{7}\times\frac{1}{2}+\frac{1}{7}\times\frac{3}{10}+\frac{4}{7}\times\frac{4}{10}$$

$$=\frac{10+3+16}{70}=\frac{29}{70}$$

24. Given, $\quad P(A)=\frac{5}{6},\ P(B)=\frac{4}{5}$ and $P(C)=\frac{3}{4}$

$$\therefore \quad P(\overline{A})=1-P(A)=1-\frac{5}{6}=\frac{1}{6},$$

$$P(\overline{B})=1-P(B)=1-\frac{4}{5}=\frac{1}{5}$$

$$\text{and} \quad P(\overline{C})=1-P(C)=1-\frac{3}{4}=\frac{1}{4}$$

(i) Probability of exactly two persons hitting the target

$$=P(AB\overline{C})+P(A\overline{B}C)+P(\overline{A}BC)$$

$$=P(A)\times P(B)\times P(\overline{C})+P(A)\times P(\overline{B})\times P(C)+P(\overline{A})\times P(B)\times P(C)$$

$$=\frac{5}{6}\times\frac{4}{5}\times\frac{1}{4}+\frac{5}{6}\times\frac{1}{5}\times\frac{3}{4}+\frac{1}{6}\times\frac{4}{5}\times\frac{3}{4}$$

$$=\frac{20+15+12}{120}=\frac{47}{120}$$

(ii) Probability of atleast one person hit the target

$= 1 - \text{Probability of none hit the target}$

$= 1 - P(\overline{A}\overline{B}\overline{C})$

$= 1 - P(\overline{A}) \times P(\overline{B}) \times P(\overline{C})$

$= 1 - \frac{1}{6} \times \frac{1}{5} \times \frac{1}{4} = 1 - \frac{1}{120} = \frac{119}{120}$

25. Given, $P(A) = 60\% = \frac{60}{100}$,

$P(\overline{A}) = 1 - P(A) = 1 - \frac{60}{100} = \frac{40}{100}$

and $P(B) = 40\% = \frac{40}{100}$,

$P(\overline{B}) = 1 - P(B) = 1 - \frac{40}{100} = \frac{60}{100}$

$\therefore$ Required probability $= P$ (A and B are contradict to each other at the same fact)

$= P(A)P(\overline{B}) + P(\overline{A})P(B)$

$= \frac{60}{100} \times \frac{40}{100} + \frac{40}{100} \times \frac{60}{100}$

$= \frac{2400}{10000} + \frac{2400}{10000} = \frac{4800}{10000} = \frac{48}{100} = 48\%$

26. Clearly, the problem will be solved, when atleast one of them solve the problem.

$\therefore$ Required probability

$= P$ (at least one of them solved the problem)

$= 1 - P$(none of them solved the problem)

$= 1 - \left(1 - \frac{1}{4}\right)\left(1 - \frac{1}{5}\right)\left(1 - \frac{1}{3}\right)$

$= 1 - \frac{3}{4} \times \frac{4}{5} \times \frac{2}{3} = 1 - \frac{2}{5} = \frac{3}{5}$

27. Total number of events $= 6 \times 6 = 36$

Total possible outcomes which have an even number on the first die or a total of 8

$= (2, 1), (2, 2), (2, 3), (2, 4), (2, 5), (2, 6), (4, 1), (4, 2), (4, 3), (4, 4), (4, 5), (4, 6), (6, 1), (6, 2), (6, 3), (6, 4), (6, 5), (6, 6), (3, 5), (5, 3) = 20$

$\therefore$ Probability of getting an even number on the first die or a total of 8 $= \frac{20}{36} = \frac{5}{9}$

28. When a pair of dice is thrown, then the total outcomes when the numbers are different $= 30$

We have to choose those pair in which the sum of numbers is 6.

Favourable pairs $= \{(1, 5), (5, 1), (4, 2), (2, 4)\}$

Number of favourable pairs $= 4$

$\therefore$ Required probability

$= \frac{\text{Number of favourable outcomes}}{\text{Number of total outcomes}} = \frac{4}{30} = \frac{2}{15}$

29. Let E = Event of drawing a spade card

F = Event of drawing an ace card.

$\therefore n(E) = 13, n(F) = 4$ and $n(E \cap F) = 1$

[$\because$ only one ace of spade card exist]

Total number of cards, $n(S) = 52$

$\therefore \quad P(E) = \frac{n(E)}{n(S)} = \frac{13}{52} = \frac{1}{4}$

$P(F) = \frac{n(F)}{n(S)} = \frac{4}{52} = \frac{1}{13}$

and $P(E \cap F) = \frac{n(E \cap F)}{n(S)} = \frac{1}{52}$

$\therefore$ Required probability $= P(E \cup F)$

$= P(E) + P(F) - P(E \cap F)$

$= \frac{1}{4} + \frac{1}{13} - \frac{1}{52} = \frac{13 + 4 - 1}{52} = \frac{16}{52} = \frac{4}{13}$

30. Given, total number of balls $= 20$

Let A = drawn ball marked with a number of multiple of 3

$= \{3, 6, 9, 12, 15, 18\}$

and B = drawn ball marked with a number of multiple of 4

$= \{4, 8, 12, 16, 20\}$

Now, marked multiples of 3 and 4 is $A \cap B = \{12\}$

$\therefore$ Required probability

$= P$ (drawn ball marked with a number of multiples of 3 or 4)

$= P(A \text{ or } B) = P(A) + P(B) - P(A \cap B)$

$= \frac{6}{20} + \frac{5}{20} - \frac{1}{20} = \frac{10}{20} = \frac{1}{2}$

31. A bag is containing three red balls and four blue balls.

(i) P (two balls are drawn of same colour)

$= P$ (both red balls) $+ P$ (both blue balls)

$= \frac{{}^3C_2}{{}^7C_2} + \frac{{}^4C_2}{{}^7C_2} = \frac{3}{7 \cdot 3} + \frac{2 \cdot 3}{7 \cdot 3} = \frac{3 + 6}{21} = \frac{9}{21} = \frac{3}{7}$

$\left[\because {}^nC_r = \frac{n!}{(n-r)!r!}\right]$

(ii) P (two balls are drawn of different colours)

$= P$ (one red ball and one blue ball)

$= \frac{{}^3C_1 \times {}^4C_1}{{}^7C_2} = \frac{3 \times 4}{\frac{7 \times 6}{2 \times 1}} = \frac{4}{7}$

32. Given, $P(A)=\frac{4}{5}, P(B)=\frac{3}{4}$ and $P(C)=\frac{2}{3}$

Then, $P(\bar{A})=1-\frac{4}{5}=\frac{1}{5}, P(\bar{B})=1-\frac{3}{4}=\frac{1}{4},$

$P(\bar{C})=1-\frac{2}{3}=\frac{1}{3}$

(i) Probability that exactly two persons hit the target

$$=P(AB\bar{C})+P(A\bar{B}C)+P(\bar{A}BC)$$

$$=P(A)P(B)P(\bar{C})+P(A)P(\bar{B})P(C)+P(\bar{A})P(B)P(C)$$

[since, A, B and C are independent events]

$$=\frac{4}{5}\times\frac{3}{4}\times\frac{1}{3}+\frac{4}{5}\times\frac{1}{4}\times\frac{2}{3}+\frac{1}{5}\times\frac{3}{4}\times\frac{2}{3}$$

$$=\frac{1}{5}+\frac{2}{15}+\frac{1}{10}=\frac{6+4+3}{30}=\frac{13}{30} \quad \text{...(i)}$$

(ii) Probability that atleast two persons hit the target

$$=P(AB\bar{C})+P(A\bar{B}C)+P(\bar{A}BC)+P(ABC)$$

$$=\frac{13}{30}+P(A)P(B)P(C) \quad \text{[from Eq. (i)]}$$

$$=\frac{13}{30}+\frac{4}{5}\times\frac{3}{4}\times\frac{2}{3}$$

$$=\frac{13}{30}+\frac{2}{5}=\frac{13+12}{30}=\frac{25}{30}=\frac{5}{6}$$

Concept Enhancer The sum of probability of occurence and non-occurence of an event is equal to 1.

33. In a given word consists of 9 different alphabets, there are 4 consonants and 5 vowels. Three alphabets are chosen at random.

∴ Probability that more than one vowel will be selected

$$=P\text{ (two vowels and one consonant)}+P\text{ (three vowels)}$$

$$=\frac{^5C_2\times{}^4C_1}{^9C_3}+\frac{^5C_3}{^9C_3}$$

$$=\frac{1}{^9C_3}\left(\frac{5\times4\times4}{2\times1}+\frac{5\times4\times3}{3\times2\times1}\right)$$

$$=\frac{3\times2\times1}{9\times8\times7}(40+10)=\frac{1}{84}\times50=\frac{25}{42}$$

34. Let S = A die has 6 numbers on it.

i.e. $\{1, 2, 3, 4, 5, 6\}$.

E_1 = Even numbers = $\{2, 4, 6\}$

E_2 = Numbers greater than 3 = $\{4, 5, 6\}$

Then, $E_1\cap E_2$ = Even numbers greater than 3 = $\{4, 6\}$

Probability that either an even number or number greater than 3 will turn up

$$=P(E_1\cup E_2)=P(E_1)+P(E_2)-P(E_1\cap E_2)$$

$$=\frac{n(E_1)}{n(S)}+\frac{n(E_2)}{n(S)}-\frac{n(E_1\cap E_2)}{n(S)}$$

$$=\frac{3}{6}+\frac{3}{6}-\frac{2}{6}=\frac{1}{2}+\frac{1}{2}-\frac{1}{3}=1-\frac{1}{3}=\frac{2}{3}$$

Concept Enhancer Using addition law of probability, $P(A\cup B)=P(A)+P(B)-P(A\cap B)$

35. Let A : Selection of Ist horse

B : Selection of IInd horse

∴ $P(A)=P$ (Ist horse selection) $=\frac{1}{4}$

and $P(B)=P$ (IInd horse selection) $=\frac{1}{3}$

(i) P (both of them will be selected)

$$=P(AB)=P(A)P(B)$$

[since, A and B are independent events]

$$=\frac{1}{4}\times\frac{1}{3}=\frac{1}{12}$$

(ii) P (only one of them will be selected)

$$=P(A\bar{B})+P(\bar{A}B)$$

$$=P(A)P(\bar{B})+P(\bar{A})P(B)$$

[if A and B independent, then A and $\bar{B}$, $\bar{A}$ and B are also independent]

$$=\frac{1}{4}\times\left(1-\frac{1}{3}\right)+\left(1-\frac{1}{4}\right)\times\frac{1}{3}$$

$$=\frac{1}{4}\times\frac{2}{3}+\frac{3}{4}\times\frac{1}{3}$$

$$=\frac{1}{6}+\frac{1}{4}=\frac{2+3}{12}=\frac{5}{12}$$

(iii) P (none of them will be selected) $=P(\overline{AB})$

$$=P(\bar{A})P(\bar{B})$$

$$=\left(1-\frac{1}{4}\right)\left(1-\frac{1}{3}\right)=\frac{3}{4}\times\frac{2}{3}=\frac{1}{2}$$

36. Total outcomes of a single throw of two dice = 36

Favourable outcomes for getting a total of 10, 11, 12 are $\{(6, 4), (4, 6), (5, 5), (6, 5), (5, 6), (6, 6)\}$.

$$P\text{ (getting a total of atleast 10)}=\frac{6}{36}=\frac{1}{6}$$

P (getting a total of atmost 9)

$= 1 - P$ (getting a total of atleast 10)

$= 1 - \frac{1}{6} = \frac{5}{6}$

37. Let E_1 = Kamal's selection after appearing for an interview

and E_2 = Monica's selection after appearing for an interview

Then, $P(E_1) = \frac{1}{3}$ and $P(E_2) = \frac{1}{5}$ [given]

P (either Kamal's or Monica's selection)

$= P(E_1 \bar{E}_2) + P(\bar{E}_1 E_2)$

$= P(E_1) P(\bar{E}_2) + P(\bar{E}_1) P(E_2)$

[since, E_1 and E_2 are independent events]

$= \frac{1}{3} \times \left(1 - \frac{1}{5}\right) + \left(1 - \frac{1}{3}\right) \times \frac{1}{5}$

$= \frac{1}{3} \times \frac{4}{5} + \frac{2}{3} \times \frac{1}{5} = \frac{4}{15} + \frac{2}{15}$

$= \frac{6}{15} = \frac{2}{5}$

38. Let A : Problem is solved by A

B : Problem is solved by B

C : Problem is solved by C

Given, $P(A) = \frac{1}{3}, P(B) = \frac{2}{7}$ and $P(C) = \frac{3}{8}$

P (only one of A, B and C solve the problem)

$= P(\bar{A}\bar{B}C) + P(\bar{A}B\bar{C}) + P(A\bar{B}\bar{C})$

$= P(\bar{A})P(\bar{B})P(C) + P(\bar{A})P(B)P(\bar{C}) + P(A)P(\bar{B})P(\bar{C})$

[since, A, B and C are independent events]

$= \left(1 - \frac{1}{3}\right)\left(1 - \frac{2}{7}\right) \times \frac{3}{8} + \left(1 - \frac{1}{3}\right) \times \frac{2}{7} \times \left(1 - \frac{3}{8}\right) + \frac{1}{3} \times \left(1 - \frac{2}{7}\right)\left(1 - \frac{3}{8}\right)$

$= \frac{2}{3} \times \frac{5}{7} \times \frac{3}{8} + \frac{2}{3} \times \frac{2}{7} \times \frac{5}{8} + \frac{1}{3} \times \frac{5}{7} \times \frac{5}{8}$

$= \frac{1}{3 \times 7 \times 8}(30 + 20 + 25)$

$= \frac{75}{3 \times 7 \times 8}$

$= \frac{25}{56}$

39. Given, tickets numbered from 1 to 20.

Let A = Numbers on tickets which are multiple of 3

$= \{3, 6, 9, 12, 15, 18\}$

and B = Numbers on tickets which are multiple of 7

$= \{7, 14\}$

Then, numbers on tickets which are multiple of 3 and 7,

$A \cap B = \phi$

$\therefore P$(ticket has a number of multiple of 3 or 7)

$= P(A \cup B)$

$= P(A) + P(B) - P(A \cap B)$

$= \frac{6}{20} + \frac{2}{20} - 0 = \frac{8}{20} = \frac{2}{5}$

40. In a leap year, there are 366 days.

i.e. 52 full weeks + 2 days extra.

For these two days, there are seven possible combinations. Which are

(i) Mon and Tue (ii) Tue and Wed

(iii) Wed and Thu (iv) Thu and Fri

(v) Fri and Sat (vi) Sat and Sun

(vii) Sun and Mon

The last two possible combinations are in favour of the event that there will be 53 Sunday.

Hence, required probability = 2/7

41. Let B_1 : 4 red and 5 black balls and second bag

B_2 : 3 red and 7 black balls

Case I 1 red ball from bag B_1 and 2 black balls from bag B_2 are drawn

$\therefore$ Probability, $P_1 = \frac{{}^4C_1}{{}^9C_1} \times \frac{{}^7C_2}{{}^{10}C_2} = \frac{4}{9} \times \frac{7 \times 6}{10 \times 9} = \frac{168}{810}$

Case II 1 black ball from bag B_1 and 1 red and 1 black ball from bag B_2 are drawn

$\therefore$ Probability, $P_2 = \frac{{}^5C_1}{{}^9C_1} \times \frac{{}^3C_1 \times {}^7C_1}{{}^{10}C_2}$

$= \frac{5}{9} \times \frac{3 \times 7}{\frac{10 \times 9}{2 \times 1}}$

$= \frac{210}{810}$

Thus, cases I and II are mutually exclusive events.

$\therefore$ Probability of event of drawing 2 black balls and 1 red ball $= P_1 + P_2 = \frac{168}{810} + \frac{210}{810} = \frac{378}{810} = \frac{7}{15}$

42. The prime numbers from 1 to 21 are $\{2, 3, 5, 7, 11, 13, 17, 19\}$.

$\therefore$ Probability of choosing a prime number $= \dfrac{8}{21}$

43. Let A : Contractor will get a plumbing contract

and B : Contractor will get an electric contract.

Given, $P(A) = \dfrac{2}{3}, P(B) = \dfrac{4}{9}$ and $P(A \cup B) = \dfrac{4}{5}$

$\therefore \; P(A \cup B) = P(A) + P(B) - P(A \cap B)$

$\Rightarrow \; \dfrac{4}{5} = \dfrac{2}{3} + \dfrac{4}{9} - P(A \cap B)$

$\Rightarrow P(A \cap B) = \dfrac{2}{3} + \dfrac{4}{9} - \dfrac{4}{5} = \dfrac{30+20-36}{45}$

$= \dfrac{50-36}{45} = \dfrac{14}{45}$

44. If n objects are arranged in a circle, then total number of ways in which they can be arranged are $(n-1)!$.
Here, $n = 10$

$\therefore$ Total number of ways in which 10 persons can be seated around a circular table $= 9!$

If two persons always sit together, then we have to arrange only 9 persons around a circular table.
[we consider two persons as a one unit]

$\therefore$ Number of ways in which 9 persons can be seated around a circular table $= 8!$

Also, these two particular persons can interchange their seats in 2 ways.

Favourable cases $= 2 \times 8!$

Probability that two particular persons always sit together out of 10 persons around a circular table

$= \dfrac{\text{Favourable cases}}{\text{Total cases}} = \dfrac{2 \times 8!}{9!} = \dfrac{2 \times 8!}{9 \times 8!} = \dfrac{2}{9}$

45. Given, 20 balls are marked from 1 to 20.

Let A : Numbers which are multiple of $5 = \{5, 10, 15, 20\}$

B : Numbers which are multiple of $7 = \{7, 14\}$

and $A \cap B$: Numbers which are multiple of 5 and $7 = \phi$

$\therefore$ Probability of a ball drawn with a number which is multiple of 5 or $7 = P(A \cup B)$

$= P(A) + P(B) - P(A \cap B)$

$= \dfrac{4}{20} + \dfrac{2}{20} - 0 = \dfrac{6}{20} = \dfrac{3}{10}$

46. Given, $P(A) = \dfrac{1}{6}, P(\bar{A}) = \dfrac{5}{6}; P(B) = \dfrac{1}{6}, P(\bar{B}) = \dfrac{5}{6};$

$P(C) = \dfrac{1}{6}, P(\bar{C}) = \dfrac{5}{6}$

Since, A starts the game.

$P(A \text{ wins}) = P(A \text{ wins of first throw})$
$+ P(A \text{ wins of fourth throw})$
$+ P(A \text{ wins on seventh throw}) + \ldots$

$= P(A) + P(\bar{A}\bar{B}\bar{C}A) + P(\bar{A}\bar{B}\bar{C}\bar{A}\bar{B}\bar{C}A) + \ldots$

$= \dfrac{1}{6} + \left(\dfrac{5}{6}\right)^3 \times \dfrac{1}{6} + \left(\dfrac{5}{6}\right)^6 \times \dfrac{1}{6} + \ldots$

$= \dfrac{1}{6}\left[1 + \left(\dfrac{5}{6}\right)^3 + \left(\dfrac{5}{6}\right)^6 + \ldots\right]$

$= \dfrac{1}{6}\left(\dfrac{1}{1-\left(\dfrac{5}{6}\right)^3}\right) \quad \left[\because a + ar + ar^2 + \ldots = \dfrac{a}{1-r}\right]$

$= \dfrac{1}{6}\left(\dfrac{216}{216-125}\right) = \dfrac{36}{91}$

$P(B \text{ wins}) = P(B \text{ wins of second throw})$
$+ P(B \text{ wins of 5th throw})$
$+ P(B \text{ wins of 8th throw}) + \ldots$

$= P(\bar{A}B) + P(\bar{A}\bar{B}\bar{C}\bar{A}B) + P(\bar{A}\bar{B}\bar{C}\bar{A}\bar{B}\bar{C}\bar{A}B)$

$= \dfrac{5}{6} \times \dfrac{1}{6} + \left(\dfrac{5}{6}\right)^4 \times \dfrac{1}{6} + \left(\dfrac{5}{6}\right)^7 \times \dfrac{1}{6} + \ldots$

$= \dfrac{5}{6} \times \dfrac{1}{6}\left(1 + \left(\dfrac{5}{6}\right)^3 + \left(\dfrac{5}{6}\right)^6 + \ldots\right)$

$= \dfrac{5}{36} \times \dfrac{1}{1 - \dfrac{125}{216}} = \dfrac{30}{91}$

$P(C \text{ wins}) = 1 - [P(A) + P(B)]$

$= 1 - \dfrac{36}{91} - \dfrac{30}{91} = \dfrac{91-66}{91} = \dfrac{25}{91}$

47. Let A be the event that the selected student has opted for Mathematics and B be the event that the selected student has opted Biology.

Total number of student $= 60$

Number of student who opted for Mathematics $= 30$

$\therefore P(A) = \dfrac{\text{Number of student who opted for Math}}{\text{Total number of student}}$

$= \dfrac{30}{60} = \dfrac{1}{2}$

and number of student who opted for Biology $= 32$

$\therefore \; P(B) = \dfrac{\text{Number of student who opted for Biology}}{\text{Total number of student}}$

$= \dfrac{32}{60} = \dfrac{8}{15}$

$\because$ Number of student who opted for both Math and Biology $= 24$

$$\therefore P(A \cap B) = \frac{\text{Number of student who opted for both Math and Biology}}{\text{Total number of students}}$$

$$= \frac{24}{60} = \frac{2}{5}$$

Now,

(i) The probability that the selected student has opted for Mathematics or Biology

$$= P(A \text{ or } B) = P(A) + P(B) - P(A \text{ and } B)$$

$$\therefore P(A \text{ or } B) = \frac{1}{2} + \frac{8}{15} - \frac{2}{5} = \frac{19}{30}$$

(ii) The probability that the selected students has neither opted for Mathematics nor Biology

$$= P(\text{not } A \text{ and not } B)$$

$$= P(A' \text{ and } B')$$

$$= P(A' \cap B')$$

[by De-Morgan's law, $(A' \cap B') = (A \cup B)'$]

$$= P(A \cup B)'$$

$$= 1 - P(A \cup B) = 1 - P(A \text{ or } B)$$

$$= 1 - \frac{19}{30} = \frac{11}{30}$$

(iii) The probability that the selected student opted for Mathematics but not for Biology

$$= P(A \cap B') = P(A) - P(A \cap B)$$

$$= \frac{1}{2} - \frac{2}{5} = \frac{5-4}{10} = \frac{1}{10}$$

48. Here, there are three cases:

Case I When the balls transferred from Urn I to Urn II are white.

Here, the probability of transferring two white balls

$$\text{from Urn I} = \frac{^{10}C_2}{^{13}C_2} = \frac{\frac{10 \times 9}{2 \times 1}}{\frac{13 \times 12}{2 \times 1}} = \frac{15}{26}$$

In Urn II, white balls $= 3 + 2 = 5$ and black balls $= 5$

$\therefore$ Probability of drawing a white ball from Urn II

$$= \frac{^5C_1}{^{10}C_1} = \frac{5}{10} = \frac{1}{2}$$

$\therefore$ Probability of these events occurring together

$$= \frac{15}{26} \times \frac{1}{2} = \frac{15}{52}.$$

Case II When one white and one black is transferred from Urn I to Urn II.

$\therefore$ The probability of transferring a white ball and a black ball from Urn I into Urn II

$$= \frac{^{10}C_1 \times {^3C_1}}{^{13}C_2} = \frac{10 \times 3}{\frac{13 \times 12}{2 \times 1}} = \frac{30}{13 \times 6} = \frac{5}{13}$$

Now, in Urn II, white balls $= 4$ and black balls $= 6$

$\therefore P$ (getting a white ball from Urn II)

$$= \frac{^4C_1}{^{10}C_1} = \frac{4}{10} = \frac{2}{5}$$

$\therefore$ Probability of these events occurring together

$$= \frac{5}{13} \times \frac{2}{5} = \frac{2}{13}$$

Case III When two black balls are transferred from Urn I to Urn II.

$\therefore$ P (transferring 2 black balls from Urn I to Urn II)

$$= \frac{^3C_2}{^{13}C_2} = \frac{3}{\frac{13 \times 12}{2 \times 1}} = \frac{3}{13 \times 6} = \frac{1}{26}$$

Now, in Urn II, white balls $= 3$ and black balls $= 5 + 2 = 7$

$$\therefore P(\text{getting a white ball}) = \frac{^3C_1}{^{10}C_1} = \frac{3}{10}$$

Now, probability of these events occurring together

$$= \frac{1}{26} \times \frac{3}{10} = \frac{3}{260}$$

Since, all the three cases are mutually exclusive. Thus, only one of them can happen at a time.

Hence, the required probability of drawing a white ball

$$= \frac{15}{52} + \frac{2}{13} + \frac{3}{260} = \frac{118}{260} = \frac{59}{130}$$

49. Given, number of boys $= 8$ and number of girls $= 6$

We have to make a committee of 4 persons.

If the committee consists of more girls than boys, then

Number of ways this can be done

$$= {^8C_0} \times {^6C_4} + {^8C_1} \times {^6C_3}$$

$$= 1 \times \frac{6!}{4!2!} + 8 \times \frac{6!}{3!3!} = \frac{6 \times 5}{2} + \frac{8 \times 6 \times 5 \times 4}{3 \times 2 \times 1}$$

$$= 15 + 160 = 175$$

$\therefore$ Total number of ways

$$= {^8C_0} \times {^6C_4} + {^8C_1} \times {^6C_3} + {^8C_2} \times {^6C_2} + {^8C_3} \times {^6C_1}$$

$$= 1 \times 15 + 8 \times 20 + 28 \times 15 + 56 \times 6 = 931$$

$$\text{Hence, required probability} = \frac{175}{931} = 0.188$$

50. Given, $P(A)=\frac{4}{5}, P(B)=\frac{3}{4}$ and $P(C)=\frac{2}{3}$

$\therefore \quad P(\bar{A})=1-P(A)=1-\frac{4}{5}=\frac{1}{5},$

$P(\bar{B})=1-P(B)=1-\frac{3}{4}=\frac{1}{4}$

and $\quad P(\bar{C})=1-P(C)=1-\frac{2}{3}=\frac{1}{3}$

(i) The probability that exactly two persons hit the target

$$=P(A\cap B\cap \bar{C})+P(A\cap \bar{B}\cap C)+P(\bar{A}\cap B\cap C)$$
$$=P(A)P(B)P(\bar{C})+P(A)P(\bar{B})P(C)+P(\bar{A})P(B)P(C)$$

[$\because A, B$ and C are independent events]

$$=\frac{4}{5}\times\frac{3}{4}\times\frac{1}{3}+\frac{4}{5}\times\frac{1}{4}\times\frac{2}{3}+\frac{1}{5}\times\frac{3}{4}\times\frac{2}{3}$$
$$=\frac{12}{60}+\frac{8}{60}+\frac{6}{60}=\frac{26}{60}=\frac{13}{30} \quad \text{...(i)}$$

(ii) The probability that atleast two persons hit the target

= Probability that exactly two persons hit the target + Probability that all three persons hit the target

$$=\frac{13}{30}+P(A\cap B\cap C) \quad \text{[from Eq. (i)]}$$
$$=\frac{13}{30}+P(A)P(B)P(C)$$
$$=\frac{13}{30}+\frac{4}{5}\times\frac{3}{4}\times\frac{2}{3}=\frac{13}{30}+\frac{12}{30}=\frac{25}{30}=\frac{5}{6}$$

(iii) The probability that none of them hit the target

$$=P(\bar{A}\cap\bar{B}\cap\bar{C})=P(\bar{A})P(\bar{B})P(\bar{C})$$
$$=\frac{1}{5}\times\frac{1}{4}\times\frac{1}{3}=\frac{1}{60}$$

51. Given, Bag I : 5 white and 4 black balls

Bag II : 7 white and 9 black balls

Case I 1 black ball from Ist Bag, 1 black and 1 white balls from IInd bag.

$$P(A)=\frac{{}^4C_1}{{}^9C_1}\times\left(\frac{{}^7C_1\times{}^9C_1}{{}^{16}C_2}\right)$$
$$=\frac{4\times7\times9\times2}{9\times16\times15}=\frac{7}{15\times2}=\frac{7}{30}$$

Case II 1 white ball from Ist bag, 2 black balls from IInd bag.

$$P(B)=\frac{{}^5C_1}{{}^9C_1}\times\left(\frac{{}^9C_2}{{}^{16}C_2}\right)=\frac{5\times9\times8\times2}{2\times9\times16\times15}=\frac{1}{6}$$

$\therefore$ Required probability $=P(A)+P(B)$

$$=\frac{7}{30}+\frac{1}{6}=\frac{12}{30}=\frac{2}{5}$$

52. Bag A : Three red balls and four white balls

Bag B : Two red balls and three white balls

(i) P (one red ball and two white balls)

$=P$ (1 white ball from bag A and 1 white and 1 red ball from bag B) $+P$ (1 red ball from bag A and 2 white balls from bag B)

$$=\frac{{}^4C_1}{{}^7C_1}\times\frac{{}^2C_1\times{}^3C_1}{{}^5C_2}+\frac{{}^3C_1}{{}^7C_1}\times\frac{{}^3C_2}{{}^5C_2}$$
$$=\frac{4}{7}\times\frac{2\times3\times2}{5\times4}+\frac{3}{7}\times\frac{3\times2}{5\times4}$$
$$=\frac{12}{35}+\frac{9}{70}=\frac{24+9}{70}=\frac{33}{70}$$

(ii) P (all balls are of same colour)

$=P$ (all white balls) $+P$ (all red balls)

$=P$ (1 white ball from bag A and 2 white balls from bag B) $+P$ (1 red ball from bag A and 2 red balls from bag B).

$$=\frac{{}^4C_1}{{}^7C_1}\times\frac{{}^3C_2}{{}^5C_2}+\frac{{}^3C_1}{{}^7C_1}\times\frac{{}^2C_2}{{}^5C_2}$$
$$=\frac{4}{7}\times\frac{3\times2}{5\times4}+\frac{3}{7}\times\frac{1\times2}{5\times4}=\frac{6}{35}+\frac{3}{70}$$
$$=\frac{12+3}{70}=\frac{15}{70}=\frac{3}{14}$$

53. Odds in favour of Aman $=3:2$

$P_1=$ Probability that Aman will solve $=\frac{3}{5}$

$\bar{P}_1=$ Probability that Aman will not solve $=1-\frac{3}{5}=\frac{2}{5}$

Odds in favour of Mohan $=4:1$

$P_2=$ Probability that Mohan will solve $=\frac{4}{5}$

$\bar{P}_2=$ Probability that Mohan will not solve $=1-\frac{4}{5}=\frac{1}{5}$

Odds in against of Bipin $=2:1$

$P_3=$ Probability that Bipin will solve $=\frac{1}{3}$

$\bar{P}_3=$ Probability that Bipin will not solve $=1-\frac{1}{3}=\frac{2}{3}$

(i) Probability that all the three persons solve the problem $=P_1\times P_2\times P_3=\frac{3}{5}\times\frac{4}{5}\times\frac{1}{3}=\frac{4}{25}$

(ii) Probability that problem will be solved

$=1-$(Problem will not be solved)

$=1-\bar{P_1}\,\bar{P_2}\,\bar{P_3}$

$=1-\frac{2}{5}\times\frac{1}{5}\times\frac{2}{3}=1-\frac{4}{75}=\frac{71}{75}$

54. Given, the box contains 30 bolts and 40 nuts. Rusted number of bolts and nuts are 15 and 20, respectively.

Total number of rusted bolts and nuts $=15+20=35$

Let A : Rusted bolts and nuts

B : Bolts

P(both items are rusted or both nuts)

$=P(A \text{ or } B)=P(A)+P(B)-P(A\cap B)$

$=\frac{^{35}C_2}{^{70}C_2}+\frac{^{30}C_2}{^{70}C_2}-\frac{^{15}C_2}{^{70}C_2}$

$=\frac{35\times34+30\times29-15\times14}{2\times{}^{70}C_2}$

$=\frac{1190+870-210}{70\times69}=\frac{1850}{4830}=\frac{185}{483}$

55. Given, a bag contains 8 red and 5 white balls.

Probability (first draw yields 3 white balls and second draw yields 3 red balls)

$=\frac{^5C_3}{^{13}C_3}\times\frac{^8C_3}{^{10}C_3}$ [without replacement]

$=\frac{5\times4\times3}{13\times12\times11}\times\frac{8\times7\times6}{10\times9\times8}$

$=\frac{60}{13\times12\times11}\times\frac{7\times6}{10\times9}=\frac{36\times7}{13\times12\times11\times9}$

$=\frac{7}{33\times13}=\frac{7}{429}$

56. Total number of ways of throwing a pair of dice

$=n(S)=36$

Let E = getting 8 as sum in pair of dice

$=\{(2,6),(3,5),(4,4),(5,3),(6,2)\}$

$P(E)=\frac{n(E)}{n(S)}=\frac{5}{36}$

$P(\bar{E})=1-P(E)=1-\frac{5}{36}=\frac{31}{36}$

Now, P (Aman wins)

$=P(E)+P(\bar{E}\bar{E}E)+P(\bar{E}\bar{E}\bar{E}\bar{E}E)+\dots$

$=\frac{5}{36}+\left(\frac{31}{36}\right)^2\times\frac{5}{36}+\left(\frac{31}{36}\right)^4\times\frac{5}{36}+\dots$

$=\frac{5}{36}\left[1+\left(\frac{31}{36}\right)^2+\left(\frac{31}{36}\right)^4+\dots\right]$

$=\frac{5}{36}\times\frac{1}{1-\left(\frac{31}{36}\right)^2}$

[$\because$ it is an infinite geometric series, $S_\infty=\frac{a}{1-r}$]

$=\frac{5}{36}\times\frac{36^2}{36^2-31^2}=\frac{5\times36}{67\times5}=\frac{36}{67}$

P (Bhuwan wins) $=P$ (Aman does not win)

$=1-P$ (Aman wins)

$=1-\frac{36}{67}=\frac{31}{67}$

57. Probability of picking either first bag or second bag $=\frac{1}{2}$

Probability of taking out copper coin from first bag

$=\frac{5}{4+5}=\frac{5}{9}$

Probability of taking out copper coin from second bag

$=\frac{7}{3+7}=\frac{7}{10}$

Probability of taking out copper from either of the bag

= Probability of taking out copper coin from first bag

+ Probability of taking out copper coin from second bag

$=\frac{1}{2}\times\frac{5}{9}+\frac{1}{2}\times\frac{7}{10}=\frac{5}{18}+\frac{7}{20}=\frac{100+126}{360}=\frac{226}{360}=\frac{113}{180}$

58. Consider the following events :

A = Akhil is selected ; B = Vijay is selected

Given, probability of Akhil's selection i.e. $P(A)=\frac{1}{4}$

Probability of Vijay's selection i.e. $P(B)=\frac{2}{3}$

Probability that only one of them will be selected for an interview $=P$ (A selected and B is not selected for the interview)

$+P$(B selected and A is not selected for the interview)

$=P(A)\times P(\bar{B})+P(B)\times P(\bar{A})$

$=\frac{1}{4}\times\left(1-\frac{2}{3}\right)+\frac{2}{3}\times\left(1-\frac{1}{4}\right)$

$=\frac{1}{4}\times\frac{1}{3}+\frac{2}{3}\times\frac{3}{4}=\frac{1}{12}+\frac{6}{12}=\frac{7}{12}$

TOPIC 2

Conditional Probability with Baye's Theorem

Conditional Probability

Let E and F be two events associated with the same sample space of a random experiment. Then, probability of occurrence of event E, when the event F has already occurred, is called conditional probability of event E over F and it is denoted by $P(E/F)$.

$$P(E/F)=\frac{P(E\cap F)}{P(F)},$$

where $P(F)\neq 0$.

Similarly, conditional probability of event F over E is given as

$$P(F/E)=\frac{P(F\cap E)}{P(E)},$$

where $P(E)\neq 0$.

Properties of Conditional Probability If E and F are two events of sample space S and G is an event of S which has already occurred such that $P(G)\neq 0$, then

(i) $P[(E\cup F)/G]=P(E/G)+P(F/G)-P[(E\cap F)/G]$

(ii) $P[(E\cup F)/G]=P(E/G)+P(F/G)$, if E and F are mutually exclusive events.

(iii) $P(E'/G)=1-P(E/G)$

(iv) $P(S/G)=P(G/G)=1$

Multiplication Theorem

If E and F are two events associated with a sample space S, then the probability of simultaneous occurrence of the events E and F is

$$P(E\cap F)=P(E)\cdot P(F/E),$$

where, $P(E)\neq 0$

or $P(E\cap F)=P(F)\cdot P(E/F)$,

where $P(F)\neq 0$.

This result is known as multiplication rule of probability.

Extension of Multiplication Theorem

For Three Events Let E, F and G be three events of sample space S.

Then, conditional probability,

$$P\left(\frac{G}{E\cap F}\right)=\frac{P(E\cap F\cap G)}{P(F)\,P\left(\frac{E}{F}\right)}$$

For n Events Let $E_1, E_2,\ldots, E_n$ and E be $n+1$ events of sample space S, then

Conditional probability,

$$P\left(\frac{E}{E_1\cap E_2\cap E_3\cap\cdots\cap E_n}\right)=\frac{P(E\cap E_1\cap E_2\cap\cdots\cap E_n)}{P(E_1)\,P\left(\frac{E_2}{E_1}\right)P\left(\frac{E_3}{E_1\cap E_2}\right)\cdots}$$

Theorem of Total Probability

Let $\{E_1, E_2,\ldots, E_n\}$ be a partition of the sample space S and suppose that each of the events $E_1, E_2,\ldots, E_n$ has non-zero probability of occurrence. Let A be any event associated with S, then

$$P(A)=P(E_1)\,P(A/E_1)+P(E_2)\,(A/E_2)+\cdots+P(E_n)\,P(A/E_n)$$

$$=\sum_{j=1}^{n}P(E_j)\,P(A/E_j)$$

Baye's Theorem

If $E_1, E_2,\ldots, E_n$ are n non-empty events, which constitute a partition of sample space S. i.e. $E_1, E_2,\ldots, E_n$ are pairwise disjoint and $E_1\cup E_2\cup\cdots\cup E_n=S$ and A is any non-zero event, then probability

$$P(E_i/A)=\frac{P(E_i)\cdot P(A/E_i)}{\sum_{j=1}^{n}P(E_j)\,P(A/E_j)}\quad\text{or}$$

Let $E_1, E_2,\ldots, E_n$ be n mutually exclusive and exhaustive events associated with a random experiment. Let A be an event which occurs together with E_i, then

$$P(E_i/A)=\frac{P(E_i)\cdot P(A/E_i)}{\sum_{j=1}^{n}P(E_j)\,P(A/E_j)}$$

Posteriori Probability Posteriori probability is a revised probability that takes account into new available information i.e. $P(A_i/A)$ is calculated only if event A has happened.

Priori Probability Probability calculated by logically examining existing information.

The largest drawback of this method (priori probability) is that it can only be applied to a finite set of events i.e. $P(A_i)$, where $i=1, 2, 3,\ldots, n$.

PYQs Previous Years Questions

1 Mark Questions

1. 50 tickets in a box are numbered 00, 01, 02, ... ,49. One ticket is drawn randomly from the box. Find the probability of the ticket having the product of its digits 7, given that the sum of the digits is 8? **ISC Specimen 2023**

2. If A and B are two events such that $P(A) > 0$ and $P(B) \neq 1$, then $P\left(\frac{\overline{A}}{\overline{B}}\right)$ is **ISC Specimen 2023**

   (a) $1 - P\left(\frac{\overline{A}}{B}\right)$ (b) $1 - P\left(\frac{A}{\overline{B}}\right)$

   (c) $\frac{1 - P(A \cup B)}{P(\overline{B})}$ (d) $\frac{P(\overline{A})}{P(B)}$

3. If A and B are two events such that $P(A) = \frac{4}{5}$ and $P(B / A) = \frac{7}{8}$, then $P(A \cap B)$ is equal to **ISC Specimen Sem-II 2022**

   (a) $\frac{7}{40}$ (b) $\frac{21}{40}$

   (c) $\frac{32}{35}$ (d) $\frac{7}{10}$

4. If $P(A) = \frac{4}{5}$ and $P(A \cap B) = \frac{7}{10}$, then the value of $P\left(\frac{B}{A}\right)$ is **ISC Specimen 2021**

   (a) $\frac{1}{8}$ (b) $\frac{4}{7}$ (c) $\frac{5}{7}$ (d) $\frac{7}{8}$

2 Marks Questions

5. Two balls are drawn from an urn containing 3 white, 5 red and 2 black balls, one by one without replacement. What is the probability that atleast one ball is red? **ISC 2019**

6. If A and B are events such that

   $P(A) = \frac{1}{2}, P(B) = \frac{1}{3}$ and $P(A \cap B) = \frac{1}{4}$, then find

   (a) $P\left(\frac{A}{B}\right)$ (b) $P\left(\frac{B}{A}\right)$ **ISC 2018**

7. A family has two children. What is the probability that both children are boys, given that at least one of them is a boy? **ISC Specimen 2018**

3/4 Marks Questions

8. A jewellery seller has precious gems in white and red colour which he has put in three boxes. The distribution of these gems is shown in the table given below **ISC 2024**

Box	Number of Gems	
	White	Red
I	1	2
II	2	3
III	3	1

He wants to gift two gems to his mother. So, he asks her to select one box at random and pick out any two gems one after the other without replacement from the selected box. The mother selects one white and one red gem.

Calculate the probability that the gems drawn are from Box II.

9. There are two boxes, Box 1 and Box 2. Each box has 8 red balls, 5 green balls and 7 blue balls. Sahil takes one ball from Box 1 and places it in Box 2. Then, he draws two balls from Box 2 simultaneously.
   (a) What is the probability of Sahil selecting a green ball from Box 1?
   (b) After Sahil transfers a ball from Box 1 to Box 2, what is the probability of drawing one red ball and one green ball simultaneously from Box 2?
   (c) Given that the balls drawn from Box 2 are red and green, what is the probability that the ball transferred from Box 1 to Box 2 was green?
   (d) Prove that the probability mentioned in (c) is less than 35%. **ISC Specimen 2024**

10. On a festival, two friends namely Shanti and Diya got identical gift bags containing 7 dark chocolates, 8 milk chocolates and 5 white chocolates each.
    (a) What is the probability of Diya drawing a dark chocolate from Shanti's bag?
    (b) While Shanti was away, Diya transferred one chocolate from Shanti's bag to hers without looking. What is the probability of drawing a dark chocolate from Diya's bag after the transfer?
    (c) Which one of the following probabilities is higher? Why?

    The probability of drawing a dark chocolate from Diya's bag after the transfer or the probability of drawing a dark chocolate from Shanti's bag before the transfer. **ISC Specimen 2024**

11. In a company, 15% of the employees are graduates and 85% of the employees are non-graduates. As per the annual report of the company, 80% of the graduate employees and 10% of the non-graduate employees are in the administrative positions. Find the probability that an employee selected at random from those working in administrative positions will be a graduate. **ISC 2023**

12. A student answers a multiple choice question with 5 alternatives, of which exactly one is correct. The probability that he knows the correct answer is $\frac{1}{5}$. If he does not know the correct answer, he randomly ticks one answer. Given that he has answered the question correctly, find the probability that he did not tick the answer randomly. **ISC Specimen 2023**

13. A bag contains 6 red and 5 blue balls and another bag contains 5 red and 8 blue balls. A ball is drawn from the first bag and without noticing its colour is placed in the second bag. If a ball is drawn from the second bag, then find the probability that the drawn ball is red in colour. **ISC Specimen Sem-II 2022**

14. A word consists of 10 different alphabets, in which there are 4 consonants and 6 vowels. Four alphabets are chosen at random. What is the probability that more than one vowel is selected? **ISC Specimen 2021**

15. Let X denote the number of hours you study during a randomly selected school day. The probability that X can take the values x has the following form, where k is some unknown constant.

$$P(X=x)=\begin{cases} 0.1, & \text{if } x=0 \\ kx, & \text{if } x=1 \text{ or } 2 \\ k(5-x), & \text{if } x=3 \text{ or } 4 \\ 0, & \text{otherwise} \end{cases}$$

(i) Find the value of k.

(ii) What is the probability that you study :

(a) at least two hours? (b) exactly two hours?

(c) at most 2 hours? **ISC Specimen 2018**

5/6 Marks Questions

16. An insurance company insured 1000 scooter drivers, 2000 car drivers and 4000 truck drivers. The probability of accidents by scooter, car and truck drivers are 0.02, 0.05 and 0.03, respectively. If one of the insured persons meets with an accident. Find the probability that he is a truck driver. **ISC Specimen Sem-II 2022**

17. In a bolt factory, machines X, Y and Z manufacture 20%, 35% and 45%, respectively of the total output. Of their output 8%, 6% and 5% respectively are defective bolts. One bolt is drawn at random from the product and is found to be defective. What is the probability that it was manufactured in the machine Y? **ISC Specimen Sem-II 2022**

18. Given three identical boxes A, B and C, box A contains 2 gold and 1 silver coin, box B contains 1 gold and 2 silver coins and box C contains 3 silver coins. A person chooses a box at random and takes out a coin. If the coin drawn is of silver, find the probability that it has been drawn from the box which has the remaining two coins also of silver. **ISC 2019**

19. Bag A contains 1 white, 2 blue and 3 red balls. Bag B contains 3 white, 3 blue and 2 red balls. Bag C contains 2 white, 3 blue and 4 red balls. One bag is selected at random and then two balls are drawn from the selected bag. Find the probability that the balls drawn are white and red. **ISC 2017**

20. A fair die is rolled. If face 1 turns up, a ball is drawn from Bag A. If face 2 or 3 turns up, a ball is drawn from Bag B. If face 4 or 5 or 6 turns up, a ball is drawn from Bag C. Bag A contains 3 red and 2 white balls, Bag B contains 3 red and 4 white balls and Bag C contains 4 red and 5 white balls. The die is rolled, a Bag is picked up and a ball is drawn. If the drawn ball is red, what is the probability that it is drawn from Bag B? **ISC 2017**

21. In an automobile factory, certain parts are to be fixed into the chassis in a section before it moves into another section. On a given day, one of the three persons A, B and C carries out this task. A has 45% chance, B has 35% chance and C has 20% chance of doing the task. The probability that A, B and C will take more than the allotted time is $\frac{1}{6}, \frac{1}{10}$ and $\frac{1}{20}$, respectively. If it is found that the time taken is more than the allotted time, then what is the probability that A has done the task? **ISC 2016**

22. Box I contains two white and three black balls. Box II contains four white and one black balls and box III contains three white and four black balls. A die having three red, two yellow and one green face, is thrown to select the box, if red face turns up, we pick up box I, if a yellow face turns up we pick up box II, otherwise, we pick up box III. Then, we draw a ball from the selected box. If the ball drawn is white, what is the probability that the dice had turned up with a red face? **ISC 2015**

23. An urn contains 2 white and 2 black balls. A ball is drawn at random. If it is white, it is not replaced into the urn. Otherwise, it is replaced with another 2 balls of the same colour. The process is repeated. Find the probability that the third ball drawn is black. **ISC 2015**

24. In a college, 70% students pass in Physics, 75% pass in Mathematics and 10% students fail in both. One student is chosen at random. What is the probability that
(i) he passes in Physics and Mathematics?
(ii) he passes Mathematics given that he passes in Physics?
(iii) he passes in Physics given that he passes in Mathematics? **ISC 2014**

25. In a bolt factory, three machines, A, B and C manufacture 25%, 35% and 40% of the total production, respectively. Of their respective outputs, 5%, 4% and 2% are defective. A bolt is drawn at random from the total production and it is found to be defective. Find the probability that it was manufactured by machine C. **ISC 2014**

KEY CONCEPT

(i) Firstly consider the events E_1, E_2, E_3 and D.

Then, determine probabilities are

$$P(E_1),\ P(E_2),\ P(E_3),\ P\left(\frac{D}{E_1}\right),\ P\left(\frac{D}{E_2}\right) \text{ and } P\left(\frac{D}{E_3}\right).$$

(ii) Further, using Baye's theorem

$$P\left(\frac{E_3}{D}\right)=\frac{P(E_3)\cdot P(D/E_3)}{P(E_1)\cdot P(D/E_1)+P(E_2)\cdot P(D/E_2)+P(E_3)\cdot P(D/E_3)}$$

26. For A, B and C the chances of being selected as the manager of a firm are 4 : 1 : 2, respectively. The probabilities for them to introduce a radical change in the marketing strategy are 0.3, 0.8 and 0.5, respectively. If a change takes place, then find the probability that it is due to the appointment of B. **ISC 2013**

27. In a class of 75 students, 15 are above average, 45 are average and the rest below average achievers. The probability that an above average achieving student fail is 0.005, that an average achieving student fails is 0.05 and the probability of a below average achieving student failing is 0.15. If a student is known to have passed, then what is the probability that he is a below average achiever? **ISC 2012**

28. Bag A contains 2 white, 1 black and 3 red balls, bag B contains 3 white, 2 black and 4 red balls and bag C contains 4 white, 3 black and 2 red balls. One bag is chosen at random and 2 balls are drawn at random from that bag. If the randomly drawn balls happen to be red and black, then what is the probability that both balls come from bag B? **ISC 2011**

29. A factory has three machines A, B and C producing 1500, 2500 and 3000 bulbs per day, respectively. Machine A produces 1.5% defective bulbs, machine B produces 2% defective bulbs and machine C produces 2.5% defective bulbs. At the end of the day, a bulb is drawn at random and is found to be defective. What is the probability that the defective bulb has been produced by machine B? **ISC 2010**

30. An insurance company insured 4000 doctors, 8000 teachers and 12000 engineers. The probability of a doctor, a teacher and an engineer dying before the age of 58 yr are 0.01, 0.03 and 0.05, respectively. If one of the insured persons dies before the age of 58 yr, then find the probability that he is a doctor. **ISC 2009**

31. A class consists of 50 students out of which there are 10 girls. In the class 2 girls and 5 boys are rank holders in an examination. If a student is selected at random from the class and is found to be a rank holder, then what is the probability that the student selected is a girl? **ISC 2008**

32. An insurance company insured 1500 scooter drivers, 2500 car drivers and 4500 truck drivers. The probability of a scooter, a car and a truck meeting with an accident is 0.01, 0.02 and 0.04, respectively. If one of the insured persons meets with an accident, then find the probability that he is a scooter driver. **(2007)**

33. The bag A contains 3 white and 2 black balls while the bag B contains 2 white and 5 black balls. One of the bags is chosen at random and a ball is drawn from it. What is the probability that the ball is white? **ISC 2007**

34. A company has two plants which manufacture scooters. Plant I manufactures 80% of the scooters while plant II manufactures 20% of the scooters. At plant I, 85 out of 100 scooters are rated as being of standard quality, while at plant II only 65 out of 100 scooters are rated as being of standard quality. If a scooter is of standard quality, what is the probability that it came from plant I? **ISC 2006**

35. A manufacturing firm produces steel pipes in three plants A, B and C with daily production of 500, 1000 and 2000 units, respectively. The fractions of defective steel pipes output produced by the plants A, B and C are respectively 0.005, 0.008 and 0.010. If a pipe is selected from a day's total production and found to be defective, then find out the probability that it came from the first plant. **ISC 2005**

Explanations

1. Total number of cases $= {}^{50}C_1 = 50$

Let A be the event of selecting ticket with sum of digits '8'.

$\therefore$ Favourable cases to A are $\{08, 17, 26, 35, 44\}$.

Let B be the event of selecting ticket with product of its digit '7'.

$\therefore$ Favourable cases to B is only $\{17\}$.

Now, $P\left(\frac{B}{A}\right) = \frac{P(A \cap B)}{P(A)} = \frac{1}{50} \times \frac{50}{5} = \frac{1}{5}$

2. (c) $\because P(A) > 0$ and $P(B) \neq 1$

$$P\left(\frac{\overline{A}}{\overline{B}}\right) = \frac{P(\overline{A} \cap \overline{B})}{P(\overline{B})} = \frac{1 - P(A \cup B)}{P(\overline{B})}$$

3. (d) Given, $P(A) = \frac{4}{5}$ and $P\left(\frac{B}{A}\right) = \frac{7}{8}$,

Now, we know that

$$P\left(\frac{B}{A}\right) = \frac{P(A \cap B)}{P(A)}$$

$$\Rightarrow P(A \cap B) = P\left(\frac{B}{A}\right) P(A) = \frac{7}{8} \times \frac{4}{5} \Rightarrow P(A \cap B) = \frac{7}{10}$$

4. (d) Given, $P(A) = \frac{4}{5}$ and $P(A \cap B) = \frac{7}{10}$

Now, $P\left(\frac{B}{A}\right) = \frac{P(A \cap B)}{P(A)} = \frac{\frac{7}{10}}{\frac{4}{5}} = \frac{7}{10} \times \frac{5}{4} = \frac{7}{8}$

5. Let A be the event of not getting a red ball in first draw and B be the event of not getting a red ball in second draw.

Then, required probability

$= $ Probability that at least one ball is red.

$= 1 -$ Probability of none is red

$= 1 - P(A \text{ and } B)$

$= 1 - P(A \cap B)$

$= 1 - P(A)P(B/A)$ ...(i)

Now, $P(A) =$ Probability of not getting a red ball in first draw

$\Rightarrow P(A) =$ Probability of getting an other colour (white or black) ball in first draw

$\Rightarrow P(A) = \frac{5}{10} = \frac{1}{2}$

When another colour ball is drawn in first draw, there are 4 other colour (white or black) balls and 5 red balls, out of which one other colour ball can be drawn in ${}^4C_1$ ways.

$$\therefore \quad P\left(\frac{B}{A}\right) = \frac{4}{9}$$

Substituting these values in Eq. (i), we get

Required probability $= 1 - P(A) \cdot P\left(\frac{B}{A}\right)$

$$= 1 - \frac{1}{2} \times \frac{4}{9} = 1 - \frac{2}{9} = \frac{7}{9}$$

6. Given, $P(A) = \frac{1}{2}$, $P(B) = \frac{1}{3}$ and $P(A \cap B) = \frac{1}{4}$

(a) $P\left(\frac{A}{B}\right) = \frac{P(A \cap B)}{P(B)} = \frac{1/4}{1/3} = \frac{3}{4}$

(b) $P\left(\frac{B}{A}\right) = \frac{P(A \cap B)}{P(A)} = \frac{1/4}{1/2} = \frac{1}{2}$

7. Given, a family has two children.

Let A be the event that both children are boys.

$\therefore \quad A = \{BB\}$

and B be the event that at least one of them is a boy.

$\therefore \quad B = \{BB, BG, GB\}$

$\therefore \quad A \cap B = \{BB\}$

Now, $P(A) = \frac{1}{4}$, $P(B) = \frac{3}{4}$, $P(A \cap B) = \frac{1}{4}$

$\therefore$ Required probability

$$= P(A/B) = \frac{P(A \cap B)}{P(B)} = \frac{1/4}{3/4} = \frac{1}{3}$$

8. Let A : one gem is white and other is red

E_1 : both gems are from Box I

E_2 : both gems are from Box II

E_3 : both gems are from Box III

Probability of selection of each box

$$= P(E_1) = P(E_2) = P(E_3) = \frac{1}{3}$$

Required probability $P\left(\frac{E_2}{A}\right)$

$$= \frac{P(A/E_2) \cdot P(E_2)}{P\left(\frac{A}{E_1}\right) \cdot P(E_1) + P\left(\frac{A}{E_2}\right) \cdot P(E_2) + P\left(\frac{A}{E_3}\right) \cdot P(E_3)},$$

[using Baye's theorem]

$$= \frac{\frac{{}^2C_1 \times {}^3C_1}{{}^5C_2} \times \frac{1}{3}}{\frac{{}^1C_1 \times {}^2C_1}{{}^3C_2} \times \frac{1}{3} + \frac{{}^2C_1 \times {}^3C_1}{{}^5C_2} \times \frac{1}{3} + \frac{{}^3C_1 \times {}^1C_1}{{}^4C_2} \times \frac{1}{3}}$$

$$= \frac{\left(\frac{6}{10}\right)}{\left(\frac{2}{3}+\frac{6}{10}+\frac{3}{6}\right)} = \frac{6}{10} \times \frac{30}{53} = \frac{18}{53}$$

Hence, the probability that the gems drawn are from Box II is $\frac{18}{53}$.

9.

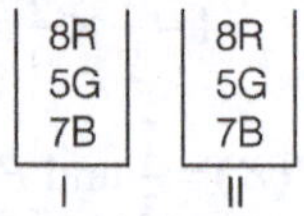

Let E_1 : red ball is transferred from bag I to bag II

E_2 : green ball is transferred from bag I to bag II

E_3 : blue ball is transferred from bag I to bag II

(a) $P(E_2) = \frac{5}{20} = \frac{1}{4}$

(b) Let A : Drawing one red ball and one green ball simultaneously from box 2

$P(E_1) = \frac{8}{20} = \frac{2}{5}, P(E_2) = \frac{5}{20} = \frac{1}{4}$ and $P(E_3) = \frac{7}{20}$

Now, $P\left(\frac{A}{E_1}\right) = \frac{{}^9C_1 \times {}^5C_1}{{}^{21}C_2} = \frac{9 \times 5}{210} = \frac{45}{210},$

$P\left(\frac{A}{E_2}\right) = \frac{{}^8C_1 \times {}^6C_1}{{}^{21}C_2} = \frac{8 \times 6}{210} = \frac{48}{210}$

and $P\left(\frac{A}{E_3}\right) = \frac{{}^8C_1 \times {}^5C_1}{{}^{21}C_2} = \frac{8 \times 5}{210} = \frac{40}{210}$

$$\therefore \quad P(A) = P(E_1)\,P\left(\frac{A}{E_1}\right) + P(E_2)\,P\left(\frac{A}{E_2}\right) + P(E_3)\,P\left(\frac{A}{E_3}\right)$$

$$= \left(\frac{8}{20} \times \frac{45}{210}\right) + \left(\frac{5}{20} \times \frac{48}{210}\right) + \left(\frac{7}{20} \times \frac{40}{210}\right)$$

$$= \frac{880}{20 \times 210} = 0.21$$

(c) $P\left(\frac{E_2}{A}\right) = \frac{P(E_2) \times P(A/E_2)}{P(A)} = \frac{\left(\frac{5}{20} \times \frac{48}{210}\right)}{0.21} = 0.27$

(d) The probability of the event mentioned in part (c) is 0.27 or 27%, which is less than 35%.

10. Let E_1 : Diya draws a dark chocolate from Shanti's bag E_2 : Diya draws a milk chocolate from Shanti's bag.

E_3 : Diya draws a white chocolate from Shanti's bag

A : Dark chocolate drawn from Diya's bag after the transfer

(a) $P(E_1) = \frac{7}{20}$

(b) $P(E_1) = \frac{7}{20}, P(E_2) = \frac{8}{20}, P(E_3) = \frac{5}{20}$

$$P\left(\frac{A}{E_1}\right) = \frac{8}{21}, P\left(\frac{A}{E_2}\right) = \frac{7}{21}, P\left(\frac{A}{E_3}\right) = \frac{7}{21}$$

$$\therefore P(A) = P(E_1)P\left(\frac{A}{E_1}\right) + P(E_2)\,P\left(\frac{A}{E_2}\right) + P(E_3)\,P\left(\frac{A}{E_3}\right)$$

$$= \left(\frac{7}{20} \times \frac{8}{21}\right) + \left(\frac{8}{20} \times \frac{7}{21}\right) + \left(\frac{5}{20} \times \frac{7}{21}\right)$$

$$= \frac{147}{420} = 0.35$$

(c) The probability of drawing a dark chocolate from Diya's bag after the transfer = 0.35 and probability of drawing a dark chocolate from Shanti's bag before the transfer $= \frac{7}{20} = 0.35$

$\therefore$ Both the probabilities are equal.

11. Consider the event

E_1 = Employees are graduate

E_2 = Employees are non-graduates

A = Employees are in the administrative position

Given, $P(E_1) = 15\% = \frac{15}{100}, \; P(E_2) = 85\% = \frac{85}{100},$

$P(A / E_1) = 80\% = \frac{80}{100}$ and $P(A / E_2) = 10\% = \frac{10}{100}$

$\therefore$ Required probability $= P(E_1 / A)$

By Baye's theorem,

$$P(E_1 / A) = \frac{P(E_1) \times P(A / E_1)}{P(E_1) \times P(A / E_1) + P(E_2) \times P(A / E_2)}$$

$$= \frac{\frac{15}{100} \times \frac{80}{100}}{\frac{15}{100} \times \frac{80}{100} + \frac{85}{100} \times \frac{10}{100}}$$

$$= \frac{1200}{1200 + 850} = \frac{1200}{2050} = \frac{120}{205} = \frac{24}{41}$$

12. Let E_1 = Students does not know the answer

E_2 = Students knows the answer

and E = Students answer correctly.

$\therefore \quad P(E_1) = 1 - \frac{1}{5} = \frac{4}{5}$ and $P(E_2) = \frac{1}{5}$

$P\left(\frac{E}{E_2}\right) = 1$ and $P\left(\frac{E}{E_1}\right) = \frac{1}{5}$

$\therefore$ The probability that student did not tick the answer randomly.

The probability that student tick the answer correctly

$$P\left(\frac{E_2}{E}\right) = \frac{P(E_2)P\left(\frac{E}{E_2}\right)}{P(E_2)P\left(\frac{E}{E_2}\right) + P(E_1)P\left(\frac{E}{E_1}\right)}$$

[by Baye's theorem]

$$= \frac{\frac{1}{5}\times 1}{\frac{1}{5}\times 1 + \frac{4}{5}\times\frac{1}{5}} = \frac{\frac{1}{5}}{\frac{5+4}{25}} = \frac{1}{5}\times\frac{25}{9} = \frac{5}{9}$$

13. Consider the following events

E_1 = transferred ball from bag I to bag II is red in colour.

E_2 = transferred ball from bag I to bag II is blue in colour.

A = ball drawn from the bag II is red in colour.

Bag I	Bag II
6 Red 5 Blue	5 Red 8 Blue

$\therefore \quad P(E_1) = \frac{6}{11}, P(E_2) = \frac{5}{11},$

$P\left(\frac{A}{E_1}\right) = \frac{6}{14}$ and $P\left(\frac{A}{E_2}\right) = \frac{5}{14}$

$\therefore$ Required probability $P(A)$ is given by

$$P(A) = P(E_1)\times P\left(\frac{A}{E_1}\right) + P(E_2)\times P\left(\frac{A}{E_2}\right)$$

$$= \left(\frac{6}{11}\times\frac{6}{14}\right) + \left(\frac{5}{11}\times\frac{5}{14}\right)$$

$$= \frac{36}{154} + \frac{25}{154}$$

$$= \frac{61}{154}$$

14. Let X denote the number of vowels.

Required probability $= P(X > 1)$

$$= 1 - [P(X=0) + P(X=1)]$$

$$= 1 - \left[\frac{{}^4C_4 \times {}^6C_0}{{}^{10}C_4} + \frac{{}^4C_3 \times {}^6C_1}{{}^{10}C_4}\right]$$

$$= 1 - \left[\frac{1\times 1}{210} + \frac{4\times 6}{210}\right]$$

$$= 1 - \left[\frac{1}{210} + \frac{24}{210}\right]$$

$$= 1 - \frac{25}{210}$$

$$= \frac{185}{210} = \frac{37}{42}$$

15. The probability distribution table for given function X is

X	0	1	2	3	4	Otherwise
P(X)	0.1	k	$2k$	$2k$	k	0

(i) We know that $\Sigma P(X) = 1$

$\Rightarrow \quad 0.1 + k + 2k + 2k + k + 0 = 1$

$\Rightarrow \quad 6k = 1 - 0.1$

$\Rightarrow \quad k = \frac{0.9}{6} = 0.15$

(ii) (a) At least two hours,

$P(X \geq 2) = 1 - P(X < 2)$

$= 1 - P(X=0) - P(X=1)$

$= 1 - 0.1 - 0.15$

$= 1 - 0.25$

$= 0.75$

(b) Exactly two hours,

$P(X=2) = 2k$

$= 2(0.15)$

$= 0.30$

(c) At most two hours,

$P(X \leq 2) = P(X=0) + P(X=1) + P(X=2)$

$= 0.1 + 0.15 + 0.30$

$= 0.55$

16. Let E_1 be the event that scooter drivers are insured.

Let E_2 be the event that car drivers are insured.

Let E_3 be the event that truck driver are insured.

$\therefore \quad P(E_1) = \frac{1000}{7000} = \frac{1}{7},$

$$P(E_2)=\frac{2000}{7000}=\frac{2}{7} \text{ and } P(E_3)=\frac{4000}{7000}=\frac{4}{7}$$

Let A be the event of drivers who meet with an accident.

$\therefore \quad P(A/E_1)=0.02,\ P(A/E_2)=0.05$

and $P(A/E_3)=0.03$

From Baye's theorem,

$$P(E_3/A)=\frac{P(E_3)\cdot P(A/E_3)}{P(E_1)\cdot P(A/E_1)+P(A/E_2)P(E_2)+P(E_3)P(A/E_3)}$$

$$=\frac{\frac{4}{7}\times 0.03}{\frac{1}{7}\times 0.02+\frac{2}{7}\times 0.05+0.03\times\frac{4}{7}}$$

$$=\frac{\frac{4}{7}\times 0.03}{\frac{0.02}{7}+\frac{0.1}{7}+\frac{0.12}{7}}$$

$$=\frac{\frac{4}{7}\times 0.03}{\frac{0.24}{7}}=\frac{\frac{0.12}{7}}{\frac{0.24}{7}}$$

$$=\frac{12}{24}=0.5$$

17. Consider the following events

E_1 = bolt is manufactured in the machine X

E_2 = bolt is manufactured in the machine Y

E_3 = bolt is manufactured in the machine Z

and A = bolt drawn from the product is defective.

$$\therefore\ P(E_1)=\frac{20}{100}=\frac{1}{5},\ P(E_2)=\frac{35}{100}=\frac{7}{20},$$

$$P(E_3)=\frac{45}{100}=\frac{9}{20},\ P\left(\frac{A}{E_1}\right)=\frac{8}{100}=\frac{2}{25},$$

$$P\left(\frac{A}{E_2}\right)=\frac{6}{100}=\frac{3}{50} \text{ and } P\left(\frac{A}{E_3}\right)=\frac{5}{100}=\frac{1}{20}$$

$\therefore$ Required probability $P\left(\frac{E_2}{A}\right)$ is given by

$$P\left(\frac{E_2}{A}\right)$$

$$=\frac{P(E_2)P\left(\frac{A}{E_2}\right)}{P(E_1)P\left(\frac{A}{E_1}\right)+P(E_2)P\left(\frac{A}{E_2}\right)+P(E_3)P\left(\frac{A}{E_3}\right)}$$

$$=\frac{\frac{7}{20}\times\frac{3}{50}}{\left(\frac{1}{5}\times\frac{2}{25}\right)+\left(\frac{7}{20}\times\frac{3}{50}\right)+\left(\frac{9}{20}\times\frac{1}{20}\right)}$$

$$=\frac{\frac{21}{1000}}{\frac{2}{125}+\frac{21}{1000}+\frac{9}{400}}$$

$$=\frac{\frac{21}{1000}}{\frac{119}{2000}}=\frac{6}{17}$$

18. Given, boxes A, B and C are identical, so each has equal probability of selecting boxes.

$$\therefore\ P(A)=\frac{1}{3},\ P(B)=\frac{1}{3} \text{ and } P(C)=\frac{1}{3}$$

Here, we see that only box C has all three silver coins.

Let E = Event of getting one silver coin.

Now, $$P\left(\frac{E}{A}\right)=\frac{1}{{}^3C_1}=\frac{1}{3},$$

$$P\left(\frac{E}{B}\right)=\frac{{}^2C_1}{{}^3C_1}=\frac{2}{3}$$

and $$P\left(\frac{E}{C}\right)=\frac{{}^3C_1}{{}^3C_1}=\frac{3}{3}$$

By using Baye's theorem,

$$P\left(\frac{C}{E}\right)=\frac{P(C)\,P\left(\frac{E}{C}\right)}{\left[P(A)\,P\left(\frac{E}{A}\right)+P(B)P\left(\frac{E}{B}\right)+P(C)\,P\left(\frac{E}{C}\right)\right]}$$

$$=\frac{\frac{1}{3}\times\frac{3}{3}}{\frac{1}{3}\times\frac{1}{3}+\frac{1}{3}\times\frac{2}{3}+\frac{1}{3}\times\frac{3}{3}}$$

$$=\frac{\frac{1}{3}}{\frac{1}{3}\left[\frac{1}{3}+\frac{2}{3}+\frac{3}{3}\right]}=\frac{1}{\frac{6}{3}}=\frac{3}{6}=\frac{1}{2}$$

19. Let E_1 be event of selecting bag A.

E_2 be event of selecting bag B.

E_3 be event of selecting bag C.

E is event of drawing two balls (white and red) which one of the three bags is selected randomly.

$$\therefore \qquad P(E_1)=\frac{1}{3},$$

$$P(E_2)=\frac{1}{3}$$

and $$P(E_3)=\frac{1}{3}$$

Now, $P(E/E_1)=$ Probability of drawing two balls, which are white and red, from bag A.

$$=\frac{1\times {}^3C_1}{{}^6C_2}$$

[$\because$ bag A contains 1 white, 2 blue and 3 red balls]

$$=\frac{1\times 3}{15}=\frac{1}{5}$$

$P(E/E_2)=$ Probability of drawing two balls, which are white and red, from bag B

$$=\frac{{}^3C_1\times {}^2C_1}{{}^8C_2}$$

[$\because$ bag B contains 3 white, 3 blue and 2 red balls]

$$=\frac{3\times 2}{28}=\frac{3}{14}$$

$P(E/E_3)=$ Probability of drawing two balls, which are white and red, from bag C

$$=\frac{{}^2C_1\times {}^4C_1}{{}^9C_2}$$

[$\because$ bag C contains 2 white, 3 blue and 4 red balls]

$$=\frac{2\times 4}{36}=\frac{2}{9}$$

Now, by using the law of total probability, we get

$$P(E)=P(E_1)P(E/E_2)+P(E_2)P(E/E_2)+P(E_3)P(E/E_3)$$

$$=\frac{1}{3}\times\frac{1}{5}+\frac{1}{3}\times\frac{3}{14}+\frac{1}{3}\times\frac{2}{9}$$

$$=\frac{1}{15}+\frac{1}{14}+\frac{2}{27}=\frac{401}{1890}$$

Concept Enhancer Using theorem of total probability

$$P(A)=P(E_1)P\left(\frac{A}{E_1}\right)+P(E_2)P\left(\frac{A}{E_2}\right)+\ldots+P(E_n)P\left(\frac{A}{E_n}\right)$$

$$=\sum_{j=1}^{n}P(E_j)P\left(\frac{A}{E_j}\right)$$

20. Let us define the following events.

E_1 : Bag A is chosen.

E_2 : Bag B is chosen.

E_3 : Bag C is chosen.

Then, $P(E_1)=\frac{1}{6}$, $P(E_2)=\frac{2}{6}=\frac{1}{3}$ and $P(E_3)=\frac{3}{6}=\frac{1}{2}$

Also, let event E : The drawn ball is red.

Then, $P(E/E_1)=\frac{3}{5}$, $P(E/E_2)=\frac{3}{7}$

and $P(E/E_3)=\frac{4}{9}$

Now, required probability

$$=P(E_2/E)$$

$$=\frac{P(E/E_2)P(E_2)}{P(E/E_2)P(E_2)+P(E/E_1)P(E_1)+P(E/E_3)P(E_3)}$$

$$P(E_2/E)=\frac{\frac{3}{7}\times\frac{1}{3}}{\frac{3}{7}\times\frac{1}{3}+\frac{3}{5}\times\frac{1}{6}+\frac{4}{9}\times\frac{1}{2}}$$

$$=\frac{\frac{1}{7}}{\frac{1}{7}+\frac{1}{10}+\frac{2}{9}}=\frac{\frac{1}{7}}{\frac{90+63+2\times 70}{630}}$$

$$=\frac{1}{7}\times\frac{630}{293}=\frac{90}{293}$$

21. Let E_1, E_2, E_3 and A be the events defined as follows

$E_1=A$ has done the task

$E_2=B$ has done the task

$E_3=C$ has done the task

and $A=$ Person takes more than the allotted time.

$$\therefore\quad P(E_1)=\frac{45}{100}=\frac{9}{20},\ P(E_2)=\frac{35}{100}=\frac{7}{20},$$

$$P(E_3)=\frac{20}{100}=\frac{4}{20},\ P(A/E_1)=\frac{1}{6},$$

$$P(A/E_2)=\frac{1}{10},\ P(A/E_3)=\frac{1}{20}$$

By using Baye's theorem, we have

$$P\left(\frac{E_1}{A}\right)=\frac{P(E_1)P(A/E_1)}{\left[P(E_1)P(A/E_1)+P(E_2)P(A/E_2)+P(E_3)P(A/E_3)\right]}$$

$$=\frac{\frac{9}{20}\times\frac{1}{6}}{\frac{9}{20}\times\frac{1}{6}+\frac{7}{20}\times\frac{1}{10}+\frac{4}{20}\times\frac{1}{20}}$$

$$=\frac{0.075}{0.075+0.035+0.01}=0.625$$

22. Let B and W denote for black and white balls.

Given, Bag I $= \{2W, 3B\}$

Bag II $= \{4W, 1B\}$

and Bag III $= \{3W, 4B\}$

Let $E_1 =$ A die have a red face,

$E_2 =$ A die have a yellow face

and $E_3 =$ A die have green face.

Total number of face is a die is six.

Then, $P(E_1) = \frac{3}{6} = \frac{1}{2}$, $P(E_2) = \frac{2}{6} = \frac{1}{3}$ and $P(E_3) = \frac{1}{6}$

Let $E =$ Event of drawing a white ball.

Now, $P\left(\frac{E}{E_1}\right) = \frac{2}{5}$, $P\left(\frac{E}{E_2}\right) = \frac{4}{5}$ and $P(E_3) = \frac{3}{7}$

$\therefore$ The probability that the white ball is selected when a die turn up red face.

$$P\left(\frac{E_1}{E}\right) = \frac{P(E_1)P\left(\frac{E}{E_1}\right)}{P(E_1)P\left(\frac{E}{E_1}\right) + P(E_2)P\left(\frac{E}{E_2}\right) + P(E_3)P\left(\frac{E}{E_3}\right)}$$

[by using Baye's theorem]

$$= \frac{\frac{1}{2}\times\frac{2}{5}}{\frac{1}{2}\times\frac{2}{5}+\frac{1}{3}\times\frac{4}{5}+\frac{1}{6}\times\frac{3}{7}} = \frac{\frac{1}{5}}{\frac{1}{5}+\frac{4}{15}+\frac{1}{14}}$$

$$= \frac{\frac{1}{5}}{\frac{113}{210}} = \frac{42}{113}$$

Concept Enhancer Using Baye's theorem,

$$P\left(\frac{E_i}{A}\right) = \frac{P(E_i)P\left(\frac{A}{E_i}\right)}{\sum_{j=1}^{n} P(E_j)P\left(\frac{A}{E_j}\right)} \text{ For any } i = 1, 2, 3, \ldots n$$

23. Let E_{pq} denote the event that the first ball drawn has colour p and second ball drawn has colour q.

Let B denote the event that the third ball drawn is black.

Now, $P(E_{ww}) = \frac{2}{4}\times\frac{1}{3} = \frac{1}{6}$, $P(E_{wb}) = \frac{2}{4}\times\frac{2}{3} = \frac{1}{3}$

$P(E_{bw}) = \frac{2}{4}\times\frac{2}{5} = \frac{1}{5}$, $P(E_{bb}) = \frac{2}{4}\times\frac{3}{5} = \frac{3}{10}$

Also, $P(B/E_{ww}) = \frac{2}{2} = 1$, $P(B/E_{wb}) = \frac{3}{4}$

$P(B/E_{bw}) = \frac{3}{4}$, $P(B/E_{bb}) = \frac{4}{6} = \frac{2}{3}$

Now, by total probability

$$P(B) = P(E_{ww})P(B/E_{ww}) + P(E_{wb}) P(B/E_{wb}) + P(E_{bw}) P P(B/E_{bw}) + P(E_{bb}) P P(B/E_{bb})$$

$$= \frac{1}{6}\times 1 + \frac{1}{3}\times\frac{3}{4} + \frac{1}{5}\times\frac{3}{4} + \frac{3}{10}\times\frac{2}{3}$$

$$= \frac{1}{6} + \frac{1}{4} + \frac{3}{20} + \frac{1}{5} = \frac{23}{30}$$

24. Consider the following events :

A : the students passed in Physics

B : the students passed in Mathematics

Given, $P(A) =$ Probability of students passed in Physics $= \frac{70}{100}$,

$P(B) =$ Probability of students passed in Mathematics $= \frac{75}{100}$

and $P(A' \cap B') =$ Probability of students fail in both $= \frac{10}{100}$

$\because P(A' \cap B') = P(A \cup B)' = 1 - P(A \cup B)$

$\Rightarrow P(A \cup B) = 1 - P(A' \cap B') = 1 - \frac{10}{100} = \frac{90}{100}$

(i) Probability of passing in Physics and Mathematics

$= P(A \cap B) = P(A) + P(B) - P(A \cup B)$

$= \frac{70}{100} + \frac{75}{100} - \frac{90}{100} = \frac{55}{100} = \frac{11}{20}$

(ii) P (he passes in Mathematics given that he passes in Physics),

$$P\left(\frac{B}{A}\right) = \frac{P(A \cap B)}{P(A)} = \frac{55/100}{70/100} = \frac{55}{70} = \frac{11}{14}$$

(iii) P (he passes in Physics given that he passes in Mathematics)

$$P\left(\frac{A}{B}\right) = \frac{P(A \cap B)}{P(B)} = \frac{55/100}{75/100} = \frac{55}{75} = \frac{11}{15}$$

25. Let E_1, E_2 and E_3 be the events of manufacturing bolt by machines A, B and C respectively, and let D be the events of manufacturing a defective bolt by machine A, B and C.

So, $P(E_1) = 25\% = \frac{25}{100}$, $P(E_2) = 35\% = \frac{35}{100}$

and $P(E_3) = 40\% = \frac{40}{100}$

Probability of defective bolt produced /manufactured by machine A,

$$P\left(\frac{D}{E_1}\right)=5\%=\frac{5}{100}$$

Probability of defective bolt produced /manufactured by machine B,

$$P\left(\frac{D}{E_2}\right)=4\%=\frac{4}{100}$$

Probability of defective bolt produced /manufactured by machine C,

$$P\left(\frac{D}{E_3}\right)=2\%=\frac{2}{100}$$

[$\because E_1, E_2$ and E_3 are mutually exclusive and exhaustive events]

Now, probability of defective bolt produced by machine C,

$$P\left(\frac{E_3}{D}\right)=\frac{P(E_3)\cdot P(D/E_3)}{P(E_1)\cdot P(D/E_1)+P(E_2)\cdot P(D/E_2)+P(E_3).P(D/E_3)}$$

[by using Baye's theorem]

$$=\frac{\frac{40}{100}\times\frac{2}{100}}{\frac{25}{100}\times\frac{5}{100}+\frac{35}{100}\times\frac{4}{100}+\frac{40}{100}\times\frac{2}{100}}$$

$$=\frac{\frac{80}{10000}}{\frac{125}{10000}+\frac{140}{10000}+\frac{80}{10000}}=\frac{\frac{80}{10000}}{\frac{125+140+80}{10000}}$$

$$=\frac{80}{10000}\times\frac{10000}{345}=\frac{80}{345}=\frac{16}{69}$$

Hence, the probability of defective bolt produced by machine C is $\frac{16}{69}$.

26. Let E_1, E_2 and E_3 be the events of chances of A, B and C being selecting as the managers, respectively and S be the event for selected person as the manager of a firm.

Since, the ratio of chances between A, B and C is 4:1:2. So, the total chances = 7

Therefore, $P(E_1)=\frac{4}{7}, P(E_2)=\frac{1}{7}$ and $P(E_3)=\frac{2}{7}$

Also given, the probability for them introduce a radical change in market strategy,

$$P\left(\frac{S}{E_1}\right)=0.3, P\left(\frac{S}{E_2}\right)=0.8, P\left(\frac{S}{E_3}\right)=0.5$$

By using Baye's theorem,

$$P\left(\frac{E_2}{S}\right)=\frac{P(E_2)\cdot P\left(\frac{S}{E_2}\right)}{P(E_1)\cdot P\left(\frac{S}{E_1}\right)+P(E_2)\cdot P\left(\frac{S}{E_2}\right)+P(E_3)\cdot P\left(\frac{S}{E_3}\right)}$$

$$=\frac{\frac{1}{7}\times 0.8}{\frac{4}{7}\times 0.3+\frac{1}{7}\times 0.8+\frac{2}{7}\times 0.5}$$

$$=\frac{\frac{0.8}{7}}{\frac{1.2}{7}+\frac{0.8}{7}+\frac{1}{7}}=\frac{\frac{8}{70}}{\frac{12}{70}+\frac{8}{70}+\frac{1}{7}}$$

$$=\frac{\frac{8}{70}}{\frac{12+8+10}{70}}=\frac{8}{70}\times\frac{70}{30}=\frac{8}{30}=\frac{4}{15}$$

27. Let E_1, E_2 and E_3 be the events of achievers for above average, average and below average respectively.

The total number of students = 75

Let A be the event of passed student.

So, $P(E_1)=\frac{15}{75}=\frac{1}{5}, P(E_2)=\frac{45}{75}=\frac{3}{5}$

and $P(E_3)=\frac{75-(15+45)}{75}=\frac{15}{75}=\frac{1}{5}$

Also, $P\left(\frac{A}{E_1}\right)=1-0.005=1-\frac{5}{1000}=\frac{995}{1000}=\frac{199}{200}$

$P\left(\frac{A}{E_2}\right)=1-0.05=1-\frac{5}{100}=\frac{95}{100}=\frac{19}{20}$

$P\left(\frac{A}{E_3}\right)=1-0.15=1-\frac{15}{100}=\frac{85}{100}=\frac{17}{20}$

The probability of below average achievers students who have passed

$$P\left(\frac{E_3}{A}\right)=\frac{P(E_3)\cdot P(A/E_3)}{P(E_1)\cdot P(A/E_1)+P(E_2)\cdot P(A/E_2)+P(E_3)\cdot P(A/E_3)}$$

$$=\frac{\frac{1}{5}\times\frac{17}{20}}{\frac{1}{5}\times\frac{199}{200}+\frac{3}{5}\times\frac{19}{20}+\frac{1}{5}\times\frac{17}{20}}$$

[by using Baye's theorem]

$$=\frac{\frac{17}{100}}{\frac{199}{1000}+\frac{57}{100}+\frac{17}{100}}$$

$$=\frac{17/100}{\frac{199+570+170}{1000}}$$

$$=\frac{17}{100}\times\frac{1000}{939}=\frac{170}{939}$$

28. Let E_1, E_2 and E_3 be the events for chosen bags A, B and C, respectively. So, $P(E_1)=P(E_2)=P(E_3)=\frac{1}{3}$

Bag A contains 2 white, 1 black and 3 red balls.
Bag B contains 3 white, 2 black and 4 red balls.
Bag C contains 4 white, 3 black and 2 red balls.
If A be the event of choosing two balls, i.e. one red and one black

$$\therefore \quad P\left(\frac{A}{E_1}\right)=\frac{{}^3C_1\times{}^1C_1}{{}^6C_2}=\frac{3\times1}{\frac{6\times5}{2\times1}}=\frac{1}{5},$$

$$P\left(\frac{A}{E_2}\right)=\frac{{}^4C_1\times{}^2C_1}{{}^9C_2}=\frac{4\times2}{\frac{9\times8}{2\times1}}=\frac{2}{9}$$

$$\text{and}\quad P\left(\frac{A}{E_3}\right)=\frac{{}^2C_1\times{}^3C_1}{{}^9C_2}=\frac{2\times3}{\frac{9\times8}{2\times1}}=\frac{1}{6}$$

Probability that both balls drawn from the bag B, having red and black balls

$$P\left(\frac{E_2}{A}\right)=\frac{P(E_2)P\left(\frac{A}{E_2}\right)}{P(E_1)P\left(\frac{A}{E_1}\right)+P(E_2)P\left(\frac{A}{E_2}\right)+P(E_3)P\left(\frac{A}{E_3}\right)}$$

$$=\frac{\frac{1}{3}\times\frac{2}{9}}{\frac{1}{3}\times\frac{1}{5}+\frac{1}{3}\times\frac{2}{9}+\frac{1}{3}\times\frac{1}{6}}$$

$$=\frac{\frac{1}{3}\times\frac{2}{9}}{\frac{1}{3}\left(\frac{1}{5}+\frac{2}{9}+\frac{1}{6}\right)}=\frac{\frac{2}{9}}{\frac{1}{5}+\frac{2}{9}+\frac{1}{6}}$$

$$=\frac{2/9}{\frac{18+20+15}{90}}=\frac{2/9}{53/90}$$

$$=\frac{2}{9}\times\frac{90}{53}=\frac{2}{53}\times10=\frac{20}{53}$$

29. Given,
The factory A production per day $=1500$
The factory B production per day $=2500$
The factory C production per day $=3000$
The total production of factores A, B and C

$$=1500+2500+3000=7000$$

Let E_1 = Event of selecting a bulb produced by A,
E_2 = Event of selecting a bulb produced by B,
E_3 = Event of selecting a bulb produced by C.
Let S be the event of selecting a defective bulb.

$$\therefore \quad P(S/E_1)=1.5\%=\frac{1.5}{100},\ P(S/E_2)=2\%=\frac{2}{100}$$

$$\text{and } P(S/E_3)=2.5\%=\frac{2.5}{100}$$

$$\text{Also,}\quad P(E_1)=\frac{1500}{7000}=\frac{3}{14},\ P(E_2)=\frac{2500}{7000}=\frac{5}{14}$$

$$\text{and}\quad P(E_3)=\frac{3000}{7000}=\frac{3}{7}$$

$\therefore$ The probability that the selecting bulb produced by B is defective,

$$P(E_2/S)=\frac{P(E_2)\cdot P(S/E_2)}{P(E_1)\cdot P(S/E_1)+P(E_2)\cdot P(S/E_2)+P(E_3)\cdot P(S/E_3)}$$

[by using Baye's theorem]

$$=\frac{\frac{5}{14}\times\frac{2}{100}}{\frac{3}{14}\times\frac{1.5}{100}+\frac{5}{14}\times\frac{2}{100}+\frac{3}{7}\times\frac{2.5}{100}}$$

$$=\frac{\frac{5}{14}\times\frac{2}{100}}{\frac{1}{100}\left(\frac{3}{14}\times1.5+\frac{5}{14}\times2+\frac{3}{7}\times2.5\right)}$$

$$=\frac{\frac{5}{14}\times2}{\frac{3}{14}\times1.5+\frac{5}{14}\times2+\frac{3}{7}\times2.5}$$

$$=\frac{\frac{10}{14}}{\frac{4.5}{14}+\frac{10}{14}+\frac{7.5}{7}}=\frac{\frac{10}{14}}{\frac{4.5+10+15}{14}}$$

$$=\frac{\frac{10}{14}}{\frac{29.5}{14}}=\frac{10}{14}\times\frac{14}{29.5}=\frac{10}{29.5}=\frac{100}{295}=\frac{20}{59}$$

30. Given, the total number of doctors insured by the insurance company = 4000

The total number of teachers insured by the insurance company = 8000

The total number of engineers insured by the insurance company =12000

The total number of insured persons

$$= 4000 + 8000 + 12000 = 24000$$

Let D be the event that an insured person die.

Let E_1 = Insured people are doctors,

E_2 = Insured people are teachers

and E_3 = Insured people are engineers

So, $P(E_1) = \frac{4000}{24000} = \frac{4}{24} = \frac{1}{6}$, $P(E_2) = \frac{8000}{24000} = \frac{8}{24} = \frac{1}{3}$

$$P(E_3) = \frac{12000}{24000} = \frac{12}{24} = \frac{1}{2}$$

Now, P (insured person die and having a doctor)

$$= P(D/E_1) = 0.01$$

P (insured person die and having a teacher)

$$= P(D/E_2) = 0.03$$

and P (insured person die and having an engineers)

$$= P(D/E_3) = 0.05$$

∴ The probability that the insured people are doctors and they die,

$$P(E_1/D) = \frac{P(E_1) \cdot P(D/E_1)}{P(E_1) \cdot P(D/E_1) + P(E_2) \cdot P(D/E_2) + P(E_3) \cdot P(D/E_3)}$$

[by using Baye's theorem]

$$= \frac{\frac{1}{6} \times 0.01}{\frac{1}{6} \times 0.01 + \frac{1}{3} \times 0.03 + \frac{1}{2} \times 0.05}$$

$$= \frac{\frac{1}{6} \times 0.01}{\frac{1}{6}(0.01 + 2 \times 0.03 + 3 \times 0.05)}$$

$$= \frac{0.01}{0.01 + 0.06 + 0.15} = \frac{0.01}{0.22} = \frac{1}{22}$$

31. Given,

The total number of students = 50

The total number of girls = 10

The total number of boys = 50 − 10 = 40

The total number of girls who achieve rank in examination = 2

The total number of boys who achieve rank in examination = 5

Rank holder/achiever students = 2 + 5 = 7

Let R = Event that the student achieve rank in examination

Let E = Event of selecting a girl

B = Event of selecting a boy

So, $P(E) = P(\text{girl}) = \frac{10}{50} = \frac{1}{5}$

and $P(B) = P(\text{boy}) = \frac{40}{50} = \frac{4}{5}$

Probability of rank holder being a girl, $P(R/E) = \frac{2}{7}$

Probability of rank holder being a boy, $P(R/B) = \frac{5}{7}$

∴ The probability that the selecting girl having rank a holder,

$$P(E/R) = \frac{P(E) \cdot (R/E)}{P(E) \cdot P(R/E) + P(B) \cdot P(R/B)}$$

[by using Baye's theorem]

$$= \frac{\frac{1}{5} \times \frac{2}{7}}{\frac{1}{5} \times \frac{2}{7} + \frac{4}{5} \times \frac{5}{7}} = \frac{\frac{2}{35}}{\frac{2}{35} + \frac{20}{35}}$$

$$= \frac{2}{35} \times \frac{35}{2 + 20} = \frac{2}{22} = \frac{1}{11}$$

32. Given,

The total number of insured scooter drivers = 1500

The total number of insured car drivers = 2500

The total number of insured truck drivers = 4500

The total number of insured drivers

$$= 1500 + 2500 + 4500 = 8500$$

Let A be event of drivers who meet with an accident.

Let E_1, E_2 and E_3 be event of insured driver of scooter, car and truck, respectively.

Then, $P(E_1) = \frac{1500}{8500} = \frac{15}{85} = \frac{3}{17}$,

$$P(E_2) = \frac{2500}{8500} = \frac{5}{17}$$

and $P(E_3) = \frac{4500}{8500} = \frac{9}{17}$

Now, probability that the drivers meets with an accident has scooter driver, $P(A/E_1) = 0.01$

Probability that the drivers meets with an accidents has a car driver $P(A/E_2) = 0.02$

Probability that the dirvers meet with an accident has a truck drivers, $P(A/E_3) = 0.04$

The probability of scooter driver meet with an accident,

$$P(E_1/A)=\frac{P(E_1)\cdot P(A/E_1)}{P(E_1)\cdot P(A/E_1)+P(E_2)P(A/E_2)+P(E_3)\cdot P(A/E_3)}$$

[by using Baye's theorem]

$$=\frac{\frac{3}{17}\times 0.01}{\frac{3}{17}\times 0.01+\frac{5}{17}\times 0.02+\frac{9}{17}\times 0.04}$$

$$=\frac{\frac{3}{17}\times 0.01}{\frac{1}{17}\times(3\times 0.01+5\times 0.02+9\times 0.04)}$$

$$=\frac{3\times 0.01}{0.03+0.10+0.36}=\frac{0.03}{0.49}=\frac{3}{49}$$

33. Bag A : 3 white and 2 black balls.

Bag B : 2 white and 5 black balls.

Probability of selecting bag A

= Probability of selecting bag B

$=\frac{1}{2}$

i.e. $P(A)=P(B)=\frac{1}{2}$

Let W : Drawing a white ball from any bag

∴ Required probability

= Probability of selecting bag A

× Probability of selecting a white ball from bag A

+ Probability of selecting bag B

× Probability of selecting a white ball from bag B

$$=P(A)\times P\left(\frac{W}{A}\right)+P(B)\times P\left(\frac{W}{B}\right)$$

$$=\frac{1}{2}\times\frac{3}{5}+\frac{1}{2}\times\frac{2}{7}=\frac{3}{10}+\frac{1}{7}=\frac{21+10}{70}=\frac{31}{70}$$

34. Let A = Scooters manufactured by plant I

B = Scooters manufactured by plant II

Let S represents the event that scooter manufactured by plants is of standard quality.

Given, plant I manufactured = 80% scooters

Plant II manufactured = 20% scooters

So, the probability of manufactured scooters by plants I and II are

$$P(A)=\frac{80}{100}=0.8 \text{ and } P(B)=\frac{20}{100}=0.2$$

Now, the probability that the scooter of standard quality manufactured by plants I and II are

$$P\left(\frac{S}{A}\right)=\frac{85}{100}=0.85 \text{ and } P\left(\frac{S}{B}\right)=\frac{65}{100}=0.65$$

The probability of selecting scooters with standard quality manufactures from plant I,

$$P(A/S)=\frac{P(A)\cdot P(S/A)}{P(A)\cdot P(S/A)+P(B)\cdot P(S/B)}$$

[by using Baye's theorem]

$$=\frac{0.8\times 0.85}{0.8\times 0.85+0.2\times 0.65}$$

$$=\frac{0.68}{0.68+0.13}=\frac{0.68}{0.81}=\frac{68}{81}\approx 0.84$$

35. Given, per day production from plant A = 500 units, per day production from plant B = 1000 units and per day production from plan C = 2000 units

Let the events, E_1 = Selecting the pipe from plant A

E_2 = Selecting the pipe from plant B

E_3 = Selecting the pipe from plant C

Let D be the event of selecting defective pipe.

Now, $P(E_1)=\frac{500}{500+1000+2000}=\frac{500}{3500}=\frac{1}{7}$,

$$P(E_2)=\frac{1000}{3500}=\frac{2}{7} \text{ and } P(E_3)=\frac{2000}{3500}=\frac{4}{7}$$

Now, the probability that defective pipe produce from plant A, $P(D/E_1)=0.005$

The probability that defective pipe produce from plant B, $P(D/E_2)=0.008$

The probability that the defective pipe produce from plant C, $P(D/E_3)=0.010$

∴ The probability that the selecting pipe produce from plant A is defective is

$$P(E_1/D)=\frac{P(E_1)\cdot P(D/E_1)}{P(E_1)\cdot P(D/E_1)+P(E_2)\cdot P(D/E_2)+P(E_3)\cdot P(D/E_3)}$$

[by using Baye's theorem]

$$=\frac{\frac{1}{7}\times 0.005}{\frac{1}{7}\times 0.005+\frac{2}{7}\times 0.008+\frac{4}{7}\times 0.010}$$

$$=\frac{\frac{1}{7}\times 0.005}{\frac{1}{7}(0.005+2\times 0.008+4\times 0.010)}$$

$$=\frac{0.005}{0.005+0.016+0.04}=\frac{0.005}{0.061}=\frac{5}{61}$$

TOPIC 3

Random Variable and Probability Distribution

Random Variable

A random variable is a real valued function, whose domain is the sample space of a random experiment.Generally, it is denoted by capital letter X.

e.g. Let a coin be tossed twice.Then, sample space,

$$S = \{(H,T), (T,H), (H,H), (T,T)\}$$

If X denotes the number of heads in two tosses, then X is a random variable.

$\therefore \quad X(H,T)=1, X(H,H)=2, X(T,H)=1, X(T,T)=0$

Clearly, the values of X are 0, 1 and 2.

Probability Distribution of a Random Variable

The system in which the values of a random variable are given along with their corresponding probability, is called **probability distribution.**

If X is a random variable and takes the values $x_1, x_2, x_3, \ldots, x_n$ with respective probabilities. $p_1, p_2, p_3, \ldots, p_n$. Then, the probability distribution of X is represented by

X	x_1	x_2	x_3	...	x_n
P(x)	p_1	p_2	p_3	...	p_n

NOTE If x_i is one of the possible values of a random variable X, then statement $X = x_i$ is true only at some point(s) of the sample space. Hence, the probability that X takes value x_i is always non-zero. i.e. $P(X = x_i) \neq 0$, where, $p_i > 0$ and $\sum_{i=1}^{n} p_i = 1; i = 1, 2, \ldots, n$.

Mean of Random Variable

Let X be a random variable taking values $x_1, x_2, x_3, \ldots, x_n$ with probabilities $p_1, p_2, p_3, \ldots, p_n$, respectively.

Then, mean of X is defined as

$$\mu (\text{or } \overline{X}) = \sum_{i=1}^{n} x_i p_i$$

The mean of a random variable X is also called the **expectation** of X, denoted by $E(X)$.

Thus, $E(X) = \mu = \sum_{i=1}^{n} x_i p_i = x_1 p_1 + x_2 p_2 + \cdots + x_n p_n$

PYQs Previous Years Questions

5 Marks Questions

1. A primary school teacher wants to teach the concept of 'larger number' to the students of Class II.

To teach this concept, he conducts an activity in his class. He asks the children to select two numbers from a set of numbers given as 2, 3, 4, 5 one after the other without replacement.

All the outcomes of this activity are tabulated in the form of ordered pairs given below. ***ISC 2024***

	2	3	4	5
2	(2, 2)	(2, 3)	(2, 4)	
3	(3, 2)	(3, 3)		(3, 5)
4	(4, 2)		(4, 4)	(4, 5)
5		(5, 3)	(5, 4)	(5, 5)

(i) Complete the table given above.

(ii) Find the total number of ordered pairs having one larger number.

(iii) Let the random variable X denote the larger of two numbers in the ordered pair.

Now, complete the probability distribution table for X given below

X	3	4	5
P(X = x)			

(iv) Find the value of $P(X < 5)$.

(v) Calculate the expected value of the probability distribution.

2. A group of class XI students designed a game for class XII students to be played at the farewell programme. They kept two sets of cards on the stage. Each set contained four cards numbered 1, 2, 3 and 4. Each student of class XII had to draw one card from each set simultaneously. The score a student received was defined as the difference between the numbers shown on the cards. The possible outcome of the score is given in the table below. ***ISC Specimen 2024***

Numbers on card 1

		1	2	3	4
Numbers on card 2	1	0	p	2	3
	2	1	0	p	2
	3	q	1	0	p
	4	3	q	1	0

(i) Calculate the values of p and q in the above table.

(ii) Reshma plays the game once. Let the random variable 'S' represents Reshma's score. Construct the probability distribution for 'S'

S				
$P(S = s)$				

(iii) Find the probability that Reshma's score is atmost 2.

(iv) Find Reshma's expected score.

3. A box contains 30 fruits, out of which 10 are rotten. Two fruits are selected at random one by one without replacement from the box. Find the probability distribution of the number of unspoiled fruits. Also, find the mean of the probability distribution. ***ISC 2023***

> **KEY CONCEPT**
> (i) Firstly determine the probability distribution of number of unspoiled fruits.
> (ii) Further, by using Mean $= \sum_{i=1}^{n} P_i X_i$.

4. A biased four-sided die with faces labelled 1, 2,3 and 4 is rolled and recorded. Let X be the result obtained when the die is rolled. The probability distribution for X is given in the following table, where p and q are constants.

x	1	2	3	4
$P(X = x)$	p	0.3	q	0.1

For the probability distribution, it is known that $E(X) = 2$. Find p and q.

Also, find $P(X > 2)$.

Ajay plays a game with this four-sided die. In this game, he is allowed a maximum of five rolls. His score is calculated by adding the results of each roll. He wins the game if his score is at least 10. After 3 rolls, Ajay has score of four points. Assuming that rolls of the die are independent, find the probability that Ajay wins the game. ***ISC Specimen 2023***

5. Five bad eggs are mixed with 10 good ones. If 3 eggs are drawn one by one with replacement, then find the probability distribution of the number of good eggs drawn. ***ISC 2010***

6. An urn contains 25 balls of which 10 balls are red and the remaining green. A ball is drawn at random from the urn, the colour is noted and the ball is replaced. If 6 balls are drawn in this way, find the probability that

(i) all the balls are red. ***(2017)***

(ii) not more than 2 balls are green.

(iii) number of red balls and green balls are equal.

7. Five dice are thrown simultaneously. If the occurrence of an odd number in a single dice is considered a success, find the probability of maximum three successes. ***(2015)***

8. On dialling certain telephone numbers, assume that on an average, one telephone number out of five is busy. Ten telephone numbers are randomly selected and dialled. Find the probability that atleast three of them will be busy. ***(2014)***

9. The probability that a bulb produced by a factory will fuse in 100 days of use is 0.05. Find the probability that out of 5 such bulbs, after 100 days of use

(i) none fuse.

(ii) no more than one fuses.

(iii) more than one fuses.

(iv) atleast one fuses. ***(2012)***

10. Five bad eggs are mixed with 10 good ones. If 3 eggs are drawn one by one with replacement, then find the probability distribution of the number of good eggs drawn. ***(2010)***

11. Eight coins are thrown simultaneously.

(i) Show that the probability of getting atleast 6 heads is $\frac{37}{256}$.

(ii) What is the probability of getting atleast 3 heads? ***(2008)***

12. The probability that a teacher will give an unannounced test during any class meeting is $\frac{1}{5}$. If a student is absent twice, find the probability that the student will miss atleast one test. ***(2008)***

Explanations

1. Given set of numbers is

$$A = \{2, 3, 4, 5\}$$

Total number of ordered pairs $= 2^{|A|} = 2^4 = 16$

(i) All outcomes of this cutting are tabulated in the form of ordered pairs given below

	2	3	4	5
2	(2, 2)	(2, 3)	(2, 4)	(2, 5)
3	(3, 2)	(3, 3)	(3, 4)	(3, 5)
4	(4, 2)	(4, 3)	(4, 4)	(4, 5)
5	(5, 2)	(5, 3)	(5, 4)	(5, 5)

(ii) The total number of pairs having one larger number

= Total number of ordered pair

– Number of ordered pair having same number

$= 16 - 4 = 12$

(iii) Let X be a random variable denotes the larger of two numbers in ordered pair.

Total number of ordered pair $= 12$

Number of ordered pair having 3 as a larger number $= 2$

$$P(X = 3) = \frac{2}{12} = \frac{1}{6}$$

Number of ordered pair having 4 as a larger number $= 4$

$$P(X = 4) = \frac{4}{12} = \frac{1}{3}$$

Also, number of ordered pair having 5 as a larger number $= 6$

$$P(X = 5) = \frac{6}{12} = \frac{1}{2}$$

(iv) Here, $P(X < 5) = P(X = 2) + P(X = 3) + P(X = 4)$

$$= 0 + \frac{1}{6} + \frac{1}{3} = \frac{1}{2}$$

(v) Excepted value of probability distribution

$$E(X) = \sum_{i=1}^{n} x_i p_i$$

$$= 2 \cdot P(X = 2) + 3 \cdot P(X = 3) + 4 \cdot P(X = 4) + 5 \cdot P(X = 5)$$

$$= 0 + 3 \times \frac{1}{6} + 4 \times \frac{1}{3} + 5 \times \frac{1}{2}$$

$$= \frac{1}{2} + \frac{4}{3} + \frac{5}{2}$$

$$= \frac{3 + 8 + 15}{6} = \frac{26}{6} = \frac{13}{3}$$

Hence, the expected value of probability distribution is $\frac{13}{3}$.

2. (i) $p = 2 - 1 = 1$

and $q = 3 - 1 = 2$

(ii) $P(S = 0) = \frac{4}{16} = \frac{1}{4}$

$P(S = 1) = \frac{6}{16} = \frac{3}{8}$

$P(S = 2) = \frac{4}{16} = \frac{1}{4}$

$P(S = 3) = \frac{2}{16} = \frac{1}{8}$

S	0	1	2	3
P(S = s)	1/4	3/8	1/4	1/8

(iii) $P(S \le 2) = \frac{1}{4} + \frac{3}{8} + \frac{1}{4} = \frac{7}{8}$

(iv) Expected score

$$= \left(0 \times \frac{1}{4}\right) + \left(1 \times \frac{3}{8}\right) + \left(2 \times \frac{1}{4}\right) + \left(3 \times \frac{1}{8}\right) = \frac{5}{4}$$

3. It is given that out of 30 fruits, 10 are rotten

$\therefore$ Number of unspoiled fruits $= 30 - 10 = 20$

2 fruits are drawn without replacement.

Let X be the random variable that denotes the number of unspoiled fruit in selected fruits.

$\therefore$ $P(X = 0) = P$ (2 spoiled and 0 unspoiled)

$$= \frac{10}{30} \times \frac{9}{29} = \frac{3}{29}$$

$P(X = 1) = P$ (1 spoiled and 1 unspoiled)

$$= \frac{10}{30} \times \frac{20}{29} + \frac{20}{30} \times \frac{10}{29}$$

$$= 2\left(\frac{20 \times 10}{30 \times 29}\right) = \frac{40}{87}$$

$P(X = 2) = P$ (0 spoiled and 2 unspoiled)

$$= \frac{20}{30} \times \frac{19}{29} = \frac{38}{87}$$

Therefore, the required probability distribution

X	0	1	2
P(X)	$\frac{3}{29}$	$\frac{40}{87}$	$\frac{38}{87}$

$$\therefore \text{ Mean} = \sum_{i=1}^{n} P_i X_i$$

$$= 0 \times \frac{3}{29} + 1 \times \frac{40}{87} + 2 \times \frac{38}{87}$$

$$= 0 + \frac{40}{87} + \frac{76}{87}$$

$$= \frac{116}{87}$$

4. Here, the probability distribution of x is given below

x	1	2	3	4
P(X = x)	p	0.3	q	0.1

$\therefore$ Mean $= E(X) = 2$

$$E(X) = \sum_{i=1}^{n} X_i P_i$$

$$\Rightarrow \quad 2 = 1 \times p + 2 \times 0.3 + 3q + 4 \times 0.1$$

$$\Rightarrow \quad 2 = p + 3q + 1$$

$$\Rightarrow \quad 1 = p + 3q \quad \ldots\text{(i)}$$

Now, $p + 0.3 + q + 0.1 = 1$

$$p + q = 1 - 0.4 = 0.6 \quad \ldots\text{(ii)}$$

From Eqs. (i) and (ii), we get

$$q = 0.2 \text{ and } p = 0.4$$

$$\therefore \quad P(X > 2) = P(X = 3) + P(X = 4)$$

$$= q + 0.1 = 0.2 + 0.1$$

$$= 0.3$$

Now, 4 points after 3 rolls can be achieved in following ways $\{(2, 1, 1), (1, 1, 2), (1, 2, 1)\}$.

$\therefore$ Probability of having 4 points after 3 rolls is

$$[P(X=2) \times P(X=1) \times P(X=1)] + [P(X=1) \times P(X=1) \times P(X=2)] + [P(X=1) \times P(X=2) \times P(X=1)]$$

$$= (0.3 \times 0.4 \times 0.4) + (0.4 \times 0.4 \times 0.3) + (0.4 \times 0.3 \times 0.4)$$

$$= 0.144$$

Now, atleast 10 points can be scored, if in the last 2 rolls atleast 6 points are scored.

$\therefore$ This can happen in following ways

$$\{(4, 3), (3, 4), (4, 4), (3, 3), (4, 2), (2, 4)\}$$

Probability of scoring atleast 6 points in the last 2 throws is

$$[P(X=4) \times P(X=3)] + [P(X=3) \times P(X=4)] + [P(X=4) \times P(X=4)] + [P(X=3) \times P(X=3)] + [P(X=4) \times P(X=2)] + [P(X=2) \times P(X=4)]$$

$$= 0.02 + 0.02 + 0.01 + 0.04 + 0.03 + 0.03$$

$$= 0.15$$

Now, the probability that Ajay wins the game

$$= 0.144 \times 0.15 = 0.0216$$

Concept Enhancer Using formula,

$$\text{Mean} = E(X) = \sum_{i=1}^{n} X_i P_i$$

5. Let the random variable be X.

Since, number of drawing eggs = 3

So, the value of X can be 0, 1, 2 and 3.

For $P(X = 0) = P$ (0 good egg)

$$= \frac{5}{15} \times \frac{5}{15} \times \frac{5}{15} = \frac{1}{3} \times \frac{1}{3} \times \frac{1}{3} = \frac{1}{27}$$

For $P(X = 1) = P$ (1 good egg)

$$= \frac{10}{15} \times \frac{5}{15} \times \frac{5}{15} + \frac{5}{15} \times \frac{10}{15} \times \frac{5}{15} + \frac{5}{15} \times \frac{5}{15} \times \frac{10}{15}$$

$$= \frac{2}{3} \times \frac{1}{3} \times \frac{1}{3} + \frac{1}{3} \times \frac{2}{3} \times \frac{1}{3} + \frac{1}{3} \times \frac{1}{3} \times \frac{2}{3}$$

$$= \frac{2}{27} + \frac{2}{27} + \frac{2}{27} = \frac{6}{27}$$

For $P(X = 2) = P$ (2 good eggs)

$$= \frac{10}{15} \times \frac{10}{15} \times \frac{5}{15} + \frac{10}{15} \times \frac{5}{15} \times \frac{10}{15} + \frac{5}{15} \times \frac{10}{15} \times \frac{10}{15}$$

$$= \frac{2}{3} \times \frac{2}{3} \times \frac{1}{3} + \frac{2}{3} \times \frac{1}{3} \times \frac{2}{3} + \frac{1}{3} \times \frac{2}{3} \times \frac{2}{3}$$

$$= \frac{4}{27} + \frac{4}{27} + \frac{4}{27}$$

$$= \frac{4+4+4}{27} = \frac{12}{27}$$

For $P(X = 3) = P$ (3 good eggs)

$$= \frac{10}{15} \times \frac{10}{15} \times \frac{10}{15}$$

$$= \frac{2}{3} \times \frac{2}{3} \times \frac{2}{3} = \frac{8}{27}$$

$\therefore$ Required probability distribution is

X	P(X)
0	1/27
1	6/27
2	12/27
3	8/27

6. Let p denote the probability of drawing red ball and q denote the probability of drawing non-red, i.e. green ball, then

$$p=\frac{10}{25}=\frac{2}{5} \text{ and } q=\frac{3}{5}$$

Let X be a random variable that denotes the number of red ball in 6 trials.

Clearly, $X \sim B(6, 2/5)$

$$\therefore P(X=x)={}^6C_x\left(\frac{2}{5}\right)^x\left(\frac{3}{5}\right)^{6-x}$$

where, $x=0,1,2,\ldots,6$

Now,

(i) P (getting all red balls)

$$=P(X=6)={}^6C_6\left(\frac{2}{5}\right)^6\left(\frac{3}{5}\right)^{6-6}=\left(\frac{2}{5}\right)^6$$

(ii) P (getting not more than 2 balls are green balls)

$$=P(X\geq 4)=P(X=4)+P(X=5)+P(X=6)$$

$$={}^6C_4\left(\frac{2}{5}\right)^4\left(\frac{3}{5}\right)^2+{}^6C_5\left(\frac{2}{5}\right)^5\left(\frac{3}{5}\right)$$

$$+{}^6C_6\left(\frac{2}{5}\right)^6\left(\frac{3}{5}\right)^0=7\left(\frac{2}{5}\right)^4$$

(iii) P (getting equal number of red and green balls)

$$=P(X=3)$$

$$={}^6C_3\left(\frac{2}{5}\right)^3\left(\frac{3}{5}\right)^{6-3}=20\left(\frac{2}{5}\right)^3\left(\frac{3}{5}\right)^3$$

7. Let $p=$ probability of occurrence of an odd number in a single die.

$$\therefore \quad p=\frac{3}{6}=\frac{1}{2}$$

[$\because$ odd number in a die are $\{1, 3, 5\}$]

$$\Rightarrow \quad q=1-\frac{1}{2}=\frac{1}{2}$$

Here, $n=5$

Using Bernoulli's theorem,

$$P(X=r)={}^nC_r\,p^r q^{n-r}$$

$\therefore$ The probability of maximum three success

$$=P(X=0)+P(X=1)+P(X=2)+P(X=3)$$

$$={}^5C_0p^0q^5+{}^5C_1p^1q^{5-1}+{}^5C_2p^2q^{5-2}+{}^5C_3p^3q^{5-3}$$

$$={}^5C_0\left(\frac{1}{2}\right)^0\left(\frac{1}{2}\right)^5+{}^5C_1\left(\frac{1}{2}\right)^1\left(\frac{1}{2}\right)^4$$

$$+{}^5C_2\left(\frac{1}{2}\right)^2\left(\frac{1}{2}\right)^3+{}^5C_3\left(\frac{1}{2}\right)^3\left(\frac{1}{2}\right)^2$$

$$=1\times\left(\frac{1}{2}\right)^5+5\left(\frac{1}{2}\right)^5+10\left(\frac{1}{2}\right)^5+10\left(\frac{1}{2}\right)^5$$

$$=\frac{1}{2^5}(1+5+10+10)=\frac{26}{32}=\frac{13}{16}$$

8. We have, the probability of a telephone number is busy $(p)=\frac{1}{5}$

The probability of a telephone number is not busy

$$(q)=1-\frac{1}{5}=\frac{5-1}{5}=\frac{4}{5}$$

Let $x=$ Number of calls dialling

Given, the total number of dialling, $n=10$

The probability of atleast three dialling out of 10 dialling is busy.

$$P(x\geq 3)=P(x=3)+P(x=4)+\cdots+P(x=10)$$

$$=1-[P(x=-0)+P(x=-1)+P(x=-2)]$$

$$=1-[{}^nC_0p^0q^{n-0}+{}^nC_1p^1q^{n-1}+{}^nC_2p^2q^{n-2}]$$

$$=1-\left[{}^{10}C_0\left(\frac{1}{5}\right)^0\left(\frac{4}{5}\right)^{10-0}+{}^{10}C_1\left(\frac{1}{5}\right)^1\left(\frac{4}{5}\right)^{10-1}+{}^{10}C_2\left(\frac{1}{5}\right)^2\left(\frac{4}{5}\right)^{10-2}\right]$$

$$\left[\because n=10,\ p=\frac{1}{5} \text{ and } q=\frac{4}{5}\right]$$

$$=1-\left[\left(\frac{4}{5}\right)^{10}+10\times\frac{4^9}{5^{10}}+45\times\frac{4^8}{5^{10}}\right]$$

$$\left[\because {}^{10}C_2=\frac{10\times 9}{2\times 1}=45\right]$$

$$=1-\frac{4^8}{5^{10}}[(4)^2+10\times(4)^1+45\times 1]$$

$$=1-\frac{4^8}{5^{10}}[16+40+45]=1-\frac{4^8}{5^{10}}[101]$$

$$=1-\frac{65536}{9765625}\times 101=1-\frac{6619136}{9765625}$$

$$=\frac{9765625-6619136}{9765625}=\frac{3146489}{9765625}=032$$

9. Let $p =$ Probability of fused bulb

$$= 0.05 = \frac{5}{100} = \frac{1}{20}$$

and $q =$ Probability of not fused bulb

$$= 1 - \frac{1}{20} = \frac{20-1}{20} = \frac{19}{20} \qquad [\because p + q = 1]$$

Let $X =$ Number of fused bulb after 100 days

Also, $n = 5$

(i) Probability that none bulb is fused,

$$P(X=0) = {}^5C_0 \left(\frac{1}{20}\right)^0 \left(\frac{19}{20}\right)^{5-0} = \left(\frac{19}{20}\right)^5$$

$$[\because P(X=r) = {}^nC_r \, p^r q^{n-r}]$$

(ii) Probability that no more than one bulb is fused,

$$P(X = 0 \text{ or } X = 1) = P(X=0) + P(X=1)$$

$$= \left(\frac{19}{20}\right)^5 + {}^5C_1 \left(\frac{1}{20}\right)^1 \left(\frac{19}{20}\right)^{5-1}$$

$$\left[\because P(X=0) = \left(\frac{19}{20}\right)^5\right]$$

$$= \left(\frac{19}{20}\right)^5 + \frac{5!}{(5-1)!} \times \frac{1}{20} \times \left(\frac{19}{20}\right)^4$$

$$= \left(\frac{19}{20}\right)^5 + 5 \times \frac{1}{20} \times \left(\frac{19}{20}\right)^4$$

$$= \left(\frac{19}{20}\right)^5 + \frac{5}{20} \times \left(\frac{19}{20}\right)^4$$

$$= \left(\frac{19}{20}\right)^4 \left(\frac{19}{20} + \frac{1}{4}\right)$$

$$= \left(\frac{19}{20}\right)^4 \left(\frac{19+5}{20}\right)$$

$$= \left(\frac{19}{20}\right)^4 \times \left(\frac{24}{20}\right)$$

$$= \left(\frac{19}{20}\right)^4 \times \frac{6}{5} \qquad \ldots\text{(i)}$$

(iii) Probability that more than one bulb is fused,

$$P(1 < X \le 5) = 1 - P(X = 0 \text{ or } X = 1)$$

$$= 1 - \frac{6}{5}\left(\frac{19}{20}\right)^4$$

$$\left[\because P(X = 0 \text{ or } X = 1) = \frac{6}{5} \times \left(\frac{19}{20}\right)^4\right]$$

(iv) Probability that for atleast one bulb is fused,

$$P(1 \le X \le 5) = 1 - P(X=0)$$

$$= 1 - \left(\frac{19}{20}\right)^5 \quad \left[\because P(X=0) = \left(\frac{19}{20}\right)^5\right]$$

10. Let the random variable be X.

Since, number of drawing eggs = 3

So, the value of X can be 0, 1, 2 and 3.

For $P(X=0) = P$ (0 good egg)

$$= \frac{5}{15} \times \frac{5}{15} \times \frac{5}{15} = \frac{1}{3} \times \frac{1}{3} \times \frac{1}{3} = \frac{1}{27}$$

For $P(X=1) = P$ (1 good egg)

$$= \frac{10}{15} \times \frac{5}{15} \times \frac{5}{15} + \frac{5}{15} \times \frac{10}{15} \times \frac{5}{15} + \frac{5}{15} \times \frac{5}{15} \times \frac{10}{15}$$

$$= \frac{2}{3} \times \frac{1}{3} \times \frac{1}{3} + \frac{1}{3} \times \frac{2}{3} \times \frac{1}{3} + \frac{1}{3} \times \frac{1}{3} \times \frac{2}{3}$$

$$= \frac{2}{27} + \frac{2}{27} + \frac{2}{27} = \frac{6}{27}$$

For $P(X=2) = P$ (2 good eggs)

$$= \frac{10}{15} \times \frac{10}{15} \times \frac{5}{15} + \frac{10}{15} \times \frac{5}{15} \times \frac{10}{15} + \frac{5}{15} \times \frac{10}{15} \times \frac{10}{15}$$

$$= \frac{2}{3} \times \frac{2}{3} \times \frac{1}{3} + \frac{2}{3} \times \frac{1}{3} \times \frac{2}{3} + \frac{1}{3} \times \frac{2}{3} \times \frac{2}{3}$$

$$= \frac{4}{27} + \frac{4}{27} + \frac{4}{27} = \frac{4+4+4}{27} = \frac{12}{27}$$

For $P(X=3) = P$ (3 good eggs)

$$= \frac{10}{15} \times \frac{10}{15} \times \frac{10}{15} = \frac{2}{3} \times \frac{2}{3} \times \frac{2}{3} = \frac{8}{27}$$

$\therefore$ Required probability distribution is

X	P(X)
0	1/27
1	6/27
2	12/27
3	8/27

11. Given,

The total number of coins $= 8 = n$

The probability of getting heads $= \frac{1}{2} = p$

$$\therefore \quad q = 1 - p = 1 - \frac{1}{2} = \frac{2-1}{2} = \frac{1}{2} \qquad [\because p + q = 1]$$

(i) By using Binomial theorem,

Required probability P (atleast 6 heads)

$$= P(x=6) + P(x=7) + P(x=8)$$

$$= {}^8C_6 \left(\frac{1}{2}\right)^6 \left(\frac{1}{2}\right)^2 + {}^8C_7 \left(\frac{1}{2}\right)^7 \left(\frac{1}{2}\right) + {}^8C_8 \left(\frac{1}{2}\right)^8$$

$$= \frac{8!}{2!6!}\left(\frac{1}{2}\right)^6\left(\frac{1}{2}\right)^2 + \frac{8!}{7!}\left(\frac{1}{2}\right)^7\left(\frac{1}{2}\right) + \left(\frac{1}{2}\right)^8$$

$$= 28\left(\frac{1}{2}\right)^8 + 8\left(\frac{1}{2}\right)^8 + \left(\frac{1}{2}\right)^8$$

$$= \left(\frac{1}{2}\right)^8 (28+8+1)$$

$$= \left(\frac{1}{2}\right)^8 (37) = \frac{1}{256} \times 37 = \frac{37}{256}$$

(ii) Required probability (atleast 3 heads)

$= 1 -$ Probability of (atmost 2 heads)

$$= 1 - [P(x=0) + P(x=1) + P(x=2)]$$

$$= 1 - \left[{}^8C_0\left(\frac{1}{2}\right)^0\left(\frac{1}{2}\right)^8 + {}^8C_1\left(\frac{1}{2}\right)\left(\frac{1}{2}\right)^7 + {}^8C_2\left(\frac{1}{2}\right)^2\left(\frac{1}{2}\right)^6\right]$$

$$= 1 - \left[\left(\frac{1}{2}\right)^8 + \frac{8!}{7!}\left(\frac{1}{2}\right)^8 + \frac{8!}{6!2!}\left(\frac{1}{2}\right)^8\right]$$

$$= 1 - \left[\left(\frac{1}{2}\right)^8 + 8\left(\frac{1}{2}\right)^8 + \frac{8\times 7}{2}\left(\frac{1}{2}\right)^8\right]$$

$$= 1 - \left(\frac{1}{2}\right)^8\left[1 + 8 + \frac{56}{2}\right]$$

$$= 1 - \left(\frac{1}{2}\right)^8 (1+8+28)$$

$$= 1 - \left(\frac{1}{2}\right)^8 \times 37$$

$$= 1 - \left(\frac{1}{256}\right) \times 37 = 1 - \frac{37}{256}$$

$$= \frac{256-37}{256} = \frac{219}{256}$$

12. Given, $p =$ Probability that a teacher will give an unannounced test during class $= \frac{1}{5}$

Then, $q = 1 - p = 1 - \frac{1}{5} = \frac{4}{5}$ $[\because p + q = 1]$

Also, given student is absent twicely i.e. $n = 2$

P (student miss only one test) $= P(X=1)$

$$= {}^2C_1 p^1 q^1 \quad [\because P(X=r) = {}^nC_r p^r q^{n-r}]$$

$$= 2 \times \left(\frac{1}{5}\right) \times \left(\frac{4}{5}\right) = \frac{8}{25}$$

P (student miss both the test) $= P(X=2)$

$$= {}^2C_2 p^2 q^0 = 1 \cdot \left(\frac{1}{5}\right)^2 \times \left(\frac{4}{5}\right)^0 = \frac{1}{25}$$

P (student miss atleast one test) $= P(X \geq 1)$

$$= P(X=1) + P(X=2)$$

$$= \frac{8}{25} + \frac{1}{25} = \frac{9}{25}$$

CHAPTER TEST

1 Mark Questions

1. If A and B are events such that $P\left(\frac{A}{B}\right)=P\left(\frac{B}{A}\right)$, then

(a) $A \subset B$ but $A \neq B$ (b) $A = B$
(c) $A \cap B = \phi$ (d) $P(A) = P(B)$

2. If A and B are two events such that $P(B)=\frac{3}{5}$, $P(A/B)=\frac{1}{2}$ and $P(A \cup B)=\frac{4}{5}$, then $P(A)$ equals to

(a) $\frac{3}{10}$ (b) $\frac{1}{5}$ (c) $\frac{1}{2}$ (d) $\frac{3}{5}$

3. If A and B are two events such that $A \subset B$ and $P(B) \neq 0$, then which of the following is correct?

(a) $P\left(\frac{B}{A}\right)=\frac{P(A)}{P(B)}$ (b) $P\left(\frac{A}{B}\right) < P(A)$
(c) $P\left(\frac{A}{B}\right) \geq P(A)$ (d) None of these

4. A flashlight has 8 batteries out of which 3 are dead. If two batteries are selected without replacement and tested, then probability that both are dead is

(a) $\frac{33}{56}$ (b) $\frac{9}{64}$ (c) $\frac{1}{14}$ (d) $\frac{3}{28}$

5. The probability of obtaining an even prime number on each die when a pair of dice is rolled is

(a) zero (b) $\frac{1}{3}$ (c) $\frac{1}{12}$ (d) $\frac{1}{36}$

3/4 Marks Questions

6. A and B throw a pair of dice alternately. A wins the game, if he gets a total of 7 and B wins the game, if he gets a total of 10. If A starts the game, then find the probability that B wins.

7. Probabilities of solving a specific problem independently by A and B are $\frac{1}{2}$ and $\frac{1}{3}$, respectively. If both try to solve problem independently, then find the probability that

(i) problem is solved.
(ii) exactly one of them solves the problem.

8. A couple has 2 children. Find the probability that both are boys, if it is known that

(i) one of them is a boy.
(ii) the older child is a boy.

9. P speaks truth in 70% of the cases and Q in 80% of the cases. In what per cent of cases are they likely to agree in stating the same fact?

10. If A and B are two independent events such that $P(\overline{A} \cap B)=\frac{2}{15}$ and $P(A \cap \overline{B})=\frac{1}{6}$, then find $P(A)$ and $P(B)$.

11. There are 4 cards numbered 1, 3, 5 and 7, one number on one card. Two cards are drawn at random without replacement. Let X denote the sum of the numbers on the two drawn cards. Find the mean.

12. The random variable X can take only the values 0, 1, 2, 3. Given that $P(X=0)=P(X=1)=p$ and $P(X=2)=P(X=3)$ such that $\Sigma p_i x_i^2 = 2\Sigma p_i x_i$, find the value of p.

13. In a game, a man wins ₹ 5 for getting a number greater than 4 and loses ₹ 1 otherwise, when a fair die is thrown. The man decided to throw a die thrice but to quit as and when he gets a number greater than 4. Find the expected value of the amount he wins/loses.

14. The random variable X can take only the values 0, 1, 2, 3. Given that $P(X=0)=P(X=1)=p$ and $P(X=2)=P(X=3)$ such that $\Sigma p_i x_i^2 = 2\Sigma p_i x_i$, find the value of p.

5/6 Marks Questions

15. In answering a question on a multiple choice test, a student either knows the answer or guesses. Let $\frac{3}{5}$ be the probability that he knows the answer and $\frac{2}{5}$ be the probability that he guesses. Assuming that a student who guesses at the answer will be correct with probability $\frac{1}{3}$. What is the probability that the student knows the answer given that he answered it correctly?

16. Assume that the chances of a patient having a heart attack is 40%. Assuming that a mediation and yoga course reduces the risk of heart attack by 30% and prescription of certain drug reduces its chance by 25%. At a time, a patient can choose anyone of the two options with equal probabilities. It is given that after going through one of the two options, the patient selected at random suffers a heart attack. Find the probability that the patient followed a course of mediation and yoga.

17. A girl throws a die. If she gets a 5 or 6, she tosses a coin three times and notes the number of heads. If she gets 1, 2, 3 or 4, she tosses a coin two times and notes the number of heads obtained. If she obtained exactly two heads, what is the probability that she threw 1, 2, 3 or 4 with the die?

18. A card from a pack of 52 cards is lost. From the remaining cards of the pack, two cards are drawn at random and are found to both of clubs. Find the probability of the lost card being of clubs.

19. A man is known to speak truth 3 out of 5 times. He throws a die and reports that it is a number greater than 4. Find the probability that it is actually a number greater than 4.

Answers

1. (d) **2.** (c) **3.** (c) **4.** (d) **5.** (d) **6.** $\frac{5}{17}$

7. (i) $\frac{2}{3}$ (ii) $\frac{1}{2}$ **8.** (i) $\frac{1}{3}$ (ii) $\frac{1}{2}$ **9.** 62%

10. $P(A)=\frac{1}{5}$ or $P(B)=\frac{1}{6}$ or $\frac{4}{5}$ **11.** Mean = 8

12. $p=\frac{3}{8}$ **13.** $\frac{19}{9}$ **14.** $P=\frac{3}{8}$ **15.** $\frac{9}{11}$

16. $\frac{14}{29}$ **17.** $\frac{4}{7}$ **18.** $\frac{11}{50}$ **19.** $\frac{3}{7}$

10 Vectors

TREND ANALYSIS 3 YEARS

		Average No. of Questions Across all Sets		
	Types of Questions	2024	2023	2020
TOPIC 01 Algebra of Vectors	1 Mark	3	—	—
	2 Marks	—	1	1
	3/4 Marks	—	—	—
	5/6 Marks	—	—	—
TOPIC 02 Scalar and Vector Product of Two Vectors	1 Mark	—	3	—
	2 Marks	2	1	—
	3/4 Marks	—	—	1
	5/6 Marks	—	—	—

TOPIC 1

Algebra of Vectors

Scalars and Vectors

Those quantities which have only magnitude and no direction, are called **scalar quantities** or **scalars**. Those quantities which have magnitude as well as direction are called **vector quantities** or **vectors**.

Representation of Vector

A directed line segment has magnitude as well as direction, so it is called vector denoted as $\overrightarrow{AB}$ or simply as $\vec{a}$. Here, the point A from where the vector $\overrightarrow{AB}$ starts is called its initial point and the point B, where it ends is called its terminal point.

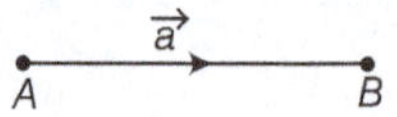

Magnitude of a Vector

The length of the vector $\overrightarrow{AB}$ or $\vec{a}$ is called magnitude of $\overrightarrow{AB}$ or $\vec{a}$ and it is represented by $|\overrightarrow{AB}|$ or $|\vec{a}|$ or a.

NOTE Since, the length is never negative, so the notation $|\vec{a}|<0$ has no meaning.

Direction of Vector

Any line which can be described by a vector, called its direction vector.

Position Vector of a Point

Let $O(0, 0, 0)$ be the origin and P be a point in space having coordinates (x, y, z) with respect to the origin O. Then, the vector $\overrightarrow{OP}$ or $\vec{r}$ is called the position vector of the point P with respect to O.

The magnitude of $\overrightarrow{OP}$ or $\vec{r}$ is given by

$$|\overrightarrow{OP}| = |\vec{r}| = \sqrt{x^2 + y^2 + z^2}.$$

NOTE Generally, the position vectors of points A, B, C, etc. with respect to origin are denoted by $\vec{a}, \vec{b}, \vec{c}$ etc., respectively.

Direction Cosines and Direction Ratios

If the angles α, β and γ made by the vector $\overrightarrow{OP}$ with the positive directions of the coordinate axes OX, OY and OZ respectively, then cosine values of these angles, i.e. $\cos\alpha$, $\cos\beta$ and $\cos\gamma$ are known as the direction cosines of $\overrightarrow{OP}$. Generally, they are denoted by the letters l, m and n respectively,

i.e. $\quad l = \cos\alpha,\ m = \cos\beta$ and $n = \cos\gamma$

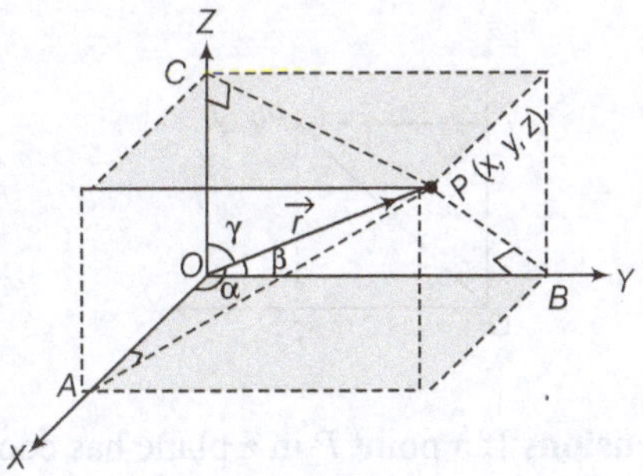

In the figure,

$$\cos\alpha = \frac{x}{|\vec{r}|},\ \cos\beta = \frac{y}{|\vec{r}|} \text{ and } \cos\gamma = \frac{z}{|\vec{r}|}$$

$$\Rightarrow \quad l = \frac{x}{|\vec{r}|},\ m = \frac{y}{|\vec{r}|} \text{ and } n = \frac{z}{|\vec{r}|}$$

$$\Rightarrow \quad x = l|\vec{r}|,\ y = m|\vec{r}| \text{ and } z = n|\vec{r}|$$

Thus, the coordinates of the point P may be expressed as

$$[l|\vec{r}|,\ m|\vec{r}|,\ n|\vec{r}|]$$

The numbers $l|\vec{r}|$, $m|\vec{r}|$ and $n|\vec{r}|$ are proportional to the direction cosines are called **direction ratios** of vector $\vec{r}$.

NOTE (i) In general, it may be noted that $l^2 + m^2 + n^2 = 1$ but $x^2 + y^2 + z^2 \neq 1$.

(ii) If $\vec{a} = a_1\hat{i} + a_2\hat{j} + a_3\hat{k}$, then a_1, a_2 and a_3 are called direction ratios of $\vec{a}$.

(iii) If it is given that l, m and n are direction cosines of a vector, then $l\hat{i} + m\hat{j} + n\hat{k} = (\cos\alpha)\hat{i} + (\cos\beta)\hat{j} + (\cos\gamma)\hat{k}$ is the unit vector in the direction of that vector, where α, β and γ are the angles made by the vector with the positive direction of X, Y and Z-axes, respectively.

Types of Vectors

(i) **Null vector or zero vector** A vector, whose initial and terminal points coincide and magnitude is zero, is called a null vector and denoted as $\vec{0}$.

NOTE Zero vector cannot be assigned a definite direction or it may be regarded as having any direction. The vectors $\overrightarrow{AA}$, $\overrightarrow{BB}$ represent the zero vector.

(ii) **Unit vector** A vector of unit length is called unit vector. The unit vector in the direction of $\vec{a}$ is $\hat{a} = \dfrac{\vec{a}}{|\vec{a}|}$.

(iii) **Coinitial vectors** Two or more vectors having the same initial point are called coinitial vectors.

(iv) **Equal vectors** Two vectors are said to be equal, if they have equal magnitudes and same direction regardless of the position of their initial points.

NOTE If $\vec{a} = \vec{b}$, then $|\vec{a}| = |\vec{b}|$ but converse may not be true.

(v) **Negative vector** A vector having the same magnitude but opposite in direction of the given vector, is called negative of the given vector. e.g. Vector $\overrightarrow{BA}$ is negative of the vector $\overrightarrow{AB}$ and written as $\overrightarrow{BA} = -\overrightarrow{AB}$.

(v) **Collinear or parallel vectors** Two or more vectors are said to be collinear, if they are parallel to the same line, irrespective of their magnitudes and directions. e.g. $\vec{a}$ and $\vec{b}$ are collinear, when $\vec{a} = \lambda\vec{b}$, where λ is some scalar.

NOTE If the value of a vector depends only on its magnitude and direction and is independent of its position in the space, such vectors are called **free vectors.**

Addition of Vectors

Triangle law of vector addition

If two vectors are represented along two sides of a triangle taken in order, then their resultant is represented by the third side taken in opposite direction, i.e. in ΔABC, by triangle law of vector addition, we have

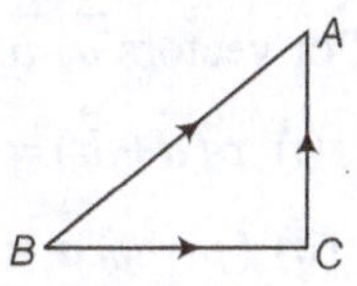

$$\overrightarrow{BC} + \overrightarrow{CA} = \overrightarrow{BA}.$$

NOTE The vector sum of three sides of a triangle taken in order is $\vec{0}$.

Parallelogram Law of vector addition

If two vectors are represented along the two adjacent sides of a parallelogram, then their resultant is represented by the diagonal of the parallelogram through the common point. In the parallelogram $OABC$, we have

$$\overrightarrow{OA} + \overrightarrow{OC} = \overrightarrow{OB}.$$

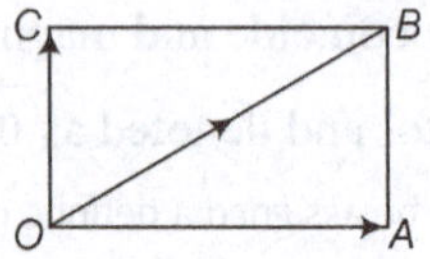

NOTE Both laws of vector addition are equivalent to each other.

Properties of vector addition

(i) **Commutative** For vectors $\vec{a}$ and $\vec{b}$, we have $\vec{a}+\vec{b}=\vec{b}+\vec{a}$.

(ii) **Associative** For vectors $\vec{a}$, $\vec{b}$ and $\vec{c}$, we have $\vec{a}+(\vec{b}+\vec{c})=(\vec{a}+\vec{b})+\vec{c}$.

(iii) **Additive identity** For any vector $\vec{a}$, a zero vector $\vec{0}$ is its additive identity as $\vec{a}+\vec{0}=\vec{a}$.

(iv) **Additive inverse** For a vector $\vec{a}$, a negative vector of $\vec{a}$ is its additive inverse as $\vec{a}+(-\vec{a})=\vec{0}$.

NOTE The associative property of vector addition enables us to write the sum of three vectors $\vec{a}, \vec{b}$ and $\vec{c}$ as $\vec{a}+\vec{b}+\vec{c}$ without using brackets.

Multiplication of a Vector by a Scalar

Let $\vec{a}$ be a given vector and λ be a scalar, then multiplication of vector $\vec{a}$ by scalar λ, denoted as $\lambda\,\vec{a}$, is also a vector, collinear to the vector $\vec{a}$ whose magnitude is $|\lambda|$ times that of vector $\vec{a}$ and direction is same as $\vec{a}$, if $\lambda > 0$; opposite of $\vec{a}$, if $\lambda < 0$ and zero vector, if $\lambda = 0$.

NOTE For any scalar λ, $\lambda \cdot \vec{0} = \vec{0}$.

Properties of Scalar Multiplication

For vectors $\vec{a}$, $\vec{b}$ and scalars p, q, we have

(i) $p(\vec{a}+\vec{b})=p\,\vec{a}+p\,\vec{b}$

(ii) $(p+q)\,\vec{a}=p\,\vec{a}+q\,\vec{a}$

(iii) $p(q\,\vec{a})=(pq)\,\vec{a}$

NOTE To prove $\vec{a}$ is parallel to $\vec{b}$, we need to show that $\vec{a}=\lambda\,\vec{b}$, where λ is a scalar.

Components of a Vector

The position vector of any point $P(x, y, z)$ with reference to O is given by $\overrightarrow{OP}$ (or $\vec{r}$) $= x\hat{i} + y\hat{j} + z\hat{k}$, where $\hat{i}, \hat{j}, \hat{k}$ are unit vectors along the X-axis, Y-axis and Z-axis. This form of any vector is called its **component form**.

Here, x, y and z are called the scalar components of $\vec{r}$ and $x\hat{i}$, $y\hat{j}$ and $z\hat{k}$ are called the vector components of $\vec{r}$ along the respective axes.

Two dimensions If a point P in a plane has coordinates (x, y), then

$$\overrightarrow{OP} = x\,\hat{i} + y\,\hat{j}$$

where $\hat{i}$ and $\hat{j}$ are unit vectors along OX and OY-axes, respectively.

Then, $|\overrightarrow{OP}| = \sqrt{x^2 + y^2}$.

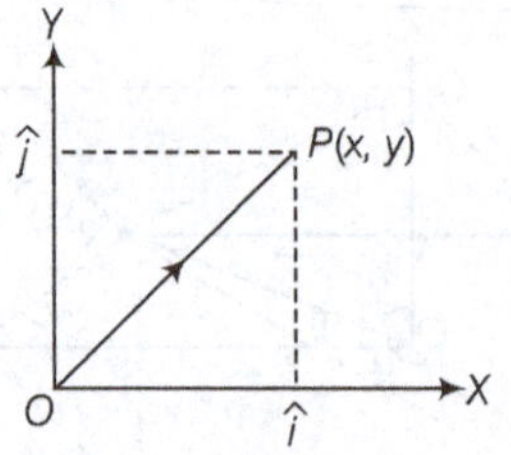

Three dimensions If a point P in a plane has coordinates (x, y, z), then $\overrightarrow{OP} = x\,\hat{i} + y\,\hat{j} + z\,\hat{k}$, where $\hat{i}, \hat{j}$ and $\hat{k}$ are unit vectors along OX, OY and OZ-axes, respectively.

Then, $|\overrightarrow{OP}| = \sqrt{x^2 + y^2 + z^2}$.

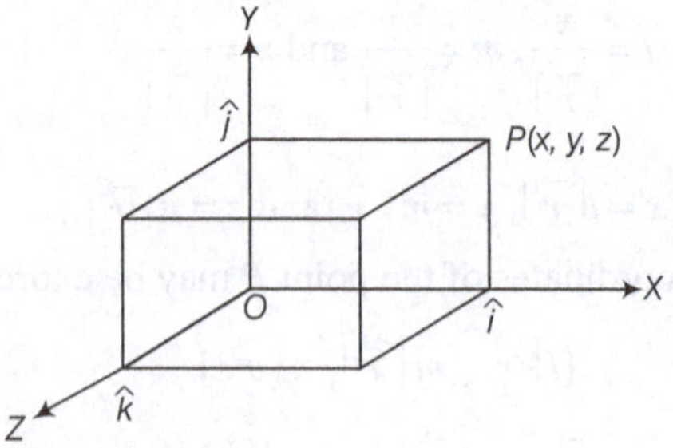

Important Facts

If we have two vectors $\vec{a}$ and $\vec{b}$, given in component form as $\vec{a} = a_1\hat{i} + a_2\hat{j} + a_3\hat{k}$ and $\vec{b} = b_1\hat{i} + b_2\hat{j} + b_3\hat{k}$ and λ any scalar, then

(i) $\vec{a} + \vec{b} = (a_1 + b_1)\hat{i} + (a_2 + b_2)\hat{j} + (a_3 + b_3)\hat{k}$

(ii) $\vec{a} - \vec{b} = (a_1 - b_1)\hat{i} + (a_2 - b_2)\hat{j} + (a_3 - b_3)\hat{k}$

(iii) $\lambda \vec{a} = (\lambda a_1)\hat{i} + (\lambda a_2)\hat{j} + (\lambda a_3)\hat{k}$

(iv) $\vec{a} = \vec{b}$ iff $a_1 = b_1, a_2 = b_2$ and $a_3 = b_3$

(v) $\vec{a}$ and $\vec{b}$ are collinear (or parallel) iff

$$\frac{a_1}{b_1} = \frac{a_2}{b_2} = \frac{a_3}{b_3} = \lambda$$

Vector Joining of Two Points

If $P_1(x_1, y_1, z_1)$ and $P_2(x_2, y_2, z_2)$ are any two points, then the vector joining P_1 and P_2 is the vector $\overrightarrow{P_1P_2}$.

$$\overrightarrow{OP_2} - \overrightarrow{OP_1} = (x_2\hat{i} + y_2\hat{j} + z_2\hat{k}) - (x_1\hat{i} + y_1\hat{j} + z_1\hat{k})$$

i.e. $\overrightarrow{P_1P_2} = (x_2 - x_1)\hat{i} + (y_2 - y_1)\hat{j} + (z_2 - z_1)\hat{k}$

and $|\overrightarrow{P_1P_2}|$ the distance between two points,

$$= \sqrt{(x_2 - x_1)^2 + (y_2 - y_1)^2 + (z_2 - z_1)^2}$$

Section Formula

Position vector of a point dividing a line segment in a given ratio Position vector $\overrightarrow{OR}$ of point R which divides the line segment joining the points A and B with position vectors $\vec{a}$ and $\vec{b}$ respectively,

Internally in the ratio $m:n$ is given by

$$\overrightarrow{OR} = \frac{m\vec{b} + n\vec{a}}{m+n}.$$

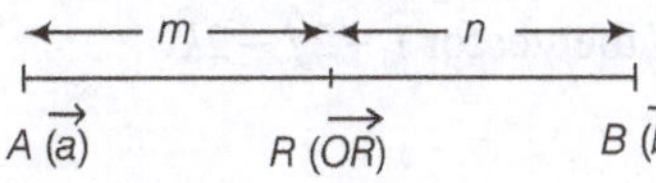

For external division

$$\overrightarrow{OR} = \frac{m\vec{b} - n\vec{a}}{m-n}.$$

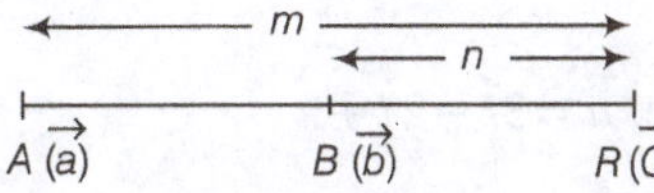

NOTE Position vector of mid-point of the line segment joining the points $A(\vec{a})$ and $B(\vec{b})$ is given by $\overrightarrow{OR} = \frac{\vec{a} + \vec{b}}{2}$.

PYQs Previous Years Questions

1 Mark Questions

1. If $\vec{a} = 3\hat{i} - 2\hat{j} + \hat{k}$ and $\vec{b} = 2\hat{i} - 4\hat{j} - 3\hat{k}$, then the value of $|\vec{a} - 2\vec{b}|$ will be *ISC 2024*

(a) $\sqrt{85}$ (b) $\sqrt{86}$ (c) $\sqrt{87}$ (d) $\sqrt{88}$

2. If $\vec{a} = 2\hat{i} + \hat{j} + 2\hat{k}$ and $\vec{b} = 5\hat{i} - 3\hat{j} + \hat{k}$, find the projection of $\vec{b}$ on $\vec{a}$. *ISC 2024*

3. Find a vector of magnitude 20 units parallel to the vector $2\hat{i} + 5\hat{j} + 4\hat{k}$. *ISC 2024*

4. Observe the vector diagram shown below and the expression that follows. *ISC Specimen 2024*

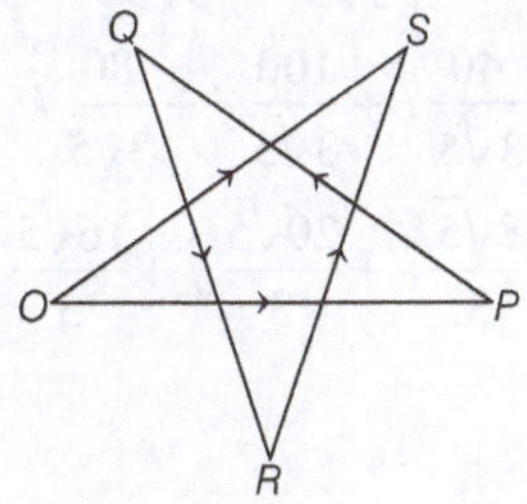

(1) $\overrightarrow{SO}$ (2) $\overrightarrow{OS}$ (3) $-\overrightarrow{SO}$ (4) $-\overrightarrow{OS}$

(a) only (1) (b) only (2)

(c) only (1) and (4) (d) only (2) and (3)

5. If $\vec{u} = \hat{i}, \vec{v} = \hat{j}$ and $\vec{w} = \hat{k}$ are unit vectors, what is the angle between $(\vec{w} \times \vec{v})$ and $\vec{u}$? *ISC Specimen 2024*

6. Find a vector of magnitude of 10 units and parallel to the vector $2\hat{i} + 3\hat{j} - \hat{k}$. *ISC Specimen 2023*

7. Find the position vector of a point R which divides the line joining the two-points $\vec{P}$ and $\vec{Q}$ with position vectors $2\hat{i} + \hat{j}$ and $\hat{i} - 2\hat{j}$, respectively in the ratio of $2:1$ externally. *ISC Specimen 2023*

8. If the vectors $a\hat{i} + 3\hat{j} - 2\hat{k}$ and $3\hat{i} - 4\hat{j} + b\hat{k}$ are collinear, then (a, b) is equal to *ISC Specimen 2021*

(a) $\left(\frac{9}{4}, \frac{8}{3}\right)$ (b) $\left(-\frac{9}{4}, \frac{8}{3}\right)$ (c) $\left(\frac{9}{4}, -\frac{8}{3}\right)$ (d) $\left(-\frac{9}{4}, -\frac{8}{3}\right)$

9. Find the unit vector parallel to the vector:
$3\hat{i}+6\hat{j}-2\hat{k}$. *ISC Specimen 2021*

2 Marks Questions

10. If $A(1, 2, -3)$ and $B(-1, -2, 1)$ are the end points of a vector $\overrightarrow{AB}$, then find the unit vector in the direction of $\overrightarrow{AB}$. *ISC 2023*

11. Write a vector of magnitude of 18 units in the direction of the vector $\hat{i}-2\hat{j}-2\hat{k}$. *ISC 2020*

3 Marks Questions

12. If $\vec{a}$ and $\vec{b}$ are non-collinear vectors, then find the value of x such that the vectors $\alpha=(x-2)\vec{a}+\vec{b}$ and $\beta=(3+2x)\vec{a}-2\vec{b}$ are collinear. *ISC 2019*

13. Find the position vector of a point which divides the join of points with position vectors $\vec{a}-2\vec{b}$ and $2\vec{a}+\vec{b}$ externally in the ratio 2:1.

14. If $\vec{a}=4\hat{i}-\hat{j}+\hat{k}$ and $\vec{b}=2\hat{i}-2\hat{j}+\hat{k}$, then find a unit vector parallel to the vector $\vec{a}+\vec{b}$.

Explanations

1. (b) We have, $\vec{a}=3\hat{i}-2\hat{j}+\hat{k}$ ...(i)

and $\vec{b}=2\hat{i}-4\hat{j}-3\hat{k}$

$\Rightarrow$ $2\vec{b}=2(2\hat{i}-4\hat{j}-3\hat{k})$ [multiplying by 2 on both sides]

$=4\hat{i}-8\hat{j}-6\hat{k}$ ...(ii)

On subtracting Eq. (ii) from Eq. (i), we get

$$\vec{a}-2\vec{b}=(3\hat{i}-2\hat{j}+\hat{k})-(4\hat{i}-8\hat{j}-6\hat{k})$$
$$=(3-4)\hat{i}+(-2+8)\hat{j}+(1+6)\hat{k}$$
$$=-\hat{i}+6\hat{j}+7\hat{k}$$

Now, $|\vec{a}-2\vec{b}|=|-\hat{i}+6\hat{j}+7\hat{k}|$

$$=\sqrt{(-1)^2+(6)^2+7^2}$$
$$=\sqrt{1+36+49}=\sqrt{86}$$

2. We have, $\vec{a}=2\hat{i}+\hat{j}+2\hat{k}$

and $\vec{b}=5\hat{i}-3\hat{j}+\hat{k}$

The projection of $\vec{b}$ on $\vec{a}$ is given by

$$=\frac{\vec{b}\cdot\vec{a}}{|\vec{a}|}$$
$$=\frac{(5\hat{i}-3\hat{j}+\hat{k})\cdot(2\hat{i}+\hat{j}+2\hat{k})}{\sqrt{2^2+1^2+2^2}}$$
$$=\frac{10-3+2}{\sqrt{4+1+4}}=\frac{9}{\sqrt{9}}=\frac{9}{3}=3$$

$\therefore$ The projection of $\vec{b}$ on $\vec{a}$ is 3.

3. We have, $\vec{a}=2\hat{i}+5\hat{j}+4\hat{k}$

$\therefore$ $|\vec{a}|=\sqrt{2^2+5^2+4^2}$

$$=\sqrt{4+25+16}=\sqrt{45}=3\sqrt{5}$$

Now, unit vector in direction of $\vec{a}=\dfrac{\vec{a}}{|\vec{a}|}$

$$\hat{a}=\frac{1}{3\sqrt{5}}[2\hat{i}+5\hat{j}+4\hat{k}]$$
$$=\frac{2}{3\sqrt{5}}\hat{i}+\frac{5}{3\sqrt{5}}\hat{j}+\frac{4}{3\sqrt{5}}\hat{k}$$

Thus, the vector with magnitude 1

$$=\frac{2}{3\sqrt{5}}\hat{i}+\frac{5}{3\sqrt{5}}\hat{j}+\frac{4}{3\sqrt{5}}\hat{k}$$

$\therefore$ Vector with magnitude 20

$$=20\times\left[\frac{2}{3\sqrt{5}}\hat{i}+\frac{5}{3\sqrt{5}}\hat{j}+\frac{4}{3\sqrt{5}}\hat{k}\right]$$
$$=\frac{40}{3\sqrt{5}}\hat{i}+\frac{100}{3\sqrt{5}}\hat{j}+\frac{80}{3\sqrt{5}}\hat{k}$$
$$=\frac{8\sqrt{5}}{3}\hat{i}+\frac{20\sqrt{5}}{3}\hat{j}+\frac{16\sqrt{5}}{3}\hat{k}$$

4. (d)

(1) $\overrightarrow{SO}$ is not follows because from the figure the initial point is O and terminal point is S.

(2) $\overrightarrow{OS}$ is follows because O is initial point and S is terminal point.

(3) $-\overrightarrow{SO}$ is follows because $-\overrightarrow{SO}$ or $\overrightarrow{OS}$ is negative vector of $\overrightarrow{SO}$.

(4) $-\overrightarrow{OS}$ does not follow because $-\overrightarrow{OS}$ or $\overrightarrow{SO}$ is negative vector of $\overrightarrow{OS}$.

5. Given, $\vec{u}=\hat{i}$, $\vec{v}=\hat{j}$ and $\vec{w}=\hat{k}$

$\therefore\ \vec{w}\times\vec{v}=(\hat{k}\times\hat{j})=-\hat{i}$

Let θ be the angle between $(\vec{w}\times\vec{v})$ and $\vec{u}$,

then $\cos\theta=\dfrac{(-\hat{i}).(\hat{i})}{\sqrt{(-1)^2}.\sqrt{(1)^2}}=\dfrac{-1}{1}=-1$

$\Rightarrow\ \cos\theta=\cos\pi \Rightarrow \theta=\pi$

6. Let $\vec{a}=\alpha\hat{i}+\beta\hat{j}+\gamma\hat{k}$ and $\vec{b}=2\hat{i}+3\hat{j}-\hat{k}$

According to the question,

$$\vec{a}=\lambda\vec{b} \quad \text{...(i)}$$

$\Rightarrow\ |\vec{a}|=|\lambda\vec{b}| \Rightarrow |\vec{a}|=\lambda|\vec{b}|$

$\Rightarrow\ 10=\lambda\sqrt{(2)^2+(3)^2+(-1)^2}$

$\Rightarrow\ \lambda=\dfrac{10}{\sqrt{14}}$

$\Rightarrow\ \vec{a}=\dfrac{10}{\sqrt{14}}(2\hat{i}+3\hat{j}-\hat{k})$ [from Eq. (i)]

$\Rightarrow\ \vec{a}=\dfrac{20}{\sqrt{14}}\hat{i}+\dfrac{30}{\sqrt{14}}\hat{j}-\dfrac{10}{\sqrt{14}}\hat{k}$

7. The position vector of point R dividing the line segment joining two points P and Q in the ratio $m:n$ is given.

For externally : $\dfrac{m\vec{Q}-n\vec{P}}{m-n}$

Position vectors of P and Q are given as

$$\overrightarrow{OP}=2\hat{i}+\hat{j} \text{ and } \overrightarrow{OQ}=\hat{i}-2\hat{j}$$

The position vector of point R which divides the line joining two points P and Q externally in the ratio 2 : 1 is given by

$$\overrightarrow{OR}=\frac{2(\hat{i}-2\hat{j})-1(2\hat{i}+\hat{j})}{2-1}$$

$\Rightarrow\ \overrightarrow{OR}=\dfrac{2\hat{i}-4\hat{j}-2\hat{i}-\hat{j}}{1}=-5\hat{j}$

8. (b) If $a\hat{i}+3\hat{j}-2\hat{k}$ and $3\hat{i}-4\hat{j}+b\hat{k}$ are collinear.

Then, $\dfrac{a}{3}=\dfrac{3}{-4}=\dfrac{-2}{b}$

Now, $\dfrac{a}{3}=\dfrac{3}{-4}$

$\Rightarrow\ -4a=9 \Rightarrow a=\dfrac{-9}{4}$

and $\dfrac{3}{-4}=\dfrac{-2}{b}$

$\Rightarrow\ 3b=8 \Rightarrow b=\dfrac{8}{3}$

Hence, $(a, b)=\left(-\dfrac{9}{4},\dfrac{8}{3}\right)$

9. Given, $\vec{r}=3\hat{i}+6\hat{j}-2\hat{k}$

Now, $|\vec{r}|=\sqrt{3^2+6^2+(-2)^2}$

$=\sqrt{9+36+4}=\sqrt{49}=7$

Thus, $\hat{r}=\dfrac{\vec{r}}{|\vec{r}|} \Rightarrow \hat{r}=\dfrac{3\hat{i}+6\hat{j}-2\hat{k}}{7}$

10. Given, $A=\hat{i}+2\hat{j}-3\hat{k}$ and $B=-\hat{i}-2\hat{j}+\hat{k}$

$\therefore\ \overrightarrow{AB}=\overrightarrow{OB}-\overrightarrow{OA}$

$=(-\hat{i}-2\hat{j}+\hat{k})-(\hat{i}+2\hat{j}-3\hat{k})$

$=-2\hat{i}-4\hat{j}+4\hat{k}$

Unit vector in $\overrightarrow{AB}=\dfrac{-2\hat{i}-4\hat{j}+4\hat{k}}{\sqrt{(-2)^2+(-4)^2+4^2}}$

$=\dfrac{-2\hat{i}-4\hat{j}+4\hat{k}}{\sqrt{4+16+16}}=\dfrac{-2\hat{i}-4\hat{j}+4\hat{k}}{\sqrt{36}}$

$=\dfrac{-2\hat{i}-4\hat{j}+4\hat{k}}{6}$

$=\dfrac{-1}{3}\hat{i}-\dfrac{2}{3}\hat{j}+\dfrac{2}{3}\hat{k}$

Concept Enhancer The unit vector in the direction of vector $\vec{a}$ is $\hat{a}=\dfrac{\vec{a}}{|\vec{a}|}$

11. Let $\vec{a} = \hat{i} - 2\hat{j} - 2\hat{k}$

The unit vector in the direction of the given vector $\vec{a}$ is

$$\hat{a} = \frac{\vec{a}}{|\vec{a}|} = \frac{\hat{i} - 2\hat{j} - 2\hat{k}}{\sqrt{1+4+4}} = \frac{1}{3}\hat{i} - \frac{2}{3}\hat{j} - \frac{2}{3}\hat{k}$$

∴ The vector having magnitude equal to 18 and in the direction of $\vec{a}$ is $18\,\hat{a}$.

$$= 18\left(\frac{1}{3}\hat{i} - \frac{2}{3}\hat{j} - \frac{2}{3}\hat{k}\right)$$

$$= 6\hat{i} - 12\hat{j} - 12\hat{k}$$

12. Given, vectors

$$\alpha = (x-2)\vec{a} + \vec{b}$$

and $\beta = (3+2x)\vec{a} - 2\vec{b}$ are collinear.

∴ $\alpha = k\beta$, where k is some scalar.

$$\Rightarrow \quad (x-2)\vec{a} + \vec{b} = k[(3+2x)\vec{a} - 2\vec{b}]$$

On comparing the coefficient of vectors $\vec{a}$ and $\vec{b}$, we get

$$x - 2 = k(3+2x) \text{ and } 1 = -2k$$

$$\Rightarrow \quad k = -\frac{1}{2}$$

$$\therefore \quad x - 2 = -\frac{1}{2}(3+2x)$$

$$\Rightarrow \quad 2x - 4 = -3 - 2x$$

$$\Rightarrow \quad 4x = 1 \Rightarrow x = \frac{1}{4}$$

13. Let given position vectors are

$$\overrightarrow{OA} = \vec{a} - 2\vec{b} \text{ and } \overrightarrow{OB} = 2\vec{a} + \vec{b}.$$

Let $\overrightarrow{OC}$ be the position vector of a point C which divides the join of points, with position vectors $\overrightarrow{OA}$ and $\overrightarrow{OB}$, externally in the ratio 2 : 1.

$$\therefore \quad \overrightarrow{OC} = \frac{2\,\overrightarrow{OB} - 1\,\overrightarrow{OA}}{2-1}$$

$$= \frac{2\,(2\vec{a}+\vec{b}) - 1\,(\vec{a} - 2\vec{b})}{1}$$

$$= 4\vec{a} + 2\vec{b} - \vec{a} + 2\vec{b} = 3\vec{a} + 4\vec{b}$$

14. Given, vectors are

$$\vec{a} = 4\hat{i} - \hat{j} + \hat{k},\ \vec{b} = 2\hat{i} - 2\hat{j} + \hat{k}.$$

Now, $\vec{a} + \vec{b} = (4\hat{i} - \hat{j} + \hat{k}) + (2\hat{i} - 2\hat{j} + \hat{k})$

$$= 6\hat{i} - 3\hat{j} + 2\hat{k}$$

and $|\vec{a} + \vec{b}| = \sqrt{(6)^2 + (-3)^2 + (2)^2}$

$$= \sqrt{36+9+4}$$

$$= \sqrt{49} = 7$$

∴ The unit vector parallel to the vector $\vec{a} + \vec{b}$ is

$$\frac{\vec{a}+\vec{b}}{|\vec{a}+\vec{b}|} = \frac{6\hat{i} - 3\hat{j} + 2\hat{k}}{7}$$

TOPIC 2

Scalar and Vector Product of Two Vectors

Dot (or scalar) Product of Two Vectors

If θ is the angle between two non-zero vectors $\vec{a}$ and $\vec{b}$, then the scalar or dot product, denoted by $\vec{a} \cdot \vec{b}$, is given by $\vec{a} \cdot \vec{b} = |\vec{a}||\vec{b}|\cos\theta$, where $0 \le \theta \le \pi$.

NOTE

(i) $\vec{a} \cdot \vec{b}$ is a real number.

(ii) If either $\vec{a} = \vec{0}$ or $\vec{b} = \vec{0}$, then θ is not defined.

(iii) $\vec{a} \cdot \vec{b} > 0$, if θ is acute.

(iv) $\vec{a} \cdot \vec{b} < 0$, if θ is obtuse

Properties of dot product of two vectors

(i) $\vec{a} \cdot \vec{b} = \vec{b} \cdot \vec{a}$ [i.e. dot product is commutative]

(ii) $(\vec{a} \cdot \vec{0}) = 0$

(iii) $\vec{a} \cdot (\vec{b} + \vec{c}) = \vec{a} \cdot \vec{b} + \vec{a} \cdot \vec{c}$ [distributive property]

(iv) If $\vec{a}$ and $\vec{b}$ are perpendicular to each other, then $\vec{a} \cdot \vec{b} = 0$, converse is also true.

(v) Projection of $\vec{a}$ on $\vec{b} = \dfrac{\vec{a}\cdot\vec{b}}{|\vec{b}|}$ and projection of $\vec{b}$ on $\vec{a} = \dfrac{\vec{a}\cdot\vec{b}}{|\vec{a}|}$.

(vi) Angle between two non-zero vectors $\vec{a}$ and $\vec{b}$ is given by $\cos\theta = \dfrac{\vec{a}\cdot\vec{b}}{|\vec{a}|\cdot|\vec{b}|}$ or $\theta = \cos^{-1}\left[\dfrac{\vec{a}\cdot\vec{b}}{|\vec{a}|\cdot|\vec{b}|}\right]$

(vii) $\vec{a}\cdot\vec{a} = |\vec{a}|^2$ [square of a vector]

(viii) $\hat{i}^2 = \hat{j}^2 = \hat{k}^2 = 1$ [orthonormal vector triad]

(ix) $\hat{i}\cdot\hat{j} = \hat{j}\cdot\hat{k} = \hat{k}\cdot\hat{i} = 0$ [orthonormal vector traid]

(x) If $\vec{a} = a_1\hat{i} + a_2\hat{j} + a_3\hat{k}$ and $\vec{b} = b_1\hat{i} + b_2\hat{j} + b_3\hat{k}$, then $\vec{a}\cdot\vec{b} = a_1b_1 + a_2b_2 + a_3b_3$.

(xi) $(\lambda\cdot\vec{a})\cdot\vec{b} = \lambda(\vec{a}\cdot\vec{b}) = \vec{a}\cdot(\lambda\cdot\vec{b})$, where λ is any scalar.

(xii) If $\theta = 0$, then $\vec{a}\cdot\vec{b} = |\vec{a}||\vec{b}|$; if $\theta = \pi$, then $\vec{a}\cdot\vec{b} = -|\vec{a}||\vec{b}|$.

(xiii) If $\vec{a}$ and $\vec{b}$ are two vectors, then $|\vec{a}+\vec{b}| \le |\vec{a}| + |\vec{b}|$ [triangle inequality]

Vector (or Cross) Product of Vectors

If θ is the angle between two non-zero non-parallel vectors $\vec{a}$ and $\vec{b}$, then the cross product of vectors, denoted by $\vec{a}\times\vec{b}$, is given by

$\vec{a}\times\vec{b} = |\vec{a}||\vec{b}|\sin\theta\,\hat{n}$, such that $0 \le \theta \le \pi$,

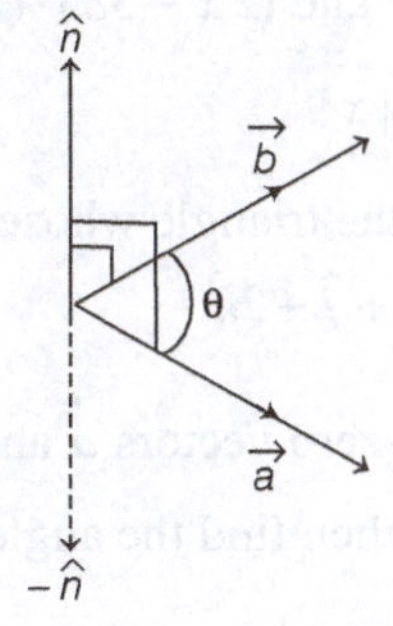

where, $\hat{n}$ is a unit vector perpendicular to both $\vec{a}$ and $\vec{b}$, such that $\vec{a}$, $\vec{b}$ and $\hat{n}$ form a right handed system.

NOTE (i) $\vec{a}\times\vec{b}$ is a vector quantity, whose magnitude is $|\vec{a}\times\vec{b}| = |\vec{a}||\vec{b}|\sin\theta$.

(ii) If either $\vec{a} = \vec{0}$ or $\vec{b} = \vec{0}$, then θ is not defined and in this case, we define $\vec{a}\times\vec{b} = \vec{0}$

Properties of cross product of two vectors

(i) Unit vector $\hat{n}$ which is perpendicular to both the vectors $\vec{a}$ and $\vec{b}$, is given by

$$\hat{n} = \frac{\vec{a}\times\vec{b}}{|\vec{a}\times\vec{b}|}.$$

(ii) For vectors $\vec{a}$ and $\vec{b}$, if $\vec{a}\times\vec{b} = \vec{0}$, then either $\vec{a} = \vec{0}$ or $\vec{b} = \vec{0}$ or $\vec{a} \parallel \vec{b}$.

(iii) Angle between two non-zero vectors is given by

$$\sin\theta = \frac{|\vec{a}\times\vec{b}|}{|\vec{a}||\vec{b}|}$$

or $$\theta = \sin^{-1}\left[\frac{|\vec{a}\times\vec{b}|}{|\vec{a}||\vec{b}|}\right].$$

(iv) $\vec{a}\times\vec{a} = \vec{0}$

(v) $\vec{a}\times\vec{b} = -\vec{b}\times\vec{a}$ [not commutative]

(vi) $\vec{a}\times(\vec{b}+\vec{c}) = \vec{a}\times\vec{b} + \vec{a}\times\vec{c}$ [distributive property]

(vii) $\lambda(\vec{a}\times\vec{b}) = (\lambda\,\vec{a})\times\vec{b} = \vec{a}\times(\lambda\,\vec{b})$

(viii) If $\vec{a}$ is parallel to $\vec{b}$, then $\vec{a}\times\vec{b} = \vec{0}$ and converse is also true.

or Two non-zero vectors $\vec{a}$, $\vec{b}$ are **collinear** iff $\vec{a}\times\vec{b} = \vec{0}$.

(ix) If $\theta = \dfrac{\pi}{2}$, then $|\vec{a}\times\vec{b}| = |\vec{a}||\vec{b}|$.

(x) If $\vec{a}$ and $\vec{b}$ represent the adjacent sides of a **parallelogram**, then its area is given by $|\vec{a}\times\vec{b}|$.

(xi) If $\vec{a}$ and $\vec{b}$ represent the adjacent sides of a **triangle,** then its area is given by $\dfrac{1}{2}|\vec{a}\times\vec{b}|$.

(xii) If $\vec{d_1}$ and $\vec{d_2}$ represent the diagonals of a **parallelogram,** then its area is given by $\frac{1}{2}|\vec{d_1} \times \vec{d_2}|$.

(xiii) $\hat{i} \times \hat{i} = \hat{j} \times \hat{j} = \hat{k} \times \hat{k} = \vec{0}$

and $\hat{i} \times \hat{j} = \hat{k}, \hat{j} \times \hat{k} = \hat{i}, \hat{k} \times \hat{i} = \hat{j}$

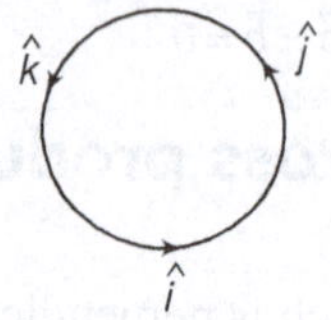

(xiv) $\hat{j} \times \hat{i} = -\hat{k}$, $\hat{k} \times \hat{j} = -\hat{i}$ and $\hat{i} \times \hat{k} = -\hat{j}$

(xv) If $\vec{a} = a_1\hat{i} + a_2\hat{j} + a_3\hat{k}$ and $\vec{b} = b_1\hat{i} + b_2\hat{j} + b_3\hat{k}$, then

$$\vec{a} \times \vec{b} = \begin{vmatrix} \hat{i} & \hat{j} & \hat{k} \\ a_1 & a_2 & a_3 \\ b_1 & b_2 & b_3 \end{vmatrix}$$

$$= (a_2b_3 - a_3b_2)\hat{i} + (a_3b_1 - a_1b_3)\hat{j} + (a_1b_2 - a_2b_1)\hat{k}$$

(xvi) If A, B and C are the position vectors of plane ABC, then the unit vector perpendicular to the plane ABC is $\frac{\vec{AB} \times \vec{AC}}{|\vec{AB} \times \vec{AC}|}$.

PYQs Previous Years Questions

1 Mark Questions

1. If $|\vec{a}| = 3$, $|\vec{b}| = \frac{\sqrt{2}}{3}$ and $\vec{a} \times \vec{b}$ is a unit vector, then the angle between $\vec{a}$ and $\vec{b}$ **ISC 2023**

(a) $\frac{\pi}{6}$ (b) $\frac{\pi}{4}$ (c) $\frac{\pi}{3}$ (d) $\frac{\pi}{2}$

2. Find the area of the parallelogram whose diagonals are $\hat{i} - 3\hat{j} + \hat{k}$ and $\hat{i} + \hat{j} + \hat{k}$. **ISC 2023**

3. If the two vectors $3\hat{i} + \alpha\hat{j} + \hat{k}$ and $2\hat{i} - \hat{j} + 8\hat{k}$ are perpendicular to each other, then find the value of α. **ISC 2023**

4. If $\vec{a} = \hat{i} + 2\hat{j} + 3\hat{k}$ and $\vec{b} = -\hat{i} + 2\hat{j} + \hat{k}$ and $\vec{c} = 3\hat{i} + \hat{j}$, find t such that $\vec{a} + t\vec{b}$ is perpendicular to $\vec{c}$ is **ISC Specimen 2023**

(a) 0 (b) 5 (c) 4 (d) 2

5. What will be the value of m, if the vector $2\hat{i} + m\hat{j} + \hat{k}$ is perpendicular to $2\hat{i} - \hat{j} + 3\hat{k}$? **ISC Specimen Sem-I 2022**

(a) 7 (b) 0 (c) 1 (d) -1

6. Find the angle between the vectors $\vec{a} = 6\hat{i} + 2\hat{j} + 3\hat{k}$, $\vec{b} = 2\hat{i} - 9\hat{j} + 6\hat{k}$. **ISC Specimen 2021**

7. If $\vec{a}$ and $\vec{b}$ are perpendicular vectors, $|\vec{a} + \vec{b}| = 13$ and $\vec{a} = 5$, then find the value of $|\vec{b}|$. **ISC Specimen 2021**

2 Marks Questions

8. If $\vec{a} \times \vec{b} = \vec{a} \times \vec{c}$ where $\vec{a}$, $\vec{b}$ and $\vec{c}$ are non-zero vectors, then prove that either $\vec{b} = \vec{c}$ or $\vec{a}$ and $(\vec{b} \cdot \vec{c})$ are parallel. **ISC 2024**

9. If $\vec{a}$ and $\vec{b}$ are two non-zero vectors such that $|\vec{a} \times \vec{b}| = \vec{a} \cdot \vec{b}$, find the angle between $\vec{a}$ and $\vec{b}$. **ISC 2024**

10. Given below are two vectors in their component form such that $|\vec{p} \times \vec{q}| = 1$. **ISC Specimen 2024**

$$\vec{p} = x\hat{i} - \frac{y}{4}\hat{j} \text{ and } \vec{q} = y\hat{i} + \frac{x}{9}\hat{j}$$

Find the relation between the variables x and y.

11. The position vectors of the points A and B are $(2, -3, 2)$ and $(2,3,1)$ respectively, then find the area of ΔOAB. **ISC Specimen 2024**

12. If $\hat{a}$ is unit vector and $(2\vec{x} - 3\hat{a}) \cdot (2\vec{x} + 3\hat{a}) = 91$, then find the value of $|\vec{x}|$. **ISC 2023**

13. Find the area of the triangle whose adjacent sides are $\hat{i} + 4\hat{j} - \hat{k}$ and $\hat{i} + \hat{j} + 2\hat{k}$. **ISC Specimen 2023**

14. For any two non-zero vectors $\vec{a}$ and $\vec{b}$, if $|\vec{a} \cdot \vec{b}| = |\vec{a} \times \vec{b}|$, then find the angle between them. **ISC Specimen 2023**

15. Find λ if the scalar projection of $\vec{a} = \lambda\hat{i} + \hat{j} + 4\hat{k}$ on $\vec{b} = 2\hat{i} + 6\hat{j} + 3\hat{k}$ is 4 units. **ISC Specimen 2021, ISC 2018**

16. If $\vec{a}$ and $\vec{b}$ are perpendicular vectors, $|\vec{a} + \vec{b}| = 13$ and $|\vec{a}| = 5$, then find the value of $|\vec{b}|$. **ISC 2019**

17. Find the area of the parallelogram whose adjacent sides are given by the vectors $\vec{a} = 3\hat{i} + \hat{j} + 4\hat{k}$ and $\vec{b} = \hat{i} - \hat{j} + \hat{k}$. **ISC Specimen 2018**

3/4 Marks Questions

18. Using vectors, find the area of the triangle whose vertices are $A(3, -1, 2)$, $B(1, -1, -3)$ and $C(4, -3, 1)$. **ISC 2020**

19. If $\vec{a} = \hat{i} - 2\hat{j} + 3\hat{k}$, $\vec{b} = 2\hat{i} + 3\hat{j} - 5\hat{k}$, then prove that $\vec{a}$ and $\vec{a} \times \vec{b}$ are perpendicular. **ISC 2019**

20. If A, B and C are three non-collinear points with position vectors $\vec{a}, \vec{b}, \vec{c}$ respectively, then show that the length of the perpendicular from C on AB is

$$\frac{|(\vec{a} \times \vec{b}) + (\vec{b} \times \vec{c}) + (\vec{c} \times \vec{a})|}{|\vec{b} - \vec{a}|}$$

ISC 2018

21. Show that $(\vec{a} \times \vec{b})^2 = \begin{vmatrix} \vec{a} \cdot \vec{a} & \vec{a} \cdot \vec{b} \\ \vec{a} \cdot \vec{b} & \vec{b} \cdot \vec{b} \end{vmatrix}$. **ISC Specimen 2018**

22. If $\vec{a}$ and $\vec{b}$ are two vectors such that $|\vec{a} + \vec{b}| = |\vec{a}|$, then show that vector $(2\vec{a} + \vec{b})$ is perpendicular to $\vec{b}$. **ISC 2004**

23. Find the unit vector perpendicular to the two vectors $\hat{i} + 2\hat{j} - \hat{k}$ and $2\hat{i} + 3\hat{j} + \hat{k}$. **ISC 2004**

24. Using vectors, show that the perpendiculars from the vertices to the opposite sides of the ΔABC are concurrent. **ISC 2003**

KEY CONCEPT

(i) First of all draw the perpendicular lines from vertices, which intersect at H and make the position vectors respectively from origin.

(ii) Then, use perpendicular property on BC and CA side of triangle by using scalar (dot) product at two vectors, then we get required result.

25. The position vectors of the vertices of a triangle are given as $2\hat{i} - \hat{j} + \hat{k}$, $\hat{i} - 3\hat{j} - 5\hat{k}$ and $3\hat{i} - 4\hat{j} - 4\hat{k}$. Prove that it is a right angled triangle. **ISC 2003, 1999**

26. Using vectors, show that the medians of a triangle meet at a point. **ISC 2002**

KEY CONCEPT

(i) First of all drawn the triangle ABC and mid-point of sides BC, AC and AB are D, E, and F, respectively.

(ii) Assume position vector of sides and mid-points of triangle and apply the property of median in triangle, then we get that medians of triangle are concurrent and position vector of the centroid is $\frac{\vec{a}+\vec{b}+\vec{c}}{3}$.

27. If $\vec{a}, \vec{b}, \vec{c}$ and $\vec{d}$ are the position vectors of four points A, B, C and D respectively and if $\vec{b} - \vec{a} = \vec{c} - \vec{d}$, show that $ABCD$ is a parallelogram. **ISC 2000**

5/6 Marks Questions

28. The given figure shows an air plant holder which is in the shape of tetrahedron. Let $A(1, 1, 1)$, $B(2, 1, 3)$, $C(3, 2, 2)$ and $D(3, 3, 4)$ are the vertices of air plant holder.

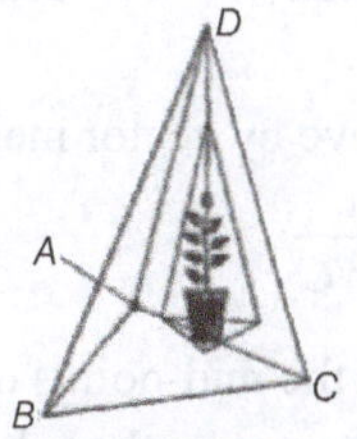

Based on the above information, answer the following questions.

(i) The vector of $\overrightarrow{AB}$ is

(a) $-\hat{i} - 2\hat{k}$ (b) $2\hat{i} + \hat{k}$ (c) $\hat{i} + 2\hat{k}$ (d) $-2\hat{i} - \hat{k}$

(ii) The vector of $\overrightarrow{AC}$ is

(a) $2\hat{i} - \hat{j} - \hat{k}$ (b) $2\hat{i} + \hat{j} + \hat{k}$
(c) $-2\hat{i} - \hat{j} + \hat{k}$ (d) $\hat{i} + 2\hat{j} + \hat{k}$

(iii) Area of ΔABC is

(a) $\frac{\sqrt{11}}{2}$ sq units (b) $\frac{\sqrt{14}}{2}$ sq units
(c) $\frac{\sqrt{13}}{2}$ sq units (d) $\frac{\sqrt{17}}{2}$ sq units

(iv) The unit vector along the $\overrightarrow{AB}$ is

(a) $\frac{-2\hat{i} - \hat{k}}{\sqrt{5}}$ (b) $\frac{-\hat{i} - 2\hat{k}}{\sqrt{5}}$ (c) $\frac{2\hat{i} + \hat{k}}{\sqrt{5}}$ (d) $\frac{\hat{i} + 2\hat{k}}{\sqrt{5}}$

29. If $\vec{a}, \vec{b}, \vec{c}$ are three mutually perpendicular vectors of equal magnitude, prove that $(\vec{a}+\vec{b}+\vec{c})$ is equally inclined with vectors $\vec{a}, \vec{b}$ and $\vec{c}$. **ISC 2017**

30. Find a unit vector perpendicular to each of the vectors $\vec{a}+\vec{b}$ and $\vec{a}-\vec{b}$, where $\vec{a}=3\hat{i}+2\hat{j}+2\hat{k}$ and $\vec{b}=\hat{i}+2\hat{j}-2\hat{k}$. **ISC 2016**

31. Using vectors, prove that angle in a semi-circle is a right angle. **ISC 2015**

32. In a ΔABC, using vectors, prove that $c^2=a^2+b^2-2ab\cos C$. **ISC 2014**

> **KEY CONCEPT**
>
> (i) Firstly, draw a ΔABC and mark the position of the vectors.
>
> (ii) Further use triangle law of addition, scalar, dot product of two vectors i.e. $\vec{a}\cdot\vec{b}=|\vec{a}||\vec{b}|\cos\theta$

33. If $\vec{a}$ and $\vec{b}$ are unit vector and θ is the angle between them, then show that $|\vec{a}-\vec{b}|=2\sin\frac{\theta}{2}$. **ISC 2013**

34. In any ΔABC, prove by vector method

$$\frac{a}{\sin A}=\frac{b}{\sin B}=\frac{c}{\sin C}.$$

ISC 2012

35. If D, E and F are the mid-points of the sides of a ΔABC, prove by vector method that

area of $\Delta DEF=\frac{1}{4}$(area of ΔABC). **ISC 2011, 01**

> **KEY CONCEPT**
>
> (i) First of all draw the triangle ABC and DEF by the mid-points of sides of ΔABC and assume position vectors at A, B and C.
>
> (ii) Find the distance of sides and put in formula of area of ΔDEF, then we get the required result.

36. In any ΔABC, prove by vector method

$$\cos B=\frac{c^2+a^2-b^2}{2ca}.$$

ISC 2010

37. Find the area of a parallelogram whose diagonals are determined by the vectors $\vec{a}=3\hat{i}+\hat{j}-2\hat{k}$ and $\vec{b}=\hat{i}-3\hat{j}+4\hat{k}$. **ISC 2009**

38. (i) Prove by vector method that the diameter of a circle will subtend a right angle at a point on its circumference.

(ii) If $\vec{a}, \vec{b}$ and $\vec{c}$ represent the position vectors of the points with coordinates $(2, -10, 2)$, $(3, 1, 2)$ and $(2, 1, 3)$, respectively, find the value of $\vec{a}\times(\vec{b}\times\vec{c})$. **ISC 2009**

39. Find $\vec{a}\cdot\vec{b}$, if $|\vec{a}|=2, |\vec{b}|=5$ and $|\vec{a}\times\vec{b}|=8$. **ISC 2008**

40. Given $\vec{a}=\hat{i}-2\hat{j}+\hat{k}$, $\vec{b}=2\hat{i}+\hat{j}+\hat{k}$ and $\vec{c}=\hat{i}+2\hat{j}-\hat{k}$. Then, find $\vec{a}\times(\vec{b}\times\vec{c})$. **ISC 2008, 02**

41. Find a unit vector perpendicular to the vectors $4\hat{i}+3\hat{j}+\hat{k}$ and $2\hat{i}-\hat{j}+2\hat{k}$. Determine the sine of the angle between these two vectors. **ISC 2007**

42. The vectors $-2\hat{i}+4\hat{j}+4\hat{k}$ and $-4\hat{i}-2\hat{k}$ represent the diagonals BD and AC of a parallelogram $ABCD$. Then, find the area of the parallelogram. **ISC 2006**

43. If $\vec{a}$ and $\vec{b}$ are unit vectors such that $2\vec{a}-4\vec{b}$ and $10\vec{a}+8\vec{b}$ are perpendicular to each other. Then, find the angle between the vectors $\vec{a}$ and $\vec{b}$. **ISC 2005**

44. Show that the sum of the squares of the sides of a parallelogram is equal to the sum of the squares of the diagonals of the parallelogram. **ISC 2004, 01**

45. The vectors $\vec{a}=3\hat{i}+x\hat{j}-\hat{k}$ and $\vec{b}=2\hat{i}+\hat{j}+y\hat{k}$ are mutually perpendicular. Given that $|\vec{a}|=|\vec{b}|$. Then, find the values of x and y. **ISC 2002**

46. Prove by the vector method that the middle point of the hypotenuse of a right angled triangle is at equidistant from the vertices of the triangle. **ISC 2000**

Explanations

1. (b) Given, $|\vec{a}|=3$ and $|\vec{b}|=\frac{\sqrt{2}}{3}$

$|\vec{a}\times\vec{b}|=1$

We know that $|\vec{a}\times\vec{b}|=|\vec{a}||\vec{b}|\sin\theta$

$$\Rightarrow \quad \sin\theta=\frac{|\vec{a}\times\vec{b}|}{|\vec{a}||\vec{b}|}=\frac{1}{3\times\frac{\sqrt{2}}{3}}=\frac{1}{\sqrt{2}}$$

$$\Rightarrow \quad \sin\theta=\frac{1}{\sqrt{2}}$$

$$\Rightarrow \quad \sin\theta=\sin\frac{\pi}{4}\Rightarrow\theta=\frac{\pi}{4}$$

2. Area of parallelogram whose diagonals are $\vec{d_1}$ and $\vec{d_2}$ is $\frac{1}{2}|\vec{d_1}\times\vec{d_2}|$.

$\therefore$ Here, $\vec{d_1}=\hat{i}-3\hat{j}+\hat{k}$ and $\vec{d_2}=\hat{i}+\hat{j}+\hat{k}$

$$\vec{d_1}\times\vec{d_2}=\begin{vmatrix}\hat{i} & \hat{j} & \hat{k}\\ 1 & -3 & 1\\ 1 & 1 & 1\end{vmatrix}$$

$$=(-3-1)\hat{i}-(1-1)\hat{j}+(1+3)\hat{k}=-4\hat{i}+4\hat{k}$$

$$\Rightarrow |\vec{d_1}\times\vec{d_2}|=\sqrt{(-4)^2+4^2}=\sqrt{16+16}=4\sqrt{2}$$

$\therefore$ Area of parallelogram $=\frac{1}{2}\times4\sqrt{2}=2\sqrt{2}$ sq units

3. Given, vectors $3\hat{i}+\alpha\hat{j}+\hat{k}$ and $2\hat{i}-\hat{j}+8\hat{k}$ are perpendicular to each other.

$\therefore \quad 3\cdot2+\alpha\cdot(-1)+1\cdot(8)=0$ $\quad [\because \vec{a}\cdot\vec{b}=0]$

$\Rightarrow \quad 6-\alpha+8=0\Rightarrow\alpha=14$

4. (b) Given, $\vec{a}=\hat{i}+2\hat{j}+3\hat{k}$, $\vec{b}=-\hat{i}+2\hat{j}+\hat{k}$

and $\quad \vec{c}=3\hat{i}+\hat{j}$

Here, $\vec{a}+t\vec{b}\perp\vec{c}\Rightarrow(\vec{a}+t\vec{b})\cdot\vec{c}=0$

$$\Rightarrow \quad \vec{a}\cdot\vec{c}+t\vec{b}\cdot\vec{c}=0$$

$$\Rightarrow \quad t=-\frac{\vec{a}\cdot\vec{c}}{\vec{b}\cdot\vec{c}}=-\frac{(\hat{i}+2\hat{j}+3\hat{k})(3\hat{i}+\hat{j})}{(-\hat{i}+2\hat{j}+\hat{k})(3\hat{i}+\hat{j})}$$

$$\Rightarrow \quad t=-\frac{(3+2)}{(-3+2)}=5$$

5. (a) Let $\vec{a}=2\hat{i}+m\hat{j}+\hat{k}$ and $\vec{b}=2\hat{i}-\hat{j}+3\hat{k}$.

For two vectors to be perpendicular, $\vec{a}\cdot\vec{b}=0$.

$\therefore \quad (2\hat{i}+m\hat{j}+\hat{k})\cdot(2\hat{i}-\hat{j}+3\hat{k})=0$

$\Rightarrow \quad 4-m+3=0$

$\Rightarrow \quad m=7$

6. Given, $\vec{a}=6\hat{i}+2\hat{j}+3\hat{k}$ and $\vec{b}=2\hat{i}-9\hat{j}+6\hat{k}$

$$\vec{a}\cdot\vec{b}=(6\hat{i}+2\hat{j}+3\hat{k})\cdot(2\hat{i}-9\hat{j}+6\hat{k})$$

$$=12-18+18=12$$

$$|\vec{a}|=\sqrt{6^2+2^2+3^2}=\sqrt{36+4+9}=\sqrt{49}=7$$

$$|\vec{b}|=\sqrt{2^2+(-9)^2+6^2}=\sqrt{4+81+36}$$

$$=\sqrt{121}=11$$

So, $\cos\theta=\frac{\vec{a}\cdot\vec{b}}{|\vec{a}||\vec{b}|}=\frac{12}{(7)(11)}=\frac{12}{77}$

or $\quad \theta=\cos^{-1}\left(\frac{12}{77}\right)$

7. Given that $\quad |\vec{a}+\vec{b}|=13$

$\Rightarrow \quad |\vec{a}+\vec{b}|^2=169$ $\quad$ [on squaring]

$\Rightarrow \quad (\vec{a}+\vec{b})\cdot(\vec{a}+\vec{b})=169$

$\Rightarrow \quad |\vec{a}|^2+2\vec{a}\cdot\vec{b}+|\vec{b}|^2=169$

$\Rightarrow \quad |\vec{a}|^2+|\vec{b}|^2=169$ $\quad [\because \vec{a}\perp\vec{b}\Rightarrow\vec{a}\cdot\vec{b}=0]$

$\Rightarrow \quad |\vec{b}|^2=169-|\vec{a}|^2=169-25=144$

$\Rightarrow \quad |\vec{b}|=12$

8. Given, $\vec{a}\times\vec{b}=\vec{a}\times\vec{c}$, where $\vec{a}$, $\vec{b}$ and $\vec{c}$ are non-zero vectors.

Since, $\quad \vec{a}\times\vec{b}=\vec{a}\times\vec{c}$

$\Rightarrow \quad \vec{a}\times\vec{b}-\vec{a}\times\vec{c}=0$

$\Rightarrow \quad \vec{a}\times(\vec{b}-\vec{c})=0$

$\Rightarrow \quad \vec{a}\,||\,(\vec{b}-\vec{c})$ or $\vec{b}-\vec{c}=0$ $\quad [\because \vec{a}\neq0]$

$\Rightarrow \quad \vec{a}\,||\,(\vec{b}-\vec{c})$ or $\vec{b}=\vec{c}$

9. Given, $\vec{a}$ and $\vec{b}$ two non-zero vectors such that

$$|\vec{a}\times\vec{b}|=\vec{a}\cdot\vec{b}$$

$$\Rightarrow \quad |\vec{a}|\cdot|\vec{b}|\sin\theta=|\vec{a}|\cdot|\vec{b}|\cos\theta$$

$$\Rightarrow \quad \sin\theta=\cos\theta$$

$$\Rightarrow \quad \frac{\sin\theta}{\cos\theta}=1$$

$$\Rightarrow \quad \tan\theta=1$$

$$\Rightarrow \quad \theta=\tan^{-1}(1)=\frac{\pi}{4}$$

Thus, the angle between $\vec{a}$ and $\vec{b}$ is $\frac{\pi}{4}$.

10. Given, $\vec{p}=x\hat{i}-\frac{y}{4}\hat{j}$, $\vec{q}=y\hat{i}+\frac{x}{9}\hat{j}$ and $|\vec{p}\times\vec{q}|=1$

$$\text{Now, } \vec{p}\times\vec{q}=\begin{vmatrix}\hat{i} & \hat{j} & \hat{k}\\ x & \frac{-y}{4} & 0\\ y & \frac{x}{9} & 0\end{vmatrix}=0-0+\hat{k}\left(\frac{x^2}{9}+\frac{y^2}{4}\right)$$

$$\Rightarrow \quad \vec{p}\times\vec{q}=\hat{k}\left(\frac{x^2}{9}+\frac{y^2}{4}\right)$$

$$\therefore \quad |\vec{p}\times\vec{q}|=\sqrt{\left(\frac{x^2}{9}+\frac{y^2}{4}\right)^2}$$

$$\Rightarrow \quad 1=\frac{x^2}{9}+\frac{y^2}{4}$$

$$\Rightarrow \quad 4x^2+9y^2=36$$

11. Given, $\overrightarrow{OA}=(2\hat{i}-3\hat{j}+2\hat{k})$ and $\overrightarrow{OB}=(2\hat{i}+3\hat{j}+\hat{k})$

$$\therefore \overrightarrow{OA}\times\overrightarrow{OB}=\begin{vmatrix}\hat{i} & \hat{j} & \hat{k}\\ 2 & -3 & 2\\ 2 & 3 & 1\end{vmatrix}$$

$$=\hat{i}(-3-6)-\hat{j}(2-4)+\hat{k}(6+6)$$

$$=-9\hat{i}+2\hat{j}+12\hat{k}$$

$$|\overrightarrow{OA}\times\overrightarrow{OB}|=\sqrt{(-9)^2+(2)^2+(12)^2}$$

$$=\sqrt{81+4+144}=\sqrt{229}$$

$$\text{Area of } \Delta OAB=\frac{1}{2}|\overrightarrow{OA}\times\overrightarrow{OB}|=\frac{1}{2}\times\sqrt{229}$$

$$=\frac{\sqrt{229}}{2} \text{ sq units}$$

12. Given, $|\hat{a}|=1$

$$\Rightarrow \quad (2\vec{x}-3\hat{a})\cdot(2\vec{x}+3\hat{a})=91$$

$$\Rightarrow \quad 4|\vec{x}|^2-9|\hat{a}|^2=91$$

$$\Rightarrow \quad 4|\vec{x}|^2=91+9 \qquad [\because |\vec{a}|=1]$$

$$\Rightarrow \quad |\vec{x}|^2=\frac{100}{4}=25$$

$$\Rightarrow \quad |\vec{x}|=\sqrt{25}\Rightarrow|\vec{x}|=5$$

13. Let $\vec{a}=\hat{i}+4\hat{j}-\hat{k}$ and $\vec{b}=\hat{i}+\hat{j}+2\hat{k}$

We know that

Area of triangle $=\frac{1}{2}|\vec{a}\times\vec{b}|$, where $\vec{a}$ and $\vec{b}$ are adjacents sides of the triangle.

$$\therefore \quad \vec{a}\times\vec{b}=\begin{vmatrix}\hat{i} & \hat{j} & \hat{k}\\ 1 & 4 & -1\\ 1 & 1 & 2\end{vmatrix}$$

$$\Rightarrow \quad \vec{a}\times\vec{b}=\hat{i}(8+1)-\hat{j}(2+1)+\hat{k}(1-4)$$

$$\Rightarrow \quad \vec{a}\times\vec{b}=9\hat{i}-3\hat{j}-3\hat{k}$$

$$\therefore \text{ Area of triangle}=\frac{1}{2}|\vec{a}\times\vec{b}|$$

$$=\frac{1}{2}\sqrt{(9)^2+(-3)^2+(-3)^2}$$

$$=\frac{1}{2}\sqrt{81+9+9}=\frac{3\sqrt{11}}{2} \text{ sq units}$$

Concept Enhancer Area of a triangle having adjacent sides $\vec{a}$ and $\vec{b}$ is $\frac{1}{2}|\vec{a}\times\vec{b}|$.

14. Given, $|\vec{a}\cdot\vec{b}|=|\vec{a}\times\vec{b}|$

$$\Rightarrow |\vec{a}||\vec{b}|\cos\theta=|\vec{a}||\vec{b}|\sin\theta$$

$$\Rightarrow \quad \tan\theta=1\Rightarrow\theta=\frac{\pi}{4}$$

Hence, the angle between a and b is $\frac{\pi}{4}$.

15. We know that, projection of $\vec{a}$ on $\vec{b}=\frac{\vec{a}\cdot\vec{b}}{|\vec{b}|}$

$$\Rightarrow \quad 4=\frac{\vec{a}\cdot\vec{b}}{|\vec{b}|} \qquad \ldots\text{(i)}$$

Now, $\vec{a}\cdot\vec{b} = 2\lambda + 6 + 12 = 2\lambda + 18$

Also, $|\vec{b}| = \sqrt{2^2 + 6^2 + 3^2} = \sqrt{4+36+9} = \sqrt{49} = 7$

On putting in Eq. (i), we obtain

$$4 = \frac{2\lambda + 18}{7}$$

$$\Rightarrow \quad 2\lambda + 18 = 28 \Rightarrow 2\lambda = 28 - 18$$

$$\Rightarrow \quad \lambda = \frac{10}{2} \Rightarrow \lambda = 5$$

Hence, the value of λ is 5.

Concept Enhancer Projection of $\vec{a}$ on $\vec{b}$ is not the value $\frac{\vec{a}\cdot\vec{b}}{|\vec{a}|}$.

16. Given, $|\vec{a} + \vec{b}| = 13, |\vec{a}| = 5$

Since, $\vec{a}$ and $\vec{b}$ are perpendicular.

$$\therefore \quad \vec{a}\cdot\vec{b} = 0$$

Now, $|\vec{a} + \vec{b}| = 13$

On squaring both sides, we get

$$(\vec{a} + \vec{b})(\vec{a} + \vec{b}) = 169 \qquad [\because |\vec{a}|^2 = \vec{a}\cdot\vec{a}]$$

$$\Rightarrow \quad |\vec{a}|^2 + |\vec{b}|^2 + 2\vec{a}\cdot\vec{b} = 169$$

$$\Rightarrow \quad (5)^2 + |\vec{b}|^2 + 2\times 0 = 169$$

$$\Rightarrow \quad |\vec{b}|^2 = 169 - 25$$

$$\Rightarrow \quad |\vec{b}|^2 = 144$$

$$\Rightarrow \quad |\vec{b}| = 12$$

[$\because$ magnitude is always positive]

Concept Enhancer If $\vec{a}$ and $\vec{b}$ two vectors are perpendicular, then $\vec{a}\cdot\vec{b} = 0$.

17. We have, adjacent side of parallelogram, given by

$$\vec{a} = 3\hat{i} + \hat{j} + 4\hat{k} \text{ and } \vec{b} = \hat{i} - \hat{j} + \hat{k}$$

$$\text{Now, } \vec{a}\times\vec{b} = \begin{vmatrix} \hat{i} & \hat{j} & \hat{k} \\ 3 & 1 & 4 \\ 1 & -1 & 1 \end{vmatrix}$$

$$= (1+4)\hat{i} - (3-4)\hat{j} + (-3-1)\hat{k}$$

$$\Rightarrow \quad \vec{a}\times\vec{b} = 5\hat{i} + \hat{j} - 4\hat{k}$$

$$\text{Area of parallelogram} = |\vec{a}\times\vec{b}| = |5\hat{i} + \hat{j} - 4\hat{k}|$$
$$= \sqrt{25+1+16}$$
$$= \sqrt{42} \text{ sq units}$$

18. We have, $\vec{A} = 3\hat{i} - \hat{j} + 2\hat{k}, \vec{B} = \hat{i} - \hat{j} - 3\hat{k}$

and $\vec{C} = 4\hat{i} - 3\hat{j} + \hat{k}$

$$\overrightarrow{AB} = -2\hat{i} - 5\hat{k} \text{ and } \overrightarrow{AC} = \hat{i} - 2\hat{j} - \hat{k}$$

The area of the given triangle is $\frac{1}{2}|\overrightarrow{AB} \times \overrightarrow{AC}|$.

$$\text{Now, } \overrightarrow{AB}\times\overrightarrow{AC} = \begin{vmatrix} \hat{i} & \hat{j} & \hat{k} \\ -2 & 0 & -5 \\ 1 & -2 & -1 \end{vmatrix} = -10\hat{i} - 7\hat{j} + 4\hat{k}$$

Therefore,

$$|\overrightarrow{AB} \times \overrightarrow{AC}| = \sqrt{100+49+16} = \sqrt{165}$$

Thus, the required area is $\frac{\sqrt{165}}{2}$ sq units.

19. Given, vectors are

$$\vec{a} = \hat{i} - 2\hat{j} + 3\hat{k} \text{ and } \vec{b} = 2\hat{i} + 3\hat{j} - 5\hat{k}.$$

$$\text{Now, } \vec{a}\times\vec{b} = \begin{vmatrix} \hat{i} & \hat{j} & \hat{k} \\ 1 & -2 & 3 \\ 2 & 3 & -5 \end{vmatrix}$$

$$= \hat{i}(10-9) - \hat{j}(-5-6) + \hat{k}(3+4)$$
$$= \hat{i} + 11\hat{j} + 7\hat{k}$$

$$\text{Now, } \vec{a}\cdot(\vec{a}\times\vec{b}) = (\hat{i} - 2\hat{j} + 3\hat{k})\cdot(\hat{i} + 11\hat{j} + 7\hat{k})$$
$$= 1 - 22 + 21 = 22 - 22 = 0$$

Hence, $\vec{a}$ is perpendicular to $\vec{a}\times\vec{b}$.

20. We have, A, B, C are three non-collinear points with position vectors $\vec{a}, \vec{b}, \vec{c}$ respectively.

Let position vector of $\overrightarrow{CD}$ be d.

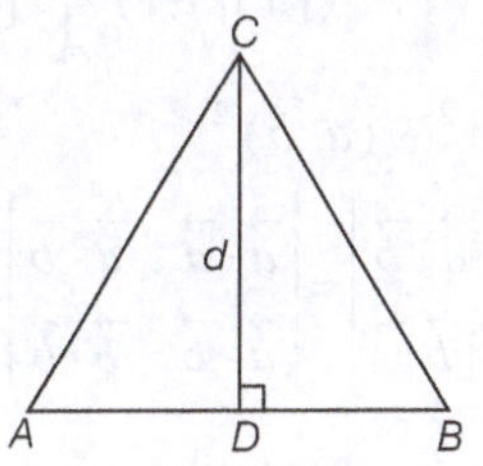

$$\overrightarrow{AB} = \vec{b} - \vec{a}$$
$$\overrightarrow{AC} = \vec{c} - \vec{a}$$
$$\overrightarrow{BC} = \vec{c} - \vec{b}$$

Now, area of ΔABC

$$= \frac{1}{2}|\overrightarrow{AB} \times \overrightarrow{AC}| = \frac{1}{2}|(\vec{b} - \vec{a}) \times (\vec{c} - \vec{a})|$$
$$= \frac{1}{2}|(\vec{b} \times \vec{c}) - (\vec{a} \times \vec{c}) - (\vec{b} \times \vec{a}) + (\vec{a} \times \vec{a})|$$
$$= \frac{1}{2}|\vec{b} \times \vec{c} + \vec{c} \times \vec{a} + \vec{a} \times \vec{b}| \quad \ldots(i)$$
$$[\because \vec{a} \times \vec{c} = -\vec{c} \times \vec{a} \text{ and } \vec{a} \times \vec{a} = 0]$$

Also, area of $\Delta ABC = \frac{1}{2}|\overrightarrow{AB}||\overrightarrow{CD}|$

$$= \frac{1}{2}|\vec{b} - \vec{a}|d \quad \ldots(ii)$$

From Eqs. (i) and (ii), we get

$$\frac{1}{2}|\vec{b} - \vec{a}|d = \frac{1}{2}|(\vec{a} \times \vec{b}) + (\vec{b} \times \vec{c}) + (\vec{c} \times \vec{a})|$$
$$\Rightarrow \quad d = \frac{|(\vec{a} \times \vec{b}) + (\vec{b} \times \vec{c}) + (\vec{c} \times \vec{a})|}{|\vec{b} - \vec{a}|}$$

Hence, length of perpendicular from C on AB is

$$\frac{|(\vec{a} \times \vec{b}) + (\vec{b} \times \vec{c}) + (\vec{c} \times \vec{a})|}{|\vec{b} - \vec{a}|}.$$

Hence proved.

21. We have to prove, $(\vec{a} \times \vec{b})^2 = \begin{vmatrix} \vec{a} \cdot \vec{a} & \vec{a} \cdot \vec{b} \\ \vec{a} \cdot \vec{b} & \vec{b} \cdot \vec{b} \end{vmatrix}$

$$\text{LHS} = (\vec{a} \times \vec{b})^2 = |\vec{a} \times \vec{b}|^2 = (\vec{a} \times \vec{b}) \cdot (\vec{a} \times \vec{b})$$
$$[\because \vec{a}^2 = \vec{a} \cdot \vec{a}]$$
$$= |\vec{a}|^2 |\vec{b}|^2 (\sin\theta)^2 \quad [\because \vec{a} \times \vec{b} = |\vec{a}||\vec{b}|\sin\theta]$$
$$= |\vec{a}|^2 |\vec{b}|^2 (1 - \cos^2\theta)$$
$$= |\vec{a}|^2 |\vec{b}|^2 \left[1 - \left(\frac{\vec{a} \cdot \vec{b}}{|\vec{a}||\vec{b}|}\right)^2\right] \quad \left[\because \cos\theta = \frac{\vec{a} \cdot \vec{b}}{|\vec{a}||\vec{b}|}\right]$$
$$= |\vec{a}|^2 |\vec{b}|^2 - (\vec{a} \cdot \vec{b})^2$$
$$= \begin{vmatrix} |\vec{a}|^2 & \vec{a} \cdot \vec{b} \\ \vec{a} \cdot \vec{b} & |\vec{b}|^2 \end{vmatrix} = \begin{vmatrix} \vec{a} \cdot \vec{a} & \vec{a} \cdot \vec{b} \\ \vec{a} \cdot \vec{b} & \vec{b} \cdot \vec{b} \end{vmatrix} = \text{RHS}$$

Hence proved.

22. Given, $|\vec{a} + \vec{b}| = |\vec{a}|$

Suppose $(2\vec{a} + \vec{b})$ is not perpendicular to $\vec{b}$.

$$\therefore \quad (2\vec{a} + \vec{b}) \cdot \vec{b} \neq 0$$
$$\Rightarrow \quad 2\vec{a} \cdot \vec{b} + \vec{b} \cdot \vec{b} \neq 0$$

On adding $|\vec{a}|^2$ both sides, we get

$$2\vec{a} \cdot \vec{b} + |\vec{b}|^2 + |\vec{a}|^2 \neq |\vec{a}|^2$$
$$\Rightarrow \quad |\vec{a} + \vec{b}|^2 \neq |\vec{a}|^2$$
$$\Rightarrow \quad |\vec{a} + \vec{b}| \neq |\vec{a}| \quad \text{[taking square root]}$$

Thus, it is a contradiction that

$$|\vec{a} + \vec{b}| = |\vec{a}| \quad \text{[given]}$$

Hence, $(2\vec{a} + \vec{b})$ is perpendicular to $\vec{b}$.

23. Let $\vec{A} = \hat{i} + 2\hat{j} - \hat{k}$ and $\vec{B} = 2\hat{i} + 3\hat{j} + \hat{k}$

We know that unit vector $\hat{n}$ is perpendicular to $\vec{A}$ and $\vec{B}$.

$$\therefore \quad \hat{n} = \frac{\vec{A} \times \vec{B}}{|\vec{A} \times \vec{B}|}$$

Now, $\vec{A} \times \vec{B} = \begin{vmatrix} \hat{i} & \hat{j} & \hat{k} \\ 1 & 2 & -1 \\ 2 & 3 & 1 \end{vmatrix}$

$$= \hat{i}(2+3) - (1+2)\hat{j} + (3-4)\hat{k}$$
$$= 5\hat{i} - 3\hat{j} - \hat{k}$$

and $|\vec{A} \times \vec{B}| = |5\hat{i} - 3\hat{j} - \hat{k}| = \sqrt{25 + 9 + 1} = \sqrt{35}$

Hence, $\quad \hat{n} = \dfrac{5\hat{i} - 3\hat{j} - \hat{k}}{\sqrt{35}}$

24. Let the perpendiculars drawn from the vertices to the opposite sides of the triangle intersect each other at H.

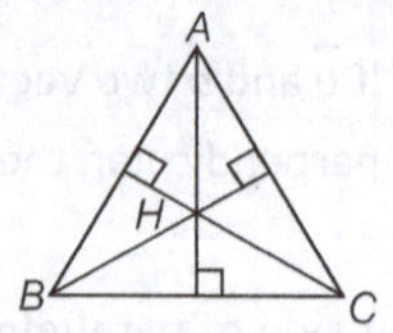

Let $\vec{a}, \vec{b}, \vec{c}$ and $\vec{h}$ be the position vectors of A, B, C and H respectively from the origin.

Since, $AH \perp BC$

Therefore, $(\vec{h} - \vec{a}) \cdot (\vec{c} - \vec{b}) = 0$

$$\Rightarrow \quad \vec{h} \cdot (\vec{c} - \vec{b}) - \vec{a} \cdot (\vec{c} - \vec{b}) = 0$$
$$\Rightarrow \quad \vec{h} \cdot \vec{c} - \vec{h} \cdot \vec{b} - \vec{a} \cdot \vec{c} + \vec{a} \cdot \vec{b} = 0 \quad \ldots(i)$$

Again, since $BH \perp CA$

Therefore, $(\vec{h} - \vec{b}) \cdot (\vec{a} - \vec{c}) = 0$

$\Rightarrow \quad \vec{h} \cdot (\vec{a} - \vec{c}) - \vec{b} \cdot (\vec{a} - \vec{c}) = 0$

$\Rightarrow \quad \vec{h} \cdot \vec{a} - \vec{h} \cdot \vec{c} - \vec{b} \cdot \vec{a} + \vec{b} \cdot \vec{c} = 0 \qquad \ldots\text{(ii)}$

On adding Eqs. (i) and (ii),we get

$\vec{h} \cdot \vec{a} - \vec{h} \cdot \vec{b} - \vec{c} \cdot \vec{a} + \vec{c} \cdot \vec{b} = 0$

$\Rightarrow \quad (\vec{h} - \vec{c}) \cdot (\vec{a} - \vec{b}) = 0$

[if $\vec{a} \perp \vec{b}$, then $\vec{a} \cdot \vec{b} = 0$]

This shows that $CH \perp BA$.

This prove that perpendiculars drawn from the vertices of a triangle to the opposite sides are concurrent.

25. Let $\vec{a}$, $\vec{b}$ and $\vec{c}$ be the position vectors of A, B and C, respectively.

Let $\vec{a} = 2\hat{i} - \hat{j} + \hat{k}$,

$\vec{b} = \hat{i} - 3\hat{j} - 5\hat{k}$

and $\vec{c} = 3\hat{i} - 4\hat{j} - 4\hat{k}$

Then, $\overrightarrow{AB} = \vec{b} - \vec{a} = (\hat{i} - 3\hat{j} - 5\hat{k}) - (2\hat{i} - \hat{j} + \hat{k})$

$= -\hat{i} - 2\hat{j} - 6\hat{k}$

$\Rightarrow |\overrightarrow{AB}| = \sqrt{(-1)^2 + (-2)^2 + (-6)^2}$

$= \sqrt{1 + 4 + 36} = \sqrt{41}$

$\overrightarrow{BC} = \vec{c} - \vec{b} = (3\hat{i} - 4\hat{j} - 4\hat{k}) - (\hat{i} - 3\hat{j} - 5\hat{k})$

$= 2\hat{i} - \hat{j} + \hat{k}$

$\Rightarrow |\overrightarrow{BC}| = \sqrt{(2)^2 + (-1)^2 + (1)^2}$

$= \sqrt{4 + 1 + 1} = \sqrt{6}$

and $\overrightarrow{CA} = \vec{a} - \vec{c} = (2\hat{i} - \hat{j} + \hat{k}) - (3\hat{i} - 4\hat{j} - 4\hat{k})$

$= -\hat{i} + 3\hat{j} + 5\hat{k}$

$\Rightarrow |\overrightarrow{CA}| = \sqrt{(-1)^2 + (3)^2 + (5)^2} = \sqrt{1 + 9 + 25}$

$= \sqrt{35}$

Now, $|\overrightarrow{AB}|^2 = 41$

and $|\overrightarrow{BC}|^2 + |\overrightarrow{CA}|^2 = 6 + 35 = 41$

$\therefore \quad |\overrightarrow{AB}|^2 = |\overrightarrow{BC}|^2 + |\overrightarrow{CA}|^2$

Hence, ABC is a right angled triangle.

26. Let ABC be the triangle and D, E and F be the mid-points of sides BC, AC and AB, respectively.

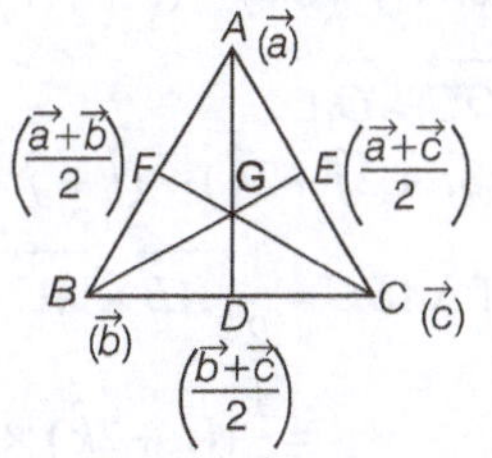

Let $\vec{a}$, $\vec{b}$ and $\vec{c}$ be the position vectors of A, B and C, respectively. Then, the position vectors of D, E and F are $\dfrac{\vec{b} + \vec{c}}{2}$, $\dfrac{\vec{a} + \vec{c}}{2}$ and $\dfrac{\vec{a} + \vec{b}}{2}$, respectively.

The position vector of a point G dividing AD in the ratio 2 : 1 is

$$\frac{1 \cdot \vec{a} + 2\left(\dfrac{\vec{b} + \vec{c}}{2}\right)}{1 + 2} = \frac{\vec{a} + \vec{b} + \vec{c}}{3}$$

Similarly, position vectors of point G dividing BE and CF in the ratio 2 : 1 and each equal to $\dfrac{\vec{a} + \vec{b} + \vec{c}}{3}$.

Thus, the point dividing AD in the ratio 2 : 1 also divides BE and CF in the same ratio.

Hence, the medians of a triangle are concurrent and the position vector of the centroid is $\dfrac{\vec{a} + \vec{b} + \vec{c}}{3}$.

27. Given, $\vec{a}$, $\vec{b}$, $\vec{c}$ and $\vec{d}$ are the position vectors of four points A, B, C and D, respectively.

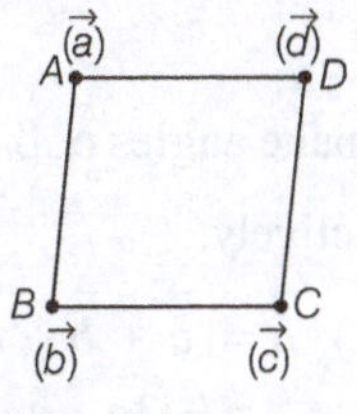

Now, $\vec{b} - \vec{a} = \overrightarrow{AB}$ and $\vec{c} - \vec{d} = \overrightarrow{DC}$

Also, given $\vec{b} - \vec{a} = \vec{c} - \vec{d}$

$\therefore \quad \overrightarrow{AB} = \overrightarrow{DC}$

$\Rightarrow \quad |\overrightarrow{AB}| = |\overrightarrow{DC}|$

[taking modulus on both sides]

and $\overrightarrow{AB} \parallel \overrightarrow{DC}$

Hence, $ABCD$ is a parallelogram.

28. (i) (c) $\overrightarrow{AB} = \overrightarrow{OB} - \overrightarrow{OA}$

$= (2\hat{i} + \hat{j} + 3\hat{k}) - (\hat{i} + \hat{j} + \hat{k}) = \hat{i} + 2\hat{k}$

(ii) (b) $\overrightarrow{AC} = \overrightarrow{OC} - \overrightarrow{OA}$

$= (3\hat{i} + 2\hat{j} + 2\hat{k}) - (\hat{i} + \hat{j} + \hat{k}) = 2\hat{i} + \hat{j} + \hat{k}$

(iii) (b) Area of $\Delta ABC = \frac{1}{2}|\overrightarrow{AB} \times \overrightarrow{AC}|$

$$= \frac{1}{2}|(\hat{i} + 2\hat{k}) \times (2\hat{i} + \hat{j} + \hat{k})|$$

$$= \begin{vmatrix} \hat{i} & \hat{j} & \hat{k} \\ 1 & 0 & 2 \\ 2 & 1 & 1 \end{vmatrix} = -2\hat{i} + 3\hat{j} + \hat{k}$$

$\therefore \quad \frac{1}{2}|\overrightarrow{AB} \times \overrightarrow{AC}| = \frac{1}{2}\sqrt{4+9+1} = \frac{\sqrt{14}}{2}$ sq units

(iv) (d) Unit vector along $\overrightarrow{AB} = \frac{\overrightarrow{AB}}{|\overrightarrow{AB}|}$

$$= \frac{\hat{i} + 2\hat{k}}{\sqrt{1^2 + 2^2}} = \frac{\hat{i} + 2\hat{k}}{\sqrt{5}}$$

29. Given, $|\vec{a}| = |\vec{b}| = |\vec{c}| = a$ (say) ...(i)

$\because \vec{a}, \vec{b}$ and $\vec{c}$ are mutually perpendicular vectors, we have

$\vec{a} \cdot \vec{b} = \vec{b} \cdot \vec{c} = \vec{c} \cdot \vec{a} = 0$ ...(ii)

Now, consider

$$|\vec{a} + \vec{b} + \vec{c}|^2 = (\vec{a} + \vec{b} + \vec{c}) \cdot (\vec{a} + \vec{b} + \vec{c})$$

$$= \vec{a} \cdot \vec{a} + \vec{b} \cdot \vec{b} + \vec{c} \cdot \vec{c} + 2(\vec{a} \cdot \vec{b} + \vec{b} \cdot \vec{c} + \vec{c} \cdot \vec{a})$$

$= |\vec{a}|^2 + |\vec{b}|^2 + |\vec{c}|^2$ [by using Eq. (ii)]

$= 3a^2$ [by Eq. (i)]

Let $(\vec{a} + \vec{b} + \vec{c})$ make angles α, β and γ with vectors $\vec{a}, \vec{b}$ and $\vec{c}$, respectively.

Then, $(\vec{a} + \vec{b} + \vec{c}) \cdot \vec{a} = |\vec{a} + \vec{b} + \vec{c}||\vec{a}|\cos\alpha$

$= (\sqrt{3}a \cdot a \cdot \cos\alpha) = \sqrt{3}a^2 \cos\alpha$

$\Rightarrow \quad (\vec{a} \cdot \vec{a} + \vec{b} \cdot \vec{a} + \vec{c} \cdot \vec{a}) = \sqrt{3}a^2 \cos\alpha$

$\Rightarrow \quad |\vec{a}|^2 = \sqrt{3}a^2 \cos\alpha$

$\Rightarrow \quad a^2 = \sqrt{3}a^2 \cos\alpha$

$\Rightarrow \quad \cos\alpha = \frac{1}{\sqrt{3}}$

$\Rightarrow \quad \alpha = \cos^{-1}\left(\frac{1}{\sqrt{3}}\right)$

Similarly, $\beta = \cos^{-1}\left(\frac{1}{\sqrt{3}}\right)$ and $\gamma = \cos^{-1}\left(\frac{1}{\sqrt{3}}\right)$

$\therefore \quad \alpha = \beta = \gamma = \cos^{-1}\left(\frac{1}{\sqrt{3}}\right)$

Thus, $(\vec{a} + \vec{b} + \vec{c})$ is equally inclined to $\vec{a}, \vec{b}$ and $\vec{c}$ and the required angle is $\cos^{-1}\left(\frac{1}{\sqrt{3}}\right)$.

30. Given, $\vec{a} = 3\hat{i} + 2\hat{j} + 2\hat{k}$

and $\vec{b} = \hat{i} + 2\hat{j} - 2\hat{k}$

Now, $\vec{a} + \vec{b} = 4\hat{i} + 4\hat{j} = \vec{c}$ [say]

and $\vec{a} - \vec{b} = 2\hat{i} + 4\hat{k} = \vec{d}$ [say]

$$\text{Now, } \vec{c} \times \vec{d} = \begin{vmatrix} \hat{i} & \hat{j} & \hat{k} \\ 4 & 4 & 0 \\ 2 & 0 & 4 \end{vmatrix}$$

$= \hat{i}(16 - 0) - \hat{j}(16 - 0) + \hat{k}(0 - 8)$

$= 16\hat{i} - 16\hat{j} - 8\hat{k}$

$\therefore$ Required unit vector $= \frac{16\hat{i} - 16\hat{j} - 8\hat{k}}{|16\hat{i} - 16\hat{j} - 8\hat{k}|}$

$$= \pm\frac{16\hat{i} - 16\hat{j} - 8\hat{k}}{\sqrt{(16)^2 + (-16)^2 + (-8)^2}}$$

$$= \pm\frac{16\hat{i} - 16\hat{j} - 8\hat{k}}{24}$$

$$= \pm\left(\frac{2}{3}\hat{i} - \frac{2}{3}\hat{j} - \frac{1}{3}\hat{k}\right)$$

31. Let O be the centre of a semi-circle and AB be a diameter of a semi-circle. Let C be a point on the circumference, then prove that $\angle ACB = 90°$.

Take O as origin and let $\overrightarrow{OB} = \vec{a}$

and $\overrightarrow{OC} = \vec{b}$, then $\overrightarrow{OA} = -\overrightarrow{OB} = -\vec{a}$

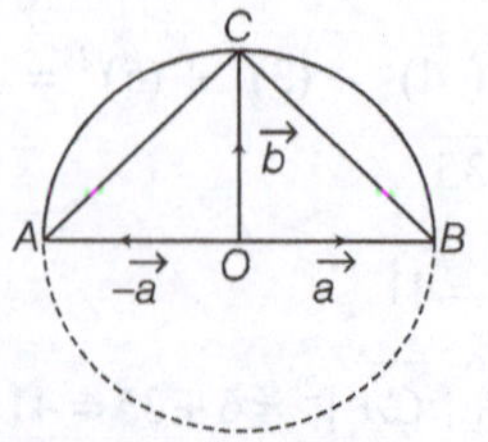

Now, $\overrightarrow{AC} = \overrightarrow{OC} - \overrightarrow{OA} = \vec{b} + \vec{a}$

$\overrightarrow{BC} = \overrightarrow{OC} - \overrightarrow{OB} = \vec{b} - \vec{a}$

$\therefore \quad \overrightarrow{AC} \cdot \overrightarrow{BC} = (\vec{b} + \vec{a}) \cdot (\vec{b} - \vec{a})$

$= \vec{b} \cdot \vec{b} - \vec{b} \cdot \vec{a} + \vec{a} \cdot \vec{b} - \vec{a} \cdot \vec{a}$

$= \vec{b} \cdot \vec{b} - \vec{a} \cdot \vec{a} = r^2 - r^2$

[where, r radius of a semi-circle]

$= 0$

$\Rightarrow \quad \overrightarrow{AC} \perp \overrightarrow{BC}$

$\therefore \quad \angle ACB = 90°$

Hence, the angle in a semi-circle is a right angle.

32. In ΔABC, let $\overrightarrow{BC} = \vec{a}$, $\overrightarrow{CA} = \vec{b}$ and $\overrightarrow{AB} = \vec{c}$

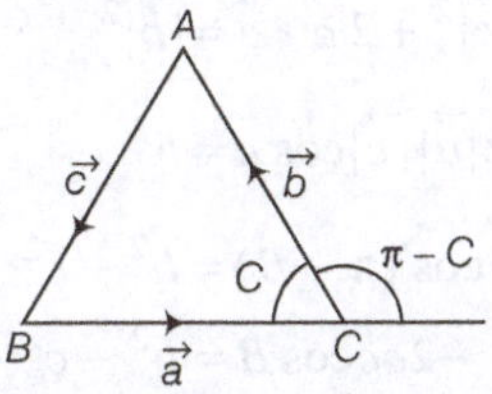

$\therefore \quad |\overrightarrow{BC}| = a, |\overrightarrow{CA}| = b$ and $|\overrightarrow{AB}| = c$

By triangle law of addition,

$\overrightarrow{BA} = \overrightarrow{BC} + \overrightarrow{CA} \Rightarrow -\vec{c} = \vec{a} + \vec{b}$

Now, $(-\vec{c}) \cdot (-\vec{c}) = (\vec{a} + \vec{b}) \cdot (\vec{a} + \vec{b})$

$\Rightarrow \quad c^2 = \vec{a} \cdot (\vec{a} + \vec{b}) + \vec{b} \cdot (\vec{a} + \vec{b})$

$\Rightarrow \quad c^2 = \vec{a} \cdot \vec{a} + \vec{a} \cdot \vec{b} + \vec{b} \cdot \vec{a} + \vec{b} \cdot \vec{b}$

$\Rightarrow \quad c^2 = a^2 + b^2 + 2\vec{a} \cdot \vec{b}$

$\Rightarrow \quad c^2 = a^2 + b^2 + 2|\vec{a}||\vec{b}| \cos(\pi - C)$

$[\because a^2 \cdot b^2 = |\vec{a}||\vec{b}| \cos(\pi - C)]$

$\Rightarrow \quad c^2 = a^2 + b^2 - 2ab \cos C$

Hence proved.

33. Given, $|\vec{a}| = 1$ and $|\vec{b}| = 1$ and θ is the angle between $\vec{a}$ and $\vec{b}$.

Now, $|\vec{a} - \vec{b}|^2 = (\vec{a} - \vec{b})^2 = a^2 + b^2 - 2\vec{a} \cdot \vec{b}$

$= a^2 + b^2 - 2|\vec{a}||\vec{b}| \cos\theta$

$[\because \vec{a} \cdot \vec{b} = |\vec{a}||\vec{b}| \cos\theta]$

$= 1 + 1 - 2\cos\theta$

$= 2 - 2\cos\theta = 2(1 - \cos\theta)$

$= 2 \times 2\sin^2 \frac{\theta}{2} = 4\sin^2 \frac{\theta}{2}$

$\left[\because (1 - \cos\theta) = 2\sin^2 \frac{\theta}{2}\right]$

$\therefore \quad |\vec{a} - \vec{b}|^2 = 4\sin^2 \frac{\theta}{2}$

$\Rightarrow \quad |\vec{a} - \vec{b}| = 2\sin \frac{\theta}{2}$ [taking positive square root]

Hence proved.

34. In ΔABC, let $\overrightarrow{BC} = \vec{a}$,

$\overrightarrow{CA} = \vec{b}$ and $\overrightarrow{AB} = \vec{c}$

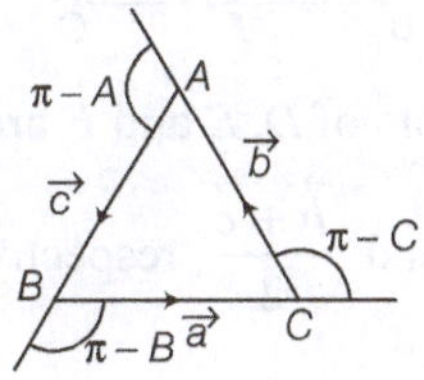

$\therefore \quad |\overrightarrow{BC}| = a, |\overrightarrow{CA}| = b$ and $|\overrightarrow{AB}| = c$

$\overrightarrow{BC} + \overrightarrow{CA} = \overrightarrow{BA}$

By triangle law of addition,

$\Rightarrow \quad \overrightarrow{BC} + \overrightarrow{CA} + \overrightarrow{AB} = \vec{0} \quad [\because \overrightarrow{BA} = -\overrightarrow{AB}]$

$\Rightarrow \quad \vec{a} + \vec{b} + \vec{c} = \vec{0}$

$\Rightarrow \quad \vec{a} \times (\vec{a} + \vec{b} + \vec{c}) = \vec{a} \times \vec{0}$

$\Rightarrow \quad (\vec{a} \times \vec{a} + \vec{a} \times \vec{b} + \vec{a} \times \vec{c}) = \vec{0}$

$\Rightarrow \quad \vec{a} \times \vec{b} = -(\vec{a} \times \vec{c})$

$[\because \vec{a} \times \vec{a} = \vec{0}]$

$\Rightarrow \quad \vec{a} \times \vec{b} = \vec{c} \times \vec{a}$

$[\because (\vec{a} \times \vec{b}) = -(\vec{b} \times \vec{a})]$ ...(i)

Similarly, $\quad \vec{c} \times \vec{a} = \vec{b} \times \vec{c}$ ...(ii)

From Eqs. (i) and (ii), we get

$\vec{a} \times \vec{b} = \vec{b} \times \vec{c} = \vec{c} \times \vec{a}$

$\Rightarrow \quad |\vec{a} \times \vec{b}| = |\vec{b} \times \vec{c}| = |\vec{c} \times \vec{a}|$

$\Rightarrow \quad ab\sin(\pi - C) = bc\sin(\pi - A) = ca\sin(\pi - B)$

$\Rightarrow \quad ab\sin C = bc\sin A = ca\sin B$

$\Rightarrow \quad \frac{\sin C}{c} = \frac{\sin A}{a} = \frac{\sin B}{b}$ [dividing by abc]

$\Rightarrow \quad \frac{a}{\sin A} = \frac{b}{\sin B} = \frac{c}{\sin C}$ [taking reciprocal]

Hence proved.

Concept Enhancer Angle between two vectors is the angle between their rays coming out.

35. Let the position vectors of A, B and C be $\vec{a}$, $\vec{b}$ and $\vec{c}$, respectively.

Given, D, E and F are the mid-points of the sides of the ΔABC.

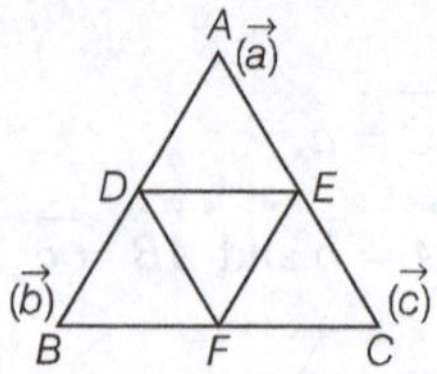

$\therefore$ Position vectors of D, E and F are

$\dfrac{\vec{a}+\vec{b}}{2}, \dfrac{\vec{a}+\vec{c}}{2}$ and $\dfrac{\vec{b}+\vec{c}}{2}$, respectively.

Now, $\overrightarrow{AB} = \vec{b} - \vec{a}$

$\overrightarrow{AC} = \vec{c} - \vec{a}$

Then, $\overrightarrow{EF} = \left(\dfrac{\vec{b}+\vec{c}}{2}\right) - \left(\dfrac{\vec{a}+\vec{c}}{2}\right) = \dfrac{1}{2}(\vec{b}-\vec{a})$

and $\overrightarrow{DF} = \left(\dfrac{\vec{b}+\vec{c}}{2}\right) - \left(\dfrac{\vec{a}+\vec{b}}{2}\right) = \dfrac{1}{2}(\vec{c}-\vec{a})$

Now, Area of $\Delta ABC = \dfrac{1}{2}|\overrightarrow{AB} \times \overrightarrow{AC}|$

$= \dfrac{1}{2}|(\vec{b}-\vec{a}) \times (\vec{c}-\vec{a})|$ ...(i)

$\therefore$ Area of $\Delta DEF = \dfrac{1}{2}|\overrightarrow{EF} \times \overrightarrow{DF}|$

$= \dfrac{1}{2}\left|\dfrac{1}{2}(\vec{b}-\vec{a}) \times \dfrac{1}{2}(\vec{c}-\vec{a})\right|$

$= \dfrac{1}{4} \times \dfrac{1}{2}|(\vec{b}-\vec{a}) \times (\vec{c}-\vec{a})|$

$= \dfrac{1}{4} \times$ Area of ΔABC [from Eq. (i)]

Hence proved.

36. Let ABC be a triangle with $\overrightarrow{BC} = \vec{a}$, $\overrightarrow{CA} = \vec{b}$ and $\overrightarrow{AB} = \vec{c}$

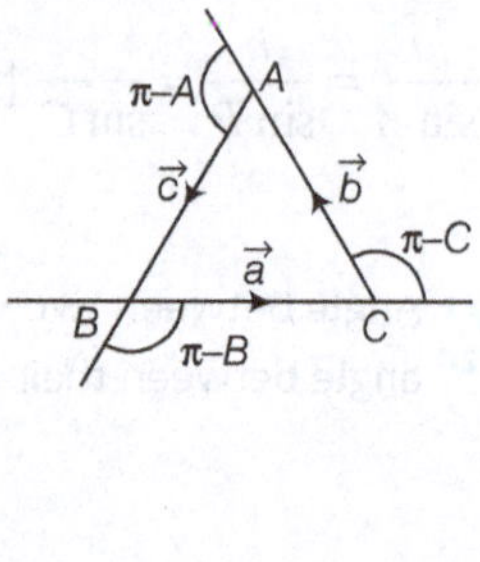

$\therefore \quad |\overrightarrow{BC}| = a, |\overrightarrow{CA}| = b$ and $|\overrightarrow{AB}| = c$

By triangle law of addition, $\overrightarrow{BC} + \overrightarrow{CA} = \overrightarrow{BA}$

$\Rightarrow \quad \overrightarrow{BC} + \overrightarrow{CA} + \overrightarrow{AB} = \vec{0}$

$\Rightarrow \quad \vec{a} + \vec{b} + \vec{c} = \vec{0}$

$\Rightarrow \quad \vec{a} + \vec{c} = -\vec{b}$

$\Rightarrow (\vec{a}+\vec{c})\cdot(\vec{a}+\vec{c}) = (-\vec{b})\cdot(-\vec{b})$

[multiply by same product]

$\Rightarrow \quad |\vec{a}|^2 + |\vec{c}|^2 + 2\vec{a}\cdot\vec{c} = |\vec{b}|^2$

$\Rightarrow a^2 + c^2 + 2|\vec{a}||\vec{c}|\cos c = b^2$

$\Rightarrow \quad 2|\vec{a}||\vec{c}|\cos(\pi - B) = b^2 - c^2 - a^2$

$\Rightarrow \quad -2ac\cos B = b^2 - c^2 - a^2$

$\Rightarrow \quad 2ac\cos B = a^2 + c^2 - b^2$

$\therefore \quad \cos B = \dfrac{a^2+c^2-b^2}{2ac}$ **Hence proved.**

37. Given, diagonals of a parallelogram are $\vec{a} = 3\hat{i} + \hat{j} - 2\hat{k}$ and $\vec{b} = \hat{i} - 3\hat{j} + 4\hat{k}$

Now, $\vec{a} \times \vec{b} = \begin{vmatrix} \hat{i} & \hat{j} & \hat{k} \\ 3 & 1 & -2 \\ 1 & -3 & 4 \end{vmatrix}$

$= [(4-6)\hat{i} - (12+2)\hat{j} + (-9-1)\hat{k}]$

$= [-2\hat{i} - 14\hat{j} - 10\hat{k}]$

$\therefore$ Area of parallelogram $= \dfrac{1}{2}|\vec{a} \times \vec{b}|$

$= \dfrac{1}{2}|-2\hat{i} - 14\hat{j} - 10\hat{k}|$

$= \dfrac{1}{2} \times \sqrt{(-2)^2 + (-14)^2 + (-10)^2}$

$= \dfrac{1}{2} \times \sqrt{4 + 196 + 100}$

$= \dfrac{1}{2} \times \sqrt{300} = \dfrac{10\sqrt{3}}{2}$

$= 5\sqrt{3}$ sq units

Concept Enhancer Area of parallelogram, if diagonals $\vec{d}_1$ and $\vec{d}_2$ given is $\frac{1}{2}|\vec{d}_1 \times \vec{d}_2|$.

38. (i) Given, AB is the diameter of the circle.

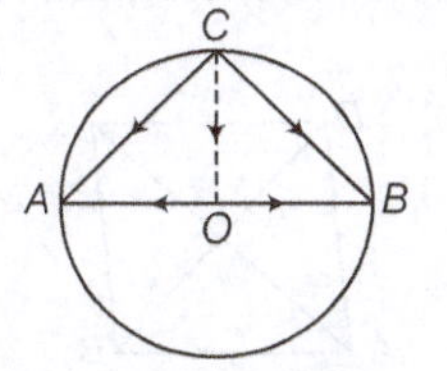

In ΔAOC, $\overrightarrow{CA} = \overrightarrow{CO} + \overrightarrow{OA}$ ...(i)

[triangle law of addition]

and in ΔBOC, $\overrightarrow{CB} = \overrightarrow{CO} + \overrightarrow{OB}$ ...(ii)

[triangle law of addition]

Now, $\overrightarrow{CA} \cdot \overrightarrow{CB} = (\overrightarrow{CO} + \overrightarrow{OA}) \cdot (\overrightarrow{CO} + \overrightarrow{OB})$

[from Eqs. (i) and (ii)]

$$= \overrightarrow{CO} \cdot \overrightarrow{CO} + \overrightarrow{CO} \cdot \overrightarrow{OB} + \overrightarrow{OA} \cdot \overrightarrow{CO} + \overrightarrow{OA} \cdot \overrightarrow{OB}$$

$$= CO^2 + \overrightarrow{CO} \cdot \overrightarrow{OB} - \overrightarrow{OB} \cdot \overrightarrow{CO} - \overrightarrow{OA} \cdot \overrightarrow{OA}$$

$[\because \overrightarrow{OB} = -\overrightarrow{OA}]$

$$= CO^2 - OA^2 = 0 \quad [\because CO = OA = \text{radius}]$$

$\therefore \quad \overrightarrow{CA} \perp \overrightarrow{CB}$

$\Rightarrow \angle ACB = 90°$

Hence, diameter of a circle will subtend a right angle at a point on its circumference.

(ii) Given, $\vec{a} = 2\hat{i} - 10\hat{j} + 2\hat{k}$, $\vec{b} = 3\hat{i} + \hat{j} + 2\hat{k}$

and $\quad \vec{c} = 2\hat{i} + \hat{j} + 3\hat{k}$

Now, $\vec{b} \times \vec{c} = \begin{vmatrix} \hat{i} & \hat{j} & \hat{k} \\ 3 & 1 & 2 \\ 2 & 1 & 3 \end{vmatrix}$

$$= (3-2)\hat{i} - (9-4)\hat{j} + (3-2)\hat{k}$$

$$= \hat{i} - 5\hat{j} + \hat{k}$$

$$\therefore \quad \vec{a} \times (\vec{b} \times \vec{c}) = \begin{vmatrix} \hat{i} & \hat{j} & \hat{k} \\ 2 & -10 & 2 \\ 1 & -5 & 1 \end{vmatrix}$$

$$= (-10+10)\hat{i} - (2-2)\hat{j} + (-10+10)\hat{k}$$

$$= 0\hat{i} + 0\hat{j} + 0\hat{k} = \vec{0}$$

39. Given, $|\vec{a} \times \vec{b}| = 8$, $|\vec{a}| = 2$, $|\vec{b}| = 5$

$\because \quad \vec{a} \times \vec{b} = |\vec{a}||\vec{b}| \sin\theta \cdot \hat{n}$

$\Rightarrow \quad |\vec{a} \times \vec{b}| = |\vec{a}||\vec{b}| \sin\theta$

$\Rightarrow \quad \sin\theta = \dfrac{|\vec{a} \times \vec{b}|}{|\vec{a}||\vec{b}|}$

$\Rightarrow \quad \sin\theta = \dfrac{8}{2 \times 5}$

$\Rightarrow \quad \sin\theta = \dfrac{4}{5}$

$\therefore \quad \cos\theta = \sqrt{1 - \sin^2\theta} = \sqrt{1 - \left(\dfrac{4}{5}\right)^2}$

$$\sqrt{1 - \left(\frac{16}{25}\right)} = \sqrt{\frac{25-16}{25}} = \sqrt{\frac{9}{25}} = \frac{3}{5}$$

Now, $\quad \vec{a} \cdot \vec{b} = |\vec{a}||\vec{b}| \cos\theta$

$$= 2 \times 5 \times \frac{3}{5} = 6$$

40. Given, $\vec{a} = \hat{i} - 2\hat{j} + \hat{k}$, $\vec{b} = 2\hat{i} + \hat{j} + \hat{k}$ and $\vec{c} = \hat{i} + 2\hat{j} - \hat{k}$

Now, $\vec{b} \times \vec{c} = (2\hat{i} + \hat{j} + \hat{k}) \times (\hat{i} + 2\hat{j} - \hat{k})$

$$= \begin{vmatrix} \hat{i} & \hat{j} & \hat{k} \\ 2 & 1 & 1 \\ 1 & 2 & -1 \end{vmatrix}$$

$$= (-1-2)\hat{i} - (-2-1)\hat{j} + (4-1)\hat{k}$$

$$= -3\hat{i} + 3\hat{j} + 3\hat{k}$$

Now, $\vec{a} \times (\vec{b} \times \vec{c}) = (\hat{i} - 2\hat{j} + \hat{k}) \times (-3\hat{i} + 3\hat{j} + 3\hat{k})$

$$= \begin{vmatrix} \hat{i} & \hat{j} & \hat{k} \\ 1 & -2 & 1 \\ -3 & 3 & 3 \end{vmatrix}$$

$$= (-6-3)\hat{i} - (3+3)\hat{j} + (3-6)\hat{k}$$

$$= -9\hat{i} - 6\hat{j} - 3\hat{k}$$

which is the required vector.

41. Let $\vec{a} = 4\hat{i} + 3\hat{j} + \hat{k}$ and $\vec{b} = 2\hat{i} - \hat{j} + 2\hat{k}$

Now, $\vec{a} \times \vec{b} = \begin{vmatrix} \hat{i} & \hat{j} & \hat{k} \\ 4 & 3 & 1 \\ 2 & -1 & 2 \end{vmatrix}$

$$= (6+1)\hat{i} - (8-2)\hat{j} + (-4-6)\hat{k}$$

$$= 7\hat{i} - 6\hat{j} - 10\hat{k}$$

Now, unit vector perpendicular to $\vec{a}$ and $\vec{b}$,

$$\hat{n} = \frac{\vec{a} \times \vec{b}}{|\vec{a} \times \vec{b}|} = \frac{7\hat{i} - 6\hat{j} - 10\hat{k}}{\sqrt{7^2 + (-6)^2 + (-10)^2}}$$

$$= \frac{7\hat{i} - 6\hat{j} - 10\hat{k}}{\sqrt{49+36+100}} = \frac{7\hat{i} - 6\hat{j} - 10\hat{k}}{\sqrt{185}}$$

Now, $|\vec{a}\times\vec{b}| = |\vec{a}||\vec{b}|\sin\theta$

$\therefore \quad \sqrt{185} = \sqrt{16+9+1}\sqrt{4+1+4}\sin\theta$

$\Rightarrow \quad \sin\theta = \dfrac{\sqrt{185}}{\sqrt{26}\sqrt{9}} = \dfrac{\sqrt{185}}{3\sqrt{26}}$

42. Given diagonals of parallelogram are

$$\overrightarrow{BD} = -2\hat{i} + 4\hat{j} + 4\hat{k}$$

and $\quad \overrightarrow{AC} = -4\hat{i} - 2\hat{k}$

Now, area of parallelogram $= \dfrac{1}{2}|\overrightarrow{BD}\times\overrightarrow{AC}|$

$$\therefore \quad \overrightarrow{BD}\times\overrightarrow{AC} = \begin{vmatrix} \hat{i} & \hat{j} & \hat{k} \\ -2 & 4 & 4 \\ -4 & 0 & -2 \end{vmatrix}$$

$$= \hat{i}(-8-0) - \hat{j}(4+16) + \hat{k}(0+16)$$

$$= -8\hat{i} - 20\hat{j} + 16\hat{k}$$

$$\Rightarrow |\overrightarrow{BD}\times\overrightarrow{AC}| = \sqrt{(-8)^2 + (-20)^2 + (16)^2}$$

$$= \sqrt{720}$$

$\therefore$ Area of parallelogram $= \dfrac{1}{2}|\overrightarrow{BD}\times\overrightarrow{AC}|$

$$= \frac{1}{2}\times\sqrt{720} = \frac{1}{2}\times 12\sqrt{5}$$

$$= 6\sqrt{5} \text{ sq units}$$

43. Given, $2\vec{a} - 4\vec{b}$ and $10\vec{a} + 8\vec{b}$ are perpendicular to each other.

$\therefore \quad (2\vec{a} - 4\vec{b})\cdot(10\vec{a} + 8\vec{b}) = 0$

$[\because \vec{a}\perp\vec{b}, \text{ then } \vec{a}\cdot\vec{b} = 0]$

$\Rightarrow \quad 20(\vec{a}\cdot\vec{a}) + 16(\vec{a}\cdot\vec{b}) - 40(\vec{b}\cdot\vec{a}) - 32(\vec{b}\cdot\vec{b}) = 0$

$\Rightarrow \quad 20|\vec{a}|^2 - 24(\vec{a}\cdot\vec{b}) - 32|\vec{b}|^2 = 0$

$\Rightarrow \quad 20 - 24(\vec{a}\cdot\vec{b}) - 32 = 0 \quad [\because |\vec{a}| = |\vec{b}| = 1]$

$\Rightarrow \quad -24\vec{a}\cdot\vec{b} - 12 = 0$

$\Rightarrow \quad 24|\vec{a}||\vec{b}|\cos\theta = -12$

$\Rightarrow \quad 24\cos\theta = -12$

$[\because |\vec{a}| = |\vec{b}| = 1]$

$\Rightarrow \quad \cos\theta = \dfrac{-12}{24} = \dfrac{-1}{2}$

$\Rightarrow \quad \theta = \pi - \dfrac{\pi}{3} = \dfrac{2\pi}{3}$

44. Given, $ABCD$ be a parallelogram as shown in figure below.

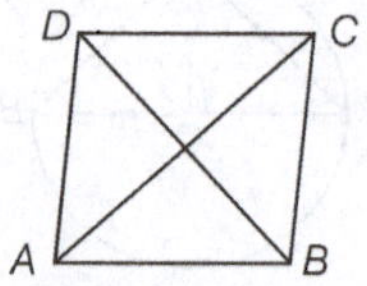

Using triangle law property,

$$\overrightarrow{AC} = \overrightarrow{AB} + \overrightarrow{BC} \quad \text{...(i)}$$

$$\overrightarrow{BD} = \overrightarrow{BA} + \overrightarrow{AD} \quad \text{...(ii)}$$

On squaring and adding of Eqs. (i) and (ii), we get

$$(\overrightarrow{AC})^2 + (\overrightarrow{BD})^2 = (\overrightarrow{AB} + \overrightarrow{BC})^2 + (\overrightarrow{BA} + \overrightarrow{AD})^2$$

$$= |\overrightarrow{AB}|^2 + |\overrightarrow{BC}|^2 + 2\overrightarrow{AB}\cdot\overrightarrow{BC}$$

$$+ |\overrightarrow{BA}|^2 + |\overrightarrow{AD}|^2 + 2\overrightarrow{BA}\cdot\overrightarrow{AD}$$

$$= AB^2 + BC^2 + 2|\overrightarrow{AB}||\overrightarrow{BC}|\cos(\angle ABC)$$

$$+ CD^2 + AD^2 + 2|\overrightarrow{BA}||\overrightarrow{AD}|\cos(\angle BAD)$$

$[\because ABCD$ is a parallelogram ; $\therefore |\overrightarrow{BA}| = |\overrightarrow{CD}|]$

$$= AB^2 + BC^2 + CD^2 + AD^2$$

$$+ 2|\overrightarrow{AB}||\overrightarrow{BC}|\cos(\angle ABC)$$

$$+ 2|\overrightarrow{AB}||\overrightarrow{BC}|\cos(\pi - \angle ABC)$$

$\left[\because |\overrightarrow{AD}| = |\overrightarrow{BC}| \text{ and } \angle ABC + \angle BAD = 180^\circ\right]$

$$= AB^2 + BC^2 + CD^2 + AD^2$$

$$+ 2|\overrightarrow{AB}||\overrightarrow{BC}|[\cos(\angle ABC) - \cos(\angle ABC)]$$

$[\because \cos(\pi - x) = -\cos x]$

$$= AB^2 + BC^2 + CD^2 + AD^2$$

$\therefore \quad AC^2 + BD^2 = AB^2 + BC^2 + CD^2 + AD^2$

Hence proved.

45. Given, $\vec{a} = 3\hat{i} + x\hat{j} - \hat{k}$ and $\vec{b} = 2\hat{i} + \hat{j} + y\hat{k}$

Now, $|\vec{a}| = \sqrt{9 + x^2 + 1}$

and $\quad |\vec{b}| = \sqrt{4 + 1 + y^2}$

Also, given $|\vec{a}| = |\vec{b}|$

$\therefore \quad |\vec{a}|^2 = |\vec{b}|^2$ [squaring both sides]

$\Rightarrow \quad 9 + x^2 + 1 = 4 + 1 + y^2$

$\Rightarrow \quad x^2 - y^2 = 5 - 10$

$\Rightarrow \quad x^2 - y^2 = -5 \quad \text{...(i)}$

Also, it is given that $\vec{a}$ and $\vec{b}$ are mutually perpendicular.

$\therefore \quad \vec{a} \cdot \vec{b} = 0$

$\Rightarrow (3\hat{i} + x\hat{j} - \hat{k}) \cdot (2\hat{i} + \hat{j} + y\hat{k}) = 0$

$\Rightarrow \quad 6 + x - y = 0$

$\Rightarrow \quad y - x = 6 \quad \text{...(ii)}$

On putting the value of y from Eq. (ii) in Eq. (i), we get

$x^2 - (6 + x)^2 = -5$

$\Rightarrow \quad x^2 - 36 - x^2 - 12x = -5$

$\Rightarrow \quad -36 - 12x = -5$

$\Rightarrow \quad 12x = -31$

$\Rightarrow \quad x = \frac{-31}{12}$

Put $x = \frac{-31}{12}$ in Eq. (ii), we get

$y - \left(\frac{-31}{12}\right) = 6$

$\Rightarrow \quad y + \frac{31}{12} = 6$

$\Rightarrow \quad y = 6 - \frac{31}{12}$

$\Rightarrow \quad y = \frac{72 - 31}{12}$

$\therefore \quad y = \frac{41}{12}$

46. Let ABC be a right angled triangle. Taking B as origin. Let the position vectors of A and C be respectively $\vec{a}$ and $\vec{b}$.

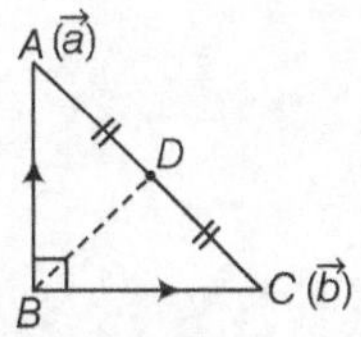

$\therefore \quad \overrightarrow{BA} = \vec{a}$ and $\overrightarrow{BC} = \vec{b}$

Let D be the mid-point of hypotenuse AC.

$\therefore \quad |\overrightarrow{DA}| = |\overrightarrow{DC}|$

Now, $\quad \overrightarrow{BA} = \overrightarrow{BD} + \overrightarrow{DA}$ and $\overrightarrow{BC} = \overrightarrow{BD} + \overrightarrow{DC}$

$\therefore \quad \overrightarrow{BA} \cdot \overrightarrow{BC} = (\overrightarrow{BD} + \overrightarrow{DA}) \cdot (\overrightarrow{BD} + \overrightarrow{DC})$

$= \overrightarrow{BD} \cdot \overrightarrow{BD} + \overrightarrow{BD} \cdot \overrightarrow{DC} + \overrightarrow{DA} \cdot \overrightarrow{BD} + \overrightarrow{DA} \cdot \overrightarrow{DC}$

But $\quad \overrightarrow{DA} = -\overrightarrow{DC}$

[since, $\overrightarrow{DA}$ and $\overrightarrow{DC}$ are equal in magnitude but opposite in direction]

$\therefore \quad \overrightarrow{BA} \cdot \overrightarrow{BC} = |\overrightarrow{BD}|^2 + \overrightarrow{BD} \cdot \overrightarrow{DC} - \overrightarrow{BD} \cdot \overrightarrow{DC} - |\overrightarrow{DA}|^2$

$= BD^2 - DA^2$

Also, $\overrightarrow{BA}$ and $\overrightarrow{BC}$ are perpendicular to each other.

$\therefore \quad \overrightarrow{BA} \cdot \overrightarrow{BC} = 0$

$\Rightarrow \quad BD^2 - DA^2 = 0$

$\Rightarrow \quad BD = DA$

Also, $\quad DA = DC \quad$ [taking square root]

$\therefore \quad BD = DA = DC$

Hence, D is equidistant from A, B and C.

Hence proved.

CHAPTER TEST

1 Mark Questions

1. If m_1, m_2, m_3 and m_4 are respectively the magnitudes of the vectors $\vec{a}_1 = 2\hat{i} - \hat{j} + \hat{k}$, $\vec{a}_2 = 3\hat{i} - 4\hat{j} - 4\hat{k}$, $\vec{a}_3 = \hat{i} + \hat{j} - \hat{k}$ and $\vec{a}_4 = -\hat{i} + 3\hat{j} + \hat{k}$, then the correct order of m_1, m_2, m_3 and m_4 is

(a) $m_3 < m_1 < m_4 < m_2$ (b) $m_3 < m_1 < m_2 < m_4$
(c) $m_3 < m_4 < m_1 < m_2$ (d) $m_3 < m_4 < m_2 < m_1$

2. If $\vec{a}$ is a non-zero vector of magnitude of a and λ is a non-zero scalar, then $\lambda\vec{a}$ is unit vector if

(a) $\lambda = 1$ (b) $\lambda = -1$
(c) $a = |\lambda|$ (d) $a = 1/|\lambda|$

3. If $|\vec{a}| = 4$ and $-3 \le \lambda \le 2$, then the range of $|\lambda\vec{a}|$ is

(a) [0, 8] (b) [−12, 8]
(c) [0, 12] (d) [8, 12]

4. The position vector of the point which divides the join of points $2\vec{a} - 3\vec{b}$ and $\vec{a} + \vec{b}$ in the ratio 3 : 1, is

(a) $\dfrac{3\vec{a} - 2\vec{b}}{2}$ (b) $\dfrac{7\vec{a} - 8\vec{b}}{4}$

(c) $\dfrac{3\vec{a}}{4}$ (d) $\dfrac{5\vec{a}}{4}$

5. The projection vector of $\vec{a}$ on $\vec{b}$ is

(a) $\left(\dfrac{\vec{a}\cdot\vec{b}}{|\vec{b}|^2}\right)\vec{b}$ (b) $\dfrac{\vec{a}\cdot\vec{b}}{|\vec{b}|}$

(c) $\dfrac{\vec{a}\cdot\vec{b}}{|\vec{a}|}$ (d) $\left(\dfrac{\vec{a}\cdot\vec{b}}{|\vec{a}|^2}\right)\hat{b}$

2 Marks Questions

6. Let $\vec{a} = \hat{i} + \hat{j} + \hat{k}$, $\vec{b} = 4\hat{i} - 2\hat{j} + 3\hat{k}$ and $\vec{c} = \hat{i} - 2\hat{j} + \hat{k}$ and find a vector of magnitude 6 units which is parallel to the vector $2\vec{a} - \vec{b} + 3\vec{c}$.

7. A vector $\vec{r}$ is inclined at equal angles to the three axes. If the magnitude of $\vec{r}$ is $2\sqrt{3}$ units, then find the value of $\vec{r}$.

8. If a unit vector $\vec{a}$ makes angle $\dfrac{\pi}{4}$ with $\hat{i}$, $\dfrac{\pi}{3}$ with $\hat{j}$ and an acute angle θ with $\hat{k}$, then find the components of $\vec{a}$ and the angle θ.

9. Find the position vector of a point C which divides the line segment joining A and B whose position vectors are $2\vec{a} + \vec{b}$ and $\vec{a} - 3\vec{b}$, externally in the ratio 1:2. Also, show that A is the mid-point of the line segment BC.

10. Points L, M and N divide the side BC, CA and AB of ΔABC in the ratio 1:4, 3:2 and 3:7, respectively. Prove that $\overrightarrow{AL} + \overrightarrow{BM} + \overrightarrow{CN}$ is a vector parallel to $\overrightarrow{CK}$, where k divides AB in the ratio 1:3.

3/4 Marks Questions

11. If $\vec{a} = 2\hat{i} + \hat{j} - 3\hat{k}$ and $\vec{b} = \hat{i} - 2\hat{j} + \hat{k}$, then find a vector of magnitude 5 perpendicular to both $\vec{a}$ and $\vec{b}$.

12. If $\vec{a} = \hat{i} + \hat{j} + \hat{k}$ and $\vec{b} = \hat{j} - \hat{k}$, then find a vector $\vec{c}$, such that $\vec{a} \times \vec{c} = \vec{b}$ and $\vec{a} \cdot \vec{c} = 3$.

13. Using vectors, find the area of triangle with vertices $A(1,1,2)$, $B(2,3,5)$ and $C(1,5,5)$.

14 If $\vec{a}$, $\vec{b}$ and $\vec{c}$ are three vectors, such that $|\vec{a}| = 5$, $|\vec{b}| = 12$, $|\vec{c}| = 13$ and $\vec{a} + \vec{b} + \vec{c} = \vec{0}$, then find the value of $\vec{a}\cdot\vec{b} + \vec{b}\cdot\vec{c} + \vec{c}\cdot\vec{a}$.

15. The diagonals AC and BD of a parallelogram $ABCD$ are represented by the vectors $\hat{i} + \hat{j} - \hat{k}$ and $\hat{i} - \hat{j} + \hat{k}$, respectively. Find the area of the parallelogram.

5/6 Marks Questions

16. $\vec{a}, \vec{b}$ and $\vec{c}$ are three vectors such that $\vec{a} \times \vec{b} = \vec{c}, \vec{b} \times \vec{c} = \vec{a}$. Prove that $\vec{a}, \vec{b}$ and $\vec{c}$ are mutually at right angle and $|\vec{b}| = 1, |\vec{c}| = |\vec{a}|$.

17. If $\vec{a}, \vec{b}$ and $\vec{c}$ are perpendicular to each other, then prove that $(\vec{a} \cdot \vec{b} \times \vec{c})^2 = a^2b^2c^2$.

18. In any ΔABC, prove by vector method, $\cos A = \dfrac{b^2 + c^2 - a^2}{2bc}$.

Answers

1. (a) **2.** (d) **3.** (c) **4.** (d) **5.** (b)

6. $2\hat{i} - 4\hat{j} + 4\hat{k}$ **7.** $\pm 2(\hat{i} + \hat{j} + \hat{k})$ **8.** $\theta = \dfrac{\pi}{3}$ and component of $a = \left(\dfrac{1}{\sqrt{2}}, \dfrac{1}{2}, \dfrac{1}{2}\right)$

9. Position vector of $\vec{c} = 3\vec{a} + 5\vec{b}$ **11.** $\dfrac{-5}{\sqrt{3}}(\hat{i} + \hat{j} + \hat{k})$ **12.** $\vec{c} = \dfrac{5}{3}\hat{i} + \dfrac{2}{3}\hat{j} + \dfrac{2}{3}\hat{k}$

13. $\dfrac{\sqrt{61}}{2}$ sq units **14.** -169 **15.** $\sqrt{2}$ sq units

11

Three Dimensional Geometry

TREND ANALYSIS 3 YEARS

Average No. of Questions Across all Sets

		Types of Questions	2024	2023	2020
TOPIC 01	Line	1 Mark	2	—	—
		2 Marks	—	—	1
		3/4 Marks	1	1	1
		5/6 Marks	—	—	—
TOPIC 02	Plane	1 Mark	—	2	—
		2 Marks	—	—	1
		3/4 Marks	1	1	—
		5/6 Marks	—	—	—

TOPIC 1

Line

Direction Cosines of a Line

If a directed line OP makes angles α, β and γ with positive X-axis, Y-axis and Z-axis respectively, then $\cos\alpha$, $\cos\beta$ and $\cos\gamma$, are called direction cosines of a line. They are denoted by l, m and n. Therefore, $l=\cos\alpha$, $m=\cos\beta$ and $n=\cos\gamma$.

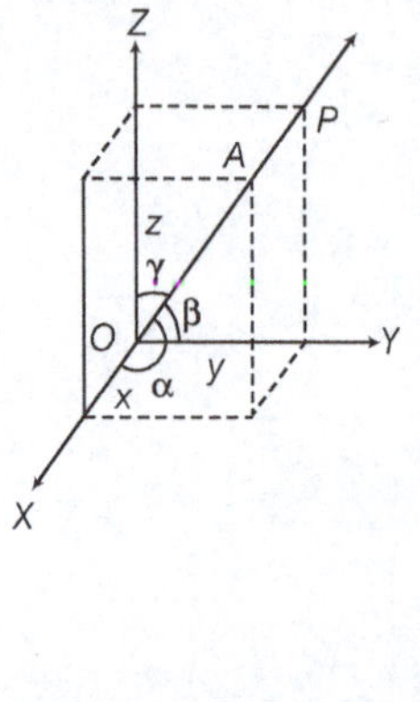

Also, sum of squares of direction cosines of a line is always 1,

i.e. $$l^2+m^2+n^2=1$$

or $\cos^2\alpha+\cos^2\beta+\cos^2\gamma=1$.

NOTE (i) Direction cosines of a directed line are unique.

(ii) Direction cosines of X, Y and Z-axes are $(1,0,0)$, $(0,1,0)$ and $(0,0,1)$.

Direction Ratios of a Line

Any three numbers a, b and c proportional to the direction cosines l, m and n respectively, are called direction ratios of the line

i.e. $$\frac{l}{a}=\frac{m}{b}=\frac{n}{c}$$

$\therefore \quad l=\frac{a}{\sqrt{a^2+b^2+c^2}}, m=\frac{b}{\sqrt{a^2+b^2+c^2}}$

and $n=\frac{c}{\sqrt{a^2+b^2+c^2}}$.

Also, direction ratios of a line PQ passing through the points $P(x_1, y_1, z_1)$ and $Q(x_2, y_2, z_2)$ are x_2-x_1, y_2-y_1 and z_2-z_1 and direction cosines are

$$\frac{x_2-x_1}{|\overrightarrow{PQ}|}, \frac{y_2-y_1}{|\overrightarrow{PQ}|}, \frac{z_2-z_1}{|\overrightarrow{PQ}|}.$$

NOTE (i) Direction ratios may be taken as (x_1-x_2), (y_1-y_2) and (z_1-z_2).
(ii) Direction ratios of two parallel lines are proportional.
(iii) Direction ratios of a line are not unique.

Straight line

A straight line is the locus of the intersection of two planes. A straight line is uniquely determined, if

(i) it passes through a given point and has a given direction.

(ii) it passes through two given points.

Equation of a Line through a Given Point and Parallel to a Given Vector

Vector form The vector equation of a line passing through a point with position vector $\vec{a}$ and parallel to a given vector $\vec{b}$ is $\vec{r}=\vec{a}+\lambda\vec{b}$

where, $\vec{a}$ = Position vector of a point through which the line is passing, $\vec{b}$ = A vector parallel to a given line.

Cartesian form The cartesian equation of a line passing through a point $A(x_1, y_1, z_1)$ and having direction ratios a, b and c is $\frac{x-x_1}{a}=\frac{y-y_1}{b}=\frac{z-z_1}{c}$.

If l, m and n are the direction cosines of the line, then the equation of the line is $\frac{x-x_1}{l}=\frac{y-y_1}{m}=\frac{z-z_1}{n}$, which is also known as symmetrical form of line.

Equation of Line Passing through Two Given Points

Vector form The vector equation of a line passing through two points A and B with position vector $\vec{a}$ and $\vec{b}$ is $\vec{r}=\vec{a}+\lambda(\vec{b}-\vec{a}), \lambda \in R$.

Cartesian form The cartesian equation of a line passing through two points $A(x_1, y_1, z_1)$ and $B(x_2, y_2, z_2)$ is $\frac{x-x_1}{x_2-x_1}=\frac{y-y_1}{y_2-y_1}=\frac{z-z_1}{z_2-z_1}$.

This is the symmetrical form of line.

Angle between Two Lines

Vector form Angle between the lines $\vec{r}=\vec{a}_1+\lambda\vec{b}_1$ and $\vec{r}=\vec{a}_2+\mu\vec{b}_2$ is given as

$$\cos\theta=\left|\frac{\vec{b}_1\cdot\vec{b}_2}{|\vec{b}_1||\vec{b}_2|}\right|,$$

where θ is the acute angle between the lines.

Cartesian form Let θ be the angle between the lines

$$\frac{x-x_1}{a_1}=\frac{y-y_1}{b_1}=\frac{z-z_1}{c_1}$$

and $$\frac{x-x_2}{a_2}=\frac{y-y_2}{b_2}=\frac{z-z_2}{c_2}.$$

Angle between Two Lines with Directions Cosines and Ratios

(i) Angle (θ) between two lines with **direction ratios**, a_1, b_1, c_1 and a_2, b_2, c_2 is given by

$$\cos\theta=\left|\frac{a_1a_2+b_1b_2+c_1c_2}{\sqrt{a_1^2+b_1^2+c_1^2}\cdot\sqrt{a_2^2+b_2^2+c_2^2}}\right|.$$

$$\text{or } \sin\theta=\frac{\sqrt{(a_1b_2-a_2b_1)^2+(b_1c_2-b_2c_1)^2+(c_1a_2-c_2a_1)^2}}{\sqrt{a_1^2+b_1^2+c_1^2}\cdot\sqrt{a_2^2+b_2^2+c_2^2}}.$$

(ii) Angle (θ) between two lines with **direction cosines**, l_1, m_1, n_1 and l_2, m_2, n_2 is given by

$$\cos\theta=|l_1l_2+m_1m_2+n_1n_2|$$

$$\text{or} \quad \sin\theta=\sqrt{(m_1n_2-m_2n_1)^2+(n_1l_2-n_2l_1)^2+(l_1m_2-l_2m_1)^2}.$$

Condition of Perpendicularity

Two lines are said to be perpendicular,

in **vector form**, if $\vec{b}_1\cdot\vec{b}_2=0$;

in **cartesian form**, if $a_1a_2+b_1b_2+c_1c_2=0$ [direction ratio form]

or $l_1l_2+m_1m_2+n_1n_2=0$ [direction cosine form]

Condition for Two Lines to be Parallel

Two lines are parallel,

in **vector form** if $\vec{b_1} = \lambda \vec{b_2}$;

in **cartesian form** if $\frac{a_1}{a_2} = \frac{b_1}{b_2} = \frac{c_1}{c_2}$ [direction ratio form]

or $\frac{l_1}{l_2} = \frac{m_1}{m_2} = \frac{n_1}{n_2}$ [direction cosine form]

Coplanar Lines

Lines which lie in the same plane are called coplanar lines. Two straight lines are coplanar, if and only if they are either parallel or intersecting.

Skew lines

Lines which are neither parallel nor intersecting lines, are called **skew lines**. In fact, such lines are non-coplanar.

Shortest Distance between Two Lines

For skew lines, the line of the shortest distance will be perpendicular to both the lines. In the figure given below i.e. PQ is the line of shortest distance.

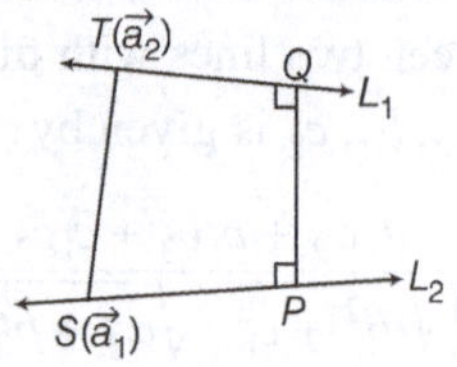

Vector form If the lines are

$$\vec{r} = \vec{a_1} + \lambda \vec{b_1} \text{ and } \vec{r} = \vec{a_2} + \mu \vec{b_2}.$$

Then, shortest distance, $d = \left| \frac{(\vec{b_1} \times \vec{b_2}) \cdot (\vec{a_2} - \vec{a_1})}{|\vec{b_1} \times \vec{b_2}|} \right|$.

Cartesian form If the lines are

$$\frac{x-x_1}{a_1} = \frac{y-y_1}{b_1} = \frac{z-z_1}{c_1} \text{ and } \frac{x-x_2}{a_2} = \frac{y-y_2}{b_2} = \frac{z-z_2}{c_2},$$

then shortest distance,

$$d = \left| \frac{\begin{vmatrix} x_2-x_1 & y_2-y_1 & z_2-z_1 \\ a_1 & b_1 & c_1 \\ a_2 & b_2 & c_2 \end{vmatrix}}{\sqrt{(b_1c_2-b_2c_1)^2 + (c_1a_2-c_2a_1)^2 + (a_1b_2-a_2b_1)^2}} \right|$$

Condition for Intersection of Two Lines

Vector Form Two lines $\vec{r_1} = \vec{a_1} + \lambda \vec{b_1}$ and $\vec{r_2} = \vec{a_2} + \mu \vec{b_2}$ intersect,

iff $\vec{b_1} \neq \vec{b_2}$ and $(\vec{a_2} - \vec{a_1}) \cdot (\vec{b_1} \times \vec{b_2}) = 0$

Cartesian Form Two lines, $\frac{x-x_1}{a_1} = \frac{y-y_1}{b_1} = \frac{z-z_1}{c_1}$

and $\frac{x-x_2}{a_2} = \frac{y-y_2}{b_2} = \frac{z-z_2}{c_2}$ intersect,

iff $a_1 : b_1 : c_1 \neq a_2 : b_2 : c_2$

The given lines are coplanar, iff $(\vec{a_2} - \vec{a_1}) \cdot (\vec{b_1} \times \vec{b_2}) = 0$

i.e. iff $\begin{vmatrix} x_2-x_1 & y_2-y_1 & z_2-z_1 \\ a_1 & b_1 & c_1 \\ a_2 & b_2 & c_2 \end{vmatrix} = 0$

Distance between Two Parallel Lines

If two lines l_1 and l_2 are parallel, then they are coplanar. Let the lines be $\vec{r} = \vec{a_1} + \lambda \vec{b}$ and $\vec{r} = \vec{a_2} + \mu \vec{b}$, then the distance between parallel lines is $\left| \frac{\vec{b} \times (\vec{a_2} - \vec{a_1})}{|\vec{b}|} \right|$.

NOTE If two lines are parallel, then they both have same or proportional direction ratios.

Distance of a Point from a Line

Length of perpendicular from a point to the line

Vector form The perpendicular distance $(\vec{d})$ of a point $P(\vec{\alpha})$ from a line $\vec{r} = \vec{a} + \alpha \vec{b}$ is given as

$$\vec{d} = \sqrt{|\vec{\alpha} - \vec{a}|^2 - \left[\frac{(\vec{\alpha} - \vec{a}) \cdot \vec{b}}{|\vec{b}|} \right]^2}$$

Cartesian form The perpendicular distance $(\vec{d})$ of a point $P(x_1, y_1, z_1)$ from a line $\frac{x-a}{l} = \frac{y-b}{m} = \frac{z-c}{n}$ is given as

$$\vec{d} = \sqrt{\begin{matrix}[(a-x_1)^2 + (b-y_1)^2 + (c-z_1)^2] \\ -[(a-x_1)l + (b-y_1)m + (c-z_1)n]^2\end{matrix}}$$

where, l, m, n are direction cosines of the line.

Distance between Two Points

The distance between two points $P(x_1, y_1, z_1)$ and $Q(x_2, y_2, z_2)$ is given by

$$PQ = \sqrt{(x_2 - x_1)^2 + (y_2 - y_1)^2 + (z_2 - z_1)^2}.$$

Mid-point of a Line

The mid-point of a line joining points $A(x_1, y_1, z_1)$ and $B(x_2, y_2, z_2)$ is given by $\left(\frac{x_1 + x_2}{2}, \frac{y_1 + y_2}{2}, \frac{z_1 + z_2}{2}\right)$.

NOTE If P is a point and P' is the image of the point with respect to the line, then mid-point of P and P' satisfy the equation of line.

Equations of Axes

Let the X, Y and Z-axes passes through the origin and have direction cosines (1, 0, 0), (0, 1, 0) and (0, 0, 1), then their equations are given as :

(i) Equation of X-axis : $\frac{x-0}{1} = \frac{y-0}{0} = \frac{z-0}{0}$

(ii) Equation of Y-axis : $\frac{x-0}{0} = \frac{y-0}{1} = \frac{z-0}{0}$

(iii) Equation of Z-axis : $\frac{x-0}{0} = \frac{y-0}{0} = \frac{z-0}{1}$

Equations of line parallel to axes

Let (α, β, γ) be any point on the line, then

(i) Equation of a line parallel to X-axis is

$$\frac{x-\alpha}{1} = \frac{y-\beta}{0} = \frac{z-\gamma}{0}$$

(ii) Equation of a line parallel to Y-axis is

$$\frac{x-\alpha}{0} = \frac{y-\beta}{1} = \frac{z-\gamma}{0}$$

(iii) Equation of a line parallel to Z-axis is

$$\frac{x-\alpha}{0} = \frac{y-\beta}{0} = \frac{z-\gamma}{1}$$

Equation of planes

(i) Equation of XY-plane is $z = 0$

(ii) Equation of YZ-plane is $x = 0$

(iii) Equation of ZY-plane is $y = 0$

PYQs Previous Years Questions

1 Mark Questions

1. If a line makes an angle α, β and γ with positive direction of the coordinate axes, then the value of $\sin^2 \alpha + \sin^2 \beta + \sin^2 \gamma$ will be *ISC 2024*

(a) 1 (b) 3
(c) – 2 (d) 2

2. In the figure given below, if the coordinates of the point P are (a, b, c), then what are the perpendicular distances of P from XY, YZ and ZX planes respectively? *ISC 2024*

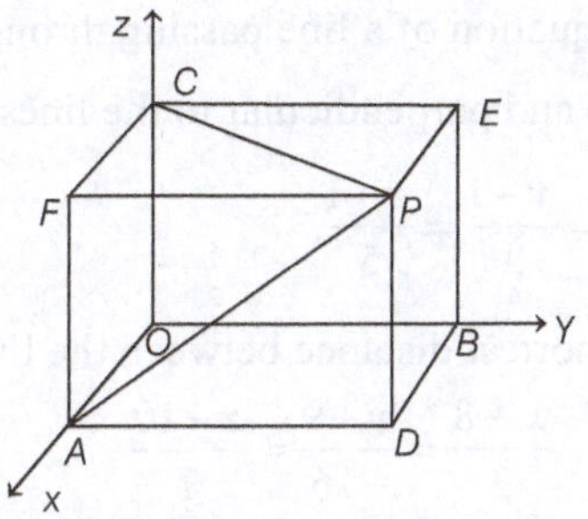

3. Prove that (1,1,1) cannot be the direction cosine of the straight line. *ISC Specimen 2024*

4. Shown below is a cube. *ISC Specimen 2024*

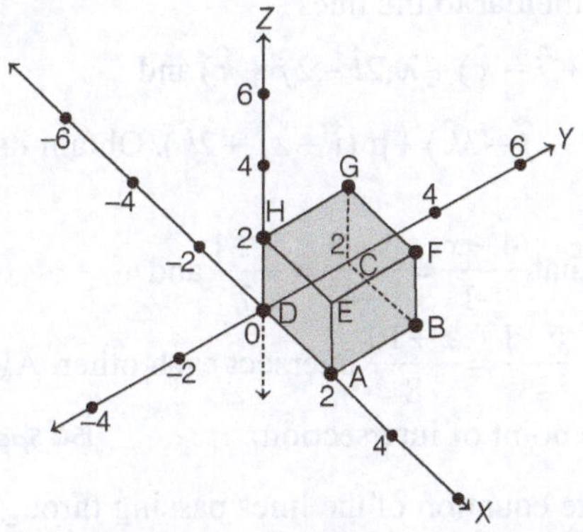

Find the equation of its diagonal which passes through the centre of the cube and also the origin.

5. The equation of the line passing (1, –1, 0) and parallel to the line $\frac{x-1}{1} = \frac{y+2}{-2} = \frac{z+1}{-1}$ is *ISC Specimen Sem-I 2022*

(a) $\frac{x-1}{1} = \frac{y+1}{-2} = \frac{z}{-1}$ (b) $\frac{x-1}{2} = \frac{y+2}{-1} = \frac{z+1}{-3}$

(c) $\frac{x-6}{1} = \frac{y-2}{-2} = \frac{z+1}{3}$ (d) $\frac{x-2}{1} = \frac{y+2}{-2} = \frac{z+3}{-1}$

6. What will be the angle between the two lines $\frac{-x+2}{-2}=\frac{y-1}{7}=\frac{z+3}{-3}$ and $\frac{x+2}{-1}=\frac{2y-8}{4}=\frac{z-5}{4}$? **ISC Specimen Sem-I 2022**

(a) $\frac{\pi}{2}$ (b) $\frac{\pi}{4}$ (c) 0 (d) π

7. What are the dirction ratios of the line passing through two points (–2, 4, 5) and (1, 2, 3)? **ISC Specimen Sem-I 2022**

(a) $<1, 2, 3>$ (b) $<-3, 2, 2>$
(c) $<2, 4, 5>$ (d) $<0, -1, 4>$

2 Marks Questions

8. Find the angle between the two lines $\frac{x+1}{2}=\frac{y-2}{5}=\frac{z+3}{4}$ and $\frac{x-1}{5}=\frac{y+2}{2}=\frac{z-1}{-5}$. **ISC 2020**

9. Find the angle between the two lines $2x=3y=-z$ and $6x=-y=-4z$. **ISC 2019**

10. The cartesian equation of a line is $2x-3=3y+1=5-6z$. Find the vector equation of a line passing through $(7,-5,0)$ and parallel to the given line. **ISC 2018**

3/4 Marks Questions

11. A line passes through the point (2, –1, 3) and is perpendicular to the lines
$\vec{r}=(\hat{i}+\hat{j}-\hat{k})+\lambda(2\hat{i}-2\hat{j}+\hat{k})$ and
$\vec{r}=(2\hat{i}-\hat{j}-3\hat{k})+\mu(\hat{i}+2\hat{j}+2\hat{k})$. Obtain its equation. **ISC 2023**

12. Show that $\frac{4-x}{-1}=\frac{y+3}{-4}=\frac{z+1}{7}$ and $\frac{x-1}{2}=\frac{y+1}{-3}=\frac{z+10}{8}$ intersect each other. Also, find out the point of intersection. **ISC Specimen 2023**

13. Find the equation of the lines passing through the point (2, 1, 3) and perpendicular to the lines $\frac{x-1}{1}=\frac{y-2}{2}=\frac{z-3}{3}$ and $\frac{x}{-3}=\frac{y}{2}=\frac{z}{5}$. **ISC Specimen 2021, 19**

14. Determine the equation of the line passing through the point (–1, –3, –2) and perpendicular to the lines $\frac{x}{1}=\frac{y}{2}=\frac{z}{3}$ and $\frac{x+2}{-3}=\frac{y-1}{2}=\frac{z+1}{5}$. **ISC 2020**

15. Find the shortest distance between the lines $\frac{x-8}{3}=\frac{y+9}{-16}=\frac{z-10}{7}$ and $\frac{x-15}{3}=\frac{y-29}{8}=\frac{z-5}{-5}$. **ISC Specimen 2018**

16. Show that the lines $\frac{x-4}{1}=\frac{y+3}{-4}=\frac{z+1}{7}$ and $\frac{x-1}{2}=\frac{y+1}{-3}=\frac{z+10}{8}$ intersect. Find the coordinates of their point of intersection. **ISC 2017**

17. Find the image of the point (2, –1, 5) in the line $\frac{x-11}{10}=\frac{y+2}{-4}=\frac{z+8}{-11}$. Also, find the length of the perpendicular from the point (2, –1, 5) to the line. **ISC 2016**

18. Find the shortest distance between the lines
$\vec{r_1}=\hat{i}+2\hat{j}+3\hat{k}+\lambda(2\hat{i}+3\hat{j}+4\hat{k})$ and
$\vec{r_2}=2\hat{i}+4\hat{j}+5\hat{k}+\mu(4\hat{i}+6\hat{j}+8\hat{k})$. **ISC 2015**

19. If a line passes through a point (1, 2, 5) then find the equation of a line parallel to
(i) X-axis (ii) Y-axis (iii) Z-axis

5/6 Marks Questions

20. Find the equation of a line passing through the points $P(-1,3,2)$ and $Q(-4,2,-2)$. Also, if the point $R(5,5,\lambda)$ is collinear with the points P and Q, then find the value of λ. **ISC 2014**

> **KEY CONCEPT**
> (i) First, determine the equation of a line passing through two point (x_1,y_1,z_1) and (x_2,y_2,z_2) which is given by $\frac{x-x_1}{x_2-x_1}=\frac{y-y_1}{y_2-y_1}=\frac{z-z_1}{z_2-z_1}=r$ (say).
> (ii) Further determine any point on the line and given point R, so that we get the required λ.

21. Find the equation of a line passing through the point $(-1,3,-2)$ and perpendicular to the lines $\frac{x}{1}=\frac{y}{2}=\frac{z}{3}$ and $\frac{x+2}{-3}=\frac{y-1}{2}=\frac{z+1}{5}$. **ISC 2013**

22. Find the shortest distance between the lines
$$\frac{x-8}{3}=\frac{y+9}{-16}=\frac{z-10}{7}$$
and $$\frac{x-15}{3}=\frac{y-29}{8}=\frac{5-z}{5}.$$ **ISC 2012**

Explanations

1. (d) We have, $\sin^2\alpha+\sin^2\beta+\sin^2\gamma$

$$=(1-\cos^2\alpha)+(1-\cos^2\beta)+(1-\cos^2\gamma)$$
$$=3-(\cos^2\alpha+\cos^2\beta+\cos^2\gamma)$$
$$=3-1$$

[$\because \cos\alpha, \cos\beta$ and $\cos\gamma$ are the direction cosines of the line]

$$=2$$

2. Let PD, PE and PF are the perpendicular distance of P from XY, YZ and ZX-planes respectively.

Now, for any point $P(a, b, c)$, a is perpendicular distance of P from YZ-plane, b is perpendicular distance of P from XZ-plane and c is perpendicular distance of P from XY-plane.

Hence, the perpendicular distances of $P(a, b, c)$ from XY, YZ and ZX-planes are c, a and b, respectively.

3. We know that if l, m and n are direction cosines of any line, then $l^2+m^2+n^2=1$

But here $1^2+1^2+1^2=3\neq 1$

So, (1, 1, 1) cannot be direction cosines for any line.

4. According to the figure, the coordinates of point D and F are (0, 0, 0) and (2, 2, 2) respectively.

Since, the centre of the cube lies on the line joining the point D and F, therefore the coordinate of the centre are

$$C\equiv\left(\frac{2+0}{2}, \frac{2+0}{2}, \frac{2+0}{2}\right)\equiv(1, 1, 1)$$

Now, the DR's of the diagonal which pass through the origin (0, 0, 0) and centre (1, 1, 1) is given by

$$\text{DR's}\equiv(1-0, 1-0, 1-0)\equiv(1, 1, 1)$$

Since, the diagonal passes through the origin with DR's (1, 1, 1). Therefore, the equation of diagonal is

$$\frac{x-0}{1}=\frac{y-0}{1}=\frac{z-0}{1} \text{ i.e. } x=y=z$$

which is the required equation of diagonal.

5. (a) Given, the required line is passing through (1, −1, 0) and parallel to the line $\frac{x-1}{1}=\frac{y+2}{-2}=\frac{z+1}{-1}$.

Direction ratios $=1, -2, -1$

We know that the cartesian equation of a line passing through a point $A(x_1, y_1, z_1)$ and having direction ratios a, b and c is given by

$$\frac{x-x_1}{a}=\frac{y-y_1}{b}=\frac{z-z_1}{c}$$

$\therefore$ The equation of the required line will be

$$\frac{x-1}{1}=\frac{y+1}{-2}=\frac{z}{-1}.$$

6. (a) We know that the angle (θ) between two lines

$$\frac{x-x_1}{a_1}=\frac{y-y_1}{b_1}=\frac{z-z_1}{c_1} \text{ and } \frac{x-x_2}{a_2}=\frac{y-y_2}{b_2}=\frac{z-z_2}{c_2}$$

with direction ratios a_1, b_1, c_1 and a_2, b_2, c_2 is given by

$$\cos\theta=\left|\frac{a_1a_2+b_1b_2+c_1c_2}{\sqrt{a_1^2+b_1^2+c_1^2}\cdot\sqrt{a_2^2+b_2^2+c_2^2}}\right|$$

Given, lines can be written as

$$\frac{x-2}{2}=\frac{y-1}{7}=\frac{z+3}{-3} \text{ and } \frac{x+2}{-1}=\frac{y-4}{2}=\frac{z-5}{4}$$

$$\therefore \cos\theta=\left|\frac{2(-1)+7(2)+(-3)(4)}{\sqrt{2^2+7^2+(-3)^2}\cdot\sqrt{(-1)^2+2^2+4^2}}\right|$$

$$=\left|\frac{-2+14-12}{\sqrt{4+49+9}\cdot\sqrt{1+4+16}}\right|=0$$

$$\Rightarrow \quad \theta=\cos^{-1}0 \Rightarrow \theta=\frac{\pi}{2}$$

7. (b) We know that direction ratios of a line PQ passing through the points $P(x_1, y_1, z_1)$ and $Q(x_2, y_2, z_2)$ are x_2-x_1, y_2-y_1 and z_2-z_1.

$\therefore$ Required direction ratios are $= <-2-1, 4-2, 5-3>$

$= <-3, 2, 2>$

8. Given lines $\frac{x+1}{2}=\frac{y-2}{5}=\frac{z+3}{4}$; $\frac{x-1}{5}=\frac{y+2}{2}=\frac{z-1}{-5}$

Here, $a_1=2, b_1=5$ and $c_1=4$

and $a_2=5, b_2=2$ and $c_2=-5$

Angle between the two lines is

$$\cos\theta=\frac{a_1a_2+b_1b_2+c_1c_2}{\sqrt{a_1^2+b_1^2+c_1^2}\sqrt{a_2^2+b_2^2+c_2^2}}$$

$$\therefore \quad \cos\theta=\frac{(2)(5)+(5)(2)+(4)(-5)}{\sqrt{2^2+5^2+4^2}\sqrt{5^2+2^2+(-5)^2}}$$

$$\Rightarrow \quad \cos\theta=0 \Rightarrow \theta=\frac{\pi}{2}$$

Concept Enhancer

Angle between the two lines is

$$\cos\theta=\frac{a_1a_2+b_1b_2+c_1c_2}{\sqrt{a_1^2+b_1^2+c_1^2}\sqrt{a_2^2+b_2^2+c_2^2}}$$

9. Given equations of lines are written as

$$\frac{x}{\frac{1}{2}}=\frac{y}{\frac{1}{3}}=\frac{z}{-1} \text{ and } \frac{x}{\frac{1}{6}}=\frac{y}{-1}=\frac{z}{-\frac{1}{4}}$$

Here, direction ratios of above lines are

$$<a_1, b_1, c_1> = <\frac{1}{2}, \frac{1}{3}, -1>$$

and $<a_2, b_2, c_2> = <\frac{1}{6}, -1, -\frac{1}{4}>$

$\because$ Angle between two lines is

$$\cos\theta = \frac{a_1a_2+b_1b_2+c_1c_2}{\sqrt{a_1^2+b_1^2+c_1^2}\sqrt{a_2^2+b_2^2+c_2^2}}$$

$$= \frac{\frac{1}{2}\times\frac{1}{6}+\frac{1}{3}\times(-1)+(-1)\times\left(-\frac{1}{4}\right)}{\sqrt{\frac{1}{4}+\frac{1}{9}+1}\sqrt{\frac{1}{36}+1+\frac{1}{16}}}$$

$$= \frac{\frac{1}{12}-\frac{1}{3}+\frac{1}{4}}{\sqrt{\frac{9+4+36}{36}}\sqrt{\frac{4+144+9}{36\times 4}}} = \frac{\frac{1-4+3}{12}}{\sqrt{\frac{49}{36}}\sqrt{\frac{157}{144}}}$$

$$\Rightarrow \quad \cos\theta = 0$$

$$\Rightarrow \quad \theta = 90^\circ$$

Hence, given lines are perpendicular.

10. Given, cartesian equation of line is

$$2x-3=3y+1=5-6z$$

$$\Rightarrow \quad \frac{x-\frac{3}{2}}{\frac{1}{2}}=\frac{y+\frac{1}{3}}{\frac{1}{3}}=\frac{z-\frac{5}{6}}{-\frac{1}{6}}$$

$$\Rightarrow \quad \frac{x-\frac{3}{2}}{3}=\frac{y+\frac{1}{3}}{2}=\frac{z-\frac{5}{6}}{-1}$$

Direction ratios of line are $(3, 2, -1)$.

Vector equation of line passing through $(7-5, 0)$ and parallel to given line is

$$\vec{r} = (7\hat{i}-5\hat{j})+\lambda(3\hat{i}+2\hat{j}-\hat{k}).$$

11. Let the equation of line passing through $(2, -1, 3)$ be

$$\vec{r} = (2\hat{i}-\hat{j}+3\hat{k})+t(\vec{b})$$

Since, this line is perpendicular to the line

$$\vec{r} = \hat{i}+\hat{j}-\hat{k}+\lambda(2\hat{i}-2\hat{j}+\hat{k})$$

and $\quad \vec{r} = 2\hat{i}-\hat{j}-3\hat{k}+\mu(\hat{i}+2\hat{j}+2\hat{k})$

Direction ratios of vector perpendicular to both vector $2\hat{i}-2\hat{j}+\hat{k}$ and $\hat{i}+2\hat{j}+2\hat{k}$ is

$$(2\hat{i}-2\hat{j}+\hat{k})\times(\hat{i}+2\hat{j}+2\hat{k}) = \begin{vmatrix}\hat{i} & \hat{j} & \hat{k}\\ 2 & -2 & 1\\ 1 & 2 & 2\end{vmatrix}$$

$$\Rightarrow \quad -6\hat{i}-3\hat{j}+6\hat{k} = -3(2\hat{i}+\hat{j}-2\hat{k})$$

$\therefore$ Equation of line is

$$\vec{r} = 2\hat{i}-\hat{j}+3\hat{k}+t(2\hat{i}+\hat{j}-2\hat{k})$$

which is equation of required line.

12. Given, $\frac{4-x}{-1}=\frac{y+3}{-4}=\frac{z+1}{7}$ and $\frac{x-1}{2}=\frac{y+1}{-3}=\frac{z+10}{8}$

Let $\quad \frac{x-4}{1}=\frac{y+3}{-4}=\frac{z+1}{7}=\lambda$

$$\Rightarrow \quad x=\lambda+4,\ y=-4\lambda-3 \text{ and } z=7\lambda-1 \quad \ldots\text{(i)}$$

Now, $\quad \frac{x-1}{2}=\frac{y+1}{-3}=\frac{z+10}{8}=\mu$

$$x=2\mu+1,\ y=-3\mu-1 \text{ and } z=8\mu-10 \quad \ldots\text{(ii)}$$

On comparing x from Eqs. (i) and (ii), we get

$$\lambda+4=2\mu+1 \Rightarrow 2\mu-\lambda=3 \quad \ldots\text{(iii)}$$

On comparing y from Eqs. (i) and (ii), we get

$$-4\lambda-3=-3\mu-1$$

$$\Rightarrow \quad 3\mu-4\lambda=2 \quad \ldots\text{(iv)}$$

On solving Eqs. (iii) and (iv), we get

$$\lambda=1 \text{ and } \mu=2$$

On substituting λ in Eq. (i), we get

$$x=1+4,\ y=-4-3 \text{ and } z=7-1$$

$$\Rightarrow \quad x=5,\ y=-7 \text{ and } z=6$$

So, the point of intersection is $(5-7, 6)$.

Common Mistake Be careful while using the cartesian form of equation of line without converting them into standard form..

13. Any line through the point $(2, 1, 3)$ is given by

$$\frac{x-2}{a}=\frac{y-1}{b}=\frac{z-3}{c}, \quad \ldots\text{(i)}$$

where a, b and c are the direction ratios of line (i).

Now, the line (i) is perpendicular to the lines

$$\frac{x-1}{1}=\frac{y-2}{2}=\frac{z-3}{3}$$

and $\quad \frac{x-0}{-3}=\frac{y-0}{2}=\frac{z-0}{5},$

where direction ratios of these two lines are (1, 2, 3) and (−3, 2, 5), respectively.

$\therefore \quad a+2b+3c=0 \quad \ldots(\text{ii})$

and $\quad -3a+2b+5c=0 \quad \ldots(\text{iii})$

[$\because$ if two lines having DR's (a_1, b_1, c_1) and (a_2, b_2, c_2) are perpendicular, then $a_1a_2+b_1b_2+c_1c_2=0$]

By cross-multiplication method, we get

$$\frac{a}{10-6}=\frac{-b}{5+9}=\frac{c}{2+6}$$

$$\Rightarrow \quad \frac{a}{4}=\frac{b}{-14}=\frac{c}{8}$$

$$\Rightarrow \quad \frac{a}{2}=\frac{b}{-7}=\frac{c}{4}=\lambda \text{ (say)}$$

$\therefore \quad a=2\lambda,\ b=-7\lambda$ and $c=4\lambda$

On putting the values of a, b and c in Eq. (i), we get

$$\frac{x-2}{2\lambda}=\frac{y-1}{-7\lambda}=\frac{z-3}{4\lambda} \Rightarrow \frac{x-2}{2}=\frac{y-1}{-7}=\frac{z-3}{4}$$

which is the required cartesian equation of the line. The required vector equation of line which passes through the point (2, 1, 3) and parallel to the vector $2\hat{i}-7\hat{j}+4\hat{k}$ is

$$\vec{r}=2\hat{i}+\hat{j}+3\hat{k}+\lambda(2\hat{i}-7\hat{j}+4\hat{k})$$

14. Let the equation of line passing through the point (−1, −3, −2) be

$$\frac{x+1}{a}=\frac{y+3}{b}=\frac{z+2}{c}$$

Since, the above line is perpendicular to the line

$$\frac{x}{1}=\frac{y}{2}=\frac{z}{3} \text{ and } \frac{x+2}{-3}=\frac{y-1}{2}=\frac{z+1}{5}$$

$\therefore \quad a+2b+3c=0 \quad \ldots(\text{i})$

and $\quad -3a+2b+5c=0 \quad \ldots(\text{ii})$

By cross-multiplication, we have

$$\frac{a}{10-6}=\frac{-b}{5+9}=\frac{c}{2+6}$$

$$\Rightarrow \quad \frac{a}{4}=\frac{b}{-14}=\frac{c}{8} \Rightarrow \frac{a}{2}=\frac{b}{-7}=\frac{c}{4}=\lambda$$

$$\Rightarrow \quad a=2\lambda,\ b=-7\lambda,\ c=4\lambda$$

$\therefore$ Equation of line is

$$\frac{x+1}{2}=\frac{y+3}{-7}=\frac{z+2}{4}$$

15. Given, lines are

$$\frac{x-8}{3}=\frac{y+9}{-16}=\frac{z-10}{7} \text{ and } \frac{x-15}{3}=\frac{y-29}{8}=\frac{z-5}{-5}$$

Here, $x_1=8,\ y_1=-9,\ z_1=10,\ a_1=3,\ b_1=-16,\ c_1=7,$ $x_2=15,\ y_2=29,\ z_2=5,\ a_2=3,\ b_2=8,\ c_2=-5$

Shortest distance between two lines is given by

$$=\left|\frac{\begin{vmatrix} x_2-x_1 & y_2-y_1 & z_2-z_1 \\ a_1 & b_1 & c_1 \\ a_2 & b_2 & c_2 \end{vmatrix}}{\sqrt{(b_1c_2-b_2c_1)^2+(c_1a_2-c_2a_1)^2+(a_1b_2-a_2b_1)^2}}\right|$$

$$=\left|\frac{\begin{vmatrix} 15-8 & 29+9 & 5-10 \\ 3 & -16 & 7 \\ 3 & 8 & -5 \end{vmatrix}}{\sqrt{(80-56)^2+(21+15)^2+(24+48)^2}}\right|$$

$$=\left|\frac{\begin{vmatrix} 7 & 38 & -5 \\ 3 & -16 & 7 \\ 3 & 8 & -5 \end{vmatrix}}{\sqrt{(24)^2+(36)^2+(72)^2}}\right|$$

$$=\left|\frac{7(80-56)-38(-15-21)-5(24+48)}{\sqrt{(24)^2+(36)^2+(72)^2}}\right|$$

$$=\left|\frac{7(24)+38(36)-5(72)}{12\sqrt{4+9+36}}\right|$$

$$=\left|\frac{12(14+114-30)}{12\times 7}\right|=\frac{98}{7}=14$$

16. Given lines are

$$\frac{x-4}{1}=\frac{y+3}{-4}=\frac{z+1}{7}=\lambda \text{ (say)} \quad \ldots(\text{i})$$

$$\frac{x-1}{2}=\frac{y+1}{-3}=\frac{z+10}{8}=\mu \text{ (say)} \quad \ldots(\text{ii})$$

The general point on line (i) is

$$M(\lambda+4,\ -4\lambda-3,\ 7\lambda-1)$$

The general point on line (ii) is

$$N(2\mu+1,\ -3\mu-1,\ 8\mu-10)$$

The given lines (i) and (ii) will intersect only when they have a common point.

This is possible when M and N coincide for some particular values of λ and μ.

$\therefore$ Given, lines will intersect only when $\lambda + 4 = 2\mu + 1$, $-4\lambda - 3 = -3\mu - 1$ and $7\lambda - 1 = 8\mu - 10$.

$\Rightarrow \quad \lambda - 2\mu = -3 \quad \ldots\text{(iii)}$

$\Rightarrow \quad -4\lambda + 3\mu = 2 \quad \ldots\text{(iv)}$

$\Rightarrow \quad 7\lambda - 8\mu = -9 \quad \ldots\text{(v)}$

On solving Eqs. (iii) and (iv), we get

$$\lambda = 1 \text{ and } \mu = 2$$

It is clear that, these values of λ and μ also satisfy Eq. (v).

$\therefore$ By putting $\lambda = 1$ in M or $\mu = 2$ in N, we get the point of intersection of the given line as $(5, -7, 6)$.

17. Given, line is $\dfrac{x-11}{10} = \dfrac{y+2}{-4} = \dfrac{z+8}{-11} \quad \ldots\text{(i)}$

Let N be the foot of perpendicular drawn from the point $P(2, -1, 5)$ to the line (i).

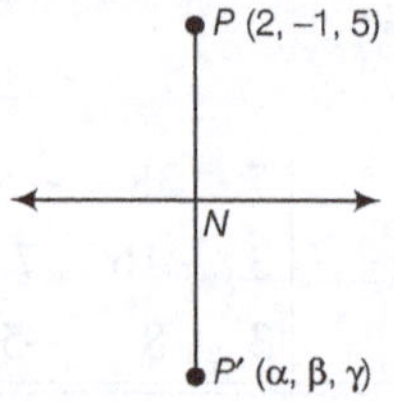

Any point on line (i) is

$$\langle 10\lambda + 11, -4\lambda - 2, -11\lambda - 8 \rangle$$

We want to find a suitable value of λ so that this point becomes N.

$\therefore$ Direction ratios of NP are

$$\langle 10\lambda + 11 - 2, -4\lambda - 2 + 1, -11\lambda - 8 - 5 \rangle$$

i.e. $\langle 10\lambda + 9, -4\lambda - 1, -11\lambda - 13 \rangle$

and direction ratios of the line (i) are $\langle 10, -4, -11 \rangle$.

$\therefore \quad 10(10\lambda + 9) - 4(-4\lambda - 1) - 11(-11\lambda - 13) = 0$

$\Rightarrow \quad 100\lambda + 90 + 16\lambda + 4 + 121\lambda + 143 = 0$

$\Rightarrow \quad 237\lambda + 237 = 0$

$\Rightarrow \quad \lambda = -1$

On substituting the value of λ in the coordinate of point N, we get $(1, 2, 3)$.

Let image of point $P(2, -1, 5)$ in the line (i) be $P'(\alpha, \beta, \gamma)$.

Also, point N is the mid-point of PP'.

$\therefore \quad 1 = \dfrac{2+\alpha}{2}, 2 = \dfrac{-1+\beta}{2}, 3 = \dfrac{5+\gamma}{2}$

$\Rightarrow \quad \alpha = 0, \beta = 5, \gamma = 1$

Hence, image of point $P(2, -1, 5)$ is $P'(0, 5, 1)$.

Required length of the perpendicular from the point $(2, -1, 5)$ to the given line

$$= \sqrt{(2-1)^2 + (-1-2)^2 + (5-3)^2}$$
$$= \sqrt{1 + 9 + 4} = \sqrt{14} \text{ units}$$

18. Given, equations of lines are

$$\vec{r} = \hat{i} + 2\hat{j} + 3\hat{k} + \lambda(2\hat{i} + 3\hat{j} + 4\hat{k})$$

and $\vec{r} = 2\hat{i} + 4\hat{j} + 5\hat{k} + \mu(4\hat{i} + 6\hat{j} + 8\hat{k})$

On comparing with $\vec{r} = \vec{a} + \lambda\vec{b}$, we get

$$\vec{a}_1 = \hat{i} + 2\hat{j} + 3\hat{k}, \vec{b}_1 = 2\hat{i} + 3\hat{j} + 4\hat{k}$$

and $\vec{a}_2 = 2\hat{i} + 4\hat{j} + 5\hat{k}, \vec{b}_2 = 4\hat{i} + 6\hat{j} + 8\hat{k}$

Now, $(\vec{a}_2 - \vec{a}_1) = (2\hat{i} + 4\hat{j} + 5\hat{k}) - (\hat{i} + 2\hat{j} + 3\hat{k})$

$$= \hat{i} + 2\hat{j} + 2\hat{k}$$

$$(\vec{b}_1 \times \vec{b}_2) = \begin{vmatrix} \hat{i} & \hat{j} & \hat{k} \\ 2 & 3 & 4 \\ 4 & 6 & 8 \end{vmatrix}$$

$$= \hat{i}(24 - 24) - \hat{j}(16 - 16) + \hat{k}(12 - 12)$$
$$= 0i - 0j + 0k$$

It means given lines are parallel.

$\therefore$ The shortest distance between two parallel lines is

$$\frac{|\vec{b} \times (\vec{a}_2 - \vec{a}_1)|}{|\vec{b}|} = \frac{|(2\hat{i} + 3\hat{j} + 4\hat{k}) \times (\hat{i} + 2\hat{j} + 2\hat{k})|}{|2\hat{i} + 3\hat{j} + 4\hat{k}|}$$

$[\because \vec{b} = \vec{b}_1 = \vec{b}_2]$

$$= \frac{\left\|\begin{matrix} \hat{i} & \hat{j} & \hat{k} \\ 2 & 3 & 4 \\ 1 & 2 & 2 \end{matrix}\right\|}{\sqrt{2^2 + 3^2 + 4^2}}$$

$$= \frac{|\hat{i}(6-8) - \hat{j}(4-4) + \hat{k}(4-3)|}{\sqrt{4 + 9 + 16}}$$

$$= \frac{|-2\hat{i} - 0\hat{j} + \hat{k}|}{\sqrt{29}} = \frac{\sqrt{(-2)^2 + 0 + (1)^2}}{\sqrt{29}}$$

$$= \frac{\sqrt{4+1}}{\sqrt{29}} = \sqrt{\frac{5}{29}}$$

19. (i) We know that if a line passes through (α, β, γ) and parallel to X-axis, then its equation is

$$\frac{x-\alpha}{1} = \frac{y-\beta}{0} = \frac{z-\gamma}{0}$$

$\therefore$ Equation of a line passing through $(1, 2, 5)$ and parallel to X-axis is

$$\frac{x-1}{1} = \frac{y-2}{0} = \frac{z-5}{0}$$

(ii) Equation of a line passing through $(1, 2, 5)$ and parallel to Y-axis is

$$\frac{x-1}{0} = \frac{y-2}{1} = \frac{z-5}{0}$$

(iii) Equation of a line passing through (1, 2, 5) and parallel to Z-axis is

$$\frac{x-1}{0}=\frac{y-2}{0}=\frac{z-5}{1}$$

20. Let the equation of line passing through $P(-1,3,2)$ and $Q(-4,2,-2)$ be

$$\frac{x+1}{-4+1}=\frac{y-3}{2-3}=\frac{z-2}{-2-2}$$

$$\left[\because \frac{x-x_1}{x_2-x_1}=\frac{y-y_1}{y_2-y_1}=\frac{z-z_1}{z_2-z_1}\right]$$

$$\Rightarrow \frac{x+1}{-3}=\frac{y-3}{-1}=\frac{z-2}{-4}$$

$$\Rightarrow \frac{x+1}{3}=\frac{y-3}{1}=\frac{z-2}{4}=r$$

[multiplying by −1]

$\therefore$ Any point on the above line PQ is

$(3r-1, r+3, 4r+2)$

Given, the point $R(5, 5, \lambda)$ lies on the line PQ.

$\therefore \quad (3r-1, r+3, 4r+2)=(5, 5, \lambda)$

$\Rightarrow \quad 3r-1=5$

$\Rightarrow \quad 3r=6$

$\Rightarrow \quad r=2$

and $\quad 4r+2=\lambda$

$\Rightarrow \quad 4\times 2+2=\lambda$

$\Rightarrow \quad 10=\lambda$

Hence, the value of λ is 10.

21. Let the direction ratios of the required line be a, b and c.

Since, the required line is perpendicular to the given lines.

Then, $\quad a+2b+3c=0 \quad$ ...(i)

$[\because a_1a_2+b_1b_2+c_1c_2=0]$

and $\quad -3a+2b+5c=0 \quad$ ...(ii)

On solving Eqs. (i) and (ii), by cross- multiplication method, we get

$$\frac{a}{10-6}=\frac{b}{-9-5}=\frac{c}{2+6}$$

$$\Rightarrow \frac{a}{4}=\frac{b}{-14}=\frac{c}{8}$$

$$\Rightarrow \frac{a}{2}=\frac{b}{-7}=\frac{c}{4}=r \quad \text{(say)}$$

As, the required line passes through $(-1, 3, -2)$ and has direction ratios proportional to $(2, -7, 4)$.

Hence, the required equation of line is

$$\frac{x+1}{2}=\frac{y-3}{-7}=\frac{z+2}{4}.$$

22. Given, lines are $\dfrac{x-8}{3}=\dfrac{y-(-9)}{-16}=\dfrac{z-10}{7}$

and $\dfrac{x-15}{3}=\dfrac{y-29}{8}=\dfrac{5-z}{5}$

or $\dfrac{x-15}{3}=\dfrac{y-29}{8}=\dfrac{z-5}{-5}$

On comparing with standard equation of line

$\dfrac{x-x_1}{a}=\dfrac{y-y_1}{b}=\dfrac{z-z_1}{c}$, we get

$x_1=8, y_1=-9, z_1=10, a_1=3, b_1=-16, c_1=7,$

$x_2=15, y_2=29, z_2=5, a_2=3, b_2=8, c_2=-5$

$\therefore$ The shortest distance between the lines

$$=\frac{\begin{vmatrix} x_2-x_1 & y_2-y_1 & z_2-z_1 \\ a_1 & b_1 & c_1 \\ a_2 & b_2 & c_2 \end{vmatrix}}{\sqrt{(b_1c_2-b_2c_1)^2+(c_1a_2-c_2a_1)^2+(a_1b_2-a_2b_1)^2}}$$

$$=\frac{\begin{vmatrix} 15-8 & 29+9 & 5-10 \\ 3 & -16 & 7 \\ 3 & 8 & -5 \end{vmatrix}}{\sqrt{(-16\times(-5)-8\times 7)^2+(7\times 3+5\times 3)^2+(3\times 8-3\times(-16))^2}}$$

$$=\frac{\begin{vmatrix} 7 & 38 & -5 \\ 3 & -16 & 7 \\ 3 & 8 & -5 \end{vmatrix}}{\sqrt{(80-56)^2+(21+15)^2+(24+48)^2}}$$

$$=\frac{7(80-56)-38(-15-21)-5(24+48)}{\sqrt{(24)^2+(36)^2+(72)^2}}$$

$$=\frac{7(24)-38(-36)-5(72)}{\sqrt{12^2(2^2+3^2+6^2)}}$$

$$=\frac{168+1368-360}{12\sqrt{4+9+36}}$$

$$=\frac{1176}{12\sqrt{49}}$$

$$=\frac{98}{7}=14 \text{ units}$$

TOPIC 2

Plane

A plane is a surface such that if two points are taken in it, straight line joining them lies completely on the surface.

Normal to the plane

A straight line which is perpendicular to every line lying on a plane is called a normal to the plane.

General Equation of Plane

An equation of the form $ax+by+cz+d=0$, where a, b and c are not all zero, is called the general equation of the first degree in x, y and z where, (a, b, c) are the direction ratios of the normal to the plane and d is any constant.

One Point Form of the Equation of the Plane

Vector Form Let $\vec{r}$ be the position vector of arbitrary point P on plane, A be a point on plane whose position vector is $\vec{a}$ and $\vec{n}$ be normal to the plane. Then, the required equation of plane is

$$(\vec{r}-\vec{a})\cdot\vec{n}=0 \text{ or } \vec{r}\cdot\vec{n}=\vec{a}\cdot\vec{n} \text{ or } \vec{r}\cdot\vec{n}=d \text{ where, } d=\vec{a}\cdot\vec{n}$$

Cartesian Form Let (x_1, y_1, z_1) be a point lies on the plane. Then, equation of the plane is

$$a(x-x_1)+b(y-y_1)+c(z-z_1)=0$$

Normal Form of the Equation of the Plane

Vector Form The equation of plane having normal unit vector $\hat{n}$ to the plane is $\vec{r}\cdot\hat{n}=d$, where d is the perpendicular distance of the plane form origin $\vec{r}$ is the position of any point P on the plane.

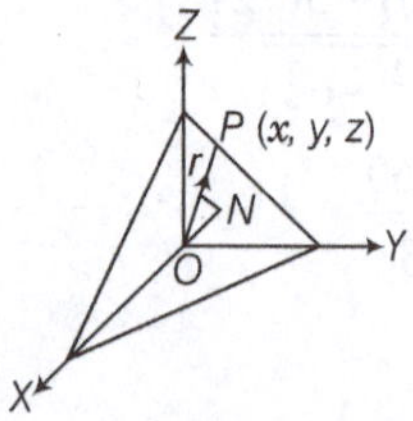

Cartesian Form If p is the length of the normal from origin to the plane and l, m and n are the direction cosines of the normal. Then, the equation of the plane is

$$lx+my+nz=p,$$

where $l^2+m^2+n^2=1$

To Reduce the General Equation to the Normal Form

Let the general equation of plane be $ax+by+cz+d=0$. Then, the normal form of plane is

$$-\frac{a}{\sqrt{\Sigma a^2}}x-\frac{b}{\sqrt{\Sigma a^2}}y-\frac{c}{\sqrt{\Sigma a^2}}z=\frac{d}{\sqrt{\Sigma a^2}}, \text{ if } d \text{ is positive.}$$

and $\dfrac{a}{\sqrt{\Sigma a^2}}x+\dfrac{b}{\sqrt{\Sigma a^2}}y+\dfrac{c}{\sqrt{\Sigma a^2}}z=\dfrac{-d}{\sqrt{\Sigma a^2}}$,

if d is negative.

Intercept Form of the Equation of the Plane

The equation of a plane, which cuts off intercepts a, b and c respectively on the axes of x, y and z is

$$\frac{x}{a}+\frac{y}{b}+\frac{z}{c}=1$$

To Reduce the General Equation to the Intercept Form

The general equation of the plane is $ax+by+cz+d=0$.

Then, the required intercept form is $\dfrac{x}{\frac{-d}{a}}+\dfrac{y}{\frac{-d}{b}}+\dfrac{z}{\frac{-d}{c}}=1.$

Equation of Plane Passing Through Three Non-Collinear Points

Vector Form The equation of plane passing through three non-collinear points with position vectors $\vec{a}$, $\vec{b}$ and $\vec{c}$ is $(\vec{r}-\vec{a})\cdot[(\vec{b}-\vec{a})\times(\vec{c}-\vec{a})]=0.$

Cartesian Form Let (x_1, y_1, z_1), (x_2, y_2, z_2) and (x_3, y_3, z_3) be the coordinates of the points R, S and T, respectively. Let (x, y, z) be the coordinates of any point P on the plane.

Then, Cartesian form of equation of plane is

$$\begin{vmatrix} x-x_1 & y-y_1 & z-z_1 \\ x_2-x_1 & y_2-y_1 & z_2-z_1 \\ x_3-x_1 & y_3-y_1 & z_3-z_1 \end{vmatrix}=0$$

NOTE The given three points must be non-collinear, if the three points are on the same line, then there will be many planes that will contain them.

Angle between Two Planes

The angle between two planes is equal to the angle between their normals.

Vector Form The angle θ between the planes $\vec{r}\cdot\vec{n_1}=d_1$ and $\vec{r}\cdot\vec{n_2}=d_2$ is given by

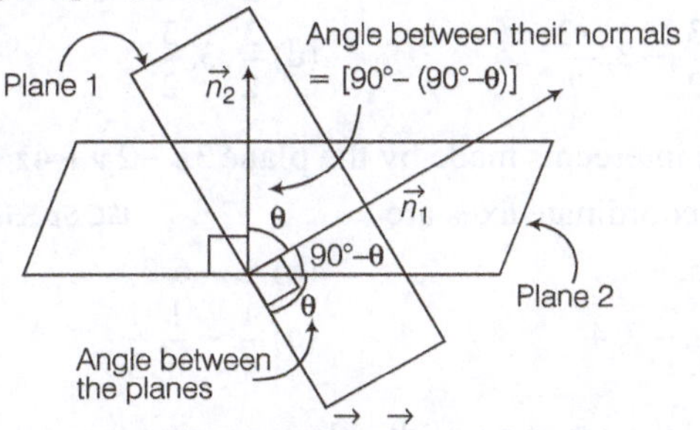

$$\cos\theta=\frac{\vec{n_1}\cdot\vec{n_2}}{|\vec{n_1}||\vec{n_2}|}$$

NOTE (i) If planes $\vec{r_1}\cdot\vec{n_1}=d_1$ and $\vec{r_2}\cdot\vec{n_2}=d_2$ are perpendicular, then $\vec{n}_1$ and $\vec{n}_2$ are perpendicular i.e. $\vec{n_1}\cdot\vec{n_2}=0$.

(ii) If planes $\vec{r_1}\cdot\vec{n_1}=d_1$ and $\vec{r_2}\cdot\vec{n_2}=d_2$ are parallel, then $\vec{n}_1$ and $\vec{n}_2$ are parallel i.e. $\vec{n_1}=\lambda\vec{n}_2$.

Cartesian Form The angle θ between the planes $a_1x+b_1y+c_1z+d_1=0$ and $a_2x+b_2y+c_2z+d_2=0$ is given by

$$\cos\theta=\frac{a_1a_2+b_1b_2+c_1c_2}{\sqrt{a_1^2+b_1^2+c_1^2}\sqrt{a_2^2+b_2^2+c_2^2}}$$

NOTE (i) If the planes are perpendicular, then $a_1a_2+b_1b_2+c_1c_2=0$.

(ii) If the planes are parallel, then $\frac{a_1}{a_2}=\frac{b_1}{b_2}=\frac{c_1}{c_2}$.

Angle between Line and a Plane

The angle between a line and a plane is the complement of the angle between the line and normal to the plane.

Vector Form Let the equation of the line be $\vec{r}=\vec{a}+\lambda\vec{b}$ and of the plane be $\vec{r}\cdot\vec{n}=d$.

If θ is the angle between the line and the plane, then $\sin\theta=\frac{|\vec{b}\cdot\vec{n}|}{|\vec{b}||\vec{n}|}$.

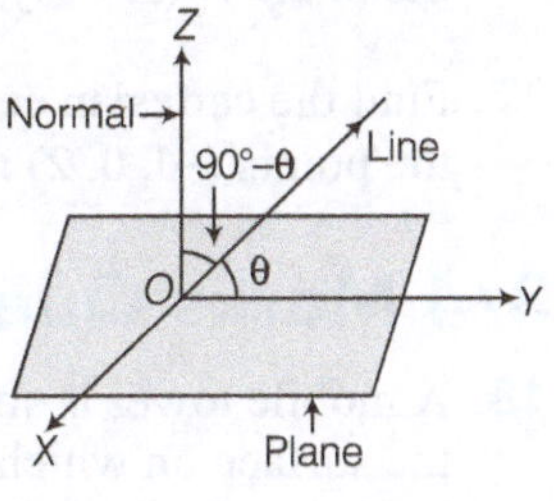

Also, the angle between the normal to the plane and line is

$$\cos\theta=\frac{|\vec{b}\cdot\vec{n}|}{|\vec{b}||\vec{n}|}$$

NOTE (i) If the line is perpendicular to the plane, then it is parallel to the normal to the plane. Therefore, $\vec{b}$ and $\vec{n}$ are parallel. i.e. $\vec{b}\times\vec{n}=\vec{0}$ or $\vec{b}=\lambda\vec{n}$ for some scalar λ.

(ii) If the line is parallel to the plane, then it is perpendicular to the normal to the plane. Therefore, $\vec{b}$ and $\vec{n}$ are perpendicular i.e. $\vec{b}\cdot\vec{n}=0$.

Cartesian Form Let the equation of line be $\frac{x-x_1}{a_1}=\frac{y-y_1}{b_1}=\frac{z-z_1}{c_1}$ and the plane be $ax+by+cz=d$.

If θ is the angle between the line and plane, then

$$\sin\theta=\frac{|aa_1+bb_1+cc_1|}{\sqrt{a^2+b^2+c^2}\sqrt{a_1^2+b_2^2+c_1^2}}$$

Also, the angle between the normal to the plane and line is

$$\cos\theta=\frac{|aa_1+bb_1+cc_1|}{\sqrt{a^2+b^2+c^2}\sqrt{a_1^2+b_1^2+c_1^2}}$$

NOTE (i) The line is parallel to the plane, if $\theta=0\Rightarrow\sin\theta=0$
$\Rightarrow aa_1+bb_1+cc_1=0$

(ii) The line is perpendicular to the plane, if it is parallel to the normal to the plane i.e. if $\frac{a}{a_1}=\frac{b}{b_1}=\frac{c}{c_1}$.

Intersection of the Line and Plane

Let the equation of the line be $\frac{x-x_1}{l}=\frac{y-y_1}{m}=\frac{z-z_1}{n}$ and that of the plane be $ax+by+cz+d=0$

There, the coordinates of point of intersection of line and plane are (x_1+lr, y_1+mr, z_1+nr),

where $r=\frac{-(ax_1+by_1+cz_1+d)}{al+bm+cn}$

Distance of a Point from a Plane

Vector Form Let $\vec{r}\cdot\vec{n}=d$ be the equation of the plane and P be any point in the space.

Let PL be the perpendicular from P on the plane, L be the foot of the perpendicular and $\vec{a}$ be the position vector of P. Then, distance of a point from a plane is

$$PL=\frac{|\vec{a}\cdot\vec{n}-d|}{|\vec{n}|}$$

Cartesian Form The length of the perpendicular from the point $P(x_1, y_1, z_1)$ to the plane $ax+by+cz+d_2=0$ is

$$d=\frac{|ax_1+by_1+cz_1+d_2|}{\sqrt{a^2+b^2+c^2}}$$

PYQs Previous Years Questions

1 Mark Questions

1. Find the intercepts on the coordinate axis cut off by the plane. **ISC Specimen 2024**

$$\vec{r}\cdot(2\hat{i}-4\hat{j}+3\hat{k})=12$$

(a) $a=6, b=-3$ and $c=4$
(b) $a=6, b=3$ and $c=4$
(c) $a=-6, b=-3$ and $c=4$
(d) $a=6, b=-3$ and $c=-4$

2. The distance of the point $2\hat{i}+\hat{j}-\hat{k}$ from the plane $\vec{r}\cdot(\hat{i}-2\hat{j}+4\hat{k})=9$ will be **ISC 2023**

(a) 13 (b) $\frac{13}{\sqrt{21}}$ (c) 21 (d) $\frac{21}{\sqrt{13}}$

3. Write the equation of the plane passing through the point (2, 4, 6) and making equal intercepts on the coordinate axes. **ISC 2023**

4. The planes $2x-y+4z=5$ and $5x-2.5y+10z=6$ are **ISC Specimen 2023**

(a) parallel (b) intersect on Y-axis
(c) perpendicular (d) pass through $\left(0, 0, \frac{5}{4}\right)$

5. Find the equation of the plane with intercept 3 on the Y-axis and parallel to XZ-plane. **ISC Specimen 2023**

6. If the intercept form of the equation of the plane $2x-3y+4z=12$ is $\frac{x}{a}+\frac{y}{b}+\frac{z}{c}=1$, then the values of a, b, c are respectively. **ISC Specimen Sem-II 2022**

(a) $a=6, b=-4, c=3$ (b) $a=-6, b=-4, c=3$
(c) $a=6, b=4, c=3$ (d) $a=6, b=4, c=-3$

7. The distance of the plane whose equation is given by $3x-4y+12z=3$, from the origin will be **ISC Specimen Sem-II 2022**

(a) $\frac{3}{13}$ (b) $\frac{-2}{13}$ (c) -3 (d) $\frac{13}{19}$

8. The equation of the plane which is parallel to $2x-3y+z=0$ and which passes through $(1,-1,2)$ is **ISC Specimen Sem-II 2022**

(a) $2x-3y+z-7=0$ (b) $2x-3y+z+7=0$
(c) $2x-3y+z-8=0$ (d) $2x-3y+z+6=0$

9. The intercepts made on the coordinate axes by the plane $2x+y-2z=3$ are **ISC Specimen Sem-II 2022**

(a) $\frac{-3}{2}, -3, \frac{-3}{2}$ (b) $\frac{3}{2}, 3, \frac{-3}{2}$
(c) $\frac{3}{2}, -3, \frac{-3}{2}$ (d) $\frac{3}{2}, 3, \frac{3}{2}$

10. The intercepts made by the plane $3x-2y+4z=12$ on the coordinate axes are **ISC Specimen 2021**

(a) 6, – 4, 3 (b) 4, – 6, 3
(c) 2, – 3, 4 (d) $\frac{1}{4}, -\frac{1}{6}, \frac{1}{3}$

11. Find the equation of the plane passing through $(-2, 1, 3)$ and perpendicular to the line having direction ratios $< 3, 1, 5 >$. **ISC Specimen 2021**

12. Find the angle between the line $\frac{x+1}{2}=\frac{y}{3}=\frac{z-3}{6}$ and the plane $2x+3y-5z=4$. **ISC Specimen 2018**

2 Marks Questions

13. Find the equation of the plane passing through the points $(-2, 6, 6)$, $(1, -1, 0)$ and $(1, 2, -1)$. **ISC Specimen Sem-II 2022**

14. Find the equation of the plane passing through the point (1, 1, 1) and is perpendicular to the line $\frac{x-1}{3}=\frac{y-2}{0}=\frac{z-3}{4}$. Also, find the distance of this plane from the origin. **ISC Specimen Sem-II 2022**

15. Find the equation of the plane passing through the point $(2, -3, 1)$ and perpendicular to the line joining the points (4, 5, 0) and $(1, -2, 4)$. **ISC 2020**

16. Find the length of the perpendicular from the origin to the plane $\vec{r}\cdot(3\hat{i}-4\hat{j}-12\hat{k})+39=0$. **ISC 2019**

17. Find the cartesian equation of the line passing through the points $(-1, 0, 2)$ and $(3, 4, 6)$. **ISC Specimen 2018**

3/4 Marks Questions

18. A mobile tower is situated at the top of a hill. Consider the surface on which the tower stands as a plane having points $A(1, 0, 2)$, $B(3, -1, 1)$ and $C(1, 2, 1)$ on it. The mobile tower is tied with three cables from the points A, B and C such that it stands vertically on the ground. The top of the tower is at point $P(2, 3, 1)$ as shown in the figure below.

The foot of the perpendicular from the point P on the plane is at the point $Q\left(\frac{43}{29}, \frac{77}{29}, \frac{9}{29}\right)$. **ISC 2024**

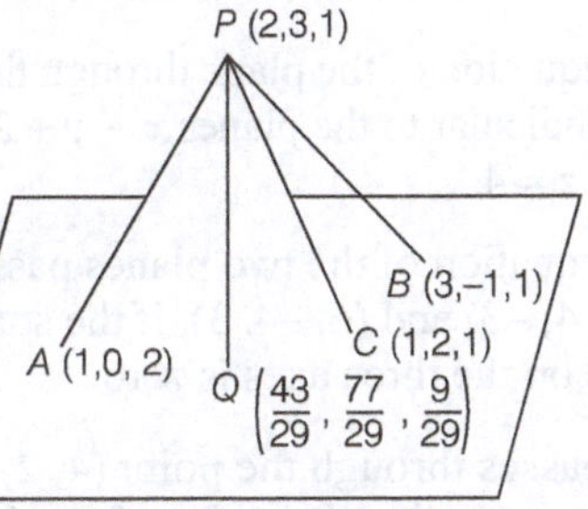

Answer the following questions.

(i) Find the equation of the plane containing the points A, B and C.

(ii) Find the equation of the line PQ.

(iii) Calculate the height of the tower.

19. Shown below are equations of two planes

Plane 1 $\frac{x}{-2} + \frac{3y}{4} - \frac{5z}{4} = 1$

Plane 2 $\frac{x}{3} - \frac{y}{4} - \frac{z}{1} = 1$

Is the point P (2, −3, 4) closer to plane 1 or plane 2? Find the angle between the planes. **ISC Specimen 2024**

20. A line with positive direction cosines passes through the point $P(-2, 3, 2)$ and makes equal angles with the coordinate axes. The line passes through the plane $3x - 4y + 2z = 11$ at point Q.

Find the length of the line segment PQ. **ISC Specimen 2024**

21. Find the equation of the plane passing through the point (1, 1, −1) and perpendicular to the planes $x + 2y + 3z = 7$ and $2x - 3y + 4z = 0$. **ISC 2023**

22. Find the equation of the plane passing through the points (0,4, −3) and (6, −4,3), if the sum of their intercepts on three axes is 0. **ISC Specimen 2023**

23. Find the distance of the point $A(3, 4, 4)$ from the point, where the line joining points $P(3, -4, -5)$ and $Q(2, -3, 1)$ intersects the plane $2x + y + z = 7$. **ISC Specimen 2021**

24. Find the equation of the plane passing through the points (2, −3, 1) and (−1, 1, −7) and perpendicular to the plane $x - 2y + 5z + 1 = 0$. **ISC 2014**

25. Find the equation of the planes parallel to the plane $2x - 4y + 4z = 7$ and which are at a distance of five units from the point (3, −1, 2). **ISC 2013**

26. Find the equation of plane through the point (−1, −1, 2) and perpendicular to the planes $3x + 2y - 3z = 1$ and $5x - 4y + z = 5$. **ISC 2004**

27. Find the angle between the line

$\frac{x-6}{3} = \frac{y-7}{2} = \frac{z-7}{-2}$ and the plane $x + y + 2z = 0$. **ISC 2004**

28. Find the cosine of the angle between the planes

$$x + 2y - 2z + 6 = 0$$

and $\quad 2x + 2y + z + 8 = 0$ **ISC 2003**

29. Find the equation of the plane passing through (1, 2, 3) and perpendicular to the straight line

$$\frac{x}{-2} = \frac{y}{-4} = \frac{z}{3}.$$ **ISC 2002**

> **KEY CONCEPT**
>
> (i) First, determine the equation of plane passing through a point (x_1, y_1, z_1) is
> $$a(x - x_1) + b(y - y_1) + c(z - z_1) = 0$$
> (ii) As plane is perpendicular to the line, then direction ratios of normal to the plane and line is proportional.
>
> (iii) Put values of a, b and c in consider equation and get the required equation.

5/6 Marks Questions

30. Find the image of a point having position vector $3\hat{i} - 2\hat{j} + \hat{k}$ in the plane $\vec{r} \cdot (3\hat{i} - \hat{j} + 4\hat{k}) = 2$. **ISC 2018, 17**

31. Find the equation of the plane passing through the point (1, −2, 1) and perpendicular to the line joining the points $A(3, 2, 1)$ and $B(1, 4, 2)$. **ISC 2017**

32. Find the equation of the plane passing through the points A (2, 1, −3), B (−3, −2, 1) and C (2, 4, −1). **ISC 2011**

> **KEY CONCEPT**
>
> Use the equation form of plane passing through three point in $\begin{vmatrix} x - x_1 & y - y_1 & z - z_1 \\ x_2 - x_1 & y_2 - y_1 & z_2 - z_1 \\ x_3 - x_1 & y_3 - y_1 & z_3 - z_1 \end{vmatrix} = 0.$
>
> Further simplify it to get the required equation.

33. Find the equation of the plane which contains the line $\frac{x-1}{2}=\frac{y+1}{-1}=\frac{z-3}{4}$ is perpendicular to the plane $x+2y+z=12$. **ISC 2009**

> **KEY CONCEPT**
>
> (i) First, consider let the equation of plane is $ax+by+cz+d=0$.
>
> (ii) Compare the equation of line with $\frac{x-x_1}{a_1}=\frac{y-y_1}{b_1}=\frac{z-z_1}{c_1}$ to get the values of (a,b,c) and (a_1,b_1,c_1).

34. Find the coordinates of the point, where the line joining the points (1, –2, 3) and (2,–1, 5) cuts the plane $x-2y+3z=19$. Hence, find the distance of this point from the point (5, 4, 1). **ISC 2008**

35. Find the equation of the plane through the point (1, 2, 3) and perpendicular to the planes $x+y+2z=3$ and $3x+2y+z=4$. **ISC 2007**

36. Find the equation of the two planes passing through the points (0, 4, –3) and (6, –4, 3), if the sum of their intercepts on the three axes is zero. **ISC 2006**

37. A plane passes through the point (4, 2, 4) and is perpendicular to the planes $2x+5y+4z+1=0$ and $4x+7y+6z+2=0$. Then, find the equation of the plane. **ISC 2005**

Explanations

1. (a) Given, $\vec{r}\cdot(2\hat{i}-4\hat{j}+3\hat{k})=12$

$\Rightarrow (x\hat{i}+y\hat{j}+z\hat{k})\cdot(2\hat{i}-4\hat{j}+3\hat{k})=12$

$\Rightarrow \quad 2x-4y+3z=12$

$\Rightarrow \quad \frac{x}{6}-\frac{y}{3}+\frac{z}{4}=1$

$\therefore$ Intercepts on the coordinate axis cut off by the plane are $a=6$, $b=-3$ and $c=4$.

2. (b) We know distance of the point $\vec{a}$ from the plane $\vec{r}\cdot\vec{n}=d$ is $\left|\frac{\vec{a}\cdot\vec{n}-d}{|\vec{n}|}\right|$.

Here, $\vec{a}=2\hat{i}+\hat{j}-\hat{k}$, $\vec{n}=\hat{i}-2\hat{j}+4\hat{k}$ and $d=9$

$$\therefore \text{Distance}=\left|\frac{(2\hat{i}+\hat{j}-\hat{k})\cdot(\hat{i}-2\hat{j}+4\hat{k})-9}{|\hat{i}-2\hat{j}+4\hat{k}|}\right|$$

$$=\left|\frac{2-2-4-9}{\sqrt{1+(-2)^2+4^2}}\right|$$

$$=\left|\frac{-13}{\sqrt{21}}\right|=\frac{13}{\sqrt{21}}$$

> **Concept Enhancer** Distance of the point $\vec{a}$ from the plane $\vec{r}\cdot\vec{n}=d$ is $\left|\frac{\vec{a}\cdot\vec{n}-d}{|\vec{n}|}\right|$.

3. Equation of plane in intercept form is

$$\frac{x}{a}+\frac{y}{b}+\frac{z}{c}=1$$

Here, $a=b=c$

$\therefore x+y+z=a$

Since, this plane is passing through (2, 4, 6).

$\therefore 2+4+6=a \Rightarrow a=12$

$\therefore$ Required equation of plane is

$$x+y+z=12$$

4. (a) Given, planes are $2x-y+4z=5$ ...(i)

and $5x-2.5y+10z=6$ ...(ii)

On multiplying both sides of Eq. (ii) by 2, we get

$$10x-5y+20z=12$$

Now, divide both sides by 5, we get

$$\Rightarrow \quad 2x-y+4z=\frac{12}{5}$$

Clearly, both planes are parallel.

5. The equation of the plane ZOX is, $y=0$

Any plane parallel to it is of the form, $y=a$

Since, the y-intercept of the plane is 3.

Therefore, $a=3$

Thus, the equation of the required plane is $y=3$

6. (a) Equation of plane $2x-3y+4z=12$

$$\frac{2x}{12}-\frac{3y}{12}+\frac{4z}{12}=1 \Rightarrow \frac{x}{6}-\frac{y}{4}+\frac{z}{3}=1$$

$\therefore \; a=6,\; b=-4$ and $c=3$

7. (a) Given, equation of plane is $3x-4y+12z=3$.

Distance of (x_1, y_1, z_1) from the plane $Ax+By+Cz+D=0$ is

$$D' = \frac{|Ax_1+By_1+Cz_1+D|}{\sqrt{A^2+B^2+C^2}}$$

Here, $(x_1, y_1, z_1) \Rightarrow (0,0,0)$

$A=3, B=-4, C=12$ and $D=-3$

$$\text{Distance, } (D') = \left|\frac{3\times0+(-4)\times0+12\times0+(-3)}{\sqrt{(3)^2+(-4)^2+(12)^2}}\right|$$

$$= \frac{|-3|}{\sqrt{9+16+144}} = \frac{3}{\sqrt{169}} = \frac{3}{13} \text{ units}$$

8. (a) Any plane parallel to the given plane is $2x-3y+z+k=0$ for some constant k. If it passes through the point $(1,-1,2)$, then

$$2(1)-3(-1)+2+k=0$$

$$\Rightarrow 2+3+2+k=0$$

$$\Rightarrow k=-7$$

Hence, the required equation of the plane is $2x-3y+z-7=0$.

9. (b) Given, $2x+y-2z=3$

$$\Rightarrow \frac{2x}{3}+\frac{y}{3}-\frac{2z}{3}=1$$

$$\Rightarrow \frac{x}{(3/2)}+\frac{y}{(3)}+\frac{z}{(-3/2)}=1$$

$\therefore$ Intercept on X-axis $=\frac{3}{2}$

Intercept on Y-axis $=3$

Intercept on Z-axis $=-\frac{3}{2}$

10. (b) Given that, $3x-2y+4z=12$

$$\Rightarrow \frac{3x}{12}+\frac{(-2)y}{12}+\frac{4z}{12}=1$$

$$\Rightarrow \frac{x}{4}+\frac{y}{-6}+\frac{z}{3}=1$$

Hence, intercepts are 4, −6, 3.

11. Here, $x_1=-2, y_1=1, z_1=3$

and $a=3, b=1, c=5$

So, required equation of plane is

$$a(x-x_1)+b(y-y_1)+c(z-z_1)=0$$

$$\Rightarrow 3(x+2)+1(y-1)+5(z-3)=0$$

$$\Rightarrow 3x+6+y-1+5z-15=0$$

$$\Rightarrow 3x+y+5z-10=0$$

$$\Rightarrow 3x+y+5z=10$$

12. We have, the line $\frac{x+1}{2}=\frac{y}{3}=\frac{z-3}{6}$

and plane $2x+3y-5z=4$.

Here, $\vec{b}=2\hat{i}+3\hat{j}+6\hat{k}$ and $\vec{n}=2\hat{i}+3\hat{j}-5\hat{k}$

Angle between line and plane is given by

$$\sin\theta = \frac{\vec{b}\cdot\vec{n}}{|\vec{b}||\vec{n}|} = \frac{(2\hat{i}+3\hat{j}+6\hat{k})\cdot(2\hat{i}+3\hat{j}-5\hat{k})}{|2\hat{i}+3\hat{j}+6\hat{k}||2\hat{i}+3\hat{j}-5\hat{k}|}$$

$$\sin\theta = \frac{4+9-30}{\sqrt{4+9+36}\sqrt{4+9+25}} = \frac{-17}{7\sqrt{38}}$$

$$\Rightarrow \theta = \sin^{-1}\left(\frac{-17}{7\sqrt{38}}\right)$$

13. Let $A(-2,6,6)$, $B(1,-1,0)$ and $C(1,2,-1)$.

Here, DR's of AB are $(3,-7,-6)$.

DR's of BC are $(0,3,-1)$.

$\therefore$ The points are non-collinear.

Since, the cartesian equation of plane passing through three points $A(x_1, y_1, z_1)$ $B(x_2, y_2, z_2)$ and $C(x_3, y_3, z_3)$ is given by

$$\begin{vmatrix} x-x_1 & y-y_1 & z-z_1 \\ x_2-x_1 & y_2-y_1 & z_2-z_1 \\ x_3-x_1 & y_3-y_1 & z_3-z_1 \end{vmatrix}=0$$

$$\Rightarrow \begin{vmatrix} (x+2) & (y-6) & (z-6) \\ 3 & -7 & -6 \\ 3 & -4 & -7 \end{vmatrix}=0$$

$$\Rightarrow (x+2)[(49)-(+24)]-(y-6)$$

$$(-21+18)+(z-6)[(-12)-(-21)]=0$$

$$\Rightarrow (x+2)(25)+3(y-6)+(z-6)9=0$$

$$\Rightarrow 25x+3y+9z=22$$

14. $\because$ The required plane is perpendicular to the line

$$\frac{x-1}{3}=\frac{y-2}{0}=\frac{z-3}{4}$$

$\therefore$ Its direction ratios are $(3,0,4)$.

Now, equation of plane passing through the point $(1,1,1)$ and having DR's 3, 0, 4 is given by

$$3(x-1)+0(y-1)+4(z-1)=0$$

$$\Rightarrow 3x-3+4z-4=0$$

$$\Rightarrow 3x+4z-7=0$$

$\therefore$ Distance of this plane from the origin is

$$= \left|\frac{3(0)+4(0)-7}{\sqrt{9+16}}\right|$$

$$= \frac{7}{5} \text{ units}$$

15. Here, direction ratios of normal to the line joining the points (4, 5, 0) and (1, –2, 4) is (1 – 4, – 2 – 5, 4 – 0) = (– 3, – 7, 4).

Equation of plane is

$$-3(x-2)-7(y+3)+4(z-1)=0$$

$$\Rightarrow \quad -3x+6-7y-21+4z-4=0$$

$$\Rightarrow \quad 3x+7y-4z+19=0$$

16. We know that the equation of plane which is at a distance of d from the origin and having unit vector $\hat{n}$ is

$$\vec{r}\cdot\hat{n}=d \qquad ...(i)$$

Given, equation of plane can be written as

$$\vec{r}\cdot(3\hat{i}-4\hat{j}-12\hat{k})=-39$$

or

$$\vec{r}\cdot(-3\hat{i}+4\hat{j}+12\hat{k})=39 \qquad ...(ii)$$

Now, $\sqrt{(-3)^2+(4)^2+(12)^2}=\sqrt{9+16+144}$

$$=\sqrt{169}=13$$

On dividing both sides of Eq. (ii) by 13, we get

$$\frac{\vec{r}\cdot(-3\hat{i}+4\hat{j}+12\hat{k})}{13}=\frac{39}{13}$$

$$\Rightarrow \quad \vec{r}\left(\frac{-3}{13}\hat{i}+\frac{4}{13}\hat{j}+\frac{12}{13}\hat{k}\right)=3 \qquad ...(iii)$$

On comparing Eqs. (i) and (iii), we get

$$d=3$$

17. Equation of line passing through the points (–1, 0, 2) and (3, 4, 6) is

$$\frac{x+1}{3+1}=\frac{y-0}{4-0}=\frac{z-2}{6-2}$$

$$\Rightarrow \quad \frac{x+1}{4}=\frac{y}{4}=\frac{z-2}{4}$$

$$\Rightarrow \quad x+1=y=z-2$$

18. (i) Given points are $A(1, 0, 2)$, $B(3, -1, 1)$ and $C(1, 2, 1)$.

Then, the equation of plane is

$$\begin{vmatrix} x-x_1 & y-y_1 & z-z_1 \\ x_2-x_1 & y_2-y_1 & z_2-z_1 \\ x_3-x_1 & y_3-y_1 & z_3-z_1 \end{vmatrix}=0$$

$$\Rightarrow \quad \begin{vmatrix} x-1 & y-0 & z-2 \\ 3-1 & -1-0 & 1-2 \\ 1-1 & 2-0 & 1-2 \end{vmatrix}=0$$

$$\Rightarrow \quad \begin{vmatrix} x-1 & y & z-2 \\ 2 & -1 & -1 \\ 0 & 2 & -1 \end{vmatrix}=0$$

$$\Rightarrow \quad (x-1)[1+2]-2[-y-2(z-2)]=0$$

$$\Rightarrow \quad (x-1)\cdot[3]-2[-y-2z+4]=0$$

$$\Rightarrow \quad 3x-3+2y+4z-8=0$$

$$\Rightarrow \quad 3x+2y+4z-11=0$$

$$\Rightarrow \quad 3x+2y+4z=11$$

(ii) The point $P(2, 3, 1)$ and the equation of the plane containing the points A, B and C is

$3x+2y+4z=11$

Thus, the equation of the line PQ is

$$\frac{x-x_1}{a}=\frac{y-y_1}{b}=\frac{z-z_1}{c}$$

$$\Rightarrow \quad \frac{x-2}{3}=\frac{y-3}{2}=\frac{z-1}{4}$$

(iii) The equation of plane is $3x+2y+4z=11$

i.e. $3x+2y+4z-11=0$

Now, the height of the top of tower $P(2, 3, 1)$ is perpendicular from the ground.

$$=\left|\frac{ax_1+by_1+cz_1-k}{\sqrt{a^2+b^2+c^2}}\right|$$

$$=\left|\frac{3(2)+2(3)+4(1)-11}{\sqrt{3^2+2^2+4^2}}\right|$$

$$=\left|\frac{6+6+4-11}{\sqrt{9+4+16}}\right|=\frac{5}{\sqrt{29}}$$

Thus, the height of the tower is $\frac{5}{\sqrt{29}}$ units.

19. Given, equation of two planes can be rewritten as $-2x+3y-5z=4$ and $4x-3y-12z=12$

Given, point is $(2, -3, 4)$ and equation of plane is $-2x+3y-5z=4$

$$\therefore \text{ Required distance }=\left|\frac{ax_1+by_1+cz_1-d}{\sqrt{a^2+b^2+c^2}}\right|$$

$$=\left|\frac{-2\times2+3\times(-3)-5\times4-4}{\sqrt{(-2)^2+(3)^2+(-5)^2}}\right|$$

$$=\left|\frac{-4-9-20-4}{\sqrt{4+9+25}}\right|=\left|\frac{-37}{\sqrt{38}}\right|=\frac{37}{\sqrt{38}}$$

and given point $(2, -3, 4)$ and equation of plane is $4x-3y-12z=12$.

$\therefore$ Required distance

$$=\left|\frac{4\times2+(-3)(-3)+(-12)(4)-12}{\sqrt{16+9+144}}\right|$$

$$=\left|\frac{8+9-48-12}{13}\right|=\left|\frac{-43}{13}\right|=\frac{43}{13}$$

Hence, the point P is closer to plane 2.

Now, given equation of the plane are

$$-2x+3y-5z-4=0$$

and $$4x-3y-12z-12=0$$

On comparing with $a_1x+b_1y+c_1z+d_1=0$ and $a_2x+b_2y+c_2z+d_2=0$, we get

$$a_1=-2,\ b_1=3,\ c_1=-5$$

and $$a_2=4,\ b_2=-3,\ c_2=-12$$

$\therefore$ Angle between two planes is given by

$$\theta=\cos^{-1}\left|\frac{a_1a_2+b_1b_2+c_1c_2}{\sqrt{a_1^2+b_1^2+c_1^2}\sqrt{a_2^2+b_2^2+c_2^2}}\right|$$

$$=\cos^{-1}\left|\frac{-2\times4+(3)(-3)+(-5)(-12)}{\sqrt{(-2)^2+(3)^2+(-5)^2}\cdot\sqrt{(4)^2+(-3)^2+(-12)^2}}\right|$$

$$=\cos^{-1}\left|\frac{-8-9+60}{\sqrt{4+9+25}\sqrt{16+9+144}}\right|$$

$$=\cos^{-1}\left|\frac{43}{\sqrt{38}\sqrt{169}}\right|=\cos^{-1}\left(\frac{43}{\sqrt{38\times13}}\right)$$

$$\Rightarrow \quad \theta=\cos^{-1}\left(\frac{43}{13\sqrt{38}}\right)$$

20. Given, a line with position direction cosines passes through the point $P(-2,3,2)$

$\therefore$ $l=\cos\alpha$, $m=\cos\alpha$ and $n=\cos\alpha$

We know that $l^2+m^2+n^2=1$

$$\Rightarrow \cos^2\alpha+\cos^2\alpha+\cos^2\alpha=1$$

$$\Rightarrow \quad 3\cos^2\alpha=1$$

$$\Rightarrow \quad \cos^2\alpha=\frac{1}{3}\Rightarrow\cos\alpha=\pm\frac{1}{\sqrt{3}}$$

$$\therefore \quad \cos\alpha=\frac{1}{\sqrt{3}}$$

$\therefore$ Equation of line is

$$\frac{x+2}{1/\sqrt{3}}=\frac{y-3}{1/\sqrt{3}}=\frac{z-2}{1/\sqrt{3}}$$

$$\Rightarrow \quad \frac{x+2}{1}=\frac{y-3}{1}=\frac{z-2}{1}=K \text{ (say)}$$

Now, any point on the line is of the form

$$Q=(K-2,K+3,K+2)$$

$\therefore$ Point Q lies on the plane $3x-4y+2z=11$

$$\Rightarrow \quad 3(K-2)-4(K+3)+2(K+2)=11$$

$$\Rightarrow \quad 3K-6-4K-12+2K+4=11$$

$$\Rightarrow \quad K-14=11\Rightarrow K=25$$

$$\therefore \quad Q=(25-2,25+3,25+2)$$

$$=(23,28,27)$$

Now, length of line segment PQ

$$=\sqrt{(23+2)^2+(28-3)^2+(27-2)^2}$$

$$=\sqrt{(25)^2+(25)^2+(25)^2}$$

$$=\sqrt{3\times(25)^2}=25\sqrt{3}\text{ units}$$

21. Let the equation of plane passing through $(1,1,-1)$ be

$$a(x-1)+b(y-1)+c(z+1)=0 \quad \ldots\text{(i)}$$

Since, this plane is perpendicular to plane

$$x+2y+3z=7 \text{ and } 2x-3y+4z=0$$

$$\therefore \quad a+2b+3c=7 \quad \ldots\text{(ii)}$$

$$2a-3b+4c=0 \quad \ldots\text{(iii)}$$

Solving Eqs. (ii) and (iii) by cross-multiplication method,

$$\frac{a}{8+9}=\frac{b}{6-4}=\frac{c}{-3-4}$$

$$\Rightarrow \quad \frac{a}{17}=\frac{b}{2}=\frac{c}{-7}=\lambda$$

$$\Rightarrow \quad a=17\lambda,\ b=2\lambda,\ c=-7\lambda$$

On putting the values of a, b, c in Eq. (i), we get

$$17(x-1)+2(y-1)-7(z+1)=0$$

$$\Rightarrow \quad 17x-17+2y-2-7z-7=0$$

$$\Rightarrow \quad 17x+2y-7z=26$$

which is equation of required plane.

22. Let the equation of plane be

$$\frac{x}{a}+\frac{y}{b}+\frac{z}{c}=1$$

As, $(0,4,-3)$ and $(6,-4,3)$ lie on it, then

$$\frac{4}{b}-\frac{3}{c}=1 \quad \ldots\text{(i)}$$

and $$\frac{6}{a}-\frac{4}{b}+\frac{3}{c}=1 \quad \ldots\text{(ii)}$$

On adding Eqs. (i) and (ii), we get

$$a=3$$

Also, $$a+b+c=0$$

$$b+c=-a=-3\Rightarrow c=-3-b$$

On putting $c=-3-b$ in Eq. (i), we get

$$\frac{4}{b}+\frac{3}{3+b}=1$$

$$\Rightarrow \quad b^2-4b-12=0$$

$$\Rightarrow \quad (b-6)(b+2)=0$$

Therefore, $b=6$ or $b=-2$

Hence, $c=-9$ or $c=-1$.

Thus, equation of planes is

$$\frac{x}{3}+\frac{y}{6}-\frac{z}{9}=1 \text{ or } \frac{x}{3}-\frac{y}{2}-\frac{z}{1}=1$$

23. The direction ratios of line joining $P(3,-4,-5)$ and $Q(2,-3,1)$ are $[(2-3),(-3+4),(1+5)]$, i.e. $(-1,1,6)$.

Now, the equation of line passing through $(3,-4,-5)$ and having DR's $(-1,1,6)$ is given by

$$\frac{x-3}{-1}=\frac{y+4}{1}=\frac{z+5}{6}$$

$$\left[\because \frac{x-x_1}{a}=\frac{y-y_1}{b}=\frac{z-z_1}{c}\right]$$

Now, let $\frac{x-3}{-1}=\frac{y+4}{1}=\frac{z+5}{6}=\lambda$ (say)

$\Rightarrow \quad x=-\lambda+3,\ y=\lambda-4$ and $z=6\lambda-5$

Thus, the general point on the line is given by

$$(3-\lambda, \lambda-4, 6\lambda-5)$$

Let the point of intersection be $(3-\lambda,\lambda-4,6\lambda-5)$ for some λ.

Since, line intersect the plane $2x+y+z=7$.

So, point $(3-\lambda,\lambda-4,6\lambda-5)$ satisfy the equation of plane.

$\therefore \quad 2(3-\lambda)+\lambda-4+6\lambda-5=7$

$\Rightarrow \quad 6-2\lambda+\lambda-4+6\lambda-5=7$

$\Rightarrow \quad 5\lambda=10$

$\therefore \quad \lambda=2$

So, the point of intersection of line and plane is $(3-2, 2-4, 6\times 2-5)$, i.e. $(1,-2,7)$.

Now, distance between $(3,4,4)$ and $(1,-2,7)$ is given by $\sqrt{(3-1)^2+(4+2)^2+(4-7)^2}=\sqrt{4+36+9}$

$=\sqrt{49}=7$ units

Concept Enhancer Distance between two points (x_1, y_1, z_1) and (x_2, y_2, z_2) is

$$d=\sqrt{(x_1-x_2)^2+(y_1-y_2)^2+(z_1-z_2)^2}$$

24. Equation of plane passing through $(2,-3,1)$ is given by

$$a(x-2)+b(y+3)+c(z-1)=0 \quad \ldots\text{(i)}$$

The given plane also passes through $(-1,1,-7)$.

$\therefore \quad a(-1-2)+b(1+3)+c(-7-1)=0$

$\Rightarrow \quad -3a+4b-8c=0$

$\Rightarrow \quad 3a-4b+8c=0 \quad \ldots\text{(ii)}$

Also, given plane (i) is perpendicular to $x-2y+5z+1=0$, then

$$a-2b+5c=0 \quad \ldots\text{(iii)}$$

$[\because$ condition for perpendicular $a_1a_2+b_1b_2+c_1c_2=0]$

On solving Eqs. (ii) and (iii), we get

$$\frac{a}{-20+16}=\frac{b}{8-15}=\frac{c}{-6+4}$$

$\Rightarrow \quad \frac{a}{-4}=\frac{b}{-7}=\frac{c}{-2}$

$\Rightarrow \quad \frac{a}{4}=\frac{b}{7}=\frac{c}{2}$

$\Rightarrow \quad a=2c$

and $\quad b=\frac{7c}{2}$

On putting $a=2c$ and $b=\frac{7c}{2}$ in Eq. (i), we get

$$2c(x-2)+\frac{7c}{2}(y+3)+c(z-1)=0$$

$\Rightarrow \quad c[4(x-2)+7(y+3)+2(z-1)]=0$

$\Rightarrow \quad 4x+7y+2z-8+21-2=0$

$\therefore \quad 4x+7y+2z+11=0$

25. The equation of the plane parallel to the plane $2x-4y+4z=7$ is given by

$$2x-4y+4z+k=0 \quad \ldots\text{(i)}$$

Since, the required plane is at a distance of 5 units from the point $(3,-1,2)$.

$\therefore \quad \left|\frac{2(3)-4(-1)+4(2)+k}{\sqrt{4+16+16}}\right|=5$

$\left[\because\right.$ perpendicular distance from (x_1,y_1,z_1) to the plane $ax+by+cz+d=0$ is $\left.d=\left|\frac{ax_1+by_1+cz_1+d}{\sqrt{a^2+b^2+c^2}}\right|\right]$

$\Rightarrow \quad \left|\frac{6+4+8+k}{\sqrt{36}}\right|=5$

$\Rightarrow \quad \frac{18+k}{6}=\pm 5$

$\Rightarrow \quad k=\pm 30-18$

$\Rightarrow \quad k=12$ or $k=-48$

$\therefore \quad k=-48$

Hence, the possible equations of required plane are $2x-4y+4z+12=0$ and $2x-4y+4z-48=0$.

[putting $k=12$ and $k=-48$ in Eq. (i)]

26. Given, plane passes through the point $(-1, -1, 2)$.
Therefore, equation of plane is

$$a(x+1)+b(y+1)+c(z-2)=0 \quad \ldots\text{(i)}$$

As, the plane is perpendicular to the planes

$$3x+2y-3z=1 \text{ and } 5x-4y+z=5 \quad \text{[given]}$$

$$\therefore \quad 3a+2b-3c=0 \quad \ldots\text{(ii)}$$

[$\because$ condition of perpendicular $a_1a_2+b_1b_2+c_1c_2=0$]

and

$$5a-4b+c=0 \quad \ldots\text{(iii)}$$

[$\because$ condition of perpendicular $a_1a_2+b_1b_2+c_1c_2=0$]

On solving Eqs. (iii) and (ii), we get

$$\frac{a}{2-12}=\frac{b}{-15-3}=\frac{c}{-12-10}$$

$$\Rightarrow \quad \frac{a}{-10}=\frac{b}{-18}=\frac{c}{-22} \Rightarrow \frac{a}{10}=\frac{b}{18}=\frac{c}{22}$$

$$\Rightarrow \quad a=\frac{5c}{11} \text{ and } b=\frac{9c}{11}$$

On putting the values of $a=\frac{5c}{11}$ and $b=\frac{9c}{11}$ in Eq. (i), we get

$$\frac{5c}{11}(x+1)+\frac{9c}{11}(y+1)+c(z-2)=0$$

$$\Rightarrow \quad \frac{c}{11}(5x+5+9y+9+11z-22)=0$$

$$\therefore \quad 5x+9y+11z-8=0$$

27. The given, equation of plane is $x+y+2z=0$ and line is $\frac{x-6}{3}=\frac{y-7}{2}=\frac{z-7}{-2}$.

The direction ratios of plane are $(1, 1, 2)$.
The direction ratios of line are $(3, 2, -2)$.

$$\because \quad \cos\theta=\frac{|aa_1+bb_1+cc_1|}{\sqrt{a^2+b^2+c^2}\sqrt{a_1^2+b_1^2+c_1^2}}$$

$$=\frac{|1\times3+1\times2+2\times(-2)|}{\sqrt{1^2+1^2+2^2}\sqrt{3^2+2^2+(-2)^2}}$$

$$=\frac{|3+2-4|}{\sqrt{6}\sqrt{17}}=\frac{1}{\sqrt{102}}$$

Concept Enhancer Angle between the two lines is

$$\cos\theta=\frac{|aa_1+bb_1+cc_1|}{\sqrt{a^2+b^2+c^2}\sqrt{a_1^2+b_1^2+c_1^2}}$$

28. The given planes are $x+2y-2z+6=0$ and $2x+2y+z+8=0$

Direction ratios of normals to these planes are $<1, 2, -2>$ and $<2, 2, 1>$, respectively.
The acute angle (θ) between these planes is given by

$$\cos\theta=\frac{|a_1a_2+b_1b_2+c_1c_2|}{\sqrt{a_1^2+b_1^2+c_1^2}\sqrt{a_2^2+b_2^2+c_2^2}}$$

$$\therefore \quad \cos\theta=\frac{|(1)(2)+2(2)+(-2)(1)|}{\sqrt{1^2+2^2+(-2)^2}\sqrt{(2)^2+(2)^2+1^2}}$$

$$=\frac{|2+4-2|}{\sqrt{9}\sqrt{9}}=\frac{4}{9}$$

29. Let the equation of plane passes through the point $(1, 2, 3)$ be

$$a(x-1)+b(y-2)+c(z-3)=0 \quad \ldots\text{(i)}$$

Given that, plane is perpendicular to the straight line $\frac{x}{-2}=\frac{y}{-4}=\frac{z}{3}$.

$\therefore$ Normal to the plane is parallel to the line.
Direction ratios of normal to the plane is proportional to the line.

$$\text{i.e.} \quad \frac{a}{-2}=\frac{b}{-4}=\frac{c}{3}=k \quad \text{(say)}$$

On putting the values of a, b and c in Eq. (i), we get

$$-2k(x-1)-4k(y-2)+3k(z-3)=0$$

$$\Rightarrow \quad -2x+2-4y+8+3z-9=0$$

$$\Rightarrow \quad -2x-4y+3z+1=0$$

$$\Rightarrow \quad 2x+4y-3z-1=0$$

[dividing by -1]

30. Let point $Q(\alpha, \beta, \gamma)$ be the image of point $P(3, -2, 1)$ in the plane $\vec{r}\cdot(3\hat{i}-\hat{j}+4\hat{k})=2$

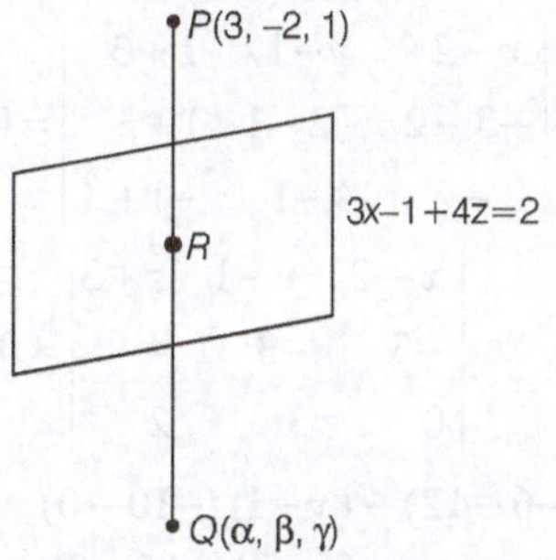

Direction ratios of normal to the plane are $(3, -1, 4)$ and direction ratios of line PQ $(\alpha-3, \beta+2, \gamma-1)$.
Line PQ is parallel to the normal of plane.

$$\therefore \quad \frac{\alpha-3}{3}=\frac{\beta+2}{-1}=\frac{\gamma-1}{4}=\lambda$$

$$\Rightarrow \quad \alpha=3\lambda+3, \beta=-\lambda-2, \gamma=4\lambda+1$$

R is mid-point of PQ.

$\therefore\ R\left(\frac{3\lambda+6}{2}, \frac{-\lambda-4}{2}, \frac{4\lambda+2}{2}\right)$

Since, R lies on plane $3x - y + 4z = 2$.

$$\therefore\ 3\left(\frac{3\lambda+6}{2}\right) - \left(\frac{-\lambda-4}{2}\right) + 4\left(\frac{4\lambda+2}{2}\right) = 2$$

$$\Rightarrow\ 9\lambda + 18 + \lambda + 4 + 16\lambda + 8 = 4 \Rightarrow \lambda = -1$$

$$\therefore\ Q(-3+3, 1-2, -4+1) = Q\,(0, -1, -3)$$

$\therefore$ Image of point $P(3, -2, 1)$ in the plane is $(0, -1, -3)$.

31. Since, the plane passes through the point $A(1, -2, 1)$, whose position vector is $a = \hat{i} - 2\hat{j} + \hat{k}$, and the normal vector n parallel to line joining points $A(3, 2, 1)$ and $B(1, 4, 2)$ is $n = \lambda(-2\hat{i} + 2\hat{j} + \hat{k})$, for some real number λ.

$\therefore$ The vector equation of the plane is

$$r \cdot n = a \cdot n$$

$$\Rightarrow\ r \cdot \lambda(-2\hat{i} + 2\hat{j} + \hat{k}) = (\hat{i} - 2\hat{j} + \hat{k}) \cdot \lambda(-2\hat{i} + 2\hat{j} + \hat{k})$$

$$\Rightarrow\ r(-2\hat{i} + 2\hat{j} + \hat{k})\lambda = (-2 - 4 + 1)\lambda$$

$$\Rightarrow\ r(-2\hat{i} + 2\hat{j} + \hat{k}) = -5$$

or $\quad -2x + 2y + z = -5$ [take $\vec{r} = x\hat{i} + y\hat{j} + z\hat{k}$]

32. We know that the equation of the plane passing through (x_1, y_1, z_1), (x_2, y_2, z_2) and (x_3, y_3, z_3) is

$$\begin{vmatrix} x - x_1 & y - y_1 & z - z_1 \\ x_2 - x_1 & y_2 - y_1 & z_2 - z_1 \\ x_3 - x_1 & y_3 - y_1 & z_3 - z_1 \end{vmatrix} = 0$$

$\therefore$ Equation of the plane passing through the points $(2, 1, -3)$, $(-3, -2, 1)$ and $(2, 4, -1)$ is

$$\begin{vmatrix} x-2 & y-1 & z+3 \\ -3-2 & -2-1 & 1+3 \\ 2-2 & 4-1 & -1+3 \end{vmatrix} = 0$$

$$\Rightarrow\ \begin{vmatrix} x-2 & y-1 & z+3 \\ -5 & -3 & 4 \\ 0 & 3 & 2 \end{vmatrix} = 0$$

$$\Rightarrow (x-2)(-6-12) - (y-1)(-10-0) + (z+3)(-15-0) = 0$$

[expanding along R_1]

$$\Rightarrow\ -18x + 36 + 10y - 10 - 15z - 45 = 0$$

$$\therefore\ 18x - 10y + 15z + 19 = 0$$

33. Let the required equation of plane be

$$ax + by + cz + d = 0 \quad \ldots(i)$$

Given, equation of plane and line are

$$x + 2y + z - 12 = 0$$

and $\quad \frac{x-1}{2} = \frac{y+1}{-1} = \frac{z-3}{4}$

Here, $(x_1, y_1, z_1) = (1, -1, 3)$ and $(a_2, b_2, c_2) = (1, 2, 1)$

Since, the required plane passing through the point $(1, -1, 3)$ and normal to the required plane is perpendicular to the line.

$$\therefore\ 2a - b + 4c = 0 \quad \ldots(ii)$$

and $\quad a - b + 3c + d = 0 \quad \ldots(iii)$

Since, required plane is perpendicular to the plane $x + 2y + z = 12$

$$\therefore\ a + 2b + c = 0 \quad [\because aa_2 + bb_2 + cc_2 = 0] \ \ldots(iv)$$

From Eqs. (ii) and (iv),

$$\frac{a}{-1-8} = \frac{b}{4-2} = \frac{c}{4+1}$$

$$\Rightarrow\ \frac{a}{9} = \frac{b}{-2} = \frac{c}{-5} = k \quad \text{(say)}$$

$$\Rightarrow\ a = 9k, b = -2k, c = -5k$$

On putting values of a, b and c in Eq. (iii), we get

$$9k + 2k - 15k + d = 0 \Rightarrow -4k + d = 0$$

$$\therefore\ d = 4k$$

Hence, equation of plane becomes

$$9kx - 2ky - 5kz + 4k = 0$$

$$\Rightarrow\ 9x - 2y - 5z + 4 = 0$$

34. The direction ratios of the line joining $(1, -2, 3)$ and $(2, -1, 5)$ are $(2-1), (-1+2), (5-3)$ i.e. $1, 1, 2$.

The equation of line joining $(1, -2, 3)$ and $(2, -1, 5)$ is

$$\frac{x-1}{1} = \frac{y+2}{1} = \frac{z-3}{2} = r \quad \text{[say]}$$

The coordinates of any point on above line are $P\,(1+r, -2+r, 3+2r) \quad \ldots(i)$

Since, this point also lies on the plane $x - 2y + 3z = 19$.

$$\therefore\ 1 + r - 2(-2+r) + 3(3+2r) = 19$$

$$\Rightarrow\ r - 2r + 6r + 1 + 4 + 9 = 19$$

$$\Rightarrow\ 5r = 19 - 14$$

$$\Rightarrow\ 5r = 5$$

$$\Rightarrow\ r = 1$$

Hence, the point P is $(2, -1, 5)$. [put $r = 1$ in Eq. (i)]

The distance between $(2, -1, 5)$ and $(5, 4, 1)$

$$= \sqrt{(5-2)^2 + (4+1)^2 + (1-5)^2}$$

$$= \sqrt{3^2 + 5^2 + 4^2}$$

$$= \sqrt{9 + 25 + 16}$$

$$= \sqrt{50} = 5\sqrt{2} \text{ units}$$

35. We know that equation of the plane passing through (x_1, y_1, z_1) is

$$a(x-x_1)+b(y-y_1)+c(z-z_1)=0$$

$\therefore$ Equation of the plane passing through the point (1, 2, 3) is

$$a(x-1)+b(y-2)+c(z-3)=0 \quad \ldots\text{(i)}$$

Since, above plane is perpendicular to the planes $x+y+2z=3$ and $3x+2y+z=4$.

$$\therefore \quad a+b+2c=0 \quad \ldots\text{(ii)}$$

and $$3a+2b+c=0 \quad \ldots\text{(iii)}$$

[$\because$ condition for perpendicular $a_1a_2+b_1b_2+c_1c_2=0$]

On solving Eqs. (ii) and (iii), we get

$$\frac{a}{1-4}=\frac{b}{6-1}=\frac{c}{2-3}$$

$$\Rightarrow \quad \frac{a}{-3}=\frac{b}{5}=\frac{c}{-1}$$

$$\therefore \quad a=3c,\ b=-5c$$

On putting the values of a and b in Eq. (i), we get

$$3c(x-1)-5c(y-2)+c(z-3)=0$$

$$\Rightarrow \quad c[3x-3-5y+10+z-3]=0$$

$$\Rightarrow \quad 3x-5y+z+4=0$$

36. Suppose the equation of the plane is

$$ax+by+cz+d=0 \quad \ldots\text{(i)}$$

Since, plane passes through the points (0, 4, –3) and (6, – 4, 3).

$$\therefore \quad 0+4b-3c+d=0 \quad \ldots\text{(ii)}$$

[put $x=0$, $y=-4$ and $x=-3$ in Eq. (i)]

and $$6a-4b+3c+d=0 \quad \ldots\text{(iii)}$$

[put $x=6$, $y=-4$ and $x=3$ in Eq. (i)]

On adding Eqs. (ii) and (iii), we get

$$6a+2d=0$$

$$\Rightarrow \quad a=\frac{-2d}{6}$$

$$\Rightarrow \quad a=\frac{-d}{3}$$

On putting $a=\frac{-d}{3}$ in Eq. (iii), we get

$$6\times\left(\frac{-d}{3}\right)-4b+3c+d=0$$

$$\Rightarrow \quad -2d-4b+3c+d=0$$

$$\Rightarrow \quad -4b+3c-d=0$$

$$\Rightarrow \quad 4b-3c=-d$$

$$\therefore \quad b=\frac{3c-d}{4}$$

Considering equation $ax+by+cz+d=0$ can be rewritten as

$$\frac{x}{-\frac{d}{a}}+\frac{y}{\frac{-d}{b}}+\frac{z}{\frac{-d}{c}}=1.$$

According to the given condition, sum of their interception the three axes is zero.

$$-\frac{d}{a}-\frac{d}{b}-\frac{d}{c}=0$$

$$\Rightarrow \quad -d\left[-\frac{3}{d}+\frac{4}{3c-d}+\frac{1}{c}\right]=0$$

$$\Rightarrow -d\left[\frac{-3c(3c-d)+4cd+d(3c-d)}{d(3c-d)c}\right]=0$$

$$\Rightarrow \quad -9c^2+3cd+4cd+3cd-d^2=0$$

$$\Rightarrow \quad 9c^2-10cd+d^2=0$$

$$\Rightarrow \quad 9c^2-9cd-cd+d^2=0$$

$$\Rightarrow \quad 9c(c-d)-d(c-d)=0$$

$$\Rightarrow \quad (9c-d)(c-d)=0$$

$$\Rightarrow \quad c=\frac{d}{9}, d$$

When $c=\frac{d}{9}$, then

$$b=\frac{3\times\frac{d}{9}-d}{4}=\left(\frac{d}{3}-d\right)\times\frac{1}{4}$$

$$=\frac{d-3d}{12}=\frac{-2d}{12}=\frac{-d}{6}$$

and when $c=d$, then

$$b=\frac{3\times d-d}{4}$$

$$=\frac{2d}{4}=\frac{d}{2}$$

Hence, required equation of planes are

$$\frac{-d}{3}\times x+\left(\frac{-d}{6}\right)y+\frac{d}{9}z+d=0$$

or $$\frac{-d(6x+3y-2z-18)}{18}=0$$

i.e. $$6x+3y-2z-18=0$$

and $$\frac{-d}{3}\times x+\left(\frac{d}{2}\right)y+d\cdot z+d=0$$

or $$\frac{-d(2x+3y-6z-6)}{6}=0$$

i.e. $$2x-3y-6z-6=0$$

37. Equation of plane passes through (4, 2, 4) is

$$a(x-4)+b(y-2)+c(z-4)=0 \quad \text{...(i)}$$

$\because$ Above plane is perpendicular to the planes $2x+5y+4z+1=0$ and $4x+7y+6z+2=0$

$\therefore$ $2a+5b+4c=0$ ...(ii)

and $4a+7b+6c=0$ ...(iii)

[$\because$ condition for perpendicular $a_1a_2+b_1b_2+c_1c_2=0$]

On multiplying Eq. (ii) by 2, we get

$$4a+10b+8c=0 \quad \text{...(iv)}$$

On subtracting Eq. (iii) from Eq. (iv), we get

$$3b+2c=0 \Rightarrow 3b=-2c \Rightarrow b=\frac{-2c}{3}$$

On putting $b=\frac{-2c}{3}$ in Eq. (ii), we get

$$2a+5\left(\frac{-2c}{3}\right)+4c=0$$

$$\Rightarrow 6a-10c+12c=0$$

$$\Rightarrow 6a+2c=0$$

$$\Rightarrow 6a=-2c$$

$$\Rightarrow a=\frac{-c}{3}$$

On putting $a=\frac{-c}{3}$ and $b=\frac{-2c}{3}$ in Eq. (i), we get

$$\frac{-c}{3}(x-4)-\frac{2}{3}c(y-2)+c(z-4)=0$$

$$\Rightarrow \frac{-c}{3}[(x-4)+2(y-2)-3(z-4)]=0$$

$$\Rightarrow x+2y-3z-4-4+12=0$$

$$\Rightarrow x+2y-3z+4=0$$

CHAPTER TEST

1 Mark Questions

1. The equation of X-axis in space is

(a) $x = 0,\ y = 0$ (b) $x = 0,\ z = 0$
(c) $x = 0$ (d) $y = 0,\ z = 0$

2. The coordinates of a point on the line $\frac{x+2}{3} = \frac{y+1}{2} = \frac{z-3}{2}$ at a distance of $\frac{6}{\sqrt{2}}$ from the point (1, 2, 3) is

(a) (56, 43, 111) (b) $\left(\frac{56}{17}, \frac{43}{17}, \frac{111}{17}\right)$
(c) (2, 1, 3) (d) (−2, −1, −3)

3. The planes $2x - y + 4z = 5$ and $5x - 2.5y + 10z = 6$ are

(a) perpendicular (b) parallel
(c) intersect along Y-axis (d) passes through $\left(0, 0, \frac{5}{4}\right)$

4. The value of k, such that $\frac{x-4}{1} = \frac{y-2}{1} = \frac{z-k}{2}$ lies in the plane $2x - 4y + z = 7$ is

(a) 7 (b) −7
(c) 4 (d) No real value

5. The sine of the angle between the straight line $\frac{x-2}{3} = \frac{y-3}{4} = \frac{z-4}{5}$ and the plane $2x - 2y + z = 5$ is

(a) $\frac{10}{6\sqrt{5}}$ (b) $\frac{4}{5\sqrt{2}}$ (c) $\frac{2\sqrt{3}}{5}$ (d) $\frac{\sqrt{2}}{10}$

2 Marks Questions

6. If a line passes through a point (−2, − 7, 3), then find the equations of a line parallel to axes.

7. Find k, so that the lines $\frac{1-x}{3} = \frac{y-2}{2k} = \frac{z-3}{2}$ and $\frac{x-1}{3k} = \frac{y-5}{1} = \frac{6-z}{5}$ are at right angles.

8. A plane meets the coordinate axes in A, B and C such that the centroid of the ΔABC is the point (p, q, r), show that the equation of the plane is $\frac{x}{p} + \frac{y}{q} + \frac{z}{r} = 3$.

9. Find the coordinates of the point, where the line passing through (5, 1, 6) and (3, 4, 1) cross YZ-plane.

10. Write the direction cosines of the normal to plane $3x + 4y + 12z = 52$.

3/4 Marks Questions

11. Prove that the lines $x = ay + b,\ z = cy + d$ and $x = a'y + b',\ z = c'y + d'$ are perpendicular, if $aa' + cc' + 1 = 0$.

12. Find the angle between the line $\vec{r} = (2\hat{i} + 2\hat{j} + \hat{k}) + \lambda(2\hat{i} - 3\hat{j} + 2\hat{k})$ and the plane $\vec{r} \cdot (3\hat{i} - 2\hat{j} + 5\hat{k}) = 4$.

13. Find the shortest distance between the lines $\vec{r} = (\hat{i} + 2\hat{j} + \hat{k}) + \lambda(\hat{i} - \hat{j} + \hat{k})$ and $\vec{r} = (2\hat{i} - \hat{j} - \hat{k}) + \mu(2\hat{i} + \hat{j} + 2\hat{k})$.

14. Show that the points whose position vectors are $(-2\hat{i} + 3\hat{j} + 5\hat{k})$, $(\hat{i} + 2\hat{j} + 3\hat{k})$ and $(7\hat{i} - \hat{k})$ are collinear.

5/6 Marks Questions

15. Find the shortest distance between the lines $l_1 : \frac{x-1}{1} = \frac{y+2}{-1} = \frac{z-1}{1}$ and $l_2 : \frac{x-2}{2} = \frac{y+1}{1} = \frac{z-1}{2}$

16. Prove that the lines $\frac{x+1}{3} = \frac{y+3}{5} = \frac{z+5}{7}$ and $\frac{x-2}{1} = \frac{y-4}{4} = \frac{z-6}{7}$ are coplanar. Also, find the plane containing these two lines.

17. Find the coordinates of foot of perpendicular drawn from the point (0, 2, 3) on line $\frac{x+3}{5} = \frac{y-1}{2} = \frac{z+4}{3}$. Also, find the length of perpendicular.

Answers

1. (d) **2.** (b) **3.** (b) **4.** (a) **5.** (d)

6. $\frac{x+2}{1} = \frac{y+7}{0} = \frac{z-3}{0}; \frac{x+2}{0} = \frac{y+7}{1} = \frac{z-3}{0}$ and $\frac{x+2}{0} = \frac{y+7}{0} = \frac{z-3}{1}$

7. $k = \frac{-10}{7}$ **9.** $\left(0, \frac{17}{2}, \frac{-13}{2}\right)$ **10.** $\frac{3}{13}, \frac{4}{13}, \frac{12}{13}$

12. $\theta = \sin^{-1}\left(\frac{22}{\sqrt{646}}\right)$ **13.** $\frac{3\sqrt{2}}{2}$ **15.** $\frac{1}{\sqrt{2}}$ **16.** $x - 2y + z = 0$

17. Foot coordinates (2, 3, −1) and length $= \sqrt{21}$

12 Application of Integrals

TREND ANALYSIS 3 YEARS

TOPIC **01** Area of Bounded Region

Average No. of Questions Across all Sets

Types of Questions	2024	2023	2020
1 Mark	—	—	—
2 Marks	—	—	—
3/4 Marks	2	1	—
5/6 Marks	—	—	1

Area of Bounded Region

The space occupied by the curve along with the axis, under the given condition is called area of bounded region.

(i) The area bounded by the curve $y = f(x)$ above the X-axis and between the lines $x = a$ and $x = b$ is given by

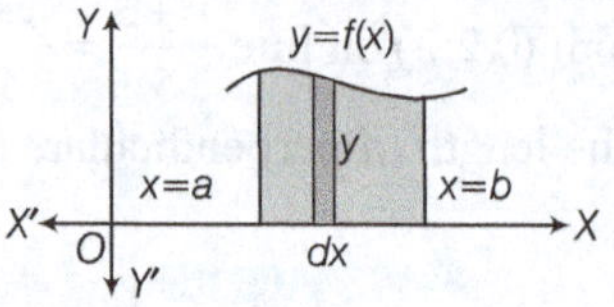

$$\int_a^b y\,dx = \int_a^b f(x)\,dx$$

(ii) If the curve is between the lines $x = a$ and $x = b$ lies below the X-axis, then the area is given by

$$\left|\int_a^b (-y)\,dx\right| = \left|-\int_a^b y\,dx\right| = \left|-\int_a^b f(x)\,dx\right|$$

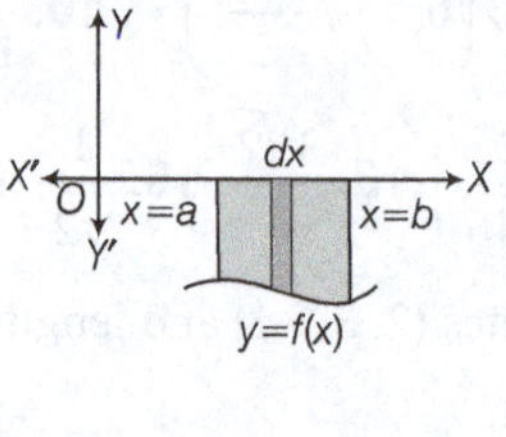

(iii) The area bounded by the curve $x = f(y)$ right to the Y-axis and the lines $y = c$ and $y = d$ is given by

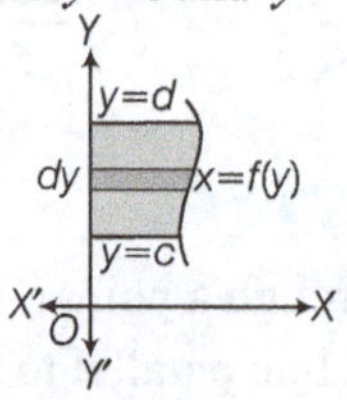

$$\int_c^d x\,dy = \int_c^d f(y)\,dy$$

(iv) If the curve is between the lines $y = c$ and $y = d$ left to the Y-axis, then the area is given by

$$\left|\int_c^d (-x)\,dy\right| = \left|-\int_c^d x\,dy\right| = \left|-\int_c^d f(y)\,dy\right|$$

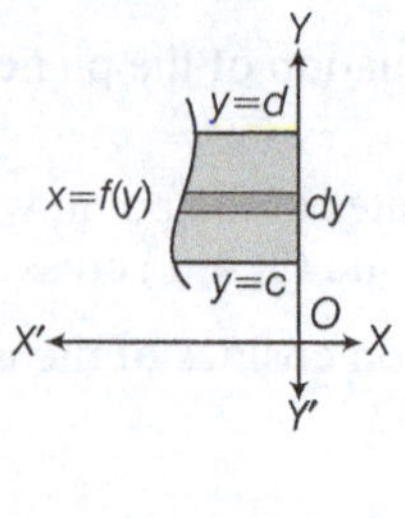

(v) Area bounded by two curves $y = f(x)$ and $y = g(x)$ between $x = a$ and $x = b$ is given by

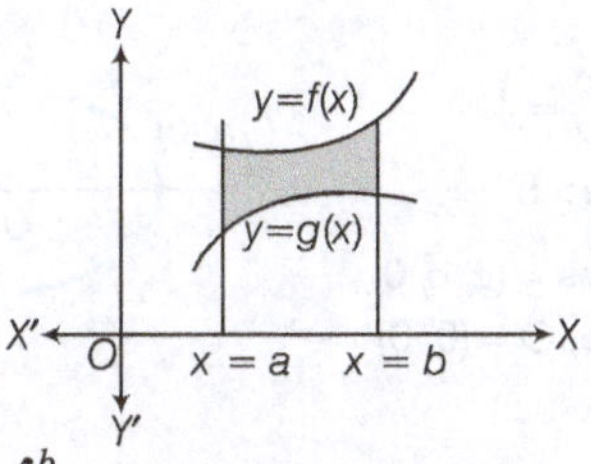

$$\int_a^b \{f(x) - g(x)\}\, dx$$

(vi) Area bounded by two curves $x = f(y)$ and $x = g(y)$ between $y = c$ and $y = d$ is given by

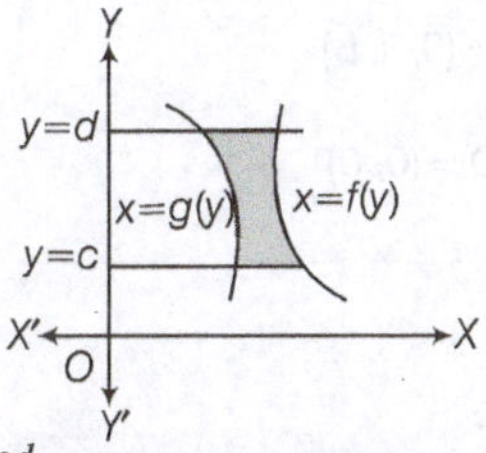

$$\int_c^d [f(y) - g(y)]\, dy$$

(vii) If $f(x) \geq g(x)$ in $[a, c]$ and $f(x) \leq g(x)$ in $[c, b]$, where $a < c < b$, then area of the region bounded by the curves is given as

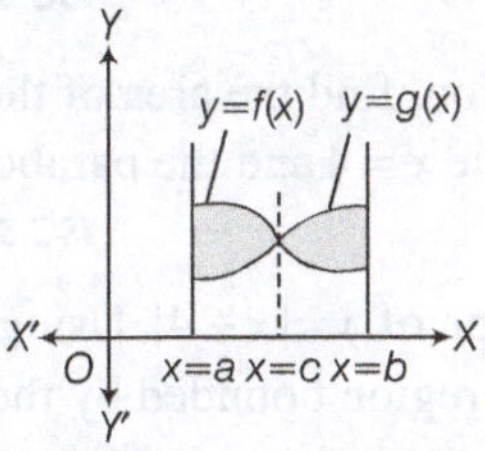

$$\text{Area} = \int_a^c \{f(x) - g(x)\}\, dx + \int_c^b \{g(x) - f(x)\}\, dx$$

Sketch of Simple Curves

	Equation of curve	Sketch
(i) (a)	**Straight lines** $x = a$ and $x = -a$, where $a > 0$	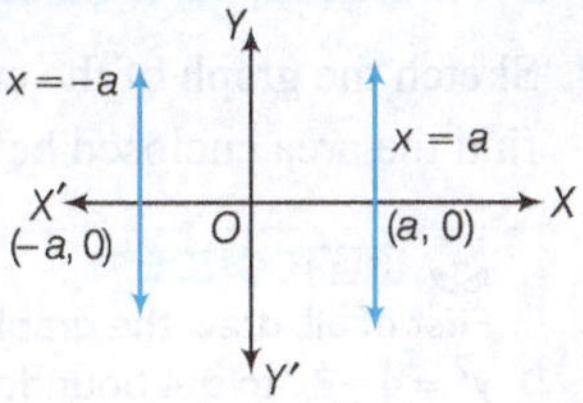
(b)	**Straight lines** $y = b$ and $y = -b$, where $b > 0$	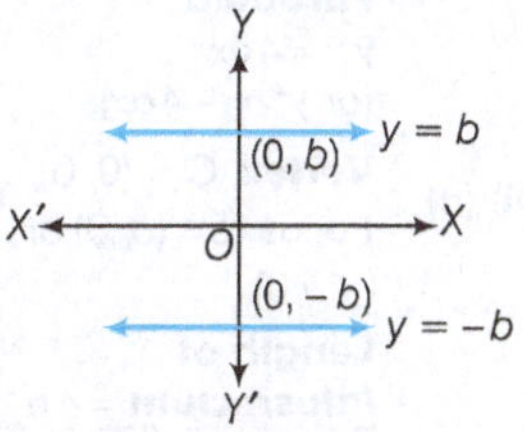
(ii)	**Straight lines** $y = x$ and $y = -x$	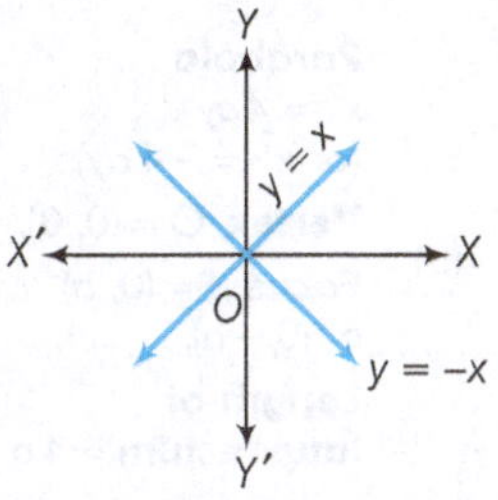
(iii)	**Straight lines** $\frac{x}{a} + \frac{y}{b} = 1,\ a \neq b$; $x + y = a,\ a = b$	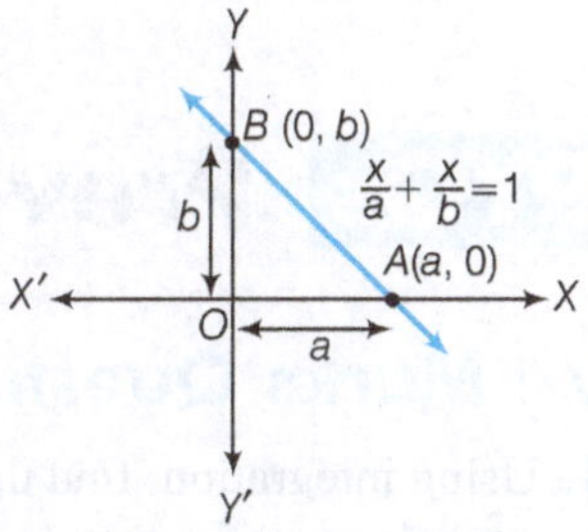
(iv)	**Modulus function** $y = \lvert x \rvert$ $y = \begin{cases} x, & \text{for } x \geq 0 \\ -x, & \text{for } x < 0 \end{cases}$	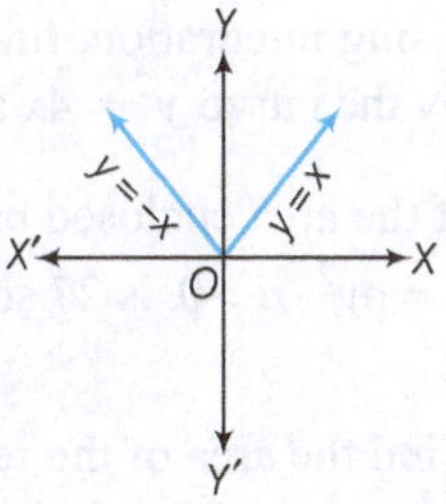
(v)	**Circle** $x^2 + y^2 = a^2$ Centre $= (0, 0)$ Radius $= a$	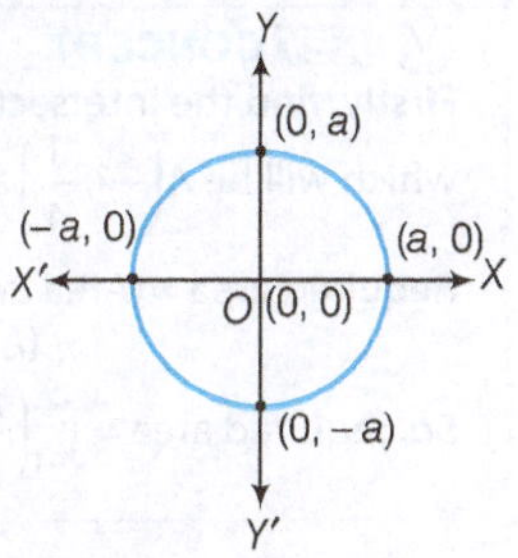

	Equation of curve	Sketch
(vi) (a)	**Parabola** $y^2 = 4ax$ (or $y^2 = -4ax$) **Vertex,** O = (0, 0), **Focus,** S = (a, 0) or (– a, 0). **Length of latusrectum** = 4a	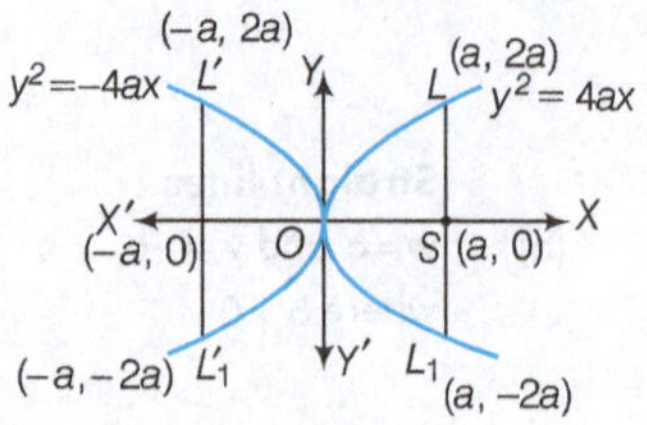
(b)	**Parabola** $x^2 = 4ay$ (or $x^2 = -4ay$) **Vertex,** O = (0, 0), **Focus,** S = (0, a) or (0, – a). **Length of latusrectum** = 4 a	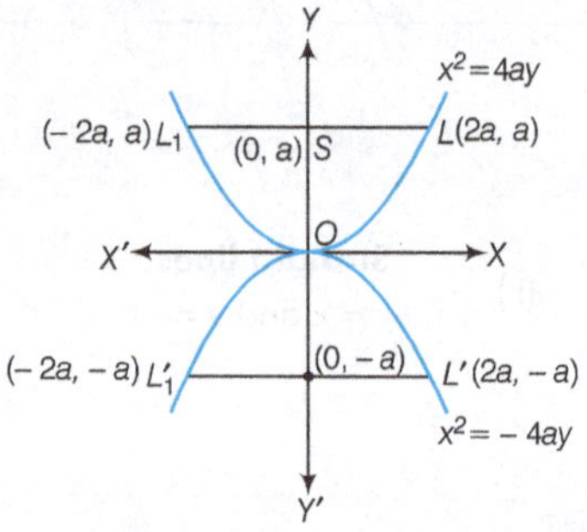
(vii) (a)	**Ellipse** $\frac{x^2}{a^2} + \frac{y^2}{b^2} = 1$, when a > b **Vertices** = (± a, 0), **Centre,** O = (0, 0)	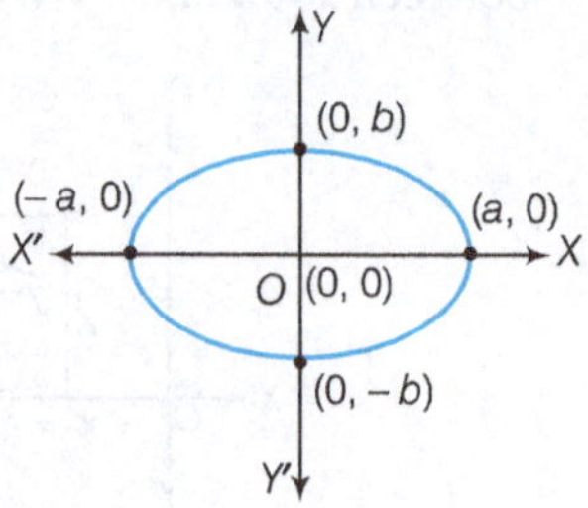
(b)	**Ellipse** $\frac{x^2}{a^2} + \frac{y^2}{b^2} = 1$, when a < b **Vertices** = (0, ± b) , **Centre,** O = (0, 0)	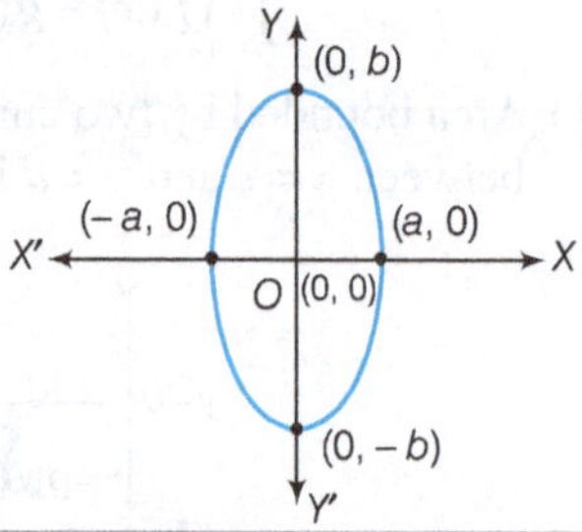

PYQs Previous Years Questions

3/4 Marks Questions

1. Using integration, find the area bounded by the curve $y^2 = 4ax$ and the line $x = a$. **ISC 2024**

2. Using integration, find the area of the region bounded by the curve $y^2 = 4x$ and $x^2 = 4y$. **ISC 2024**

3. If the area enclosed between the curves $y = ax^2$ and $x = ay^2$, $a > 0$, is 27 sq unit, find the value of a. **ISC Specimen 2024**

4. Find the area of the region bounded by the curve $x^2 = 4y$ and the line $x = 4y - 2$. **ISC 2023**

> **KEY CONCEPT**
> Firstly, find the intersection point of line and parabola, which will be $A\left(-1, \frac{1}{4}\right)$ and $B(2, 1)$.
> Required area = (Area under the line $x = 4y - 2$) – (Area under the parabola $x^2 = 4y$)
> So, required area $= \int_{-1}^{2} \left(\frac{x+2}{4}\right) dx - \int_{-1}^{2} \frac{x^2}{4} dx$

5. If the area is bounded by the parabola $y^2 = 16x$ and the line $y = 4mx$ is $\frac{1}{12}$ sq unit, then using integration, find the value of m, $(m > 0)$. **ISC Specimen 2023**

6. Find the area of the region bounded by the curves $y = x^2 + 2$, $y = x$, $x = 0$ and $x = 3$. **ISC Specimen Sem-II 2022**

7. Using integration, find the area of the region bounded between the line $x = 4$ and the parabola $y^2 = 16x$. **ISC Specimen Sem-II 2022**

8. Sketch the graph of $y = |x + 4|$. Using integration, find the area of the region bounded by the curve $y = |x + 4|$ and $x = -6$ and $x = 0$. **ISC Specimen 2021, ISC 2018**

9. Draw a rough sketch of the curve and find the area of the region bounded by curve $y^2 = 8x$ and the line $x = 2$. **ISC 2018**

5/6 Marks Questions

10. Sketch the graph of the curve $y^2 = x$ and $y^2 = 4 - 3x$ and find the area enclosed between them. **ISC 2020, 14, 07**

> **KEY CONCEPT**
> First of all, draw the graph of given curves $y^2 = x$ and $y^2 = 4 - 3x$ to get bounded region. Then, apply the concept of area bounded by two curves to get the required area.

11. Draw a rough sketch and find the area bounded by the curve $x^2 = y$ and $x + y = 2$. **ISC 2019**

12. Using integration, find the area of the following region : $\left\{(x, y): \frac{x^2}{9} + \frac{y^2}{4} \le 1 \le \frac{x}{3} + \frac{y}{2}\right\}$. **ISC Specimen 2018**

13. Draw a rough sketch of the curve $y^2 = 4x$ and find the area of g the region enclosed by the curve and the line $y = x$. **ISC 2017**

14. Find the area of the region bounded by the curves $y = 6x - x^2$ and $y = x^2 - 2x$. **ISC 2016**

15. Find the smaller area enclosed by the circle $x^2 + y^2 = 4$ and the line $x + y = 2$. **ISC 2015**

> **KEY CONCEPT**
>
> Firstly, find the point of intersection of given circle and line and draw the graph.
>
> Further apply the concept of area bounded by curve and line to get required area.

16. Find the area bounded by the curves $y = 2x - x^2$ and the line $y = x$. **ISC 2013**

17. Find the area of the region bounded by the curves $x = 4y - y^2$ and the Y-axis. **ISC 2012**

18. Draw a rough sketch of the curve $y = (x-1)^2$ and $y = |x - 1|$. Hence, find the area of the region bounded by these curves. **ISC 2011**

> **KEY CONCEPT**
>
> First of all, draw the graph of given curve i.e. $y = (x-1)^2$ which represents a parabola with vertex (1,0) and $y = |x-1|$, which is a modulus function, further find the intersection point of these curves and then apply the concept of area bounded by curves to get required area.

19. Draw a rough sketch of the curve $y = x^2 - 5x + 6$ and find the area bounded by curve and the X-axis. **ISC 2010**

20. Draw a rough sketch of the curve $x^2 + y = 9$ and find the area enclosed by the curve, the X-axis and the lines $x + 1 = 0$ and $x - 2 = 0$. **ISC 2009**

21. Draw a rough sketch of the curve $y^2 + 1 = x, x \le 2$.

Find the area enclosed by the curve and the line $x = 2$. **ISC 2008**

22. Sketch and shade the area of the region lying in first quadrant and bounded by $y = 9x^2, x = 0, y = 1$ and $y = 4$. Find the area of the shaded region. **ISC 2004**

23. Show that the area enclosed between the X-axis and the curve $a^2y = x^2(x + a)$ is $a^2/12$. **ISC 2003**

Explanations

1. Shaded part of the following figure shows area enclosed by curve $y^2 = 4ax$ and the line $x = a$.

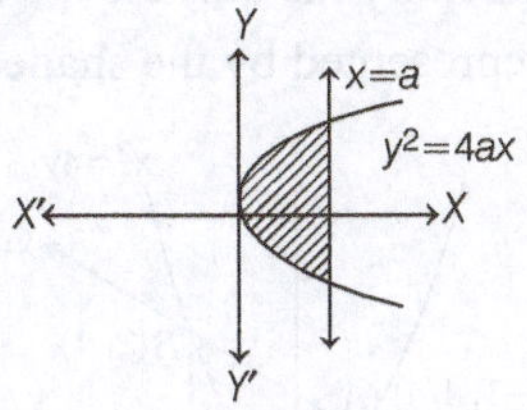

Thus, the required area $= 2\int_{x=0}^{x=a} y\,dx = 2\int_0^a \sqrt{4ax}\,dx$

$$= 4\sqrt{a}\int_0^a \sqrt{x}\,dx$$

$$= 4\sqrt{a}\cdot\left[\frac{x^{3/2}}{3/2}\right]_0^a$$

$$= 4\sqrt{a} \times \frac{2}{3}[a^{3/2} - 0^{3/2}]$$

$$= \frac{8\sqrt{a}}{3}\cdot a^{3/2}$$

$$= \frac{8}{3}a^2 \text{ sq units}$$

2. We have two parabolas,

$$y^2 = 4x \text{ and } x^2 = 4y$$

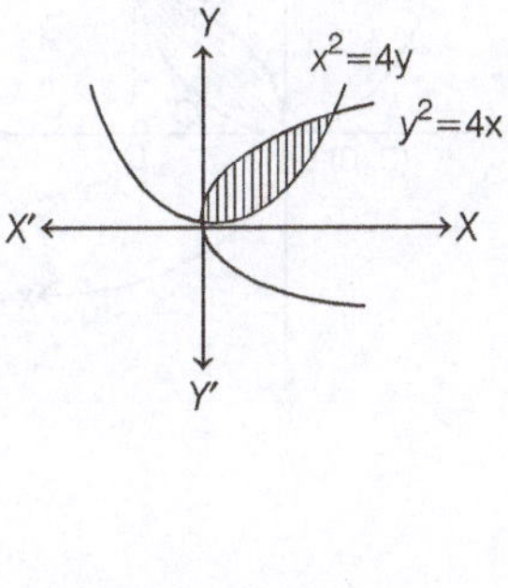

Since, $y^2 = 4x$

$\Rightarrow \left(\frac{x^2}{4}\right)^2 = 4x \quad \left[\because \frac{x^2}{4} = y\right]$

$\Rightarrow \frac{x^4}{16} = 4x$

$\Rightarrow x^4 - 64x = 0$

$\Rightarrow x(x^3 - 64) = 0$

$\Rightarrow x = 0, x^3 = 64$

$\Rightarrow x = 0, x = 4$

When $x = 0$, then $y = 0$

When $x = 4$, then $y = 4$

$\therefore$ Required area $= \int_{x=0}^{x=4} [y \text{ (parabola } y^2 = 4x)$

$- y \text{ (parabola } 4y = x^2)] \, dx$

$= \int_0^4 \left[\sqrt{4x} - \frac{x^2}{4}\right] dx$

$= \int_0^4 \left[2\sqrt{x} - \frac{x^2}{4}\right] dx$

$= \left[2 \cdot \frac{2}{3} \cdot x^{3/2}\right]_0^4 - \frac{1}{4}\left[\frac{x^3}{3}\right]_0^4$

$= \frac{4}{3}[4^{3/2} - 0] - \frac{1}{12}[4^3 - 0]$

$= \frac{4}{3}[8 - 0] - \frac{1}{12}[64 - 0]$

$= \frac{32}{3} - \frac{64}{12}$

$= \frac{16}{3}$ sq units

3. We have two parabolas,

$y = ax^2 \quad \ldots\text{(i)}$

and $x = ay^2 \quad \ldots\text{(ii)}$

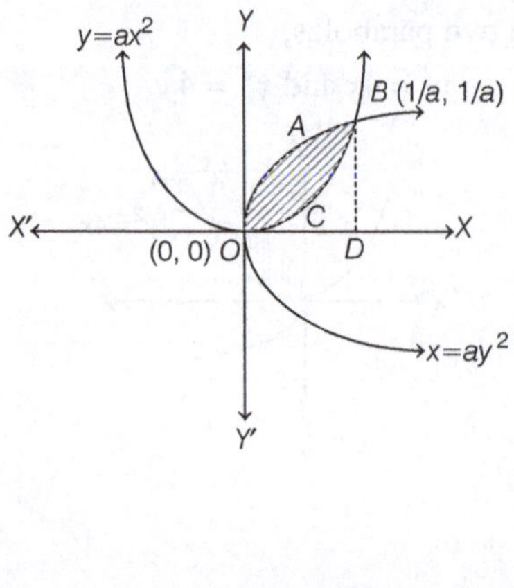

On putting the value of y from Eq. (i) in Eq. (ii), we get

$x = a(ax^2)^2$

$\Rightarrow x = a^3x^4$

$\Rightarrow x(1 - a^3x^3) = 0$

$\Rightarrow x = 0 \text{ or } 1 - a^3x^3 = 0$

$\Rightarrow x = 0 \text{ or } x = \frac{1}{a}$

When $x = 0$, then $y = 0$ [from Eq. (i)]

When $x = \frac{1}{a}$, then $y = \frac{1}{a}$ [from Eq. (i)]

So, the point of intersection are O (0, 0) and $B\left(\frac{1}{a}, \frac{1}{a}\right)$.

$\therefore$ Required area = Area of bounded region $OABCO$

$= \int_0^{1/a} \left(\sqrt{\frac{x}{a}} - ax^2\right) dx = 27 \text{ (given)}$

$\Rightarrow \left[\frac{1}{\sqrt{a}} \frac{x^{3/2}}{3/2} - \frac{ax^3}{3}\right]_0^{1/a} = 27$

$\Rightarrow \frac{2}{3a^2} - \frac{1}{3a^2} = 27$

$\Rightarrow \frac{1}{3a^2} = 27$

$\Rightarrow 3a^2 = \frac{1}{27}$

$\Rightarrow a^2 = \frac{1}{81}$

$\Rightarrow a = \frac{1}{9} \quad [\because a > 0]$

4. The area bounded by the curve $x^2 = 4y$ and line $x = 4y - 2$ is represented by the shaded area $OBAO$.

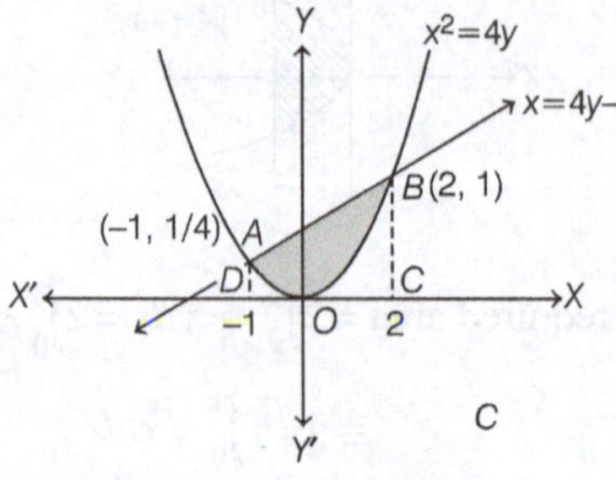

C

Let A and B be the intersection point of line and parabola, where $A\left(-1, \frac{1}{4}\right)$ and B (2, 1).

$\therefore$ Area of shaded region

$$= [\text{ar}(ABCDA) - \text{ar}(AOBCDA)]$$

$$= \int_{-1}^{2} (y_{\text{line}} - y_{\text{parabola}}) = \int_{-1}^{2} \left(\frac{x+2}{4} - \frac{x^2}{4} \right) dx$$

$$= \frac{1}{4}\left[\frac{x^2}{2} + 2x\right]_{-1}^{2} - \frac{1}{4}\left[\frac{x^3}{3}\right]_{-1}^{2}$$

$$= \frac{1}{4}\left[\left(\frac{4}{2}+4\right) - \left(\frac{1}{2}-2\right) - \left(\frac{8}{3}+\frac{1}{3}\right)\right]$$

$$= \frac{1}{4}\left[\left(2+4+\frac{3}{2}\right) - \left(\frac{9}{3}\right)\right]$$

$$= \frac{1}{4}\left[\frac{15}{2} - 3\right] = \frac{15-6}{8}$$

$$= \frac{9}{8} \text{ sq units}$$

5. Let $y^2 = 16x$ ...(i)

and $y = 4mx$ ...(ii)

From Eqs. (i) and (ii), we get

$$16m^2x^2 = 16x \Rightarrow x = \frac{1}{m^2} \text{ or } x = 0$$

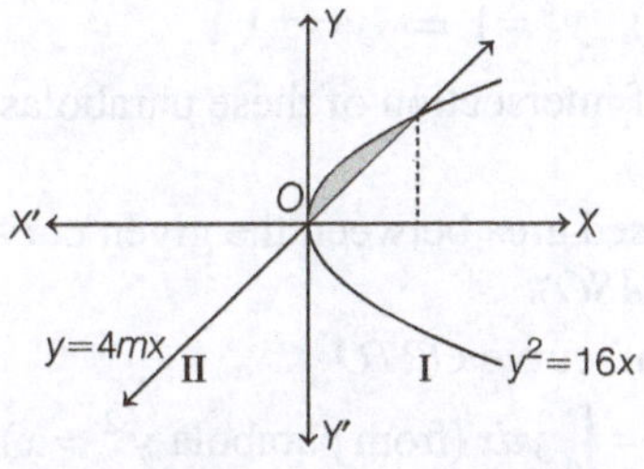

According to question, area bounded by the curves,

$$\int_0^{\frac{1}{m^2}} (y_{\text{I}} - y_{\text{II}}) dx = \frac{1}{12}$$

$$\Rightarrow \int_0^{\frac{1}{m^2}} (\sqrt{16x} - 4mx) dx = \frac{1}{12}$$

$$\Rightarrow \left[\frac{4x^{\frac{1}{2}+1}}{\frac{1}{2}+1} - \frac{4mx^2}{2}\right]_0^{\frac{1}{m^2}} = \frac{1}{12}$$

$$\Rightarrow \left[2 \times \frac{4x^{\frac{3}{2}}}{3} - \frac{4m}{2}x^2\right]_0^{\frac{1}{m^2}} = \frac{1}{12}$$

$$\Rightarrow \frac{2\times 4}{3}\left(\frac{1}{m^2}\right)^{\frac{3}{2}} - 2m\left(\frac{1}{m^2}\right)^2 = \frac{1}{12}$$

$$\Rightarrow \frac{8}{3}\frac{1}{m^3} - \frac{2}{m^3} = \frac{1}{12} \Rightarrow \frac{8-6}{3m^3} = \frac{1}{12}$$

$$\Rightarrow m^3 = \frac{2\times 12}{3} = 8$$

$$\therefore \quad m = 2$$

6. Given, curve $y = x^2 + 2$ i.e. $y - 2 = x^2$ represents a parabola whose vertex is (0, 2) and it is symmetric about Y-axis.

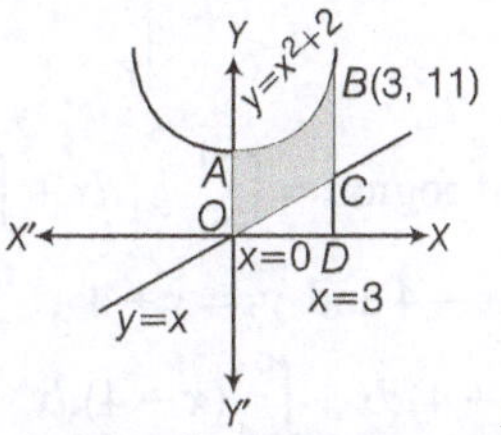

The area bounded by the curves $y = x^2 + 2$, $y = x$, $x = 0$ and $x = 3$ is represented by the shaded region.

$\therefore$ Required area (shaded region)

$$= \text{area}(OABDO) - \text{area}(OCDO)$$

$$= \int_0^3 (x^2 + 2)\, dx - \int_0^3 x\, dx$$

$$= \left[\frac{x^3}{3} + 2x\right]_0^3 - \left[\frac{x^2}{2}\right]_0^3$$

$$= \left[\frac{3^3}{3} + 6 - 0\right] - \left[\frac{3^2}{2} - 0\right]$$

$$= 9 + 6 - \frac{9}{2} = \frac{21}{2} \text{ sq units.}$$

7. Given, $y^2 = 16x$ ...(i)

$x = 4$ ...(ii)

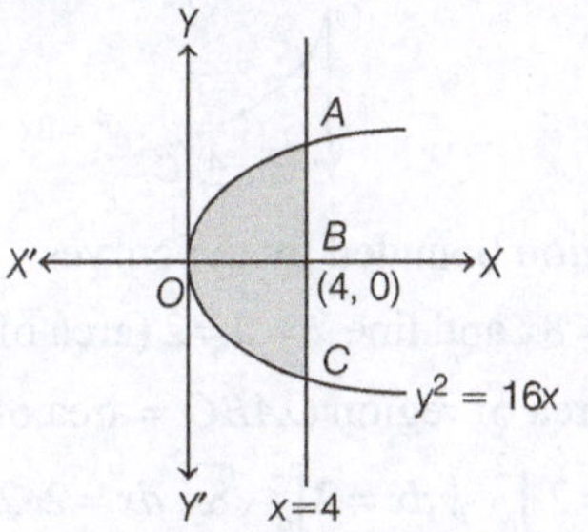

$$\therefore \text{ Required area} = 2\int_0^4 y\, dx = 2\int_0^4 \sqrt{16x}\, dx$$

$$= 8\int_0^4 \sqrt{x}\, dx = 8 \times \frac{2}{3}[x^{3/2}]_0^4$$

$$= \frac{16}{3} \times 8 = \frac{128}{3} \text{ sq units}$$

8. Given, $y=|x+4| \Rightarrow y=\begin{cases}-(x+4), & x<-4 \\ x+4 & x \geq -4\end{cases}$

Graph of $y=|x+4|$ is given below

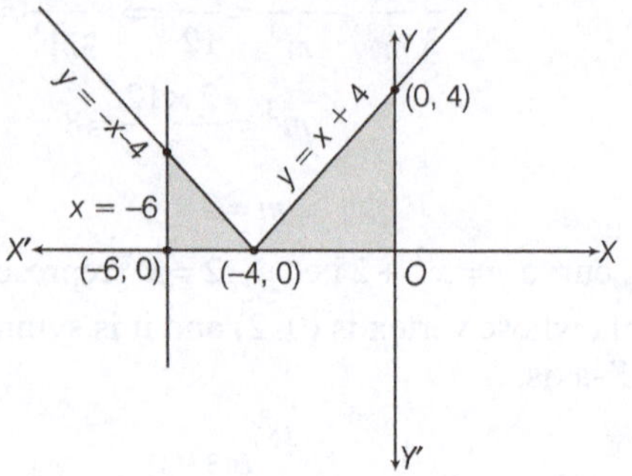

Area of shaded region $=\int_{-6}^{-4} y_1 dx+\int_{-4}^{0} y_2 dx$

where, $y_1=-x-4$ and $y_2=x+4$

$\therefore \ A=\int_{-6}^{-4}-(x+4)dx+\int_{-4}^{0}(x+4)dx$

$$=-\left[\frac{x^2}{2}+4x\right]_{-6}^{-4}+\left[\frac{x^2}{2}+4x\right]_{-4}^{0}$$

$$=-\left[\left(\frac{16}{2}-16\right)-\left(\frac{36}{2}-24\right)\right]+\left[0-\left(\frac{16}{2}\right)+16\right]$$

$=-8+16+18-24-8+16$

$=10$ sq units

9. Given, curves $y^2=8x$ and line $x=2$.

Let B and C be the intersection point of line and curve, where B (2, 4) and C (2, – 4).

The graph of curves $y^2=8x$ and $x=2$ are given below

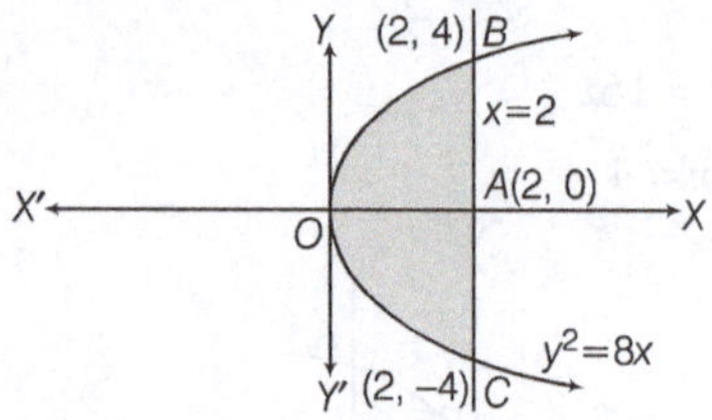

Area of region bounded by the curves

$y^2=8x$ and line $x=2=2$ (area of region $OABO$)

[$\because$ area of region $OABO$ = area of region $OACO$]

$$=2\int_0^2 y\,dx=2\int_0^2\sqrt{8x}\,dx=2\cdot 2\sqrt{2}\int_0^2\sqrt{x}\,dx$$

$$=4\sqrt{2}\left[\frac{2}{3}(x)^{\frac{3}{2}}\right]_0^2=\frac{8\sqrt{2}}{3}\{(2)^{3/2}-0\}$$

$$=\frac{8\sqrt{2}}{3}\times 2\sqrt{2}=\frac{32}{3}\text{ sq units}$$

10. Given, curves are $y^2=x$ ...(i)

and $y^2=4-3x \Rightarrow y^2=-3(x-4/3)$

This is the form of $Y^2=-4aX$.

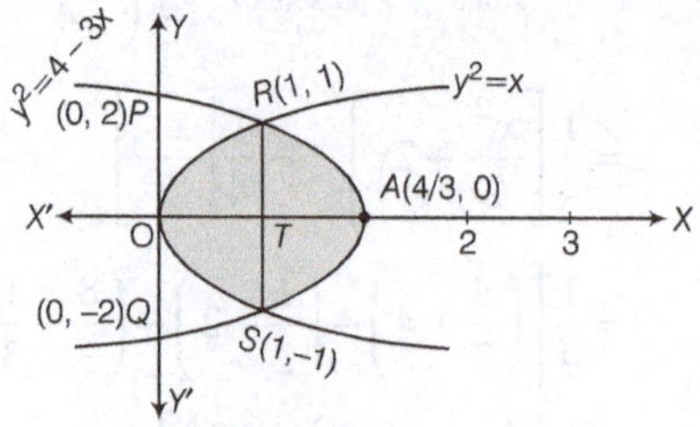

Vertex of this parabola is A $(4/3, 0)$.

and intersect at Y-axis

i.e. $y^2=4 \Rightarrow y=\pm 2$

$\therefore$ Point of intersection on Y-axis are P (0, 2) and Q (0, – 2).

So, the parabola $y^2=4-3x$ cuts Y-axis at P (0, 2) and Q (0, – 2) and opens towards the left.

Now, $y^2=x$ has its vertex at the origin O and is open towards the right.

Now, from Eqs. (i) and (ii),

$$x=4-3x \Rightarrow 4x=4 \Rightarrow x=1$$

From Eq. (i), $y^2=1 \Rightarrow y=\pm 1$

The point of intersection of these parabolas are R (1,1) and S (1,–1).

Now, enclosed area between the given curve is equal to area ($ORASO$).

Now, area of curve $ORTO$

$$=\int_0^1 y\,dx \text{ (from parabola } y^2=x)$$

$$=\int_0^1\sqrt{x}\,dx=\left[\frac{x^{3/2}}{3/2}\right]_0^1$$

$$=\frac{2}{3}[x^{3/2}]_0^1=\frac{2}{3}[1-0]=\frac{2}{3}$$

Area of curve $RATR$

$$=\int_1^{4/3} y\,dx \text{ (from parabola } y^2=4-3x)$$

$$=\int_1^{4/3}\sqrt{4-3x}\,dx=\left[\frac{(4-3x)^{3/2}}{3/2}\cdot\left(-\frac{1}{3}\right)\right]_1^{4/3}$$

$$=-\frac{2}{9}[(4-3x)^{3/2}]_1^{4/3}$$

$$=-\frac{2}{9}\left[\left(4-3\times\frac{4}{3}\right)^{3/2}-(4-3)^{3/2}\right]$$

$$=-\frac{2}{9}[0-1]=\frac{2}{9}$$

Area of curve $ORATO$ = Area of curve $(ORTO + RATR)$

$$= \frac{2}{3} + \frac{2}{9} = \frac{8}{9}$$

$\therefore$ Required area $(ORASO) = 2 \times$ Area of curve $ORATO$

$$= 2 \times \frac{8}{9} = \frac{16}{9} \text{ sq units}$$

11. Given, equation of the curve $x^2 = y$ is a parabola having vertex (0, 0) and it opens upward.
Again, given equation of line is $x + y = 2$, which intercept the coordinate axes at (2, 0) and (0, 2).
Now, intersection point of the curve and line is

$$x + x^2 = 2$$
$$\Rightarrow x^2 + x - 2 = 0$$
$$\Rightarrow x^2 + 2x - x - 2 = 0$$
$$\Rightarrow x(x+2) - 1(x+2) = 0$$
$$\Rightarrow (x-1)(x+2) = 0$$
$$\Rightarrow x = 1, -2$$

When $x = 1$, then $y = (1)^2 = 1$

When $x = -2$, then $y = (-2)^2 = 4$

Hence, the points of intersection are $A(1, 1)$ and $B(-2, 4)$.

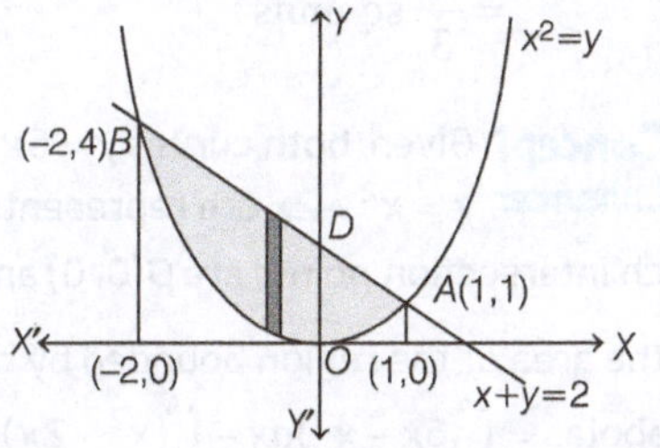

$\therefore$ Required area = Area of shaded region $(AOBDA)$

$$= \int_{-2}^{1} [y\,(\text{line}) - y\,(\text{parabola})]\, dx$$
$$= \int_{-2}^{1} [(2 - x) - (x^2)]\, dx$$
$$= \int_{-2}^{1} (2 - x - x^2)\, dx$$
$$= \left[2x - \frac{x^2}{2} - \frac{x^3}{3}\right]_{-2}^{1}$$
$$= 2 - \frac{1}{2} - \frac{1}{3} - \left(-4 - \frac{4}{2} + \frac{8}{3}\right)$$
$$= \frac{7}{6} - \left(-6 + \frac{8}{3}\right) = \frac{7}{6} + 6 - \frac{8}{3}$$
$$= \frac{7 + 36 - 16}{6} = \frac{27}{6} = \frac{9}{2}$$

12. Given, curve is $\frac{x^2}{9} + \frac{y^2}{4} = 1$ ...(i)

It is an ellipse with centre (0, 0) and given equation of line is $\frac{x}{3} + \frac{y}{2} = 1$.

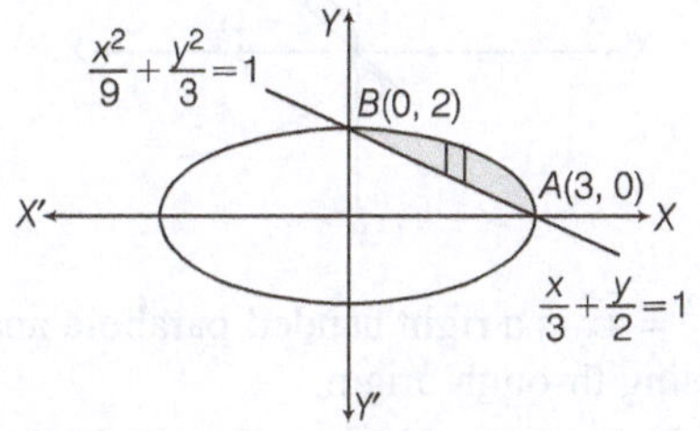

For finding the points of intersection of ellipse and line, putting the value of $\frac{x}{3}$ from Eq. (ii) in Eq. (i), we get

$$\left(1 - \frac{y}{2}\right)^2 + \frac{y^2}{4} = 1 \Rightarrow \frac{y^2}{4} + 1 - y + \frac{y^2}{4} = 1$$
$$\Rightarrow y^2 - 2y = 0 \Rightarrow y = 0, 2$$

When $y = 0$, then $\frac{x}{3} + \frac{0}{2} = 1 \Rightarrow x = 3$

When $y = 2$, then $\frac{x}{3} + \frac{2}{2} = 1 \Rightarrow x = 0$

So, the points of intersection are $A(3, 0)$ and $B(0, 2)$.

$\therefore$ Required area $= \int_0^3 [y\,(\text{ellipse}) - y\,(\text{line})]\, dx$

$$= \int_0^3 2\sqrt{1 - \frac{x^2}{9}}\, dx - \int_0^3 2\left(1 - \frac{x}{3}\right) dx$$
$$= \frac{2}{3}\int_0^3 \sqrt{3^2 - x^2}\, dx - \frac{2}{3}\int_0^3 (3 - x)\, dx$$
$$= \frac{2}{3}\left[\frac{x}{2}\sqrt{3^2 - x^2} + \frac{9}{2}\sin^{-1}\frac{x}{3}\right]_0^3 - \frac{2}{3}\left[3x - \frac{x^2}{2}\right]_0^3$$
$$\left[\because \int \sqrt{a^2 - x^2}\, dx = \frac{x}{2}\sqrt{a^2 - x^2} + \frac{a^2}{2}\sin^{-1}\frac{x}{a}\right]$$
$$= \frac{2}{3}\left[0 + \frac{9}{2}\sin^{-1}(1) - 0\right] - \frac{2}{3}\left[9 - \frac{9}{2} - 0\right]$$
$$= 3\left(\frac{\pi}{2}\right) - (3) = 3\left(\frac{\pi}{2} - 1\right) \text{ sq units}$$

Hence, the required area is $3\left(\frac{\pi}{2} - 1\right)$ sq units.

13. The given equations are

$$y^2 = 4x \quad \text{...(i)}$$

and

$$y = x \quad \text{...(ii)}$$

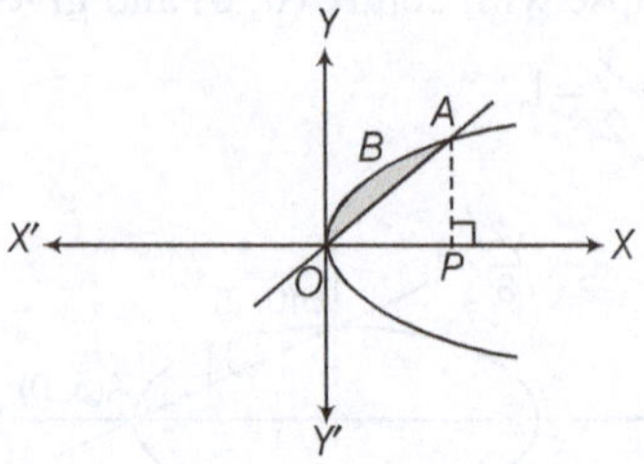

Here, $y^2 = 4x$ is a right handed parabola and $y = x$ is a line passing through origin.

We can find points of intersection of the given parabola and given line, by solving Eqs. (i) and (ii).

On putting $y = x$ in Eq. (i), we get

$$x^2 = 4x$$

$$\Rightarrow \quad x^2 - 4x = 0 \Rightarrow x(x-4) = 0$$

$$\Rightarrow \quad x = 0 \text{ or } x = 4$$

Thus, the points of intersections are O (0, 0) and A (4, 4).

Now, draw AP perpendicular to OX.

Clearly, required area

$$= (\text{area } OBAPO) - (\text{area } OAPO)$$

$$= \int_0^4 (y \text{ for the parabola})\, dx - \int_0^4 (y \text{ for the line})\, dx$$

$$= \int_0^4 2\sqrt{x}\, dx - \int_0^4 x\, dx$$

$$= 2 \cdot \frac{2}{3} [x^{\frac{3}{2}}]_0^4 - \frac{1}{2}[x^2]_0^4$$

$$= \frac{4}{3}[4^{\frac{3}{2}} - 0] - \frac{1}{2}[4^2 - 0]$$

$$= \left(\frac{4}{3} \times 8\right) - \left(\frac{1}{2} \times 16\right) = \frac{32}{3} - 8 = \frac{8}{3} \text{ sq units}$$

$\therefore$ The required area is $\frac{8}{3}$ sq units.

14. Given, curves are

$$y = 6x - x^2 \quad \text{...(i)}$$

and

$$y = x^2 - 2x \quad \text{...(ii)}$$

Eq. (i) can be written as

$$x^2 - 6x + 9 = -y + 9$$

$$\Rightarrow \quad (x-3)^2 = -(y-9),$$

which represents a downward parabola with vertex at (3, 9). Now, Eq. (ii) can be written as $(x^2+1)^2 = y + 1$, which represents an upward parabola with vertex at (1, – 1).

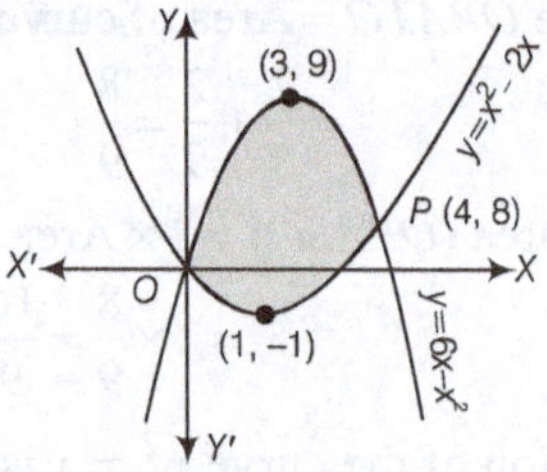

On solving Eqs. (i) and (ii), we get

$$6x - x^2 = x^2 - 2x$$

$$\Rightarrow \quad 2x^2 - 8x = 0$$

$$\Rightarrow \quad x(x-4) = 0$$

$$\Rightarrow \quad x = 0, x = 4$$

So, the points of intersection are O (0, 0) and P(4, 8).

$\therefore$ Required area = Area of the shaded region

$$= \int_0^4 [(6x - x^2) - (x^2 - 2x)]\, dx$$

$$= \int_0^4 (8x - 2x^2)\, dx = \left[8 \cdot \frac{x^2}{2} - 2 \cdot \frac{x^3}{3}\right]_0^4$$

$$= \left(64 - \frac{128}{3}\right) - 0$$

$$= \frac{64}{3} \text{ sq units}$$

> **Concept Enhancer** Given, both curves $y = 6x - x^2$ and $y = x^2 - 2x$ are represents parabola, which intersection points are $O(0, 0)$ and $P(4, 8)$.
>
> So, the area of the region bounded by both parabolas $= \int_0^4 (6x - x^2)dx - \int_0^4 (x^2 - 2x)dx$

15. Given, equation of circle is

$$x^2 + y^2 = 4 \quad \text{...(i)}$$

with centre (0, 0) and radius 2.

and given equation of line is

$$x + y = 2 \quad \text{...(ii)}$$

The point of intersection of

$$x^2 + y^2 = 4 \text{ and } x + y = 2 \text{ is}$$

$$\Rightarrow \quad x^2 + (2-x)^2 = 4 \quad [\because y = 2 - x]$$

$$\Rightarrow \quad x^2 + 4 + x^2 - 4x = 4$$

$$\Rightarrow \quad 2x^2 - 4x = 0$$

$$\Rightarrow \quad 2x(x-2) = 0$$

$$\therefore \quad x = 0 \text{ or } 2$$

When $x = 0$, then $y = 2 - 0 = 2$

and when $x = 2$, then $y = 2 - 2 = 0$

So, points of intersection are (0, 2) and (2,0).

Rough sketch for the above region is given as

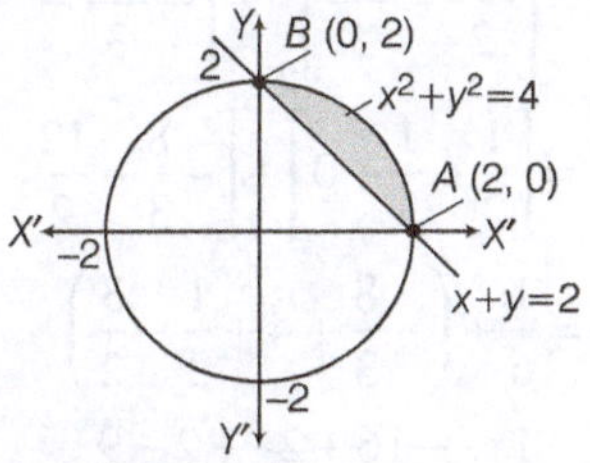

Required area of region

$$= \int_0^2 [y dx \text{ (from circle)} - y dx \text{ (from line)}] dx$$

$$= \int_0^2 [\sqrt{4-x^2} - (2-x) dx]$$

$$\left[\because x^2+y^2=4, \Rightarrow y=\sqrt{4-x^2}\right]$$

$$= \int_0^2 \sqrt{4-x^2}\, dx - \int_0^2 (2-x)\, dx$$

$$= \left[\frac{x}{2}\sqrt{4-x^2} + \frac{4}{2}\sin^{-1}\frac{x}{2}\right]_0^2 - \left[2x - \frac{x^2}{2}\right]_0^2$$

$$\left[\because \int \sqrt{a^2-x^2}\, dx = \left\{\frac{x}{2}\sqrt{a^2-x^2} + \frac{a^2}{2}\sin^{-1}\left(\frac{x}{a}\right)\right\}\right]$$

$$= \left[\frac{x}{2}\sqrt{4-x^2} + 2\sin^{-1}\frac{x}{2}\right]_0^2 - \left[2x - \frac{x^2}{2}\right]_0^2$$

$$= \left[\frac{2}{2}\sqrt{4-4} + 2\sin^{-1}\left(\frac{2}{2}\right) - 0 - 2\sin^{-1} 0\right]$$

$$- \left[4 - \frac{4}{2} - 0\right]$$

$$= (2\sin^{-1} 1 - 0) - \left(4 - \frac{4}{2}\right)$$

$$= 2\sin^{-1}\left(\sin\frac{\pi}{2}\right) - 2 \qquad \left[\because 1 = \sin\frac{\pi}{2}\right]$$

$$= 2\frac{\pi}{2} - 2 = \pi - 2$$

$\therefore$ Area of region is $(\pi - 2)$ sq units

16. Given, curves are $y = 2x - x^2$ ...(i)

and $y = x$ ...(ii)

From Eqs. (i) and (ii),

$$x = 2x - x^2$$

$$\Rightarrow \quad x^2 = x$$

$$\Rightarrow \quad (x-1)x = 0$$

$$\Rightarrow \quad x = 0, 1$$

When $x = 0$, then $y = 0$

When $x = 1$, then $y = 1$

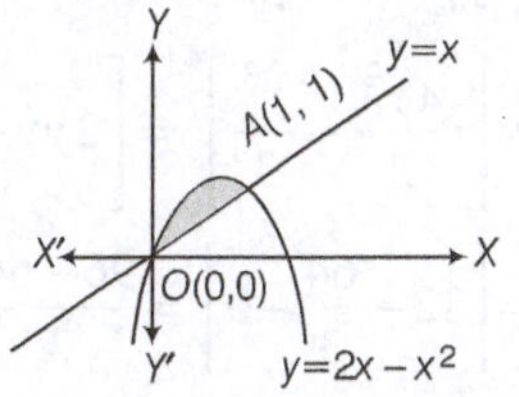

$\therefore$ The point of intersection of two curves are O (0,0) and A (1,1).

$$\text{Required area} = \int_0^1 [y dx \text{ (From parabola)} - y dx \text{(From line)}] dx$$

$$= \int_0^1 (2x - x^2 - x)\, dx$$

$$= \int_0^1 (x - x^2)\, dx = \left[\frac{x^2}{2} - \frac{x^3}{3}\right]_0^1$$

$$= \left(\frac{1}{2} - \frac{1}{3} - 0\right) = \frac{3-2}{6} = \frac{1}{6} \text{ sq unit}$$

17. Given, curve is $x = 4y - y^2$

$$\Rightarrow \quad x = -(y^2 - 4y) \qquad \text{...(i)}$$

$$\Rightarrow \quad x = -(y^2 - 4y + 4) + 4$$

$$\Rightarrow \quad x = -(y-2)^2 + 4$$

$$\Rightarrow \quad (y-2)^2 = 4 - x = -(x-4)$$

Let $y - 2 = Y$ and $(x - 4) = X$

Then, $Y^2 = -X$

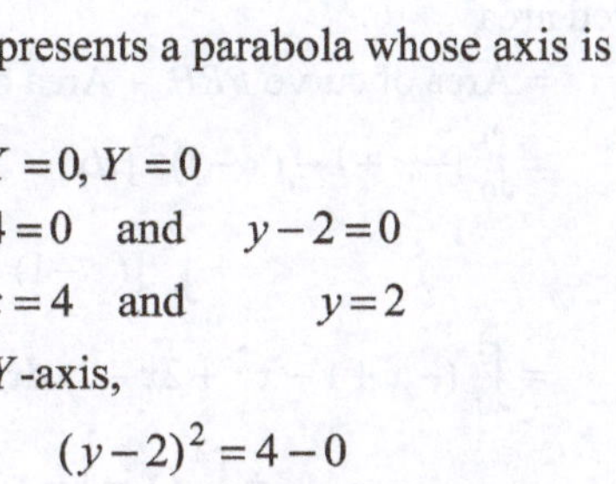

which represents a parabola whose axis is parallel to X-axis.

Vertex $X = 0, Y = 0$

i.e. $x - 4 = 0$ and $y - 2 = 0$

$\Rightarrow \quad x = 4$ and $y = 2$

Also, at Y-axis,

$$(y-2)^2 = 4 - 0 \qquad [\because x = 0]$$

$$\Rightarrow \quad y - 2 = \pm 2$$

$$\Rightarrow \quad y = 4, 0$$

Area bounded between parabola and Y-axis

$$=\int_0^4 x\,dy=\int_0^4 (4y-y^2)\,dy \quad \text{[from Eq. (i)]}$$

$$=\left[\frac{4y^2}{2}-\frac{y^3}{3}\right]_0^4=\left[2y^2-\frac{y^3}{3}\right]_0^4$$

$$=\left[32-\frac{64}{3}-0\right]=\frac{96-64}{3}=\frac{32}{3} \text{ sq units}$$

18. Given, curves are $=(x-1)^2$ ...(i)

and $y=|x-1|$ ...(ii)

$$=\begin{cases} x-1, & x\ge 1 \\ -x+1, & x<1 \end{cases}$$

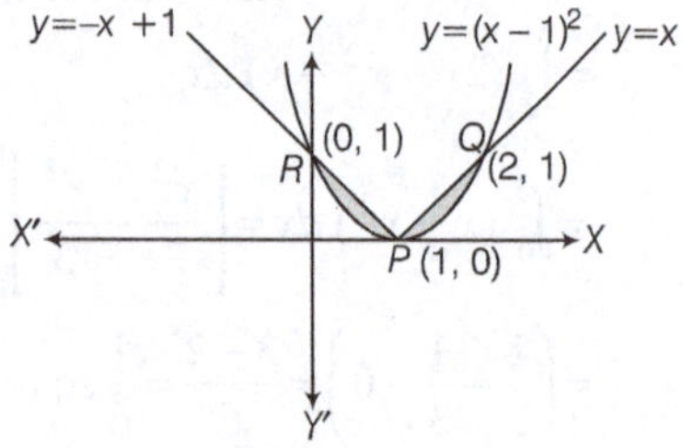

Now, from $y=(x-1)^2$ and $y=x-1$, $(x-1)=(x-1)^2$

$\Rightarrow$ $(x-1)^2-(x-1)=0 \Rightarrow (x-1)(x-1-1)=0$

$\Rightarrow$ $(x-2)(x-1)=0 \Rightarrow x=2$ or 1

When $x=2$, then $y=(2-1)^2=1$

When $x=1$, then $y=(1-1)^2=0$

Thus, the points of intersection are $P(1,0)$ and $Q(2,1)$.

From equations

$y=(x-1)^2$ and $y=-x+1$

$(x-1)^2=-x+1 \Rightarrow x^2-2x+1=-x+1$

$\Rightarrow$ $x^2-x=0 \Rightarrow x(x-1)=0$

$\Rightarrow$ $x=0$ or 1

When $x=0$, then $y=(0-1)^2=1$

When $x=1$, then $y=(1-1)^2=0$

Thus, the points of intersection are $R(0,1)$ and $P(1,0)$.

$\therefore$ Required area

= Area of curve PRP + Area of curve PQP

$$=\int_0^1 [-x+1-(x-1)^2]\,dx + \int_1^2 [(x-1)-(x-1)^2]dx$$

$$=\int_0^1 (-x+1-x^2+2x-1)\,dx + \int_1^2 (x-1-x^2+2x-1)\,dx$$

$$=\int_0^1 (x-x^2)\,dx+\int_1^2 (-x^2+3x-2)\,dx$$

$$=\left[\frac{x^2}{2}-\frac{x^3}{3}\right]_0^1+\left[-\frac{x^3}{3}+\frac{3x^2}{2}-2x\right]_1^2$$

$$=\left[\frac{1}{2}-\frac{1}{3}+0\right]+\left[-\frac{8}{3}+\frac{12}{2}-4+\frac{1}{3}-\frac{3}{2}+2\right]$$

$$=\frac{1}{6}+\left(-\frac{8}{3}+4+\frac{1}{3}-\frac{3}{2}\right)$$

$$=\frac{1}{6}+\frac{-16+24+2-9}{6}$$

$$=\frac{1}{6}+\frac{1}{6}=\frac{1}{3} \text{ sq unit}$$

19. Given, curve is $y=x^2-5x+6$

$$y=x^2-3x-2x+6=x(x-3)-2(x-3)$$

$$y=(x-3)(x-2)$$

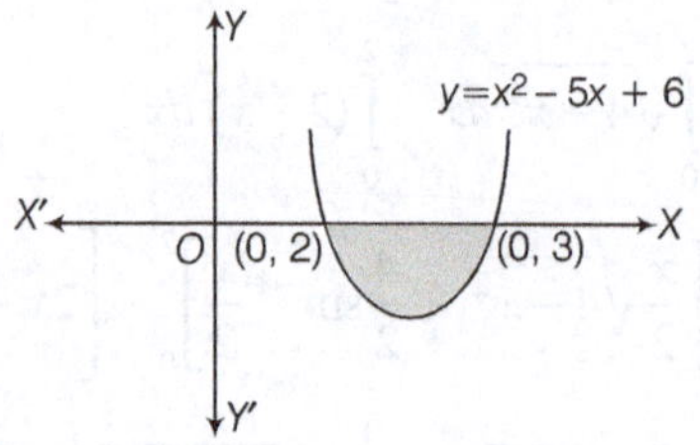

We know that, at X-axis, $y=0$

$\therefore$ $0=(x-3)(x-2)$

$\Rightarrow$ $x-3=0$ or $x-2=0 \Rightarrow x=3$ or 2

$\therefore$ Required area $=\left|\int_2^3 -y\,dx\right|$

$$=\left|\int_2^3 -(x^2-5x+6)\,dx\right|$$

$$=\left|-\left[\frac{x^3}{3}-\frac{5x^2}{2}+6x\right]_2^3\right|$$

$$=\left|-\left(\frac{27}{3}-\frac{45}{2}+18-\frac{8}{3}+10-12\right)\right|$$

$$=\left|-\left(9-\frac{45}{2}-\frac{8}{3}+16\right)\right|$$

$$=\left|-\left(\frac{150-135-16}{6}\right)\right|$$

$$=\left|\frac{-(150-151)}{6}\right|$$

$$=\frac{1}{6} \text{ sq unit}$$

20. Given, curves are $x^2+y=9$, $x+1=0$

and $x-2=0$

Now, $x^2=-(y-9)$

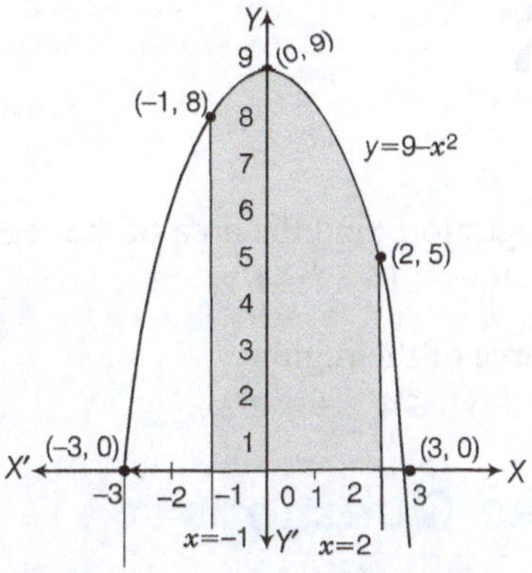

This represents a parabola having vertex (0, 9) and open downwards.

$\therefore$ Required area $= \int_{-1}^{2} y\,dx = \int_{-1}^{2} (9 - x^2)\,dx$

$$= \left[9x - \frac{x^3}{3}\right]_{-1}^{2} = \left(18 - \frac{8}{3}\right) - \left(-9 + \frac{1}{3}\right)$$

$$= 27 - \frac{8}{3} - \frac{1}{3} = 27 - 3 = 24 \text{ sq units}$$

21. Given, curves are $y^2 + 1 = x, x \le 2$ ...(i)

and $x = 2$ ...(ii)

Now, $y^2 = x - 1$

$\Rightarrow$ $y = \pm\sqrt{x-1}$ ...(iii)

which is defined only when $x - 1 \ge 0$ or $x \ge 1$

$y^2 = x - 1$

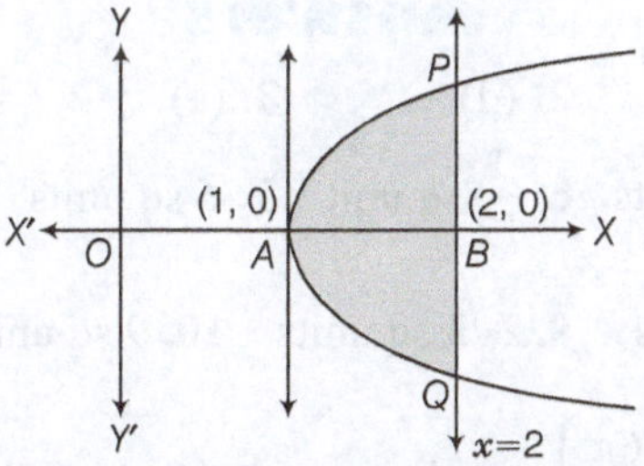

Now, $y^2 = x - 1$ is a right open parabola with vertex (1, 0).

$\therefore$ Required area = 2 (Area of curve ABP)

$$= 2\int_1^2 y\,dx = 2\int_1^2 \sqrt{x-1}\,dx$$

[from Eq. (iii)]

On putting $x - 1 = t^2 \Rightarrow dx = 2t\,dt$

Upper limit, when $x = 2$, then $t = 1$

Lower limit, when $x = 1$, then $t = 0$

$\therefore$ Required area $= 4\int_0^1 t \cdot t\,dt = 4\int_0^1 t^2\,dt$

$$= 4\left[\frac{t^3}{3}\right]_0^1 = 4\left[\frac{1}{3} - 0\right] = \frac{4}{3} \text{ sq units}$$

22. Given, curve is $y = 9x^2 \Rightarrow x^2 = \frac{y}{9}$, which represents a parabola.

Now, at $x = 0$, $y = 0$

At $y = 1$, $x = \pm\sqrt{\frac{1}{9}} = \pm\frac{1}{3}$ and At $y = 4$, $x = \pm\sqrt{\frac{4}{9}} = \pm\frac{2}{3}$

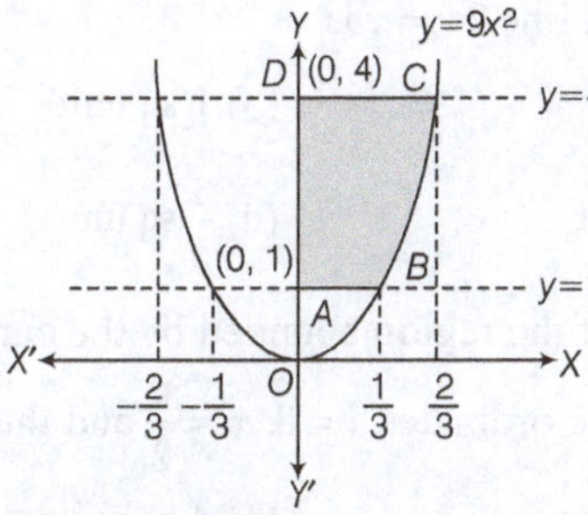

$\therefore$ Required area = Area of shaded region ($ABCDA$)

$$= \int_1^4 x\,dy \text{ (for parabola)}$$

$$= \int_1^4 \frac{y^{1/2}}{3}\,dy = \frac{1}{3}\left(\frac{y^{3/2}}{3/2}\right)_1^4$$

$$= \frac{2}{9}(4^{3/2} - 1) = \frac{2}{9}(8 - 1)$$

$$= \frac{14}{9} \text{ sq units}$$

23. Given, curve is $a^2 y = x^2 (x + a)$ ...(i)

At X-axis, $y = 0$

Then, $x^2 (x + a) = 0$

$\Rightarrow$ $x = 0$ or $x = -a$

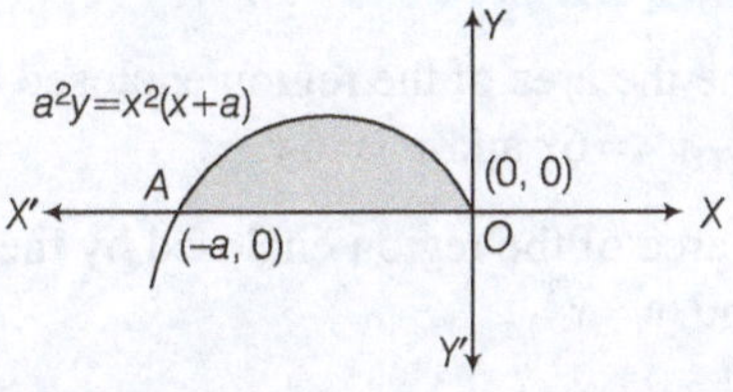

$\therefore$ Required area $= \int_{-a}^{0} y\,dx = \int_{-a}^{0} \left(\frac{x^3 + ax^2}{a^2}\right) dx$

$$= \frac{1}{a^2}\left[\frac{x^4}{4} + \frac{ax^3}{3}\right]_{-a}^{0}$$

$$= \frac{1}{a^2}\left[0 - \frac{a^4}{4} + \frac{a^4}{3}\right]$$

$$= \frac{1}{a^2}\left[\frac{(-3+4)}{12}a^4\right]$$

$$= \frac{1}{a^2}\left[\frac{a^4}{12}\right] = \frac{a^2}{12} \text{ sq units}$$

CHAPTER TEST

1 Mark Questions

1. The area of the region bounded by parabola $y^2 = x$ and the straight line $2y = x$ is

(a) $\frac{4}{3}$ sq units (b) 1 sq unit

(c) $\frac{2}{3}$ sq unit (d) $\frac{1}{3}$ sq unit

2. The area of the region bounded by the curve $y = \sin x$ between the ordinates $x = 0$, $x = \frac{\pi}{2}$ and the X-axis is

(a) 2 sq units (b) 4 sq units
(c) 3 sq units (d) 1 sq unit

3. The area bounded by the lines $y = 4x + 5$, $y = 5 - x$ and $4y = x + 5$ is

(a) $\frac{15}{2}$ sq units (b) $\frac{9}{2}$ sq units

(c) $\frac{13}{2}$ sq units (d) None of these

4. The area enclosed between the curves $y = ax^2$ and $x = ay^2$, $(a > 0)$ is 1 sq unit. Then, the value of a is

(a) $\frac{1}{\sqrt{3}}$ (b) $\frac{1}{2}$ (c) 1 (d) $\frac{1}{3}$

2 Marks Questions

5. Determine the area of the region enclosed by the parabolas $y^2 = 6x$ and $x^2 = 6y$.

6. Find the area of the region enclosed by the curves $y = x^2$ and $y = x^3$.

7. Find the area of the region bounded by the curve $x = 2y + 3$ and the lines $y = 1$, $y = -1$.

8. Find the area of the region bounded by the curve $y = x + 1$ and the lines $x = 2$, $x = 3$.

3/4 Marks Questions

9. Using integration, find the area of the triangle formed by positive X-axis and tangent and normal to the circle $x^2 + y^2 = 4$ at $(1, \sqrt{3})$.

10. Sketch the graph of $y = |x + 3|$ and evaluate the area under the curve $y = |x + 3|$ above X-axis and between $x = -6$ to $x = 0$.

11. Using integration, find the area of the region $\{(x, y): x^2 + y^2 \leq 16, x^2 \leq 6y\}$.

12. Find the area of the region $\{(x, y): x^2 + y^2 \leq 4, x + y \geq 2\}$.

5/6 Marks Questions

13. Using integration, find the area of the triangular region whose sides have the equations $y = 2x + 1$, $y = 3x + 1$ and $x = 4$.

14. Find the area of the region bounded by ellipse $\frac{x^2}{a^2} + \frac{y^2}{b^2} = 1$ and the straight line $\frac{x}{a} + \frac{y}{b} = 1$.

15. Find the area of the region included between the curve $4y = 3x^2$ and the line $2y = 3x + 12$.

16. Sketch the region bounded by the curve $y = \sqrt{5 - x^2}$ and $y = |x - 1|$ and find its area.

17. Find the area of the region enclosed between the two circles $x^2 + y^2 = 9$ and $(x - 3)^2 + y^2 = 9$.

18. Find the area of the region bounded by the curves $y = x^2 + 2$, $y = x$, $x = 0$ and $x = 3$.

Answers

1. (a) **2.** (d) **3.** (a) **4.** (a)

5. 12 sq units **6.** $\frac{1}{12}$ sq unit **7.** 6 sq units

8. $\frac{7}{2}$ sq units **9.** $2\sqrt{3}$ sq units **10.** 9 sq units

11. $\left(\frac{4\sqrt{3}}{3} + \frac{16\pi}{3}\right)$ sq units **12.** $(\pi - 2)$ sq units

13. 8 sq units **14.** $\left(\frac{\pi}{4} - \frac{1}{2}\right)ab$ sq units

15. 27 sq units

16. $\left[\frac{5}{2}\left(\sin^{-1}\frac{2}{\sqrt{5}} + \sin^{-1}\frac{1}{\sqrt{5}}\right) - \frac{1}{2}\right]$ sq units

17. $\left(6\pi - \frac{9\sqrt{3}}{2}\right)$ sq units

18. $\frac{21}{2}$ sq units

13

Application of Calculus

TREND ANALYSIS 3 YEARS

TOPIC 01 Application of Calculus

Average No. of Questions Across all Sets

Types of Questions	2024	2023	2020
1 Mark	3	3	—
2 Marks	2	2	2
3/4 Marks	—	—	1
5/6 Marks	—	1	—

Cost Function

If x denotes the quantity produced of a certain commodity at total cost c, then the total cost function is expressed as $C = c(x)$, explicitly and $f(c, x) = 0$ is the implicit form. The total cost is broken into two parts, the fixed cost and the variable cost.

(i) Fixed Cost

Fixed costs are those which incurred regardless of the level of production-like interest, rent, wages of permanent staff etc.

Thus, Total Fixed Cost (TFC) = TC, when $x = 0$

Fixed cost does not change whether there is any increase or decrease in level of production.

(ii) Variable Cost

Variable costs are those which vary with output. e.g. Raw materials and wages of casual labour etc.

Thus, Total Cost = Total Fixed Cost + Total Variable Cost

or TC = TFC + TVC

Average Cost

The average cost represents the cost per unit, i.e. $\text{AC} = \dfrac{C}{x}$.

(where, C = total cost, x = number of commodities)

Demand Function

The demand function represents the functional relationship between demand and price of a commodity.

If p denotes the price per unit and x is the number of units demanded by a consumer at that price, then demand function in explicit form will be written as $x = f(p)$ and in implicit form as $f(x, p) = 0$.

$\therefore$ Price (p) is shown against demand x in following figure

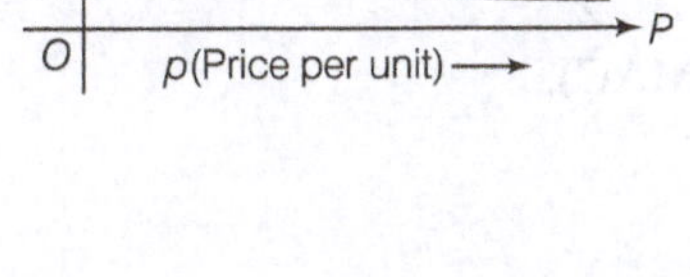

NOTE (i) If the demand of the item depends upon the price of the item, then the demand function is $x = f(p)$.

(ii) If the price of the item depends upon the demand of the item, then the demand is $p = f(x)$.

Revenue Function

Revenue means the amount received by a company on selling a certain number of units of a commodity. Let p be the price per unit and x be the number of units sold. Then, total revenue

$$R \text{ or } R(x) = p \cdot x$$

Total revenue = Selling price per unit of the commodity × Quantity sold

Profit Function

Profit function is the difference of revenue function and cost function

i.e. $$P(x) = R(x) - C(x)$$

Breakeven Point

The break-even point is that point, where total revenue equals to total cost incurred i.e. $R(x) = C(x)$. At break-even point, a company begins to earn a profit.

Marginal cost

The marginal cost is the rate of change of the total cost with respect to x (output).

i.e. $$\text{MC} = \frac{d}{dx}(C) = \frac{dC}{dx}$$

Relation between Average cost and Marginal cost

If C is the total cost of producing and marketing x units of commodity, then

$$\frac{d}{dx}(\text{AC}) = \frac{1}{x}(\text{MC} - \text{AC})$$

Here, three cases arise.

(i) For MC > AC ⇒ AC increases with x and AC curve is rising.

(ii) For MC = AC ⇒ AC is constant at all levels of output.

(iii) For MC < AC ⇒ AC decreases with x and AC curve is falling.

Average Revenue and Marginal Revenue

(i) **Average Revenue** is the revenue generated per unit of output sold. It is denoted by AR

i.e. $$\text{AR} = \frac{\text{Total revenue}}{\text{Number of units sold}}$$

$$= \frac{R}{x} = \frac{p \cdot x}{x} = p$$

(ii) **Marginal Revenue** is the rate of change of total revenue with respect to quantity sold

i.e. $$\text{MR} = \frac{dR}{dx} = \frac{d}{dx}(px)$$

PYQs Previous Years Questions

1 Mark Questions

1. A company sells hand towels at ₹ 100 per unit. The fixed cost for the company to manufacture hand towels is ₹ 35000 and variable cost is estimated to be 30% of total revenue. What will be the total cost function for manufacturing hand towels? **ISC 2024**

(a) $35000 + 3x$ (b) $35000 + 30x$

(c) $35000 + 100x$ (d) $35000 + 10x$

2. If the total cost function is given by $C = x + 2x^3 - \frac{7}{2}x^2$, find the Marginal Average Cost function (MAC). **ISC 2024**

3. The manufacturer of a pen fixes its selling price at ₹ 45, and the cost function is $C(x) = 30x + 240$. The manufacturer will begin to earn profit, if he sells more than 16 pens. Why? Give one reason. **ISC 2024**

4. At a toy factory, the production cost per day for x number of toys is given by the following function

$$C(x) = 0.0001x^3 - 0.01x^2 - 20x + 3500$$

Which of these represents the approximate additional cost to produce 201st toy? **ISC Specimen 2024**

(a) $C(200)$ (b) AC(201)

(c) MC(200) (d) MC(201)

5. The marginal revenue of a manufacturing facility is given by the function $MR(x) = 408 - 17x$

The manufacturer should limit the production to 24 units. Why? **ISC Specimen 2024**

6. Vishwanath runs a company that produces and sells a particular model of laptop.

Its revenue function is given by $R(x) = 4x^3 + \frac{1}{5}x^2 + x$, where x is the number of laptops demanded and $R(x)$ is in rupees.

What is the ideal unit price (in rupees) for Vishwanath to charge for each laptop, if there is a demand for 100 laptops? **ISC Specimen 2024**

7. If the demand function is given by $p(x) = 1500 - 2x - x^2$, then find the marginal revenue when $x = 10$. **ISC 2023**

(a) 1160 (b) 1600 (c) 1100 (d) 1200

8. The fixed cost of a product is ₹ 30000 and its variable cost per unit is ₹ 800. If the demand function is $p(x) = 4500 - 100x$, then find the break-even values. **ISC 2023**

9. The cost function $C(x) = 3x^2 - 6x + 5$. Find the average cost when $x = 2$. **ISC 2023**

10. Which relation is correct for break-even point, where $R(X)$ is revenue function and $C(X)$ is cost function? **ISC Specimen 2023**

(a) $R(X) > C(X)$ (b) $R(X) < C(X)$
(c) $R(X) = C(X)$ (d) $R(X) > 2C(X)$

11. Average revenue of a commodity is given by $AR(x) = a + \frac{b}{x}$. Find the demand function, when marginal revenue is zero. **ISC Specimen 2023**

12. If $R(X) = 36x + 3x^2 + 5$, then find actual revenue from selling 50th item. **ISC Specimen 2023**

13. A company sells its product for ₹ 20 per unit. Fixed costs for the company is ₹ 45000 and variable costs is estimated to run 25% of total revenue. If x denotes number of units produced, then what will be the total cost function? **ISC Specimen Sem-I 2022**

(a) $45000 + 5x$ (b) $15000 + 4x$
(c) $45000 + 2x$ (d) $4500 + 20x$

14. The demand function for the certain commodity is given by $p = 4000 - 100x$. What will be the total revenue from the sale of 3 units? **ISC Specimen Sem-I 2022**

(a) 11100 (b) 1000 (c) 4500 (d) 2000

15. A company sells x packets of biscuits each day at ₹ 10 a packet. The cost of manufacturing these packets is ₹ 5 per packet plus a fixed daily overhead cost of ₹ 700. What will be the profit function? **ISC Specimen Sem-I 2022**

(a) $6x - 400$ (b) $5x - 700$
(c) $10x - 500$ (d) $5x - 10$

16. The cost function of a firm is given by $(x) = 3x^2 - 2x + 6$. The average cost of the firm at $x = 3$ is **ISC Specimen Sem-I 2022**

(a) 11 (b) 17 (c) 9 (d) 27

17. The demand function of a monopolist is given by $x = 100 - 4p$. The quantity at which MR=0 will be **ISC Specimen 2021**

(a) 25 (b) 10 (c) 50 (d) 30

18. Find the marginal cost function (MC), if the cost function is $C(x) = \frac{x^3}{3} + 5x^2 - 16x + 2$. **ISC Specimen 2021**

19. If revenue function $R(x) = 3x^3 + 8x - 2$, then find the average revenue function. **ISC Specimen 2021**

2 Marks Questions

20. The average cost function associated with producing and marketing x units of an item is given by $AC = x + 5 + \frac{36}{x}$.

(i) Find the total cost function.
(ii) Find the range of values of x for which average cost is increasing. **ISC 2024**

21. A monopolist's demand function is $x = 60 - \frac{p}{5}$. At what level of output will marginal revenue be zero? **ISC 2024**

22. A bicycle spare parts manufacturing company decided to upgrade its production unit by installing advanced machinery. As a result of this investment, the cost of producing spare parts increased. The company used to sell 1000 spare parts daily at ₹ 50 per unit. The increased daily cost of production $C(x)$ for x number of spare parts is given by

$$C(x) = \frac{99}{2}x + 525$$

If the selling price remains the same, find how many more spare parts must the company sell daily to ensure no loss? **ISC Specimen 2024**

23. The government's department of Culture is organising an art and craft exhibition cum sale to promote local artists and their work.

They want to charge a nominal amount as entry fee. Profit, in rupees, generated by the entry tickets can be calculated using the function

$P(x) = -8x^3 + 29400x - 60000$, where x is the price of each ticket.

What is the ideal price for each ticket that the department should set to maximise the profit? ***ISC Specimen 2024***

24. The total cost function for x units is given by $C(x) = \sqrt{6x+5} + 2500$. Show that the marginal cost decreases as the output x increases. ***ISC 2023***

25. The average revenue function is given by $\text{AR} = 25 - \dfrac{x}{4}$.

Find total revenue function and marginal revenue function. ***ISC 2023***

26. The total revenue function $R(x) = x + 2x^3 - 3.5x^2$. Find the point, where marginal revenue curve cuts the coordinate axis. ***IS Specimen 2023***

27. For the revenue function $R(x) = \dfrac{bx}{a+x}$, show that the marginal revenue function is increasing for all $b < 0$ and $a > 0$. ***ISC Specimen 2023***

28. The total cost function for a production is given by $C(x) = \dfrac{3}{4}x^2 - 7x + 27$. Find the number of units produced for which MC = AC.

(MC = Marginal Cost and AC = Average Cost) ***ISC Specimen 2021, ISC 2019***

29. The selling price of a commodity is fixed at ₹ 60 and its cost function is $C(x) = 35x + 250$. ***ISC 2020***

(i) Determine the profit function.

(ii) Find the break-even points.

30. The revenue function is given by $R(x) = 100x - x^2 - x^3$. Find ***ISC 2020***

(i) the demand function.

(ii) marginal revenue function.

31. A company produces a commodity with ₹ 24000 as fixed cost. The variable cost, estimated to be 25% of the total revenue received on selling the product, is at the rate of ₹ 8 per unit. Find the break-even point. ***ISC 2019***

32. Given, the total cost function for x units of a commodity as : $C(x) = \dfrac{1}{3}x^3 + 3x^2 - 16x + 2$. ***ISC 2018***

Find (i) marginal cost function

(ii) average cost function

33. The average cost function associated with producing and marketing x units of an item is given by $AC = 2x - 11 + \dfrac{50}{x}$. Find the range of values of the output x, for which AC is increasing. ***ISC 2018***

34. Find the cost of increasing from 100 to 200 units if the marginal cost (in rupees per unit) is given by the function $\text{MC} = 0.003x^2 - 0.01x + 2.5$. ***ISC Specimen 2018***

35. The total variable cost of manufacturing x units in a firm is ₹$\left(3x + \dfrac{x^5}{25}\right)$. Show that average variable cost increases with output x. ***ISC Specimen 2018***

3/4 Marks Questions

36. The total cost function of a firm is given by $C(x) = \dfrac{1}{3}x^3 - 5x^2 + 30x - 15$, where the selling price per unit is given as ₹ 6. Find for what value of x will the profit be maximum. ***ISC 2020***

37. The cost function of a product is given by $C(x) = \dfrac{x^3}{3} - 45x^2 - 900x + 36$, where x is the number of units produced. How many units should be produced to minimise the marginal cost? ***ISC 2019***

38. A product can be manufactured at a total cost $C(x) = \dfrac{x^2}{100} + 100x + 40$, where x is the number of units produced. The price at which each unit can be sold is given by $P = \left(200 - \dfrac{x}{400}\right)$. Determine the production level x at which the profit is maximum. What is the price per unit and total profit at the level of production? ***ISC 2018***

39. If the demand function is given by $x = \dfrac{600 - P}{8}$, where the price is ₹ P per unit and the manufacturer produces x unit per week at the total cost of ₹ $x^2 + 78x + 2500$, find the value of x for which the profit is maximum. ***ISC Specimen 2018***

40. The fixed cost of new product is ₹ 35000 and the variable cost per unit is ₹ 500. If the demand function : $P = 5000 - 100x$, find the break-even value(s)? **ISC Specimen 2018**

5/6 Marks Questions

41. The demand function for a certain product is represented by the equation $p = ax^2 + bx + c$, where x is the number of units demanded and p is the price per unit. **ISC 2023**

On the basis of above information, answer the following questions.

(i) The revenue function $R(x)$ is

(a) $ax^3 + bx^2 + cx$ (b) $ax + b + \frac{c}{x}$

(c) $ax^3 + bx^2 + cx + d$ (d) $2ax + b$

(ii) The marginal revenue MR (x) is

(a) $a - \frac{c}{x^2}$ (b) $3ax^2 + 2bx + c$

(c) $3ax^3 + 2bx^2 + c$ (d) $2a$

(iii) The slope of the marginal revenue is

(a) 0 (b) $6ax + 2b$ (c) $\frac{2c}{x^3}$ (d) $9ax^2 + 4bx$

(iv) Values of x, for which marginal revenue increases is

(a) $x > \frac{-b}{3a}$ (b) $x < \frac{-b}{3a}$ (c) $x = \frac{-b}{3a}$ (d) $x \le \frac{-b}{3a}$

42. The demand for a certain product is represented by the equation $p = 500 + 25x - \frac{x^2}{3}$ in rupees where x is the number of units and p is the price per unit. Find

(i) marginal revenue function.

(ii) the marginal revenue when 10 units are sold. **ISC 2017**

43. The demand function is $x = \frac{24 - 2p}{3}$, where x is the number of units demanded and p is the price per unit.

(i) Find the revenue function R in terms of p.

(ii) Find the price and the number of units demanded for which the revenue is maximum. **ISC 2016**

44. The average cost function AC for a commodity is given by $\text{AC} = x + 5 + \frac{36}{x}$ in terms of output x, find the

(i) marginal cost as the function of x.

(ii) output for which AC increases. **ISC 2015, 10**

45. A firm has the cost function, $C = \frac{x^3}{3} - 7x^2 + 111x + 50$ and demand function, $x = 100 - P$.

(i) Write the total revenue in terms of x.

(ii) Formulate the total profit function P in terms of x.

(iii) Find the profit maximising level of output x. **ISC 2014**

Explanations

1. (b) Let the number of units of manufacturing hand towels be x and selling price per unit = ₹ 100

Thus, the revenue generated on selling particular number of units is

$$R(x) = 100 \times x = 100x$$

Also, variable cost = 30% of total revenue

$$= \frac{30}{100} \text{ of } R(x)$$

$$= \frac{30}{100} \times 100x = 30x$$

∴ Total cost = Fixed cost + Variable cost = $35000 + 30x$

∴ The total cost function for manufacturing hand towels is $35000 + 30x$.

2. Given, total cost function is

$$C(x) = x + 2x^3 - \frac{7}{2}x^2$$

Thus, the average cost is

$$\text{AC} = \frac{C(x)}{x} = \frac{x + 2x^3 - \frac{7}{2}x^2}{x}$$

$$= 1 + 2x^2 - \frac{7}{2}x$$

Here, the marginal average cost function is

$$\text{MAC} = \frac{d}{dx}(\text{AC})$$

$$= \frac{d}{dx}\left(1 + 2x^2 - \frac{7}{2}x\right)$$

$$= 0 + 2(2x) - \frac{7}{2} = 4x - \frac{7}{2}$$

Thus, the Marginal Average Cost function (MAC) is $4x - \frac{7}{2}$.

3. Selling price of pen fixed at ₹ 45.

The cost function is $C(x) = 30x + 240$

and the revenue function is $R(x) = 45x$

So, the profit is

$$P(x) = R(x) - C(x) = 45x - (30x + 240)$$
$$= 45x - 30x - 240 = 15x - 240$$

For break even point, we put $P(x) = 0$

$$P(x) = 0 \Rightarrow 15x - 240 = 0$$
$$\Rightarrow \quad 15x = 240 \Rightarrow x = \frac{240}{15} = 16$$

Since, the break even point is 16.

Therefore, the manufacturer will begin to earn profit, if he sells more than 16 pens.

4. (d) We know that, marginal cost is interpreted as the approximate cost of one additional unit of output.

$\therefore$ MC (201) will represent the approximate additional cost to produce 201st toy.

5. On substituting $x = 24$ into MR $(x) = 408 - 17x$,

We have, MR $(24) = 408 - 17 \times 24 = 408 - 408 = 0$

If more than 24 units will be produced, then the marginal revenue will be negative and manufacturer will face loss. So, the manufacturer should limit the production to 24 units.

6. On substituting $x = 100$ into the revenue function

$$R(x) = 4x^3 + \frac{1}{5}x^2 + x, \text{ we get}$$
$$R(100) = 4 \times (100)^3 + \frac{1}{5}(100)^2 + 100$$
$$= 4000000 + 2000 + 100$$
$$= 4002100$$

So, ideal unit price = average revenue

$$= \frac{4002100}{100}$$
$$= ₹\ 40021$$

Hence, Vishwanath should charge 40021 rupees for each laptop.

7. (a) Given, $p(x) = 1500 - 2x - x^2$

$$\therefore \quad R(x) = p(x) \cdot x \Rightarrow R(x) = 1500x - 2x^2 - x^3$$

$\therefore$ Marginal revenue (MR) $= \dfrac{dR}{dx} = 1500 - 4x - 3x^2$

$$\left(\frac{dR}{dx}\right)_{x=10} = 1500 - 4(10) - 3(10)^2$$
$$= 1500 - 40 - 300$$
$$= 1160$$

8. Given, fixed cost = ₹ 30000

Variable cost = ₹ 800 per unit

$\therefore$ Cost function, $C(x) = 800x + 30000$

and Demand function, $p(x) = 4500 - 100x$

$\therefore$ Revenue function, $R(x) = p(x) \cdot x$

$$= (4500 - 100x)\,x$$
$$= 4500x - 100x^2$$

Concept Enhancer The break-even point is that point, where the total revenue equals to total cost incurred $R(x) = C(x)$.

For break-even point,

$$R(x) = C(x)$$
$$\Rightarrow \quad 4500x - 100x^2 = 800x + 30000$$
$$\Rightarrow \quad 100x^2 - 3700x + 30000 = 0$$
$$\Rightarrow \quad x^2 - 37x + 300 = 0$$
$$\Rightarrow \quad x^2 - 25x - 12x + 300 = 0$$
$$\Rightarrow \quad (x - 25)(x - 12) = 0$$
$$\Rightarrow \quad x = 25, 12$$

Break-even values = 25, 12

9. Given, $C(x) = 3x^2 - 6x + 5$

$\therefore$ Average cost (AC) $= \dfrac{C(x)}{x} = \dfrac{3x^2 - 6x + 5}{x} = 3x - 6 + \dfrac{5}{x}$

Average cost at $x = 2$ is

$$3(2) - 6 + \frac{5}{2} = 6 - 6 + \frac{5}{2} = \frac{5}{2}$$

10. (c) We know that the break-even point at which total revenue is equal to total cost

$$R(x) = C(x)$$

11. Given, AR $(x) = a + \dfrac{b}{x}$ ...(i)

$$\Rightarrow \quad \frac{dR}{dx} = a + \frac{b}{x}$$
$$\Rightarrow \quad dR = \left(a + \frac{b}{x}\right)dx$$

On integerating both sides, we get

$$\int dR = \int \left(a + \frac{b}{x}\right)dx$$
$$\therefore \quad R = ax + b\log x + C \quad \text{...(ii)}$$

When $R = 0$ and $x = 0$

$$0 = a \times 0 + b\log 0 + C$$
$$\Rightarrow \quad C = 0$$
$$R = ax + b\log x \quad \text{[from Eq. (ii)]}$$

12. Given, $R(x)=36x+3x^2+5$

Actual revenue received on selling 50th item

$$=R(50)-R(49)$$
$$=(36\times 50+3(50)^2+5)-(36\times 49+3(49)^2+5)$$
$$=(1800+7500+5)-(1764+7203+5)$$
$$=9305-8972=333$$

13. (a) Given, selling price of product = ₹ 20 per unit

Fixed cost = ₹ 45000

and variable cost is estimated to run 25% of total revenue.

Revenue function $(R)=px=20x$

Cost function (C) = Fixed cost + variable cost

$$\therefore \quad C=45000+\frac{25}{100}R$$
$$=45000+\frac{1}{4}(20x)$$
$$=45000+5x$$

14. (a) Given, $p=4000-100x$

Total revenue $=px=4000x-100x^2$

At $x=3$,

Total revenue $=4000(3)-100(3)^2$

$$=12000-900$$
$$=11100$$

15. (b) Given, a company sells x packets of biscuits each day at ₹ 10 per packet.

Manufacturing cost of one packet = ₹ 5

Total fixed cost = ₹ 700

$\therefore$ Revenue function, $R(x)=10(x)$ ...(i)

Cost function $C(x)$ = Variable cost + Fixed cost

$\therefore \quad C(x)=700+5(x)$ ...(ii)

We know that profit function $P(x)=R(x)-C(x)$

On substituting the values of $R(x)$ and $C(x)$ from Eqs. (i) and (ii) respectively, we have

$$P(x)=10x-(700+5x)$$
$$=10x-700-5x$$
$$=5x-700$$

16. (c) Given, cost function, $x=3x^2-2x+6$

We know that, average cost (AC) $=\frac{C}{x}$,

where C is cost function.

and x = Number of commodities.

$$\therefore \quad AC=\frac{3x^2-2x+6}{x} \quad \text{...(i)}$$

On substituting $x=3$ into Eq. (i), we have

$$AC=\frac{3(3)^2-2(3)+6}{3}$$
$$=\frac{27-6+6}{3}=9$$

17. (c) Given that, $x=100-4p$

So, $p=25-\frac{x}{4}$

Here, $R=p\times x=\left(25-\frac{x}{4}\right)x=25x-\frac{x^2}{4}$

Now, $\text{MR}=\frac{dR}{dx}$

$$\Rightarrow \quad 0=\frac{d}{dx}\left(25x-\frac{x^2}{4}\right)$$
$$\Rightarrow \quad 0=25-\frac{2x}{4}$$
$$\Rightarrow \quad 0=25-\frac{x}{2}$$
$$\Rightarrow \quad \frac{x}{2}=25 \Rightarrow x=50$$

18. Given that, $C(x)=\frac{x^3}{3}+5x^2-16x+2$

Now, $\text{MC}=\frac{d}{dx}\{C(x)\}$

$$=\frac{d}{dx}\left\{\frac{x^3}{3}+5x^2-16x+2\right\}$$
$$=\frac{3x^2}{3}+10x-16=x^2+10x-16$$

19. Given that, $R(x)=3x^3+8x-2$

So, Average revenue function $(p)=\frac{R(x)}{x}$

$$=\frac{3x^3+8x-2}{x}$$
$$=3x^2+8-\frac{2}{x}$$

20. Given, average cost function is

$$AC=x+5+\frac{36}{x}$$

(i) We know that

$$\text{Average cost}=\frac{\text{Total cost}}{x}$$
$$\Rightarrow \quad AC=\frac{C(x)}{x}$$

$$\Rightarrow x+5+\frac{36}{x}=\frac{C(x)}{x}$$

$$\Rightarrow \quad C(x)=x\left(x+5+\frac{36}{x}\right)$$

$$=x^2+5x+36$$

Thus, the total cost function is $x^2+5x+36$.

(ii) Since, $AC=x+5+\frac{36}{x}$

$$\frac{d}{dx}(AC)=\frac{d}{dx}\left(x+5+\frac{36}{x}\right)$$

$$=1+0-\frac{36}{x^2}$$

$$=1-\frac{36}{x^2}$$

For AC to be increasing,

$$\frac{d}{dx}(AC)>0$$

$$\Rightarrow \quad 1-\frac{36}{x^2}>0$$

$$\Rightarrow \quad x^2-36>0$$

$$\Rightarrow \quad (x-6)(x+6)>0$$

$$\Rightarrow \quad x<-6, x>6$$

Hence, the average cost function increases, if the value of $x>6$ i.e. $(6, \infty)$

21. Given monopolist's demand function is

$$x=60-\frac{p}{5}$$

$$\Rightarrow \quad 5x=300-p$$

$$\Rightarrow \quad p=300-5x$$

Thus, the revenue function = Profit function × x

$$\Rightarrow \quad R(x)=p\times x$$

$$=(300-5x)x=300x-5x^2$$

Now, marginal revenue $=\frac{dR}{dx}$

$$=\frac{d}{dx}[300x-5x^2]$$

$$=300-10x$$

Then, the marginal revenue = 0

$$\Rightarrow \quad 300-10x=0$$

$$\Rightarrow \quad 10x=300$$

$$\Rightarrow \quad x=30$$

Thus, at output level $x=30$, the marginal revenue would be zero.

22. The increased daily cost of production for 1000 spare parts $=C(1000)=\frac{99}{2}\times 1000+525$

$$=99\times 500+525$$

$$=49500+525=₹\,50025$$

Now,the company must have to sell ₹ 50025 of spare parts more daily at ₹ 50 per unit to ensure no loss.

∴ The required numbers of spares parts to be sold

$$=\frac{50025}{50}=1000.5$$

Hence, atleast 1001 more spare parts must be sold by the company to ensure no loss.

23. Given, $P(x)=-8x^3+29400x-60000$

$$\therefore \quad \frac{d(P(x))}{dx}=-24x^2+29400$$

For profit to be maximum, put $\frac{d(P(x))}{dx}=0$

$$\therefore \quad -24x^2+29400=0 \Rightarrow 24x^2-29400=0$$

$$\Rightarrow \quad x^2=\frac{29400}{24}$$

$$\Rightarrow \quad x^2=1225 \Rightarrow x=\pm 35$$

Now, $\frac{d^2(P(x))}{dx^2}=\frac{d(-24x^2+29400)}{dx}=-48x$

At $x=-35$, $\frac{d^2p}{dx^2}=(-48)\times(-35)=1680>0$

At $x=35$, $\frac{d^2P}{dx^2}=-48\times 35=-1680<0$

Hence, at $x=35$, the profit will be maximum.

24. Given, $C(x)=\sqrt{6x+5}+2500$

∴ Marginal cost (MC) $=\frac{dC}{dx}$

$$=\frac{3}{\sqrt{6x+5}}=6(6x+5)^{-\frac{1}{2}}$$

Now, $\frac{d(MC)}{dx}=-\frac{3}{2}(6x+5)^{\frac{-1}{2}-1}\times 6$

$$=-9(6x+5)^{-3/2}$$

$$=\frac{-9}{(6x+5)^{3/2}}<0,$$

for all positive values of x.

Hence, the marginal cost falls continuously as the output increases.

25. Given, average revenue function $(AR) = 25 - \frac{x}{4}$

$\therefore$ Revenue function $R(x) = (AR)(x)$

$$\Rightarrow \quad R(x) = \left(25 - \frac{x}{4}\right)x$$

$$= 25x - \frac{x^2}{4}$$

$\therefore$ Marginal revenue $(MR) = \frac{dR}{dx} = 25 - \frac{2x}{4}$

$$= 25 - \frac{x}{2}$$

26. Given, total revenue function,

$$R(x) = x + 2x^3 - 3.5x^2$$

$$\therefore \quad MR = \frac{d}{dx}(R(x)) = \frac{d}{dx}(x + 2x^3 - 3.5x^2)$$

$$\Rightarrow MR = 1 + 6x^2 - 7x$$

Put $MR = 0$

$$\Rightarrow \quad 1 + 6x^2 - 7x = 0$$

$$\Rightarrow \quad 6x^2 - 7x + 1 = 0 \Rightarrow 6x^2 - 6x - x + 1 = 0$$

$$\Rightarrow 6x(x-1) - 1(x-1) = 0 \Rightarrow (x-1)(6x-1) = 0$$

$$\Rightarrow \quad x - 1 = 0 \text{ or } 6x - 1 = 0$$

$$\Rightarrow \quad x = 1 \text{ or } \frac{1}{6}$$

Hence, marginal revenue curve cuts the coordinate axis at $x = 1, \frac{1}{6}$.

Concept Enhancer Marginal revenue is the rate of change of total revenue with respect to quantity sold

$$MR = \frac{dR}{dx} = \frac{d}{dx}(px)$$

27. Given, revenue function,

$$R(x) = \frac{bx}{a+x}$$

$\therefore$ Marginal revenue,

$$(MR) = \frac{dR(x)}{dx} = \frac{d}{dx}\left(\frac{bx}{a+x}\right)$$

$$= \frac{(a+x)\frac{d}{dx}(bx) - bx\frac{d}{dx}(a+x)}{(a+x)^2}$$

$$= \frac{(a+x)\cdot b - bx \cdot 1}{(a+x)^2} = \frac{ab}{(a+x)^2}$$

$$\Rightarrow \quad MR = ab(a+x)^{-2}$$

To show that MR is increasing we will show that

$$\frac{d}{dx}(MR) = \frac{-2ab}{(a+x)^3}$$

Since, $b < 0$ and $a > 0$, so ab is –ve and so $-2ab$ is +ve.

Also, $(a+x)^3$ is positive, since a and x both are positive.

Thus, the expression $-2ab$ is '+ ve' for all values of a, b.

Common Mistake When $b < 0$ and $a > 0$, then always ab will be negative and if $(a + x)^3$ is positive the assume always a and x both are positive.

28. We have, $C(x) = \frac{3}{4}x^2 - 7x + 27$

Now, marginal cost $= \frac{d}{dx}\left(\frac{3}{4}x^2 - 7x + 27\right)$

$$= \frac{3}{4} \times 2x - 7 = \frac{3}{2}x - 7$$

and average cost $= \dfrac{\frac{3}{4}x^2 - 7x + 27}{x}$

$$= \frac{3}{4}x - 7 + \frac{27}{x}$$

According to the given condition,

Marginal Cost = Average Cost

$$\frac{3}{2}x - 7 = \frac{3}{4}x - 7 + \frac{27}{x}$$

$$\Rightarrow \quad \frac{3}{2}x - \frac{3}{4}x = \frac{27}{x}$$

$$\Rightarrow \quad \frac{3}{4}x = \frac{27}{x}$$

$$\Rightarrow \quad x^2 = \frac{27 \times 4}{3}$$

$$\Rightarrow \quad x^2 = 9 \times 4$$

$$\Rightarrow \quad x = 3 \times 2 \quad [\because x \text{ cannot be negative}]$$

$$\Rightarrow \quad x = 6$$

29. We have, price of commodity = ₹ 60

$$R(x) = px = 60x$$

$$C(x) = 35x + 250$$

(i) Profit function $P(x) = R(x) - C(x)$

$$\Rightarrow \quad P(x) = 60x - 35x - 250 = 25x - 250$$

(ii) At break-even point,

$$R(x) = C(x)$$

$$\therefore \quad 60x = 35x + 250$$

$$\Rightarrow \quad 25x = 250 \Rightarrow x = 10$$

Hence, the break-even points at $x = 10$

30. Given, $R(x)=100x-x^2-x^3$

(i) Demand function, $p=\dfrac{R(x)}{x}$

$$=\frac{100x-x^2-x^3}{x}=100-x-x^2$$

(ii) Marginal revenue function (MR) $=\dfrac{d(R(x))}{dx}$

$$=\frac{d(100x-x^2-x^3)}{dx}$$

$$=100-2x-3x^2$$

31. Given, fixed cost of the commodity = ₹ 24000

Let the number of units produced by company be x and p be the price per unit.

Then, total revenue $R=xp=$ ₹ $8x$

Since, the variable cost is 25% of the total revenue.

Thus, variable cost = 25% of $8x$

$$=\frac{25}{100}\times 8x=\frac{1}{4}\times 8x=₹\,2x$$

Total cost $C(x)$ = Fixed cost of the commodity + Variable cost of the commodity

$$=24000+2x$$

For break-even point, $R(x)=C(x)$

$\Rightarrow\quad 8x=24000+2x$ $\quad[\because R(x)=8x \text{ and } C(x)=24000+2x]$

$\Rightarrow\quad 8x-2x=24000$

$\Rightarrow\quad 6x=24000$

$\therefore\quad x=\dfrac{24000}{6}=4000$

Hence, the break-even point is 4000.

32. Given, $C(x)=\dfrac{1}{3}x^3+3x^2-16x+2$

(i) Marginal Cost (MC) $=\dfrac{dC}{dx}$

$\therefore\quad \text{MC}=\dfrac{d}{dx}\left(\dfrac{1}{3}x^3+3x^2-16x+2\right)$

$$\text{MC}=x^2+6x-16$$

(ii) Average Cost (AC) $=\dfrac{C}{x}$

$$\text{AC}=\frac{\frac{1}{3}x^3+3x^2-16x+2}{x}$$

$\Rightarrow\quad \text{AC}=\dfrac{x^2}{3}+3x-16+\dfrac{2}{x}$

33. Given, Average cost $AC=2x-11+\dfrac{50}{x}$

On differentiating w.r.t. x, we get

$$\frac{d}{dx}(AC)=2-\frac{50}{x^2}$$

For average cost is increasing

$$\frac{d}{dx}(AC)>0$$

$\therefore\quad 2-\dfrac{50}{x^2}>0$

$\Rightarrow\quad 2x^2-50>0$ $\quad[\because x^2>0]$

$\Rightarrow\quad x^2>25$

$\Rightarrow\quad x>5$

Hence, the average cost increase, if the output $x>5$.

34. We have, $\text{MC}=0.003x^2-0.01x+2.5$

$$C(x)=\int \text{MC}\,dx$$

Now, cost of increasing from 100 to 200 units is

$$\int_{100}^{200}(0.003x^2-0.01x+2.5)dx$$

$$=\left[\frac{0.003x^3}{3}-\frac{0.01x^2}{2}+2.5x\right]_{100}^{200}$$

$$=0.001(8000000-1000000)$$

$$-\frac{0.01}{2}(40000-10000)+2.5(200-100)$$

$$=7000-150+250$$

$$=7100$$

35. We have, total variable cost $=3x+\dfrac{x^5}{25}$

Average variable cost $=\dfrac{\text{TVC}}{x}$

$\therefore\quad \text{AVC}=\dfrac{3x+\frac{x^5}{25}}{x}$

$\Rightarrow\quad \text{AVC}=3+\dfrac{x^4}{25}$

On differentiating w.r.t. x, we get

$$\frac{d\,(\text{AVC})}{dx}=\frac{4x^3}{25}\geq 0,\ \forall x$$

Hence, AVC increases with output x.

36. Given, $C(x)=\dfrac{1}{3}x^3-5x^2+30x-15$

$$R(x)=px$$

$\therefore\quad R(x)=6x$ $\quad[\because p=6]$

Profit function

$$P(x)=R(x)-C(x)$$

$$P(x)=6x-\frac{1}{3}x^3+5x^2-30x+15$$

$$P(x)=-\frac{1}{3}x^3+5x^2-24x+15$$

$$\frac{dP(x)}{dx}=-x^2+10x-24$$

For maxima or minima $\frac{dP(x)}{dx}=0$

$\Rightarrow \quad -x^2+10x-24=0$

$\Rightarrow \quad x^2-10x+24=0$

$\Rightarrow \quad (x-6)(x-4)=0$

$\Rightarrow \quad x=6, 4$

$\Rightarrow \quad \frac{d^2P(x)}{dx^2}=-2x+10$

$\Rightarrow \quad \left(\frac{d^2P(x)}{dx^2}\right)_{x=6}=-12+10=-2<0$

and $\quad \left(\frac{d^2P(x)}{dx^2}\right)_{x=4}=-8+10=2>0$

Hence, profit is maximum when $x=6$

37. Given, cost function is

$$C(x)=\frac{x^3}{3}-45x^2-900x+36$$

$\therefore$ Marginal Cost, $\text{MC}=\frac{dC}{dx}$

$$=\frac{d}{dx}\left(\frac{x^3}{3}-45x^2-900x+36\right)$$

$$=\frac{3x^2}{3}-90x-900$$

$\Rightarrow \quad \text{MC}=x^2-90x-900 \quad \ldots\text{(i)}$

On differentiating Eq. (i) w.r.t. x, we get

$$\frac{d(\text{MC})}{dx}=2x-90 \text{ and } \frac{d^2(\text{MC})}{dx^2}=2$$

For minimum marginal cost, put $\frac{d(\text{MC})}{dx}=0$

$\Rightarrow \quad 2x-90=0 \Rightarrow x=45$

At $x=45$, $\frac{d^2(\text{MC})}{dx^2}=2>0$

Hence, it produce 45 units, to minimise the marginal cost.

Concept Enhancer Marginal cost $=\frac{d}{dx}$(cost function)

$$\text{MC}=\frac{d}{dx}C(x)$$

For minimum marginal cost, $\frac{d}{dx}(\text{MC})=0$

38. Given, total cost $C(x)=\frac{x^2}{100}+100x+40$

Price of each unit can be sold $P=200-\frac{x}{400}$

Price of x unit sold $R(x)=P(x)=200x-\frac{x^2}{400}$

Profit, $P(x)=R(x)-C(x)$

$$=200x-\frac{x^2}{400}-\frac{x^2}{100}-100x-40$$

$\Rightarrow \quad P(x)=-\frac{x^2}{80}+100x-40$

On differentiating w.r.t. x, we get

$$P'(x)=-\frac{2x}{80}+100=-\frac{x}{40}+100$$

For maxima or minima put $P'(x)=0$

$\Rightarrow \quad -\frac{x}{40}+100=0 \Rightarrow x=4000$

Now, $\quad P''(x)=-\frac{1}{40}<0$

Hence, $P(x)$ is maximum when $x=4000$.

Total profit at $x=4000$,

$$P(4000)=\frac{-(4000)^2}{80}+100(4000)-40$$

$$=-200000+400000-40=199960$$

Total profit = ₹ 199960

Concept Enhancer Profit function $P(x)$

= Revenue function − Cost function

$$P(x)=R(x)-C(x)$$

For maxima and minima, $P'(x)=0$

39. Given, demand function $x=\frac{600-P}{8} \Rightarrow P=600-8x$

Revenue function $R(x)=Px$

$$=(600-8x)x=600x-8x^2$$

Also, we have cost function $C(x)=x^2+78x+2500$

Now, profit function $P(x)=R(x)-C(x)$

$\Rightarrow \quad P(x)=600x-8x^2-x^2-78x-2500$

$\Rightarrow \quad P(x)=-9x^2+522x-2500$

On differentiating w.r.t. x, we get

$$P'(x) = -18x + 522$$

For maxima or minima put $P'(x) = 0$

$$-18x + 522 = 0$$

$$x = \frac{522}{18} = 29$$

and $\quad P''(x) = -18 < 0$

$\therefore$ Profit is maximum when $x = 29$

40. We have, fixed cost = ₹ 35000

Variable cost per cent = ₹ 500

Total cost of x units = Fixed cost + Total variable cost of x unit

$$\therefore \quad TC = 35000 + 500x$$

Also, we have demand function, $p = 5000 - 100x$

$\therefore$ Revenue function $R(x) = px$

$$R(x) = (5000 - 100x)x$$

$$\Rightarrow \quad R(x) = 5000x - 100x^2$$

Profit function $P(x) = R(x) - TC$

$$P(x) = 5000x - 100x^2 - 35000 - 500x$$

$$P(x) = -100x^2 + 4500x - 35000$$

At break-even value,

$$P(x) = 0$$

$$\Rightarrow \quad -100x^2 + 4500x - 35000 = 0$$

$$\Rightarrow \quad x^2 - 45x + 350 = 0 \quad \text{[divide by } -100\text{]}$$

$$\Rightarrow \quad (x - 35)(x - 10) = 0$$

$$\Rightarrow \quad x = 35, 10$$

Hence, the break-even values are $x = 35$ and $x = 10$.

41. Given, demand function is $p = ax^2 + bx + c$, where x is the number of units demanded and p is the price per unit.

(i) (a) We know that revenue function $R = p \cdot x$, where p is the price per unit and x is the number of units.

$$\therefore \; R(x) = (ax^2 + bx + c)x$$

$$= ax^3 + bx^2 + cx$$

(ii) (b) We know that, marginal revenue (MR) $= \dfrac{dR(x)}{dx}$

$$\therefore \; \text{MR}(x) = \frac{d(ax^3 + bx^2 + cx)}{dx} = 3ax^2 + 2bx + c$$

(iii) (b) We know that

Slope of marginal revenue (MR) $= \dfrac{d(\text{MR})}{dx}$

$$\therefore \; \frac{d(\text{MR})}{dx} = \frac{d(3ax^2 + 2bx + c)}{dx} = 6ax + 2b$$

(iv) (a) For increasing marginal revenue, $\dfrac{d(\text{MR})}{dx} > 0$

$$\therefore \quad 6ax + 2b > 0$$

$$\Rightarrow \quad 6ax > -2b$$

$$\Rightarrow \quad x > \frac{-2b}{6a} \Rightarrow x > \frac{-b}{3a}$$

42. Given, $p = 500 + 25x - \dfrac{x^2}{3}$

Clearly, total revenue

$$R(x) = px = \left(500 + 25x - \frac{x^2}{3}\right)x$$

$$= 500x + 25x^2 - \frac{x^3}{3}$$

(i) We know that,

Marginal revenue $= \dfrac{dR(x)}{dx} = 500 + 50x - x^2$

(ii) Marginal revenue at $x = 10$, is given by

$$\left.\frac{dR}{dx}\right|_{x=10} = 500 + 50(10) - (10)^2$$

$$= 500 + 500 - 100 = 900$$

43. (i) Given, demand function, $x = \dfrac{24 - 2p}{3}$

Revenue function, $R(p)$

= Demand function × Per unit price

$$= \frac{24 - 2p}{3} \times p = \frac{(24 - 2p)p}{3}$$

(ii) For revenue to be maximum, put

$$\frac{dR(p)}{dp} = 0$$

$$\therefore \quad \frac{d}{dp}\left[\frac{(24 - 2p)p}{3}\right] = 0$$

$$\Rightarrow \quad \frac{d}{dp}\left[\frac{24p - 2p^2}{3}\right] = 0$$

$$\Rightarrow \quad \frac{1}{3}(24 - 4p) = 0$$

$$\Rightarrow \quad p = 6$$

Now, $\dfrac{d^2R}{dp^2} = -\dfrac{4}{3} < 0$

$\therefore$ Revenue is maximum when $p =$ ₹ 6.

Hence, number of units demanded for maximum revenue is

$$x = \frac{24 - 2 \times 6}{3} = \frac{12}{3} = 4 \text{ units}$$

44. Given, the average cost function of the commodity is

$$(\text{AC}) = x + 5 + \frac{36}{x}$$

We know that,

$$\text{Average cost (AC)} = \frac{\text{Cost function}}{x}$$

$$\Rightarrow \quad C = x\,(\text{AC})$$

$$\Rightarrow \quad C = x\left(x + 5 + \frac{36}{x}\right)$$

$$\Rightarrow \quad C = x^2 + 5x + 36$$

(i) Marginal Cost function

$$(\text{MC}) = \frac{dC}{dx} = \frac{d}{dx}(x^2 + 5x + 36)$$

$$\Rightarrow \quad \text{MC} = 2x + 5$$

(ii) Condition for increasing of AC,

$$\frac{d}{dx}(\text{AC}) > 0$$

$$\Rightarrow \quad \frac{d}{dx}\left(x + 5 + \frac{36}{x}\right) > 0 \Rightarrow 1 - \frac{36}{x^2} > 0$$

$$\Rightarrow \quad \frac{x^2 - 36}{x^2} > 0$$

$$\Rightarrow \quad (x^2 - 6^2) > 0 \Rightarrow (x+6)(x-6) > 0$$

$$[\because a^2 - b^2 = (a+b)(a-b)]$$

$$\therefore \quad x < -6 \text{ or } x > 6$$

So, the average cost of the commodity increases, when the output $x > 6$.

45. Given, cost function, $C = \dfrac{x^3}{3} - 7x^2 + 111x + 50$

and demand function, $x = 100 - P$

We know that,

(i) Revenue function, $R = xP$

From equation of demand function,

$$x = 100 - P$$

$$\therefore \quad P = 100 - x$$

Now, we put the value of $P = 100 - x$ in equation of revenue function, we get

$$R = x(100 - x) \Rightarrow R = 100x - x^2$$

(ii) Also, profit function

$$P(x) = \text{Revenue} - \text{Cost}$$

$$= 100x - x^2 - \left(\frac{x^3}{3} - 7x^2 + 111x + 50\right)$$

$$= 100x - x^2 - \frac{x^3}{3} + 7x^2 - 111x - 50$$

$$= \frac{-x^3}{3} + 7x^2 - x^2 - 111x + 100x - 50$$

$$= \frac{-x^3}{3} + 6x^2 - 11x - 50$$

Hence, profit function,

$$P(x) = \frac{-x^3}{3} + 6x^2 - 11x - 50$$

(iii) For the profit maximising level of output x, $\dfrac{dP}{dx} = 0$

$$\therefore \quad \frac{d(P)}{d(x)} = 0$$

$$\Rightarrow \quad \frac{d}{dx}\left(\frac{-x^3}{3} + 6x^2 - 11x - 50\right) = 0$$

$$\Rightarrow \quad \frac{-3x^2}{3} + 2 \times 6x - 11 = 0$$

$$\Rightarrow \quad -x^2 + 12x - 11 = 0$$

$$\Rightarrow \quad -(x^2 - 12x + 11) = 0$$

$$\Rightarrow \quad x^2 - 12x + 11 = 0$$

$$\Rightarrow \quad x^2 - 11x - x + 11 = 0$$

$$\Rightarrow \quad x(x - 11) - 1(x - 11) = 0$$

$$\Rightarrow \quad (x-1)(x-11) = 0$$

$$\Rightarrow \quad x - 1 = 0 \text{ and } x - 11 = 0$$

$$\therefore \quad x = 1 \text{ and } x = 11$$

Now, $$\frac{d^2P}{dx^2} = \frac{d}{dx}\left(\frac{dP}{dx}\right)$$

$$\Rightarrow \quad \frac{d^2P}{dx^2} = \frac{d}{dx}(-x^2 + 12x - 11)$$

$$\Rightarrow \quad \frac{d^2P}{dx^2} = -2x + 12$$

At $x = 1$, $$\frac{d^2P}{dx^2} = -2 \times 1 + 12$$

$$= -2 + 12 = 10 > 0$$

At $x = 11$, $$\frac{d^2P}{dx^2} = -2 \times 11 + 12$$

$$= -22 + 12 = -10 < 0$$

At $x = 11$, the profit will be maximum.

CHAPTER TEST

2 Marks Questions

1. The fixed cost of a new product is ₹ 30000 and the variable cost per unit is ₹ 800. If the demand function is $P(x) = 4500 - 100x$, then find the break-even values.

2. The total cost $C(x)$ of a company is given as $C(x) = 1000 + 25x + 2x^2$, where x is the output. Determine
(i) average cost.
(ii) marginal cost.
(iii) marginal cost when $x = 15$.

3. The demand function for a product is given as $P = 30 + 2x - 5x^2$, where x is the number of units demanded and P is the price per unit. Find
(i) total revenue.
(ii) marginal revenue.
(iii) MR when $x = 3$.

4. The demand function for a product is given by $P = \frac{5}{x+3}$. Show that the marginal revenue function is a decreasing function.

5. The marginal revenue function for a firm is given by $\text{MR} = \frac{2}{x+3} - \frac{2x}{(x+3)^2} + 5$. Show that the demand function is $P = \frac{2}{x+3} + 5$.

3/4 Marks Questions

6. The average cost function (AC) for a product is given by $\text{AC} = x + 5 + \frac{36}{x}$, where x is the output. Find the output for which AC is increasing and the output for which AC is decreasing with increasing output. Also find the total cost C and the marginal cost MC.

7. The demand function for a product marketed by a company is $p = \frac{80 - x}{4}$, where x is the number of units and p is the price per unit. At what value of x will there be maximum revenue? What is the maximum revenue?

8. A firm has found from past experience that its profit in terms of number of units x produced, is given by $P(x) = -\frac{x^3}{3} + 729x + 2700, 0 \le x \le 35$.
Compute
(i) the value of x that maximises the profit.
(ii) the profit per unit of the product, when this maximum level is achieved.

5/6 Marks Questions

9. A company produced a commodity with ₹ 20000 fixed costs. The variable cost estimated to 35% of the total revenue when it is sold at a rate of ₹ 6 per unit. Find the total revenue, total cost and profit function of revenue when it is sold.

10. A manufacturer can sell x items of commodity at price of ₹ $(330 - x)$ each. Find the revenue function. If the cost of producing x items is ₹ $(x^2 + 10x + 12)$, determine the profit function.

11. A company has fixed cost of ₹ 10000 and cost of producing one unit of its product is ₹ 50. If each unit sells for ₹ 75, then find the break-even point, also find the value of x for which the company result in profit.

12. A profit making company wants to launch a new product. It observes that the fixed cost of the new product is ₹ 35000 and the variable cost per unit is ₹ 500. The revenue received on the sale of x units is given by $5000x - 100x^2$. Find
(i) profit function. (ii) break-even points.

13. Given, the total cost function for x units of a commodity as $C(x) = \frac{1}{3}x^3 + x^2 - 15x + 3$. Find
(i) marginal cost function.
(ii) average cost function.

14. The cost function $C(x)$ of a firm is given by $C(x) = 3x^2 - 6x + 5$. Find
(i) the average cost.
(ii) the marginal cost when $x = 2$.

15. The total revenue received from the sale of x units of a product is given by $R(x) = 20x - 0.5x^2$. Find
(i) the average revenue.
(ii) the marginal revenue.
(iii) the average revenue and marginal revenue at $x \ne 0$.

16. Suppose the demand per month for a commodity is 24, if the price is ₹ 16 and 12, if the price is ₹ 22. Assuming that the demand curve is linear.

Determine

(i) the demand function.

(ii) the total revenue function.

(iii) the marginal revenue function.

17. In a factory it is found that the number of units (x) produced in a day depends upon the number of workers (n) and is obtained by the relation $x = 5n/\sqrt{n+5}$. The demand function of the product is $P = 2/x + x$.

Determine the marginal revenue when $n = 20$.

Answers

1. 12 units, 25 units

2. (i) $\frac{1000}{x} + 25 + 2x$ (ii) $25 + 4x$ (iii) 85

3. (i) $30x + 2x^2 - 5x^3$ (ii) $30 + 4x - 15x^2$ (iii) 177

6. $x > 6, 0 < x < 6, x^2 + 5x + 36, 2x + 5$

7. 40; 400

8. (i) 27 (ii) ₹ 586

9. $R(x) = 6x, C(x) = 20000 + \frac{21x}{10}, P(x) = \frac{39x}{10} - 20000$

10. $R(x) = 330x - x^2,\ P(x) = 320x - 12 - 2x^2$

11. Break-even point, 400 units

12. (i) $P(x) = 4500x - 100x^2 - 35000$ (ii) Breakeven points = 10 and 35

13. (i) $\text{MC}(x) = x^2 + 2x - 15$ (ii) $\text{AC}(x) = \frac{1}{3}x^2 + x - 15 + \frac{3}{x}$

14. (i) $\text{AC}_{\text{at } x=2} = 2.5$ (ii) $\text{MC}_{\text{at } x=2} = 6$

15. (i) $\text{AR}(x) = 20 - 0.5x$ (ii) $\text{MR}(x) = 20 - x$ (iii) $\text{AR}_{\text{at } x=100} = 15, \text{MR}_{\text{at } x=10} = 10$

16. (i) Demand function $f(x) = 56 - 2x$ (ii) Revenue $(x) = 56x - 2x^2$ (iii) $\text{MR} = 56 - 4x$

17. $\text{MR}_{\text{at } n=20} = 40$

14 Linear Regression

TREND ANALYSIS 3 YEARS

TOPIC 01 Linear Regression

Average No. of Questions Across all Sets

Types of Questions	2024	2023	2020
1 Mark	2	2	—
2 Marks	—	—	1
3/4 Marks	2	2	2
5/6 Marks	—	—	—

Linear Regression

It helps to estimate or predict the unknown value of one variable from the known value of the other value of the related variables called regression.

Line of Regression

A line of regression is the straight line which gives the best fit in the least square sense to the given sets of data.

Scatter Diagram

It is a technique for visually examining the form of relationship, without calculating any numerical value. To construct a scatter diagram, x variable is taken on X-axis and y variable is taken on Y-axis. The cluster of points, plotted is referred to as a scatter diagram.

e.g. Let us draw a scatter diagram for observations,

(2, 8), (3, 7), (4, 6), (5, 5), (6, 4), (7, 3), (8, 2)

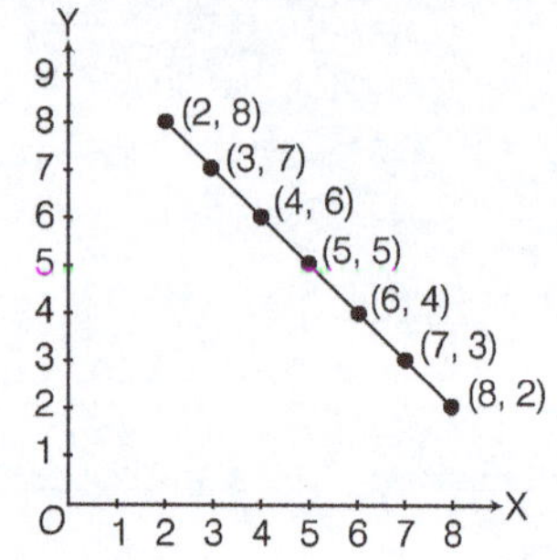

Curve Fitting

If data $(x_1, y_1), (x_2, y_2), \ldots, (x_n, y_n)$ is plotted on a scatter diagram and then visualise a smooth curve which is approximating the data is called curve fitting. The main purpose of curve fitting is to estimate one of the variable from the other. It is shown in the following diagram.

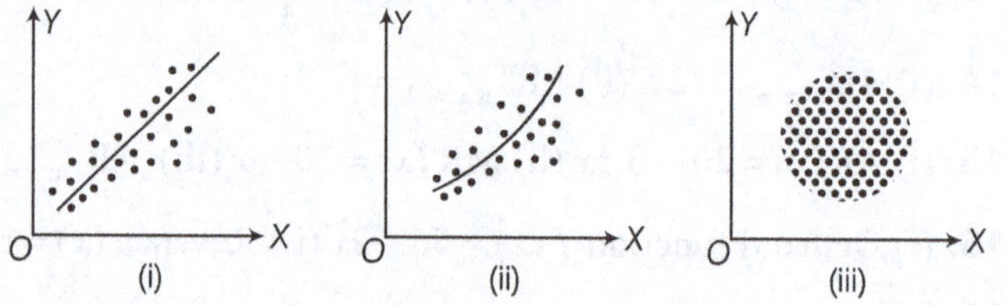

In above diagram the function $y = f(x)$ is called regression function. Also, the best fitting line is called **regression line** of y on x.

Least Squares Method

Under this method a regression line is fitted through different points in such a way that the sum of squares of the deviations of the observed value from the fitted line shall be least. The line drawn by this method is called **line of best fit**.

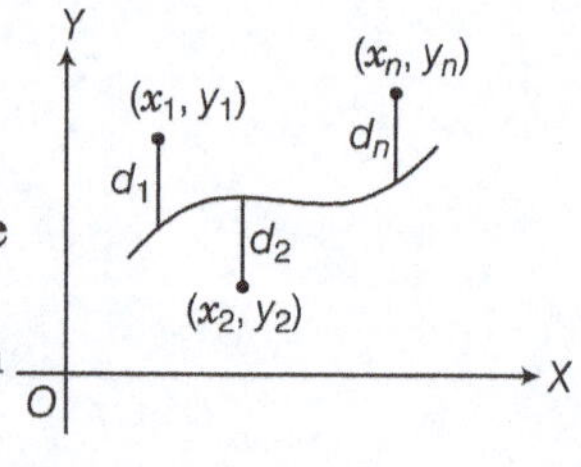

In the following diagram, clearly all the curves approximately a given set of data point, where $d_1^2 + d_2^2 + \ldots + d_n^2$ is minimum and it is best fitting curve. It is estimating correctly (very least error) on average.

Regression Coefficient For Two Variables x and y

There are two regression coefficients.

(i) **Regression Coefficient of y on x** It is a unit change in the value of x variable and the average change in the value of y variable. Thus, it is represented by b_{yx}.

$$\therefore \quad b_{yx} = r \cdot \frac{\sigma_y}{\sigma_x} = \frac{\Sigma xy - \dfrac{\Sigma x \cdot \Sigma y}{n}}{\Sigma x^2 - \dfrac{(\Sigma x)^2}{n}},$$

where r represents correlation coefficient.

The value of b_{yx} can also be found out by other formulae.

(ii) **Regression Coefficient of x on y** It is a unit change in the value of y-variable, and the average change in the value of x-variable. It is represented by b_{xy}.

$$\therefore \quad b_{xy} = r \cdot \frac{\sigma_x}{\sigma_y} = \frac{\Sigma xy - \dfrac{\Sigma x \cdot \Sigma y}{n}}{\Sigma y^2 - \dfrac{(\Sigma y)^2}{n}},$$

where r represents correlation coefficient.

The value of b_{xy} can also be found out by other formulae.

Relation between regression coefficients of y on x and x on y

$$b_{xy} \times b_{yx} = r^2, 0 \le b_{xy} \times b_{yx} \le 1$$

and r is known as correlation coefficient.

NOTE Correlation studies and measures the direction and intensities of relationship between two variables in which change in the value of one variable, are associated with changes in the value of the other variable.

Types of Correlation

(i) **Positive Correlation** When two related variables move together in the same direction, it is said to be positive correlation.

(ii) **Negative Correlation** When two variables move in the opposite direction, it is said to be negative correlation.

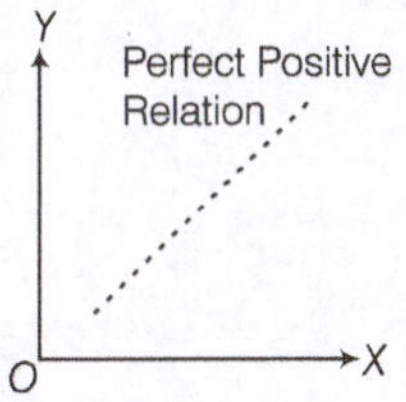

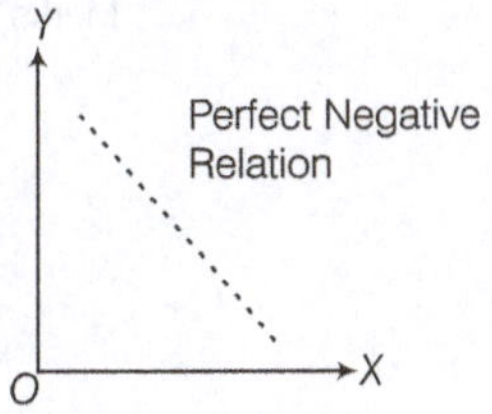

Regression Equation (Equation of line of Regression)

Regression equations are the algebraic formulation of regression lines. Regression equations represent regression lines.

Lines of regression can be fixed in following ways.

(i) **Lines of regression Equation of y on x** This equation is used to estimate the probable values of y on the basis of the given values of x.

i.e. $\quad y = a + bx$

where, a and b are constants.

Line of regression of y on x can also be written as

or $\quad y - \bar{y} = b_{yx}(x - \bar{x}) \quad \left[\text{where, } \bar{x} = \dfrac{\Sigma x}{n}, \bar{y} = \dfrac{\Sigma y}{n}\right]$

where, b_{yx} = Regression coefficient of y on x.

(ii) **Lines of regression Equation of x on y.** This equation is used to estimate the probable values of x on the basis of the given values of y.

i.e. $\quad x = a_0 + b_0 y$

where, a_0 and b_0 are constants.

Line of regression of x on y can also be written as

or $\quad x - \bar{x} = b_{xy}(y - \bar{y}) \quad \left[\text{where, } \bar{x} = \dfrac{\Sigma x}{n}, \bar{y} = \dfrac{\Sigma y}{n}\right]$

where, b_{xy} = Regression coefficient of x on y.

Identification of Regression Equations

Suppose two equations $a_1 x + b_1 y + c_1 = 0$ and $a_2 x + b_2 y + c_2 = 0$ are given and we have to identify the regression line of y on x or x on y, we use the following steps

Step I First, we consider any one of the equations say first, i.e. $a_1 x + b_1 y + c_1 = 0$ as y on x and other equation say second, i.e. $a_2 x + b_2 y + c_2 = 0$ as x on y.

Step II Adjust the first equation y on x such that y should be on left side with coefficient 1 and rest of the terms be on right side (i.e. $y = -\dfrac{a_1}{b_1}x - \dfrac{c_1}{b_1}$). The coefficient of x will considered as regression coefficient y on x, i.e. $b_{yx} = \dfrac{-a_1}{b_1}$.

Similarly, for another equation x on y, adjust equation like as $x = -\frac{b_2}{a_2}y - \frac{c_2}{a_2}$. The coefficient of y will give regression coefficient of x on y

i.e. $b_{xy} = \frac{-b_2}{a_2}$

Step III If b_{xy} and b_{yx} are not of same sign, then we do not determine the regression line. If they have the same sign, then determine coefficient by using the formula.

$$r = \sqrt{b_{yx} \times b_{xy}}, 0 \le b_{yx} \times b_{xy} \le 1$$

Step IV If the value of r lies from 0 to 1, then our consideration is true, otherwise we have to change the considering equations.

Properties of Regression Coefficient and Lines of Regression

(i) **Coefficient of correlation** is the geometric mean of the regression coefficients,

i.e. $r = \sqrt{b_{xy} \times b_{yx}}$

(ii) Both the regression coefficients must have the same algebraic signs.

(iii) The **coefficient of correlation** will have the same sign as that of regression coefficients.

(iv) Both the regression coefficients cannot be greater than unity.

(v) Arithmetic mean of two regression coefficients is either equal to or greater than the **correlation coefficient**

i.e. $\frac{b_{yx} + b_{xy}}{2} \ge r$

(vi) The two regression lines coincide if and only if there is perfect linear relation between X and Y.

i.e. $\rho(X, Y) = \pm 1$

(vii) The intersection point of two regression lines is $(\bar{X}, \bar{Y})$.

PYQs Previous Years Questions

1 Mark Questions

1. If the correlation coefficient of two sets of variables (X, Y) is $\frac{-3}{4}$, which one of the following statements is true for the same set of variables? *ISC 2024*

(a) Only one of the two regression lines has a negative coefficient.

(b) Both regression coefficients are positive.

(c) Both regression coefficients are negative.

(d) One of the lines of regression is parallel to the X-axis.

2. The equations of two lines of regression are $4x + 3y + 7 = 0$ and $3x + 4y + 8 = 0$. Find the mean value of x and y. *ISC 2024*

3. At FNG High School, teachers plotted students' scores in Science and Social Studies with respect to their scores in Maths and English, from their 10th grade final examination.

The graphs plotted by the teachers are shown below

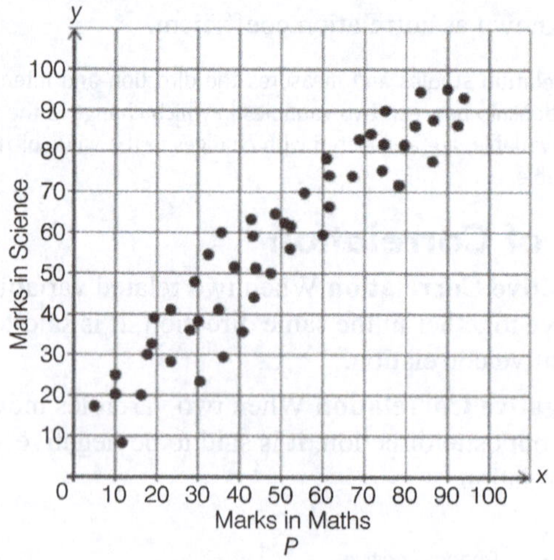

P

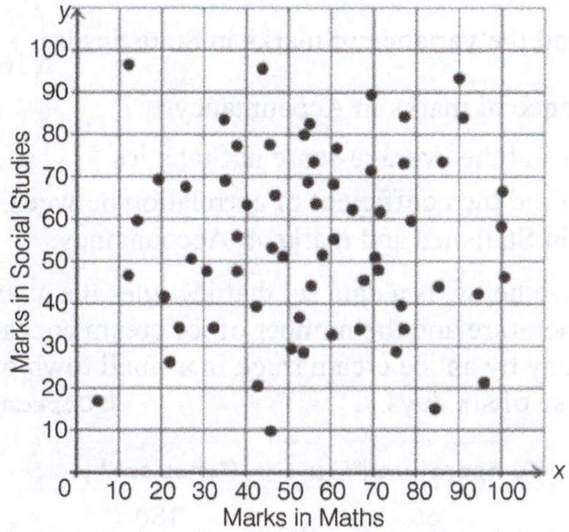

Q

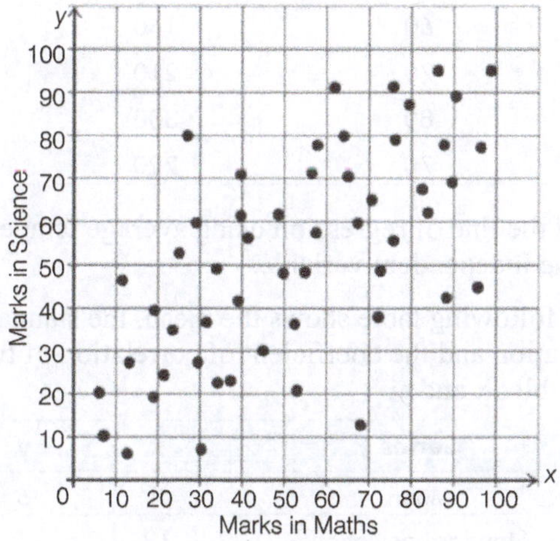

R

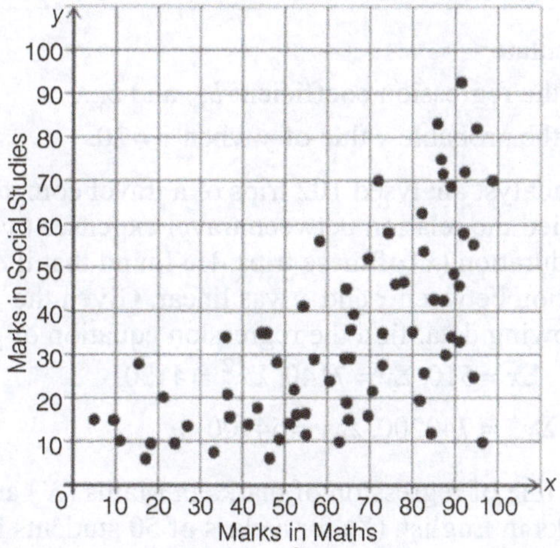

S

Which one of the given graphs could a line of best fit be drawn for? ***ISC Specimen 2024***

(a) Only *P* (b) Only *P* and *S*
(c) Only *P*, *R* and *S* (d) All *P*, *Q*, *R* and *S*

4. Given below are two regression lines for the same dataset. ***ISC Specimen 2024***

$$L_1 : 2x = 5y - 2$$
$$L_2 : 3y = 2x + 1$$

Identify the regression line of *x* on *y*.

5. If the two regression coefficients are 0.8 and 0.2, then the value of coefficients of correlation *r* will be ***ISC 2023***

(a) ± 0.4 (b) ± 0.16 (c) 0.4 (d) 0.16

6. Out of the two regression lines $x + 2y - 5 = 0$ and $2x + 3y = 8$, find the line of regression of *y* on *x*. ***ISC 2023***

7. If correlation coefficient $r = 0$, then regression lines are ***ISC Specimen 2023***

(a) parallel to each other
(b) not mutually perpendicular
(c) parallel to coordinate axis
(d) overlapping lines

8. For a given bivariant distribution, the mean of variable $x = 4$ and the mean of variable $y = 6$. Find the point of intersection of two regression lines. ***ISC Specimen 2023***

9. If the two regression coefficients b_{xy} and b_{yx} are -0.8 and -0.2 respectively, then the correlation coefficient (ρ) will be ***ISC Specimen Sem-II 2022***

(a) 0.16 (b) − 0.16 (c) 0.4 (d) − 0.4

10. The line of regression of *y* on *x* is, $4x - 5y + 33 = 0$ and the line of regression of *x* on *y* is, $20x - 9y - 107 = 0$, then the value of *x* when $y = 7$ is ***ISC Specimen Sem-II 2022***

(a) 8.5 (b) − 8.5 (c) 0.5 (d) − 0.5

11. If $\bar{x} = 40$, $\bar{y} = 6$, $\sigma_x = 10$, $\sigma_y = 1.5$ and $r = 0.9$ for the two sets of data *x* and *y*, then the regression line of *x* on *y* will be ***ISC Specimen Sem-II 2022***

(a) $x - 6y - 4 = 0$ (b) $x + 6y - 4 = 0$
(c) $x - 6y + 4 = 0$ (d) $x + 6y + 4 = 0$

12. If the regression line of *x* on *y* is, $9x + 3y - 46 = 0$ and *y* on *x* is, $3x + 12y - 7 = 0$, then the correlation coefficient *r* is equal to ***ISC Specimen Sem-II 2022***

(a) $\frac{-1}{12}$ (b) $\frac{1}{12}$ (c) $\frac{-1}{2\sqrt{3}}$ (d) $\frac{1}{2\sqrt{3}}$

13. If the lines of regression are parallel to coordinate axes, then the coefficient of correlation is ***ISC Specimen 2021***

(i) 1 (b) 0 (c) − 1 (d) $\frac{1}{2}$

14. If $\sigma_x = 3, \sigma_y = 4$ and $b_{xy} = \frac{1}{3}$, then find the value of correlation coefficient (r). **ISC Specimen 2021**

2 Marks Questions

15. The mean and standard deviation of the two variables x and y are given as $\bar{x} = 6, \bar{y} = 8, \sigma_x = 4$ and $\sigma_y = 12$. The correlation coefficient is given as $r = \frac{2}{3}$. Find the regression line of x on y. **ISC Specimen Sem-II 2022**

16. For 5 observation of pairs (x, y) of variables X and Y, the following results are obtained $\Sigma x = 15, \Sigma y = 25, \Sigma x^2 = 55, \Sigma y^2 = 135$ and $\Sigma xy = 83$. Calculate the value of b_{xy} and b_{yx}. **ISC Specimen Sem-II 2022**

17. For the lines of regression $4x - 2y = 4$ and $2x - 3y + 6 = 0$, find the mean of x and the mean of y. **ISC 2020**

18. If $\bar{x} = 18, \bar{y} = 100, \sigma_x = 14, \sigma_y = 20$ and correlation coefficient $r_{xy} = 0.8$, find the regression equation of y on x. **ISC 2019**

19. Find the coefficient of correlation from the regression lines $x - 2y + 3 = 0$ and $4x - 5y + 1 = 0$. **ISC 2018**

20. If two lines of regression are $4x + 2y - 3 = 0$ and $3x + 6y + 5 = 0$, find the correlation coefficient between x and y. **ISC 2018**

3/4 Marks Questions

21. *XYZ* company plans to advertise some vacancies. The Manager is asked to suggest the monthly salary for these vacancies based on the years of experience. To do so, the Manager studies the years of service and the monthly salary drawn by the existing employees in the company. **ISC 2024**

Following is the data that the Manager refers to

Years of service (X)	11	7	9	5	8	6	10
Monthly salary (in ₹ 1000) (Y)	10	8	6	5	9	7	11

(a) Find the regression equation of monthly salary on the years of service.

(b) If a person with 13 years of experience applies for a job in this company, what monthly salary will be suggested by the Manager?

22. The line of regression of marks in Statistics (X) and marks in Accountancy (Y) for a class of 50 students is $3y - 5x + 180 = 0$. The average score in Accountancy is 44 and the variance of marks in Statistics is $\left(\frac{9}{16}\right)$th of variance of marks in Accountancy. **ISC 2024**

(a) Find the average score in Statistics

(b) Find the coefficient of correlation between marks in Statistics and marks in Accountancy.

23. Shown below is a data set that includes the average temperature and the number of ice cream cones sold per day by an ice cream truck in a small town over the course of six days. **ISC Specimen 2024**

Temperature (°F) **x**	**Cones sold y**
65	180
75	250
60	160
70	210
80	300
70	220

Find the line of regression using average temperature as the independent variable.

24. The following table shows the mean, the standard deviation and the coefficient of correlation of two variables x and y. **ISC 2023**

Series	**x**	**y**
Mean	8	6
Standard deviation	12	4
Coefficient of correlation	0.6	

Calculate

(a) the regression coefficient b_{xy} and b_{yx}.

(b) the probable value of y when $x = 20$.

25. An analyst analysed 102 trips of a travel company. He studied the relation between travel expenses (y) and the duration (x) of these trips. He found that the relation between x and y was linear. Given the following data, find the regression equation of y on x.

$$\Sigma x = 510, \Sigma y = 7140, \Sigma x^2 = 4150,$$
$$\Sigma y^2 = 740200, \Sigma xy = 54900$$ **ISC 2023**

26. The line of regression of marks in Maths (X) and marks in English (Y) for a class of 50 students is $3y - 5x + 180 = 0$. The average score in English is 44 and variance of marks in Maths is $\frac{9}{16}$ th of the variance of marks in English. Find the average score in Maths. Also, find out the coefficient of correlation between marks in Maths and English. **ISC Specimen 2023**

27. Find the equation of the regression line of y on x, if the observations (x, y) are as follows
(1, 4), (2, 8), (3, 2) (4, 12), (5, 10), (6, 14),
(7, 16), (8, 6), (9, 18)
Also, find the estimated value of y when $x = 14$. *ISC Specimen 2021, ISC 2019*

28. The correlation coefficient between x and y is 0.6. If the variance of x is 225, the variance of y is 400, mean of x is 10 and mean of y is 20, find
(i) the equations of two regression lines.
(ii) the expected value of y when $x = 2$. *ISC 2020*

29. Find the regression coefficients b_{yx}, b_{xy} and correlation coefficient r for the following data (2, 8), (6, 8), (4, 5), (7, 6), (5, 2). *ISC 2020, ISC Specimen 2018*

30. The following results were obtained with respect to two variables x and y
$\Sigma x = 15, \Sigma y = 25, \Sigma xy = 83, \Sigma x^2 = 55,$
$\Sigma y^2 = 135$ and $n = 5$. *ISC 2019*
(i) Find the regression coefficient b_{xy}.
(ii) Find the regression equation of x on y.

31. Find the line of regression of y on x from the following table. *ISC 2018*

x	1	2	3	4	5
y	7	6	5	4	3

Hence, estimate the value of y when $x = 6$.

32. From the given data *ISC 2018*

Variable	x	y
Mean	6	8
Standard Deviation	4	6

and correlation coefficient $\frac{2}{3}$. Find
(i) regression coefficients b_{yx} and b_{xy}.
(ii) regression line x on y.
(iii) most likely value of x, when $y = 14$.

33. Given that the observations are
(9, – 4), (10, – 3), (11, – 1), (13, 1), (14, 3), (15, 5), (16, 8), find the two lines of regression. Estimate the value of y when $x = 13.5$. *ISC Specimen 2018*

34. By using the data $\bar{x} = 25$, $\bar{y} = 30$, $b_{yx} = 1.6$ and $b_{xy} = 0.4$, find
(i) the regression equation y on x.
(ii) what is the most likely value of y when $x = 60$?
(iii) what is the coefficient of correlation between x and y? *ISC 2017*

35. The two lines of regressions are $x + 2y - 5 = 0$ and $2x + 3y - 8 = 0$ and the variance of x is 12. Find the coefficient of correlation. *ISC 2016*

36. For the given lines of regression, $3x - 2y = 5$ and $x - 4y = 7$, find
(i) regression coefficients b_{yx} and b_{xy}.
(ii) coefficient of correlation $r(x, y)$. *ISC 2014*

KEY CONCEPT
(i) First, convert the given equations y on x and x on y in standard form and find their regression coefficients, respectively.
(ii) Further use the formula for coefficient of correlation, $r = \sqrt{b_{yx} \times b_{xy}}$ and taking '+' or '–' sign as outside the as per the sign of regression coefficients.

37. Two regression lines represented by $4x + 10y = 9$ and $6x + 3y = 4$. Then, find the line of regression of y on x. *ISC 2013*

KEY CONCEPT
(i) First, determine the intersection point of two lines say $(\bar{x}, \bar{y})$.
(ii) Second determine the regression coefficients of y on x from first equation
(iii) Further use the formula for line of regression on y on x i.e. $y - \bar{y} = b_{yx}(x - \bar{x})$.

5/6 Marks Questions

38. Find the line of best fit for the following data, treating x as dependent variable (Regression equation x on y).

x	14	12	13	14	16	10	13	12
y	14	23	17	24	18	25	23	24

Hence, estimate the value of x when $y = 16$. *ISC 2017*

39. The marks obtained by 10 candidates in English and Mathematics are given below:

Marks in English	20	13	18	21	11	12	17	14	19	15
Marks in Mathematics	17	12	23	25	14	8	19	21	22	19

Estimate the probable score for Mathematics, if the marks obtained in English are 24. *ISC 2016*

40. Given that the observations are

$(9, -4), (10, -3), (11, -1), (12, 0), (13, 1),$
$(14, 3), (15, 5), (16, 8).$

Find the two lines of regression and estimate the value of y, when $x = 13.5$. **ISC 2015**

41. The following results were obtained with respect to two variables x and y.

$$\Sigma x = 30, \Sigma y = 42, \Sigma xy = 199, \Sigma x^2 = 184,$$
$$\Sigma y^2 = 318 \text{ and } n = 6$$

Find the following :

(i) The regression coefficients.

(ii) Correlation coefficient between x and y.

(iii) Regression equation of y on x.

(iv) The likely value of y when $x = 10$. **ISC 2012**

Explanations

1. (c) The value of correlation coefficient r lies between -1 and 1 where, -1 indicates a perfect negative linear relationship and 1 indicates a perfect positive linear relationship. Since, the correlation coefficient of two sets of variables (X, Y) is $\frac{-3}{4}$, which is negative linear relationship between the variables X and Y.

Thus, both regression coefficients are negative.

2. Given two lines of regression are $4x + 3y + 7 = 0$ and $3x + 4y + 8 = 0$

Now, to find the mean value of x and y, we solve the system of equations formed by the two given lines of regression.

$$3x + 4y + 8 = 0 \quad \ldots\text{(i)}$$
$$4x + 3y + 7 = 0 \quad \ldots\text{(ii)}$$

On multiplying Eq. (i) by 4 and Eq. (ii) by 3, we get

$$12x + 16y + 32 = 0 \quad \ldots\text{(iii)}$$
$$12x + 9y + 21 = 0 \quad \ldots\text{(iv)}$$

Now, subtract Eq. (iv) from Eq. (iii), we get

$$x = \frac{-4}{7} \text{ and } y = \frac{-11}{7}$$

So, the mean value of x is $\frac{-4}{7}$ and the mean value of y is $\frac{-11}{7}$.

3. (a) A line of best fit is a straight line that minimises the distance between it and some data.

From the given graph it can be observed that only P could be a line best fit be drawn for.

4. We know that the regression line of x on y is represented by $x = a + by$ and it gives the most probable value of x for the given value of y.

Here, x is dependent and y is independent variable.

So, the line L_1 is the regression line of x on y.

5. (a) We know, $r^2 = b_{xy} \cdot b_{yx}$

$$\therefore \quad r^2 = 0.8 \times 0.2 = 0.16$$
$$\Rightarrow \quad r = \pm\sqrt{0.16} = \pm 0.4$$

6. Assuming $x + 2y - 5 = 0$ to be regression line of y on x

$$2y = -x + 5$$
$$\Rightarrow \quad y = -\frac{1}{2}x + \frac{5}{2}$$
$$\Rightarrow \quad b_{yx} = -\frac{1}{2}$$

Then, $2x + 3y = 8$ is regression line of x on y.

$$\therefore \quad 2x = -3y + 8$$
$$\Rightarrow \quad x = \frac{-3}{2}y + \frac{8}{2}$$
$$\Rightarrow \quad b_{xy} = \frac{-3}{2}$$

Now, $b_{yx} \cdot b_{xy} = \left(-\frac{1}{2}\right)\left(\frac{-3}{2}\right) = \frac{3}{4} < 1$

$\therefore$ Regression line of y on x is $x + 2y - 5 = 0$.

7. (c) If the correlation coefficient $r_{xy} = 0$, then the lines of regression are parallel to the coordinate axes.

8. Given, the mean of variable $x = 4$

i.e. $\bar{x} = 4$ and mean of variable $y = 6$

i.e. $\bar{y} = 6$

We know that point of intersection of two regression line $= (\bar{x}, \bar{y})$ i.e. $(4, 6)$.

9. (d) Given that $b_{xy} = -0.8$ and $b_{yx} = -0.2$

We know that

$$r = \pm\sqrt{b_{yx} \cdot b_{xy}}$$
$$\Rightarrow \quad r = \pm\sqrt{-0.8 \times -0.2}$$
$$= \pm\sqrt{0.16}$$
$$\Rightarrow \quad r = -0.4$$

10. (a) Consider equation

$$20x - 9y - 107 = 0$$

$$20x = 9y + 107$$

$$\Rightarrow \quad x = \frac{9y+107}{20}$$

$$\Rightarrow \quad x = \frac{9\times 7+107}{20}$$

$$= \frac{170}{20} = \frac{17}{2} = 8.5$$

11. (a) Given, $\bar{x} = 40, \bar{y} = 6, \sigma_x = 10, \sigma_y = 1.5$ and $r = 0.9$

$$\therefore \quad b_{xy} = r\frac{\sigma_x}{\sigma_y} = \frac{0.9\times 10}{1.5} = 6$$

$\therefore$ Regression line of x on y is

$$x - \bar{x} = b_{xy}(y - \bar{y})$$

$$\Rightarrow \quad x - 40 = 6(y-6)$$

$$\Rightarrow \quad x - 40 = 6y - 36$$

$$\Rightarrow \quad x - 6y - 4 = 0$$

12. (c) Given, regression line of x on y is

$$9x + 3y - 46 = 0$$

$$\Rightarrow \quad x = \frac{-3}{9}y + \frac{46}{9}$$

$$\therefore \quad b_{xy} = \frac{-3}{9} = \frac{-1}{3}$$

and the regression line of y on x is $3x + 12y - 7 = 0$

$$\Rightarrow \quad y = \frac{-3}{12}x + \frac{7}{12}$$

$$\therefore \quad b_{yx} = \frac{3}{12} = \frac{1}{4}$$

$\therefore$ Correlation coefficient $r = -\sqrt{b_{yx}\times b_{xy}}$

$$= -\sqrt{\left(\frac{-1}{4}\right)\times\left(\frac{-1}{3}\right)}$$

$$= -\sqrt{\frac{1}{12}} = -\frac{1}{2\sqrt{3}}$$

13. (b) If the lines of regression are parallel to coordinate axes, then r_{xy} will be zero.

14. Given that $b_{xy} = \frac{1}{3}$, $\sigma_x = 3$ and $\sigma_y = 4$

$$\text{Now,} \quad b_{xy} = r\times\frac{\sigma_x}{\sigma_y} \Rightarrow \frac{1}{3} = r\times\frac{3}{4}$$

$$\Rightarrow \quad r = \frac{1}{3}\times\frac{4}{3} \Rightarrow r = \frac{4}{9}$$

15. Given, $\bar{x} = 6$, $\bar{y} = 8$, $r = \frac{2}{3}$, $\sigma_x = 4$, $\sigma_y = 12$

Regression line x on y is

$$x - \bar{x} = b_{xy}(y - \bar{y})$$

$$x - 6 = b_{xy}(y-8)$$

$$\text{Now,} \quad b_{xy} = r.\frac{\sigma_x}{\sigma_y} = \frac{2}{3}\times\frac{4}{12} = \frac{2}{9}$$

$$\Rightarrow \quad (x-6) = \frac{2}{9}(y-8)$$

$$\Rightarrow \quad 9x - 54 = 2y - 16$$

$$\Rightarrow \quad 9x - 2y = -16 + 54$$

$$\Rightarrow \quad 9x - 2y = 38$$

16. Given for 5 observation,

$$\Sigma x = 15, \Sigma y = 25, \Sigma x^2 = 55, \Sigma y^2 = 135,$$

$$\Sigma xy = 83 \text{ and } n = 5$$

$$\therefore \quad \bar{x} = \frac{\Sigma x}{n} = \frac{15}{5} = 3, \; \bar{y} = \frac{\Sigma y}{n} = \frac{25}{5} = 5$$

$$\text{Now, } b_{xy} = \frac{\Sigma xy - \frac{\Sigma x\cdot\Sigma y}{n}}{\Sigma y^2 - \frac{(\Sigma y)^2}{n}} = \frac{83 - \frac{1}{5}(15)(25)}{135 - \frac{1}{5}(25)^2}$$

$$= \frac{83-75}{135-125} = \frac{8}{10} = 0.8$$

$$\text{Now, } b_{yx} = \frac{\Sigma xy - \frac{1}{n}\Sigma x\cdot\Sigma y}{\Sigma x^2 - \frac{1}{n}(\Sigma x)^2}$$

$$= \frac{83 - \frac{1}{5}(15)(25)}{55 - \frac{1}{5}(15)^2}$$

$$= \frac{83-75}{55-45} = \frac{8}{10} = 0.8$$

17. Given, lines of regression are

$$4x - 2y = 4$$

$$\text{and} \quad 2x - 3y + 6 = 0$$

We know that $(\bar{x}, \bar{y})$ is common point of two regression lines.

Solving the equation $4x - 2y = 4$ and $2x - 3y + 6 = 0$, we get

$$x = 3, \; y = 4$$

$\therefore$ Mean of $x\,(\bar{x}) = 3$ and mean of $y\,(\bar{y}) = 4$

18. Given, $\bar{x}=18, \bar{y}=100, \sigma_x=14, \sigma_y=20$ and $r_{xy}=0.8$

Now, regression equation of y on x is

$$(y-\bar{y})=r\frac{\sigma_y}{\sigma_x}(x-\bar{x})$$

$$\therefore \quad y-100=0.8\times\frac{20}{14}(x-18)$$

$$\Rightarrow \quad y-100=\frac{8}{7}(x-18)$$

$$\Rightarrow \quad 7y-700=8x-144 \Rightarrow 7y=8x+556$$

19. Given, regression line $x-2y+3=0$

$$\Rightarrow \quad y=\frac{1}{2}x+\frac{3}{2}$$

Regression coefficient of y on x is $b_{yx}=\frac{1}{2}$

and $\quad 4x-5y+1=0 \Rightarrow x=\frac{5}{4}y-\frac{1}{4}$

Regression coefficient of x on y is $b_{xy}=\frac{5}{4}$.

$\therefore$ Coefficient of correlation

$$r=\sqrt{b_{yx}\cdot b_{xy}}=\sqrt{\frac{1}{2}\times\frac{5}{4}}=\sqrt{\frac{5}{8}}=0.791$$

20. Given lines of regression are

$$4x+2y-3=0$$

$$\Rightarrow \quad x=\frac{-1}{2}y+\frac{3}{4}$$

$\therefore$ Regression coefficients, $b_{xy}=\frac{-1}{2}$

and $\quad 3x+6y+5=0 \Rightarrow y=\frac{-1}{2}x-\frac{5}{6}$

$\therefore$ Regression coefficients, $b_{yx}=-\frac{1}{2}$

Coefficient of correlation $(r)=-\sqrt{b_{xy}b_{yx}}$

[$\because$ both regression coefficients are negative, so we take '–' sign for correlation coefficient]

$$r=-\sqrt{\frac{-1}{2}\times\frac{-1}{2}} \Rightarrow r=-\frac{1}{2}$$

21. (a) The given data is

Years of service (X)	11	7	9	5	8	6	10
Monthly salary (in ₹ 1000) (Y)	10	8	6	5	9	7	11

Sum of $X=56$

Sum of $Y=56$

So, Mean $(X)=\frac{\Sigma X}{n}=\frac{56}{7}=8=M_X$

and Mean $(Y)=\frac{\Sigma Y}{n}=\frac{56}{7}=8=M_Y$

X	Y	$X-M_x$	$Y-M_Y$	$(X-M_x)^2$	$(X-M_x)(Y-M_Y)$
11	10	3	+2	9	6
7	8	−1	0	1	0
9	6	1	−2	1	−2
5	5	−3	−3	9	9
8	9	0	1	0	0
6	7	−2	−1	4	2
10	11	2	3	4	6

Thus, using the above table,

Sum of squares, $SS_x=\Sigma(X-M_x)^2=28$

Sum of products, $SP=\Sigma(X-M_x)(Y-M_y)=21$

$$\therefore \quad b=\frac{SP}{SS_x}=\frac{21}{28}=0.75$$

and $a=M_y-bM_x=8-0.75\times8=2$

Since, regression equation $\hat{y}=bX+a$

$\therefore \quad \hat{y}=0.75X+2$

(b) Using part (a) $\hat{y}=0.75X+2$

Since, $X=13$

Thus, $\quad \hat{y}=0.75\times13+2=11.75$

$\therefore$ If a person with 13 years of experience applies for a job in the company, then the monthly salary will be suggested by the manager is ₹ 11750.

22. Given, $n=50$, $X=$ Marks in Statistics,

$Y=$ Marks in Accountancy

Regression equation of X on Y is

$$3y-5x+180=0$$

$$\bar{y}=44, \sigma_X^2=\frac{9}{14}\sigma_Y^2$$

(a) Since, regression equation is

$$3y-5x+180=0$$

$$\Rightarrow \quad 5x=3y+180$$

$$\Rightarrow \quad x=\frac{3}{5}y+36$$

On comparing it with $x=b_{XY}y+a$, we get

$$b_{XY}=\frac{3}{5}, a=36$$

So, $\quad a=\bar{x}-b_{XY}\bar{y}$

$$\Rightarrow \quad 36=\bar{x}-\frac{3}{5}\times44$$

$$\Rightarrow \quad \bar{x}=62.4$$

Thus, $\bar{x}=$ Average score in Statistics $=62.4$

(b) Since, $\sigma_X^2 = \frac{9}{16}\sigma_Y^2$

$$\Rightarrow \frac{\sigma_X^2}{\sigma_Y^2} = \frac{9}{16} \Rightarrow \frac{\sigma_X}{\sigma_Y} = \frac{3}{4}$$

and we know that

$$b_{XY} = r \times \frac{\sigma_X}{\sigma_Y}$$

$$\Rightarrow \frac{3}{5} = r \times \frac{3}{4} \Rightarrow r = \frac{4}{5} = 0.8$$

Thus, the correlation coefficient (r) between marks in Statistics and Accountancy is 0.8.

23. Let us construct the table

Temperature (°F) x	Cones sold y	x^2	xy
65	180	4225	11700
75	250	5625	18750
60	160	3600	9600
70	210	4900	14700
80	300	6400	24000
70	220	4900	15400
$\Sigma x = 420$	$\Sigma y = 1320$	$\Sigma x^2 =$ 29650	$\Sigma xy =$ 94150

Here, $\bar{x} = \frac{\Sigma x}{n} = \frac{420}{6} = 70$ and $\bar{y} = \frac{\Sigma y}{n} = \frac{1320}{6} = 220$

Regression coefficient of y on x,

i.e. $$b_{yx} = \frac{\Sigma xy - \frac{\Sigma x \cdot \Sigma y}{n}}{\Sigma x^2 - \frac{(\Sigma x)^2}{n}}$$

$$\Rightarrow b_{yx} = \frac{94150 - \frac{420 \cdot 1320}{6}}{29650 - \frac{176400}{6}} = \frac{94150 - 92400}{29650 - 29400}$$

$$\Rightarrow b_{yx} = \frac{1750}{250} = 7$$

Equation of line of regression of y on x is

$$y - \bar{y} = b_{yx}(x - \bar{x})$$
$$\Rightarrow y - 220 = 7(x - 70)$$
$$\Rightarrow y - 220 = 7x - 490$$
$$\Rightarrow y = 7x - 270$$

24. (a) Given, $\bar{x} = 8, \bar{y} = 6, \sigma_x = 12, \sigma_y = 4$ and $r = 0.6$

$$\therefore b_{yx} = r \cdot \frac{\sigma_y}{\sigma_x} = 0.6 \times \frac{4}{12} = 0.2$$

$$\therefore b_{xy} = r \cdot \frac{\sigma_x}{\sigma_y} = 0.6 \times \frac{12}{4} = 1.8$$

(b) Regression equation of y on x is

$$y - \bar{y} = b_{yx}(x - \bar{x})$$
$$\Rightarrow y - 6 = 0.2(x - 8)$$
$$\Rightarrow y = 0.2x - 1.6 + 6$$
$$\Rightarrow y = 0.2x + 4.4$$

Putting $x = 20$, we get

$$y = 0.2\,(20) + 4.4 = 4 + 4.4 = 8.4$$

25. Given, $\Sigma x = 510, \Sigma y = 7140, \Sigma x^2 = 4150,$

$\Sigma y^2 = 740200, \Sigma xy = 54900$ and $n = 102$

We know, $\bar{x} = \frac{\Sigma x}{n} = \frac{510}{102} = 5$

and $\bar{y} = \frac{\Sigma y}{n} = \frac{7140}{102} = 70$

$$\therefore b_{yx} = \frac{\Sigma xy - \frac{1}{n}\Sigma x \Sigma y}{\Sigma x^2 - \frac{1}{n}(\Sigma x)^2}$$

$$= \frac{54900 - \frac{1}{102} \times 510 \times 7140}{4150 - \frac{1}{102}(510)^2}$$

$$= \frac{54900 - 35700}{4150 - 2550} = \frac{19200}{1600} = 12$$

$\therefore$ Regression equation of y on x is

$$y - \bar{y} = b_{yx}(x - \bar{x})$$
$$\Rightarrow y - 70 = 12(x - 5)$$
$$\Rightarrow y - 70 = 12x - 60$$
$$\Rightarrow 12x - y + 10 = 0$$

26. Given, $h = 50$

Regression line of x on y is

$$3y - 5x + 180 = 0 \quad \text{...(i)}$$
$$\Rightarrow 5x = 3y + 180$$
$$\Rightarrow x = \frac{3}{5}y + \frac{180}{5}$$

$\therefore b_{xy} =$ coefficient of $y = \frac{3}{5}$

Let variance of marks in Maths $= \sigma_{x^2}$

and variance of marks in English $= \sigma_{y^2}$

From given condition, we have

$$\sigma_{x^2} = \frac{9}{16}\sigma_{y^2} \Rightarrow \frac{\sigma_{x^2}}{\sigma_{y^2}} = \frac{9}{16} \Rightarrow \frac{\sigma_x}{\sigma_y} = \frac{3}{4}$$

We have, $b_{xy} = r \cdot \frac{\sigma_x}{\sigma_y} \Rightarrow \frac{3}{5} = r \times \frac{3}{4} \Rightarrow r = \frac{4}{5}$

Given, $\bar{y} = 44$

On substituting $y = 44$ in Eq. (i), we get

$\Rightarrow \quad 3(44) - 5x + 180 = 0$

$\Rightarrow \quad 132 - 5x + 180 = 0$

$\Rightarrow \quad 5x = 180 + 132 \Rightarrow x = \frac{312}{5} = 62.4$

$\therefore \quad \bar{x} = 62.4$

$\therefore$ Mean marks in Maths, $\bar{x} = 62.4$

27. Let us construct the following table for given data

x	y	x^2	y^2	xy
1	4	1	16	4
2	8	4	64	16
3	2	9	4	6
4	12	16	144	48
5	10	25	100	50
6	14	36	196	84
7	16	49	256	112
8	6	64	36	48
9	18	81	324	162
$\Sigma x = 45$	$\Sigma y = 90$	$\Sigma x^2 = 285$	$\Sigma y^2 = 1140$	$\Sigma xy = 530$

Here, $n = 9$

$\therefore \quad \bar{x} = \frac{\Sigma x}{n} = \frac{45}{9} = 5$ and $\bar{y} = \frac{\Sigma y}{y} = \frac{90}{9} = 10$

$\therefore$ Regression coefficient of y on x is

$$b_{yx} = \frac{\Sigma xy - \frac{1}{n}\Sigma x\, \Sigma y}{\Sigma x^2 - \frac{1}{n}(\Sigma x)^2}$$

$$= \frac{530 - \frac{1}{9} \times 45 \times 90}{285 - \frac{1}{9} \times (45)^2}$$

$$= \frac{530 - 450}{285 - 225} = \frac{80}{60} = \frac{4}{3}$$

Now, regression equation of y on x is

$$(y - \bar{y}) = b_{yx}(x - \bar{x})$$

$\because \quad y - 10 = \frac{4}{3}(x - 5) \Rightarrow 4x - 3y + 10 = 0$

Now, estimated value of y when $x = 14$ is

$4 \times 14 - 3y + 10 = 0$

$\Rightarrow \quad 3y = 56 + 10$

$\Rightarrow \quad y = \frac{66}{3}$

$\Rightarrow \quad y = 22$

28. Given, $\quad r = \sqrt{b_{xy}\, b_{yx}} = 0.6$

$(\sigma_x)^2 = 225, (\sigma_y)^2 = 400$

$\bar{x} = 10, \bar{y} = 20$

We know that $b_{xy} = r.\frac{\sigma_x}{\sigma_y}$

$$b_{xy} = 0.6\frac{\sqrt{225}}{\sqrt{400}}$$

$$= \frac{0.6 \times 15}{20} = \frac{9}{20}$$

and $\quad b_{yx} = r.\frac{\sigma_y}{\sigma_x}$

$$b_{yx} = 0.6 \times \frac{20}{15} = \frac{12}{15} = \frac{4}{5}$$

(i) Given, $r = 0.6$, $(\sigma_x)^2 = 225$, $(\sigma_y)^2 = 400$

$\bar{x} = 10$ and $\bar{y} = 20$

Now, $b_{xy} = r\frac{\sigma_x}{\sigma_y} = 0.6 \times \frac{15}{20} = \frac{9}{20}$

The equation of regression line of x on y is

$$x - \bar{x} = b_{xy}(y - \bar{y})$$

$\Rightarrow \quad x - 10 = \frac{9}{20}(y - 20)$

$\Rightarrow \quad 20x - 200 = 9y - 180$

$\Rightarrow \quad 20x - 9y = 20$

$\Rightarrow \quad x = \frac{9y}{20} + 1$

The equation of regression line of y on x is

$$y - \bar{y} = b_{yx}(x - \bar{x})$$

$\Rightarrow \quad y - 20 = \frac{4}{5}(x - 10)$

$\Rightarrow \quad 5y - 100 = 4x - 40$

$\Rightarrow \quad 5y - 4x = 60$

$\Rightarrow \quad y = \frac{4}{5}x + 12$

(ii) The expected value of y when $x = 2$

Equation of regression line of y on x is

$$y = \frac{4}{5}x + 12$$

Putting $x = 2$, we get

$$y = \frac{4}{5}(2) + 12$$

$\Rightarrow \quad y = 1.6 + 12$

$= 13.6$

29. Given, data (2, 8), (6, 8), (4, 5), (7, 6) (5, 2)

We construct the following table

x	y	x^2	y^2	xy
2	8	4	64	16
6	8	36	64	48
4	5	16	25	20
7	6	49	36	42
5	2	25	4	10
$\Sigma x = 24$	$\Sigma y = 29$	$\Sigma x^2 = 130$	$\Sigma y^2 = 193$	$\Sigma xy = 136$

$$b_{yx} = \frac{\Sigma xy - \frac{1}{n}\Sigma x \Sigma y}{\Sigma x^2 - \frac{1}{n}(\Sigma x)^2}$$

$$= \frac{136 - \frac{1}{5} \times 24 \times 29}{130 - \frac{1}{5}(24)^2}$$

$$= \frac{136 - 139.2}{130 - 115.2} = \frac{-3.2}{14.8} = \frac{-8}{37}$$

$$b_{xy} = \frac{\Sigma xy - \frac{1}{n}\Sigma x \Sigma y}{\Sigma y^2 - \frac{1}{n}(\Sigma y)^2}$$

$$= \frac{136 - \frac{1}{5}(24)(29)}{193 - \frac{1}{5}(29)^2} = \frac{136 - 139.2}{193 - 168.2} = \frac{-3.2}{24.8} = \frac{-4}{31}$$

$$r = \sqrt{b_{yx} \times b_{xy}}$$

$$= -\sqrt{\frac{8}{37} \times \frac{-4}{31}} = -\sqrt{\frac{32}{1147}} = -0.167$$

[∵ both regression coefficients are negative, so we take negative sign outside the root]

30. We have, $\Sigma x = 15, \Sigma y = 25, \Sigma xy = 83,$

$\Sigma x^2 = 55, \Sigma y^2 = 135$ and $n = 5$

(i) Regression coefficient,

$$b_{xy} = \frac{\Sigma xy - \frac{1}{n}\Sigma x \Sigma y}{\Sigma y^2 - \frac{1}{n}(\Sigma y)^2}$$

$$= \frac{83 - \frac{1}{5}(15) \times (25)}{135 - \frac{1}{5}(25)^2}$$

$$= \frac{83 - 75}{135 - 125} = \frac{8}{10} = \frac{4}{5}$$

(ii) Now, regression equation of x on y is

$$x - \bar{x} = b_{xy}(y - \bar{y})$$

$$\Rightarrow \quad x - \frac{\Sigma x}{n} = \frac{4}{5}\left(y - \frac{\Sigma y}{n}\right)$$

$$\Rightarrow \quad x - \frac{15}{5} = \frac{4}{5}\left(y - \frac{25}{5}\right)$$

$$\Rightarrow \quad x - 3 = \frac{4}{5}(y - 5)$$

$$\Rightarrow \quad 5x - 15 = 4y - 20$$

$$\Rightarrow \quad 5x - 4y = -5$$

31. Given data (1, 7), (2, 6), (3, 5), (4, 4), (5, 3)

Now, we construct the following table

x	y	x^2	xy
1	7	1	7
2	6	4	12
3	5	9	15
4	4	16	16
5	3	25	15
$\Sigma x = 15$	$\Sigma y = 25$	$\Sigma x^2 = 55$	$\Sigma xy = 65$

Here, $\bar{x} = \frac{\Sigma x}{n} = \frac{15}{5} = 3$ and $\bar{y} = \frac{\Sigma y}{n} = \frac{25}{5} = 5$

Regression coefficient of y on x

$$\text{i.e. } b_{yx} = \frac{\Sigma xy - \frac{\Sigma x \cdot \Sigma y}{n}}{\Sigma x^2 - \frac{(\Sigma x)^2}{n}}$$

$$\Rightarrow \quad b_{yx} = \frac{65 - \frac{15 \times 25}{5}}{55 - \frac{(15)^2}{5}}$$

$$= \frac{65 - 75}{55 - 45} = \frac{-10}{10} = -1$$

Equation of line of regression of y on x is

$$y - \bar{y} = b_{yx}(x - \bar{x})$$

$$\Rightarrow \quad y - 5 = -1(x - 3)$$

$$\Rightarrow \quad x + y - 8 = 0 \qquad \ldots\text{(i)}$$

On substituting $x = 6$ into Eq. (i), we get

$$6 + y - 8 = 0$$

$$\Rightarrow \quad y = 8 - 6 = 2$$

32. Given data is

Variable	x	y
Mean	6	8
Standard Deviation	4	6

and $r=\frac{2}{3}$

(i) Regression coefficient

$$b_{yx}=r\frac{\sigma_y}{\sigma_x}=\frac{2}{3}\left(\frac{6}{4}\right) \quad [\because \sigma_y=6, \sigma_x=4]$$

$$b_{yx}=1$$

and $b_{xy}=r\frac{\sigma_x}{\sigma_y}=\frac{2}{3}\left(\frac{4}{6}\right)=\frac{4}{9}$

(ii) Regression line x on y is

$$x-\bar{x}=b_{xy}(y-\bar{y})$$

$\Rightarrow$ $x-6=\frac{4}{9}(y-8)$ $[\because \bar{x}=6, \bar{y}=8]$

$\Rightarrow$ $9x-4y-22=0$

(iii) Most likely value of x when $y=14$ is

$$x=\frac{4}{9}(14)+\frac{22}{9}$$

$\Rightarrow$ $x=\frac{56+22}{9}=\frac{78}{9}$

33. Given data $(9, -4)$, $(10, -3)$, $(11, -1)$, $(13, 1)$, $(14, 3)$, $(15, 5)$, $(16, 8)$

Now, we construct the following table

x	y	x^2	y^2	xy
9	–4	81	16	–36
10	–3	100	9	–30
11	–1	121	1	–11
13	1	169	1	13
14	3	196	9	42
15	5	225	25	75
16	8	256	64	128
$\Sigma x=88$	$\Sigma y=9$	$\Sigma x^2=1148$	$\Sigma y^2=125$	$\Sigma xy=181$

Here, $n=7$, $\Sigma x=88$, $\Sigma y=9$

$\therefore$ $\bar{x}=\frac{\Sigma x}{n}=\frac{88}{7}$ and $\bar{y}=\frac{\Sigma y}{n}=\frac{9}{7}$

Now, $b_{yx}=\dfrac{\Sigma xy-\dfrac{\Sigma x\times\Sigma y}{n}}{\Sigma x^2-\dfrac{(\Sigma x)^2}{n}}=\dfrac{181-\dfrac{88\times 9}{7}}{1148-\dfrac{(88)^2}{7}}$

$$b_{yx}=\frac{1267-792}{8036-7744}=\frac{475}{292}$$

$\therefore$ Equation of line of regression of y on x is

$$y-\bar{y}=b_{yx}(x-\bar{x})$$

$$y-\frac{9}{7}=\frac{475}{292}\left(x-\frac{88}{7}\right)$$

Now, $b_{xy}=\dfrac{\Sigma xy-\dfrac{\Sigma x\times\Sigma y}{n}}{\Sigma y^2-\dfrac{(\Sigma y)^2}{n}}$

$$=\frac{181-\dfrac{88\times 9}{7}}{125-\dfrac{81}{7}}=\frac{1267-792}{875-81}=\frac{475}{794}$$

Equation of line of regression of x on y is

$$x-\bar{x}=b_{xy}(y-\bar{y})$$

$\Rightarrow$ $x-\frac{88}{7}=\frac{475}{794}\left(y-\frac{9}{7}\right)$

Now, equation of line regression of y on x is

$$y-\frac{9}{7}=\frac{475}{292}\left(x-\frac{88}{7}\right)$$

Given, $x=13.5$

We get

$$y=\frac{475}{292}\left(13.5-\frac{88}{7}\right)+\frac{9}{7}$$

$$y=1.63(13.5-12.57)+1.28$$

$$=1.52+1.28$$

$$y=2.8$$

34. We have, $\bar{x}=25$, $\bar{y}=30$, $b_{yx}=1.6$ and $b_{xy}=0.4$

(i) The regression equation y on x is

$$y-\bar{y}=b_{yx}(x-\bar{x})$$

$\Rightarrow$ $y-30=1.6(x-25)$

$\Rightarrow$ $y=1.6x-40+30$

$\Rightarrow$ $y=1.6x-10$

(ii) When $x=60$, then

$$y=1.6\times 60-10$$

$$=96-10=86$$

(iii) Coefficient of correlation between x and y

$$=\sqrt{b_{xy}\times b_{yx}}$$

$$=\sqrt{0.4\times 1.6}$$

$$=\sqrt{0.64}=0.8$$

[$\because$ coefficient of correlation has the same sign as regression coefficients]

35. Given, two regression lines are

$$x+2y-5=0 \quad \ldots(i)$$

and $$2x+3y-8=0 \quad \ldots(ii)$$

Clearly, line (i) represents regression line of y on x and line (ii) represents regression line of x on y.

From Eq. (i), we get

$$b_{yx}=-\frac{1}{2}$$

From Eq. (ii), we get

$$b_{xy}=-\frac{3}{2}$$

Now, $$r^2=b_{xy}\times b_{yx}$$

$$\Rightarrow \quad r^2=-\frac{1}{2}\times\left(-\frac{3}{2}\right)=\frac{3}{4}$$

$$\Rightarrow \quad r=\pm\sqrt{\frac{3}{4}}=\pm\frac{\sqrt{3}}{2}$$

But r has same sign as that of b_{yx} and b_{xy}.

$$\therefore \quad r=-\frac{\sqrt{3}}{2}$$

36. (i) Given regression lines are

$$3x-2y=5 \quad \ldots(i)$$

and $$x-4y=7 \quad \ldots(ii)$$

Let the line of regression x on y is

$$3x=2y+5$$

i.e. $$x=\frac{2}{3}y+\frac{5}{3}$$

$\therefore$ Regression coefficient x on y is

$$b_{xy}=\frac{2}{3} \quad [\because b_{xy}=\text{coefficient of } y]$$

Let the line of regression y on x is

$$4y=x-7$$

i.e. $$y=\frac{1}{4}x-\frac{7}{4}$$

$\therefore$ Regression coefficient of y on x is

$$b_{yx}=\frac{1}{4} \quad [\because b_{yx}=\text{coefficient of } x]$$

(ii) Coefficient of correlation,

$$r=\sqrt{b_{xy}\times b_{yx}}$$

$$=\sqrt{\frac{2}{3}\times\frac{1}{4}}$$

$$\therefore \quad r=\frac{1}{\sqrt{6}}$$

37. Given regression lines are

$$4x+10y=9 \quad \ldots(i)$$

and $$6x+3y=4 \quad \ldots(ii)$$

On multiplying Eq. (i) by 6 and Eq. (ii) by 4 and then subtracting Eq. (ii) from Eq. (i), we get

$$24x+60y-(24x+12y)=54-16$$

$$\Rightarrow \quad 48y=38$$

$$\Rightarrow \quad y=\frac{38}{48}=\frac{19}{24}$$

Put $y=\frac{19}{24}$ in Eq. (i),we get

$$4x+10\times\frac{19}{24}=9$$

$$\Rightarrow \quad 4x+\frac{190}{24}=9$$

$$\Rightarrow \quad 4x=9-\frac{190}{24}=\frac{216-190}{24}=\frac{26}{24}$$

$$\therefore \quad x=\frac{26}{4\times24}=\frac{13}{48}$$

Mean of $x=(\bar{x})=\frac{13}{48}$

and mean of $y=(\bar{y})=\frac{19}{24}$

From Eq. (i), $y=\frac{-4}{10}x+\frac{9}{10}$

So, regression coefficient of y on x is $b_{yx}=\frac{-4}{10}$.

Line of regression, y on x is

$$y-\bar{y}=b_{yx}(x-\bar{x})$$

$$\Rightarrow \quad y-\frac{19}{24}=\frac{-4}{10}\left(x-\frac{13}{48}\right)$$

$$\Rightarrow \quad 10y-\frac{190}{24}=-4x+\frac{52}{48}$$

$$\Rightarrow \quad 4x+10y=\frac{190}{24}+\frac{52}{48}$$

$$\Rightarrow \quad 4x+10y=\frac{380+52}{48}$$

$$\Rightarrow \quad 4x+10y=\frac{432}{48}$$

$$\Rightarrow \quad 4x+10y=9$$

Hence, line of regression y on x is

$$4x+10y=9$$

38. Let us construct the following table.

x	x^2	y	y^2	xy
14	196	14	196	196
12	144	23	529	276
13	169	17	289	221
14	196	24	576	336
16	256	18	324	288
10	100	25	625	250
13	169	23	529	299
12	144	24	576	288
$\Sigma x = 104$	$\Sigma x^2 = 1374$	$\Sigma y = 168$	$\Sigma y^2 = 3644$	$\Sigma xy = 2154$

$$\bar{x} = \frac{\Sigma X}{n} = \frac{104}{8} = 13,\ \bar{y} = \frac{168}{8} = 21$$

Regression line of x on y is

$$x - \bar{x} = b_{xy}(y - \bar{y})$$

$$b_{xy} = \frac{\Sigma xy - \frac{1}{8}\Sigma x \cdot \Sigma y}{\Sigma y^2 - \frac{1}{8}(\Sigma y)^2}$$

$$= \frac{2154 - \frac{1}{8} \times 104 \times 168}{3644 - \frac{1}{8} \times (168)^2}$$

$$= \frac{2154 - 104 \times 21}{3644 - 168 \times 21}$$

$$= \frac{-30}{116} = -0.25862$$

$\therefore$ Regression line of x on y is

$$x - 13 = -0.25862(y - 21)$$

$$\Rightarrow \quad x = -0.25862y + 5.43102 + 13$$

$$\Rightarrow \quad x = -0.25862y + 18.43102$$

When $y = 16$, then $x = 14.2931$.

39. The marks of 10 candidates in English and Mathematics are given below:

Marks in English(x)	Marks in Mathematics (y)	x^2	xy
20	17	400	340
13	12	169	156
18	23	324	414
21	25	441	525
11	14	121	154
12	8	144	96
17	19	289	323
14	21	196	294
19	22	361	418
15	19	225	285
$\Sigma x = 160$	$\Sigma y = 180$	$\Sigma x^2 = 2670$	$\Sigma xy = 3005$

$$b_{yx} = \frac{\Sigma xy - \frac{1}{N}\Sigma x \Sigma y}{\Sigma x^2 - \frac{1}{N}(\Sigma x)^2}$$

$$= \frac{3005 - \frac{1}{10} \times 160 \times 180}{2670 - \frac{1}{10} \times (160)^2}$$

$$= \frac{3005 - 2880}{2670 - 2560} = \frac{125}{110} = 1.14$$

$$\therefore \quad \bar{x} = \frac{\Sigma x}{N} = \frac{160}{10} = 16$$

and $\bar{y} = \dfrac{\Sigma y}{N} = \dfrac{180}{10} = 18$

Now, regression line of y on x is

$$(y - \bar{y}) = b_{yx}(x - \bar{x})$$

$$\Rightarrow \quad (y - 18) = 1.14(x - 16)$$

$$\Rightarrow \quad y - 18 = 1.14x - 18.24$$

$$\Rightarrow \quad y = 1.14x - 18.24 + 18$$

$$\Rightarrow \quad y = 1.14x - 0.24$$

When $x = 24$, then

$$y = 1.14 \times 24 - 0.24$$

$$\Rightarrow \quad y = 27.12$$

40. We construct the table for given data

x	y	x^2	y^2	xy
9	−4	81	16	−36
10	−3	100	9	−30
11	−1	121	1	−11
12	0	144	0	0
13	1	169	1	13
14	3	196	9	42
15	5	225	25	75
16	8	256	64	128
Total 100	9	1292	125	181

Here, $n=8$, $\Sigma x=100$, $\Sigma y=9$, $\Sigma x^2=1292$, $\Sigma y^2=125$ and $\Sigma xy=181$

Now, mean of x, $\bar{x}=\frac{\Sigma x}{n}=\frac{100}{8}=12.5$

and mean of y, $\bar{y}=\frac{\Sigma y}{n}=\frac{9}{8}$

Regression coefficients of y on x is

$$b_{yx}=\frac{\Sigma xy-\frac{1}{n}\Sigma x\Sigma y}{\Sigma x^2-\frac{1}{n}(\Sigma x)^2}=\frac{181-\frac{1}{8}(100\times 9)}{1292-\frac{1}{8}(100)^2}$$

$$=\frac{181-\frac{900}{8}}{1292-\frac{10000}{8}}=\frac{1448-900}{10336-10000}=\frac{548}{336}=\frac{137}{84}$$

and regression coefficients of x on y is

$$b_{xy}=\frac{\Sigma xy-\frac{1}{n}\Sigma x\Sigma y}{\Sigma y^2-\frac{1}{n}(\Sigma y)^2}$$

$$=\frac{181-\frac{1}{8}(100\times 9)}{125-\frac{1}{8}(9)^2}=\frac{1448-900}{1000-81}=\frac{548}{919}$$

$\therefore$ Regression line of x on y is $x-\bar{x}=b_{xy}(y-\bar{y})$

$$\therefore \quad (x-12.5)=\frac{548}{919}\left(y-\frac{9}{8}\right)$$

$$\Rightarrow \quad 919x-11487.5=548y-616.5$$

$$\Rightarrow \quad 919x-548y=10871$$

And regression line of y on x is

$$y-\bar{y}=b_{yx}(x-\bar{x})$$

$$\therefore \quad y-\frac{9}{8}=\frac{137}{84}(x-12.5)$$

$$\Rightarrow \quad 84\left(y-\frac{9}{8}\right)=137x-1712.5$$

$$\Rightarrow \quad 84y-94.5=137x-1712.5$$

$$\Rightarrow \quad 137x-84y=1618$$

Since, the regression line of y on x is

$$137x-84y=1618$$

For $x=13.5$,

$$137\times 13.5-84y=1618$$

$$\Rightarrow \quad 84y=1849.5-1618$$

$$\Rightarrow \quad 84y=231.5$$

$$\Rightarrow \quad y=2.76$$

41. (i) We have, $\Sigma x=30$, $\Sigma y=42$, $\Sigma xy=199$, $\Sigma x^2=184$, $\Sigma y^2=318$ and $n=6$

$\therefore$ Regression coefficient of x on y is

$$b_{xy}=\frac{\Sigma xy-\frac{\Sigma x\cdot\Sigma y}{n}}{\Sigma y^2-\frac{(\Sigma y)^2}{n}}=\frac{199-\frac{30\times 42}{6}}{318-\frac{42\times 42}{6}}$$

$$=\frac{199-210}{318-294}=-\frac{11}{24}=-0.458$$

and regression coefficient of y on x is

$$b_{yx}=\frac{\Sigma xy-\frac{\Sigma x\,\Sigma y}{n}}{\Sigma x^2-\frac{(\Sigma x)^2}{n}}=\frac{199-210}{184-\frac{900}{6}}$$

$$=\frac{199-210}{184-150}=\frac{-11}{34}=-0.324$$

(ii) Since, b_{yx} and b_{xy} both are negative, so r also be negative.

$$\therefore \quad r=-\sqrt{b_{yx}\times b_{xy}}$$

$$=-\sqrt{-\frac{11}{24}\times\frac{(-11)}{34}}$$

$$=-\frac{11}{\sqrt{24\times 34}}=-\frac{11}{\sqrt{816}}$$

$$=-\frac{11}{28.6}=-0.38$$

(iii) Regression equation of y on x is

$$y-\bar{y}=b_{yx}(x-\bar{x}).$$

Now, mean, $\bar{x}=\frac{\Sigma x}{n}=\frac{30}{6}=5$, $\bar{y}=\frac{\Sigma y}{n}=\frac{42}{6}=7$

Also, $b_{yx}=-\frac{11}{34}$

Regression equation of y on x is

$$y-7=-\frac{11}{34}(x-5)$$

$$\Rightarrow \quad 34y-238=-11x+55$$

$$\Rightarrow \quad 11x+34y-293=0 \quad \ldots(i)$$

(iv) When $x=10$

Then, from Eq. (i),

$$11\times 10+34y-293=0$$

$$\Rightarrow \quad 34y=293-110$$

$$\Rightarrow \quad 34y=183$$

$$\Rightarrow \quad y=\frac{183}{34}=5.382$$

Hence, the likely value of y when $x=10$ is 5.382.

CHAPTER TEST

2 Marks Questions

1. If the two coefficients of regression are –0.6 and –1.4, then find the coefficient of correlation.

2. Find the coefficient of correlation from the following regression lines $x-2y+3=0$, $4x-5y+1=0$.

3. Fit a straight line to the following data, treating y as the dependent variable.

x	1	2	3	4	5
y	7	6	5	4	3

Hence, estimate the value of y when $x=3.5$.

4. Is the following statement true? Give reasons.

$40x-18y=5$ and $8x-10y+6=0$ are respectively the regression equations of y on x and x on y.

3/4 Marks Questions

5. Find the equations of two lines of regression for the data

x	1	2	3	4	5
y	7	6	5	4	3

and hence find an estimate of y for $x=3.5$ from the appropriate line of regression.

6. Show that if five students get respectively 1, 2, 3, 4, 5 marks (X) out of 10 in subject A, and 3, 3, 5, 7, 6 marks (Y) out of 10 in subject B, the regression equation of y on x can be written as $y=1.8+x$.

7. If x and y are a pair of correlated variables. Ten observations of their values (x_i, y_i) have the following results.

$$\Sigma x_i=55, \Sigma y_i=55, \Sigma x_i y_i=350, \Sigma x_i^2=385$$

Predict the value of y when the value of x is 6.

5/6 Marks Questions

8. Given the observations (10, –5), (10, –3), (11, –2), (11, 0), (12, 1), (15, 6), (16, 4), (11, –2), predict the value of Y corresponding to the value 14 of X and predict the value of X when the value of Y is 3.

9. Heights (in centimeters) of a sample of 12 fathers and their eldest sons are given below:

Heights of Father	165	160	170	163	173	158	178	168	173	170	175	180
Heights of Son	173	168	173	165	175	168	173	165	180	170	173	178

(i) Find the least squares regression lines? Construct scatter diagram.

(ii) What is the correlation coefficient?

10. The two lines of regression for a distribution (x, y) are $3x+2y=7$ and $x+4y=9$. Then, find the regression coefficient b_{yx} and b_{xy}.

11. If $\bar{x}=18$, $\bar{y}=100$, $\sigma_x=14$, $\sigma_y=20$ and $r(X,Y)=0.8$, Find the regression lines. Estimate the value of y when $x=70$ and that of x when $y=90$.

12. Fit a least square line to the data in the following table using:

(i) x as the independent variable.

(ii) y as the independent variable.

Find y when $x=5$ and also find x when $y=7$.

x	3	5	6	8	9	11
y	2	3	4	6	5	8

13. Find two regression equation from the following data:

x	38	48	43	40	41
y	31	38	43	33	35

14. Using the following data, determine the estimated value of x when $y=22$ with the help of suitable regression line:

x	4	5	8	9	11	12	14
y	16	10	8	7	6	5	4

Answers

1. –0.916 **2.** 0.790 **3.** 4.5 **4.** The statement is false, because $b_{yx} \cdot b_{xy} > 1$

5. $x+y=8, x+y=8$; 4.5 **7.** 5.79

8. 2.875 and 13.778. **9.** (i) $y=0.477x+90.936$ and $x=1.016y-5.12$ (ii) 0.696

10. $b_{yx}=-\frac{1}{4}, b_{xy}=-\frac{2}{3}$

11. $y=1.143x+79.43, x=0.56y-38$, when $x=70$, $y=159.44$ and when $y=90$, $x=12.4$.

12. $x=5$, $y=3.22$ and $x=10.03$, $y=7$

13. $x=0.52y+23.18$, $y=0.79x+2.69$

14. $98x=1530-81y, -\frac{18}{7}$

15

Linear Programming

TREND ANALYSIS 3 YEARS

TOPIC **01** Linear Programming

Average No. of Questions Across all Sets

Types of Questions	2024	2023	2020
1 Mark	—	—	—
2 Marks	—	—	—
3/4 Marks	1	1	—
5/6 Marks	—	—	1

Linear Programming is a method to achieve the best outcome (such as maximum profit or lowest cost) in a mathematical model whose requirements are represented by linear relationships. Linear programming is a special case of mathematical programming (mathematical optimisation).

Linear Inequalities

An inequality or inequation is said to be linear, if each variable occurs in first degree only and there is no term involving the product of the variables.

e.g. $ax + b \leq 0$, $ay + bx > 4$ etc.

Linear Inequality in One Variable

The statement of any of the following types $x < a, x \leq a, x > a, x \geq a$, where $a \in R$ is called a linear inequation (or inequality) in one variable.

Linear Inequality in Two Variables

The statement of any of the following types:

$ax + by + c < 0$, $ax + by + c \leq 0$, $ax + by + c > 0$ and $ax + by + c \geq 0$, where $a, b, c \in R$

is called linear inequation (or inequality) in two variables.

Some important definitions related to inequality

- **Half Plane** A straight line divides the cartesian plane into two parts. Each part is called half plane.
- **Solution Set** The set of all ordered pairs which satisfy a given inequation is called the solution set.
- **Solution Region** The set of points whose coordinates satisfy a given inequation is called the solution region.

Graphical Solution of Linear Inequation

To solve a linear inequation, we proceed as follows:

(i) Write the given linear inequation in the form of linear equation.

(ii) Draw the straight line which divides the coordinate plane into two halves.

(iii) The region which satisfies the given inequality is the required solution region.

(iv) Shade the solution region of given inequation.

Graphical Solution of System of Linear Inequations

To solve a system of linear inequations (in one or two variables), we proceed as follows:

(i) Draw the graphs (or solution regions) of all the given linear inequations.

(ii) Find the common part of the coordinate plane which satisfies all the given linear inequations.

(iii) This common part of the coordinate plane is the required solution of the given system of linear inequations.

Linear Programming Problem

A linear programming problem is one that is concerned with finding the optimal value (maximum or minimum value) of a linear function of several variables, subject to the constraints that the variables are non-negative and satisfy a set of linear inequalities.

The following definitions and concepts are very helpful in understanding the problems of linear programming problem

- **Optimal Value** The maximum value of an objective function is known as the optimal value of LPP.
- **Objective Function** If $k_1, k_2, \ldots, k_n$ are constants and $x_1, x_2, \ldots, x_n$ are variables, then the linear function $z = k_1x_1 + k_2x_2 + \ldots + k_nx_n$ which is to be maximised or minimised is called the objective function.
- **Constraints** The inequations or equations in the variables of a linear programming problem which describe the conditions under which the optimisation (maximisation or minimisation) is to be accomplished are called constraints.
- **Optimisation Problem** A problem which seeks to maximise or minimise a linear function subject to certain constraints as determined by a set of linear inequalities is called an optimisation problem. Linear programming problems are special type of optimisation problems.
- **Non-negative Restrictions** These are the constraints which describe that the variables involved in a linear programming problem are non-negative.
- **Convex Region** A region is called convex region, if on choosing any two points in the region, we get the line segment joining these two points in that region as shown in the figure.

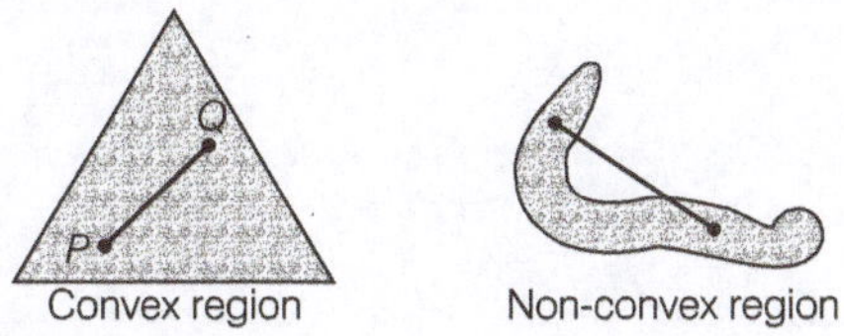

- **Feasible and Infeasible Region** The common region determined by all the constraints including non-negative constraints $x \geq 0$, $y \geq 0$ of a linear programming problem is called a feasible region. The region other than the feasible region is called infeasible region.
- **Bounded and Unbounded Region** A feasible region of a system of linear inequalities is said to be bounded, if it can be enclosed within a circle. Otherwise, it is said to be unbounded region.
- **Feasible and Infeasible Solution** The set of all points available in the feasible region (including its boundary) is called a feasible solution of linear programming problem. The region of feasible solution is always common set. Any point outside the feasible region is called an infeasible solution of linear programming problem.
- **Optimal Feasible Solution** A feasible solution of a linear programming problem is said to be an optimal feasible solution, if it optimises the objective function.

Advantages of Linear Programming

(i) Linear programming is used in solving different problems like diet problems, manufacturing problems, investment problems, transportation problems, blending problems and advertising media selection problems.

(ii) It is used in determining shortest routes for **travelling salesmen**.

(iii) It helps a farmer to produce the best crop by minimising risk and maximising profit.

(iv) It helps to choose the best alternative amongst a set of alternatives, so that the profit is maximised or cost is minimised.

(v) It is not only about considering internal factors like machine, budget, manpower, storage etc., but also external factors like market demand, purchasing power of the customer etc.

Limitations of Linear Programming

(i) It deals with optimising a single objective only.

(ii) The assumption that input and output variables are directly proportional is not strictly true.

(iii) In practice, many decision variables assume integral values. e.g. Number of workers.
Linear programming deals with variables having continuous values.

Formulation of Linear Programming Problem and its Solution

There are three steps followed in the mathematical formulation of an LPP and its solution, as given below:

Step I Identify the objective function as a linear combination of variables (x and y) and to construct all constraints.

Thus, an LPP can be stated mathematically as Maximise (or minimise) $Z = ax + by$ subject to the conditions (constraints)

$$a_i x + b_i y \leq (\text{or} \geq \text{or} = \text{or} > \text{or} <)\ c_i,$$

where $i = 1$ to n and the non-negative restrictions $x \geq 0, y \geq 0$.

Step II Find the solutions and feasible region of the inequations by mathematical method.

Step III Find the optimal solution i.e. select particular values of the variables x and y obtained in Step II that give the desired value (maximum/minimum) of the objective function.

The following theorems are fundamental in solving LPP

- **Theorem 1** Let R be the feasible region for an LPP and $Z = ax + by$ be the objective function. When Z has an optimal value (maximum or minimum), subject to the constraints described by linear inequalities, this optimal value must occur at a corner point (vertex) of the feasible region.
- **Theorem 2** Let R be the feasible region for an LPP and $Z = ax + by$ be the objective function. If R is bounded, then the objective function Z has both a maximum and a minimum value on R and each of these occurs at a corner point (vertex) of R.

REMARK If R (the feasible region) is unbounded, then a maximum or a minimum value of the objective function may not exist. However, if it exists, then it must occur at a corner point of R.

Graphical Method of Solving LPP

The graphical method is suitable for solving linear programming problems containing two variables only. This method of solving programming problem is referred to as corner point method.

Method to solve LPP To solve a linear programming problem (LPP), we use the following steps:

Step I First, write the given LPP in mathematical form by using mathematical formulation (if not given in mathematical form).

Step II Consider all constraints as linear equations.

Step III Draw the graph of each linear equation obtained in Step II and find their intersection points (if any).

Step IV Shade the common region of all the linear inequalities i.e. find feasible region and check that feasible region is bounded or unbounded.

Step V Now, find the corner points of feasible region and calculate the value of objective function at each corner point.

Step VI
- If region is bounded, then maximum (say M) or minimum (say m) value out of these values obainted in Step V, is the required maximum or minimum value of the objective function.
- If region is unbounded, then no need to go next step. Then, maximum (say M) or minimum (say m) value out of these values obtained in Step V may or may not be required maximum or minimum value of the objective function. Then, we go to next step.

Step VII Suppose the given objective function is $ax + by$, then drawn graph of inequalities has no point in common with the feasible region obtained in Step VI, then M or m is the required maximum or minimum value. Otherwise, objective function has no maximum or no minimum value.

PYQs Previous Years Questions

3/4 Marks Questions

1. Aman has ₹ 1500 to purchase rice and wheat for his grocery shop. Each sack of rice and wheat costs ₹ 180 and ₹ 120 respectively. He can store a maximum number of 10 bags in his shop. He will earn a profit of ₹ 11 per bag of rice and ₹ 9 per bag of wheat.
   (i) Formulate a linear programming problem to maximise Aman's profit.
   (ii) Calculate the maximum profit. **ISC 2024**

2. Maximise $Z = 4x - 3y$,
   Subject to the following constraints
   $$2x + y \leq 20,\ 3x - 2y \geq 16,$$
   $$x \leq 9,\ y \geq 1$$
   Also, find Z's maximum value. **ISC Specimen 2024**

3. A soap company manufactures two varieties of soap using two machines. The time taken on each machine to manufacture one batch of each variety of soap is given below. **ISC Specimen 2024**

	Machine 1	Machine 2
Soap A	1 h	1 h
Soap B	2 h	1 h

   Machine 1 and Machine 2 cannot be operational for more than 12 and 10 hours in a day, respectively. The profit earned from one batch of Soap A and one batch of Soap B is ₹ 3000 and ₹ 4000, respectively.
   Find the number of batches of each kind of soap that should be made daily to maximise the profit.

4. Solve the following linear programming problem graphically. **ISC 2023**
   Maximise $Z = 5x + 2y$ subject to
   $$x - 2y \leq 2,\ 3x + 2y \leq 12,\ -3x + 2y \leq 3,\ x \geq 0,\ y \geq 0$$

5. Solve the following linear programming problem graphically and interpret your result of $Z = 2x - 5y$ subject to the constraints $x + y \geq 2$, $x - y \geq 0$, $x \leq 1$, $x \geq 0$, $y \geq 0$. **ISC Specimen 2023**

6. The standard weight of a special purpose brick is 5 kg and it must contain two basic ingredients B_1 and B_2. B_1 costs ₹ 5 per kg and B_2 costs ₹ 8 per kg. Strength considerations dictate that the brick should not contain more than 4 kg of B_1 and minimum 2 kg of B_2. Since, the demand for the product is likely to be related to the price of the bricks, find the minimum cost of the brick satisfying the above conditions. Formulate this situation as an LPP and solve it graphically. **ISC Specimen 2023**

7. A manufacturer has two machines X and Y that may run at the most 360 min in a day to produce two types of toys A and B.
   To produce each toy A, machines X and Y need to run at the most 12 min and 6 min, respectively.
   To produce each toy B, machines X and Y need to run at the most 6 min and 9 min, respectively.
   By selling the toys A and B, the manufacturer makes the profits of ₹ 30 and ₹ 20, respectively.
   Formulate a linear programming problem and find the number of toys A and B that should be manufactured in a day to get maximum profit. **ISC Specimen Sem-II 2022**

8. A manufacturer wishes to produce two commodities A and B. The number of units of material, labour and equipment needed to produce one unit of each commodity is shown in the table given below. Also shown is the available number of units of each item, material, labour, and equipment.

Items	Commodity A	Commodity B	Available Number of Units
Material	1	2	8
Labour	3	2	12
Equipment	1	1	10

   Find the maximum profit, if each unit of commodity A earns a profit of ₹ 2 and each unit of B earns a profit of ₹ 3. **ISC Specimen Sem-II 2022**

9. A farm is engaged in breeding hens. The hens are fed products A and B grown in the farm which contains nutrients P, Q and R. One kilogram of product A contains 36 units, 3 units and 20 units of nutrients P, Q and R respectively, whereas one kilogram of product B contains 6 units, 12 units and 10 units of nutrients P, Q and R respectively. The minimum requirement of nutrients P, Q and R for a hen is 108, 36 and 100 units respectively. Product A costs ₹ 20 per kilogram and product B costs ₹ 40 per kilogram. Using linear programming, find the number of kilograms of products A and B to be produced to minimize the total cost. Identify the feasible region from the rough sketch. **ISC Specimen 2021**

5/6 Marks Questions

10. A carpenter has 90, 80 and 50 running feet respectively, of teak wood, plywood and rosewood which is used to produce product *A* and product *B*. Each unit of product A requires 2, 1 and 1 running feet and each unit of product *B* requires 1, 2 and 1 running feet of teak wood, plywood and rosewood, respectively. If product *A* is sold for ₹ 48 per unit and product *B* is sold for ₹ 40 per unit, how many units of product *A* and product *B* should be produced and sold by the carpenter, in order to obtain the maximum gross income?

Formulate the above as a linear programming problem and solve it, indicating clearly the feasible region in the graph. **ISC Specimen 2021, ISC 2019**

11. A company uses three machines to manufacture two types of shirts, half sleeves and full sleeves. The number of hours required per week on machine M_1, M_2 and M_3 for one shirt of each type is given in the following table

	M_1	M_2	M_3
Half sleeves	1	2	8/5
Full sleeves	2	1	8/5

None of the machines can be in operations for more than 40 h/week. The profit on each half sleeve shirt is ₹ 1 and the profit on each full sleeve shirt is ₹ 1.50. How many of each type of shirts should be made per week to maximise the company's profit? **ISC 2020**

12. A manufacturing company makes two types of teaching aids *A* and *B* of Mathematics for Class *X*. Each type of *A* requires 9 labour hours for fabricating and 1 labour hour for finishing. Each type of *B* requires 12 labour hours for fabricating and 3 labour hours for finishing. For fabricating and finishing, the maximum labour hours available per week are 180 and 30, respectively.

The company makes a profit of ₹ 80 on each piece of type *A* and ₹ 120 on each piece of type *B*. How many pieces of type *A* and type *B* should be manufactured per week to get a maximum profit? Formulate this as linear programming problem and solve it. Identify the feasible region from the rough sketch. **ISC 2018**

13. A toy company manufactures two types of dolls *A* and *B*. Market test and available resources have indicated that the combined production level should not exceed 1200 dolls per week and the demands for the dolls of type *B* is atmost half of that for dolls of type *A*. Further, the production level of type *A* can exceed three times the production of dolls of other type be at most 600 units. If the company makes profit of ₹ 12 and ₹ 16 per doll respectively on dolls *A* and *B*, how many of each type of dolls should be produced weekly, in order to maximise the profit? **ISC Specimen 2018**

14. A farmer has a supply of chemical fertilizer of type *A* which contains 10% nitrogen and 6% phosphoric acid and of type *B* which contains 5% nitrogen and 10% phosphoric acid. After soil test, it is found that at least 7 kg of nitrogen and same quantity of phosphoric acid is required for a good crop. The fertilizer of type *A* costs ₹ 5.00 per kg and the type *B* costs ₹ 8.00 per kg. Using linear programming, find how many kilograms of each type of the fertilizer should be bought to meet the requirement and for the cost to be minimum. Find the feasible region in the graph. **ISC 2017**

15. A company manufactures two types of products *A* and *B*. Each unit of *A* requires 3 g of nickel and 1 g of chromium, while each unit of *B* requires 1 g of nickel and 2 g of chromium. The firm can produce 9 g of nickel and 8 g of chromium. The profit is ₹ 40 on each unit of product of type *A* and ₹ 50 on each unit of type *B*. How many units of each type should the company manufacture so as to earn maximum profit? Use linear programming to find the solution. **ISC 2016**

16. A dietician wishes to mix two kinds of food *X* and *Y* in such a way that the mixture contains at least 10 units of vitamin *A*, 12 units of vitamin *B* and 8 units of vitamin *C*. The vitamin contents of one kg food is given below:

Food	Vitamin A	Vitamin B	Vitamin C
X	1 unit	2 units	3 units
Y	2 units	2 units	1 unit

One kg food of *X* costs ₹ 24 and one kg food of *Y* costs ₹ 36. Using linear programming, find the least cost of the total mixture which will contain the required vitamins. **ISC 2015**

17. A company manufactures two types of toys A and B. A toy of type A requires 5 min for cutting and 10 min for assembling. A toy of type B requires 8 min for cutting and 8 min for assembling. There are 3 h available for cutting and 4 h available for assembling the toys in a day. The profit is ₹ 50 each on a toy of type A and ₹ 60 each on a toy of type B. How many toys of each type should company manufacture in a day to maximise the profit? Use linear programming to find the solution. ***ISC 2014***

KEY CONCEPT

(i) First, write the given condition as inequations and form LPP.

(ii) Second, draw the graph of inequation and find the feasible region.

(iii) Further, find the objective value at each corner points and get the maximum value.

18. A mill owner buys two types of machines A and B for his mill. Machine A occupies 1000 sq m of area and requires 12 men to operate it, while machine B occupies 1200 sq m of area and requires 8 men to operate it. The owner has 7600 sq m of area available and 72 men to operate the machines. If machine A produces 50 units and machine B produces 40 units daily, how many machines of each type should he buy to maximize the daily output? Use linear programming to find the solution. ***ISC 2013***

KEY CONCEPT

(i) First of all, to get maximised profit assume type A machine is x and type of B machine is y.

(ii) Make two inqualities according to the question and put values of $x=0$ and $y=0$ to get the points.

(iii) By getting points make the feasible region $OAEDO$.

(iv) Get corner points of ($OAEDO$) feasible region to get the required maximised profit.

19. Two tailors P and Q earn ₹ 150 and ₹ 200 per day respectively. P can stitch 6 shirts and 4 trousers a day, while Q can stitch 10 shirts and 4 trousers per day. How many days should each work to produce atleast 60 shirts and 32 trousers at minimum labour cost? ***ISC 2012***

KEY CONCEPT

(i) First, write the given condition as inequations and form LPP.

(ii) Second, draw the graph of inequation and find unbounded feasible region.

(iii) Find the objective value at each corner points.

(iv) Now, in unbounded feasible region, we draw a graph of inequality objective function $<m$, where m minimum value.

(v) Further, check the graph of this inequality has no common point with feasible region.

Explanations

1. (i) Let the number of wheat and rice bags be x and y. Since, each sack of rice and wheat cost ₹ 180 and ₹ 120, Aman has total ₹ 1500.

Therefore, $120x + 180y \le 1500$ ...(i)

Also, he can store maximum number of 10 bags.

$\therefore \quad x + y \le 10$ ...(ii)

Thus, the linear programming to maximise Aman's profit is

Maximise, $Z = 9x + 11y$

Subject to the constraints

$$120x + 180y \le 1500$$
$$x + y \le 10$$
$$x \ge 0,\ y \ge 0$$

(ii) To calculate the maximum profit, we draw the feasible region using given constraints.

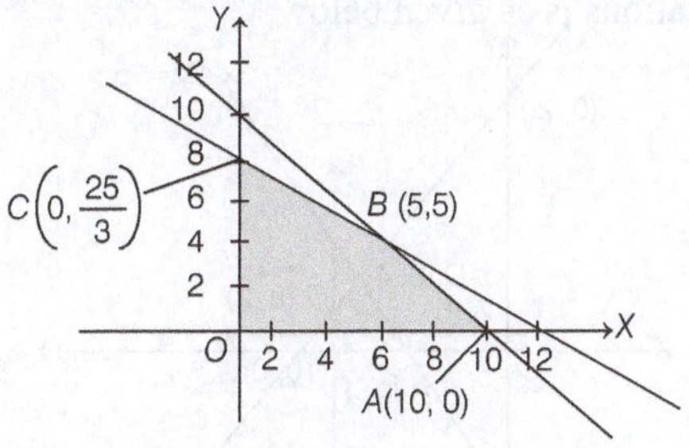

Feasible region is $OABCO$.

Thus, the corner points of feasible region are

$O(0, 0)$, $A(10, 0)$, $B(5, 5)$ and $C\left(0, \dfrac{25}{3}\right)$.

The value of Z at corner point is

Corner point	$Z = 9x + 11y$
O(0, 0)	0
A(10, 0)	90
B(5, 5)	100 (Maximum)
$C\left(0, \frac{25}{3}\right)$	91.67

The maximum value of Z is 100 at point (5, 5).

$\therefore$ The maximum profit is ₹ 100.

2. We have, the following LPP

Maximise $Z = 4x - 3y$

Subjected to the constraints

$$2x + y \le 20,\ 3x - 2y \ge 16,$$
$$x \le 9 \text{ and } y \ge 1$$

Now, considering the inequations as equations, we get

$$2x + y = 20 \quad \ldots\text{(i)}$$

and $$3x - 2y = 16 \quad \ldots\text{(ii)}$$

Table for line $2x + y = 20$ is

x	0	10
y	20	0

So, the line is passing through the points (0, 20) and (10, 0).

On putting (0, 0) in the inequality $2x + y \le 20$, we get $0 + 0 \le 20$, which is true.

So, half plane is towards the origin.

Table for line $3x - 2y = 16$ is

x	0	16/3
y	−8	0

So, the line is passing through the points (0, − 8) and (16 / 3, 0).

On putting (0, 0) in the inequality $3x - 2y \ge 16$, we get $0 - 0 \ge 16$, which is false.

So, the half plane is away from the origin.

The graphical representation of the system of the inequations is as given below

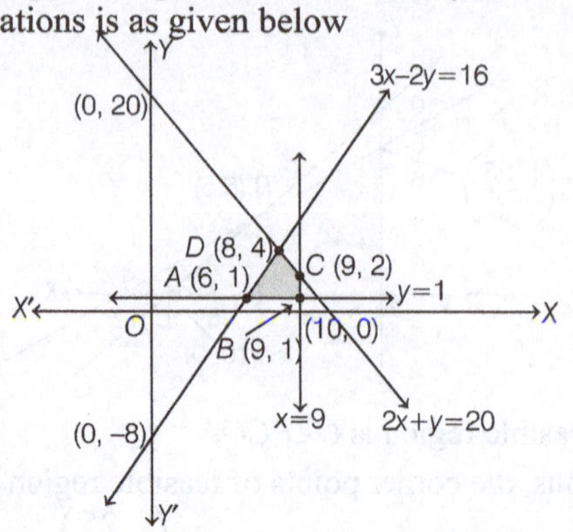

Clearly, the feasible region is $ABCDA$, where the corner points are A (6, 1), B (9, 1), C (9, 2) and D (8, 4).

Now, the values of Z at corner points are as follow

Corner points	$Z = 4x - 3y$
A(6, 1)	$Z = 24 - 3 = 21$
B(9, 1)	$Z = 36 - 3 = 33$ (Maximum)
C(9, 2)	$Z = 36 - 6 = 30$
D(8, 4)	$Z = 32 - 12 = 20$

Hence, the maximum value of Z is 33, which occurs at (9, 1).

3. Let the number of batches of Soap A be x and of Soap B be y.

$\therefore$ Objective function is maximise,

$$Z = 3000x + 4000y.$$

Machine 1 cannot be operational for more than 12 h.

So, first constraint is $x + 2y \le 12$.

Machine 2 cannot be operational for more than 10 h.

So, second constraint is $x + y \le 10$.

Also, the number of batches of each kind of soap cannot be negative.

So, non-negative restrictions or constraints are

$$x \ge 0,\ y \ge 0$$

Hence, the linear programming problem for the given problem is as follows :

Maximise $Z = 3000x + 4000y$

Subjecte to constraints $x + 2y \le 12$,

$$x + y \le 10,$$
$$x \ge 0 \text{ and } y \ge 0$$

Now, table for the line $x + 2y = 12$ is

x	0	12
y	6	0

So, the line is passing through the points (0, 6) and (12, 0).

On putting (0, 0) in the inequality $x + 2y \le 12$, we get $0 + 0 \le 12$, which is true

So, half plane is towards the origin.

Table for the line $x + y = 10$ is

x	0	10
y	10	0

So, the line is passing through the points (0, 10) and (10, 0).

On putting (0, 0) in the inequality $x + y \le 10$, we get

$0 + 0 \le 10$, which is true

So, half plane is towards the origin.

Since, $x \ge 0$ and $y \ge 0$

So, the feasible region lies in the first quadrant.

On solving equations $x+2y=12$ and $x+y=10$, we get $B\,(8, 2)$.

The graphical representation of the obtained system of inequalities is as follows.

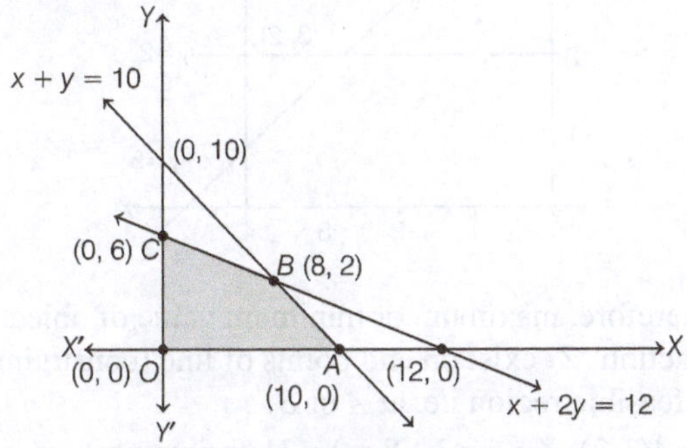

Clearly, the feasible region is $OABCO$.

The corner points of the feasible region are $O(0, 0)$, $A(10, 0)$, $B\,(8, 2)$ and $C\,(0, 6)$.

Now, the value of Z at these points are as follows.

Corner points	$Z = 3000x + 4000y$
O(0, 0)	$Z = 0 + 0 = 0$
A(10, 0)	$Z = 30000 + 0 = 30000$
B(8, 2)	$Z = 24000 + 8000 = 32000$ (maximum)
C(0, 6)	$Z = 0 + 24000 = 24000$

Thus, the maximum value of Z is ₹ 32000, which occurs at $B\,(8, 2)$.

Hence, 8 batches of Soap A and 2 batches of Soap B should be made daily to maximise the profit.

4. We have, Maximize $Z = 5x + 2y$

Subject to constraints,

$$x - 2y \le 2 \quad \text{...(i)}$$
$$3x + 2y \le 12 \quad \text{...(ii)}$$
$$-3x + 2y \le 3 \quad \text{...(iii)}$$
and $$x \ge 0,\ y \ge 0 \quad \text{...(iv)}$$

Given constraints can be written in equation form as

$$x - 2y = 2 \quad \text{...(v)}$$
$$3x + 2y = 12 \quad \text{...(vi)}$$
$$-3x + 2y = 3 \quad \text{...(vii)}$$
and $$x = 0,\ y = 0 \quad \text{...(viii)}$$

Table for line $x - 2y = 2$

x	0	2
y	−1	0

On putting (0, 0) in the inequality $x - 2y \le 2$, we get $0 - 0 \le 2$, which is true.

So, the half plane is toward the origin.

Table for line $3x + 2y = 12$

x	0	4
y	6	0

On putting (0, 0) in the inequality $3x + 2y \le 12$, we get $0 + 0 \le 12$, which is true.

So, the half plane is toward the origin.

Table for line $-3x + 2y = 3$

x	0	−1
y	3/2	0

On putting (0, 0) in the inequality $-3x + 2y \le 3$, we get $0 + 0 \le 3$, which is true.

So, the half plane is toward the origin.

On drawing graph, we have

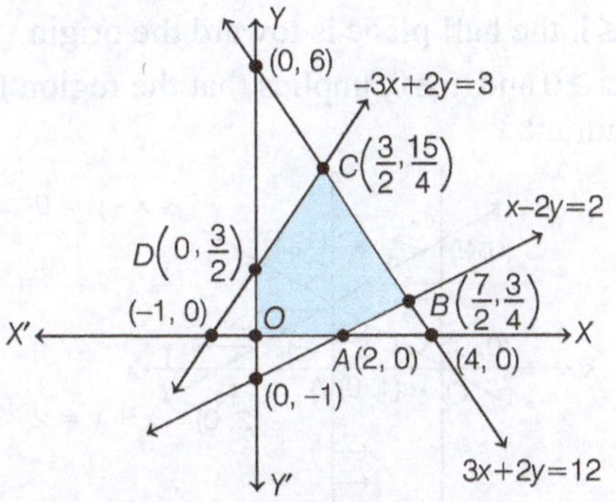

The corner points of the feasible region are $O(0, 0)$, $A(2, 0)$, $B\left(\frac{7}{2}, \frac{3}{4}\right)$, $C\left(\frac{3}{2}, \frac{15}{4}\right)$ and $D\left(0, \frac{3}{2}\right)$

Corner points	$Z = 5x + 2y$
O(0, 0)	0
A(2, 0)	10
$B\left(\frac{7}{2}, \frac{3}{4}\right)$	19 (Maximum)
$C\left(\frac{3}{2}, \frac{15}{4}\right)$	15
$D\left(0, \frac{3}{2}\right)$	3

Hence, maximum value of Z is 19 at $B\left(\frac{7}{2}, \frac{3}{4}\right)$.

5. Given, objective function $Z = 2x - 5y$

Subject to constraints,

$$x + y \geq 2 \quad \ldots\text{(i)}$$
$$x - y \geq 0 \quad \ldots\text{(ii)}$$
$$x \leq 1, x \geq 0, y \geq 0 \quad \ldots\text{(iii)}$$

and table for line $x + y = 2$

x	0	2
y	2	0

So, the line is passing through the points (2, 0) and (0, 2).

On putting (0, 0) in the inequality $x + y \geq 2$, we get

$0 + 0 \geq 2$, which is false.

So, the half plane is away from the origin.

Table for line $x - y \geq 0$

x	0	1	2
y	0	1	2

So, the line is passing through the origin.

For $x \leq 1$, the half plane is toward the origin.

Also, $x \geq 0$ and $y \geq 0$, implies that the region lies in the Ist quadrant.

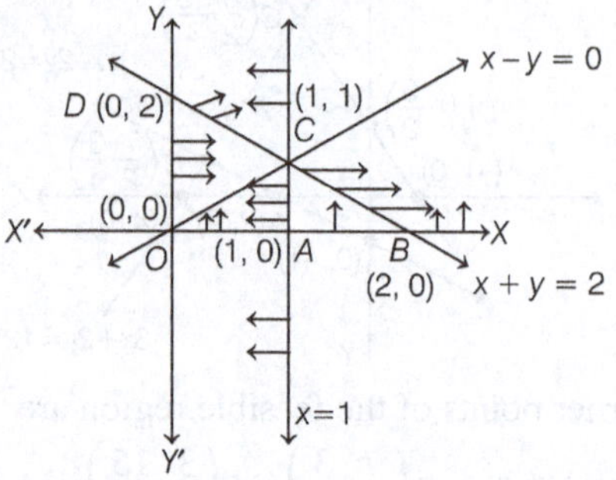

On drawing the graph there will no common region bounded and $C(1, 1)$ is the only common point in the region.

So, $Z = 2 \times 1 - 5 \times 1 = 2 - 5 = -3$.

6. Let x kg of B_1 and y kg of B_2 are taken for making brick.

Here, $Z = 5x + 8y$ is the cost which is objective function and is to be maximise subject to constraints are

$$x + y = 5 \quad \ldots\text{(i)}$$
$$x \leq 4 \quad \ldots\text{(ii)}$$
$$y \geq 2 \quad \ldots\text{(iii)}$$
$$x, y \geq 0 \quad \ldots\text{(iv)}$$

In this case constraints (i) is a line passing through the feasible region by constraints (ii), (iii) and (iv).

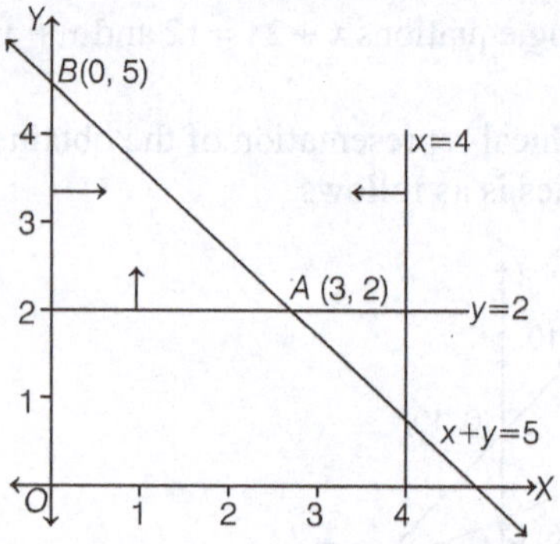

Therefore, maximum or minimum value of objective function 'Z' exist on end points of line (constraints) (i) in feasible region i.e. at A or B.

At $A(3, 2)$, $Z = 5 \times 3 + 8 \times 2 = 31$ (minimum)

At $B(0, 5)$, $Z = 5 \times 0 + 8 \times 5 = 40$ (maximum)

Hence, cost of brick is minimum when 3 kg of B_1 and 2 kg of B_2 are taken.

7. Let x and y be the number of toys of type A and type B respectively.

The data given in the problem can be summarized in the following tabular form.

Type of toys	Machine X	Machine Y
A	12	6
B	6	9
Maximum time available	360	360

Since, the profit is to be maximized.

$\therefore$ Maximise, $Z = 30x + 20y$

Subject to the constraints are

$$12x + 6y \leq 360, \quad \ldots\text{(i)}$$
$$6x + 9y \leq 360 \quad \ldots\text{(ii)}$$
$$\text{and} \quad x \geq 0, \quad \ldots\text{(iii)}$$
$$y \geq 0 \quad \ldots\text{(iv)}$$

Table for graph $12x + 6y \leq 360$

x	0	30
y	60	0

Put (0, 0) in the inequality $12x + 6y \leq 360$, we get

$0 + 0 \leq 360 \Rightarrow 0 \leq 360$, which is true.

So, the half plane is towards the origin.

Table for graph line $6x + 9y \leq 360$

x	0	60
y	40	0

Put (0, 0) in the equality $6x+9y\le 360$, we get

$$0+0\le 360 \Rightarrow 0\le 360, \text{ which is true.}$$

So, the half plane is towards the origin.

Also, $x\ge 0$ $y\ge 0$. So, the feasible region lies in the first quadrant.

On solving Eqs. (i) and (ii), we get intersection point $C(15, 30)$.

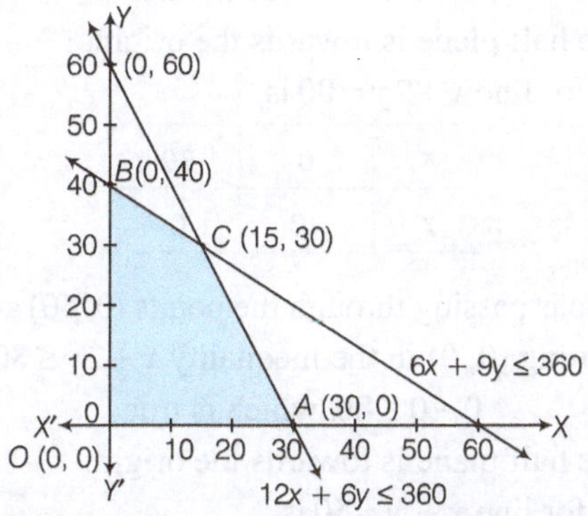

The shaded region represents the feasible region

Corner Points	$Z = 30x + 20y$
O (0, 0)	$Z = 30\times 0 + 20\times 0 = 0$
A (30, 0)	$Z = 30\times 30 + 20\times 0 = 900$
B (0, 40)	$Z = 30\times 0 + 20\times 40 = 800$
C (15, 30)	$Z = 30\times 15 + 20\times 30 = 1050$

Maximum profit is ₹ 1050 at C (15, 30).

Type $A=15$ toys and type $B=30$ toys should be manufactured in a day to maximize the profit.

8. Let x be the number of units of commodity A produced and y be the number of units of commodity B produced.

Maximise, $Z=2x+3y$

$\therefore$ $x+2y\le 8$ [material constraint]

$3x+2y\le 12$ [labour constraint]

$x+y\le 10$ [equipment constraint]

$x, y\ge 0$ [non-negative constraint]

Now, consider the inequations as equation

$\therefore$ Table for line $x+2y=8$

x	8	0
y	0	4

On putting (0, 0) in $x+2y\le 8$, we get

$$0+0\le 8, \text{ which is true}$$

So, half plane is towards the origin.

Table for line $3x+2y=12$

x	4	0
y	0	6

On putting (0, 0) in $3x+2y\le 12$, we get

$$0+0\le 12, \text{ which is true}$$

So, half plane is towards the origin.

Table for line $x+y=10$

x	10	0
y	0	10

On putting (0, 0) in $x+y\le 10$, we get

$$0+0\le 10, \text{ which is true}$$

So, half plane is towards the origin.

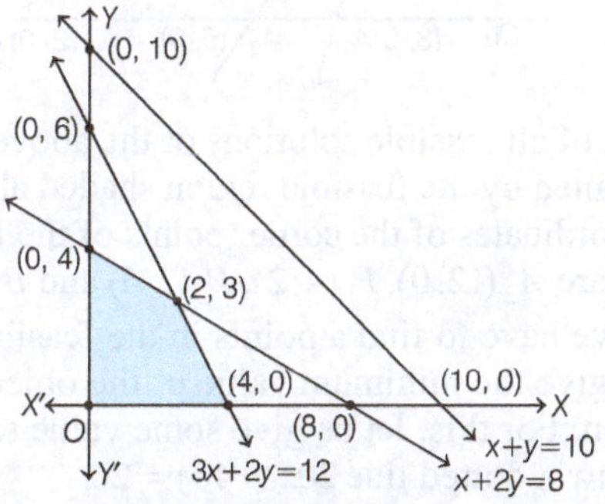

Now, we have to maximise $Z=2x+3y$

Corner Points	Value of $Z = 2x + 3y$
(0, 0)	0
(4, 0)	8
(2, 3)	13 (Maximum)
(0, 4)	12

Hence, the maximum profit is ₹ 13 at (2, 3).

9. The data given in the problem can be summarised in the following tabular form

Product	Nutrient Constituent P	Q	R	Cost in (₹)
A	36	3	20	20
B	6	12	10	40
Minimum Requirement	108	36	100	

Let x units of product A and y units of products B are bought to fulfill the minimum requirement of P, Q and R and to minimise the cost.

The mathematical formulation of the above problem is as follows

Minimise $Z=20x+40y$

Subject to $36x+6y\ge 108$

$3x+12y\ge 36$

$20x+10y\ge 100$

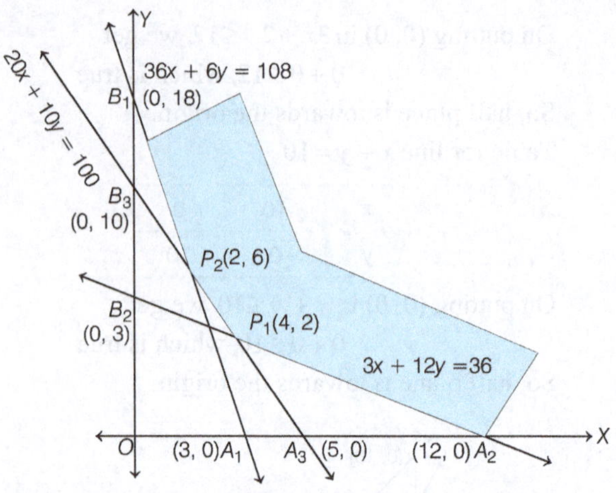

The set of all feasible solutions of the above LPP is represented by the feasible region shaded above figure. The coordinates of the corner points of the feasible region are $A_2(12, 0)$, $P_1(4, 2)$, $P_2(2, 6)$ and $B_1(0, 18)$.

Now, we have to find a points in the feasible region which give the minimum value of the objective function. For this, let us give some value to Z, say 20 and draw a dotted line $20x + 40y = 20$.

Now, draw line parallel to this line which have at least on point common to the feasible region and locate a line which is nearest to the origin and has at least one point common to the feasible region.

Clearly, such as line is $Z_1 = 20x + 40y$ and it has a point $P_1(4, 2)$ common with the feasible region. Thus, $Z_1 = 20x + 40y$ is the minimum value of Z, and the feasible solution which gives this value of Z is the corner $P_1(4, 2)$ of the shaded region. The values of the variables for the optimal solution are $x = 4$, $y = 2$. substituting these values in $Z = 20x + 40y$, we get $Z = 160$ as the optimal value of Z.

Hence, 2 units of product A and 4 units of product B are sufficient to fulfill the minimum requirement at a minimum cost of ₹ 160.

10. Let x units of product A and y units of product B will be produced.

Type	Number	Teak wood	Plywood	Rosewood
A	x	$2x$	$1x$	$1x$
B	y	$1y$	$2y$	$1y$

∴ The objective function is to maximise

$$Z = 48x + 40y$$

Subject to constraints are

$$2x + y \le 90,\ x + 2y \le 80,\ x + y \le 50 \text{ and } x, y \ge 0$$

Consider the constraints as linear equations

$$2x + y = 90 \quad \ldots(i)$$
$$x + 2y = 80 \quad \ldots(ii)$$
$$x + y = 50 \quad \ldots(iii)$$
and $$x = y = 0 \quad \ldots(iv)$$

Table for line $2x + y = 90$ is

x	0	45
y	90	0

So, line is passing through the points (0, 90) and (45, 0).
On putting (0, 0) in the inequality $2x + y \le 90$, we get $0 + 0 \le 90$, which is true.

So, the half plane is towards the origin.

Table for line $x + 2y = 80$ is

x	0	80
y	40	0

So, line is passing through the points (0, 40) and (80, 0).
On putting (0, 0) in the inequality $x + 2y \le 80$, we get $0 + 0 \le 80$, which is true

So, the half plane is towards the origin.

Table for line $x + y = 50$ is

x	0	50
y	50	0

So, line is passing through the points (0, 50) and (50, 0).
On putting (0, 0) in the inequality $x + y \le 50$, we get $0 + 0 \le 50 \Rightarrow 0 \le 50$, which is true.

So, the half plane is towards the origin.

Also, $x, y \ge 0$, implies the feasible region lies in the Ist quadrant.

Now, the points of intersection of lines (i) and (iii); (ii) and (iii), are respectively, $C(40, 10)$ and $B(20, 30)$.

The graphical representation of these lines is given below

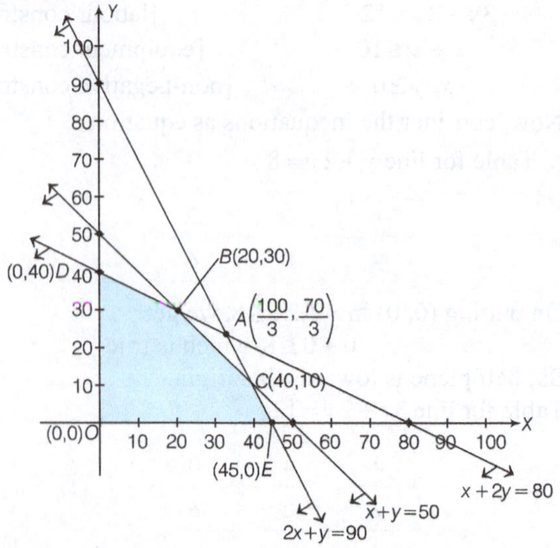

The shaded region *OECBDO* represents the feasible region and its corner points are $O(0, 0)$, $B(20, 30)$, $C(40, 10)$, $D(0, 40)$ and $E(45, 0)$.

The values of Z at the corner points are given below

Corner points	$Z = 48x + 40y$
O(0,0)	$Z = 48\times0+40\times0=0$
B(20,30)	$Z=48\times20+40\times30=2160$
C(40,10)	$Z=48\times40+40\times10=2320$ (max)
D(0,40)	$Z=48\times0+40\times40=1600$
E(45,0)	$Z=48\times45+40\times0=2160$

Thus, Z is maximum at $x=40$, $y=10$ and maximum value of Z is 2320.

Hence, the product A produce 40 quantity and product B produce 10 quantity to obtain maximum gross income.

11. Let the number of half sleeves shirt $= x$ and the number of full sleeves shirt $= y$

Maximise profit $Z = x + 1.5y$ ...(i)

Subject to constraints

$$x+2y \le 40 \quad \text{...(ii)}$$

$$\Rightarrow \quad 2x+y \le 40 \quad \text{...(iii)}$$

$$\frac{8}{5}x+\frac{8}{5}y \le 40$$

$$\Rightarrow \quad x+y \le 25 \quad \text{...(iv)}$$

$$x, y \ge 0$$

Now, table for line $x+2y=40$ is

x	0	40
y	20	0

So, line is passing through the points (0, 20) and (40, 0) on putting (0, 0) in the inequality $x+2y\le 40$, we get

$$0+0\le 40, \text{ which is true}$$

So, the half plane is towards the origin.

Table for line $2x+y=40$ is

x	0	20
y	40	0

So, line is passing through the points (0, 40) and (20, 0) on putting (0, 0) in the inequality $2x+y\le 40$, we get

$$0+0\le 40, \text{ which is true.}$$

So, the half plane is towards the origin.

Now, table for the line $x+y=25$ is

x	0	25
y	25	0

So, line is passing through the points (0, 25) and (25, 0). On putting (0, 0) in the inequality $x+y\le 25$, we get $0+0\le 25$, which is true.

So, the half plane is towards the origin also, $x, y\ge 0$ implies the feasible region in the Ist quadrant.

Now, draw the lines $x+2y=40$, $2x+y=40$ and $x+y=25$.

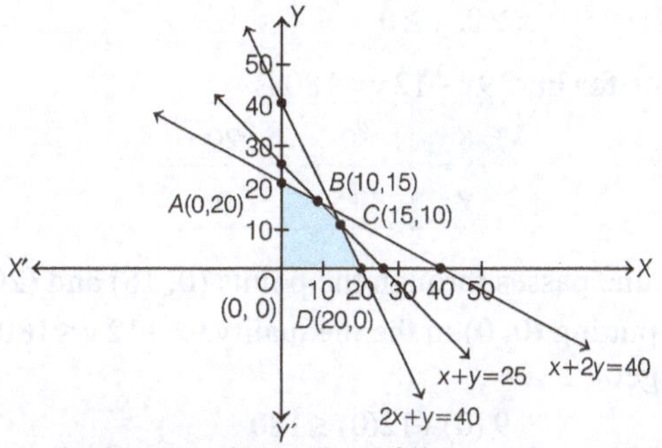

Now, the intersection point of line $x+2y=40$ and $x+y=25$ is $B(10, 15)$ and intersection point of lines $x+y=25$ and $2x+y=40$ is $C(15, 10)$.

The shaded region *OABCDO* represents the feasible region and its corner points are

$O(0, 0)$, $A(0, 20)$, $B(10, 15)$, $C(15, 10)$ and $D(20, 0)$

The values of Z at the corner points are given

Corner points	$Z = x + 1.5y$
O(0, 0)	$0+1.5\times0=0$
A (0, 20)	$0+1.5\times20=30$
B (10, 15)	$10+1.5\times15=32.5$ (max)
C (15, 10)	$15+1.5\times10=30$
D (20, 0)	$20+1.5\times0=20$

Here, maximum value of $Z=32.5$ at

$$x=10, y=15$$

$\therefore$ Number of half sleeves shirt $=10$ and Number of full sleeves shirt $=15$

12. Let the number of pieces of two types of teaching aids A and B be x and y, respectively.

We construct the following table.

Items	Number of pieces	Time on fabricating (in h)	Time on finishing (in h)	Profit (in ₹)
A	x	$9x$	x	$80x$
B	y	$12y$	$3y$	$120y$
Total	$x+y$	$9x+12y$	$x+3y$	$80x+120y$
Availability		180	30	

The profit on type A is ₹ 80 and on type B is ₹ 120.
Our objective is to maximise,

$$Z = 80x + 120y \quad \text{...(i)}$$

Subject to constraints,

$$9x + 12y \leq 180 \text{ or } 3x + 4y \leq 60 \quad \text{...(ii)}$$

$$x + 3y \leq 30 \quad \text{...(iii)}$$

and $\quad x \geq 0, y \geq 0 \quad$ ...(iv)

Table for line $9x + 12y = 180$ is

x	0	20
y	15	0

So, line passes through the points (0, 15) and (20, 0).
On putting (0, 0) in the inequality $9x + 12y \leq 180$, we get

$$9(0) + 12(0) \leq 180$$

$\Rightarrow \quad 0 \leq 180$, which is true.

So, the half plane is towards the origin.
Table for line $x + 3y = 30$ is

x	0	30
y	10	0

So, line passes through the points (0,10) and (30,0).
On putting (0,0) in the inequality $x + 3y \leq 30$, we get

$$0 + 3(0) \leq 30$$

$\Rightarrow \quad 0 \leq 30$, which is true.

So, the half plane is towards the origin.
Also, $x \geq 0$ and $y \geq 0$, so the region lies in the Ist quadrant.
On solving Eqs. (ii) and (iii), we get the point of intersection is B (12,6).
The graphical representation of the lines is given below

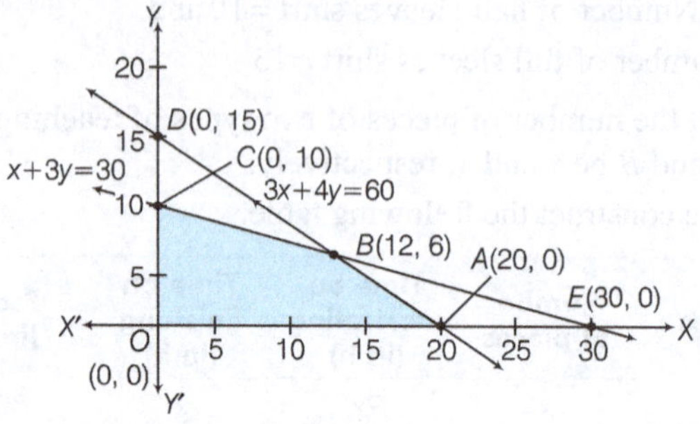

∴ Feasible region is $OABCO$.
The corner points of the feasible region are $O(0,0)$, $A(20,0)$, $B(12,6)$ and $C(0,10)$.

Corner points	$Z = 80x + 120y$
O(0,0)	$Z = 80(0) + 120(0) = 0$
A(20, 0)	$Z = 80(20) + 120(0) = 1600$
B(12, 6)	$Z = 80(12) + 120(6) = 1680$
C(0, 10)	$Z = 80(0) + 120(10) + 1200$

Hence, the maximum value of Z is ₹ 1680 at B (12, 6).
Thus, the number of pieces of types $A = 12$ and types $B = 6$ should be manufactured per week to get a maximum profit.

13. Let the company manufactures x dolls of type A and y dolls of type B, then

$$x \geq 0, y \geq 0 \quad \text{...(i)}$$

$$x + y \leq 1200 \quad \text{...(ii)}$$

$$y \leq \frac{x}{2} \Rightarrow x - 2y \geq 0 \quad \text{...(iii)}$$

$$x \leq 3y + 600 \Rightarrow x - 3y \leq 600 \quad \text{...(iv)}$$

Let Z be the total profit, then

$$Z = 12x + 16y$$

Firstly, draw the graph of the line $x + y = 1200$

x	1200	0
y	0	1200

On putting (0, 0) in the inequality $x + y \leq 1200$, we get

$$0 + 0 \leq 1200 \Rightarrow 0 \leq 1200, \text{ which is true}$$

So, the half plane is towards the origin.
Secondly, draw the graph of the line $x - 2y = 0$

x	0	2
y	0	1

On putting (200, 0) in the inequality $x - 2y \geq 0$, we have

$$200 - 2 \times 0 \geq 0 \Rightarrow 200 \geq 0, \text{ which is true}$$

So, the half plane is towards the X-axis.
Thirdly, draw the graph of the line $x - 3y = 600$

x	600	0
y	0	−200

On putting (0, 0) in the inequality $x - 3y \leq 600$, we get

$$0 - 3 \times 0 \leq 600 \Rightarrow 0 \leq 600, \text{ which is true}$$

So, the half plane is towards the origin.
Since, $x, y \geq 0$.
So, the feasible region lies in the first quadrant.

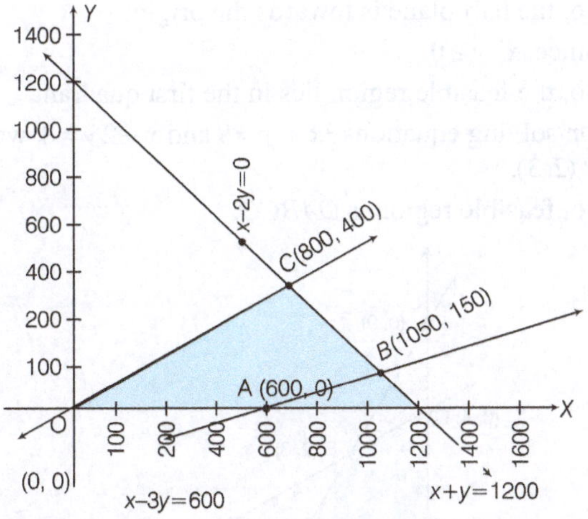

The point of intersection of lines $x-3y=600$ and $x+y=1200$ is $B(1050,150)$; of lines $x=2y$ and $x+y=1200$ is $C(800, 400)$.

$\therefore$ Feasible region is $OABCO$.

The corner points of the feasible region are $O(0,0)$, $A(600, 0)$, $B(1050,150)$ and $C(800, 400)$. The values of Z at these points are as follows

Corner point	$Z = 12x + 16y$
O(0, 0)	0
A(600, 0)	7200
B(1050, 150)	15000
C(800, 400)	16000 $\rightarrow$ maximum

The maximum value of Z is 16000 at $C(800, 400)$.

Thus, 800 and 400 dolls of type A and type B should be produced respectively, so that company get the maximum profit of ₹ 16000.

14. Let the farmer uses x kg of type A fertilizer and y kg of type B fertilizer. Then, we have the following table

Type	Quantity (in kg)	Nitrogen	Phosphoric acid	Cost in (₹)
A	x	$\frac{10}{100}x=\frac{1}{10}x$	$\frac{6}{100}x$	$5x$
B	y	$\frac{5}{100}y=\frac{1}{20}y$	$\frac{10}{100}y$	$8y$
Total	$x+y$	$\frac{x}{10}+\frac{y}{20}$	$\frac{6x}{100}+\frac{10y}{100}$	$5x+8y$
Requirement (in kg)		7	7	

Total cost of fertilizers $=5x+8y$

Since, we have to minimise the cost

i.e. $\qquad Z=5x+8y \qquad \ldots$(i)

Subject to constraints

$$\frac{x}{10}+\frac{y}{20}\geq 7 \Rightarrow 2x+y\geq 140 \qquad \ldots\text{(ii)}$$

$$\frac{6x}{100}+\frac{10y}{100}\geq 7 \Rightarrow 3x+5y\geq 350 \qquad \ldots\text{(iii)}$$

and $\qquad x\geq 0,\ y\geq 0 \qquad \ldots$(iv)

Firstly, draw the graph of the line

$$2x+y=140$$

x	0	70
y	140	0

Putting (0, 0) in the inequality $2x+y\geq 140$, we get

$2\times 0+0\geq 140 \Rightarrow 0\geq 140$, which is false

So, the half plane is away from the origin.

Since, $x,\ y\geq 0$

So, the feasible region lies in the first quadrant.

Secondly, draw the graph of the line

$$3x+5y=350$$

x	0	350/3
y	70	0

Putting (0, 0) in the inequality $3x+5y\geq 350$, we get

$3\times 0+5\times 0\geq 350 \Rightarrow 0\geq 350$, which is false

So, the half plane is away from the origin.

On solving the equations $2x+y=140$ and $3x+5y=350$, we get $B(50, 40)$.

It can be seen that the feasible region is unbounded.

The corner points of the feasible region are $A\left(\frac{350}{3},0\right)$, $B(50, 40)$ and $C(0,140)$. The values of Z at these points are as follows

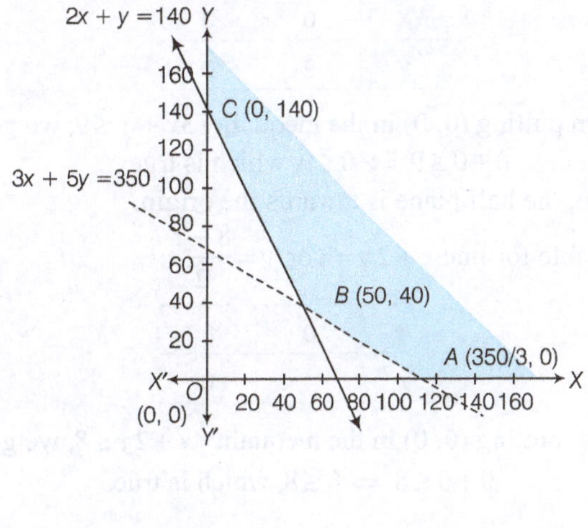

The values of Z at the corner points are given

Corner Point	$Z = 5x + 8y$
$A\left(\frac{350}{3}, 0\right)$	$Z = 5\left(\frac{350}{3}\right) + 8(0) = \frac{1750}{3} \approx 583$
$B(50, 40)$	$Z = 5(50) + 8(40) = 570$ (Minimum)
$C(0, 140)$	$Z = 5(0) + 8(140) = 1120$

As the feasible region is unbounded therefore, 570 may or may not be the minimum value of Z. For this, we draw a graph of the inequality, $5x + 8y < 570$ and check, whether the resulting half plane has points in common with the feasible region or not.

It can be seen that the feasible region has no common point with $5x + 8y < 570$.

Therefore, 50 kg of fertilizer A and 40 kg of fertilizer B should be used to minimize the cost. The minimum cost is ₹570.

15. Let the company manufactures x units of product A and y units of product B.

We construct the following table:

Type	Unit	Nickel (in g)	Chromium (in g)	Profit
A	x	$3x$	x	$40x$
B	y	y	$2y$	$50y$
Total	$x + y$	$3x + y$	$x + 2y$	$40x + 50y$
Availability		9	8	

Since, the profit is to be maximised

i.e. $Z = 40x + 50y$ ...(i)

Subject to the constraints are

$3x + y \le 9$ ...(ii)

$x + 2y \le 8$ ...(iii)

and $x \ge 0, y \ge 0$ ...(iv)

Table for line $3x + y = 9$ or $y = 9 - 3x$

x	0	3
y	9	0

On putting (0, 0) in the inequality $3x + y \le 9$, we get

$0 + 0 \le 9 \Rightarrow 0 \le 9$, which is true

So, the half plane is towards the origin.

Table for line $x + 2y = 8$ or $y = \frac{8 - x}{2}$

x	0	8
y	4	0

On putting (0, 0) in the inequality $x + 2y \le 8$, we get

$0 + 0 \le 8 \Rightarrow 0 \le 8$, which is true.

So, the half plane is towards the origin.

Since, $x, y \ge 0$

So, the feasible region lies in the first quadrant.

On solving equations $3x + y = 9$ and $x + 2y = 8$, we get B (2, 3).

So, feasible region is $OABCO$.

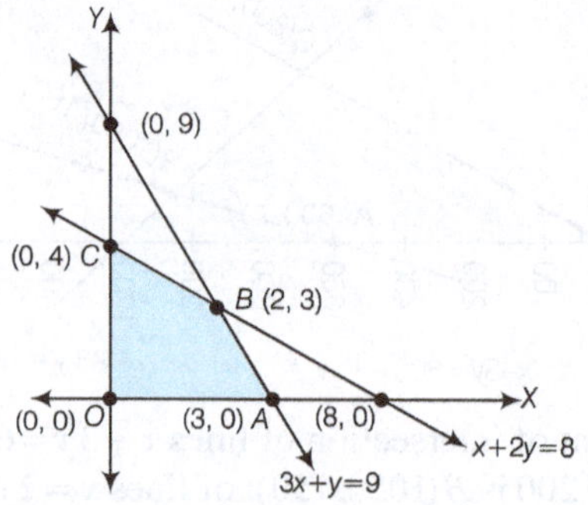

The corner points of the feasible region are $O(0, 0)$, $A(3, 0)$, $B(2, 3)$ and $C(0, 4)$. Now, the values of Z at these points are as follows:

Corner point	$Z = 40x + 50y$
$O(0, 0)$	$Z = 40(0) + 50(0) = 0$
$A(3, 0)$	$Z = 40(3) + 50(0) = 120$
$B(2, 3)$	$Z = 40(2) + 50(3) = 230$ (Maximum)
$C(0, 4)$	$Z = 40(0) + 50(4) = 200.$

Hence, the maximum value of Z is ₹230 at B (2, 3).

Thus, 2 units of type A and 3 units of type B should be produced, to get the maximum profit of ₹230.

16. Let x kg of food F_1 and y kg of food F_2 produce the required diet. Then, the problem can be formulated as an LPP as

Minimum, $Z = 24x + 36y$ ...(i)

Subject to the constraints are

$x + 2y \ge 10$ ...(ii)

$2x + 2y \ge 12$ or $x + y \ge 6$ ...(iii)

$3x + y \ge 8$ ...(iv)

and $x \ge 0, y \ge 0$ ...(v)

Table for graph of the line $x + 2y = 10$

x	10	0
y	0	5

So, line passes through (10, 0) and (0, 5).

On putting (0, 0) in the inequality $x + 2y \ge 10$, we get

$0 + 0 \ge 10$, which is false

So, the half plane is away from the origin.

Table for line $x + y = 6$

x	6	0
y	0	6

So, line passes through (6, 0) and (0, 6).

On putting (0,0) in the inequality $x + y \geq 6$, we get

$0 + 0 \geq 6$, which is false

So, the half plane is away from the origin.

Table for graph of the line $3x + y = 8$

x	8/3	0
y	0	8

So, line passes through $\left(\frac{8}{3}, 0\right)$ and (0, 8).

On putting (0, 0) in the inequality $3x + y \geq 8$, we get

$0 + 0 \geq 8$, which is false

So, the half plane is away from the origin.

Also, $x \geq 0$, $y \geq 0$, so shaded region lies in Ist quadrant.

The intersection point of lines (ii), (iii) and (iv), we get $B(1, 5)$ and $C(2, 4)$.

The graph is shown below

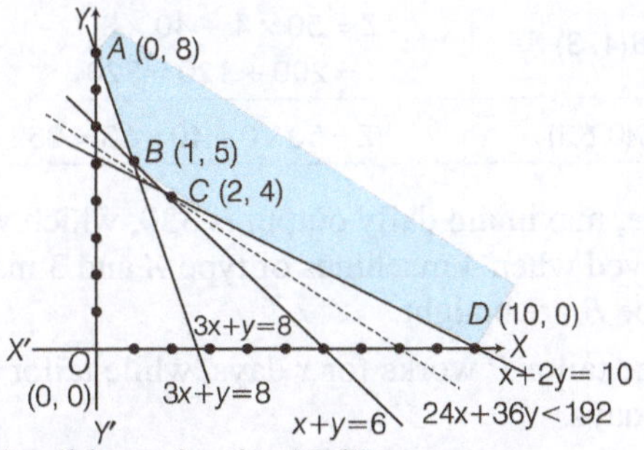

The feasible region is $ABCD$.

The corner points of feasible region are

$A(0, 8)$, $B(1, 5)$, $C(2, 4)$ and $D(10, 0)$.

Corner points	$Z = 24x + 36y$
$A(0, 8)$	$Z = 0 + 36 \times 8 = 288$
$B(1, 5)$	$Z = 24 \times 1 + 36 \times 5$ $= 24 + 180 = 204$
$C(2, 4)$	$Z = 24 \times 2 + 36 \times 4$ $= 48 + 144 = 192$ (least)
$D(10, 0)$	$Z = 24 \times 10 + 36 \times 0 = 240$ (Maximum)

The least value of Z is 192 at $C(2, 4)$. As, the feasible region is unbounded, so we draw the graph of the half plane $24x + 36y < 192$ and note that there is no point common with the feasible region. Therefore, Z has minimum value and the minimum value is ₹ 192.

17. Let the total number of toys manufactured by the company, A type to be x and B type to be y.

Since, the profit is to be maximised.

$\therefore$ Maximise profit $(P) = 50x + 60y$ ...(i)

So, we can arrange the given data in the following table

Types of toys	Total number	Required time for cutting	Required time for assembling	Profit
A	x	$5x$ min	$10x$ min	₹ $50x$
B	y	$8y$ min	$8y$ min	₹ $60y$
Total		$(5x + 8y)$ min	$(10x + 8y)$ min	₹ $(50x + 60y)$

Given, total time for cutting ≤ 180 min

and total time for assembling ≤ 240 min

$\therefore$ $5x + 8y \leq 180$ ...(ii)

and $10x + 8y \leq 240$

or $(5x + 4y) \leq (120)$ ...(iii)

and $x \geq 0, y \geq 0$ ...(iv)

Table for graph of the line $5x + 8y = 180$.

x	0	36
y	45/2	0

Put (0,0) in the inequality $5x + 8y \leq 180$, we get

$0 + 0 \leq 180$, which is true

So, the half plane is towards the origin.

Table for graph of the line $5x + 4y = 120$.

x	0	24
y	30	0

Put (0, 0) in the inequality $5x + 4y \leq 120$, we get

$0 + 0 \leq 120$, which is true

So, the half plane is towards the origin.

Also, $x \geq 0, y \geq 0$, so the feasible region lies in the first qradrant.

The point of intersection of Eqs. (ii) and (iii) is E (12, 15).

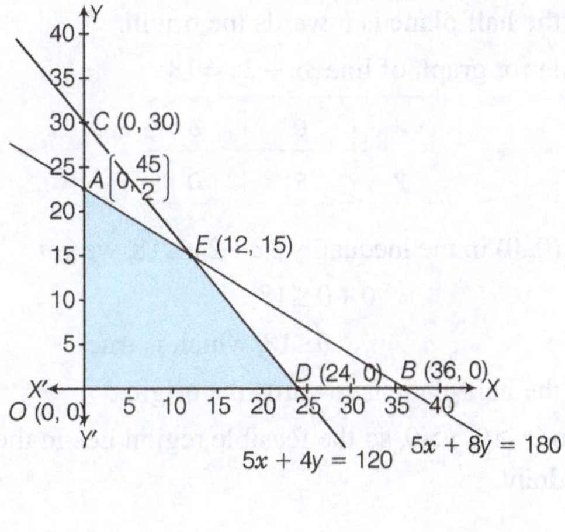

The shaded region represents the feasible region and its corner points are

$$O(0,0), A\left(0, \frac{45}{2}\right), D(24, 0) \text{ and } E(12, 15).$$

Corner points	$P = 50x + 60y$
O (0,0)	$P = 50 \times 0 + 60 \times 0 = 0$
$A\left(0, \frac{45}{2}\right)$	$P = 50 \times 0 + 60 \times \frac{45}{2}$ $= 30 \times 45 = 1350$
D (24, 0)	$P = 50 \times 24 + 60 \times 0$ $= 50 \times 24 = 1200$
E (12, 15)	$P = 50 \times 12 + 60 \times 15$ $= 600 + 900 = 1500$

Hence, the profit of the company is maximum of ₹1500 for manufacturing 12 toys of type *A* and 15 toys of type *B*.

18. Let the number of type *A* machines be *x* and the total number of type *B* machines be *y*.

Since, the profit is to be maximised.

$\therefore$ Maximise, $Z = 50x + 40y$ ...(i)

Subject to the constraints are

$1000x + 1200y \le 7600$ or $5x + 6y \le 38$ ...(ii)

$12x + 8y \le 72$ or $3x + 2y \le 18$ ...(iii)

$x \ge 0$ and $y \ge 0$ ...(iv)

Table for graph of line $5x + 6y = 38$.

x	0	38/5
y	19/3	0

Put (0, 0) in the ineqality $5x + 6y \le 38$, we get

$0 + 0 \le 38$

$\Rightarrow$ $0 \le 38$, which is true

So, the half plane is towards the origin.

Table for graph of line $3x + 2y = 18$

x	0	6
y	9	0

Put (0, 0) in the inequality $3x + 2y \le 18$, we get

$0 + 0 \le 18$

$\Rightarrow$ $0 \le 18$, which is true

So, the half plane is towards the origin.

Also, $x \ge 0$, $y > 0$, so the feasible region lies in the first quadrant.

The point of intersection of Eqs. (ii) and (iii) is *B* (4,3).

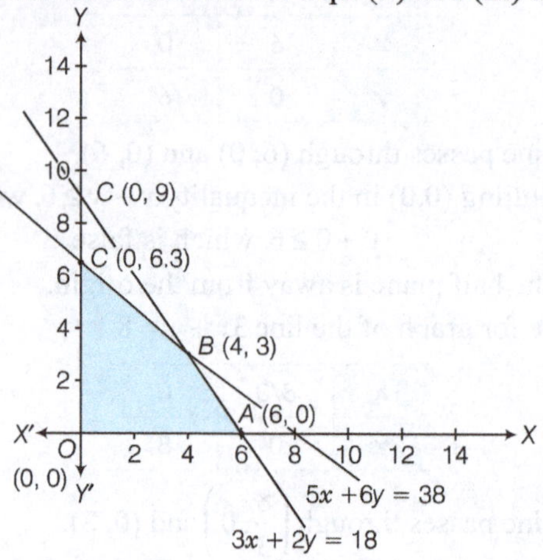

The shaded region represents a bounded feasible region and its corner point are $O(0,0)$, $A(6, 0)$, $B(4, 3)$, $C(0, 6.3)$.

Corner points	$Z = 50x + 40y$
O (0,0)	$Z = 50 \times 0 + 40 \times 0 = 0$
A (6, 0)	$Z = 50 \times 6 + 40 \times 0 = 300$
B(4, 3)	$Z = 50 \times 4 + 40 \times 3$ $= 200 + 120 = 320$
C (0,6.3)	$Z = 50 \times 0 + 40 \times 6.3 = 252$

Hence, maximum daily output is 320, which will be achieved when 4 machines of type *A* and 3 machines of type *B* are bought.

19. Let the tailor *P* works for *x* days, while tailor *Q* works for *y* days.

Since, the cost is to be minimised.

$\therefore$ Minimise $(Z) = 150x + 200y$ ...(i)

Subject to the constraints are

$6x + 10y \ge 60$

or $3x + 5y \ge 30$ ...(ii)

$4x + 4y \ge 32$ or $x + y \ge 8$ ...(iii)

$x \ge 0, y \ge 0$ ...(iv)

Table for graph of line $3x + 5y = 30$.

x	0	10
y	6	0

Put (0, 0) in the inequality $3x + 5y \ge 30$, we get

$0 + 0 \ge 30 \Rightarrow 0 \ge 30$, which is false

So, the half plane is away from the origin.

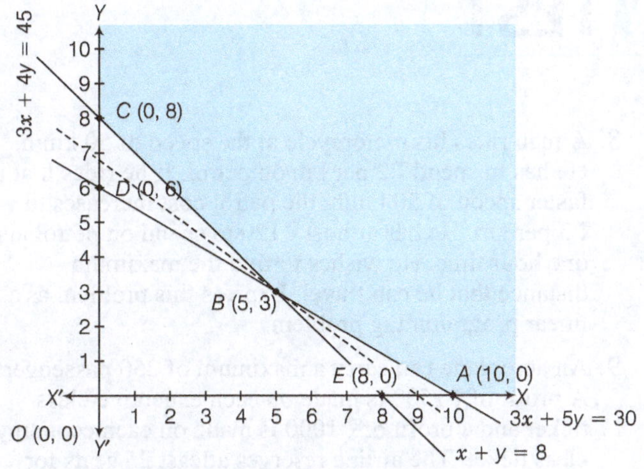

Table for graph of the line $x + y = 8$.

x	0	8
y	8	0

Put (0, 0) in the inequality $x + y \geq 8$, we get

$0 + 0 \geq 8 \Rightarrow 0 \geq 8$, which is false

So, the half plane is away from the origin.

Also, $x \geq 0$, $y \geq 0$, so the feasible region lies in the first quadrant. The intersection point of lines (i) and (ii) is B (5,3).

The shaded region represents an unbounded feasible region and its corner points are A (10,0), B (5,3) and C(0,8).

Corner points	$Z = 150x + 200y$
A (10, 0)	$Z = 150 \times 10 + 200 \times 0 = 1500$
B (5, 3)	$Z = 150 \times 5 + 200 \times 3$ $= 750 + 600 = 1350$
C (0, 8)	$Z = 150 \times 0 + 200 \times 8 = 1600$

The cost is minimum at B (5, 3).

But the feasible region is unbounded, therefore 1350 may or may not be the minimum value of Z.

Now, we draw the graph of the inequality $150x + 200y < 1350$, i.e. $3x + 4y < 27$ and check whether the open half plane has points in common with feasible region or not. From the graph, we see that the open half plane $3x + 4y < 27$ has no points in common with the feasible region.

So, the minimum value of Z is 1350 at B (5,3).

Hence,tailor P should works for 5 days and tailor Q should work for 3 days to minimise the labour cost.

CHAPTER TEST

1 Mark Questions

1. The variables x and y in a linear programming problem are called

(a) decision variables (b) linear variables
(c) optimal variables (d) None of these

2. The linear inequalities or equations or restrictions on the variables of a linear programming problem are called

(a) linear relations
(b) constraints
(c) functions
(d) objective functions

3. The objective function of an LPP is

(a) a constraint
(b) a function to be optimised
(c) a relation between the variables
(d) None of the above

4. Which of the term is not used in a linear programming problem?

(a) Optimal solution (b) Feasible solution
(c) Concave region (d) Objective function

5. Which of the following sets are not convex?

(a) $\{(x, y): 8x^2 + 6y^2 \le 24\}$
(b) $\{(x, y): 6 \le x^2 + y^2 \le 36\}$
(c) $\{(x, y): y \ge 3, y \ge 30\}$
(d) $\{(x, y): x^2 \le y\}$

6. The optimal value of the objective function is attained at the point is

(a) given by intersection of inequations with axes only
(b) given by intersection of inequations with X-axis only
(c) given by corner points of the feasible region
(d) None of the above

2 Marks Questions

7. A diet for a sick person must contain atleast 4000 units of vitamins, 50 units of minerals and 1400 calories. Two foods A and B are available at a cost of ₹ 4 and ₹ 3 per unit, respectively. Food A contains 200 units of vitamins, 1 unit of minerals and 40 calories. Food B contains 100 units of vitamins, 2 units of minerals and 40 calories. Express this problem as a linear programming problem.

8. A man rides his motorcycle at the speed of 50 km/h. He has to spend ₹ 2 per km on petrol. If he rides it at a faster speed of 80 km/h, the petrol cost increases to ₹ 3 per km. He has atmost ₹ 120 to spend on petrol and one hour time. He wishes to find the maximum distance that he can travel. Express this problem as a linear programming problem.

9. An aeroplane can carry a maximum of 250 passengers. A profit of ₹ 1500 is made on each executive class ticket and a profit of ₹ 1000 is made on each economy class ticket. The airline reserves atleast 25 seats for executive class. However, atleast 3 times as many passenger prefer to travel by economy class than by executive class.

Frame the linear programming problem to determine how many tickets of each type must be sold in order to maximise the profit for the airline?

10. A small firm manufactures necklaces and bracelets. The total number of necklaces and bracelets that it can handle per day is at most 24. It takes one hour to make a bracelet and half an hour to make a necklace. The maximum number of hours available per day is 16. If the profit on a necklace is ₹ 100 and that on a bracelet is ₹ 300. Formulate linear programming problem for finding how many, each should be produced daily to maximise the profit, if it is being given that atleast one of each must be produced?

11. Two tailors A and B earn ₹ 300 and ₹ 400 per day, respectively. A can stitch 6 shirts and 4 pairs of trousers while B can stitch 10 shirts and 4 pairs of trousers per day. To find how many days should each of them work and if it is desired to produce atleast 60 shirts and 32 pairs of trousers at a minimum labour cost, formulate this as an LPP.

5/6 Marks Questions

12. A manufacturer makes two products A and B. Product A sells at ₹ 200 each and takes 1/2 h to make. Product B sells at ₹ 300 each and takes 1 h to make. There is a permanent order for 14 numbers of product A and 16 numbers of product B. A working week consists of 60 h of production and the weekly turnover must not be less than ₹10000. If the profit on each product of A is ₹ 20 and on product of B ₹ 30, then how many of each should produce, so that the profit is maximum? Also, find the profit.

13. A dealer wishes to purchase a number of fans and sewing machines. He has only ₹ 57600 to invest and has space for at most 20 items. A fan costs him ₹ 3600 and a sewing machine ₹ 2400. He expects to sell a fan at a profit of ₹ 220 and a sewing machine at a profit of ₹ 180. Assuming that he can sell all the items that he buys, how should he invest his money to maximise the profit? Solve graphically and find the maximum profit.

14. A gardener has a supply of fertiliser of type I which consists of 10% nitrogen and 6% phosphoric acid and type II fertiliser which consists of 5% nitrogen and 10% phosphoric acid. After testing the soil conditions he finds that he needs at least 14 kg of nitrogen and 14 kg of phosphoric acid for his crop. If the type 1 fertiliser costs 60 paise per kg and type II fertiliser costs 40 paise per kg. Determine how many kilograms of each fertiliser should be used, so that nutrient requirements are met at a minimum cost? What is the minimum cost?

15. A manufacturer produces two products A and B. Both the products are processed on two different machines. The available capacity of the first machine is 12 h and that of second machine is 9 h. Each unit of product A requires 3 h on both machines and each unit of product B requires 2 h on first machine and 1 h on the second machine. Each unit of product A is sold at a profit of ₹ 5 and B at a profit of ₹ 6, find the production level for maximum profit graphically.

16. Every gram of wheat provides 0.1 g, of protein and 0.25 g of carbohydrates. The corresponding values for rice are 0.05 g and 0.5 g, respectively. Wheat costs ₹ 4 per kg and rice ₹ 6 per kg. The minimum daily requirements of protein and carbohydrates for an average child are 50 g and 200 g, respectively. In what quantities should wheat and rice be mixed in the daily diet, so as to provide the maximum daily requirements of protein and carbohydrates at minimum cost?

Answers

1. (a) **2.** (b) **3.** (b) **4.** (c) **5.** (b) **6.** (c)

7. Minimise $Z = 4x + 3y$, subject to constraints $200x + 100y \geq 4000$, $x + 2y \geq 50$, $40x + 40y \geq 1400$ and $x \geq 0$, $y \geq 0$.

8. Maximise $Z = x + y$, subject to constraints are $2x + 3y \leq 120$, $8x + 5y \leq 400$ and $x \geq 0$, $y \geq 0$.

9. Maximum profit $P = (1500x + 1000y)$, subject to constraints are $x + y \leq 250$, $x > 25$, $y \geq 3x$ and $x, y \geq 0$,

10. Maximum $Z = 100x + 300y$, subject to constraints are $x + y \leq 24$, $\frac{x}{2} + y \leq 16$ and $x \geq 1$, $y \geq 1$

11. Minimum $Z = 300x + 400y$, subject to constraints are $6x + 10y \geq 60$, $4x + 4y \geq 32$ and $x \geq 0$, $y \geq 0$

12. Product $A = 88$ units, Product $B = 16$ units, maximum profit = ₹2240

13. Maximum profit is ₹ 3920 for 8 fans and 12 sewing machines.

14. Type I = 100 kg, Type II = 80 kg, Minimum cost = ₹ 92

15. Maximum profit = ₹ 36, Product $A = 0$ unit, Product $B = 6$ units

16. Minimum cost profit = ₹ 2.8, Wheat = 400g, Rice = 200 g

ISC

CHAPTERWISE - TOPICWISE
QUESTION BANK

Assertion-Reason Questions

Assertion-Reason Questions

Directions *In these questions, a statement of Assertion (A) is followed by a statement of Reason (R). Choose the correct option as given below.*

(a) Both A and R are correct and R is the correct explanation of A.
(b) Both A and R are correct but R is not the correct explanation of A.
(c) A is correct but R is incorrect.
(d) R is correct but A is incorrect.

1. Relations and Functions

1. **Assertion** (A) The relation R in the set $A = \{1, 2, 3, 4, 5, 6\}$ defined as $R = \{(x, y) : y \text{ is divisible by } x\}$ is not an equivalence relation.

Reason (R) The relation R will be an equivalence relation, if it is reflexive, symmetric and transitive.

2. **Assertion** (A) The relation R on the set $N \times N$ defined by $(a, b)\, R\, (c, d) \Leftrightarrow a + d = b + c$, for all $(a, b), (c, d) \in N \times N$ is an equivalence relation.

Reason (R) Any relation R is an equivalence relation, if it is reflexive, symmetric and transitive.

3. **Assertion** (A) Let A and B be sets. Then, the function $f : A \times B \to B \times A$ such that $f(a, b) = (b, a)$ is bijective.

Reason (R) A function f is said to be bijective, if it is both one-one and onto.

4. **Assertion** (A) The function $f : R \to R$ given by $f(x) = x^3$ is injective.

Reason (R) The function $f : X \to Y$ is injective, if $f(x) = f(y) \Rightarrow x = y$ for all $x, y \in X$.

2. Inverse Trigonometric Functions

5. **Assertion** (A) cosec^{-1} is define as a function whose domain is $R - (-1, 1)$ and range could be any of the intervals $\left[\frac{-\pi}{2}, \frac{\pi}{2}\right] - \{0\}$, $\left[\frac{-3\pi}{2}, \frac{-\pi}{2}\right] - \{-\pi\}$, $\left[\frac{\pi}{2}, \frac{3\pi}{2}\right] - \{\pi\}$ etc.

Reason (R) If cosec function is bijective, then the intervals $\left[\frac{-3\pi}{2}, \frac{-\pi}{2}\right] - \{-\pi\}$, $\left[\frac{-\pi}{2}, \frac{\pi}{2}\right] - \{0\}$, $\left[\frac{\pi}{2}, \frac{3\pi}{2}\right] - \{\pi\}$ etc. are the domain and range is the set of all real numbers $R - (-1, 1)$.

6. **Assertion** (A) $\tan^{-1}$ is defined as a function if the domain is R and range is any of the intervals $\left(\frac{-3\pi}{2}, \frac{-\pi}{2}\right), \left(\frac{-\pi}{2}, \frac{\pi}{2}\right) \left(\frac{\pi}{2}, \frac{3\pi}{2}\right)$ and so on.

Reason (R) The principal value branch of $\tan^{-1}$ is $\left(\frac{-\pi}{2}, \frac{\pi}{2}\right)$.

7. **Assertion** (A) The value of $\cos^{-1}\left[\cos\left(\frac{13\pi}{6}\right)\right]$ is $\frac{\pi}{6}$.

Reason (R) $\cos^{-1}(\cos x) = x ; x \in [0, \pi]$.

8. **Assertion** (A) If $\tan^{-1}\frac{x-1}{x-2} + \tan^{-1}\frac{x+1}{x+2} = \frac{\pi}{4}$, then the value of x is $\pm\frac{1}{\sqrt{2}}$.

Reason (R) The value of $\tan^{-1}\left(\tan\frac{3\pi}{4}\right)$ is $\frac{\pi}{4}$.

3. Matrices

9. **Assertion** (A) Matrix $A = \begin{bmatrix} 0 \\ \sqrt{3} \\ -1 \\ 1/2 \end{bmatrix}$ is a column matrix of order 4×1.

Reason (R) If $A = [a_{ij}]_{m \times 1}$ is a column matrix, then its order is $m \times 1$.

10. Assertion (A) If $A=\begin{bmatrix}3 & 1\\ -5 & x\end{bmatrix}$, then $(-A)$ is given by $\begin{bmatrix}-3 & -1\\ 5 & -x\end{bmatrix}$.

Reason (R) The negative of a matrix is denoted by $-A$ and is defined as $-A=(-1)\,A$.

11. Assertion (A) A 2×2 matrix $A=[a_{ij}]$, whose elements are given by $a_{ij}=i\times j$ is $\begin{bmatrix}1 & 2\\ 2 & 4\end{bmatrix}$.

Reason (R) If A is a 4×2 matrix, then the elements in A is 5.

12. Assertion (A) Scalar matrix $A=[a_{ij}]=\begin{cases}k; & i=j\\ 0; & i\neq j\end{cases}$, where k is a scalar, is an identity matrix when $k=1$.

Reason (R) Every identity matrix is not a scalar matrix.

4. Determinants

13. Assertion (A) $\Delta=\begin{vmatrix}a_1 & a_2 & a_3\\ b_1 & b_2 & b_3\\ ka_1 & ka_2 & ka_3\end{vmatrix}=0$

Reason (R) If corresponding elements of any two rows of a determinant are proportional, then its value is zero.

14. Assertion (A) The points $A\,(a, b+c)$, $B\,(b, c+a)$ and $C\,(c, a+b)$ are collinear.

Reason (R) Area of a triangle with three collinear points is zero.

15. Assertion (A) $\Delta=a_{11}A_{11}+a_{12}A_{12}+a_{13}A_{13}$ where, A_{ij} is cofactor of a_{ij}.

Reason (R) $\Delta=$ Sum of the products of elements of any row (or column) with their corresponding cofactors.

16. Assertion (A) The matrix $A=\begin{bmatrix}1 & 2\\ 4 & 8\end{bmatrix}$ is singular.

Reason (R) A square matrix A is said to be singular, if $|A|=0$.

5. Continuity and Differentiability

17. Assertion (A) If a function f is discontinuous at c, then c is called a point of discontinuity.

Reason (R) A function is continuous at $x=c$, if the function is defined at $x=c$ and the value of the function at $x=c$ equals the limit of the function at $x=c$.

18. Assertion (A) If $f(x)=\dfrac{\sin(ax+b)}{\cos(cx+d)}$, then

$$f'(x)=a\cos(ax+b)\sec(cx+d)+c\sin(ax+b)\tan(cx+d)\sec(cx+d).$$

Reason (R) If $f(x)=\dfrac{u}{v}$, then $f'(x)=\dfrac{vu'-uv'}{v^2}$

19. Assertion (A) If $xy=e^{x-y}$, then $\dfrac{dy}{dx}=\dfrac{y\,(x-1)}{x\,(1+y)}$.

Reason (R) $\dfrac{d}{dx}(u\cdot v)=u\dfrac{d}{dx}v+v\dfrac{d}{dx}u$

20. Assertion (A) $\dfrac{d^2}{dx^2}(e^{6x}\cos 3x)=9\,e^{6x}\,(3\cos 3x-4\sin 3x)$

Reason (R) $\dfrac{d}{dx}(u\cdot v)=u\dfrac{d}{dx}v+v\dfrac{d}{dx}u$

6. Application of Derivatives

21. Assertion (A) A balloon, which always remains spherical, has a variable radius. The rate, at which its volume is increasing with the radius when the radius is 10 cm, is $400\,\pi$ cm^3 / cm.

Reason (R) Rate of change of volume (v) of balloon with respect to radius (r) is $\dfrac{dv}{dr}=\left(\dfrac{2}{3}\pi\right)\cdot 3r^2$

22. Assertion (A) $f(x)=2x^3-9x^2+12x-3$ is increasing outside the interval (1, 2).

Reason (R) $f'(x)<0$ for $x\in(1, 2)$.

Then, which of the following is true?

23. Assertion (A) The tangents to curve $y=7x^3+11$ at the points, where $x=2$ and $x=-2$ are parallel.

Reason (R) The slope of the tangents at the points, where $x=2$ and $x=-2$, are equal.

24. Assertion (A) If the length of three sides of a trapezium other than base are equal to 10 cm, then the area of trapezium when it is maximum, is $75\sqrt{3}$ cm^2.

Reason (R) Area of trapezium is maximum at $x=5$.

7. Integrals

25. If $f(x)=2x$, then $\int f(x)\,dx=x^2+C$

Assertion (A) We get different integrals for different values of C.

Reason (R) Here, x^2+C represents a family of integrals.

26. **Assertion** (A) $\int \frac{x^3}{x+1}dx = x - \frac{x^2}{2} + \frac{x^3}{3} - \log|x+1| + C.$

Reason (R) $\frac{d}{dx}[x - \frac{x^2}{2} + \frac{x^3}{3} - \log|x+1| + C] = \frac{x^2}{x+1}$

27. **Assertion** (A) $\int [\sin(\log x) + \cos(\log x)]\,dx = x\sin(\log x) + C.$

Reason (R) $\frac{d}{dx}[x\sin(\log x)] = \sin(\log x) + \cos(\log x).$

28. **Assertion** (A) $\int_0^{2a} f(x)\,dx = 2\int_0^a f(x)\,dx$

Reason (R) $f(2a - x) = f(x)$

8. Differential Equations

29. **Assertion** (A) The degree of the differential equation $\frac{d^3y}{dx^3} + 2\left(\frac{d^2y}{dx^2}\right)^2 - \frac{dy}{dx} + y = 0$ can be defined.

Reason (R) The degree of a differential equation can be defined, if it is a polynomial equation in derivatives.

30. **Assertion** (A) The degree of the differential equation $\frac{d^2y}{dx^2} + 3\left(\frac{dy}{dx}\right)^2 = x^2 \log\left(\frac{d^2y}{dx^2}\right)$ is not defined.

Reason (R) If the differential equation is a polynomial in terms of its derivatives, then its degree is defined.

31. **Assertion** (A) The differential equations

$$\frac{dx}{dy} + x = \cos y \text{ and } \frac{dx}{dy} + \frac{-2x}{y} = y^2e^{-y}$$

are first order linear differential equations.

Reason (R) The differential equation of the form

$$\frac{dx}{dy} + P_1x = Q_1$$

where, P_1 and Q_1 are constants or functions of y only, is called first order linear differential equation.

32. Consider the differential equation

$$\frac{dy}{dx} - \frac{\tan y}{x} = \frac{\tan y \sin y}{x^2}$$

Assertion (A) Its solution is $\frac{x}{\sin y} + \log x = C.$

Reason (R) Its solution is x.

9. Probability

33. Consider the two events E and F which are associated with the sample space of a random experiment.

Assertion (A) $P(E/F) = \frac{n(E \cap F)}{n(F)}.$

Reason (R) $P(E/F) = \frac{P(E \cap F)}{P(F)}.$

34. Consider the following statements

Two coins are tossed once.

Assertion (A) If E : tail appears on one coin and F : one coin shows head, then $P(E/F)$ is 1.

Reason (R) If E : no tail appears and F : no head appears, then $P(E/F)$ is 0.

35. **Assertion** (A) If A and B are two events such that $P(A) = \frac{1}{2}, P(B) = \frac{1}{3}$ and $P(A/B) = \frac{1}{4}$, then $P(A' \cap B')$ is equal to $\frac{1}{4}$.

Reason (R) If $P(A) = 0.4, P(B) = 0.8$ and $P(B/A) = 0.6$, then $P(A \cup B)$ is equal to 0.96.

36. **Assertion** (A) Let A and B be two independent events. Then, $P(A \cap B) = P(A) + P(B)$.

Reason (R) Three events A, B and C are said to be pairwise independent, if $P(A \cap B \cap C) = P(A)P(B)P(C)$.

Solutions

1. (a) Here, $R = \{(x, y) : y \text{ is divisible by } x\}$ is a relation in the set $A = \{1, 2, 3, 4, 5, 6\}$.

For reflexive, we know that x is divisible by x, which is true for all $x \in A$.

$\therefore \quad (x, x) \in R$ for all $x \in A$. So, R is reflexive.

For symmetry, we observe that 6 is divisible by 2. This means that $(2, 6) \in R$ but $(6, 2) \notin R$. So, R is not symmetric.

For transitivity, let $(x, y) \in R$ and $(y, z) \in R$

$\Rightarrow y$ is divisible by x and z is divisible by y.

$\Rightarrow z$ is divisible by x.

$\Rightarrow (x, z) \in R$

For example, 2 is divisible by 1 and 4 is divisible by 2.

So, 4 is divisible by 1. So, R is transitive.

2. (a) Let (a, b) be an arbitrary element of $N \times N$.

Then, $\quad (a, b) \in N \times N$

$\Rightarrow \quad a, b \in N$

$\Rightarrow \quad a + b = b + a$

(by commutativity of addition in N)

$\Rightarrow \quad (a, b)\, R\, (a, b)$

$\Rightarrow R$ is reflexive on $N \times N$.

Let $(a, b), (c, d) \in N \times N$ be such that $(a, b)\, R\, (c, d)$

$\Rightarrow \quad a + d = b + c$

$\Rightarrow \quad b + c = a + d$

$\Rightarrow \quad c + b = d + a$

$\Rightarrow \quad (c, d)\, R\, (a, b)$

$\Rightarrow R$ is symmetric on $N \times N$.

Now, let $(a, b), (c, d), (e, f) \in N \times N$ such that $(a, b)\, R\, (c, d)$ and $(c, d)\, R\, (e, f)$.

$\because \quad (a, b)\, R\, (c, d)$

$\Rightarrow \quad a + d = b + c$

$\because \quad (c, d)\, R\, (e, f)$

$\Rightarrow \quad c + f = d + e$

$\Rightarrow \quad (a + d) + (c + f) = (b + c) + (d + e)$

$\Rightarrow \quad a + f = b + e$

$\Rightarrow \quad (a, b)\, R\, (e, f)$

Thus, $(a, b)\, R\, (c, d)$ and $(c, d)\, R\, (e, f)$

$\Rightarrow (a, b)\, R\, (e, f)$ for all $(a, b), (c, d), (e, f) \in N \times N$

$\Rightarrow R$ is transitive on $N \times N$.

$\Rightarrow R$ is an equivalence relation on $N \times N$.

3. (a) Here, $f : A \times B \to B \times A$ is defined as $f(a, b) = (b, a)$.

Let $(a_1, b_1), (a_2, b_2) \in A \times B$ such that

$$f(a_1, b_1) = f(a_2, b_2)$$

$\Rightarrow \quad (b_1, a_1) = (b_2, a_2)$

$\Rightarrow \quad b_1 = b_2$ and $a_1 = a_2$

$\Rightarrow \quad (a_1, b_1) = (a_2, b_2)$

Therefore, f is one-one. Now, let $(b, a) \in B \times A$ be any element.

Then, there exists $(a, b) \in A \times B$ such that

$f(a, b) = (b, a)$ (definition of f)

Therefore, f is onto.

Hence, f is bijective.

4. (a) Here, $f : R \to R$ is given as $f(x) = x^3$.

Suppose $\quad f(x) = f(y)$,

where $\quad x, y \in R \Rightarrow x^3 = y^3$ ...(i)

Now, we try to show that $x = y$.

Suppose $x \neq y$, their cubes will also be not equal.

$$x^3 \neq y^3$$

However, this will be a contradiction to Eq. (i).

Therefore, $x = y$.

Hence, f is injective.

5. (a) If we restrict the domain of cosec function to $\left[\frac{-\pi}{2}, \frac{\pi}{2}\right] - \{0\}$, then it is one to one and onto and its range as the set $R - (-1, 1)$. Actually, cosec function restricted to any of the intervals $\left[\frac{-3\pi}{2}, \frac{-\pi}{2}\right] - \{-\pi\}$, $\left[\frac{-\pi}{2}, \frac{\pi}{2}\right] - \{0\}$, $\left[\frac{\pi}{2}, \frac{3\pi}{2}\right] - \{\pi\}$ etc., is bijective and its range is the set of all real numbers $R - (-1, 1)$. Thus, cosec^{-1} can be defined as a function whose domain is $R - (-1, 1)$ and range could be any of the intervals $\left[\frac{-\pi}{2}, \frac{\pi}{2}\right] - \{0\}$, $\left[\frac{-3\pi}{2}, \frac{-\pi}{2}\right] - \{-\pi\}$, $\left[\frac{\pi}{2}, \frac{3\pi}{2}\right] - \{\pi\}$ etc.

6. (b) $\tan^{-1}$ can be defined as a function whose domain is R and range could be any of the intervals $\left(\frac{-3\pi}{2}, \frac{-\pi}{2}\right), \left(\frac{-\pi}{2}, \frac{\pi}{2}\right), \left(\frac{\pi}{2}, \frac{3\pi}{2}\right)$ and so on.

These intervals give different branches of the function $\tan^{-1}$. The branch with range $\left(\frac{-\pi}{2}, \frac{\pi}{2}\right)$ is called the principal value branch of the function $\tan^{-1}$.

7. (a) Let $\theta = \cos^{-1}\left[\cos\left(\frac{13\pi}{6}\right)\right] \neq \frac{13\pi}{6} \quad \left[\because \frac{13\pi}{6} \notin [0, \pi]\right]$

Now, $\theta = \cos^{-1}\left[\cos\left(2\pi + \frac{\pi}{6}\right)\right]$

$[\because \text{range of } \cos^{-1} x \text{ is } [0, \pi]]$

$= \cos^{-1}\left[\cos\frac{\pi}{6}\right] \quad [\because \cos[2\pi + x] = \cos x]$

$= \frac{\pi}{6} \quad [\because \cos^{-1}(\cos x) = x, \text{ if } x \in [0, \pi]]$

$\therefore$ Both A and R are correct; R is correct explanation of A.

8. (c) Given, $\tan^{-1}\frac{x-1}{x-2} + \tan^{-1}\frac{x+1}{x+2} = \frac{\pi}{4}$

$$\Rightarrow \tan^{-1}\left(\frac{\frac{x-1}{x-2} + \frac{x+1}{x+2}}{1 - \left(\frac{x-1}{x-2}\right)\left(\frac{x+1}{x+2}\right)}\right) = \frac{\pi}{4}$$

$\left[\because \tan^{-1} x + \tan^{-1} y = \tan^{-1}\left(\frac{x+y}{1-xy}\right)\right]$

$$\Rightarrow \tan^{-1}\left(\frac{\frac{(x-1)(x+2) + (x+1)(x-2)}{(x-2)(x+2)}}{\frac{(x-2)(x+2) - (x-1)(x+1)}{(x-2)(x+2)}}\right) = \frac{\pi}{4}$$

$$\Rightarrow \frac{(x-1)(x+2) + (x+1)(x-2)}{(x-2)(x+2) - (x-1)(x+1)} = \tan\frac{\pi}{4}$$

$$\Rightarrow \frac{2x^2 - 4}{(x^2-4) - (x^2-1)} = 1 \quad \left[\because \tan\frac{\pi}{4} = 1\right]$$

$$\Rightarrow 2x^2 - 4 = -3$$

$$\Rightarrow 2x^2 = 1$$

$$\Rightarrow x^2 = \frac{1}{2} \Rightarrow x = \pm\frac{1}{\sqrt{2}}$$

Now, $\tan^{-1}\left(\tan\frac{3\pi}{4}\right) = \tan^{-1}\left[\tan\left(\pi - \frac{\pi}{4}\right)\right]$

$= \tan^{-1}\left(-\tan\frac{\pi}{4}\right)$

$[\because \tan(\pi - \theta) = -\tan\theta]$

$= \tan^{-1}\left[\tan\left(-\frac{\pi}{4}\right)\right]$

$[\because -\tan\theta = \tan(-\theta)]$

$= -\frac{\pi}{4}$ which lies in the range $\left(-\frac{\pi}{2}, \frac{\pi}{2}\right)$.

9. (a) $A = \begin{bmatrix} 0 \\ \sqrt{3} \\ -1 \\ 1/2 \end{bmatrix}$ is a column matrix of order 4×1.

In general, $A = [a_{ij}]_{m \times 1}$ is a column matrix, of order $m \times 1$.

10. (a) **Negative of a matrix** The negative of a matrix is denoted by $-A$. We define $-A = (-1)A$.

If $A = \begin{bmatrix} 3 & 1 \\ -5 & x \end{bmatrix}$, then $-A$ is given by

$-A = (-1)A$

$= (-1)\begin{bmatrix} 3 & 1 \\ -5 & x \end{bmatrix} = \begin{bmatrix} -3 & -1 \\ 5 & -x \end{bmatrix}$

11. **Assertion** In general, the matrix A of order 2×2 is given by $A = \begin{bmatrix} a_{11} & a_{12} \\ a_{21} & a_{22} \end{bmatrix}$.

Now, $a_{ij} = i \times j$, $i = 1, 2$ and $j = 1, 2$

$\therefore \quad a_{11} = 1, a_{12} = 2, a_{21} = 2$ and $a_{22} = 4$

Thus, matrix A is $\begin{bmatrix} 1 & 2 \\ 2 & 4 \end{bmatrix}$

Reason If A is a 4×2 matrix, then A has $4 \times 2 = 8$ elements.

12. A scalar matrix $A = [a_{ij}] = \begin{cases} k; & i = j \\ 0; & i \neq j \end{cases}$ is an identity matrix when $k = 1$.

But every identity matrix is clearly a scalar matrix.

13. (a) If corresponding elements of any two rows (or columns) of a determinant are proportional (in the same ratio), then its value is zero.

Thus, $\Delta = \begin{vmatrix} a_1 & a_2 & a_3 \\ b_1 & b_2 & b_3 \\ k a_1 & k a_2 & k a_3 \end{vmatrix} = 0$

$[\because R_1 \text{ and } R_3 \text{ are proportional}]$

14. (a) We know that, the area of triangle with three collinear points is zero.

Now, consider

Area of $\Delta ABC = \frac{1}{2}\begin{vmatrix} a & b+c & 1 \\ b & c+a & 1 \\ c & a+b & 1 \end{vmatrix}$

$= \frac{1}{2}| a\{(c+a) \times 1 - (a+b) \times 1\} - (b+c)\{b \times 1 - 1 \times c\}$

$+ 1\{b \times (a+b) - (c+a) \times c\}|$

$$=\frac{1}{2}|a(c+a-a-b)-(b+c)(b-c)+1(ab+b^2-c^2-ac)|$$

$$=\frac{1}{2}|ac-ab-b^2+c^2+ab+b^2-c^2-ac|=\frac{1}{2}\times 0=0$$

Since, area of $\Delta ABC=0$.

Hence, points $A(a, b+c)$, $B(b, c+a)$ and $C(c, a+b)$ are collinear.

15. (a) By expanding the determinant

$$\Delta=\begin{vmatrix} a_{11} & a_{12} & a_{13} \\ a_{21} & a_{22} & a_{23} \\ a_{31} & a_{32} & a_{33} \end{vmatrix} \text{ along } R_1, \text{ we have}$$

$$\Delta=(-1)^{1+1}a_{11}\begin{vmatrix} a_{22} & a_{23} \\ a_{32} & a_{33} \end{vmatrix}+(-1)^{1+2}a_{12}\begin{vmatrix} a_{21} & a_{23} \\ a_{31} & a_{33} \end{vmatrix}+(-1)^{1+3}a_{13}\begin{vmatrix} a_{21} & a_{22} \\ a_{31} & a_{32} \end{vmatrix}$$

$$=a_{11}A_{11}+a_{12}A_{12}+a_{13}A_{13},$$

where A_{ij} is cofactor of a_{ij}.

= Sum of products of elements of R_1 with their corresponding cofactors

Similarly, Δ can be calculated by other five ways of expansion that is along R_2, R_3, C_1, C_2 and C_3.

Hence, Δ = sum of the products of elements of any row (or column) with their corresponding cofactors

16. (a) The determinant of the matrix $A=\begin{bmatrix} 1 & 2 \\ 4 & 8 \end{bmatrix}$ is

$$|A|=\begin{vmatrix} 1 & 2 \\ 4 & 8 \end{vmatrix}=8-8=0$$

Hence, A is a singular matrix.

17. (b) A function is continuous at $x=c$, if the function is defined at $x=c$ and if the value of the function at $x=c$ equals the limit of the function at $x=c$. And if f is not continuous at c, we say f is discontinuous at c and c is called a point of discontinuity of f.

18. (a) Let $y=\dfrac{\sin(ax+b)}{\cos(cx+d)}$

On differentiating both sides w.r.t. x, we get

$$\frac{dy}{dx}=\frac{d}{dx}\left(\frac{\sin(ax+b)}{\cos(cx+d)}\right)$$

$$=\frac{\cos(cx+d)\frac{d}{dx}\{\sin(ax+b)\}-\sin(ax+b)\frac{d}{dx}\cos(cx+d)}{[\cos(cx+d)]^2}$$

[by quotient rule]

$$=\frac{\cos(cx+d)\cos(ax+b).(a+0)+\sin(ax+b)\sin(cx+d)(c+0)}{\cos^2(cx+d)}$$

[by chain rule,

$\frac{d}{dx}\sin(ax+b)=\cos(ax+b)\frac{d}{dx}(ax+b)$
$=\cos(ax+b)\times(a\times1+0)$

$\frac{d}{dx}\cos(cx+d)=-\sin(cx+d)\frac{d}{dx}(cx+d)$
$=-\sin(cx+d)\times(c\times1+0)$]

$$=\frac{a\cos(cx+d)\cos(ax+b)+c\sin(ax+b)\sin(cx+d)}{\cos^2(cx+d)}$$

$$=\frac{a\cos(cx+d)\cos(ax+b)}{\cos^2(cx+d)}+\frac{c\sin(ax+b)\sin(cx+d)}{\cos^2(cx+d)}$$

$$=\frac{a\cos(ax+b)}{\cos(cx+d)}+\frac{c\sin(ax+b)\sin(cx+d)}{\cos(cx+d)\cos(cx+d)}$$

$$=a\cos(ax+b)\sec(cx+d)+c\sin(ax+b)\tan(cx+d)\sec(cx+d)$$

19. (b) Given, $xy=e^{(x-y)}$

On differentiating both sides w.r.t. x, we get

$$\frac{d}{dx}(xy)=\frac{d}{dx}(e^{x-y})$$

$$\Rightarrow \quad x\frac{dy}{dx}+y.1=e^{x-y}\frac{d}{dx}(x-y)$$

[using product rule in LHS and chain rule in RHS]

$$\Rightarrow \quad x\frac{dy}{dx}+y=e^{x-y}\left(1-\frac{dy}{dx}\right)$$

$$\Rightarrow \quad x\frac{dy}{dx}+e^{x-y}\frac{dy}{dx}=e^{x-y}-y$$

$$\Rightarrow \quad (x+e^{x-y})\frac{dy}{dx}=e^{x-y}-y$$

$$\Rightarrow \quad \frac{dy}{dx}=\frac{e^{x-y}-y}{x+e^{x-y}}=\frac{xy-y}{x+xy}$$

[$\because e^{x-y}=xy$ is given]

$$=\frac{y(x-1)}{x(1+y)}$$

Also, $\dfrac{d}{dx}(u\cdot v)=u\dfrac{dv}{dx}+v\dfrac{du}{dx}$

20. (b) Let $y=e^{6x}\cos 3x$

On differentiating twice w.r.t. x, we get

$$\frac{dy}{dx}=\frac{d}{dx}(e^{6x}\cos 3x)$$

$$= e^{6x}\frac{d}{dx}(\cos 3x) + \cos 3x \frac{d}{dx}(e^{6x})$$
$$= e^{6x}(-\sin 3x . 3) + (\cos 3x)\, e^{6x} . 6$$
$$= e^{6x}\{-3\sin 3x + 6\cos 3x\}$$

and $\frac{d^2y}{dx^2} = \frac{d}{dx}\{e^{6x}(-3\sin 3x + 6\cos 3x)\}$

$$= e^{6x}\frac{d}{dx}(-3\sin 3x + 6\cos 3x) + (-3\sin 3x + 6\cos 3x)\frac{d}{dx}e^{6x}$$
$$= e^{6x}(-3\cos 3x . 3 - 6\sin 3x . 3) + (-3\sin 3x + 6\cos 3x)\, e^{6x} . 6$$
$$= e^{6x}\{-9\cos 3x - 18\sin 3x - 18\sin 3x + 36\cos 3x\}$$
$$= e^{6x}\{27\cos 3x - 36\sin 3x\}$$
$$= 9e^{6x}\{3\cos 3x - 4\sin 3x\}$$

21. (c) Let r be the radius of spherical balloon and V be its volume.

Then, $r = 10$ cm and $V = \frac{4}{3}\pi r^3$,

Rate of change of volume w.r.t. radius r,

$$\frac{dV}{dr} = \left(\frac{4}{3}\pi\right)3r^2$$ [differentiating w.r.t. r]

$$= 4\pi r^2 = 4\pi(10)^2 = 400\pi \quad [\because r = 10 \text{ cm}]$$

Hence, the volume of the balloon is increasing at the rate of 400π cm^3/cm.

22. (b) $f'(x) = 6x^2 - 18x + 12$

For increasing function, $f'(x) \geq 0$

$\therefore \quad 6(x^2 - 3x + 2) \geq 0$

$\Rightarrow \quad 6(x-2)(x-1) \geq 0$

$\Rightarrow \quad x \leq 1$ and $x \geq 2$

$\therefore f(x)$ is increasing outside the interval (1, 2), therefore it is true statement.

Now, $\quad f'(x) < 0$

$\Rightarrow \quad 6(x-2)(x-1) < 0$

$\Rightarrow \quad 1 < x < 2$

$\therefore$ A and R are both true but R is not the correct explanation of A.

23. The equation of the given curve is

$$y = 7x^3 + 11 \qquad \ldots(i)$$

$\Rightarrow \quad \frac{dy}{dx} = 7 \times 3x^2 = 21x^2$ [differentiating w.r.t. x]

$\because$ The slope of the tangent to the curve at (x_0, y_0) is $\left(\frac{dy}{dx}\right)_{(x_0, y_0)}$

$\therefore$ Slope of tangent at $x = 2$ is

$$\left(\frac{dy}{dx}\right)_{x=2} = 21(2)^2 = 84$$

Slope of tangent at $x = -2$ is

$$\left(\frac{dy}{dx}\right)_{x=-2} = 21(-2)^2 = 84$$

It is observed that the slopes of the tangents at the points where, $x = 2$ and $x = -2$ are equal.

Hence, the two tangents are parallel.

Hence, both Assertion and Reason are true and Reason is the correct explanation of Assertion.

24. (a) The required trapezium is as given in figure. Draw perpendiculars DP and CQ on AB.

Let $AP = x$ cm.

Note that $\Delta APD \sim \Delta BQC$.

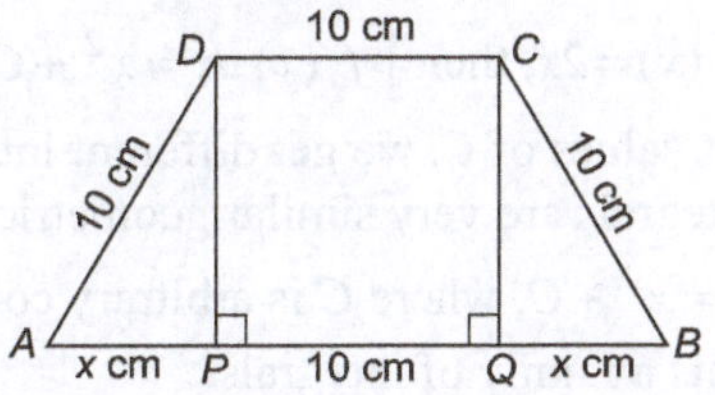

Therefore, $QB = x$ cm.

Also, by Pythagoras theorem, $DP = QC = \sqrt{100 - x^2}$.

Let A be the area of the trapezium.

Then,

$$A \equiv A(x) = \frac{1}{2}\text{(Sum of parallel sides)} \times \text{(Height)}$$
$$= \frac{1}{2}(2x + 10 + 10)(\sqrt{100 - x^2})$$
$$= (x + 10)(\sqrt{100 - x^2})$$

or $A'(x) = (x+10)\frac{(-2x)}{2\sqrt{100 - x^2}} + \sqrt{100 - x^2}$

$$= \frac{-2x^2 - 10x + 100}{\sqrt{100 - x^2}}$$

Now, $A'(x) = 0$ gives $2x^2 + 10x - 100 = 0$,

i.e. $x = 5$ and $x = -10$.

Since, x represents distance, it cannot be negative.

So, $x = 5$.

Now,

$$A''(x) = \frac{\left(\sqrt{100-x^2}(-4x-10) - (-2x^2-10x+100)\frac{(-2x)}{2\sqrt{100-x^2}}\right)}{100-x^2}$$

$$= \frac{2x^3 - 300x - 1000}{(100-x^2)^{3/2}} \quad \text{(on simplification)}$$

or $$A''(5) = \frac{2(5)^3 - 300(5) - 1000}{(100-(5)^2)^{\frac{3}{2}}}$$

$$= \frac{-2250}{75\sqrt{75}} = \frac{-30}{\sqrt{75}} < 0$$

Thus, area of trapezium is maximum at $x = 5$ and the area is given by

$$A(5) = (5+10)\sqrt{100-(5)^2}$$

$$= 15\sqrt{75}$$

$$= 75\sqrt{3}\ \text{cm}^2$$

25. (b) If $f(x) = 2x$, then $\int f(x)\,dx = x^2 + C$. For different values of C, we get different integrals. But these integrals are very similar geometrically.

Thus, $y = x^2 + C$, where C is arbitrary constant, represents a family of integrals.

By assigning different values to C, we get different members of the family. These together constitute the indefinite integral.

26. (c) $$\frac{d}{dx}\left(x - \frac{x^2}{2} + \frac{x^3}{3} - \log|x+1| + C\right)$$

$$= 1 - \frac{2x}{2} + \frac{3x^2}{3} - \frac{1}{x+1}$$

$$= 1 - x + x^2 - \frac{1}{x+1} = \frac{x^3}{x+1}$$

Thus, $$x - \frac{x^2}{2} + \frac{x^3}{3} - \log|x+1| + C = \int \frac{x^3}{x+1}\,dx$$

27. (a) Here, $I = \int [\sin(\log x) + \cos(\log x)]\,dx$ ...(i)

By using inspection method,

$$\frac{d}{dx}\{x\sin(\log x)\} = x\frac{d}{dx}\sin(\log x) + \sin(\log x)\frac{d}{dx}(x)$$

$$= x\cos(\log x) \times \frac{1}{x} + \sin(\log x)$$

$$= \cos(\log x) + \sin(\log x) \quad \text{...(ii)}$$

From Eqs. (i) and (ii), we get

$$I = \int \frac{d}{dx}\{x\sin(\log x)\}\,dx$$

$$= x\sin(\log x) + C$$

28. (b) Using $\int_0^{2a} f(x)\,dx = \int_0^a f(x)\,dx + \int_0^a f(2a-x)\,dx$ ...(i)

Now , if $f(2a-x) = f(x)$, then Eq. (i) becomes

$$\int_0^{2a} f(x)\,dx = \int_0^a f(x)\,dx + \int_0^a f(x)\,dx, = 2\int_0^a f(x)\,dx$$

and if $f(2a-x) = -f(x)$, then (1) becomes

$$\int_0^{2a} f(x)\,dx = \int_0^a f(x)\,dx - \int_0^a f(x)\,dx = 0$$

29. (a) To study the degree of a differential equation the key point is that the differential equation must be a polynomial equation in derivatives,

i.e. y', y'', y''' etc.

The given differential equation is

$$\frac{d^3y}{dx^3} + 2\left(\frac{d^2y}{dx^2}\right)^2 - \frac{dy}{dx} + y = 0$$

This is a polynomial equation in y''', y'' and y'

$\therefore$ Its degree can be defined.

30. (a) The given differential equation is

$$\frac{d^2y}{dx^2} + 3\left(\frac{dy}{dx}\right)^2 = x^2\log\left(\frac{d^2y}{dx^2}\right)$$

This is not a polynomial equation in terms of its derivatives.

$\therefore$ Its degree is not defined.

31. (a) Another form of first order linear differential equation is $\frac{dx}{dy} + P_1x = Q_1$.

where, P_1 and Q_1 are constants or functions of y only.

This type of differential equation are

$$\frac{dx}{dy} + x = \cos y$$

$$\frac{dx}{dy} + \frac{-2x}{y} = y^2e^{-y}$$

32. (c) Given, $$\frac{dy}{dx} - \frac{\tan y}{x} = \frac{\tan y \sin y}{x^2}$$

$$\Rightarrow \cot y \operatorname{cosec} y\frac{dy}{dx} - \frac{\operatorname{cosec} y}{x} = \frac{1}{x^2} \quad \text{...(i)}$$

Put $-\operatorname{cosec} y = t \Rightarrow \cot y \operatorname{cosec} y\frac{dy}{dx} = \frac{dt}{dx}$

$\therefore \quad \frac{dt}{dx}+\frac{t}{x}=\frac{1}{x^2}$ [from Eq. (i)]

$\therefore \quad \text{IF}=e^{\int P\,dx}=e^{\int \frac{1}{x}dx}=x$

$\therefore$ Solution is $tx=\int x\cdot\frac{1}{x^2}\,dx-C$

$\Rightarrow \quad -\text{cosec }y\cdot x=\log x-C \Rightarrow \frac{x}{\sin y}+\log x=C$

33. (a) **Assertion** The conditional probability of E given that F has occurred is

$$P\left(\frac{E}{F}\right)=\frac{\text{Number of elementary events favourable to } E\cap F}{\text{Numer of elementary events which are favourable } F}$$

$$=\frac{n(E\cap F)}{n(F)}$$

Dividing the numerator and the denominator by total number of elementary events of the sample space, we see that $P\left(\frac{E}{F}\right)$ can also be written as

$$P\left(\frac{E}{F}\right)=\frac{\frac{n(E\cap F)}{n(S)}}{\frac{n(F)}{n(S)}}=\frac{P(E\cap F)}{P(F)} \quad \ldots\text{(i)}$$

Note that I is valid only when $P(F)\neq 0$ i.e., $F\neq\phi$.

Reason If E and F are two events associated with the same sample space of a random experiment, the conditional probability of the event E given that F has occurred, i.e. $P\left(\frac{E}{F}\right)$ is given by

$$P\left(\frac{E}{F}\right)=\frac{P(E\cap F)}{P(F)} \text{ provided } P(F)\neq 0$$

34. (b) If two coins are tossed once, then the sample space $S=\{HH, HT, TH, TT\}$

Assertion E = Set of events having tail on one coin $=\{HT, TH\}$

F = Set of events having one coin showing head $=\{HT, TH\}$

and $\quad E\cap F=\{HT, TH\}$

$\therefore \quad P(E)=\frac{2}{4}=\frac{1}{2}, P(F)=\frac{2}{4}=\frac{1}{2}$

and $\quad P(E\cap F)=\frac{2}{4}=\frac{1}{2}$

$\therefore \quad P\left(\frac{E}{F}\right)=\frac{P(E\cap F)}{P(F)}=\frac{1/2}{1/2}=1$

Reason E = Set of events having no tail = $\{HH\}$,

F = Set of events having no head = $\{TT\}$

and $\quad E\cap F=\phi$

$P(E)=\frac{1}{4}, P(F)=\frac{1}{4}$

and $\quad P(E\cap F)=\frac{0}{4}=0.$

$P\left(\frac{E}{F}\right)=\frac{P(E\cap F)}{P(F)}=\frac{0}{1/4}=0.$

35. (b) **Assertion** Given that,

$P(A)=\frac{1}{2}, P(B)=\frac{1}{3}$ and $P\left(\frac{A}{B}\right)=\frac{1}{4}$

$\because \quad P\left(\frac{A}{B}\right)=\frac{P(A\cap B)}{P(B)}$

$\therefore \quad \frac{1}{4}=\frac{P(A\cap B)}{\frac{1}{3}}$

$\Rightarrow \quad P(A\cap B)=\frac{1}{4\times 3} \Rightarrow P(A\cap B)=\frac{1}{12}$

Now, $\quad P(A\cup B)=P(A)+P(B)-P(A\cap B)$

$=\frac{1}{2}+\frac{1}{3}-\frac{1}{12}=\frac{6+4-1}{12}=\frac{9}{12}=\frac{3}{4}$

We know that,

$P(A'\cap B')=\overline{P(A\cup B)}$

$=1-P(A\cup B)=1-\frac{3}{4}=\frac{1}{4}$

Reason Given that,

$P(A)=0.4, P(B)=0.8$

and $\quad P\left(\frac{B}{A}\right)=0.6$

$\because \quad P\left(\frac{B}{A}\right)=\frac{P(A\cap B)}{P(A)}$

$\therefore \quad 0.6=\frac{P(A\cap B)}{0.4}$

$\Rightarrow \quad P(A\cap B)=0.6\times 0.4=0.24$

Now, $\quad P(A\cup B)=P(A)+P(B)-P(A\cap B)$

$=0.4+0.8-0.24$

$=1.20-0.24=0.96$

36. (d) **Assertion** False. If A and B are independent events, then $P(A\cap B)=P(A)\cdot P(B)$

Reason False. Reason is that A, B, C will be independent, if they are pairwise independent and $P(A\cap B\cap C)=P(A)\,P(B)\,P(C)$.

ISC

SAMPLE PAPER 01

Time : 3 hrs
Marks : 80

Mathematics

General Instructions

1. The Question Paper consists of three Sections A, B and C.
2. Candidates are required to attempt all questions from Section A and all questions either from Section B or Section C.
3. Section A Internal choice has been provided in two questions of two marks each, two questions of four marks each and two questions of six marks each.
4. Section B Internal choice has been provided in one question of two marks and one question of four marks.
5. Section C Internal choice has been provided in one question of two marks and one question of four marks.
6. All working, including rough work, should be done on the same sheet as, and adjacent to the rest of the answer.
7. The intended marks for questions or parts of questions are given in brackets [ ].
8. Mathematical tables and graph papers are provided.

Section A **[65 Marks]**

1. In sub-parts (i) to (x) choose the correct option and in sub-parts (xi) to (xv), answer the questions as instructed. **[15 × 1]**

(i) Let $f : R \to R$ be defined by $f(x) = x^2 + 1$. Then, pre-images of 17 and -3 respectively, are

(a) ϕ, $\{4, -4\}$ (b) $\{3, -3\}$, ϕ
(c) $\{4\}$, ϕ (d) $\{4, -4\}$, $\{2, -2\}$

(ii) The value of $\tan^2(\sec^{-1} 2) + \cot^2(\text{cosec}^{-1} 3)$ is

(a) 5 (b) 13 (c) 11 (d) 15

(iii) The equation of tangent drawn to the curve $y = \sin x$ at the point (0, 0), is

(a) $y = x$ (b) $2x + 3y = 0$
(c) $y \sin x + 2x = 0$ (d) None of these

(iv) The equation of the normal to the curve $y = \sin x$ at (0, 0) is

(a) $x = 0$ (b) $y = 0$ (c) $x + y = 0$ (d) $x - y = 0$

(v) If $f(x) = \cos^{-1}(\sin x)$, then $f'(x)$ is equal to

(a) 0 (b) 1
(c) -1 (d) None of these

(vi) If the determinant of matrix A of order 3×3 is of value 4. Then, the value of $|3A|$ is equal to

(a) 107 (b) 108 (c) 106 (d) 105

(vii) The value of x such that

$$[1 \;\; 2 \;\; 1]\begin{bmatrix} 1 & 2 & 0 \\ 2 & 0 & 1 \\ 1 & 0 & 2 \end{bmatrix}\begin{bmatrix} 0 \\ 2 \\ x \end{bmatrix} = 0 \text{ is}$$

(a) 1 (b) 0 (c) -1 (d) 3

(viii) The range of the function $f(x) = x^2 + 2x + 2$ is

(a) $(1, \infty)$ (b) $(2, \infty)$
(c) $(0, \infty)$ (d) $[1, \infty)$

(ix) **Statement I** If A is skew-symmetric matrix of order 3, then $|A| = 0$.

Statement II The value of $\begin{vmatrix} 1 & 1 & 17 \\ 0 & 3 & 3 \\ 1 & 4 & 6 \end{vmatrix}$ is -42.

Which of the following option is correct?

(a) Both the statements are true.
(b) Both the statements are false.
(c) Statement I is true and Statement II is false.
(d) Statement I is false and Statement II is true.

(x) **Assertion** (A) If A and B are two independent events such that $P(A)=\frac{1}{2}$ and $P(B)=\frac{1}{3}$, then $P(\text{neither } A \text{ nor } B)=\frac{1}{3}$.

Reason (R) $P\left(\frac{E}{F}\right)=\frac{P(E\cap F)}{P(F)}$.

(a) Both A and R are true and R is the correct explanation of A.
(b) Both A and R are true but R is not the correct explanation of A.
(c) A is true but R is false.
(d) A is false but R is true.

(xi) The sum of the order and degree of the differential equation $1+\left(\frac{dy}{dx}\right)^4=7\left(\frac{d^2y}{dx^2}\right)^3$ is

(a) 5 (b) 6 (c) 7 (d) 8

(xii) Let $A=\{a, b, c\}$ and the relation R be defined on A as $R=\{(a,a),(b,c),(a,b)\}$. Then, write minimum number of ordered pairs to be added in R to make R reflexive and transitive.

(xiii) Find a matrix X such that $3A-2B+X=O$, where $A=\begin{bmatrix}4 & 2\\ 1 & 3\end{bmatrix}$, $B=\begin{bmatrix}-2 & 1\\ 3 & 2\end{bmatrix}$.

(xiv) A die is tossed thrice. Find the probability of getting an even number atleast once.

(xv) If $P(A)=0.4$, $P(B)=0.8$ and $P\left(\frac{B}{A}\right)=0.6$, then find $P(A\cup B)$. **[2]**

2. (i) Prove that the greatest integer function defined by $f(x)=[x], 0<x<3$ is non-differentiable at $x=1$. **[2]**

Or

(ii) Discuss the continuity of the function $f(x)=\sin x\cdot\cos x$.

3. If the function f in $A=R-\left\{\frac{2}{3}\right\}$ defined as $f(x)=\frac{4x+3}{6x-4}$, then find f^{-1}.

4. (i) Evaluate $\int\left(\log(\log x)+\frac{1}{(\log x)^2}\right)dx$. **[2]**

Or

(ii) Evaluate $\int_0^{\pi/4}(\tan x+\cot x)^{-2}\,dx$.

5. Show that the function $f(x)=\tan x-x$ is always increasing in $x\in R$. **[2]**

6. Solve $\frac{dy}{dx}+y=\cos x-\sin x$. **[2]**

7. The equation of tangent at $(2,3)$ on the curve $y^2=ax^3+b$ is $y=4x-5$, find the values of a and b. **[4]**

8. Show that $\tan\left(\frac{1}{2}\sin^{-1}\frac{3}{4}\right)=\frac{4-\sqrt{7}}{3}$. **[4]**

Or

Prove that $\tan^{-1}\left(\frac{\sqrt{1+x}-\sqrt{1-x}}{\sqrt{1+x}+\sqrt{1-x}}\right)=\frac{\pi}{4}-\frac{1}{2}\cos^{-1}x$, where $-\frac{1}{\sqrt{2}}\le x\le 1$.

9. (i) Find $\int\frac{2\cos x}{(1-\sin x)(1+\sin^2 x)}\,dx$. **[4]**

Or

(ii) Evaluate $\int_0^{\pi/4}\log(1+\tan\theta)\,d\theta$.

10. In a factory which manufactures bolts, machines A, B and C manufacture respectively 30%, 50% and 20% of the bolts of their outputs, 3%, 4% and 1% respectively are defective bolts.

(i) What is the probability that bolt is manufactured by machine A?
(ii) What is the probability that bolt is manufactured by machine C?
(iii) What is the probability of getting defective bolt if it is manufactured by machine B?
(iv) A bolt is drawn at random from the product and is found to be defective. Find the probability that this is not manufactured by machine B? **[4]**

11. (i) Solve the following differential equation.

$$x(x^2-1)\frac{dy}{dx}=1,\ y=0,\text{ when } x=2$$ **[6]**

Or

(ii) Solve the following differential equation.

$$(3xy+y^2)\,dx+(x^2+xy)\,dy=0$$

12. (i) Prove that the semi-vertical angle of the right circular cone of given volume and least curved surface area is $\cot^{-1}\sqrt{2}$. **[6]**

Or

(ii) Consider an open box with square base is to be made of a given quantity of cardboard of area c^2.

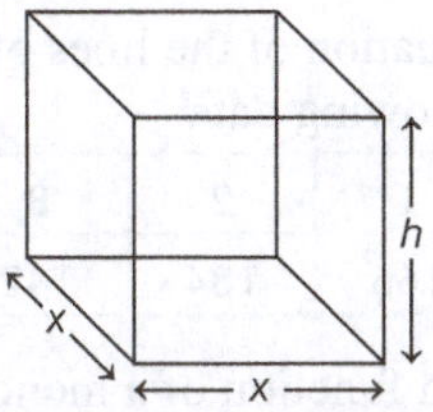

(a) Find the height of the box in terms of c and x.

(b) Show that the volume of the box is $\frac{1}{4}(c^2x - x^3)$.

(c) Find the value of x, for which the volume of the box is maximum.

(d) Calculate the maximum volume of the box.

13. The sum of three number is 6. If we multiply third number by 3 and add second number to it, we get 11. By adding first and third numbers, we get double of the second number.

(i) Form a set of simultaneous equations for the above information.

(ii) Solve the set of equations formed in (i) by matrix method.

(iii) Find the product of three numbers. **[6]**

14. Consider the throw of a pair of dice.

All outcomes of this throw are tabulated in the form of ordered pairs given below

(1, 1)	(1, 2)	(1, 3)	(1, 4)	(1, 5)	(1, 6)
(2, 1)	(2, 2)	(2, 3)	(2, 4)	(2, 5)	(2, 6)
(3, 1)	(3, 2)	(3, 3)	(3, 4)	(3, 5)	(3, 6)
(4, 1)	(4, 2)	(4, 3)	(4, 4)	(4, 5)	(4, 6)
(5, 1)	(5, 2)	(5, 3)	(5, 4)	(5, 5)	(5, 6)
(6, 1)	(6, 2)	(6, 3)	(6, 4)	(6, 5)	(6, 6)

If the total number of throws is four, then answer the following questions.

(i) Find the probability distribution.

	0	1	2	3	4

(ii) Calculate $P(1 \le X < 4)$.

(iii) Find mean.

(iv) $P(X \ge 4) = ?$ **[6]**

Section B **[15 Marks]**

15. In sub-parts (i) and (ii) choose the correct option and in sub-parts (iii) to (v), answer the questions as instructed.

(i) The projection of $\vec{a} = 3\hat{i} - \hat{j} + 5\hat{k}$ on $\vec{b} = 2\hat{i} + 3\hat{j} + \hat{k}$ is

(a) $\frac{8}{\sqrt{35}}$ (b) $\frac{8}{\sqrt{39}}$

(c) $\frac{8}{\sqrt{14}}$ (d) $\sqrt{14}$ **[1]**

(ii) If the lines $\frac{1-x}{3} = \frac{y-2}{2\alpha} = \frac{z-3}{2}$ and $\frac{x-1}{3\alpha} = y-1 = \frac{6-z}{5}$ are perpendicular, then the value of α is

(a) $\left(\frac{-10}{7}\right)$ (b) $\left(\frac{7}{10}\right)$

(c) $\left(\frac{10}{7}\right)$ (d) None of these **[1]**

(iii) Vectors $\vec{a}, \vec{b}$ and $\vec{c}$ are such that $\vec{a} + \vec{b} + \vec{c} = 0$ and $|\vec{a}| = 3, |\vec{b}| = 5$ and $|\vec{c}| = 7$, find the angle between $\vec{a}$ and $\vec{b}$. **[1]**

(iv) Find a vector in the direction of vector $\vec{a} = \hat{i} - 2\hat{j}$ that has magnitude 7 units. **[2]**

16. (i) Show that the vectors $\vec{a} = 3\hat{i} - 2\hat{j} + \hat{k}$, $\vec{b} = \hat{i} - 3\hat{j} + 5\hat{k}$ and $\vec{c} = 2\hat{i} + \hat{j} - 4\hat{k}$ from a right angled triangle. **[2]**

Or

(ii) Let $\vec{a} = \hat{i} + 4\hat{j} + 2\hat{k}$, $\vec{b} = 3\hat{i} - 2\hat{j} + 7\hat{k}$ and $\vec{c} = 2\hat{i} - \hat{j} + 4\hat{k}$. Find the vector $\vec{p}$ which is perpendicular to both $\vec{a}$ and $\vec{b}$ and $\vec{p} \cdot \vec{c} = 18$.

17. Consider the points $A(2, 1, -3)$, $B(-3, -2, 1)$ and $C(2, 4, -1)$.

(i) Find the equation of the plane passing through the points.

(ii) Find the equation of straight line passing through the points A and C.

(iii) Find the distance between the points A and B. **[4]**

18. Using integration, find the area of the circle $x^2 + y^2 = 16$ which is exterior to the parabola $y^2 = 6x$. **[4]**

Or

Sketch the graph of the curve $y^2 = x$ and $y^2 = 4 - 3x$ and find the area enclosed between them.

Section C **[15 Marks]**

19. In sub-parts (i) and (ii) choose the correct option and in sub-parts (iii) to (v), answer the questions as instructed.

(i) If the demand function is $p = \sqrt{6 - x}$, then the total revenue is equal to

(a) $x\sqrt{6-x}$ (b) $\frac{\sqrt{6-x}}{x}$

(c) $x^2\sqrt{6-x}$ (d) None of these **[1]**

(ii) If $b_{yx} = 0.8$, $r = 0.6$, $\sigma_x = 3$, then the value of σ_y is

(a) 4 (b) 5 (c) 3 (d) 2 **[1]**

(iii) The manufacturing cost of an item consists of ₹ 6000 as over heads, material cost ₹ 5 per unit and labour cost ₹ $\frac{x^2}{60}$ for x units produced. Find how many units must be produced so that the average cost is minimum. **[3]**

20. (i) The following observation are given (1, 4), (2, 8), (3, 2), (4, 12), (5, 10), (6, 14), (7, 16), (8, 6), (9, 18). Estimate the value of y when the value of x is 10 and also estimate the value of x when the value of y is 5. **[2]**

Or

(ii) Find the equation of the lines of regression on the basis of following data.

x	1	2	3	4	5
y	166	184	142	180	338

21. (i) The demand function of a monopolist is given by $p = 1500 - 2x - x^2$. Find the marginal revenue for any level of output x. Also, find the marginal revenue (MR) when $x = 10$ **[4]**

Or

(ii) A company charges ₹ 700 for a ratio set on an order of 60 or less sets. The charge is reduced by ₹ 10 per set for each set ordered in excess of 60. Find the largest size order company should allow so as to receive a maximum revenue.

22. An aeroplane can carry a maximum of 200 passengers. A profit of ₹1000 is made on each first class ticket and a profit of ₹600 is made on each economy class ticket. The airline reserves atleast 20 seats for first class. However, atleast 4 times as many passengers prefer to travel by economy class to the first class. Determine how many tickets of each type must be sold in order to maximise the profit for the airline. What is the maximum profit? **[4]**

1. (i) (c) (ii) (c) (iii) (a) (iv) (c) (v) (c)
(vi) (b) (vii) (c) (viii) (d) (ix) (a) (x) (b)
(xi) (a) (xii) {(b, b), (c, c), (a, c)} (xiii) $x=\begin{bmatrix}-16 & -4\\ 3 & -5\end{bmatrix}$ (xiv) $\frac{7}{8}$ (xv) 0.96

2. (ii) $f(x)$ is continuous **3.** $f^{-1}(x)=\frac{4x+3}{6x-4}$ **4.** (i) $x\left(\log(\log x)-\frac{1}{\log x}\right)+C$ *Or* (ii) $\pi/32$

6. $ye^x=e^x\cos x+C$ **7.** $a=-2,\ b=25$

9. (i) $\left[\tan^{-1}(\sin x)+\log\left|\frac{\sqrt{1+\sin^2 x}}{1-\sin x}\right|+C\right.$ *Or* (ii) $\frac{\pi}{8}\log 2$ **10.** (i) 0.3 (ii) 0.2 (iii) 0.04 (iv) $\frac{11}{31}$

11. (i) $y=-\log|x|+\frac{1}{2}\log|x-1|+\frac{1}{2}\log|x+1|+\log\frac{2}{\sqrt{3}}$ *Or* (ii) $y(y+2x)=\frac{c}{x^2}$

12. (ii) (a) $h=\frac{C^2-x^2}{4x}$ (c) $x=\frac{C}{\sqrt{3}}$ (d) $V_{max}=\frac{C^3}{6\sqrt{3}}$ cu units

13. (i) $x+y+z=6,\ y+3z=1,\ x-2y+z=0$ (ii) $x=1,\ y=2$ and $z=3$ (iii) 6

14. (i)

X	0	1	2	3	4
P(X)	$\frac{625}{1296}$	$\frac{500}{1296}$	$\frac{150}{1296}$	$\frac{20}{1296}$	$\frac{1}{1296}$

(ii) $\frac{670}{1296}$ (iii) $\frac{2}{3}$ (iv) $\frac{1}{1296}$

15. (i) (c) (ii) (a) (iii) $\frac{\pi}{3}$ (iv) $\frac{7}{\sqrt{5}}\hat{i}-\frac{14}{\sqrt{5}}\hat{j}$

16. *Or* (ii) $64\hat{i}-2\hat{j}-28\hat{k}$ **17.** (i) $18x-10y+5z+19=0$ (ii) $\frac{x-2}{-5}=\frac{y-1}{-3}=\frac{z+3}{4}$ (iii) $5\sqrt{2}$ units

18. $\left(\frac{10}{\sqrt{3}}+\frac{8\pi}{3}\right)$ sq units *Or* $\frac{16}{9}$ sq units

19. (i) (a) (ii) (a) (iii) 600 units

20. (i) $\frac{50}{3},\frac{10}{3}$ *Or* (ii) $y=34x+100,\ x=0.014\,y+0.172$

21. (i) $MR=1500-4x-3x^2$, MR=1160 when $x=10$ *Or* (ii) 65 sets

22. Maximum profit = ₹136000 at (40, 160) and minimum value = 1350 at (5, 3)

ISC

SAMPLE PAPER 02

Time : 3 hrs
Marks : 80

Mathematics

General Instructions

1. The Question Paper consists of three Sections A, B and C.
2. Candidates are required to attempt all questions from Section A and all questions either from Section B or Section C.
3. Section A Internal choice has been provided in two questions of two marks each, two questions of four marks each and two questions of six marks each.
4. Section B Internal choice has been provided in one question of two marks and one question of four marks.
5. Section C Internal choice has been provided in one question of two marks and one question of four marks.
6. All working, including rough work, should be done on the same sheet as, and adjacent to the rest of the answer.
7. The intended marks for questions or parts of questions are given in brackets [ ].
8. Mathematical tables and graph papers are provided.

Section A [65 Marks]

1. In sub-parts (i) to (x) choose the correct option and in sub-parts (xi) to (xv), answer the questions as instructed. **[15 × 1]**

(i) If $\cos^{-1} x > \sin^{-1} x$, then x belongs to the interval

(a) $(-\infty, 0)$ (b) $(-1, 0)$
(c) $\left[0, \frac{1}{\sqrt{2}}\right)$ (d) $\left[-1, \frac{1}{\sqrt{2}}\right)$

(ii) A relation f from C to R is defined by $x\ f\ y \Leftrightarrow |x| = y$. Then, the correct option is

(a) $(2+i)\ f\ 3$ (b) $3\ f\ (-3)$
(c) $i\ f\ 1$ (d) $(2+3i)\ f\ (13)$

(iii) The general solution of $e^x \sin y\, dy = 0$ is

(a) $e^x \cos y = k$ (b) $e^x \sin y = k$
(c) $e^x = \cos y$ (d) $e^x = k \sin y$

(iv) The tangent to the curve $y = e^{2x}$ at the point (0, 1) meets X-axis at

(a) (0, 1) (b) $\left(-\frac{1}{2}, 0\right)$ (c) (2, 0) (d) (0, 2)

(v) If A and B are two mutually exclusive events, then $P(A \text{ and } B)$ is equal to

(a) 1 (b) $\frac{1}{2}$ (c) $-\frac{1}{2}$ (d) 0

(vi) Let R be the relation in the set N given by $R = \{(a, b): a = b - 2, b > 6\}$. Then, the correct option is

(a) $(2,4 \in R)$ (b) $(3,8 \in R)$
(c) $(6,8 \in R)$ (d) $(8,7 \in R)$

(vii) The maximum number of equivalence relations on the set $A = \{1,2,3\}$ are

(a) 1 (b) 2
(c) 4 (d) 5

(viii) If A is square matix, A' is its transpose, then $\frac{1}{2}(A - A')$ is

(a) a symmetric matrix (b) a skew-symmetric matrix
(c) a unit matrix (d) an elementary matrix

(ix) **Statement I** If A is matrix of order 3 such that $A\,(\text{adj}\,A) = 10\,I$, then $|\text{adj}\,A| = 100$.

Statement II If A is skew-symmetric matrix of odd order x, then $|A| = -1$.

Which of the following option is correct?
(a) Both the statements are true.
(b) Both the statements are false.
(c) Statement I is true and Statement II is false.
(d) Statement II is false and Statement II is true.

(x) **Assertion** (A) If $A=\begin{bmatrix}2 & 3\\5 & 1\end{bmatrix}$, then $A^{-1}=\frac{1}{13}\begin{bmatrix}1 & 3\\5 & 2\end{bmatrix}$.

Reason (R) If the points (a_1, b_1), (a_2, b_2) and (a_1+a_2, b_1+b_2) are collinear, then $a_1b_2=a_2b_1$.
(a) Both A and R are true and R is the correct explanation of A.
(b) Both A and R are true but R is not the correct explanation of A.
(c) A is true but R is false.
(d) A is false but R is true.

(xi) If $x=a(\cos t+t\sin t)$ and $y=a(\sin t-t\cos t)$, then the value of $\frac{d^2y}{dx^2}$ at $x=\frac{\pi}{4}$ is
(a) $\frac{8\sqrt{2}}{a\pi}$ (b) $\frac{6\sqrt{2}}{a\pi}$ (c) $\frac{4\sqrt{2}}{a\pi}$ (d) $\frac{3\sqrt{2}}{a\pi}$

(xii) The elements a_{ij} of 3×3 matrix are given by $a_{ij}=\frac{1}{2}|-3\hat{i}+\hat{j}|$. Write the value of element a_{32}.

(xiii) Find the inverse of the function $f(x)=(x-3)^3$.

(xiv) The probability that atleast one of the two events A and B occurs is 0.6. If A and B occur simultaneously with probability 0.3, then evaluate $P(\bar{A})+P(\bar{B})$.

(xv) Given two independent events A and B such that $P(A)=0.3$ and $P(B)=0.6$.
Find (a) $P(A \text{ and not } B)$ (b) $P(A \text{ or } B)$ **[2]**

2. (i) If $f(x)=\sin 2x-\cos 2x$, then find $f'\left(\frac{\pi}{6}\right)$. **[2]**

Or

(ii) If $x=a\cos\theta+b\sin\theta$ and $y=a\sin\theta-b\cos\theta$, then show that $y^2\frac{d^2y}{dx^2}-x\frac{dy}{dx}+y=0$.

3. Consider $f:\{1,2,3\}\to\{a,b,c\}$ given by $f(1)=a$, $f(2)=b$, $f(3)=c$. Find f^{-1} and show that $(f^{-1})^{-1}=f$.

4. (i) Evaluate $\int\log|1+x^2|\,dx$. **[2]**

Or

(ii) Evaluate $\int\frac{1}{\sqrt{x^2-4x}}\,dx$.

5. If a function f is differentiable at a point C, then prove that it is also continuous at that point. **[2]**

6. Solve $(x-1)\frac{dy}{dx}=2x^3y$ **[2]**

7. Solve for x: $\tan^{-1}3x+\tan^{-1}2x=\frac{\pi}{4}$. **[4]**

8. Find the point on the curve $9y^2=x^3$, where the normal to the curve makes equal intercepts on the axes. **[4]**

Or

Show that the surface area of a closed cuboid with square base and given volume is minimum, when it is a cube.

9. (i) Evaluate $\int e^{2x}\sin x\,dx$. **[4]**

Or

(ii) Evaluate $\int\frac{e^x(2+\sin 2x)}{\cos^2 x}\,dx$.

10. The bag A contains 3 white and 2 black balls while the bag B contains 2 white and 5 black balls. One of the bags is chosen at random and a ball is drawn from it. What is the probability that the ball is white? **[4]**

11. (i) Evaluate $\int\frac{\cos x}{\cos 3x}\,dx$. **[6]**

Or

(ii) Evaluate $\int_0^{\pi/2}\frac{x}{(\sin x+\cos x)}\,dx$.

12. (i) A cone is inscribed in a sphere of radius 12 cm. If the volume of the cone is maximum, find its height. **[6]**

Or

(ii) The sum of surface area of a sphere and a cuboid with sides $\frac{x}{3}$, x and $2x$ is constant (K).

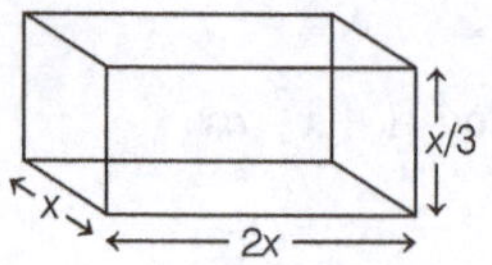

Cuboid

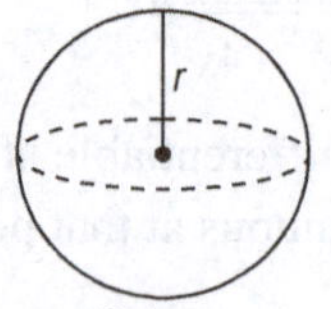

Sphere

(a) Express radius of sphere r in terms of x and K using surface areas.

(b) Prove that the sum of volumes is $\frac{4}{3}\pi\left(\frac{K-6x^2}{4\pi}\right)^{3/2}+\frac{2}{3}x^3$

(c) Prove that $x = 3r$ for which the sum of their volumes is minimum.

(d) Prove that $x = 3\sqrt{\frac{K-6x^2}{4\pi}}$

13. An amount of ₹ 5000 is put into three investments at the rate of interest of 6%, 7% and 8% per annum respectively. The total annual income is ₹ 358 and the combined income from the first two investments is ₹ 70 more than the income from the third.

(i) From a set of simultaneous equations for the above information.

(ii) Solve the set of equations formed in (i) by matrix method.

(iii) Find the amount invested at the rate of 70%. **[6]**

14. Bag A contains three red and four white balls; Bag B contains two red and three white balls.

(i) What is the probability of getting a red ball from bag A?

(ii) What is the probability of getting a white ball from bag B?

(iii) If one ball is draw from bag A and two balls from bag B. What is the probability that one ball is red and two balls are white?

(iv) If one ball is drawn from bag A and two balls from bag B, what is the probability that all the three balls are of the same colour? **[6]**

(v) What is the probability that all the bulls are not of same colour?

Section B **[15 Marks]**

15. In sub-parts (i) and (ii) choose the correct option and in sub-parts (iii) to (v), answer the questions as instructed.

(i) If $|\vec{a}|=1, |\vec{b}|=4, \vec{a}\cdot\vec{b}=2$ and $\vec{c}=2\vec{a}\times\vec{b}-3\vec{b}$, then the angle between $\vec{b}$ and $\vec{c}$ is

(a) $\frac{\pi}{6}$ (b) $\frac{5\pi}{6}$

(c) $\frac{\pi}{3}$ (d) $\frac{2\pi}{3}$ **[1]**

(ii) If the plane $3x+y+2z+6=0$ is parallel to the line $\frac{3x-1}{2b}=3-y=\frac{z-1}{a}$, then the value of $3a+3b$ is

(a) $\frac{1}{2}$ (b) $\frac{3}{2}$

(c) 3 (d) 4 **[1]**

(iii) If $\vec{a}=(3\hat{i}+\hat{j}-4\hat{k})$ and $\vec{b}=(6\hat{i}+5\hat{j}-2\hat{k})$, find $(\vec{a}\times\vec{b})$ and $|\vec{a}\times\vec{b}|$. **[1]**

(iv) Find the value of λ for which the points $A(-1,3,2), B(-4,2,-2)$ and $C(5,5,\lambda)$ are collinear. **[2]**

16. (i) If $\vec{a}+\vec{b}+\vec{c}=\vec{0}$, prove that $(\vec{a}\times\vec{b})=(\vec{b}\times\vec{c})=(\vec{c}\times\vec{a})$. **[2]**

Or

(ii) Find the area of the triangle whose vertices are $P(-1,2,-1), Q(3,-1,2)$ and $R(2,3,-1)$. **[2]**

17. Consider the point $A(-2,3,-4)$

Straight line $L: \frac{x+2}{3}=\frac{2y+3}{4}=\frac{3z+4}{5}$

and the plane $P: 4x+12y-3z+1=0$

Answer the following questions.

(i) Find the distance of point $(-2,3,-4)$ from the line measured parallel to the plane $4x+12y-3z+1=0$.

(ii) Find the perpendicular distance of a point (3, 4, 5) from the given plane P.

(iii) Find the equation of the plane containing the lines L and $\frac{x-2}{1}=\frac{y-4}{4}=\frac{z-6}{7}$. **[4]**

18. (i) Find the area of the region bounded by the curve $y = x^2 + 2$ and the lines $y = x$, $x = 0$ and $x = 3$. **[4]**

Or

(ii) Using integration, find the area of the region bounded by the ellipse $\frac{x^2}{a^2} + \frac{y^2}{b^2} = 1$.

Section C **[15 Marks]**

19. In sub-parts (i) and (ii) choose the correct option and in sub-parts (iii) to (v), answer the questions as instructed.

(i) The total revenue received from the sale of x unit of a product is given by $R(x) = 20x - 0.5x^2$. The average revenue where $x = 10$, is

(a) 15 (b) −15 (c) 10 (d) −10 **[1]**

(ii) If two regression coefficients are 0.8 and 0.2, what would be the value of coefficient of correlation?

(a) −0.4 (b) 0.4 (c) 0.6 (d) − 0.6 **[1]**

(iii) The demand for a certain product is represented by the equation $p = 300 + 24x - \frac{x^3}{4}$ in rupees, where x is the number of units and p is the price per unit. Find the marginal revenue when 8 units are sold. **[3]**

20. (i) Find the equation of two lines of regression for the following observations.

(3, 6), (4, 5), (5, 4), (6, 3), (7, 2). Find an estimate of y for $x = 2.5$. **[2]**

Or

(ii) The data for marks on Physics and History obtained by ten students are given below

Marks in Physics	Marks in History
15	10
12	25
8	17
8	11
7	13
7	17
7	20
6	13
5	9
3	15

(a) Find the line of regression in which Physics is taken as the independent.

(b) A candidate has score 10 marks in Physics but was absent from the History test. Estimate his probable score for the lattest test.

21. (i) The following table shows the sales and advertisement expenditure of a firm

	Sales (in crore)	Advertisement expenditure (in crore)
Mean	40	6
Standard deviation	10	1.5

Coefficient of correlation, $r = 0.9$. Estimate the likely sales for a proposed advertisement expenditure of ₹ 10 crore. **[4]**

Or

(ii) The marginal revenue function of a commodity is given by $MR = 9 - 2x + 4x^2$. Find the demand function.

22. A manufacturing company makes two types of teaching aids A and B of Mathematics for Class XII. Each type of A requires 9 labour hours of fabricating and 1 labour hour for finishing. Each type of B requires 12 labour hours for fabricating and 3 labour hours for finishing. For fabricating and finishing, the maximum labour hours available per week are 180 and 30, respectively. The company makes a profit of ₹ 80 on each piece of type A and ₹ 120 on each piece of type B. How many pieces of type A and type B should be manufactured per week to get a maximum profit? Make it as an LPP and solve it graphically. What is the maximum profit per week? **[4]**

Answers

1. (i) (d) (ii) (c) (iii) (a)
   (iv) (b) (v) d
   (vi) (c) (vii) (d) (viii) (b)
   (ix) (c) (x) (d)
   (xi) (a) (xii) $\frac{7}{2}$ (xiii) $3+x^{1/3}$
   (xiv) 1.1 (xv) (a) 0.12 (b) 0.72
2. (i) $1+\sqrt{3}$
3. $\{(a,1),(b,2),(c,3)\}$
4. (i) $x\log|1+x^2|-2x+\tan^{-1}x+C$ *Or* (ii) $\log[|x-2|+\sqrt{x^2-4x}]+C$
6. $\log|y|=2\left(\frac{x^3}{3}+\frac{x^2}{2}+x+\log|x-1|\right)+C$
7. $\frac{1}{6}$ and -1
8. $\left(4,\frac{8}{3}\right)$ and $\left(4,\frac{-8}{3}\right)$
9. (i) $\frac{e^{2x}}{5}[2\sin x-\cos x]+C$ *Or* (ii) $2e^x\tan x+C$
10. 31/70
11. (i) $\frac{1}{2\sqrt{3}}\log\left|\frac{1+\sqrt{3}\tan x}{1-\sqrt{3}\tan x}\right|+C$
    Or (ii) $\frac{\pi}{4\sqrt{2}}\log\left|\frac{\sqrt{2}+1}{\sqrt{2}-1}\right|$
12. (i) $h=16$ cm *Or* (ii) (a) $r=\sqrt{\frac{k-6x^2}{4\pi}}$
13. (i) $x+y+z=5000,\ 6x+7y+8z=35800,$ $6x+7y-8z=7000$
    (ii) Three investments are of ₹ 1000, ₹ 2200 and ₹ 1800 respectively.
    (iii) ₹ 2200
14. (i) $\frac{3}{7}$ (ii) $\frac{3}{5}$ (iii) $\frac{33}{70}$ (iv) $\frac{3}{14}$ (v) $\frac{11}{14}$
15. (i) (b) (ii) (b) (iii) $18\hat{i}-18\hat{j}+9\hat{k}$, 27
    (iv) 10
16. *Or* (ii) $-3\hat{i}+9\hat{j}+13\hat{k}$
17. (i) 8.5 units (ii) 46/13 units (iii) $3x+8y-5z-8=0$
18. (i) $\frac{21}{2}$ sq units *Or* (ii) πab sq units
19. (i) (a) (ii) (b) (iii) 172
20. (i) $y=-x+9, x=-y+9$, 6.5 *Or* (ii) (a) $y=0.208x+13.38$ (b) 15.46
21. (i) ₹ 64 crore *Or* (ii) $9-x+\frac{4}{3}x^2$
22. ₹ 1680

ISC

SAMPLE PAPER 03

Time : 3 hrs
Marks : 80

Mathematics

General Instructions

1. The Question Paper consists of three Sections A, B and C.
2. Candidates are required to attempt all questions from Section A and all questions either from Section B or Section C.
3. Section A Internal choice has been provided in two questions of two marks each, two questions of four marks each and two questions of six marks each.
4. Section B Internal choice has been provided in one question of two marks and one question of four marks.
5. Section C Internal choice has been provided in one question of two marks and one question of four marks.
6. All working, including rough work, should be done on the same sheet as, and adjacent to the rest of the answer.
7. The intended marks for questions or parts of questions are given in brackets [ ].
8. Mathematical tables and graph papers are provided.

Section A **[65 Marks]**

1. In sub-parts (i) to (x) choose the correct option and in sub-parts (xi) to (xv), answer the questions as instructed. **[15 × 1]**

(i) If $\sin^{-1} x+\sin^{-1} y+\sin^{-1} z=\frac{3\pi}{2}$, then $xy+yz-xz$ is equal to

(a) 0 (b) −1 (c) 1 (d) 2

(ii) The normal at the point (1, 1) on the curve $2y+x^2=3$ is

(a) $x+y=0$ (b) $x-y=0$
(c) $x+y+1=0$ (d) $x-y+1=0$

(iii) If $P(A)=\frac{1}{2}$, $P(B)=0$, then $P\left(\frac{A}{B}\right)$ is

(a) 0 (b) $\frac{1}{2}$
(c) not defined (d) 1

(iv) Function $f(x)=|x+2|-1$ has

(a) −1 as minimum value
(b) 2 as maximum value
(c) −2 as maximum value
(d) 1 as minimum value

(v) The relation R in the set of natural numbers N defined as $R=\{(x, y): y=x+5 \text{ and } x<4\}$ is

(a) reflexive (b) symmetric
(c) transitive (d) None of these

(vi) An integrating factor of the differential equation $(1+x^2)\frac{dy}{dx}+xy=x$ is

(a) $\frac{x}{1+x^2}$ (b) $\sqrt{1+x^2}$ (c) $\frac{1}{2}\log(1+x^2)$ (d) $5x$

(vii) Write the correct option from the following if $R=\{(a, b): a \text{ and } b \text{ both are either even or odd}\}$ in the set $A=\{1, 2, 3, 4, 5, 6, 7\}$.

(a) No relation (b) Trivial
(c) Equivalence relation (d) Not symmetric

(viii) If $A=\begin{bmatrix} x & 1 \\ 1 & 0 \end{bmatrix}$ and A^2 is the identity matrix, then x is equal to

(a) −1 (b) 0 (c) 1 (d) 2

(ix) **Statement I** If $\begin{vmatrix} x & 2 \\ 8 & x \end{vmatrix}=\begin{vmatrix} 6 & 2 \\ 18 & 6 \end{vmatrix}$, then $x=55$.

Statement II If matrix $A=\begin{vmatrix} 6 & x \\ 12 & 4 \end{vmatrix}$ is a singular matrix, then $x=-2$.

Which one of the following option is correct?
(a) Both the statements are true.
(b) Both the statements are false.
(c) Statement I is true and Statement II is false.
(d) Statement I is false and Statement II is true.

(x) **Assertion** (A) The value of $\begin{vmatrix} \sec\theta & \tan\theta \\ \tan\theta & \sec\theta \end{vmatrix} = 1.$

Reason (R) $\begin{vmatrix} a & b \\ c & d \end{vmatrix} = ad + bc.$

(a) Both A and R are true and R is the correct explanation of A.
(b) Both A and R are true but R is not the correct explanation of A.
(c) A is true but R is false.
(d) A is false but R is true.

(xi) $A = \begin{bmatrix} 0 & b & -2 \\ 3 & 1 & 3 \\ 2a & 3 & -1 \end{bmatrix}$ is symmetric matrix, the sum of values of a and b is
(a) 2 (b) 5 (c) 3 (d) 4

(xii) Show that the function $f : R \to R$ given by $f(x) = \cos x, \forall x \in R$ is neither one-one nor onto.

(xiii) Verify that $y = e^{-x} + Ax + B$ is a solution of differential equation $e^x \left(\frac{d^2y}{dx^2}\right) = 1.$

(xiv) If $P(A) = \frac{7}{13}$ and $P(B) = \frac{9}{13}$ and $P(A \cap B) = \frac{4}{13}$, then find
(a) $P(\bar{A} / B)$ (b) $P(\bar{A} / \bar{B})$

(xv) P speaks truth in 70% of cases and Q in 80% of the cases. In what percent of cases are they likely to agree in stating the same fact.

2. (i) If $y = e^x \sin 5x$, then find $\frac{d^2y}{dx^2}$. **[2]**

Or

(ii) If the following function is differentiable at $x = 2$, then find the values of a and b.

$$f(x) = \begin{cases} x^2, & \text{if } x \le 2 \\ ax + b, & \text{if } x > 2 \end{cases}$$

3. Let $f : N \to Y$ be a function defined as $f(x) = 4x + 3$, where $y = \{y \in N : y = 4x + 3 \text{ for some } x \in N\}$. Show that f is invertible. Also, find the inverse. **[2]**

4. (i) Write the value of a for which

$f(x) = \begin{cases} 5x - 4 & 0 < x \le 1 \\ 4x^2 + 3ax & 1 < x < 2 \end{cases}$ is continuous at $x = 1$. **[2]**

Or

(ii) If $y = e^x + e^{-x}$, then prove that $\frac{dy}{dx} = \sqrt{y^2 - 4}.$

5. Find the particular solution of the differential equation $e^x \tan y \, dx + (2 - e^x) \sec^2 y \, dy = 0$ given that $y = \frac{\pi}{4}$, when $x = 0$. **[2]**

6. Evaluate $\int e^x \left(\frac{1 - \sin x}{1 - \cos x}\right) dx.$ **[2]**

7. Find the greatest and least value of $(\sin^{-1} x)^2 + (\cos^{-1} x)^2$. **[4]**

8. For the curve $y = 4x^3 - 2x^5$, find all the points on the curve at which the tangent passes through the origin. **[4]**

Or

Prove that the curve $x = y^2$ and $xy = k$ cuts at right angles, if $8k^2 = 1$.

9. (i) Evaluate $\int_{-2}^{2} \frac{x^2}{1 + 5^x} dx.$ **[4]**

Or

(ii) Evaluate $\int_0^{\pi} \frac{x \tan x}{\sec x + \tan x} dx.$

10. An urn contains 2 white and 2 black balls. A ball is drawn at random. If it is white, it is not replaced into the urn. Otherwise, it is replaced with another ball of the same colour. The process is repeated. Find the probability that the third ball drawn is black.

11. (i) Show that the differential equation

$\frac{dy}{dx} = \frac{y^2}{xy - x^2}$ is homogeneous and also solve it. **[6]**

Or

(ii) Find the general solution of differential equation $(x^3 - 3xy^2) \, dx = (y^3 - 3x^2 y) \, dy.$

12. (i) Show that the rectangle of maximum perimeter which can be inscribed in a circle of radius 10 cm is a square of side $10\sqrt{2}$ cm. [6]

Or

(ii) Deepchand has bought a conical shaped toy. The radius is r and slant height is l as shown in the figure.

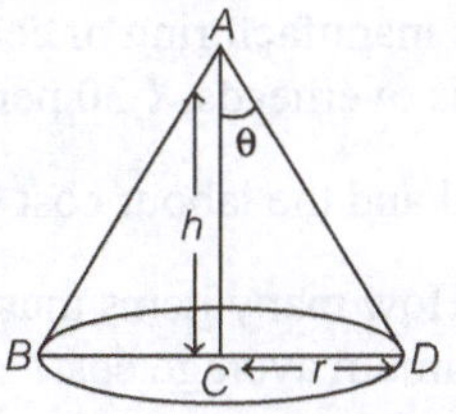

(a) Express the volume of cone in terms of l and h.

(b) Find the value of h (in terms of l) for which volume is maximum.

(c) Prove that the semi-vertical angle of cone is $\tan^{-1}\sqrt{2}$.

(d) Prove that the maximum volume (in term of h) is $\frac{2}{3}\pi h^3$. [6]

13. The cost of 4 kg onion, 3 kg wheat and 2 kg rice is ₹ 60. The cost of 2 kg onion, 4 kg wheat and 6 kg rice is ₹ 90. The cost of 6 kg onion, 2 kg wheat and 3 kg rice is ₹ 70.

(i) Form a set of simultaneous equation for the above information.

(ii) Solve the set of equations formed in (i) by matrix method.

(iii) Find the sum of cost of each item per kg. [6]

14. Three persons A, B and C apply for a job of manager in a private company. Chances of their selections (A, B and C) are in the ratio 1 : 2 : 4. The probability that A, B and can introduce charges to improve profits of the company are 0.8, 0.5 and 0.3, respectively.

(i) What is the probability of selecting person A?

(ii) What is the probability of selecting person C?

(iii) What is the probability that person B introduce the changes in their profits?

(iv) If the changes does not take places, what is the probability that it is due to the appointment of C?

(v) Find the sum of the probabilities of not selecting person A and person C. [6]

Section B [15 Marks]

15. In sub-parts (i) and (ii) choose the correct option and in sub-parts (iii) to (v), answer the questions as instructed.

(i) The distance of the plane $6x-3y+2z-14=0$ from the origin is

(a) 2 (b) 1 (c) 14 (d) 8 [1]

(ii) If $\vec{a}\cdot\vec{b}=0$ and $\vec{a}+\vec{b}$ makes an angle of 60° with $\vec{a}$, then

(a) $|\vec{a}|=2|\vec{b}|$

(b) $2|\vec{a}|=|\vec{b}|$

(c) $|\vec{a}|=\sqrt{3}|\vec{b}|$

(d) $\sqrt{3}|\vec{a}|=|\vec{b}|$ [1]

(iii) P and Q are two points with position vectors $3\vec{a}-2\vec{b}$ and $\vec{a}+\vec{b}$, respectively.

Write the position vector of a point R which divides the line segment PQ externally in the ratio 2:1. [1]

(iv) If the lines $\frac{x-1}{-2}=\frac{y-4}{3p}=\frac{z-3}{4}$ and $\frac{x-2}{4p}=\frac{y-5}{2}=\frac{z-1}{-7}$ are perpendicular to each other, then find the value of p. [2]

16. (i) If $\vec{PQ}+\vec{OQ}=\vec{QO}+\vec{OR}$, then show that the points P, Q and R are collinear. [2]

Or

(ii) Using vectors, find the area of triangle whose vertices are A (1, 2, 3), B(2, –1, 4) and C(4, 5, –1). [2]

17. It is given that

The coordinates of a point A are (3, 4, 5).

The equation of the plane P is $x+y+z=2$

and the equation of line is $2x=y=z$

Now, answer the following questions.

(i) Find the distance of the point A from the plane P measured parallel to the line $2x=y=z$.

(ii) Find the distance of a point (1, 2, 3) from the plane P.

(iii) Distance between the point P and (1, 2, 3). [4]

18. (i) Find the area of region in the first quadrant enclosed by the Y-axis, the line $y = x$ and the circle $x^2 + y^2 = 32$, using integration. **[4]**

Or

(ii) Draw the graph of $y = |x+1|$ and using integration find the area between $y = |x+1|$ above X–axis and between $x = -4$ to $x = 2$. **[4]**

Section C **[15 Marks]**

19. In sub-parts (i) and (ii) choose the correct option and in sub-parts (iii) to (v), answer the questions as instructed.

(i) If total cost function of a firm is $C = \frac{1}{3}x^3 - 5x^2 + 30x + 15$, then profit function is **[1]**

(a) $\frac{1}{3}x^3 + 5x^2 - 24x$ (b) $-\frac{1}{3}x^3 + 5x^2 - 24x - 15$

(c) $-\frac{1}{3}x^3 + 5x^2 + 24x + 15$ (d) None of these

(ii) The regression coefficient b_{yx} for the data $\Sigma x = 55$, $\Sigma y = 88$, $\Sigma x^2 = 385$, $\Sigma xy = 586$ and $n = 10$ is **[1]**

(a) 1.32
(b) 1.48
(c) 1.24
(d) None of the above

(iii) The demand function for TV sets is $P = 20000 - 100x$. Determine the total revenue and average revenue by selling 20 sets. **[3]**

20. (i) Find the correlation coefficient between x and y from the following data

$\Sigma x = 40$, $\Sigma y = 50$, $\Sigma xy = 220$, $\Sigma x^2 = 200$, $\Sigma y^2 = 262$, $n = 10$. **[2]**

Or

(ii) If we have the following data.

Arithmetic Mean	36	85
Standard deviation	11	8

Correlation coefficient between x and y is 0.66. Find (a) the two regression coefficients.

(b) the two regression equations.

21. (i) The cost of manufacturing of certain items consists of ₹ 1600 as overheads, ₹ 30 per item as the cost of the material and the labour cost ₹ $\frac{x^2}{100}$ for x items produced. How many items must be produced to have a minimum average cost? **[4]**

Or

(ii) A firm has the cost function,

$C = \frac{x^3}{3} - 7x^2 + 111x + 50$ and demand function $x = 100 - P$

(a) Write the total revenue in terms of x.

(b) Formulate the total profit function P in terms of x.

22. A dietician wishes to mix two types of food in such a way that the vitamin contents of the mixture contain atleast 8 units of vitamin A and 10 units of vitamin C. Food I contains 2 units/kg of vitamin A and 1 unit/kg of vitamin C Food II contains 1 unit/kg of vitamin A and 2 units/kg of vitamin C. It costs ₹ 50 per kg to purchase food I and ₹ 70 per kg to purchase food II. Determine the minmum cost of such a mixture. Formulate this is as linear programming problem and solve it. Identify the feasible region from the rough sketch. **[4]**

Answers

1. (i) (c) (ii) (b) (iii) (c)
(iv) (a) (v) (c)
(vi) (b) (vii) (c) (viii) (b)
(ix) (b) (x) (c)
(xi) (a) (xiv) (a) $\frac{5}{9}$ (b) $\frac{1}{4}$ (xv) 62%

2. (i) $2e^x[5\cos 5x - 12\sin 5x]$ *Or* (ii) $a=4, b=-4$ 3. $f^{-1}(x)=\frac{x-3}{4}$ 4. (i) 1 5. $y=2-e^x$ 6. $-e^x\cot\frac{x}{2}+C$

7. Greatest value $=\frac{5\pi^2}{4}$, least value $=\frac{\pi^2}{8}$ 8. (0, 0), (1, 2) (−1, −2) 9. (i) $\frac{8}{3}$ *Or* (ii) $\frac{\pi}{2}(\pi-2)$ 10. $\frac{23}{30}$

11. (i) $\frac{y}{x}-\log|y|=C$ *Or* (ii) $x^2-y^2=C(x^2+y^2)^2$

12. (ii) (a) $V=\frac{\pi}{3}(l^2h-h^3)$ (b) $h=\frac{l}{\sqrt{3}}$

13. (i) $4x+3y+2z=60,\ 2x+4y+6z=90,$ $6x+2y+3z=70$
(ii) Price of onion per kg is ₹ 5, wheat per kg is ₹ 8 and rice per kg is ₹ 8. (iii) ₹ 21 per kg.

14. (i) $\frac{1}{7}$ (ii) $\frac{4}{7}$ (iii) 0.5 (iv) 0.7 (v) $\frac{5}{7}$

15. (i) (a) (ii) (d) (iii) $4\vec{b}-\vec{a}$ (iv) $p=-14$

16. *Or* (ii) $\frac{5a}{2}$ 17. (i) 6 units (ii) $\frac{4}{\sqrt{3}}$ units (iii) $2\sqrt{3}$ units

18. (i) 4π *Or* (ii) 9 sq units

19. (i) (b) (ii) (c) (iii) TR = ₹ 360000, AR = ₹ 18000

20. (i) 0.91 *Or* (ii) (a) $b_{yx}=0.48, b_{xy}=0.9075$ (b) $y=0.48x+67.72, x=0.9075\,y-41.41$

21. (i) 400 items *Or* (ii) (a) $R=100x-x^2$ (b) Profit function $=\frac{-x^3}{3}+6x^2-11x-50$

22. 2 kg of food I, 4 kg of food II; Minimum cost ₹ 380

ISC

Time : 3 hrs
Marks : 80

Latest Specimen Paper

Mathematics

General Instructions

1. The Question Paper consists of three Sections A, B and C.
2. Candidates are required to attempt all questions from Section A and all questions either from Section B or Section C.
3. Section A Internal choice has been provided in two questions of two marks each, two questions of four marks each and two questions of six marks each.
4. Section B Internal choice has been provided in one question of two marks and one question of four marks.
5. Section C Internal choice has been provided in one question of two marks and one question of four marks.
6. All working, including rough work, should be done on the same sheet as, and adjacent to the rest of the answer.
7. The intended marks for questions or parts of questions are given in brackets [ ].
8. Mathematical tables and graph papers are provided.

Section A [65 Marks]

1. In subparts (i) to (xi) choose the correct options and in subparts (xii) to (xv), answer the questions as instructed.

(i) A matrix which is both symmetric and skew-symmetric matrix is a/ an • *Understanding*

(a) triangular matrix
(b) identity matrix
(c) diagonal matrix
(d) null matrix

(ii) The value of $\int a^x \cdot e^x dx$ equals • *Recall* [1]

(a) $(a^x \cdot \log_e a)e^x + c$ (b) $\dfrac{a^x \cdot e^x}{\log_e (ae)} + c$

(c) $\dfrac{a^x \cdot e^x}{\log_{ae} e} + c$ (d) $\log_e (ae)(ae)^x + c$

(iii) The trigonometric equation $\tan^{-1} x = 3 \tan^{-1} a$ has solution for • *Application* [1]

(a) $|a| \le \dfrac{1}{\sqrt{3}}$ (b) $|a| > \dfrac{1}{\sqrt{3}}$

(c) $|a| < \dfrac{1}{\sqrt{3}}$ (d) all real value of a.

(iv) **Assertion** Degree of the differential equation $a\left(\dfrac{dy}{dx}\right)^2 + b\dfrac{dx}{dy} = c$, is 3.

Reason If each term involving derivatives of a differential equation is a polynomial (or can be expressed as polynomial), then highest exponent of the highest order derivative is called the degree of the differential equation. • *Analysis* [1]

Which of the following is correct?

(a) Both Assertion and Reason are true and Reason is the correct explanation for Assertion.
(b) Both Assertion and Reason are true but Reason is not the correct explanation for Assertion.
(c) Assertion is true and Reason is false.
(d Assertion is false and Reason is true.

(v) Five numbers x_1, x_2, x_3, x_4 and x_5 are randomly selected from the numbers 1, 2, 3, ..., 18 and are arranged in the increasing order such that $x_1 < x_2 < x_3 < x_4 < x_5$. What is the probability that $x_2 = 7$ and $x_4 = 11$? • *Application* [1]

(a) $\dfrac{26}{51}$ (b) $\dfrac{3}{104}$ (c) $\dfrac{1}{68}$ (d) $\dfrac{1}{34}$

(vi) If $\begin{vmatrix} a & b & c \\ m & n & p \\ x & y & z \end{vmatrix} = k$, then what is the value of $\begin{vmatrix} 6a & 2b & 2c \\ 3m & n & p \\ 3x & y & z \end{vmatrix}$? • *Understanding* [1]

(a) $\frac{k}{6}$ (b) $2k$

(c) $3k$ (d) $6k$

(vii) Consider the graph $y = x^{\frac{1}{3}}$

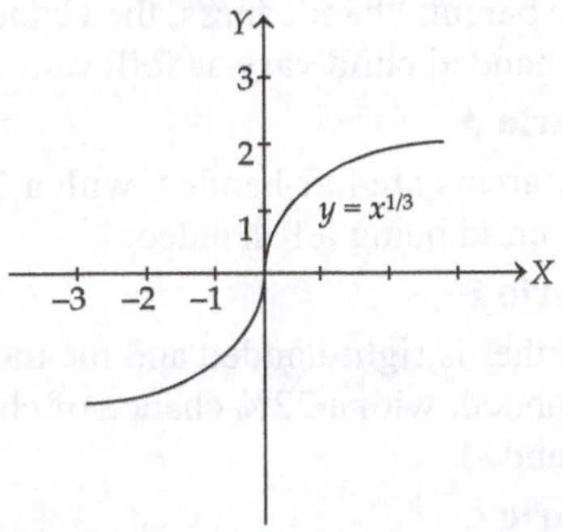

Statement I The above graph is continuous at $x = 0$.

Statement II The above graph is differentiable at $x = 0$ • *Application* [1]

Which of the following is correct?

(a) Statement I is true and Statement II is false.

(b) Statement II is true and Statement I is false.

(c) Both the statements are true.

(d) Both the statements are false.

(viii) The value of $\frac{dy}{dx}$, if $y = |x-1| + |x-4|$ at $x = 3$ is

(a) – 2 (b) 0

(c) 2 (d) 4

(ix) **Statement I** The intersection of two equivalence relations is always an equivalence relation.

Statement II The Union of two equivalence relations is always an equivalence relation. • *Understanding* [1]

Which one of the following is correct?

(a) Statement I implies Statement II.

(b) Statement II implies Statement I.

(c) Statement I is true only if Statement II is true.

(d) Statement I and II are independent of each other.

(x) In a third order matrix a_{ij} denotes the element of the ith row and the jth column.

$$A = a_{ij} = \begin{cases} 0, & \text{for } i = j \\ 1, & \text{for } i > j \\ -1, & \text{for } i < j \end{cases}$$

Assertion Matrix A is not invertible.

Reason Determinant of $A = 0$

Which of the following is correct? • *Application* [1]

(a) Both Assertion and Reason are true and Reason is the correct explanation for Assertion.

(b) Both Assertion and Reason are true but Reason is not the correct explanation for Assertion.

(c) Assertion is true and Reason is false.

(d) Assertion is false and Reason is true.

(xi) Given two events A and B such that $P\left(\frac{A}{B}\right) = 0.25$ and $P(A \cap B) = 0.12$. The value of $P(A \cap B')$ is • *Understanding* [1]

(a) 0.36

(b) 0.48

(c) 0.88

(d) 0.036

(xii) The value of the determinant of a matrix A of order 3 is 3. If C is the matrix of co-factors of the matrix A, then what is the value of determinant of C^2? • *Analysis* [1]

(xiii) If a relation R on the set $\{a, b, c\}$ defined by $R = \{(b, b)\}$, then classify the relation. • *Understanding* [1]

(xiv)

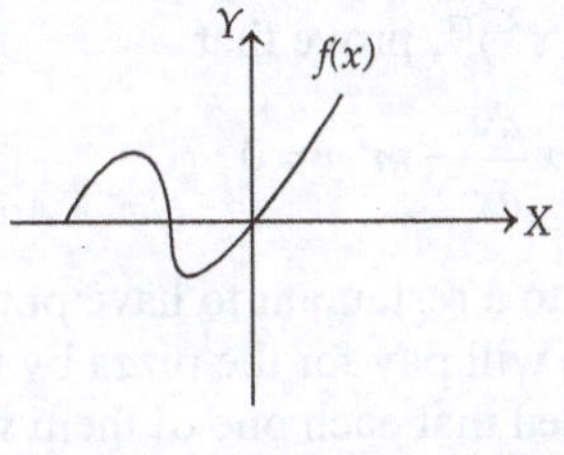

The given function $f: R \to R$ is not onto function. Give reason. • *Understanding* [1]

(xv) There are three machines and 2 of them are faulty. They are tested one by one in a random order till both the faulty machines are identified. What is the probability that only two tests are needed to identify the faulty machines? • *Application* [1]

2. (i) If $x^y = y^x$, then find $\frac{dy}{dx}$. • *Understanding* [2]

Or

(ii) Find the interval in which the function $f(x) = x^2 e^{-x}$ is strictly increasing or decreasing. • *Understanding* [2]

3. Evaluate $\int_0^{\sqrt{2}} [x^2] dx$ • *Evaluate* [2]

4. Find the equation to the tangent at (0, 0) on the curve $y = 4x^2 - 2x^3$. • *Analysis* [2]

5. (i) Evaluate $\int \frac{2x^3 - 1}{x^4 + x} dx$ • *Evaluate* [2]

Or

(ii) Evaluate $\int e^x \operatorname{cosec} x(1 - \cot x) dx$ • *Evaluate* [2]

6. Find the value of $\tan^{-1}\left(\frac{x}{y}\right) + \tan^{-1}\left(\frac{y - x}{y + x}\right)$ • *Application* [2]

7. Solve $\sin^{-1}(x) + \sin^{-1}(1 - x) = \cos^{-1} x$ • *Application* [4]

8. Evaluate $\int \sqrt{\sec \frac{x}{2} - 1}\, dx$ • *Application* [4]

9. (i) A kite is being pulled down by a string that goes through a ring on the ground 8 m away from the person pulling it. If the string is pulled in at 1 m per second, how fast is the kite coming down when it is 15 m high? • *Application* [4]

Or

(ii) If $y = (x + \sqrt{a^2 + x^2})^m$, prove that

$$(a^2 + x^2)\frac{d^2y}{dx^2} + x\frac{dy}{dx} - m^2 y = 0$$ • *Analysis* [4]

10. (i) Three friends go to a restaurant to have pizza. They decide who will pay for the pizza by tossing a coin. It is decided that each one of them will toss a coin and if one person gets a different result (heads or tails) than the other two, that person would pay. If all three get the same result (all heads or all tails), they will toss again until they get a different result. • *Analysis* [4]

(a) What is the probability that all three friends will get the same result (all heads or all tails) in one round of tossing?

(b) What is the probability that they will get a different result in one round of tossing?

(c) What is the probability that they will need exactly four rounds of tossing to determine who would pay?

Or

(ii) Students of under graduation submitted a case study on 'Understanding the Probability of Left-Handedness in Children Based on Parental Handedness'.

Following recent studies suggest that roughly 12% of the world population is left-handed. Depending on the parents' handedness, the chances of having a left-handed child vary as follows:

Scenario A

Both parents are left-handed, with a 24% chance of the child being left-handed.

Scenario B

The father is right-handed and the mother is left-handed, with a 22% chance of child being left-handed.

Scenario C

The father is left-handed and the mother is right-handed, with a 17% chance of child being left-handed.

Scenario D

Both parents are right-handed, with a 9% chance of having a left-handed child.

Assuming that scenarios A, B, C and D are equally likely and L denotes the event that the child is left-handed, answer the following questions.

(a) What is the overall probability that a randomly selected child is left-handed?

(b) Given that exactly one parent is left-handed, what is the probability that a randomly selected child is left-handed?

(c) If a child is left-handed, what is the probability that both parents are left-handed?

11. To raise money for an orphanage, students of three schools *A*, *B* and *C* organised an exhibition in their residential colony, where they sold paper bags, scrap books and pastel sheets made by using recycled paper. Students of school *A* sold 30 paper bags, 20 scrap books and 10 pastel sheets and raised ₹ 410. Students of school *B* sold 20 paper bags, 10 scrap books and 20 pastel sheets and raised ₹ 290.

Students of school C sold 20 paper bags, 20 scrap books and 20 pastel sheets and raised ₹ 440.

Answer the following question.

(i) Translate the problem into a system of equations.

(ii) Solve the system of equation by using matrix method.

(iii) Hence, find the cost of one paper bag, one scrap book and one pastel sheet. • *Application* [6]

12. (i) Solve the differential equation.

$$(xdy - ydx)\, y \sin\left(\frac{y}{x}\right) = (ydx + xdy)\, x \cos\left(\frac{y}{x}\right).$$

Find the particular solution satisfying the condition that $y = \pi$ when $x = 1$. • *Application* [6]

Or

(ii) Evaluate $\int_0^{\pi} (\sin^4 x + \cos^4 x) dx$ and hence evaluate

$$\int_{-2\pi}^{2\pi} \frac{\sin^4 x + \cos^4 x}{1 + e^x} dx.$$

• *Evaluate*

13. (i) A cone of maximum volume is inscribed in a given sphere. Then, prove that ratio of the height of the cone to the diameter of the sphere is equal to 2 / 3. • *Application*

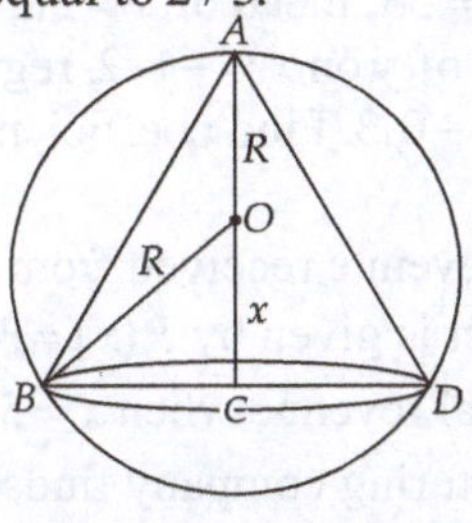

Or (ii) A given quantity of metal is to be cast into a solid half circular cylinder with a rectangular base and semi-circular ends. If the total surface area is minimum, then prove that the ratio of the length of cylinder to the diameter of semi-circular ends is $\pi : \pi + 2$. • *Application*

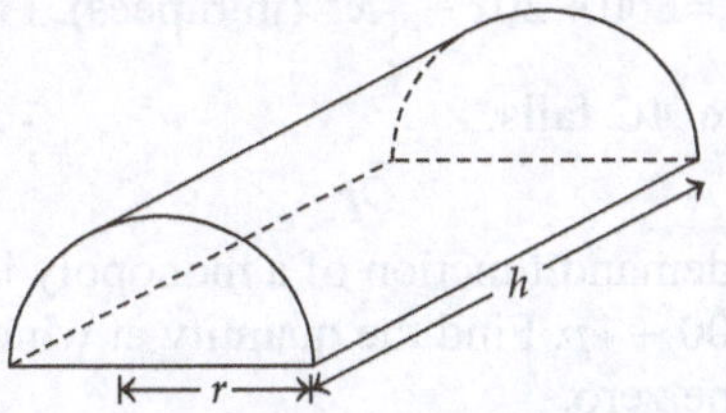

14. Kiran plays a game of throwing a fair die 3 times but to quit as and when she gets a six. Kiran gets + 1 point for a six and – 1 for any other number. • *Analysis* [6]

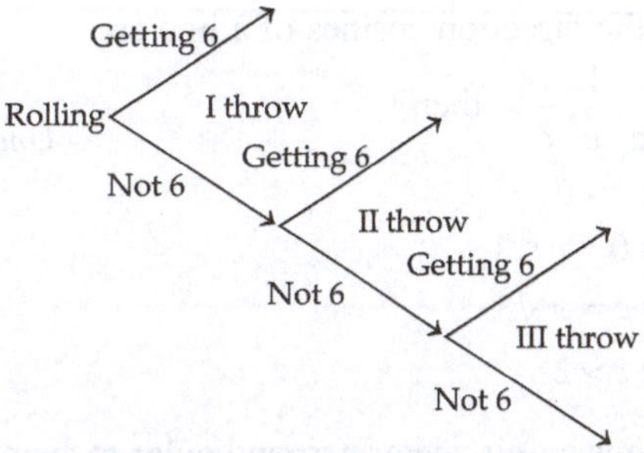

(i) If X denotes the random variable 'points earned' then what are the possible values X can take?

(ii) Find the probability distribution of this random variable X.

(iii) Find the expected value of the points she gets.

Section B

[15 Marks]

15. In subparts (i) and (iii) choose the correct options and in subparts (iv) to (v), answer the questions as instructed.

(i) Consider the following statements and choose the correct option.

Statement I If $\vec{a}$ and $\vec{b}$ represent two adjacent sides of a parallelogram, then the diagonals are represented by $\vec{a} + \vec{b}$ and F$\vec{a} - \vec{b}$.

Statement II If $\vec{a}$ and $\vec{b}$ represents two diagonals of a parallelogram, then the adjacent sides are represented by $2(\vec{a} + \vec{b})$ and $2(\vec{a} - \vec{b})$.

• *Recall*

Which of the following is correct?

(a) Only Statement I

(b) Only Statement II

(c) Both Statements I and II

(d) Neither Statement I nor Statement II

(ii) The distance of the plane through (1, 1, 1) and perpendicular to the line $\frac{x-1}{3} = \frac{y-1}{0} = \frac{z-1}{4}$ from the origin is • *Application*

(a) $\frac{3}{4}$ (b) $\frac{4}{3}$

(c) $\frac{7}{5}$ (d) 1

(iii) If the direction cosines of a line are $<\frac{1}{c}, \frac{1}{c}, \frac{1}{c}>$, then • *Understanding*

(a) $c > 0$

(b) $0 < c < 1$

(c) $c = \pm\sqrt{3}$

(d) $c > 2$

(iv) If $\hat{a}$ is a unit vector perpendicular to $\vec{b}$ and $(\vec{a} + 2\vec{b}) \cdot (3\vec{a} - \vec{b}) = -5$, find $|\vec{b}|$ • *Understanding*

(v) Shown below is a cuboid. Find $\overrightarrow{BA} \cdot \overrightarrow{BC}$

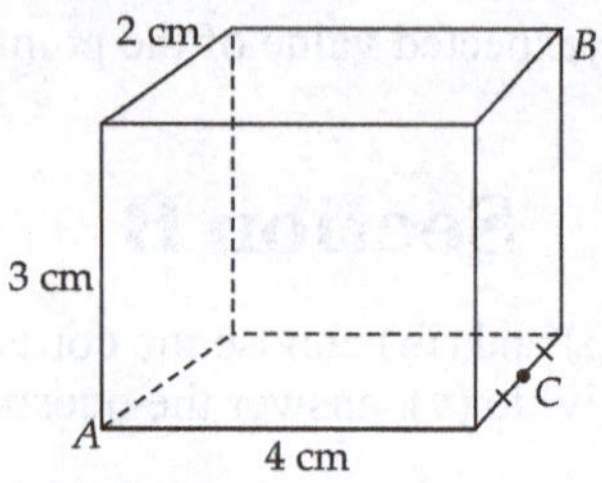

16. (i) Find a vector of magnitude 9 units and perpendicular to the vectors $\vec{a} = 4\hat{i} - \hat{j} + \hat{k}$ and $\vec{b} = -2\hat{i} + \hat{j} - 2\hat{k}$ • *Application*

Or

(ii) What are the values of x for which the angle between the vectors? $2x^2\hat{i} + 3x\hat{j} + \hat{k}$ and $\hat{i} - 2\hat{j} + x^2\hat{k}$ is obtuse? • *Application*

17. (i) Show that the line whose vector equation is $\vec{r} = (2\hat{i} - 2\hat{j} + 3\hat{k}) + \lambda(\hat{i} - \hat{j} + 4\hat{k})$ is parallel to the plane whose vector equation is $\vec{r} \cdot (\hat{i} + 5\hat{j} + \hat{k}) = 5$. Also, find the distance between them. • *Application*

Or

(ii) Find the equation of the plane containing the line $\frac{x}{-2} = \frac{y-1}{3} = \frac{1-z}{1}$ and the point $(-1, 0, 2)$. • *Application*

18. (i) Sketch the region enclosed bounded by the curve, $y = x|x|$ and the coordinates $x = -1$ and $x = 1$.

(ii) Evaluate $\int_0^1 x^2 dx$.

(iii) Hence, find the area bounded by the curve, $y = x|x|$ and the coordinates $x = -1$ and $x = 1$.

Section C [15 Marks]

19. In subparts (i) and (ii) choose the correct options and in subparts (iii) to (v), answer the questions as instructed.

(i) Which condition is true if Average Cost (AC) is constant at all levels of out put • *Recall*

(a) $MC > AC$ (b) $MC = AC$

(c) $MC < AC$ (d) $MC = \frac{1}{2}AC$

(ii) Read the following statements and choose the correct option.

(I) If $r = 0$, then regression lines are not defined.

(II) If $r = 0$, then regression lines are parallel.

(III) If $r = 0$, then regression lines are perpendicular.

(IV) If $r = \pm 1$, then regression lines coincide. • *Recall*

Which of the following is correct?

(a) Only IV is correct.

(b) Only I and II are correct.

(c) Only I and IV are correct.

(d) Only III and IV are correct.

(iii) Mean of $x = 53$, mean of $y = 28$, regression coefficient of y on $x = -1 \cdot 2$, regression coefficient of x on $y = -0.3$. Find coefficient of correlation (r). • *Understanding*

(iv) The total revenue received from the sale of x unit of a product is given by $R(x) = 3x^2 + 36x + 5$. Find the marginal revenue when $x = 5$. • *Understanding*

(v) A manufacturing company finds that the daily cost of producing x item of product is given by $C(x) = 210x + 7000$. Find the minimum number that must be produced and sold daily, if each item is sold for ₹ 280. • *Understanding*

20. (i) The cost function of a commodity is $C(x) = 200 + 20x - \frac{1}{2}x^2$ (in rupees). Find the range where AC falls. • *Application* [2]

Or

(ii) The demand function of a monopoly is given by $x = 100 - 4p$. Find the quantity at which the MR will be zero. • *Application*

21. (i) A survey of 50 families to study the relationships between expenditure on accommodation in (₹ x) and expenditure on food and entertainment (₹ y) gave the following results.

$\Sigma x = 8500, \Sigma y = 9600, \sigma_x = 60, \sigma_y = 20, r = 0.6$

Estimate the expenditure on food and entertainment when expenditure on accommodation is ₹ 200. • *Application*

Or

(ii) The random variables have regression lines $3x + 2y - 26 = 0$ and $6x + y - 31 = 0$

Calculate

(a) Mean value of x and y.

(b) Coefficient of correlations. • *Application*

22. A linear programming problem is given by $Z = px + qy$ where $p, q > 0$ subject to the constraints: • *Analysis* [4]

$x + y \le 60, 5x + y \le 100, x \ge 0$ and $y \ge 0$

(i) Solve graphically to find the corner points of the feasible region.

(ii) If $Z = px + qy$ is maximum at (0, 60) and (10, 50), find the relation of p and q.

Also mention the number of optimal solution(s) in this case.

Solutions

1. (i) (d) Let A be a matrix.

$\because A$ is symmetric,

$$\Rightarrow \quad A = A^T \quad \text{...(i)}$$

and A is skew-symmetric

$$\Rightarrow \quad A = -A^T \quad \text{...(ii)}$$

On adding Eqs. (i) and (ii), we get

$$\Rightarrow \quad A + A = A^T - A^T$$

$$\Rightarrow \quad 2A = O \Rightarrow A = O$$

which is null matrix.

(ii) (b) Let $I = \int \underset{\text{I}}{a^x} \cdot \underset{\text{II}}{e^x}\, dx$ ...(i)

On integrating by parts, we get

$$I = a^x \int e^x dx - \int \left(\frac{d}{dx} a^x \cdot \int e^x dx \right) dx + C$$

$$= a^x \cdot e^x - \int a^x \log_e a \cdot e^x \cdot dx + C$$

$$= a^x e^x - \log_e a \cdot \int a^x \cdot e^x \, dx + C$$

From Eq. (i), we get

$$I = a^x e^x - \log_e a \cdot I + C$$

$$(1 + \log_e a) I = a^x e^x + C$$

$$\therefore \quad I = \frac{a^x e^x}{1 + \log_e a} + C$$

$$= \frac{a^x e^x}{\log_e e + \log_e a} + C \quad [\because \log_e e = 1]$$

$$= \frac{a^x e^x}{\log_e (ae)} + C$$

$[\because \log m + \log n = \log mn]$

(iii) (c) We have, $\tan^{-1} x = 3 \tan^{-1} a$

We know that

$$3 \tan^{-1} \theta = \tan^{-1} \left(\frac{3\theta - \theta^3}{1 - 3\theta^2} \right)$$

$$\therefore \quad \tan^{-1} x = \tan^{-1} \left(\frac{3a - a^3}{1 - 3a^2} \right)$$

$$\Rightarrow \quad x = \frac{3a - a^3}{1 - 3a^2}$$

For the tangent inverse function to be defined, the argument must be real.

So, $\quad 1 - 3a^2 \ne 0$

$$\Rightarrow \quad 1 \ne 3a^2$$

$$\Rightarrow \quad a^2 \ne \frac{1}{3}$$

$$\Rightarrow \quad |a| \ne \frac{1}{\sqrt{3}}$$

So, the solution is valid for $|a| < \frac{1}{\sqrt{3}}$.

(iv) (d) **Assertion** (A) The given differential equation

$$a\left(\frac{dy}{dx}\right)^2 + b\left(\frac{dy}{dx}\right) = C$$

The power of the heighest order derivative = 2

$\therefore$ The degree of the given differential equation is 2.

So, Assertion is false and reason is true.

(v) (c) Given, five numbers x_1, x_2, x_3, x_4 and x_5 randomly selected from the numbers 1, 2, 3, ..., 18.

$\therefore$ Total number of ways to choose 5 numbers out of

$$18 = {}^{18}C_5$$

$$= \frac{18!}{5!13!}$$

$$= \frac{18 \times 17 \times 16 \times 15 \times 14}{5 \times 4 \times 3 \times 2}$$

$$= 18 \times 17 \times 2 \times 14$$

These number arranged in the increasing pattern

$x_1 < x_2 < x_3 < x_4 < x_5$,

On fixing $x_2 = 7$ and $x_4 = 11$

Then, number of ways of choosing x_1 from (1, 2, ..., 6) = 6 ways.

Number of ways choosing x_3 from {8, 9, 10} = 3 ways.

and number of ways of choosing x_5 from {12, 13, ..., 18} = 7 ways

Now, the number of favourable outcomes

$$= 6 \times 3 \times 7$$

$$= 126 \text{ ways}$$

$\therefore$ Required probability

$$= \frac{\text{Number of favourable outcomes}}{\text{Total number of outcomes}}$$

$$= \frac{126}{18 \times 17 \times 2 \times 14} = \frac{1}{17 \times 2 \times 2} = \frac{1}{68}$$

Hence, the probability that $x_2 = 7$ and $x_4 = 11$ is $\frac{1}{68}$.

(vi) (d) Given, $\begin{vmatrix} a & b & c \\ m & n & p \\ x & y & z \end{vmatrix} = k$ ...(i)

Then, $\Delta = \begin{vmatrix} 6a & 2b & 2c \\ 3m & n & p \\ 3x & y & z \end{vmatrix}$

On taking 2 as common from first row, we get

$$\Delta = 2 \begin{vmatrix} 3a & b & c \\ 3m & n & p \\ 3x & y & z \end{vmatrix}$$

Now, taking 3 as common from first "Column" we get

$$\Delta = 2 \times 3 \begin{vmatrix} a & b & c \\ m & n & p \\ x & y & z \end{vmatrix}$$

$$\Delta = 6k \quad \text{[using Eq. (i)]}$$

Hence, $\begin{vmatrix} 6a & 2b & 2c \\ 3m & n & p \\ 3x & y & z \end{vmatrix} = 6k$

(vii) (a) Given, $y = x^{\frac{1}{3}}$

To check the continuity at $x = 0$, we find

$$\text{LHL} = \lim_{x \to 0^-} f(x) = \lim_{h \to 0} f(0 - h)$$

$$= \lim_{h \to 0} (-h)^{1/3} = 0$$

$$\text{RHL} = \lim_{x \to 0^+} f(x) = \lim_{h \to 0} f(0 + h)$$

$$= \lim_{h \to 0} h^{1/3} = 0$$

$$f(0) = 0$$

Here, LHL = RHL = $f(0)$

Hence, $f(x) = x^{\frac{1}{3}}$ is continuous at $x = 0$.

Now, $y = x^{\frac{1}{3}}$

On differentiating w.r.t. x, we get

$$\frac{dy}{dx} = \frac{1}{3} x^{-\frac{2}{3}}$$

at $x = 0$,

$$\left.\frac{dy}{dx}\right|_{x=0} = \left.\frac{1}{3x^{\frac{2}{3}}}\right|_{x=0}$$

which is not define.

Hence, the function is not differentiable at $x = 0$.

(viii) (b) We have, $y = |x - 1| + |x - 4|$

for $x = 3$, $y = (x - 1) - (x - 4)$

$$y = x - 1 - x + 4$$

$$\Rightarrow \quad y = 3$$

On differentiating w.r.t. x, we get

$$\frac{dy}{dx} = \frac{d}{dx}(3) = 0 \quad \left[\because \frac{d}{dx}(\text{constant}) = 0\right]$$

(ix) (c) **Statement I** An equivalence relation on a set is a relation which is reflexive, symmetric and transitive.

Reflexivity Let R and S be two equivalence relations on set A, then for any $a \in A$, $(a, a) \in R$ and $(a, a) \in S$. Thus, $(a, a) \in R \cap S$. Therefore, $R \cap S$ is reflexive.

Symmetry If $(a, b) \in R \cap S \Rightarrow (a, b) \in R$ and $(a, b) \in S$. Since, R and S are symmetric, therefore $(b, a) \in R$ and $(b, a) \in S$.

$\Rightarrow \quad (b, a) \in R \cap S$

Therefore, $R \cap S$ is symmetric.

Transitivity If $(a, b) \in R \cap S$ and $(b, c) \in R \cap S$, then $(a, b) \in R$, $(a, b) \in S$ and $(b, c) \in R$, $(b, c) \in S$ $\Rightarrow (a, c) \in R$ and $(a, c) \in S \Rightarrow (a, c) \in R \cap S$

Therefore, $R \cap S$ is transitive.

Thus, the intersection of two equivalence relation is also an equivalence relation. So, Statement I is true.

The union of two equivalence relations is not necessarily an equivalence relation.

If the union of two equivalence relations is an equivalence relation, then intersection also will be an equivalence relation.

So, Statement I is true only if Statement II is true.

(x) (a) Given a_{ij} denotes the elements of ith row and j^{th} column.

and $A = a_{ij} = \begin{cases} 0 & \text{for } i = j \\ 1 & \text{for } i > j \\ -1 & \text{for } i < j \end{cases}$

Let $A = \begin{bmatrix} a_{11} & a_{12} & a_{13} \\ a_{21} & a_{22} & a_{23} \\ a_{31} & a_{32} & a_{33} \end{bmatrix}$

Then, $A = \begin{bmatrix} 0 & -1 & -1 \\ 1 & 0 & -1 \\ 1 & 1 & 0 \end{bmatrix}$

$\because \quad |A| = \begin{vmatrix} 0 & -1 & -1 \\ 1 & 0 & -1 \\ 1 & 1 & 0 \end{vmatrix}$

$= 0\,(0+1) + 1(0+1) - 1(1-0) = 0 + 1 - 1 = 0$

So, A is not invertible.

and Reason is the correct explanation of A.

(xi) (a) Given, $P\left(\dfrac{A}{B}\right) = 0.25$ and $P\,(A \cap B) = 0.12$

$\because \quad P\left(\dfrac{A}{B}\right) = \dfrac{P\,(A \cap B)}{P\,(A)}$

$\Rightarrow \quad P\,(A) = \dfrac{P\,(A \cap B)}{P\left(\dfrac{A}{B}\right)} = \dfrac{0.12}{0.25} = 0.48$

Now, we know that

$$P\,(A) = P\,(A \cap B) + P\,(A \cap B')$$

$\Rightarrow P\,(A \cap B') = P\,(A) - P\,(A \cap B)$

$= 0.48 - 0.12 = 0.36$

Hence, $P\,(A \cap B') = 0.36$

(xii) Given, $|A| = 3$

$\because \quad C = (\text{adj}\, A)^T$

$\Rightarrow \quad |C| = \left| (\text{adj}\, A)^T \right|$

$= |\text{adj}\, A| = |A|^{3-1}$

$[\because |\text{adj}\, A| = |A|^{n-1}$, where n is the order of $A]$

$= 3^{3-1} = 3^2 = 9$

Hence, $|C^2| = |C| \cdot |C| = 9 \times 9 = 81$

(xiii) Given, R is a relation on set $\{a, b, c\}$ and $R = \{(b, b)\}$

Reflexivity Since, $(a, a) \notin R$ and $(c, c) \notin R$, therefore the relation R is not reflexive.

Symmetry If a relation is symmetric, then $(a, b) \in R \Rightarrow (b, a) \in R$.

Here, $(b, b) \in R$, so it is symmetric.

Transitivity R is not transitive.

Hence, the relation R is symmetric but not reflexive and transitive.

(xiv) Given function, $f: R \rightarrow R$.

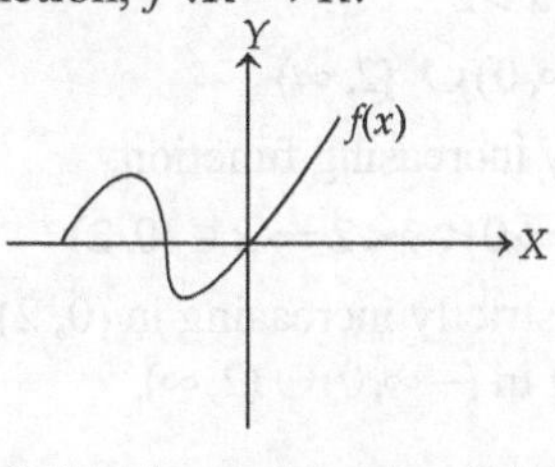

Since, each line in co-domain of the function parallel to X-axis, does not cuts the graph of function at least one point, therefore $f\,(x)$ is not an onto function.

(xv) Given, total number of machines = 3

Number of faulty machines = 2

Number of good machines = 3 − 2 = 1

Two test will be required and outcome will be first machine is faulty and second is good or both machines are faulty.

$\therefore$ Probability that only two tests are needed

$= \dfrac{2}{3} \times \dfrac{1}{2} + \dfrac{2}{3} \times \dfrac{1}{2} = \dfrac{1}{3} + \dfrac{1}{3} = \dfrac{2}{3}$

2. (i) We have, $x^y = y^x$

On taking log both sides, we get

$$y \log x = x \log y$$

On differentiating both sides, we get

$$\frac{d}{dx}(y \log x) = \frac{d}{dx}(x \log y)$$

$$\Rightarrow \quad y \cdot \frac{1}{x} + \log x \frac{dy}{dx} = x \cdot \frac{1}{y}\frac{dy}{dx} + \log y$$

$$\Rightarrow \quad \frac{dy}{dx}\left(\log x - \frac{x}{y}\right) = \log y - \frac{y}{x}$$

$$\therefore \quad \frac{dy}{dx} = \frac{\log y - \frac{y}{x}}{\log x - \frac{x}{y}}$$

Or

(ii) We have, $f(x) = x^2 e^{-x}$

On differentiating both sides, we get

$$f'(x) = -x^2 e^{-x} + e^{-x} \cdot 2x$$

$$= e^{-x}(-x)[x-2] = -e^{-x}[x(x-2)]$$

$\because$ e^x is always positive.

$\therefore$ $x(x-2) = 0 \Rightarrow x = 0$ or $x = 2$

For strictly decreasing function, $f'(x) < 0$

$\Rightarrow x < 0$ or $x > 2$

$\therefore$ $x \in (-\infty, 0) \cup (2, \infty)$

For strictly increasing function,

$f'(x) > 0 \Rightarrow 0 < x < 2 \Rightarrow x \in (0, 2)$

$\therefore f(x)$ is strictly increasing in (0, 2) and strictly decreasing in $(-\infty, 0) \cup (2, \infty)$.

3. Let $I = \int_0^{\sqrt{2}} [x^2]\, dx$

We know that if $n \le x < n+1$ for any integer n, then $[x] = n$

$$\therefore \int_0^{\sqrt{2}} [x^2]\, dx = \int_0^1 0\, dx + \int_1^{\sqrt{2}} 1\, dx = (x)_1^{\sqrt{2}} = \sqrt{2} - 1$$

4. Given, the equation of the curve is $y = 4x^2 - 2x^3$

On differentiating w.r.t. x, we get

$$\frac{dy}{dx} = 8x - 6x^2 = 2x(4 - 3x)$$

Slope of the tangent to the curve at origin.

$$m = \left(\frac{dy}{dx}\right)_{(0,\,0)} = 0$$

Now, the equation of tangent to the curve at (0, 0) is

$$y - y_1 = m(x - x_1)$$

$$\Rightarrow \quad y - 0 = 0(x - 0)$$

$$\Rightarrow \quad y = 0$$

Hence, X-axis is the tangent to the curve.

5. (i) Let $I = \int \frac{2x^3 - 1}{x^4 + x}\, dx$

On dividing both numerator and denominator by x^2, we get

$$= \int \frac{\left(2x - \frac{1}{x^2}\right)}{x^2 + \frac{1}{x}}\, dx$$

On putting $x^2 + \frac{1}{x} = t$,

$$\Rightarrow \quad \left(2x - \frac{1}{x^2}\right) dx = dt$$

We get, $\quad I = \int \frac{1}{t}\, dt = \ln|t| + C$

$$\therefore \quad I = \ln\left|x^2 + \frac{1}{x}\right| + C$$

Or

(ii) Let $I = \int e^x \operatorname{cosec} x (1 - \cot x)\, dx$

$$= \int e^x (\operatorname{cosec} x - \operatorname{cosec} x \cdot \cot x)\, dx$$

$$= \int e^x (\operatorname{cosec} x + (-\operatorname{cosec} x \cdot \cot x))\, dx$$

$$\therefore \quad I = e^x \operatorname{cosec} x + C$$

$$\left[\because \int e^x (f(x) + f'(x))\, dx = e^x f(x) + C\right]$$

6. We have, $\tan^{-1}\left(\frac{x}{y}\right) + \tan^{-1}\left(\frac{y-x}{y+x}\right)$

$$= \tan^{-1}\left(\frac{x}{y}\right) + \tan^{-1}\left(\frac{1 - \frac{x}{y}}{1 + \frac{x}{y}}\right)$$

$$= \tan^{-1}\left(\frac{x}{y}\right) + \tan^{-1}(1) - \tan^{-1}\left(\frac{x}{y}\right)$$

$$\left[\because \tan^{-1} a - \tan^{-1} b = \tan^{-1}\left(\frac{a-b}{1+ab}\right)\right]$$

$$= \tan^{-1}(1) = \frac{\pi}{4}$$

7. We have, $\sin^{-1}(x)+\sin^{-1}(1-x)=\cos^{-1}x$

$\Rightarrow \sin^{-1}(x)+\sin^{-1}(1-x)=\dfrac{\pi}{2}-\sin^{-1}x,$

$$\left[\because \cos^{-1}a+\sin^{-1}a=\frac{\pi}{2}\right]$$

$\Rightarrow \sin^{-1}(1-x)=\dfrac{\pi}{2}-2\sin^{-1}x$

$\Rightarrow (1-x)=\sin\left(\dfrac{\pi}{2}-2\sin^{-1}x\right)$

$\Rightarrow (1-x)=\cos(2\sin^{-1}x)$

$$\left[\because \sin\left(\frac{\pi}{2}-\theta\right)=\cos\theta\right]$$

$\Rightarrow (1-x)=\cos(\cos^{-1}(1-2x^2))$

$$[\because 2\sin^{-1}a=\cos^{-1}(1-2a^2)]$$

$\Rightarrow (1-x)=1-2x^2$

$\Rightarrow 2x^2-x=0 \Rightarrow x(2x-1)=0$

$\therefore \quad x=0,\dfrac{1}{2}$

8. Let $I=\displaystyle\int\sqrt{\sec\frac{x}{2}-1}\,dx$

$$=\int\sqrt{\frac{1-\cos\frac{x}{2}}{\cos\frac{x}{2}}}\,dx$$

$$=\int\sqrt{\frac{\left(1-\cos\frac{x}{2}\right)\left(1+\cos\frac{x}{2}\right)}{\cos\frac{x}{2}\left(1+\cos\frac{x}{2}\right)}}\,dx$$

$$=\int\frac{\sin\frac{x}{2}}{\sqrt{\cos^2\frac{x}{2}+\cos\frac{x}{2}}}\,dx$$

Put $\quad \cos\dfrac{x}{2}=t$

$\Rightarrow -\sin\dfrac{x}{2}\cdot\dfrac{1}{2}\,dx=dt$

$\Rightarrow \sin\dfrac{x}{2}\cdot dx=-2dt$

Then, $\quad I=-2\displaystyle\int\frac{dt}{\sqrt{t^2+t}}$

$$=-2\int\frac{dt}{\sqrt{\left(t+\frac{1}{2}\right)^2-\left(\frac{1}{2}\right)^2}}$$

$$=-2\log_e\left|\left(t+\frac{1}{2}\right)+\sqrt{t^2+t}\right|+C$$

$$=-2\log_e\left|\left(\cos\frac{x}{2}+\frac{1}{2}\right)+\sqrt{\cos^2\frac{x}{2}+\cos\frac{x}{2}}\right|+C$$

$$\left[\because t=\cos\frac{x}{2}\right]$$

9. (i) Let $y(t)$ be the height of the kite at time t, x be the horizontal distance between the person and the ring on the ground, which is given as 8 m and $s(t)$ be the length of the string between the kite and the ring at time t.

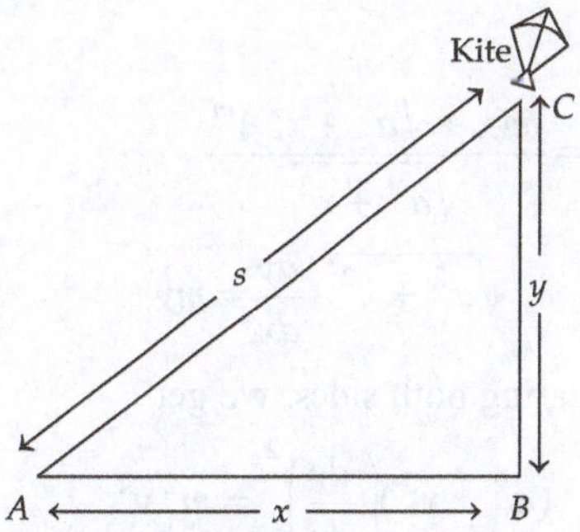

Given, $\dfrac{ds}{dt}=-1$ m/sec

In ΔABC, using Pythagoras theorem,

$$s^2=x^2+y^2$$

$\Rightarrow \quad s^2=8^2+y^2 \quad \ldots$(i)

On differentiating w.r.t t, we get

$$2s\frac{ds}{dt}=2y\frac{dy}{dt}$$

$\Rightarrow \quad s\dfrac{ds}{dt}=y\dfrac{dy}{dt} \quad \ldots$(ii)

From Eq. (i), when $y=15$, we get

$$s^2=8^2+15^2$$

$$=64+225=289$$

$\Rightarrow \quad s=17$ m

Now, from Eq. (ii), putting $\dfrac{ds}{dt}=-1$ m/sec,

$s=17$ m and $y=15$, we get

$$17(-1)=15\frac{dy}{dt}$$

$$\therefore \quad \frac{dy}{dt}=-\frac{17}{15}\text{ m/sec}$$

Hence, the kite is coming down at $\frac{17}{15}$ m/sec.

Or

(ii) We have, $y=(x+\sqrt{a^2+x^2})^m$ ...(i)

On differentiating w.r.t. x, we get

$$\frac{dy}{dx}=m(x+\sqrt{a^2+x^2})^{m-1}\cdot\left(1+\frac{2x}{2\sqrt{a^2+x^2}}\right)$$

$$\Rightarrow \frac{dy}{dx}=m(x+\sqrt{a^2+x^2})^{m-1}\cdot\left(\frac{x+\sqrt{a^2+x^2}}{\sqrt{a^2+x^2}}\right) \quad \text{...(ii)}$$

$$\frac{dy}{dx}=\frac{m(x+\sqrt{a^2+x^2})^m}{\sqrt{a^2+x^2}}$$

$$\Rightarrow \quad \sqrt{a^2+x^2}\cdot\frac{dy}{dx}=my$$

On squaring both sides, we get

$$\Rightarrow \quad (a^2+x^2)\left(\frac{dy}{dx}\right)^2=m^2y^2$$

Again, differentiating w.r.t. x, we get

$$2x\cdot\left(\frac{dy}{dx}\right)^2+(a^2+x^2)\cdot 2\cdot\frac{dy}{dx}\frac{d^2y}{dx^2}=2m^2y\cdot\frac{dy}{dx}$$

On dividing by $2\cdot\frac{dy}{dx}$ both sides, we get

$$x\cdot\frac{dy}{dx}+(a^2+x^2)\cdot\frac{d^2y}{dx^2}=m^2y$$

$$\therefore \quad (a^2+x^2)\frac{d^2y}{dx^2}+x\frac{dy}{dx}-m^2y=0$$ **Hence proved.**

10. Total number of possible outcomes, when a coin tossed three times $=2^3=8$.

$S=\{HHH, HHT, HTT, HTH, TTH, THT, THH, TTT\}$

(a) If all three friends will get the same result, then

$S_1=\{HHH, TTT\}$

Number of favourable outcomes $=2$

$\therefore$ Probability that all three friends will get same result.

i.e. P (no odd person)

$$=\frac{\text{Number of favourable outcomes}}{\text{Total number of outcomes}}=\frac{2}{8}=\frac{1}{4}$$

(b) Probability that they will get a different result in one round of tossing $=1-P$ (no odd person)

$$=1-\frac{1}{4}=\frac{3}{4}$$

(c) Probability that they will need exactly four rounds of tossing to determine who would pay

$=P$ (no odd person) $\times P$ (no odd person) $\times P$ (no odd person) $\times P$ (odd person)

$$=\frac{1}{4}\times\frac{1}{4}\times\frac{1}{4}\times\frac{3}{4}=\frac{3}{256}$$

Or

(ii) Let us define the events,

$L=$ The event that the child is left-handed.

$A=$ If both parents are left-handed with a 24% chance of the child being left handed.

$B=$ If father is right-handed and the mother is left-handed with a 22% chance of child being left handed.

$C=$ If father is left-handed and mother is right-handed with a 17% chance of child being left-handed.

$D=$ Both parents are right-handed with a 9% chance of having a left handed-child.

Given that the events A, B, C and D are equally likely.

Therefore, $P(A)=P(B)=P(C)=P(D)=\frac{1}{4}$.

Now, $P\left(\frac{L}{A}\right)=\frac{24}{100}=0.24$, $P\left(\frac{L}{B}\right)=\frac{22}{100}=0.22$,

$P\left(\frac{L}{C}\right)=\frac{17}{100}=0.17$ and $P\left(\frac{L}{D}\right)=\frac{9}{100}=0.09$

(a) Probability that a randomly selected child is left-handed

$$=P(A)\times P\left(\frac{L}{A}\right)+P(B)\times P\left(\frac{L}{B}\right)+P(C)\times P\left(\frac{L}{C}\right)+P(D)\times P\left(\frac{L}{D}\right)$$

$$=\frac{1}{4}\times\frac{24}{100}+\frac{1}{4}\times\frac{22}{100}+\frac{1}{4}\times\frac{17}{100}+\frac{1}{4}\times\frac{9}{100}$$

$$=\frac{1}{4}\times\frac{72}{100}=\frac{18}{100}=0.18$$

(b) The probability that a randomly selected child is left-handed given that exactly one of the parents is left handed $= P\left(\frac{L}{B}\right) + P\left(\frac{L}{C}\right)$

$$= \frac{22}{100} + \frac{17}{100}$$

$$= \frac{39}{100} = 0.39$$

(c) If a child is left handed, then the probability that both parents are left handed

$$P\left(\frac{A}{L}\right) = \frac{P(A) \times P\left(\frac{L}{A}\right)}{P(A) \times P\left(\frac{L}{A}\right) + P(B) \times P\left(\frac{L}{B}\right) + P(C) \times P\left(\frac{L}{C}\right) + P(D) \times P\left(\frac{L}{D}\right)}$$

$$= \frac{\frac{1}{4} \times \frac{24}{100}}{\frac{1}{4} \times \frac{72}{100}} \quad \text{[using part (i)]}$$

$$= \frac{24}{72} = \frac{1}{3}$$

11. Let x, y and z be the cost of one paper bag, one scrapbook and one pastel sheet respectively.

	Paper bags	Scrap books	Pastel sheets	Fund raised
School A	30	20	10	₹ 410
School B	20	10	20	₹ 290
School C	20	20	20	₹ 440

(i) Now, setting up the above information into a system of equations.

$$30x + 20y + 10z = 410$$
$$20x + 10y + 20z = 290$$
$$20x + 20y + 20z = 440$$

(ii) We have, $30x + 20y + 10z = 410$

$$20x + 10y + 20z = 290$$
$$20x + 20y + 20z = 440$$

Rewrite the system in matrix form $MX = N$ ...(i)

where $M = \begin{bmatrix} 30 & 20 & 10 \\ 20 & 10 & 20 \\ 20 & 20 & 20 \end{bmatrix}$, $X = \begin{bmatrix} x \\ y \\ z \end{bmatrix}$ and $N = \begin{bmatrix} 410 \\ 290 \\ 440 \end{bmatrix}$

$$\because |M| = \begin{vmatrix} 30 & 20 & 10 \\ 20 & 10 & 20 \\ 20 & 20 & 20 \end{vmatrix}$$

$$= 30(200 - 400) - 20(400 - 400) + 10(400 - 200)$$

$$= 30 \times (-200) + 10 \times 200$$

$$= -6000 + 2000 = -4000 \neq 0$$

$\therefore M^{-1}$ exists.

The cofactors of matrix M are

$$M_{11} = -200,\ M_{12} = 0,\ M_{13} = 200$$
$$M_{21} = -200,\ M_{22} = 400,\ M_{23} = -200$$
$$M_{31} = 300,\ M_{32} = -400,\ M_{33} = -100$$

$$\because \text{adj}(M) = \begin{bmatrix} -200 & 0 & 200 \\ -200 & 400 & -200 \\ 300 & -400 & -100 \end{bmatrix}^T$$

$$= \begin{bmatrix} -200 & -200 & 300 \\ 0 & 400 & -400 \\ 200 & -200 & -100 \end{bmatrix}$$

$$\therefore \quad M^{-1} = \frac{1}{|M|} \text{adj}(M)$$

$$= \frac{-1}{4000} \begin{bmatrix} -200 & -200 & 300 \\ 0 & 400 & -400 \\ 200 & -200 & -100 \end{bmatrix}$$

Now, from Eq. (i), we get $X = M^{-1}N$

$$= -\frac{1}{4000} \begin{bmatrix} -200 & -200 & 300 \\ 0 & 400 & -400 \\ 200 & -200 & -100 \end{bmatrix} \begin{bmatrix} 410 \\ 290 \\ 440 \end{bmatrix}$$

$$= -\frac{1}{40} \begin{bmatrix} -2 & -2 & 3 \\ 0 & 4 & -4 \\ 2 & -2 & -1 \end{bmatrix} \begin{bmatrix} 410 \\ 290 \\ 440 \end{bmatrix}$$

$$= -\frac{1}{4} \begin{bmatrix} -2 & -2 & 3 \\ 0 & 4 & -4 \\ 2 & -2 & -1 \end{bmatrix} \begin{bmatrix} 41 \\ 29 \\ 44 \end{bmatrix}$$

$$= -\frac{1}{4}\begin{bmatrix} -82-58+132 \\ 0+116-176 \\ 82-58-44 \end{bmatrix}$$

$$= -\frac{1}{4}\begin{bmatrix} -8 \\ -60 \\ -20 \end{bmatrix} = \begin{bmatrix} 2 \\ 15 \\ 5 \end{bmatrix}$$

Hence, $x = 2$, $y = 15$ and $z = 5$

(iii) The cost of one paper bag is ₹ 2,
the cost of one scrap book is ₹ 15,
and the cost of one pastel sheet is ₹ 5.

12. (i) **Method 1**

We have,

$$(xdy - ydx)y\sin\left(\frac{y}{x}\right) = (ydx + xdy)x\cos\left(\frac{y}{x}\right).$$

$$\Rightarrow \frac{dy}{dx} = \frac{(xy)\cos\left(\frac{y}{x}\right) + y^2\sin\left(\frac{y}{x}\right)}{(xy)\sin\left(\frac{y}{x}\right) - x^2\cos\left(\frac{y}{x}\right)}$$

$$\Rightarrow \frac{dy}{dx} = \frac{1 + \left(\frac{y}{x}\right)\tan\left(\frac{y}{x}\right)}{\tan\left(\frac{y}{x}\right) - \frac{1}{\left(\frac{y}{x}\right)}},$$

which is homogenous differential equation of type $\frac{dy}{dx} = f\left(\frac{y}{x}\right)$.

Let $y = vx \Rightarrow \frac{dy}{dx} = v + x\frac{dv}{dx}$

$$\Rightarrow \quad v + x\frac{dv}{dx} = \frac{1 + v\tan v}{\tan v - \frac{1}{v}}$$

$$\Rightarrow \left(\tan v - \frac{1}{v}\right)dv = 2\frac{dx}{x},$$

which is variable separable form where variables are v and x.

On integrating both sides, we get

$$\Rightarrow \quad \int\left(\tan v - \frac{1}{v}\right)dv = 2\int\frac{dx}{x}$$

$$\Rightarrow \log|\sec v| - \log|v| = 2\log|x| + \log c$$

$$\Rightarrow \quad \log|\sec v| = \log|v \cdot x^2 \cdot c|$$

$$\Rightarrow \quad \sec v = cx^2 v \Rightarrow \sec\left(\frac{y}{x}\right) = c\,(xy)$$

Given that $y = \pi$ when $x = 1$

Then, $\sec\pi = c\pi$

$$\Rightarrow \quad c = -\frac{1}{\pi}$$

Hence, required particular solution is

$$\sec\left(\frac{y}{x}\right) = -\frac{1}{\pi}(xy)$$

Alternate

The given differential equation is

$$(xdy - ydx)\,y\sin\left(\frac{y}{x}\right) = (ydx + xdy)\,x\cos\left(\frac{y}{x}\right).$$

$$\Rightarrow (xdy - ydx)\frac{\sin\left(\frac{y}{x}\right)}{\cos\left(\frac{y}{x}\right)} = \frac{(ydx + xdy)x}{y}$$

On dividing both sides by x^2, we get

$$\Rightarrow \frac{(xdy - ydx)}{x^2}\tan\left(\frac{y}{x}\right) = \frac{(ydx + xdy)x}{x^2 y}$$

$$\Rightarrow \frac{(xdy - ydx)}{x^2}\tan\left(\frac{y}{x}\right) = \frac{(ydx + xdy)}{xy}$$

$$\Rightarrow \quad \tan\left(\frac{y}{x}\right)d\left(\frac{y}{x}\right) = \frac{d(xy)}{xy}$$

which is variable separable form where variables are $\frac{y}{x}$ and xy.

On integrating both sides, we get

$$\Rightarrow \quad \int\tan\frac{y}{x}\cdot d\left(\frac{y}{x}\right) = \int\frac{d(xy)}{xy}$$

$$\Rightarrow \quad \log\left|\sec\left(\frac{y}{x}\right)\right| = \log(xy) + \log c$$

$$\Rightarrow \quad \sec\left(\frac{y}{x}\right) = c\,(xy)$$

Given that $y = \pi$ when $x = 1$

So that $c = -\frac{1}{\pi}$.

Hence, required particular solution is

$$\sec\left(\frac{y}{x}\right) = -\frac{1}{\pi}(xy).$$

Or

(ii) We have, $\int_0^\pi (\sin^4 x + \cos^4 x)dx$

$$[\because \sin^4 x + \cos^4 x = 1 - \frac{1}{2}\sin^2 2x = \frac{1}{4}(3 + \cos 4x)]$$

$$\therefore \int_0^\pi (\sin^4 x + \cos^4 x)\,dx = \frac{1}{4}\int_0^\pi (3 + \cos 4x)dx$$

$$= \frac{1}{4}\left[3x + \frac{\sin 4x}{4}\right]_0^\pi = \frac{3\pi}{4}$$

Let $I = \int_{-2\pi}^{2\pi} \frac{\sin^4 x + \cos^4 x}{1 + e^x} dx$ ...(i)

$$= \int_{-2\pi}^{2\pi} \frac{\sin^4(-x) + \cos^4(-x)}{1 + e^{-x}} dx$$

$$[\because \int_a^b f(x)dx = \int_a^b f(a + b - x)dx]$$

$$= \int_{-2\pi}^{2\pi} \frac{\sin^4 x + \cos^4 x}{1 + e^{-x}} dx$$

$I = \int_{-2\pi}^{2\pi} \frac{e^x(\sin^4 x + \cos^4 x)}{1 + e^x} dx$ ...(ii)

On adding Eqs. (i) and (ii), we get

$$I + I = \int_{-2\pi}^{2\pi} \frac{\sin^4 x + \cos^4 x}{1 + e^x} dx + \int_{-2\pi}^{2\pi} \frac{e^x(\sin^4 x + \cos^4 x)}{1 + e^x} dx$$

$$\therefore 2I = \int_{-2\pi}^{2\pi} (\sin^4 x + \cos^4 x)dx$$

$$= 2\int_0^{2\pi} (\sin^4 x + \cos^4 x)dx$$

$$[\because \int_{-a}^a f(x)dx = 2\int_0^a f(x)dx, \text{ if } f(-x) = f(x)]$$

$$\therefore I = \int_0^{2\pi} (\sin^4 x + \cos^4 x)dx$$

$$= 2\int_0^\pi (\sin^4 x + \cos^4 x)dx$$

$$[\because \int_0^{2a} f(x)dx = 2\int_0^a f(x)dx, \text{ if } f(2a - x) = f(x)]$$

$$= 2 \cdot \frac{3\pi}{4} = \frac{3\pi}{2} \quad \left[\because \int_0^\pi (\sin^4 x + \cos^4 x)\,dx = \frac{3\pi}{4}\right]$$

13. (i) Given radius of sphere be R.

Let radius and height of cone be r and h.

Then, height of cone, $h = R + x$

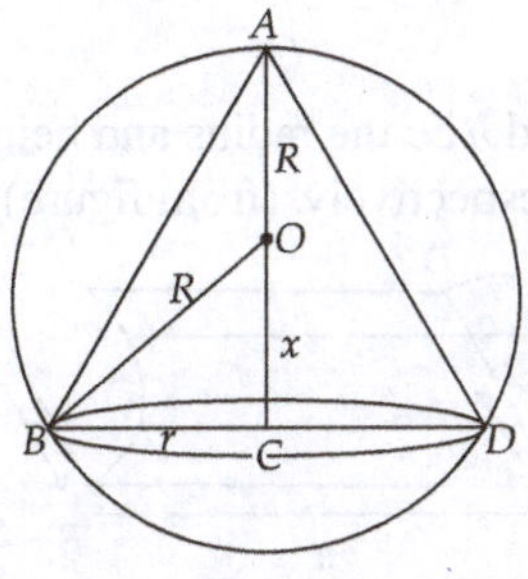

From the diagram

In ΔOCB, $r^2 + x^2 = R^2$

[using Pythagoras theorem] ...(i)

Volume of cone, $V = \frac{1}{3}\pi r^2 h = \frac{1}{3}\pi r^2 (R + x)$

$$= \frac{1}{3}\pi(R + x)(R^2 - x^2)$$

[from Eq. (i)]

$$\frac{dV}{dx} = \frac{1}{3}\pi[(R^2 - x^2)(1) + (R + x)(-2x)]$$

$$\frac{dV}{dx} = \frac{1}{3}\pi(R + x)(R - 3x)$$

and $\frac{d^2V}{dx^2} = \frac{1}{3}\pi[1(R - 3x) + (R + x)(-3)]$

$$= \frac{1}{3}\pi(-2R - 6x)$$

For maxima and minima, $\frac{dV}{dx} = 0$

$$\Rightarrow \frac{1}{3}\pi(R + x)(R - 3x) = 0$$

$$\Rightarrow R = 3x \text{ or } x = \frac{R}{3}$$

Now, applying the second derivative test, we have

$\frac{d^2V}{dx^2} = \frac{1}{3}\pi[-2R - 6x] < 0$, at $x = \frac{R}{3}$

Volume is maximum at $x = \frac{R}{3}$

Height of cone, $h = R + x = R + \frac{R}{3} = \frac{4R}{3}$

$\therefore$ Ratio of height of cone to diameter of sphere

$$= \frac{h}{2R} = \frac{\frac{4R}{3}}{2R} = \frac{2}{3}$$

Or

(ii) Given r and h be the radius and height of the cylinder, respectively. (from figure)

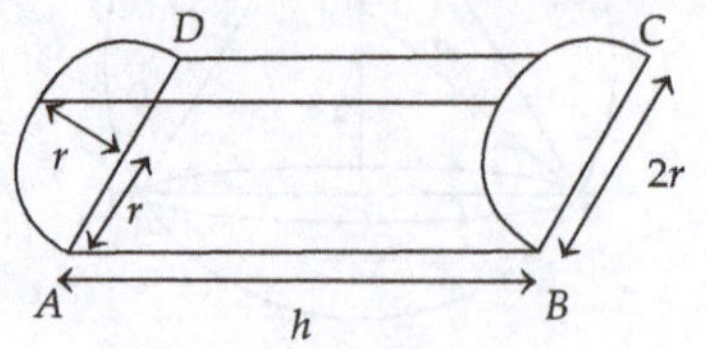

Volume of half cylinder $= \frac{1}{2}\pi r^2 h = V$

$$\Rightarrow \quad h = \frac{2V}{\pi r^2}$$

and total surface area $S = \pi r^2 + \pi rh + 2rh$

$$= \pi r^2 + \pi r \cdot \frac{2V}{\pi r^2} + 2r \cdot \frac{2V}{\pi r^2}$$

$$= \pi r^2 + \frac{1}{r}\left(2V + \frac{4V}{\pi}\right)$$

On differentiating two times w.r.t. r, we get

$$\frac{dS}{dr} = 2\pi r - \frac{1}{r^2}\left(2V + \frac{4V}{\pi}\right)$$

and $\quad \frac{d^2S}{dr^2} = 2\pi + \frac{2}{r^3}\left(2V + \frac{4V}{\pi}\right)$

For maximum and minimum, $\frac{dS}{dr} = 0$

$$\Rightarrow \quad 2\pi r - \frac{1}{r^2}\left(2V + \frac{4V}{\pi}\right) = 0$$

$$\Rightarrow \quad 2\pi r = \frac{1}{r^2}\left(2V + \frac{4V}{\pi}\right)$$

$$\Rightarrow \quad \pi r^3 = V\left(\frac{\pi + 2}{\pi}\right) \Rightarrow \quad r^3 = \frac{V}{\pi}\left(\frac{\pi + 2}{\pi}\right)$$

At $r^3 = \frac{V}{\pi}\left(\frac{\pi+2}{\pi}\right)$,

$$\frac{d^2S}{dr^2} = 2\pi + \frac{2}{r^3}\left(2V + \frac{4}{\pi}\right) > 0$$

$\therefore$ Surface area is minimum.

Now, on putting the value of V in Eq. (i), we get

$$\pi r^3 = \frac{1}{2}\pi r^2 h \cdot \frac{\pi + 2}{\pi} \Rightarrow \frac{2r}{h} = \frac{\pi + 2}{\pi}$$

Hence, ratio of the length of cylinder to the diameter of semi-circular ends is $\pi : \pi + 2$.

14. The random variable X denotes the points earned by Kiran. The possible values of X depends on the outcomes of the die rolls.

(i) If Kiran get a six on the first throw, then

$X = 1$ [$\because$ she gets $+1$ for the six]

If Kiran does not get a six on the first throw but get a six on the second throw, then

$X = -1 + 1 = 0$

If Kiran does not get a six on the first two throws but gets a six on the third throw, then

$$X = -1 - 1 + 1 = -1$$

If Kiran does not get a six on any of the three throws.

$$X = -1 - 1 - 1 = -3$$

Therefore, the possible values X can take are

$$X = 1, 0, -1, -3$$

(ii) Probability that Kiran does not get a six on any of the three throws, then

$$P(X = -3) = \frac{5}{6} \times \frac{5}{6} \times \frac{5}{6} = \frac{125}{216}$$

Probability that Kiran gets a six on the third thrown, then

$$P(X = -1) = \frac{5}{6} \times \frac{5}{6} \times \frac{1}{6} = \frac{25}{216}$$

Probability that Kiran gets a six on the second thrown, then

$$P(X = 0) = \frac{5}{6} \times \frac{1}{6} = \frac{5}{36}$$

Probability that Kiran gets a six on the first throw, then

$$P(X = 1) = \frac{1}{6}$$

Hence, required probability distribution

X	-3	-1	0	1
$P(X)$	$\frac{125}{216}$	$\frac{25}{216}$	$\frac{5}{36}$	$\frac{1}{6}$

(iii) Required expected value $= \Sigma P_i X_i = (-3)\left(\frac{125}{216}\right)$

$$+ (-1)\left(\frac{25}{216}\right) + 0 + \left(\frac{1}{6}\right)$$

$$= -\frac{91}{54} = -1\frac{37}{54} \approx -1.69$$

15. (i) (a) **Statement I** If $\vec{a}$ and $\vec{b}$ represent two adjacent sides of a parallelogram, then the diagonals are represented as

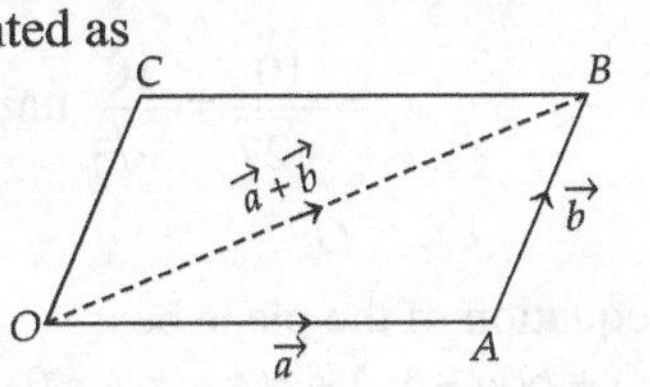

Here, the diagonals $\overrightarrow{OB} = \vec{a} + \vec{b}$

and diagonal $\overrightarrow{AC} = \vec{a} - \vec{b}$

So, Statement I is correct.

Statement II We know that the diagonals of a parallelogram intersects each other at the mid point. Therefore, the sides of the parallelogram are actually represented by $\frac{1}{2}(\vec{a} + \vec{b})$ and $\frac{1}{2}(\vec{a} - \vec{b})$.

So, Statement II is incorrect.

(ii) (c) Given, plane passes through the point $P \equiv (1, 1, 1)$ and the equation of line is

$$\frac{x-1}{3} = \frac{y-1}{0} = \frac{z-1}{4}$$

Since, the line is perpendicular to the plane, therefore the normal of the plane is parallel to the line.

$\Rightarrow$ The direction ratios of the plane

= The direction ratios of the line = (3, 0, 4)

The equation of plane

$$a(x-x_1)+b(y-y_1)+c(z-z_1)=0$$

$$\Rightarrow \quad 3(x-1)+0(y-1)+4(z-1)=0$$

$$\Rightarrow \quad 3x-3+4z-4=0$$

$$\Rightarrow \quad 3x-4z-7=0$$

The distance of the plane from the origin

$$d = \left|\frac{3\times 0+4\times 0-7}{\sqrt{3^2+4^2}}\right|$$

$$d = \left|\frac{-7}{\sqrt{25}}\right| = \left|\frac{-7}{5}\right| = \frac{7}{5} \text{ units}$$

(iii) (c) Given, the direction cosines of the line are $<\frac{1}{c}, \frac{1}{c}, \frac{1}{c}>$.

We know that

$$l^2+m^2+n^2=1$$

$$\Rightarrow \quad \left(\frac{1}{c}\right)^2+\left(\frac{1}{c}\right)^2+\left(\frac{1}{c}\right)^2=1$$

$$\Rightarrow \quad \frac{3}{c^2}=1 \Rightarrow c^2=3$$

$$\therefore \quad c=|\sqrt{3}| \Rightarrow c=\pm\sqrt{3}$$

(iv) Given, $\hat{a}$ is a unit vector

$$\Rightarrow \quad |\hat{a}|=1$$

and $\vec{a}$ is perpendicular to $\vec{b}$

$$\Rightarrow \quad \vec{a}\cdot\vec{b}=0$$

$$\because \quad (\vec{a}+2\vec{b})\cdot(3\vec{a}-\vec{b})=-5$$

$$\because 3|\vec{a}|^2-\vec{a}\cdot\vec{b}+6\vec{b}\cdot\vec{a}-2|\vec{b}|^2=-5$$

$$\Rightarrow \quad 3-2|\vec{b}|^2=-5$$

$[\because \vec{a}\cdot\vec{b}=\vec{b}\cdot\vec{a}=0]$

$$\Rightarrow \quad 8=2|\vec{b}|^2 \Rightarrow |\vec{b}|^2=4$$

$$\therefore \quad |\vec{b}|=2$$

(v) Placing the coordinate axes as illustrated, coordinates of A are (2, 0, 0), B are (0, 4, 3) and C are (1, 4, 0).

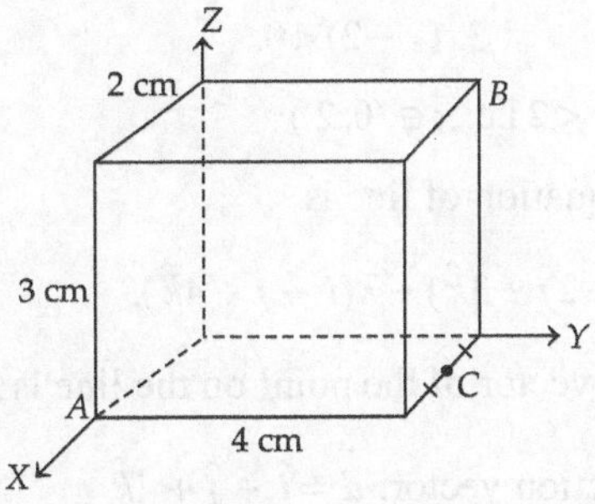

$$\therefore \quad \overrightarrow{BA}=\overrightarrow{OA}-\overrightarrow{OB}=2\hat{i}-4\hat{j}-3\hat{k}$$

and $\overrightarrow{BC}=\overrightarrow{OC}-\overrightarrow{OB}=\hat{i}-3\hat{k}$

Now, $\overrightarrow{BA}\cdot\overrightarrow{BC}=(2\hat{i}-4\hat{j}-3\hat{k})\cdot(\hat{i}-3\hat{k})=2+9=11$

16. (i) Given, $\vec{a}=4\hat{i}-\hat{j}+\hat{k}$ and $\vec{b}=-2\hat{i}+\hat{j}-2\hat{k}$

$$\vec{a}\times\vec{b}=\begin{vmatrix}\hat{i} & \hat{j} & \hat{k}\\ 4 & -1 & 1\\ -2 & 1 & -2\end{vmatrix}$$

$$=\hat{i}(2-1)-\hat{j}(-8+2)+\hat{k}(4-2)$$

$$=\hat{i}+6\hat{j}+2\hat{k}$$

and $\left|\vec{a} \times \vec{b}\right| = \sqrt{(1)^2 + 6^2 + 2^2} = \sqrt{41}$

A vector of magnitude 9 units and perpendicular to the vectors $\vec{a}$ and $\vec{b}$ is $9\left(\dfrac{\vec{a} \times \vec{b}}{\left|\vec{a} \times \vec{b}\right|}\right)$

Hence, required vector is $\dfrac{9}{\sqrt{41}}(\hat{i} + 6\hat{j} + 2\hat{k})$.

Or

(ii) Let $\vec{a} = 2x^2\hat{i} + 3x\hat{j} + \hat{k}$

and $\vec{b} = \hat{i} - 2\hat{j} + x^2\hat{k}$

$\because$ Angle between the vectors is obtuse

$\Rightarrow \quad \cos\theta < 0$

$\Rightarrow \quad \dfrac{\vec{a} \cdot \vec{b}}{|\vec{a}||\vec{b}|} < 0$

$\Rightarrow \quad \vec{a} \cdot \vec{b} < 0$

$\Rightarrow \quad 2x^2 - 6x + x^2 < 0$

$\Rightarrow \quad 3x(x-2) < 0$

$\therefore 0 < x < 2$ i.e. $x \in (0, 2)$

17. Given equation of line is

$\vec{r} = (2\hat{i} - 2\hat{j} + 3\hat{k}) + \lambda(\hat{i} - \hat{j} + 4\hat{k})$.

Position vector of the point on the line is $2\hat{i} - 2\hat{j} + 3\hat{k}$

and direction vector, $\vec{d} = \hat{i} - \hat{j} + 4\hat{k}$

Given plane is $\vec{r} \cdot (\hat{i} + 5\hat{j} + \hat{k}) - 5 = 0$.

$\therefore$ Normal vector of the plane is $\vec{n} = \hat{i} + 5\hat{j} + \hat{k}$

If straight line and plane are parallel to each other, then direction vector of line and normal vector of the plane are perpendicular to each other.

Now, $\vec{n} \cdot \vec{d} = (\hat{i} - \hat{j} + 4\hat{k})(\hat{i} + 5\hat{j} + \hat{k})$

$= 1 - 5 + 4 = 0$

$\Rightarrow$ They are perpendicular to each other.

$\therefore$ Straight line and plane are parallel to each other.

$\therefore$ Required distance $= \dfrac{(2\hat{i} - 2\hat{j} + 3\hat{k}) \cdot (\hat{i} + 5\hat{j} + \hat{k}) - 5}{\sqrt{1 + 25 + 1}}$

$= \dfrac{10}{\sqrt{27}} = \dfrac{10}{3\sqrt{3}}$ units

Or

(ii) Let the equation of the plane be $a(x - x_1) + b(y - y_1) + c(z - z_1) = 0$, which is passing through $(-1, 0, 2)$.

$\therefore \quad a(x+1) + b(y-0) + c(z-2) = 0$ ...(i)

Given line $\dfrac{x-0}{-2} = \dfrac{y-1}{3} = \dfrac{z-1}{-1}$ is passing through the point (0, 1, 1) and having direction ratios $<-2, 3, -1>$

Since, the plane contains the line and the point, then

$a(1) + b(1) + c(1-2) = 0 \Rightarrow a + b - c = 0$ ...(ii)

Also, the line and normal to the plane are perpendicular

$\therefore \quad -2a + 3b - c = 0$ ...(iii)

On solving Eqs. (ii) and (iii), we get

$$\frac{a}{\begin{vmatrix} 1 & -1 \\ 3 & -1 \end{vmatrix}} = \frac{b}{\begin{vmatrix} -1 & 1 \\ -1 & -2 \end{vmatrix}} = \frac{c}{\begin{vmatrix} 1 & 1 \\ -2 & 3 \end{vmatrix}}$$

$$\frac{a}{2} = \frac{b}{3} = \frac{c}{5} = k \text{ (say)}$$

Hence, required equation of the plane is

$2(x+1) + 3(y-0) + 5(z-2) = 0$

or $\quad 2x + 3y + 5z - 8 = 0$

18. (i) Given, the equation of the curve is $y = x|x|$.

$$\therefore y = \begin{cases} -x^2, & x < 0 \\ x^2, & x \geq 0 \end{cases}$$

Hence, sketch of the region enclosed bounded by the curve, $y = x|x|$ and the ordinates $x = -1$ and $x = 1$ is as follows.

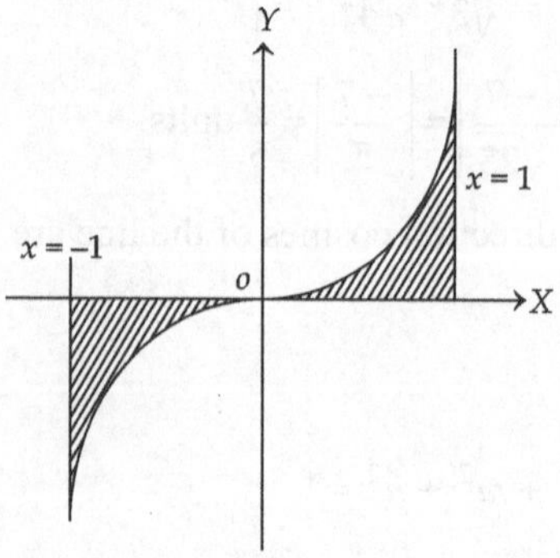

(ii) $\int_0^1 x^2 dx = \left[\frac{x^3}{3}\right]_0^1 = \frac{1}{3}$

(iii) Area of the shaded region $= 2 \times$ Area of shaded region is Ist quadratnt $= 2\int_0^1 x^2 dx = \frac{2}{3}$ sq units

19. (i) (b) If the average cost (AC) is constant at all level of output, it means that the marginal cost (MC) is equal to the average cost (AC).
So, MC = AC

(ii) (d) If $r = 0$, then the regression lines are perpendicular to each other and if $r = \pm 1$, then regression lines are coincide.
Hence, only III and IV statements are correct.

(iii) Given, $\bar{x} = 53$, $\bar{y} = 28$, $b_{yx} = -1.2$ and $b_{xy} = -0.3$

We know that $r^2 = b_{yx} \times b_{xy} = (-1.2) \times (-0.3) = 0.36$

$\Rightarrow \quad r = -0.6$

[b_{xy} and b_{yx} both are negative]

(iv) Given, $\quad R(x) = 36x + 3x^2 + 5$

$\Rightarrow \quad MR = \frac{d}{dx}(36x + 3x^2 + 5) = 36 + 6x$

$\therefore \; MR(x = 5) = 66$

(v) Given, $C(x) = 210x + 7000$ and $R(x) = 280x$
Minimum number must be produced and sold daily when $R(x) = C(x)$

$\Rightarrow \quad 210x + 7000 = 280x$

$\Rightarrow \quad 70x = 7000$

$\Rightarrow \quad x = 100$

Hence, minimum number that must be produced and sold is 100.

20. (i) Given, $C(x) = 200 + 20x - \frac{1}{2}x^2$

We know that average cost

$$AC = \frac{C(x)}{x}$$

$$\Rightarrow \quad AC = \frac{200}{x} + 20 - \frac{1}{2}x$$

To find AC falls,

$$\frac{d}{dx}(AC) = \frac{d}{dx}\left(\frac{200}{x} + 20 - \frac{1}{2}x\right)$$

$$= -\frac{200}{x^2} - \frac{1}{2} = -\left(\frac{200}{x^2} + \frac{1}{2}\right) < 0, \forall\, x > 0.$$

Hence, AC falls continuously.

Or

(ii) Given, $x = 100 - 4p$

$$\Rightarrow \quad p = \frac{100 - x}{4}$$

$$\therefore \text{ Revenue}, R(x) = px = \frac{100x - x^2}{4}$$

Then, $\quad MR = \frac{d}{dx}(Rx) = \frac{d}{dx}\left(\frac{100x - x^2}{4}\right) = \frac{100 - 2x}{4}$

$\because \quad MR = 0$

$$\Rightarrow \quad \frac{100 - 2x}{4} = 0$$

$\Rightarrow \quad 100 = 2x$

$\therefore \quad x = 50$

21. (i) Given,

Number of families, $n = 50$

Expenditure on accommodation = ₹ x

Expenditure on food and entertainment = ₹ y

$\Sigma x = 8500$, $\Sigma y = 9600$

$\sigma_x = 60$, $\sigma_y = 20$ and $r = 0.6$.

Now, $\quad \bar{x} = \frac{\Sigma x}{n} = \frac{8500}{50} = 170,$

$\quad \bar{y} = \frac{\Sigma y}{n} = \frac{9600}{50} = 192,$

and $b_{yx} = r\frac{\sigma_y}{\sigma_x} = 0.6 \times \frac{20}{60} = 0.2$

Regression equation y on x is

$$y - \bar{y} = b_{yx}(x - \bar{x})$$

$$y - 192 = 0.2(x - 170)$$

$\Rightarrow \quad y - 192 = 0.2x - 34$

$\Rightarrow \quad y = 0.2x + 158$

When $\quad x = 200$

Then, $\quad y = 0.2(200) + 158 = 198$

$\therefore$ Expenditure on food and entertainment is ₹ 198.

Or

(ii) (a) Given, linear regression $3x + 2y - 26 = 0$ ...(i)

and $\quad 6x + y - 31 = 0$ ...(ii)

Let $\bar{x}$ and $\bar{y}$ be the mean value of x and y.

Then, $(\bar{x}, \bar{y})$ satisfies the Eqs. (i) and (ii), we get

$3\bar{x} + 2\bar{y} - 26 = 0$ ...(iii)

$6\bar{x} + \bar{y} - 31 = 0$ ...(iv)

By cross-multiplication method, we get

$$\frac{\bar{x}}{\begin{matrix}2 & -26\\ 1 & -31\end{matrix}} = \frac{\bar{y}}{\begin{matrix}-26 & 3\\ -31 & 6\end{matrix}} = \frac{1}{\begin{matrix}3 & 2\\ 6 & 1\end{matrix}}$$

$$\Rightarrow \quad \frac{\bar{x}}{-36} = \frac{\bar{y}}{-63} = \frac{1}{-9}$$

or $\quad \frac{\bar{x}}{4} = \frac{\bar{y}}{7} = \frac{1}{1}$

$\Rightarrow \bar{x} = 4$ and $\bar{y} = 7$

Hence, the mean values of x and y are 4 and 7.

(b) We have,

$$3x + 2y - 26 = 0 \qquad \text{...(i)}$$

$$6x + y - 31 = 0 \qquad \text{...(ii)}$$

From Eq. (i)

$$2y = -3x + 26$$

$$y = -\frac{3}{2}x + 13$$

$$\therefore \quad b_{xy} = -\frac{3}{2}$$

From Eq. (ii), we get

$$6x = -y + 31$$

$$\Rightarrow \quad x = \frac{-1}{6}y + \frac{31}{6}$$

$$\Rightarrow \quad x = \frac{-1}{6}y + \frac{31}{6}$$

$$\therefore \quad b_{yx} = \frac{-1}{6}$$

Now, $r^2 = b_{yx} \times b_{xy} = \left(-\frac{3}{2}\right) \times \left(\frac{-1}{6}\right) = \frac{1}{4}$

$$\therefore \quad r^2 = \frac{1}{4}$$

$$\Rightarrow \quad r = \frac{\pm 1}{2}$$

We know that b_{yx}, b_{xy} and r have same sign, therefore $r = -\frac{1}{2}$.

22. Given, $Z = px + qy$, $p, q > 0$

Subject to constraints $x + y \leq 60$

$$5x + y \leq 100 \text{ and } x, y \geq 0$$

Table for $x + y = 60$ is ...(i)

x	0	60
y	60	0

The line passes through the points (0, 60) and (60, 0).

At (0, 0),

$$0 + 0 \leq 60$$

$$\Rightarrow \quad 0 \leq 6 \text{ (true)}$$

So, the half plane lies towards the origin.

Table for $5x + y = 100$ is ...(ii)

x	0	20
y	100	0

The line passes through the points (0, 100) and (20, 0).

At (0, 0),

$$0 + 0 \leq 100$$

$$\Rightarrow \quad 0 \leq 100 \text{ (true)}$$

So, the half plane lies towards the origin.

On solving Eqs. (i) and (ii), we get

$$x = 10 \text{ and } y = 50$$

On plating the graph, we get the feasible region $ABCD$ as shown below

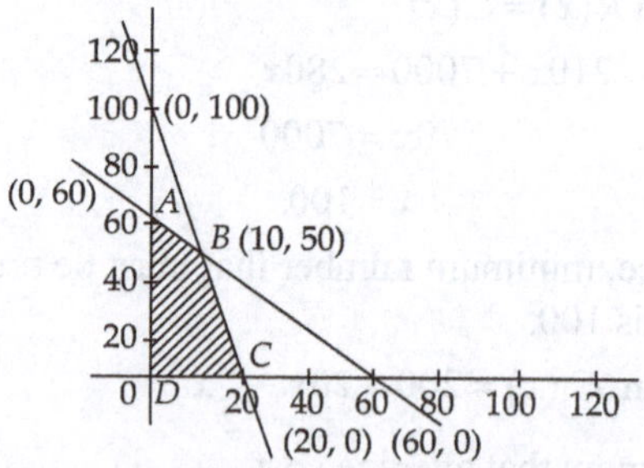

Thus, the corner points of the feasible region are $A(0, 60)$, $B(10, 50)$, $C(20, 0)$ and $D(0, 0)$.

(ii) We have, $Z = px + qy$

Given, Z is maximum at (0, 60) and (10, 50)

$$\therefore \quad 0 \cdot p + 60 \cdot q = 10 \cdot p + 50 \cdot q$$

$$\Rightarrow \quad 10p = 10q$$

$$\Rightarrow \quad p = q$$

which is the required relation. Also, there can be infinite number of optimal solutions.

ISC

Examination Paper 2025

Time : 3 hrs
Marks : 80

Mathematics

General Instructions

1. The Question Paper consists of three Sections A, B and C.
2. Candidates are required to attempt all questions from Section A and all questions either from Section B or Section C.
3. Section A Internal choice has been provided in two questions of two marks each, two questions of four marks each and two questions of six marks each.
4. Section B Internal choice has been provided in one question of two marks and one question of four marks.
5. Section C Internal choice has been provided in one question of two marks and one question of four marks.
6. All working, including rough work, should be done on the same sheet as, and adjacent to the rest of the answer.
7. The intended marks for questions or parts of questions are given in brackets [ ].
8. Mathematical tables and graph papers are provided.

Section A [65 Marks]

1. In subparts (i) to (xi), choose the correct options and in subparts (xii) to (xv), answer the questions as instructed. **[15]**

(i) If $A=\begin{bmatrix}0 & a\\ 0 & 0\end{bmatrix}$ then A^{16} is

(a) unit matrix (b) null matrix
(c) diagonal matrix (d) skew-symmetric matrix

(ii) Which of the following is a homogeneous differential equation?

(a) $(4x^2+6y+5)\,dy-(3y^2+2x+4)\,dx=0$
(b) $(xy)\,dx-(x^3+y^3)\,dy=0$
(c) $(x^3+2y^2)\,dx+2xy\,dy=0$
(d) $y^2dx+(x^2-xy-y^2)\,dy=0$

(iii) Consider the graph of the function $f(x)$ shown below

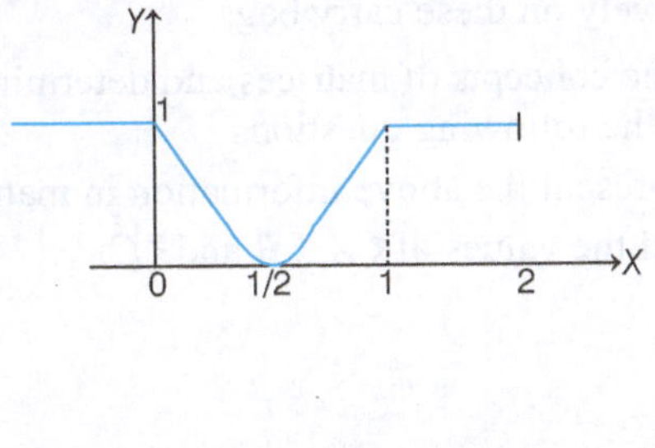

Statement I The function $f(x)$ is increasing in $\left(\frac{1}{2},2\right)$

Statement II The function $f(x)$ is strictly increasing in $\left(\frac{1}{2},1\right)$

Which of the following is correct with respect to the above statements?

(a) Statement I is true and Statement II is false.
(b) Statement II is true and Statement I is false.
(c) Both the statements are true.
(d) Both the statements are false.

(iv) $\int_0^1 \frac{x^4-1}{x^2+1}\,dx$ is equal to

(a) $\frac{2}{3}$
(b) $\frac{1}{3}$
(c) $\frac{-2}{3}$
(d) 0

(v) **Assertion** Consider the two events A and B such that $n(A) = n(B)$ and $P\left(\frac{A}{B}\right) = P\left(\frac{B}{A}\right)$.

Reason The events A and B are mutually exclusive.

(a) Both Assertion and Reason are true and Reason is the correct explanation for Assertion.
(b) Both Assertion and Reason are true but Reason is not the correct explanation for Assertion.
(c) Assertion is true and Reason is false.
(d) Assertion is false and Reason is true.

(vi) The existence of unique solution of the system of equations $x + y = \lambda$ and $5x + ky = 2$ depends on

(a) λ only (b) $\frac{\lambda}{k} = 1$
(c) Both k and λ (d) k only

(vii) A cylindrical popcorn tub of radius 10 cm is being filled with popcorns at the rate of 314 cm^3 per minute. The level of the popcorns in the tub is increasing at the rate of

(a) 1 cm/min (b) 0.1 cm/min
(c) 1.1 cm/min (d) 0.5 cm/min

(viii) If $f(x) = \begin{cases} x+2, & x<0 \\ -x^2-2, & 0 \le x < 1 \\ x, & x \ge 1 \end{cases}$ then the number of point(s) of discontinuity of $f(x)$, is/are

(a) 1 (b) 3
(c) 2 (d) 0

(ix) **Assertion** If set A has m elements, set B has n elements and $n < m$ then the number of one-one function(s) from $A \to B$ is zero.

Reason A function $f: A \to B$ is defined only if all elements in set A have an image in set B.

(a) Both Assertion and Reason are true and Reason is the correct explanation for Assertion.
(b) Both Assertion and Reason are true but Reason is not the correct explanation for Assertion.
(c) Assertion is true and Reason is false.
(d) Assertion is false and Reason is true.

(x) Let X be a discrete random variable. The probability distribution of X is given below.

X	30	10	−10
$P(X)$	$\frac{1}{5}$	$\frac{3}{10}$	$\frac{1}{2}$

Then, $E(X)$ will be

(a) 1 (b) 4 (c) 2 (d) 30

(xi) **Statement I** If A is an invertible matrix then $(A^2)^{-1} = (A^{-1})^2$.

Statement II If A is an invertible matrix then $|A^{-1}| = |A|^{-1}$.

(a) Statement I is true and Statement II is false.
(b) Statement II is true and Statement I is false.
(c) Both the statements are true.
(d) Both the statements are false.

(xii) Write the smallest equivalence relation from the set A to set A, where $A = \{1, 2, 3\}$.

(xiii) For what value of x, is $A = \begin{bmatrix} 0 & 1 & -2 \\ -1 & 0 & 3 \\ x & -3 & 0 \end{bmatrix}$ a skew-symmetric matrix?

(xiv) Three critics review a book. Odds in favour of the book are 5 : 2, 4 : 3 and 3 : 4 respectively for the three critics. Find the probability that all critics are in favour of the book.

(xv) Evaluate $\int \frac{5}{\sqrt{2x+7}}\,dx$

2. Find the point on the curve $y = 2x^2 - 6x - 4$ at which the tangent is parallel to the X-axis. **[2]**

3. Find the value of $\tan^{-1} x - \cot^{-1} x$ if $(\tan^{-1} x)^2 - (\cot^{-1} x)^2 = \frac{5\pi}{8}$. **[2]**

4. (i) If $x^y = e^{x-y}$, prove that $\frac{dy}{dx} = \frac{\log x}{(1+\log x)^2}$. **[2]**

Or

(ii) If $f(x) = \log(1+x) + \frac{1}{1+x}$, show that $f(x)$ attains its minimum value at $x = 0$. **[2]**

5. Three shopkeepers Gaurav, Rizwan and Jacob use carry bags made of polythene, handmade paper and newspaper. The number of polythene bags, handmade bags and newspaper bags used by Gaurav, Rizwan and Jacob are (20, 30, 40), (30, 40, 20) and (40, 20, 30), respectively. One polythene bag costs ₹1, one handmade bag is for ₹5 and one newspaper bag costs ₹2. Gaurav, Rizwan and Jacob spend ₹ A, ₹ B and ₹ C respectively on these carry bags.

Using the concepts of matrices and determinants, answer the following questions

(i) Represent the above information in matrix form.
(ii) Find the values of ₹ A, ₹ B and ₹ C. **[2]**

6. (i) Differentiate $\sin^{-1}\left(\frac{2^{x+1}\,3^{x}}{1+(36)^{x}}\right)$ with respect to x. **[2]**

Or

(ii) Show that $\tan^{-1}x+\tan^{-1}y=C$ is the general solution of the differential equation $(1+x^2)\,dy+(1+y^2)\,dx=0$. **[2]**

7. If $x+y+z=0$ then show that $\begin{vmatrix} 1 & 1 & 1 \\ x & y & z \\ x^3 & y^3 & z^3 \end{vmatrix}=0$, using properties of determinant. **[4]**

8. (i) Evaluate $\int \frac{\cos x}{3\cos x-5}\,dx$ **[4]**

Or

(ii) Evaluate $\int (\log x)^2\,dx$ **[4]**

9. (i) If $x=\tan\left(\frac{1}{a}\log y\right)$ then show that $(1+x^2)\frac{d^2y}{dx^2}+(2x-a)\frac{dy}{dx}=0.$ **[4]**

Or

(ii) The graph of $f(x)=-x^3+27x-2$ is given below. **[4]**

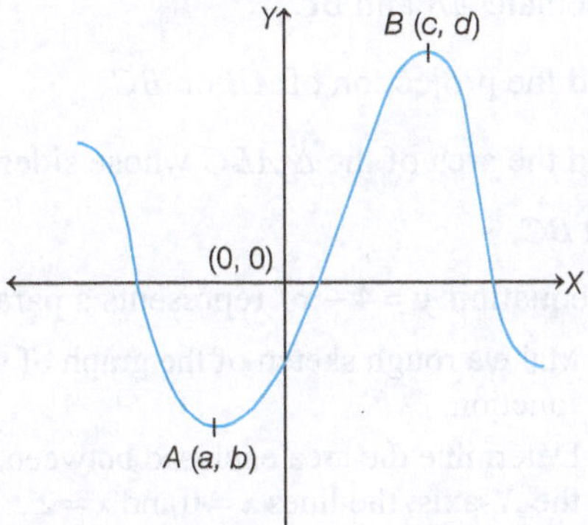

(a) Find the slope of the above graph.
(b) Find the coordinates of turning points A and B.
(c) Evaluate $f''(-2)$, $f(0)$ and $f'(3)$ and arrange them in ascending order.

10. Pia, Sia and Dia displayed their paintings in an art exhibition. The three artists displayed 15, 5 and 10 of their paintings, respectively. A person bought three paintings from the exhibition.

(i) Find the probability that he bought one painting from each of them.

(ii) Find the probability that he bought all the three paintings from the same person. **[4]**

11. (i) Prove $\int_{\pi/4}^{3\pi/4} \frac{x\,dx}{1+\sin x}=(\sqrt{2}-1)\,\pi$ **[6]**

Or (ii) Evaluate $\int \frac{x^2}{(x-1)^2\,(x^2+1)}\,dx$ **[6]**

12. (i) Solve the differential equation $(x+5y^2)\frac{dy}{dx}=y$ when $x=2$ and $y=1$. **[6]**

Or

(ii) Find the particular solution of the differential equation $(x^2-2y^2)\,dx+2xy\,dy=0$, when $x=1$ and $y=1$. **[6]**

13. Observe the two graphs, Graph 1 and Graph 2 given below and answer the questions that follow.

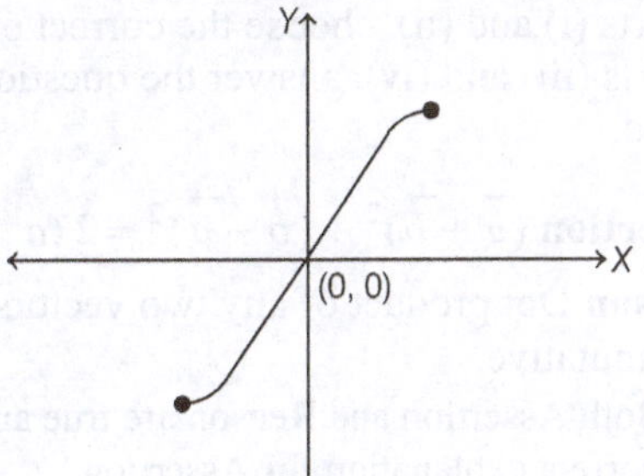

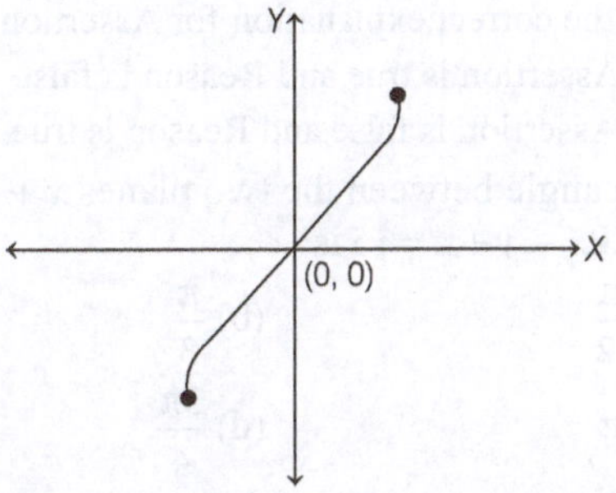

(i) Which one of the graphs represents $y=\sin^{-1}x$?

(ii) Write the domain and range of $y=\sin^{-1}x$.

(iii) Prove that $\sin^{-1}\frac{1}{\sqrt{5}}+\sin^{-1}\frac{2}{\sqrt{5}}=\frac{\pi}{2}$.

(iv) Find the value of $\tan^{-1}\left[2\sin\left(2\cos^{-1}\frac{\sqrt{3}}{2}\right)\right]$. **[6]**

14. An international conference takes place in a metropolitan city. International leaders, scientists and industrialists participate in it.

The organisers of the conference appoint three agencies namely X, Y and Z for the security of the participants. The track record of the success of X, Y and Z in providing security services is 99%, 98.5% and 98%, respectively. The organisers assign the responsibility of ensuring the security of 1000 people to agency X, 2000 people to agency Y and 3000 people to agency Z.

At the end of the conference, one participant goes missing from the conference room.

What is the probability that the missing participant was placed under the responsibility of the security agency X? **[6]**

Section B **[15 Marks]**

15. In subparts (i) and (ii), choose the correct options and in subparts (iii) and (iv), answer the questions as instructed.

(i) **Assertion** $(\vec{a}+\vec{b})^2+(\vec{b}-\vec{a})^2=2(\vec{a}^2+\vec{b}^2)$

Reason Dot product of any two vectors is commutative.

(a) Both Assertion and Reason are true and Reason is the correct explanation for Assertion.

(b) Both Assertion and Reason are true but Reason is not the correct explanation for Assertion.

(c) Assertion is true and Reason is false.

(d) Assertion is false and Reason is true. **[1]**

(ii) The angle between the two planes $x+y+2z=9$ and $2x-y+z=15$ is **[1]**

(a) $\frac{\pi}{2}$ (b) $\frac{\pi}{3}$

(c) π (d) $\frac{3\pi}{4}$

(iii) Show that points $P(-2, 3, 5)$, $Q(1, 2, 3)$ and $R(7, 0, -1)$ are collinear. **[1]**

(iv) Two honeybees are flying parallel to each other in the garden to collect the nectar. The path traced by the bees is given in the form of a straight line.

The equation of the path traced by one honeybee is $\vec{r}=(\hat{i}+2\hat{i}+3\hat{k})+\lambda(2\hat{i}+3\hat{j}+4\hat{k})$.

(a) Write the above mentioned equation in cartesian form. **[1]**

(b) Find the equation of the path traced by the other honeybee passing through the point (2, 4, 5). **[1]**

16. (i) Find the equation of the plane passing through the points (2, 2, – 1), (3, 4, 2) and (7, 0, 6). **[2]**

Or

(ii) Find the equation of the plane passing through the points (2, 3, 1), (4, –5, 3) and parallel to X-axis. **[2]**

17. Consider the position vectors of A, B and C as

$\vec{OA}=2\hat{i}-2\hat{j}+\hat{k}$, $\vec{OB}=\hat{i}+2\hat{j}-2\hat{k}$

and $\vec{OC}=2\hat{i}-\hat{j}+4\hat{k}$.

(i) Calculate $\vec{AB}$ and $\vec{BC}$.

(ii) Find the projection of $\vec{AB}$ on $\vec{BC}$.

(iii) Find the area of the ΔABC whose sides are $\vec{AB}$ and $\vec{BC}$. **[4]**

18. (i) The equation $y=4-x^2$ represents a parabola.

(a) Make a rough sketch of the graph of the given function.

(b) Determine the area enclosed between the curve, the X-axis, the lines $x=0$ and $x=2$.

(c) Hence, find the area bounded by the parabola and the X-axis. **[4]**

Or

(ii) A farmer has a field bounded by three lines $x+2y=2$, $y-x=1$, $2x+y=7$. Using integration, find the area of the region bounded by these lines. **[4]**

Section C [15 Marks]

19. In subparts (i) and (ii), choose the correct options and in subpart (iii), answer the questions as instructed.

(i) The total revenue received from the sale of x units of a product is $R(x) = 36x + 3x^2 + 5$. Then, the actual revenue for selling the 10th item will be [1]

(a) 27 (b) 90
(c) 93 (d) 33

(ii) Read the following statements and choose the correct option.

(I) The correlation coefficient and the regression coefficients are of the same sign.

(II) The correlation coefficient is the arithmetic mean between the regression coefficients.

(III) The product of two regression coefficients is always equal to 1.

(IV) Both the regression coefficients cannot be numerically greater than unity.

(a) Only (IV) is correct.
(b) Only (I) and (II) are correct.
(c) Only (I) and (IV) are correct.
(d) Only (III) and (IV) are correct. [1]

(iii) Consider the following data:

x	1	2	3	6
y	6	5	4	1
$x-\bar{x}$				
$y-\bar{y}$				

(a) Calculate $\bar{x}$ and $\bar{y}$. (b) Complete the table.
(c) Calculate b_{xy}. [1 + 1 + 1]

20. (i) Find the regression line of best fit from the following data.

$\Sigma x = 24$, $\Sigma y = 44$, $\Sigma xy = 306$, $\Sigma x^2 = 164$, $\Sigma y^2 = 576$, $n = 4$ [2]

Or

(ii) Two lines of regression are given as $4x + 3y + 7 = 0$ and $3x + 4y + 8 = 0$. Identify the line of regression of x on y. [2]

21. (i) A utensil manufacturer produces x dinner sets per week and sells each set at ₹ p, where $x = \dfrac{600 - p}{8}$.

The cost of production of x sets is ₹$x^2 + 78x + 2000$.

(a) Write the revenue function.
(b) Write the profit function.
(c) Calculate the number of dinner sets to be produced and sold per week to ensure maximum profit. [4]

Or

(ii) The average cost of producing x units of commodity is given by AC $= \dfrac{x^2}{200} - \dfrac{x}{50} - 30 + \dfrac{5000}{x}$.

(a) Find the cost function.
(b) Find the marginal cost function.
(c) Find the marginal average cost function.
(d) Verify that $\dfrac{d}{dx}(\text{AC}) = \dfrac{\text{MC} - \text{AC}}{x}$. [4]

22. Two different types of books have to be stacked in the shelf of a library. The first type of book weighs 1 kg and has a thickness of 6 cm. The second type of book weighs 1.5 kg and has a thickness of 4 cm. The shelf is 96 cm long and can support a maximum weight of 21 kg.

How should both the types of books be placed in the shelf to include the maximum number of books? Formulate a LPP and solve it graphically. [4]

Solutions

1. (i) (b) We have, $A=\begin{bmatrix}0 & a\\ 0 & 0\end{bmatrix}$

Now, $A^2 = A\cdot A$

$$=\begin{bmatrix}0 & a\\ 0 & 0\end{bmatrix}\begin{bmatrix}0 & a\\ 0 & 0\end{bmatrix}$$

$$=\begin{bmatrix}0+0 & 0+0\\ 0+0 & 0+0\end{bmatrix}=\begin{bmatrix}0 & 0\\ 0 & 0\end{bmatrix}$$

$\therefore$ A^2 is a null matrix.

Since, A^2 is a null matrix. So, any higher power of A will also be a null matrix.

$\therefore$ $A^{16}=(A^2)^8$

$$=\begin{bmatrix}0 & 0\\ 0 & 0\end{bmatrix}^8=\begin{bmatrix}0 & 0\\ 0 & 0\end{bmatrix}$$

So, A^{16} is a null matrix.

(ii) (d) From option (a), we have,

$(4x^2+6y+5)\,dy-(3y^2+2x+4)\,dx=0$

$$\Rightarrow \frac{dy}{dx}=\frac{3y^2+2x+4}{4x^2+6y+5}$$

It is not a homogeneous differential equation because degree of numerator and denominator are not same.

From option (b), we have,

$(xy)\,dx-(x^3+y^3)\,dy=0$

$$\Rightarrow \frac{dy}{dx}=\frac{xy}{x^3+y^3}$$

It is not a homogeneous differential equation because degree of numerator and denominator are not same.

From option(c), we have, $(x^3+2y^2)\,dx+2xy\,dy=0$

$$\Rightarrow \frac{dy}{dx}=-\left(\frac{x^3+2y^2}{2xy}\right)$$

It is not a homogeneous differential equation because degree of numerator and denominator are not same.

From option (d), we have, $y^2dx+(x^2-xy-y^2)\,dy=0$

$$\Rightarrow \frac{dy}{dx}=-\frac{y^2}{x^2-xy-y^2}$$

It is a homogeneous differential equation because degree of numerator and denominator are same.

(iii) (b) From the graph, it is clear that $f(x)$ is strictly increasing in $\left(\frac{1}{2},1\right)$

So, Statement I is false and Statement II is true.

(iv) (c) Let $I=\int_0^1 \frac{x^4-1^4}{x^2+1}\,dx$

$$=\int_0^1 \frac{(x^2)^2-(1^2)^2}{x^2+1}\,dx$$

$$=\int_0^1 \frac{(x^2+1)(x^2-1)}{x^2+1}\,dx$$

$$=\int_0^1 (x^2-1)\,dx=\left[\frac{x^3}{3}-x\right]_0^1$$

$$=\frac{1^3}{3}-1-(0-0)=\frac{1}{3}-1=-\frac{2}{3}$$

(v) (c) **Assertion** $P\left(\frac{A}{B}\right)=\frac{P(A\cap B)}{P(B)}$

and $P\left(\frac{B}{A}\right)=\frac{P(B\cap A)}{P(A)}$

Now, we have, $P\left(\frac{A}{B}\right)=P\left(\frac{B}{A}\right)$

$$\Rightarrow \frac{P(A\cap B)}{P(B)}=\frac{P(B\cap A)}{P(A)}$$

$$\Rightarrow \frac{P(A\cap B)}{P(B)}=\frac{P(A\cap B)}{P(A)}$$

$[\because P(A\cap B)=P(B\cap A)]$

$$\Rightarrow P(A)=P(B)$$

$$\Rightarrow \frac{n(A)}{n(S)}=\frac{n(B)}{n(S)}$$

$\Rightarrow$ $n(A)=n(B)$, which is given.

$\therefore$ Assertion is true.

Reason If A and B are mutually exclusive then $P(A\cap B)=0$.

If $P(A\cap B)=0$ then $P\left(\frac{A}{B}\right)=\frac{0}{P(B)}=0$

and $P\left(\frac{B}{A}\right)=\frac{0}{P(A)}=0$

Thus, $P\left(\frac{A}{B}\right)=P\left(\frac{B}{A}\right)=0$

However, this does not mean that events A and B have to be mutually exclusive for $P\left(\frac{A}{B}\right)=P\left(\frac{B}{A}\right)$ to hold true.

As shown in Assertion, $P\left(\frac{A}{B}\right)=P\left(\frac{B}{A}\right)$ if $P(A)=P(B)$ which means $n(A)=n(B)$.

$\therefore$ Reason is false.

(vi) (d) The given system of equations is

$$x+y=\lambda \text{ and } 5x+ky=2.$$

The given system of equations can be written in matrix form as $AX=B$,

where $A=\begin{bmatrix}1 & 1\\ 5 & k\end{bmatrix}$, $X=\begin{bmatrix}x\\ y\end{bmatrix}$ and $B=\begin{bmatrix}\lambda\\ 2\end{bmatrix}$

We know that the system of equations has a unique solution if the determinant of the matrix is non-zero.

$\therefore \quad |A|\neq 0$

$\Rightarrow \quad \begin{vmatrix}1 & 1\\ 5 & k\end{vmatrix}\neq 0$

$\Rightarrow \quad k-5\neq 0$

$\Rightarrow \quad k\neq 5$

So, the existence of unique solution depends on the value of k.

(vii) (a) Let r be radius, h be the height and V be the volume of the cylindrical popcorn.

$\therefore \quad r=10$ cm, $\frac{dV}{dt}=314\text{ cm}^3/\text{min}$

Now, $V=\pi r^2 h=\pi(10)^2 h=100\pi h$

On differentiating both sides w.r.t. t, we get

$$\frac{dV}{dt}=100\pi\frac{dh}{dt}$$

$\Rightarrow \quad 314=100\pi\frac{dh}{dt}$

$\Rightarrow \quad \frac{dh}{dt}=\frac{314}{100\pi}=\frac{314}{100\times 3.14}$

$\Rightarrow \quad \frac{dh}{dt}=1$

So, the level of the popcorns in the tub is increasing at the rate of 1 cm/min.

(viii) (c) We have,

$$f(x)=\begin{cases}x+2, & x<0\\ -x^2-2, & 0\leq x<1\\ x, & x\geq 1\end{cases}$$

At $x=0$,

$\text{LHL}=\lim_{x\to 0^-} f(x)=\lim_{h\to 0} f(0-h)$

$=\lim_{h\to 0} f(-h)$

$=\lim_{h\to 0} -h+2=-0+2=2$

$\text{RHL}=\lim_{x\to 0^+} f(x)=\lim_{h\to 0} f(0+h)$

$=\lim_{h\to 0} f(h)$

$=\lim_{h\to 0} -(h)^2-2=0-2=-2$

$\because \quad \text{LHL}\neq\text{RHL}$

$\therefore f(x)$ is discontinuous at $x=0$.

At $x=1$,

$\text{LHL}=\lim_{x\to 1^-} f(x)=\lim_{h\to 0} f(1-h)$

$=\lim_{h\to 0} -(1-h)^2-2$

$=-(1-0)^2-2=-1-2=-3$

$\text{RHL}=\lim_{x\to 1^+} f(x)=\lim_{h\to 0} f(1+h)$

$=\lim_{h\to 0} f(1+h)=1+0=1$

$\because$ LHL $\neq$ RHL

$\therefore f(x)$ is discontinuous at $x=0$.

So, the number of points of discontinuity of $f(x)$ is 2.

(ix) (b) If A has n elements, B has m elements and $n<m$ then the number of one-one function from A to B is zero because if $n<m$, it is impossible to map each element of A to distinct element of B.

Clearly, Reason is true.

Hence, both Assertion and Reason are true but Reason is not the correct explanation for Assertion.

(x) (b) We know that $E(X)=\Sigma x_i p_i$

$$=30\times\frac{1}{5}+10\times\frac{3}{10}+(-10)\times\frac{1}{2}$$

$$=6+3-5=4$$

(xi) (c) **Statement I** $(A^2)^{-1} = (A \cdot A)^{-1}$

$$= A^{-1} \cdot A^{-1} \quad [\because (AB)^{-1} = B^{-1}A^{-1}]$$

$$= (A^{-1})^2$$

$\therefore$ Statement I is true.

Statement II We know that $AA^{-1} = I$

$$\Rightarrow \quad |AA^{-1}| = |I|$$

$$\Rightarrow \quad |A||A^{-1}| = 1$$

$$[\because |AB| = |A||B| \text{ and } |I| = 1]$$

$$\Rightarrow \quad |A^{-1}| = \frac{1}{|A|}$$

$$\Rightarrow \quad |A^{-1}| = |A|^{-1}$$

$\therefore$ Statement II is true.

(xii) We have, $A = \{1, 2, 3\}$

The smallest equivalence relation from the set A to set A is $R = \{(1, 1), (2, 2), (3, 3)\}$.

(xiii) We have, $A = \begin{bmatrix} 0 & 1 & -2 \\ -1 & 0 & 3 \\ x & -3 & 0 \end{bmatrix}$

$$\therefore \quad A' = \begin{bmatrix} 0 & -1 & x \\ 1 & 0 & -3 \\ -2 & 3 & 0 \end{bmatrix}$$

and $-A = \begin{bmatrix} 0 & -1 & 2 \\ 1 & 0 & -3 \\ -x & 3 & 0 \end{bmatrix}$

Since, A is a skew-symmetric matrix.

$$\therefore \quad A' = -A$$

$$\Rightarrow \begin{bmatrix} 0 & -1 & x \\ 1 & 0 & -3 \\ -2 & 3 & 0 \end{bmatrix} = \begin{bmatrix} 0 & -1 & 2 \\ 1 & 0 & -3 \\ -x & 3 & 0 \end{bmatrix}$$

On equating the corresponding element, we get

$$x = 2$$

(xiv) Let A, B and C denote the events that the book be favoured by the first, second and third critic, respectively.

$$\therefore \quad P(A) = \frac{5}{2+5} = \frac{5}{7},$$

$$P(B) = \frac{4}{4+3} = \frac{4}{7}$$

and $P(C) = \frac{3}{3+4} = \frac{3}{7}$

$\therefore$ Required probability $= \frac{5}{7} \times \frac{4}{7} \times \frac{3}{7} = \frac{60}{343}$

(xv) Let $I = \int \frac{5}{\sqrt{2x+7}}\, dx$

Put $2x + 7 = t \Rightarrow 2 = \frac{dt}{dx}$

$$\Rightarrow \quad dx = \frac{dt}{2}$$

$$\therefore \quad I = \int \frac{5}{\sqrt{t}} \times \frac{dt}{2} = \frac{5}{2}\int t^{-\frac{1}{2}}\, dt$$

$$= \frac{5}{2}\frac{t^{\frac{1}{2}}}{\frac{1}{2}} + C \quad \left[\because \int x^n\, dx = \frac{x^{n+1}}{n+1} + C\right]$$

$$= 5\sqrt{t} + C = 5\sqrt{2x+7} + C$$

2. We have,

$$y = 2x^2 - 6x - 4 \quad \ldots(i)$$

On differentiating both sides w.r.t. x, we get

$$\frac{dy}{dx} = 4x - 6$$

$\therefore$ Slope of tangent is $4x - 6$.

Since, the tangent is parallel to X-axis.

$$\therefore \quad \frac{dy}{dx} = 0$$

$$\Rightarrow \quad 4x - 6 = 0$$

$$\Rightarrow \quad 4x = 6 \Rightarrow x = \frac{3}{2}$$

On putting the value of x in Eq. (i), we get

$$y = 2\left(\frac{3}{2}\right)^2 - 6\left(\frac{3}{2}\right) - 4$$

$$= 2 \times \frac{9}{4} - 9 - 4$$

$$\Rightarrow \quad y = \frac{9}{2} - 13 = -\frac{17}{2}$$

So, the point on the curve $y = 2x^2 - 6x - 4$ at which the tangent is parallel to X-axis is $\left(\frac{3}{2}, -\frac{17}{2}\right)$.

3. We have, $(\tan^{-1} x)^2 - (\cot^{-1} x)^2 = \frac{5\pi}{8}$

$$\Rightarrow \quad (\tan^{-1} x + \cot^{-1} x)(\tan^{-1} x - \cot^{-1} x) = \frac{5\pi}{8}$$

$$[\because a^2 - b^2 = (a+b)(a-b)]$$

$$\Rightarrow \quad \frac{\pi}{2}(\tan^{-1}x-\cot^{-1}x)=\frac{5\pi}{8}$$

$$\left[\because \tan^{-1}\theta+\cot^{-1}\theta=\frac{\pi}{2}\right]$$

$$\Rightarrow \quad \tan^{-1}x-\cot^{-1}x=\frac{5\pi}{8}\times\frac{2}{\pi}=\frac{5}{4}$$

4. (i) We have, $x^y=e^{x-y}$

On taking log both sides, we get

$$\log x^y=\log e^{x-y}$$

$$\Rightarrow \quad y\cdot\log x=(x-y)\log e$$

$$[\because \log a^b=b\cdot\log a]$$

$$\Rightarrow \quad y\cdot\log x=x-y \quad \text{...(i)}$$

On differentiating both sides w.r.t. x, we get

$$\frac{dy}{dx}\log x+y\times\frac{1}{x}=1-\frac{dy}{dx}$$

$$\Rightarrow \quad \frac{dy}{dx}\log x+\frac{dy}{dx}=1-\frac{y}{x}$$

$$\Rightarrow \quad \frac{dy}{dx}(\log x+1)=\frac{x-y}{x}$$

$$\Rightarrow \quad \frac{dy}{dx}(\log x+1)=\frac{y\log x}{x} \quad \text{[from Eq. (i)]}$$

$$\Rightarrow \quad \frac{dy}{dx}=\frac{y\log x}{x(\log x+1)}$$

$$\Rightarrow \quad \frac{dy}{dx}=\frac{\log x}{(1+\log x)^2}$$ **Hence proved.**

$$\left[\text{from Eq. (i)}, \frac{y}{x}=\frac{1}{1+\log x}\right]$$

Or

(ii) We have,

$$f(x)=\log(1+x)+\frac{1}{1+x} \quad \text{...(i)}$$

On differentiating both sides w.r.t. x, we get

$$f'(x)=\frac{1}{1+x}-\frac{1}{(1+x)^2}$$

Again, on differentiating both sides w.r.t. x, we get

$$f''(x)=\frac{-1}{(1+x)^2}+\frac{2}{(1+x)^3}$$

For maxima or minima, put $f'(x)=0$

$$\Rightarrow \quad \frac{1}{1+x}-\frac{1}{(1+x)^2}=0$$

$$\Rightarrow \quad \frac{1}{1+x}=\frac{1}{(1+x)^2}\Rightarrow 1=\frac{1}{1+x}$$

$$\Rightarrow \quad 1+x=1$$

$$\Rightarrow \quad x=0$$

Now, $f''(0)=\dfrac{-1}{(1+0)^2}+\dfrac{2}{(1+0)^3}=\dfrac{-1}{1}+\dfrac{2}{1}$

$=1>0$

So, $f(x)$ attains its minimum value at $x=0$.

Hence proved.

5. (i) Let the matrix M represent the bags used and the matrix N represent the costs.

$$\therefore \quad M=\begin{bmatrix}20&30&40\\30&40&20\\40&20&30\end{bmatrix} \text{ and } N=\begin{bmatrix}1\\5\\2\end{bmatrix}$$

(ii) Now, $MN=\begin{bmatrix}20&30&40\\30&40&20\\40&20&30\end{bmatrix}\begin{bmatrix}1\\5\\2\end{bmatrix}$

$$\Rightarrow \quad \begin{bmatrix}A\\B\\C\end{bmatrix}=\begin{bmatrix}20+150+80\\30+200+40\\40+100+60\end{bmatrix}=\begin{bmatrix}250\\270\\200\end{bmatrix}$$

Since, matrices are equal.

So, their corresponding elements are also equal.

$\therefore \quad A=₹250, B=₹270$ and $C=₹200$

6. (i) Let $y=\sin^{-1}\left(\dfrac{2^{x+1}\cdot 3^x}{1+36^x}\right)$

$$=\sin^{-1}\left(\frac{2^x\cdot 2\cdot 3^x}{1+(6^2)^x}\right)=\sin^{-1}\left(\frac{2\cdot 6^x}{1+(6^x)^2}\right)$$

Put $6^x=\tan\theta$

$$\Rightarrow \quad \theta=\tan^{-1}(6^x)$$

$$\therefore \quad y=\sin^{-1}\left(\frac{2\cdot\tan\theta}{1+\tan^2\theta}\right)$$

$$\Rightarrow \quad y=\sin^{-1}(\sin 2\theta) \quad \left[\because \sin 2x=\frac{2\tan x}{1+\tan^2 x}\right]$$

$$\Rightarrow \quad y=2\theta$$

$$\Rightarrow \quad y=2\tan^{-1}(6^x)$$

On differentiating both sides w.r.t. x, we get

$$\frac{dy}{dx}=\frac{2}{(1+(6^x)^2)}\times\frac{d}{dx}(6^x)$$

$$=\frac{2}{1+(6^2)^x}\times 6^x\log 6$$

$$=\frac{2\times 2^x\times 3^x\log 6}{1+(36)^x}=\frac{2^{x+1}3^x\log 6}{1+(36)^x}$$

OR

(ii) Given equation is

$\tan^{-1} x + \tan^{-1} y = C$

On differentiating both sides w.r.t. x, we get

$$\frac{1}{1+x^2} + \frac{1}{1+y^2}\frac{dy}{dx} = 0$$

$$\Rightarrow \quad \frac{dy}{dx}\left(\frac{1}{1+y^2}\right) = -\frac{1}{1+x^2}$$

$$\Rightarrow \quad (1+x^2)\,dy = -(1+y^2)\,dx$$

$$\Rightarrow \quad (1+x^2)\,dy + (1+y^2)\,dx = 0$$

So, $\tan^{-1} x + \tan^{-1} y = C$ is the general solution of the differential equation $(1+x^2)\,dy + (1+y^2)\,dx = 0$. **Hence Proved**

7. We have, $x + y + z = 0$

$$\text{LHS} = \begin{vmatrix} 1 & 1 & 1 \\ x & y & z \\ x^3 & y^3 & z^3 \end{vmatrix}$$

Applying $C_1 \to C_1 - C_2$ and $C_2 \to C_2 - C_3$, we get

$$= \begin{vmatrix} 0 & 0 & 1 \\ x-y & y-z & z \\ x^3 - y^3 & y^3 - z^3 & z^3 \end{vmatrix}$$

$$= \begin{vmatrix} 0 & 0 & 1 \\ x-y & y-z & z \\ (x-y)(x^2+xy+y^2) & (y-z)(y^2+yz+z^2) & z^3 \end{vmatrix}$$

On taking common $(x-y)$ from C_1 and $(y-z)$ from C_2, we get

$$(x-y)(y-z)\begin{vmatrix} 0 & 0 & 1 \\ 1 & 1 & z \\ x^2+xy+y^2 & y^2+yz+z^2 & z^3 \end{vmatrix}$$

Expanding along R_1, we get

$$(x-y)(y-z)[1(y^2+yz+z^2) - (x^2+xy+y^2)]$$

$$= (x-y)(y-z)[y^2+yz+z^2-x^2-xy-y^2]$$

$$= (x-y)(y-z)[(yz-xy)+(z^2-x^2)]$$

$$= (x-y)(y-z)[y(z-x)+(z-x)(z+x)]$$

$$= (x-y)(y-z)[(z-x)(x+y+z)]$$

$$= (x-y)(y-z)(z-x)\times 0 \quad [\because x+y+z=0]$$

$= 0 = \text{RHS}$ **Hence proved.**

8. (i) Let $I = \int \frac{\cos x}{3\cos x - 5}\,dx$

$$= \frac{1}{3}\int \frac{3\cos x}{3\cos x - 5}\,dx = \frac{1}{3}\int \frac{3\cos x - 5 + 5}{3\cos x - 5}\,dx$$

$$= \frac{1}{3}\int \frac{3\cos x - 5}{3\cos x - 5}\,dx + \frac{1}{3}\int \frac{5}{3\cos x - 5}\,dx$$

$$= \frac{1}{3}\int 1\,dx + \frac{5}{3}\int \frac{1}{3\left(\dfrac{1-\tan^2\frac{x}{2}}{1+\tan^2\frac{x}{2}}\right) - 5}\,dx$$

$$= \frac{x}{3} + \frac{5}{3}\int \frac{1}{\dfrac{3 - 3\tan^2\frac{x}{2} - 5 - 5\tan^2\frac{x}{2}}{1+\tan^2\frac{x}{2}}}\,dx$$

$$= \frac{x}{3} + \frac{5}{3}\int \frac{\sec^2\frac{x}{2}}{-2 - 8\tan^2\frac{x}{2}}\,dx$$

$$= \frac{x}{3} - \frac{5}{6}\int \frac{\sec^2\frac{x}{2}}{1 + 4\tan^2\frac{x}{2}}\,dx$$

Put $\tan\frac{x}{2} = t$

$$\Rightarrow \quad \sec^2\frac{x}{2}\times\frac{1}{2} = \frac{dt}{dx} \Rightarrow \sec^2\frac{x}{2}\,dx = 2dt$$

$$\therefore \quad I = \frac{x}{3} - \frac{5}{6}\int \frac{2}{1+4t^2}\,dt$$

$$= \frac{x}{3} - \frac{5\times 2}{6\times 4}\int \frac{1}{\left(\frac{1}{2}\right)^2 + t^2}\,dt$$

$$= \frac{x}{3} - \frac{5}{12}\times\frac{1}{\frac{1}{2}}\tan^{-1}\left(\frac{t}{\frac{1}{2}}\right) + C$$

$$\left[\because \int \frac{1}{a^2+x^2}\,dx = \frac{1}{a}\tan^{-1}\frac{x}{a} + C\right]$$

$$= \frac{x}{3} - \frac{5}{6}\tan^{-1}\left(2\tan\frac{x}{2}\right) + C$$

OR

(ii) Let $I = \int \underset{\text{I}}{(\log x)^2} \cdot \underset{\text{II}}{1}\, dx$

$$= (\log x)^2 \int 1\, dx - \int \left[\frac{d}{dx} (\log x)^2 \int 1\, dx \right] dx$$

[integration by parts]

$$= x \cdot (\log x)^2 - \int 2 \cdot \log x \times \frac{1}{x} \times x\, dx$$

$$= x \cdot (\log x)^2 - 2 \int \underset{\text{I}}{\log x} \cdot \underset{\text{II}}{1}\, dx$$

$$= x (\log x)^2 - 2 \left[\log x \int 1\, dx - \int \left(\frac{d}{dx} \log x \int 1\, dx \right) dx \right]$$

$$= x (\log x)^2 - 2 \left[x \log x - \int \frac{1}{x} \times x\, dx \right]$$

$$= x (\log x)^2 - 2 [x \log x - \int 1\, dx]$$

$$= x (\log x)^2 - 2 [x \log x - x] + C$$

$$= x (\log x)^2 - 2x \log x + 2x + C$$

$$= x (\log x)^2 + 2x(1 - \log x) + C$$

9. (i) We have, $x = \tan \left(\frac{1}{a} \log y \right)$

$$\Rightarrow \quad \tan^{-1} x = \frac{1}{a} \log y$$

$$\Rightarrow \quad a \tan^{-1} x = \log y$$

On differentiating both sides w.r.t. x, we get

$$\frac{a}{1 + x^2} = \frac{1}{y} \frac{dy}{dx}$$

$$\Rightarrow \quad \frac{dy}{dx} = \frac{ay}{1 + x^2}$$

$$\Rightarrow \quad (1 + x^2) \frac{dy}{dx} = ay$$

Again, on differentiating both sides w.r.t. x, we get

$$(1 + x^2) \frac{d^2 y}{dx^2} + \frac{dy}{dx} (0 + 2x) = a \frac{dy}{dx}$$

$$\Rightarrow (1 + x^2) \frac{d^2 y}{dx^2} + 2x \frac{dy}{dx} - a \frac{dy}{dx} = 0$$

$$\Rightarrow \quad (1 + x^2) \frac{d^2 y}{dx^2} + (2x - a) \frac{dy}{dx} = 0$$

OR

(ii) (a) We have,

$$f(x) = -x^3 + 27x - 2$$

On differentiating both sides w.r.t. x, we get

$$f'(x) = -3x^2 + 27 \quad \ldots \text{(i)}$$

$\therefore$ The slope of the given graph is $-3x^2 + 27$

(b) For the turning point, put $f'(x) = 0$

$$\Rightarrow \quad -3x^2 + 27 = 0$$

$$\Rightarrow \quad 3x^2 = 27$$

$$\Rightarrow \quad x^2 = 9 \Rightarrow x = \pm 3$$

On putting $x = 3$ into $f(x)$, we get

$$f(3) = -(3)^3 + 27 \times 3 - 2$$

$$= -27 + 81 - 2 = 52$$

and on putting $x = -3$ into $f(x)$, we get

$$f(-3) = -(-3)^3 + 27 \times (-3) - 2$$

$$= 27 - 81 - 2 = -56$$

So, point A is $(-3, -56)$ and point B is $(3, 52)$.

(c) We have, $f'(x) = -3x^2 + 27$

On differentiating both sides w.r.t. x, we get

$$f''(x) = -6x$$

$$\therefore \quad f''(-2) = -6 \times (-2) = 12$$

Now, $\quad f(0) = -(0)^3 + 27 \times 0 - 2 = -2$

and $\quad f'(3) = -3(3)^2 + 27$

$$= -27 + 27 = 0$$

Hence, ascending order of $f''(-2)$, $f(0)$ and $f'(3)$ is $f(0) < f'(3) < f''(-2)$.

10. Given, number of paintings Pia has $= 15$,

number of paintings Sia has $= 5$

and number of paintings Dia has $= 10$

$\therefore$ Total number of paintings $= 15 + 5 + 10 = 30$

Total number of ways to select 3 paintings from 30 paintings

$$= {}^{30}C_3 = \frac{30 \times 29 \times 28}{3 \times 2 \times 1}$$

$$= 4060$$

(i) Number of ways to select 1 painting from Pia

$$= {}^{15}C_1 = 15,$$

number of ways to select 1 painting from Sia $= {}^{5}C_1 = 5$

and number of ways to select 1 painting from Dia

$$= {}^{10}C_1 = 10$$

$\therefore$ Number of ways to select 1 painting from each artist

$$= 15 \times 5 \times 10 = 750$$

$\therefore$ Required probability $= \frac{750}{4060} = \frac{75}{406}$

(ii) Number of ways to select 3 paintings from Pia

$= {}^{15}C_3 = \frac{15\times14\times13}{3\times2\times1} = 455,$

number of ways to select 3 paintings from Sia

$= {}^{5}C_3 = \frac{5\times4\times3}{3\times2} = 10$

and number of ways to select 3 paintings from Dia

$= {}^{10}C_3 = \frac{10\times9\times8}{3\times2\times1} = 120$

∴ Number of ways to select all three paintings from the same artist

$= 455 + 10 + 120 = 585$

∴ Required probability $= \frac{585}{4060} = \frac{117}{812}$

11. (i) Let $I = \int_{\frac{\pi}{4}}^{\frac{3\pi}{4}} \frac{x}{1+\sin x}\,dx$ ...(i)

$$= \int_{\frac{\pi}{4}}^{\frac{3\pi}{4}} \frac{\left(\frac{3\pi}{4}+\frac{\pi}{4}-x\right)}{1+\sin\left(\frac{3\pi}{4}+\frac{\pi}{4}-x\right)}\,dx$$

$$\left[\because \int_a^b f(x)\,dx = \int_a^b f(a+b-x)\,dx\right]$$

$$= \int_{\frac{\pi}{4}}^{\frac{3\pi}{4}} \frac{\pi-x}{1+\sin(\pi-x)}\,dx = \int_{\frac{\pi}{4}}^{\frac{3\pi}{4}} \frac{\pi-x}{1+\sin x}\,dx \quad \text{...(ii)}$$

On adding Eqs. (i) and (ii), we get

$$2I = \int_{\frac{\pi}{4}}^{\frac{3\pi}{4}} \frac{x}{1+\sin x}\,dx + \int_{\frac{\pi}{4}}^{\frac{3\pi}{4}} \frac{\pi-x}{1+\sin x}\,dx$$

$$= \int_{\frac{\pi}{4}}^{\frac{3\pi}{4}} \frac{x}{1+\sin x}\,dx + \int_{\frac{\pi}{4}}^{\frac{3\pi}{4}} \frac{\pi}{1+\sin x}\,dx - \int_{\frac{\pi}{4}}^{\frac{3\pi}{4}} \frac{x}{1+\sin x}\,dx$$

$$= \pi \int_{\frac{\pi}{4}}^{\frac{3\pi}{4}} \frac{1}{1+\sin x}\,dx$$

$$\Rightarrow I = \frac{\pi}{2}\int_{\frac{\pi}{4}}^{\frac{3\pi}{4}} \left(\frac{1}{1+\sin x}\times\frac{1-\sin x}{1-\sin x}\right)dx$$

$$\Rightarrow I = \frac{\pi}{2}\int_{\frac{\pi}{4}}^{\frac{3\pi}{4}} \frac{1-\sin x}{1-\sin^2 x}\,dx = \frac{\pi}{2}\int_{\frac{\pi}{4}}^{\frac{3\pi}{4}} \frac{1-\sin x}{\cos^2 x}\,dx$$

$$= \frac{\pi}{2}\int_{\frac{\pi}{4}}^{\frac{3\pi}{4}} \left(\sec^2 x - \frac{\sin x}{\cos^2 x}\right)dx$$

$$I = \frac{\pi}{2}\int_{\frac{\pi}{4}}^{\frac{3\pi}{4}} \sec^2 x\,dx - \frac{\pi}{2}\int_{\frac{\pi}{4}}^{\frac{3\pi}{4}} \frac{\sin x}{\cos^2 x}\,dx$$

Put $\cos x = t$

$\Rightarrow -\sin x = \frac{dt}{dx} \Rightarrow \sin x dx = -dt$

Lower limit When $x = \frac{\pi}{4}$ then $t = \cos\frac{\pi}{4} = \frac{1}{\sqrt{2}}$

Upper limit When $x = \frac{3\pi}{4}$ then $t = -\frac{1}{\sqrt{2}}$

$$\therefore \quad I = \frac{\pi}{2}[\tan x]_{\frac{\pi}{4}}^{\frac{3\pi}{4}} - \frac{\pi}{2}\int_{\frac{1}{\sqrt{2}}}^{-\frac{1}{\sqrt{2}}} \frac{-dt}{t^2}$$

$$= \frac{\pi}{2}\left[\tan\frac{3\pi}{4} - \tan\frac{\pi}{4}\right] + \frac{\pi}{2}\left[-\frac{1}{t}\right]_{\frac{1}{\sqrt{2}}}^{-\frac{1}{\sqrt{2}}}$$

$$= \frac{\pi}{2}[-1-1] - \frac{\pi}{2}[-\sqrt{2}-\sqrt{2}]$$

$$= -\frac{2\pi}{2} + \frac{\pi}{2}\times 2\sqrt{2}$$

$$= -\pi + \pi\sqrt{2} = \pi(\sqrt{2}-1)$$ **Hence Proved**

OR

(ii) Let $I = \int \frac{x^2}{(x-1)^2(x^2+1)}\,dx$

Here, integrand is a proper rational function.

So, by the form of partial fraction, we get

$$\frac{x^2}{(x-1)^2(x^2+1)} = \frac{A}{x-1} + \frac{B}{(x-1)^2} + \frac{Cx+D}{x^2+1}$$

$$\Rightarrow x^2 = A(x-1)(x^2+1) + B(x^2+1) + (Cx+D)(x-1)^2 \quad \text{...(i)}$$

On putting $x=1$ in Eq. (i), we get

$$1^2 = A(0)(1^2+1) + B(1^2+1) + (C(1)+D)(0)$$

$$\Rightarrow \quad 1 = 2B \Rightarrow \quad B = \frac{1}{2}$$

On putting $x=0$ Eq. (i), we get

$$0 = A(-1)(1) + B(1) + (0+D)(-1)^2$$

$$\Rightarrow \quad 0 = -A + B + D$$

$$\Rightarrow D - A = -B$$

$$\Rightarrow D - A = -\frac{1}{2} \quad \ldots\text{(ii)}$$

On putting $x=-1$ in Eq. (i), we get

$$(-1)^2 = A(-1-1)((-1)^2+1) + B((-1)^2+1) + (C(-1)+D)(-1-1)^2$$

$$\Rightarrow \quad 1 = -2A(2) + 2B + (-C+D)(4)$$

$$\Rightarrow \quad 1 = -4A + 2B - 4C + 4D$$

$$\Rightarrow \quad 1 = -4A + 2\times\frac{1}{2} - 4C + 4D$$

$$\Rightarrow \quad 4(D-A) - 4C = 0 \quad \ldots\text{(iii)}$$

On putting $x=2$ in Eq. (i), we get

$$2^2 = A(2-1)(2^2+1) + B(2^2+1) + (2C+D)(2-1)^2$$

$$\Rightarrow \quad 4 = 5A + 5B + 2C + D$$

$$\Rightarrow \quad 4 = 5A + 5\times\frac{1}{2} + 2C + D$$

$$\Rightarrow \quad 4 - \frac{5}{2} = 5A + 2C + D$$

$$\Rightarrow \quad \frac{3}{2} = 5A + 2C + D \quad \ldots\text{(iv)}$$

On solving Eqs. (ii) and (iii), we get

$$C = -\frac{1}{2}$$

On putting the value of C in Eqs. (iii) and (iv), we get

$$4(D-A) - 4\times\left(-\frac{1}{2}\right) = 0$$

$$\Rightarrow \quad 4D - 4A + 2 = 0$$

$$\Rightarrow \quad 2D - 2A = -1 \quad \ldots\text{(v)}$$

and

$$\frac{3}{2} = 5A + 2\left(-\frac{1}{2}\right) + D$$

$$\Rightarrow \quad 5A + D = \frac{3}{2} + 1 = \frac{5}{2}$$

$$\Rightarrow \quad 10A + 2D = 5 \quad \ldots\text{(vi)}$$

On solving Eqs. (v) and (vi), we get

$$A = \frac{1}{2}, D = 0$$

Now,

$$\frac{x^2}{(x-1)^2(x^2+1)} = \frac{\frac{1}{2}}{x-1} + \frac{\frac{1}{2}}{(x-1)^2} + \frac{-\frac{1}{2}x+0}{x^2+1}$$

$$\therefore I = \int \frac{x^2}{(x-1)(x^2+1)}\,dx = \frac{1}{2}\int\frac{1}{x-1}\,dx + \frac{1}{2}\int\frac{1}{(x-1)^2}\,dx - \frac{1}{2}\int\frac{x}{x^2+1}\,dx$$

$$= \frac{1}{2}\int\frac{1}{x-1}\,dx + \frac{1}{2}\int(x-1)^{-2}\,dx - \frac{1}{4}\int\frac{2x}{x^2+1}\,dx$$

$$= \frac{1}{2}\log|x-1| + \frac{1}{2}\left(\frac{(x-1)^{-1}}{-1}\right) - \frac{1}{4}\log|x^2+1| + C$$

$$= \frac{1}{2}\log|x-1| - \frac{1}{2(x-1)} - \frac{1}{4}\log|x^2+1| + C$$

12. (i) Given differential equation is

$$(x+5y^2)\frac{dy}{dx} = y$$

$$\Rightarrow \quad \frac{dx}{dy} = \frac{x+5y^2}{y}$$

$$\Rightarrow \quad \frac{dx}{dy} = \frac{x}{y} + 5y$$

$$\Rightarrow \quad \frac{dx}{dy} - \frac{x}{y} = 5y$$

On comparing above equation with linear differential equation $\frac{dx}{dy} + Px = Q$, we get

$$P = -\frac{1}{y} \text{ and } Q = 5y$$

$$\therefore \quad \text{IF} = e^{\int P dy} = e^{-\int \frac{1}{y} dy}$$

$$= e^{-\log|y|} = e^{\log\frac{1}{|y|}} = \frac{1}{y}$$

The solution is $x \times \text{IF} = \int (Q \times \text{IF})\,dy + C$

$$\Rightarrow \quad \frac{x}{y} = \int \frac{5y}{y}\,dy + C$$

$\Rightarrow \quad \dfrac{x}{y} = 5\int dy + C$

$\Rightarrow \quad \dfrac{x}{y} = 5y + C$

$\Rightarrow \quad x = 5y^2 + yC \quad \ldots(i)$

Also given, $x = 2$ and $y = 1$, therefore from Eq. (i), we get

$2 = 5(1)^2 + C$

$\Rightarrow \quad C = 2 - 5 = -3$

On putting the value of C in Eq. (i), we get

$x = 5y^2 - 3y,$

which is the required solution.

OR

(ii) Given, $(x^2 - 2y^2)\,dx + 2xy\,dy = 0$

$\Rightarrow \quad 2xy\,dy = -(x^2 - 2y^2)\,dx$

$\Rightarrow \quad \dfrac{dy}{dx} = \dfrac{2y^2 - x^2}{2xy},$

which is a homogeneous differential equation.

Put $y = vx$

$\Rightarrow \quad \dfrac{dy}{dx} = v + x\dfrac{dv}{dx}$

$\therefore \quad v + x\dfrac{dv}{dx} = \dfrac{2v^2x^2 - x^2}{2x\,vx} = \dfrac{2v^2 - 1}{2v}$

$\Rightarrow \quad x\dfrac{dv}{dx} = \dfrac{2v^2 - 1}{2v} - v$

$\Rightarrow \quad x\dfrac{dv}{dx} = \dfrac{2v^2 - 1 - 2v^2}{2v}$

$\Rightarrow \quad x\dfrac{dv}{dx} = -\dfrac{1}{2v}$

$\Rightarrow \quad 2v\,dv = -\dfrac{1}{x}\,dx$

On integrating both sides, we get

$\int 2v\,dv = \int -\dfrac{1}{x}\,dx$

$\Rightarrow \quad v^2 = -\log|x| + C$

$\Rightarrow \quad \dfrac{y^2}{x^2} = -\log|x| + C \quad \left[\because v = \dfrac{y}{x}\right]$

$\Rightarrow \quad y^2 = x^2(-\log|x| + C) \quad \ldots(i)$

Also given, when $x = 2$ and $y = 1$, therefore from Eq. (i), we get

$1 = 4(-\log 1 + C)$

$\Rightarrow \quad C = \dfrac{1}{4}$

On putting the value of C in Eq. (i), we get

$y^2 = x^2\left(\dfrac{1}{4} - \log x\right),$

which is the required solution.

13. (i) Graph 2 represents $y = \sin^{-1} x$.

(ii) Domain of $y = \sin^{-1} x$ is $[-1, 1]$.

Range of $y = \sin^{-1} x$ is $\left[-\dfrac{\pi}{2}, \dfrac{\pi}{2}\right]$.

(iii) $\text{LHS} = \sin^{-1}\dfrac{1}{\sqrt{5}} + \sin^{-1}\dfrac{2}{\sqrt{5}}$

$= \sin^{-1}\left[\dfrac{1}{\sqrt{5}}\sqrt{1 - \left(\dfrac{2}{\sqrt{5}}\right)^2} + \dfrac{2}{\sqrt{5}}\sqrt{1 - \left(\dfrac{1}{\sqrt{5}}\right)^2}\right]$

$[\because \sin^{-1} x + \sin^{-1} y = \sin^{-1}[x\sqrt{1 - y^2} + y\sqrt{1 - x^2}]$

$= \sin^{-1}\left[\dfrac{1}{\sqrt{5}}\sqrt{\dfrac{5-4}{5}} + \dfrac{2}{\sqrt{5}}\sqrt{\dfrac{5-1}{5}}\right]$

$= \sin^{-1}\left[\dfrac{1}{\sqrt{5}} \times \dfrac{1}{\sqrt{5}} + \dfrac{2}{\sqrt{5}} \times \dfrac{2}{\sqrt{5}}\right]$

$= \sin^{-1}\left[\dfrac{1}{5} + \dfrac{4}{5}\right] = \sin^{-1}(1)$

$= \sin^{-1}\left(\sin\dfrac{\pi}{2}\right) = \dfrac{\pi}{2} = \text{RHS}$ **Hence proved.**

(iv) We have, $\tan^{-1}\left[2\sin\left(2\cos^{-1}\dfrac{\sqrt{3}}{2}\right)\right]$

$= \tan^{-1}\left[2\sin\left(2\cos^{-1}\left(\cos\dfrac{\pi}{6}\right)\right)\right]$

$= \tan^{-1}\left[2\sin\left(2 \times \dfrac{\pi}{6}\right)\right]$

$= \tan^{-1}\left[2\sin\dfrac{\pi}{3}\right]$

$= \tan^{-1}\left(2 \times \dfrac{\sqrt{3}}{2}\right) = \tan^{-1}(\sqrt{3})$

$= \tan^{-1}\left(\tan\dfrac{\pi}{3}\right) = \dfrac{\pi}{3}$

14. Let X, Y and Z be the events that the missing person was the responsibility of agencies X, Y and Z respectively and A be the event that a person is missing.

$$P(X)=\frac{1000}{1000+2000+3000}=\frac{1000}{6000}=\frac{1}{6},$$

$$P(Y)=\frac{2000}{6000}=\frac{1}{3}$$

$$\text{and } P(Z)=\frac{3000}{6000}=\frac{1}{2}$$

$$\text{Also, } P(A/X)=1-\frac{99}{100}$$
$$=1-0.99=0.01,$$

$$P(A/Y)=1-\frac{98.5}{100}$$
$$=1-0.985=0.015$$

$$\text{and } \quad P(A/Z)=1-\frac{98}{100}$$
$$=1-0.98=0.02$$

$\therefore$ Required probability $= P(X/A)$

$$=\frac{P(X)\,P(A/X)}{P(X)\,P(A/X)+P(Y)\,P(A/Y)+P(Z)\,P(A/Z)}$$

$$=\frac{\frac{1}{6}\times 0.01}{\frac{1}{6}\times 0.01+\frac{1}{3}\times 0.015+\frac{1}{2}\times 0.02}$$

$$=\frac{0.00167}{0.00167+0.005+0.01}=\frac{0.00167}{0.01667}$$

$$=0.1001$$

Section B

15. (i) (a) We have,

$$(\vec{a}+\vec{b})^2+(\vec{b}-\vec{a})^2=2(\vec{a}^2+\vec{b}^2)$$

$$\text{LHS}=(\vec{a}+\vec{b})^2+(\vec{b}-\vec{a})^2$$

$$=(\vec{a}^2+2\vec{a}\cdot\vec{b}+\vec{b}^2)+(\vec{b}^2-2\vec{b}\cdot\vec{a}+\vec{a}^2)$$

$$=2\vec{a}^2+2\vec{b}^2+2\vec{a}\cdot\vec{b}-2\vec{a}\cdot\vec{b} \quad [\because \vec{a}\cdot\vec{b}=\vec{b}\cdot\vec{a}]$$

$$=2(\vec{a}^2+\vec{b}^2)=\text{RHS}$$

Thus, Assertion is true.

We know that dot product of any two vectors is commutative.

Hence, both Assertion and Reason are true and Reason is the correct explanation for Assertion.

(ii) (b) Given equations of planes are

$x+y+2z-9=0$ and $2x-y+z-15=0$

On comparing with $a_1x+b_1y+c_1z+d_1=0$

and $a_2x+b_2y+c_2z+d=0$, we get

$$a_1=1, b_1=1, c_1=2$$

and $\quad a_2=2, b_2=-1, c_2=1$

Now, the angle between two planes is given by

$$\theta=\cos^{-1}\left|\frac{a_1a_2+b_1b_2+c_1c_2}{\sqrt{a_1^2+b_1^2+c_1^2}\sqrt{a_2^2+b_2^2+c_2^2}}\right|$$

$$=\cos^{-1}\left|\frac{1\times 2+1\times(-1)+2\times 1}{\sqrt{1+1+(2)^2}\sqrt{(2)^2+1+1}}\right|$$

$$=\cos^{-1}\left|\frac{2-1+2}{\sqrt{6}\sqrt{6}}\right|$$

$$=\cos^{-1}\left(\frac{3}{6}\right)=\cos^{-1}\left(\frac{1}{2}\right)=\frac{\pi}{3}$$

(iii) Given points are $P(-2, 3, 5)$, $Q(1, 2, 3)$ and $R(7, 0, -1)$.

Direction ratios of line joining P and Q are $(1-(-2), 2-3, 3-5)$ i.e. $(3, -1, -2)$.

Direction ratios of line joining Q and R are $(7-1, 0-2, -1-3)$ i.e. $(6, -2, -4)$.

Now, ratios of direction ratios of PQ and QR are

$$\frac{3}{6}, \frac{-1}{-2}, \frac{-2}{-4} \text{ i.e. } \frac{1}{2}, \frac{1}{2}, \frac{1}{2}$$

Thus, the direction ratios of PQ and QR are proportional. So, PQ is parallel to QR but Q is common to both PQ and QR. Hence, P, Q and R are collinear points.

(iv) (a) The given vector equation of the path traced by one honeybee is

$$\vec{r}=(\hat{i}+2\hat{j}+3\hat{k})+\lambda(2\hat{i}+3\hat{j}+4\hat{k})$$

$$\text{Let} \quad \vec{r}=x\hat{i}+y\hat{j}+z\hat{k}$$

Then, $x\hat{i}+y\hat{j}+z\hat{k}=(\hat{i}+2\hat{j}+3\hat{k})+\lambda(2\hat{i}+3\hat{j}+4\hat{k})$

$$\Rightarrow \quad x\hat{i}+y\hat{j}+z\hat{k}=(1+2\lambda)\hat{i}+(2+3\lambda)\hat{j}+(3+4\lambda)\hat{k}$$

On comparing the coefficients of $\hat{i}\ \hat{j}$ and $\hat{k}$, we get

$x=1+2\lambda,\ y=2+3\lambda,\ z=3+4\lambda$

$\Rightarrow\quad \lambda=\dfrac{x-1}{2},\ \lambda=\dfrac{y-2}{3},\ \lambda=\dfrac{z-3}{4}$

$\therefore\quad \dfrac{x-1}{2}=\dfrac{y-2}{3}=\dfrac{z-3}{4}=\lambda$

Thus, the required cartesian equation of the given line is

$\dfrac{x-1}{2}=\dfrac{y-2}{3}=\dfrac{z-3}{4}$

(b) Since, the other honeybee flies parallel to the first one. So, it has the same direction ratios i.e. 2, 3, 4.

$\therefore$ The equation of the line passing through the point (2, 4, 5) with direction ratios 2, 3 and 4 is

$\dfrac{x-2}{2}=\dfrac{y-4}{3}=\dfrac{z-5}{4}$

Hence, the equation of the path traced by the other honeybee is $\dfrac{x-2}{2}=\dfrac{y-4}{3}=\dfrac{z-5}{4}$.

16. (i) Let the three points be $A(2, 2, -1)$, $B(3, 4, 2)$ and $C(7, 0, 6)$.

Now, direction ratios of AB are (1, 2, 3) and direction ratios of BC are (4, –4, 4).

$\because$ Direction ratios of AB and BC are not proportional.

$\therefore$ The points are non collinear.

We know that, the cartesian equation of plane passing through three points $A(x_1, y_1, z_1)$, $B(x_2, y_2, z_2)$ and $C(x_3, y_3, z_3)$ is given by

$$\begin{vmatrix} x-x_1 & y-y_1 & z-z_1 \\ x_2-x_1 & y_2-y_1 & z_2-z_1 \\ x_3-x_1 & y_3-y_1 & z_3-z_1 \end{vmatrix}=0$$

$$\therefore\quad \begin{vmatrix} x-2 & y-2 & z+1 \\ 3-2 & 4-2 & 2+1 \\ 7-2 & 0-2 & 6+1 \end{vmatrix}=0$$

$$\Rightarrow\quad \begin{vmatrix} x-2 & y-2 & z+1 \\ 1 & 2 & 3 \\ 5 & -2 & 7 \end{vmatrix}=0$$

Expanding along R_1, we get

$(x-2)(14+6)-(y-2)(7-15)$

$+(z+1)(-2-10)=0$

$\Rightarrow 20(x-2)+8(y-2)-12(z+1)=0$

$\Rightarrow\quad 5(x-2)+2(y-2)-3(z+1)=0$

$\Rightarrow\quad 5x-10+2y-4-3z-3=0$

$\Rightarrow\quad 5x+2y-3z=17,$

which is the required equation of the plane in cartesian form.

OR

(ii) The equation of plane passing through (2, 3, 1) is

$a(x-2)+b(y-3)+c(z-1)=0$ ...(i)

This plane also passes through (4, –5, 3).

So, $a(4-2)+b(-5-3)+c(3-1)=0$

$\Rightarrow\quad 2a-8b+2c=0$ ...(ii)

Also given plane (i) is parallel to X-axis.

It means the, plane (i) is perpendicular to the YZ-plane whose equation is $x=0$.

$\therefore\quad a(1)+b(0)+c(0)=0$ ...(iii)

$[\because a_1a_2+b_1b_2+c_1c_2=0]$

On solving Eqs. (i), (ii) and (iii), we get

$$\begin{vmatrix} x-2 & y-3 & z-1 \\ 2 & -8 & 2 \\ 1 & 0 & 0 \end{vmatrix}=0$$

$\Rightarrow\quad 0-0+2(y-3)+8(z-1))=0$

$\Rightarrow\quad 2y-6+8z-8=0$

$\Rightarrow\quad 2y+8z-14=0$

$\Rightarrow\quad y+4z-7=0,$

which is the required equation of plane.

17. Given position vectors of A, B and C are

$\overrightarrow{OA}=2\hat{i}-2\hat{j}+\hat{k},\ \overrightarrow{OB}=\hat{i}+2\hat{j}-2\hat{k}$

and $\overrightarrow{OC}=2\hat{i}-\hat{j}+4\hat{k}$

(i) Here, $\overrightarrow{AB}=\overrightarrow{OB}-\overrightarrow{OA}$

$=(\hat{i}+2\hat{j}-2\hat{k})-(2\hat{i}-2\hat{j}+\hat{k})$

$=-\hat{i}+4\hat{j}-3\hat{k}$

and $\overrightarrow{BC}=\overrightarrow{OC}-\overrightarrow{OB}$

$=(2\hat{i}-\hat{j}+4\hat{k})-(\hat{i}+2\hat{j}-2\hat{k})$

$=\hat{i}-3\hat{j}+6\hat{k}$

(ii) Projection of $\overrightarrow{AB}$ on $\overrightarrow{BC}$ is given by

$$\frac{\overrightarrow{AB}\cdot\overrightarrow{BC}}{|\overrightarrow{BC}|}=\frac{(-\hat{i}+4\hat{j}-3\hat{k})\cdot(\hat{i}-3\hat{j}+6\hat{k})}{\sqrt{1^2+(-3)^2+6^2}}$$

$$=\frac{-1-12-18}{\sqrt{1+9+36}}=\frac{-31}{\sqrt{46}}$$

(iii) Area of ΔABC, whose sides are $\overrightarrow{AB}$ and $\overrightarrow{BC}$ is given by

$$= \frac{1}{2} |\overrightarrow{AB} \times \overrightarrow{BC}|$$

Now, $$\overrightarrow{AB} \times \overrightarrow{BC} = \begin{vmatrix} \hat{i} & \hat{j} & \hat{k} \\ -1 & 4 & -3 \\ 1 & -3 & 6 \end{vmatrix}$$

$$= \hat{i}\,(24-9) - \hat{j}\,(-6+3) + \hat{k}\,(3-4)$$

$$= 15\hat{i} + 3\hat{j} - \hat{k}$$

$$|\overrightarrow{AB} \times \overrightarrow{AC}| = \sqrt{(15)^2 + (3)^2 + (-1)^2}$$

$$= \sqrt{225+9+1} = \sqrt{235}$$

$\therefore$ Area of $\Delta ABC = \frac{1}{2} \times \sqrt{235} = \frac{\sqrt{235}}{2}$ sq. units

18. (i) (a) Given equation is $y = 4 - x^2$

$$\Rightarrow \quad x^2 = 4 - y$$

$$\Rightarrow \quad x^2 = -(y-4)$$

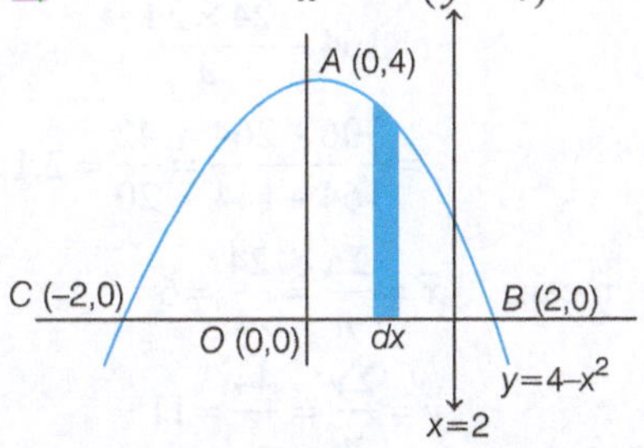

which is the parabola of the form $X^2 = -4AY$.

Its vertex is (0, 4) and it is symmetrical about X-axis.

(b) Area enclosed between the curve, X-axis, the lines $x = 0$ and $x = 2$

= Area of region $OABO$

$$= \int_0^2 y\,dx = \int_0^2 (4 - x^2)\,dx$$

$$= \left[4x - \frac{x^3}{3}\right]_0^2 = \left[4(2) - \frac{2^3}{3}\right] - \left[4(0) - \frac{0}{3}\right]$$

$$= 8 - \frac{8}{3} = \frac{24-8}{3} = \frac{16}{3} \text{ sq. units}$$

(c) Area bounded by the parabola and the X-axis

= Area of region $CABC$

= 2 (Area of region $OABO$)

$$= 2 \times \frac{16}{3} = \frac{32}{3} \text{ sq. units}$$

OR

(ii) Given equations of lines are

$$x + 2y = 2 \quad \ldots\text{(i)}$$

$$y - x = 1 \quad \ldots\text{(ii)}$$

$$2x + y = 7 \quad \ldots\text{(iii)}$$

Table for line (i) is

x	0	2
y	1	0

So, line (i) passes through the points (0, 1) and (2, 0).

Table for line (ii) is

x	0	–1
y	1	0

So, line (ii) passes through the points (0, 1) and (–1, 0).

Table for line (iii) is

x	0	3.5
y	7	0

So, line (iii) passes through the points (0, 7) and (3.5, 0).

On plotting these lines, we get the following graph.

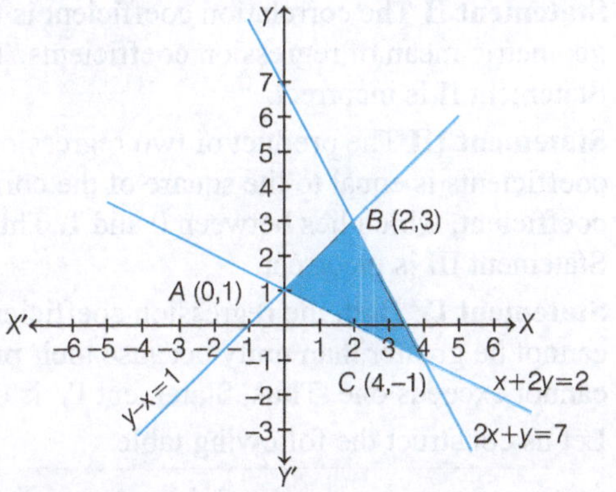

On solving the lines (ii) and (iii) and lines (i) and (iii), we get the intersection point $B(2, 3)$ and $C(4, -1)$, respectively.

$\therefore$ Required area

$$= \int_{-1}^{3} x_{BC}\,dy - \int_{-1}^{1} x_{AC}\,dy - \int_{1}^{3} x_{AB}\,dy$$

$$= \frac{1}{2}\int_{-1}^{3} (7-y)\,dy - \int_{-1}^{1} (2-2y)\,dy - \int_{1}^{3} (y-1)\,dy$$

$$= \frac{1}{2}\left[7y - \frac{y^2}{2}\right]_{-1}^{3} - 2\left[y - \frac{y^2}{2}\right]_{-1}^{1} - \left[\frac{y^2}{2} - y\right]_{1}^{3}$$

$$=\frac{1}{2}\left[\left(21-\frac{9}{2}\right)-\left(-7-\frac{1}{2}\right)\right]$$

$$-2\left[\left(1-\frac{1}{2}\right)-\left(-1-\frac{1}{2}\right)\right]-\left[\left(\frac{9}{2}-3\right)-\left(\frac{1}{2}-1\right)\right]$$

$$=\frac{1}{2}\left(\frac{33}{2}+\frac{15}{2}\right)-2\left(\frac{1}{2}+\frac{3}{2}\right)-\left(\frac{3}{2}+\frac{1}{2}\right)$$

$$=\frac{1}{2}\times 24-2\times 2-2$$

$$=12-4-2=6 \text{ sq. units}$$

Section C

19. (i) (c) Given, $R(x)=36x+3x^2+5$

Actual revenue received on selling 10th item

$= R(10)-R(9)$

$=[36(10)+3(10)^2+5]-[36(9)+3(9)^2+5]$

$=36(10-9)+3(10^2-9^2)=36+3\times 19$

$=36+57=93$

(ii) (c) **Statement I** The correlation coefficients will have the same sign as that of regression coefficients i.e. b_{yx} and b_{xy} have the same sign as that of r. Thus, Statement I is correct.

Statement II The correlation coefficient is the geometric mean of regression coefficients. Thus, Statement II is incorrect.

Statement III The product of two regression coefficients is equal to the square of the correlation coefficient, which lies between 0 and 1. Thus, Statement III is incorrect.

Statement IV Both the regression coefficients cannot be greater than unity because their product cannot exceeds one. Thus, Statement IV is correct.

(iii) Let us construct the following table.

x	y	$x-\bar{x}$	$y-\bar{y}$	y^2	xy
1	6	–2	2	36	6
2	5	–1	1	25	10
3	4	0	0	16	12
6	1	3	–3	1	6
$\Sigma x=12$	$\Sigma y=16$			$\Sigma y^2=78$	$\Sigma xy=34$

(a) Here, $\bar{x}=\frac{\Sigma x}{n}=\frac{12}{4}=3$

and $\bar{y}=\frac{\Sigma y}{n}=\frac{16}{4}=4$

(b) The complete table is shown above.

(c) $b_{xy}=\dfrac{\Sigma xy-\frac{1}{n}\Sigma x\cdot\Sigma y}{\Sigma y^2-\frac{1}{n}(\Sigma y)^2}$

$$=\frac{34-\frac{1}{4}\times 12\times 16}{78-\frac{1}{4}\times 16\times 16}$$

$$=\frac{34-48}{78-64}=\frac{-14}{14}=-1$$

20. (i) We have, $\Sigma x=24$, $\Sigma y=44$, $\Sigma xy=306$, $\Sigma x^2=164$, $\Sigma y^2=576$, $n=4$

Now, regression of y on x is

$$b_{yx}=\frac{\Sigma xy-\frac{\Sigma x\,\Sigma y}{n}}{\Sigma x^2-\frac{(\Sigma x)^2}{n}}$$

$$=\frac{306-\frac{24\times 44}{4}}{164-\frac{24\times 24}{4}}$$

$$=\frac{306-264}{164-144}=\frac{42}{20}=2.1$$

Now, mean, $\bar{x}=\frac{\Sigma x}{n}=\frac{24}{4}=6$

and $\bar{y}=\frac{\Sigma y}{n}=\frac{44}{4}=11$

$\therefore$ Regression equation of y on x is

$$y-\bar{y}=b_{yx}(x-\bar{x})$$

$\Rightarrow$ $y-11=2.1(x-6)$

$\Rightarrow$ $y-11=2.1x-12.6$

$\Rightarrow$ $2.1x-y-1.6=0$

OR

(ii) Assuming $4x+3y+7=0$ to be regression of x on y

$\therefore$ $4x=-3y-7$

$\Rightarrow$ $x=-\frac{3}{4}y-\frac{7}{4}$

$\Rightarrow$ $b_{xy}=-\frac{3}{4}$

Then, $3x+4y+8=0$ is regression line of y on x.

$\therefore$ $4y=-3x-8$

$\Rightarrow$ $y=-\frac{3}{4}x-\frac{8}{4}$

$$\Rightarrow \quad b_{yx} = \frac{-3}{4}$$

Now, $b_{xy} \cdot b_{yx} = \left(\frac{-3}{4}\right)\left(\frac{-3}{4}\right) = \frac{9}{16} < 1$

$\therefore$ Regression line of x on y is

$$4x + 3y + 7 = 0.$$

21. (i) Given, cost function,

$$C = x^2 + 78x + 2000$$

and demand function, $x = \frac{600 - p}{8}$

(a) We know that
revenue function, $R = xp$
From equation of demand function,

$$x = \frac{600 - p}{8}$$

$$\therefore \quad p = 600 - 8x$$

Now, we put $p = 600 - 8x$ in equation of revenue function, we get

$$R = x(600 - 8x)$$

$$\Rightarrow \quad R = 600x - 8x^2$$

(b) Also, profit function,

$$P(x) = \text{Revenue} - \text{Cost}$$

$$= (600x - 8x^2) - (x^2 + 78x + 2000)$$

$$= 600x - 8x^2 - x^2 - 78x - 2000$$

$$= -9x^2 + 522x - 2000$$

(c) For the profit maximising level of output x, $\frac{dP}{dx} = 0.$

$$\therefore \quad \frac{d(P)}{dx} = 0$$

$$\Rightarrow \quad \frac{d}{dx}(-9x^2 + 522x - 2000) = 0$$

$$\Rightarrow \quad -18x + 522 = 0$$

$$\Rightarrow \quad 18x = 522$$

$$\Rightarrow \quad x = 29$$

Now, $\frac{d^2P}{dx^2} = \frac{d}{dx}\left(\frac{dP}{dx}\right) = \frac{d}{dx}(-18x + 522)$

$$= -18 < 0$$

Hence, the number of dinner sets to maximise profit is 29.

OR

(ii) Given, average cost function is

$$AC = \frac{x^2}{200} - \frac{x}{50} - 30 + \frac{5000}{x} \quad \ldots(i)$$

(a) We know that

$$\text{Average cost (AC)} = \frac{\text{Cost function } (C)}{x}$$

$$\Rightarrow \quad C = x(\text{AC})$$

$$\Rightarrow \quad C = x\left(\frac{x^2}{200} - \frac{x}{50} - 30 + \frac{5000}{x}\right)$$

$$\Rightarrow \quad C = \frac{x^3}{200} - \frac{x^2}{50} - 30x + 5000 \quad \ldots(ii)$$

(b) Marginal cost (MC) $= \frac{dC}{dx}$

$$= \frac{d}{dx}\left(\frac{x^3}{200} - \frac{x^2}{50} - 30x + 5000\right)$$

$$= \frac{3x^2}{200} - \frac{2x}{50} - 30$$

$$\text{MC} = \frac{3x^2}{200} - \frac{x}{25} - 30 \quad \ldots(iii)$$

(c) Marginal average cost (MAC)

$$= \frac{d}{dx}(\text{AC})$$

$$= \frac{d}{dx}\left(\frac{x^2}{200} - \frac{x}{50} - 30 + \frac{5000}{x}\right)$$

$$= \frac{2x}{200} - \frac{1}{50} - \frac{5000}{x^2}$$

$$\Rightarrow \quad \text{MAC} = \frac{x}{100} - \frac{1}{50} - \frac{5000}{x^2} \quad \ldots(iv)$$

(d) We have to verify $\frac{d}{dx}(\text{AC}) = \frac{\text{MC} - \text{AC}}{x}$

$$\text{LHS} = \frac{d}{dx}(\text{AC}) = \frac{x}{100} - \frac{1}{50} - \frac{5000}{x^2}$$

[from Eq. (iv)]

$$\text{RHS} = \frac{\text{MC} - \text{AC}}{x}$$

$$= \frac{\left(\frac{3x^2}{200} - \frac{x}{25} - 30\right) - \left(\frac{x^2}{200} - \frac{x}{50} - 30 + \frac{5000}{x}\right)}{x}$$

[from q.s (i) and (iii)]

$$= \frac{1}{x}\left[\frac{3x^2}{200} - \frac{x^2}{200} - \frac{x}{25} + \frac{x}{50} - 30 + 30 - \frac{5000}{x}\right]$$

$$= \frac{1}{x}\left[\frac{2x^2}{200} - \frac{x}{50} - \frac{5000}{x}\right]$$

$$= \frac{x}{100} - \frac{1}{50} - \frac{5000}{x^2}$$

Thus, LHS = RHS **Hence verified.**

22. Let x and y be the numbers of books of the first and second type, respectively.

So, our problem is to maximise

$$Z = x + y \quad \ldots(i)$$

Subject to constraints,

$$x + 1.5y \le 21 \quad \ldots(ii)$$
$$6x + 4y \le 96 \quad \ldots(iii)$$
$$\text{and } x \ge 0,\ y \ge 0 \quad \ldots(iv)$$

Table for line $x + 1.5y = 21$ is

x	0	21
y	14	0

So, line is passing through the points (0, 14) and (21, 0).

On putting (0, 0) in the inequality $x + 1.5y \le 21$, we get

$$0 + 0 \le 21$$

$\Rightarrow 0 \le 21$, which is true.

So, the half plane is towards the origin.

Table for line $6x + 4y = 96$

x	0	16
y	24	0

So, line is passing through the points (0, 24) and (16, 0).

On putting (0, 0) in the inequality

$6x + 4y \le 96$, we get

$$0 + 0 \le 96$$

$\Rightarrow \quad 0 \le 96$, which is true.

So, the half plane is towards the origin.

On plotting these lines, we get the following graph

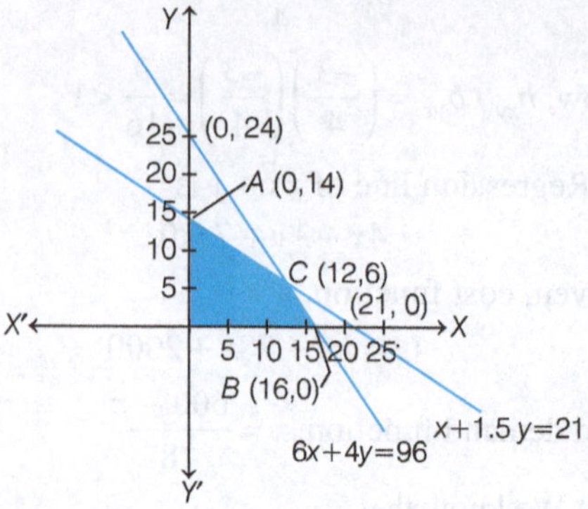

The intersection point of lines (ii) and (iii) is $C(12, 6)$.

Clearly, the feasible region is $OBCAO$, where the corner points are $O(0, 0)$, $B(16, 0)$, $C(12, 6)$ and $A(0, 14)$.

Now, the value of Z at corner points are as follow.

Corner points	$Z = x + y$
$O(0, 0)$	$Z = 0 + 0 = 0$
$A(0, 14)$	$Z = 0 + 14 = 14$
$B(16, 0)$	$Z = 16 + 0 = 16$
$C(12, 6)$	$Z = 12 + 6 = 18$ (Maximum)

The maximum value of Z is 18 at (12, 6).

Hence, the maximum number of books to be placed by placing 12 books of first type and 6 books of second type.